The Sporting News

PRO FOOTBALL
REGISTER

2001 EDITION

Editors/Pro Football Register
JEFF PAUR
DAVID WALTON

CONTENTS

EXPLANATION OF ABBREVIATIONS AND TERMS

LEAGUES: AFL: American Football League. **Ar.FL., Arena Football:** Arena Football League. **CFL:** Canadian Football League. **CoFL:** Continental Football League. **NFL:** National Football League. **NFLE:** NFL Europe League. **USFL:** United States Football League. **WFL:** World Football League. **W.L.:** World League. **WLAF:** World League of American Football.

TEAMS: Birm.: Birmingham. **Jack., Jax.:** Jacksonville. **L.A. Raiders:** Los Angeles Raiders. **L.A. Rams:** Los Angeles Rams. **New Eng.:** New England. **N.Y. Giants:** New York Giants. **N.Y. Jets:** New York Jets. **N.Y./N.J.:** New York/New Jersey. **San Ant.:** San Antonio. **San Fran.:** San Francisco. **Sask.:** Saskatchewan. **StL.:** St. Louis.

STATISTICS: Att.: Attempts. **Avg.:** Average. **Blk.:** Blocked punts. **Cmp.:** Completions. **FGA:** Field goals attempted. **FGM:** Field goals made. **50+:** Field goals of 50 yards or longer. **F., Fum.:** Fumbles. **G:** Games. **In. 20:** Punts inside 20-yard line. **Int.:** Interceptions. **Lg.:** Longest made field goal. **L:** Lost. **Net avg.:** Net punting average. **No.:** Number. **Rat.:** Passer rating. **Pct.:** Percentage. **Pts.:** Points scored. **T:** Tied. **TD:** Touchdowns. **2-pt.:** Two-point conversions. **W:** Won. **XPA:** Extra points attempted. **XPM:** Extra points made. **Yds.:** Yards.

POSITIONS: C: Center. **CB:** Cornerback. **DB:** Defensive back. **DE:** Defensive end. **DT:** Defensive tackle. **FB:** Fullback. **G:** Guard. **K:** Kicker. **LB:** Linebacker. **OL:** Offensive lineman. **OT:** Offensive tackle. **P:** Punter. **QB:** Quarterback. **RB:** Running back. **S:** Safety. **TE:** Tight end. **WR:** Wide receiver.

SINGLE GAME HIGHS (regular season): If a player reached a single game high on numerous occasions—had one rushing touchdown in a game, for example—the most recent occurrence is listed.

EXPLANATION OF AWARDS

AWARDS: Butkus Award: Nation's top college linebacker. **Chuck Bednarik Award:** Nation's top defensive player. **Davey O'Brien Award:** Nation's top college quarterback. **Doak Walker Award:** Nation's top college junior or senior running back. **Fred Biletnikoff Award:** Nation's top college wide receiver. **Harlon Hill Trophy:** Nation's top college Division II player. **Heisman Trophy:** Nation's top college player. **Jim Thorpe Award:** Nation's top college defensive back. **Lombardi Award:** Nation's top college lineman. **Lou Groza Award:** Nation's top college kicker. **Maxwell Award:** Nation's top college player. **Outland Trophy:** Nation's top college interior lineman. **Walter Payton Award:** Nation's top college Division I-AA player.

ON THE COVER: Donovan McNabb. (Both photos by Bob Leverone/THE SPORTING NEWS.) Spine photo of Dick Vermeil (File photo).

VETERAN PLAYERS

Please note for statistical comparisons: In 1982, only nine of 16 games were played due to the cancellation of games because of a player's strike. In 1987, only 15 of 16 games were played due to the cancellation of games in the third week because of a player's strike. Most NFL players also missed games scheduled in the fourth, fifth and sixth weeks.

Sacks became an official NFL statistic in 1982.

Two-point conversions became an official NFL statistic in 1994.

* Indicates league leader.	† Indicates tied for league lead.	... Statistics unavailable, unofficial, or mathematically impossible to calculate.
‡ Indicates NFC leader.	§ Indicates AFC leader.	
∞ Indicates tied for NFC lead.	▲ Indicates tied for AFC lead.	

ABDULLAH, RABIH — RB — BUCCANEERS

PERSONAL: Born April 27, 1975, in Martinsville, Va. ... 6-1/227. ... Name pronounced RAH-bee ab-DUE-lah.
HIGH SCHOOL: Barham Clark (Roselle, N.J.).
COLLEGE: Lehigh.
TRANSACTIONS/CAREER NOTES: Signed as non-drafted free agent by Tampa Bay Buccaneers (April 20, 1998). ... Inactive for all 16 games (1998). ... On injured reserve with thumb injury (December 28, 1999-remainder of season). ... Granted free agency (March 2, 2001).
PRO STATISTICS: 2000—Returned one kickoff for 16 yards.
SINGLE GAME HIGHS (regular season): Attempts—10 (December 3, 2000, vs. Dallas); yards—38 (December 3, 2000, vs. Dallas); and rushing touchdowns—0.

			RUSHING				RECEIVING				TOTALS			
Year Team	G	GS	Att.	Yds.	Avg.	TD	No.	Yds.	Avg.	TD	TD	2pt.	Pts.	Fum.
1999—Tampa Bay NFL	15	1	5	12	2.4	0	2	11	5.5	0	0	0	0	0
2000—Tampa Bay NFL	12	0	16	70	4.4	0	2	14	7.0	0	0	0	0	0
Pro totals (2 years)	27	1	21	82	3.9	0	4	25	6.3	0	0	0	0	0

ABDULLAH, RAHIM — LB — BROWNS

PERSONAL: Born March 22, 1976, in Jacksonville. ... 6-5/251. ... Full name: Rahim Fahim Abdullah. ... Name pronounced ra-HEEM ab-DUE-lah.
HIGH SCHOOL: Fletcher (Neptune Beach, Fla.).
COLLEGE: Clemson.
TRANSACTIONS/CAREER NOTES: Selected after junior season by Cleveland Browns in second round (45th pick overall) of 1999 NFL draft. ... Signed by Browns (July 22, 1999).
PLAYING EXPERIENCE: Cleveland NFL, 1999 and 2000. ... Games/Games started: 1999 (16/13), 2000 (13/4). Total: 29/17.
PRO STATISTICS: 1999—Intercepted one pass for no yards. 2000—Credited with two sacks.

ABRAHAM, DONNIE — CB — BUCCANEERS

PERSONAL: Born October 8, 1973, in Orangeburg, S.C. ... 5-10/192. ... Full name: Nathaniel Donnell Abraham.
HIGH SCHOOL: Orangeburg-Wilkinson (Orangeburg, S.C.).
COLLEGE: East Tennessee State (degree in business management, 1995).
TRANSACTIONS/CAREER NOTES: Selected by Tampa Bay Buccaneers in third round (71st pick overall) of 1996 NFL draft. ... Signed by Buccaneers (July 13, 1996).
CHAMPIONSHIP GAME EXPERIENCE: Played in NFC championship game (1999 season).
HONORS: Played in Pro Bowl (2000 season).
PRO STATISTICS: 1996—Recovered two fumbles for three yards. 1997—Recovered one fumble for two yards. 1998—Recovered two fumbles. 1999—Credited with two sacks. 2000—Returned blocked field goal for 53 yards and a touchdown.

			INTERCEPTIONS			
Year Team	G	GS	No.	Yds.	Avg.	TD
1996—Tampa Bay NFL	16	12	5	27	5.4	0
1997—Tampa Bay NFL	16	16	5	16	3.2	0
1998—Tampa Bay NFL	13	13	1	3	3.0	0
1999—Tampa Bay NFL	16	16	†7	115	16.4	†2
2000—Tampa Bay NFL	16	16	7	82	11.7	0
Pro totals (5 years)	77	73	25	243	9.7	2

ABRAHAM, JOHN — LB — JETS

PERSONAL: Born May 6, 1978, in Timmonsville, S.C. ... 6-4/250.
HIGH SCHOOL: Lamar (Timmonsville, S.C.).
COLLEGE: South Carolina.
TRANSACTIONS/CAREER NOTES: Selected by New York Jets in first round (13th pick overall) of 2000 NFL draft. ... Signed by Jets (July 10, 2000). ... On injured reserve with hernia (November 17, 2000-remainder of season).

Year Team	G	GS	SACKS
2000—New York Jets NFL	6	0	4.5

ACKERMAN, TOM   G   SAINTS

PERSONAL: Born September 6, 1972, in Bellingham, Wash. ... 6-3/296. ... Full name: Thomas Michael Ackerman.
HIGH SCHOOL: Nooksack (Wash.) Valley.
COLLEGE: Eastern Washington.
TRANSACTIONS/CAREER NOTES: Selected by New Orleans Saints in fifth round (145th pick overall) of 1996 NFL draft. ... Signed by Saints (July 14, 1996). ... Granted free agency (February 12, 1999). ... Re-signed by Saints (April 14, 1999). ... Granted unconditional free agency (February 11, 2000). ... Re-signed by Saints (February 15, 2000).
PLAYING EXPERIENCE: New Orleans NFL, 1996-2000. ... Games/Games started: 1996 (2/0), 1997 (14/0), 1998 (15/10), 1999 (16/8), 2000 (15/0). Total: 62/18.

ADAMS, FLOZELL   OT   COWBOYS

PERSONAL: Born May 18, 1975, in Chicago. ... 6-7/335. ... Full name: Flozell Jootin Adams. ... Cousin of Hersey Hawkins, guard, Charlotte Hornets.
HIGH SCHOOL: Proviso West (Hillside, Ill.).
COLLEGE: Michigan State.
TRANSACTIONS/CAREER NOTES: Selected by Dallas Cowboys in second round (38th pick overall) of 1998 NFL draft. ... Signed by Cowboys (July 17, 1998).
PLAYING EXPERIENCE: Dallas NFL, 1998-2000. ... Games/Games started: 1998 (16/12), 1999 (16/16), 2000 (16/16). Total: 48/44.
HONORS: Named offensive tackle on THE SPORTING NEWS college All-America third team (1997).
PRO STATISTICS: 1998—Recovered one fumble. 1999—Recovered one fumble.

ADAMS, SAM   DT   RAVENS

PERSONAL: Born June 13, 1973, in Houston. ... 6-3/330. ... Full name: Sam Aaron Adams. ... Son of Sam Adams Sr., guard with New England Patriots (1972-80) and New Orleans Saints (1981).
HIGH SCHOOL: Cypress Creek (Houston).
COLLEGE: Texas A&M.
TRANSACTIONS/CAREER NOTES: Selected after junior season by Seattle Seahawks in first round (eighth pick overall) of 1994 NFL draft. ... Signed by Seahawks (July 30, 1994). ... Granted unconditional free agency (February 11, 2000). ... Signed by Baltimore Ravens (April 17, 2000).
CHAMPIONSHIP GAME EXPERIENCE: Played in AFC championship game (2000 season). ... Member of Super Bowl championship team (2000 season).
HONORS: Named defensive lineman on THE SPORTING NEWS college All-America first team (1993). ... Played in Pro Bowl (2000 season).
PRO STATISTICS: 1996—Recovered one fumble for two yards. 1998—Intercepted one pass for 25 yards and a touchdown and recovered one fumble. 1999—Recovered one fumble. 2000—Recovered one fumble.

Year Team	G	GS	SACKS
1994—Seattle NFL	12	7	4.0
1995—Seattle NFL	16	5	3.5
1996—Seattle NFL	16	15	5.5
1997—Seattle NFL	16	16	7.0
1998—Seattle NFL	16	11	2.0
1999—Seattle NFL	13	13	1.0
2000—Baltimore NFL	16	16	2.0
Pro totals (7 years)	105	83	25.0

AGNEW, RAY   DT   RAMS

PERSONAL: Born December 9, 1967, in Winston-Salem, N.C. ... 6-3/285. ... Full name: Raymond Mitchell Agnew.
HIGH SCHOOL: Carver (Winston-Salem, N.C.).
COLLEGE: North Carolina State.
TRANSACTIONS/CAREER NOTES: Selected by New England Patriots in first round (10th pick overall) of 1990 NFL draft. ... Signed by Patriots (July 19, 1990). ... On injured reserve with knee injury (December 29, 1990-remainder of season). ... Granted unconditional free agency (February 17, 1995). ... Signed by New York Giants (March 10, 1995). ... Released by Giants (June 4, 1997). ... Signed by Carolina Panthers (June 12, 1997). ... Released by Panthers (August 19, 1997). ... Signed by Giants (August 21, 1997). ... Granted unconditional free agency (February 13, 1998). ... Signed by St. Louis Rams (March 5, 1998). ... Released by Rams (February 21, 2001). ... Re-signed by Rams (April 6, 2001).
CHAMPIONSHIP GAME EXPERIENCE: Played in NFC championship game (1999 season). ... Member of Super Bowl championship team (1999 season).
PRO STATISTICS: 1990—Recovered one fumble. 1992—Recovered one fumble. 1995—Recovered one fumble. 1996—Intercepted one pass for 34 yards and a touchdown. 1997—Recovered one fumble. 1998—Intercepted one pass for no yards and recovered one fumble.

Year Team	G	GS	SACKS
1990—New England NFL	12	9	2.5
1991—New England NFL	13	10	2.0
1992—New England NFL	14	14	1.0
1993—New England NFL	16	1	1.5
1994—New England NFL	11	3	0.5
1995—New York Giants NFL	16	15	1.0
1996—New York Giants NFL	13	2	0.5
1997—New York Giants NFL	15	0	2.0
1998—St. Louis NFL	16	12	5.0
1999—St. Louis NFL	16	16	2.5
2000—St. Louis NFL	15	15	4.0
Pro totals (11 years)	157	97	22.5

AGUIAR, LOUIE   P

PERSONAL: Born June 30, 1966, in Livermore, Calif. ... 6-2/218. ... Full name: Louis Raymond Aguiar. ... Name pronounced AG-ee-ar.
HIGH SCHOOL: Granada (Livermore, Calif.).
JUNIOR COLLEGE: Chabot College (Calif.).
COLLEGE: Utah State.
TRANSACTIONS/CAREER NOTES: Signed as non-drafted free agent by Buffalo Bills (May 8, 1989). ... Released by Bills (August 14, 1989). ... Re-signed by Bills (March 27, 1990). ... Released by Bills (August 7, 1990). ... Signed by WLAF (January 8, 1991). ... Selected by Barcelona Dragons in first round (first punter) of 1991 WLAF positional draft. ... Signed by New York Jets (June 14, 1991). ... Granted free agency (February 17, 1994). ... Signed by Kansas City Chiefs (April 1994). ... Granted unconditional free agency (February 14, 1997). ... Re-signed by Chiefs (April 18, 1997). ... Released by Chiefs (September 5, 1999). ... Signed by Green Bay Packers (September 15, 1999). ... Granted free agency (February 11, 2000). ... Signed by St. Louis Rams (August 1, 2000). ... Released by Rams (August 21, 2000). ... Signed by Chicago Bears (October 18, 2000). ... Granted unconditional free agency (March 2, 2001).
PRO STATISTICS: NFL: 1991—Made one of two field goal attempts (23 yards), rushed once for 18 yards and recovered one fumble. 1993— Rushed three times for minus 27 yards, attempted two passes without a completion and an interception, fumbled twice and recovered one fumble for minus 10 yards. 1997— Rushed twice for 11 yards and completed only pass attempt for 35 yards. 1998—Recovered one fumble. 2000—Completed only pass attempt for 13 yards.

				PUNTING			
Year Team	G	No.	Yds.	Avg.	Net avg.	In. 20	Blk.
1991—Barcelona W.L.	10	49	2029	41.4	33.7	15	1
—New York Jets NFL	16	64	2521	39.4	34.6	14	0
1992—New York Jets NFL	16	73	2993	41.0	37.6	21	0
1993—New York Jets NFL	16	73	2806	38.4	34.3	21	0
1994—Kansas City NFL	16	85	3582	42.1	34.5	15	0
1995—Kansas City NFL	16	91	3990	43.8	36.5	†29	0
1996—Kansas City NFL	16	88	3667	41.7	33.7	25	0
1997—Kansas City NFL	16	82	3465	42.3	38.2	▲28	0
1998—Kansas City NFL	16	75	3226	43.0	34.4	20	1
1999—Green Bay NFL	15	75	2954	39.4	33.9	20	0
2000—Chicago NFL	9	52	2017	38.8	34.9	8	0
W.L. totals (1 year)	10	49	2029	41.4	33.7	15	1
NFL totals (10 years)	152	758	31221	41.2	35.3	201	1
Pro totals (11 years)	162	807	33250	41.2	35.2	216	2

AHANOTU, CHIDI   DE

PERSONAL: Born October 11, 1970, in Modesto, Calif. ... 6-2/285. ... Full name: Chidi Obioma Ahanotu. ... Name pronounced CHEE-dee a-HA-noe-too.
HIGH SCHOOL: Berkeley (Calif.).
COLLEGE: California (degree in physical education).
TRANSACTIONS/CAREER NOTES: Selected by Tampa Bay Buccaneers in sixth round (145th pick overall) of 1993 NFL draft. ... Signed by Buccaneers (July 9, 1993). ... Granted free agency (February 16, 1996). ... Re-signed by Buccaneers (February 20, 1996). ... On injured reserve with shoulder injury (October 27, 1998-remainder of season). ... Designated by Buccaneers as franchise player (February 12, 1999). ... Re-signed by Buccaneers (July 30, 1999). ... Released by Buccaneers (April 20, 2001).
CHAMPIONSHIP GAME EXPERIENCE: Played in NFC championship game (1999 season).
PRO STATISTICS: 1996—Recovered one fumble. 1997—Recovered two fumbles. 2000—Recovered one fumble.

Year Team	G	GS	SACKS
1993—Tampa Bay NFL	16	10	1.5
1994—Tampa Bay NFL	16	16	1.0
1995—Tampa Bay NFL	16	15	3.0
1996—Tampa Bay NFL	13	13	5.5
1997—Tampa Bay NFL	16	15	10.0
1998—Tampa Bay NFL	4	4	0.0
1999—Tampa Bay NFL	16	15	6.5
2000—Tampa Bay NFL	16	16	3.5
Pro totals (8 years)	113	104	31.0

AIKMAN, TROY   QB

PERSONAL: Born November 21, 1966, in West Covina, Calif. ... 6-4/220. ... Full name: Troy Kenneth Aikman.
HIGH SCHOOL: Henryetta (Okla.).
COLLEGE: Oklahoma, then UCLA.
TRANSACTIONS/CAREER NOTES: Selected by Dallas Cowboys in first round (first pick overall) of 1989 NFL draft. ... Signed by Cowboys (April 20, 1989). ... On injured reserve with shoulder injury (December 28, 1990-remainder of season). ... Released by Cowboys (March 7, 2001). ... Announced retirement (April 9, 2001).
CHAMPIONSHIP GAME EXPERIENCE: Played in NFC championship game (1992-1995 seasons). ... Member of Super Bowl championship team (1992, 1993 and 1995 seasons).
HONORS: Named quarterback on THE SPORTING NEWS college All-America second team (1987). ... Davey O'Brien Award winner (1988). ... Named quarterback on THE SPORTING NEWS college All-America first team (1988). ... Played in Pro Bowl (1991, 1992 and 1994 seasons). ... Named Most Valuable Player of Super Bowl XXVII (1992 season). ... Named quarterback on THE SPORTING NEWS NFL All-Pro team (1993). ... Named to play in Pro Bowl (1993 season); replaced by Bobby Hebert due to injury. ... Named to play in Pro Bowl (1995 season); replaced by Warren Moon due to injury. ... Named to play in Pro Bowl (1996 season); replaced by Gus Frerotte due to injury.
POST SEASON RECORDS: Holds Super Bowl career record for highest percentage of passes completed (minimum 40 attempts)—70.0. ... Holds NFL postseason single-game record for longest pass completion (to Alvin Harper)—94 yards (January 8, 1995, vs. Green Bay).
PRO STATISTICS: 1989—Caught one pass for minus 13 yards, fumbled six times and recovered three fumbles. 1990—Fumbled five times and recovered one fumble. 1991—Caught one pass for minus six yards and fumbled four times. 1992—Fumbled four times and recovered one fumble. 1993—Fumbled seven times and recovered three fumbles for minus three yards. 1994—Fumbled twice and recovered two fumbles.

A

1995—Fumbled five times and recovered two fumbles for minus 15 yards. 1996—Fumbled six times and recovered two fumbles for minus eight yards. 1997—Fumbled six times for minus five yards. 1998—Fumbled three times for minus 20 yards. 1999—Fumbled eight times and recovered two fumbles for minus 12 yards. 2000—Fumbled twice.

SINGLE GAME HIGHS (regular season): Attempts—57 (November 26, 1998, vs. Minnesota); completions—34 (November 26, 1998, vs. Minnesota); yards—455 (November 26, 1998, vs. Minnesota); and touchdown passes—5 (September 12, 1999, vs. Washington).

STATISTICAL PLATEAUS: 300-yard passing games: 1989 (1), 1990 (1), 1991 (1), 1993 (1), 1994 (1), 1995 (2), 1996 (1), 1997 (2), 1998 (1), 1999 (1), 2000 (1). Total: 13.

MISCELLANEOUS: Regular-season record as starting NFL quarterback: 94-71 (.570). ... Postseason record as starting NFL quarterback: 11-4 (.733). ... Holds Dallas Cowboys all-time record for most yards passing (32,942) and most touchdown passes (165).

				PASSING								RUSHING				TOTALS	
Year Team	G	GS	Att.	Cmp.	Pct.	Yds.	TD	Int.	Avg.	Rat.	Att.	Yds.	Avg.	TD	TD	2pt.	Pts.
1989—Dallas NFL	11	11	293	155	52.9	1749	9	18	5.97	55.7	38	302	7.9	0	0	0	0
1990—Dallas NFL	15	15	399	226	56.6	2579	11	∞18	6.46	66.6	40	172	4.3	1	1	0	6
1991—Dallas NFL	12	12	363	237	‡65.3	2754	11	10	7.59	86.7	16	5	0.3	1	1	0	6
1992—Dallas NFL	16	16	473	∞302	63.8	3445	23	14	7.28	89.5	37	105	2.8	1	1	0	6
1993—Dallas NFL	14	14	392	271	*69.1	3100	15	6	7.91	99.0	32	125	3.9	0	0	0	0
1994—Dallas NFL	14	14	361	233	64.5	2676	13	12	7.41	84.9	30	62	2.1	1	1	0	6
1995—Dallas NFL	16	16	432	280	64.8	3304	16	7	7.65	93.6	21	32	1.5	1	1	0	6
1996—Dallas NFL	15	15	465	296	63.7	3126	12	13	6.72	80.1	35	42	1.2	1	1	0	6
1997—Dallas NFL	16	16	‡518	292	56.4	3283	19	12	6.34	78.0	25	79	3.2	0	0	0	0
1998—Dallas NFL	11	11	315	187	59.4	2330	12	5	7.40	88.5	22	69	3.1	2	2	0	12
1999—Dallas NFL	14	14	442	263	59.5	2964	17	12	6.71	81.1	21	10	0.5	1	1	0	6
2000—Dallas NFL	11	11	262	156	59.5	1632	7	14	6.23	64.3	10	13	1.3	0	0	0	0
Pro totals (12 years)	165	165	4715	2898	61.5	32942	165	141	6.99	81.6	327	1016	3.1	9	9	0	54

AKERS, DAVID   K   EAGLES

PERSONAL: Born December 9, 1974, in Lexington, Ky. ... 5-10/200. ... Full name: David Roy Akers. ... Name pronounced A-kers.
HIGH SCHOOL: Tates Creek (Lexington, Ky.).
COLLEGE: Louisville.
TRANSACTIONS/CAREER NOTES: Signed as non-drafted free agent by Carolina Panthers (April 19, 1997). ... Released by Panthers (August 17, 1997). ... Signed by Atlanta Falcons (April 28, 1998). ... Released by Falcons (July 7, 1998). ... Re-signed by Falcons (July 21, 1998). ... Released by Falcons (August 24, 1998). ... Signed by Washington Redskins to practice squad (September 1, 1998). ... Activated (September 15, 1998). ... Released by Redskins (September 22, 1998). ... Signed by Philadelphia Eagles (January 11, 1999). ... Assigned by Eagles to Berlin Thunder in 1999 NFL Europe enhancement allocation program (February 22, 1999).
PRO STATISTICS: 2000—Rushed once for 15 yards.

					KICKING				
Year Team	G	XPM	XPA	FGM	FGA	Lg.	50+	Pts.
1998—Washington NFL	1	2	2	0	2	0	0-0	2
1999—Berlin NFLE	...	3	3	10	15	0	2-5	33
—Philadelphia NFL	16	2	2	3	6	∞53	1-3	11
2000—Philadelphia NFL	16	34	36	29	33	51	1-1	121
NFL Europe totals (1 year)	...	3	3	10	15	0	2-5	33
NFL totals (3 years)	33	38	40	32	41	53	2-4	134
Pro totals (4 years)	...	41	43	42	56	53	4-0	167

AKINS, CHRIS   S   PACKERS

PERSONAL: Born November 29, 1976, in Little Rock, Ark. ... 5-11/195. ... Full name: Christopher Drew Akins. ... Second cousin of Jackie Harris, tight end, Dallas Cowboys. ... Name pronounced A-kenz.
HIGH SCHOOL: Little Rock (Ark.) Hall.
COLLEGE: Arkansas, then Arkansas-Pine Bluff.
TRANSACTIONS/CAREER NOTES: Selected by Green Bay Packers in seventh round (212th pick overall) of 1999 NFL draft. ... Signed by Packers (June 1, 1999). ... Released by Packers (September 5, 1999). ... Re-signed by Packers to practice squad (September 14, 1999). ... Signed by Dallas Cowboys off Packers practice squad (October 27, 1999). ... Assigned by Cowboys to Rhein Fire in 2000 NFL Europe enhancement allocation program (February 18, 2000). ... Claimed on waivers by Packers (November 2, 2000).
PLAYING EXPERIENCE: Dallas NFL, 1999; Rhein NFLE, 2000; Dallas (8)-Green Bay (2) NFL, 2000. ... Games/Games started: 1999 (9/0), NFLE 2000 (games played unavailable), NFL 2000 (Dal.-8; G.B.-2; Total: 10/0). Total NFL: 19/0.
PRO STATISTICS: NFLE: 2000—Intercepted one pass for 13 yards.

AL-JABBAR, ABDUL-KARIM   RB   COLTS

PERSONAL: Born June 28, 1974, in Los Angeles. ... 5-10/205. ... Formerly known as Sharmon Shah.
HIGH SCHOOL: Dorsey (Los Angeles).
COLLEGE: UCLA.
TRANSACTIONS/CAREER NOTES: Selected after junior season by Miami Dolphins in third round (80th pick overall) of 1996 NFL draft. ... Signed by Dolphins (July 18, 1996). ... Granted free agency (February 12, 1999). ... Re-signed by Dolphins (April 13, 1999). ... Traded by Dolphins to Cleveland Browns for sixth-round pick (DT Earnest Grant) in 2000 draft and conditional fifth-round pick in 2001 draft (October 19, 1999). ... Granted unconditional free agency (February 11, 2000). ... Signed by Indianapolis Colts (July 14, 2000). ... On injured reserve with knee injury (October 2, 2000-remainder of season).
HONORS: Named running back on THE SPORTING NEWS college All-America second team (1995).
PRO STATISTICS: 1998—Recovered one fumble. 1999—Recovered one fumble.
SINGLE GAME HIGHS (regular season): Attempts—33 (September 20, 1998, vs. Pittsburgh); yards—152 (December 22, 1996, vs. New York Jets); and rushing touchdowns—3 (November 23, 1997, vs. New England).
STATISTICAL PLATEAUS: 100-yard rushing games: 1996 (4), 1997 (2), 1998 (3). Total: 9.

Year Team	G	GS	RUSHING Att.	Yds.	Avg.	TD	RECEIVING No.	Yds.	Avg.	TD	TOTALS TD	2pt.	Pts.	Fum.
1996—Miami NFL	16	14	307	1116	3.6	11	23	139	6.0	0	11	0	66	4
1997—Miami NFL	16	14	283	892	3.2	†15	29	261	9.0	1	*16	0	†96	3
1998—Miami NFL	15	15	270	960	3.6	6	21	102	4.9	0	6	0	36	2
1999—Miami NFL	3	3	28	95	3.4	1	4	25	6.3	0	1	0	6	0
—Cleveland NFL	10	6	115	350	3.0	0	13	59	4.5	1	1	0	6	0
2000—Indianapolis NFL	1	0	1	-2	-2.0	0	0	0	0.0	0	0	0	0	0
Pro totals (5 years)	61	52	1004	3411	3.4	33	90	586	6.5	2	35	0	210	9

A

ALBRIGHT, ETHAN   OL   REDSKINS

PERSONAL: Born May 1, 1971, in Greensboro, N.C. ... 6-5/268. ... Full name: Lawrence Ethan Albright.
HIGH SCHOOL: Grimsley (Greensboro, N.C.).
COLLEGE: North Carolina.
TRANSACTIONS/CAREER NOTES: Signed as non-drafted free agent by Miami Dolphins (April 28, 1994). ... Released by Dolphins (August 22, 1994). ... Re-signed by Dolphins to practice squad (August 29, 1994). ... Released by Dolphins (September 14, 1994). ... Re-signed by Dolphins to practice squad (September 28, 1994). ... Released by Dolphins (November 2, 1994). ... Re-signed by Dolphins (February 16, 1995). ... On injured reserve with knee injury (November 15, 1995-remainder of season). ... Released by Dolphins (August 20, 1996). ... Signed by Buffalo Bills (August 26, 1996). ... Granted free agency (February 13, 1998). ... Re-signed by Bills (April 15, 1998). ... Granted unconditional free agency (February 12, 1999). ... Re-signed by Bills (April 1, 1999). ... Released by Bills (March 1, 2001). ... Signed by Washington Redskins (March 9, 2001).
PLAYING EXPERIENCE: Miami NFL, 1995; Buffalo NFL, 1996-2000. ... Games/Games started: 1995 (10/0), 1996 (16/0), 1997 (16/0), 1998 (16/0), 1999 (16/0), 2000 (16/0). Total: 90/0.
PRO STATISTICS: 1998—Recovered one fumble. 1999—Fumbled once for minus eight yards. 2000—Recovered one fumble for 19 yards.

ALDRIDGE, ALLEN   LB   LIONS

PERSONAL: Born May 30, 1972, in Houston. ... 6-1/254. ... Full name: Allen Ray Aldridge. ... Son of Allen Aldridge, defensive end with Houston Oilers (1971-72) and Cleveland Browns (1974).
HIGH SCHOOL: Willowridge (Sugar Land, Texas).
COLLEGE: Houston.
TRANSACTIONS/CAREER NOTES: Selected by Denver Broncos in second round (51st pick overall) of 1994 NFL draft. ... Signed by Broncos (July 12, 1994). ... Granted free agency (February 14, 1997). ... Re-signed by Broncos (April 15, 1997). ... Granted unconditional free agency (February 13, 1998). ... Signed by Detroit Lions (February 14, 1998).
CHAMPIONSHIP GAME EXPERIENCE: Played in AFC championship game (1997 season). ... Member of Super Bowl championship team (1997 season).
PRO STATISTICS: 1995—Recovered one fumble. 1998—Recovered one fumble. 1999—Fumbled once and recovered one fumble for eight yards and a touchdown. 2000—Intercepted one pass for four yards and recovered one fumble.

Year Team	G	GS	SACKS
1994—Denver NFL	16	2	0.0
1995—Denver NFL	16	12	1.5
1996—Denver NFL	16	16	0.0
1997—Denver NFL	16	15	0.0
1998—Detroit NFL	16	15	3.0
1999—Detroit NFL	16	14	3.0
2000—Detroit NFL	16	14	2.0
Pro totals (7 years)	112	88	9.5

ALEXANDER, BRENT   S   STEELERS

PERSONAL: Born July 10, 1971, in Gallatin, Tenn. ... 5-11/196. ... Full name: Ronald Brent Alexander.
HIGH SCHOOL: Gallatin (Tenn.).
COLLEGE: Tennessee State.
TRANSACTIONS/CAREER NOTES: Signed as non-drafted free agent by Arizona Cardinals (April 28, 1994). ... Granted unconditional free agency (February 13, 1998). ... Signed by Carolina Panthers (March 20, 1998). ... Released by Panthers (April 18, 2000). ... Signed by Pittsburgh Steelers (May 30, 2000).
PRO STATISTICS: 1995—Credited with 1/2 sack and recovered one fumble. 1998—Recovered one fumble for 12 yards. 2000—Credited with 1 1/2 sacks and recovered one fumble.

Year Team	G	GS	INTERCEPTIONS No.	Yds.	Avg.	TD
1994—Arizona NFL	16	7	0	0	0.0	0
1995—Arizona NFL	16	13	2	14	7.0	0
1996—Arizona NFL	16	15	2	3	1.5	0
1997—Arizona NFL	16	15	0	0	0.0	0
1998—Carolina NFL	16	16	0	0	0.0	0
1999—Carolina NFL	16	16	2	18	9.0	0
2000—Pittsburgh NFL	16	16	3	31	10.3	0
Pro totals (7 years)	112	98	9	66	7.3	0

ALEXANDER, DERRICK   DE   BROWNS

PERSONAL: Born November 13, 1973, in Jacksonville. ... 6-4/286.
HIGH SCHOOL: Raines (Jacksonville).
COLLEGE: Florida State.

TRANSACTIONS/CAREER NOTES: Selected after junior season by Minnesota Vikings in first round (11th pick overall) of 1995 NFL draft. ... Signed by Vikings (August 16, 1995). ... Granted unconditional free agency (February 12, 1999). ... Signed by Cleveland Browns (April 17, 1999). ... On physically unable to perform list with knee injury (July 27-August 11, 1999). ... On injured reserve with ankle injury (August 28, 2000-entire season).
CHAMPIONSHIP GAME EXPERIENCE: Played in NFC championship game (1998 season).
HONORS: Named defensive lineman on THE SPORTING NEWS college All-America second team (1994).
PRO STATISTICS: 1995—Recovered one fumble. 1996—Recovered one fumble for three yards. 1997—Recovered one fumble.

Year Team	G	GS	SACKS
1995—Minnesota NFL	15	12	2.0
1996—Minnesota NFL	12	9	3.5
1997—Minnesota NFL	14	14	4.5
1998—Minnesota NFL	16	16	7.5
1999—Cleveland NFL	16	16	2.5
2000—Cleveland NFL			Did not play.
Pro totals (5 years)	73	67	20.0

ALEXANDER, DERRICK   WR   CHIEFS

PERSONAL: Born November 6, 1971, in Detroit. ... 6-2/200. ... Full name: Derrick Scott Alexander.
HIGH SCHOOL: Benedictine (Detroit).
COLLEGE: Michigan (degree in sports management).
TRANSACTIONS/CAREER NOTES: Selected by Cleveland Browns in first round (29th pick overall) of 1994 NFL draft. ... Signed by Browns (August 3, 1994). ... Browns franchise moved to Baltimore and renamed Ravens for 1996 season (March 11, 1996). ... Granted unconditional free agency (February 13, 1998). ... Signed by Kansas City Chiefs (March 2, 1998).
PRO STATISTICS: 1995—Fumbled three times and recovered one fumble. 1997—Fumbled once.
SINGLE GAME HIGHS (regular season): Receptions—9 (November 5, 2000, vs. Oakland); yards—198 (December 1, 1996, vs. Pittsburgh); and touchdown receptions—2 (November 5, 2000, vs. Oakland).
STATISTICAL PLATEAUS: 100-yard receiving games: 1994 (3), 1996 (3), 1997 (3), 1998 (2), 1999 (4), 2000 (6). Total: 21.
MISCELLANEOUS: Shares Baltimore Ravens all-time records for most touchdowns (18) and touchdown receptions (18).

			RUSHING				RECEIVING				PUNT RETURNS				KICKOFF RETURNS				TOTALS		
Year Team	G	GS	Att.	Yds.	Avg.	TD	No.	Yds.	Avg.	TD	No.	Yds.	Avg.	TD	No.	Yds.	Avg.	TD	TD	2pt.	Pts.
1994—Cleveland NFL	14	12	4	38	9.5	0	48	828	17.3	2	0	0	0.0	0	0	0	0.0	0	2	1	14
1995—Cleveland NFL	14	2	1	29	29.0	0	15	216	14.4	0	9	122	13.6	†1	21	419	20.0	0	1	0	6
1996—Baltimore NFL	15	14	3	0	0.0	0	62	1099	17.7	9	1	15	15.0	0	1	13	13.0	0	9	1	56
1997—Baltimore NFL	15	13	1	0	0.0	0	65	1009	15.5	9	1	34	34.0	0	0	0	0.0	0	9	0	54
1998—Kansas City NFL	15	14	0	0	0.0	0	54	992	18.4	4	0	0	0.0	0	0	0	0.0	0	4	0	24
1999—Kansas City NFL	16	15	2	82	41.0	1	54	832	15.4	2	0	0	0.0	0	0	0	0.0	0	3	0	18
2000—Kansas City NFL	16	16	3	45	15.0	0	78	1391	§17.8	10	0	0	0.0	0	0	0	0.0	0	10	0	60
Pro totals (7 years)	105	86	14	194	13.9	1	376	6367	16.9	36	11	171	15.5	1	22	432	19.6	0	38	2	232

ALEXANDER, ELIJAH   LB   RAIDERS

PERSONAL: Born August 2, 1970, in Fort Worth, Texas. ... 6-2/235. ... Full name: Elijah Alfred Alexander III.
HIGH SCHOOL: Dunbar Senior (Fort Worth, Texas).
COLLEGE: Kansas State (degree in accounting).
TRANSACTIONS/CAREER NOTES: Selected by Tampa Bay Buccaneers in 10th round (254th pick overall) of 1992 NFL draft. ... Signed by Buccaneers (June 3, 1992). ... Released by Buccaneers (August 31, 1992). ... Re-signed by Buccaneers (September 1, 1992). ... Released by Buccaneers (October 16, 1992). ... Re-signed by Buccaneers to practice squad (October 22, 1992). ... Activated (November 10, 1992). ... Claimed on waivers by Denver Broncos (August 31, 1993). ... On injured reserve with shoulder injury (November 22, 1995-remainder of season). ... Granted unconditional free agency (February 16, 1996). ... Signed by Indianapolis Colts (August 6, 1996). ... Selected by Cleveland Browns from Colts in NFL expansion draft (February 9, 1999). ... Released by Browns (June 1, 1999). ... Signed by Oakland Raiders (March 14, 2000).
CHAMPIONSHIP GAME EXPERIENCE: Played in AFC championship game (2000 season).
PRO STATISTICS: 1994—Recovered one fumble for nine yards. 1998—Recovered two fumbles.

			INTERCEPTIONS				SACKS
Year Team	G	GS	No.	Yds.	Avg.	TD	No.
1992—Tampa Bay NFL	12	0	0	0	0.0	0	0.0
1993—Denver NFL	16	0	0	0	0.0	0	0.0
1994—Denver NFL	16	16	1	2	2.0	0	1.0
1995—Denver NFL	9	8	2	5	2.5	0	0.5
1996—Indianapolis NFL	14	3	0	0	0.0	0	1.0
1997—Indianapolis NFL	13	11	1	43	43.0	1	1.0
1998—Indianapolis NFL	13	9	1	12	12.0	0	0.0
1999—					Did not play.		
2000—Oakland NFL	16	16	0	0	0.0	0	2.0
Pro totals (8 years)	109	63	5	62	12.4	1	5.5

ALEXANDER, SHAUN   RB   SEAHAWKS

PERSONAL: Born August 30, 1977, in Florence, Ky. ... 5-11/218.
HIGH SCHOOL: Boone County (Ky.).
COLLEGE: Alabama (degree in marketing, 1999).
TRANSACTIONS/CAREER NOTES: Selected by Seattle Seahawks in first round (19th pick overall) of 2000 NFL draft. ... Signed by Seahawks (July 20, 2000).
HONORS: Named running back on THE SPORTING NEWS college All-America second team (1999).
SINGLE GAME HIGHS (regular season): Attempts—11 (October 2, 2000, vs. Kansas City); yards—74 (October 2, 2000, vs. Kansas City); and rushing touchdowns—1 (December 16, 2000, vs. Oakland).

Year Team	G	GS	RUSHING Att.	Yds.	Avg.	TD	RECEIVING No.	Yds.	Avg.	TD	TOTALS TD	2pt.	Pts.	Fum.
2000—Seattle NFL	16	1	64	313	4.9	2	5	41	8.2	0	2	0	12	2

ALEXANDER, STEPHEN   TE   REDSKINS   A

PERSONAL: Born November 7, 1975, in Chickasha, Okla. ... 6-4/246.
HIGH SCHOOL: Chickasha (Okla.).
COLLEGE: Oklahoma.
TRANSACTIONS/CAREER NOTES: Selected by Washington Redskins in second round (48th pick overall) of 1998 NFL draft. ... Signed by Redskins (July 13, 1998).
HONORS: Played in Pro Bowl (2000 season).
SINGLE GAME HIGHS (regular season): Receptions—7 (December 13, 1998, vs. Carolina); yards—86 (September 19, 1999, vs. New York Giants); and touchdown receptions—2 (September 19, 1999, vs. New York Giants).

Year Team	G	GS	RECEIVING No.	Yds.	Avg.	TD	TOTALS TD	2pt.	Pts.	Fum.
1998—Washington NFL	15	5	37	383	10.4	4	4	0	24	2
1999—Washington NFL	15	15	29	324	11.2	3	3	0	18	0
2000—Washington NFL	16	16	47	510	10.9	2	2	0	12	2
Pro totals (3 years)	46	36	113	1217	10.8	9	9	0	54	4

ALFORD, DARNELL   OT   CHIEFS

PERSONAL: Born June 11, 1977, in Fredricksburg, Va. ... 6-4/328. ... Full name: Darnell LaShawn Alford.
HIGH SCHOOL: Chancellor (Fredricksburg, Va.).
COLLEGE: Boston College.
TRANSACTIONS/CAREER NOTES: Selected by Kansas City Chiefs in sixth round (188th pick overall) of 2000 NFL draft. ... Signed by Chiefs (July 20, 2000).
PLAYING EXPERIENCE: Kansas City NFL, 2000. ... Games/Games started: 2000 (1/0).

ALLEN, ERIC   DB   RAIDERS

PERSONAL: Born November 22, 1965, in San Diego. ... 5-10/185. ... Full name: Eric Andre Allen.
HIGH SCHOOL: Point Loma (San Diego).
COLLEGE: Arizona State (degree in broadcasting, 1988).
TRANSACTIONS/CAREER NOTES: Selected by Philadelphia Eagles in second round (30th pick overall) of 1988 NFL draft. ... Signed by Eagles (July 19, 1988). ... Granted free agency (February 1, 1992). ... Re-signed by Eagles (September 2, 1992). ... Granted roster exemption (September 2-4, 1992). ... Designated by Eagles as transition player (February 25, 1993). ... Tendered offer sheet by New Orleans Saints (March 20, 1995). ... Eagles declined to match offer (March 27, 1995). ... Traded by Saints to Oakland Raiders for fourth-round pick (DB Fred Weary) in 1998 draft (March 5, 1998). ... On injured reserve with knee injury (November 18, 1998-remainder of season).
CHAMPIONSHIP GAME EXPERIENCE: Played in AFC championship game (2000 season).
HONORS: Played in Pro Bowl (1989 and 1991-1995 seasons).
RECORDS: Shares NFL single-season record for most touchdowns by interception—4 (1993). ... Shares NFL single-game record for most touchdowns by interception—2 (December 26, 1993, vs. New Orleans).
PRO STATISTICS: 1989—Fumbled once for seven yards. 1990—Returned one kickoff for two yards and recovered one fumble. 1991—Recovered one fumble. 1992—Recovered two fumbles. 1993—Credited with two sacks. 1994—Recovered one fumble for 30 yards. 1999—Recovered one fumble. 2000—Credited with one sack.
MISCELLANEOUS: Shares Philadelphia Eagles all-time record for most interceptions (34).

Year Team	G	GS	INTERCEPTIONS No.	Yds.	Avg.	TD
1988—Philadelphia NFL	16	16	5	76	15.2	0
1989—Philadelphia NFL	15	15	‡8	38	4.8	0
1990—Philadelphia NFL	16	15	3	37	12.3	1
1991—Philadelphia NFL	16	16	5	20	4.0	0
1992—Philadelphia NFL	16	16	4	49	12.3	0
1993—Philadelphia NFL	16	16	6	*201	33.5	*4
1994—Philadelphia NFL	16	16	3	61	20.3	0
1995—New Orleans NFL	16	16	2	28	14.0	0
1996—New Orleans NFL	16	16	1	33	33.0	0
1997—New Orleans NFL	16	16	2	27	13.5	0
1998—Oakland NFL	10	10	5	59	11.8	0
1999—Oakland NFL	16	16	3	33	11.0	0
2000—Oakland NFL	16	15	6	145	24.2	*3
Pro totals (13 years)	201	199	53	807	15.2	8

ALLEN, JAMES   RB   BEARS

PERSONAL: Born March 28, 1975, in Wynnewood, Okla. ... 5-10/215.
HIGH SCHOOL: Wynnewood (Okla.).
COLLEGE: Oklahoma.
TRANSACTIONS/CAREER NOTES: Signed as non-drafted free agent by Tennessee Oilers (May 14, 1997). ... Released by Oilers (August 20, 1997). ... Signed by Philadelphia Eagles to practice squad (August 27, 1997). ... Released by Eagles (September 2, 1997). ... Re-signed by Eagles to practice squad (September 10, 1997). ... Signed by Chicago Bears off Eagles practice squad (December 9, 1997). ... Inactive for two games (1997). ... Released by Bears (August 25, 1998). ... Re-signed by Bears to practice squad (August 31, 1998). ... Activated (October 13, 1998). ... Granted free agency (March 2, 2001). ... Re-signed by Bears (April 24, 2001).

PRO STATISTICS: 1998—Recovered two fumbles.
SINGLE GAME HIGHS (regular season): Attempts—37 (December 10, 2000, vs. New England); yards—163 (December 20, 1998, vs. Baltimore); and rushing touchdowns—1 (December 10, 2000, vs. New England).
STATISTICAL PLATEAUS: 100-yard rushing games: 1998 (1), 2000 (1). Total: 2.

Year Team	G	GS	RUSHING				RECEIVING				TOTALS			
			Att.	Yds.	Avg.	TD	No.	Yds.	Avg.	TD	TD	2pt.	Pts.	Fum.
1997—Chicago NFL								Did not play.						
1998—Chicago NFL	6	2	58	270	4.7	1	8	77	9.6	1	2	0	12	1
1999—Chicago NFL	12	3	32	119	3.7	0	9	91	10.1	0	0	0	0	0
2000—Chicago NFL	16	15	290	1120	3.9	2	39	291	7.5	1	3	0	18	5
Pro totals (3 years)	34	20	380	1509	4.0	3	56	459	8.2	2	5	0	30	6

ALLEN, LARRY   G   COWBOYS

PERSONAL: Born November 27, 1971, in Los Angeles. ... 6-3/326. ... Full name: Larry Christopher Allen.
HIGH SCHOOL: Vintage (Napa, Calif.).
JUNIOR COLLEGE: Butte College (Calif.).
COLLEGE: Sonoma State (Calif.).
TRANSACTIONS/CAREER NOTES: Selected by Dallas Cowboys in second round (46th pick overall) of 1994 NFL draft. ... Signed by Cowboys (July 16, 1994).
PLAYING EXPERIENCE: Dallas NFL, 1994-2000. ... Games/Games started: 1994 (16/10), 1995 (16/16), 1996 (16/16), 1997 (16/16), 1998 (16/16), 1999 (11/11), 2000 (16/16). Total: 107/101.
CHAMPIONSHIP GAME EXPERIENCE: Played in NFC championship game (1994 and 1995 seasons). ... Member of Super Bowl championship team (1995 season).
HONORS: Named guard on THE SPORTING NEWS NFL All-Pro team (1995-97, 1999 and 2000). ... Played in Pro Bowl (1995-1998 and 2000 seasons). ... Named to play in Pro Bowl (1999 season); replaced by Adam Timmerman due to injury. ... Named offensive tackle on THE SPORTING NEWS NFL All-Pro team (1998).
PRO STATISTICS: 1995—Recovered one fumble. 2000—Recovered two fumbles.

ALLEN, TAJE   CB   CHIEFS

PERSONAL: Born November 6, 1973, in Lubbock, Texas. ... 5-11/185. ... Full name: Taje LaQuane Allen.
HIGH SCHOOL: Estacado (Lubbock, Texas).
COLLEGE: Texas.
TRANSACTIONS/CAREER NOTES: Selected by St. Louis Rams in fifth round (158th pick overall) of 1997 NFL draft. ... Signed by Rams (July 3, 1997). ... Granted free agency (February 11, 2000). ... Re-signed by Rams (June 2, 2000). ... Granted unconditional free agency (March 2, 2001). ... Signed by Kansas City Chiefs (April 17, 2001).
PLAYING EXPERIENCE: St. Louis NFL, 1997-2000. ... Games/Games started: 1997 (14/1), 1998 (16/0), 1999 (16/2), 2000 (11/1). Total: 57/4.
CHAMPIONSHIP GAME EXPERIENCE: Played in NFC championship game (1999 season). ... Member of Super Bowl championship team (1999 season); did not play.
PRO STATISTICS: 1999—Intercepted two passes for 76 yards and credited with $1/2$ sack.

ALLEN, TERRY   RB

PERSONAL: Born February 21, 1968, in Commerce, Ga. ... 5-10/208. ... Full name: Terry Thomas Allen Jr.
HIGH SCHOOL: Banks County (Homer, Ga.).
COLLEGE: Clemson.
TRANSACTIONS/CAREER NOTES: Selected after junior season by Minnesota Vikings in ninth round (241st pick overall) of 1990 NFL draft. ... Signed by Vikings (July 2, 1990). ... On injured reserve with knee injury (August 28, 1990-entire season). ... On injured reserve with knee injury (August 23, 1993-entire season). ... Released by Vikings (May 8, 1995). ... Signed by Washington Redskins (June 15, 1995). ... Granted free agency (February 16, 1996). ... Re-signed by Redskins (July 17, 1996). ... Granted unconditional free agency (February 14, 1997). ... Re-signed by Redskins (February 26, 1997). ... Released by Redskins (April 19, 1999). ... Signed by New England Patriots (August 27, 1999). ... Released by Patriots (February 14, 2000). ... Signed by New Orleans Saints (November 14, 2000). ... Granted unconditional free agency (March 2, 2001).
HONORS: Played in Pro Bowl (1996 season).
PRO STATISTICS: 1991—Returned one kickoff for 14 yards and recovered one fumble. 1992—Recovered two fumbles. 1994—Recovered two fumbles for four yards. 1995—Recovered one fumble. 1997—Recovered one fumble. 1998—Recovered one fumble. 1999—Recovered one fumble. 2000—Ran six yards with lateral from kickoff return.
SINGLE GAME HIGHS (regular season): Attempts—36 (September 28, 1997, vs. Jacksonville); yards—172 (December 20, 1992, vs. Pittsburgh); and rushing touchdowns—3 (December 22, 1996, vs. Dallas).
STATISTICAL PLATEAUS: 100-yard rushing games: 1991 (1), 1992 (3), 1994 (3), 1995 (4), 1996 (5), 1997 (3), 1999 (2). Total: 21. ... 100-yard receiving games: 1992 (1).

Year Team	G	GS	RUSHING				RECEIVING				TOTALS			
			Att.	Yds.	Avg.	TD	No.	Yds.	Avg.	TD	TD	2pt.	Pts.	Fum.
1990—Minnesota NFL								Did not play.						
1991—Minnesota NFL	15	6	120	563	‡4.7	2	6	49	8.2	1	3	0	18	4
1992—Minnesota NFL	16	16	266	1201	4.5	13	49	478	9.8	2	15	0	90	9
1993—Minnesota NFL								Did not play.						
1994—Minnesota NFL	16	16	255	1031	4.0	8	17	148	8.7	0	8	1	50	3
1995—Washington NFL	16	16	338	1309	3.9	10	31	232	7.5	1	11	0	66	6
1996—Washington NFL	16	16	347	1353	3.9	*21	32	194	6.1	0	*21	0	126	4
1997—Washington NFL	10	10	210	724	3.4	4	20	172	8.6	1	5	0	30	2
1998—Washington NFL	10	10	148	700	4.7	2	17	128	7.5	0	2	0	12	4
1999—New England NFL	16	13	254	896	3.5	8	14	125	8.9	1	9	0	54	8
2000—New Orleans NFL	4	3	46	179	3.9	2	1	7	7.0	0	2	1	14	0
Pro totals (9 years)	119	106	1984	7956	4.0	70	187	1533	8.2	6	76	2	460	40

ALLRED, JOHN   TE

PERSONAL: Born September 9, 1974, in Del Mar, Calif. ... 6-4/249.
HIGH SCHOOL: Torrey Pines (Encinitas, Calif.).
COLLEGE: Southern California.
TRANSACTIONS/CAREER NOTES: Selected by Chicago Bears in second round (38th pick overall) of 1997 NFL draft. ... Signed by Bears (July 14, 1997). ... Granted free agency (February 11, 2000). ... Re-signed by Bears (April 20, 2000). ... On injured reserve with knee injury (October 10, 2000-remainder of season). ... Granted unconditional free agency (March 2, 2001).
PRO STATISTICS: 1997—Returned two kickoffs for 21 yards.
SINGLE GAME HIGHS (regular season): Receptions—4 (October 1, 2000, vs. Green Bay); yards—36 (September 3, 2000, vs. Minnesota); and touchdown receptions—1 (September 3, 2000, vs. Minnesota).

| | | | RECEIVING | | | | TOTALS | | | |
Year Team	G	GS	No.	Yds.	Avg.	TD	TD	2pt.	Pts.	Fum.
1997—Chicago NFL	15	4	8	70	8.8	0	0	0	0	0
1998—Chicago NFL	3	0	0	0	0.0	0	0	0	0	0
1999—Chicago NFL	16	5	13	102	7.8	1	1	0	6	0
2000—Chicago NFL	5	3	9	109	12.1	1	1	0	6	0
Pro totals (4 years)	39	12	30	281	9.4	2	2	0	12	0

ALSTOTT, MIKE   FB   BUCCANEERS

PERSONAL: Born December 21, 1973, in Joliet, Ill. ... 6-1/248. ... Full name: Michael Joseph Alstott.
HIGH SCHOOL: Joliet (Ill.) Catholic.
COLLEGE: Purdue (degree in business, 1995).
TRANSACTIONS/CAREER NOTES: Selected by Tampa Bay Buccaneers in second round (35th pick overall) of 1996 NFL draft. ... Signed by Buccaneers (July 21, 1996).
CHAMPIONSHIP GAME EXPERIENCE: Played in NFC championship game (1999 season).
HONORS: Played in Pro Bowl (1997-2000 seasons).
PRO STATISTICS: 1996—Returned one kickoff for 14 yards. 1997—Returned one kickoff for no yards. 1998—Attempted one pass without a completion and returned one kickoff for eight yards. 1999—Returned one kickoff for 19 yards. 2000—Attempted one pass without a completion and recovered one fumble.
SINGLE GAME HIGHS (regular season): Attempts—25 (November 7, 1999, vs. New Orleans); yards—131 (September 26, 1999, vs. Denver); and rushing touchdowns—3 (December 27, 1998, vs. Cincinnati).
STATISTICAL PLATEAUS: 100-yard rushing games: 1998 (2), 1999 (2). Total: 4.

| | | | RUSHING | | | | RECEIVING | | | | TOTALS | | | |
Year Team	G	GS	Att.	Yds.	Avg.	TD	No.	Yds.	Avg.	TD	TD	2pt.	Pts.	Fum.
1996—Tampa Bay NFL	16	16	96	377	3.9	3	65	557	8.6	3	6	0	36	4
1997—Tampa Bay NFL	15	15	176	665	3.8	7	23	178	7.7	3	10	0	60	5
1998—Tampa Bay NFL	16	16	215	846	3.9	8	22	152	6.9	1	9	0	54	5
1999—Tampa Bay NFL	16	16	242	949	3.9	7	27	239	8.9	2	9	0	54	6
2000—Tampa Bay NFL	13	13	131	465	3.5	5	13	93	7.2	0	5	0	30	3
Pro totals (5 years)	76	76	860	3302	3.8	30	150	1219	8.1	9	39	0	234	23

AMBROSE, ASHLEY   CB   FALCONS

PERSONAL: Born September 17, 1970, in New Orleans. ... 5-10/185. ... Full name: Ashley Avery Ambrose.
HIGH SCHOOL: Fortier (New Orleans).
COLLEGE: Mississippi Valley State (degree in industrial technology).
TRANSACTIONS/CAREER NOTES: Selected by Indianapolis Colts in second round (29th pick overall) of 1992 NFL draft. ... Signed by Colts (August 11, 1992). ... On injured reserve with leg injury (September 14-October 29, 1992); on practice squad (October 21-29, 1992). ... Granted free agency (February 17, 1995). ... Re-signed by Colts (April 29, 1995). ... Granted unconditional free agency (February 16, 1996). ... Signed by Cincinnati Bengals (February 25, 1996). ... Granted unconditional free agency (February 12, 1999). ... Signed by New Orleans Saints (July 13, 1999). ... Granted unconditional free agency (February 11, 2000). ... Signed by Atlanta Falcons (February 12, 2000).
CHAMPIONSHIP GAME EXPERIENCE: Played in AFC championship game (1995 season).
HONORS: Played in Pro Bowl (1996 season).
PRO STATISTICS: 1992—Returned eight kickoffs for 126 yards. 1994—Recovered one fumble. 1997—Credited with one sack and recovered two fumbles. 1999—Recovered two fumbles for 29 yards.

| | | | INTERCEPTIONS | | | |
Year Team	G	GS	No.	Yds.	Avg.	TD
1992—Indianapolis NFL	10	2	0	0	0.0	0
1993—Indianapolis NFL	14	6	0	0	0.0	0
1994—Indianapolis NFL	16	4	2	50	25.0	0
1995—Indianapolis NFL	16	0	3	12	4.0	0
1996—Cincinnati NFL	16	16	8	63	7.9	1
1997—Cincinnati NFL	16	16	3	56	18.7	0
1998—Cincinnati NFL	15	15	2	0	0.0	0
1999—New Orleans NFL	16	16	6	27	4.5	0
2000—Atlanta NFL	16	16	4	‡139	34.8	1
Pro totals (9 years)	135	91	28	347	12.4	2

ANDERS, KIMBLE   RB

PERSONAL: Born September 10, 1966, in Galveston, Texas. ... 5-11/226. ... Full name: Kimble Lynard Anders.
HIGH SCHOOL: Ball (Galveston, Texas).
COLLEGE: Houston.

TRANSACTIONS/CAREER NOTES: Signed as non-drafted free agent by Pittsburgh Steelers (April 25, 1990). ... Released by Steelers (September 3, 1990). ... Signed by Kansas City Chiefs (March 13, 1991). ... On injured reserve with hand injury (September 15, 1991-remainder of season). ... On injured reserve with knee injury (September 12-October 17, 1992); on practice squad (October 7-17, 1992). ... Granted unconditional free agency (February 16, 1996). ... Re-signed by Chiefs (April 1, 1996). ... On injured reserve with Achilles' tendon injury (September 20, 1999-remainder of season). ... Released by Chiefs (February 23, 2001).
CHAMPIONSHIP GAME EXPERIENCE: Played in AFC championship game (1993 season).
HONORS: Played in Pro Bowl (1995-1997 seasons).
PRO STATISTICS: 1994—Recovered two fumbles. 1997—Recovered one fumble. 1998—Recovered one fumble.
SINGLE GAME HIGHS (regular season): Attempts—22 (September 19, 1999, vs. Denver); yards—142 (September 19, 1999, vs. Denver); and rushing touchdowns—2 (October 22, 2000, vs. St. Louis).
STATISTICAL PLATEAUS: 100-yard rushing games: 1999 (1), 2000 (1). Total: 2.

Year Team	G	GS	RUSHING				RECEIVING				KICKOFF RETURNS				TOTALS			
			Att.	Yds.	Avg.	TD	No.	Yds.	Avg.	TD	No.	Yds.	Avg.	TD	TD	2pt.	Pts.	Fum.
1991—Kansas City NFL	2	0	0	0	0.0	0	2	30	15.0	0	0	0	0.0	0	0	0	0	0
1992—Kansas City NFL	11	2	1	1	1.0	0	5	65	13.0	0	1	20	20.0	0	0	0	0	1
1993—Kansas City NFL	16	13	75	291	3.9	0	40	326	8.2	1	1	47	47.0	0	1	0	6	1
1994—Kansas City NFL	16	13	62	231	3.7	0	67	525	7.8	1	2	36	18.0	0	3	0	18	1
1995—Kansas City NFL	16	13	58	398	6.9	2	55	349	6.3	1	0	0	0.0	0	3	0	18	1
1996—Kansas City NFL	16	15	54	201	3.7	2	60	529	8.8	2	2	37	18.5	0	4	0	24	0
1997—Kansas City NFL	15	14	79	397	5.0	0	59	453	7.7	2	1	0	0.0	0	2	0	12	3
1998—Kansas City NFL	16	15	58	230	4.0	1	64	462	7.2	2	1	16	16.0	0	3	0	18	6
1999—Kansas City NFL	2	2	32	181	5.7	0	2	14	7.0	0	0	0	0.0	0	0	0	0	1
2000—Kansas City NFL	15	7	76	331	4.4	2	15	76	5.1	0	1	14	14.0	0	2	0	12	1
Pro totals (10 years)	125	94	495	2261	4.6	9	369	2829	7.7	9	9	170	18.9	0	18	0	108	15

ANDERSEN, JASON   C   DOLPHINS

PERSONAL: Born September 3, 1975, in Hayward, Calif. ... 6-6/315. ... Full name: Jason Allen Andersen.
HIGH SCHOOL: Piedmont (Calif.).
COLLEGE: Brigham Young.
TRANSACTIONS/CAREER NOTES: Selected by New England Patriots in seventh round (211th pick overall) of 1998 NFL draft. ... Signed by Patriots (June 18, 1998). ... Active for seven games (1998); did not play. ... Released by Patriots (October 21, 2000). ... Signed by Miami Dolphins (November 14, 2000). ... Inactive for six games with Miami (2000).
PLAYING EXPERIENCE: New England NFL, 1999 and 2000. ... Games/Games started: 1999 (9/0), 2000 (7/0). Total: 16/0.

ANDERSEN, MORTEN   K

PERSONAL: Born August 19, 1960, in Copenhagen, Denmark. ... 6-2/225.
HIGH SCHOOL: Ben Davis (Indianapolis).
COLLEGE: Michigan State (degrees in communications and German).
TRANSACTIONS/CAREER NOTES: Selected by New Orleans Saints in fourth round (86th pick overall) of 1982 NFL draft. ... On injured reserve with sprained ankle (September 15-November 20, 1982). ... Designated by Saints as transition player (February 25, 1993). ... Released by Saints (July 19, 1995). ... Signed by Atlanta Falcons (July 21, 1995). ... Granted unconditional free agency (March 2, 2001).
CHAMPIONSHIP GAME EXPERIENCE: Played in NFC championship game (1998 season). ... Played in Super Bowl XXXIII (1998 season).
HONORS: Named kicker on THE SPORTING NEWS college All-America first team (1981). ... Named kicker on THE SPORTING NEWS NFL All-Pro team (1985-1987 and 1995). ... Played in Pro Bowl (1985-1988, 1990, 1992 and 1995 seasons).
RECORDS: Holds NFL career records for most consecutive games scoring—269 (December 11, 1983-present); and for most made field goals of 50 or more yards—37. ... Holds NFL single-season record for most made field goals of 50 or more yards—8 (1995). ... Holds NFL single-game record for most made field goals of 50 or more yards—3 (December 11, 1983, at Philadelphia).

Year Team	G	KICKING						
		XPM	XPA	FGM	FGA	Lg.	50+	Pts.
1982—New Orleans NFL	8	6	6	2	5	45	0-1	12
1983—New Orleans NFL	16	37	38	18	24	52	3-4	91
1984—New Orleans NFL	16	34	34	20	27	53	2-3	94
1985—New Orleans NFL	16	27	29	31	35	§55	3-4	120
1986—New Orleans NFL	16	30	30	26	30	53	2-5	108
1987—New Orleans NFL	12	37	37	*28	*36	52	2-6	121
1988—New Orleans NFL	16	32	33	26	36	51	1-4	110
1989—New Orleans NFL	16	44	45	20	29	49	0-4	104
1990—New Orleans NFL	16	29	29	21	27	52	3-4	92
1991—New Orleans NFL	16	38	38	25	32	*60	2-4	113
1992—New Orleans NFL	16	33	34	29	34	52	3-3	∞120
1993—New Orleans NFL	16	33	33	28	35	56	1-5	117
1994—New Orleans NFL	16	32	32	28	†39	48	0-6	116
1995—Atlanta NFL	16	29	30	‡31	37	*59	8-9	122
1996—Atlanta NFL	16	31	31	22	29	∞54	1-5	97
1997—Atlanta NFL	16	35	35	23	27	∞55	2-3	104
1998—Atlanta NFL	16	51	52	23	28	53	2-2	120
1999—Atlanta NFL	16	34	34	15	21	49	0-1	79
2000—Atlanta NFL	16	23	23	25	31	51	2-3	98
Pro totals (19 years)	292	615	623	441	562	60	37-76	1938

ANDERSON, GARY   K   VIKINGS

PERSONAL: Born July 16, 1959, in Parys, Orange Free State, South Africa. ... 5-11/170. ... Full name: Gary Allan Anderson. ... Son of Rev. Douglas Anderson, former professional soccer player in England.
HIGH SCHOOL: Brettonwood (Durban, South Africa).
COLLEGE: Syracuse (degree in management and accounting, 1982).

TRANSACTIONS/CAREER NOTES: Selected by Buffalo Bills in seventh round (171st pick overall) of 1982 NFL draft. ... Signed by Bills for 1982 season. ... Claimed on waivers by Pittsburgh Steelers (September 7, 1982). ... Designated by Steelers as transition player (February 15, 1994). ... On reserve/did not report list (August 23-25, 1994). ... Free agency status changed by Steelers from transition to unconditional (February 17, 1995). ... Signed by Philadelphia Eagles (July 23, 1995). ... Released by Eagles (April 22, 1997). ... Signed by San Francisco 49ers (June 11, 1997). ... Granted unconditional free agency (February 13, 1998). ... Signed by Minnesota Vikings (February 20, 1998).

CHAMPIONSHIP GAME EXPERIENCE: Played in AFC championship game (1984 and 1994 seasons). ... Played in NFC championship game (1997 and 1998 seasons). ... Member of Vikings for NFC Championship game (2000 season); did not play.

HONORS: Played in Pro Bowl (1983, 1985, 1993 and 1998 seasons). ... Named kicker on THE SPORTING NEWS NFL All-Pro team (1998).

RECORDS: Holds NFL career record for most points—2,059. ... Holds NFL career record for most field goals made—461; and most consecutive field goals made—40. ... Holds NFL single-season records for most PATs made without a miss—59 (1998); and most points scored without a touchdown—164 (1998). ... Shares NFL career record for most seasons with 100 or more points—13 (1983-85, 1988, 1991-94 and 1996-2000). ... Shares NFL single-season record for highest field-goal percentage—100.0 (1998).

POST SEASON RECORDS: Holds NFL postseason career record for most made field goals—26. ... Holds NFL postseason record for most consecutive made field goals—16 (1989-95).

PRO STATISTICS: 1994—Rushed once for three yards.

Year Team	G	XPM	XPA	FGM	FGA	Lg.	50+	Pts.
1982—Pittsburgh NFL	9	22	22	10	12	48	0-1	52
1983—Pittsburgh NFL	16	38	39	27	31	49	0-0	§119
1984—Pittsburgh NFL	16	45	45	▲24	32	55	2-3	§117
1985—Pittsburgh NFL	16	40	40	*33	*42	52	1-4	§139
1986—Pittsburgh NFL	16	32	32	21	32	45	0-3	95
1987—Pittsburgh NFL	12	21	21	22	27	52	2-2	87
1988—Pittsburgh NFL	16	34	35	28	36	52	1-2	118
1989—Pittsburgh NFL	16	28	28	21	30	49	0-0	91
1990—Pittsburgh NFL	16	32	32	20	25	48	0-2	92
1991—Pittsburgh NFL	16	31	31	23	33	54	1-6	100
1992—Pittsburgh NFL	16	29	31	28	36	49	0-2	113
1993—Pittsburgh NFL	16	32	32	28	30	46	0-0	*116
1994—Pittsburgh NFL	16	32	32	24	29	50	1-2	104
1995—Philadelphia NFL	16	32	33	22	30	43	0-3	98
1996—Philadelphia NFL	16	40	40	25	29	46	0-0	115
1997—San Francisco NFL	16	38	38	29	36	51	1-3	125
1998—Minnesota NFL	16	*59	*59	‡35	∞35	53	2-2	*164
1999—Minnesota NFL	16	46	46	19	30	44	0-2	103
2000—Minnesota NFL	16	‡45	‡45	22	23	49	0-1	111
Pro totals (19 years)	293	676	681	461	578	55	11-38	2059

ANDERSON, JAMAL   RB   FALCONS

PERSONAL: Born September 30, 1972, in Woodland Hills, Calif. ... 5-11/237. ... Full name: Jamal Sharif Anderson.

HIGH SCHOOL: El Camino Real (Woodland Hills, Calif.).

JUNIOR COLLEGE: Moorpark (Calif.) Junior College.

COLLEGE: Utah.

TRANSACTIONS/CAREER NOTES: Selected by Atlanta Falcons in seventh round (201st pick overall) of 1994 NFL draft. ... Signed by Falcons (June 21, 1994). ... On injured reserve with knee injury (September 22, 1999-remainder of season).

CHAMPIONSHIP GAME EXPERIENCE: Played in NFC championship game (1998 season). ... Played in Super Bowl XXXIII (1998 season).

HONORS: Named running back on THE SPORTING NEWS NFL All-Pro team (1998). ... Played in Pro Bowl (1998 season).

RECORDS: Holds NFL single-season record for most rushing attempts—410 (1998).

PRO STATISTICS: 1996—Recovered one fumble. 1997—Attempted four passes with one completion for 27 yards and one touchdown and an interception and recovered one fumble. 1998—Attempted two passes without a completion and recovered one fumble. 2000—Recovered one fumble.

SINGLE GAME HIGHS (regular season): Attempts—33 (December 21, 1997, vs. Arizona); yards—188 (November 29, 1998, vs. St. Louis); and rushing touchdowns—3 (October 6, 1996, vs. Detroit).

STATISTICAL PLATEAUS: 100-yard rushing games: 1996 (3), 1997 (2), 1998 (12), 2000 (2). Total: 19.

Year Team	G	GS	RUSHING Att.	Yds.	Avg.	TD	RECEIVING No.	Yds.	Avg.	TD	KICKOFF RETURNS No.	Yds.	Avg.	TD	TOTALS TD	2pt.	Pts.	Fum.
1994—Atlanta NFL	3	0	2	-1	-0.5	0	0	0	0.0	0	1	11	11.0	0	0	0	0	0
1995—Atlanta NFL	16	0	39	161	4.1	0	4	42	10.5	0	24	541	22.5	0	1	0	6	0
1996—Atlanta NFL	16	12	232	1055	4.5	5	49	473	9.7	1	4	80	20.0	0	6	0	36	4
1997—Atlanta NFL	16	15	290	1002	3.5	7	29	284	9.8	3	0	0	0.0	0	10	0	60	4
1998—Atlanta NFL	16	16	*410	‡1846	4.5	‡14	27	319	11.8	2	0	0	0.0	0	16	1	98	5
1999—Atlanta NFL	2	2	19	59	3.1	0	2	34	17.0	0	0	0	0.0	0	0	0	0	0
2000—Atlanta NFL	16	16	282	1024	3.6	6	42	382	9.1	0	0	0	0.0	0	6	1	38	6
Pro totals (7 years)	85	61	1274	5146	4.0	33	153	1534	10.0	6	29	632	21.8	0	39	2	238	19

ANDERSON, MIKE   RB   BRONCOS

PERSONAL: Born September 21, 1973, in Winnsboro, S.C. ... 6-0/230. ... Full name: Michael Moschello Anderson.

HIGH SCHOOL: Fairfield (S.C.).

JUNIOR COLLEGE: Mount San Jacinto Community College (Calif.).

COLLEGE: Utah.

TRANSACTIONS/CAREER NOTES: Selected by Denver Broncos in sixth round (189th pick overall) of 2000 NFL draft. ... Signed by Broncos (July 14, 2000).

SINGLE GAME HIGHS (regular season): Attempts—37 (December 3, 2000, vs. New Orleans); yards—251 (December 3, 2000, vs. New Orleans); and rushing touchdowns—4 (December 3, 2000, vs. New Orleans).

STATISTICAL PLATEAUS: 100-yard rushing games: 2000 (6).

Year Team	G	GS	RUSHING Att.	Yds.	Avg.	TD	RECEIVING No.	Yds.	Avg.	TD	TOTALS TD	2pt.	Pts.	Fum.
2000—Denver NFL	16	12	297	1487	§5.0	§15	23	169	7.3	0	15	▲1	92	4

ANDERSON, RASHARD   DB   PANTHERS

PERSONAL: Born June 14, 1977, in Forest, Miss. ... 6-2/204.
HIGH SCHOOL: Forest (Miss.).
COLLEGE: Jackson State.
TRANSACTIONS/CAREER NOTES: Selected by Carolina Panthers in first round (23rd pick overall) of 2000 NFL draft. ... Signed by Panthers (July 17, 2000).
PLAYING EXPERIENCE: Carolina NFL, 2000. ... Games/Games started: 2000 (12/0).

ANDERSON, RICHIE   FB   JETS

PERSONAL: Born September 13, 1971, in Sandy Spring, Md. ... 6-2/230. ... Full name: Richard Darnoll Anderson II.
HIGH SCHOOL: Sherwood (Sandy Spring, Md.).
COLLEGE: Penn State.
TRANSACTIONS/CAREER NOTES: Selected after junior season by New York Jets in sixth round (144th pick overall) of 1993 NFL draft. ... Signed by Jets (June 10, 1993). ... On injured reserve with ankle injury (December 31, 1993-remainder of season). ... On injured reserve with ankle injury (November 30, 1995-remainder of season).
CHAMPIONSHIP GAME EXPERIENCE: Member of Jets for AFC championship game (1998 season); did not play.
HONORS: Played in Pro Bowl (2000 season).
PRO STATISTICS: 1993—Recovered one fumble. 1994—Recovered one fumble. 1995—Attempted one pass without a completion. 1996—Recovered one fumble. 1997—Recovered one fumble.
SINGLE GAME HIGHS (regular season): Attempts—9 (November 13, 1994, vs. Green Bay); yards—74 (November 13, 1994, vs. Green Bay); and rushing touchdowns—1 (October 27, 1996, vs. Arizona).
STATISTICAL PLATEAUS: 100-yard receiving games: 2000 (3).

Year Team	G	GS	RUSHING Att.	Yds.	Avg.	TD	RECEIVING No.	Yds.	Avg.	TD	KICKOFF RETURNS No.	Yds.	Avg.	TD	TOTALS TD	2pt.	Pts.	Fum.
1993—New York Jets NFL......	7	0	0	0	0.0	0	0	0	0.0	0	4	66	16.5	0	0	0	0	1
1994—New York Jets NFL......	13	5	43	207	4.8	1	25	212	8.5	1	3	43	14.3	0	2	0	12	1
1995—New York Jets NFL......	10	0	5	17	3.4	0	5	26	5.2	0	0	0	0.0	0	0	0	0	2
1996—New York Jets NFL......	16	13	47	150	3.2	1	44	385	8.8	0	0	0	0.0	0	1	0	6	0
1997—New York Jets NFL......	16	3	21	70	3.3	0	26	150	5.8	1	0	0	0.0	0	1	0	6	2
1998—New York Jets NFL......	8	2	1	2	2.0	0	3	12	4.0	0	0	0	0.0	0	0	0	0	0
1999—New York Jets NFL......	16	9	16	84	5.3	0	29	302	10.4	3	0	0	0.0	0	3	0	18	0
2000—New York Jets NFL......	16	10	27	63	2.3	0	88	853	9.7	2	0	0	0.0	0	2	0	12	2
Pro totals (8 years)...............	102	42	160	593	3.7	2	220	1940	8.8	7	7	109	15.6	0	9	0	54	8

ANDERSON, WILLIE   OT   BENGALS

PERSONAL: Born July 11, 1975, in Mobile, Ala. ... 6-5/340. ... Full name: Willie Aaron Anderson.
HIGH SCHOOL: Vigor (Prichard, Ala.).
COLLEGE: Auburn.
TRANSACTIONS/CAREER NOTES: Selected after junior season by Cincinnati Bengals in first round (10th pick overall) of 1996 NFL draft. ... Signed by Bengals (August 5, 1996).
PLAYING EXPERIENCE: Cincinnati NFL, 1996-2000. ... Games/Games started: 1996 (16/10), 1997 (16/16), 1998 (16/16), 1999 (14/14), 2000 (16/16). Total: 78/72.
PRO STATISTICS: 1998—Recovered one fumble. 1999—Recovered one fumble. 2000—Recovered one fumble.

ANDRUZZI, JOE   G   PATRIOTS

PERSONAL: Born August 23, 1975, in Brooklyn, N.Y. ... 6-3/315. ... Full name: Joseph Dominick Andruzzi. ... Name pronounced ann-DROOZ-ee.
HIGH SCHOOL: Tottenville (Staten Island, N.Y.).
COLLEGE: Southern Connecticut State.
TRANSACTIONS/CAREER NOTES: Signed as non-drafted free agent by Green Bay Packers (April 25, 1997). ... Inactive for all 16 games (1997). ... Assigned by Packers to Scottish Claymores in 1998 NFL Europe enhancement allocation program (February 18, 1998). ... On injured reserve with knee injury (November 23, 1999-remainder of season). ... Released by Packers (August 27, 2000). ... Signed by New England Patriots (September 9, 2000). ... On injured reserve with knee injury (December 7, 2000-remainder of season).
PLAYING EXPERIENCE: Scottish NFLE, 1998; Green Bay NFL, 1998 and 1999; New England NFL, 2000. ... Games/Games started: NFLE 1998 (10/10), NFL 1998 (15/1), 1999 (8/3), 2000 (11/11). Total NFLE: 10/10. Total NFL: 34/15. Total Pro: 44/24.
CHAMPIONSHIP GAME EXPERIENCE: Member of Packers for NFC championship game (1997 season); inactive. ... Member of Packers for Super Bowl XXXII (1997 season); inactive.
PRO STATISTICS: NFL: 1998—Recovered one fumble. 2000—Recovered one fumble for two yards.

ANTHONY, REIDEL   WR   BUCCANEERS

PERSONAL: Born October 20, 1976, in South Bay, Fla. ... 5-11/180. ... Full name: Reidel Clarence Anthony. ... Name pronounced REE-dell.
HIGH SCHOOL: Glades Central (Belle Glade, Fla.).
COLLEGE: Florida.
TRANSACTIONS/CAREER NOTES: Selected after junior season by Tampa Bay Buccaneers in first round (16th pick overall) of 1997 NFL draft. ... Signed by Buccaneers (July 20, 1997).
CHAMPIONSHIP GAME EXPERIENCE: Member of Buccaneers for NFC championship game (1999 season); inactive.
HONORS: Named wide receiver on THE SPORTING NEWS college All-America first team (1996).
PRO STATISTICS: 1998—Recovered one fumble.

SINGLE GAME HIGHS (regular season): Receptions—7 (October 3, 1999, vs. Minnesota); yards—126 (November 15, 1998, vs. Jacksonville); and touchdown receptions—2 (November 15, 1998, vs. Jacksonville).
STATISTICAL PLATEAUS: 100-yard receiving games: 1998 (1).

			RUSHING				RECEIVING				KICKOFF RETURNS				TOTALS			
Year Team	G	GS	Att.	Yds.	Avg.	TD	No.	Yds.	Avg.	TD	No.	Yds.	Avg.	TD	TD	2pt.	Pts.	Fum.
1997—Tampa Bay NFL..........	16	12	5	84	16.8	0	35	448	12.8	4	25	592	23.7	0	4	0	24	0
1998—Tampa Bay NFL..........	15	13	4	43	10.8	0	51	708	13.9	7	46	1118	24.3	0	7	1	44	0
1999—Tampa Bay NFL..........	13	7	1	2	2.0	0	30	296	9.9	1	21	434	20.7	0	1	0	6	1
2000—Tampa Bay NFL..........	16	1	0	0	0.0	0	15	232	15.5	4	3	88	29.3	0	4	0	24	0
Pro totals (4 years)...............	60	33	10	129	12.9	0	131	1684	12.9	16	95	2232	23.5	0	16	1	98	1

A

ARCHAMBEAU, LESTER   DE

PERSONAL: Born June 27, 1967, in Montville, N.J. ... 6-5/275. ... Full name: Lester Milward Archambeau. ... Name pronounced ar-sham-bow.
HIGH SCHOOL: Montville (N.J.).
COLLEGE: Stanford (degree in industrial engineering).
TRANSACTIONS/CAREER NOTES: Selected by Green Bay Packers in seventh round (186th pick overall) of 1990 NFL draft. ... Signed by Packers (July 22, 1990). ... On injured reserve with back injury (October 6, 1990-remainder of season). ... Granted free agency (February 1, 1992). ... Re-signed by Packers (August 12, 1992). ... Traded by Packers to Atlanta Falcons for WR James Milling (June 3, 1993). ... Granted unconditional free agency (February 17, 1994). ... Re-signed by Falcons (March 7, 1994). ... Granted unconditional free agency (February 14, 1997). ... Re-signed by Falcons (March 3, 1997). ... Granted unconditional free agency (February 11, 2000). ... Signed by Denver Broncos (February 23, 2000). ... Released by Broncos (June 4, 2001).
CHAMPIONSHIP GAME EXPERIENCE: Played in NFC championship game (1998 season). ... Played in Super Bowl XXXIII (1998 season).
PRO STATISTICS: 1995—Recovered one fumble. 1997—Intercepted one pass for no yards and recovered three fumbles. 1998—Recovered two fumbles.

Year Team	G	GS	SACKS
1990—Green Bay NFL..............	4	0	0.0
1991—Green Bay NFL..............	16	0	4.5
1992—Green Bay NFL..............	16	0	1.0
1993—Atlanta NFL..............	15	11	0.0
1994—Atlanta NFL..............	16	12	2.0
1995—Atlanta NFL..............	16	7	3.0
1996—Atlanta NFL..............	15	15	2.0
1997—Atlanta NFL..............	16	16	8.5
1998—Atlanta NFL..............	15	15	10.0
1999—Atlanta NFL..............	15	15	5.5
2000—Denver NFL..............	3	0	0.0
Pro totals (11 years)...............	147	91	36.5

ARMOUR, JOJUAN   S   BENGALS

PERSONAL: Born July 10, 1976, in Toledo, Ohio. ... 5-11/220. ... Name pronounced JOE-wan.
HIGH SCHOOL: Central Catholic (Cleveland).
COLLEGE: Miami of Ohio.
TRANSACTIONS/CAREER NOTES: Selected by Oakland Raiders in seventh round (224th pick overall) of 1999 NFL draft. ... Signed by Raiders (July 24, 1999). ... Claimed on waivers by Jacksonville Jaguars (September 7, 1999). ... Inactive for two games with Jaguars (1999). ... Claimed on waivers by Cincinnati Bengals (September 21, 1999). ... Released by Bengals (October 15, 1999). ... Re-signed by Bengals to practice squad (October 16, 1999). ... Activated (December 16, 1999). ... Released by Bengals (August 27, 2000). ... Re-signed by Bengals to practice squad (August 28, 2000). ... Activated (October 2, 2000). ... Assigned by Bengals to Barcelona Dragons in 2001 NFL Europe enhancement allocation program (February 19, 2001).
PLAYING EXPERIENCE: Cincinnati NFL, 1999 and 2000. ... Games/Games started: 1999 (2/0), 2000 (4/0). Total: 6/0.
HONORS: Named outside linebacker on THE SPORTING NEWS college All-America second team (1997).

ARMOUR, PHILLIP   C   COLTS

PERSONAL: Born December 9, 1976, in Denton, Texas ... 6-3/318.
HIGH SCHOOL: Ryan (Denton, Texas).
COLLEGE: North Texas State.
TRANSACTIONS/CAREER NOTES: Signed as non-drafted free agent by Indianapolis Colts (April 22, 1999). ... On injured reserve with foot injury (August 3, 1999-entire season).
PLAYING EXPERIENCE: Indianapolis NFL, 2000. ... Games/Games started: 2000 (3/0).

ARMSTEAD, JESSIE   LB   GIANTS

PERSONAL: Born October 26, 1970, in Dallas. ... 6-1/240. ... Full name: Jessie W. Armstead.
HIGH SCHOOL: David W. Carter (Dallas).
COLLEGE: Miami, Fla. (degree in criminal justice, 1992).
TRANSACTIONS/CAREER NOTES: Selected by New York Giants in eighth round (207th pick overall) of 1993 NFL draft. ... Signed by Giants (July 19, 1993).
CHAMPIONSHIP GAME EXPERIENCE: Played in NFC championship game (2000 season). ... Played in Super Bowl XXXV (2000 season).
HONORS: Named outside linebacker on THE SPORTING NEWS NFL All-Pro team (1997). ... Played in Pro Bowl (1997-2000 seasons).
PRO STATISTICS: 1995—Recovered one fumble. 1996—Fumbled once and recovered two fumbles. 1997—Recovered one fumble. 2000—Recovered one fumble.

A

Year Team	G	GS	INTERCEPTIONS No.	Yds.	Avg.	TD	SACKS No.
1993—New York Giants NFL	16	0	1	0	0.0	0	0.0
1994—New York Giants NFL	16	0	1	0	0.0	0	3.0
1995—New York Giants NFL	16	2	1	58	58.0	1	0.5
1996—New York Giants NFL	16	16	2	23	11.5	0	3.0
1997—New York Giants NFL	16	16	2	57	28.5	1	3.5
1998—New York Giants NFL	16	16	2	4	2.0	0	5.0
1999—New York Giants NFL	16	16	2	35	17.5	0	9.0
2000—New York Giants NFL	16	16	1	-2	-2.0	0	5.0
Pro totals (8 years)	128	82	12	175	14.6	2	29.0

ARMSTRONG, BRUCE　　　OT

PERSONAL: Born September 7, 1965, in Miami. ... 6-4/295. ... Full name: Bruce Charles Armstrong.
HIGH SCHOOL: Miami Central.
COLLEGE: Louisville.
TRANSACTIONS/CAREER NOTES: Selected by New England Patriots in first round (23rd pick overall) of 1987 NFL draft. ... Signed by Patriots (July 23, 1987). ... On injured reserve with knee injury (November 2, 1992-remainder of season). ... On physically unable to perform list with knee injury (July 16-27, 1993). ... Granted unconditional free agency (February 13, 1998). ... Re-signed by Patriots (February 13, 1998). ... Released by Patriots (February 10, 2000). ... Re-signed by Patriots (July 16, 2000). ... Granted unconditional free agency (March 2, 2001).
PLAYING EXPERIENCE: New England NFL, 1987-2000. ... Games: 1987 (12/12), 1988 (16/16), 1989 (16/16), 1990 (16/16), 1991 (16/16), 1992 (8/8), 1993 (16/16), 1994 (16/16), 1995 (16/16), 1996 (16/16), 1997 (16/16), 1998 (16/16), 1999 (16/16), 2000 (16/16). Total: 212/212.
CHAMPIONSHIP GAME EXPERIENCE: Played in AFC championship game (1996 season). ... Played in Super Bowl XXXI (1996 season).
HONORS: Named offensive tackle on THE SPORTING NEWS NFL All-Pro team (1988). ... Played in Pro Bowl (1990, 1991 and 1994-1997 seasons).
PRO STATISTICS: 1990—Recovered two fumbles for four yards. 1992—Recovered one fumble. 1993—Recovered one fumble for one yard. 1995—Recovered one fumble. 1998—Recovered three fumbles. 1999—Recovered one fumble.

ARMSTRONG, TRACE　　　DE　　　RAIDERS

PERSONAL: Born October 5, 1965, in Bethesda, Md. ... 6-4/270. ... Full name: Raymond Lester Armstrong.
HIGH SCHOOL: John Carroll (Birmingham, Ala.).
COLLEGE: Arizona State, then Florida (degree in psychology, 1989).
TRANSACTIONS/CAREER NOTES: Selected by Chicago Bears in first round (12th pick overall) of 1989 NFL draft. ... Signed by Bears (August 18, 1989). ... On injured reserve with knee injury (September 24-November 3, 1991). ... Granted free agency (March 1, 1993). ... Re-signed by Bears (March 14, 1993). ... Traded by Bears to Miami Dolphins for second- (P Todd Sauerbrun) and third-round (G Evan Pilgrim) picks in 1995 draft (April 4, 1995). ... Granted unconditional free agency (March 2, 2001). ... Signed by Oakland Raiders (March 5, 2001).
HONORS: Named defensive lineman on THE SPORTING NEWS college All-America first team (1988). ... Played in Pro Bowl (2000 season).
PRO STATISTICS: 1989—Recovered one fumble. 1990—Recovered two fumbles. 1992—Recovered one fumble. 1993—Recovered three fumbles for three yards. 1995—Recovered one fumble. 1996—Recovered two fumbles. 1997—Recovered three fumbles. 1998—Recovered one fumble for two yards.

Year Team	G	GS	SACKS
1989—Chicago NFL	15	14	5.0
1990—Chicago NFL	16	16	10.0
1991—Chicago NFL	12	12	1.5
1992—Chicago NFL	14	14	6.5
1993—Chicago NFL	16	16	11.5
1994—Chicago NFL	15	15	7.5
1995—Miami NFL	15	0	4.5
1996—Miami NFL	16	9	12.0
1997—Miami NFL	16	16	5.5
1998—Miami NFL	16	0	10.5
1999—Miami NFL	16	2	7.5
2000—Miami NFL	16	0	§16.5
Pro totals (12 years)	183	114	98.5

ARRINGTON, LaVAR　　　LB　　　REDSKINS

PERSONAL: Born June 20, 1978, in Pittsburgh. ... 6-3/250. ... Full name: LaVar RaShad Arrington.
HIGH SCHOOL: North Hills (Pittsburgh).
COLLEGE: Penn State.
TRANSACTIONS/CAREER NOTES: Selected after junior season by Washington Redskins in first round (second pick overall) of 2000 NFL draft. ... Signed by Redskins (July 22, 2000).
HONORS: Named linebacker on THE SPORTING NEWS college All-America first team (1998 and 1999). ... Butkus Award winner (1999). ... Chuck Bednarik Award winner (1999).
PRO STATISTICS: 2000—Returned one kickoff for 39 yards.

Year Team	G	GS	INTERCEPTIONS No.	Yds.	Avg.	TD	SACKS No.
2000—Washington NFL	16	11	0	0	0.0	0	4.0

ASHMORE, DARRYL　　　G/OT　　　RAIDERS

PERSONAL: Born November 1, 1969, in Peoria, Ill. ... 6-7/310. ... Full name: Darryl Allan Ashmore.
HIGH SCHOOL: Peoria (Ill.) Central.
COLLEGE: Northwestern (degree in business).

TRANSACTIONS/CAREER NOTES: Selected by Los Angeles Rams in seventh round (171st pick overall) of 1992 NFL draft. ... Signed by Rams (July 13, 1992). ... On injured reserve with knee injury (September 3-October 7, 1992). ... On practice squad (October 7, 1992-remainder of season). ... Granted free agency (February 17, 1995). ... Rams franchise moved to St. Louis (April 12, 1995). ... Re-signed by Rams (July 20, 1995). ... Released by Rams (October 14, 1996). ... Signed by Washington Redskins (October 26, 1996). ... Granted unconditional free agency (February 14, 1997). ... Re-signed by Redskins (May 9, 1997). ... Granted unconditional free agency (February 13, 1998). ... Signed by Oakland Raiders (April 25, 1998). ... Granted unconditional free agency (February 11, 2000). ... Re-signed by Raiders (February 22, 2000).
PLAYING EXPERIENCE: Los Angeles Rams NFL, 1993 and 1994; St. Louis NFL, 1995; St. Louis (6)-Washington (5) NFL, 1996; Washington NFL, 1997; Oakland NFL, 1998-2000. ... Games/Games started: 1993 (9/7), 1994 (11/3), 1995 (16/15), 1996 (St.L-6/0; Wash.-5/0; Total: 11/0), 1997 (11/2), 1998 (15/4), 1999 (16/2), 2000 (16/0). Total: 105/33.
CHAMPIONSHIP GAME EXPERIENCE: Played in AFC championship game (2000 season).
PRO STATISTICS: 1998—Recovered one fumble for one yard and a touchdown. 1999—Returned one kickoff for no yards.

ATKINS, COREY LB FALCONS

PERSONAL: Born November 11, 1976, in Greenville, S.C. ... 6-0/232.
HIGH SCHOOL: Southside (Greenville, S.C.).
COLLEGE: Southern California.
TRANSACTIONS/CAREER NOTES: Signed as non-drafted free agent by Dallas Cowboys (April 17, 2000). ... Released by Cowboys (August 27, 2000). ... Signed by Atlanta Falcons to practice squad (August 30, 2000). ... Activated (September 19, 2000).
PLAYING EXPERIENCE: Atlanta NFL, 2000. ... Games/Games started: 2000 (12/0).

ATKINS, JAMES OT LIONS

PERSONAL: Born January 28, 1970, in Amite, La. ... 6-6/306.
HIGH SCHOOL: Woodland (Amite, La.).
COLLEGE: Southwestern Louisiana.
TRANSACTIONS/CAREER NOTES: Signed as non-drafted free agent by Houston Oilers (May 26, 1993). ... Released by Oilers (August 31, 1993). ... Signed by Seattle Seahawks to practice squad (October 11, 1993). ... Released by Seahawks (February 27, 1998). ... Signed by Baltimore Ravens (March 25, 1998). ... Granted unconditional free agency (February 11, 2000). ... Signed by Detroit Lions (August 5, 2000). ... Released by Lions (December 22, 2000). ... Re-signed by Lions (April 19, 2001).
PLAYING EXPERIENCE: Seattle NFL, 1994-1997; Baltimore NFL, 1998 and 1999; Detroit NFL, 2000. ... Games/Games started: 1994 (4/2), 1995 (16/16), 1996 (16/16), 1997 (13/3), 1998 (9/6), 1999 (2/1), 2000 (2/1). Total: 62/45.
PRO STATISTICS: 1995—Recovered one fumble. 1996—Recovered two fumbles. 1997—Recovered one fumble. 1998—Caught one pass for no yards.

ATKINS, LARRY LB CHIEFS

PERSONAL: Born July 21, 1975, in Santa Monica, Calif. ... 6-3/225. ... Full name: Larry Tabay Atkins III.
HIGH SCHOOL: Venice (Los Angeles).
COLLEGE: UCLA.
TRANSACTIONS/CAREER NOTES: Selected by Kansas City Chiefs in third round (84th pick overall) of 1999 NFL draft. ... Signed by Chiefs (July 15, 1999).
PLAYING EXPERIENCE: Kansas City NFL, 1999 and 2000. ... Games/Games started: 1999 (9/0), 2000 (15/0). Total: 24/0.
HONORS: Named free safety on THE SPORTING NEWS college All-America second team (1998).
PRO STATISTICS: 2000—Recovered one fumble.

AUSTIN, BILLY DB COLTS

PERSONAL: Born March 8, 1975, in Washington, D.C. ... 5-10/195.
HIGH SCHOOL: Kempner (Sugar Land, Texas).
COLLEGE: New Mexico.
TRANSACTIONS/CAREER NOTES: Signed as non-drafted free agent by St. Louis Rams (April 20, 1998). ... Released by Rams (July 8, 1998). ... Re-signed by Rams (July 21, 1998). ... Released by Rams (August 24, 1998). ... Signed by Indianapolis Colts to practice squad (September 9, 1998). ... Activated (December 16, 1998).
PLAYING EXPERIENCE: Indianapolis NFL, 1998-2000. ... Games/Games started: 1998 (1/0), 1999 (16/0), 2000 (16/0). Total: 33/0.
PRO STATISTICS: 1999—Returned one kickoff for no yards and recovered one fumble.

AUTRY, DARNELL RB EAGLES

PERSONAL: Born June 19, 1976, in Weisbaden, West Germany ... 5-10/210. ... Full name: Harrington Darnell Autry.
HIGH SCHOOL: Tempe (Ariz.).
COLLEGE: Northwestern.
TRANSACTIONS/CAREER NOTES: Selected after junior season by Chicago Bears in fourth round (105th pick overall) of 1997 NFL draft. ... Signed by Bears (July 14, 1997). ... Released by Bears (August 24, 1998). ... Signed by Philadelphia Eagles (September 9, 1998). ... Announced retirement (October 5, 1998). ... Reinstated to active roster by Eagles (February 23, 1999).
HONORS: Named running back on THE SPORTING NEWS college All-America second team (1995 and 1996).
PRO STATISTICS: 2000—Recovered one fumble.
SINGLE GAME HIGHS (regular season): Attempts—26 (December 14, 1997, vs. St. Louis); yards—65 (November 5, 2000, vs. Dallas); and rushing touchdowns—1 (December 10, 2000, vs. Cleveland).

Year Team	G	GS	RUSHING				RECEIVING				TOTALS			
			Att.	Yds.	Avg.	TD	No.	Yds.	Avg.	TD	TD	2pt.	Pts.	Fum.
1997—Chicago NFL	13	3	112	319	2.8	1	9	59	6.6	0	1	1	8	2
1998—							Did not play.							
1999—							Did not play.							
2000—Philadelphia NFL	11	7	112	334	3.0	3	24	275	11.5	1	4	0	24	2
Pro totals (2 years)	24	10	224	653	2.9	4	33	334	10.1	1	5	1	32	4

AYANBADEJO, OBAFEMI   FB   RAVENS

PERSONAL: Born March 5, 1975, in Chicago. ... 6-2/235. ... Name pronounced oh-BUH-fem-me eye-an-buh-DAY-ho.
HIGH SCHOOL: Santa Cruz (Calif.).
JUNIOR COLLEGE: Cabrillo College (Calif.).
COLLEGE: San Diego State.
TRANSACTIONS/CAREER NOTES: Signed as non-drafted free agent by Minnesota Vikings (April 25, 1997). ... Released by Vikings (August 18, 1997). ... Re-signed by Vikings (February 6, 1998). ... Assigned by Vikings to England Monarchs in 1998 NFL Europe enhancement allocation program (February 17, 1998). ... Released by Vikings (August 24, 1998). ... Re-signed by Vikings to practice squad (August 31, 1998). ... Activated (December 1, 1998). ... Released by Vikings (December 23, 1998). ... Re-signed by Vikings to practice squad (December 24, 1998). ... Released by Vikings (September 21, 1999). ... Signed by Baltimore Ravens (September 27, 1999). ... On injured reserve with toe injury (November 28, 2000-remainder of season).
PLAYING EXPERIENCE: England Monarchs NFLE, 1998; Minnesota NFL, 1998; Minnesota (2)-Baltimore (12) NFL, 1999; Baltimore NFL, 2000. ... Games/Games started: NFLE 1998 (games played unavailable), NFL 1998 (1/0), 1999 (Min.-2/0; Balt.-12/0; Total: 14/0), 2000 (8/4). Total NFL: 23/4.
PRO STATISTICS: NFLE: 1998—Caught two passes for 28 yards. NFL: 1999—Caught one pass for two yards. 2000—Rushed 15 times for 37 yards and a touchdown and caught 23 passes for 168 yards.
SINGLE GAME HIGHS (regular season): Attempts—4 (September 24, 2000, vs. Cincinnati); yards—9 (September 24, 2000, vs. Cincinnati); and rushing touchdowns—1 (September 24, 2000, vs. Cincinnati).

AZUMAH, JERRY   CB   BEARS

PERSONAL: Born September 1, 1977, in Worcester, Mass. ... 5-10/195. ... Name pronounced ah-ZOO-muh.
HIGH SCHOOL: St. Peter-Marian (Worcester, Mass.).
COLLEGE: New Hampshire.
TRANSACTIONS/CAREER NOTES: Selected by Chicago Bears in fifth round (147th pick overall) of 1999 NFL draft. ... Signed by Bears (June 8, 1999).
PLAYING EXPERIENCE: Chicago NFL, 1999 and 2000. ... Games/Games started: 1999 (16/2), 2000 (14/4). Total: 30/6.
HONORS: Walter Payton Award winner (1998).
PRO STATISTICS: 2000—Intercepted one pass for two yards.

BADGER, BRAD   OT   VIKINGS

PERSONAL: Born January 11, 1975, in Corvallis, Ore. ... 6-4/319.
HIGH SCHOOL: Corvallis (Ore.).
COLLEGE: Stanford.
TRANSACTIONS/CAREER NOTES: Selected by Washington Redskins in fifth round (162nd pick overall) of 1997 NFL draft. ... Signed by Redskins (May 5, 1997). ... Granted free agency (February 11, 2000). ... Tendered offer sheet by Minnesota Vikings (April 10, 2000). ... Redskins declined to match offer (April 11, 2000).
PLAYING EXPERIENCE: Washington NFL, 1997-1999; Minnesota NFL, 2000. ... Games/Games started: 1997 (12/2), 1998 (16/16), 1999 (14/4), 2000 (16/0). Total: 58/22.
CHAMPIONSHIP GAME EXPERIENCE: Member of Vikings for NFC Championship game (2000 season); did not play.
PRO STATISTICS: 2000—Recovered one fumble.

BAILEY, CHAMP   CB   REDSKINS

PERSONAL: Born June 22, 1978 ... 6-1/184. ... Full name: Roland Champ Bailey.
HIGH SCHOOL: Charlton County (Folkson, Ga.).
COLLEGE: Georgia.
TRANSACTIONS/CAREER NOTES: Selected after junior season by Washington Redskins in first round (seventh pick overall) of 1999 NFL draft. ... Signed by Redskins (July 24, 1999).
HONORS: Named cornerback on THE SPORTING NEWS college All-America second team (1998). ... Played in Pro Bowl (2000 season).
PRO STATISTICS: 2000—Rushed once for seven yards and one touchdown, caught three passes for 78 yards and returned one punt for 65 yards.

Year Team	G	GS	INTERCEPTIONS				SACKS
			No.	Yds.	Avg.	TD	No.
1999—Washington NFL	16	16	5	55	11.0	1	1.0
2000—Washington NFL	16	16	5	48	9.6	0	0.0
Pro totals (2 years)	32	32	10	103	10.3	1	1.0

BAILEY, KARSTEN   WR   SEAHAWKS

PERSONAL: Born April 26, 1977, in Newnan, Ga. ... 5-10/201. ... Full name: Karsten Mario Bailey.
HIGH SCHOOL: East Coweta (Sharpsburg, Ga.).
COLLEGE: Auburn.

TRANSACTIONS/CAREER NOTES: Selected by Seattle Seahawks in third round (82nd pick overall) of 1999 NFL draft. ... Signed by Seahawks (July 29, 1999).
PLAYING EXPERIENCE: Seattle NFL, 1999 and 2000. ... Games/Games started: 1999 (2/0), 2000 (9/0). Total: 11/0.
PRO STATISTICS: 2000—Caught six passes for 62 yards and a touchdown.
SINGLE GAME HIGHS (regular season): Receptions—2 (December 23, 2000, vs. Buffalo); yards—34 (December 23, 2000, vs. Buffalo); and touchdown receptions—1 (October 15, 2000, vs. Indianapolis).

BAILEY, ROBERT — CB — LIONS

PERSONAL: Born September 3, 1968, in Barbados. ... 5-10/182. ... Full name: Robert Martin Luther Bailey.
HIGH SCHOOL: Miami Southridge Senior.
COLLEGE: Miami, Fla. (degree in science).
TRANSACTIONS/CAREER NOTES: Selected by Los Angeles Rams in fourth round (107th pick overall) of 1991 NFL draft. ... Signed by Rams (July 17, 1991). ... On injured reserve with broken hand (August 27-October 11, 1991). ... On injured reserve with finger injury (November 19, 1991-remainder of season). ... On injured reserve with knee injury (December 11, 1993-remainder of season). ... Granted free agency (February 17, 1994). ... Re-signed by Rams (June 10, 1994). ... Released by Rams (August 22, 1995). ... Signed by Washington Redskins (September 11, 1995). ... Released by Redskins (October 17, 1995). ... Signed by Dallas Cowboys (October 19, 1995). ... Granted unconditional free agency (February 16, 1996). ... Signed by Miami Dolphins (March 7, 1996). ... Released by Dolphins (March 20, 1997). ... Signed by Detroit Lions (April 24, 1997). ... Released by Lions (June 20, 1997). ... Re-signed by Lions (July 22, 1997). ... Granted unconditional free agency (February 13, 1998). ... Re-signed by Lions (March 6, 1998). ... Granted unconditional free agency (February 11, 2000). ... Signed by Baltimore Ravens (March 16, 2000). ... Released by Ravens (March 13, 2001). ... Signed by Lions (May 17, 2001).
CHAMPIONSHIP GAME EXPERIENCE: Played in NFC championship game (1995 season). ... Member of Super Bowl championship team (1995 and 2000 seasons). ... Played in AFC championship game (2000 season).
RECORDS: Holds NFL record for longest punt return—103 yards, touchdown (October 23, 1994, at New Orleans).
PRO STATISTICS: 1994—Returned one punt for 103 yards and a touchdown and recovered one fumble. 1996—Credited with one sack. 1997—Credited with two sacks. 1999—Credited with two sacks. 2000—Recovered one fumbles for 27 yards.

| | | | INTERCEPTIONS | | | |
Year Team	G	GS	No.	Yds.	Avg.	TD
1991—Los Angeles Rams NFL	6	0	0	0	0.0	0
1992—Los Angeles Rams NFL	16	6	3	61	20.3	1
1993—Los Angeles Rams NFL	9	3	2	41	20.5	0
1994—Los Angeles Rams NFL	16	2	0	0	0.0	0
1995—Washington NFL	4	0	0	0	0.0	0
—Dallas NFL	9	0	0	0	0.0	0
1996—Miami NFL	14	0	0	0	0.0	0
1997—Detroit NFL	15	0	1	0	0.0	0
1998—Detroit NFL	16	0	0	0	0.0	0
1999—Detroit NFL	16	11	2	39	19.5	0
2000—Baltimore NFL	16	0	0	0	0.0	0
Pro totals (10 years)	137	22	8	141	17.6	1

BAKER, EUGENE — WR — FALCONS

PERSONAL: Born March 18, 1976, in Monroeville, Pa. ... 6-0/170.
HIGH SCHOOL: Shady Side Academy (Monroeville, Pa.).
COLLEGE: Kent.
TRANSACTIONS/CAREER NOTES: Selected by Atlanta Falcons in fifth round (164th pick overall) of 1999 NFL draft. ... Signed by Falcons (July 7, 1999). ... Released by Falcons (September 5, 1999). ... Re-signed by Falcons to practice squad (September 7, 1999). ... Activated (December 13, 1999).
PLAYING EXPERIENCE: Atlanta NFL, 1999 and 2000. ... Games/Games started: 1999 (3/1), 2000 (12/0). Total: 15/1.
PRO STATISTICS: 1999—Caught seven passes for 118 yards.
SINGLE GAME HIGHS (regular season): Receptions—5 (December 19, 1999, vs. Tennessee); yards—66 (December 19, 1999, vs. Tennessee); and touchdown receptions—0.

BAKER, JOHN — P — RAMS

PERSONAL: Born April 22, 1977, in Brenham, Texas. ... 6-3/223.
HIGH SCHOOL: Brenham (Texas).
JUNIOR COLLEGE: Blinn College (Texas).
COLLEGE: North Texas State.
TRANSACTIONS/CAREER NOTES: Signed as non-drafted free agent by Indianapolis Colts (April 16, 2000). ... Traded by Colts to St. Louis Rams for undisclosed draft pick (August 22, 2000).

| | | | | PUNTING | | |
Year Team	G	No.	Yds.	Avg.	Net avg.	In. 20	Blk.
2000—St. Louis NFL	15	43	1736	40.4	34.2	13	1

BANIEWICZ, MARK — OT — JAGUARS

PERSONAL: Born March 24, 1977, in Fairport, N.Y. ... 6-6/304. ... Full name: Mark Jeffrey Baniewicz. ... Name pronounced BAN-uh-wits.
HIGH SCHOOL: Penfield (Fairport, N.Y.).
COLLEGE: Syracuse (degree in finance, 1999).
TRANSACTIONS/CAREER NOTES: Selected by Jacksonville Jaguars in seventh round (247th pick overall) of 2000 NFL draft. ... Signed by Jaguars (May 24, 2000). ... Active for four games (2000); did not play. ... On injured reserve with knee injury (November 14, 2000-remainder of season).

BANKS, ANTONIO   CB   VIKINGS

PERSONAL: Born March 12, 1973, in Ivor, Va. ... 5-10/195. ... Full name: Antonio Dontral Banks.
HIGH SCHOOL: Warwick (Newport News, Va.).
COLLEGE: Virginia Tech.
TRANSACTIONS/CAREER NOTES: Selected by Minnesota Vikings in fourth round (113th pick overall) of 1997 NFL draft. ... Signed by Vikings (June 9, 1997). ... On injured reserve with foot injury (August 18, 1997-entire season). ... Assigned by Vikings to Amsterdam Admirals in 1998 NFL Europe enhancement allocation program (February 18, 1998). ... Released by Vikings (August 30, 1998). ... Signed by Winnipeg Blue Bombers of CFL (September 24, 1998). ... Released by Blue Bombers (October 21, 1998). ... Signed by Vikings to practice squad (November 10, 1998). ... Activated (December 3, 1998). ... Released by Vikings (September 21, 1999). ... Re-signed by Vikings (November 24, 1999). ... Assigned by Vikings to Amsterdam Admirals in 2000 NFL Europe enhancement allocation program (February 18, 2000).
PLAYING EXPERIENCE: Amsterdam Admirals NFLE, 1998 and 2000; Winnipeg Blue Bombers CFL, 1998; Minnesota NFL, 1998-2000. ... Games/Games started: NFLE 1998 (games played unavailable), CFL 1998 (4/-games started unavailable), NFL 1998 (4/0), 1999 (6/1), NFLE 2000 (-), NFL 2000 (14/0). Total NFL: 24/1.
CHAMPIONSHIP GAME EXPERIENCE: Played in NFC championship game (1998 and 2000 seasons).
PRO STATISTICS: NFLE: 1998—Credited with three sacks. CFL: 1998—Intercepted one pass and recovered one fumble for seven yards and a touchdown. NFL: 1999—Recovered one fumble. NFLE: 2000—Intercepted two passes for 29 yards.

BANKS, CHRIS   G   FALCONS

PERSONAL: Born April 4, 1973, in Lexington, Mo. ... 6-1/315. ... Full name: Warren Christopher Banks.
HIGH SCHOOL: Lexington (Mo.).
COLLEGE: Kansas.
TRANSACTIONS/CAREER NOTES: Selected by Denver Broncos in seventh round (226th pick overall) of 1996 NFL draft. ... Signed by Broncos (July 16, 1996). ... On injured reserve with knee injury (August 25-September 6, 1996). ... Released by Broncos (September 6, 1996). ... Re-signed by Broncos (January 29, 1997). ... Assigned by Broncos to Barcelona Dragons in 1997 World League enhancement allocation program (February 19, 1997). ... Released by Broncos (August 24, 1997). ... Re-signed by Broncos to practice squad (August 25, 1997). ... Released by Broncos (January 26, 1998). ... Re-signed by Broncos to practice squad (January 30, 1998). ... Claimed on waivers by Atlanta Falcons (August 28, 2000).
PLAYING EXPERIENCE: Barcelona W.L., 1997; Denver NFL, 1998 and 1999; Atlanta NFL, 2000. ... Games/Games started: W.L. 1997 (games played unavailable), 1998 (4/0), 1999 (16/1), 2000 (8/4). Total NFL: 28/5.
CHAMPIONSHIP GAME EXPERIENCE: Member of Broncos for AFC championship game (1998 season); inactive. ... Member of Super Bowl championship team (1998 season); inactive.

BANKS, TONY   QB   COWBOYS

PERSONAL: Born April 5, 1973, in San Diego. ... 6-4/225. ... Full name: Anthony Lamar Banks. ... Cousin of Chip Banks, linebacker with Cleveland Browns (1982-86), San Diego Chargers (1987) and Indianapolis Colts (1989-92).
HIGH SCHOOL: Herbert Hoover (San Diego).
JUNIOR COLLEGE: San Diego Mesa College.
COLLEGE: Michigan State.
TRANSACTIONS/CAREER NOTES: Selected by St. Louis Rams in second round (42nd pick overall) of 1996 NFL draft. ... Signed by Rams (July 15, 1996). ... On injured reserve list with knee injury (December 14, 1998-remainder of season). ... Granted free agency (February 12, 1999). ... Re-signed by Rams (April 17, 1999). ... Traded by Rams to Baltimore Ravens for fifth-round pick (G Cameron Spikes) in 1999 draft and seventh-round pick (traded to Chicago) in 2000 draft (April 17, 1999). ... Granted unconditional free agency (February 11, 2000). ... Re-signed by Ravens (February 17, 2000). ... Released by Ravens (March 1, 2001). ... Signed by Dallas Cowboys (March 28, 2001).
CHAMPIONSHIP GAME EXPERIENCE: Member of Ravens for AFC championship game (2000 season); did not play. ... Member of Super Bowl championship team (2000 season).
RECORDS: Holds NFL single-season record for most fumbles—21 (1996).
PRO STATISTICS: 1996—Led league with 21 fumbles and recovered four fumbles for minus 17 yards. 1997—Tied for NFC lead with 15 fumbles and recovered three fumbles for minus 27 yards. 1998—Fumbled 10 times and recovered eight fumbles for minus 23 yards. 1999—Fumbled 11 times and recovered two fumbles. 2000—Fumbled five times and recovered two fumbles for minus two yards.
SINGLE GAME HIGHS (regular season): Attempts—49 (September 28, 1997, vs. Oakland); completions—29 (September 6, 1998, vs. New Orleans); yards—401 (November 2, 1997, vs. Atlanta); and touchdown passes—5 (September 10, 2000, vs. Jacksonville).
STATISTICAL PLATEAUS: 300-yard passing games: 1996 (2), 1997 (1), 1999 (1). Total: 4.
MISCELLANEOUS: Regular-season record as starting NFL quarterback: 25-36 (.410).

					PASSING						RUSHING				TOTALS	
Year Team	G	GS	Att.	Cmp.	Pct.	Yds.	TD	Int.	Avg.	Rat.	Att.	Yds.	Avg.	TD	TD	2pt.	Pts.
1996—St. Louis NFL	14	13	368	192	52.2	2544	15	15	6.91	71.0	61	212	3.5	0	0	1	2
1997—St. Louis NFL	16	16	487	252	51.7	3254	14	13	6.68	71.5	47	186	4.0	1	1	0	2
1998—St. Louis NFL	14	14	408	241	59.1	2535	7	14	6.21	68.6	40	156	3.9	3	3	1	20
1999—Baltimore NFL	12	10	320	169	52.8	2136	17	8	6.68	81.2	24	93	3.9	0	0	0	0
2000—Baltimore NFL	11	8	274	150	54.7	1578	8	8	5.76	69.3	19	57	3.0	0	0	0	0
Pro totals (5 years)	67	61	1857	1004	54.1	12047	61	58	6.49	72.1	191	704	3.7	4	4	2	28

RECORD AS BASEBALL PLAYER

TRANSACTIONS/CAREER NOTES: Threw right, batted right. ... Selected by Minnesota Twins organization in 10th round of free-agent draft (June 3, 1991).

						BATTING								FIELDING			
Year Team (League)	Pos.	G	AB	R	H	2B	3B	HR	RBI	Avg.	BB	SO	SB	PO	A	E	Avg.
1991—GC Twins (GCL)	DH	17	57	7	13	3	0	0	1	.228	4	16	2	...	...	...	...

BANKSTON, MICHAEL   DE

PERSONAL: Born March 12, 1970, in East Bernard, Texas. ... 6-5/285.
HIGH SCHOOL: East Bernard (Texas).
COLLEGE: Sam Houston State.

TRANSACTIONS/CAREER NOTES: Selected by Phoenix Cardinals in fourth round (100th pick overall) of 1992 NFL draft. ... Signed by Cardinals (July 20, 1992). ... Cardinals franchise renamed Arizona Cardinals for 1994 season. ... Granted free agency (February 14, 1997). ... Re-signed by Cardinals (April 2, 1997). ... Granted unconditional free agency (February 13, 1998). ... Signed by Cincinnati Bengals (February 13, 1998). ... Granted unconditional free agency (March 2, 2001).

PRO STATISTICS: 1993—Recovered five fumbles for 16 yards. 1994—Recovered one fumble for two yards. 1995—Intercepted one pass for 28 yards and fumbled once. 1996—Recovered one fumble. 1998—Recovered one fumble for five yards.

Year Team	G	GS	SACKS
1992—Phoenix NFL	16	6	2.0
1993—Phoenix NFL	16	12	3.0
1994—Arizona NFL	16	16	7.0
1995—Arizona NFL	16	16	2.0
1996—Arizona NFL	16	16	0.5
1997—Arizona NFL	16	16	2.0
1998—Cincinnati NFL	16	16	4.5
1999—Cincinnati NFL	16	9	6.0
2000—Cincinnati NFL	16	14	0.0
Pro totals (9 years)	144	121	27.0

B

BANTA, BRADFORD　　　　TE　　　　LIONS

PERSONAL: Born December 14, 1970, in Baton Rouge, La. ... 6-6/255. ... Full name: Dennis Bradford Banta.
HIGH SCHOOL: University (Baton Rouge, La.).
COLLEGE: Southern California.
TRANSACTIONS/CAREER NOTES: Selected by Indianapolis Colts in fourth round (106th pick overall) of 1994 NFL draft. ... Signed by Colts (July 22, 1994). ... Granted free agency (February 14, 1997). ... Re-signed by Colts (May 14, 1997). ... Granted unconditional free agency (February 11, 2000). ... Re-signed by Colts (March 9, 2000). ... Released by Colts (August 27, 2000). ... Signed by New York Jets (August 29, 2000). ... Granted unconditional free agency (March 2, 2001). ... Signed by Detroit Lions (April 19, 2001).
PLAYING EXPERIENCE: Indianapolis NFL, 1994-1999; New York Jets NFL, 2000. ... Games/Games started: 1994 (16/0), 1995 (16/2), 1996 (13/0), 1997 (15/0), 1998 (16/0), 1999 (16/0), 2000 (16/0). Total: 108/2.
CHAMPIONSHIP GAME EXPERIENCE: Played in AFC championship game (1995 season).
PRO STATISTICS: 1995—Caught one pass for six yards. 1998—Caught one pass for seven yards and recovered one fumble.
SINGLE GAME HIGHS (regular season): Receptions—1 (November 1, 1998, vs. New England); yards—7 (November 1, 1998, vs. New England); and touchdown receptions—0.

BARBER, RONDE　　　　CB　　　　BUCCANEERS

PERSONAL: Born April 7, 1975, in Roanoke, Va. ... 5-10/184. ... Full name: Jamael Oronde Barber. ... Twin brother of Tiki Barber, running back, New York Giants. ... Name pronounced RON-day.
HIGH SCHOOL: Cave Spring (Roanoke, Va.).
COLLEGE: Virginia (degree in commerce, 1996).
TRANSACTIONS/CAREER NOTES: Selected after junior season by Tampa Bay Buccaneers in third round (66th pick overall) of 1997 NFL draft. ... Signed by Buccaneers (July 18, 1997). ... Granted free agency (February 11, 2000). ... Re-signed by Buccaneers (June 13, 2000). ... Granted unconditional free agency (March 2, 2001). ... Re-signed by Buccaneers (April 9, 2001).
CHAMPIONSHIP GAME EXPERIENCE: Played in NFC championship game (1999 season).
PRO STATISTICS: 1998—Returned one punt for 23 yards and a touchdown. 2000—Recovered one fumble for 24 yards and a touchdown.

Year Team	G	GS	INTERCEPTIONS No.	Yds.	Avg.	TD	SACKS No.
1997—Tampa Bay NFL	1	0	0	0	0.0	0	0.0
1998—Tampa Bay NFL	16	9	2	67	33.5	0	3.0
1999—Tampa Bay NFL	16	15	2	60	30.0	0	1.0
2000—Tampa Bay NFL	16	16	2	46	23.0	1	5.5
Pro totals (4 years)	49	40	6	173	28.8	1	9.5

BARBER, SHAWN　　　　LB　　　　REDSKINS

PERSONAL: Born January 14, 1975, in Richmond, Va. ... 6-2/224.
HIGH SCHOOL: Hermitage (Richmond, Va.).
COLLEGE: Richmond.
TRANSACTIONS/CAREER NOTES: Selected by Washington Redskins in fourth round (113th pick overall) of 1998 NFL draft. ... Signed by Redskins (May 13, 1998). ... Granted free agency (March 2, 2001). ... Re-signed by Redskins (June 1, 2001).
PRO STATISTICS: 1999—Credited with one sack. 2000—Credited with two sacks and recovered three fumbles.

Year Team	G	GS	INTERCEPTIONS No.	Yds.	Avg.	TD
1998—Washington NFL	16	1	1	0	0.0	0
1999—Washington NFL	16	16	2	70	35.0	1
2000—Washington NFL	14	14	0	0	0.0	0
Pro totals (3 years)	46	31	3	70	23.3	1

BARBER, TIKI　　　　RB　　　　GIANTS

PERSONAL: Born April 7, 1975, in Roanoke, Va. ... 5-10/200. ... Full name: Atiim Kiambu Barber. ... Twin brother of Ronde Barber, cornerback, Tampa Bay Buccaneers. ... Name pronounced TEE-kee.
HIGH SCHOOL: Cave Spring (Roanoke, Va.).
COLLEGE: Virginia.

TRANSACTIONS/CAREER NOTES: Selected by New York Giants in second round (36th pick overall) of 1997 NFL draft. ... Signed by Giants for 1997 season. ... Granted free agency (February 11, 2000). ... Re-signed by Giants (June 8, 2000). ... Granted unconditional free agency (March 2, 2001). ... Re-signed by Giants (March 8, 2001).
CHAMPIONSHIP GAME EXPERIENCE: Played in NFC championship game (2000 season). ... Played in Super Bowl XXXV (2000 season).
PRO STATISTICS: 1997—Fumbled three times. 1998—Fumbled once. 1999—Fumbled five times and recovered five fumbles. 2000—Fumbled nine times and recovered five fumbles.
SINGLE GAME HIGHS (regular season): Attempts—24 (December 23, 2000, vs. Jacksonville); yards—144 (September 3, 2000, vs. Arizona); and rushing touchdowns—2 (September 3, 2000, vs. Arizona).
STATISTICAL PLATEAUS: 100-yard rushing games: 1997 (1), 2000 (1). Total: 2. ... 100-yard receiving games: 1999 (1).

Year Team	G	GS	RUSHING				RECEIVING				PUNT RETURNS				KICKOFF RETURNS				TOTALS		
			Att.	Yds.	Avg.	TD	No.	Yds.	Avg.	TD	No.	Yds.	Avg.	TD	No.	Yds.	Avg.	TD	TD	2pt.	Pts.
1997—NY Giants NFL	12	6	136	511	3.8	3	34	299	8.8	1	0	0	0.0	0	0	0	0.0	0	4	1	26
1998—NY Giants NFL	16	4	52	166	3.2	0	42	348	8.3	3	0	0	0.0	0	14	250	17.9	0	3	0	18
1999—NY Giants NFL	16	1	62	258	4.2	0	66	609	9.2	2	∞44	‡506	11.5	∞1	12	266	22.2	0	3	0	18
2000—NY Giants NFL	16	12	213	1006	4.7	8	70	719	10.3	1	‡39	332	8.5	0	1	28	28.0	0	9	0	54
Pro totals (4 years)	60	23	463	1941	4.2	11	212	1975	9.3	7	83	838	10.1	1	27	544	20.1	0	19	1	116

BARKER, BRYAN — P — REDSKINS

PERSONAL: Born June 28, 1964, in Jacksonville Beach, Fla. ... 6-2/199. ... Full name: Bryan Christopher Barker.
HIGH SCHOOL: Miramonte (Orinda, Calif.).
COLLEGE: Santa Clara (degree in economics).
TRANSACTIONS/CAREER NOTES: Signed as non-drafted free agent by Denver Broncos (May 1988). ... Released by Broncos (July 19, 1988). ... Signed by Seattle Seahawks (1989). ... Released by Seahawks (August 30, 1989). ... Signed by Kansas City Chiefs (May 1, 1990). ... Released by Chiefs (August 28, 1990). ... Re-signed by Chiefs (September 26, 1990). ... Granted unconditional free agency (February 1-April 1, 1991). ... Re-signed by Chiefs for 1991 season. ... Granted unconditional free agency (February 1-April 1, 1992). ... Re-signed by Chiefs for 1992 season. ... Released by Chiefs (1994). ... Signed by Minnesota Vikings (May 18, 1994). ... Released by Vikings (August 30, 1994). ... Signed by Philadelphia Eagles (October 11, 1994). ... Granted unconditional free agency (February 17, 1995). ... Signed by Jacksonville Jaguars (March 7, 1995). ... Granted unconditional free agency (March 2, 2001). ... Signed by Washington Redskins (April 12, 2001).
CHAMPIONSHIP GAME EXPERIENCE: Played in AFC championship game (1993, 1996 and 1999 seasons).
HONORS: Played in Pro Bowl (1997 season).
PRO STATISTICS: 1997—Rushed once for no yards, attempted one pass with a completion for 22 yards and fumbled once for minus 19 yards. 1999—Rushed once for six yards.

Year Team	G	PUNTING					
		No.	Yds.	Avg.	Net avg.	In. 20	Blk.
1990—Kansas City NFL	13	64	2479	38.7	33.3	16	0
1991—Kansas City NFL	16	57	2303	40.4	35.0	14	0
1992—Kansas City NFL	15	75	3245	43.3	35.2	16	1
1993—Kansas City NFL	16	76	3240	42.6	35.3	19	1
1994—Philadelphia NFL	11	66	2696	40.8	‡36.2	20	0
1995—Jacksonville NFL	16	82	3591	43.8	*38.6	19	0
1996—Jacksonville NFL	16	69	3016	43.7	35.6	16	0
1997—Jacksonville NFL	16	66	2964	44.9	38.8	27	0
1998—Jacksonville NFL	16	85	3824	45.0	38.5	28	0
1999—Jacksonville NFL	16	78	3260	41.8	36.9	32	0
2000—Jacksonville NFL	16	76	3194	42.0	34.4	29	0
Pro totals (11 years)	167	794	33812	42.6	36.3	236	2

BARKER, ROY — DE

PERSONAL: Born February 24, 1969, in New York. ... 6-5/290.
HIGH SCHOOL: Central Islip (N.Y.).
COLLEGE: North Carolina (degree in speech communications, 1991).
TRANSACTIONS/CAREER NOTES: Selected by Minnesota Vikings in fourth round (98th pick overall) of 1992 NFL draft. ... Signed by Vikings (July 16, 1992). ... On injured reserve with knee injury (September 1-30, 1992). ... Granted unconditional free agency (February 16, 1996). ... Signed by San Francisco 49ers (February 28, 1996). ... Traded by 49ers with TE Irv Smith to Cleveland Browns for past considerations (February 12, 1999). ... Claimed on waivers by Green Bay Packers (December 21, 1999). ... Released by Packers (December 27, 1999). ... Signed by Vikings (October 3, 2000). ... Released by Vikings (November 15, 2000).
CHAMPIONSHIP GAME EXPERIENCE: Played in NFC championship game (1997 season).
PRO STATISTICS: 1993—Recovered one fumble. 1994—Recovered one fumble. 1995—Intercepted one pass for minus two yards. 1998—Intercepted one pass for minus four yards. 1999—Intercepted one pass for 14 yards.

Year Team	G	GS	SACKS
1992—Minnesota NFL	8	0	0.0
1993—Minnesota NFL	16	16	6.0
1994—Minnesota NFL	16	15	3.5
1995—Minnesota NFL	16	16	3.0
1996—San Francisco NFL	16	16	12.5
1997—San Francisco NFL	13	12	5.5
1998—San Francisco NFL	16	16	12.0
1999—Cleveland NFL	12	3	2.0
—Green Bay NFL	1	0	0.0
2000—Minnesota NFL	4	0	0.0
Pro totals (9 years)	118	94	44.5

BARLOW, REGGIE　　　　WR/PR/KR　　　　RAIDERS

PERSONAL: Born January 22, 1973, in Montgomery, Ala. ... 6-0/186. ... Full name: Reggie Devon Barlow.
HIGH SCHOOL: Lanier (Montgomery, Ala.).
COLLEGE: Alabama State.
TRANSACTIONS/CAREER NOTES: Selected by Jacksonville Jaguars in fourth round (110th pick overall) of 1996 NFL draft. ... Signed by Jaguars (May 28, 1996). ... Granted free agency (February 12, 1999). ... Re-signed by Jaguars (March 23, 1999). ... Released by Jaguars (February 27. 2001). ... Signed by Oakland Raiders (March 22, 2001).
CHAMPIONSHIP GAME EXPERIENCE: Played in AFC championship game (1996 and 1999 seasons).
PRO STATISTICS: 1997—Recovered one fumble. 1998—Recovered one fumble. 1999—Recovered one fumble.
SINGLE GAME HIGHS (regular season): Receptions—4 (December 2, 1999, vs. Pittsburgh); yards—50 (October 12, 1998, vs. Miami); and touchdown receptions—0.

			RECEIVING				PUNT RETURNS				KICKOFF RETURNS				TOTALS			
Year　Team	G	GS	No.	Yds.	Avg.	TD	No.	Yds.	Avg.	TD	No.	Yds.	Avg.	TD	TD	2pt.	Pts.	Fum.
1996—Jacksonville NFL.........	7	0	0	0	0.0	0	0	0	0.0	0	0	0	0.0	0	0	0	0	0
1997—Jacksonville NFL.........	16	0	5	74	14.8	0	36	412	11.4	0	10	267	26.7	▲1	2	0	12	2
1998—Jacksonville NFL.........	16	2	11	168	15.3	0	43	*555	§12.9	1	30	747	24.9	0	1	0	6	1
1999—Jacksonville NFL.........	14	2	16	202	12.6	0	38	414	10.9	1	19	396	20.8	0	1	0	6	4
2000—Jacksonville NFL.........	16	0	1	28	28.0	0	29	200	6.9	0	11	224	20.4	0	0	0	0	0
Pro totals (5 years)...............	69	4	33	472	14.3	0	146	1581	10.8	2	70	1634	23.3	1	4	0	24	7

B

BARNDT, TOM　　　　DT　　　　BENGALS

PERSONAL: Born March 14, 1972, in Mentor, Ohio. ... 6-3/293. ... Full name: Thomas Allen Barndt.
HIGH SCHOOL: Mentor (Ohio).
COLLEGE: Pittsburgh.
TRANSACTIONS/CAREER NOTES: Selected by Kansas City Chiefs in sixth round (207th pick overall) of 1995 NFL draft. ... Signed by Chiefs for the 1995 season. ... Released by Chiefs (August 27, 1995). ... Re-signed by Chiefs to practice squad (August 29, 1995). ... Assigned by Chiefs to Scottish Claymores in 1996 World League enhancement allocation program (February 19, 1996). ... Granted free agency (February 12, 1999). ... Re-signed by Chiefs (June 16, 1999). ... Granted unconditional free agency (February 11, 2000). ... Signed by Cincinnati Bengals (February 18, 2000).
PRO STATISTICS: 1998—Recovered two fumbles. 1999—Recovered one fumble. 2000—Recovered one fumble.

Year　Team	G	GS	SACKS
1995—Kansas City NFL		Did not play.	
1996—Scottish W.L.	...	...	0.0
—Kansas City NFL	13	0	0.0
1997—Kansas City NFL	16	1	2.0
1998—Kansas City NFL	16	16	3.5
1999—Kansas City NFL	16	13	2.5
2000—Cincinnati NFL	14	5	0.0
W.L. totals (1 year)..	...	...	0.0
NFL totals (4 years)...	75	35	8.0
Pro totals (5 years)..	...	...	8.0

BARNES, LIONEL　　　　DE　　　　COLTS

PERSONAL: Born April 19, 1976, in New Orleans. ... 6-4/274. ... Full name: Lionel Barnes Jr.
HIGH SCHOOL: Lakenheath American (Suffolk, England).
JUNIOR COLLEGE: Barton County Community College, Kan. (did not play football).
COLLEGE: Northeast Louisiana.
TRANSACTIONS/CAREER NOTES: Selected by St. Louis Rams in sixth round (176th pick overall) of 1999 NFL draft. ... Signed by Rams (July 19, 1999). ... Claimed on waivers by Indianapolis Colts (October 12, 2000).
PLAYING EXPERIENCE: St. Louis NFL, 1999; St. Louis (1) and Indianapolis (1) NFL, 2000. ... Games/Games started: 1999 (3/0), 2000 (St.L-1/0; Ind.-1/0; Total: 2/0). Total: 5/0.
CHAMPIONSHIP GAME EXPERIENCE: Member of Rams for NFC championship game (1999 season); inactive. ... Member of Super Bowl championship team (1999 season); inactive.

BARNES, MARLON　　　　RB　　　　BEARS

PERSONAL: Born March 13, 1976, in Memphis, Tenn. ... 5-9/215.
HIGH SCHOOL: Balla Vista (Tenn.).
COLLEGE: Colorado.
TRANSACTIONS/CAREER NOTES: Signed as non-drafted free agent by Oakland Raiders (April 22, 1999). ... Released by Raiders (October 20, 1999). ... Re-signed by Raiders to practice squad (October 27, 1999). ... Released by Raiders (October 31, 1999). ... Signed by Miami Dolphins to practice squad (January 5, 2000). ... Released by Dolphins (January 24, 2000). ... Signed by Chicago Bears (January 25, 2000).
SINGLE GAME HIGHS (regular season): Attempts—5 (November 5, 2000); yards—30 (December 24, 2000); and rushing touchdowns—0.

			RUSHING				RECEIVING				TOTALS			
Year　Team	G	GS	Att.	Yds.	Avg.	TD	No.	Yds.	Avg.	TD	TD	2pt.	Pts.	Fum.
2000—Chicago NFL	13	0	15	81	5.4	0	1	7	7.0	0	0	0	0	1

BARNES, RASHIDI   DB   BROWNS

PERSONAL: Born June 26, 1978, in Berkeley, Calif. ... 5-11/205.
HIGH SCHOOL: Berkeley (Calif.).
COLLEGE: Colorado.
TRANSACTIONS/CAREER NOTES: Selected by Cleveland Browns in seventh round (225th pick overall) of 2000 NFL draft. ... Signed by Browns (July 10, 2000).
PLAYING EXPERIENCE: Cleveland NFL, 2000. ... Games/Games started: 2000 (14/0).
PRO STATISTICS: 2000—Returned one punt for no yards.

BARNHARDT, TOMMY   P

B

PERSONAL: Born June 11, 1963, in China Grove, N.C. ... 6-2/228. ... Full name: Tommy Ray Barnhardt.
HIGH SCHOOL: South Rowan (China Grove, N.C.).
COLLEGE: East Carolina, then North Carolina (degree in industrial relations, 1986).
TRANSACTIONS/CAREER NOTES: Selected by Baltimore Stars in 1986 USFL territorial draft. ... Selected by Tampa Bay Buccaneers in ninth round (223rd pick overall) of 1986 NFL draft. ... Signed by Buccaneers (July 16, 1986). ... Released by Buccaneers (August 25, 1986). ... Re-signed by Buccaneers (February 6, 1987). ... Released by Buccaneers (August 5, 1987). ... Signed as replacement player by New Orleans Saints (September 23, 1987). ... Released by Saints (November 3, 1987). ... Signed by Chicago Bears (December 16, 1987). ... Released by Bears (August 24, 1988). ... Signed by Washington Redskins (September 9, 1988). ... On injured reserve with pulled quadricep (October 11, 1988-remainder of season). ... Granted unconditional free agency (February 1-April 1, 1989). ... Re-signed by Redskins (May 11, 1989). ... Released by Redskins (June 27, 1989). ... Signed by Detroit Lions (July 20, 1989). ... Released by Lions (August 30, 1989). ... Signed by Saints (October 11, 1989). ... Granted unconditional free agency (February 1-April 1, 1992). ... Re-signed by Saints for 1992 season. ... Granted unconditional free agency (March 1, 1993). ... Re-signed by Saints (July 15, 1993). ... Granted unconditional free agency (February 17, 1995). ... Signed by Carolina Panthers (March 2, 1995). ... Released by Panthers (May 7, 1996). ... Signed by Buccaneers (May 13, 1996). ... On injured reserve with broken collarbone (October 9, 1997-remainder of season). ... Granted unconditional free agency (February 12, 1999). ... Signed by Saints (June 28, 1999). ... Released by Saints (April 6, 2000). ... Signed by Washington Redskins (May 8, 2000). ... Granted unconditional free agency (March 2, 2001).
PRO STATISTICS: 1987—Rushed once for minus 13 yards. 1991—Rushed once for no yards. 1992—Rushed four times for minus two yards and fumbled twice for minus 16 yards. 1993—Rushed once for 18 yards and completed only pass attempt for seven yards. 1994—Rushed once for 21 yards and attempted one pass without a completion. 1996—Rushed twice for 27 yards. 1997—Completed only pass attempt for 25 yards. 1999—Rushed once for four yards, fumbled once and recovered one fumble. 2000—Rushed once for 11 yards.

				PUNTING				
Year Team	G	No.	Yds.	Avg.	Net avg.	In. 20	Blk.	
1987—New Orleans NFL	3	11	483	43.9	0	4	0	
—Chicago NFL	2	6	236	39.3	35.2	2	0	
1988—Washington NFL	4	15	628	41.9	34.2	1	0	
1989—New Orleans NFL	11	55	2179	39.6	35.0	17	0	
1990—New Orleans NFL	16	70	2990	42.7	36.2	20	1	
1991—New Orleans NFL	16	86	*3743	43.5	35.2	20	1	
1992—New Orleans NFL	16	67	2947	44.0	37.7	19	0	
1993—New Orleans NFL	16	77	3356	43.6	37.5	26	0	
1994—New Orleans NFL	16	67	2920	43.6	33.5	14	0	
1995—Carolina NFL	16	‡95	‡3906	41.1	35.2	27	0	
1996—Tampa Bay NFL	16	70	3015	43.1	37.7	24	1	
1997—Tampa Bay NFL	6	29	1304	45.0	39.1	12	0	
1998—Tampa Bay NFL	16	81	3340	41.2	35.3	19	0	
1999—New Orleans NFL	16	82	3262	39.8	35.1	14	0	
2000—Washington NFL	16	79	3160	40.0	34.4	23	0	
Pro totals (14 years)	186	890	37469	42.1	35.3	242	3	

BARRETT, DAVID   CB   CARDINALS

PERSONAL: Born December 22, 1977, in Osceola, Ark. ... 5-11/198.
HIGH SCHOOL: Osceola (Ark.).
COLLEGE: Arkansas.
TRANSACTIONS/CAREER NOTES: Selected by Arizona Cardinals in fourth round (102nd pick overall) of 2000 NFL draft. ... Signed by Cardinals (June 15, 2000).
PLAYING EXPERIENCE: Arizona NFL, 2000. ... Games/Games started: 2000 (16/0).
PRO STATISTICS: 2000—Recovered one fumble and ran 46 yards with lateral from kickoff return.

BARROW, MIKE   LB   GIANTS

PERSONAL: Born April 19, 1970, in Homestead, Fla. ... 6-2/240. ... Full name: Micheal Colvin Barrow.
HIGH SCHOOL: Homestead (Fla.) Senior.
COLLEGE: Miami, Fla. (degree in accounting, 1992).
TRANSACTIONS/CAREER NOTES: Selected by Houston Oilers in second round (47th pick overall) of 1993 NFL draft. ... Signed by Oilers (July 30, 1993). ... Granted free agency (February 16, 1996). ... Re-signed by Oilers (August 9, 1996). ... Granted unconditional free agency (February 14, 1997). ... Signed by Carolina Panthers (February 20, 1997). ... Released by Panthers (February 22, 2000). ... Signed by New York Giants (March 2, 2000).
CHAMPIONSHIP GAME EXPERIENCE: Played in NFC championship game (2000 season). ... Played in Super Bowl XXXV (2000 season).
HONORS: Named linebacker on THE SPORTING NEWS college All-America first team (1992).
PRO STATISTICS: 1995—Recovered one fumble. 1996—Recovered one fumble. 1997—Recovered two fumbles. 1998—Intercepted one pass for 10 yards and recovered two fumbles. 1999—Recovered one fumble. 2000—Intercepted one pass for seven yards and recovered one fumble.

Year Team	G	GS	SACKS
1993—Houston NFL	16	0	1.0
1994—Houston NFL	16	16	2.5
1995—Houston NFL	13	12	3.0
1996—Houston NFL	16	16	6.0
1997—Carolina NFL	16	16	8.5
1998—Carolina NFL	16	16	4.0
1999—Carolina NFL	16	16	4.0
2000—New York Giants NFL	15	15	3.5
Pro totals (8 years)	**124**	**107**	**32.5**

BARTEE, WILLIAM — CB — CHIEFS

PERSONAL: Born June 25, 1977, in Daytona Beach, Fla. ... 6-1/196.
HIGH SCHOOL: Atlantic (Daytona Beach, Fla.).
JUNIOR COLLEGE: Butler County Community College (Kan.).
COLLEGE: Oklahoma.
TRANSACTIONS/CAREER NOTES: Selected by Kansas City Chiefs in second round (54th pick overall) of 2000 NFL draft. ... Signed by Chiefs (July 21, 2000).

Year Team	G	GS	SACKS
2000—Kansas City NFL	16	3	1.0

BARTHOLOMEW, BRENT — P — BEARS

PERSONAL: Born October 22, 1976, in Birmingham, Ala. ... 6-2/220. ... Full name: Brent Robert Bartholomew.
HIGH SCHOOL: Apopka (Fla.).
COLLEGE: Ohio State.
TRANSACTIONS/CAREER NOTES: Selected by Miami Dolphins in sixth round (192nd pick overall) of 1999 NFL draft. ... Signed by Dolphins (July 27, 1999). ... On injured reserve with knee injury (September 27, 1999-remainder of season). ... Traded by Dolphins to Chicago Bears for seventh-round pick (DB Jeff Harris) in 2000 draft and undisclosed pick in 2001 draft (April 16, 2000). ... On injured reserve with knee injury (October 18, 2000-remainder of season).

Year Team	G	No.	Yds.	Avg.	Net avg.	In. 20	Blk.
1999—Miami NFL	2	7	308	44.0	32.6	1	0
2000—Chicago NFL	7	44	1607	36.5	32.2	12	0
Pro totals (2 years)	**9**	**51**	**1915**	**37.5**	**32.3**	**13**	**0**

(header: PUNTING)

BARTON, ERIC — LB — RAIDERS

PERSONAL: Born September 29, 1977, in Alexandria, Va. ... 6-2/245.
HIGH SCHOOL: Thomas A. Edison (Alexandria, Va.).
COLLEGE: Maryland.
TRANSACTIONS/CAREER NOTES: Selected by Oakland Raiders in fifth round (146th pick overall) of 1999 NFL draft. ... Signed by Raiders for 1999 season.
CHAMPIONSHIP GAME EXPERIENCE: Member of Raiders for AFC Championship game (2000 season); inactive.

Year Team	G	GS	SACKS
1999—Oakland NFL	16	3	3.0
2000—Oakland NFL	4	0	0.0
Pro totals (2 years)	**20**	**3**	**3.0**

BARTRUM, MIKE — TE — EAGLES

PERSONAL: Born June 23, 1970, in Gallipolis, Ohio. ... 6-4/245. ... Full name: Michael Weldon Bartrum.
HIGH SCHOOL: Meigs (Pomeroy, Ohio).
COLLEGE: Marshall (degree in education).
TRANSACTIONS/CAREER NOTES: Signed as non-drafted free agent by Kansas City Chiefs (May 5, 1993). ... Released by Chiefs (August 30, 1993). ... Re-signed by Chiefs to practice squad (August 31, 1993). ... Activated (October 27, 1993). ... Released by Chiefs (August 23, 1994). ... Signed by Green Bay Packers (January 20, 1995). ... On injured reserve with broken arm (October 11, 1995-remainder of season). ... Traded by Packers with DE Walter Scott to New England Patriots for past considerations (August 25, 1996). ... On injured reserve with forearm injury (November 12, 1997-remainder of season). ... Granted unconditional free agency (February 13, 1998). ... Re-signed by Patriots (April 7, 1998). ... Released by Patriots (April 10, 2000). ... Signed by Philadelphia Eagles (April 17, 2000).
PLAYING EXPERIENCE: Kansas City NFL, 1993; Green Bay NFL, 1995; New England NFL, 1996-1999; Philadelphia NFL, 2000. ... Games/Games started: 1993 (3/0), 1995 (4/0), 1996 (16/0), 1997 (9/0), 1998 (16/0), 1999 (16/0), 2000 (16/0). Total: 80/0.
CHAMPIONSHIP GAME EXPERIENCE: Member of Chiefs for AFC championship game (1993 season); inactive. ... Played in AFC championship game (1996 season). ... Played in Super Bowl XXXI (1996 season).
PRO STATISTICS: 1996—Caught one pass for one yard and a touchdown. 1999—Caught one pass for one yard and a touchdown and fumbled once for minus seven yards. 2000—Recovered one fumble.
SINGLE GAME HIGHS (regular season): Receptions—1 (January 2, 2000, vs. Baltimore); yards—1 (January 2, 2000, vs. Baltimore); and touchdown receptions—1 (January 2, 2000, vs. Baltimore).

BATCH, CHARLIE　　　　　QB　　　　　LIONS

PERSONAL: Born December 5, 1974, in Homestead, Pa. ... 6-2/220. ... Full name: Charles D'Donte Batch.
HIGH SCHOOL: Steel Valley (Munhall, Pa.).
COLLEGE: Eastern Michigan (degree in business, 1997).
TRANSACTIONS/CAREER NOTES: Selected by Detroit Lions in second round (60th pick overall) of 1998 NFL draft. ... Signed by Lions (July 19, 1998). ... On injured reserve with back injury (December 24, 1998-remainder of season).
RECORDS: Holds NFL rookie-season record for lowest interception percentage—1.98.
PRO STATISTICS: 1998—Fumbled twice. 1999—Fumbled four times. 2000—Fumbled six times and recovered one fumbled for minus five yards.
SINGLE GAME HIGHS (regular season): Attempts—44 (October 1, 2000, vs. Minnesota); completions—26 (September 17, 2000, vs. Tampa Bay); yards—277 (September 17, 2000, vs. Tampa Bay); and touchdown passes—3 (November 19, 2000, vs. New York Giants).
MISCELLANEOUS: Regular-season record as starting NFL quarterback: 19-18 (.514).

				PASSING						RUSHING				TOTALS		
Year　Team	G	GS	Att.	Cmp.	Pct.	Yds.	TD	Int.	Avg.	Rat.	Att.	Yds.	Avg.	TD	TD	2pt.	Pts.
1998—Detroit NFL	12	12	303	173	57.1	2178	11	6	7.19	83.5	41	229	5.6	1	1	0	6
1999—Detroit NFL	11	10	270	151	55.9	1957	13	7	7.25	84.1	28	87	3.1	2	2	0	12
2000—Detroit NFL	15	15	412	221	53.6	2489	13	15	6.04	67.3	44	199	4.5	2	2	0	12
Pro totals (3 years)	38	37	985	545	55.3	6624	37	28	6.72	76.9	113	515	4.6	5	5	0	30

BATES, D'WAYNE　　　　　WR　　　　　BEARS

PERSONAL: Born December 4, 1975, in Aiken, S.C. ... 6-2/215. ... Full name: D'Wayne Lavoris Bates.
HIGH SCHOOL: Silver Bluff (Aiken, S.C.).
COLLEGE: Northwestern.
TRANSACTIONS/CAREER NOTES: Selected by Chicago Bears in third round (71st pick overall) of 1999 NFL draft. ... Signed by Bears (July 22, 1999).
PLAYING EXPERIENCE: Chicago NFL, 1999 and 2000. ... Games/Games started: 1999 (7/1), 2000 (5/0). Total: 12/1.
PRO STATISTICS: 1999—Caught two passes for 19 yards. 2000—Rushed once for minus two yards and caught four passes for 42 yards.
SINGLE GAME HIGHS (regular season): Receptions—2 (October 8, 2000, vs. New Orleans); yards—18 (October 8, 2000, vs. New Orleans); and touchdown receptions—0.
MISCELLANEOUS: Selected by Toronto Blue Jays organization in 53rd round of free-agent draft (June 2, 1994); did not sign.

BATES, MARIO　　　　　RB

PERSONAL: Born January 16, 1973, in Tucson, Ariz. ... 6-2/237. ... Full name: Mario Doniel Bates. ... Brother of Michael Bates, running back/kick returner with Seattle Seahawks (1992-94), Cleveland Browns (1995) and Carolina Panthers (1996-2000).
HIGH SCHOOL: Amphitheater (Tucson, Ariz.).
COLLEGE: Arizona State.
TRANSACTIONS/CAREER NOTES: Selected after junior season by New Orleans Saints in second round (44th pick overall) of 1994 NFL draft. ... Signed by Saints (July 6, 1994). ... Granted free agency (February 14, 1997). ... Re-signed by Saints (June 12, 1997). ... Granted unconditional free agency (February 13, 1998). ... Signed by Arizona Cardinals (March 6, 1998). ... Released by Cardinals (August 24, 2000). ... Signed by Detroit Lions (August 29, 2000). ... Granted unconditional free agency (March 2, 2001).
PRO STATISTICS: 1994—Recovered one fumble. 1995—Recovered one fumble. 1997—Attempted one pass with a completion for 21 yards and a touchdown. 1999—Recovered one fumble.
SINGLE GAME HIGHS (regular season): Attempts—32 (December 15, 1996, vs. New York Giants); yards—162 (September 21, 1997, vs. Detroit); and rushing touchdowns—3 (December 4, 1994, vs. Los Angeles Rams).
STATISTICAL PLATEAUS: 100-yard rushing games: 1994 (1), 1995 (3), 1996 (1), 1997 (1). Total: 6.

			RUSHING				RECEIVING				KICKOFF RETURNS				TOTALS			
Year　Team	G	GS	Att.	Yds.	Avg.	TD	No.	Yds.	Avg.	TD	No.	Yds.	Avg.	TD	TD	2pt.	Pts.	Fum.
1994—New Orleans NFL	11	7	151	579	3.8	6	8	62	7.8	0	1	20	20.0	0	6	0	36	3
1995—New Orleans NFL	16	16	244	951	3.9	7	18	114	6.3	0	0	0	0.0	0	7	0	42	2
1996—New Orleans NFL	14	10	164	584	3.6	4	13	44	3.4	0	0	0	0.0	0	4	0	24	4
1997—New Orleans NFL	12	7	119	440	3.7	4	5	42	8.4	0	0	0	0.0	0	4	0	24	2
1998—Arizona NFL	16	1	60	165	2.8	6	1	14	14.0	0	0	0	0.0	0	6	0	36	0
1999—Arizona NFL	16	2	72	202	2.8	9	5	34	6.8	0	52	1231	23.7	0	9	0	54	2
2000—Detroit NFL	13	0	31	127	4.1	2	15	109	7.3	0	0	0	0.0	0	2	0	12	0
Pro totals (7 years)	98	43	841	3048	3.6	38	65	419	6.4	0	53	1251	23.6	0	38	0	228	13

BATES, MICHAEL　　　　　RB/KR

PERSONAL: Born December 19, 1969, in Tucson, Ariz. ... 5-10/189. ... Full name: Michael Dion Bates. ... Brother of Mario Bates, running back with New Orleans Saints (1994-97), Arizona Cardinals (1998 and 1999) and Detroit Lions (2000).
HIGH SCHOOL: Amphitheater (Tucson, Ariz.).
COLLEGE: Arizona.
TRANSACTIONS/CAREER NOTES: Selected after sophomore season by Seattle Seahawks in sixth round (151st pick overall) of 1992 NFL draft. ... Missed 1992 season due to contract dispute. ... Signed by Seahawks (March 7, 1993). ... Claimed on waivers by Carolina Panthers (August 28, 1995). ... Traded by Panthers to Cleveland Browns for LB Travis Hill (August 29, 1995). ... Granted unconditional free agency (February 16, 1996). ... Signed by Panthers (March 12, 1996). ... Granted unconditional free agency (February 13, 1998). ... Re-signed by Panthers (March 4, 1998). ... Granted unconditional free agency (March 2, 2001).
CHAMPIONSHIP GAME EXPERIENCE: Played in NFC championship game (1996 season).
HONORS: Named kick returner on THE SPORTING NEWS NFL All-Pro team (1996 and 1997). ... Played in Pro Bowl (1996-2000 seasons).

PRO STATISTICS: 1993—Rushed twice for 12 yards and recovered two fumbles for three yards. 1994—Rushed twice for minus four yards. 1997—Returned one punt for eight yards and recovered two fumbles. 1999—Rushed three times for 12 yards. 2000—Rushed five times for 13 yards, returned seven punts for 31 yards and recovered one fumble.
SINGLE GAME HIGHS (regular season): Attempts—2 (December 3, 2000, vs. St. Louis); yards—14 (November 7, 1999, vs. Philadelphia); and rushing touchdowns—0.
MISCELLANEOUS: Won bronze medal in 200-meter dash in 1992 Summer Olympics.

Year Team	G	GS	RECEIVING				KICKOFF RETURNS				TOTALS			
			No.	Yds.	Avg.	TD	No.	Yds.	Avg.	TD	TD	2pt.	Pts.	Fum.
1992—Seattle NFL							Did not play.							
1993—Seattle NFL	16	1	1	6	6.0	0	30	603	20.1	0	0	0	0	1
1994—Seattle NFL	15	0	5	112	22.4	1	26	508	19.5	0	1	0	6	3
1995—Cleveland NFL	13	0	0	0	0.0	0	9	176	19.6	0	0	0	0	0
1996—Carolina NFL	14	0	0	0	0.0	0	33	998	*30.2	1	1	0	6	2
1997—Carolina NFL	16	0	0	0	0.0	0	47	1281	*27.3	0	0	0	0	4
1998—Carolina NFL	14	0	0	0	0.0	0	59	1480	25.1	1	1	0	6	1
1999—Carolina NFL	16	0	1	2	2.0	0	52	1287	24.8	†2	2	0	12	1
2000—Carolina NFL	16	0	5	38	7.6	0	42	941	22.4	1	1	0	6	4
Pro totals (8 years)	120	1	12	158	13.2	1	298	7274	24.4	5	6	0	36	16

B

BATTAGLIA, MARCO   TE   BENGALS

PERSONAL: Born January 25, 1973, in Howard Beach, N.Y. ... 6-3/252. ... Name pronounced buh-TAG-lee-uh.
HIGH SCHOOL: St. Francis (Fresh Meadows, N.Y.).
COLLEGE: Rutgers.
TRANSACTIONS/CAREER NOTES: Selected by Cincinnati Bengals in second round (39th pick overall) of 1996 NFL draft. ... Signed by Bengals (July 15, 1996). ... Granted free agency (February 12, 1999). ... Re-signed by Bengals (May 25, 1999).
HONORS: Named tight end on THE SPORTING NEWS college All-America first team (1995).
PRO STATISTICS: 1996—Returned one kickoff for eight yards and recovered one fumble. 1997—Recovered two fumbles. 1998—Returned one kickoff for five yards and recovered three fumbles.
SINGLE GAME HIGHS (regular season): Receptions—3 (November 7, 1999, vs. Seattle); yards—42 (December 21, 1997, vs. Baltimore); and touchdown receptions—1 (November 1, 1998, vs. Denver).

Year Team	G	GS	RECEIVING				TOTALS			
			No.	Yds.	Avg.	TD	TD	2pt.	Pts.	Fum.
1996—Cincinnati NFL	16	0	8	79	9.9	0	0	0	0	0
1997—Cincinnati NFL	16	0	12	149	12.4	1	1	0	6	2
1998—Cincinnati NFL	16	0	10	47	4.7	1	1	0	6	1
1999—Cincinnati NFL	16	0	14	153	10.9	0	0	0	0	0
2000—Cincinnati NFL	10	9	13	105	8.1	0	0	0	0	0
Pro totals (5 years)	74	9	57	533	9.4	2	2	0	12	3

BATTLES, AINSLEY   S   STEELERS

PERSONAL: Born November 6, 1977, in Lilburn, Ga. ... 5-10/190.
HIGH SCHOOL: Parkview (Lilburn, Ga.).
COLLEGE: Vanderbilt.
TRANSACTIONS/CAREER NOTES: Signed as non-drafted free agent by Pittsburgh Steelers (April 21, 2000).
PLAYING EXPERIENCE: Pittsburgh NFL, 2000. ... Games/Games started: 2000 (16/1).
PRO STATISTICS: 2000—Fumbled once, recovered two fumbles for minus one yard and credited with one sack.

BAXTER, FRED   TE   BEARS

PERSONAL: Born June 14, 1971, in Brundidge, Ala. ... 6-3/265. ... Full name: Frederick Denard Baxter.
HIGH SCHOOL: Pike County (Brundidge, Ala.).
COLLEGE: Auburn.
TRANSACTIONS/CAREER NOTES: Selected by New York Jets in fifth round (115th pick overall) of 1993 NFL draft. ... Signed by Jets (July 13, 1993). ... On injured reserve with broken hand (November 21-December 23, 2000). ... Released by Jets (December 23, 2000). ... Signed by Chicago Bears (February 22, 2001).
CHAMPIONSHIP GAME EXPERIENCE: Played in AFC championship game (1998 season).
PRO STATISTICS: 1994—Returned one kickoff for 20 yards and recovered one fumble. 1995—Returned six kickoffs for 36 yards and recovered two fumbles for eight yards. 1997—Returned one kickoff for no yards. 1998—Returned one kickoff for eight yards and recovered one fumble. 1999—Recovered one fumble. 2000—Returned one kickoff for 15 yards and recovered one fumble.
SINGLE GAME HIGHS (regular season): Receptions—6 (September 17, 1995, vs. Jacksonville); yards—99 (September 17, 1995, vs. Jacksonville); and touchdown receptions—1 (October 29, 2000, vs. Buffalo).

Year Team	G	GS	RECEIVING				TOTALS			
			No.	Yds.	Avg.	TD	TD	2pt.	Pts.	Fum.
1993—New York Jets NFL	7	0	3	48	16.0	1	1	0	6	0
1994—New York Jets NFL	11	1	3	11	3.7	1	1	0	6	0
1995—New York Jets NFL	15	3	18	222	12.3	1	1	0	6	1
1996—New York Jets NFL	16	4	7	114	16.3	0	0	0	0	1
1997—New York Jets NFL	16	9	27	276	10.2	3	3	0	18	1
1998—New York Jets NFL	14	1	3	50	16.7	0	0	0	0	0
1999—New York Jets NFL	14	8	8	66	8.3	2	2	0	12	0
2000—New York Jets NFL	9	6	4	22	5.5	2	2	0	12	0
Pro totals (8 years)	102	32	73	809	11.1	10	10	0	60	3

BEAN, ROBERT · CB · BENGALS

PERSONAL: Born January 6, 1978, in Atlanta. ... 5-11/178. ... Full name: Robert D. Bean Jr.
HIGH SCHOOL: Lakeside (Atlanta).
JUNIOR COLLEGE: Georgia Military College.
COLLEGE: Mississippi State.
TRANSACTIONS/CAREER NOTES: Selected by Cincinnati Bengals in fifth round (133rd pick overall) of 2000 NFL draft. ... Signed by Bengals (June 16, 2000).

			INTERCEPTIONS			
Year Team	G	GS	No.	Yds.	Avg.	TD
2000—Cincinnati NFL	12	4	1	0	0.0	0

BEASLEY, AARON · CB · JAGUARS

PERSONAL: Born July 7, 1973, in Pottstown, Pa. ... 6-0/195. ... Full name: Aaron Bruce Beasley.
HIGH SCHOOL: Pottstown (Pa.), then Valley Forge Military Academy (Wayne, Pa.).
COLLEGE: West Virginia.
TRANSACTIONS/CAREER NOTES: Selected by Jacksonville Jaguars in third round (63rd pick overall) of 1996 NFL draft. ... Signed by Jaguars (May 24, 1996). ... Granted free agency (February 12, 1999). ... Re-signed by Jaguars (March 3, 1999). ... Granted unconditional free agency (February 11, 2000). ... Re-signed by Jaguars (February 11, 2000).
CHAMPIONSHIP GAME EXPERIENCE: Played in AFC championship game (1996 and 1999 seasons).
PRO STATISTICS: 1998—Recovered one fumble for 90 yards and a touchdown and ran 30 yards on a lateral from punt return. 2000—Recovered one fumble.
MISCELLANEOUS: Holds Jacksonville Jaguars all-time record for most interceptions (12).

			INTERCEPTIONS				SACKS
Year Team	G	GS	No.	Yds.	Avg.	TD	No.
1996—Jacksonville NFL	9	7	1	0	0.0	0	1.0
1997—Jacksonville NFL	9	7	1	5	5.0	0	0.0
1998—Jacksonville NFL	16	15	3	35	11.7	0	0.0
1999—Jacksonville NFL	16	16	6	*200	§33.3	†2	1.5
2000—Jacksonville NFL	14	14	1	39	39.0	0	5.0
Pro totals (5 years)	64	59	12	279	23.3	2	7.5

BEASLEY, FRED · FB · 49ERS

PERSONAL: Born September 18, 1974, in Montgomery, Ala. ... 6-0/235. ... Full name: Frederick Jerome Beasley.
HIGH SCHOOL: Robert E. Lee (Montgomery, Ala.).
COLLEGE: Auburn.
TRANSACTIONS/CAREER NOTES: Selected by San Francisco 49ers in sixth round (180th pick overall) of 1998 NFL draft. ... Signed by 49ers (July 18, 1998). ... Granted free agency (March 2, 2001).
PRO STATISTICS: 1999—Recovered two fumbles.
SINGLE GAME HIGHS (regular season): Attempts—12 (December 26, 1999, vs. Washington); yards—65 (December 26, 1999, vs. Washington); and rushing touchdowns—2 (December 12, 1999, vs. Atlanta).

			RUSHING				RECEIVING				TOTALS			
Year Team	G	GS	Att.	Yds.	Avg.	TD	No.	Yds.	Avg.	TD	TD	2pt.	Pts.	Fum.
1998—San Francisco NFL	16	0	0	0	0.0	0	1	11	11.0	0	0	0	0	0
1999—San Francisco NFL	13	11	58	276	4.8	4	32	282	8.8	0	4	0	24	2
2000—San Francisco NFL	15	15	50	147	2.9	3	31	233	7.5	3	6	0	36	0
Pro totals (3 years)	44	26	108	423	3.9	7	64	526	8.2	3	10	0	60	2

BECHT, ANTHONY · TE · JETS

PERSONAL: Born August 8, 1977, in Drexel Hill, Pa. ... 6-5/267.
HIGH SCHOOL: Monsignor Bonner (Drexel Hill, Pa.).
COLLEGE: West Virginia (degree in business, 1999).
TRANSACTIONS/CAREER NOTES: Selected by New York Jets in first round (27th pick overall) of 2000 NFL draft. ... Signed by Jets (May 26, 2000).
PRO STATISTICS: 2000—Fumbled once and returned two kickoffs for no yards.
SINGLE GAME HIGHS (regular season): Receptions—3 (November 11, 2000, vs. Denver); yards—41 (November 5, 2000, vs. Denver); and touchdown receptions—1 (November 26, 2000, vs. Chicago).

			RECEIVING			
Year Team	G	GS	No.	Yds.	Avg.	TD
2000—New York Jets NFL	14	10	16	144	9.0	2

BECKETT, ROGERS · S · CHARGERS

PERSONAL: Born January 31, 1977, in Apopka, Fla. ... 6-3/205.
HIGH SCHOOL: Apopka (Fla.).
COLLEGE: Marshall (degree in political science).
TRANSACTIONS/CAREER NOTES: Selected by San Diego Chargers in second round (43rd pick overall) of 2000 NFL draft. ... Signed by Chargers (July 24, 2000).

			INTERCEPTIONS				SACKS
Year Team	G	GS	No.	Yds.	Avg.	TD	No.
2000—San Diego NFL	16	3	1	7	7.0	0	1.0

BEDELL, BRAD — OL — BROWNS

PERSONAL: Born February 12, 1977, in Arcadia, Calif. ... 6-4/299.
HIGH SCHOOL: Arcadia (Calif.).
JUNIOR COLLEGE: Mount San Antonio College (Calif.).
COLLEGE: Colorado.
TRANSACTIONS/CAREER NOTES: Selected by Cleveland Browns in sixth round (206th pick overall) of 2000 NFL draft. ... Signed by Browns (July 10, 2000).
PLAYING EXPERIENCE: Cleveland NFL, 2000. ... Games/Games started: 2000 (12/0).

BEEDE, FRANK — G — SEAHAWKS

PERSONAL: Born May 1, 1973, in Antioch, Calif. ... 6-4/296. ... Name pronounced BEE-dee.
HIGH SCHOOL: Antioch (Calif.).
COLLEGE: Panhandle State (Okla.).
TRANSACTIONS/CAREER NOTES: Signed as non-drafted free agent by Seattle Seahawks (April 22, 1996). ... On injured reserve with knee injury (August 25, 1998-entire season). ... Granted free agency (February 12, 1999). ... Re-signed by Seahawks (April 7, 1999). ... Granted unconditional free agency (February 11, 2000). ... Re-signed by Seahawks (June 9, 2000).
PLAYING EXPERIENCE: Seattle NFL, 1996, 1997, 1999 and 2000. ... Games/Games started: 1996 (14/2), 1997 (16/6), 1999 (10/0), 2000 (7/0). Total: 47/8.
PRO STATISTICS: 1997—Returned one kick for no yards and fumbled once.

BELL, MYRON — S — STEELERS

PERSONAL: Born September 15, 1971, in Toledo, Ohio. ... 5-11/203. ... Full name: Myron Corey Bell.
HIGH SCHOOL: Macomber-Whitney (Toledo, Ohio).
COLLEGE: Michigan State.
TRANSACTIONS/CAREER NOTES: Selected by Pittsburgh Steelers in fifth round (140th pick overall) of 1994 NFL draft. ... Signed by Steelers (July 18, 1994). ... Granted free agency (February 14, 1997). ... Re-signed by Steelers (April 15, 1997). ... Granted unconditional free agency (February 13, 1998). ... Signed by Cincinnati Bengals (June 26, 1998). ... Granted unconditional free agency (February 11, 2000). ... Signed by Steelers (December 20, 2000).
CHAMPIONSHIP GAME EXPERIENCE: Played in AFC championship game (1994, 1995 and 1997 seasons). ... Played in Super Bowl XXX (1995 season).
PRO STATISTICS: 1995—Recovered one fumble. 1996—Recovered two fumbles. 1997—Recovered one fumble.

				INTERCEPTIONS			SACKS
Year Team	G	GS	No.	Yds.	Avg.	TD	No.
1994—Pittsburgh NFL	15	0	0	0	0.0	0	0.0
1995—Pittsburgh NFL	16	9	2	4	2.0	0	0.0
1996—Pittsburgh NFL	16	4	0	0	0.0	0	2.0
1997—Pittsburgh NFL	16	8	1	10	10.0	0	1.5
1998—Cincinnati NFL	16	2	0	0	0.0	0	1.0
1999—Cincinnati NFL	16	16	1	5	5.0	0	2.0
2000—Pittsburgh NFL	1	0	0	0	0.0	0	0.0
Pro totals (7 years)	96	39	4	19	4.8	0	6.5

BELLAMY, JAY — S — SAINTS

PERSONAL: Born July 8, 1972, in Perth Amboy, N.J. ... 5-11/199. ... Full name: John Lee Bellamy. ... Name pronounced BELL-a-me.
HIGH SCHOOL: Matawan Regional (Aberdeen, N.J.).
COLLEGE: Rutgers.
TRANSACTIONS/CAREER NOTES: Signed as non-drafted free agent by Seattle Seahawks (April 27, 1994). ... On injured reserve with shoulder injury (November 11, 1994-remainder of season). ... Granted unconditional free agency (March 2, 2001). ... Signed by New Orleans Saints (April 4, 2001).
PRO STATISTICS: 1997—Credited with two sacks. 1998—Credited with one sack and recovered two fumbles. 1999—Recovered one fumble. 2000—Credited with two sacks.

			INTERCEPTIONS			
Year Team	G	GS	No.	Yds.	Avg.	TD
1994—Seattle NFL	3	0	0	0	0.0	0
1995—Seattle NFL	14	0	0	0	0.0	0
1996—Seattle NFL	16	0	3	18	6.0	0
1997—Seattle NFL	16	7	1	13	13.0	0
1998—Seattle NFL	16	16	3	40	13.3	0
1999—Seattle NFL	16	16	4	4	1.0	0
2000—Seattle NFL	16	16	4	132	33.0	1
Pro totals (7 years)	97	55	15	207	13.8	1

BELSER, JASON — DB

PERSONAL: Born May 28, 1970, in Kansas City, Mo. ... 5-9/196. ... Full name: Jason Daks Belser. ... Son of Caeser Belser, defensive back with Kansas City Chiefs (1968-71) and linebacker with San Francisco 49ers (1974). ... Name pronounced BELL-sir.
HIGH SCHOOL: Raytown (Mo.) South.
COLLEGE: Oklahoma.

TRANSACTIONS/CAREER NOTES: Selected by Indianapolis Colts in eighth round (197th pick overall) of 1992 NFL draft. ... Signed by Colts (July 22, 1992). ... Granted free agency (February 17, 1995). ... Tendered offer sheet by Carolina Panthers (April 17, 1995). ... Offer matched by Colts (April 19, 1995). ... Granted unconditional free agency (March 2, 2001).

CHAMPIONSHIP GAME EXPERIENCE: Played in AFC championship game (1995 season).

PRO STATISTICS: 1992—Fumbled once and recovered two fumbles. 1993—Recovered three fumbles. 1995—Returned one kickoff for 15 yards and recovered two fumbles. 1996—Recovered one fumble. 1998—Returned one punt for 53 yards and recovered one fumble. 2000— Recovered one fumble.

				INTERCEPTIONS			SACKS
Year Team	G	GS	No.	Yds.	Avg.	TD	No.
1992—Indianapolis NFL	16	2	3	27	9.0	0	0.0
1993—Indianapolis NFL	16	16	1	14	14.0	0	0.0
1994—Indianapolis NFL	13	12	1	31	31.0	0	0.0
1995—Indianapolis NFL	16	16	1	0	0.0	0	0.0
1996—Indianapolis NFL	16	16	4	81	20.3	†2	1.0
1997—Indianapolis NFL	16	16	2	121	60.5	1	1.0
1998—Indianapolis NFL	16	16	1	19	19.0	0	1.0
1999—Indianapolis NFL	16	16	0	0	0.0	0	1.0
2000—Indianapolis NFL	16	16	0	0	0.0	0	5.0
Pro totals (9 years)	141	126	13	293	22.5	3	9.0

BENNETT, BRANDON   RB   BENGALS

PERSONAL: Born February 3, 1973, in Taylors, S.C. ... 5-11/220.

HIGH SCHOOL: Riverside (Greer, S.C.).

COLLEGE: South Carolina.

TRANSACTIONS/CAREER NOTES: Signed as non-drafted free agent by Cleveland Browns (July 25, 1995). ... Released by Browns (August 18, 1995). ... Signed by Chicago Bears to practice squad (December 6, 1995). ... Released by Bears (August 19, 1996). ... Re-signed by Bears to practice squad (September 24, 1996). ... Released by Bears (November 1, 1996). ... Signed by Miami Dolphins to practice squad (November 5, 1996). ... Activated (December 17, 1996); did not play. ... Released by Dolphins (August 12, 1997). ... Signed by Cincinnati Bengals (April 20, 1998). ... Released by Bengals (August 30, 1998). ... Re-signed by Bengals (September 7, 1998). ... Released by Bengals (June 3, 1999). ... Re-signed by Bengals (March 2, 2001).

PRO STATISTICS: 1998—Recovered one fumble. 2000—Recovered one fumble.

SINGLE GAME HIGHS (regular season): Attempts—25 (December 20, 1998, vs. Pittsburgh); yards—87 (December 13, 1998, vs. Indianapolis); and rushing touchdowns—1 (December 3, 2000, vs. Arizona).

STATISTICAL PLATEAUS: 100-yard receiving games: 1998 (1).

			RUSHING				RECEIVING				KICKOFF RETURNS				TOTALS			
Year Team	G	GS	Att.	Yds.	Avg.	TD	No.	Yds.	Avg.	TD	No.	Yds.	Avg.	TD	TD	2pt.	Pts.	Fum.
1995—Chicago NFL							Did not play.											
1996—Miami NFL							Did not play.											
1997—							Did not play.											
1998—Cincinnati NFL	14	1	77	243	3.2	2	8	153	19.1	0	3	61	20.3	0	2	0	12	1
2000—Cincinnati NFL	16	0	90	324	3.6	3	19	168	8.8	0	0	0	0.0	0	3	0	18	2
Pro totals (2 years)	30	1	167	567	3.4	5	27	321	11.9	0	3	61	20.3	0	5	0	30	3

BENNETT, CORNELIUS   LB

PERSONAL: Born August 25, 1965, in Birmingham, Ala. ... 6-3/240. ... Full name: Cornelius O'landa Bennett.

HIGH SCHOOL: Ensley (Birmingham, Ala.).

COLLEGE: Alabama.

TRANSACTIONS/CAREER NOTES: Selected by Indianapolis Colts in first round (second pick overall) of 1987 NFL draft. ... Placed on reserve/unsigned list (August 31-October 30, 1987). ... Rights traded by Colts to Buffalo Bills in exchange for Bills trading first-round pick (RB Gaston Green) in 1988 draft, first-(RB Cleveland Gary) and second-round (CB Darryl Henley) picks in 1989 draft and RB Greg Bell to Los Angeles Rams (October 31, 1987); Rams also traded RB Eric Dickerson to Colts for first-(WR Aaron Cox) and second-round (LB Fred Strickland) picks in 1988 draft, second-round pick (LB Frank Stams) in 1989 draft and RB Owen Gill. ... Signed by Bills (October 31, 1987). ... Granted roster exemption (October 31-November 7, 1987). ... Granted free agency (February 1, 1992). ... Re-signed by Bills (August 31, 1992). ... Designated by Bills as franchise player (February 15, 1995). ... Granted unconditional free agency (February 16, 1996). ... Signed by Atlanta Falcons (March 1, 1996). ... Released by Falcons (February 17, 1999). ... Signed by Indianapolis Colts (March 1, 1999). ... On physically unable to perform list with knee injury (July 14-August 7, 2000). ... Released by Colts (March 1, 2001).

CHAMPIONSHIP GAME EXPERIENCE: Played in AFC championship game (1988 and 1990-1993 seasons). ... Played in Super Bowl XXV (1990 season), Super Bowl XXVI (1991 season), Super Bowl XXVII (1992 season), Super Bowl XXVIII (1993 season) and Super Bowl XXXIII (1998 season). ... Played in NFC championship game (1998 season).

HONORS: Named linebacker on THE SPORTING NEWS college All-America first team (1984-1986). ... Lombardi Award winner (1986). ... Named outside linebacker on THE SPORTING NEWS NFL All-Pro team (1988). ... Played in Pro Bowl (1988 and 1990-1993 seasons).

PRO STATISTICS: 1988—Recovered three fumbles. 1989—Recovered two fumbles for five yards. 1990—Returned blocked field-goal attempt 80 yards for a touchdown and recovered two fumbles. 1991—Recovered two fumbles for nine yards and one touchdown. 1992—Recovered three fumbles. 1993—Recovered two fumbles for 40 yards and fumbled once. 1994—Recovered three fumbles for 14 yards. 1995— Recovered two fumbles. 1996—Recovered two fumbles. 1997—Recovered one fumble. 1998—Recovered two fumbles for 10 yards. 1999— Recovered one fumble. 2000—Recovered one fumble.

				INTERCEPTIONS			SACKS
Year Team	G	GS	No.	Yds.	Avg.	TD	No.
1987—Buffalo NFL	8	7	0	0	0.0	0	8.5
1988—Buffalo NFL	16	16	2	30	15.0	0	9.5
1989—Buffalo NFL	12	12	2	5	2.5	0	5.5
1990—Buffalo NFL	16	16	0	0	0.0	0	4.0
1991—Buffalo NFL	16	16	0	0	0.0	0	9.0
1992—Buffalo NFL	15	15	0	0	0.0	0	4.0
1993—Buffalo NFL	16	16	1	5	5.0	0	5.0
1994—Buffalo NFL	16	16	0	0	0.0	0	5.0

Year Team	G	GS	INTERCEPTIONS No.	Yds.	Avg.	TD	SACKS No.
1995—Buffalo NFL	14	14	1	69	69.0	▲1	2.0
1996—Atlanta NFL	13	13	1	3	3.0	0	3.0
1997—Atlanta NFL	16	16	0	0	0.0	0	7.0
1998—Atlanta NFL	16	16	0	0	0.0	0	1.0
1999—Indianapolis NFL	16	16	0	0	0.0	0	5.0
2000—Indianapolis NFL	16	15	0	0	0.0	0	3.0
Pro totals (14 years)	206	204	7	112	16.0	1	71.5

BENNETT, DARREN   P   CHARGERS

PERSONAL: Born January 9, 1965, in Sydney, Australia. ... 6-5/235. ... Full name: Darren Leslie Bennett.
HIGH SCHOOL: Applecross (Perth, Western Australia).
COLLEGE: None.
TRANSACTIONS/CAREER NOTES: Played Australian Rules Football (1987-1993). ... Signed as non-drafted free agent by San Diego Chargers (April 14, 1994). ... Released by Chargers (August 28, 1994). ... Re-signed by Chargers to practice squad (August 29, 1994). ... Assigned by Chargers to Amsterdam Admirals in 1995 World League enhancement allocation program (February 20, 1995). ... Granted unconditional free agency (February 11, 2000). ... Re-signed by Chargers (March 7, 2000).
HONORS: Named punter on THE SPORTING NEWS NFL All-Pro team (1995). ... Played in Pro Bowl (1995 and 2000 seasons).
PRO STATISTICS: 1998—Fumbled once and recovered one fumble.

Year Team	G	No.	Yds.	PUNTING Avg.	Net avg.	In. 20	Blk.
1994—San Diego NFL				Did not play.			
1995—Amsterdam W.L.	10	60	2296	38.3	35.1	24	1
—San Diego NFL	16	72	3221	44.7	36.6	28	0
1996—San Diego NFL	16	87	3967	45.6	37.2	23	0
1997—San Diego NFL	16	89	3972	44.6	37.7	26	1
1998—San Diego NFL	16	95	4174	43.9	36.8	27	0
1999—San Diego NFL	16	89	3910	43.9	*38.7	32	0
2000—San Diego NFL	16	92	4248	*46.2	36.2	23	0
W.L. totals (1 year)	10	60	2296	38.3	35.1	24	1
NFL totals (5 years)	96	524	23492	44.8	37.2	159	1
Pro totals (6 years)	106	584	25788	44.2	37.0	183	2

BENNETT, DONNELL   FB   REDSKINS

PERSONAL: Born September 14, 1972, in Fort Lauderdale, Fla. ... 6-0/245.
HIGH SCHOOL: Cardinal Gibbons (Fort Lauderdale, Fla.).
COLLEGE: Miami (Fla.).
TRANSACTIONS/CAREER NOTES: Selected after junior season by Kansas City Chiefs in second round (58th pick overall) of 1994 NFL draft. ... Signed by Chiefs (May 6, 1994). ... On injured reserve with knee injury (December 20, 1994-remainder of season). ... On physically unable to perform list with knee injury (August 22-October 31, 1995). ... Granted free agency (February 14, 1997). ... Re-signed by Chiefs (April 22, 1997). ... Granted unconditional free agency (March 2, 2001). ... Signed by Washington Redskins (May 4, 2001).
PRO STATISTICS: 1994—Returned one kickoff for 12 yards and recovered one fumble. 1999—Returned three kickoffs for 51 yards.
SINGLE GAME HIGHS (regular season): Attempts—30 (September 20, 1998, vs. San Deigo); yards—115 (September 6, 1998, vs, Oakland); and rushing touchdowns—3 (September 27, 1998, vs. Philadelphia).
STATISTICAL PLATEAUS: 100-yard rushing games: 1998 (1).

Year Team	G	GS	RUSHING Att.	Yds.	Avg.	TD	RECEIVING No.	Yds.	Avg.	TD	TOTALS TD	2pt.	Pts.	Fum.
1994—Kansas City NFL	15	0	46	178	3.9	2	7	53	7.6	0	2	0	12	2
1995—Kansas City NFL	3	1	7	11	1.6	0	1	12	12.0	0	0	0	0	0
1996—Kansas City NFL	16	0	36	166	4.6	0	8	21	2.6	0	0	0	0	0
1997—Kansas City NFL	14	1	94	369	3.9	1	7	5	0.7	0	1	0	6	0
1998—Kansas City NFL	16	10	148	527	3.6	5	16	91	5.7	1	6	0	36	4
1999—Kansas City NFL	15	1	161	627	3.9	8	10	41	4.1	0	8	0	48	1
2000—Kansas City NFL	7	2	27	24	0.9	1	2	17	8.5	0	1	0	6	0
Pro totals (7 years)	86	15	519	1902	3.7	17	51	240	4.7	1	18	0	108	7

BENNETT, SEAN   RB   GIANTS

PERSONAL: Born November 9, 1975, in Evansville, Ind. ... 6-1/230. ... Full name: William Sean Bennett.
HIGH SCHOOL: Harrison (Evansville, Ind.).
COLLEGE: Illinois (did not play football), then Evansville, then Northwestern.
TRANSACTIONS/CAREER NOTES: Selected by New York Giants in fourth round (112th pick overall) of 1999 NFL draft. ... Signed by Giants (July 27, 1999). ... On injured reserve with knee injury (August 25, 2000-entire season).
SINGLE GAME HIGHS (regular season): Attempts—13 (September 12, 1999, vs. Tampa Bay); yards—45 (September 19, 1999, vs. Washington); and rushing touchdowns—1 (November 28, 1999, vs. Arizona).

Year Team	G	GS	RUSHING Att.	Yds.	Avg.	TD	RECEIVING No.	Yds.	Avg.	TD	TOTALS TD	2pt.	Pts.	Fum.
1999—New York Giants NFL	9	2	29	126	4.3	1	4	27	6.8	0	1	0	6	0
2000—New York Giants NFL					Did not play.									
Pro totals (1 years)	9	2	29	126	4.3	1	4	27	6.8	0	1	0	6	0

BENNETT, TOMMY — S — CARDINALS

PERSONAL: Born February 19, 1973, in Las Vegas, Nev. ... 6-2/212.
HIGH SCHOOL: Samuel F.B. Morse (San Diego).
COLLEGE: UCLA.
TRANSACTIONS/CAREER NOTES: Signed as a non-drafted free agent by Arizona Cardinals (April 23, 1996). ... Granted free agency (February 12, 1999). ... Re-signed by Cardinals (June 16, 1999). ... Granted unconditional free agency (February 11, 2000). ... Re-signed Cardinals (July 21, 2000). ... Granted unconditional free agency (March 2, 2001). ... Re-signed by Cardinals (June 1, 2001).
PRO STATISTICS: 1997—Recovered blocked punt in end zone for a touchdown. 1999—Recovered one fumble. 2000—Returned one kickoff for 17 yards.

| | | | | INTERCEPTIONS | | | | TOTALS | | | |
Year Team	G	GS	No.	Yds.	Avg.	TD	TD	2pt.	Pts.	Fum.
1996—Arizona NFL	16	1	0	0	0.0	0	0	0	0	0
1997—Arizona NFL	13	7	1	0	0.0	0	1	0	6	0
1998—Arizona NFL	16	16	2	100	50.0	1	1	0	6	0
1999—Arizona NFL	15	15	1	13	13.0	0	0	0	0	0
2000—Arizona NFL	11	0	0	0	0.0	0	0	0	0	0
Pro totals (5 years)	71	39	4	113	28.3	1	2	0	12	0

BENTLEY, SCOTT — K — REDSKINS

PERSONAL: Born April 10, 1974, in Dallas. ... 6-0/203.
HIGH SCHOOL: Aurora (Colo.).
COLLEGE: Florida State.
TRANSACTIONS/CAREER NOTES: Signed as non-drafted free agent by Arizona Cardinals (April 21, 1997). ... Released by Cardinals (August 19, 1997). ... Signed by Denver Broncos to practice squad (October 1, 1997). ... Activated (October 6, 1997). ... Released by Broncos (October 7, 1997). ... Signed by Atlanta Falcons to practice squad (December 2, 1997). ... Activated (December 14, 1997). ... Granted free agency (February 13, 1998). ... Signed by Denver Broncos to practice squad (October 7, 1998). ... Released by Broncos (October 13, 1998). ... Signed by Tampa Bay Buccaneers (April 7, 1999). ... Claimed on waivers by Baltimore Ravens (April 21, 1999). ... Released by Ravens (September 4, 1999). ... Signed by Kansas City Chiefs (November 10, 1999). ... Released by Chiefs (November 22, 1999). ... Signed by Broncos (October 14, 2000). ... Released by Broncos (October 16, 2000). ... Signed by Washington Redskins (November 9, 2000).

| | | | | KICKING | | | | |
Year Team	G	XPM	XPA	FGM	FGA	Lg.	50+	Pts.
1997—Denver NFL	1	4	4	2	3	33	0-0	10
—Atlanta NFL	2	0	0	0	0	0	0-0	0
1998—				Did not play.				
1999—Kansas City NFL	2	0	0	0	0	0	0-0	0
2000—Denver NFL	1	0	0	0	0	0	0-0	0
—Washington NFL	6	0	0	1	1	50	1-1	3
Pro totals (3 years)	12	4	4	3	4	50	1-1	13

BERCICH, PETE — LB

PERSONAL: Born December 23, 1971, in Joliet, Ill. ... 6-1/239. ... Full name: Peter James Bercich. ... Son of Bob Bercich, safety with Dallas Cowboys (1960 and 1961); and cousin of Bryan Rekar, pitcher, Tampa Bay Devil Rays. ... Name pronounced Burr-sitch.
HIGH SCHOOL: Providence Catholic (New Lenox, Ill.).
COLLEGE: Notre Dame (degree in finance, 1993).
TRANSACTIONS/CAREER NOTES: Selected by Minnesota Vikings in seventh round (211th pick overall) of 1994 NFL draft. ... Signed by Vikings (July 11, 1994). ... Released by Vikings (August 28, 1994). ... Re-signed by Vikings to practice squad (August 29, 1994). ... Granted free agency (February 13, 1998). ... Re-signed by Vikings (April 27, 1998). ... Granted unconditional free agency (February 12, 1999). ... Re-signed by Vikings (April 16, 1999). ... On injured reserve with knee injury (September 5, 1999-entire season). ... Granted unconditional free agency (February 11, 2000). ... Re-signed by Vikings (August 15, 2000). ... Released by Vikings (August 28, 2000). ... Re-signed by Vikings (November 25, 2000). ... Granted unconditional free agency (March 2, 2001).
PLAYING EXPERIENCE: Minnesota NFL, 1995-1998 and 2000. ... Games/Games started: 1995 (9/0), 1996 (15/1), 1997 (16/0), 1998 (15/1), 2000 (2/0). Total: 57/2.
CHAMPIONSHIP GAME EXPERIENCE: Played in NFC championship game (1998 and 2000 seasons).
PRO STATISTICS: 1996—Recovered one fumble.

BERGER, MITCH — P — VIKINGS

PERSONAL: Born June 24, 1972, in Kamloops, B.C. ... 6-4/228.
HIGH SCHOOL: North Delta (Vancouver).
JUNIOR COLLEGE: Tyler (Texas) Junior College.
COLLEGE: Colorado.
TRANSACTIONS/CAREER NOTES: Selected by Philadelphia Eagles in sixth round (193rd pick overall) of 1994 NFL draft. ... Signed by Eagles (July 11, 1994). ... Released by Eagles (October 10, 1994). ... Signed by Cincinnati Bengals to practice squad (October 13, 1994). ... Released by Bengals (November 30, 1994). ... Signed by Chicago Bears (March 7, 1995). ... Released by Bears (May 4, 1995). ... Signed by Indianapolis Colts (May 16, 1995). ... Claimed on waivers by Green Bay Packers (August 24, 1995). ... Released by Packers (August 27, 1995). ... Signed by Bears (November 7, 1995). ... Released by Bears (November 13, 1995). ... Signed by Minnesota Vikings (April 19, 1996). ... Granted unconditional free agency (February 11, 2000). ... Re-signed by Vikings (February 27, 2000).
CHAMPIONSHIP GAME EXPERIENCE: Played in NFC championship game (1998 and 2000 seasons).
HONORS: Named punter on THE SPORTING NEWS NFL All-Pro team (1999). ... Played in Pro Bowl (1999 season).
PRO STATISTICS: 1997—Rushed once for no yards and fumbled once for minus nine yards. 1999—Recovered one fumble. 2000—Had only pass attempt intercepted.

Year Team	G	PUNTING No.	Yds.	Avg.	Net avg.	In. 20	Blk.
1994—Philadelphia NFL	5	25	951	38.0	31.3	8	0
1995—			Did not play.				
1996—Minnesota NFL	16	88	3616	41.1	32.3	26	2
1997—Minnesota NFL	14	73	3133	42.9	34.1	22	0
1998—Minnesota NFL	16	55	2458	44.7	37.0	17	0
1999—Minnesota NFL	16	61	2769	‡45.4	‡38.4	18	0
2000—Minnesota NFL	16	62	2773	‡44.7	36.2	16	0
Pro totals (6 years)	83	364	15700	43.1	35.0	107	2

BERRY, GARY   S

PERSONAL: Born October 24, 1977, in Columbus, Ohio. ... 5-11/199. ... Full name: Gary John Berry II.
HIGH SCHOOL: Worthington (Ohio), then St. Francis DeSales (Columbus, Ohio).
COLLEGE: Ohio State.
TRANSACTIONS/CAREER NOTES: Selected by Green Bay Packers in fourth round (126th pick overall) of 2000 NFL draft. ... Signed by Packers (July 18, 2000). ... On injured reserve with neck injury (October 31, 2000-remainder of season). ... Released by Packers (June 5, 2001).
PLAYING EXPERIENCE: Green Bay NFL, 2000. ... Games/Games started: 2000 (4/0).
PRO STATISTICS: 2000—Returned one kickoff for 22 yards.

BETTIS, JEROME   RB   STEELERS

PERSONAL: Born February 16, 1972, in Detroit. ... 5-11/250. ... Full name: Jerome Abram Bettis. ... Nickname: The Bus.
HIGH SCHOOL: Mackenzie (Detroit).
COLLEGE: Notre Dame.
TRANSACTIONS/CAREER NOTES: Selected after junior season by Los Angeles Rams in first round (10th pick overall) of 1993 NFL draft. ... Signed by Rams (July 22, 1993). ... Rams franchise moved to St. Louis (April 12, 1995). ... Traded by Rams with third-round pick (LB Steven Conley) in 1996 draft to Pittsburgh Steelers for second-round pick (TE Ernie Conwell) in 1996 draft and fourth-round pick (traded to Miami) in 1997 draft (April 20, 1996). ... Granted unconditional free agency (February 14, 1997). ... Re-signed by Steelers (February 17, 1997). ... Granted unconditional free agency (March 2, 2001). ... Re-signed by Steelers (March 2, 2001).
CHAMPIONSHIP GAME EXPERIENCE: Played in AFC championship game (1997 season).
HONORS: Named NFL Rookie of the Year by THE SPORTING NEWS (1993). ... Played in Pro Bowl (1993, 1994, 1996 and 1997 seasons).
PRO STATISTICS: 1994—Recovered three fumbles. 1995—Recovered two fumbles. 1996—Recovered one fumble. 1999—Completed only pass attempt for 21 yards and a touchdown and recovered three fumbles for one yard. 2000—Attempted two passes without a completion and one interception and recovered one fumble.
SINGLE GAME HIGHS (regular season): Attempts—39 (January 2, 1994, vs. Chicago); yards—212 (December 12, 1993, vs. New Orleans); and rushing touchdowns—3 (November 30, 1997, vs. Arizona).
STATISTICAL PLATEAUS: 100-yard rushing games: 1993 (7), 1994 (4), 1996 (10), 1997 (10), 1998 (6), 1999 (2), 2000 (7). Total: 46.

Year Team	G	GS	RUSHING Att.	Yds.	Avg.	TD	RECEIVING No.	Yds.	Avg.	TD	TOTALS TD	2pt.	Pts.	Fum.
1993—Los Angeles Rams NFL	16	12	‡294	1429	4.9	7	26	244	9.4	0	7	0	42	4
1994—Los Angeles Rams NFL	16	16	319	1025	3.2	3	31	293	9.5	1	4	∞2	28	5
1995—St. Louis NFL	15	13	183	637	3.5	3	18	106	5.9	0	3	0	18	4
1996—Pittsburgh NFL	16	12	320	1431	4.5	11	22	122	5.5	0	11	0	66	7
1997—Pittsburgh NFL	15	15	*375	1665	4.4	7	15	110	7.3	2	9	0	54	6
1998—Pittsburgh NFL	15	15	316	1185	3.8	3	16	90	5.6	0	3	0	18	2
1999—Pittsburgh NFL	16	16	299	1091	3.6	7	21	110	5.2	0	7	0	42	2
2000—Pittsburgh NFL	16	16	355	1341	3.8	8	13	97	7.5	0	8	0	48	1
Pro totals (8 years)	125	115	2461	9804	4.0	49	162	1172	7.2	3	52	2	316	31

BEUERLEIN, STEVE   QB   BRONCOS

PERSONAL: Born March 7, 1965, in Hollywood, Calif. ... 6-3/220. ... Full name: Stephen Taylor Beuerlein. ... Name pronounced BURR-line.
HIGH SCHOOL: Servite (Anaheim, Calif.).
COLLEGE: Notre Dame (degree in American studies, 1987).
TRANSACTIONS/CAREER NOTES: Selected by Los Angeles Raiders in fourth round (110th pick overall) of 1987 NFL draft. ... Signed by Raiders (July 24, 1987). ... On injured reserve with elbow and shoulder injuries (September 7, 1987-entire season). ... Granted free agency (February 1, 1990). ... Re-signed by Raiders (September 3, 1990). ... Granted roster exemption (September 3-16, 1990). ... Inactive for all 16 games (1990). ... Granted free agency (February 1, 1991). ... Re-signed by Raiders (July 8, 1991). ... Traded by Raiders to Dallas Cowboys for fourth-round pick (traded to Indianapolis) in 1992 draft (August 25, 1991). ... Granted unconditional free agency (March 1, 1993). ... Signed by Phoenix Cardinals (April 21, 1993). ... Cardinals franchise renamed Arizona Cardinals for 1994 season. ... Selected by Jacksonville Jaguars from Cardinals in NFL expansion draft (February 15, 1995). ... Granted free agency (February 16, 1996). ... Signed by Carolina Panthers (April 10, 1996). ... Released by Panthers (March 19, 2001). ... Signed by Denver Broncos (May 30, 2001).
CHAMPIONSHIP GAME EXPERIENCE: Member of Raiders for AFC championship game (1990 season); inactive. ... Played in NFC championship game (1992 season). ... Member of Super Bowl championship team (1992 season). ... Member of Panthers for NFC championship game (1996 season); did not play.
HONORS: Played in Pro Bowl (1999 season).
PRO STATISTICS: 1988—Caught one pass for 21 yards, fumbled six times and recovered two fumbles for minus one yard. 1989—Fumbled six times and recovered three fumbles for minus eight yards. 1993—Fumbled eight times and recovered two fumbles. 1994—Fumbled eight times and recovered three fumbles for minus 13 yards. 1995—Fumbled three times. 1996—Fumbled nine times and recovered two fumbles for minus seven yards. 1997—Fumbled once. 1998—Fumbled 13 times and recovered five fumbles for minus 19 yards. 1999—Tied for NFC lead with 12 fumbles for minus four yards. 2000—Fumbled nine times for minus five yards.
SINGLE GAME HIGHS (regular season): Attempts—53 (December 19, 1993, vs. Seattle); completions—34 (December 19, 1993, vs. Seattle); yards—431 (December 19, 1993, vs. Seattle); and touchdown passes—5 (January 2, 2000, vs. New Orleans).
STATISTICAL PLATEAUS: 300-yard passing games: 1988 (1), 1993 (2), 1999 (5), 2000 (3). Total: 11.
MISCELLANEOUS: Regular-season record as starting NFL quarterback: 45-52 (.463). ... Postseason record as starting NFL quarterback: 1-1 (.500). ... Holds Carolina Panthers all-time records for most passing yards (12,690) and touchdown passes (86).

Year Team	G	GS	PASSING								RUSHING				TOTALS		
			Att.	Cmp.	Pct.	Yds.	TD	Int.	Avg.	Rat.	Att.	Yds.	Avg.	TD	TD	2pt.	Pts.
1987—L.A. Raiders NFL........							Did not play.										
1988—L.A. Raiders NFL........	10	8	238	105	44.1	1643	8	7	6.90	66.6	30	35	1.2	0	0	0	0
1989—L.A. Raiders NFL........	10	7	217	108	49.8	1677	13	9	7.73	78.4	16	39	2.4	0	0	0	0
1990—L.A. Raiders NFL........							Did not play.										
1991—Dallas NFL..................	8	4	137	68	49.6	909	5	2	6.64	77.2	7	-14	-2.0	0	0	0	0
1992—Dallas NFL..................	16	0	18	12	66.7	152	0	1	8.44	69.7	4	-7	-1.8	0	0	0	0
1993—Phoenix NFL................	16	14	418	258	61.7	3164	18	17	7.57	82.5	22	45	2.0	0	0	0	0
1994—Arizona NFL	9	7	255	130	51.0	1545	5	9	6.06	61.6	22	39	1.8	1	1	0	6
1995—Jacksonville NFL	7	6	142	71	50.0	952	4	7	6.70	60.5	5	32	6.4	0	0	0	0
1996—Carolina NFL	8	4	123	69	56.1	879	8	2	7.15	93.5	12	17	1.4	0	0	0	0
1997—Carolina NFL	7	3	153	89	58.2	1032	6	3	6.75	83.6	4	32	8.0	0	0	0	0
1998—Carolina NFL	12	12	343	216	63.0	2613	17	12	7.62	88.2	22	26	1.2	0	0	0	0
1999—Carolina NFL	16	16	571	*343	60.1	*4436	36	15	7.77	94.6	27	124	4.6	2	2	0	12
2000—Carolina NFL	16	16	533	324	60.8	3730	19	18	7.00	79.7	44	106	2.4	1	1	1	8
Pro totals (12 years)	135	97	3148	1793	57.0	22732	139	102	7.22	80.9	215	474	2.2	4	4	1	26

BEVERLY, ERIC — C — LIONS

PERSONAL: Born March 28, 1974, in Cleveland. ... 6-3/294. ... Full name: Eric Raymonde Beverly.
HIGH SCHOOL: Bedford Heights (Ohio).
COLLEGE: Miami of Ohio.
TRANSACTIONS/CAREER NOTES: Signed as non-drafted free agent by Detroit Lions (April 24, 1997). ... Released by Lions (August 24, 1997). ... Re-signed by Lions to practice squad (August 26, 1997). ... Activated (December 20, 1997). ... Active for one game (1997); did not play. ... Granted free agency (March 2, 2001). ... Tendered offer sheet by Miami Dolphins (March 8, 2001). ... Offer matched by Lions (March 15, 2001).
PLAYING EXPERIENCE: Detroit NFL, 1998-2000. ... Games/Games started: 1998 (16/0), 1999 (16/2), 2000 (16/7). Total: 48/9.
PRO STATISTICS: 2000—Returned one kickoff for no yards.

BIAKABUTUKA, TSHIMANGA — RB — PANTHERS

PERSONAL: Born January 24, 1974, in Kinsasha, Zaire. ... 6-0/215. ... Name pronounced tee-MON-guh bee-ock-a-ba-TWO-kah. ... Nickname: Tim.
HIGH SCHOOL: John Jacques Rosseau (Longueuil, Que.).
JUNIOR COLLEGE: Vanier College (Montreal).
COLLEGE: Michigan.
TRANSACTIONS/CAREER NOTES: Selected after junior season by Carolina Panthers in first round (eighth pick overall) of 1996 NFL draft. ... Signed by Panthers (August 16, 1996). ... On injured reserve with knee injury (October 1, 1996-remainder of season).
SINGLE GAME HIGHS (regular season): Attempts—31 (November 28, 1999, vs. Atlanta); yards—142 (October 3, 1999, vs. Washington); and rushing touchdowns—3 (October 3, 1999, vs. Washington).
STATISTICAL PLATEAUS: 100-yard rushing games: 1997 (1), 1998 (2), 1999 (2), 2000 (1). Total: 6.
MISCELLANEOUS: Holds Carolina Panthers all-time record for most yards rushing (2,300). ... Shares Carolina Panthers all-time record for rushing touchdowns (13).

Year Team	G	GS	RUSHING				RECEIVING				TOTALS			
			Att.	Yds.	Avg.	TD	No.	Yds.	Avg.	TD	TD	2pt.	Pts.	Fum.
1996—Carolina NFL	4	4	71	229	3.2	0	0	0	0.0	0	0	0	0	0
1997—Carolina NFL	8	2	75	299	4.0	2	0	0	0.0	0	2	0	12	1
1998—Carolina NFL	11	3	101	427	4.2	3	8	138	17.3	1	4	0	24	1
1999—Carolina NFL	11	11	138	718	5.2	6	23	189	8.2	0	6	0	36	3
2000—Carolina NFL	12	11	173	627	3.6	2	34	341	10.0	2	4	0	24	4
Pro totals (5 years)	46	31	558	2300	4.1	13	65	668	10.3	3	16	0	96	9

BIDWELL, JOSH — P — PACKERS

PERSONAL: Born March 13, 1976, in Roseburg, Ore. ... 6-3/225. ... Full name: Joshua John Bidwell.
HIGH SCHOOL: Douglas (Winston, Ore.).
COLLEGE: Oregon (degree in English).
TRANSACTIONS/CAREER NOTES: Selected by Green Bay Packers in fourth round (133rd pick overall) of 1999 NFL draft. ... Signed by Packers (July 27, 1999). ... On non-football illness list with cancer (September 5, 1999-entire season).
HONORS: Named punter on THE SPORTING NEWS college All-America second team (1998).
PRO STATISTICS: 2000—Fumbled once and recovered one fumble.

Year Team	G	PUNTING					
		No.	Yds.	Avg.	Net avg.	In. 20	Blk.
1999—Green Bay NFL				Did not play.			
2000—Green Bay NFL	16	78	3003	38.5	34.6	22	0
Pro totals (1 years)	16	78	3003	38.5	34.6	22	0

BIEKERT, GREG — LB — RAIDERS

PERSONAL: Born March 14, 1969, in Iowa City, Iowa. ... 6-2/255. ... Name pronounced BEEK-ert.
HIGH SCHOOL: Longmont (Colo.).
COLLEGE: Colorado (degree in marketing, 1992).
TRANSACTIONS/CAREER NOTES: Selected by Los Angeles Raiders in seventh round (181st pick overall) of 1993 NFL draft. ... Signed by Raiders (July 13, 1993). ... Raiders franchise moved to Oakland (July 21, 1995).

CHAMPIONSHIP GAME EXPERIENCE: Played in AFC championship game (2000 season).
PRO STATISTICS: 1994—Intercepted one pass for 11 yards. 1996—Recovered one fumble. 1997—Returned one kickoff for 16 yards. 1998—Recovered one fumble. 1999—Intercepted two passes for 57 yards. 2000—Recovered two fumbles.

Year Team	G	GS	SACKS
1993—Los Angeles Raiders NFL	16	0	0.0
1994—Los Angeles Raiders NFL	16	14	1.5
1995—Oakland NFL	16	14	1.0
1996—Oakland NFL	16	15	0.0
1997—Oakland NFL	16	16	2.5
1998—Oakland NFL	16	16	3.0
1999—Oakland NFL	16	16	2.0
2000—Oakland NFL	16	16	2.0
Pro totals (8 years)	128	107	12.0

BINN, DAVID   C   CHARGERS

PERSONAL: Born February 6, 1972, in San Mateo, Calif. ... 6-3/245. ... Full name: David Aaron Binn.
HIGH SCHOOL: San Mateo (Calif.).
COLLEGE: California (degree in ecology and the social system, 1993).
TRANSACTIONS/CAREER NOTES: Signed as non-drafted free agent by San Diego Chargers (April 28, 1994). ... Granted unconditional free agency (February 13, 1998). ... Re-signed by Chargers (February 25, 1998). ... Granted unconditional free agency (February 11, 2000). ... Re-signed by Chargers (February 11, 2000).
PLAYING EXPERIENCE: San Diego NFL, 1994-2000. ... Games/Games started: 1994 (16/0), 1995 (16/0), 1996 (16/0), 1997 (16/0), 1998 (15/0), 1999 (16/0), 2000 (16/0). Total: 111/0.
CHAMPIONSHIP GAME EXPERIENCE: Played in AFC championship game (1994 season). ... Played in Super Bowl XXIX (1994 season).
PRO STATISTICS: 1999—Fumbled once for minus 36 yards.

BIRK, MATT   C   VIKINGS

PERSONAL: Born July 23, 1976, in St. Paul, Minn. ... 6-4/308. ... Full name: Matthew Robert Birk.
HIGH SCHOOL: Cretin-Derham Hall (St. Paul, Minn.).
COLLEGE: Harvard (degree in economics, 1998).
TRANSACTIONS/CAREER NOTES: Selected by Minnesota Vikings in sixth round (173rd pick overall) of 1998 NFL draft. ... Signed by Vikings (June 24, 1998). ... Granted free agency (March 2, 2001). ... Re-signed by Vikings (March 6, 2001).
PLAYING EXPERIENCE: Minnesota NFL, 1998-2000. ... Games/Games started: 1998 (7/0), 1999 (15/0), 2000 (16/16). Total: 38/16.
CHAMPIONSHIP GAME EXPERIENCE: Member of Vikings for NFC championship game (1998 season); did not play. ... Played in NFC championship game (2000 season).
HONORS: Played in Pro Bowl (2000 season).
PRO STATISTICS: 2000—Fumbled once.

BISHOP, BLAINE   S   TITANS

PERSONAL: Born July 24, 1970, in Indianapolis. ... 5-9/203. ... Full name: Blaine Elwood Bishop.
HIGH SCHOOL: Cathedral (Indianapolis).
COLLEGE: Saint Joseph's College (Ind.), then Ball State (degree in insurance, 1993).
TRANSACTIONS/CAREER NOTES: Selected by Houston Oilers in eighth round (214th pick overall) of 1993 NFL draft. ... Signed by Oilers (July 16, 1993). ... Granted free agency (February 16, 1996). ... Re-signed by Oilers (June 17, 1996). ... Designated by Oilers as franchise player (February 14, 1997). ... Re-signed by Oilers (August 27, 1997). ... Oilers franchise moved to Tennessee for 1997 season. ... Oilers franchise renamed Tennessee Titans for 1999 season (December 26, 1998).
CHAMPIONSHIP GAME EXPERIENCE: Played in AFC championship game (1999 season). ... Played in Super Bowl XXXIV (1999 season).
HONORS: Played in Pro Bowl (1995, 1997 and 2000 seasons). ... Named to play in Pro Bowl (1996 season); replaced by Tyrone Braxton due to injury.
PRO STATISTICS: 1993—Fumbled once and recovered one fumble. 1994—Returned two kickoffs for 18 yards and recovered one fumble. 1995—Recovered four fumbles for six yards. 1997—Recovered two fumbles. 1998—Recovered one fumble. 1999—Recovered two fumbles.

			INTERCEPTIONS				SACKS
Year Team	G	GS	No.	Yds.	Avg.	TD	No.
1993—Houston NFL	16	2	1	1	1.0	0	1.0
1994—Houston NFL	16	13	1	21	21.0	0	1.5
1995—Houston NFL	16	16	1	62	62.0	▲1	1.5
1996—Houston NFL	15	15	1	6	6.0	0	0.0
1997—Tennessee NFL	14	14	0	0	0.0	0	1.5
1998—Tennessee NFL	13	13	1	13	13.0	0	3.0
1999—Tennessee NFL	15	15	0	0	0.0	0	2.5
2000—Tennessee NFL	16	16	0	0	0.0	0	2.5
Pro totals (8 years)	121	104	5	103	20.6	1	13.5

BISHOP, MICHAEL   QB   PATRIOTS

PERSONAL: Born May 15, 1976, in Galveston, Texas. ... 6-2/217. ... Full name: Michael Paul Bishop.
HIGH SCHOOL: Willis (Texas).
JUNIOR COLLEGE: Blinn College (Texas).
COLLEGE: Kansas State.

TRANSACTIONS/CAREER NOTES: Selected by New England Patriots in seventh round (227th pick overall) of 1999 NFL draft. ... Signed by Patriots (June 25, 1999). ... Active for one game (1999); did not play. ... Assigned by Patriots to Frankfurt Galaxy in 2001 NFL Europe enhancement allocation program (February 19, 2001).

HONORS: Davey O'Brien Award winner (1998). ... Named quarterback on THE SPORTING NEWS college All-America first team (1998).

SINGLE GAME HIGHS (regular season): Attempts—6 (October 15, 2000, vs. New York Jets); completions—2 (October 15, 2000, vs. New York Jets); yards—44 (October 8, 2000, vs. Indianapolis); and touchdown passes—1 (October 8, 2000, vs. Indianapolis).

				PASSING							RUSHING				TOTALS	
Year Team	G	GS	Att.	Cmp.	Pct.	Yds.	TD	Int.	Avg.	Rat.	Att.	Yds.	Avg.	TD	TD	2pt.	Pts.
1999—New England NFL........									Did not play.								
2000—New England NFL........	8	0	9	3	33.3	80	1	1	8.89	64.4	7	-1	-0.1	0	0	0	0
Pro totals (1 years)	8	0	9	3	33.3	80	1	1	8.89	64.4	7	-1	-0.1	0	0	0	0

BJORNSON, ERIC   TE   RAIDERS

PERSONAL: Born December 15, 1971, in San Francisco. ... 6-4/236. ... Name pronounced be-YORN-son.
HIGH SCHOOL: Bishop O'Dowd (Oakland).
COLLEGE: Washington.
TRANSACTIONS/CAREER NOTES: Selected by Dallas Cowboys in fourth round (110th pick overall) of 1995 NFL draft. ... Signed by Cowboys (July 18, 1995). ... Granted free agency (February 13, 1998). ... Re-signed by Cowboys (July 13, 1998). ... Granted unconditional free agency (February 11, 2000). ... Signed by New England Patriots (February 26, 2000). ... Released by Patriots (November 15, 2000). ... Signed by Oakland Raiders (March 1, 2001).
CHAMPIONSHIP GAME EXPERIENCE: Played in NFC championship game (1995 season). ... Member of Super Bowl championship team (1995 season).
PRO STATISTICS: 1998—Rushed once for seven yards and a touchdown. 1999—Rushed once for 20 yards and a touchdown. 2000— Recovered one fumble.
SINGLE GAME HIGHS (regular season): Receptions—8 (November 10, 1996, vs. San Francisco); yards—71 (October 5, 1997, vs. New York Giants); and touchdown receptions—1 (October 8, 2000, vs. Indianapolis).

			RECEIVING				TOTALS			
Year Team	G	GS	No.	Yds.	Avg.	TD	TD	2pt.	Pts.	Fum.
1995—Dallas NFL..............................	14	1	7	53	7.6	0	0	0	0	0
1996—Dallas NFL..............................	14	10	48	388	8.1	3	3	1	20	1
1997—Dallas NFL..............................	14	14	47	442	9.4	0	0	1	2	2
1998—Dallas NFL..............................	16	4	15	218	14.5	1	2	0	12	0
1999—Dallas NFL..............................	16	6	10	131	13.1	0	1	0	6	0
2000—New England NFL....................	8	6	20	152	7.6	2	2	0	12	0
Pro totals (6 years)	82	41	147	1384	9.4	6	8	2	52	3

BLACK, AVION   WR   BILLS

PERSONAL: Born April 24, 1977, in Nashville. ... 5-11/181. ... Full name: Avion Carlos Black.
HIGH SCHOOL: Maplewood (Nashville).
COLLEGE: Tennessee State.
TRANSACTIONS/CAREER NOTES: Selected by Buffalo Bills in fourth round (121st pick overall) of 2000 NFL draft. ... Signed by Bills (July 10, 2000).

			KICKOFF RETURNS				TOTALS			
Year Team	G	GS	No.	Yds.	Avg.	TD	TD	2pt.	Pts.	Fum.
2000—Buffalo NFL	2	0	9	165	18.3	0	0	0	0	0

BLACKSHEAR, JEFF   G   CHIEFS

PERSONAL: Born March 29, 1969, in Fort Pierce, Fla. ... 6-6/316. ... Full name: Jeffrey Leon Blackshear.
HIGH SCHOOL: Westwood Christian (Miami).
JUNIOR COLLEGE: Northwest Mississippi Junior College.
COLLEGE: Northeast Louisiana.
TRANSACTIONS/CAREER NOTES: Selected by Seattle Seahawks in eighth round (197th pick overall) of 1993 NFL draft. ... Signed by Seahawks (July 15, 1993). ... Traded by Seahawks to Cleveland Browns for fourth-round pick (traded to Atlanta) in 1997 draft (March 12, 1996). ... Browns franchise moved to Baltimore and renamed Ravens for 1996 season (March 11, 1996). ... Granted unconditional free agency (February 14, 1997). ... Re-signed by Ravens (March 13, 1997). ... Released by Ravens (February 23, 2000). ... Signed by Kansas City Chiefs (May 4, 2000).
PLAYING EXPERIENCE: Seattle NFL, 1993 and 1994; Cleveland NFL, 1995; Baltimore NFL, 1996-1999; Kansas City NFL, 2000. ... Games/Games started: 1993 (15/2), 1994 (16/16), 1995 (16/3), 1996 (16/12), 1997 (16/16), 1998 (16/16), 1999 (16/16), 2000 (16/15). Total: 127/96.

BLACKWELL, WILL   WR   STEELERS

PERSONAL: Born July 9, 1975, in Texarkana, Texas. ... 6-0/190. ... Full name: William Herman Blackwell Jr.
HIGH SCHOOL: Skyline (Oakland).
COLLEGE: San Diego State.
TRANSACTIONS/CAREER NOTES: Selected after junior season by Pittsburgh Steelers in second round (53rd pick overall) of 1997 NFL draft. ... Signed by Steelers (July 15, 1997). ... On injured reserve with foot injury (December 6, 1999-remainder of season). ... Granted free agency (February 11, 2000). ... Re-signed by Steelers (March 17, 2000). ... On physically unable to perform list with knee injury (August 21-November 20, 2000). ... Granted unconditional free agency (March 2, 2001). ... Re-signed by Steelers (May 7, 2001).
CHAMPIONSHIP GAME EXPERIENCE: Played in AFC championship game (1997 season).
PRO STATISTICS: 1997—Recovered two fumbles.
SINGLE GAME HIGHS (regular season): Receptions—4 (November 21, 1999, vs. Tennessee); yards—68 (September 28, 1997, vs. Tennessee); and touchdown receptions—1 (November 26, 1998, vs. Detroit).

Year Team	G	GS	RECEIVING No.	Yds.	Avg.	TD	PUNT RETURNS No.	Yds.	Avg.	TD	KICKOFF RETURNS No.	Yds.	Avg.	TD	TOTALS TD	2pt.	Pts.	Fum.
1997—Pittsburgh NFL............	14	0	12	168	14.0	1	23	149	6.5	0	32	791	24.7	▲1	2	0	12	3
1998—Pittsburgh NFL............	16	2	32	297	9.3	1	4	22	5.5	0	20	382	19.1	0	1	1	8	1
1999—Pittsburgh NFL............	11	1	20	186	9.3	0	1	39	39.0	0	14	282	20.1	0	0	0	0	1
2000—Pittsburgh NFL............	5	0	2	23	11.5	0	0	0	0.0	0	10	281	28.1	▲1	1	0	6	0
Pro totals (4 years)...............	46	3	66	674	10.2	2	28	210	7.5	0	76	1736	22.8	2	4	1	26	5

BLAISE, KERLIN   G   LIONS

PERSONAL: Born December 25, 1974, in Orlando, Fla. ... 6-5/323.
HIGH SCHOOL: Maynard Evans (Orlando, Fla.).
COLLEGE: Miami (Fla.).
TRANSACTIONS/CAREER NOTES: Signed as non-drafted free agent by Detroit Lions (April 24, 1998). ... Released by Lions (August 30, 1998). ... Re-signed by Lions to practice squad (September 1, 1998). ... Activated (October 27, 1998); did not play. ... On injured reserve with knee injury (December 1, 1998-remainder of season). ... Granted free agency (March 2, 2001). ... Re-signed by Lions (April 26, 2001).
PLAYING EXPERIENCE: Detroit NFL, 1999 and 2000. ... Games/Games started: 1999 (16/4), 2000 (12/0). Total: 28/4.

BLAKE, JEFF   QB   SAINTS

PERSONAL: Born December 4, 1970, in Daytona Beach, Fla. ... 6-0/210. ... Son of Emory Blake, running back with Toronto Argonauts of CFL (1974).
HIGH SCHOOL: Seminole (Sanford, Fla.).
COLLEGE: East Carolina.
TRANSACTIONS/CAREER NOTES: Selected by New York Jets in sixth round (166th pick overall) of 1992 NFL draft. ... Signed by Jets (July 14, 1992). ... Inactive for all 16 games (1993). ... Claimed on waivers by Cincinnati Bengals (August 29, 1994). ... Granted free agency (February 17, 1995). ... Re-signed by Bengals (May 8, 1995). ... On injured reserve with wrist injury (December 24, 1998-remainder of season). ... Granted unconditional free agency (February 11, 2000). ... Signed by New Orleans Saints (February 11, 2000). ... On injured reserve with broken foot (November 20, 2000-remainder of season).
HONORS: Played in Pro Bowl (1995 season).
PRO STATISTICS: 1992—Fumbled once. 1994—Fumbled six times. 1995—Fumbled 10 times for minus seven yards. 1996—Fumbled seven times and recovered one fumble for minus five yards. 1997—Fumbled seven times. 1998—Fumbled once. 1999—Fumbled 12 times and recovered seven fumbles for minus 28 yards. 2000—Fumbled seven times and recovered three fumbles for minus two yards.
SINGLE GAME HIGHS (regular season): Attempts—46 (September 10, 2000, vs. San Diego); completions—33 (September 10, 2000, vs. San Diego); yards—387 (November 6, 1994, vs. Seattle); and touchdown passes—4 (December 5, 1999, vs. San Francisco).
STATISTICAL PLATEAUS: 300-yard passing games: 1994 (2), 1995 (1), 1996 (2), 1997 (1), 1998 (1), 1999 (1). Total: 8.
MISCELLANEOUS: Regular-season record as starting NFL quarterback: 32-45 (.416).

Year Team	G	GS	PASSING Att.	Cmp.	Pct.	Yds.	TD	Int.	Avg.	Rat.	RUSHING Att.	Yds.	Avg.	TD	TOTALS TD	2pt.	Pts.
1992—New York Jets NFL......	3	0	9	4	44.4	40	0	1	4.44	18.1	2	-2	-1.0	0	0	0	0
1993—New York Jets NFL......						Did not play.											
1994—Cincinnati NFL............	10	9	306	156	51.0	2154	14	9	7.04	76.9	37	204	5.5	1	1	1	8
1995—Cincinnati NFL............	16	16	567	§326	57.5	3822	§28	17	6.74	82.1	53	309	5.8	2	2	1	14
1996—Cincinnati NFL............	16	16	549	308	56.1	3624	24	14	6.60	80.3	72	317	4.4	2	2	0	12
1997—Cincinnati NFL............	11	11	317	184	58.0	2125	8	7	6.70	77.6	45	234	5.2	3	3	0	18
1998—Cincinnati NFL............	9	2	93	51	54.8	739	3	3	7.95	78.2	15	103	6.9	0	0	0	0
1999—Cincinnati NFL............	14	12	389	215	55.3	2670	16	12	6.86	77.6	63	332	5.3	2	2	0	12
2000—New Orleans NFL.......	11	11	302	184	60.9	2025	13	9	6.71	82.7	57	243	4.3	1	1	0	6
Pro totals (8 years)...............	90	77	2532	1428	56.4	17199	106	72	6.79	79.5	344	1740	5.1	11	11	2	70

BLANCHARD, CARY   K   CARDINALS

PERSONAL: Born November 5, 1968, in Fort Worth, Texas. ... 6-2/222. ... Full name: Robert Cary Blanchard.
HIGH SCHOOL: L.D. Bell (Hurst, Texas).
COLLEGE: Oklahoma State.
TRANSACTIONS/CAREER NOTES: Signed as non-drafted free agent by Dallas Cowboys (April 25, 1991). ... Released by Cowboys (August 4, 1991). ... Signed by Sacramento Surge of World League (1992). ... Signed by New Orleans Saints (July 7, 1992). ... Released by Saints (August 31, 1992). ... Re-signed by Saints to practice squad (September 7, 1992). ... Activated (September 14, 1992). ... Active for one game with Saints (1992); did not play. ... Claimed on waivers by New York Jets (September 29, 1992). ... Released by Jets (June 24, 1994). ... Signed by Minnesota Vikings (July 12, 1994). ... Released by Vikings (August 28, 1994). ... Signed by Saints (April 18, 1995). ... Released by Saints (August 27, 1995). ... Signed by Indianapolis Colts (October 3, 1995). ... Released by Colts (August 30, 1998). ... Signed by Washington Redskins (September 22, 1998). ... Granted unconditional free agency (February 12, 1999). ... Re-signed by Redskins (April 20, 1999). ... Released by Redskins (August 30, 1999). ... Signed by New York Giants (October 20, 1999). ... Granted unconditional free agency (February 11, 2000). ... Signed by Arizona Cardinals (February 28, 2000).
CHAMPIONSHIP GAME EXPERIENCE: Played in AFC championship game (1995 season).
HONORS: Named kicker on THE SPORTING NEWS NFL All-Pro team (1996). ... Played in Pro Bowl (1996 season).
RECORDS: Shares NFL single-game record for most field goals made, one quarter—4 (September 21, 1997, vs. Buffalo, second quarter).
PRO STATISTICS: 1998—Punted three times for 113 yards.

Year Team	G	KICKING XPM	XPA	FGM	FGA	Lg.	50+	Pts.
1992—Sacramento W.L.	4	17	17	5	8	42	0-0	32
—New York Jets NFL.............................	11	17	17	16	22	47	0-1	65
1993—New York Jets NFL.............................	16	31	31	17	26	45	0-2	82
1994—				Did not play.				
1995—Indianapolis NFL	12	25	25	19	24	50	1-1	82
1996—Indianapolis NFL	16	27	27	§36	§40	52	5-5	§135

Year—Team	G	KICKING						
		XPM	XPA	FGM	FGA	Lg.	50+	Pts.
1997—Indianapolis NFL	16	21	21	§32	†41	50	1-3	117
1998—Washington NFL	13	30	31	11	17	54	1-2	63
1999—New York Giants NFL	10	19	19	18	21	48	0-0	73
2000—Arizona NFL	16	18	19	16	23	54	2-4	66
W.L. totals (1 year)	4	17	17	5	8	42	0-0	32
NFL totals (8 years)	110	188	190	165	214	54	10-18	683
Pro totals (9 years)	114	205	207	170	222	54	10-0	715

BLEDSOE, DREW — QB — PATRIOTS

PERSONAL: Born February 14, 1972, in Ellensburg, Wash. ... 6-5/240.
HIGH SCHOOL: Walla Walla (Wash.).
COLLEGE: Washington State.
TRANSACTIONS/CAREER NOTES: Selected after junior season by New England Patriots in first round (first pick overall) of 1993 NFL draft. ... Signed by Patriots (July 6, 1993).
CHAMPIONSHIP GAME EXPERIENCE: Played in AFC championship game (1996 season). ... Played in Super Bowl XXXI (1996 season).
HONORS: Played in Pro Bowl (1994, 1996 and 1997 seasons).
RECORDS: Holds NFL single-season record for most passes attempted—691 (1994). ... Holds NFL single-game records for most passes completed—45; most passes attempted—70; and most passes attempted without an interception—70 (November 13, 1994, vs. Minnesota).
POST SEASON RECORDS: Shares Super Bowl single-game record for most passes intercepted—4 (January 26, 1997, vs. Green Bay).
PRO STATISTICS: 1993—Fumbled eight times and recovered five fumbles for minus 23 yards. 1994—Fumbled nine times and recovered three fumbles for minus five yards. 1995—Caught one pass for minus nine yards, fumbled 11 times and recovered one fumble for minus eight yards. 1996—Fumbled nine times and recovered one fumble for minus two yards. 1997—Fumbled four times and recovered three fumbles for minus four yards. 1998—Fumbled nine times and recovered four fumbles for minus 10 yards. 1999—Fumbled eight times and recovered six fumbles for minus 13 yards. 2000—Fumbled nine times and recovered three fumbles for minus 20 yards.
SINGLE GAME HIGHS (regular season): Attempts—70 (November 13, 1994, vs. Minnesota); completions—45 (November 13, 1994, vs. Minnesota); yards—426 (November 13, 1994, vs. Minnesota); and touchdown passes—4 (October 1, 2000, vs. Denver).
STATISTICAL PLATEAUS: 300-yard passing games: 1993 (1), 1994 (6), 1995 (2), 1996 (4), 1997 (3), 1998 (4), 1999 (5), 2000 (1). Total: 26.
MISCELLANEOUS: Regular-season record as starting NFL quarterback: 63-58 (.521). ... Postseason record as starting NFL quarterback: 3-3 (.500). ... Holds New England Patriots all-time record for most yards passing (29,257).

Year—Team	G	GS	PASSING								RUSHING				TOTALS		
			Att.	Cmp.	Pct.	Yds.	TD	Int.	Avg.	Rat.	Att.	Yds.	Avg.	TD	TD	2pt.	Pts.
1993—New England NFL	13	12	429	214	49.9	2494	15	15	5.81	65.0	32	82	2.6	0	0	0	0
1994—New England NFL	16	16	*691	*400	57.9	*4555	25	*27	6.59	73.6	44	40	0.9	0	0	0	0
1995—New England NFL	15	15	*636	323	50.8	3507	13	16	5.51	63.7	20	28	1.4	0	0	0	0
1996—New England NFL	16	16	*623	*373	59.9	4086	27	15	6.56	83.7	24	27	1.1	0	0	0	0
1997—New England NFL	16	16	522	314	60.2	3706	28	15	7.10	87.7	28	55	2.0	0	0	0	0
1998—New England NFL	14	14	481	263	54.7	3633	20	14	7.55	80.9	28	44	1.6	0	0	0	0
1999—New England NFL	16	16	§539	305	56.6	3985	19	§21	7.39	75.6	42	101	2.4	0	0	0	0
2000—New England NFL	16	16	531	312	58.8	3291	17	13	6.20	77.3	47	158	3.4	2	2	0	12
Pro totals (8 years)	122	121	4452	2504	56.2	29257	164	136	6.57	75.9	265	535	2.0	2	2	0	12

BLEVINS, DARRIUS — WR — RAMS

PERSONAL: Born April 21, 1976, in Morristown, Tenn. ... 6-2/215.
HIGH SCHOOL: East High (Morristown, Tenn.).
COLLEGE: Memphis State.
TRANSACTIONS/CAREER NOTES: Signed as non-drafted free agent by St. Louis Rams (June 10, 1999). ... Released by Rams (September 5, 1999). ... Re-signed by Rams to practice squad (September 6, 1999). ... Released by Rams (August 27, 2000). ... Re-signed by Rams to practice squad (November 22, 2000). ... Activated (November 24, 2000).
PLAYING EXPERIENCE: St. Louis NFL, 2000. ... Games/Games started: 2000 (5/0).
PRO STATISTICS: 2000—Returned nine kickoffs for 173 yards.

BLEVINS, TONY — DB — COLTS

PERSONAL: Born January 29, 1975, in Rockford, Ill. ... 6-0/165.
HIGH SCHOOL: Rockhurst (Kansas City, Mo.).
COLLEGE: Kansas.
TRANSACTIONS/CAREER NOTES: Signed as non-drafted free agent by San Francisco 49ers (April 24, 1998). ... Released by 49ers (August 25, 1998). ... Re-signed by 49ers to practice squad (September 1, 1998). ... Activated (September 26, 1998). ... Released by 49ers (September 29, 1998). ... Re-signed by 49ers to practice squad (October 1, 1998). ... Activated (October 7, 1998). ... Claimed on waivers by Indianapolis Colts (October 30, 1998).
PLAYING EXPERIENCE: San Francisco (2)-Indianapolis (3) NFL, 1998, Indianapolis NFL, 1999 and 2000. ... Games/Games started: 1998 (S.F.-2/0; Ind.-3/0; Total: 5/0), 1999 (15/0), 2000 (16/1). Total: 36/1.
PRO STATISTICS: 1999—Intercepted two passes for 115 yards and one touchdown, credited with one sack and recovered two fumbles for two yards. 2000—Recovered one fumble.

BLY, DRE' — CB — RAMS

PERSONAL: Born May 22, 1977, in Chesapeake, Va. ... 5-9/185. ... Full name: Donald Andre Bly.
HIGH SCHOOL: Western Branch (Chesapeake, Va.).
COLLEGE: North Carolina (degree in exercise and sports science).

TRANSACTIONS/CAREER NOTES: Selected after junior season by St. Louis Rams in second round (41st pick overall) of 1999 NFL draft. ... Signed by Rams (July 16, 1999).
CHAMPIONSHIP GAME EXPERIENCE: Played in NFC championship game (1999 season). ... Member of Super Bowl championship team (1999 season).
HONORS: Named cornerback on THE SPORTING NEWS college All-America first team (1996). ... Named cornerback on THE SPORTING NEWS college All-America third team (1997).
PRO STATISTICS: 1999—Returned one kickoff for one yard. 2000—Returned nine kickoffs for 163 yards, credited with one sack, fumbled once and recovered one fumble.

				INTERCEPTIONS		
Year Team	G	GS	No.	Yds.	Avg.	TD
1999—St. Louis NFL	16	2	3	53	17.7	1
2000—St. Louis NFL	16	3	3	44	14.7	0
Pro totals (2 years)	32	5	6	97	16.2	1

BOBO, ORLANDO   G

PERSONAL: Born February 9, 1974, in Westpoint, Miss. ... 6-3/300.
HIGH SCHOOL: Westpoint (Miss.).
JUNIOR COLLEGE: East Mississippi Community College.
COLLEGE: Northeast Louisiana.
TRANSACTIONS/CAREER NOTES: Signed as non-drafted free agent by Minnesota Vikings (April 26, 1996). ... Released by Vikings (August 20, 1996). ... Re-signed by Vikings to practice squad (August 26, 1996). ... Released by Vikings (August 27, 1997). ... Re-signed by Vikings to practice squad (August 29, 1997). ... Activated (September 12, 1997). ... On injured reserve with leg injury (October 27, 1998-remainder of season). ... Selected by Cleveland Browns from Vikings in NFL expansion draft (February 9, 1999). ... Granted free agency (February 11, 2000). ... Signed by Baltimore Ravens (April 7, 2000). ... Granted unconditional free agency (March 2, 2001).
PLAYING EXPERIENCE: Minnesota NFL, 1997 and 1998; Cleveland NFL, 1999; Baltimore NFL, 2000. ... Games/Games started: 1997 (5/0), 1998 (4/0), 1999 (9/1), 2000 (7/0). Total: 25/1.
CHAMPIONSHIP GAME EXPERIENCE: Member of Ravens for AFC Championship game (2000 season); inactive. ... Member of Super Bowl championship team (2000 season); inactive.
PRO STATISTICS: 1999—Caught one pass for three yards.

BOCK, JOHN   G

PERSONAL: Born February 11, 1971, in Chicago. ... 6-3/295. ... Full name: John Matthew Bock. ... Nephew of Wayne Bock, tackle with Chicago Cardinals (1957).
HIGH SCHOOL: Crystal Lake (Ill.).
COLLEGE: Louisville, then Indiana State (degree in sociology).
TRANSACTIONS/CAREER NOTES: Signed as non-drafted free agent by Buffalo Bills (May 7, 1994). ... Released by Bills (August 22, 1994). ... Selected by Amsterdam Admirals in 1995 World League draft. ... Signed by New York Jets (June 22, 1995). ... Released by Jets (August 29, 1996). ... Signed by Miami Dolphins (October 16, 1996). ... Granted unconditional free agency (February 12, 1999). ... Re-signed by Dolphins (March 23, 1999). ... On injured reserve with knee injury (November 2, 1999-remainder of season). ... Granted unconditional free agency (February 11, 2000). ... Re-signed by Dolphins (March 2, 2000). ... On injured reserve with shoulder injury (October 25, 2000-remainder of season). ... Granted unconditional free agency (March 2, 2001).
PLAYING EXPERIENCE: Amsterdam W.L., 1995; New York Jets NFL, 1995; Miami NFL, 1996-2000. ... Games/Games started: W.L. 1995 (10/10), NFL 1995 (10/7), 1996 (2/0), 1997 (14/3), 1998 (16/6), 1999 (7/0), 2000 (6/1). Total W.L.: 10/10. Total NFL: 55/17. Total Pro: 65/27.
PRO STATISTICS: 1995—Fumbled once for minus one yard.

BOIREAU, MICHAEL   DE   VIKINGS

PERSONAL: Born July 24, 1978, in Miami. ... 6-4/274. ... Full name: Michael Innocent Boireau.
HIGH SCHOOL: North Miami Beach.
JUNIOR COLLEGE: Northeast Mississippi Community College.
COLLEGE: Miami (Fla.).
TRANSACTIONS/CAREER NOTES: Selected by Minnesota Vikings in second round (56th pick overall) of 2000 NFL draft. ... Signed by Vikings (July 21, 2000). ... On injured reserve with knee and hand injuries (October 3, 2000-remainder of season).

Year Team	G	GS	SACKS
2000—Minnesota NFL	Did not play.		

BOOKER, MARTY   WR   BEARS

PERSONAL: Born July 31, 1976, in Marrero, La. ... 5-11/215.
HIGH SCHOOL: Jonesboro-Hodge (Jonesboro, La.).
COLLEGE: Northeastern Louisiana.
TRANSACTIONS/CAREER NOTES: Selected by Chicago Bears in third round (78th pick overall) of 1999 NFL draft. ... Signed by Bears (July 22, 1999).
PRO STATISTICS: 1999—Rushed once for eight yards. 2000—Rushed twice for minus one yard and recovered one fumble.
SINGLE GAME HIGHS (regular season): Receptions—7 (December 24, 2000, vs. Detroit); yards—134 (November 14, 1999, vs. Minnesota); and touchdown receptions—2 (November 14, 1999, vs. Minnesota).
STATISTICAL PLATEAUS: 100-yard receiving games: 1999 (1).

			RECEIVING				TOTALS			
Year Team	G	GS	No.	Yds.	Avg.	TD	TD	2pt.	Pts.	Fum.
1999—Chicago NFL	9	4	19	219	11.5	3	3	0	18	0
2000—Chicago NFL	15	7	47	490	10.4	2	2	0	12	2
Pro totals (2 years)	24	11	66	709	10.7	5	5	0	30	2

BOOKER, MICHAEL   CB

PERSONAL: Born April 27, 1975, in Oceanside, Calif. ... 6-2/200. ... Full name: Michael Allen Booker.
HIGH SCHOOL: El Camino (Calif.).
COLLEGE: Nebraska.
TRANSACTIONS/CAREER NOTES: Selected by Atlanta Falcons in first round (11th pick overall) of 1997 NFL draft. ... Signed by Falcons (July 16, 1997). ... Released by Falcons (August 27, 2000). ... Signed by Tennessee Titans (August 30, 2000). ... Granted unconditional free agency (March 2, 2001).
CHAMPIONSHIP GAME EXPERIENCE: Played in NFC championship game (1998 season). ... Played in Super Bowl XXXIII (1998 season).
PRO STATISTICS: 1998—Fumbled once and recovered one fumble for five yards.

			INTERCEPTIONS		
Year Team	G	GS	No.	Yds.	Avg.	TD
1997—Atlanta NFL	15	2	3	16	5.3	0
1998—Atlanta NFL	14	6	1	27	27.0	0
1999—Atlanta NFL	13	1	2	10	5.0	0
2000—Tennessee NFL	15	1	1	2	2.0	0
Pro totals (4 years)	57	10	7	55	7.9	0

BOOKER, VAUGHN   DE   BENGALS

PERSONAL: Born February 24, 1968, in Cincinnati. ... 6-5/300. ... Full name: Vaughn Jamel Booker.
HIGH SCHOOL: Taft (Cincinnati).
COLLEGE: Cincinnati.
TRANSACTIONS/CAREER NOTES: Signed by Winnipeg Blue Bombers of CFL (June 1992). ... Granted free agency after 1993 season. ... Signed as non-drafted free agent by Kansas City Chiefs (May 2, 1994). ... Traded by Chiefs to Green Bay Packers for DT Darius Holland (May 13, 1998). ... Granted unconditional free agency (February 11, 2000). ... Signed by Cincinnati Bengals (February 16, 2000). ... On injured reserve with knee injury (December 7, 2000-remainder of season).
PRO STATISTICS: CFL: 1992—Recovered four fumbles and returned one kickoff for three yards. NFL: 1994—Recovered two fumbles for six yards and returned two kickoffs for 10 yards. 1995—Recovered one fumble for 14 yards and a touchdown. 1996—Recovered one fumble. 1997—Recovered one fumble.
MISCELLANEOUS: Served in U.S. Army (1988-90).

Year Team	G	GS	SACKS
1992—Winnipeg CFL	15	...	2.0
1993—Winnipeg CFL	9	...	4.0
1994—Kansas City NFL	13	0	0.0
1995—Kansas City NFL	16	10	1.5
1996—Kansas City NFL	14	12	1.0
1997—Kansas City NFL	13	13	4.0
1998—Green Bay NFL	16	4	3.0
1999—Green Bay NFL	14	14	3.5
2000—Cincinnati NFL	9	9	0.0
CFL totals (2 years)	24	...	6.0
NFL totals (7 years)	95	62	13.0
Pro totals (9 years)	119	...	19.0

BOOSE, DORIAN   DE

PERSONAL: Born January 29, 1974, in Frankfurt, West Germany. ... 6-5/292. ... Full name: Dorian Alexander Boose.
HIGH SCHOOL: Henry Foss (Tacoma, Wash.).
JUNIOR COLLEGE: Walla Walla (Wash.) Community College.
COLLEGE: Washington State.
TRANSACTIONS/CAREER NOTES: Selected by New York Jets in second round (56th pick overall) of 1998 NFL draft. ... Signed by Jets (July 8, 1998). ... Released by Jets (May 17, 2001).
PLAYING EXPERIENCE: New York Jets NFL, 1998-2000. ... Games/Games started: 1998 (12/0), 1999 (12/0), 2000 (10/0). Total: 34/0.
CHAMPIONSHIP GAME EXPERIENCE: Member of Jets for AFC championship game (1998 season); inactive.
PRO STATISTICS: 1999—Recovered one fumble.

BORDANO, CHRIS   LB

PERSONAL: Born December 30, 1974, in San Antonio. ... 6-1/241.
HIGH SCHOOL: Southwest (San Antonio).
COLLEGE: Southern Methodist.
TRANSACTIONS/CAREER NOTES: Selected by New Orleans Saints in sixth round (161st pick overall) of 1998 NFL draft. ... Signed by Saints (June 11, 1998). ... Traded by Saints to Dallas Cowboys for CB Kevin Mathis (April 26, 2000). ... Released by Cowboys (August 28, 2000). ... Signed by Atlanta Falcons (September 6, 2000). ... On injured reserve with neck injury (September 19, 2000-remainder of season). ... Granted unconditional free agency (March 2, 2001).
PLAYING EXPERIENCE: New Orleans NFL, 1998 and 1999; Atlanta NFL, 2000. ... Games/Games started: 1998 (16/6), 1999 (15/12), 2000 (2/0). Total: 33/18.
PRO STATISTICS: 1998—Credited with one sack.

BOSELLI, TONY   OT   JAGUARS

PERSONAL: Born April 17, 1972, in Boulder, Colo. ... 6-7/318. ... Full name: Don Anthony Boselli Jr.
HIGH SCHOOL: Fairview (Boulder, Colo.).

COLLEGE: Southern California (degree in business administration, 1995).
TRANSACTIONS/CAREER NOTES: Selected by Jacksonville Jaguars in first round (second pick overall) of 1995 NFL draft. ... Signed by Jaguars (June 1, 1995). ... On injured reserve with knee injury (January 4, 2000-remainder of playoffs).
PLAYING EXPERIENCE: Jacksonville NFL, 1995-2000. ... Games/Games started: 1995 (13/12), 1996 (16/16), 1997 (12/12), 1998 (15/15), 1999 (16/16), 2000 (16/16). Total: 88/87.
CHAMPIONSHIP GAME EXPERIENCE: Played in AFC championship game (1996 season).
HONORS: Named offensive lineman on THE SPORTING NEWS college All-America first team (1994). ... Played in Pro Bowl (1996-1998 seasons). ... Named offensive tackle on THE SPORTING NEWS NFL All-Pro team (1997-99). ... Named to play in Pro Bowl (1999 season); replaced by Walter Jones due to injury. ... Named to play in Pro Bowl (2000 season); replaced by Lincoln Kennedy due to injury.
PRO STATISTICS: 1996—Recovered one fumble. 1998—Recovered one fumble for two yards. 1999—Recoverd three fumbles.

BOSTIC, JASON   S   EAGLES

PERSONAL: Born June 30, 1976, in Lauderhill, Fla. ... 5-9/181. ... Full name: Jason Devon Bostic.
HIGH SCHOOL: Cardinal Gibbons (Lauderhill, Fla.).
COLLEGE: Georgia Tech.
TRANSACTIONS/CAREER NOTES: Signed as non-drafted free agent by Philadelphia Eagles (April 19, 1999). ... Released by Eagles (September 5, 1999). ... Re-signed by Eagles to practice squad (September 8, 1999). ... Activated (December 27, 1999).
PLAYING EXPERIENCE: Philadelphia NFL, 1999 and 2000. ... Games/Games started: 1999 (1/0), 2000 (16/0). Total: 17/0.
PRO STATISTICS: 2000—Fumbled once and returned one punt for no yards.

BOSTON, DAVID   WR   CARDINALS

PERSONAL: Born August 19, 1978, in Humble, Texas. ... 6-2/211.
HIGH SCHOOL: Humble (Texas).
COLLEGE: Ohio State.
TRANSACTIONS/CAREER NOTES: Selected after junior season by Arizona Cardinals in first round (eighth pick overall) of 1999 NFL draft. ... Signed by Cardinals (August 2, 1999).
HONORS: Named wide receiver on THE SPORTING NEWS college All-America second team (1998).
PRO STATISTICS: 1999—Recovered one fumble. 2000—Recovered one fumble.
SINGLE GAME HIGHS (regular season): Receptions—9 (December 3, 2000, vs. Cincinnati); yards—184 (December 3, 2000, vs. Cincinnati); and touchdown receptions—2 (December 3, 2000, vs. Cincinnati).
STATISTICAL PLATEAUS: 100-yard receiving games: 1999 (1), 2000 (4). Total: 5.

			RUSHING				RECEIVING				PUNT RETURNS				TOTALS		
Year Team	G	GS	Att.	Yds.	Avg.	TD	No.	Yds.	Avg.	TD	No.	Yds.	Avg.	TD	TD	2pt.	Pts. Fum.
1999—Arizona NFL	16	8	5	0	0.0	0	40	473	11.8	2	7	62	8.9	0	2	0	12 2
2000—Arizona NFL	16	16	3	9	3.0	0	71	1156	16.3	7	0	0	0.0	0	7	0	42 2
Pro totals (2 years)	32	24	8	9	1.1	0	111	1629	14.7	9	7	62	8.9	0	9	0	54 4

BOULWARE, PETER   LB   RAVENS

PERSONAL: Born December 18, 1974, in Columbia, S.C. ... 6-4/255. ... Full name: Peter Nicholas Boulware. ... Name pronounced BOWL-ware.
HIGH SCHOOL: Spring Valley (Columbia, S.C.).
COLLEGE: Florida State (degree in management information systems, 1997).
TRANSACTIONS/CAREER NOTES: Selected after junior season by Baltimore Ravens in first round (fourth pick overall) of 1997 NFL draft. ... Signed by Ravens (August 16, 1997).
CHAMPIONSHIP GAME EXPERIENCE: Played in AFC championship game (2000 season). ... Member of Super Bowl championship team (2000 season).
HONORS: Named defensive end on THE SPORTING NEWS college All-America first team (1996). ... Played in Pro Bowl (1998 and 1999 seasons).
PRO STATISTICS: 1998—Recovered one fumble.

Year Team	G	GS	SACKS
1997—Baltimore NFL	16	16	11.5
1998—Baltimore NFL	16	16	8.5
1999—Baltimore NFL	16	11	10.0
2000—Baltimore NFL	16	15	7.0
Pro totals (4 years)	64	58	37.0

BOWDEN, JOE   LB   COWBOYS

PERSONAL: Born February 25, 1970, in Dallas. ... 5-11/235. ... Full name: Joseph Tarrod Bowden.
HIGH SCHOOL: North Mesquite (Mesquite, Texas).
COLLEGE: Oklahoma.
TRANSACTIONS/CAREER NOTES: Selected by Houston Oilers in fifth round (133rd pick overall) of 1992 NFL draft. ... Signed by Oilers (July 16, 1992). ... Granted free agency (February 17, 1995). ... Re-signed by Oilers (June 6, 1995). ... Granted unconditional free agency (February 16, 1996). ... Re-signed by Oilers (March 4, 1996). ... Oilers franchise moved to Tennessee for 1997 season. ... Oilers franchise renamed Tennessee Titans for 1999 season (December 26, 1998). ... Granted unconditional free agency (February 11, 2000). ... Signed by Dallas Cowboys (May 4, 2000). ... Released by Cowboys (February 28, 2001). ... Re-signed by Cowboys (April 1, 2001).
CHAMPIONSHIP GAME EXPERIENCE: Played in AFC championship game (1999 season). ... Played in Super Bowl XXXIV (1999 season).
PRO STATISTICS: 1993—Recovered one fumble. 1995—Returned one kickoff for six yards and recovered one fumble. 1997—Recovered one fumble. 1998—Intercepted one pass for one yard and a touchdown and recovered two fumbles for 17 yards and one touchdown. 1999—Intercepted one pass for 29 yards and recovered three fumbles for 11 yards.

Year Team	G	GS	SACKS
1992—Houston NFL	14	0	0.0
1993—Houston NFL	16	6	1.0
1994—Houston NFL	14	1	0.0
1995—Houston NFL	16	14	1.0
1996—Houston NFL	16	16	3.0
1997—Tennessee NFL	16	16	2.5
1998—Tennessee NFL	16	16	1.5
1999—Tennessee NFL	15	15	3.5
2000—Dallas NFL	16	0	0.0
Pro totals (9 years)	139	84	12.5

BOWEN, MATT — S — RAMS

PERSONAL: Born November 12, 1976, in Glen Ellyn, Ill. ... 6-1/208.
HIGH SCHOOL: Glenbard West (Glen Ellyn, Ill.).
COLLEGE: Iowa.
TRANSACTIONS/CAREER NOTES: Selected by St. Louis Rams in sixth round (198th pick overall) of 2000 NFL draft. ... Signed by Rams (July 7, 2000).
PLAYING EXPERIENCE: St. Louis NFL, 2000. ... Games/Games started: 2000 (16/2).

BOWENS, DAVID — DE — PACKERS

PERSONAL: Born July 3, 1977, in Denver. ... 6-2/261. ... Full name: David Walter Bowens.
HIGH SCHOOL: St. Mary's (Orchard Lake, Mich.).
COLLEGE: Michigan, then Western Illinois.
TRANSACTIONS/CAREER NOTES: Selected after junior season by Denver Broncos in fifth round (158th pick overall) of 1999 NFL draft. ... Signed by Broncos (July 22, 1999). ... Traded by Broncos to Green Bay Packers for fourth-round pick (C Ben Hamilton) in 2001 draft (February 24, 2000).
PRO STATISTICS: 1999—Recovered one fumble. 2000—Returned one kickoff for 12 yards and recovered one fumble.

Year Team	G	GS	SACKS
1999—Denver NFL	16	0	1.0
2000—Green Bay NFL	14	0	3.5
Pro totals (2 years)	30	0	4.5

BOWENS, TIM — DT — DOLPHINS

PERSONAL: Born February 7, 1973, in Okolona, Miss. ... 6-4/320. ... Full name: Timothy L. Bowens.
HIGH SCHOOL: Okolona (Miss.).
JUNIOR COLLEGE: Itawamba Community College (Miss.).
COLLEGE: Mississippi.
TRANSACTIONS/CAREER NOTES: Selected after junior season by Miami Dolphins in first round (20th pick overall) of 1994 NFL draft. ... Signed by Dolphins (June 2, 1994). ... Designated by Dolphins as franchise player (February 13, 1998). ... Re-signed by Dolphins (August 21, 1998). ... On injured reserve with torn biceps muscle (January 3, 1999-remainder of playoffs).
HONORS: Named to play in Pro Bowl (1998 season); replaced by Cortez Kennedy due to injury.
PRO STATISTICS: 1994—Recovered one fumble. 1995—Recovered two fumbles. 1996—Recovered one fumble. 1997—Recovered one fumble in end zone for a touchdown. 2000—Intercepted one pass for no yards.

Year Team	G	GS	SACKS
1994—Miami NFL	16	15	3.0
1995—Miami NFL	16	16	2.0
1996—Miami NFL	16	16	3.0
1997—Miami NFL	16	16	5.0
1998—Miami NFL	16	16	0.0
1999—Miami NFL	16	15	1.5
2000—Miami NFL	15	15	2.5
Pro totals (7 years)	111	109	17.0

BOWNES, FABIEN — WR — SEAHAWKS

PERSONAL: Born February 29, 1972, in Aurora, Ill. ... 5-11/192. ... Name pronounced FAY-bee-en BOW-ens.
HIGH SCHOOL: Waubonsie Valley (Aurora, Ill.).
COLLEGE: Western Illinois.
TRANSACTIONS/CAREER NOTES: Signed as non-drafted free agent by Chicago Bears (April 27, 1995). ... Released by Bears (August 27, 1995). ... Re-signed by Bears to practice squad (August 29, 1995). ... Activated (December 14, 1995). ... Released by Bears (August 19, 1996). ... Re-signed by Bears to practice squad (October 15, 1996). ... Claimed on waivers by Seattle Seahawks (September 6, 1999). ... Granted free agency (February 11, 2000). ... Re-signed by Seahawks (May 1, 2000). ... Granted unconditional free agency (March 2, 2001). ... Re-signed by Seahawks (April 19, 2001).
PRO STATISTICS: 1997—Recovered one fumble. 1999—Rushed once for minus 14 yards.
SINGLE GAME HIGHS (regular season): Receptions—4 (November 2, 1997, vs. Washington); yards—56 (September 27, 1998, vs. Minnesota); and touchdown receptions—1 (September 19, 1999, vs. Chicago).

Year Team	G	GS	RECEIVING				KICKOFF RETURNS				TOTALS			
			No.	Yds.	Avg.	TD	No.	Yds.	Avg.	TD	TD	2pt.	Pts.	Fum.
1995—Chicago NFL	1	0	0	0	0.0	0	0	0	0.0	0	0	0	0	0
1996—Chicago NFL							Did not play.							
1997—Chicago NFL	16	0	12	146	12.2	0	19	396	20.8	0	0	0	0	0
1998—Chicago NFL	16	0	5	69	13.8	1	1	19	19.0	0	1	0	6	0
1999—Seattle NFL	15	0	4	68	17.0	1	2	40	20.0	0	1	0	6	0
2000—Seattle NFL	16	0	0	0	0.0	0	3	83	27.7	0	0	0	0	0
Pro totals (5 years)	64	0	21	283	13.5	2	25	538	21.5	0	2	0	12	0

BOYD, LaVELL   WR   BENGALS

PERSONAL: Born September 12, 1976, in Louisville, Ky. ... 6-3/215.
HIGH SCHOOL: Doss (Louisville, Ky.).
COLLEGE: Louisville.
TRANSACTIONS/CAREER NOTES: Signed as non-drafted free agent by Cincinnati Bengals (April 17, 2000). ... Released by Bengals (August 27, 2000). ... Re-signed by Bengals to practice squad (August 28, 2000). ... Activated (November 29, 2000).
PLAYING EXPERIENCE: Cincinnati NFL, 2000. ... Games/Games started: 2000 (2/0).

BOYD, STEPHEN   LB   LIONS

PERSONAL: Born August 22, 1972, in Valley Stream, N.Y. ... 6-0/242. ... Full name: Stephen Gerard Boyd.
HIGH SCHOOL: Valley Stream (N.Y.).
COLLEGE: Boston College (degree in human development).
TRANSACTIONS/CAREER NOTES: Selected by Detroit Lions in fifth round (141st pick overall) of 1995 NFL draft. ... Signed by Lions (July 19, 1995). ... Granted free agency (February 13, 1998). ... Re-signed by Lions (April 17, 1998). ... On injured reserve with shoulder injury (December 23, 1998-remainder of season). ... Granted unconditional free agency (February 12, 1999). ... Re-signed by Lions (February 23, 1999).
PLAYING EXPERIENCE: Detroit NFL, 1995-2000. ... Games/Games started: 1995 (16/0), 1996 (8/5), 1997 (16/16), 1998 (13/13), 1999 (14/14), 2000 (15/15). Total: 82/63.
HONORS: Named linebacker on THE SPORTING NEWS college All-America first team (1994). ... Played in Pro Bowl (1999 season). ... Named to play in Pro Bowl (2000 season); replaced by Brian Urlacher due to injury.
RECORDS: Shares NFL single-game record for most opponents' fumbles recovered—3 (October 4, 1998, vs. Chicago).
PRO STATISTICS: 1997—Intercepted one pass for four yards and recovered one fumble for 42 yards and a touchdown. 1998—Credited with four sacks and recovered four fumbles for one yard. 1999—Intercepted one pass for 18 yards. 2000—Intercepted one pass for no yards, credited with $1/2$ sack and recovered one fumble.

BOYER, BRANT   LB   BROWNS

PERSONAL: Born June 27, 1971, in Ogden, Utah. ... 6-1/230. ... Full name: Brant T. Boyer.
HIGH SCHOOL: North Summit (Coalville, Utah).
JUNIOR COLLEGE: Snow College (Utah).
COLLEGE: Arizona.
TRANSACTIONS/CAREER NOTES: Selected by Miami Dolphins in sixth round (177th pick overall) of 1994 NFL draft. ... Signed by Dolphins (July 11, 1994). ... Released by Dolphins (September 21, 1994). ... Re-signed by Dolphins to practice squad (September 22, 1994). ... Activated (October 5, 1994). ... Selected by Jacksonville Jaguars from Dolphins in NFL expansion draft (February 15, 1995). ... Released by Jaguars (August 27, 1995). ... Re-signed by Jaguars (December 13, 1995). ... Released by Jaguars (August 25, 1996). ... Re-signed by Jaguars (September 24, 1996). ... Released by Jaguars (September 25, 1996). ... Re-signed by Jaguars (September 27, 1996). ... Granted free agency (February 13, 1998). ... Re-signed by Jaguars (March 18, 1998). ... On injured reserve with neck injury (December 2, 1998-remainder of season). ... Granted unconditional free agency (February 12, 1999). ... Re-signed by Jaguars (March 15, 1999). ... Released by Jaguars (March 1, 2001). ... Signed by Cleveland Browns (March 12, 2001).
PLAYING EXPERIENCE: Miami NFL, 1994; Jacksonville NFL, 1995-2000. ... Games/Games started: 1994 (14/0), 1995 (2/0), 1996 (12/0), 1997 (16/2), 1998 (11/0), 1999 (15/0), 2000 (12/5). Total: 82/7.
CHAMPIONSHIP GAME EXPERIENCE: Played in AFC championship game (1996 and 1999 seasons).
PRO STATISTICS: 1997—Credited with $1^{1}/_{2}$ sacks. 1998—Credited with one sack. 1999—Intercepted one pass for five yards and credited with four sacks. 2000—Intercepted one pass for 12 yards and credited with $3^{1}/_{2}$ sacks.

BRACKENS, TONY   DE   JAGUARS

PERSONAL: Born December 26, 1974, in Fairfield, Texas. ... 6-4/271. ... Full name: Tony Lynn Brackens Jr.
HIGH SCHOOL: Fairfield (Texas).
COLLEGE: Texas.
TRANSACTIONS/CAREER NOTES: Selected after junior season by Jacksonville Jaguars in second round (33rd pick overall) of 1996 NFL draft. ... Signed by Jaguars (May 28, 1996). ... Designated by Jaguars as franchise player (February 11, 2000). ... Re-signed by Jaguars (August 25, 2000).
CHAMPIONSHIP GAME EXPERIENCE: Played in AFC championship game (1996 and 1999 seasons).
HONORS: Named defensive lineman on THE SPORTING NEWS college All-America first team (1995). ... Played in Pro Bowl (1999 season).
PRO STATISTICS: 1996—Intercepted one pass for 27 yards and recovered three fumbles. 1997—Recovered one fumble. 1998—Recovered three fumbles for eight yards. 1999—Intercepted two passes for 16 yards and one touchdown and recovered two fumbles for six yards. 2000—Intercepted one pass for seven yards and recovered two fumbles for 15 yards.
MISCELLANEOUS: Holds Jacksonville Jaguars all-time record for most sacks (37).

Year Team	G	GS	SACKS
1996—Jacksonville NFL	16	1	7.0
1997—Jacksonville NFL	15	3	7.0
1998—Jacksonville NFL	12	8	3.5
1999—Jacksonville NFL	16	15	12.0
2000—Jacksonville NFL	16	16	7.5
Pro totals (5 years)	75	43	37.0

BRADFORD, COREY   WR   PACKERS

PERSONAL: Born December 8, 1975, in Baton Rouge, La. ... 6-1/197. ... Full name: Corey Lamon Bradford.
HIGH SCHOOL: Clinton (La.).
JUNIOR COLLEGE: Hinds Community College (Miss.).
COLLEGE: Jackson State.
TRANSACTIONS/CAREER NOTES: Selected by Green Bay Packers in fifth round (150th pick overall) of 1998 NFL draft. ... Signed by Packers (July 17, 1998). ... Granted free agency (March 2, 2001).
PRO STATISTICS: 1998—Returned two kickoffs for 33 yards.
SINGLE GAME HIGHS (regular season): Receptions—6 (November 21, 1999, vs. Detroit); yards—106 (November 1, 1999, vs. Seattle); and touchdown receptions—1 (November 29, 1999, vs. San Francisco).
STATISTICAL PLATEAUS: 100-yard receiving games: 1999 (1).

Year Team	G	GS	RECEIVING No.	Yds.	Avg.	TD	TOTALS TD	2pt.	Pts.	Fum.
1998—Green Bay NFL	8	0	3	27	9.0	0	0	0	0	1
1999—Green Bay NFL	16	2	37	637	17.2	5	5	1	32	1
2000—Green Bay NFL	2	2	0	0	0.0	0	0	0	0	0
Pro totals (3 years)	26	4	40	664	16.6	5	5	1	32	2

BRADFORD, RONNIE   CB   FALCONS

PERSONAL: Born October 1, 1970, in Minot, N.D. ... 5-10/198. ... Full name: Ronald L. Bradford.
HIGH SCHOOL: Adams City (Commerce City, Colo.).
COLLEGE: Colorado.
TRANSACTIONS/CAREER NOTES: Selected by Miami Dolphins in fourth round (105th pick overall) of 1993 NFL draft. ... Signed by Dolphins (July 14, 1993). ... Released by Dolphins (August 24, 1993). ... Signed by Denver Broncos to practice squad (September 1, 1993). ... Activated (October 12, 1993). ... On injured reserve with knee injury (September 28, 1995-remainder of season). ... Released by Broncos (August 25, 1996). ... Signed by Arizona Cardinals (August 27, 1996). ... Granted unconditional free agency (February 14, 1997). ... Signed by Atlanta Falcons (April 11, 1997). ... Granted unconditional free agency (February 12, 1999). ... Re-signed by Falcons (March 11, 1999).
CHAMPIONSHIP GAME EXPERIENCE: Played in NFC championship game (1998 season). ... Played in Super Bowl XXXIII (1998 season).
PRO STATISTICS: 1993—Returned one punt for no yards and fumbled once. 1994—Credited with one sack and recovered two fumbles. 1996—Recovered one fumble. 1998—Credited with a safety and recovered one fumble.

Year Team	G	GS	INTERCEPTIONS No.	Yds.	Avg.	TD	TOTALS TD	2pt.	Pts.	Fum.
1993—Denver NFL	10	3	1	0	0.0	0	0	0	0	1
1994—Denver NFL	12	0	0	0	0.0	0	0	0	0	0
1995—Denver NFL	4	0	0	0	0.0	0	0	0	0	0
1996—Arizona NFL	15	11	1	0	0.0	0	0	0	0	0
1997—Atlanta NFL	16	15	4	9	2.3	0	0	0	0	0
1998—Atlanta NFL	14	10	3	11	3.7	1	1	0	8	0
1999—Atlanta NFL	16	16	0	0	0.0	0	0	0	0	0
2000—Atlanta NFL	16	15	3	25	8.3	0	0	0	0	0
Pro totals (8 years)	103	70	12	45	3.8	1	1	0	8	1

BRADY, KYLE   TE   JAGUARS

PERSONAL: Born January 14, 1972, in New Cumberland, Pa. ... 6-6/277. ... Full name: Kyle James Brady.
HIGH SCHOOL: Cedar Cliff (Camp Hill, Pa.).
COLLEGE: Penn State.
TRANSACTIONS/CAREER NOTES: Selected by New York Jets in first round (ninth pick overall) of 1995 NFL draft. ... Signed by Jets (July 17, 1995). ... Designated by Jets as transition player (February 12, 1999). ... Tendered offer sheet by Jacksonville Jaguars (February 16, 1999). ... Jets declined to match offer (February 18, 1999).
CHAMPIONSHIP GAME EXPERIENCE: Played in AFC championship game (1998 and 1999 seasons).
HONORS: Named tight end on THE SPORTING NEWS college All-America second team (1994).
PRO STATISTICS: 1995—Returned two kickoffs for 25 yards. 1996—Returned two kickoffs for 26 yards. 1998—Returned one kickoff for 20 yards.
SINGLE GAME HIGHS (regular season): Receptions—10 (October 29, 2000, vs. Dallas); yards—138 (October 29, 2000, vs. Dallas); and touchdown receptions—2 (October 19, 1998, vs. New England).
STATISTICAL PLATEAUS: 100-yard receiving games: 2000 (2).

Year Team	G	GS	RECEIVING No.	Yds.	Avg.	TD	TOTALS TD	2pt.	Pts.	Fum.
1995—New York Jets NFL	15	11	26	252	9.7	2	2	0	12	0
1996—New York Jets NFL	16	16	15	144	9.6	1	1	1	8	1
1997—New York Jets NFL	16	14	22	238	10.8	2	2	0	12	1
1998—New York Jets NFL	16	16	30	315	10.5	5	5	0	30	1
1999—Jacksonville NFL	13	12	32	346	10.8	1	1	1	8	0
2000—Jacksonville NFL	16	15	64	729	11.4	3	3	▲1	20	0
Pro totals (6 years)	92	84	189	2024	10.7	14	14	3	90	3

BRADY, TOM — QB — PATRIOTS

PERSONAL: Born August 3, 1977, in San Mateo, Calif. ... 6-4/210.
HIGH SCHOOL: Serra (San Mateo, Calif.).
COLLEGE: Michigan.
TRANSACTIONS/CAREER NOTES: Selected by New England Patriots in sixth round (199th pick overall) of 2000 NFL draft. ... Signed by Patriots (July 14, 2000).
PLAYING EXPERIENCE: New England NFL, 2000. ... Games/Games started: 2000 (1/0).
PRO STATISTICS: 2000—Attempted three passes with one completion for six yards.
SINGLE GAME HIGHS (regular season): Attempts—3 (November 23, 2000, vs. Detroit); completions—1 (November 23, 2000, vs. Detroit); yards—6 (November 23, 2000, vs. Detroit); and touchdown passes—0.
MISCELLANEOUS: Selected by Montreal Expos organization in 18th round of free-agent draft (June 1, 1995); did not sign.

BRAHAM, RICH — C — BENGALS

B

PERSONAL: Born November 6, 1970, in Morgantown, W.Va. ... 6-4/305. ... Name pronounced BRAY-um.
HIGH SCHOOL: University (Morgantown, W.Va.).
COLLEGE: West Virginia (degree in finance).
TRANSACTIONS/CAREER NOTES: Selected by Arizona Cardinals in third round (76th pick overall) of 1994 NFL draft. ... Signed by Cardinals (July 30, 1994). ... Claimed on waivers by Cincinnati Bengals (November 18, 1994). ... On injured reserve with ankle injury (August 29, 1995-entire season). ... Granted free agency (February 14, 1997). ... Tendered offer sheet by New England Patriots (April 8, 1997). ... Offer matched by Bengals (April 15, 1997). ... On injured reserve with knee injury (December 3, 1998-remainder of season). ... Granted unconditional free agency (March 2, 2001). ... Signed by Cincinnati Bengals (March 12, 2001).
PLAYING EXPERIENCE: Cincinnati NFL, 1994 and 1996-2000. ... Games/Games started: 1994 (3/0), 1996 (16/16), 1997 (16/16), 1998 (12/12), 1999 (16/16), 2000 (9/9). Total: 72/69.
HONORS: Named offensive lineman on THE SPORTING NEWS college All-America second team (1993).
PRO STATISTICS: 1999—Recovered one fumble. 2000—Fumbled once for minus 16 yards.

BRANCH, CALVIN — S — RAIDERS

PERSONAL: Born May 8, 1974, in Lexington, Ky. ... 5-11/195. ... Full name: Calvin Stanley Branch.
HIGH SCHOOL: Klein (Spring, Texas).
COLLEGE: Iowa State, then Colorado State.
TRANSACTIONS/CAREER NOTES: Selected by Oakland Raiders in sixth round (172nd pick overall) of 1997 NFL draft. ... Signed by Raiders (July 21, 1997). ... Assigned by Raiders to Barcelona Dragons in 1999 NFL Europe enhancement allocation program (February 22, 1999).
PLAYING EXPERIENCE: Oakland NFL, 1997-2000; Barcelona Dragons NFLE, 1999. ... Games/Games started: 1997 (6/0), 1998 (16/0), NFLE 1999 (games played unavailable), NFL 1999 (16/1), 2000 (16/0). Total NFL: 54/1.
CHAMPIONSHIP GAME EXPERIENCE: Played in AFC championship game (2000 season).
PRO STATISTICS: 1998—Returned five kickoffs for 70 yards, fumbled once and recovered one fumble. 1999—Returned six kickoffs for 96 yards. 2000—Returned two kickoffs for 48 yards and recovered one fumble for six yards.

BRATZKE, CHAD — DE — COLTS

PERSONAL: Born September 15, 1971, in Brandon, Fla. ... 6-5/272. ... Full name: Chad Allen Bratzke. ... Name pronounced BRAT-ski.
HIGH SCHOOL: Bloomingdale (Valcro, Fla.).
COLLEGE: Eastern Kentucky.
TRANSACTIONS/CAREER NOTES: Selected by New York Giants in fifth round (155th pick overall) of 1994 NFL draft. ... Signed by Giants (July 17, 1994). ... On injured reserve with knee injury (November 12, 1997-remainder of season). ... Granted unconditional free agency (February 12, 1999). ... Signed by Indianapolis Colts (March 1, 1999).
PRO STATISTICS: 1996—Recovered two fumbles. 1997—Recovered two fumbles. 1998—Recovered one fumble. 1999—Fumbled once and recovered one fumble for three yards. 2000—Credited with one safety and recovered one fumble.

Year Team	G	GS	SACKS
1994—New York Giants NFL	2	0	0.0
1995—New York Giants NFL	6	0	0.0
1996—New York Giants NFL	16	16	5.0
1997—New York Giants NFL	10	10	3.5
1998—New York Giants NFL	16	16	11.0
1999—Indianapolis NFL	16	16	12.0
2000—Indianapolis NFL	16	16	7.5
Pro totals (7 years)	82	74	39.0

BRAZZELL, CHRIS — WR — COWBOYS

PERSONAL: Born May 22, 1976, in Fort Worth, Texas. ... 6-2/193. ... Name pronounced BRA-zel.
HIGH SCHOOL: Alice (Texas).
JUNIOR COLLEGE: Blinn College (Texas).
COLLEGE: Angelo State (Texas).
TRANSACTIONS/CAREER NOTES: Selected by New York Jets in sixth round (174th pick overall) of 1998 NFL draft. ... Signed by Jets (May 29, 1998). ... Released by Jets (August 30, 1998). ... Re-signed by Jets to practice squad (August 31, 1998). ... Claimed on waivers by Dallas Cowboys (September 6, 1999). ... Released by Cowboys (October 14, 1999). ... Re-signed by Cowboys to practice squad (October 16, 1999). ... Activated (December 10, 1999).
PLAYING EXPERIENCE: Dallas NFL, 1999 and 2000. ... Games/Games started: 1999 (5/0), 2000 (9/0). Total: 14/0.
PRO STATISTICS: 1999—Caught five passes for 114 yards. 2000—Caught two passes for 12 yards.
SINGLE GAME HIGHS (regular season): Receptions—2 (December 19, 1999, vs. New York Jets); yards—62 (December 19, 1999, vs. New York Jets); and touchdown receptions—0.

BRIEN, DOUG   K

PERSONAL: Born November 24, 1970, in Bloomfield, N.J. ... 6-0/180. ... Full name: Douglas Robert Zachariah Brien.
HIGH SCHOOL: De La Salle Catholic (Concord, Calif.).
COLLEGE: California (degree in political economies).
TRANSACTIONS/CAREER NOTES: Selected by San Francisco 49ers in third round (85th pick overall) of 1994 NFL draft. ... Signed by 49ers (July 27, 1994). ... Released by 49ers (October 16, 1995). ... Signed by New Orleans Saints (October 31, 1995). ... Granted free agency (February 14, 1997). ... Re-signed by Saints (July 17, 1997). ... Released by Saints (March 1, 2001).
CHAMPIONSHIP GAME EXPERIENCE: Played in NFC championship game (1994 season). ... Member of Super Bowl championship team (1994 season).
POST SEASON RECORDS: Shares Super Bowl single-game record for most extra points—7 (January 29, 1995, vs. San Diego).
PRO STATISTICS: 1998—Punted twice for 72 yards. 1999—Punted once for 20 yards.

					KICKING			
Year Team	G	XPM	XPA	FGM	FGA	Lg.	50+	Pts.
1994—San Francisco NFL	16	*60	*62	15	20	48	0-1	105
1995—San Francisco NFL	6	19	19	7	12	51	1-1	40
—New Orleans NFL	8	16	16	12	17	47	0-1	52
1996—New Orleans NFL	16	18	18	21	25	‡54	3-4	81
1997—New Orleans NFL	16	22	22	23	27	53	4-5	91
1998—New Orleans NFL	16	31	31	20	22	56	4-6	91
1999—New Orleans NFL	16	20	21	24	29	52	2-2	92
2000—New Orleans NFL	16	37	37	23	29	48	0-2	106
Pro totals (7 years)	110	223	226	145	181	56	14-22	658

BRIGANCE, O.J.   LB

PERSONAL: Born September 29, 1969, in Houston. ... 6-0/236. ... Full name: Orenthial James Brigance.
HIGH SCHOOL: Willowridge (Sugar Land, Texas).
COLLEGE: Rice (degree in managerial studies).
TRANSACTIONS/CAREER NOTES: Signed by B.C. Lions of CFL (May 1991). ... Granted free agency (February 1994). ... Signed by Baltimore Stallions of CFL (April 1994). ... Granted free agency (February 16, 1996). ... Signed as non-drafted free agent by Miami Dolphins (May 17, 1996). ... Granted free agency (February 12, 1999). ... Re-signed by Dolphins (May 20, 1999). ... On physically unable to perform list with back injury (July 30-August 25, 1999). ... Granted unconditional free agency (February 11, 2000). ... Signed by Baltimore Ravens (June 15, 2000). ... Granted unconditional free agency (March 2, 2001).
CHAMPIONSHIP GAME EXPERIENCE: Played in AFC championship game (2000 season). ... Member of Super Bowl championship team (2000 season).
PRO STATISTICS: CFL: 1991—Intercepted one pass for seven yards. 1992—Returned five kickoffs for 40 yards and recovered three fumbles. 1993—Recovered one fumble for 27 yards. 1994—Recovered two fumbles. 1995—Intercepted one pass for 13 yards and recovered three fumbles for 10 yards. NFL: 1997—Recovered one fumble. 2000—Recovered one fumble.

Year Team	G	GS	SACKS
1991—British Columbia CFL	18	...	2.0
1992—British Columbia CFL	18	...	0.0
1993—British Columbia CFL	18	...	20.0
1994—Baltimore CFL	18	...	6.0
1995—Baltimore CFL	18	...	7.0
1996—Miami NFL	12	0	0.0
1997—Miami NFL	16	0	0.0
1998—Miami NFL	16	0	0.0
1999—Miami NFL	16	0	0.0
2000—Baltimore NFL	16	0	0.0
CFL totals (5 years)	90	...	35.0
NFL totals (5 years)	76	0	0.0
Pro totals (10 years)	166	...	35.0

BRIGHAM, JEREMY   TE   RAIDERS

PERSONAL: Born March 22, 1975, in Boston. ... 6-6/255.
HIGH SCHOOL: Saguara (Scottsdale, Ariz.).
COLLEGE: Washington.
TRANSACTIONS/CAREER NOTES: Selected by Oakland Raiders in fifth round (127th pick overall) of 1998 NFL draft. ... Signed by Raiders (July 18, 1998).
PLAYING EXPERIENCE: Oakland NFL, 1998-2000. ... Games/Games started: 1998 (2/0), 1999 (16/2), 2000 (15/3). Total: 33/5.
CHAMPIONSHIP GAME EXPERIENCE: Played in AFC championship game (2000 season).
PRO STATISTICS: 1999—Caught eight passes for 108 yards. 2000—Caught 13 passes for 107 yards and two touchdowns.
SINGLE GAME HIGHS (regular season): Receptions—2 (December 24, 2000, vs. Carolina); yards—39 (September 19, 1999, vs. Minnesota); and touchdown receptions—2 (December 24, 2000, vs. Carolina).

BRISBY, VINCENT   WR

PERSONAL: Born January 25, 1971, in Houston. ... 6-3/193. ... Full name: Vincent Cole Brisby.
HIGH SCHOOL: Washington-Marion Magnet (Lake Charles, La.).
COLLEGE: Northeast Louisiana (degree in business administration, 1993).
TRANSACTIONS/CAREER NOTES: Selected by New England Patriots in second round (56th pick overall) of 1993 NFL draft. ... Signed by Patriots (July 30, 1993). ... Granted free agency (February 16, 1996). ... Re-signed by Patriots (May 31, 1996). ... On injured reserve with broken

finger and hamstring injury (November 21, 1998-remainder of season). ... Released by Patriots (August 14, 2000). ... Signed by New York Jets (August 16, 2000). ... Released by Jets (October 21, 2000).
CHAMPIONSHIP GAME EXPERIENCE: Played in AFC championship game (1996 season). ... Played in Super Bowl XXXI (1996 season).
PRO STATISTICS: 1993—Recovered one fumble.
SINGLE GAME HIGHS (regular season): Receptions—9 (October 1, 1995, vs. Atlanta); yards—161 (October 1, 1995, vs. Atlanta); and touchdown receptions—2 (December 18, 1994, vs. Buffalo).
STATISTICAL PLATEAUS: 100-yard receiving games: 1994 (2), 1995 (3). Total: 5.

			RECEIVING				TOTALS			
Year Team	G	GS	No.	Yds.	Avg.	TD	TD	2pt.	Pts.	Fum.
1993—New England NFL	16	12	45	626	13.9	2	2	0	12	1
1994—New England NFL	14	11	58	904	15.6	5	5	0	30	1
1995—New England NFL	16	16	66	974	14.8	3	3	0	18	0
1996—New England NFL	3	0	0	0	0.0	0	0	0	0	0
1997—New England NFL	16	4	23	276	12.0	2	2	0	12	0
1998—New England NFL	6	1	7	96	13.7	2	2	0	12	0
1999—New England NFL	12	1	18	266	14.8	0	0	0	0	0
2000—New York Jets NFL	3	1	4	60	15.0	0	0	0	0	0
Pro totals (8 years)	86	46	221	3202	14.5	14	14	0	84	2

BRISTER, BUBBY   QB   CHIEFS

PERSONAL: Born August 15, 1962, in Alexandria, La. ... 6-3/215. ... Full name: Walter Andrew Brister III.
HIGH SCHOOL: Neville (Monroe, La.).
COLLEGE: Tulane, then Northeast Louisiana.
TRANSACTIONS/CAREER NOTES: Selected by Pittsburgh Steelers in third round (67th pick overall) of 1986 NFL draft. ... Selected by New Jersey Generals in 11th round (80th pick overall) of 1986 USFL draft; did not sign. ... Signed by Steelers (July 25, 1986). ... Granted free agency (February 1, 1992). ... Re-signed by Steelers (June 16, 1992). ... Released by Steelers (June 4, 1993). ... Signed by Philadelphia Eagles (July 19, 1993). ... Granted unconditional free agency (February 17, 1994). ... Re-signed by Eagles (April 6, 1994). ... Granted unconditional free agency (February 17, 1995). ... Signed by New York Jets (March 17, 1995). ... Released by Jets (February 29, 1996). ... Signed by Denver Broncos (April 7, 1997). ... Released by Broncos (March 29, 2000). ... Signed by Minnesota Vikings (April 10, 2000). ... Granted unconditional free agency (March 2, 2001). ... Signed by Kansas City Chiefs (April 20, 2001).
CHAMPIONSHIP GAME EXPERIENCE: Member of Broncos for AFC championship game (1997 season); did not play. ... Member of Super Bowl championship team (1997 season); did not play. ... Member of Broncos for AFC championship game (1998 season); did not play. ... Member of Super Bowl championship team (1998 season). ... Member of Vikings for NFC championship game (2000 season); did not play.
PRO STATISTICS: 1986—Fumbled once. 1988—Recovered two fumbles. 1989—Caught one pass for minus 10 yards, fumbled eight times and recovered one fumble. 1990—Fumbled nine times. 1991—Fumbled four times and recovered two fumbles. 1992—Fumbled twice and recovered two fumbles for minus two yards. 1993—Fumbled three times. 1995—Caught one pass for two yards, fumbled four times and recovered three fumbles for minus nine yards. 1998—Fumbled twice and recovered one fumble for minus one yard. 2000—Fumbled once and recovered one fumble.
SINGLE GAME HIGHS (regular season): Attempts—48 (December 12, 1993, vs. Buffalo); completions—28 (December 12, 1993, vs. Buffalo); yards—353 (October 14, 1990, vs. Denver); and touchdown passes—4 (October 4, 1998, vs. Philadelphia).
STATISTICAL PLATEAUS: 300-yard passing games: 1988 (2), 1993 (1), 1994 (1). Total: 4.
MISCELLANEOUS: Regular-season record as starting NFL quarterback: 37-38 (.493). ... Postseason record as starting NFL quarterback: 1-1 (.500).

				PASSING							RUSHING				TOTALS		
Year Team	G	GS	Att.	Cmp.	Pct.	Yds.	TD	Int.	Avg.	Rat.	Att.	Yds.	Avg.	TD	TD	2pt.	Pts.
1986—Pittsburgh NFL	2	2	60	21	35.0	291	0	2	4.85	37.6	6	10	1.7	1	1	0	6
1987—Pittsburgh NFL	2	0	12	4	33.3	20	0	3	1.67	2.8	0	0	0.0	0	0	0	0
1988—Pittsburgh NFL	13	13	370	175	47.3	2634	11	14	7.12	65.3	45	209	4.6	6	6	0	36
1989—Pittsburgh NFL	14	14	342	187	54.7	2365	9	10	6.92	73.1	27	25	0.9	0	0	0	0
1990—Pittsburgh NFL	16	16	387	223	57.6	2725	20	14	7.04	81.6	25	64	2.6	0	0	0	0
1991—Pittsburgh NFL	8	8	190	103	54.2	1350	9	9	7.11	72.9	11	17	1.5	0	0	0	0
1992—Pittsburgh NFL	6	4	116	63	54.3	719	2	5	6.20	61.0	10	16	1.6	0	0	0	0
1993—Philadelphia NFL	10	8	309	181	58.6	1905	14	5	6.17	84.9	20	39	2.0	0	0	0	0
1994—Philadelphia NFL	7	2	76	51	67.1	507	2	1	6.67	89.1	1	7	7.0	0	0	0	0
1995—New York Jets NFL	9	4	170	93	54.7	726	4	8	4.27	53.7	16	18	1.1	0	0	0	0
1997—Denver NFL	1	0	9	6	66.7	48	0	0	5.33	79.9	4	2	0.5	0	0	0	0
1998—Denver NFL	7	4	131	78	59.5	986	10	3	7.53	99.0	19	102	5.4	1	1	0	6
1999—Denver NFL	2	0	20	12	60.0	87	0	3	4.35	30.6	2	17	8.5	0	0	0	0
2000—Minnesota NFL	2	0	20	10	50.0	82	0	1	4.10	40.0	5	20	4.0	0	0	0	0
Pro totals (14 years)	99	75	2212	1207	54.6	14445	81	78	6.53	72.3	191	546	2.9	8	8	0	48

RECORD AS BASEBALL PLAYER

TRANSACTIONS/CAREER NOTES: Threw right, batted right. ... Selected by Detroit Tigers organization in fourth round of free-agent draft (June 8, 1981). ... On suspended list (June 22, 1982-entire season). ... Placed on restricted list (October 7, 1982).

				BATTING										FIELDING			
Year Team (League)	Pos.	G	AB	R	H	2B	3B	HR	RBI	Avg.	BB	SO	SB	PO	A	E	Avg.
1981—Bristol (Appal.)	OF-SS	39	111	12	20	7	0	0	10	.180	16	27	5	46	11	9	.864
1982—					Did not play.												

BROCKERMEYER, BLAKE   OT   BEARS

PERSONAL: Born April 11, 1973, in Fort Worth, Texas. ... 6-4/300. ... Full name: Blake Weeks Brockermeyer.
HIGH SCHOOL: Arlington Heights (Texas).
COLLEGE: Texas.
TRANSACTIONS/CAREER NOTES: Selected after junior season by Carolina Panthers in first round (29th pick overall) of 1995 NFL draft. ... Signed by Panthers (July 14, 1995). ... Granted unconditional free agency (February 12, 1999). ... Signed by Chicago Bears (February 27, 1999).

PLAYING EXPERIENCE: Carolina NFL, 1995-1998; Chicago NFL, 1999 and 2000. ... Games/Games started: 1995 (16/16), 1996 (12/12), 1997 (16/13), 1998 (14/14), 1999 (15/15), 2000 (15/14). Total: 88/84.
CHAMPIONSHIP GAME EXPERIENCE: Played in NFC championship game (1996 season).
HONORS: Named offensive lineman on THE SPORTING NEWS college All-America first team (1994).
PRO STATISTICS: 1998—Recovered two fumbles.

BROMELL, LORENZO   DE   DOLPHINS

PERSONAL: Born September 23, 1975, in Georgetown, S.C. ... 6-6/275. ... Full name: Lorenzo Alexis Bromell.
HIGH SCHOOL: Choppee (Georgetown, S.C.).
JUNIOR COLLEGE: Georgia Military College.
COLLEGE: Clemson.
TRANSACTIONS/CAREER NOTES: Selected by Miami Dolphins in fourth round (102nd pick overall) of 1998 draft. ... Signed by Dolphins (July 10, 1998). ... Granted free agency (March 2, 2001). ... Re-signed by Dolphins (April 19, 2001).
PRO STATISTICS: 1998—Recovered one fumble.

Year Team	G	GS	SACKS
1998—Miami NFL	14	0	8.0
1999—Miami NFL	15	1	5.0
2000—Miami NFL	8	0	2.0
Pro totals (3 years)	37	1	15.0

BRONSON, ZACK   S   49ERS

PERSONAL: Born January 28, 1974, in Jasper, Texas. ... 6-1/195. ... Full name: Robert Bronson.
HIGH SCHOOL: Jasper (Texas).
COLLEGE: McNeese State.
TRANSACTIONS/CAREER NOTES: Signed as non-drafted free agent by San Francisco 49ers (May 2, 1997). ... On injured reserve with foot injury (December 29, 1999-remainder of season). ... Granted free agency (February 11, 2000). ... Re-signed by 49ers (June 15, 2000). ... Granted unconditional free agency (March 2, 2001). ... Re-signed by 49ers (May 15, 2001).
CHAMPIONSHIP GAME EXPERIENCE: Played in NFC championship game (1997 season).
PRO STATISTICS: 1997—Recovered one fumble for three yards.

Year Team	G	GS	INTERCEPTIONS No.	Yds.	Avg.	TD
1997—San Francisco NFL	16	0	1	22	22.0	0
1998—San Francisco NFL	11	0	4	34	8.5	0
1999—San Francisco NFL	15	2	0	0	0.0	0
2000—San Francisco NFL	9	7	3	75	25.0	0
Pro totals (4 years)	51	9	8	131	16.4	0

BROOKING, KEITH   LB   FALCONS

PERSONAL: Born October 30, 1975, in Senoia, Ga. ... 6-2/245. ... Full name: Keith Howard Brooking.
HIGH SCHOOL: East Coweta (Sharpsburg, Ga.).
COLLEGE: Georgia Tech.
TRANSACTIONS/CAREER NOTES: Selected by Atlanta Falcons in first round (12th pick overall) of 1998 NFL draft. ... Signed by Falcons (June 29, 1998). ... On injured reserve with foot injury (November 1, 2000-remainder of season).
PLAYING EXPERIENCE: Atlanta NFL, 1998-2000. ... Games/Games started: 1998 (15/0), 1999 (13/13), 2000 (5/5). Total: 33/18.
CHAMPIONSHIP GAME EXPERIENCE: Played in NFC championship game (1998 season). ... Played in Super Bowl XXXIII (1998 season).
PRO STATISTICS: 1998—Intercepted one pass for 12 yards. 1999—Credited with two sacks. 2000—Credited with one sack.

BROOKS, AARON   QB   SAINTS

PERSONAL: Born March 24, 1976, in Newport News, Va. ... 6-4/205. ... Full name: Aaron Lafette Brooks.
HIGH SCHOOL: Homer L. Ferguson (Newport News, Va.).
COLLEGE: Virginia (degree in anthropology).
TRANSACTIONS/CAREER NOTES: Selected by Green Bay Packers in fourth round (131st pick overall) of 1999 NFL draft. ... Signed by Packers (July 27, 1999). ... Traded by Packers with TE Lamont Hall to New Orleans Saints for LB K.D. Williams and third-round pick (traded to San Francisco) in 2001 draft (July 31, 2000).
PRO STATISTICS: 2000—Fumbled four times for minus four yards.
SINGLE GAME HIGHS (regular season): Attempts—48 (December 3, 2000, vs. Denver); completions—30 (December 3, 2000, vs. Denver); yards—441 (December 3, 2000, vs. Denver); and touchdown passes—2 (December 24, 2000, vs. St. Louis).
STATISTICAL PLATEAUS: 300-yard passing games: 2000 (1). ... 100-yard rushing games: 2000 (1).
MISCELLANEOUS: Regular-season record as starting NFL quarterback: 3-2 (.600). ... Postseason record as starting NFL quarterback: 1-1 (.500).

Year Team	G	GS	PASSING Att.	Cmp.	Pct.	Yds.	TD	Int.	Avg.	Rat.	RUSHING Att.	Yds.	Avg.	TD	TOTALS TD	2pt.	Pts.
1999—Green Bay NFL	1	0	0	0	0.0	0	0	0	0.0	...	0	0	0.0	0	0	0	0
2000—New Orleans NFL	8	5	194	113	58.2	1514	9	6	7.80	85.7	41	170	4.1	2	2	0	12
Pro totals (2 years)	9	5	194	113	58.2	1514	9	6	7.80	85.7	41	170	4.1	2	2	0	12

BROOKS, BARRETT   OT

PERSONAL: Born May 5, 1972, in St. Louis. ... 6-4/326.
HIGH SCHOOL: McCluer North (Florissant, Mo.).
COLLEGE: Kansas State.
TRANSACTIONS/CAREER NOTES: Selected by Philadelphia Eagles in second round (58th pick overall) of 1995 NFL draft. ... Signed by Eagles (July 19, 1995). ... Granted free agency (February 13, 1998). ... Re-signed by Eagles (April 21, 1998). ... Granted unconditional free agency (February 12, 1999). ... Signed by Detroit Lions (April 12, 1999). ... Granted unconditional free agency (March 2, 2001).
PLAYING EXPERIENCE: Philadelphia NFL, 1995-1998; Detroit NFL, 1999 and 2000. ... Games/Games started: 1995 (16/16), 1996 (16/15), 1997 (16/14), 1998 (16/1), 1999 (16/12), 2000 (15/4). Total: 95/62.
PRO STATISTICS: 1996—Returned one kickoff for no yards and recovered one fumble. 1997—Recovered two fumbles. 1998—Returned one kickoff for seven yards.

BROOKS, BOBBY   LB   RAIDERS

PERSONAL: Born March 3, 1976, in Vallejo, Calif. ... 6-2/240.
HIGH SCHOOL: Hogan (Vallejo, Calif.).
COLLEGE: Fresno State.
TRANSACTIONS/CAREER NOTES: Signed as non-drafted free agent by Oakland Raiders (April 1999). ... Released by Raiders (September 5, 1999). ... Re-signed by Raiders to practice squad (October 20, 1999). ... Activated (December 1999).
PLAYING EXPERIENCE: Oakland NFL, 1999 and 2000. ... Games/Games started: 1999 (1/0), 2000 (16/0). Total: 17/0.
CHAMPIONSHIP GAME EXPERIENCE: Played in AFC championship game (2000 season).

BROOKS, DERRICK   LB   BUCCANEERS

PERSONAL: Born April 18, 1973, in Pensacola, Fla. ... 6-0/235. ... Full name: Derrick Dewan Brooks.
HIGH SCHOOL: Booker T. Washington (Pensacola, Fla.).
COLLEGE: Florida State (degree in communications, 1994).
TRANSACTIONS/CAREER NOTES: Selected by Tampa Bay Buccaneers in first round (28th pick overall) of 1995 NFL draft. ... Signed by Buccaneers (May 3, 1995).
CHAMPIONSHIP GAME EXPERIENCE: Played in NFC championship game (1999 season).
HONORS: Named linebacker on THE SPORTING NEWS college All-America first team (1993 and 1994). ... Played in Pro Bowl (1997-2000 seasons). ... Named linebacker on THE SPORTING NEWS NFL All-Pro team (1999 and 2000).
PRO STATISTICS: 1997—Fumbled once and recovered one fumble. 1999—Recovered two fumbles for four yards.

| | | | INTERCEPTIONS | | | | SACKS |
Year Team	G	GS	No.	Yds.	Avg.	TD	No.
1995—Tampa Bay NFL	16	13	0	0	0.0	0	1.0
1996—Tampa Bay NFL	16	16	1	6	6.0	0	0.0
1997—Tampa Bay NFL	16	16	2	13	6.5	0	1.5
1998—Tampa Bay NFL	16	16	1	25	25.0	0	0.0
1999—Tampa Bay NFL	16	16	4	61	15.3	0	2.0
2000—Tampa Bay NFL	16	16	1	34	34.0	1	1.0
Pro totals (6 years)	96	93	9	139	15.4	1	5.5

BROOKS, ETHAN   OT   BRONCOS

PERSONAL: Born April 27, 1972, in Hartford, Conn. ... 6-6/297.
HIGH SCHOOL: Westminster (Simsbury, Conn.).
COLLEGE: Williams, Conn. (degree in psychology, 1995).
TRANSACTIONS/CAREER NOTES: Selected by Atlanta Falcons in seventh round (229th pick overall) of 1996 NFL draft. ... Signed by Falcons (June 7, 1996). ... Assigned by Falcons to Frankfurt Galaxy in 1997 World League enhancement allocation program (February 19, 1997). ... Released by Falcons (August 27, 1997). ... Signed by St. Louis Rams (November 20, 1997). ... Inactive for five games (1997). ... Released by Rams (July 19, 1999). ... Signed by Arizona Cardinals (February 3, 2000). ... Granted unconditional free agency (March 2, 2001). ... Signed by Denver Broncos (March 15, 2001).
PLAYING EXPERIENCE: Atlanta NFL, 1996; Frankfurt W.L., 1997; St. Louis NFL, 1998; Arizona NFL, 2000. ... Games/Games started: 1996 (2/0), 1997 (games played unavailable), 1998 (15/0), 2000 (14/3). Total NFL: 31/3.

BROOKS, MACEY   WR

PERSONAL: Born February 2, 1975, in Hampton, Va. ... 6-5/215. ... Full name: Barry Macey Brooks.
HIGH SCHOOL: Kecoughtan (Hampton, Va.).
COLLEGE: James Madison.
TRANSACTIONS/CAREER NOTES: Selected by Dallas Cowboys in fourth round (127th pick overall) of 1997 NFL draft. ... Signed by Cowboys (July 14, 1997). ... On injured reserve with arm injury (August 27, 1997-entire season). ... Released by Cowboys (August 30, 1998). ... Signed by Chicago Bears to practice squad (September 1, 1998). ... Activated (October 7, 1998); did not play. ... On injured reserve with knee injury (November 10, 1999-remainder of season). ... Granted free agency (February 11, 2000). ... Re-signed by Bears (April 17, 2000). ... Granted unconditional free agency (March 2, 2001).
PLAYING EXPERIENCE: Chicago NFL, 1999 and 2000. ... Games/Games started: 1999 (9/2), 2000 (16/3). Total: 25/5.
PRO STATISTICS: 1999—Rushed once for seven yards, caught 14 passes for 160 yards and recovered one fumble. 2000—Caught 26 passes for 216 yards.
SINGLE GAME HIGHS (regular season): Receptions—5 (October 22, 2000, vs. Philadelphia); yards—51 (September 26, 1999, vs. Oakland); and touchdown receptions—0.
MISCELLANEOUS: Selected by San Francisco Giants organization in second round of free-agent draft (June 2, 1993); did not sign. ... Selected by Kansas City Royals organization in 55th round of free-agent draft (June 4, 1996); did not sign.

BROOKS, ROBERT　　　WR

PERSONAL: Born June 23, 1970, in Greenwood, S.C. ... 6-0/180. ... Full name: Robert Darren Brooks.
HIGH SCHOOL: Greenwood (S.C.).
COLLEGE: South Carolina (bachelor of science degree in retailing).
TRANSACTIONS/CAREER NOTES: Selected by Green Bay Packers in third round (62nd pick overall) of 1992 NFL draft. ... Signed by Packers (July 22, 1992). ... Granted free agency (February 17, 1995). ... Re-signed by Packers (June 1, 1995). ... On injured reserve with knee injury (October 26, 1996-remainder of season). ... Granted unconditional free agency (February 13, 1998). ... Re-signed by Packers (February 13, 1998). ... Announced retirement (August 2, 1999). ... Signed by Denver Broncos (August 14, 2000). ... Released by Broncos (November 14, 2000).
CHAMPIONSHIP GAME EXPERIENCE: Played in NFC championship game (1995 and 1997 seasons). ... Member of Super Bowl championship team (1996 season); inactive. ... Played in Super Bowl XXXII (1997 season).
RECORDS: Shares NFL record for longest pass reception (from Brett Favre)—99 yards, touchdown (September 11, 1995, at Chicago).
POST SEASON RECORDS: Holds NFL posteason career record for highest average punt return (minimum 10 returns)—15.3.
PRO STATISTICS: 1993—Fumbled once and recovered one fumble. 1994—Fumbled four times and recovered one fumble.
SINGLE GAME HIGHS (regular season): Receptions—11 (December 24, 1995, vs. Pittsburgh); yards—164 (September 28, 1997, vs. Detroit); and touchdown receptions—2 (September 9, 1996, vs. Philadelphia).
STATISTICAL PLATEAUS: 100-yard receiving games: 1994 (1), 1995 (9), 1996 (2), 1997 (1). Total: 13.

			RUSHING				RECEIVING				PUNT RETURNS				KICKOFF RETURNS				TOTALS		
Year　Team	G	GS	Att.	Yds.	Avg.	TD	No.	Yds.	Avg.	TD	No.	Yds.	Avg.	TD	No.	Yds.	Avg.	TD	TD	2pt.	Pts.
1992—Green Bay NFL....	16	1	2	14	7.0	0	12	126	10.5	1	11	102	9.3	0	18	338	18.8	0	1	0	6
1993—Green Bay NFL....	14	0	3	17	5.7	0	20	180	9.0	0	16	135	8.4	0	23	611	*26.6	†1	1	0	6
1994—Green Bay NFL....	16	16	1	0	0.0	0	58	648	11.2	4	40	352	8.8	1	9	260	28.9	1	6	0	36
1995—Green Bay NFL....	16	15	4	21	5.3	0	102	1497	14.7	13	0	0	0.0	0	1	28	28.0	0	13	0	78
1996—Green Bay NFL....	7	7	4	2	0.5	0	23	344	15.0	4	0	0	0.0	0	0	0	0.0	0	4	0	24
1997—Green Bay NFL....	15	15	2	19	9.5	0	60	1010	‡16.8	7	0	0	0.0	0	0	0	0.0	0	7	0	42
1998—Green Bay NFL....	12	12	1	2	2.0	0	31	420	13.5	3	0	0	0.0	0	0	0	0.0	0	3	0	18
1999—								Did not play.													
2000—Denver NFL........	4	0	0	0	0.0	0	3	51	17.0	0	0	0	0.0	0	0	0	0.0	0	0	0	0
Pro totals (8 years)........	100	66	17	75	4.4	0	309	4276	13.8	32	67	589	8.8	1	51	1237	24.3	2	35	0	210

BROUGHTON, LUTHER　　　TE　　　PANTHERS

PERSONAL: Born November 30, 1974, in Charleston, S.C. ... 6-2/248. ... Full name: Luther Rashard Broughton Jr.
HIGH SCHOOL: Cainhoy (Huger, S.C.).
COLLEGE: Furman.
TRANSACTIONS/CAREER NOTES: Selected by Philadelphia Eagles in fifth round (155th pick overall) of 1997 NFL draft. ... Signed by Eagles (July 15, 1997). ... Active for one game with Eagles (1997); did not play. ... Released by Eagles (November 5, 1997). ... Re-signed by Eagles to practice squad (November 5, 1997). ... Signed by Carolina Panthers from Eagles practice squad (December 15, 1997). ... Inactive for one game with Panthers (1997). ... Traded by Panthers to Philadelphia Eagles for seventh-round pick (TE Mike Roberg) in 2001 draft (September 5, 1999). ... Granted free agency (February 11, 2000). ... Re-signed by Eagles (April 10, 2000). ... Granted unconditional free agency (March 2, 2001). ... Signed by Panthers (May 8, 2001).
PRO STATISTICS: 1998—Recovered one fumble. 1999—Returned one kickoff for five yards and recovered one fumble. 2000—Returned one kickoff for 20 yards.
SINGLE GAME HIGHS (regular season): Receptions—4 (November 21, 1999, vs. Indianapolis); yards—78 (December 20, 1998, vs. St. Louis); and touchdown receptions—2 (November 28, 1999, vs. Washington).

			RECEIVING				TOTALS			
Year　Team	G	GS	No.	Yds.	Avg.	TD	TD	2pt.	Pts.	Fum.
1997—Philadelphia NFL					Did not play.					
1998—Carolina NFL	16	4	6	142	23.7	1	1	0	6	0
1999—Philadelphia NFL	16	3	26	295	11.3	4	4	0	24	0
2000—Philadelphia NFL	15	1	12	104	8.7	0	0	0	0	1
Pro totals (3 years)	47	8	44	541	12.3	5	5	0	30	2

BROWN, BOBBY　　　WR　　　BROWNS

PERSONAL: Born March 26, 1977, in Fort Lauderdale, Fla. ... 6-2/197. ... Full name: Braynard Ontawyn Brown.
HIGH SCHOOL: St. Thomas Aquinas (Fla.).
COLLEGE: Notre Dame.
TRANSACTIONS/CAREER NOTES: Signed as non-drafted free agent by Green Bay Packers (April 20, 2000). ... Released by Packers (August 27, 2000). ... Signed by Cleveland Browns to practice squad (August 29, 2000). ... Activated (November 11, 2000).
PLAYING EXPERIENCE: Cleveland NFL, 2000. ... Games/Games started: 2000 (6/0).
PRO STATISTICS: 2000—Caught two passes for 14 yards.
SINGLE GAME HIGHS (regular season): Receptions—1 (December 17, 2000, vs. Tennessee); yards—8 (December 10, 2000, vs. Philadelphia); and touchdown receptions—0.

BROWN, CHAD　　　LB　　　SEAHAWKS

PERSONAL: Born July 12, 1970, in Altadena, Calif. ... 6-2/240. ... Full name: Chadwick Everett Brown.
HIGH SCHOOL: John Muir (Pasadena, Calif.).
COLLEGE: Colorado (degree in marketing, 1992).
TRANSACTIONS/CAREER NOTES: Selected by Pittsburgh Steelers in second round (44th pick overall) of 1993 NFL draft. ... Signed by Steelers (July 26, 1993). ... Granted unconditional free agency (February 14, 1997). ... Signed by Seattle Seahawks (February 15, 1997).
CHAMPIONSHIP GAME EXPERIENCE: Played in AFC championship game (1994 and 1995 seasons). ... Played in Super Bowl XXX (1995 season).

HONORS: Named linebacker on THE SPORTING NEWS NFL All-Pro team (1996 and 1998). ... Played in Pro Bowl (1996, 1998 and 1999 seasons).
PRO STATISTICS: 1996—Fumbled once and recovered two fumbles. 1997—Recovered four fumbles for 68 yards and two touchdowns. 1998—Recovered one fumble. 1999—Recovered one fumble. 2000—Recovered three fumbles for 16 yards.

				INTERCEPTIONS			SACKS
Year Team	G	GS	No.	Yds.	Avg.	TD	No.
1993—Pittsburgh NFL	16	9	0	0	0.0	0	3.0
1994—Pittsburgh NFL	16	16	1	9	9.0	0	8.5
1995—Pittsburgh NFL	10	10	0	0	0.0	0	5.5
1996—Pittsburgh NFL	14	14	2	20	10.0	0	13.0
1997—Seattle NFL	15	15	0	0	0.0	0	6.5
1998—Seattle NFL	16	16	1	11	11.0	0	7.5
1999—Seattle NFL	15	15	0	0	0.0	0	5.5
2000—Seattle NFL	16	16	1	0	0.0	0	6.0
Pro totals (8 years)	118	111	5	40	8.0	0	55.5

BROWN, CORNELL   LB

PERSONAL: Born March 15, 1975, in Englewood, N.J. ... 6-0/240. ... Full name: Cornell Desmond Brown. ... Brother of Ruben Brown, guard, Buffalo Bills.
HIGH SCHOOL: E.C. Glass (Lynchburg, Va.).
COLLEGE: Virginia Tech.
TRANSACTIONS/CAREER NOTES: Selected by Baltimore Ravens in sixth round (194th pick overall) of 1997 NFL draft. ... Signed by Ravens (July 10, 1997). ... Granted free agency (February 11, 2000). ... Re-signed by Ravens (April 25, 2000) ... Granted unconditional free agency (March 2, 2001).
PLAYING EXPERIENCE: Baltimore NFL, 1997-2000. ... Games/Games started: 1997 (16/1), 1998 (16/1), 1999 (16/5), 2000 (16/1). Total: 64/8.
CHAMPIONSHIP GAME EXPERIENCE: Member of Ravens for AFC Championship game (2000 season); inactive. ... Member of Super Bowl championship team (2000 season).
HONORS: Named defensive lineman on THE SPORTING NEWS college All-America first team (1995).
PRO STATISTICS: 1997—Intercepted one pass for 21 yards and credited with $1/2$ sack. 1999—Credited with one sack. 2000—Credited with three sacks, returned one kickoff for no yards and fumbled once.

BROWN, CORWIN   S

PERSONAL: Born April 25, 1970, in Chicago. ... 6-1/205. ... Full name: Corwin Alan Brown.
HIGH SCHOOL: Percy L. Julian (Chicago).
COLLEGE: Michigan (degree in English).
TRANSACTIONS/CAREER NOTES: Selected by New England Patriots in fourth round (110th pick overall) of 1993 NFL draft. ... Signed by Patriots (July 16, 1993). ... Granted free agency (February 16, 1996). ... Re-signed by Patriots (February 27, 1996). ... Released by Patriots (August 24, 1997). ... Signed by New York Jets (August 25, 1997). ... Released by Jets (September 5, 1999). ... Signed by Detroit Lions (October 4, 1999). ... Granted unconditional free agency (February 11, 2000). ... Re-signed by Lions (April 25, 2000). ... Granted unconditional free agency (March 2, 2001).
PLAYING EXPERIENCE: New England NFL, 1993-1996; New York Jets NFL, 1997 and 1998; Detroit NFL, 1999 and 2000. ... Games/Games started: 1993 (15/12), 1994 (16/0), 1995 (16/2), 1996 (14/0), 1997 (16/0), 1998 (16/1), 1999 (13/1), 2000 (14/4). Total: 120/20.
CHAMPIONSHIP GAME EXPERIENCE: Played in AFC championship game (1996 and 1998 seasons). ... Played in Super Bowl XXXI (1996 season).
PRO STATISTICS: 1993—Recovered one fumble. 1995—Recovered one fumble. 1996—Recovered one fumble for 42 yards and a touchdown. 1997—Caught one pass for 26 yards. 1998—Intercepted one pass for no yards and recovered one fumble for 16 yards. 2000—Intercepted two passes for 12 yards and credited with $1/2$ sack.

BROWN, COURTNEY   DE   BROWNS

PERSONAL: Born February 14, 1978, in Charleston, S.C. ... 6-4/266. ... Full name: Courtney Lanair Brown.
HIGH SCHOOL: Macedonia (Alvin, S.C.).
COLLEGE: Penn State (degree in integrative arts, 1999).
TRANSACTIONS/CAREER NOTES: Selected by Cleveland Browns in first round (first pick overall) of 2000 NFL draft. ... Signed by Browns (May 10, 2000).
HONORS: Named defensive end on THE SPORTING NEWS college All-America first team (1999).
PRO STATISTICS: 2000—Recovered one fumble.

Year Team	G	GS	SACKS
2000—Cleveland NFL	16	16	4.5

BROWN, DAVE   QB   CARDINALS

PERSONAL: Born February 25, 1970, in Summit, N.J. ... 6-6/230. ... Full name: David Michael Brown.
HIGH SCHOOL: Westfield (N.J.).
COLLEGE: Duke (degrees in history and political science, 1992).
TRANSACTIONS/CAREER NOTES: Selected by New York Giants in first round of 1992 NFL supplemental draft. ... Signed by Giants (August 12, 1992). ... On injured reserve with thumb injury (December 18, 1992-remainder of season). ... Granted unconditional free agency (February 16, 1996). ... Re-signed by Giants (May 3, 1996). ... Released by Giants (February 20, 1998). ... Signed by Arizona Cardinals (April 29, 1998). ... Granted unconditional free agency (February 11, 2000). ... Re-signed by Cardinals (February 23, 2000).

PRO STATISTICS: 1994—Punted twice for 57 yards, fumbled 11 times and recovered four fumbles for minus 15 yards. 1995—Punted once for 15 yards, fumbled 10 times and recovered two fumbles for minus eight yards. 1996—Fumbled nine times and recovered one fumble for minus three yards. 1997—Fumbled once. 1999—Fumbled four times and recovered one fumble. 2000—Fumbled twice for minus three yards.
SINGLE GAME HIGHS (regular season): Attempts—50 (September 17, 1995, vs. Green Bay); completions—28 (September 14, 1997, vs. Baltimore); yards—299 (November 5, 1995, vs. Seattle); and touchdown passes—2 (September 28, 1997, vs. New Orleans).
MISCELLANEOUS: Regular-season record as starting NFL quarterback: 26-34 (.433).

Year Team	G	GS	Att.	Cmp.	Pct.	Yds.	TD	Int.	Avg.	Rat.	Att.	Yds.	Avg.	TD	TD	2pt.	Pts.
					PASSING							RUSHING				TOTALS	
1992—N.Y. Giants NFL..........	2	0	7	4	57.1	21	0	0	3.00	62.2	2	-1	-0.5	0	0	0	0
1993—N.Y. Giants NFL..........	1	0	0	0	0.0	0	0	0	0.0	...	3	-4	-1.3	0	0	0	0
1994—N.Y. Giants NFL..........	15	15	350	201	57.4	2536	12	16	7.25	72.5	60	196	3.3	2	2	0	12
1995—N.Y. Giants NFL..........	16	16	456	254	55.7	2814	11	10	6.17	73.1	45	228	5.1	4	4	0	24
1996—N.Y. Giants NFL..........	16	16	398	214	53.8	2412	12	20	6.06	61.3	50	170	3.4	0	0	0	0
1997—N.Y. Giants NFL..........	8	6	180	93	51.7	1023	5	3	5.68	71.1	17	29	1.7	1	1	0	6
1998—Arizona NFL	1	0	5	2	40.0	31	0	0	6.20	61.3	1	2	2.0	0	0	0	0
1999—Arizona NFL	8	5	169	84	49.7	944	2	6	5.59	55.9	13	49	3.8	0	0	0	0
2000—Arizona NFL	6	2	69	40	58.0	467	2	3	6.77	70.1	1	0	0.0	0	0	0	0
Pro totals (9 years)	73	60	1634	892	54.6	10248	44	58	6.27	67.9	192	669	3.5	7	7	0	42

BROWN, ERIC   S   BRONCOS

PERSONAL: Born March 20, 1975, in San Antonio. ... 6-0/210. ... Full name: Eric Jon Brown.
HIGH SCHOOL: Judson (Converse, Texas).
JUNIOR COLLEGE: Blinn College (Texas).
COLLEGE: Mississippi State.
TRANSACTIONS/CAREER NOTES: Selected by Denver Broncos in second round (61st pick overall) of 1998 NFL draft. ... Signed by Broncos (July 16, 1998). ... On injured reserve with knee injury (November 18, 1999-remainder of season).
PLAYING EXPERIENCE: Denver NFL, 1998-2000. ... Games/Games started: 1998 (11/10), 1999 (10/10), 2000 (16/16). Total: 37/36.
CHAMPIONSHIP GAME EXPERIENCE: Member of Broncos for AFC championship game (1998 season); inactive. ... Member of Super Bowl championship team (1998 season); inactive.
PRO STATISTICS: 1998—Recovered one fumble. 1999—Intercepted one pass for 13 yards, credited with 1 1/2 sacks, fumbled twice and recovered one fumble. 2000—Intercepted three passes for nine yards, credited with one sack and recovered three fumbles for eight yards.

BROWN, FAKHIR   CB   CHARGERS

PERSONAL: Born September 21, 1977, in Detroit. ... 5-11/192. ... Full name: Fakhir Hamin Brown. ... Name pronounced fah-KEAR.
HIGH SCHOOL: Mansfield (La.).
COLLEGE: Grambling State.
TRANSACTIONS/CAREER NOTES: Signed by Toronto Argonauts of CFL (April 6, 1998). ... Signed as non-drafted free agent by San Diego Chargers (April 20, 1999). ... Released by Chargers (September 4, 1999). ... Re-signed by Chargers to practice squad (September 7, 1999). ... Activated (October 9, 1999). ... Released by Chragers (October 15, 1999). ... Re-signed by Chargers to practice squad (October 16, 1999). ... Activated (October 22, 2000).
PLAYING EXPERIENCE: Toronto CFL, 1998; San Diego NFL, 1999 and 2000. ... Games/Games started: 1998 (6/games started unavailable), 1999 (9/3), 2000 (9/8). Total NFL: 18/11. Total Pro: 24/-.
PRO STATISTICS: CFL: 1998—Intercepted one pass for no yards. 2000—Intercepted one pass for no yards.

BROWN, GILBERT   DT   PACKERS

PERSONAL: Born February 22, 1971, in Detroit. ... 6-2/339. ... Full name: Gilbert Jesse Brown.
HIGH SCHOOL: Mackenzie (Detroit).
COLLEGE: Kansas.
TRANSACTIONS/CAREER NOTES: Selected by Minnesota Vikings in third round (79th pick overall) of 1993 NFL draft. ... Signed by Vikings (July 16, 1993). ... Claimed on waivers by Green Bay Packers (August 31, 1993). ... On injured reserve with knee injury (December 6, 1994-remainder of season). ... Granted unconditional free agency (February 14, 1997). ... Re-signed by Packers (February 18, 1997). ... Granted unconditional free agency (February 11, 2000). ... Re-signed by Packers (March 23, 2001).
CHAMPIONSHIP GAME EXPERIENCE: Played in NFC championship game (1995-97 seasons). ... Member of Super Bowl championship team (1996 season). ... Played in Super Bowl XXXII (1997 season).

Year Team	G	GS	SACKS
1993—Green Bay NFL..	2	0	0.0
1994—Green Bay NFL..	13	1	3.0
1995—Green Bay NFL..	13	7	0.0
1996—Green Bay NFL..	16	16	1.0
1997—Green Bay NFL..	12	12	3.0
1998—Green Bay NFL..	16	16	0.0
1999—Green Bay NFL..	16	15	0.0
2000—		Did not play.	
Pro totals (7 years)..	88	67	7.0

BROWN, J.B.   CB

PERSONAL: Born January 5, 1967, in Washington, D.C. ... 6-0/191. ... Full name: James Harold Brown.
HIGH SCHOOL: DeMatha Catholic (Hyattsville, Md.).
COLLEGE: Maryland.

TRANSACTIONS/CAREER NOTES: Selected by Miami Dolphins in 12th round (315th pick overall) of 1989 NFL draft. ... Signed by Dolphins (July 16, 1989). ... Granted free agency (February 1, 1991). ... Re-signed by Dolphins to practice squad (August 29, 1991). ... Activated (September 7, 1991). ... Granted free agency (March 1, 1993). ... Re-signed by Dolphins (July 21, 1993). ... Released by Dolphins (February 3, 1997). ... Signed by Pittsburgh Steelers (February 7, 1997). ... Traded by Steelers to Arizona Cardinals for seventh-round pick (K Kris Brown) in 1999 draft (August 25, 1998). ... Signed by Cardinals after 1998 season. ... Signed by Detroit Lions (July 20, 1999). ... Granted unconditional free agency (February 11, 2000). ... Re-signed by Lions (December 4, 2000). ... Granted unconditional free agency (March 2, 2001).
CHAMPIONSHIP GAME EXPERIENCE: Played in AFC championship game (1992 and 1997 seasons).
PRO STATISTICS: 1990—Credited with one sack. 1992—Recovered one fumble. 1993—Fumbled once. 1995—Fumbled once and recovered two fumbles. 1998—Recovered one fumble.

			INTERCEPTIONS			
Year Team	G	GS	No.	Yds.	Avg.	TD
1989—Miami NFL	16	0	0	0	0.0	0
1990—Miami NFL	16	16	0	0	0.0	0
1991—Miami NFL	15	11	1	0	0.0	0
1992—Miami NFL	16	16	4	119	29.8	1
1993—Miami NFL	16	16	5	43	8.6	0
1994—Miami NFL	16	16	3	82	27.3	0
1995—Miami NFL	13	12	2	20	10.0	0
1996—Miami NFL	14	1	1	29	29.0	0
1997—Pittsburgh NFL	13	0	0	0	0.0	0
1998—Arizona NFL	15	6	0	0	0.0	0
1999—Detroit NFL	13	3	0	0	0.0	0
2000—Detroit NFL	3	0	0	0	0.0	0
Pro totals (12 years)	166	97	16	293	18.3	1

BROWN, JAMES   OT

PERSONAL: Born November 30, 1970, in Philadelphia. ... 6-6/325. ... Full name: James Lamont Brown.
HIGH SCHOOL: Mastbaum Area Vo-Tech (Philadelphia).
COLLEGE: Virginia State.
TRANSACTIONS/CAREER NOTES: Selected by Dallas Cowboys in third round (82nd pick overall) of 1992 NFL draft. ... Signed by Cowboys (July 15, 1992). ... Released by Cowboys (August 17, 1992). ... Signed by Indianapolis Colts (August 19, 1992). ... Released by Colts (August 31, 1992). ... Signed by New York Jets to practice squad (September 2, 1992). ... Traded by Jets to Miami Dolphins for fifth-round pick (DB Raymond Austin) in 1997 draft (March 4, 1996). ... Granted unconditional free agency (February 13, 1998). ... Re-signed by Dolphins (March 3, 1998). ... Released by Dolphins (June 15, 2000). ... Signed by Cleveland Browns (July 13, 2000). ... Granted unconditional free agency (March 2, 2001).
PLAYING EXPERIENCE: New York Jets NFL, 1993-1995; Miami NFL, 1996-1999; Cleveland NFL, 2000. ... Games/Games started: 1993 (14/1), 1994 (16/6), 1995 (14/12), 1996 (16/16), 1997 (16/16), 1998 (16/16), 1999 (15/14), 2000 (7/5). Total: 114/86.
PRO STATISTICS: 1994—Recovered one fumble.

BROWN, KRIS   K   STEELERS

PERSONAL: Born December 23, 1976, in Southlake, Texas. ... 5-10/204.
HIGH SCHOOL: Carroll (Southlake, Texas).
COLLEGE: Nebraska.
TRANSACTIONS/CAREER NOTES: Selected by Pittsburgh Steelers in seventh round (228th pick overall) of 1999 NFL draft. ... Signed by Steelers (June 29, 1999).

		KICKING						
Year Team	G	XPM	XPA	FGM	FGA	Lg.	50+	Pts.
1999—Pittsburgh NFL	16	30	31	25	29	51	1-1	105
2000—Pittsburgh NFL	16	32	33	25	30	52	1-2	107
Pro totals (2 years)	32	62	64	50	59	52	2-3	212

BROWN, LOMAS   OT   GIANTS

PERSONAL: Born March 30, 1963, in Miami. ... 6-4/280. ... Full name: Lomas Brown Jr. ... Cousin of Joe Taylor, defensive back with Chicago Bears (1967-74); cousin of Guy McIntyre, guard with San Francisco 49ers (1984-93), Green Bay Packers (1994) and Philadelphia Eagles (1995 and 1996); and cousin of Eric Curry, defensive end with Tampa Bay Buccaneers (1993-97) and Jacksonville Jaguars (1998 and 1999).
HIGH SCHOOL: Miami Springs Senior.
COLLEGE: Florida (degree in public recreation, 1996).
TRANSACTIONS/CAREER NOTES: Selected by Orlando Renegades in second round (18th pick overall) of 1985 USFL draft. ... Selected by Detroit Lions in first round (sixth pick overall) of 1985 NFL draft. ... Signed by Lions (August 9, 1985). ... Designated by Lions as franchise player (February 25, 1993). ... Granted roster exemption (September 1-3, 1993). ... Designated by Lions as franchise player (February 15, 1995). ... Re-signed by Lions (September 7, 1995). ... Granted unconditional free agency (February 16, 1996). ... Signed by Arizona Cardinals (February 28, 1996). ... Granted unconditional free agency (February 12, 1999). ... Signed by Cleveland Browns (March 9, 1999). ... On injured reserve with knee injury (December 14, 1999-remainder of season). ... Released by Browns (February 8, 2000). ... Signed by New York Giants (February 2, 2000).
PLAYING EXPERIENCE: Detroit NFL, 1985-1995; Arizona NFL, 1996-1998; Cleveland NFL, 1999; New York Giants NFL, 2000. ... Games/Games started: 1985 (16/16), 1986 (16/16), 1987 (11/11), 1988 (16/16), 1989 (16/16), 1990 (16/16), 1991 (15/15), 1992 (16/16), 1993 (11/11), 1994 (16/16), 1995 (14/14), 1996 (16/16), 1997 (14/14), 1998 (16/16), 1999 (10/10), 2000 (16/16). Total: 236/235.
CHAMPIONSHIP GAME EXPERIENCE: Played in NFC championship game (1991 and 2000 season). ... Played in Super Bowl XXXV (2000 season).
HONORS: Named tackle on THE SPORTING NEWS college All-America first team (1984). ... Played in Pro Bowl (1990-1996 seasons). ... Named offensive tackle on THE SPORTING NEWS NFL All-Pro team (1992).
PRO STATISTICS: 1989—Rushed once for three yards and recovered one fumble. 1991—Recovered one fumble. 2000—Recovered one fumble.

BROWN, MIKE   S   BEARS

PERSONAL: Born February 13, 1978, in Scottsdale, Ariz. ... 5-10/202.
HIGH SCHOOL: Saguaro (Scottsdale, Ariz.).
COLLEGE: Nebraska.
TRANSACTIONS/CAREER NOTES: Selected by Chicago Bears in second round (39th pick overall) of 2000 NFL draft. ... Signed by Bears (July 23, 2000).
PRO STATISTICS: 2000—Recovered one fumble for 12 yards.

			INTERCEPTIONS		
Year Team	G	GS	No.	Yds.	Avg.	TD
2000—Chicago NFL	16	16	1	35	35.0	1

B

BROWN, NA   WR   EAGLES

PERSONAL: Born February 22, 1977, in Reidsville, N.C. ... 6-0/196. ... Full name: Na Orlando Brown. ... Name pronounced NAY.
HIGH SCHOOL: Reidsville (N.C.).
COLLEGE: North Carolina.
TRANSACTIONS/CAREER NOTES: Selected by Philadelphia Eagles in fourth round (130th pick overall) of 1999 NFL draft. ... Signed by Eagles (July 28, 1999).
SINGLE GAME HIGHS (regular season): Receptions—4 (December 5, 1999, vs. Arizona); yards—60 (December 19, 1999, vs. New England); and touchdown receptions—1 (December 8, 2000, vs. Washington).

			RECEIVING				TOTALS			
Year Team	G	GS	No.	Yds.	Avg.	TD	TD	2pt.	Pts.	Fum.
1999—Philadelphia NFL	12	5	18	188	10.4	1	1	0	6	0
2000—Philadelphia NFL	14	2	9	80	8.9	1	1	0	6	0
Pro totals (2 years)	26	7	27	268	9.9	2	2	0	12	0

BROWN, RALPH   CB   GIANTS

PERSONAL: Born September 9, 1978, in Hacienda Heights, Calif. ... 5-10/185. ... Full name: Ralph Brown II.
HIGH SCHOOL: Bishop Amat (La Puente, Calif.).
COLLEGE: Nebraska.
TRANSACTIONS/CAREER NOTES: Selected by New York Giants in fifth round (140th pick overall) of 2000 NFL draft. ... Signed by Giants (July 18, 2000). ... On injured reserve with kidney injury (October 3, 2000-remainder of season).
HONORS: Named cornerback on THE SPORTING NEWS college All-America first team (1999).

			INTERCEPTIONS		
Year Team	G	GS	No.	Yds.	Avg.	TD
2000—New York Giants NFL	2	0	0	0	0.0	0

BROWN, RAY   G   49ERS

PERSONAL: Born December 12, 1962, in Marion, Ark. ... 6-5/318. ... Full name: Leonard Ray Brown Jr.
HIGH SCHOOL: Marion (Ark.).
COLLEGE: Memphis State, then Arizona State, then Arkansas State.
TRANSACTIONS/CAREER NOTES: Selected by St. Louis Cardinals in eighth round (201st pick overall) of 1986 NFL draft. ... Signed by Cardinals (July 14, 1986). ... On injured reserve with knee injury (October 17-November 21, 1986). ... Released by Cardinals (September 7, 1987). ... Re-signed by Cardinals as replacement player (September 25, 1987). ... On injured reserve with finger injury (November 12-December 12, 1987). ... Cardinals franchise moved to Phoenix (March 15, 1988). ... Granted unconditional free agency (February 1, 1989). ... Signed by Washington Redskins (March 10, 1989). ... On injured reserve with knee injury (September 5-November 4, 1989). ... On injured reserve with knee injury (September 4, 1990-January 4, 1991). ... Granted unconditional free agency (February 1-April 1, 1991). ... Re-signed by Redskins for 1991 season. ... On injured reserve with elbow injury (August 27, 1991-entire season). ... Granted unconditional free agency (February 16, 1996). ... Signed by San Francisco 49ers (March 1, 1996).
PLAYING EXPERIENCE: St. Louis NFL, 1986 and 1987; Phoenix NFL, 1988; Washington NFL, 1989, 1992-1995; San Francisco NFL, 1996-2000. ... Games/Games started: 1986 (11/4), 1987 (7/3), 1988 (15/1), 1989 (7/0), 1992 (16/8), 1993 (16/14), 1994 (16/16), 1995 (16/16), 1996 (16/16), 1997 (15/15), 1998 (16/16), 1999 (16/16), 2000 (16/16). Total: 183/141.
CHAMPIONSHIP GAME EXPERIENCE: Played in NFC championship game (1997 season).
PRO STATISTICS: 1999—Recovered two fumbles. 2000—Recovered one fumble.

BROWN, REGGIE   FB   SEAHAWKS

PERSONAL: Born June 26, 1973, in Highland Park, Mich. ... 6-0/244. ... Full name: Regilyn Brown.
HIGH SCHOOL: Henry Ford (Detroit).
JUNIOR COLLEGE: College of the Desert (Calif.).
COLLEGE: Fresno State.
TRANSACTIONS/CAREER NOTES: Selected by Seattle Seahawks in third round (91st pick overall) of 1996 NFL draft. ... Signed by Seahawks (July 17, 1996). ... On injured reserve with knee injury (October 23, 1996-remainder of season). ... On injured reserve with knee injury (December 17, 1997-remainder of season). ... Granted free agency (February 12, 1999). ... Re-signed by Seahawks (April 14, 1999). ... Granted unconditional free agency (February 11, 2000). ... Re-signed by Seahawks (May 19, 2000).
SINGLE GAME HIGHS (regular season): Attempts—4 (October 17, 1999, vs. San Diego); yards—9 (September 26, 1999, vs. Pittsburgh); and rushing touchdowns—0.

Year Team	G	GS	RUSHING				RECEIVING				KICKOFF RETURNS				TOTALS			
			Att.	Yds.	Avg.	TD	No.	Yds.	Avg.	TD	No.	Yds.	Avg.	TD	TD	2pt.	Pts.	Fum.
1996—Seattle NFL	7	0	0	0	0.0	0	0	0	0.0	0	4	51	12.8	0	0	0	0	0
1997—Seattle NFL	11	0	0	0	0.0	0	0	0	0.0	0	1	16	16.0	0	0	0	0	0
1998—Seattle NFL	15	1	1	2	2.0	0	0	0	0.0	0	4	44	11.0	0	0	0	0	0
1999—Seattle NFL	16	8	14	38	2.7	0	34	228	6.7	1	0	0	0.0	0	1	0	6	1
2000—Seattle NFL	12	1	3	6	2.0	0	2	9	4.5	0	2	19	9.5	0	0	0	0	0
Pro totals (5 years)	61	10	18	46	2.6	0	36	237	6.6	1	11	130	11.8	0	1	0	6	1

BROWN, RUBEN   G   BILLS

PERSONAL: Born February 13, 1972, in Englewood, N.J. ... 6-3/304. ... Full name: Ruben Pernell Brown. ... Brother of Cornell Brown, linebacker with Baltimore Ravens (1997-2000).
HIGH SCHOOL: E.C. Glass (Lynchburg, Va.).
COLLEGE: Pittsburgh.
TRANSACTIONS/CAREER NOTES: Selected by Buffalo Bills in first round (14th pick overall) of 1995 NFL draft. ... Signed by Bills (June 20, 1995). ... Granted unconditional free agency (February 11, 2000). ... Re-signed by Bills (March 31, 2000).
PLAYING EXPERIENCE: Buffalo NFL, 1995-2000. ... Games/Games started: 1995 (16/16), 1996 (14/14), 1997 (16/16), 1998 (13/13), 1999 (14/14), 2000 (16/16). Total: 89/89.
HONORS: Named offensive lineman on THE SPORTING NEWS college All-America second team (1994). ... Played in Pro Bowl (1996-2000 seasons).
PRO STATISTICS: 1997—Recovered one fumble.

BROWN, TIM   WR   RAIDERS

PERSONAL: Born July 22, 1966, in Dallas. ... 6-0/195. ... Full name: Timothy Donell Brown.
HIGH SCHOOL: Woodrow Wilson (Dallas).
COLLEGE: Notre Dame (degree in sociology).
TRANSACTIONS/CAREER NOTES: Selected by Los Angeles Raiders in first round (sixth pick overall) of 1988 NFL draft. ... Signed by Raiders (July 14, 1988). ... On injured reserve with knee injury (September 12, 1989-remainder of season). ... Granted free agency (February 1, 1992). ... Re-signed by Raiders (August 13, 1992). ... Designated by Raiders as transition player (February 25, 1993). ... Tendered offer sheet by Denver Broncos (March 11, 1994). ... Offer matched by Raiders (March 16, 1994). ... Raiders franchise moved to Oakland (July 21, 1995).
CHAMPIONSHIP GAME EXPERIENCE: Played in AFC championship game (1990 and 2000 seasons).
HONORS: Named wide receiver on THE SPORTING NEWS college All-America first team (1986 and 1987). ... Heisman Trophy winner (1987). ... Named College Football Player of the Year by THE SPORTING NEWS (1987). ... Named kick returner on THE SPORTING NEWS NFL All-Pro team (1988). ... Played in Pro Bowl (1988, 1991 and 1993-1997 seasons). ... Named wide receiver on THE SPORTING NEWS NFL All-Pro team (1997). ... Named to play in Pro Bowl (1999 season); replaced by Terry Glenn due to injury.
RECORDS: Holds NFL rookie-season record for most combined yards gained—2,317 (1988).
PRO STATISTICS: 1988—Fumbled five times and recovered one fumble for seven yards. 1989—Fumbled once. 1990—Fumbled three times. 1991—Fumbled once. 1992—Fumbled six times and recovered one fumble. 1993—Fumbled once. 1994—Fumbled three times. 1995—Recovered one fumble for three yards. 1996—Fumbled three times and recovered one fumble. 1997—Fumbled once. 1998—Fumbled three times and recovered two fumbles.
SINGLE GAME HIGHS (regular season): Receptions—14 (December 21, 1997, vs. Jacksonville); yards—190 (October 24, 1999, vs. New York Jets); and touchdown receptions—3 (August 31, 1997, vs. Tennessee).
STATISTICAL PLATEAUS: 100-yard receiving games: 1988 (1), 1991 (1), 1992 (1), 1993 (4), 1994 (4), 1995 (6), 1996 (2), 1997 (7), 1998 (3), 1999 (6), 2000 (2). Total: 37.
MISCELLANEOUS: Holds Raiders franchise all-time record for most receptions (846), most yards receiving (12,072) and receiving touchdowns (86).

Year Team	G	GS	RUSHING				RECEIVING				PUNT RETURNS				KICKOFF RETURNS				TOTALS		
			Att.	Yds.	Avg.	TD	No.	Yds.	Avg.	TD	No.	Yds.	Avg.	TD	No.	Yds.	Avg.	TD	TD	2pt.	Pts.
1988—LA Raiders NFL	16	9	14	50	3.6	1	43	725	16.9	5	§49	§444	9.1	0	†41	*1098	*26.8	†1	7	0	42
1989—LA Raiders NFL	1	1	0	0	0.0	0	1	8	8.0	0	4	43	10.8	0	3	63	21.0	0	0	0	0
1990—LA Raiders NFL	16	0	0	0	0.0	0	18	265	14.7	3	34	295	8.7	0	0	0	0.0	0	3	0	18
1991—LA Raiders NFL	16	1	5	16	3.2	0	36	554	15.4	5	29	§330	11.4	▲1	1	29	29.0	0	6	0	36
1992—LA Raiders NFL	15	12	3	-4	-1.3	0	49	693	14.1	7	37	383	10.4	0	2	14	7.0	0	7	0	42
1993—LA Raiders NFL	16	16	2	7	3.5	0	80	§1180	14.8	7	40	§465	11.6	1	0	0	0.0	0	8	0	48
1994—LA Raiders NFL	16	16	0	0	0.0	0	89	§1309	14.7	9	40	*487	12.2	0	0	0	0.0	0	9	0	54
1995—Oakland NFL	16	16	0	0	0.0	0	89	§1342	15.1	10	36	364	10.1	0	0	0	0.0	0	10	0	60
1996—Oakland NFL	16	16	6	35	5.8	0	90	1104	12.3	9	32	272	8.5	0	1	24	24.0	0	9	0	54
1997—Oakland NFL	16	16	5	19	3.8	0	†104	§1408	13.5	5	0	0	0.0	0	1	7	7.0	0	5	1	32
1998—Oakland NFL	16	16	1	-7	-7.0	0	81	1012	12.5	9	3	23	7.7	0	0	0	0.0	0	9	0	54
1999—Oakland NFL	16	16	1	4	4.0	0	90	1344	14.9	6	0	0	0.0	0	0	0	0.0	0	6	0	36
2000—Oakland NFL	16	16	3	12	4.0	0	76	1128	14.8	11	0	0	0.0	0	0	0	0.0	0	11	0	66
Pro totals (13 years)	192	151	40	132	3.3	1	846	12072	14.3	86	304	3106	10.2	2	49	1235	25.2	1	90	1	542

BROWN, TRAVIS   QB   SEAHAWKS

PERSONAL: Born July 17, 1977, in Phoenix. ... 6-3/218.
HIGH SCHOOL: Moon Valley (Phoenix).
COLLEGE: Northern Arizona.
TRANSACTIONS/CAREER NOTES: Signed as non-drafted free agent by Philadelphia Eagles (April 19, 2000). ... Released by Eagles (August 27, 2000). ... Signed by Seattle Seahawks to practice squad (August 30, 2000). ... Activated (November 21, 2000).
PLAYING EXPERIENCE: Pittsburgh NFL, 2000. ... Games/Games started: 2000 (1/0).
PRO STATISTICS: 2000—Attempted one pass without a completion.
SINGLE GAME HIGHS (regular season): Attempts—1 (December 16, 2000, vs. Oakland); completions—0; yards—0; and touchdown passes—0.

BROWN, TROY — WR — PATRIOTS

PERSONAL: Born July 2, 1971, in Barnwell, S.C. ... 5-10/190. ... Full name: Troy Fitzgerald Brown.
HIGH SCHOOL: Blackville-Hilda (Blackville, S.C.).
JUNIOR COLLEGE: Lees-McRae College (N.C.).
COLLEGE: Marshall.
TRANSACTIONS/CAREER NOTES: Selected by New England Patriots in eighth round (198th pick overall) of 1993 NFL draft. ... Signed by Patriots (July 16, 1993). ... On injured reserve with quadriceps injury (December 31, 1993-remainder of season). ... Released by Patriots (August 28, 1994). ... Re-signed by Patriots (October 19, 1994). ... Granted unconditional free agency (February 14, 1997). ... Re-signed by Patriots (March 10, 1997). ... Granted unconditional free agency (February 11, 2000). ... Re-signed by Patriots (February 26, 2000).
CHAMPIONSHIP GAME EXPERIENCE: Played in AFC championship game (1996 season). ... Member of Patriots for Super Bowl XXXI (1996 season); inactive.
PRO STATISTICS: 1993—Recovered one fumble. 1994—Recovered two fumbles. 1995—Recovered one fumble for 75 yards and a touchdown. 1997—Rushed once for minus 18 yards. 1999—Attempted one pass without a completion and recovered two fumbles. 2000—Rushed six times for 46 yards.
SINGLE GAME HIGHS (regular season): Receptions—12 (December 4, 2000, vs. Kansas City); yards—125 (October 19, 1997, vs. New York Jets); and touchdown receptions—2 (October 1, 2000, vs. Denver).
STATISTICAL PLATEAUS: 100-yard receiving games: 1997 (2), 1999 (1), 2000 (4). Total: 7.

			RECEIVING				PUNT RETURNS				KICKOFF RETURNS				TOTALS		
Year Team	G	GS	No.	Yds.	Avg.	TD	No.	Yds.	Avg.	TD	No.	Yds.	Avg.	TD	TD	2pt.	Pts. Fum.
1993—New England NFL	12	0	2	22	11.0	0	25	224	9.0	0	15	243	16.2	0	0	0	0 2
1994—New England NFL	9	0	0	0	0.0	0	24	202	8.4	0	1	14	14.0	0	0	0	0 2
1995—New England NFL	16	0	14	159	11.4	0	0	0	0.0	0	31	672	21.7	0	1	0	6 1
1996—New England NFL	16	0	21	222	10.6	0	0	0	0.0	0	29	634	21.9	0	0	0	0 0
1997—New England NFL	16	6	41	607	14.8	6	0	0	0.0	0	0	0	0.0	0	6	0	36 0
1998—New England NFL	10	0	23	346	15.0	1	17	225	13.2	0	0	0	0.0	0	1	0	6 0
1999—New England NFL	13	1	36	471	13.1	1	38	405	10.7	0	8	271	33.9	0	1	0	6 1
2000—New England NFL	16	15	83	944	11.4	4	39	504	12.9	1	2	15	7.5	0	5	0	30 2
Pro totals (8 years)	108	22	220	2771	12.6	12	143	1560	10.9	1	86	1849	21.5	0	14	0	84 8

BROWNING, JOHN — DT — CHIEFS

PERSONAL: Born September 30, 1973, in Miami. ... 6-4/289.
HIGH SCHOOL: North Miami.
COLLEGE: West Virginia.
TRANSACTIONS/CAREER NOTES: Selected by Kansas City Chiefs in third round (68th pick overall) of 1996 NFL draft. ... Signed by Chiefs (July 24, 1996). ... On injured reserve with Achilles' tendon injury (September 1, 1999-entire season). ... Granted unconditional free agency (February 11, 2000). ... Re-signed by Chiefs (February 11, 2000).
PRO STATISTICS: 1997—Recovered one fumble. 2000—Intercepted one pass for no yards and recovered one fumble.

Year Team	G	GS	SACKS
1996—Kansas City NFL	13	2	2.0
1997—Kansas City NFL	14	13	4.0
1998—Kansas City NFL	8	8	0.0
1999—Kansas City NFL		Did not play.	
2000—Kansas City NFL	16	16	6.0
Pro totals (4 years)	51	39	12.0

BRUCE, ISAAC — WR — RAMS

PERSONAL: Born November 10, 1972, in Fort Lauderdale, Fla. ... 6-0/188. ... Full name: Isaac Isidore Bruce. ... Cousin of Derrick Moore, running back with Detroit Lions (1993 and 1994) and Carolina Panthers (1995).
HIGH SCHOOL: Dillard (Fort Lauderdale, Fla.).
JUNIOR COLLEGE: West Los Angeles Junior College, then Santa Monica (Calif.) Junior College.
COLLEGE: Memphis State.
TRANSACTIONS/CAREER NOTES: Selected by Los Angeles Rams in second round (33rd pick overall) of 1994 NFL draft. ... Signed by Rams (July 13, 1994). ... On injured reserve with sprained right knee (December 9, 1994-remainder of season). ... Rams franchise moved to St. Louis (April 12, 1995). ... On injured reserve with hamstring injury (December 9, 1998-remainder of season).
CHAMPIONSHIP GAME EXPERIENCE: Played in NFC championship game (1999 season). ... Member of Super Bowl championship team (1999 season).
HONORS: Named wide receiver on THE SPORTING NEWS NFL All-Pro team (1999). ... Played in Pro Bowl (1996 and 1999 season). ... Named to play in Pro Bowl (2000 season); replaced by Torry Holt due to injury.
PRO STATISTICS: 1995—Ran 52 yards with lateral from punt return and recovered one fumble. 1996—Attempted two passes with one completion for 15 yards and one interception.
SINGLE GAME HIGHS (regular season): Receptions—15 (December 24, 1995, vs. Miami); yards—233 (November 2, 1997, vs. Atlanta); and touchdown receptions—4 (October 10, 1999, vs. San Francisco).
STATISTICAL PLATEAUS: 100-yard receiving games: 1995 (9), 1996 (4), 1997 (2), 1998 (2), 1999 (4), 2000 (4). Total: 25.

			RUSHING				RECEIVING				TOTALS		
Year Team	G	GS	Att.	Yds.	Avg.	TD	No.	Yds.	Avg.	TD	TD	2pt.	Pts. Fum.
1994—Los Angeles Rams NFL	12	0	1	2	2.0	0	21	272	13.0	3	3	0	18 0
1995—St. Louis NFL	16	16	3	17	5.7	0	119	1781	15.0	13	13	1	80 2
1996—St. Louis NFL	16	16	1	4	4.0	0	84	*1338	15.9	7	7	0	42 1
1997—St. Louis NFL	12	12	0	0	0.0	0	56	815	14.6	5	5	0	30 1
1998—St. Louis NFL	5	5	1	30	30.0	0	32	457	14.3	1	1	0	6 0
1999—St. Louis NFL	16	16	5	32	6.4	0	77	1165	15.1	12	12	1	74 0
2000—St. Louis NFL	16	16	1	11	11.0	0	87	1471	16.9	9	9	0	54 1
Pro totals (7 years)	93	81	12	96	8.0	0	476	7299	15.3	50	50	2	304 5

BRUENER, MARK   TE   STEELERS

PERSONAL: Born September 16, 1972, in Olympia, Wash. ... 6-4/261. ... Full name: Mark Frederick Bruener. ... Name pronounced BREW-ner.
HIGH SCHOOL: Aberdeen (Wash.).
COLLEGE: Washington (degree in economics).
TRANSACTIONS/CAREER NOTES: Selected by Pittsburgh Steelers in first round (27th pick overall) of 1995 NFL draft. ... Signed by Steelers (July 25, 1995). ... On injured reserve with knee injury (November 29, 1996-remainder of season).
CHAMPIONSHIP GAME EXPERIENCE: Played in AFC championship game (1995 and 1997 seasons). ... Played in Super Bowl XXX (1995 season).
PRO STATISTICS: 1995—Returned two kickoffs for 19 yards. 1998—Lost seven yards with lateral from kickoff return. 1999—Recovered two fumbles for four yards.
SINGLE GAME HIGHS (regular season): Receptions—5 (December 13, 1997, vs. New England); yards—51 (November 28, 1999, vs. Cincinnati); and touchdown receptions—1 (December 3, 2000, vs. Oakland).

B

| | | | RECEIVING | | | | TOTALS | | |
Year Team	G	GS	No.	Yds.	Avg.	TD	TD	2pt.	Pts.	Fum.
1995—Pittsburgh NFL	16	13	26	238	9.2	3	3	0	18	0
1996—Pittsburgh NFL	12	12	12	141	11.8	0	0	1	2	0
1997—Pittsburgh NFL	16	16	18	117	6.5	6	6	0	36	1
1998—Pittsburgh NFL	16	16	19	157	8.3	2	2	0	12	0
1999—Pittsburgh NFL	14	14	18	176	9.8	0	0	0	0	0
2000—Pittsburgh NFL	16	16	17	192	11.3	3	3	0	18	0
Pro totals (6 years)	90	87	110	1021	9.3	14	14	1	86	1

BRUNELL, MARK   QB   JAGUARS

PERSONAL: Born September 17, 1970, in Los Angeles. ... 6-1/217. ... Full name: Mark Allen Brunell.
HIGH SCHOOL: St. Joseph (Santa Maria, Calif.).
COLLEGE: Washington (degree in history).
TRANSACTIONS/CAREER NOTES: Selected by Green Bay Packers in fifth round (118th pick overall) of 1993 NFL draft. ... Signed by Packers (July 1, 1993). ... Traded by Packers to Jacksonville Jaguars for third- (FB William Henderson) and fifth-round (RB Travis Jervey) picks in 1995 draft (April 21, 1995).
CHAMPIONSHIP GAME EXPERIENCE: Played in AFC championship game (1996 and 1999 seasons).
HONORS: Played in Pro Bowl (1996, 1997 and 1999 seasons). ... Named Outstanding Player of Pro Bowl (1996 season).
PRO STATISTICS: 1994—Fumbled once. 1995—Fumbled five times and recovered three fumbles. 1996—Led AFC with 14 fumbles and recovered five fumbles for minus 14 yards. 1997—Fumbled four times for minus five yards. 1998—Fumbled three times and recovered two fumbles for minus one yard. 1999—Fumbled six times and recovered three fumbles for minus two yards. 2000—Fumbled seven times and recovered three fumbles for minus two yards.
SINGLE GAME HIGHS (regular season): Attempts—52 (October 20, 1996, vs. St. Louis); completions—37 (October 20, 1996, vs. St. Louis); yards—432 (September 22, 1996, vs. New England); and touchdown passes—4 (November 29, 1998, vs. Cincinnati).
STATISTICAL PLATEAUS: 300-yard passing games: 1995 (2), 1996 (6), 1997 (3), 1998 (2), 1999 (3), 2000 (3). Total: 19.
MISCELLANEOUS: Regular-season record as starting NFL quarterback: 51-33 (.607). ... Postseason record as starting NFL quarterback: 4-4 (.500). ... Holds Jacksonville Jaguars all-time record for most yards passing (19,117) and most touchdown passes (106).

| | | | PASSING | | | | | | | RUSHING | | | | TOTALS | | |
Year Team	G	GS	Att.	Cmp.	Pct.	Yds.	TD	Int.	Avg.	Rat.	Att.	Yds.	Avg.	TD	TD	2pt.	Pts.
1993—Green Bay NFL							Did not play.										
1994—Green Bay NFL	2	0	27	12	44.4	95	0	0	3.52	53.8	6	7	1.2	1	1	0	6
1995—Jacksonville NFL	13	10	346	201	58.1	2168	15	7	6.27	82.6	67	480	7.2	4	4	0	24
1996—Jacksonville NFL	16	16	557	353	§63.4	*4367	19	§20	*7.84	84.0	80	396	5.0	3	3	2	22
1997—Jacksonville NFL	14	14	435	264	60.7	3281	18	7	§7.54	§91.2	48	257	5.4	2	2	0	12
1998—Jacksonville NFL	13	13	354	208	58.8	2601	20	9	7.35	89.9	49	192	3.9	0	0	0	0
1999—Jacksonville NFL	15	15	441	259	58.7	3060	14	9	6.94	82.0	47	208	4.4	1	1	†1	8
2000—Jacksonville NFL	16	16	512	311	60.7	3640	20	14	7.11	84.0	48	236	4.9	2	2	0	12
Pro totals (7 years)	89	84	2672	1608	60.2	19212	106	66	7.19	85.1	345	1776	5.1	13	13	3	84

BRUSCHI, TEDY   LB   PATRIOTS

PERSONAL: Born June 9, 1973, in San Francisco. ... 6-1/245. ... Full name: Tedy Lacap Bruschi. ... Stepson of Ronald Sandys, former professional tennis player. ... Name pronounced BREW-ski.
HIGH SCHOOL: Roseville (Calif.).
COLLEGE: Arizona (degree in communications).
TRANSACTIONS/CAREER NOTES: Selected by New England Patriots in third round (86th pick overall) of 1996 NFL draft. ... Signed by Patriots (July 17, 1996). ... Granted free agency (February 12, 1999). ... Re-signed by Patriots (June 1, 1999). ... Granted unconditional free agency (February 11, 2000). ... Re-signed by Patriots (March 22, 2000).
CHAMPIONSHIP GAME EXPERIENCE: Played in AFC championship game (1996 season). ... Played in Super Bowl XXXI (1996 season).
HONORS: Named defensive lineman on THE SPORTING NEWS college All-America first team (1994 and 1995).
PRO STATISTICS: 1996—Returned blocked punt four yards for a touchdown. 1997—Recovered two fumbles. 1998—Returned one kickoff for four yards. 1999—Intercepted one pass for one yard and recovered one fumble. 2000—Returned two kickoffs for 13 yards.

Year Team	G	GS	SACKS
1996—New England NFL	16	0	4.0
1997—New England NFL	16	1	4.0
1998—New England NFL	16	7	2.0
1999—New England NFL	14	14	2.0
2000—New England NFL	16	16	1.0
Pro totals (5 years)	78	38	13.0

BRYANT, FERNANDO CB JAGUARS

PERSONAL: Born March 26, 1977, in Albany, Ga. ... 5-10/176. ... Full name: Fernando Antoneiyo Bryant. ... Nephew of Don Griffin, cornerback with San Francisco 49ers (1986-93), Cleveland Browns (1994 and 1995) and Philadelphia Eagles (1996); and nephew of James Griffin, defensive back with Cincinnati Bengals (1983-85) and Detroit Lions (1986-89).

HIGH SCHOOL: Riverdale (Murfreesboro, Tenn.).

COLLEGE: Alabama.

TRANSACTIONS/CAREER NOTES: Selected by Jacksonville Jaguars in first round (26th pick overall) of 1999 NFL draft. ... Signed by Jaguars (August 9, 1999).

CHAMPIONSHIP GAME EXPERIENCE: Played in AFC championship game (1999 season).

PRO STATISTICS: 1999—Recovered three fumbles for 27 yards. 2000—Recovered one fumble for five yards.

				INTERCEPTIONS		
Year Team	G	GS	No.	Yds.	Avg.	TD
1999—Jacksonville NFL	16	16	2	0	0.0	0
2000—Jacksonville NFL	14	14	1	0	0.0	0
Pro totals (2 years)	30	30	3	0	0.0	0

BRYANT, JUNIOR DT 49ERS

PERSONAL: Born January 16, 1971, in Omaha, Neb. ... 6-4/278. ... Full name: Edward E. Bryant.

HIGH SCHOOL: Creighton Prep (Omaha, Neb.).

COLLEGE: Notre Dame.

TRANSACTIONS/CAREER NOTES: Signed as non-drafted free agent by San Francisco 49ers (May 3, 1993). ... Released by 49ers (August 30, 1993). ... Re-signed by 49ers to practice squad (August 31, 1993). ... Released by 49ers (August 27, 1994). ... Re-signed by 49ers to practice squad (August 31, 1994). ... Granted unconditional free agency (February 11, 2000). ... Re-signed by 49ers (February 17, 2000). ... Placed on injured reserve with neck injury (October 10, 2000-remainder of season).

CHAMPIONSHIP GAME EXPERIENCE: Played in NFC championship game (1997 season).

PRO STATISTICS: 1996—Recovered one fumble. 1999—Recovered one fumble in end zone for a touchdown.

Year Team	G	GS	SACKS
1993—San Francisco NFL	Did not play.		
1994—San Francisco NFL	Did not play.		
1995—San Francisco NFL	16	4	1.0
1996—San Francisco NFL	16	1	0.5
1997—San Francisco NFL	16	3	2.5
1998—San Francisco NFL	16	16	5.0
1999—San Francisco NFL	16	16	4.5
2000—San Francisco NFL	3	3	0.0
Pro totals (6 years)	83	43	13.5

BRYANT, TONY DE RAIDERS

PERSONAL: Born September 3, 1976, in Marathon, Fla. ... 6-6/275.

HIGH SCHOOL: Marathon (Fla.).

JUNIOR COLLEGE: Copiah-Lincoln Junior College (Miss.).

COLLEGE: Florida State.

TRANSACTIONS/CAREER NOTES: Selected by Oakland Raiders in second round (40th pick overall) of 1999 NFL draft. ... Signed by Raiders (July 22, 1999).

CHAMPIONSHIP GAME EXPERIENCE: Played in AFC championship game (2000 season).

PRO STATISTICS: 2000—Recovered one fumble for three yards.

Year Team	G	GS	SACKS
1999—Oakland NFL	10	0	4.5
2000—Oakland NFL	16	16	5.5
Pro totals (2 years)	26	16	10.0

BRYSON, SHAWN RB BILLS

PERSONAL: Born November 30, 1976, in Franklin, N.C. ... 6-1/233. ... Full name: Adrian Shawn Bryson.

HIGH SCHOOL: Franklin (N.C.).

COLLEGE: Tennessee.

TRANSACTIONS/CAREER NOTES: Selected by Buffalo Bills in third round (86th pick overall) of 1999 NFL draft. ... Signed by Bills (July 27, 1999). ... On injured reserve with knee injury (August 30, 1999-entire season).

SINGLE GAME HIGHS (regular season): Attempts—19 (December 17, 2000, vs. New England); yards—88 (December 3, 2000, vs. Miami); and rushing touchdowns—0.

			RUSHING				RECEIVING				KICKOFF RETURNS				TOTALS			
Year Team	G	GS	Att.	Yds.	Avg.	TD	No.	Yds.	Avg.	TD	No.	Yds.	Avg.	TD	TD	2pt.	Pts.	Fum.
1999—Buffalo NFL								Did not play.										
2000—Buffalo NFL	16	7	161	591	3.7	0	32	271	8.5	2	8	122	15.3	0	2	▲1	14	1
Pro totals (1 years)	16	7	161	591	3.7	0	32	271	8.5	2	8	122	15.3	0	2	1	14	1

BRZEZINSKI, DOUG   G   EAGLES

PERSONAL: Born March 11, 1976, in Livonia, Mich. ... 6-4/305. ... Full name: Douglas Gregory Brzezinski. ... Name pronounced bruh-ZHIN-skee.
HIGH SCHOOL: Detroit Catholic Central.
COLLEGE: Boston College.
TRANSACTIONS/CAREER NOTES: Selected by Philadelphia Eagles in third round (64th pick overall) of 1999 NFL draft. ... Signed by Eagles (July 28, 1999).
PLAYING EXPERIENCE: Philadelphia NFL, 1999 and 2000. ... Games/Games started: 1999 (16/16), 2000 (16/0). Total: 32/16.
HONORS: Named offensive guard on THE SPORTING NEWS college All-America first team (1998).

BUCHANAN, RAY   CB   FALCONS

B

PERSONAL: Born September 29, 1971, in Chicago. ... 5-9/186. ... Full name: Raymond Louis Buchanan.
HIGH SCHOOL: Proviso East (Maywood, Ill.).
COLLEGE: Louisville.
TRANSACTIONS/CAREER NOTES: Selected by Indianapolis Colts in third round (65th pick overall) of 1993 NFL draft. ... Signed by Colts (July 26, 1993). ... Designated by Colts as transition player (February 13, 1997). ... Tendered offer sheet by Atlanta Falcons (February 25, 1997). ... Colts declined to match offer (March 3, 1997). ... Granted unconditional free agency (March 2, 2001). ... Re-signed by Falcons (March 2, 2001).
CHAMPIONSHIP GAME EXPERIENCE: Played in AFC championship game (1995 season). ... Played in NFC championship game (1998 season). ... Played in Super Bowl XXXIII (1998 season).
HONORS: Played in Pro Bowl (1998 season).
PRO STATISTICS: 1994 —Credited with one sack and recovered one fumble. 1995—Returned one kickoff for 22 yards, credited with one sack and recovered two fumbles. 1996—Returned one kickoff for 20 yards. 1997—Ran 37 yards with lateral from punt return. 1999—Credited with one sack. 2000—Recovered two fumbles for one yard.

				INTERCEPTIONS				PUNT RETURNS				TOTALS		
Year Team	G	GS	No.	Yds.	Avg.	TD	No.	Yds.	Avg.	TD	TD	2pt.	Pts.	Fum.
1993—Indianapolis NFL	16	5	4	45	11.3	0	0	0	0.0	0	0	0	0	0
1994—Indianapolis NFL	16	16	8	221	27.6	†3	0	0	0.0	0	3	0	18	0
1995—Indianapolis NFL	16	16	2	60	30.0	0	16	113	7.1	0	0	0	0	1
1996—Indianapolis NFL	13	13	2	32	16.0	0	12	201	16.8	0	0	0	0	0
1997—Atlanta NFL	16	16	5	49	9.8	0	0	37	0.0	0	0	0	0	0
1998—Atlanta NFL	16	16	7	102	14.6	0	1	4	4.0	0	0	0	0	0
1999—Atlanta NFL	16	16	4	81	20.3	1	0	0	0.0	0	1	0	6	0
2000—Atlanta NFL	16	16	6	114	19.0	0	0	0	0.0	0	0	0	0	0
Pro totals (8 years)	125	114	38	704	18.5	4	29	355	12.2	0	4	0	24	1

BUCKLEY, TERRELL   CB

PERSONAL: Born June 7, 1971, in Pascagoula, Miss. ... 5-10/180. ... Full name: Douglas Terrell Buckley.
HIGH SCHOOL: Pascagoula (Miss.).
COLLEGE: Florida State.
TRANSACTIONS/CAREER NOTES: Selected after junior season by Green Bay Packers in first round (fifth pick overall) of 1992 NFL draft. ... Signed by Packers (September 11, 1992). ... Granted roster exemption for one game (September 1992). ... Traded by Packers to Miami Dolphins for past considerations (April 3, 1995). ... Granted unconditional free agency (February 11, 2000). ... Signed by Denver Broncos (July 20, 2000). ... Granted unconditional free agency (March 2, 2001).
HONORS: Named defensive back on THE SPORTING NEWS college All-America second team (1990). ... Jim Thorpe Award winner (1991). ... Named defensive back on THE SPORTING NEWS college All-America first team (1991).
PRO STATISTICS: 1992—Recovered four fumbles. 1994—Recovered one fumble. 1995—Returned one kickoff for 16 yards. 1996—Returned one kickoff for 48 yards and recovered two fumbles. 1997—Recovered two fumbles for 23 yards and one touchdown. 1998—Recovered two fumbles. 1999—Credited with one sack.

				INTERCEPTIONS				PUNT RETURNS				TOTALS		
Year Team	G	GS	No.	Yds.	Avg.	TD	No.	Yds.	Avg.	TD	TD	2pt.	Pts.	Fum.
1992—Green Bay NFL	14	12	3	33	11.0	1	21	211	10.0	1	2	0	12	7
1993—Green Bay NFL	16	16	2	31	15.5	0	11	76	6.9	0	0	0	0	1
1994—Green Bay NFL	16	16	5	38	7.6	0	0	0	0.0	0	0	0	0	1
1995—Miami NFL	16	4	1	0	0.0	0	0	0	0.0	0	0	0	0	0
1996—Miami NFL	16	16	6	*164	27.3	1	3	24	8.0	0	1	0	6	1
1997—Miami NFL	16	16	4	26	6.5	0	4	58	14.5	0	1	0	6	0
1998—Miami NFL	16	16	8	157	19.6	1	29	354	12.2	0	1	0	6	1
1999—Miami NFL	16	11	3	3	1.0	0	8	13	1.6	0	0	0	0	1
2000—Denver NFL	16	16	6	110	18.3	1	2	10	5.0	0	1	0	6	0
Pro totals (9 years)	142	123	38	562	14.8	4	78	746	9.6	1	6	0	36	11

BUCKNER, BRENTSON   DT   PANTHERS

PERSONAL: Born September 30, 1971, in Columbus, Ga. ... 6-2/305. ... Full name: Brentson Andre Buckner. ... Name pronounced BRENT-son.
HIGH SCHOOL: Carver (Columbus, Ga.).
COLLEGE: Clemson (degree in English, 1993).
TRANSACTIONS/CAREER NOTES: Selected by Pittsburgh Steelers in second round (50th pick overall) of 1994 NFL Draft. ... Signed by Steelers (July 23, 1994). ... Traded by Steelers to Kansas City Chiefs for seventh-round pick (traded to San Diego) in 1997 draft (April 4, 1997). ... Claimed on waivers by Cincinnati Bengals (August 25, 1997). ... Granted unconditional free agency (February 13, 1998). ... Signed by San Francisco 49ers (May 26, 1998). ... On physically unable to perform list with pulled quadricep muscle (July 17-August 15, 1998). ... Granted unconditional free agency (February 12, 1999). ... Re-signed by 49ers (April 7, 1999). ... Granted unconditional free agency (February 11, 2000). ... Re-signed by 49ers (August 8, 2000). ... Granted unconditional free agency (March 2, 2001). ... Signed by Carolina Panthers (April 21, 2001).

CHAMPIONSHIP GAME EXPERIENCE: Played in AFC championship game (1994 and 1995 seasons). ... Played in Super Bowl XXX (1995 season).

PRO STATISTICS: 1994—Recovered one fumble. 1995—Recovered one fumble for 46 yards and a touchdown. 1996—Fumbled once and recovered one fumble for 13 yards. 1998—Recovered one fumble.

Year Team	G	GS	SACKS
1994—Pittsburgh NFL	13	5	2.0
1995—Pittsburgh NFL	16	16	3.0
1996—Pittsburgh NFL	15	14	3.0
1997—Cincinnati NFL	14	5	0.0
1998—San Francisco NFL	13	0	0.5
1999—San Francisco NFL	16	5	1.0
2000—San Francisco NFL	16	16	7.0
Pro totals (7 years)	103	61	16.5

BULLUCK, KEITH — LB — TITANS

PERSONAL: Born April 4, 1977, in Suffern, N.Y. ... 6-3/232. ... Full name: Keith J. Bulluck.
HIGH SCHOOL: Clarkstown (New City, N.Y.).
COLLEGE: Syracuse.
TRANSACTIONS/CAREER NOTES: Selected by Tennessee Titans in first round (30th pick overall) of 2000 NFL draft. ... Signed by Titans (July 19, 2000).

Year Team	G	GS	INTERCEPTIONS No.	Yds.	Avg.	TD	TOTALS TD	2pt.	Pts.	Fum.
2000—Tennessee NFL	16	1	1	8	8.0	1	1	0	6	0

BUNDREN, JIM — C — BROWNS

PERSONAL: Born October 6, 1974, in Pontiac, Mich. ... 6-3/303. ... Full name: Jim G. Bundren.
HIGH SCHOOL: Alexis I. Dupont (Greenville, Del.), then Valley Forge Military Academy (Wayne, Pa.).
COLLEGE: Clemson.
TRANSACTIONS/CAREER NOTES: Selected by Miami Dolphins in seventh round (210th pick overall) of 1998 NFL draft. ... Signed by Dolphins (July 15, 1998). ... Claimed on waivers by New York Jets (September 1, 1998). ... Inactive for all 16 games (1998). ... Selected by Cleveland Browns from Jets in NFL expansion draft (February 9, 1999). ... On injured reserve with ankle injury (November 14, 2000-remainder of season). ... Granted free agency (March 2, 2001). ... Re-signed by Browns (March 21, 2001).
PLAYING EXPERIENCE: Cleveland NFL, 1999 and 2000. ... Games/Games started: 1999 (16/1), 2000 (11/9). Total: 27/8.
CHAMPIONSHIP GAME EXPERIENCE: Member of Jets for AFC championship game (1998 season); inactive.
HONORS: Named offensive tackle on THE SPORTING NEWS college All-America third team (1997).
PRO STATISTICS: 2000—Recovered one fumble.

BURKE, THOMAS — DE — CARDINALS

PERSONAL: Born October 12, 1976, in Poplar, Wis. ... 6-3/275.
HIGH SCHOOL: Northwestern (Maple, Wis.).
COLLEGE: Wisconsin.
TRANSACTIONS/CAREER NOTES: Selected by Arizona Cardinals in third round (83rd pick overall) of 1999 NFL draft. ... Signed by Cardinals (June 18, 1999). ... On injured reserve with abdominal injury (December 15, 2000-remainder of season).
HONORS: Named defensive end on THE SPORTING NEWS college All-America first team (1998).

Year Team	G	GS	SACKS
1999—Arizona NFL	16	3	2.5
2000—Arizona NFL	3	0	0.0
Pro totals (2 years)	19	3	2.5

BURKS, DIAELLO — WR

PERSONAL: Born July 7, 1974, in LaGrange, Ga. ... 6-2/181.
HIGH SCHOOL: LaGrange (Ga.).
COLLEGE: Eastern Kentucky.
TRANSACTIONS/CAREER NOTES: Signed as non-drafted free agent by Carolina Panthers (July 13, 1999). ... Released by Panthers (September 5, 1999). ... Re-signed by Panthers to practice squad (September 7, 1999). ... Released by Panthers (October 3, 2000).
PLAYING EXPERIENCE: Carolina NFL, 2000. ... Games/Games started: 2000 (1/0).
PRO STATISTICS: 2000—Returned one kickoff for 25 yards.

BURNETT, CHESTER — LB — BROWNS

PERSONAL: Born April 15, 1975, in Denver. ... 5-10/230. ... Full name: Chester Dean Burnett.
HIGH SCHOOL: J.K. Mullen (Denver).
COLLEGE: Arizona.
TRANSACTIONS/CAREER NOTES: Selected by Minnesota Vikings in seventh round (208th pick overall) of 1998 NFL draft. ... Signed by Vikings (July 14, 1998). ... On physically unable to perform list with knee injury (July 27-August 3, 1998). ... Released by Vikings (September 4, 1998). ... Signed by Washington Redskins to practice squad (October 7, 1998). ... Activated (November 27, 1998). ... Released by Redskins (September 4, 1999). ... Signed by Jacksonville Jaguars (September 29, 1999). ... Inactive for three games (1999). ... Released by Jaguars (October 19, 1999). ... Re-signed by Jaguars to practice squad (December 28, 1999). ... Activated (January 4, 2000). ... On injured reserve

with hamstring injury (August 27-September 11, 2000). ... Released by Jaguars (September 11, 2000). ... Signed by Cleveland Browns to practice squad (October 25, 2000). ... Activated (November 1, 2000).
PLAYING EXPERIENCE: Washington NFL, 1998; Cleveland NFL, 2000. ... Games/Games started: 1998 (5/0), 2000 (7/0).
CHAMPIONSHIP GAME EXPERIENCE: Member of Jaguars for AFC championship game (1999 season); inactive.
PRO STATISTICS: 1998—Returned one kickoff for five yards. 2000—Returned one kickoff for 18 yards.

BURNETT, ROB　　　　　　　DE　　　　　　　RAVENS

PERSONAL: Born August 27, 1967, in Livingston, N.J. ... 6-4/270. ... Full name: Robert Barry Burnett.
HIGH SCHOOL: Newfield (Selden, N.Y.).
COLLEGE: Syracuse (degree in economics).
TRANSACTIONS/CAREER NOTES: Selected by Cleveland Browns in fifth round (129th pick overall) of 1990 NFL draft. ... Signed by Browns (July 22, 1990). ... Granted free agency (March 1, 1993). ... Re-signed by Browns (June 11, 1993). ... Browns franchise moved to Baltimore and renamed Ravens for 1996 season (March 11, 1996). ... Granted unconditional free agency (February 11, 2000). ... Re-signed by Ravens (February 17, 2000).
CHAMPIONSHIP GAME EXPERIENCE: Played in AFC championship game (2000 season). ... Member of Super Bowl championship team (2000 season).
HONORS: Played in Pro Bowl (1994 season).
PRO STATISTICS: 1991—Recovered one fumble for nine yards. 1992—Recovered two fumbles. 1993—Recovered two fumbles. 1994—Recovered one fumble. 1995—Recovered one fumble. 1997—Recovered one fumble. 1998—Credited with a safety and recovered one fumble. 2000—Intercepted one pass for three yards and recovered five fumbles.

Year Team	G	GS	SACKS
1990—Cleveland NFL	16	6	2.0
1991—Cleveland NFL	13	8	3.0
1992—Cleveland NFL	16	16	9.0
1993—Cleveland NFL	16	16	9.0
1994—Cleveland NFL	16	16	10.0
1995—Cleveland NFL	16	16	7.5
1996—Baltimore NFL	6	6	3.0
1997—Baltimore NFL	15	15	4.0
1998—Baltimore NFL	16	16	2.5
1999—Baltimore NFL	16	16	6.5
2000—Baltimore NFL	16	16	10.5
Pro totals (11 years)	162	147	67.0

BURNS, KEITH　　　　　　　LB

PERSONAL: Born May 16, 1972, in Greelyville, S.C. ... 6-2/245. ... Full name: Keith Bernard Burns.
HIGH SCHOOL: T. C. Williams (Alexandria, Va.).
JUNIOR COLLEGE: Navarro College (Texas).
COLLEGE: Oklahoma State.
TRANSACTIONS/CAREER NOTES: Selected by Denver Broncos in seventh round (210th pick overall) of 1994 NFL draft. ... Signed by Broncos (July 12, 1994). ... Granted free agency (February 14, 1997). ... Re-signed by Broncos (June 30, 1997). ... Granted unconditional free agency (February 12, 1999). ... Signed by Chicago Bears (April 6, 1999). ... Released by Bears (August 27, 2000). ... Signed by Broncos (September 19, 2000). ... Granted unconditional free agency (March 2, 2001).
PLAYING EXPERIENCE: Denver NFL, 1994-1998 and 2000; Chicago NFL, 1999. ... Games/Games started: 1994 (11/1), 1995 (16/0), 1996 (16/0), 1997 (16/0), 1998 (16/0), 1999 (15/0), 2000 (13/0). Total: 103/1.
CHAMPIONSHIP GAME EXPERIENCE: Played in AFC championship game (1997 and 1998 seasons). ... Member of Super Bowl championship team (1997 and 1998 seasons).
PRO STATISTICS: 1995—Credited with 1$^{1}/_{2}$ sacks, returned one kickoff for five yards and recovered two fumbles. 1997—Returned four kickoffs for 45 yards. 1998—Returned two kickoffs for 17 yards, fumbled once and recovered one fumble. 1999—Intercepted one pass for 15 yards and recovered one fumble. 2000—Recovered one fumble.

BURRESS, PLAXICO　　　　　　WR　　　　　　STEELERS

PERSONAL: Born August 12, 1977, in Norfolk, Va. ... 6-5/229.
HIGH SCHOOL: Green Run (Virginia Beach, Va.).
COLLEGE: Michigan State.
TRANSACTIONS/CAREER NOTES: Selected after junior season by Pittsburgh Steelers in first round (eighth pick overall) of 2000 NFL draft. ... Signed by Steelers (July 20, 2000). ... On injured reserve with wrist injury (December 1, 2000-remainder of season).
PRO STATISTICS: 2000—Fumbled once.
SINGLE GAME HIGHS (regular season): Receptions—4 (October 15, 2000, vs. Cincinnati); yards—77 (September 3, 2000, vs. Baltimore); and touchdown receptions—0.

Year Team	G	GS	RECEIVING No.	Yds.	Avg.	TD
2000—Pittsburgh NFL	12	9	22	273	12.4	0

BURRIS, JEFF　　　　　　　DB　　　　　　　COLTS

PERSONAL: Born June 7, 1972, in Rock Hill, S.C. ... 6-0/190. ... Full name: Jeffrey Lamar Burris.
HIGH SCHOOL: Northwestern (Rock Hill, S.C.).
COLLEGE: Notre Dame.

TRANSACTIONS/CAREER NOTES: Selected by Buffalo Bills in first round (27th pick overall) of 1994 NFL draft. ... Signed by Bills (July 18, 1994). ... On injured reserve with knee injury (November 20, 1995-remainder of season). ... Granted unconditional free agency (February 13, 1998). ... Signed by Indianapolis Colts (February 18, 1998).

HONORS: Named defensive back on THE SPORTING NEWS college All-America second team (1993).

PRO STATISTICS: 1994—Recovered one fumble. 1996—Recovered one fumble. 1997—Returned one kickoff for 10 yards and recovered one fumble. 1999—Credited with two sacks. 2000—Credited with three sacks.

Year Team	G	GS	INTERCEPTIONS				PUNT RETURNS				TOTALS			
			No.	Yds.	Avg.	TD	No.	Yds.	Avg.	TD	TD	2pt.	Pts.	Fum.
1994—Buffalo NFL	16	0	2	24	12.0	0	32	332	10.4	0	0	0	0	2
1995—Buffalo NFL	9	9	1	19	19.0	0	20	229	11.5	0	0	0	0	0
1996—Buffalo NFL	15	15	1	28	28.0	0	27	286	10.6	0	0	0	0	1
1997—Buffalo NFL	14	14	2	19	9.5	0	21	198	9.4	0	0	0	0	3
1998—Indianapolis NFL	14	14	1	0	0.0	0	0	0	0.0	0	0	0	0	0
1999—Indianapolis NFL	16	16	2	83	41.5	0	0	0	0.0	0	0	0	0	0
2000—Indianapolis NFL	16	16	4	38	9.5	1	0	0	0.0	0	1	0	6	0
Pro totals (7 years)	100	84	13	211	16.2	1	100	1045	10.5	0	1	0	6	6

BURROUGH, JOHN   DE

PERSONAL: Born May 17, 1972, in Laramie, Wyo. ... 6-5/276.

HIGH SCHOOL: Pinedale (Wyo.).

COLLEGE: Wyoming.

TRANSACTIONS/CAREER NOTES: Selected by Atlanta Falcons in seventh round (245th pick overall) of 1995 NFL draft. ... Signed by Falcons (June 30, 1995). ... Granted free agency (February 13, 1998). ... Re-signed by Falcons (April 1, 1998). ... Granted unconditional free agency (February 12, 1999). ... Signed by Minnesota Vikings (February 17, 1999). ... Released by Vikings (March 1, 2001).

PLAYING EXPERIENCE: Atlanta NFL, 1995-1998; Minnesota NFL, 1999 and 2000. ... Games/Games started: 1995 (16/0), 1996 (16/1), 1997 (16/1), 1998 (16/3), 1999 (10/3), 2000 (14/6). Total: 88/14.

CHAMPIONSHIP GAME EXPERIENCE: Played in NFC championship game (1998 and 2000 seasons). ... Played in Super Bowl XXXIII (1998 season).

PRO STATISTICS: 1997—Returned one kickoff for six yards and credited with one sack. 1998—Credited with 1/2 sack and recovered one fumble. 1999—Returned one kickoff for nine yards and credited with one sack. 2000—Credited with two sacks.

BURTON, SHANE   DE/DT   JETS

PERSONAL: Born January 18, 1974, in Logan, W.Va. ... 6-6/305. ... Full name: Franklin Shane Burton.

HIGH SCHOOL: Bandys (Catawba, N.C.).

COLLEGE: Tennessee.

TRANSACTIONS/CAREER NOTES: Selected by Miami Dolphins in fifth round (150th pick overall) of 1996 NFL draft. ... Signed by Dolphins (June 18, 1996). ... Granted free agency (February 12, 1999). ... Re-signed by Dolphins (April 13, 1999). ... Claimed on waivers by Chicago Bears (August 24, 1999). ... Granted unconditional free agency (February 11, 2000). ... Signed by New York Jets (March 20, 2000).

PRO STATISTICS: 1996—Recovered one fumble. 1997—Recovered one fumble. 1998—Recovered one fumble. 1999—Intercepted one pass for 37 yards. 2000—Recovered one fumble for four yards.

Year Team	G	GS	SACKS
1996—Miami NFL	16	8	3.0
1997—Miami NFL	16	4	4.0
1998—Miami NFL	15	0	2.0
1999—Chicago NFL	15	0	3.0
2000—New York Jets NFL	16	16	1.0
Pro totals (5 years)	78	28	13.0

BUSH, DEVIN   S   RAMS

PERSONAL: Born July 3, 1973, in Miami. ... 6-0/210.

HIGH SCHOOL: Hialeah (Fla.) Miami Lakes.

COLLEGE: Florida State.

TRANSACTIONS/CAREER NOTES: Selected after junior season by Atlanta Falcons in first round (26th pick overall) of 1995 NFL draft. ... Signed by Falcons (August 8, 1995). ... Granted unconditional free agency (February 12, 1999). ... Signed by St. Louis Rams (February 18, 1999).

CHAMPIONSHIP GAME EXPERIENCE: Member of Falcons for NFC championship game (1998 season); inactive. ... Played in Super Bowl XXXII (1998 season). ... Played in NFC championship game (1999 season). ... Member of Super Bowl championship team (1999 season).

PRO STATISTICS: 1995—Recovered one fumble. 1996—Recovered one fumble. 1997—Recovered one fumble. 1999—Recovered two fumbles for 31 yards. 2000—Credited with one sack and recovered one fumble for 15 yards and a touchdown.

Year Team	G	GS	INTERCEPTIONS			
			No.	Yds.	Avg.	TD
1995—Atlanta NFL	11	5	1	0	0.0	0
1996—Atlanta NFL	16	15	1	2	2.0	0
1997—Atlanta NFL	16	16	1	4	4.0	0
1998—Atlanta NFL	13	0	0	0	0.0	0
1999—St. Louis NFL	16	7	2	45	22.5	1
2000—St. Louis NFL	13	12	0	0	0.0	0
Pro totals (6 years)	85	55	5	51	10.2	1

BUSH, LEW — LB — CHIEFS

PERSONAL: Born December 2, 1969, in Atlanta. ... 6-2/247. ... Full name: Lewis Fitzgerald Bush.
HIGH SCHOOL: Washington (Tacoma, Wash.).
COLLEGE: Washington State.
TRANSACTIONS/CAREER NOTES: Selected by San Diego Chargers in fourth round (99th pick overall) of 1993 NFL draft. ... Signed by Chargers (July 9, 1993). ... Granted free agency (February 16, 1996). ... Re-signed by Chargers (June 14, 1996). ... Granted unconditional free agency (February 14, 1997). ... Re-signed by Chargers (May 13, 1997). ... On injured reserve with knee injury (December 26, 1998-remainder of season). ... Released by Chargers (March 1, 2000). ... Signed by Kansas City Chiefs (March 4, 2000).
PLAYING EXPERIENCE: San Diego NFL, 1993-1999; Kansas City NFL, 2000. ... Games/Games started: 1993 (16/0), 1994 (16/0), 1995 (16/15), 1996 (16/16), 1997 (14/13), 1998 (10/10), 1999 (16/14), 2000 (16/8). Total: 120/76.
CHAMPIONSHIP GAME EXPERIENCE: Played in AFC championship game (1994 season). ... Played in Super Bowl XXIX (1994 season).
PRO STATISTICS: 1994—Recovered one fumble. 1995—Intercepted one pass and recovered two fumbles. 1996—Credited with one sack and recovered two fumbles. 1998—Credited with one sack. 1999—Credited with one sack and recovered one fumble. 2000—Credited with one sack, intercepted one pass for 33 yards and recovered one fumble.

B

BUSH, STEVE — TE/FB

PERSONAL: Born July 4, 1974, in Phoenix. ... 6-3/258. ... Full name: Steven Jack Bush.
HIGH SCHOOL: Paradise Valley (Phoenix).
COLLEGE: Arizona State.
TRANSACTIONS/CAREER NOTES: Signed as non-drafted free agent by Cincinnati Bengals (April 25, 1997). ... Granted free agency (February 11, 2000). ... Re-signed by Bengals (April 25, 2000). ... Granted unconditional free agency (March 2, 2001).
PLAYING EXPERIENCE: Cincinnati NFL, 1997-2000. ... Games/Games started: 1997 (16/0), 1998 (12/2), 1999 (13/0), 2000 (16/0). Total: 57/2.
PRO STATISTICS: 1998—Caught four passes for 39 yards. 1999—Caught one pass for four yards. 2000—Caught three passes for 39 yards and returned three kickoffs for 18 yards.
SINGLE GAME HIGHS (regular season): Receptions—2 (December 24, 2000, vs. Philadelphia); yards—31 (December 24, 2000, vs. Philadelphia); and touchdown receptions—0.

BUTLER, LEROY — S — PACKERS

PERSONAL: Born July 19, 1968, in Jacksonville. ... 6-0/203. ... Full name: LeRoy Butler III. ... Name pronounced luh-ROY.
HIGH SCHOOL: Robert E. Lee Senior (Jacksonville).
COLLEGE: Florida State.
TRANSACTIONS/CAREER NOTES: Selected by Green Bay Packers in second round (48th pick overall) of 1990 NFL draft. ... Signed by Packers (July 25, 1990). ... On suspended list (December 9, 1992). ... Designated by Packers as transition player (February 15, 1994).
CHAMPIONSHIP GAME EXPERIENCE: Played in NFC championship game (1995-1997 seasons). ... Member of Super Bowl championship team (1996 season). ... Played in Super Bowl XXXII (1997 season).
HONORS: Named strong safety on THE SPORTING NEWS NFL All-Pro team (1993 and 1996-1998). ... Played in Pro Bowl (1993 and 1996-1998 seasons).
PRO STATISTICS: 1991—Recovered one fumble. 1992—Recovered one fumble for 17 yards. 1993—Ran 25 yards with lateral from fumble recovery for a touchdown. 1996—Recovered two fumbles for two yards. 1997—Recovered one fumble. 1998—Recovered two fumbles for 32 yards and one touchdown. 1999—Recovered one fumble. 2000—Recovered one fumble.

| | | | INTERCEPTIONS | | | | SACKS |
Year Team	G	GS	No.	Yds.	Avg.	TD	No.
1990—Green Bay NFL	16	0	3	42	14.0	0	0.0
1991—Green Bay NFL	16	16	3	6	2.0	0	0.0
1992—Green Bay NFL	15	15	1	0	0.0	0	0.0
1993—Green Bay NFL	16	16	6	131	21.8	0	1.0
1994—Green Bay NFL	13	13	3	68	22.7	0	1.0
1995—Green Bay NFL	16	16	5	105	21.0	0	1.0
1996—Green Bay NFL	16	16	5	149	29.8	1	6.5
1997—Green Bay NFL	16	16	5	4	0.8	0	3.0
1998—Green Bay NFL	16	16	3	3	1.0	0	4.0
1999—Green Bay NFL	16	16	2	0	0.0	0	1.0
2000—Green Bay NFL	16	16	2	25	12.5	0	2.0
Pro totals (11 years)	172	156	38	533	14.0	1	19.5

BYNUM, KENNY — RB

PERSONAL: Born May 29, 1974, in Gainesville, Fla. ... 5-11/191. ... Full name: Kenneth Bernard Bynum.
HIGH SCHOOL: Gainesville (Fla.).
COLLEGE: South Carolina State.
TRANSACTIONS/CAREER NOTES: Selected by San Diego Chargers in fifth round (138th pick overall) of 1997 NFL draft. ... Signed by Chargers (June 16, 1997). ... Assigned by Chargers to Rhein Fire in 1999 NFL Europe enhancement allocation program (February 22, 1999). ... Granted free agency (February 11, 2000). ... Re-signed by Chargers (June 2, 2000). ... Granted unconditional free agency (March 2, 2001).
PRO STATISTICS: 1998—Recovered two fumbles. 1999—Recovered three fumbles.
SINGLE GAME HIGHS (regular season): Attempts—17 (December 5, 1999, vs. Cleveland); yards—64 (November 23, 1997, vs. San Francisco); and rushing touchdowns—1 (December 5, 1999, vs. Cleveland).

Year Team	G	GS	RUSHING				RECEIVING				KICKOFF RETURNS				TOTALS			
			Att.	Yds.	Avg.	TD	No.	Yds.	Avg.	TD	No.	Yds.	Avg.	TD	TD	2pt.	Pts.	Fum.
1997—San Diego NFL	13	0	30	97	3.2	0	2	4	2.0	0	38	814	21.4	0	0	0	0	0
1998—San Diego NFL	10	0	11	23	2.1	0	4	27	6.8	0	19	345	18.2	0	0	0	0	3
1999—Rhein NFLE	...	...	194	960	4.9	5	10	86	8.6	1	0	0	0.0	0	6	0	36	0
—San Diego NFL	16	5	92	287	3.1	1	16	209	13.1	2	37	781	21.1	0	3	0	18	3
2000—San Diego NFL	14	0	7	26	3.7	0	2	13	6.5	0	13	242	18.6	0	0	0	0	0
NFL Europe totals (1 year)	...	...	194	960	4.9	5	10	86	8.6	1	0	0	0.0	0	6	0	36	0
NFL totals (4 years)	53	5	140	433	3.1	1	24	253	10.5	2	107	2182	20.4	0	3	0	18	6
Pro totals (5 years)	...	...	334	1393	4.2	6	34	339	10.0	3	107	2182	20.4	0	9	0	54	6

BYRD, ISAAC   WR

PERSONAL: Born November 16, 1974, in St. Louis. ... 6-1/188. ... Full name: Isaac Byrd III. ... Brother of Israel Byrd, defensive back with New Orleans Saints (1994 and 1995).
HIGH SCHOOL: Parkway Central (Chesterfield, Mo.).
COLLEGE: Kansas.
TRANSACTIONS/CAREER NOTES: Selected by Kansas City Chiefs in sixth round (195th pick overall) of 1997 NFL draft. ... Signed by Chiefs (May 6, 1997). ... Released by Chiefs (August 23, 1997). ... Re-signed by Chiefs to practice squad (August 25, 1997). ... Signed by Tennessee Oilers off Chiefs practice squad (November 7, 1997). ... Oilers franchise renamed Tennessee Titans for 1999 season (December 26, 1998). ... Granted free agency (February 11, 2000). ... Re-signed by Titans (June 6, 2000). ... Claimed on waivers by Carolina Panthers (August 29, 2000). ... Granted unconditional free agency (March 2, 2001).
CHAMPIONSHIP GAME EXPERIENCE: Played in AFC championship game (1999 season). ... Played in Super Bowl XXXIV (1999 season).
PRO STATISTICS: 1998—Recovered one fumble. 1999—Returned two punts for eight yards and returned two kickoffs for 16 yards. 2000—Returned one punt for 10 yards, returned nine kickoffs for 172 yards and recovered one fumble.
SINGLE GAME HIGHS (regular season): Receptions—6 (October 8, 2000, vs. Seattle); yards—84 (December 19, 1999, vs. Atlanta); and touchdown receptions—1 (December 17, 2000, vs. San Diego).

Year Team	G	GS	RECEIVING				TOTALS			
			No.	Yds.	Avg.	TD	TD	2pt.	Pts.	Fum.
1997—Tennessee NFL	2	0	0	0	0.0	0	0	0	0	0
1998—Tennessee NFL	4	3	6	71	11.8	0	0	0	0	0
1999—Tennessee NFL	12	6	14	261	18.6	2	2	0	12	1
2000—Carolina NFL	15	4	22	241	11.0	2	2	0	12	0
Pro totals (4 years)	33	13	42	573	13.6	4	4	0	24	1

RECORD AS BASEBALL PLAYER

TRANSACTIONS/CAREER NOTES: Batted right, threw right. ... Selected by San Diego Padres organization in 24th round of free-agent draft (June 3, 1993); did not sign. ... Selected by St. Louis Cardinals organization in 11th round of free agent draft (June 2, 1996).

Year Team (League)	Pos.	G	BATTING											FIELDING			
			AB	R	H	2B	3B	HR	RBI	Avg.	BB	SO	SB	PO	A	E	Avg.
1996— Johnson City (Appal.).......	OF	24	94	16	26	6	1	2	15	.277	8	19	5	37	1	1	.974

CADREZ, GLENN   LB   CHIEFS

PERSONAL: Born January 2, 1970, in El Centro, Calif. ... 6-3/240. ... Full name: Glenn E. Cadrez. ... Name pronounced ku-DREZ.
HIGH SCHOOL: El Centro Central Union (El Centro, Calif.).
JUNIOR COLLEGE: Chaffey College (Calif.).
COLLEGE: Houston.
TRANSACTIONS/CAREER NOTES: Selected by New York Jets in sixth round (154th pick overall) of 1992 NFL draft. ... Signed by Jets (July 13, 1992). ... Released by Jets (September 19, 1995). ... Signed by Denver Broncos (September 27, 1995). ... Released by Broncos (May 2, 2001). ... Signed by Kansas City Chiefs (June 6, 2001).
CHAMPIONSHIP GAME EXPERIENCE: Played in AFC championship game (1997 and 1998 seasons). ... Member of Super Bowl championship team (1997 and 1998 seasons).
PRO STATISTICS: 1992—Recovered one fumble. 1994—Returned one kickoff for 10 yards and recovered one fumble. 1995—Recovered one fumble. 1996—Recovered one fumble. 1998—Intercepted two passes for 11 yards. 1999—Recovered four fumbles for 74 yards and one touchdown.

Year Team	G	GS	SACKS
1992—New York Jets NFL	16	0	0.0
1993—New York Jets NFL	16	0	0.0
1994—New York Jets NFL	16	0	0.0
1995—New York Jets NFL	1	0	0.0
—Denver NFL	10	7	2.0
1996—Denver NFL	16	0	0.0
1997—Denver NFL	16	0	0.0
1998—Denver NFL	16	15	4.0
1999—Denver NFL	16	15	7.0
2000—Denver NFL	16	3	0.0
Pro totals (9 years)	139	40	13.0

CALDWELL, MIKE   LB   EAGLES

PERSONAL: Born August 31, 1971, in Oak Ridge, Tenn. ... 6-2/237. ... Full name: Mike Isiah Caldwell. ... Nickname: Zeke.
HIGH SCHOOL: Oak Ridge (Tenn.).
COLLEGE: Middle Tennessee State (degree in business administration, 1996).
TRANSACTIONS/CAREER NOTES: Selected by Cleveland Browns in third round (83rd pick overall) of 1993 NFL draft. ... Signed by Browns (July 14, 1993). ... Granted free agency (February 16, 1996). ... Browns franchise moved to Baltimore and renamed Ravens for 1996 season

(March 11, 1996). ... Re-signed by Ravens for 1996 season. ... Granted unconditional free agency (February 14, 1997). ... Signed by Arizona Cardinals (July 16, 1997). ... Granted unconditional free agency (February 13, 1998). ... Signed by Philadelphia Eagles (April 9, 1998).
PRO STATISTICS: 1993—Recovered one fumble. 1994—Returned one punt for two yards. 1999—Recovered one fumble.

				INTERCEPTIONS				SACKS
Year Team	G	GS	No.	Yds.	Avg.	TD		No.
1993—Cleveland NFL	15	1	0	0	0.0	0		0.0
1994—Cleveland NFL	16	1	1	0	0.0	0		0.0
1995—Cleveland NFL	16	6	2	24	12.0	▲1		0.0
1996—Baltimore NFL	9	9	1	45	45.0	0		4.5
1997—Arizona NFL	16	0	1	5	5.0	0		2.0
1998—Philadelphia NFL	16	8	1	33	33.0	0		1.0
1999—Philadelphia NFL	14	2	1	12	12.0	0		1.0
2000—Philadelphia NFL	16	3	1	26	26.0	1		0.0
Pro totals (8 years)	118	30	8	145	18.1	3		8.5

CALLOWAY, CHRIS   WR

PERSONAL: Born March 29, 1968, in Chicago. ... 5-10/182. ... Full name: Christopher Fitzpatrick Calloway.
HIGH SCHOOL: Mount Carmel (Chicago).
COLLEGE: Michigan (degree in communications and film, 1990).
TRANSACTIONS/CAREER NOTES: Selected by Pittsburgh Steelers in fourth round (97th pick overall) of 1990 NFL draft. ... Signed by Steelers (July 18, 1990). ... On injured reserve with knee injury (November 25, 1991-remainder of season). ... Granted unconditional free agency (February 1, 1992). ... Signed by New York Giants (April 1, 1992). ... Granted unconditional free agency (February 17, 1994). ... Re-signed by Giants (July 18, 1994). ... Granted unconditional free agency (February 16, 1996). ... Re-signed by Giants (April 2, 1996). ... Released by Giants (February 17, 1999). ... Signed by Atlanta Falcons (March 3, 1999). ... Released by Falcons (May 23, 2000). ... Signed by New England Patriots (August 14, 2000). ... Released by Patriots (October 21, 2000).
PRO STATISTICS: 1991—Recovered one fumble. 1992—Returned two kickoffs for 29 yards. 1993—Returned six kickoffs for 89 yards and recovered one fumble. 1996—Recovered one fumble for seven yards.
SINGLE GAME HIGHS (regular season): Receptions—9 (October 20, 1996, vs. Washington); yards—145 (October 19, 1997, vs. Detroit); and touchdown receptions—2 (December 27, 1998, vs. Philadelphia).
STATISTICAL PLATEAUS: 100-yard receiving games: 1995 (1), 1996 (1), 1997 (1). Total: 3.

			RUSHING				RECEIVING				TOTALS			
Year Team	G	GS	Att.	Yds.	Avg.	TD	No.	Yds.	Avg.	TD	TD	2pt.	Pts.	Fum.
1990—Pittsburgh NFL	16	2	0	0	0.0	0	10	124	12.4	1	1	0	6	0
1991—Pittsburgh NFL	12	0	0	0	0.0	0	15	254	16.9	1	1	0	6	0
1992—New York Giants NFL	16	1	0	0	0.0	0	27	335	12.4	1	1	0	6	0
1993—New York Giants NFL	16	9	0	0	0.0	0	35	513	14.7	3	3	0	18	0
1994—New York Giants NFL	16	14	8	77	9.6	0	43	666	15.5	2	2	0	12	1
1995—New York Giants NFL	16	15	2	-9	-4.5	0	56	796	14.2	3	3	0	18	0
1996—New York Giants NFL	16	15	1	2	2.0	0	53	739	13.9	4	4	0	24	1
1997—New York Giants NFL	16	16	1	-1	-1.0	0	58	849	14.6	8	8	0	48	0
1998—New York Giants NFL	16	16	0	0	0.0	0	62	812	13.1	6	6	0	36	1
1999—Atlanta NFL	11	6	0	0	0.0	0	22	314	14.3	1	1	0	6	0
2000—New England NFL	7	2	0	0	0.0	0	5	95	19.0	0	0	0	0	0
Pro totals (11 years)	158	96	12	69	5.8	0	386	5497	14.2	30	30	0	180	3

CAMPBELL, DAN   TE   GIANTS

PERSONAL: Born April 13, 1976, in Glen Rose, Texas. ... 6-5/260. ... Full name: Daniel Allen Campbell.
HIGH SCHOOL: Glen Rose (Texas).
COLLEGE: Texas A&M.
TRANSACTIONS/CAREER NOTES: Selected by New York Giants in third round (79th pick overall) of 1999 NFL draft. ... Signed by Giants (July 29, 1999).
PLAYING EXPERIENCE: New York Giants NFL, 1999 and 2000. ... Games/Games started: 1999 (12/1), 2000 (16/5). Total: 28/6.
CHAMPIONSHIP GAME EXPERIENCE: Played in NFC championship game (2000 season). ... Played in Super Bowl XXXV (2000 season).
PRO STATISTICS: 2000—Caught eight passes for 46 yards and three touchdowns and fumbled once.
SINGLE GAME HIGHS (regular season): Receptions—1 (December 23, 2000, vs. Jacksonville); yards—13 (September 17, 2000, vs. Chicago); and touchdown receptions—1 (November 26, 2000, vs. Arizona).

CAMPBELL, LAMAR   CB   LIONS

PERSONAL: Born August 29, 1976, in Chester, Pa. ... 5-11/183.
HIGH SCHOOL: Strath Haven (Wallingford, Pa.).
COLLEGE: Wisconsin.
TRANSACTIONS/CAREER NOTES: Signed as non-drafted free agent by Detroit Lions (April 24, 1998). ... Granted free agency (March 2, 2001). ... Re-signed by Lions (April 19, 2001).
PLAYING EXPERIENCE: Detroit NFL, 1998-2000. ... Games/Games started: 1998 (12/0), 1999 (15/2), 2000 (16/2). Total: 43/4.
PRO STATISTICS: 2000—Intercepted one pass for 42 yards and a touchdown.

CAMPBELL, MARK   TE   BROWNS

PERSONAL: Born December 6, 1975, in Clawson, Mich. ... 6-6/253.
HIGH SCHOOL: Bishop Foley (Madison Heights, Mich.).
COLLEGE: Michigan.

TRANSACTIONS/CAREER NOTES: Signed as non-drafted free agent by Cleveland Browns (April 23, 1999). ... On injured reserve with ankle injury (December 14, 1999-remainder of season).
PRO STATISTICS: 1999—Recovered two fumbles.
SINGLE GAME HIGHS (regular season): Receptions—3 (December 10, 2000, vs. Philadelphia); yards—33 (December 12, 1999, vs. Cincinnati); and touchdown receptions—1 (September 10, 2000, vs. Cincinnati).

Year Team	G	GS	RECEIVING				KICKOFF RETURNS				TOTALS			
			No.	Yds.	Avg.	TD	No.	Yds.	Avg.	TD	TD	2pt.	Pts.	Fum.
1999—Cleveland NFL	14	4	9	131	14.6	0	3	28	9.3	0	0	0	0	0
2000—Cleveland NFL	16	10	12	80	6.7	1	3	30	10.0	0	1	0	6	0
Pro totals (2 years)	30	14	21	211	10.0	1	6	58	9.7	0	1	0	6	0

CAMPBELL, MATT   G   REDSKINS

PERSONAL: Born July 14, 1972, in North Augusta, S.C. ... 6-4/300. ... Full name: Mathew Thomas Campbell.
HIGH SCHOOL: North Augusta (S.C.).
COLLEGE: South Carolina.
TRANSACTIONS/CAREER NOTES: Signed as non-drafted free agent by New Orleans Saints (April 28, 1994). ... Released by Saints (August 23, 1994). ... Re-signed by Saints to practice squad (August 30, 1994). ... Released by Saints (September 20, 1994). ... Signed by Carolina Panthers (December 15, 1994). ... Granted free agency (February 13, 1998). ... Tendered offer sheet by Miami Dolphins (February 20, 1998). ... Offer matched by Panthers (February 27, 1998). ... Granted unconditional free agency (March 2, 2001). ... Signed by Washington Redskins (May 8, 2001).
PLAYING EXPERIENCE: Carolina NFL, 1995-2000. ... Games/Games started: 1995 (10/1), 1996 (9/8), 1997 (16/14), 1998 (10/10), 1999 (10/10), 2000 (14/14). Total: 69/47.
CHAMPIONSHIP GAME EXPERIENCE: Played in NFC championship game (1996 season).
PRO STATISTICS: 1995—Caught three passes for 32 yards and fumbled once.
MISCELLANEOUS: Played tight end during 1995 season.

CANIDATE, TRUNG   RB   RAMS

PERSONAL: Born March 3, 1977, in Phoenix. ... 5-11/205. ... Full name: Trung Jered Canidate.
HIGH SCHOOL: Central (Phoenix).
COLLEGE: Arizona.
TRANSACTIONS/CAREER NOTES: Selected by St. Louis Rams in first round (31st pick overall) of 2000 NFL draft. ... Signed by Rams (July 20, 2000). ... On injured reserve with wrist injury (November 13, 2000-remainder of season).
SINGLE GAME HIGHS (regular season): Attempts—2 (November 12, 2000, vs. New York Giants); yards—5 (November 12, 2000, vs. New York Giants); and rushing touchdowns—0.

Year Team	G	GS	RUSHING				RECEIVING				TOTALS			
			Att.	Yds.	Avg.	TD	No.	Yds.	Avg.	TD	TD	2pt.	Pts.	Fum.
2000—St. Louis NFL	3	0	3	6	2.0	0	1	4	4.0	0	0	0	0	0

CANNIDA, JAMES   DT   BUCCANEERS

PERSONAL: Born January 3, 1975, in Savannah, Ga. ... 6-2/291. ... Full name: James Thomas Cannida II.
HIGH SCHOOL: American (Fremont, Calif.).
COLLEGE: Nevada-Reno.
TRANSACTIONS/CAREER NOTES: Selected by Tampa Bay Buccaneers in sixth round (175th pick overall) of 1998 NFL draft. ... Signed by Buccaneers (June 4, 1998). ... Granted free agency (March 2, 2001).
PLAYING EXPERIENCE: Tampa Bay NFL, 1998-2000. ... Games/Games started: 1998 (10/0), 1999 (2/1), 2000 (16/0). Total: 28/1.
CHAMPIONSHIP GAME EXPERIENCE: Member of Buccaneers for NFC championship game (1999 season); inactive.
PRO STATISTICS: 2000—Credited with two sacks.

CANTRELL, BARRY   P

PERSONAL: Born November 2, 1976, in Margate, Fla. ... 6-1/195.
HIGH SCHOOL: St. Thomas Aquinas (Margate, Fla.).
COLLEGE: Fordham.
TRANSACTIONS/CAREER NOTES: Signed as non-drafted free agent by Dallas Cowboys (April 21, 1998). ... Released by Cowboys (August 19, 1998). ... Signed by Philadelphia Eagles (February 18, 1999). ... Assigned by Eagles to Frankfurt Galaxy in 1999 NFL Europe enhancement allocation program (February 22, 1999). ... Released by Eagles (July 12, 1999). ... Signed by Cowboys (April 11, 2000). ... Released by Cowboys (August 21, 2000). ... Re-signed by Cowboys (November 15, 2000). ... Released by Cowboys (November 29, 2000).

Year Team	G	PUNTING					
		No.	Yds.	Avg.	Net avg.	In. 20	Blk.
1999—Frankfurt NFLE	...	39	1602	41.1	34.5	12	0
2000—Dallas NFL	2	10	367	36.7	33.3	3	0
NFL Europe totals (1 year)	...	39	1602	41.1	34.5	12	0
NFL totals (1 year)	2	10	367	36.7	33.3	3	0
Pro totals (2 years)	...	49	1969	40.2	34.3	15	0

CANTY, CHRIS   CB

PERSONAL: Born March 30, 1976, in Long Beach, Calif. ... 5-9/185. ... Full name: Christopher Shawn Patrick Canty.
HIGH SCHOOL: Eastern (Voorhees, N.J.).
COLLEGE: Kansas State.

TRANSACTIONS/CAREER NOTES: Selected after junior season by New England Patriots in first round (29th pick overall) of 1997 NFL draft. ... Signed by Patriots (July 17, 1997). ... Released by Patriots (June 7, 1999). ... Signed by Chicago Bears (July 21, 1999). ... Claimed on waivers by Seattle Seahawks (September 6, 1999). ... Granted free agency (February 11, 2000). ... Re-signed by Seahawks (April 17, 2000). ... Released by Seahawks (November 28, 2000). ... Signed by New Orleans Saints (November 29, 2000). ... Granted unconditional free agency (March 2, 2001).
HONORS: Named defensive back on THE SPORTING NEWS college All-America first team (1995). ... Named cornerback on THE SPORTING NEWS college All-America first team (1996).
PRO STATISTICS: 1997—Recovered two fumbles for nine yards.

			INTERCEPTIONS				SACKS	PUNT RETURNS				KICKOFF RETURNS				TOTALS			
Year	Team	G	GS	No.	Yds.	Avg.	TD	No.	No.	Yds.	Avg.	TD	No.	Yds.	Avg.	TD	TD	2pt.	Pts.	Fum.
1997—New England NFL		16	1	0	0	0.0	0	2.0	0	0	0.0	0	4	115	28.8	0	0	0	0	0
1998—New England NFL		16	9	1	12	12.0	0	1.0	16	170	10.6	0	11	198	18.0	0	0	0	0	2
1999—Seattle NFL		14	1	3	26	8.7	0	0.0	0	0	0.0	0	0	0	0.0	0	0	0	0	0
2000—Seattle NFL		12	1	0	0	0.0	0	0.0	4	21	5.3	0	0	0	0.0	0	0	0	0	0
—New Orleans NFL		3	0	0	0	0.0	0	0.0	9	45	5.0	0	0	0	0.0	0	0	0	0	0
Pro totals (4 years)		61	12	4	38	9.5	0	3.0	29	236	8.1	0	15	313	20.9	0	0	0	0	2

CARLISLE, COOPER G/OT BRONCOS

PERSONAL: Born August 11, 1977, in Greenville, Miss. ... 6-5/295. ... Full name: Cooper Morrison Carlisle.
HIGH SCHOOL: McComb (Miss.).
COLLEGE: Florida.
TRANSACTIONS/CAREER NOTES: Selected by Denver Broncos in fourth round (112th pick overall) of 2000 NFL draft. ... Signed by Broncos (July 19, 2000).
PLAYING EXPERIENCE: Denver NFL, 2000. ... Games/Games started: 2000 (14/0).

CARMAN, JON OT BILLS

PERSONAL: Born January 14, 1976, in Sterling, Va. ... 6-7/335. ... Full name: Jonathon Daniel Carman.
HIGH SCHOOL: Herndon (Va.).
COLLEGE: Georgia Tech.
TRANSACTIONS/CAREER NOTES: Signed as non-drafted free agent by Buffalo Bills (April 22, 2000).
PLAYING EXPERIENCE: Buffalo NFL, 2000. ... Games/Games started: 2000 (3/0).

CARNEY, JOHN K

PERSONAL: Born April 20, 1964, in Hartford, Conn. ... 5-11/170. ... Full name: John Michael Carney.
HIGH SCHOOL: Cardinal Newman (West Palm Beach, Fla.).
COLLEGE: Notre Dame (degree in marketing, 1987).
TRANSACTIONS/CAREER NOTES: Signed as non-drafted free agent by Cincinnati Bengals (May 1, 1987). ... Released by Bengals (August 10, 1987). ... Signed as replacement player by Tampa Bay Buccaneers (September 24, 1987). ... Released by Buccaneers (October 14, 1987). ... Re-signed by Buccaneers (April 5, 1988). ... Released by Buccaneers (August 23, 1988). ... Re-signed by Buccaneers (November 22, 1988). ... Granted unconditional free agency (February 1-April 1, 1989). ... Re-signed by Buccaneers (April 13, 1989). ... Released by Buccaneers (September 5, 1989). ... Re-signed by Buccaneers (December 13, 1989). ... Granted unconditional free agency (February 1, 1990). ... Signed by San Diego Chargers (April 1, 1990). ... Released by Chargers (August 28, 1990). ... Signed by Los Angeles Rams (September 21, 1990). ... Released by Rams (September 26, 1990). ... Signed by Chargers (October 3, 1990). ... Granted free agency (February 1, 1992). ... Re-signed by Chargers (July 27, 1992). ... Granted free agency (March 1, 1993). ... Re-signed by Chargers (June 9, 1993). ... Granted unconditional free agency (February 17, 1994). ... Re-signed by Chargers (April 6, 1994). ... On injured reserve with knee injury (November 15, 1997-remainder of season). ... Granted unconditional free agency (March 2, 2001).
CHAMPIONSHIP GAME EXPERIENCE: Played in AFC championship game (1994 season). ... Played in Super Bowl XXIX (1994 season).
HONORS: Named kicker on THE SPORTING NEWS NFL All-Pro team (1994). ... Played in Pro Bowl (1994 season).
PRO STATISTICS: 1993—Punted four times for 155 yards. 1999—Recovered one fumble.

				KICKING				
Year	Team	G	XPM	XPA	FGM	FGA	Lg.	50+	Pts.
1988—Tampa Bay NFL	4	6	6	2	5	29	0-0	12
1989—Tampa Bay NFL	1	0	0	0	0	0	0-0	0
1990—Los Angeles Rams NFL	1	0	0	0	0	0	0-0	0
—San Diego NFL	12	27	28	19	21	43	0-1	84
1991—San Diego NFL	16	31	31	19	29	54	2-4	88
1992—San Diego NFL	16	35	35	26	32	50	1-3	113
1993—San Diego NFL	16	31	33	31	40	51	2-3	124
1994—San Diego NFL	16	33	33	†34	§38	50	2-2	*135
1995—San Diego NFL	16	32	33	21	26	45	0-2	95
1996—San Diego NFL	16	31	31	29	36	53	3-3	118
1997—San Diego NFL	4	5	5	7	7	41	0-0	26
1998—San Diego NFL	16	19	19	26	30	54	2-3	97
1999—San Diego NFL	16	22	23	31	36	50	1-1	115
2000—San Diego NFL	16	27	27	18	25	▲54	2-4	81
Pro totals (13 years)	166	299	304	263	325	54	15-26	1088

CARPENTER, KEION S BILLS

PERSONAL: Born October 31, 1977, in Baltimore. ... 5-11/205. ... Full name: Keion Eric Carpenter.
HIGH SCHOOL: Woodlawn (Baltimore).
COLLEGE: Virginia Tech.
TRANSACTIONS/CAREER NOTES: Signed as non-drafted free agent by Buffalo Bills (April 19, 1999).
PLAYING EXPERIENCE: Buffalo NFL, 1999 and 2000. ... Games/Games started: 1999 (10/0), 2000 (12/12). Total: 22/12.
PRO STATISTICS: 2000—Intercepted five passes for 63 yards.

CARRIER, MARK   S

PERSONAL: Born April 28, 1968, in Lake Charles, La. ... 6-1/190. ... Full name: Mark Anthony Carrier III. ... Related to Mark Carrier, wide receiver with Tampa Bay Buccaneers (1987-92), Cleveland Browns (1993 and 1994) and Carolina Panthers (1995-98).
HIGH SCHOOL: Polytechnic (Pasadena, Calif.).
COLLEGE: Southern California (degree in communications).
TRANSACTIONS/CAREER NOTES: Selected after junior season by Chicago Bears in first round (sixth pick overall) of 1990 NFL draft. ... Signed by Bears (April 22, 1990). ... Designated by Bears as transition player (February 25, 1993). ... Released by Bears (June 1, 1997). ... Signed by Detroit Lions (June 20, 1997). ... Granted unconditional free agency (February 11, 2000). ... Signed by Washington Redskins (February 17, 2000). ... Released by Redskins (June 5, 2001).
HONORS: Named defensive back on THE SPORTING NEWS college All-America second team (1988). ... Jim Thorpe Award winner (1989). ... Named defensive back on THE SPORTING NEWS college All-America first team (1989). ... Played in Pro Bowl (1990, 1991 and 1993 seasons). ... Named free safety on THE SPORTING NEWS NFL All-Pro team (1991).
PRO STATISTICS: 1990—Recovered two fumbles for 16 yards. 1991—Recovered one fumble for two yards. 1992—Recovered two fumbles. 1995—Recovered one fumble. 1996—Recovered one fumble. 1997—Returned one punt for no yards and fumbled once. 1998—Fumbled once. 1999—Recovered one fumble for six yards.
STATISTICAL PLATEAUS: 100-yard receiving games: 1995 (3).

| | | | | INTERCEPTIONS | | |
Year Team	G	GS	No.	Yds.	Avg.	TD
1990—Chicago NFL	16	16	*10	39	3.9	0
1991—Chicago NFL	16	16	2	54	27.0	0
1992—Chicago NFL	16	14	0	0	0.0	0
1993—Chicago NFL	16	16	4	94	23.5	1
1994—Chicago NFL	16	15	2	10	5.0	0
1995—Chicago NFL	16	15	0	0	0.0	0
1996—Chicago NFL	13	13	2	0	0.0	0
1997—Detroit NFL	16	16	5	94	18.8	0
1998—Detroit NFL	13	13	3	33	11.0	0
1999—Detroit NFL	15	15	3	16	5.3	0
2000—Washington NFL	15	15	1	30	30.0	0
Pro totals (11 years)	168	164	32	370	11.6	1

CARSON, LEONARDO   DT   CHARGERS

PERSONAL: Born February 11, 1977, in Mobile, Ala. ... 6-2/285. ... Full name: Leonardo Tremayne Carson.
HIGH SCHOOL: Shaw (Mobile, Ala.).
COLLEGE: Auburn.
TRANSACTIONS/CAREER NOTES: Selected by San Diego Chargers in fourth round (113th pick overall) of 2000 NFL draft. ... Signed by Chargers (July 20, 2000). ... On injured reserve with shoulder injury (November 17, 2000-remainder of season).
PLAYING EXPERIENCE: San Diego NFL, 2000. ... Games/Games started: 2000 (4/0).

CARSWELL, DWAYNE   TE   BRONCOS

PERSONAL: Born January 18, 1972, in Jacksonville. ... 6-3/260.
HIGH SCHOOL: University Christian (Jacksonville).
COLLEGE: Liberty (Va.).
TRANSACTIONS/CAREER NOTES: Signed as non-drafted free agent by Denver Broncos (May 2, 1994). ... Released by Broncos (August 26, 1994). ... Re-signed by Broncos to practice squad (August 30, 1994). ... Activated (November 25, 1994).
CHAMPIONSHIP GAME EXPERIENCE: Played in AFC championship game (1997 and 1998 seasons). ... Member of Super Bowl championship team (1997 and 1998 seasons).
PRO STATISTICS: 1994—Returned one kickoff for no yards and recovered one fumble. 1997—Recovered one fumble. 2000—Returned one kickoff for no yards.
SINGLE GAME HIGHS (regular season): Receptions—6 (December 25, 1999, vs. Detroit); yards—68 (October 22, 2000, vs. Cincinnati); and touchdown receptions—1 (December 3, 2000, vs. New Orleans).

| | | | RECEIVING | | | | TOTALS | | | |
Year Team	G	GS	No.	Yds.	Avg.	TD	TD	2pt.	Pts.	Fum.
1994—Denver NFL	4	0	0	0	0.0	0	0	0	0	0
1995—Denver NFL	9	2	3	37	12.3	0	0	0	0	0
1996—Denver NFL	16	2	15	85	5.7	0	0	0	0	0
1997—Denver NFL	16	3	12	96	8.0	1	1	0	6	0
1998—Denver NFL	16	1	4	51	12.8	0	0	0	0	0
1999—Denver NFL	16	11	24	201	8.4	2	2	0	12	0
2000—Denver NFL	16	16	49	495	10.1	3	3	0	18	0
Pro totals (7 years)	93	35	107	965	9.0	6	6	0	36	0

CARTER, CHRIS   S

PERSONAL: Born September 27, 1974, in Tyler, Texas. ... 6-2/209. ... Full name: Christopher Cary Carter. ... Cousin of Joe Carter, first baseman/outfielder with five major league baseball teams (1984-98).
HIGH SCHOOL: John Tyler (Tyler, Texas).
COLLEGE: Texas.
TRANSACTIONS/CAREER NOTES: Selected by New England Patriots in third round (89th pick overall) of 1997 NFL draft. ... Signed by Patriots (July 15, 1997). ... Granted free agency (February 11, 2000). ... Re-signed by Patriots (July 14, 2000). ... Claimed on waivers by Cincinnati Bengals (August 28, 2000). ... Granted unconditional free agency (March 2, 2001).
PLAYING EXPERIENCE: New England NFL, 1997-1999; Cincinnati NFL, 2000. ... Games/Games started: 1997 (16/0), 1998 (16/0), 1999 (15/15), 2000 (16/10). Total: 63/25.
PRO STATISTICS: 1998—Credited with one sack. 1999—Intercepted three passes for 13 yards, credited with one sack and recovered two fumbles. 2000—Intercepted one pass for six yards, credited with one sack and recovered one fumble.

CARTER, CRIS   WR   VIKINGS

PERSONAL: Born November 25, 1965, in Troy, Ohio. ... 6-3/208. ... Full name: Christopher D. Carter. ... Brother of Butch Carter, head coach, Toronto Raptors (February 13, 1998-99).
HIGH SCHOOL: Middletown (Ohio).
COLLEGE: Ohio State.
TRANSACTIONS/CAREER NOTES: Selected by Philadelphia Eagles in fourth round of 1987 NFL supplemental draft (September 4, 1987). ... Signed by Eagles (September 17, 1987). ... Granted roster exemption (September 17-October 26, 1987). ... Claimed on waivers by Minnesota Vikings (September 4, 1990). ... Granted free agency (February 1, 1991). ... Re-signed by Vikings (July 9, 1991). ... Granted free agency (February 1, 1992). ... Re-signed by Vikings (July 26, 1992). ... On injured reserve with broken collarbone (December 4-30, 1992).
CHAMPIONSHIP GAME EXPERIENCE: Played in NFC championship game (1998 and 2000 seasons).
HONORS: Played in Pro Bowl (1993-2000 seasons). ... Named wide receiver on THE SPORTING NEWS NFL All-Pro team (1994).
PRO STATISTICS: 1987—Attempted one pass without a completion and returned 12 kickoffs for 241 yards. 1988—Recovered one fumble in end zone for a touchdown. 1989—Recovered one fumble. 1993—Recovered one fumble. 1996—Returned one kickoff for three yards and recovered one fumble. 2000—Recovered two fumbles.
SINGLE GAME HIGHS (regular season): Receptions—14 (October 2, 1994, vs. Arizona); yards—168 (September 10, 2000, vs. Miami); and touchdown receptions—3 (November 14, 1999, vs. Chicago).
STATISTICAL PLATEAUS: 100-yard receiving games: 1988 (1), 1989 (1), 1990 (2), 1991 (4), 1992 (1), 1993 (3), 1994 (5), 1995 (5), 1996 (1), 1997 (4), 1998 (3), 1999 (5), 2000 (6). Total: 41.
MISCELLANEOUS: Active NFC leader for career receptions (1,620), receiving yards (12,962) and touchdowns (124). ... Holds Minnesota Vikings all-time records for most receptions (931), most yards receiving (11,412), most touchdowns (104) and most touchdown receptions (104).

| | | | RUSHING | | | | RECEIVING | | | | TOTALS | | |
Year Team	G	GS	Att.	Yds.	Avg.	TD	No.	Yds.	Avg.	TD	TD	2pt.	Pts.	Fum.
1987—Philadelphia NFL	9	0	0	0	0.0	0	5	84	16.8	2	2	0	12	0
1988—Philadelphia NFL	16	16	1	1	1.0	0	39	761	19.5	6	7	0	42	0
1989—Philadelphia NFL	16	15	2	16	8.0	0	45	605	13.4	11	11	0	66	1
1990—Minnesota NFL	16	5	2	6	3.0	0	27	413	15.3	3	3	0	18	0
1991—Minnesota NFL	16	16	0	0	0.0	0	72	962	13.4	5	5	0	30	1
1992—Minnesota NFL	12	12	5	15	3.0	0	53	681	12.8	6	6	0	36	1
1993—Minnesota NFL	16	16	0	0	0.0	0	86	1071	12.5	9	9	0	54	0
1994—Minnesota NFL	16	16	0	0	0.0	0	*122	1256	10.3	7	7	2	46	4
1995—Minnesota NFL	16	16	1	0	0.0	0	122	1371	11.2	†17	17	0	102	0
1996—Minnesota NFL	16	16	0	0	0.0	0	96	1163	12.1	10	10	0	60	1
1997—Minnesota NFL	16	16	0	0	0.0	0	89	1069	12.0	*13	13	3	84	3
1998—Minnesota NFL	16	16	1	-1	-1.0	0	78	1011	13.0	12	12	0	72	0
1999—Minnesota NFL	16	16	0	0	0.0	0	90	1241	13.8	*13	13	0	78	0
2000—Minnesota NFL	16	16	0	0	0.0	0	96	1274	13.3	9	9	0	54	3
Pro totals (14 years)	213	192	12	37	3.1	0	1020	12962	12.7	123	124	5	754	14

CARTER, KEVIN   DE   TITANS

PERSONAL: Born September 21, 1973, in Miami. ... 6-5/280. ... Full name: Kevin Louis Carter. ... Brother of Bernard Carter, linebacker with Jacksonville Jaguars (1995).
HIGH SCHOOL: Lincoln (Tallahassee, Fla.).
COLLEGE: Florida.
TRANSACTIONS/CAREER NOTES: Selected by St. Louis Rams in first round (sixth pick overall) of 1995 NFL draft. ... Signed by Rams (July 17, 1995). ... Designated by Rams as franchise player (February 22, 2001). ... Traded by Rams to Tennessee Titans for first-round pick (DT Ryan Pickett) in 2001 draft (March 28, 2001).
CHAMPIONSHIP GAME EXPERIENCE: Played in NFC championship game (1999 season). ... Member of Super Bowl championship team (1999 season).
HONORS: Named defensive lineman on THE SPORTING NEWS college All-America first team (1994). ... Named defensive end on THE SPORTING NEWS NFL All-Pro team (1999). ... Played in Pro Bowl (1999 season).
PRO STATISTICS: 1995—Recovered one fumble. 1996—Recovered two fumbles. 1997—Recovered two fumbles for five yards. 1999—Recovered two fumbles. 2000—Fumbled once and recovered one fumble.

Year Team	G	GS	SACKS
1995—St. Louis NFL	16	16	6.0
1996—St. Louis NFL	16	16	9.5
1997—St. Louis NFL	16	16	7.5
1998—St. Louis NFL	16	16	12.0
1999—St. Louis NFL	16	16	*17.0
2000—St. Louis NFL	16	13	10.5
Pro totals (6 years)	96	93	62.5

CARTER, MARTY   S   FALCONS

PERSONAL: Born December 17, 1969, in La Grange, Ga. ... 6-1/213. ... Full name: Marty LaVincent Carter.
HIGH SCHOOL: La Grange (Ga.).
COLLEGE: Middle Tennessee State.
TRANSACTIONS/CAREER NOTES: Selected by Tampa Bay Buccaneers in eighth round (207th pick overall) of 1991 NFL draft. ... Signed by Buccaneers (July 19, 1991). ... Granted unconditional free agency (February 17, 1995). ... Signed by Chicago Bears (March 3, 1995). ... Granted unconditional free agency (February 12, 1999). ... Signed by Atlanta Falcons (March 12, 1999). ... On injured reserve with knee injury (November 30, 1999-remainder of season).
PRO STATISTICS: 1993—Recovered two fumbles. 1994—Caught one pass for 21 yards and returned one kickoff for no yards. 1995—Recovered one fumble. 1998—Recovered two fumbles. 1999—Recovered one fumble. 2000—Recovered two fumbles.

Year Team	G	GS	INTERCEPTIONS				SACKS
			No.	Yds.	Avg.	TD	No.
1991—Tampa Bay NFL	14	11	1	5	5.0	0	0.0
1992—Tampa Bay NFL	16	16	3	1	0.3	0	2.0
1993—Tampa Bay NFL	16	14	1	0	0.0	0	0.0
1994—Tampa Bay NFL	16	14	0	0	0.0	0	1.0
1995—Chicago NFL	16	16	2	20	10.0	0	0.0
1996—Chicago NFL	16	16	3	34	11.3	0	0.0
1997—Chicago NFL	15	15	1	14	14.0	0	1.0
1998—Chicago NFL	16	16	0	0	0.0	0	0.0
1999—Atlanta NFL	11	11	1	4	4.0	0	0.0
2000—Atlanta NFL	16	16	0	0	0.0	0	2.0
Pro totals (10 years)	152	145	12	78	6.5	0	6.0

CARTER, TOM — CB — BENGALS

PERSONAL: Born September 5, 1972, in St. Petersburg, Fla. ... 6-0/190. ... Full name: Thomas Carter III.
HIGH SCHOOL: Lakeland (Fla.).
COLLEGE: Notre Dame (degree in finance, 1996).
TRANSACTIONS/CAREER NOTES: Selected after junior season by Washington Redskins in first round (17th pick overall) of 1993 NFL draft. ... Signed by Redskins for 1993 season. ... Designated by Redskins as transition player (February 15, 1994). ... Designated by Redskins as transition player (February 12, 1997). ... Tendered offer sheet by Chicago Bears (March 31, 1997). ... Redskins declined to match offer (April 7, 1997). ... On injured reserve with broken collarbone (September 30, 1998-remainder of season). ... Claimed on waivers by Cincinnati Bengals (December 14, 1999). ... Released by Bengals (March 1, 2001). ... Re-signed by Bengals (April 9, 2001).
PRO STATISTICS: 1999—Recovered one fumble for 21 yards.

Year Team	G	GS	INTERCEPTIONS			
			No.	Yds.	Avg.	TD
1993—Washington NFL	14	11	6	54	9.0	0
1994—Washington NFL	16	16	3	58	19.3	0
1995—Washington NFL	16	16	4	116	29.0	1
1996—Washington NFL	16	16	5	24	4.8	0
1997—Chicago NFL	16	16	3	12	4.0	0
1998—Chicago NFL	4	4	2	20	10.0	0
1999—Chicago NFL	12	6	1	36	36.0	0
—Cincinnati NFL	2	2	1	0	0.0	0
2000—Cincinnati NFL	16	11	2	40	20.0	0
Pro totals (8 years)	112	98	27	360	13.3	1

CARTER, TONY — FB — BRONCOS

PERSONAL: Born August 23, 1972, in Columbus, Ohio. ... 6-0/235. ... Full name: Antonio Marcus Carter.
HIGH SCHOOL: South (Columbus, Ohio).
COLLEGE: Minnesota.
TRANSACTIONS/CAREER NOTES: Signed as non-drafted free agent by Chicago Bears (April 28, 1994). ... Granted unconditional free agency (February 13, 1998). ... Signed by New England Patriots (February 25, 1998). ... Granted unconditional free agency (March 2, 2001). ... Signed by Denver Broncos (May 4, 2001).
PRO STATISTICS: 1996—Recovered one fumble. 1997—Recovered one fumble. 1999—Recovered one fumble.
SINGLE GAME HIGHS (regular season): Attempts—9 (December 17, 2000, vs. Buffalo); yards—37 (October 13, 1996, vs. New Orleans); and rushing touchdowns—1 (December 24, 2000, vs. Miami).

Year Team	G	GS	RUSHING				RECEIVING				KICKOFF RETURNS				TOTALS			
			Att.	Yds.	Avg.	TD	No.	Yds.	Avg.	TD	No.	Yds.	Avg.	TD	TD	2pt.	Pts.	Fum.
1994—Chicago NFL	14	0	0	0	0.0	0	1	24	24.0	0	6	99	16.5	0	0	0	0	0
1995—Chicago NFL	16	11	10	34	3.4	0	40	329	8.2	1	3	24	8.0	0	1	0	6	1
1996—Chicago NFL	16	11	11	43	3.9	0	41	233	5.7	0	0	0	0.0	0	0	0	0	1
1997—Chicago NFL	16	10	9	56	6.2	0	24	152	6.3	0	2	34	17.0	0	0	0	0	0
1998—New England NFL	11	7	2	3	1.5	0	18	166	9.2	0	0	0	0.0	0	0	0	0	0
1999—New England NFL	16	14	6	26	4.3	0	20	108	5.4	0	0	0	0.0	0	0	0	0	0
2000—New England NFL	16	6	37	90	2.4	2	9	73	8.1	0	1	16	16.0	0	2	0	12	0
Pro totals (7 years)	105	59	75	252	3.4	2	153	1085	7.1	1	12	173	14.4	0	3	0	18	2

CARTER, TYRONE — S — VIKINGS

PERSONAL: Born March 31, 1976, in Pompano Beach, Fla. ... 5-8/190.
HIGH SCHOOL: Ely (Pompano Beach, Fla.).
COLLEGE: Minnesota.
TRANSACTIONS/CAREER NOTES: Selected by Minnesota Vikings in fourth round (118th pick overall) of 2000 NFL draft. ... Signed by Vikings (July 5, 2000).
CHAMPIONSHIP GAME EXPERIENCE: Played in NFC championship game (2000 season).
HONORS: Jim Thorpe Award winner (1999). ... Named strong safety on THE SPORTING NEWS college All-America first team (1999).

Year Team	G	GS	INTERCEPTIONS				KICKOFF RETURNS				TOTALS			
			No.	Yds.	Avg.	TD	No.	Yds.	Avg.	TD	TD	2pt.	Pts.	Fum.
2000—Minnesota NFL	15	7	0	0	0.0	0	17	389	22.9	0	0	0	0	0

CARTY, JOHNDALE　　　　　S　　　　　FALCONS

PERSONAL: Born August 27, 1977, in Miami. ... 6-0/196.
HIGH SCHOOL: Hialeah (Fla.) Miami Lakes.
COLLEGE: Utah State.
TRANSACTIONS/CAREER NOTES: Selected by Atlanta Falcons in fourth round (126th pick overall) of 1999 NFL draft. ... Signed by Falcons (July 8, 1999).
PLAYING EXPERIENCE: Atlanta NFL, 1999 and 2000. ... Games/Games started: 1999 (14/0), 2000 (15/0). Total: 29/0.

CASE, STONEY　　　　　QB

PERSONAL: Born July 7, 1972, in Odessa, Texas. ... 6-3/201. ... Full name: Stoney Jarrod Case.
HIGH SCHOOL: Permian (Odessa, Texas).
COLLEGE: New Mexico (degree in biology, 1995).
TRANSACTIONS/CAREER NOTES: Selected by Arizona Cardinals in third round (80th pick overall) of 1995 NFL draft. ... Signed by Cardinals for 1995 season. ... Inactive for all 16 games (1996). ... Assigned by Cardinals to Barcelona Dragons in 1997 World League enhancement allocation program (February 19, 1997). ... Granted free agency (February 13, 1998). ... Re-signed by Cardinals (April 28, 1998). ... Granted unconditional free agency (February 12, 1999). ... Signed by Indianapolis Colts (March 4, 1999). ... Released by Colts (August 11, 1999). ... Signed by Baltimore Ravens (August 17, 1999). ... Granted unconditional free agency (February 11, 2000). ... Signed by Detroit Lions (June 13, 2000). ... Granted unconditional free agency (March 2, 2001).
PRO STATISTICS: 1997—Fumbled three times. 1999—Fumbled twice and recovered two fumbles for minus three yards. 2000—Fumbled once.
SINGLE GAME HIGHS (regular season): Attempts—37 (October 21, 1999, vs. Kansas City); completions—23 (November 30, 2000, vs. Minnesota); yards—230 (November 30, 2000, vs. Minnesota); and touchdown passes—2 (October 3, 1999, vs. Atlanta).
MISCELLANEOUS: Regular-season record as starting NFL quarterback: 2-4 (.333).

Year Team	G	GS	PASSING Att.	Cmp.	Pct.	Yds.	TD	Int.	Avg.	Rat.	RUSHING Att.	Yds.	Avg.	TD	TOTALS TD	2pt.	Pts.
1995—Arizona NFL	2	0	2	1	50.0	19	0	1	9.50	43.8	1	4	4.0	0	0	0	0
1996—Arizona NFL							Did not play.										
1997—Arizona NFL	3	1	55	29	52.7	316	0	2	5.75	54.8	7	8	1.1	1	1	0	6
1998—Arizona NFL	1	0	0	0	0.0	0	0	0	0.0		0	0	0.0	0	0	0	0
1999—Baltimore NFL	10	4	170	77	45.3	988	3	8	5.81	50.3	36	141	3.9	3	3	0	18
2000—Detroit NFL	5	1	91	56	61.5	503	1	4	5.53	61.7	16	117	7.3	1	1	0	6
Pro totals (5 years)	21	6	318	163	51.3	1826	4	15	5.74	53.3	60	270	4.5	5	5	0	30

C

CAVIL, KWAME　　　　　WR　　　　　BILLS

PERSONAL: Born May 3, 1979, in Waco, Texas. ... 6-2/203. ... Cousin of Ben Cavil, offensive guard with Baltimore Ravens (1997 and 1998).
HIGH SCHOOL: Waco (Texas).
COLLEGE: Texas.
TRANSACTIONS/CAREER NOTES: Signed as non-drafted free agent by Buffalo Bills (April 22, 2000).
PLAYING EXPERIENCE: Buffalo NFL, 2000. ... Games/Games started: 2000 (16/0).
PRO STATISTICS: 2000—Caught four passes for 66 yards and returned one kickoff for one yard.
SINGLE GAME HIGHS (regular season): Receptions—2 (October 22, 2000, vs. Minnesota); yards—39 (December 23, 2000, vs. Seattle); and touchdown receptions—0.

CENTERS, LARRY　　　　　RB　　　　　BILLS

PERSONAL: Born June 1, 1968, in Tatum, Texas. ... 6-0/225. ... Full name: Larry E. Centers.
HIGH SCHOOL: Tatum (Texas).
COLLEGE: Stephen F. Austin State.
TRANSACTIONS/CAREER NOTES: Selected by Phoenix Cardinals in fifth round (115th pick overall) of 1990 NFL draft. ... Signed by Cardinals (July 23, 1990). ... On injured reserve with broken foot (September 11-October 30, 1991). ... Granted free agency (February 1, 1992). ... Re-signed by Cardinals (July 23, 1992). ... Granted unconditional free agency (February 17, 1994). ... Re-signed by Cardinals (March 15, 1994). ... Cardinals franchise renamed Arizona Cardinals for 1994 season. ... Granted unconditional free agency (February 14, 1997). ... Re-signed by Cardinals (March 14, 1997). ... Released by Cardinals (June 18, 1999). ... Signed by Washington Redskins (July 6, 1999). ... Released by Redskins (April 20, 2001). ... Signed by Buffalo Bills (May 8, 2001).
HONORS: Played in Pro Bowl (1995 and 1996 seasons).
PRO STATISTICS: 1991—Returned five punts for 30 yards and recovered two fumbles. 1993—Recovered two fumbles. 1994—Recovered two fumbles for 27 yards. 1995—Had only pass attempt intercepted and recovered one fumble. 1996—Recovered one fumble. 1999—Recovered one fumble. 2000—Recovered one fumble.
SINGLE GAME HIGHS (regular season): Attempts—15 (September 4, 1994, vs. Los Angeles Rams); yards—62 (November 26, 1995, vs. Atlanta); and rushing touchdowns—2 (December 4, 1994, vs. Houston).
STATISTICAL PLATEAUS: 100-yard receiving games: 1995 (2), 1996 (1). Total: 3.
MISCELLANEOUS: Holds Cardinals franchise all-time record for most receptions (535).

Year Team	G	GS	RUSHING Att.	Yds.	Avg.	TD	RECEIVING No.	Yds.	Avg.	TD	KICKOFF RETURNS No.	Yds.	Avg.	TD	TOTALS TD	2pt.	Pts.	Fum.
1990—Phoenix NFL	6	0	0	0	0.0	0	0	0	0.0	0	16	272	17.0	0	0	0	0	1
1991—Phoenix NFL	9	2	14	44	3.1	0	19	176	9.3	0	16	330	20.6	0	0	0	0	4
1992—Phoenix NFL	16	1	37	139	3.8	0	50	417	8.3	2	0	0	0.0	0	2	0	12	1
1993—Phoenix NFL	16	9	25	152	6.1	0	66	603	9.1	3	0	0	0.0	0	3	0	18	1
1994—Arizona NFL	16	5	115	336	2.9	5	77	647	8.4	2	0	0	0.0	0	7	0	42	2
1995—Arizona NFL	16	10	78	254	3.3	2	101	962	9.5	2	1	15	15.0	0	4	0	24	2
1996—Arizona NFL	16	14	116	425	3.7	2	99	766	7.7	7	0	0	0.0	0	9	0	54	1

Year Team	G	GS	RUSHING				RECEIVING				KICKOFF RETURNS				TOTALS			
			Att.	Yds.	Avg.	TD	No.	Yds.	Avg.	TD	No.	Yds.	Avg.	TD	TD	2pt	Pts.	Fum.
1997—Arizona NFL	15	14	101	276	2.7	1	54	409	7.6	1	0	0	0.0	0	2	0	12	1
1998—Arizona NFL	16	12	31	110	3.5	0	69	559	8.1	2	0	0	0.0	0	2	0	12	1
1999—Washington NFL	16	12	13	51	3.9	0	69	544	7.9	3	0	0	0.0	0	3	0	18	2
2000—Washington NFL	15	5	19	103	5.4	0	81	600	7.4	3	0	0	0.0	0	3	0	18	1
Pro totals (11 years)	157	84	549	1890	3.4	10	685	5683	8.3	25	33	617	18.7	0	35	0	210	17

CERCONE, MATT — TE — VIKINGS

PERSONAL: Born November 30, 1975, in Bakersfield, Calif. ... 6-5/252. ... Full name: Matthew Anthony Cercone.
HIGH SCHOOL: South High (Calif.).
COLLEGE: Arizona State.
TRANSACTIONS/CAREER NOTES: Signed as non-drafted free agent by Minnesota Vikings (April 30, 1999). ... Released by Vikings (August 27, 1999). ... Re-signed by Vikings (February 1, 2000). ... Released by Vikings (August 27, 2000). ... Re-signed by Vikings to practice squad (August 28, 2000). ... Released by Vikings (September 5, 2000). ... Re-signed by Vikings to practice squad (September 25, 2000). ... Activated (November 15, 2000). ... Released by Vikings (December 5, 2000). ... Re-signed by Vikings to practice squad (December 6, 2000).
PLAYING EXPERIENCE: Minnesota NFL, 2000. ... Games/Games started: 2000 (2/0).

CHAMBERLAIN, BYRON — TE — VIKINGS

C

PERSONAL: Born October 17, 1971, in Honolulu. ... 6-1/264.
HIGH SCHOOL: Eastern Hills (Fort Worth, Texas).
COLLEGE: Missouri, then Wayne State (Neb.).
TRANSACTIONS/CAREER NOTES: Selected by Denver Broncos in seventh round (222nd pick overall) of 1995 NFL draft. ... Signed by Broncos (August 27, 1995). ... Released by Broncos (August 27, 1995). ... Re-signed by Broncos to practice squad (August 28, 1995). ... Activated (November 24, 1995). ... Assigned by Broncos to Rhein Fire in 1996 World League enhancement allocation program (February 19, 1996). ... Granted unconditional free agency (March 2, 2001). ... Signed by Minnesota Vikings (March 15, 2001).
CHAMPIONSHIP GAME EXPERIENCE: Played in AFC championship game (1997 and 1998 seasons). ... Member of Super Bowl championship team (1997 season); did not play. ... Member of Super Bowl championship team (1998 season).
PRO STATISTICS: W.L.: 1996—Rushed once for four yards and returned one kickoff for eight yards. NFL: 1996—Returned three kickoffs for 49 yards. 1997—Returned one kickoff for 13 yards. 2000—Returned two kickoffs for 25 yards.
SINGLE GAME HIGHS (regular season): Receptions—6 (October 8, 2000, vs. San Diego); yards—123 (October 17, 1999, vs. Green Bay); and touchdown receptions—1 (November 13, 2000, vs. Oakland).
STATISTICAL PLATEAUS: 100-yard receiving games: 1999 (1).

Year Team	G	GS	RECEIVING				TOTALS			
			No.	Yds.	Avg.	TD	TD	2pt.	Pts.	Fum.
1995—Denver NFL	5	0	1	11	11.0	0	0	0	0	0
1996—Rhein W.L.	10	10	58	685	11.8	8	8	0	48	0
—Denver NFL	11	0	12	129	10.8	0	0	0	0	1
1997—Denver NFL	10	0	2	18	9.0	0	0	0	0	1
1998—Denver NFL	16	0	3	35	11.7	0	0	0	0	0
1999—Denver NFL	16	0	32	488	15.3	2	2	0	12	0
2000—Denver NFL	15	0	22	283	12.9	1	1	0	6	0
W.L. totals (1 year)	10	10	58	685	11.8	8	8	0	48	0
NFL totals (6 years)	73	0	72	964	13.4	3	3	0	18	2
Pro totals (7 years)	83	10	130	1649	12.7	11	11	0	66	2

CHAMBERLIN, FRANK — LB — TITANS

PERSONAL: Born January 2, 1978, in Paranus, N.J. ... 6-1/250. ... Full name: Frank Jacob Chamberlin.
HIGH SCHOOL: Mahwah (N.J.).
COLLEGE: Boston College.
TRANSACTIONS/CAREER NOTES: Selected by Tennessee Titans in fifth round (160th pick overall) of 2000 NFL draft. ... Signed by Titans (July 7, 2000).
PLAYING EXPERIENCE: Tennessee NFL, 2000. ... Games/Games started: 2000 (12/0).

CHANCEY, ROBERT — RB

PERSONAL: Born September 7, 1972, in Macon, Ala. ... 6-0/252. ... Full name: Robert Dewayne Chancey. ... Name pronounced CHAN-see.
HIGH SCHOOL: Stanhope Elmore (Millbrook, Ala.).
COLLEGE: None.
TRANSACTIONS/CAREER NOTES: Signed as non-drafted free agent by San Diego Chargers (April 7, 1997). ... Released by Chargers (August 24, 1997). ... Re-signed by Chargers to practice squad (August 25, 1997). ... Activated (November 4, 1997). ... Released by Chargers (July 23, 1998). ... Signed by Chicago Bears (July 26, 1998). ... Released by Bears (September 5, 1999). ... Signed by Dallas Cowboys (October 5, 1999). ... Granted free agency (February 11, 2000). ... Signed by Chargers (February 28, 2000). ... Released by Chargers (February 28, 2001).
PRO STATISTICS: 1998—Returned two kickoffs for 18 yards. 2000—Attempted one pass without a completion.
SINGLE GAME HIGHS (regular season): Attempts—23 (September 3, 2000, vs. Oakland); yards—74 (September 3, 2000, vs. Oakland) and rushing touchdowns—1 (September 10, 2000, vs. New Orleans).

Year Team	G	GS	RUSHING				RECEIVING				TOTALS			
			Att.	Yds.	Avg.	TD	No.	Yds.	Avg.	TD	TD	2pt.	Pts.	Fum.
1997—San Diego NFL................	6	0	0	0	0.0	0	0	0	0.0	0	0	0	0	0
1998—Chicago NFL	16	1	29	122	4.2	2	11	102	9.3	0	2	0	12	2
1999—Dallas NFL	3	0	14	57	4.1	0	0	0	0.0	0	0	0	0	0
2000—San Diego NFL................	4	3	42	141	3.4	2	1	6	6.0	0	2	0	12	0
Pro totals (4 years)	29	4	85	320	3.8	4	12	108	9.0	0	4	0	24	2

RECORD AS BASEBALL PLAYER

TRANSACTIONS/CAREER NOTES: Selected by Baltimore Orioles organization in sixth round of free-agent draft (June 1, 1992). ... Released by Orioles (September 30, 1993). ... Signed by New York Mets organization (April 15, 1996). ... On Pittsfield temporarily inactive list (May 10-June 10, 1996). ... Released by Mets (July 1, 1996).

STATISTICAL NOTES: Led Gulf Coast League outfielders with seven errors (1992).

								BATTING							FIELDING		
Year	Team (League)	Pos.	G	AB	R	H	2B	3B	HR	RBI	Avg.	BB	SO	SB	PO	A	E	Avg.
1992— GC Orioles (GCL).......		OF	43	141	22	41	3	3	1	23	.291	7	50	13	70	5	*7	.915
1993— GC Orioles (GCL)		OF	29	84	7	12	3	0	0	3	.143	4	39	3	31	3	6	.850
1996— Kingsport (Appal.)■ ..		OF	6	19	4	5	0	0	1	3	.263	2	5	1	7	0	1	.875

CHANDLER, CHRIS   QB   FALCONS

PERSONAL: Born October 12, 1965, in Everett, Wash. ... 6-4/226. ... Full name: Christopher Mark Chandler. ... Brother of Greg Chandler, catcher with San Francisco Giants organization (1978); and son-in-law of John Brodie, quarterback with San Francisco 49ers (1957-73).
HIGH SCHOOL: Everett (Wash.).
COLLEGE: Washington (degree in economics, 1988).
TRANSACTIONS/CAREER NOTES: Selected by Indianapolis Colts in third round (76th pick overall) of 1988 NFL draft. ... Signed by Colts (July 23, 1988). ... On injured reserve with knee injury (October 3, 1989-remainder of season). ... Traded by Colts to Tampa Bay Buccaneers for first round pick (LB Quentin Coryatt) in 1992 draft (August 7, 1990). ... Claimed on waivers by Phoenix Cardinals (November 6, 1991). ... Granted unconditional free agency (February 17, 1994). ... Signed by Los Angeles Rams (May 6, 1994). ... Granted unconditional free agency (February 17, 1995). ... Signed by Houston Oilers (March 10, 1995). ... Traded by Oilers to Atlanta Falcons for fourth- (WR Derrick Mason) and sixth-round (traded to New Orleans) picks in 1997 draft (February 24, 1997).
CHAMPIONSHIP GAME EXPERIENCE: Played in NFC championship game (1998 season). ... Played in Super Bowl XXXIII (1998 season).
HONORS: Played in Pro Bowl (1997 and 1998 seasons).
PRO STATISTICS: 1988—Fumbled eight times and recovered five fumbles for minus six yards. 1990—Fumbled five times and recovered one fumble for minus two yards. 1991—Fumbled six times and recovered two fumbles for minus seven yards. 1992—Fumbled nine times and recovered two fumbles for minus 11 yards. 1993—Fumbled twice. 1994—Fumbled three times. 1995—Tied for AFC lead with 12 fumbles and recovered five fumbles for minus nine yards. 1996—Fumbled eight times and recovered three fumbles for minus four yards. 1997—Fumbled nine times and recovered three fumbles for minus 18 yards. 1998—Caught one pass for 22 yards, fumbled six times and recovered one fumble for minus four yards. 1999—Fumbled seven times and recovered four fumbles for minus 14 yards. 2000—Caught one pass for minus four yards, fumbled seven times and recovered four fumbles for minus 13 yards.
SINGLE GAME HIGHS (regular season): Attempts—47 (October 1, 1995, vs. Jacksonville); completions—28 (September 20, 1992, vs. Dallas); yards—383 (September 20, 1992, vs. Dallas); and touchdown passes—4 (November 28, 1999, vs. Carolina).
STATISTICAL PLATEAUS: 300-yard passing games: 1992 (1), 1995 (1), 1998 (1), 1999 (2). Total: 5.
MISCELLANEOUS: Regular-season record as starting NFL quarterback: 56-67 (.455). ... Postseason record as starting NFL quarterback: 2-1 (.667).

				PASSING							RUSHING				TOTALS		
Year	Team	G	GS	Att.	Cmp.	Pct.	Yds.	TD	Int.	Avg.	Rat.	Att.	Yds.	Avg.	TD	TD	2pt.	Pts.
1988—Indianapolis NFL		15	13	233	129	55.4	1619	8	12	6.95	67.2	46	139	3.0	3	3	0	18
1989—Indianapolis NFL		3	3	80	39	48.8	537	2	3	6.71	63.4	7	57	8.1	1	1	0	6
1990—Tampa Bay NFL		7	3	83	42	50.6	464	1	6	5.59	41.4	13	71	5.5	1	1	0	6
1991—Tampa Bay NFL		6	3	104	53	51.0	557	4	8	5.36	47.6	18	79	4.4	0	0	0	0
—Phoenix NFL		3	2	50	25	50.0	289	1	2	5.78	57.8	8	32	4.0	0	0	0	0
1992—Phoenix NFL...............		15	13	413	245	59.3	2832	15	15	6.86	77.1	36	149	4.1	1	1	0	6
1993—Phoenix NFL...............		4	2	103	52	50.5	471	3	2	4.57	64.8	3	2	0.7	0	0	0	0
1994—L.A. Rams NFL		12	6	176	108	61.4	1352	7	2	7.68	93.8	18	61	3.4	1	1	0	6
1995—Houston NFL		13	13	356	225	63.2	2460	17	10	6.91	87.8	28	58	2.1	2	2	1	14
1996—Houston NFL		12	12	320	184	57.5	2099	16	11	6.56	79.7	28	113	4.0	0	0	0	0
1997—Atlanta NFL		14	14	342	202	59.1	2692	20	7	7.87	95.1	43	158	3.7	0	0	0	0
1998—Atlanta NFL		14	14	327	190	58.1	3154	25	12	*9.65	100.9	36	121	3.4	2	2	0	12
1999—Atlanta NFL		12	12	307	174	56.7	2339	16	11	7.62	83.5	16	57	3.6	1	1	0	6
2000—Atlanta NFL		14	13	331	192	58.0	2236	10	12	6.76	73.5	21	60	2.9	0	0	0	0
Pro totals (13 years)		144	123	3225	1860	57.7	23101	145	113	7.16	80.4	321	1157	3.6	12	12	1	74

CHANOINE, ROGER   OT   BROWNS

PERSONAL: Born August 11, 1976, in Newark, N.J. ... 6-4/295. ... Full name: Roger Chanoine Jr. ... Name pronounced SHAN-wah.
HIGH SCHOOL: Linden (N.J.).
COLLEGE: Temple.
TRANSACTIONS/CAREER NOTES: Signed as non-drafted free agent by St. Louis Rams (April 20, 1998). ... On injured reserve with ankle injury (August 25, 1998-entire season). ... Released by Rams (August 30, 1999). ... Signed by Cleveland Browns to practice squad (September 7, 1999). ... Activated (December 8, 1999).
PLAYING EXPERIENCE: Cleveland NFL, 1999 and 2000. ... Games/Games started: 1999 (1/0), 2000 (7/0). Total: 8/0.
PRO STATISTICS: 2000—Recovered one fumble.

CHAPMAN, DOUG   RB   VIKINGS

PERSONAL: Born August 22, 1977, in Chesterfield, Va. ... 5-10/213.
HIGH SCHOOL: Lloyd C. Bird (Chesterfield, Va.).
COLLEGE: Marshall.
TRANSACTIONS/CAREER NOTES: Selected by Minnesota Vikings in third round (88th pick overall) of 2000 NFL draft. ... Signed by Vikings (July 23, 2000). ... Inactive for all 16 games (2000).
CHAMPIONSHIP GAME EXPERIENCE: Member of Vikings for NFC championship game (2000 season); inactive.

			RUSHING				RECEIVING				TOTALS		
Year	Team	G	GS	Att.	Yds.	Avg.	TD	No.	Yds.	Avg.	TD	TD	2pt.	Pts.	Fum.
2000—Minnesota NFL								Did not play.						

CHAPMAN, LAMAR   DB   BROWNS

PERSONAL: Born November 6, 1976, in Liberal, Kan. ... 6-0/186.
HIGH SCHOOL: Liberal (Kan.).
COLLEGE: Kansas State.
TRANSACTIONS/CAREER NOTES: Selected by Cleveland Browns in fifth round (146th pick overall) of 2000 NFL draft. ... Signed by Browns (June 16, 2000).
HONORS: Named free safety on THE SPORTING NEWS college All-America second team (1999).
PRO STATISTICS: 2000—Returned one punt for five yards and fumbled once.

				INTERCEPTIONS		
Year Team	G	GS	No.	Yds.	Avg.	TD
2000—Cleveland NFL	7	0	1	0	0.0	0

CHARLTON, IKE   S   SEAHAWKS

PERSONAL: Born October 6, 1977, in Orlando, Fla. ... 5-11/205. ... Full name: Isaac C. Charlton IV.
HIGH SCHOOL: Dr. Phillips (Orlando, Fla.).
COLLEGE: Virginia Tech.
TRANSACTIONS/CAREER NOTES: Selected after junior season by Seattle Seahawks in second round (52nd pick overall) of 2000 NFL draft. ... Signed by Seahawks (July 20, 2000).
PLAYING EXPERIENCE: Seattle NFL, 2000. ... Games/Games started: 2000 (16/0).

C

CHASE, MARTIN   DT   SAINTS

PERSONAL: Born December 19, 1974, in Lawton, Okla. ... 6-2/310. ... Full name: Cecil Martin Chase.
HIGH SCHOOL: Eisenhower (Lawton, Okla.).
COLLEGE: Oklahoma.
TRANSACTIONS/CAREER NOTES: Selected by Baltimore Ravens in fifth round (124th pick overall) of 1998 NFL draft. ... Signed by Ravens (July 17, 1998). ... On injured reserve with ankle injury (August 25, 1998-entire season). ... Assigned by Ravens to Frankfurt Galaxy in 2000 NFL Europe enhancement allocation program (February 18, 2000). ... Claimed on waivers by New Orleans Saints (August 28, 2000). ... Granted free agency (March 2, 2001).
PLAYING EXPERIENCE: Baltimore NFL, 1999; Frankfurt NFLE, 2000; New Orleans NFL, 2000. ... Games/Games started: 1999 (3/0), NFLE 2000 (games played unavailable), NFL 2000 (9/0). Total NFL: 12/0.

CHATHAM, MATT   LB   PATRIOTS

PERSONAL: Born June 28, 1977, in Sioux City, Iowa. ... 6-4/240.
HIGH SCHOOL: Sioux City (Iowa).
COLLEGE: South Dakota.
TRANSACTIONS/CAREER NOTES: Signed as non-drafted free agent by St. Louis Rams (April 26, 1999). ... Released by Rams (June 26, 1999). ... Signed by Rams (February 11, 2000). ... Claimed on waivers by New England Patriots (August 28, 2000).
PLAYING EXPERIENCE: New England NFL, 2000. ... Games/Games started: 2000 (6/0).

CHAVOUS, COREY   CB   CARDINALS

PERSONAL: Born January 15, 1976, in Aiken, S.C. ... 6-1/202. ... Cousin of Fred Vinson, cornerback, Seattle Seahawks. ... Name pronounced CHAY-vus.
HIGH SCHOOL: Silver Bluff (Aiken, S.C.).
COLLEGE: Vanderbilt.
TRANSACTIONS/CAREER NOTES: Selected by Arizona Cardinals in second round (33rd pick overall) of 1998 NFL draft. ... Signed by Cardinals (July 23, 1998). ... Granted free agency (March 2, 2001).
PRO STATISTICS: 1998—Recovered one fumble.

				INTERCEPTIONS		
Year Team	G	GS	No.	Yds.	Avg.	TD
1998—Arizona NFL	16	5	2	0	0.0	0
1999—Arizona NFL	15	4	1	1	1.0	0
2000—Arizona NFL	16	1	1	0	0.0	0
Pro totals (3 years)	47	10	4	1	0.3	0

CHERRY, Je'ROD   S

PERSONAL: Born May 30, 1973, in Charlotte. ... 6-1/205. ... Full name: Je'Rod L. Cherry. ... Name pronounced juh-ROD.
HIGH SCHOOL: Berkeley (Calif.).
COLLEGE: California (degree in political science, 1995).
TRANSACTIONS/CAREER NOTES: Selected by New Orleans Saints in second round (40th pick overall) of 1996 NFL draft. ... Signed by Saints (July 3, 1996). ... Granted free agency (February 12, 1999). ... Re-signed by Saints (July 21, 1999). ... Granted unconditional free agency (February 11, 2000). ... Signed by Oakland Raiders (February 19, 2000). ... Released by Raiders (August 27, 2000). ... Signed by Philadelphia Eagles (September 20, 2000). ... Granted unconditional free agency (March 2, 2001).
PLAYING EXPERIENCE: New Orleans NFL, 1996-1999; Philadelphia NFL, 2000. ... Games/Games started: 1996 (13/0), 1997 (16/0), 1998 (14/0), 1999 (16/0), 2000 (13/0). Total: 72/0.
PRO STATISTICS: 1996—Recovered one fumble. 1998—Credited with two sacks. 2000—Recovered one fumble.

CHESTER, LARRY　　　DT　　　PANTHERS

PERSONAL: Born October 17, 1975, in Hammond, La. ... 6-2/310.
HIGH SCHOOL: Hammond (La.).
JUNIOR COLLEGE: Southwest Mississippi Junior College.
COLLEGE: Temple.
TRANSACTIONS/CAREER NOTES: Signed as non-drafted free agent by Indianapolis Colts (April 24, 1998). ... Released by Colts (August 31, 1998). ... Re-signed by Colts to practice squad (September 2, 1998). ... Activated (September 11, 1998). ... Granted free agency (March 2, 2001). ... Signed by Carolina Panthers (May 15, 2001).
PRO STATISTICS: 1999—Recovered one fumble. 2000—Recovered one fumble.

Year Team	G	GS	SACKS
1998—Indianapolis NFL	14	2	3.0
1999—Indianapolis NFL	16	8	1.0
2000—Indianapolis NFL	16	0	2.5
Pro totals (3 years)	46	10	6.5

CHIAVERINI, DARRIN　　　WR　　　BROWNS

PERSONAL: Born October 12, 1977, in Orange County, Calif. ... 6-2/210. ... Name pronounced SHEVV-er-re-nee.
HIGH SCHOOL: Corona (Calif.).
COLLEGE: Colorado.
TRANSACTIONS/CAREER NOTES: Selected by Cleveland Browns in fifth round (148th pick overall) of 1999 NFL draft. ... Signed by Browns (July 22, 1999).
PRO STATISTICS: 1999—Returned two kickoffs for 35 yards and recovered one fumble.
SINGLE GAME HIGHS (regular season): Receptions—10 (December 19, 1999, vs. Jacksonville); yards—108 (December 19, 1999, vs. Jacksonville); and touchdown receptions—1 (September 24, 2000, vs. Oakland).
STATISTICAL PLATEAUS: 100-yard receiving games: 1999 (1).

			RECEIVING				TOTALS			
Year Team	G	GS	No.	Yds.	Avg.	TD	TD	2pt.	Pts.	Fum.
1999—Cleveland NFL	16	8	44	487	11.1	4	4	0	24	0
2000—Cleveland NFL	10	2	8	68	8.5	1	1	0	6	1
Pro totals (2 years)	26	10	52	555	10.7	5	5	0	30	1

CHREBET, WAYNE　　　WR　　　JETS

PERSONAL: Born August 14, 1973, in Garfield, N.J. ... 5-10/188. ... Name pronounced kra-BET.
HIGH SCHOOL: Garfield (N.J.).
COLLEGE: Hofstra.
TRANSACTIONS/CAREER NOTES: Signed as non-drafted free agent by New York Jets (April 25, 1995).
CHAMPIONSHIP GAME EXPERIENCE: Played in AFC championship game (1998 season).
PRO STATISTICS: 1995—Rushed once for one yard. 1996—Recovered two fumbles. 1997—Returned one kickoff for five yards. 2000—Rushed three times for minus three yards and recovered one fumble.
SINGLE GAME HIGHS (regular season): Receptions—12 (October 13, 1996, vs. Jacksonville); yards—162 (October 13, 1996, vs. Jacksonville); and touchdown receptions—2 (October 23, 2000, vs. Miami).
STATISTICAL PLATEAUS: 100-yard receiving games: 1996 (1), 1997 (1), 1998 (5), 1999 (1), 2000 (2). Total: 10.

			RECEIVING				PUNT RETURNS				TOTALS			
Year Team	G	GS	No.	Yds.	Avg.	TD	No.	Yds.	Avg.	TD	TD	2pt.	Pts.	Fum.
1995—New York Jets NFL	16	16	66	726	11.0	4	0	0	0.0	0	4	0	24	1
1996—New York Jets NFL	16	9	84	909	10.8	3	28	139	5.0	0	3	0	18	5
1997—New York Jets NFL	16	1	58	799	13.8	3	0	0	0.0	0	3	0	18	0
1998—New York Jets NFL	16	15	75	1083	14.4	8	0	0	0.0	0	8	0	48	0
1999—New York Jets NFL	11	11	48	631	13.1	3	0	0	0.0	0	3	0	18	0
2000—New York Jets NFL	16	16	69	937	13.6	8	0	0	0.0	0	8	0	48	0
Pro totals (6 years)	91	68	400	5085	12.7	29	28	139	5.0	0	29	0	174	6

CHRISTIAN, BOB　　　FB　　　FALCONS

PERSONAL: Born November 14, 1968, in St. Louis. ... 5-11/232. ... Full name: Robert Douglas Christian.
HIGH SCHOOL: McCluer North (Florissant, Mo.).
COLLEGE: Northwestern.
TRANSACTIONS/CAREER NOTES: Selected by Atlanta Falcons in 12th round (310th pick overall) of 1991 NFL draft. ... Signed by Falcons (July 18, 1991). ... Released by Falcons (August 20, 1991). ... Selected by London Monarchs in 16th round (175th pick overall) of 1992 World League draft. ... Signed by San Diego Chargers (July 10, 1992). ... Released by Chargers (August 25, 1992). ... Signed by Chicago Bears to practice squad (September 8, 1992). ... Activated (December 18, 1992). ... On injured reserve with knee injury (December 2, 1994-remainder of season). ... Selected by Carolina Panthers from Bears in NFL expansion draft (February 15, 1995). ... Granted free agency (February 16, 1996). ... Re-signed by Panthers (July 19, 1996). ... On injured reserve with shoulder injury (August 25, 1996-entire season). ... Granted unconditional free agency (February 14, 1997). ... Signed by Falcons (March 6, 1997). ... On injured reserve with knee injury (December 15, 1998-remainder of season).
PRO STATISTICS: 1995—Recovered one fumble. 1997—Recovered one fumble. 1998—Recovered two fumbles. 2000—Recovered one fumble for 10 yards.
SINGLE GAME HIGHS (regular season): Attempts—9 (December 26, 1999, vs. Arizona); yards—54 (December 26, 1998, vs. Arizona); and rushing touchdowns—2 (December 26, 1999, vs. Arizona).

C

Year—Team	G	GS	RUSHING Att.	Yds.	Avg.	TD	RECEIVING No.	Yds.	Avg.	TD	TOTALS TD	2pt.	Pts.	Fum.
1992—Chicago NFL	2	0	0	0	0.0	0	0	0	0.0	0	0	0	0	0
1993—Chicago NFL	14	1	8	19	2.4	0	16	160	10.0	0	0	0	0	0
1994—Chicago NFL	12	0	7	29	4.1	0	2	30	15.0	0	0	0	0	0
1995—Carolina NFL	14	12	41	158	3.9	0	29	255	8.8	1	1	1	8	1
1996—Carolina NFL							Did not play.							
1997—Atlanta NFL	16	12	7	8	1.1	0	22	154	7.0	1	1	0	6	3
1998—Atlanta NFL	14	11	8	21	2.6	2	19	214	11.3	1	3	0	18	1
1999—Atlanta NFL	16	14	38	174	4.6	5	40	354	8.9	2	7	0	42	1
2000—Atlanta NFL	16	14	9	19	2.1	0	44	315	7.2	0	0	0	0	0
Pro totals (8 years)	104	64	118	428	3.6	7	172	1482	8.6	5	12	1	74	6

CHRISTIE, STEVE — K — BILLS

PERSONAL: Born November 13, 1967, in Oakville, Ont. ... 6-0/190. ... Full name: Geoffrey Stephen Christie.
HIGH SCHOOL: Trafalgar (Oakville, Ont.).
COLLEGE: William & Mary.
TRANSACTIONS/CAREER NOTES: Signed as non-drafted free agent by Tampa Bay Buccaneers (May 8, 1990). ... Granted unconditional free agency (February 1, 1992). ... Signed by Buffalo Bills (February 5, 1992). ... Granted unconditional free agency (March 2, 2001). ... Re-signed by Bills (April 21, 2001).
CHAMPIONSHIP GAME EXPERIENCE: Played in AFC championship game (1992 and 1993 seasons). ... Played in Super Bowl XXVII (1992 season) and Super Bowl XXVIII (1993 season).
POST SEASON RECORDS: Holds Super Bowl single-game record for longest field goal—54 yards (January 30, 1994, vs. Dallas). ... Shares NFL postseason single-game record for most field goals made—5; and most field goals attempted—6 (January 17, 1993, at Miami).
PRO STATISTICS: 1994—Recovered one fumble. 1999—Recovered one fumble.

Year—Team	G	KICKING XPM	XPA	FGM	FGA	Lg.	50+	Pts.
1990—Tampa Bay NFL	16	27	27	23	27	54	2-2	96
1991—Tampa Bay NFL	16	22	22	15	20	49	0-0	67
1992—Buffalo NFL	16	§43	§44	24	30	†54	3-5	115
1993—Buffalo NFL	16	36	37	23	32	*59	1-6	105
1994—Buffalo NFL	16	§38	§38	24	28	52	2-2	110
1995—Buffalo NFL	16	33	35	31	40	51	2-5	126
1996—Buffalo NFL	16	33	33	24	29	48	0-1	105
1997—Buffalo NFL	16	21	21	24	30	†55	1-2	93
1998—Buffalo NFL	16	41	41	33	*41	52	1-3	§140
1999—Buffalo NFL	16	33	33	25	34	52	3-3	108
2000—Buffalo NFL	16	31	31	26	35	48	0-1	109
Pro totals (11 years)	176	358	362	272	346	59	15-30	1174

CHRISTY, JEFF — C — BUCCANEERS

PERSONAL: Born February 3, 1969, in Natrona Heights, Pa. ... 6-2/285. ... Full name: Jeffrey Allen Christy. ... Brother of Greg Christy, offensive tackle with Buffalo Bills (1985).
HIGH SCHOOL: Freeport (Pa.) Area.
COLLEGE: Pittsburgh.
TRANSACTIONS/CAREER NOTES: Selected by Phoenix Cardinals in fourth round (91st pick overall) of 1992 NFL draft. ... Signed by Cardinals (July 21, 1992). ... Released by Cardinals (August 31, 1992). ... Signed by Minnesota Vikings (March 16, 1993). ... On injured reserve with ankle injury (November 26, 1997-remainder of season). ... Granted unconditional free agency (February 11, 2000). ... Signed by Tampa Bay Buccaneers (February 15, 2000).
PLAYING EXPERIENCE: Minnesota NFL, 1993-1999; Tampa Bay NFL, 2000. ... Games/Games started: 1993 (9/0), 1994 (16/16), 1995 (16/16), 1996 (16/16), 1997 (12/12), 1998 (16/16), 1999 (16/16), 2000 (16/16). Total: 117/108.
CHAMPIONSHIP GAME EXPERIENCE: Played in NFC championship game (1998 season).
HONORS: Played in Pro Bowl (1998-2000 seasons).

CLAIBORNE, CHRIS — LB — LIONS

PERSONAL: Born July 26, 1978, in Riverdale, Calif. ... 6-3/255.
HIGH SCHOOL: John W. North (Riverside, Calif.).
COLLEGE: Southern California.
TRANSACTIONS/CAREER NOTES: Selected after junior season by Detroit Lions in first round (ninth pick overall) of 1999 NFL draft. ... Signed by Lions (July 24, 1999).
HONORS: Butkus Award winner (1998). ... Named inside linebacker on THE SPORTING NEWS college All-America first team (1998).
PRO STATISTICS: 1999—Recovered three fumbles for 27 yards. 2000—Intercepted one pass for one yard.

Year—Team	G	GS	SACKS
1999—Detroit NFL	15	13	1.5
2000—Detroit NFL	16	14	0.5
Pro totals (2 years)	31	27	2.0

CLANCY, KENDRICK — NT — STEELERS

PERSONAL: Born September 17, 1978, in Tuscaloosa, Ala. ... 6-1/280.
HIGH SCHOOL: Holt (Tuscaloosa, Ala.).
JUNIOR COLLEGE: East Central Community College (Miss.).
COLLEGE: Mississippi.
TRANSACTIONS/CAREER NOTES: Selected by Pittsburgh Steelers in third round (72nd pick overall) of 2000 NFL draft. ... Signed by Steelers (July 16, 2000).
PLAYING EXPERIENCE: Pittsburgh NFL, 2000. ... Games/Games started: 2000 (9/0).

C

CLARIDGE, TRAVIS · OT/G · FALCONS

PERSONAL: Born March 23, 1978, in Detroit. ... 6-5/300.
HIGH SCHOOL: Fort Vancouver (Vancouver, Wash.).
COLLEGE: Southern California.
TRANSACTIONS/CAREER NOTES: Selected by Atlanta Falcons in second round (37th pick overall) of 2000 NFL draft. ... Signed by Falcons (May 16, 2000).
PLAYING EXPERIENCE: Atlanta NFL, 2000. ... Games/Games started: 2000 (16/16).

CLARK, DANNY · LB · JAGUARS

PERSONAL: Born May 9, 1977, in Blue Island, Ill. ... 6-2/240. ... Full name: Daniel Clark IV.
HIGH SCHOOL: Hillcrest (Ill.).
COLLEGE: Illinois (degree in speech communications).
TRANSACTIONS/CAREER NOTES: Selected by Jacksonville Jaguars in seventh round (245th pick overall) of 2000 NFL draft. ... Signed by Jaguars (June 6, 2000).
PLAYING EXPERIENCE: Jacksonville NFL, 2000. ... Games/Games started: 2000 (16/0).
PRO STATISTICS: 2000—Recovered two fumbles for 44 yards.

CLARK, DESMOND · TE · BRONCOS

PERSONAL: Born April 20, 1977, in Bartow, Fla. ... 6-3/255. ... Full name: Desmond Darice Clark.
HIGH SCHOOL: Kathleen (Lakeland, Fla.).
COLLEGE: Wake Forest.
TRANSACTIONS/CAREER NOTES: Selected by Denver Broncos in sixth round (179th pick overall) of 1999 NFL draft. ... Signed by Broncos (June 14, 1999).
SINGLE GAME HIGHS (regular season): Receptions—6 (October 22, 2000, vs. Cincinnati); yards—73 (November 26, 2000, vs. Seattle); and touchdown receptions—1 (November 26, 2000, vs. Seattle).

				RECEIVING				TOTALS		
Year Team	G	GS	No.	Yds.	Avg.	TD	TD	2pt.	Pts.	Fum.
1999—Denver NFL	9	0	1	5	5.0	0	0	0	0	0
2000—Denver NFL	16	2	27	339	12.6	3	3	0	18	0
Pro totals (2 years)	25	2	28	344	12.3	3	3	0	18	0

CLARK, GREG · TE · 49ERS

PERSONAL: Born April 7, 1972, in Centerville, Utah. ... 6-4/251. ... Full name: Gregory Jay Clark.
HIGH SCHOOL: Viewmont (Bountiful, Utah).
JUNIOR COLLEGE: Ricks College (Idaho).
COLLEGE: Stanford (degree in psychology, 1996).
TRANSACTIONS/CAREER NOTES: Selected by San Francisco 49ers in third round (77th pick overall) of 1997 NFL draft. ... Signed by 49ers (July 17, 1997). ... Granted free agency (February 11, 2000). ... Re-signed by 49ers (June 7, 2000).
CHAMPIONSHIP GAME EXPERIENCE: Played in NFC championship game (1997 season).
POST SEASON RECORDS: Shares NFL postseason career record for most two-point conversions—1.
PRO STATISTICS: 2000—Recovered one fumble.
SINGLE GAME HIGHS (regular season): Receptions—5 (December 18, 1999, vs. Carolina); yards—62 (December 3, 2000, vs. San Diego); and touchdown receptions—1 (December 17, 2000, vs. Chicago).

				RECEIVING				TOTALS		
Year Team	G	GS	No.	Yds.	Avg.	TD	TD	2pt.	Pts.	Fum.
1997—San Francisco NFL	15	4	8	96	12.0	1	1	0	6	0
1998—San Francisco NFL	13	8	12	124	10.3	1	1	1	8	0
1999—San Francisco NFL	12	11	34	347	10.2	0	0	0	0	1
2000—San Francisco NFL	15	15	38	342	9.0	2	2	0	12	1
Pro totals (4 years)	55	38	92	909	9.9	4	4	1	26	2

CLARKE, PHIL · LB · SAINTS

PERSONAL: Born January 9, 1977, in Miami. ... 6-0/241.
HIGH SCHOOL: South Miami.
COLLEGE: Pittsburgh.
TRANSACTIONS/CAREER NOTES: Signed as non-drafted free agent by New Orleans Saints (May 17, 1999). ... Released by Saints (September 5, 1999). ... Re-signed by Saints to practice squad (September 6, 1999). ... Activated (November 10, 1999).
PLAYING EXPERIENCE: New Orleans NFL, 1999 and 2000. ... Games/Games started: 1999 (8/3), 2000 (14/4). Total: 22/7.
PRO STATISTICS: 2000—Credited with one sack and recovered one fumble.

CLEELAND, CAM · TE · SAINTS

PERSONAL: Born April 15, 1975, in Sedro Woolley, Wash. ... 6-4/272. ... Full name: Cameron Cleeland. ... Nephew of Phil Misley, pitcher in Milwaukee Braves organization (1956-58).
HIGH SCHOOL: Sedro Woolley (Wash.).
COLLEGE: Washington.

C

TRANSACTIONS/CAREER NOTES: Selected by New Orleans Saints in second round (40th pick overall) of 1998 NFL draft. ... Signed by Saints (June 9, 1998). ... On injured reserve with Achilles' tendon injury (August 22, 2000-entire season). ... Granted free agency (March 2, 2001).
PRO STATISTICS: 1998—Recovered two fumbles for seven yards.
SINGLE GAME HIGHS (regular season): Receptions—10 (December 27, 1998, vs. Buffalo); yards—112 (December 27, 1998, vs. Buffalo); and touchdown receptions—1 (December 12, 1999, vs. New Orleans).
STATISTICAL PLATEAUS: 100-yard receiving games: 1998 (1).

				RECEIVING				TOTALS		
Year Team	G	GS	No.	Yds.	Avg.	TD	TD	2pt.	Pts.	Fum.
1998—New Orleans NFL	16	16	54	684	12.7	6	6	0	36	1
1999—New Orleans NFL	11	8	26	325	12.5	1	1	†1	8	1
2000—New Orleans NFL					Did not play.					
Pro totals (2 years)	27	24	80	1009	12.6	7	7	1	44	2

CLEMENT, ANTHONY   OT   CARDINALS

PERSONAL: Born April 10, 1976, in Lafayette, La. ... 6-8/351.
HIGH SCHOOL: Cecilia (La.).
COLLEGE: Southwestern Louisiana.
TRANSACTIONS/CAREER NOTES: Selected by Arizona Cardinals in second round (36th pick overall) of 1998 NFL draft. ... Signed by Cardinals (June 16, 1998). ... On injured reserve with back injury (November 17, 1998-remainder of season). ... Granted free agency (March 2, 2001).
PLAYING EXPERIENCE: Arizona NFL, 1998-2000. ... Games/Games started: 1998 (1/0), 1999 (16/14), 2000 (16/16). Total: 33/30.
PRO STATISTICS: 2000—Recovered one fumble.

C

CLEMONS, CHARLIE   LB   SAINTS

PERSONAL: Born July 4, 1972, in Griffin, Ga. ... 6-2/250. ... Full name: Charlie Fitzgerald Clemons.
HIGH SCHOOL: Griffin (Ga.).
JUNIOR COLLEGE: Northeast Oklahoma Junior College.
COLLEGE: Georgia (degree in recreation and leisure studies, 1993).
TRANSACTIONS/CAREER NOTES: Signed by Winnipeg Blue Bombers of CFL (May 1994). ... Transferred to Ottawa Rough Riders of CFL (August 1995). ... Transferred back to Blue Bombers (January 1996). ... Signed as non-drafted free agent by St. Louis Rams (February 19, 1997). ... On injured reserve with hamstring injury (November 24, 1997-remainder of season). ... Granted free agency (February 11, 2000). ... Tendered offer sheet by New Orleans Saints (February 16, 2000). ... Rams declined to match offer (February 22, 2000). ... On injured reserve with Achilles' tendon injury (October 2, 2000-remainder of season).
CHAMPIONSHIP GAME EXPERIENCE: Played in NFC championship game (1999 season). ... Member of Super Bowl championship team (1999 season).
PRO STATISTICS: CFL: 1994—Recovered one fumble. 1995—Returned one kickoff for 10 yards. NFL: 1998—Returned one kickoff for no yards. 1999—Intercepted one pass for no yards and recovered one fumble.

Year Team	G	GS	SACKS
1994—Winnipeg CFL	7	...	0.0
1995—Winnipeg CFL	6	...	3.0
—Ottawa CFL	7	...	3.0
1996—Winnipeg CFL	14	...	6.0
1997—St. Louis NFL	5	0	0.0
1998—St. Louis NFL	16	0	2.0
1999—St. Louis NFL	16	0	3.0
2000—New Orleans NFL		Did not play.	
CFL totals (3 years)	34	...	12.0
NFL totals (3 years)	37	0	5.0
Pro totals (6 years)	71	...	17.0

CLEMONS, DUANE   DE   CHIEFS

PERSONAL: Born May 23, 1974, in Riverside, Calif. ... 6-5/277.
HIGH SCHOOL: John W. North (Riverside, Calif.).
COLLEGE: California (degree in ethnic studies, 1993).
TRANSACTIONS/CAREER NOTES: Selected after junior season by Minnesota Vikings in first round (16th pick overall) of 1996 NFL draft. ... Signed by Vikings (July 25, 1996). ... Granted unconditional free agency (February 11, 2000). ... Signed by Kansas City Chiefs (March 24, 2000).
CHAMPIONSHIP GAME EXPERIENCE: Played in NFC championship game (1998 season).
PRO STATISTICS: 1996—Recovered one fumble for eight yards. 1997—Recovered one fumble. 1999—Recovered four fumbles. 2000—Recovered one fumble.

Year Team	G	GS	SACKS
1996—Minnesota NFL	13	0	0.0
1997—Minnesota NFL	13	3	7.0
1998—Minnesota NFL	16	4	2.5
1999—Minnesota NFL	16	9	9.0
2000—Kansas City NFL	12	12	7.5
Pro totals (5 years)	70	28	26.0

CLIFTON, CHAD   OT   PACKERS

PERSONAL: Born June 26, 1976, in Martin, Tenn. ... 6-5/325. ... Full name: Jeffrey Chad Clifton.
HIGH SCHOOL: Westview (Martin, Tenn.).
COLLEGE: Tennessee.

TRANSACTIONS/CAREER NOTES: Selected by Green Bay Packers in second round (44th pick overall) of 2000 NFL draft. ... Signed by Packers (July 24, 2000).
PLAYING EXPERIENCE: Green Bay NFL, 2000. ... Games/Games started: 2000 (13/10).
HONORS: Named offensive tackle on THE SPORTING NEWS college All-America second team (1999).

CLOUD, MIKE — RB — CHIEFS

PERSONAL: Born July 1, 1975, in Charleston, S.C. ... 5-10/205. ... Full name: Michael Alexander Cloud.
HIGH SCHOOL: Portsmouth (R.I.).
COLLEGE: Boston College.
TRANSACTIONS/CAREER NOTES: Selected by Kansas City Chiefs in second round (54th pick overall) of 1999 NFL draft. ... Signed by Chiefs (July 30, 1999).
SINGLE GAME HIGHS (regular season): Attempts—11 (November 28, 1999, vs. Oakland); yards—58 (November 28, 1999, vs. Oakland); and rushing touchdowns—1 (October 2, 2000, vs. San Francisco).
PRO STATISTICS 2000—Returned blocked punt for six yards and a touchdown.

			RUSHING				RECEIVING				KICKOFF RETURNS				TOTALS		
Year Team	G	GS	Att.	Yds.	Avg.	TD	No.	Yds.	Avg.	TD	No.	Yds.	Avg.	TD	TD	2pt.	Pts. Fum.
1999—Kansas City NFL	11	0	35	128	3.7	0	3	25	8.3	0	2	28	14.0	0	0	0	0 0
2000—Kansas City NFL	16	4	30	84	2.8	1	2	16	8.0	0	36	779	21.6	0	2	0	12 0
Pro totals (2 years)	27	4	65	212	3.3	1	5	41	8.2	0	38	807	21.2	0	2	0	12 0

COADY, RICH — S — RAMS

PERSONAL: Born January 26, 1976, in Dallas. ... 6-0/203. ... Full name: Richard Joseph Coady IV. ... Son of Rich Coady, tight end/center with Chicago Bears (1970-74).
HIGH SCHOOL: J.J. Pearce (Richardson, Texas).
COLLEGE: Texas A&M.
TRANSACTIONS/CAREER NOTES: Selected by St. Louis Rams in third round (68th pick overall) of 1999 NFL draft. ... Signed by Rams (July 16, 1999). ... On injured reserve with neck injury (December 13, 2000-remainder of season).
PLAYING EXPERIENCE: St. Louis NFL, 1999 and 2000. ... Games/Games started: 1999 (16/0), 2000 (12/2). Total: 28/2.
CHAMPIONSHIP GAME EXPERIENCE: Played in NFC championship game (1999 season). ... Member of Super Bowl championship team (1999 season).

COAKLEY, DEXTER — LB — COWBOYS

PERSONAL: Born October 20, 1972, in Charleston, S.C. ... 5-10/228. ... Full name: William Dexter Coakley.
HIGH SCHOOL: Wando (Mt. Pleasant, S.C.), then Fork Union (Va.) Military Academy.
COLLEGE: Appalachian State.
TRANSACTIONS/CAREER NOTES: Selected by Dallas Cowboys in third round (65th pick overall) of 1997 NFL draft. ... Signed by Cowboys (July 14, 1997). ... Granted free agency (February 11, 2000). ... Re-signed by Cowboys (April 28, 2000). ... Granted unconditional free agency (March 2, 2001). ... Re-signed by Cowboys (March 7, 2001).
HONORS: Played in Pro Bowl (1999 season).
PRO STATISTICS: 1997—Recovered one fumble for 16 yards and a touchdown. 1998—Recovered one fumble. 1999—Returned one kickoff for three yards. 2000—Rushed once for 26 yards and recovered one fumble for eight yards.

			INTERCEPTIONS				SACKS
Year Team	G	GS	No.	Yds.	Avg.	TD	No.
1997—Dallas NFL	16	16	1	6	6.0	0	2.5
1998—Dallas NFL	16	16	1	18	18.0	0	2.0
1999—Dallas NFL	16	16	4	119	29.8	1	1.0
2000—Dallas NFL	16	16	0	0	0.0	0	0.0
Pro totals (4 years)	64	64	6	143	23.8	1	5.5

COATES, BEN — TE

PERSONAL: Born August 16, 1969, in Greenwood, S.C. ... 6-5/245. ... Full name: Ben Terrence Coates.
HIGH SCHOOL: Greenwood (S.C.).
COLLEGE: Livingstone College, N.C. (degree in sports management).
TRANSACTIONS/CAREER NOTES: Selected after junior season by New England Patriots in fifth round (124th pick overall) of 1991 NFL draft. ... Signed by Patriots (April 25, 1991). ... Granted free agency (February 17, 1994). ... Re-signed by Patriots (April 2, 1994). ... Released by Patriots (February 9, 2000). ... Signed by Baltimore Ravens (July 24, 2000). ... Granted unconditional free agency (March 2, 2001).
CHAMPIONSHIP GAME EXPERIENCE: Played in AFC championship game (1996 and 2000 seasons). ... Played in Super Bowl XXXI (1996 season). ... Member of Super Bowl championship team (2000 season).
HONORS: Named tight end on THE SPORTING NEWS NFL All-Pro team (1994 and 1995). ... Played in Pro Bowl (1994-1998 seasons).
RECORDS: Holds NFL single-season record for most receptions by tight end—96 (1994).
PRO STATISTICS: 1991—Rushed once for minus six yards and returned one kickoff for six yards. 1992—Rushed once for two yards. 1994—Rushed once for no yards and recovered two fumbles. 1997—Returned one kickoff for 20 yards.
SINGLE GAME HIGHS (regular season): Receptions—12 (November 27, 1994, vs. Indianapolis); yards—161 (September 4, 1994, vs. Miami); and touchdown receptions—3 (November 26, 1995, vs. Buffalo).
STATISTICAL PLATEAUS: 100-yard receiving games: 1993 (1), 1994 (5), 1995 (1), 1996 (1), 1998 (1). Total: 9.

Year Team	G	GS	RECEIVING				TOTALS			
			No.	Yds.	Avg.	TD	TD	2pt.	Pts.	Fum.
1991—New England NFL	16	2	10	95	9.5	1	1	0	6	0
1992—New England NFL	16	2	20	171	8.6	3	3	0	18	1
1993—New England NFL	16	10	53	659	12.4	8	8	0	48	0
1994—New England NFL	16	16	§96	1174	12.2	7	7	0	42	2
1995—New England NFL	16	15	84	915	10.9	6	6	0	36	4
1996—New England NFL	16	15	62	682	11.0	9	9	1	56	1
1997—New England NFL	16	16	66	737	11.2	8	8	0	48	0
1998—New England NFL	14	14	67	668	10.0	6	6	0	36	0
1999—New England NFL	16	15	32	370	11.6	2	2	0	12	0
2000—Baltimore NFL	16	8	9	84	9.3	0	0	▲1	2	0
Pro totals (10 years)	158	113	499	5555	11.1	50	50	2	304	8

COCHRAN, ANTONIO — DT — SEAHAWKS

PERSONAL: Born June 21, 1976, in Montezuma, Ga. ... 6-4/297. ... Full name: Antonio Desez Cochran.
HIGH SCHOOL: Macon County (Montezuma, Ga.).
JUNIOR COLLEGE: Middle Georgia College.
COLLEGE: Georgia.
TRANSACTIONS/CAREER NOTES: Selected by Seattle Seahawks in fourth round (115th pick overall) of 1999 NFL draft. ... Signed by Seahawks (July 27, 1999).
PLAYING EXPERIENCE: Seattle NFL, 1999 and 2000. ... Games/Games started: 1999 (4/0), 2000 (15/0). Total: 19/0.
PRO STATISTICS: 2000—Credited with $1/2$ sack.

CODIE, NAKIA — DB — STEELERS

PERSONAL: Born January 20, 1976, in Cleburne, Texas. ... 6-2/208.
HIGH SCHOOL: Cleburne (Texas).
COLLEGE: Baylor.
TRANSACTIONS/CAREER NOTES: Signed as non-drafted free agent by Pittsburgh Steelers (April 4, 2000). ... Released by Steelers (August 22, 2000). ... Re-signed by Steelers to practice squad (August 29, 2000). ... Activated (November 18, 2000).
PLAYING EXPERIENCE: Pittsburgh NFL, 2000. ... Games/Games started: 2000 (6/0).
PRO STATISTICS: 2000—Intercepted one pass for 14 yards.

CODY, MAC — WR

PERSONAL: Born August 7, 1972, in St. Louis. ... 5-11/182. ... Full name: Maclin Cody.
HIGH SCHOOL: Vashon (St. Louis).
COLLEGE: Memphis State.
TRANSACTIONS/CAREER NOTES: Signed as non-drafted free agent by Indianapolis Colts (April 1994). ... Released by Colts (August 1994). ... Signed by Winnipeg Blue Bombers of CFL (September 1994). ... Released by Blue Bombers (September 1994). ... Signed by Ottawa Roughriders of CFL (September 17, 1994). ... Released by Roughriders (September 29, 1994). ... Signed by Birmingham Barracudas of CFL (May 1995). ... Selected by Hamilton Tiger-Cats of CFL in 1996 U.S. Team Dispersal Draft. ... Played with Orlando Predators of Arena League (1997). ... Signed by Montreal Alouettes of CFL (May 22, 1998). ... Signed by St. Louis Rams (February 25, 1999). ... Claimed on waivers by Arizona Cardinals (September 5, 1999). ... Released by Cardinals (February 19, 2001).
PRO STATISTICS: CFL: 1996—Rushed once for one yard. NFL: 1999—Recovered one fumble. 2000—Recovered one fumble.
SINGLE GAME HIGHS (regular season): Receptions—3 (October 1, 2000, vs. San Francisco); yards—44 (September 24, 2000, vs. Green Bay); and touchdown receptions—1 (January 2, 2000, vs. Green Bay).

Year Team	G	GS	RECEIVING				PUNT RETURNS				KICKOFF RETURNS				TOTALS			
			No.	Yds.	Avg.	TD	No.	Yds.	Avg.	TD	No.	Yds.	Avg.	TD	TD	2pt.	Pts.	Fum.
1994—Ottawa CFL	2	...	0	0	0.0	0	13	100	7.7	0	13	276	21.2	0	0	0	0	0
1995—Birmingham CFL	15	...	31	452	14.6	3	26	278	10.7	0	18	334	18.6	0	3	0	18	0
1996—Hamilton CFL	17	...	80	1426	17.8	11	17	123	7.2	0	20	333	16.7	0	11	0	66	0
1997—Orlando Arena Football									Statistics unavailable.									
1998—Montreal CFL	12	...	33	479	14.5	5	7	30	4.3	0	6	115	19.2	0	5	0	30	0
1999—Arizona NFL	13	0	6	60	10.0	1	32	373	‡11.7	0	4	76	19.0	0	1	0	6	2
2000—Arizona NFL	15	1	17	212	12.5	0	31	222	7.2	0	1	18	18.0	0	0	0	0	4
CFL totals (4 years)	46	...	144	2357	16.4	19	63	531	8.4	0	57	1058	18.6	0	19	0	114	0
NFL totals (2 years)	28	1	23	272	11.8	1	63	595	9.4	0	5	94	18.8	0	1	0	6	6
Pro totals (6 years)	74	...	167	2629	15.7	20	126	1126	8.9	0	62	1152	18.6	0	20	0	120	6

COGHILL, GEORGE — S — BRONCOS

PERSONAL: Born March 30, 1970, in Fredericksburg, Va. ... 6-0/210.
HIGH SCHOOL: James Madison (Vienna, Va.).
COLLEGE: Wake Forest.
TRANSACTIONS/CAREER NOTES: Signed as non-drafted free agent by New Orleans Saints (April 27, 1993). ... On injured reserve with knee injury (August 12, 1993-entire season). ... Released by Saints (August 22, 1994). ... Played for Scottish Claymores of World League (1995-1997). ... Signed by Denver Broncos (July 16, 1997). ... Released by Broncos (August 24, 1997). ... Re-signed by Broncos to practice squad (August 25, 1997). ... Released by Broncos (January 26, 1998). ... Re-signed by Broncos (January 28, 1998).
PLAYING EXPERIENCE: Scottish Claymores W.L., 1995-1997; Denver NFL, 1998-2000. ... Games/Games started: 1995 (games played unavailable), 1996 (-), 1997 (-), 1998 (9/0), 1999 (13/5), 2000 (16/0). Total NFL: 38/5.
CHAMPIONSHIP GAME EXPERIENCE: Played in AFC championship game (1998 season). ... Member of Super Bowl championship team (1998 season).
PRO STATISTICS: 1998—Intercepted one pass for 20 yards and returned three punts for 20 yards. 1999—Intercepted one pass for no yards and returned three punts for 25 yards.

COLE, CHRIS   WR   BRONCOS

PERSONAL: Born November 12, 1977, in Orange, Texas. ... 6-0/195. ... Full name: Charles Christopher Cole.
HIGH SCHOOL: West Orange-Stark (Orange, Texas).
COLLEGE: Texas A&M.
TRANSACTIONS/CAREER NOTES: Selected by Denver Broncos in third round (70th pick overall) of 2000 NFL draft. ... Signed by Broncos (July 21, 2000).
PLAYING EXPERIENCE: Denver NFL, 2000. ... Games/Games started: 2000 (8/0).
PRO STATISTICS: 2000—Returned 11 kickoffs for 264 yards.

COLEMAN, BEN   G/OT

PERSONAL: Born May 18, 1971, in South Hill, Va. ... 6-5/327. ... Full name: Benjamin Leon Coleman.
HIGH SCHOOL: Park View Senior (South Hill, Va.).
COLLEGE: Wake Forest.
TRANSACTIONS/CAREER NOTES: Selected by Phoenix Cardinals in second round (32nd pick overall) of 1993 NFL draft. ... Signed by Cardinals (July 6, 1993). ... Cardinals franchise renamed Arizona Cardinals for 1994 season. ... Claimed on waivers by Jacksonville Jaguars (September 27, 1995). ... Granted free agency (February 16, 1996). ... Re-signed by Jaguars (June 6, 1996). ... Granted unconditional free agency (February 14, 1997). ... Re-signed by Jaguars (March 3, 1997). ... Granted unconditional free agency (February 11, 2000). ... Signed by San Diego Chargers (June 15, 2000). ... Granted unconditional free agency (March 2, 2001).
PLAYING EXPERIENCE: Phoenix NFL, 1993; Arizona NFL, 1994; Arizona (3)-Jacksonville (10) NFL, 1995; Jacksonville NFL, 1996-1999; San Diego NFL, 2000. ... Games/Games started: 1993 (12/0), 1994 (15/13), 1995 (Ariz.-3/0; Jack.-10/5; Total: 13/5), 1996 (16/16), 1997 (16/16), 1998 (16/16), 1999 (16/12), 2000 (16/16). Total: 120/94.
CHAMPIONSHIP GAME EXPERIENCE: Played in AFC championship game (1996 and 1999 seasons).
PRO STATISTICS: 1995—Recovered one fumble.

COLEMAN, CHRIS   WR   TITANS

PERSONAL: Born May 8, 1977, in Shelby, N.C. ... 6-0/202.
HIGH SCHOOL: Crest (Shelby, N.C.).
COLLEGE: North Carolina State.
TRANSACTIONS/CAREER NOTES: Signed as non-drafted free agent by Tennessee Titans (April 18, 2000). ... Claimed on waivers by Green Bay Packers (August 23, 2000). ... Releasd by Packers (August 25, 2000). ... Signed by Titans to practice squad (August 29, 2000). ... Released by Titans (September 5, 2000). ... Re-signed by Titans to practice squad (September 8, 2000). ... Activated (September 29, 2000).
PLAYING EXPERIENCE: Tennessee NFL, 2000. ... Games/Games started: 2000 (13/0).
PRO STATISTICS: 2000—Returned two kickoffs for 54 yards.

COLEMAN, COSEY   G   BUCCANEERS

PERSONAL: Born October 27, 1978, in Clarkston, Ga. ... 6-4/322. ... Full name: Cosey Clinton Coleman.
HIGH SCHOOL: DeKalb (Clarkston, Ga.).
COLLEGE: Tennessee.
TRANSACTIONS/CAREER NOTES: Selected after junior season by Tampa Bay Buccaneers in second round (51st pick overall) of 2000 NFL draft. ... Signed by Buccaneers (July 23, 2000).
PLAYING EXPERIENCE: Tampa Bay NFL, 2000. ... Games/Games started: 2000 (8/0).

COLEMAN, KaRON   RB   BRONCOS

PERSONAL: Born May 22, 1978, in Missouri City, Texas. ... 5-7/198.
HIGH SCHOOL: Elkins (Missouri City, Texas).
COLLEGE: Stephen F. Austin State.
TRANSACTIONS/CAREER NOTES: Signed as non-drafted free agent by Denver Broncos (April 17, 2000). ... Released by Broncos (August 27, 2000). ... Re-signed by Broncos to practice squad (August 28, 2000). ... Activated (September 9, 2000). ... Released by Broncos (September 12, 2000). ... Re-signed by Broncos to practice squad (September 9, 2000). ... Activated (October 4, 2000).
PLAYING EXPERIENCE: Denver NFL, 2000. ... Games/Games started: 2000 (9/0).
PRO STATISTICS: 2000—Rushed 54 times for 183 yards and one touchdown, caught one pass for five yards, fumbled twice and recovered one fumble.
SINGLE GAME HIGHS (regular season): Attempts—14 (October 8, 2000, vs. San Diego); yards—52 (December 23, 2000, vs. San Francisco); and rushing touchdowns—1 (December 23, 2000, vs. San Francisco).

COLEMAN, MARCO   DE   REDSKINS

PERSONAL: Born December 18, 1969, in Dayton, Ohio. ... 6-3/267. ... Full name: Marco Darnell Coleman.
HIGH SCHOOL: Patterson Co-op (Dayton, Ohio).
COLLEGE: Georgia Tech.
TRANSACTIONS/CAREER NOTES: Selected after junior season by Miami Dolphins in first round (12th pick overall) of 1992 NFL draft. ... Signed by Dolphins (August 1, 1992). ... Designated by Dolphins as transition player (February 25, 1993). ... Tendered offer sheet by San Diego Chargers (February 28, 1996). ... Dolphins declined to match offer (March 7, 1996). ... Granted unconditional free agency (February 12, 1999). ... Signed by Washington Redskins (June 3, 1999). ... Granted unconditional free agency (February 11, 2000). ... Re-signed by Redskins (February 29, 2000).

C

CHAMPIONSHIP GAME EXPERIENCE: Played in AFC championship game (1992 season).
HONORS: Named linebacker on THE SPORTING NEWS college All-America second team (1991). ... Played in Pro Bowl (2000 season).
PRO STATISTICS: 1997—Intercepted one pass for two yards. 1998—Recovered two fumbles. 1999—Recovered one fumble for 42 yards and a touchdown.

Year Team	G	GS	SACKS
1992—Miami NFL	16	15	6.0
1993—Miami NFL	15	15	5.5
1994—Miami NFL	16	16	6.0
1995—Miami NFL	16	16	6.5
1996—San Diego NFL	16	15	4.0
1997—San Diego NFL	16	16	2.0
1998—San Diego NFL	16	16	3.5
1999—Washington NFL	16	16	6.5
2000—Washington NFL	16	16	12.0
Pro totals (9 years)	143	141	52.0

COLEMAN, MARCUS   CB   JETS

PERSONAL: Born May 24, 1974, in Dallas. ... 6-2/210.
HIGH SCHOOL: Lake Highlands (Dallas).
COLLEGE: Texas Tech.
TRANSACTIONS/CAREER NOTES: Selected by New York Jets in fifth round (133rd pick overall) of 1996 NFL draft. ... Signed by Jets (July 11, 1996). ... Granted unconditional free agency (February 11, 2000). ... Re-signed by Jets (February 14, 2000).
CHAMPIONSHIP GAME EXPERIENCE: Played in AFC championship game (1998 season).
PRO STATISTICS: 1997—Recovered one fumble. 1999—Recovered one fumble. 2000—Caught one pass for 45 yards and a touchdown, converted two-point conversion and recovered one fumble.

			INTERCEPTIONS			
Year Team	G	GS	No.	Yds.	Avg.	TD
1996—New York Jets NFL	13	4	1	23	23.0	0
1997—New York Jets NFL	16	2	1	24	24.0	0
1998—New York Jets NFL	14	0	0	0	0.0	0
1999—New York Jets NFL	16	10	6	165	27.5	1
2000—New York Jets NFL	16	16	4	6	1.5	0
Pro totals (5 years)	75	32	12	218	18.2	1

COLEMAN, RODERICK   DE   RAIDERS

PERSONAL: Born August 16, 1976, in Philadelphia. ... 6-2/265.
HIGH SCHOOL: Simon Gratz (Philadelphia).
COLLEGE: East Carolina.
TRANSACTIONS/CAREER NOTES: Selected by Oakland Raiders in fifth round (153rd pick overall) of 1999 NFL draft. ... Signed by Raiders (July 24, 1999).
PLAYING EXPERIENCE: Oakland NFL, 1999 and 2000. ... Games/Games started: 1999 (3/0), 2000 (13/1). Total: 16/1.
CHAMPIONSHIP GAME EXPERIENCE: Played in AFC championship game (2000 season).
PRO STATISTICS: 2000—Credited with six sacks and recovered one fumble.

COLES, LAVERANUES   WR/KR   JETS

PERSONAL: Born December 29, 1977, in Jacksonville. ... 5-11/190.
HIGH SCHOOL: Jean Ribault (Jacksonville).
COLLEGE: Florida State.
TRANSACTIONS/CAREER NOTES: Selected by New York Jets in third round (78th pick overall) of 2000 NFL draft. ... Signed by Jets (May 1, 2000).
SINGLE GAME HIGHS (regular season): Receptions—6 (October 15, 2000, vs. New England); yards—131 (October 29, 2000, vs. Buffalo); and touchdown receptions—1 (October 23, 2000, vs. Miami).
STATISTICAL PLATEAUS: 100-yard receiving games: 2000 (1).

			RUSHING				RECEIVING				KICKOFF RETURNS				TOTALS			
Year Team	G	GS	Att.	Yds.	Avg.	TD	No.	Yds.	Avg.	TD	No.	Yds.	Avg.	TD	TD	2pt.	Pts.	Fum.
2000—New York Jets NFL	13	3	2	15	7.5	0	22	370	16.8	1	11	207	18.8	0	1	▲1	8	0

COLINET, STALIN   DT   BROWNS

PERSONAL: Born July 19, 1974, in Bronx, N.Y. ... 6-6/288.
HIGH SCHOOL: Cardinal Hayes (Bronx, N.Y.).
COLLEGE: Boston College (degree in sociology, 1996).
TRANSACTIONS/CAREER NOTES: Selected by Minnesota Vikings in third round (78th pick overall) of 1997 NFL draft. ... Signed by Vikings (June 30, 1997). ... Traded by Vikings to Cleveland Browns for DT Jerry Ball (September 28, 1999). ... Granted free agency (February 11, 2000). ... Re-signed by Browns (April 18, 2000). ... Granted unconditional free agency (March 2, 2001). ... Re-signed by Browns (March 2, 2001).
PLAYING EXPERIENCE: Minnesota NFL, 1997 and 1998; Minnesota (3)-Cleveland (11) NFL, 1999; Cleveland NFL, 2000. ... Games/games started: 1997 (10/2), 1998 (11/3), 1999 (Min.-3/1; Cle.-11/9; Total: 14/10), 2000 (16/16). Total: 51/31.
CHAMPIONSHIP GAME EXPERIENCE: Played in NFC championship game (1998 season).
PRO STATISTICS: 1998—Credited with one sack. 2000—Credited with $3^1/_2$ sacks and recovered one fumble.

COLLINS, BOBBY   TE   BILLS

PERSONAL: Born August 26, 1976, in York, Ala. ... 6-4/248. ... Full name: Bobby Eugene Collins.
HIGH SCHOOL: Sumter County (York, Ala.).
JUNIOR COLLEGE: East Mississippi Junior College.
COLLEGE: North Alabama.
TRANSACTIONS/CAREER NOTES: Selected by Buffalo Bills in fourth round (122nd pick overall) of 1999 NFL draft. ... Signed by Bills (July 12, 1999).
PRO STATISTICS: 1999—Returned one kickoff for six yards.
SINGLE GAME HIGHS (regular season): Receptions—3 (September 17, 2000, vs. New York Jets); yards—45 (November 28, 1999, vs. New England); and touchdown receptions—1 (January 2, 2000, vs. Indianapolis).

			RECEIVING			
Year Team	G	GS	No.	Yds.	Avg.	TD
1999—Buffalo NFL	14	4	9	124	13.8	2
2000—Buffalo NFL	12	2	6	72	12.0	0
Pro totals (2 years)	26	6	15	196	13.1	2

COLLINS, CALVIN   C   FALCONS

PERSONAL: Born January 5, 1974, in Beaumont, Texas. ... 6-2/310. ... Full name: Calvin Lewis Collins.
HIGH SCHOOL: West Brook (Beaumont, Texas).
COLLEGE: Texas A&M.
TRANSACTIONS/CAREER NOTES: Selected by Atlanta Falcons in sixth round (180th pick overall) of 1997 NFL draft. ... Signed by Falcons (June 22, 1997). ... Granted free agency (February 11, 2000). ... Re-signed by Falcons (May 24, 2000).
PLAYING EXPERIENCE: Atlanta NFL, 1997-2000. ... Games/Games started: 1997 (15/13), 1998 (16/16), 1999 (14/8), 2000 (16/16). Total: 61/53.
CHAMPIONSHIP GAME EXPERIENCE: Played in NFC championship game (1998 season). ... Played in Super Bowl XXXIII (1998 season).
PRO STATISTICS: 1998—Recovered one fumble.

COLLINS, KERRY   QB   GIANTS

PERSONAL: Born December 30, 1972, in Lebanon, Pa. ... 6-5/245. ... Full name: Kerry Michael Collins.
HIGH SCHOOL: Wilson (West Lawn, Pa.).
COLLEGE: Penn State.
TRANSACTIONS/CAREER NOTES: Selected by Carolina Panthers in first round (fifth pick overall) of 1995 NFL draft. ... Signed by Panthers (July 17, 1995). ... Granted free agency (February 13, 1998). ... Re-signed by Panthers (July 24, 1998). ... Claimed on waivers by New Orleans Saints (October 14, 1998). ... Granted unconditional free agency (February 12, 1999). ... Signed by New York Giants (February 19, 1999).
CHAMPIONSHIP GAME EXPERIENCE: Played in NFC championship game (1996 and 2000 season). ... Played in Super Bowl XXXV (2000 season).
HONORS: Maxwell Award winner (1994). ... Davey O'Brien Award winner (1994). ... Named quarterback on THE SPORTING NEWS college All-America first team (1994). ... Played in Pro Bowl (1996 season).
PRO STATISTICS: 1995—Fumbled 13 times and recovered four fumbles for minus 15 yards. 1996—Fumbled six times and recovered one fumble. 1997—Fumbled eight times and recovered two fumbles for minus 14 yards. 1998—Caught one pass for minus 11 yards, fumbled 13 times and recovered two fumbles for minus nine yards. 1999—Fumbled 11 times and recovered two fumbles for minus 27 yards. 2000—Fumbled seven times and recovered one fumble for minus 13 yards.
SINGLE GAME HIGHS (regular season): Attempts—53 (September 27, 1998, vs. Green Bay); completions—31 (December 26, 1999, vs. Minnesota); passing yards—350 (November 19, 2000, vs. Detroit); and touchdown passes—3 (November 12, 2000, vs. St. Louis).
STATISTICAL PLATEAUS: 300-yard passing games: 1995 (2), 1996 (1), 1997 (1), 1998 (2), 1999 (2), 2000 (3). Total: 11.
MISCELLANEOUS: Selected by Detroit Tigers organization in 26th round of free-agent draft (June 4, 1990); did not sign. ... Selected by Toronto Blue Jays organization in 58th round of free-agent draft (June 4, 1994); did not sign. ... Regular-season record as starting NFL quarterback: 38-34 (.528). ... Postseason record as starting NFL quarterback: 3-2 (.600).

			PASSING							RUSHING				TOTALS		
Year Team	G	GS	Att.	Cmp.	Pct.	Yds.	TD	Int.	Avg.	Rat.	Att.	Yds.	Avg.	TD	TD	2pt.	Pts.
1995—Carolina NFL	15	13	433	214	49.4	2717	14	19	6.27	61.9	42	74	1.8	3	3	0	18
1996—Carolina NFL	13	12	364	204	56.0	2454	14	9	6.74	79.4	32	38	1.2	0	0	1	2
1997—Carolina NFL	13	13	381	200	52.5	2124	11	*21	5.57	55.7	26	65	2.5	1	1	0	6
1998—Carolina NFL	4	4	162	76	46.9	1011	8	5	6.24	70.8	7	40	5.7	0	0	1	2
—New Orleans NFL	7	7	191	94	49.2	1202	4	10	6.29	54.5	23	113	4.9	1	1	0	6
1999—N.Y. Giants NFL	10	7	331	190	57.4	2318	8	11	7.00	73.3	19	36	1.9	2	2	†1	14
2000—N.Y. Giants NFL	16	16	529	311	58.8	3610	22	13	6.82	83.1	41	65	1.6	1	1	0	6
Pro totals (6 years)	78	72	2391	1289	53.9	15436	81	88	6.46	69.9	190	431	2.3	8	8	3	54

COLLINS, MO   OT   RAIDERS

PERSONAL: Born September 22, 1976, in Charlotte. ... 6-4/325. ... Full name: Damon Jamal Collins.
HIGH SCHOOL: West Charlotte.
COLLEGE: Florida.
TRANSACTIONS/CAREER NOTES: Selected after junior season by Oakland Raiders in first round (23rd pick overall) of 1998 NFL draft. ... Signed by Raiders (July 15, 1998).
PLAYING EXPERIENCE: Oakland NFL, 1998-2000. ... Games/Games started: 1998 (16/11), 1999 (13/12), 2000 (16/16). Total: 45/39.
CHAMPIONSHIP GAME EXPERIENCE: Played in AFC championship game (2000 season).

COLLINS, TODD — LB — RAMS

PERSONAL: Born May 27, 1970, in New Market, Tenn. ... 6-2/248. ... Full name: Todd Franklin Collins.
HIGH SCHOOL: Jefferson County (Dandridge, Tenn.).
COLLEGE: Georgia (did not play football), then Tennessee (did not play football), then Carson-Newman (Tenn.).
TRANSACTIONS/CAREER NOTES: Selected after junior season by New England Patriots in third round (64th pick overall) of 1992 NFL draft. ... Signed by Patriots (July 23, 1992). ... On injured reserve with neck injury (October 16-November 13, 1992); on practice squad (November 11-13, 1992). ... On injured reserve with knee injury (November 15, 1994-remainder of season). ... Granted free agency (February 17, 1995). ... Re-signed by Patriots (April 20, 1995). ... On reserved/retired list (July 21, 1995-April 16, 1996). ... Granted unconditional free agency (February 14, 1997). ... Re-signed by Patriots (April 4, 1997). ... Granted unconditional free agency (February 12, 1999). ... Signed by St. Louis Rams (March 11, 1999).
PLAYING EXPERIENCE: New England NFL, 1992-1994 and 1996-1998; St. Louis NFL, 1999 and 2000. ... Games/Games started: 1992 (10/0), 1993 (16/12), 1994 (7/7), 1996 (16/9), 1997 (15/15), 1998 (12/10), 1999 (16/13), 2000 (14/11). Total: 106/77.
CHAMPIONSHIP GAME EXPERIENCE: Played in AFC championship game (1996 season). ... Played in Super Bowl XXXI (1996 season). ... Played in NFC championship game (1999 season). ... Member of Super Bowl championship team (1999 season).
PRO STATISTICS: 1992—Recovered two fumbles. 1993—Credited with one sack, intercepted one pass for eight yards and recovered one fumble for two yards. 1996—Intercepted one pass for seven yards. 1997—Credited with $1^1/_2$ sacks. 2000—Credited with one sack.

COLMAN, DOUG — LB — JETS

C

PERSONAL: Born June 4, 1973, in Somers Point, N.J. ... 6-2/250.
HIGH SCHOOL: Ocean City (N.J.).
COLLEGE: Nebraska.
TRANSACTIONS/CAREER NOTES: Selected by New York Giants in sixth round (171st pick overall) of 1996 NFL draft. ... Signed by Giants (June 18, 1996). ... Granted free agency (February 12, 1999). ... Re-signed by Giants (June 8, 1999). ... Released by Giants (September 5, 1999). ... Signed by Tennessee Titans (September 9, 1999). ... Granted unconditional free agency (February 11, 2000). ... Signed by Oakland Raiders (May 24, 2000). ... Released by Raiders (August 22, 2000). ... Signed by Cleveland Browns (September 20, 2000). ... On injured reserve with hamstring injury (November 1-7, 2000). ... Released by Browns (November 7, 2000). ... Signed by New York Jets (April 4, 2001).
PLAYING EXPERIENCE: New York Giants NFL, 1996-1998; Tennessee NFL, 1999; Cleveland NFL, 2000. ... Games/Games started: 1996 (13/0), 1997 (14/0), 1998 (16/0), 1999 (16/1), 2000 (5/0). Total: 64/1.
CHAMPIONSHIP GAME EXPERIENCE: Played in AFC championship game (1999 season). ... Played in Super Bowl XXXIV (1999 season).

COLVIN, ROSEVELT — LB — BEARS

PERSONAL: Born September 5, 1977, in Indianapolis. ... 6-3/254.
HIGH SCHOOL: Broad Ripple (Indianapolis).
COLLEGE: Purdue.
TRANSACTIONS/CAREER NOTES: Selected by Chicago Bears in fourth round (111th pick overall) of 1999 NFL draft. ... Signed by Bears (July 21, 1999).
PRO STATISTICS: 1999—Recovered one fumble. 2000—Recovered one fumble.

Year Team	G	GS	SACKS
1999—Chicago NFL	11	0	2.0
2000—Chicago NFL	13	8	3.0
Pro totals (2 years)	24	8	5.0

COMBS, CHRIS — DE — STEELERS

PERSONAL: Born December 15, 1976, in Roanoke, Va. ... 6-4/284. ... Full name: Christopher Brandon Combs. ... Son of Glen Combs, guard with five American Basketball Association teams (1968-69 through 1974-75).
HIGH SCHOOL: Patrick Henry (Roanoke, Va.).
COLLEGE: Duke (degree in sociology).
TRANSACTIONS/CAREER NOTES: Selected by Pittsburgh Steelers in sixth round (173rd pick overall) of 2000 NFL draft. ... Signed by Steelers (July 16, 2000).
PLAYING EXPERIENCE: Pittsburgh NFL, 2000. ... Games/Games started: 2000 (6/0).

COMELLA, GREG — FB — GIANTS

PERSONAL: Born July 29, 1975, in Wellesley, Mass. ... 6-1/248. ... Name pronounced Ka-MELL-uh.
HIGH SCHOOL: Xaverian Brothers (Westwood, Mass.).
COLLEGE: Stanford.
TRANSACTIONS/CAREER NOTES: Signed as non-drafted free agent by New York Giants (April 24, 1998). ... Granted free agency (March 2, 2001).
PLAYING EXPERIENCE: New York Giants NFL, 1998-2000. ... Games/Games started: 1998 (16/0), 1999 (16/3), 2000 (16/12). Total: 48/15.
CHAMPIONSHIP GAME EXPERIENCE: Played in NFC championship game (2000 season). ... Played in Super Bowl XXXV (2000 season).
PRO STATISTICS: 1998—Rushed once for six yards, caught one pass for three yards, returned one kickoff for 12 yards and recovered one fumble. 1999—Rushed once for nine yards, caught eight passes for 39 yards and returned two kickoffs for 31 yards. 2000—Rushed 10 times for 45 yards, caught 36 passes for 274 yards, returned two kickoffs for 20 yards, returned one punt for no yards and fumbled twice.
SINGLE GAME HIGHS (regular season): Attempts—3 (November 5, 2000, vs. Cleveland); yards—19 (September 10, 2000, vs. Philadelphia); and rushing touchdowns—0.

COMPTON, MIKE　　　　　OL　　　　　PATRIOTS

PERSONAL: Born September 18, 1970, in Richlands, Va. ... 6-6/300. ... Full name: Michael Eugene Compton.
HIGH SCHOOL: Richlands (Va.).
COLLEGE: West Virginia.
TRANSACTIONS/CAREER NOTES: Selected by Detroit Lions in third round (68th pick overall) of 1993 NFL draft. ... Signed by Lions (June 4, 1993). ... Granted unconditional free agency (March 2, 2001). ... Signed by New England Patriots (April 2, 2001).
PLAYING EXPERIENCE: Detroit NFL, 1993-2000. ... Games/Games started: 1993 (8/0), 1994 (2/0), 1995 (16/8), 1996 (15/15), 1997 (16/16), 1998 (16/16), 1999 (15/15), 2000 (16/16). Total: 104/86.
HONORS: Named center on The Sporting News college All-America first team (1992).
PRO STATISTICS: 1996—Fumbled once. 1999—Recovered two fumbles for eight yards.

CONATY, BILLY　　　　　C　　　　　BILLS

PERSONAL: Born March 8, 1973, in Baltimore. ... 6-2/300. ... Full name: William B. Conaty. ... Name pronounced CON-uh-tee.
HIGH SCHOOL: Milford (Conn.) Academy, then Camden Catholic (Cherry Hill, N.J.).
COLLEGE: Virginia Tech.
TRANSACTIONS/CAREER NOTES: Signed as non-drafted free agent by Buffalo Bills (April 25, 1997). ... Released by Bills (August 24, 1997). ... Re-signed by Bills to practice squad (August 26, 1997). ... Activated (September 6, 1997). ... Released by Bills (September 22, 1997). ... Re-signed by Bills to practice squad (September 24, 1997). ... Granted free agency (March 2, 2001).
PLAYING EXPERIENCE: Buffalo NFL, 1997-2000. ... Games/Games started: 1997 (1/0), 1998 (15/1), 1999 (7/1), 2000 (16/0). Totals: 39/2.
HONORS: Named center on The Sporting News college All-America first team (1996).

C

CONNELL, ALBERT　　　　　WR　　　　　SAINTS

PERSONAL: Born May 13, 1974, in Fort Lauderdale, Fla. ... 6-0/179. ... Full name: Albert Gene Anthony Connell.
HIGH SCHOOL: Piper (Fort Lauderdale, Fla.).
JUNIOR COLLEGE: Trinity Valley Community College (Texas).
COLLEGE: Texas A&M.
TRANSACTIONS/CAREER NOTES: Selected by Washington Redskins in fourth round (115th pick overall) of 1997 NFL draft. ... Signed by Redskins (May 28, 1997). ... Granted free agency (February 11, 2000). ... Re-signed by Redskins (April 21, 2000). ... Granted unconditional free agency (March 2, 2001). ... Signed by New Orleans Saints (March 5, 2001).
PRO STATISTICS: 1997—Rushed once for three yards. 1999—Rushed once for eight yards and recovered one fumble.
SINGLE GAME HIGHS (regular season): Receptions—8 (October 17, 1999, vs. Arizona); yards—211 (October 22, 2000, vs. Jacksonville); and touchdown receptions—3 (October 22, 2000, vs. Jacksonville).
STATISTICAL PLATEAUS: 100-yard receiving games: 1998 (1), 1999 (4), 2000 (2). Total: 7.

			RECEIVING				TOTALS		
Year　Team	G	GS	No.	Yds.	Avg.	TD	TD	2pt.	Pts.	Fum.
1997—Washington NFL	5	1	9	138	15.3	2	2	0	12	0
1998—Washington NFL	14	5	28	451	16.1	2	2	0	12	0
1999—Washington NFL	15	14	62	1132	18.3	7	7	0	42	1
2000—Washington NFL	16	13	39	762	19.5	3	3	0	18	0
Pro totals (4 years)	50	33	138	2483	18.0	14	14	0	84	1

CONWAY, BRETT　　　　　K　　　　　REDSKINS

PERSONAL: Born March 8, 1975, in Atlanta. ... 6-2/192. ... Full name: Brett Alan Conway.
HIGH SCHOOL: Parkview (Lilburn, Ga.).
COLLEGE: Penn State.
TRANSACTIONS/CAREER NOTES: Selected by Green Bay Packers in third round (90th pick overall) of 1997 NFL draft. ... Signed by Packers (July 8, 1997). ... On injured reserve with thigh injury (September 3, 1997-entire season). ... Traded by Packers to New York Jets for an undisclosed draft pick (August 21, 1998). ... Released by Jets (August 30, 1998). ... Re-signed by Jets to practice squad (September 1, 1998). ... Released by Jets (September 23, 1998). ... Signed by Washington Redskins (November 12, 1998). ... Granted free agency (February 11, 2000). ... Re-signed by Redskins (May 31, 2000). ... Released by Redskins (September 20, 2000). ... Signed by Oakland Raiders (November 11, 2000). ... Released by Raiders (November 21, 2000). ... Signed by Jets (December 18, 2000). ... Granted unconditional free agency (March 2, 2001). ... Signed by Redskins (March 15, 2001).
PRO STATISTICS: 1999—Attempted one pass without a completion and recovered one fumble.

				KICKING				
Year　Team	G	XPM	XPA	FGM	FGA	Lg.	50+	Pts.
1997—Green Bay NFL				Did not play.				
1998—Washington NFL	6	0	0	0	0	0	0-0	0
1999—Washington NFL	16	49	50	22	∞32	51	3-9	115
2000—Washington NFL	2	3	3	3	3	26	0-0	12
—Oakland NFL	1	3	3	1	1	19	0-0	6
—New York Jets NFL	1	2	2	2	2	40	0-0	8
Pro totals (3 years)	26	57	58	28	38	51	3-9	141

CONWAY, CURTIS　　　　　WR　　　　　CHARGERS

PERSONAL: Born March 13, 1971, in Los Angeles. ... 6-1/196. ... Full name: Curtis LaMont Conway.
HIGH SCHOOL: Hawthorne (Calif.).
JUNIOR COLLEGE: El Camino College (Calif.).
COLLEGE: Southern California.

TRANSACTIONS/CAREER NOTES: Selected after junior season by Chicago Bears in first round (seventh pick overall) of 1993 NFL draft. ... Signed by Bears (May 24, 1993). ... Granted free agency (February 16, 1996). ... Re-signed by Bears (March 4, 1996). ... On injured reserve with shoulder injury (December 22, 1999-remainder of season). ... Granted unconditional free agency (February 11, 2000). ... Signed by San Diego Chargers (February 22, 2000).

HONORS: Named kick returner on THE SPORTING NEWS college All-America second team (1992).

PRO STATISTICS: 1993—Fumbled once. 1994—Completed only pass attempt for 23 yards and a touchdown, fumbled twice and recovered one fumble. 1994—Returned eight punts for 63 yards. 1995—Attempted one pass without a completion. 1996—Completed only pass attempt for 33 yards and a touchdown. 1997—Attempted one pass without a completion. 1998—Attempted one pass without a completion and recovered one fumble.

SINGLE GAME HIGHS (regular season): Receptions—9 (September 12, 1999, vs. Kansas City); yards—148 (September 12, 1994, vs. Philadelphia); and touchdown receptions—3 (October 15, 1995, vs. Jacksonville).

STATISTICAL PLATEAUS: 100-yard receiving games: 1994 (1), 1995 (3), 1996 (4), 1997 (3), 1999 (1), 2000 (2). Total: 14.

			RUSHING				RECEIVING				KICKOFF RETURNS				TOTALS			
Year Team	G	GS	Att.	Yds.	Avg.	TD	No.	Yds.	Avg.	TD	No.	Yds.	Avg.	TD	TD	2pt.	Pts.	Fum.
1993—Chicago NFL	16	7	5	44	8.8	0	19	231	12.2	2	21	450	21.4	0	2	0	12	1
1994—Chicago NFL	13	12	6	31	5.2	0	39	546	14.0	2	10	228	22.8	0	2	1	14	2
1995—Chicago NFL	16	16	5	77	15.4	0	62	1037	16.7	12	0	0	0.0	0	12	0	72	0
1996—Chicago NFL	16	16	8	50	6.3	0	81	1049	13.0	7	0	0	0.0	0	7	0	42	1
1997—Chicago NFL	7	7	3	17	5.7	0	30	476	15.9	1	0	0	0.0	0	1	0	6	0
1998—Chicago NFL	15	15	5	48	9.6	0	54	733	13.6	3	0	0	0.0	0	3	0	18	1
1999—Chicago NFL	9	8	1	-2	-2.0	0	44	426	9.7	4	0	0	0.0	0	4	0	24	2
2000—San Diego NFL	14	14	3	31	10.3	0	53	712	13.4	5	0	0	0.0	0	5	0	30	0
Pro totals (8 years)	106	95	36	296	8.2	0	382	5210	13.6	36	31	678	21.9	0	36	1	218	7

C

CONWELL, ERNIE　　　　TE　　　　RAMS

PERSONAL: Born August 17, 1972, in Renton, Wash. ... 6-2/265. ... Full name: Ernest Harold Conwell.
HIGH SCHOOL: Kentwood (Kent, Wash.).
COLLEGE: Washington (degree in sociology, 1995).
TRANSACTIONS/CAREER NOTES: Selected by St. Louis Rams in second round (59th pick overall) of 1996 NFL draft. ... Signed by Rams (June 25, 1996). ... On injured reserve with knee injury (October 28, 1998-remainder of season). ... On physically unable to perform list with knee injury (August 30-November 9, 1999). ... Granted unconditional free agency (February 11, 2000). ... Re-signed by Rams (February 11, 2000).
CHAMPIONSHIP GAME EXPERIENCE: Played in NFC championship game (1999 season). ... Member of Super Bowl championship team (1999 season).
PRO STATISTICS: 1996—Recovered one fumble. 1997—Recovered one fumble. 2000—Rushed twice for 23 yards.
SINGLE GAME HIGHS (regular season): Receptions—5 (September 13, 1998, vs. Minnesota); yards—75 (November 23, 1997, vs. Carolina); and touchdown receptions—1 (December 20, 1997, vs. Carolina).

			RECEIVING				TOTALS			
Year Team	G	GS	No.	Yds.	Avg.	TD	TD	2pt.	Pts.	Fum.
1996—St. Louis NFL	10	8	15	164	10.9	0	0	0	0	0
1997—St. Louis NFL	16	16	38	404	10.6	4	4	0	24	0
1998—St. Louis NFL	7	7	15	105	7.0	0	0	0	0	0
1999—St. Louis NFL	3	0	1	11	11.0	0	0	0	0	0
2000—St. Louis NFL	16	1	5	40	8.0	0	0	0	0	0
Pro totals (5 years)	52	32	74	724	9.8	4	4	0	24	0

COOK, RASHARD　　　　S　　　　EAGLES

PERSONAL: Born April 18, 1977, in San Diego. ... 5-11/197.
HIGH SCHOOL: Samuel F.B. Morse (San Diego).
COLLEGE: Southern California.
TRANSACTIONS/CAREER NOTES: Selected by Chicago Bears in sixth round (184th pick overall) of 1999 NFL draft. ... Signed by Bears (June 25, 1999). ... Claimed on waivers by Philadelphia Eagles (September 7, 1999).
PLAYING EXPERIENCE: Philadelphia NFL, 1999 and 2000. ... Games/Games started: 1999 (13/0), 2000 (14/0). Total: 27/0.
PRO STATISTICS: 1999—Intercepted one pass for 29 yards and credited with one sack.

COPELAND, JOHN　　　　DE　　　　BENGALS

PERSONAL: Born September 20, 1970, in Lanett, Ala. ... 6-3/280.
HIGH SCHOOL: Valley (Ala.).
JUNIOR COLLEGE: Hinds Community College (Miss.).
COLLEGE: Alabama.
TRANSACTIONS/CAREER NOTES: Selected by Cincinnati Bengals in first round (fifth pick overall) of 1993 NFL draft. ... Signed by Bengals (August 13, 1993). ... Granted unconditional free agency (February 13, 1998). ... Re-signed by Bengals (February 20, 1998). ... On physically unable to perform list with heel injury (August 25-November 17, 1998). ... Released by Bengals (April 23, 2000). ... Re-signed by Bengals (May 24, 2001).
HONORS: Named defensive lineman on THE SPORTING NEWS college All-America first team (1992).
PRO STATISTICS: 1997—Recovered two fumbles for 25 yards and one touchdown. 1998—Intercepted one pass for three yards. 1999—Intercepted two passes for 16 yards. 2000—Recovered one fumble for four yards.

Year Team	G	GS	SACKS
1993—Cincinnati NFL	14	14	3.0
1994—Cincinnati NFL	12	12	1.0
1995—Cincinnati NFL	16	16	9.0
1996—Cincinnati NFL	13	13	3.0
1997—Cincinnati NFL	15	15	3.0
1998—Cincinnati NFL	5	0	0.0
1999—Cincinnati NFL	16	16	4.0
2000—Cincinnati NFL	16	16	1.0
Pro totals (8 years)	107	102	24.0

COTA, CHAD   DB   COLTS

PERSONAL: Born August 8, 1971, in Ashland, Ore. ... 6-0/196. ... Full name: Chad Garrett Cota.
HIGH SCHOOL: Ashland (Ore.).
COLLEGE: Oregon (degree in sociology).
TRANSACTIONS/CAREER NOTES: Selected by Carolina Panthers in seventh round (209th pick overall) of 1995 NFL draft. ... Signed by Panthers (July 14, 1995). ... Granted free agency (February 13, 1998). ... Tendered offer sheet by New Orleans Saints (March 11, 1998). ... Panthers declined to match offer (March 19, 1998). ... Granted unconditional free agency (February 12, 1999). ... Signed by Indianapolis Colts (February 23, 1999).
CHAMPIONSHIP GAME EXPERIENCE: Played in NFC championship game (1996 season).
PRO STATISTICS: 1995—Recovered one fumble. 1996—Credited with one sack, fumbled once and recovered one fumble. 1997—Credited with one sack and recovered one fumble. 1998—Credited with two sacks and recovered one fumble. 1999—Recovered one fumble for 25 yards and a touchdown.

				INTERCEPTIONS		
Year Team	G	GS	No.	Yds.	Avg.	TD
1995—Carolina NFL	16	0	0	0	0.0	0
1996—Carolina NFL	16	2	5	63	12.6	0
1997—Carolina NFL	16	16	2	28	14.0	0
1998—New Orleans NFL	16	16	4	16	4.0	0
1999—Indianapolis NFL	15	15	0	0	0.0	0
2000—Indianapolis NFL	16	16	2	3	1.5	0
Pro totals (6 years)	95	65	13	110	8.5	0

COUCH, TIM   QB   BROWNS

PERSONAL: Born July 31, 1977, in Hyden, Ky. ... 6-4/227. ... Full name: Timothy Scott Couch.
HIGH SCHOOL: Leslie County (Hyden, Ky.).
COLLEGE: Kentucky.
TRANSACTIONS/CAREER NOTES: Selected after junior season by Cleveland Browns in first round (first pick overall) of 1999 NFL draft. ... Signed by Browns (April 17, 1999). ... On injured reserve with broken thumb (October 20, 2000-remainder of season).
HONORS: Named quarterback on THE SPORTING NEWS college All-America third team (1998).
PRO STATISTICS: 1999—Fumbled 14 times and recovered four fumbles for minus 11 yards. 2000—Fumbled twice for minus eight yards.
SINGLE GAME HIGHS (regular season): Attempts—46 (November 21, 1999, vs. Carolina); completions—29 (November 21, 1999, vs. Carolina); passing yards—316 (September 17, 2000, vs. Pittsburgh); and touchdown passes—3 (October 31, 1999, vs. New Orleans).
STATISTICAL PLATEAUS: 300-yard passing games: 2000 (1).
MISCELLANEOUS: Regular-season record as starting NFL quarterback: 4-17 (.190).

			PASSING							RUSHING				TOTALS		
Year Team	G	GS	Att.	Cmp.	Pct.	Yds.	TD	Int.	Avg.	Rat.	Att.	Yds.	Avg.	TD	TD	2pt.	Pts.
1999—Cleveland NFL	15	14	399	223	55.9	2447	15	13	6.13	73.2	40	267	6.7	1	1	†1	8
2000—Cleveland NFL	7	7	215	137	63.7	1483	7	9	6.90	77.3	12	45	3.8	0	0	0	0
Pro totals (2 years)	22	21	614	360	58.6	3930	22	22	6.40	74.6	52	312	6.0	1	1	1	8

COUSIN, TERRY   CB   DOLPHINS

PERSONAL: Born April 11, 1975, in Miami. ... 5-9/182.
HIGH SCHOOL: Miami Beach Senior.
COLLEGE: South Carolina.
TRANSACTIONS/CAREER NOTES: Signed as non-drafted free agent by Chicago Bears (April 25, 1997). ... Released by Bears (August 24, 1997). ... Re-signed by Bears to practice squad (August 26, 1997). ... Activated (October 25, 1997). ... Released by Bears (October 28, 1997). ... Re-signed by Bears to practice squad (October 30, 1997). ... Activated (November 15, 1997). ... Granted free agency (February 11, 2000). ... Re-signed by Bears (April 18, 2000). ... Claimed on waivers by Atlanta Falcons (August 28, 2000). ... Granted unconditional free agency (March 2, 2001). ... Signed by Miami Dolphins (March 15, 2001).
PRO STATISTICS: 1998—Recovered two fumbles. 1999—Recovered one fumble.

				INTERCEPTIONS		
Year Team	G	GS	No.	Yds.	Avg.	TD
1997—Chicago NFL	6	0	0	0	0.0	0
1998—Chicago NFL	16	12	1	0	0.0	0
1999—Chicago NFL	16	9	2	1	0.5	0
2000—Atlanta NFL	15	0	0	0	0.0	0
Pro totals (4 years)	53	21	3	1	0.3	0

COWART, SAM   LB   BILLS

PERSONAL: Born February 26, 1975, in Jacksonville. ... 6-2/245.
HIGH SCHOOL: Mandarin (Jacksonville).
COLLEGE: Florida State.
TRANSACTIONS/CAREER NOTES: Selected by Buffalo Bills in second round (39th pick overall) of 1998 NFL draft. ... Signed by Bills (July 20, 1998).
PLAYING EXPERIENCE: Buffalo NFL, 1998 and 1999. ... Games/Games started: 1998 (16/11), 1999 (16/16), 2000 (12/12). Total: 44/39.
HONORS: Named outside linebacker on THE SPORTING NEWS college All-America first team (1997). ... Played in Pro Bowl (2000 season).
PRO STATISTICS: 1998—Intercepted two passes for 23 yards. 1999—Recovered one fumble and credited with one sack. 2000—Intercepted two passes for four yards, credited with $5^1/_2$ sacks and recovered two fumbles for three yards.

C

COX, BRYAN — LB

PERSONAL: Born February 17, 1968, in St. Louis. ... 6-4/250. ... Full name: Bryan Keith Cox.
HIGH SCHOOL: East St. Louis (Ill.) Senior.
COLLEGE: Western Illinois (bachelor of science degree in mass communications).
TRANSACTIONS/CAREER NOTES: Selected by Miami Dolphins in fifth round (113th pick overall) of 1991 NFL draft. ... Signed by Dolphins (July 11, 1991). ... On injured reserve with sprained ankle (October 5-November 2, 1991). ... Granted unconditional free agency (February 16, 1996). ... Signed by Chicago Bears (February 20, 1996). ... On injured reserve with thumb injury (November 5, 1996-remainder of season). ... Released by Bears (June 2, 1998). ... Signed by New York Jets (August 1, 1998). ... On injured reserve with abdominal injury (December 10, 1999-remainder of season). ... On injured reserve with broken leg (December 18, 2000-remainder of season). ... Released by Jets (February 21, 2001).
CHAMPIONSHIP GAME EXPERIENCE: Played in AFC championship game (1992 and 1998 seasons).
HONORS: Played in Pro Bowl (1992, 1994 and 1995 seasons).
PRO STATISTICS: 1992—Recovered one fumble. 1993—Recovered four fumbles for one yard. 1995—Recovered one fumble. 1996—Recovered three fumbles, including one in end zone for a touchdown. 1997—Recovered one fumble. 1998—Credited with a safety. 1999—Recovered one fumble. 2000—Recovered two fumbles.

				INTERCEPTIONS			SACKS
Year Team	G	GS	No.	Yds.	Avg.	TD	No.
1991—Miami NFL	13	13	0	0	0.0	0	2.0
1992—Miami NFL	16	16	1	0	0.0	0	14.0
1993—Miami NFL	16	16	1	26	26.0	0	5.0
1994—Miami NFL	16	16	0	0	0.0	0	3.0
1995—Miami NFL	16	16	1	12	12.0	0	7.5
1996—Chicago NFL	9	9	0	0	0.0	0	3.0
1997—Chicago NFL	16	15	0	0	0.0	0	5.0
1998—New York Jets NFL	16	10	0	0	0.0	0	6.0
1999—New York Jets NFL	12	11	1	27	27.0	1	0.0
2000—New York Jets NFL	15	15	0	0	0.0	0	6.0
Pro totals (10 years)	145	137	4	65	16.3	1	51.5

CRAFT, JASON — CB — JAGUARS

PERSONAL: Born February 13, 1976, in Denver. ... 5-10/178. ... Full name: Jason Donell Andre Craft.
HIGH SCHOOL: Denver East.
JUNIOR COLLEGE: Denver Community College.
COLLEGE: Colorado State.
TRANSACTIONS/CAREER NOTES: Selected by Jacksonville Jaguars in fifth round (160th pick overall) of 1999 NFL draft. ... Signed by Jaguars (May 18, 1999).
PLAYING EXPERIENCE: Jacksonville NFL, 1999 and 2000. ... Games/Games started: 1999 (16/0), 2000 (16/3). Total: 32/3.
CHAMPIONSHIP GAME EXPERIENCE: Played in AFC championship game (1999 season).
PRO STATISTICS: 1999—Recovered one fumble for 23 yards and a touchdown. 2000—Recovered one fumble for four yards.

CRAIG, DAMEYUNE — QB — PANTHERS

PERSONAL: Born April 19, 1974, in Mobile, Ala. ... 6-1/200. ... Full name: Dameyune Vashon Craig. ... Name pronounced DAME-ee-un.
HIGH SCHOOL: Blunt (Pritchard, Ala.).
COLLEGE: Auburn.
TRANSACTIONS/CAREER NOTES: Signed as non-drafted free agent by Carolina Panthers (April 18, 1998). ... Released by Panthers (August 30, 1998). ... Re-signed by Panthers to practice squad (September 1, 1998). ... Activated (December 5, 1998); did not play. ... Assigned by Panthers to Scottish Claymores in 1999 NFL Europe enhancement allocation program (February 22, 1999). ... Inactive for all 16 games (1999).
PRO STATISTICS: 2000—Rushed twice for four yards and caught two passes for four yards.

			PASSING								RUSHING				TOTALS		
Year Team	G	GS	Att.	Cmp.	Pct.	Yds.	TD	Int.	Avg.	Rat.	Att.	Yds.	Avg.	TD	TD	2pt.	Pts.
1999—Scottish NFLE	...	...	339	198	58.4	2932	21	12	8.65	92.7	53	276	5.2	3	3	0	18
2000—Carolina NFL	4	0	0	0	0.0	0	0	0	0.0	...	2	4	2.0	0	0	0	0
NFL Europe totals (1 year)	...	...	339	198	58.4	2932	21	12	8.65	92.7	53	276	5.2	3	3	0	18
NFL totals (1 year)	4	0	0	0	0.0	0	0	0	0.0		2	4	2.0	0	0	0	0
Pro totals (2 years)	...	...	339	198	58.4	2932	21	12	8.65	92.7	55	280	5.1	3	3	0	18

CRAWFORD, CASEY — TE — PANTHERS

PERSONAL: Born August 1, 1977, in Washington, D.C. ... 6-6/255. ... Full name: Casey Stuart Crawford.
HIGH SCHOOL: Bishop O'Connell (Arlington, Va.).
COLLEGE: Virginia.
TRANSACTIONS/CAREER NOTES: Signed as non-drafted free agent by Carolina Panthers (April 25, 2000).
PLAYING EXPERIENCE: Carolina NFL, 2000. ... Games/Games started: 2000 (8/0).
PRO STATISTICS: 2000—Caught four passes for 47 yards and one touchdown.
SINGLE GAME HIGHS (regular season): Receptions—1 (December 10, 2000, vs. Kansas City); yards—16 (November 5, 2000, vs. St. Louis); and touchdown receptions—1 (November 5, 2000, vs. St. Louis).

CRISS, SHAD   CB   JAGUARS

PERSONAL: Born January 11, 1976, in Sherman, Texas. ... 5-11/184. ... Full name: Shadwick Leon Criss.
HIGH SCHOOL: Denison (Texas).
COLLEGE: Missouri.
TRANSACTIONS/CAREER NOTES: Signed as non-drafted free agent by San Diego Chargers (January 18, 2000). ... Released by Chargers (July 19, 2000). ... Re-signed by Chargers (July 21, 2000). ... Released by Chargers (August 27, 2000). ... Signed by Jacksonville Jaguars to practice squad (September 6, 2000). ... Activated (October 21, 2000). ... Released by Jaguars (October 24, 2000). ... Re-signed by Jaguars to practice squad (October 25, 2000). ... Activated (November 11, 2000).
PLAYING EXPERIENCE: Jacksonville NFL, 2000. ... Games/Games started: 2000 (3/0).

CROCKETT, HENRI   LB   BRONCOS

PERSONAL: Born October 28, 1974, in Pompano Beach, Fla. ... 6-2/238. ... Full name: Henri W. Crockett. ... Brother of Zack Crockett, fullback, Oakland Raiders.
HIGH SCHOOL: Ely (Pompano Beach, Fla.).
COLLEGE: Florida State (degree in criminology, 1996).
TRANSACTIONS/CAREER NOTES: Selected by Atlanta Falcons in fourth round (100th pick overall) of 1997 NFL draft. ... Signed by Falcons (July 14, 1997). ... Granted free agency (February 11, 2000). ... Re-signed by Falcons (June 1, 2000). ... Granted unconditional free agency (March 2, 2001). ... Signed by Denver Broncos (May 4, 2001).
CHAMPIONSHIP GAME EXPERIENCE: Played in NFC championship game (1998 season). ... Played in Super Bowl XXXIII (1998 season).
PRO STATISTICS: 1997—Recovered one fumble.

Year Team	G	GS	SACKS
1997—Atlanta NFL	16	10	2.0
1998—Atlanta NFL	10	10	1.0
1999—Atlanta NFL	16	14	1.5
2000—Atlanta NFL	15	12	2.0
Pro totals (4 years)	57	46	6.5

CROCKETT, RAY   CB   CHIEFS

PERSONAL: Born January 5, 1967, in Dallas. ... 5-10/184. ... Full name: Donald Ray Crockett.
HIGH SCHOOL: Duncanville (Texas).
COLLEGE: Baylor.
TRANSACTIONS/CAREER NOTES: Selected by Detroit Lions in fourth round (86th pick overall) of 1989 NFL draft. ... Signed by Lions (July 18, 1989). ... Granted unconditional free agency (February 17, 1994). ... Signed by Denver Broncos (March 9, 1994). ... Granted unconditional free agency (March 2, 2001). ... Signed by Kansas City Chiefs (April 5, 2001).
CHAMPIONSHIP GAME EXPERIENCE: Played in NFC championship game (1991 season). ... Played in AFC championship game (1997 and 1998 seasons). ... Member of Super Bowl championship team (1997 and 1998 seasons).
PRO STATISTICS: 1989—Returned one kickoff for eight yards and recovered one fumble. 1990—Recovered two fumbles for 22 yards and a touchdown. 1992—Recovered one fumble for 15 yards. 1993—Recovered one fumble. 1994—Recovered two fumbles for 43 yards. 1995—Ran four yards with lateral from punt return and recovered one fumble for 50 yards and a touchdown. 1999—Recovered one fumble.

Year Team	G	GS	INTERCEPTIONS No.	Yds.	Avg.	TD	SACKS No.
1989—Detroit NFL	16	0	1	5	5.0	0	0.0
1990—Detroit NFL	16	6	3	17	5.7	0	1.0
1991—Detroit NFL	16	16	∞6	141	23.5	∞1	1.0
1992—Detroit NFL	15	15	4	50	12.5	0	1.0
1993—Detroit NFL	16	16	2	31	15.5	0	1.0
1994—Denver NFL	14	14	2	6	3.0	0	0.0
1995—Denver NFL	16	16	0	0	0.0	0	3.0
1996—Denver NFL	15	15	2	34	17.0	0	4.0
1997—Denver NFL	16	16	4	18	4.5	0	0.0
1998—Denver NFL	16	16	3	105	35.0	1	0.5
1999—Denver NFL	16	16	2	14	7.0	0	2.0
2000—Denver NFL	13	11	4	31	7.8	1	1.0
Pro totals (12 years)	185	157	33	452	13.7	3	14.5

CROCKETT, ZACK   FB   RAIDERS

PERSONAL: Born December 2, 1972, in Pompano Beach, Fla. ... 6-2/240. ... Brother of Henri Crockett, linebacker, Denver Broncos.
HIGH SCHOOL: Ely (Pompano Beach, Fla.).
JUNIOR COLLEGE: Hinds Community College (Miss.).
COLLEGE: Florida State.
TRANSACTIONS/CAREER NOTES: Selected by Indianapolis Colts in third round (79th pick overall) of 1995 NFL draft. ... Signed by Colts (July 21, 1995). ... On injured reserve with knee injury (October 22, 1996-remainder of season). ... Granted free agency (February 13, 1998). ... Re-signed by Colts (July 23, 1998). ... Claimed on waivers by Jacksonville Jaguars (October 21, 1998). ... Granted unconditional free agency (February 12, 1999). ... Signed by Oakland Raiders (March 16, 1999).
CHAMPIONSHIP GAME EXPERIENCE: Played in AFC championship game (1995 and 2000 seasons).
PRO STATISTICS: 2000—Recovered one fumble.
SINGLE GAME HIGHS (regular season): Attempts—17 (November 19, 2000, vs. New Orleans); yards—81 (November 2, 1997, vs. Tampa Bay); and rushing touchdowns—2 (November 19, 2000, vs. New Orleans).

C

Year Team	G	GS	RUSHING Att.	Yds.	Avg.	TD	RECEIVING No.	Yds.	Avg.	TD	TOTALS TD	2pt.	Pts.	Fum.
1995—Indianapolis NFL	16	0	1	0	0.0	0	2	35	17.5	0	0	0	0	0
1996—Indianapolis NFL	5	5	31	164	5.3	0	11	96	8.7	1	1	0	6	2
1997—Indianapolis NFL	16	12	95	300	3.2	1	15	112	7.5	0	1	0	6	3
1998—Indianapolis NFL	2	1	2	5	2.5	0	1	1	1.0	0	0	0	0	1
—Jacksonville NFL	10	1	0	0	0.0	0	1	4	4.0	0	0	0	0	0
1999—Oakland NFL	13	1	45	91	2.0	4	8	56	7.0	1	5	0	30	0
2000—Oakland NFL	16	4	43	130	3.0	7	10	62	6.2	0	7	0	42	0
Pro totals (6 years)	78	24	217	690	3.2	12	48	366	7.6	2	14	0	84	6

CROSS, HOWARD — TE — GIANTS

PERSONAL: Born August 8, 1967, in Huntsville, Ala. ... 6-5/270. ... Full name: Howard E. Cross.
HIGH SCHOOL: New Hope (Ala.).
COLLEGE: Alabama.
TRANSACTIONS/CAREER NOTES: Selected by New York Giants in sixth round (158th pick overall) of 1989 NFL draft. ... Signed by Giants (July 24, 1989). ... Granted free agency (February 1, 1991). ... Re-signed by Giants (July 24, 1991). ... Granted free agency (March 1, 1993). ... Re-signed by Giants (July 16, 1993). ... Designated by Giants as transition player (February 15, 1994).
CHAMPIONSHIP GAME EXPERIENCE: Played in NFC championship game (1990 and 2000 season). ... Member of Super Bowl championship team (1990 season). ... Played in Super Bowl XXXV (2000 season).
PRO STATISTICS: 1992—Recovered one fumble. 1993—Recovered one fumble. 1994—Recovered one fumble. 1997—Recovered one fumble.
SINGLE GAME HIGHS (regular season): Receptions—6 (September 13, 1992, vs. Dallas); yards—77 (September 13, 1992, vs. Dallas); and touchdown receptions—2 (September 11, 1994, vs. Arizona).

Year Team	G	GS	RECEIVING No.	Yds.	Avg.	TD	KICKOFF RETURNS No.	Yds.	Avg.	TD	TOTALS TD	2pt.	Pts.	Fum.
1989—New York Giants NFL	16	4	6	107	17.8	1	0	0	0.0	0	1	0	6	1
1990—New York Giants NFL	16	8	8	106	13.3	0	1	10	10.0	0	0	0	0	1
1991—New York Giants NFL	16	16	20	283	14.2	2	1	11	11.0	0	2	0	12	1
1992—New York Giants NFL	16	16	27	357	13.2	2	0	0	0.0	0	2	0	12	2
1993—New York Giants NFL	16	16	21	272	13.0	5	2	15	7.5	0	5	0	30	0
1994—New York Giants NFL	16	16	31	364	11.7	4	0	0	0.0	0	4	0	24	0
1995—New York Giants NFL	15	15	18	197	10.9	0	0	0	0.0	0	0	0	0	0
1996—New York Giants NFL	16	16	22	178	8.1	1	0	0	0.0	0	1	0	6	1
1997—New York Giants NFL	16	16	21	150	7.1	2	0	0	0.0	0	2	0	12	1
1998—New York Giants NFL	16	16	13	90	6.9	0	0	0	0.0	0	0	0	0	2
1999—New York Giants NFL	16	15	9	55	6.1	0	0	0	0.0	0	0	0	0	0
2000—New York Giants NFL	16	11	4	30	7.5	0	0	0	0.0	0	0	0	0	0
Pro totals (12 years)	191	165	200	2189	10.9	17	4	36	9.0	0	17	0	102	8

CROWELL, GERMANE — WR — LIONS

PERSONAL: Born September 13, 1976, in Winston-Salem, N.C. ... 6-3/216. ... Full name: Germane L. Crowell.
HIGH SCHOOL: North Forsyth (Winston-Salem, N.C.).
COLLEGE: Virginia.
TRANSACTIONS/CAREER NOTES: Selected by Detroit Lions in second round (50th pick overall) of 1998 NFL draft. ... Signed by Lions (July 20, 1998).
PRO STATISTICS: 1999—Recovered one fumble.
SINGLE GAME HIGHS (regular season): Receptions—8 (October 1, 2000, vs. Minnesota); yards—163 (November 7, 1999, vs. St. Louis); and touchdown receptions—2 (September 12, 1999, vs. Seattle).
STATISTICAL PLATEAUS: 100-yard receiving games: 1999 (6).

Year Team	G	GS	RUSHING Att.	Yds.	Avg.	TD	RECEIVING No.	Yds.	Avg.	TD	TOTALS TD	2pt.	Pts.	Fum.
1998—Detroit NFL	14	2	1	35	35.0	0	25	464	18.6	3	3	0	18	1
1999—Detroit NFL	16	15	5	38	7.6	0	81	1338	16.5	7	7	†1	44	1
2000—Detroit NFL	9	7	1	12	12.0	0	34	430	12.6	3	3	0	18	0
Pro totals (3 years)	39	24	7	85	12.1	0	140	2232	15.9	13	13	1	80	2

CULPEPPER, BRAD — DT

PERSONAL: Born May 8, 1969, in Tallahassee, Fla. ... 6-1/270. ... Full name: John Broward Culpepper.
HIGH SCHOOL: Leon (Tallahassee, Fla.).
COLLEGE: Florida (degree in history, 1991).
TRANSACTIONS/CAREER NOTES: Selected by Minnesota Vikings in 10th round (264th pick overall) of 1992 NFL draft. ... Signed by Vikings (July 20, 1992). ... On injured reserve with toe injury (November 23, 1992-remainder of season). ... Claimed on waivers by Tampa Bay Buccaneers (August 30, 1994). ... Released by Buccaneers (August 21, 2000). ... Signed by Chicago Bears (August 23, 2000). ... Released by Bears (February 27, 2001).
CHAMPIONSHIP GAME EXPERIENCE: Played in NFC championship game (1999 season).
HONORS: Named defensive lineman on THE SPORTING NEWS college All-America first team (1991).
PRO STATISTICS: 1994—Returned two kickoffs for 30 yards and recovered one fumble. 1995—Recovered one fumble for 12 yards. 1998—Recovered one fumble. 1999—Credited with a safety.

Year—Team	G	GS	SACKS
1992—Minnesota NFL	11	2	0.0
1993—Minnesota NFL	15	0	0.0
1994—Tampa Bay NFL	16	15	4.0
1995—Tampa Bay NFL	16	4	4.0
1996—Tampa Bay NFL	13	13	1.5
1997—Tampa Bay NFL	16	16	8.5
1998—Tampa Bay NFL	16	16	9.0
1999—Tampa Bay NFL	16	16	6.0
2000—Chicago NFL	12	1	1.0
Pro totals (9 years)	131	83	34.0

CULPEPPER, DAUNTE QB VIKINGS

PERSONAL: Born January 28, 1977, in Ocala, Fla. ... 6-4/260.
HIGH SCHOOL: Vanguard (Ocala, Fla.).
COLLEGE: Central Florida.
TRANSACTIONS/CAREER NOTES: Selected by Minnesota Vikings in first round (11th pick overall) of 1999 NFL draft. ... Signed by Vikings (July 30, 1999).
CHAMPIONSHIP GAME EXPERIENCE: Played in NFC championship game (2000 season).
HONORS: Played in Pro Bowl (2000 season).
PRO STATISTICS: 1999—Fumbled once and recovered one fumble for minus two yards. 2000—Led NFC with 11 fumbles and recovered five fumbles for minus 23 yards.
SINGLE GAME HIGHS (regular season): Attempts—53 (October 29, 2000, vs. Tampa Bay); completions—29 (October 29, 2000, vs. Tampa Bay); yards—357 (November 19, 2000, vs. Carolina); and touchdown passes—3 (December 17, 2000, vs. Green Bay).
STATISTICAL PLATEAUS: 300-yard passing games: 2000 (5).
MISCELLANEOUS: Selected by New York Yankees organization in 26th round of free-agent baseball draft (June 1, 1995); did not sign. ... Regular-season record as starting NFL quarterback: 11-5 (.688). ... Postseason record as starting NFL quarterback: 1-1 (.500).

			PASSING							RUSHING				TOTALS		
Year—Team	G	GS	Att.	Cmp.	Pct.	Yds.	TD	Int.	Avg.	Rat.	Att.	Yds.	Avg.	TD	TD	2pt.	Pts.
1999—Minnesota NFL	1	0	0	0	0.0	0	0	0	0.0	...	3	6	2.0	0	0	0	0
2000—Minnesota NFL	16	16	474	297	62.7	3937	33	16	8.31	98.0	89	470	5.3	7	7	0	42
Pro totals (2 years)	17	16	474	297	62.7	3937	33	16	8.31	98.0	92	476	5.2	7	7	0	42

CUNNINGHAM, RANDALL QB RAVENS

PERSONAL: Born March 27, 1963, in Santa Barbara, Calif. ... 6-4/213. ... Brother of Sam Cunningham, running back with New England Patriots (1973-79 and 1981).
HIGH SCHOOL: Santa Barbara (Calif.).
COLLEGE: UNLV.
TRANSACTIONS/CAREER NOTES: Selected by Arizona Outlaws in 1985 USFL territorial draft. ... Selected by Philadelphia Eagles in second round (37th pick overall) of 1985 NFL draft. ... Signed by Eagles (July 22, 1985). ... On injured reserve with knee injury (September 3, 1991-remainder of season). ... Granted unconditional free agency (February 16, 1996). ... On retired list (August 30, 1996-April 15, 1997). ... Signed by Minnesota Vikings (April 15, 1997). ... Granted unconditional free agency (February 13, 1998). ... Re-signed by Vikings (March 24, 1998). ... Released by Vikings (June 2, 2000). ... Signed by Dallas Cowboys (June 8, 2000). ... Granted unconditional free agency (March 2, 2001). ... Signed by Baltimore Ravens (May 29, 2001).
CHAMPIONSHIP GAME EXPERIENCE: Played in NFC championship game (1998 season).
HONORS: Named punter on THE SPORTING NEWS college All-America first team (1984). ... Played in Pro Bowl (1988-1990 and 1998 seasons). ... Named Outstanding Player of Pro Bowl (1988 season).
RECORDS: Holds NFL single-season record for most times sacked—72 (1986). ... Shares NFL single-game records for most own fumbles recovered—4 (November 30, 1986, OT, at Los Angeles Raiders); and most own and opponents' fumbles recovered—4 (November 30, 1986, OT, at Los Angeles Raiders).
PRO STATISTICS: 1985—Fumbled three times. 1986—Punted twice for 54 yards, fumbled seven times and recovered four fumbles. 1987—Caught one pass for minus three yards, led league with 12 fumbles and recovered six fumbles for minus seven yards. 1988—Punted three times for 167 yards, led league with 12 fumbles and recovered six fumbles. 1989—Punted six times for 319 yards, led the NFC with 17 fumbles and recovered four fumbles for minus six yards. 1990—Fumbled nine times and recovered three fumbles for minus four yards. 1992—Led league with 13 fumbles and recovered three fumbles. 1993—Fumbled three times. 1994—Punted once for 80 yards, fumbled 10 times and recovered two fumbles for minus 15 yards. 1995—Fumbled three times and recovered one fumble for minus five yards. 1997—Fumbled four times and recovered two fumbles. 1998—Caught one pass for minus three yards and fumbled twice. 1999—Fumbled twice for minus one yard. 2000—Fumbled four times and recovered three fumbles for minus two yards.
SINGLE GAME HIGHS (regular season): Attempts—62 (October 2, 1989, vs. Chicago); completions—34 (September 17, 1989, vs. Washington); passing yards—447 (September 17, 1989, vs. Washington); and touchdown passes—5 (September 17, 1989, vs. Washington).
STATISTICAL PLATEAUS: 300-yard passing games: 1987 (1), 1988 (2), 1989 (3), 1992 (1), 1993 (1), 1994 (4), 1998 (4), 1999 (2). Total: 18. ... 100-yard rushing games: 1986 (1), 1990 (1), 1992 (1). Total: 3.
MISCELLANEOUS: Regular-season record as starting NFL quarterback: 80-52-1 (.602). ... Postseason record as starting NFL quarterback: 3-6 (.333).

			PASSING							RUSHING				TOTALS		
Year—Team	G	GS	Att.	Cmp.	Pct.	Yds.	TD	Int.	Avg.	Rat.	Att.	Yds.	Avg.	TD	TD	2pt.	Pts.
1985—Philadelphia NFL	6	4	81	34	42.0	548	1	8	6.77	29.8	29	205	7.1	0	0	0	0
1986—Philadelphia NFL	15	5	209	111	53.1	1391	8	7	6.66	72.9	66	540	8.2	5	5	0	30
1987—Philadelphia NFL	12	12	406	223	54.9	2786	23	12	6.86	83.0	76	505	6.6	3	3	0	18
1988—Philadelphia NFL	16	16	‡560	301	53.8	3808	24	16	6.80	77.6	93	624	6.7	6	6	0	36
1989—Philadelphia NFL	16	16	532	290	54.5	3400	21	15	6.39	75.5	104	621	*6.0	4	4	0	24
1990—Philadelphia NFL	16	16	465	271	58.3	3466	‡30	13	7.45	91.6	118	942	*8.0	5	5	0	30
1991—Philadelphia NFL	1	1	4	1	25.0	19	0	0	4.75	46.9	0	0	0.0	0	0	0	0
1992—Philadelphia NFL	15	15	384	233	60.7	2775	19	11	7.23	87.3	87	549	6.3	5	5	0	30
1993—Philadelphia NFL	4	4	110	76	69.1	850	5	5	7.73	88.1	18	110	6.1	1	1	0	6
1994—Philadelphia NFL	14	14	490	265	54.1	3229	16	13	6.59	74.4	65	288	4.4	3	3	0	18

			PASSING								RUSHING				TOTALS		
Year Team	G	GS	Att.	Cmp.	Pct.	Yds.	TD	Int.	Avg.	Rat.	Att.	Yds.	Avg.	TD	TD	2pt.	Pts.
1995—Philadelphia NFL	7	4	121	69	57.0	605	3	5	5.00	61.5	21	98	4.7	0	0	0	0
1996—								Did not play.									
1997—Minnesota NFL	6	3	88	44	50.0	501	6	4	5.69	71.3	19	127	6.7	0	0	0	0
1998—Minnesota NFL	15	14	425	259	60.9	3704	34	10	8.72	*106.0	32	132	4.1	1	1	1	8
1999—Minnesota NFL	6	6	200	124	62.0	1475	8	9	7.38	79.1	10	58	5.8	0	0	0	0
2000—Dallas NFL	6	3	125	74	59.2	849	6	4	6.79	82.4	23	89	3.9	1	1	0	6
Pro totals (15 years)	155	133	4200	2375	56.5	29406	204	132	7.00	81.5	761	4888	6.4	34	34	1	206

CUNNINGHAM, RICHIE   K   BENGALS

PERSONAL: Born August 18, 1970, in Terrebonne, La. ... 5-10/167. ... Full name: Richard Anthony Cunningham.
HIGH SCHOOL: Terrebonne (La.).
COLLEGE: Southwestern Louisiana (degree in marketing).
TRANSACTIONS/CAREER NOTES: Signed as non-drafted free agent by Dallas Cowboys (May 2, 1994). ... Released by Cowboys (August 17, 1994). ... Signed by Green Bay Packers (April 22, 1996). ... Released by Packers (August 19, 1996). ... Signed by Cowboys (April 15, 1997). ... Released by Cowboys (December 7, 1999). ... Signed by Carolina Panthers (December 14, 1999). ... Released by Panthers (February 10, 2000). ... Re-signed by Panthers (August 18, 2000). ... Released by Panthers (October 3, 2000). ... Signed by Cincinnati Bengals (March 16, 2001).
HONORS: Named kicker on The Sporting News NFL All-Pro team (1997).

				KICKING				
Year Team	G	XPM	XPA	FGM	FGA	Lg.	50+	Pts.
1997—Dallas NFL	16	24	24	*34	∞37	53	1-1	‡126
1998—Dallas NFL	16	40	40	29	35	54	1-3	127
1999—Dallas NFL	12	31	31	12	22	47	0-1	67
—Carolina NFL	3	13	14	3	3	43	0-0	22
2000—Carolina NFL	4	9	9	5	7	39	0-0	24
Pro totals (4 years)	51	117	118	83	104	54	2-5	366

CURTIS, CANUTE   LB   BENGALS

PERSONAL: Born August 4, 1974, in Amityville, N.Y. ... 6-2/257. ... Name pronounced kuh-NOOT.
HIGH SCHOOL: Farmingdale (N.Y.).
COLLEGE: West Virginia.
TRANSACTIONS/CAREER NOTES: Selected by Cincinnati Bengals in sixth round (176th pick overall) of 1997 NFL draft. ... Signed by Bengals (July 11, 1997). ... Released by Bengals (August 24, 1997). ... Re-signed by Bengals to practice squad (August 26, 1997). ... Activated (October 21, 1997). ... Released by Bengals (August 30, 1998). ... Re-signed by Bengals to practice squad (August 31, 1998). ... Activated (November 10, 1998). ... Granted free agency (February 11, 2000). ... Re-signed by Bengals (March 1, 2000).
PLAYING EXPERIENCE: Cincinnati NFL, 1997-2000. ... Games/games started: 1997 (3/0), 1998 (5/0), 1999 (15/0), 2000 (15/0). Total: 38/0.
HONORS: Named outside linebacker on The Sporting News college All-America first team (1996).
PRO STATISTICS: 1999—Credited with one sack. 2000—Credited with two sacks and recovered one fumble.

CUSHING, MATT   TE   STEELERS

PERSONAL: Born July 2, 1975, in Chicago ... 6-3/258. ... Full name: Matt Jay Cushing.
HIGH SCHOOL: Mount Carmel (Chicago).
COLLEGE: Illinois.
TRANSACTIONS/CAREER NOTES: Signed as non-drafted free agent by Pittsburgh Steelers (April 24, 1998). ... Released by Steelers (August 24, 1998). ... Re-signed by Steelers (February 22, 1999). ... Assigned by Steelers to Amsterdam Admirals in 1999 NFL Europe enhancement allocation program (February 22, 1999). ... Released by Steelers (September 5, 1999). ... Re-signed by Steelers (October 28, 1999). ... Released by Steelers (August 27, 2000). ... Re-signed by Steelers (November 7, 2000).
SINGLE GAME HIGHS (regular season): Receptions—2 (November 19, 2000, vs. Jacksonville); yards—29 (January 2, 2000, vs. Tennessee); and touchdown receptions—0.

			RECEIVING				TOTALS			
Year Team	G	GS	No.	Yds.	Avg.	TD	TD	2pt.	Pts.	Fum.
1999—Amsterdam NFLE	...	...	6	62	10.3	0	0	0	0	0
—Pittsburgh NFL	7	1	2	29	14.5	0	0	0	0	0
2000—Pittsburgh NFL	7	1	4	17	4.3	0	0	0	0	0
NFL Europe totals (1 year)	...	...	6	62	10.3	0	0	0	0	0
NFL totals (2 years)	14	2	6	46	7.7	0	0	0	0	0
Pro totals (3 years)	...	...	12	108	9.0	0	0	0	0	0

DALMAN, CHRIS   C

PERSONAL: Born March 15, 1970, in Salinas, Calif. ... 6-3/297. ... Full name: Christopher William Dalman.
HIGH SCHOOL: Palma (Salinas, Calif.).
COLLEGE: Stanford (degree in political science, 1992).
TRANSACTIONS/CAREER NOTES: Selected by San Francisco 49ers in sixth round (166th pick overall) of 1993 NFL draft. ... Signed by 49ers (June 24, 1993). ... Granted unconditional free agency (February 14, 1997). ... Re-signed by 49ers (April 25, 1997). ... On injured reserve with neck injury (August 22, 2000-entire season). ... Announced retirement (June 4, 2001).
PLAYING EXPERIENCE: San Francisco NFL, 1993-1999. ... Games/Games started: 1993 (15/0), 1994 (16/4), 1995 (15/1), 1996 (16/16), 1997 (13/13), 1998 (15/15), 1999 (15/15). Total: 105/64.
CHAMPIONSHIP GAME EXPERIENCE: Played in NFC championship game (1993, 1994 and 1997 seasons). ... Member of Super Bowl championship team (1994 season).
PRO STATISTICS: 1993—Recovered one fumble. 1994—Fumbled once. 1995—Caught one pass for minus one yard, returned three kickoffs for 29 yards and recovered one fumble. 1997—Recovered one fumble.

DALTON, ANTICO   LB   PATRIOTS

PERSONAL: Born December 31, 1975, in Eden, N.C. ... 6-1/240.
HIGH SCHOOL: J.M. Morehead (Eden, N.C.).
COLLEGE: Hampton University.
TRANSACTIONS/CAREER NOTES: Selected by Minnesota Vikings in sixth round (199th pick overall) of 1999 NFL draft. ... Signed by Vikings (June 8, 1999). ... Released by Vikings (October 12, 1999). ... Re-signed by Vikings to practice squad (October 13, 1999). ... Released by Vikings (August 27, 2000). ... Signed by New England Patriots to practice squad (November 28, 2000). ... Activated (December 7, 2000).
PLAYING EXPERIENCE: Minnesota NFL, 1999; New England NFL, 2000. ... Games/Games started: 1999 (2/0), 2000 (3/0). Total: 5/0.
PRO STATISTICS: 2000—Recovered one fumble.

DALTON, LIONAL   DT   RAVENS

PERSONAL: Born February 21, 1975, in Detroit. ... 6-1/309.
HIGH SCHOOL: Cooley (Detroit).
COLLEGE: Eastern Michigan.
TRANSACTIONS/CAREER NOTES: Signed as non-drafted free agent by Baltimore Ravens (April 23, 1998). ... Granted free agency (March 2, 2001).
PLAYING EXPERIENCE: Baltimore NFL, 1998-2000. ... Games/Games started: 1998 (2/1), 1999 (16/2), 2000 (16/1). Total: 34/4.
CHAMPIONSHIP GAME EXPERIENCE: Played in AFC championship game (2000 season). ... Member of Super Bowl championship team (2000 season).
PRO STATISTICS: 1999—Credited with one sack.

DALUISO, BRAD   K

PERSONAL: Born December 31, 1967, in San Diego. ... 6-1/180. ... Full name: Bradley William Daluiso.
HIGH SCHOOL: Valhalla (El Cajon, Calif.).
JUNIOR COLLEGE: Grossmont College (Calif.).
COLLEGE: San Diego State, then UCLA.
TRANSACTIONS/CAREER NOTES: Signed as non-drafted free agent by Green Bay Packers (May 2, 1991). ... Traded by Packers to Atlanta Falcons for an undisclosed pick in 1992 draft (August 26, 1991). ... Claimed on waivers by Buffalo Bills (September 10, 1991). ... Granted unconditional free agency (February 1, 1992). ... Signed by Dallas Cowboys (February 18, 1992). ... Claimed on waivers by Denver Broncos (September 1, 1992). ... Released by Broncos (August 23, 1993). ... Signed by New York Giants (September 1, 1993). ... Granted free agency (February 17, 1994). ... Re-signed by Giants (June 21, 1994). ... Granted unconditional free agency (February 17, 1995). ... Re-signed by Giants (February 22, 1995). ... Granted unconditional free agency (February 13, 1998). ... Re-signed by Giants (February 13, 1998). ... On injured reserve with knee injury (October 20, 1999-remainder of season). ... Granted unconditional free agency (March 2, 2001).
CHAMPIONSHIP GAME EXPERIENCE: Played in AFC championship game (1991 season). ... Played in Super Bowl XXVI (1991 season). ... Played in NFC championship game (2000 season). ... Played in Super Bowl XXXV (2000 season).
PRO STATISTICS: 1992—Punted 10 times for 467 yards.

| | | | | KICKING | | | | |
Year Team	G	XPM	XPA	FGM	FGA	Lg.	50+	Pts.
1991—Atlanta NFL	2	2	2	2	3	23	0-0	8
—Buffalo NFL	14	0	0	0	0	0	0-0	0
1992—Denver NFL	16	0	0	0	1	0	0-1	0
1993—New York Giants NFL	15	0	0	1	3	54	1-3	3
1994—New York Giants NFL	16	5	5	11	11	52	1-1	38
1995—New York Giants NFL	16	28	28	20	28	51	2-2	88
1996—New York Giants NFL	16	22	22	24	27	46	0-0	94
1997—New York Giants NFL	16	27	29	22	32	52	1-4	93
1998—New York Giants NFL	16	32	32	21	27	51	1-1	95
1999—New York Giants NFL	6	9	9	7	9	36	0-0	30
2000—New York Giants NFL	14	34	34	17	23	46	0-0	85
Pro totals (10 years)	147	159	161	125	164	54	6-12	534

DANIELS, PHILLIP   DE   BEARS

PERSONAL: Born March 4, 1973, in Donaldsonville, Ga. ... 6-5/290. ... Full name: Phillip Bernard Daniels.
HIGH SCHOOL: Seminole County (Donaldsonville, Ga.).
COLLEGE: Georgia.
TRANSACTIONS/CAREER NOTES: Selected by Seattle Seahawks in fourth round (99th pick overall) of 1996 NFL draft. ... Signed by Seahawks (July 17, 1996). ... Granted free agency (February 12, 1999). ... Re-signed by Seahawks (April 6, 1999). ... Granted unconditional free agency (February 11, 2000). ... Signed by Chicago Bears (February 12, 2000). ... On injured reserve with ankle injury (December 13, 2000-remainder of season).
PRO STATISTICS: 1996—Recovered one fumble. 1997—Returned one kickoff for minus two yards and fumbled once. 1998—Recovered two fumbles. 2000—Recovered one fumble.

Year Team	G	GS	SACKS
1996—Seattle NFL	15	0	2.0
1997—Seattle NFL	13	10	4.0
1998—Seattle NFL	16	15	6.5
1999—Seattle NFL	16	16	9.0
2000—Chicago NFL	14	14	6.0
Pro totals (5 years)	74	55	27.5

D

DARCHE, JEAN-PHILIPPE   TE   SEAHAWKS

PERSONAL: Born February 28, 1975, in Montreal. ... 6-0/242.
COLLEGE: McGill (Montreal).
TRANSACTIONS/CAREER NOTES: Signed as non-drafted free agent by Seattle Seahawks (May 11, 2000).
PLAYING EXPERIENCE: Seattle NFL, 2000. ... Games/Games started: 2000 (16/0).

DARDEN, TONY   CB   PACKERS

PERSONAL: Born August 11, 1975, in Baton Rouge, La. ... 5-11/193. ... Full name: Tony Dwayne Darden.
HIGH SCHOOL: Holmes (San Antonio).
COLLEGE: Texas Tech.
TRANSACTIONS/CAREER NOTES: Selected by Minnesota Vikings in seventh round (225th pick overall) of 1998 NFL draft. ... Signed by Vikings (July 20, 1998). ... Inactive for seven games (1998). ... On injured reserve with foot injury (October 30, 1998-remainder of season). ... Released by Vikings (September 5, 1999). ... Signed by San Diego Chargers (January 18, 2000). ... Claimed on waivers by Green Bay Packers (April 26, 2001).

			INTERCEPTIONS				RECEIVING				TOTALS		
Year Team	G	GS	No.	Yds.	Avg.	TD	No.	Yds.	Avg.	TD	TD	2pt.	Pts. Fum.
2000—San Diego NFL	16	3	0	0	0.0	0	0	0	0.0	0	0	0	0 0

DARIUS, DONOVIN   S   JAGUARS

PERSONAL: Born August 12, 1975, in Camden, N.J. ... 6-1/216. ... Full name: Donovin Lee Darius.
HIGH SCHOOL: Woodrow Wilson (Camden, N.J.).
COLLEGE: Syracuse (degree in exercise science, 1997).
TRANSACTIONS/CAREER NOTES: Selected by Jacksonville Jaguars in first round (25th pick overall) of 1998 NFL draft. ... Signed by Jaguars (July 23, 1998).
PLAYING EXPERIENCE: Jacksonville NFL, 1998-2000. ... Games/Games started: 1998 (14/14), 1999 (16/16), 2000 (16/16). Total: 46/46.
CHAMPIONSHIP GAME EXPERIENCE: Played in AFC championship game (1999 season).
HONORS: Named free safety on THE SPORTING NEWS college All-America first team (1997).
PRO STATISTICS: 1998—Recovered one fumble for 83 yards and a touchdown. 1999—Intercepted four passes for 37 yards. 2000—Intercepted two passes for 26 yards and credited with one sack.

DARLING, JAMES   LB   JETS

PERSONAL: Born December 29, 1974, in Denver. ... 6-0/250. ... Full name: James Jackson Darling.
HIGH SCHOOL: Kettle Falls (Wash.).
COLLEGE: Washington State.
TRANSACTIONS/CAREER NOTES: Selected by Philadelphia Eagles in second round (57th pick overall) of 1997 NFL draft. ... Signed by Eagles (July 16, 1997). ... Granted free agency (February 11, 2000). ... Re-signed by Eagles (April 10, 2000). ... Granted unconditional free agency (March 2, 2001). ... Signed by New York Jets (March 21, 2001).
PLAYING EXPERIENCE: Philadelphia NFL, 1997-2000. ... Games/Games started: 1997 (16/6), 1998 (12/8), 1999 (15/10), 2000 (16/0). Total: 59/24.
HONORS: Named inside linebacker on THE SPORTING NEWS college All-America second team (1996).
PRO STATISTICS: 1998—Credited with two sacks. 1999—Intercepted one pass for 33 yards. 2000—Credited with 1/2 sack.

DAVIDDS-GARRIDO, NORBERTO   OT   CARDINALS

PERSONAL: Born October 4, 1972, in La Puente, Calif. ... 6-6/336. ... Full name: Norberto Davidds-Garrido Jr. ... Formerly known as Norberto Garrido.
HIGH SCHOOL: Workman (City of Industry, Calif.).
JUNIOR COLLEGE: Mount San Antonio College (Calif.).
COLLEGE: Southern California.
TRANSACTIONS/CAREER NOTES: Selected by Carolina Panthers in fourth round (106th pick overall) of 1996 NFL draft. ... Signed by Panthers (June 17, 1996). ... On injured reserve with ankle injury (December 15, 1997-remainder of season). ... Granted free agency (February 12, 1999). ... Re-signed by Panthers (July 27, 1999). ... Granted unconditional free agency (February 11, 2000). ... Signed by Arizona Cardinals (April 18, 2000).
PLAYING EXPERIENCE: Carolina NFL, 1996-1999; Arizona NFL, 2000. ... Games/Games started: 1996 (12/8), 1997 (15/15), 1998 (16/16), 1999 (16/0), 2000 (9/2). Total: 68/41.
CHAMPIONSHIP GAME EXPERIENCE: Played in NFC championship game (1996 season).
PRO STATISTICS: 1998—Recovered one fumble.

DAVIS, ANTHONY   LB

PERSONAL: Born March 7, 1969, in Kennewick, Wash. ... 6-0/235. ... Full name: Anthony D. Davis.
HIGH SCHOOL: Pasco (Wash.).
JUNIOR COLLEGE: Spokane Falls Community College (Wash.).
COLLEGE: Utah.
TRANSACTIONS/CAREER NOTES: Selected by Houston Oilers in 11th round (301st pick overall) of 1992 NFL draft. ... Signed by Oilers for 1992 season. ... Released by Oilers (August 24, 1992). ... Re-signed by Oilers to practice squad (September 2, 1992). ... Released by Oilers (October 6, 1992). ... Signed by Seattle Seahawks to practice squad (December 9, 1992). ... Released by Seahawks (August 30, 1993). ...

D

Re-signed by Seahawks to practice squad (September 1, 1993). ... Activated (October 11, 1993). ... Released by Seahawks (August 22, 1994). ... Signed by Kansas City Chiefs (November 24, 1994). ... Granted unconditional free agency (February 12, 1999). ... Signed by Green Bay Packers (July 29, 1999). ... On injured reserve with hamstring injury (January 1, 2000-remainder of season). ... Granted unconditional free agency (February 11, 2000). ... Signed by Baltimore Ravens (July 23, 2000) ... Granted unconditional free agency (March 2, 2001).

CHAMPIONSHIP GAME EXPERIENCE: Played in AFC championship game (2000 season). ... Member of Super Bowl championship team (2000 season).

PRO STATISTICS: 1997—Recovered one fumble for two yards.

Year Team	G	GS	INTERCEPTIONS No.	Yds.	Avg.	TD	SACKS No.
1993—Seattle NFL	10	0	0	0	0.0	0	0.0
1994—Kansas City NFL	5	0	0	0	0.0	0	0.0
1995—Kansas City NFL	16	2	1	11	11.0	0	2.0
1996—Kansas City NFL	16	15	2	37	18.5	0	2.5
1997—Kansas City NFL	15	15	0	0	0.0	0	3.5
1998—Kansas City NFL	16	16	2	27	13.5	0	4.5
1999—Green Bay NFL	14	1	0	0	0.0	0	0.0
2000—Baltimore NFL	14	0	0	0	0.0	0	0.0
Pro totals (8 years)	106	49	5	75	15.0	0	12.5

DAVIS, BILLY   WR

PERSONAL: Born July 6, 1972, in El Paso, Texas. ... 6-1/205. ... Full name: William Augusta Davis III.

HIGH SCHOOL: Irvin (El Paso, Texas).

COLLEGE: Pittsburgh.

TRANSACTIONS/CAREER NOTES: Signed as non-drafted free agent by Dallas Cowboys (April 27, 1995). ... Granted free agency (February 13, 1998). ... Re-signed by Cowboys (February 27, 1998). ... Released by Cowboys (June 1, 1999). ... Signed by Baltimore Ravens (June 18, 1999). ... Granted unconditional free agency (February 11, 2000). ... Re-signed by Ravens (April 28, 2000). ... Released by Ravens (March 13, 2001).

CHAMPIONSHIP GAME EXPERIENCE: Played in NFC championship game (1995 season). ... Member of Super Bowl championship team (1995 and 2000 seasons). ... Played in AFC championship game (2000 season).

PRO STATISTICS: 1998—Rushed four times for 15 yards, returned one kickoff for 10 yards and recovered one fumble. 1999—Recovered one fumble.

SINGLE GAME HIGHS (regular season): Receptions—4 (December 27, 1998, vs. Washington); yards—87 (September 27, 1998, vs. Oakland); and touchdown receptions—1 (November 22, 1998, vs. Seattle).

D

Year Team	G	GS	RECEIVING No.	Yds.	Avg.	TD	TOTALS TD	2pt.	Pts.	Fum.
1995—Dallas NFL	16	0	0	0	0.0	0	0	0	0	0
1996—Dallas NFL	13	0	0	0	0.0	0	0	0	0	0
1997—Dallas NFL	16	0	3	33	11.0	0	0	0	0	0
1998—Dallas NFL	16	11	39	691	17.7	3	3	0	18	1
1999—Baltimore NFL	16	0	6	121	20.2	0	0	0	0	0
2000—Baltimore NFL	16	1	3	62	20.7	0	0	0	0	0
Pro totals (6 years)	93	12	51	907	17.8	3	3	0	18	1

DAVIS, DON   LB   RAMS

PERSONAL: Born December 17, 1972, in Olathe, Kan. ... 6-1/234.

HIGH SCHOOL: Olathe (Kan.) South.

COLLEGE: Kansas.

TRANSACTIONS/CAREER NOTES: Signed as non-drafted free agent by New York Jets (April 28, 1995). ... Released by Jets (August 27, 1995). ... Signed by Kansas City Chiefs (January 9, 1996). ... Released by Chiefs (August 20, 1996). ... Signed by New Orleans Saints to practice squad (August 27, 1996). ... Activated (October 4, 1996). ... On injured reserve with wrist injury (November 19, 1997-remainder of season). ... Claimed on waivers by Tampa Bay Buccaneers (November 25, 1998). ... Granted free agency (February 12, 1999). ... Re-signed by Buccaneers (May 21, 1999). ... Released by Buccaneers (October 9, 1999). ... Re-signed by Buccaneers (October 19, 1999). ... Granted unconditional free agency (February 11, 2000). ... Re-signed by Buccaneers (July 1, 2000). ... Granted unconditional free agency (March 2, 2001). ... Signed by St. Louis Rams (March 3, 2001).

PLAYING EXPERIENCE: New Orleans NFL, 1996 and 1997; New Orleans (4)-Tampa Bay (5) NFL, 1998; Tampa Bay NFL, 1999 and 2000. ... Games/Games started: 1996 (11/0), 1997 (11/0), 1998 (N.O.-4/0; T.B.-5/0; Total: 9/0), 1999 (14/0), 2000 (16/0). Total: 61/0.

CHAMPIONSHIP GAME EXPERIENCE: Played in NFC championship game (1999 season).

PRO STATISTICS: 1996—Recovered one fumble.

DAVIS, ERIC   CB

PERSONAL: Born January 26, 1968, in Anniston, Ala. ... 5-11/185. ... Full name: Eric Wayne Davis.

HIGH SCHOOL: Anniston (Ala.).

COLLEGE: Jacksonville (Ala.) State.

TRANSACTIONS/CAREER NOTES: Selected by San Francisco 49ers in second round (53rd pick overall) of 1990 NFL draft. ... Signed by 49ers (July 28, 1990). ... On injured reserve with shoulder injury (September 11, 1991-remainder of season). ... Granted free agency (March 1, 1993). ... Re-signed by 49ers (July 20, 1993). ... Granted unconditional free agency (February 16, 1996). ... Signed by Carolina Panthers (February 21, 1996). ... Released by Panthers (February 28, 2001).

CHAMPIONSHIP GAME EXPERIENCE: Played in NFC championship game (1990, 1992-1994 and 1996 seasons). ... Member of Super Bowl championship team (1994 season).

HONORS: Played in Pro Bowl (1995 and 1996 seasons).

POST SEASON RECORDS: Shares NFL postseason career record for most consecutive games with one or more interception—3.

PRO STATISTICS: 1990—Returned five punts for 38 yards and recovered one fumble for 34 yards. 1992—Recovered two fumbles. 1993—Recovered one fumble for 47 yards and a touchdown. 1994—Recovered two fumbles. 1995—Credited with one sack. 1997—Recovered one fumble for two yards. 1998—Credited with one sack and recovered one fumble. 1999—Fumbled once and recovered one fumble. 2000—Returned two punts for 24 yards, fumbled once and recovered one fumble.

MISCELLANEOUS: Holds Carolina Panthers all-time record for most interceptions (25).

				INTERCEPTIONS		
Year Team	G	GS	No.	Yds.	Avg.	TD
1990—San Francisco NFL	16	0	1	13	13.0	0
1991—San Francisco NFL	2	2	0	0	0.0	0
1992—San Francisco NFL	16	16	3	52	17.3	0
1993—San Francisco NFL	16	16	4	45	11.3	1
1994—San Francisco NFL	16	16	1	8	8.0	0
1995—San Francisco NFL	15	15	3	84	28.0	1
1996—Carolina NFL	16	16	5	57	11.4	0
1997—Carolina NFL	14	14	5	25	5.0	0
1998—Carolina NFL	16	16	5	81	16.2	2
1999—Carolina NFL	16	16	5	49	9.8	0
2000—Carolina NFL	16	16	5	14	2.8	0
Pro totals (11 years)	159	143	37	428	11.6	4

DAVIS, JOHN — TE — VIKINGS

PERSONAL: Born May 14, 1973, in Jasper, Texas. ... 6-4/271.
HIGH SCHOOL: Jasper (Texas).
JUNIOR COLLEGE: Cisco (Texas) Junior College.
COLLEGE: Emporia (Kan.) State.
TRANSACTIONS/CAREER NOTES: Selected by Dallas Cowboys in fifth round of 1994 supplemental draft. ... Signed by Cowboys for 1994 season. ... Released by Cowboys (August 28, 1994). ... Re-signed by Cowboys to practice squad (August 30, 1994). ... On injured reserve with ankle injury (prior to 1995 season-October 31, 1995). ... Released by Cowboys (October 31, 1995). ... Signed by New Orleans Saints (June 3, 1996). ... Released by Saints (August 12, 1996). ... Signed by Tampa Bay Buccaneers (January 20, 1997). ... Granted free agency (February 12, 1999). ... Re-signed by Buccaneers (April 18, 1999). ... Granted unconditional free agency (February 11, 2000). ... Signed by Minnesota Vikings (May 31, 2000).
CHAMPIONSHIP GAME EXPERIENCE: Played in NFC championship game (1999 and 2000 seasons).
SINGLE GAME HIGHS (regular season): Receptions—4 (October 1, 2000, vs. Detroit); yards—42 (September 10, 2000, vs. Miami); and touchdown receptions—1 (October 9, 2000, vs. Tampa Bay).

			RECEIVING				TOTALS			
Year Team	G	GS	No.	Yds.	Avg.	TD	TD	2pt.	Pts.	Fum.
1997—Tampa Bay NFL	8	2	3	35	11.7	0	0	0	0	0
1998—Tampa Bay NFL	16	0	2	12	6.0	1	1	0	6	0
1999—Tampa Bay NFL	16	0	2	7	3.5	1	1	0	6	0
2000—Minnesota NFL	15	9	17	202	11.9	1	1	0	6	0
Pro totals (4 years)	55	11	24	256	10.7	3	3	0	18	0

DAVIS, REGGIE — TE — CHARGERS

PERSONAL: Born September 3, 1976, in Long Beach, Calif. ... 6-3/233. ... Full name: Reginald DeSean Davis.
HIGH SCHOOL: Brethren Christian (Huntington Beach, Calif.).
COLLEGE: Washington.
TRANSACTIONS/CAREER NOTES: Signed as non-drafted free agent by San Diego Chargers (May 12, 1999).
PRO STATISTICS: 1999—Recovered one fumble. 2000—Recovered one fumble.
SINGLE GAME HIGHS (regular season): Receptions—6 (November 21, 1999, vs. Chicago); yards—46 (September 26, 1999, vs. Indianapolis); and touchdown receptions—1 (November 21, 1999, vs. Chicago).

			RECEIVING				TOTALS			
Year Team	G	GS	No.	Yds.	Avg.	TD	TD	2pt.	Pts.	Fum.
1999—San Diego NFL	16	3	12	137	11.4	1	1	0	6	0
2000—San Diego NFL	10	0	1	8	8.0	0	0	0	0	0
Pro totals (2 years)	26	3	13	145	11.2	1	1	0	6	0

DAVIS, ROB — C — PACKERS

PERSONAL: Born December 10, 1968, in Washington, D.C. ... 6-3/286. ... Full name: Robert Emmett Davis.
HIGH SCHOOL: Eleanor Roosevelt (Greenbelt, Md.).
COLLEGE: Shippensburg, Pa. (degree in criminal justice/law enforcement).
TRANSACTIONS/CAREER NOTES: Signed as non-drafted free agent by New York Jets (April 27, 1993). ... Released by Jets (August 24, 1993). ... Re-signed by Jets (April 29, 1994). ... Released by Jets (August 22, 1994). ... Signed by Baltimore Stallions of CFL (April 1995). ... Signed by Kansas City Chiefs (April 22, 1996). ... Released by Chiefs (August 20, 1996). ... Signed by Chicago Bears (August 28, 1996). ... Released by Bears (August 27, 1997). ... Signed by Green Bay Packers (November 4, 1997). ... On physically unable to perform list with back injury (July 18-August 10, 1998). ... Granted unconditional free agency (March 2, 2001). ... Re-signed by Packers (March 20, 2001).
PLAYING EXPERIENCE: Baltimore CFL, 1995; Chicago NFL, 1996; Green Bay NFL, 1997-2000. ... Games/Games started: 1995 (18/games started unavailable), 1996 (16/0), 1997 (7/0), 1998 (16/0), 1999 (16/0), 2000 (16/0). Total CFL: 18/-. Total NFL: 71/0. Total Pro: 89/-.
CHAMPIONSHIP GAME EXPERIENCE: Played in NFC championship game (1997 season). ... Played in Super Bowl XXXII (1997 season).
PRO STATISTICS: 2000—Recovered one fumble.

DAVIS, RUSSELL   DT   CARDINALS

PERSONAL: Born March 28, 1975, in Fayetteville, N.C. ... 6-4/295. ... Full name: Russell Morgan Davis.
HIGH SCHOOL: E.E. Smith (Fayetteville, N.C.).
COLLEGE: North Carolina.
TRANSACTIONS/CAREER NOTES: Selected by Chicago Bears in second round (48th pick overall) of 1999 NFL draft. ... Signed by Bears (July 22, 1999). ... Claimed on waivers by Arizona Cardinals (August 28, 2000).

Year Team	G	GS	SACKS
1999—Chicago NFL	11	8	2.0
2000—Arizona NFL	13	9	0.5
Pro totals (2 years)	24	17	2.5

DAVIS, SHOCKMAIN   WR   PATRIOTS

PERSONAL: Born August 20, 1977, in Port Arthur, Texas. ... 6-0/205. ... Full name: Shockmain Nastase Davis.
HIGH SCHOOL: Port Arthur (Texas).
COLLEGE: Angelo State.
TRANSACTIONS/CAREER NOTES: Signed as non-drafted free agent by New England Patriots (April 25, 2000).
PLAYING EXPERIENCE: New England NFL, 2000. ... Games/Games started: 2000 (12/1).
PRO STATISTICS: 2000—Caught two passes for 12 yards and returned two kickoffs for 45 yards.
SINGLE GAME HIGHS (regular season): Receptions—2 (November 23, 2000, vs. Detroit); yards—12 (November 23, 2000, vs. Detroit); and touchdown receptions—0.

DAVIS, STEPHEN   RB   REDSKINS

PERSONAL: Born March 1, 1974, in Spartanburg, S.C. ... 6-0/234.
HIGH SCHOOL: Spartanburg (S.C.).
COLLEGE: Auburn (degree in vocational education, 1995).
TRANSACTIONS/CAREER NOTES: Selected by Washington Redskins in fourth round (102nd pick overall) of 1996 NFL draft. ... Signed by Redskins (July 16, 1996). ... Granted free agency (February 12, 1999). ... Re-signed by Redskins (May 12, 1999). ... Designated by Redskins as franchise player (February 11, 2000).
HONORS: Played in Pro Bowl (1999 and 2000 seasons).
PRO STATISTICS: 1997—Returned three kickoffs for 62 yards and recovered one fumble. 1999—Recovered two fumbles. 2000—Recovered one fumble.
SINGLE GAME HIGHS (regular season): Attempts—37 (December 12, 1999, vs. Arizona); yards—189 (December 12, 1999, vs. Arizona); and rushing touchdowns—3 (September 26, 1999, vs. New York Jets).
STATISTICAL PLATEAUS: 100-yard rushing games: 1999 (6), 2000 (5). Total: 11. ... 100-yard receiving games: 1998 (1).

			RUSHING				RECEIVING				TOTALS			
Year Team	G	GS	Att.	Yds.	Avg.	TD	No.	Yds.	Avg.	TD	TD	2pt.	Pts.	Fum.
1996—Washington NFL	12	0	23	139	6.0	2	0	0	0.0	0	2	0	12	0
1997—Washington NFL	14	6	141	567	4.0	3	18	134	7.4	0	3	0	18	1
1998—Washington NFL	16	12	34	109	3.2	0	21	263	12.5	2	2	0	12	0
1999—Washington NFL	14	14	290	‡1405	4.8	*17	23	111	4.8	0	†17	†1	104	4
2000—Washington NFL	15	15	332	1318	4.0	11	33	313	9.5	0	11	0	66	4
Pro totals (5 years)	71	47	820	3538	4.3	33	95	821	8.6	2	35	1	212	9

DAVIS, TERRELL   RB   BRONCOS

PERSONAL: Born October 28, 1972, in San Diego. ... 5-11/210.
HIGH SCHOOL: Abraham Lincoln Prep (San Diego).
COLLEGE: Long Beach State, then Georgia.
TRANSACTIONS/CAREER NOTES: Selected by Denver Broncos in sixth round (196th pick overall) of 1995 NFL draft. ... Signed by Broncos (June 30, 1995). ... On injured reserve with knee injury (October 6, 1999-remainder of season).
CHAMPIONSHIP GAME EXPERIENCE: Played in AFC championship game (1997 and 1998 seasons). ... Member of Super Bowl championship team (1997 and 1998 seasons).
HONORS: Named running back on THE SPORTING NEWS NFL All-Pro team (1996-1998). ... Played in Pro Bowl (1996 and 1997 seasons). ... Named Most Valuable Player of Super Bowl XXXII (1997 season). ... Named to play in Pro Bowl (1998 season); replaced by Curtis Martin due to injury. ... Named NFL Player of the Year by The Sporting News (1998).
POST SEASON RECORDS: Holds Super Bowl single-game record for most rushing touchdowns—3 (January 25, 1998, vs. Green Bay). ... Shares Super Bowl single-game records for most points—18; and most touchdowns—3 (January 25, 1998, vs. Green Bay). ... Holds NFL postseason career record for highest average gain—5.41. ... Holds NFL postseason record for most consecutive games with 100 or more yards rushing—7 (1997-present). ... Shares NFL postseason career record for most games with 100 or more yards rushing—7.
PRO STATISTICS: 1995—Recovered one fumble. 1996—Recovered two fumbles. 1997—Recovered two fumbles for minus seven yards. 1998—Recovered one fumble. 1999—Recovered one fumble.
SINGLE GAME HIGHS (regular season): Attempts—42 (October 26, 1997, vs. Buffalo); yards—215 (September 21, 1997, vs. Cincinnati); and rushing touchdowns—3 (December 6, 1998, vs. Kansas City).
STATISTICAL PLATEAUS: 100-yard rushing games: 1995 (3), 1996 (6), 1997 (10), 1998 (11), 2000 (1). Total: 31.
MISCELLANEOUS: Holds Denver Broncos all-time records for most yards rushing (6,906), most touchdowns (65) and most rushing touchdowns (60).

Year Team		G	GS	RUSHING Att.	Yds.	Avg.	TD	RECEIVING No.	Yds.	Avg.	TD	TOTALS TD	2pt.	Pts.	Fum.
1995—Denver NFL		14	14	237	1117	§4.7	7	49	367	7.5	1	8	0	48	5
1996—Denver NFL		16	16	§345	§1538	4.5	13	36	310	8.6	2	15	0	90	5
1997—Denver NFL		15	15	369	§1750	4.7	†15	42	287	6.8	0	15	3	†96	4
1998—Denver NFL		16	16	§392	*2008	*5.1	*21	25	217	8.7	2	*23	0	138	2
1999—Denver NFL		4	4	67	211	3.1	2	3	26	8.7	0	2	0	12	1
2000—Denver NFL		5	4	78	282	3.6	2	2	4	2.0	0	2	0	12	1
Pro totals (6 years)		70	69	1488	6906	4.6	60	157	1211	7.7	5	65	3	396	18

DAVIS, THABITI — WR — GIANTS

PERSONAL: Born March 24, 1975, in Charlotte, N.C. ... 6-2/205.
HIGH SCHOOL: Olympic (Charlotte, N.C.).
COLLEGE: Wake Forest.
TRANSACTIONS/CAREER NOTES: Signed as non-drafted free agent by New York Giants (June 29, 2000).
PLAYING EXPERIENCE: New York Giants NFL, 2000. ... Games/Games started: 2000 (13/0).
CHAMPIONSHIP GAME EXPERIENCE: Played in NFC championship game (2000 season). ... Played in Super Bowl XXXV (2000 season).
PRO STATISTICS: 2000—Caught two passes for 40 yards.
SINGLE GAME HIGHS (regular season): Receptions—1 (November 19, 2000, vs. Detroit); yards—27 (November 19, 2000, vs. Detriot); and touchdown receptions—0.

DAVIS, TYRONE — TE — PACKERS

PERSONAL: Born June 30, 1972, in Halifax, Va. ... 6-4/260.
HIGH SCHOOL: Halifax County (South Boston, Va.), then Fork Union (Va.) Military Academy.
COLLEGE: Virginia.
TRANSACTIONS/CAREER NOTES: Selected by New York Jets in fourth round (107th pick overall) of 1995 NFL draft. ... Signed by Jets (June 14, 1995). ... Released by Jets (September 13, 1995). ... Re-signed by Jets to practice squad (September 15, 1995). ... Activated (December 11, 1995). ... Granted free agency (February 14, 1997). ... Re-signed by Jets for 1997 season. ... Traded by Jets to Green Bay Packers for past considerations (August 25, 1997). ... Released by Packers (September 24, 1997). ... Re-signed by Packers (September 29, 1997). ... Granted unconditional free agency (March 2, 2001). ... Re-signed by Packers (March 21, 2001).
CHAMPIONSHIP GAME EXPERIENCE: Played in NFC championship game (1997 season). ... Played in Super Bowl XXXII (1997 season).
PRO STATISTICS: 1997—Recovered one fumble in end zone for a touchdown.
SINGLE GAME HIGHS (regular season): Receptions—5 (September 17, 2000, vs. Philadelphia); yards—83 (November 15, 1998, vs. New York Giants); and touchdown receptions—2 (November 22, 1998, vs. Minnesota).

Year Team		G	GS	RECEIVING No.	Yds.	Avg.	TD	TOTALS TD	2pt.	Pts.	Fum.
1995—New York Jets NFL		4	0	1	9	9.0	0	0	0	0	0
1996—New York Jets NFL		2	0	1	6	6.0	0	0	0	0	0
1997—Green Bay NFL		13	0	2	28	14.0	1	2	0	12	0
1998—Green Bay NFL		13	1	18	250	13.9	7	7	0	42	1
1999—Green Bay NFL		16	13	20	204	10.2	2	2	0	12	0
2000—Green Bay NFL		14	9	19	177	9.3	2	2	1	14	2
Pro totals (6 years)		62	23	61	674	11.0	12	13	1	80	3

DAWKINS, BRIAN — S — EAGLES

PERSONAL: Born October 13, 1973, in Jacksonville. ... 5-11/200.
HIGH SCHOOL: Raines (Jacksonville).
COLLEGE: Clemson (degree in education, 1995).
TRANSACTIONS/CAREER NOTES: Selected by Philadelphia Eagles in second round (61st pick overall) of 1996 NFL draft. ... Signed by Eagles (July 17, 1996).
HONORS: Named defensive back on THE SPORTING NEWS college All-America second team (1995). ... Played in Pro Bowl (1999 season).
PRO STATISTICS: 1996—Recovered two fumbles for 23 yards. 1998—Recovered one fumble. 1999—Recovered two fumbles. 2000—Recovered two fumbles.

Year Team		G	GS	INTERCEPTIONS No.	Yds.	Avg.	TD	SACKS No.
1996—Philadelphia NFL		14	13	3	41	13.7	0	1.0
1997—Philadelphia NFL		15	15	3	76	25.3	1	0.0
1998—Philadelphia NFL		14	14	2	39	19.5	0	1.0
1999—Philadelphia NFL		16	16	4	127	31.8	1	1.5
2000—Philadelphia NFL		13	13	4	62	15.5	0	2.0
Pro totals (5 years)		72	71	16	345	21.6	2	5.5

DAWKINS, SEAN — WR — JAGUARS

PERSONAL: Born February 3, 1971, in Red Bank, N.J. ... 6-4/218. ... Full name: Sean Russell Dawkins.
HIGH SCHOOL: Homestead (Cupertino, Calif.).
COLLEGE: California.
TRANSACTIONS/CAREER NOTES: Selected after junior season by Indianapolis Colts in first round (16th pick overall) of 1993 NFL draft. ... Signed by Colts (August 4, 1993). ... Granted unconditional free agency (February 13, 1998). ... Signed by New Orleans Saints (May 1, 1998). ... Granted unconditional free agency (February 12, 1999). ... Signed by Seattle Seahawks (April 15, 1999). ... Released by Seahawks (June 8, 2000). ... Re-signed by Seahawks (July 26, 2000). ... Released by Seahawks (March 1, 2001). ... Signed by Jacksonville Jaguars (May 30, 2001).

CHAMPIONSHIP GAME EXPERIENCE: Played in AFC championship game (1995 season).
HONORS: Named wide receiver on THE SPORTING NEWS college All-America first team (1992).
SINGLE GAME HIGHS (regular season): Receptions—8 (November 22, 1998, vs. San Francisco); yards—148 (November 22, 1998, vs. San Francisco); and touchdown receptions—2 (December 10, 2000, vs. Denver).
STATISTICAL PLATEAUS: 100-yard receiving games: 1993 (1), 1994 (1), 1995 (2), 1997 (1), 1998 (3), 1999 (2), 2000 (1). Total: 11.

			RECEIVING				TOTALS			
Year Team	G	GS	No.	Yds.	Avg.	TD	TD	2pt.	Pts.	Fum.
1993—Indianapolis NFL	16	7	26	430	16.5	1	1	0	6	0
1994—Indianapolis NFL	16	16	51	742	14.5	5	5	0	30	1
1995—Indianapolis NFL	16	13	52	784	15.1	3	3	0	18	1
1996—Indianapolis NFL	15	14	54	751	13.9	1	1	0	6	1
1997—Indianapolis NFL	14	12	68	804	11.8	2	2	0	12	0
1998—New Orleans NFL	15	15	53	823	15.5	1	1	0	6	2
1999—Seattle NFL	16	13	58	992	17.1	7	7	0	42	1
2000—Seattle NFL	16	16	63	731	11.6	5	5	0	30	0
Pro totals (8 years)	124	106	425	6057	14.3	25	25	0	150	6

DAWSON, DERMONTTI   C

PERSONAL: Born June 17, 1965, in Lexington, Ky. ... 6-2/292. ... Full name: Dermontti Farra Dawson. ... Cousin of Marc Logan, running back with four NFL teams (1987-97); and cousin of George Adams, running back with New York Giants (1985-89) and New England Patriots (1990-91).
HIGH SCHOOL: Bryan Station (Lexington, Ky.).
COLLEGE: Kentucky (degree in kinesiology and health promotions, 1988).
TRANSACTIONS/CAREER NOTES: Selected by Pittsburgh Steelers in second round (44th pick overall) of 1988 NFL draft. ... Signed by Steelers (August 1, 1988). ... On injured reserve with knee injury (September 26-November 26, 1988). ... Designated by Steelers as transition player (February 25, 1993). ... On injured reserve with hamstring injury (December 14, 1999-remainder of season). ... Released by Steelers (February 28, 2001).
PLAYING EXPERIENCE: Pittsburgh NFL, 1988-2000. ... Games: 1988 (8/5), 1989 (16/16), 1990 (16/16), 1991 (16/16), 1992 (16/16), 1993 (16/16), 1994 (16/16), 1995 (16/16), 1996 (16/16), 1997 (16/16), 1998 (16/16), 1999 (7/7), 2000 (9/9). Total: 184/181.
CHAMPIONSHIP GAME EXPERIENCE: Played in AFC championship game (1994, 1995 and 1997 seasons). ... Played in Super Bowl XXX (1995 season).
HONORS: Played in Pro Bowl (1992-1998 seasons). ... Named center on THE SPORTING NEWS NFL All-Pro team (1994-1998).
PRO STATISTICS: 1991—Fumbled twice and recovered one fumble for two yards. 1993—Fumbled once. 1998—Fumbled once for minus 25 yards.

DAWSON, JAJUAN   WR   BROWNS

PERSONAL: Born November 5, 1977, in Houston. ... 6-1/197. ... Full name: JaJuan LaTroy Dawson.
HIGH SCHOOL: H.L. Bourgeois (Gibson, La.).
COLLEGE: Tulane.
TRANSACTIONS/CAREER NOTES: Selected by Cleveland Browns in third round (79th pick overall) of 2000 NFL draft. ... Signed by Browns (June 3, 2000). ... On injured reserve with clavicle injury (September 20, 2000-remainder of season).
SINGLE GAME HIGHS (regular season): Receptions—6 (September 3, 2000, vs. Jacksonville); yards—83 (September 3, 2000, vs. Jacksonville); and touchdown receptions—1 (September 3, 2000, vs. Jacksonville).

			RECEIVING			
Year Team	G	GS	No.	Yds.	Avg.	TD
2000—Cleveland NFL	2	2	9	97	10.8	1

DAWSON, PHIL   K   BROWNS

PERSONAL: Born January 23, 1975, in West Palm Beach, Fla. ... 5-11/190.
HIGH SCHOOL: Lake Highlands (Dallas).
COLLEGE: Texas.
TRANSACTIONS/CAREER NOTES: Signed as non-drafted free agent by Oakland Raiders (April 24, 1998). ... Claimed on waivers by New England Patriots (August 21, 1998). ... Released by Patriots (August 30, 1998). ... Re-signed by Patriots to practice squad (August 31, 1998). ... Granted free agency after 1998 season. ... Signed by Cleveland Browns (March 25, 1999).
PRO STATISTICS: 1999—Rushed once for four yards and a touchdown.

				KICKING				
Year Team	G	XPM	XPA	FGM	FGA	Lg.	50+	Pts.
1999—Cleveland NFL	15	23	24	8	12	49	0-0	47
2000—Cleveland NFL	16	17	17	14	17	45	0-0	59
Pro totals (2 years)	31	40	41	22	29	49	0-0	106

DAYNE, RON   RB   GIANTS

PERSONAL: Born March 14, 1978, in Berlin, N.J. ... 5-10/253.
HIGH SCHOOL: Overbrook (Berlin, N.J.).
COLLEGE: Wisconsin.
TRANSACTIONS/CAREER NOTES: Selected by New York Giants in first round (11th pick overall) of 2000 NFL draft. ... Signed by Giants (July 21, 2000).

CHAMPIONSHIP GAME EXPERIENCE: Played in NFC championship game (2000 season). ... Played in Super Bowl XXXV (2000 season).
HONORS: Heisman Trophy winner (1999). ... Doak Walker Award winner (1999). ... Maxwell Award winner (1999). ... Named running back on THE SPORTING NEWS college All-America first team (1999). ... Named College Football Player of the Year by THE SPORTING NEWS (1999).
SINGLE GAME HIGHS (regular season): Attempts—25 (October 29, 2000, vs. Philadelphia); yards—108 (October 15, 2000, vs. Dallas); and rushing touchdowns—1 (November 26, 2000, vs. Arizona).
STATISTICAL PLATEAUS: 100-yard rushing games: 2000 (1).

				RUSHING				RECEIVING				TOTALS		
Year	Team	G	GS	Att.	Yds.	Avg.	TD	No.	Yds.	Avg.	TD	TD	2pt.	Pts.	Fum.
2000—New York Giants NFL		16	4	228	770	3.4	5	3	11	3.7	0	5	0	30	1

DEESE, DERRICK   OT   49ERS

PERSONAL: Born May 17, 1970, in Culver City, Calif. ... 6-3/289.
HIGH SCHOOL: Culver City (Calif.).
JUNIOR COLLEGE: El Camino Junior College (Calif.).
COLLEGE: Southern California.
TRANSACTIONS/CAREER NOTES: Signed as non-drafted free agent by San Francisco 49ers (May 8, 1992). ... On injured reserve with elbow injury (August 4, 1992-entire season). ... Inactive for six games (1993). ... On injured reserve with broken wrist (October 23, 1993-remainder of season). ... Granted free agency (February 17, 1995). ... Tendered offer sheet by St. Louis Rams (April 20, 1995). ... Offer matched by 49ers (April 21, 1995). ... Granted unconditional free agency (February 16, 1996). ... Re-signed by 49ers (June 4, 1996). ... Granted unconditional free agency (February 14, 1997). ... Re-signed by 49ers (April 22, 1997).
PLAYING EXPERIENCE: San Francisco NFL, 1994-2000. ... Games/Games started: 1994 (16/15), 1995 (2/2), 1996 (16/0), 1997 (16/13), 1998 (16/16), 1999 (16/16), 2000 (13/13). Total: 95/75.
CHAMPIONSHIP GAME EXPERIENCE: Played in NFC championship game (1994 and 1997 seasons). ... Member of Super Bowl championship team (1994 season).
PRO STATISTICS: 1996—Returned two kickoffs for 20 yards. 1997—Recovered one fumble. 1998—Recovered one fumble. 1999—Recovered four fumbles.

DEL GRECO, AL   K

PERSONAL: Born March 2, 1962, in Providence, R.I. ... 5-10/202. ... Full name: Albert Louis Del Greco Jr.
HIGH SCHOOL: Coral Gables (Fla.).
COLLEGE: Auburn (degree in business transportation).
TRANSACTIONS/CAREER NOTES: Signed as non-drafted free agent by Miami Dolphins (May 17, 1984). ... Released by Dolphins (August 27, 1984). ... Signed by Green Bay Packers (October 17, 1984). ... Released by Packers (November 25, 1987). ... Signed by St. Louis Cardinals (December 8, 1987). ... Cardinals franchise moved to Phoenix (March 15, 1988). ... Granted unconditional free agency (February 1-April 1, 1991). ... Re-signed by Cardinals (July 1, 1991). ... Released by Cardinals (August 19, 1991). ... Signed by Houston Oilers (November 5, 1991). ... Granted unconditional free agency (February 1-April 1, 1992). ... Re-signed by Oilers for 1992 season. ... Granted unconditional free agency (February 17, 1995). ... Re-signed by Oilers (June 2, 1995). ... Oilers franchise moved to Tennessee for 1997 season. ... Oilers franchise renamed Tennessee Titans for 1999 season (December 26, 1998). ... Released by Titans (March 1, 2001).
CHAMPIONSHIP GAME EXPERIENCE: Played in AFC championship game (1999 season). ... Played in Super Bowl XXXIV (1999 season).
PRO STATISTICS: 1988—Rushed once for eight yards. 1990—Recovered one fumble. 1995—Punted once for 15 yards. 1997—Punted once for 32 yards.

					KICKING					
Year	Team	G	XPM	XPA	FGM	FGA	Lg.	50+	Pts.
1984—Green Bay NFL		9	34	34	9	12	45	0-1	61
1985—Green Bay NFL		16	38	40	19	26	46	0-1	95
1986—Green Bay NFL		16	29	29	17	27	50	2-4	80
1987—Green Bay NFL		5	11	11	5	10	47	0-0	26
—St. Louis NFL		3	8	9	4	5	37	0-0	20
1988—Phoenix NFL		16	42	44	12	21	51	1-2	78
1989—Phoenix NFL		16	28	29	18	26	50	1-2	82
1990—Phoenix NFL		16	31	31	17	27	50	2-6	82
1991—Houston NFL		7	16	16	10	13	52	1-1	46
1992—Houston NFL		16	41	41	21	27	†54	1-1	104
1993—Houston NFL		16	39	40	29	34	52	4-7	126
1994—Houston NFL		16	18	18	16	20	50	1-3	66
1995—Houston NFL		16	33	33	27	31	53	1-3	114
1996—Houston NFL		16	35	35	32	38	*56	1-3	131
1997—Tennessee NFL		16	32	32	27	35	52	2-2	113
1998—Tennessee NFL		16	28	28	*36	39	48	0-0	136
1999—Tennessee NFL		16	43	43	21	25	50	1-1	106
2000—Tennessee NFL		16	37	38	27	33	50	1-1	118
Pro totals (17 years)		248	543	551	347	449	56	21-40	1584

DeLONG, GREG   TE

PERSONAL: Born April 3, 1973, in Orefield, Pa. ... 6-4/255. ... Full name: Gregory A. DeLong.
HIGH SCHOOL: Parkland Senior (Orefield, Pa.).
COLLEGE: North Carolina.
TRANSACTIONS/CAREER NOTES: Signed as non-drafted free agent by Cleveland Browns (May 2, 1995). ... Released by Browns (August 21, 1995). ... Signed by Minnesota Vikings to practice squad (August 28, 1995). ... Activated (November 15, 1995). ... Granted free agency (February 13, 1998). ... Re-signed by Vikings (April 23, 1998). ... Granted unconditional free agency (February 12, 1999). ... Signed by Baltimore Ravens (February 26, 1999). ... Released by Ravens (August 27, 2000). ... Signed by Jacksonville Jaguars (September 5, 2000). ... Released by Jaguars (October 3, 2000).

CHAMPIONSHIP GAME EXPERIENCE: Played in NFC championship game (1998 season).
PRO STATISTICS: 1996—Returned one kickoff for three yards and recovered one fumble. 1999—Returned one kickoff for 11 yards.
SINGLE GAME HIGHS (regular season): Receptions—4 (November 21, 1999, vs. Cincinnati); yards—28 (September 20, 1998, vs. Detroit); and touchdown receptions—1 (November 21, 1999, vs. Cincinnati).

				RECEIVING			TOTALS			
Year Team	G	GS	No.	Yds.	Avg.	TD	TD	2pt.	Pts.	Fum.
1995—Minnesota NFL	2	2	6	38	6.3	0	0	0	0	0
1996—Minnesota NFL	16	8	8	34	4.3	0	0	0	0	0
1997—Minnesota NFL	16	3	8	75	9.4	0	0	0	0	1
1998—Minnesota NFL	15	5	8	58	7.3	0	0	0	0	0
1999—Baltimore NFL	16	7	13	52	4.0	1	1	0	6	0
2000—Jacksonville NFL	4	1	0	0	0.0	0	0	0	0	0
Pro totals (6 years)	69	26	43	257	6.0	1	1	0	6	1

DENNIS, PAT   CB   CHIEFS

PERSONAL: Born June 3, 1978, in Shreveport, La. ... 6-0/207. ... Full name: Patrick Dennis.
HIGH SCHOOL: Southwood (Shreveport, La.).
COLLEGE: Louisiana-Monroe.
TRANSACTIONS/CAREER NOTES: Selected after junior season by Kansas City Chiefs in fifth round (162nd pick overall) of 2000 NFL draft. ... Signed by Chiefs (July 20, 2000).
PRO STATISTICS: 2000—Recovered two fumbles for minus five yards.

			INTERCEPTIONS			
Year Team	G	GS	No.	Yds.	Avg.	TD
2000—Kansas City NFL	16	13	1	0	0.0	0

DENSON, AUTRY   RB   DOLPHINS

PERSONAL: Born December 8, 1976, in Davie, Fla. ... 5-10/193. ... Full name: Autry Lamont Denson.
HIGH SCHOOL: Nova (Fort Lauderdale, Fla.).
COLLEGE: Notre Dame.
TRANSACTIONS/CAREER NOTES: Selected by Tampa Bay Buccaneers in seventh round (233rd pick overall) of 1999 NFL draft. ... Signed by Buccaneers (July 29, 1999). ... Released by Buccaneers (September 5, 1999). ... Re-signed by Buccaneers to practice squad (September 6, 1999). ... Signed by Miami Dolphins off Buccaneers practice squad (October 20, 1999).
PRO STATISTICS: 2000—Returned 20 kickoffs for 495 yards.
SINGLE GAME HIGHS (regular season): Attempts—21 (January 2, 2000, vs. Washington); yards—80 (January 2, 2000, vs. Washington); and rushing touchdowns—0.

			RUSHING				RECEIVING				TOTALS			
Year Team	G	GS	Att.	Yds.	Avg.	TD	No.	Yds.	Avg.	TD	TD	2pt.	Pts.	Fum.
1999—Miami NFL	6	1	28	98	3.5	0	4	28	7.0	0	0	0	0	0
2000—Miami NFL	11	0	31	108	3.5	0	14	105	7.5	0	0	0	0	1
Pro totals (2 years)	17	1	59	206	3.5	0	18	133	7.4	0	0	0	0	1

DENTON, TIM   DB   CHARGERS

PERSONAL: Born February 2, 1973, in Galveston, Texas ... 5-11/182.
HIGH SCHOOL: Ball (Galveston, Texas).
JUNIOR COLLEGE: Blinn College (Texas).
COLLEGE: Oklahoma, then Sam Houston State.
TRANSACTIONS/CAREER NOTES: Signed as non-drafted free agent by Atlanta Falcons (April 22, 1996). ... Released by Falcons (August 31, 1996). ... Re-signed by Falcons (February 10, 1997). ... Released by Falcons (August 18, 1997). ... Re-signed by Falcons to practice squad (August 26, 1997). ... Granted free agency after 1997 season. ... Signed by Washington Redskins (February 18, 1998). ... Assigned by Redskins to Rhein Fire in 1998 NFL Europe enhancement allocation program (February 18, 1998). ... Released by Redskins (August 27, 2000). ... Signed by San Diego Chargers (October 18, 2000). ... Granted free agency (March 2, 2001).
PLAYING EXPERIENCE: Rhein Fire NFLE, 1998; Washington NFL, 1998 and 1999; San Diego NFL, 2000. ... Games/Games started: NFLE 1998 (games played unavailable), NFL 1998 (16/0), 1999 (16/0), 2000 (5/0). Total NFL: 37/0.
PRO STATISTICS: NFLE: 1998—Intercepted two passes for no yards.

DERCHER, DAN   OT   49ERS

PERSONAL: Born June 2, 1976, in Kansas City, Kan. ... 6-5/293. ... Full name: Daniel Lawrence Dercher.
HIGH SCHOOL: Bishop Miege (Mission, Kan.).
COLLEGE: Kansas.
TRANSACTIONS/CAREER NOTES: Signed as non-drafted free agent by San Francisco 49ers (April 23, 1999). ... Inactive for 13 games (2000).
PLAYING EXPERIENCE: San Francisco NFL, 1999 and 2000. ... Games/Games started: 1999 (9/0), 2000 (2/0). Total: 11/0.

DETMER, KOY   QB   EAGLES

PERSONAL: Born July 5, 1973, in San Antonio. ... 6-1/195. ... Brother of Ty Detmer, quarterback, Cleveland Browns.
HIGH SCHOOL: Mission (Texas).
COLLEGE: Colorado (degree in communications, 1996).

TRANSACTIONS/CAREER NOTES: Selected by Philadelphia Eagles in seventh round (207th pick overall) of 1997 NFL draft. ... Signed by Eagles (June 4, 1997). ... On injured reserve with knee injury (August 22, 1997-entire season). ... Granted free agency (February 11, 2000). ... Re-signed by Eagles (April 17, 2000).
PRO STATISTICS: 1998—Fumbled once.
SINGLE GAME HIGHS (regular season): Attempts—43 (December 20, 1998, vs. Dallas); completions—24 (December 20, 1998, vs. Dallas); yards—231 (December 20, 1998, vs. Dallas); and touchdown passes—3 (December 19, 1999, vs. New England).
MISCELLANEOUS: Regular-season record as starting NFL quarterback: 2-4 (.333).

Year Team	G	GS	Att.	Cmp.	Pct.	Yds.	TD	Int.	Avg.	Rat.	Att.	Yds.	Avg.	TD	TD	2pt.	Pts.
					PASSING							RUSHING				TOTALS	
1997—Philadelphia NFL							Did not play.										
1998—Philadelphia NFL	8	5	181	97	53.6	1011	5	5	5.59	67.7	7	20	2.9	0	0	0	0
1999—Philadelphia NFL	1	1	29	10	34.5	181	3	2	6.24	62.6	2	-2	-1.0	0	0	0	0
2000—Philadelphia NFL	16	0	1	0	0.0	0	0	1	0.0	0.0	1	8	8.0	0	0	0	0
Pro totals (3 years)	25	6	211	107	50.7	1192	8	8	5.65	64.7	10	26	2.6	0	0	0	0

DETMER, TY QB BROWNS

PERSONAL: Born October 30, 1967, in San Marcos, Texas. ... 6-0/194. ... Full name: Ty Hubert Detmer. ... Brother of Koy Detmer, quarterback, Philadelphia Eagles.
HIGH SCHOOL: Southwest (San Antonio).
COLLEGE: Brigham Young (degree in recreation administration, 1991).
TRANSACTIONS/CAREER NOTES: Selected by Green Bay Packers in ninth round (230th pick overall) of 1992 NFL draft. ... Signed by Packers (July 22, 1992). ... Active for two games (1992); did not play. ... Active for five games (1994); did not play. ... On injured reserve with thumb injury (November 8, 1995-remainder of season). ... Granted unconditional free agency (February 16, 1996). ... Signed by Philadelphia Eagles (March 1, 1996). ... Granted unconditional free agency (February 13, 1998). ... Signed by San Francisco 49ers (March 12, 1998). ... Traded by 49ers with fourth-round pick (LB Wali Rainer) in 1999 draft to Cleveland Browns for fourth- (traded to Indianapolis) and fifth-round (traded to Miami) picks in 1999 draft (February 23, 1999). ... On injured reserve with Achilles' tendon injury (August 16, 2000-entire season).
HONORS: Heisman Trophy winner (1990). ... Maxwell Award winner (1990). ... Davey O'Brien Award winner (1990 and 1991). ... Named quarterback on THE SPORTING NEWS college All-America first team (1990 and 1991).
PRO STATISTICS: 1995—Fumbled once and recovered one fumble. 1996—Fumbled seven times and recovered one fumble. 1997—Fumbled six times and recovered one fumble for minus two yards. 1998—Fumbled once.
SINGLE GAME HIGHS (regular season): Attempts—45 (September 28, 1997, vs. Minnesota); completions—28 (September 28, 1997, vs. Minnesota); yards—342 (October 27, 1996, vs. Carolina); and touchdown passes—4 (October 20, 1996, vs. Miami).
STATISTICAL PLATEAUS: 300-yard passing games: 1996 (3).
MISCELLANEOUS: Regular-season record as starting NFL quarterback: 10-11 (.476). ... Postseason record as starting NFL quarterback: 0-1.

Year Team	G	GS	Att.	Cmp.	Pct.	Yds.	TD	Int.	Avg.	Rat.	Att.	Yds.	Avg.	TD	TD	2pt.	Pts.
					PASSING							RUSHING				TOTALS	
1992—Green Bay NFL							Did not play.										
1993—Green Bay NFL	3	0	5	3	60.0	26	0	0	5.20	73.8	1	-2	-2.0	0	0	0	0
1994—Green Bay NFL							Did not play.										
1995—Green Bay NFL	4	0	16	8	50.0	81	1	1	5.06	59.6	3	3	1.0	0	0	0	0
1996—Philadelphia NFL	13	11	401	238	59.4	2911	15	13	7.26	80.8	31	59	1.9	1	1	0	6
1997—Philadelphia NFL	8	7	244	134	54.9	1567	7	6	6.42	73.9	14	46	3.3	1	1	0	6
1998—San Francisco NFL	16	1	38	24	63.2	312	4	3	8.21	91.1	8	7	0.9	0	0	0	0
1999—Cleveland NFL	5	2	91	47	51.6	548	4	2	6.02	75.7	6	38	6.3	1	1	0	6
2000—Cleveland NFL							Did not play.										
Pro totals (6 years)	49	21	795	454	57.1	5445	31	25	6.85	78.1	63	151	2.4	3	3	0	18

DeVRIES, JARED DE LIONS

PERSONAL: Born June 11, 1976, in Aplington, Iowa. ... 6-4/280.
HIGH SCHOOL: Aplington-Parkersburg (Aplington, Iowa).
COLLEGE: Iowa.
TRANSACTIONS/CAREER NOTES: Selected by Detroit Lions in third round (70th pick overall) of 1999 NFL draft. ... Signed by Lions (July 28, 1999).
PLAYING EXPERIENCE: Detroit NFL, 1999 and 2000. ... Games/Games started: 1999 (2/0), 2000 (15/1). Total: 17/1.
HONORS: Named defensive tackle on THE SPORTING NEWS college All-America third team (1997). ... Named defensive tackle on THE SPORTING NEWS college All-America first team (1998).
PRO STATISTICS: 2000—Recovered one fumble.

DEXTER, JAMES OL

PERSONAL: Born March 3, 1973, in Fort Ord, Calif. ... 6-7/320.
HIGH SCHOOL: West Springfield (Va.).
COLLEGE: South Carolina (degree in criminal justice, 1996).
TRANSACTIONS/CAREER NOTES: Selected by Arizona Cardinals in fifth round (137th pick overall) of 1996 NFL draft. ... Signed by Cardinals (July 21, 1996). ... Granted free agency (February 12, 1999). ... Re-signed by Cardinals (May 21, 1999). ... Granted unconditional free agency (February 11, 2000). ... Signed by Carolina Panthers (April 25, 2000). ... Released by Panthers (February 28, 2001).
PLAYING EXPERIENCE: Arizona NFL, 1996-1999; Carolina NFL, 2000. ... Games/Games started: 1996 (6/1), 1997 (10/9), 1998 (16/16), 1999 (9/5), 2000 (9/2). Total: 50/33.
PRO STATISTICS: 1998—Recovered two fumbles. 2000—Recovered one fumble.

DIAZ, JORGE   G

PERSONAL: Born November 15, 1973, in New York. ... 6-4/315. ... Full name: Jorge Armando Diaz. ... Name pronounced George.
HIGH SCHOOL: Katy (Texas).
JUNIOR COLLEGE: Kilgore (Texas) College.
COLLEGE: Texas A&M-Kingsville.
TRANSACTIONS/CAREER NOTES: Signed as a non-drafted free agent by Tampa Bay Buccaneers (April 23, 1996). ... Released by Buccaneers (March 17, 2000). ... Signed by Dallas Cowboys (March 31, 2000). ... Released by Cowboys (March 1, 2001).
PLAYING EXPERIENCE: Tampa Bay NFL, 1996-1999; Dallas NFL, 2000. ... Games/Games started: 1996 (11/6), 1997 (16/16), 1998 (12/12), 1999 (13/11), 2000 (9/0). Total: 61/45.
CHAMPIONSHIP GAME EXPERIENCE: Played in NFC championship game (1999 season).
PRO STATISTICS: 1997—Recovered one fumble. 1999—Recovered one fumble.

DIGGS, NA'IL   LB   PACKERS

PERSONAL: Born July 8, 1978, in Phoenix. ... 6-4/234. ... Full name: Na'il Ronald Diggs.
HIGH SCHOOL: Dorsey (Los Angeles).
COLLEGE: Ohio State.
TRANSACTIONS/CAREER NOTES: Selected after junior season by Green Bay Packers in fourth round (98th pick overall) of 2000 NFL draft. ... Signed by Packers (June 19, 2000).
PLAYING EXPERIENCE: Green Bay NFL, 2000. ... Games/Games started: 2000 (13/12).
PRO STATISTICS: 2000—Recovered one fumble for 52 yards.

DILFER, TRENT   QB

PERSONAL: Born March 13, 1972, in Santa Cruz, Calif. ... 6-4/229. ... Full name: Trent Farris Dilfer.
HIGH SCHOOL: Aptos (Calif.).
COLLEGE: Fresno State.
TRANSACTIONS/CAREER NOTES: Selected after junior season by Tampa Bay Buccaneers in first round (sixth pick overall) of 1994 NFL draft. ... Signed by Buccaneers (August 3, 1994). ... Granted unconditional free agency (January 25, 2000). ... Signed by Baltimore Ravens (March 8, 2000). ... Granted unconditional free agency (March 2, 2001).
CHAMPIONSHIP GAME EXPERIENCE: Member of Buccaneers for NFC championship game (1999 season); inactive. ... Played in AFC championship game (2000 season). ... Member of Super Bowl championship team (2000 season).
HONORS: Played in Pro Bowl (1997 season).
PRO STATISTICS: 1994—Fumbled twice. 1995—Fumbled 13 times and recovered one fumble for minus nine yards. 1996—Fumbled 10 times and recovered four fumbles for minus four yards. 1997—Fumbled nine times and recovered three fumbles for minus 22 yards. 1998—Fumbled nine times and recovered two fumbles for minus five yards. 1999—Fumbled six times for minus four yards. 2000—Fumbled eight times, recovered one fumble for minus seven yards and caught one pass for minus one yard.
SINGLE GAME HIGHS (regular season): Attempts—48 (November 26, 1995, vs. Green Bay); completions—30 (November 17, 1996, vs. San Diego); yards—327 (November 17, 1996, vs. San Diego); and touchdown passes—4 (September 21, 1997, vs. Miami).
STATISTICAL PLATEAUS: 300-yard passing games: 1995 (1), 1996 (1), 1999 (1). Total: 3.
MISCELLANEOUS: Regular-season record as starting NFL quarterback: 45-39 (.535). ... Postseason record as starting NFL quarterback: 5-1 (.833).

			PASSING							RUSHING				TOTALS		
Year Team	G	GS	Att.	Cmp.	Pct.	Yds.	TD	Int.	Avg.	Rat.	Att.	Yds.	Avg.	TD	TD	2pt.	Pts.
1994—Tampa Bay NFL	5	2	82	38	46.3	433	1	6	5.28	36.3	2	27	13.5	0	0	0	0
1995—Tampa Bay NFL	16	16	415	224	54.0	2774	4	18	6.68	60.1	23	115	5.0	2	2	0	12
1996—Tampa Bay NFL	16	16	482	267	55.4	2859	12	19	5.93	64.8	32	124	3.9	0	0	0	0
1997—Tampa Bay NFL	16	16	386	217	56.2	2555	21	11	6.62	82.8	33	99	3.0	1	1	0	6
1998—Tampa Bay NFL	16	16	429	225	52.4	2729	21	15	6.36	74.0	40	141	3.5	2	2	0	12
1999—Tampa Bay NFL	10	10	244	146	59.8	1619	11	11	6.64	75.8	35	144	4.1	0	0	0	0
2000—Baltimore NFL	11	8	226	134	59.3	1502	12	11	6.65	76.6	20	75	3.8	0	0	0	0
Pro totals (7 years)	90	84	2264	1251	55.3	14471	82	91	6.39	70.1	185	725	3.9	5	5	0	30

DILGER, KEN   TE   COLTS

PERSONAL: Born February 2, 1971, in Mariah Hill, Ind. ... 6-5/253. ... Full name: Kenneth Ray Dilger. ... Name pronounced DIL-gur.
HIGH SCHOOL: Heritage Hills (Lincoln City, Ind.).
COLLEGE: Illinois (degree in marketing).
TRANSACTIONS/CAREER NOTES: Selected by Indianapolis Colts in second round (48th pick overall) of 1995 NFL draft. ... Signed by Colts (July 15, 1995).
CHAMPIONSHIP GAME EXPERIENCE: Played in AFC championship game (1995 season).
PRO STATISTICS: 1998—Returned one kickoff for 14 yards. 1999—Recovered one fumble. 2000—Returned one kickoff for no yards.
SINGLE GAME HIGHS (regular season): Receptions—8 (September 10, 2000, vs. Oakland); yards—156 (September 8, 1996, vs. New York Jets); and touchdown receptions—3 (December 14, 1997, vs. Miami).
STATISTICAL PLATEAUS: 100-yard receiving games: 1995 (1), 1996 (1), 1997 (1). Total: 3.

			RECEIVING				TOTALS			
Year Team	G	GS	No.	Yds.	Avg.	TD	TD	2pt.	Pts.	Fum.
1995—Indianapolis NFL	16	13	42	635	15.1	4	4	0	24	0
1996—Indianapolis NFL	16	16	42	503	12.0	4	4	0	24	1
1997—Indianapolis NFL	14	14	27	380	14.1	3	3	0	18	0
1998—Indianapolis NFL	16	16	31	303	9.8	1	1	1	8	0
1999—Indianapolis NFL	15	15	40	479	12.0	2	2	0	12	1
2000—Indianapolis NFL	16	16	47	538	11.4	3	3	0	18	1
Pro totals (6 years)	93	90	229	2838	12.4	17	17	1	104	3

DILLON, COREY   RB   BENGALS

PERSONAL: Born October 24, 1975, in Seattle. ... 6-1/225.
HIGH SCHOOL: Franklin (Seattle).
JUNIOR COLLEGE: Garden City (Kan.) Community College, then Dixie College (Utah).
COLLEGE: Washington.
TRANSACTIONS/CAREER NOTES: Selected after junior season by Cincinnati Bengals in second round (43rd pick overall) of 1997 NFL draft. ... Signed by Bengals (July 21, 1997). ... Granted free agency (February 11, 2000). ... Re-signed by Bengals (August 9, 2000). ... Designated by Bengals as transition player (February 12, 2001). ... Re-signed by Bengals (May 11, 2001).
HONORS: Named running back on THE SPORTING NEWS college All-America second team (1996). ... Played in Pro Bowl (1999 and 2000 seasons).
PRO STATISTICS: 1997—Recovered one fumble for four yards. 1999—Recovered one fumble.
SINGLE GAME HIGHS (regular season): Attempts—39 (December 4, 1997, vs. Tennessee); yards—278 (October 22, 2000, vs. Denver); and rushing touchdowns—4 (December 4, 1997, vs. Tennessee).
STATISTICAL PLATEAUS: 100-yard rushing games: 1997 (4), 1998 (4), 1999 (5), 2000 (5). Total: 18.
MISCELLANEOUS: Selected by San Diego Padres organization in 34th round of free agent draft (June 3, 1993); did not sign.

			RUSHING				RECEIVING				KICKOFF RETURNS				TOTALS			
Year Team	G	GS	Att.	Yds.	Avg.	TD	No.	Yds.	Avg.	TD	No.	Yds.	Avg.	TD	TD	2pt.	Pts.	Fum.
1997—Cincinnati NFL............	16	6	233	1129	4.8	10	27	259	9.6	0	6	182	30.3	0	10	0	60	1
1998—Cincinnati NFL............	15	15	262	1130	4.3	4	28	178	6.4	1	0	0	0.0	0	5	0	30	2
1999—Cincinnati NFL............	15	15	263	1200	4.6	5	31	290	9.4	1	1	4	4.0	0	6	0	36	3
2000—Cincinnati NFL............	16	16	315	1435	4.6	7	18	158	8.8	0	0	0	0.0	0	7	0	42	4
Pro totals (4 years)................	62	52	1073	4894	4.6	26	104	885	8.5	2	7	186	26.6	0	28	0	168	10

DINGLE, ADRIAN   DE   CHARGERS

PERSONAL: Born June 25, 1977, in Holly Hill, S.C. ... 6-3/272. ... Full name: Adrian Kennell Dingle.
HIGH SCHOOL: Holly Hill (S.C.)-Roberts.
COLLEGE: Clemson.
TRANSACTIONS/CAREER NOTES: Selected by San Diego Chargers in fifth round (139th pick overall) of 1999 NFL draft. ... Signed by Chargers (July 23, 1999). ... On physically unable to perform list with knee injury (August 31-November 17, 1999). ... Active for two games (1999); did not play.
PLAYING EXPERIENCE: San Diego NFL, 2000. ... Games/Games started: 2000 (14/1).
PRO STATISTICS: 2000—Credited with 2$\frac{1}{2}$ sacks.

DISHMAN, CHRIS   G   CARDINALS

PERSONAL: Born February 27, 1974, in Cozad, Neb. ... 6-3/338.
HIGH SCHOOL: Cozad (Neb.).
COLLEGE: Nebraska.
TRANSACTIONS/CAREER NOTES: Selected by Arizona Cardinals in fourth round (106th pick overall) of 1997 NFL draft. ... Signed by Cardinals (July 9, 1997). ... Granted free agency (February 11, 2000). ... Re-signed by Cardinals (April 28, 2000) ... Granted unconditional free agency (March 2, 2001). ... Re-signed by Cardinals (March 2, 2001).
PLAYING EXPERIENCE: Arizona NFL, 1997-2000. ... Games/Games started: 1997 (8/0), 1998 (12/11), 1999 (13/10), 2000 (14/12). Total: 47/33.
PRO STATISTICS: 1998—Recovered one fumble. 1999—Returned one kickoff for nine yards. 2000—Fumbled once and recovered one fumble.

DISHMAN, CRIS   CB

PERSONAL: Born August 13, 1965, in Louisville, Ky. ... 6-0/196. ... Full name: Cris Edward Dishman.
HIGH SCHOOL: DeSales (Louisville, Ky.).
COLLEGE: Purdue.
TRANSACTIONS/CAREER NOTES: Selected by Houston Oilers in fifth round (125th pick overall) of 1988 NFL draft. ... Signed by Oilers (July 15, 1988). ... Granted free agency (February 1, 1991). ... Re-signed by Oilers (August 18, 1991). ... Granted free agency (February 1, 1992). ... Re-signed by Oilers (September 10, 1992). ... Designated by Oilers as transition player (February 15, 1994). ... Free agency status changed by Oilers from transitional to franchise player (February 15, 1996). ... Granted unconditional free agency (February 14, 1997). ... Signed by Washington Redskins (April 5, 1997). ... Released by Redskins (April 19, 1999). ... Signed by Kansas City Chiefs (May 13, 1999). ... Released by Chiefs (August 27, 2000). ... Signed by Vikings (August 28, 2000). ... Released by Vikings (November 26, 2000).
HONORS: Played in Pro Bowl (1991 and 1997 seasons).
PRO STATISTICS: 1988—Returned blocked punt 10 yards for a touchdown and recovered one fumble. 1989—Returned blocked punt seven yards for a touchdown and recovered one fumble. 1991—Recovered three fumbles for 19 yards and one touchdown. 1993—Recovered two fumbles for 69 yards and one touchdown. 1994—Returned one punt for no yards and recovered one fumble for 29 yards. 1995—Recovered two fumbles for 15 yards. 1996—Credited with 1$\frac{1}{2}$ sacks and recovered one fumble. 1999—Recovered three fumbles for 40 yards and one touchdown.

			INTERCEPTIONS				TOTALS			
Year Team	G	GS	No.	Yds.	Avg.	TD	TD	2pt.	Pts.	Fum.
1988—Houston NFL	15	2	0	0	0.0	0	1	0	6	0
1989—Houston NFL	16	0	4	31	7.8	0	1	0	6	0
1990—Houston NFL	16	14	4	50	12.5	0	0	0	0	0
1991—Houston NFL	15	15	6	61	10.2	0	1	0	6	0
1992—Houston NFL	15	15	3	34	11.3	0	0	0	0	0
1993—Houston NFL	16	16	6	74	12.3	0	1	0	6	0
1994—Houston NFL	16	16	4	74	18.5	1	1	0	6	0
1995—Houston NFL	15	15	3	17	5.7	0	0	0	0	0
1996—Houston NFL	16	16	1	7	7.0	0	0	0	0	0

Year Team	G	GS	INTERCEPTIONS No.	Yds.	Avg.	TD	TOTALS TD	2pt.	Pts.	Fum.
1997—Washington NFL	16	15	4	47	11.8	1	1	0	6	0
1998—Washington NFL	16	16	2	60	30.0	0	0	0	0	0
1999—Kansas City NFL	16	16	5	95	19.0	1	2	0	12	0
2000—Minnesota NFL	11	9	1	0	0.0	0	0	0	0	0
Pro totals (13 years)	199	165	43	550	12.8	3	8	0	48	0

DIXON, DAVID   G   VIKINGS

PERSONAL: Born January 5, 1969, in Papakura, New Zealand. ... 6-5/359. ... Full name: David Tukatahi Dixon.
HIGH SCHOOL: Pukekohe (New Zealand).
JUNIOR COLLEGE: Ricks College (Idaho).
COLLEGE: Arizona State.
TRANSACTIONS/CAREER NOTES: Selected by New England Patriots in ninth-round (232nd pick overall) of 1992 draft. ... Signed by Patriots for 1992 season. ... Released by Patriots (August 1992). ... Signed by Minnesota Vikings to practice squad (October 20, 1992). ... Released by Vikings (August 23, 1993). ... Signed by Dallas Cowboys to practice squad (September 8, 1993). ... Granted free agency after 1993 season. ... Signed by Vikings (July 12, 1994). ... Granted free agency (February 14, 1997). ... Re-signed by Vikings (May 1, 1997). ... Granted unconditional free agency (February 13, 1998). ... Re-signed by Vikings (February 17, 1998). ... On physically unable to perform list with knee injury (August 1-10, 1999).
PLAYING EXPERIENCE: Minnesota NFL, 1994-2000. ... Games/Games started: 1994 (1/0), 1995 (15/6), 1996 (13/6), 1997 (13/13), 1998 (16/16), 1999 (16/16), 2000 (16/16). Total: 90/73.
CHAMPIONSHIP GAME EXPERIENCE: Played in NFC championship game (1998 and 2000 seasons).
PRO STATISTICS: 1998—Recovered one fumble. 2000—Recovered one fumble.

DIXON, GERALD   •   LB   CHARGERS

PERSONAL: Born June 20, 1969, in Charlotte. ... 6-3/250. ... Full name: Gerald Scott Dixon.
HIGH SCHOOL: Rock Hill (S.C.).
JUNIOR COLLEGE: Garden City (Kan.) Community College.
COLLEGE: South Carolina.
TRANSACTIONS/CAREER NOTES: Selected by Cleveland Browns in third round (78th pick overall) of 1992 NFL draft. ... Signed by Browns (July 15, 1992). ... On injured reserve with ankle injury (September 2, 1992-entire season). ... Granted free agency (February 17, 1995). ... Re-signed by Browns for 1995 season. ... Granted unconditional free agency (February 16, 1996). ... Signed by Cincinnati Bengals (March 14, 1996). ... Granted unconditional free agency (February 13, 1998). ... Signed by San Diego Chargers (March 24, 1998). ... Granted unconditional free agency (February 11, 2000). ... Re-signed by Chargers (March 15, 2000).
PRO STATISTICS: 1995—Intercepted two passes for 48 yards and one touchdown, returned one kickoff for 10 yards and recovered one fumble. 1999—Recovered one fumble for 27 yards and a touchdown. 2000—Intercepted one pass for 36 yards and a touchdown and recovered one fumble.

Year Team	G	GS	SACKS
1992—Cleveland NFL	Did not play.		
1993—Cleveland NFL	11	0	0.0
1994—Cleveland NFL	16	0	1.0
1995—Cleveland NFL	16	9	0.0
1996—Cincinnati NFL	16	1	0.0
1997—Cincinnati NFL	15	12	8.5
1998—San Diego NFL	16	6	2.5
1999—San Diego NFL	14	1	4.0
2000—San Diego NFL	16	16	5.0
Pro totals (8 years)	120	45	21.0

DIXON, MARK   G   DOLPHINS

PERSONAL: Born November 26, 1970, in Charlottesville, N.C. ... 6-4/300. ... Full name: Mark Keller Dixon.
HIGH SCHOOL: Ragsdale (Jamestown, N.C.).
COLLEGE: Virginia.
TRANSACTIONS/CAREER NOTES: Signed as non-drafted free agent by Philadelphia Eagles (April 1994). ... Released by Eagles (August 1994). ... Played with Frankfurt Galaxy of World League (1995). ... Signed by Atlanta Falcons (July 18, 1995). ... Released by Falcons (August 21, 1995). ... Signed by Baltimore Stallions of CFL (August 30, 1995). ... Signed by Miami Dolphins (January 22, 1998). ... On injured reserve with neck injury (November 24, 1998-remainder of season).
PLAYING EXPERIENCE: Frankfurt W.L., 1995; Baltimore Stallions CFL, 1995; Montreal Alouettes CFL, 1996 and 1997; Miami NFL, 1998-2000. ... Games/Games started: W.L. 1995 (games played unavailable), CFL 1995 (9/5), 1996 (18/18), 1997 (7/7), 1998 (11/10), 1999 (13/13), 2000 (15/15). Total CFL: 33/30. Total NFL 39/38. Total Pro: 72/68.
CHAMPIONSHIP GAME EXPERIENCE: Member of CFL championship team (1995).
PRO STATISTICS: 1998—Recovered two fumbles.

DIXON, RON   WR/KR   GIANTS

PERSONAL: Born May 28, 1976, in Wildwood, Fla. ... 6-0/190. ... Full name: Ronald Dixon.
HIGH SCHOOL: Wildwood (Fla.).
JUNIOR COLLEGE: Itawamba Community College (Miss.).
COLLEGE: West Georgia, then Lambuth University.
TRANSACTIONS/CAREER NOTES: Selected by New York Giants in third round (73rd pick overall) of 2000 NFL draft. ... Signed by Giants (July 23, 2000).

CHAMPIONSHIP GAME EXPERIENCE: Played in NFC championship game (2000 season). ... Played in Super Bowl XXXV (2000 season).
PRO STATISTICS: 2000—Rushed twice for 13 yards.
SINGLE GAME HIGHS (regular season): Receptions—1 (December 3, 2000, vs. Washington); yards—34 (September 17, 2000, vs. Chicago); and touchdown receptions—1 (September 17, 2000, vs. Chicago).

				RECEIVING				KICKOFF RETURNS				TOTALS		
Year Team	G	GS	No.	Yds.	Avg.	TD	No.	Yds.	Avg.	TD	TD	2pt.	Pts.	Fum.
2000—New York Giants NFL............................	12	0	6	92	15.3	1	31	658	21.2	0	1	0	6	0

DONNALLEY, KEVIN   G   PANTHERS

PERSONAL: Born June 10, 1968, in St. Louis. ... 6-5/310. ... Full name: Kevin Thomas Donnalley. ... Brother of Rick Donnalley, center with Pittsburgh Steelers (1982 and 1983), Washington Redskins (1984 and 1985) and Kansas City Chiefs (1986 and 1987).
HIGH SCHOOL: Athens Drive Senior (Raleigh, N.C.).
COLLEGE: Davidson, then North Carolina (degree in economics).
TRANSACTIONS/CAREER NOTES: Selected by Houston Oilers in third round (79th pick overall) of 1991 NFL draft. ... Signed by Oilers (July 10, 1991). ... Granted free agency (February 17, 1994). ... Tendered offer sheet by Los Angeles Rams (March 17, 1994). ... Offer matched by Oilers (March 23, 1994). ... Oilers franchise moved to Tennessee for 1997 season. ... Granted unconditional free agency (February 13, 1998). ... Signed by Miami Dolphins (February 17, 1998). ... Released by Dolphins (June 2, 2000). ... Re-signed by Dolphins (June 13, 2000). ... Granted unconditional free agency (March 2, 2001). ... Signed by Carolina Panthers (March 16, 2001).
PLAYING EXPERIENCE: Houston NFL, 1991-1996; Tennessee NFL, 1997; Miami NFL, 1998-2000. ... Games/Games started: 1991 (16/0), 1992 (16/2), 1993 (16/6), 1994 (13/11), 1995 (16/16), 1996 (16/16), 1997 (16/16), 1998 (14/14), 1999 (16/9), 2000 (16/16). Total: 155/106.
PRO STATISTICS: 1995—Recovered one fumble. 1998—Recovered one fumble.

DORSETT, ANTHONY   S   RAIDERS

PERSONAL: Born September 14, 1973, in Aliquippa, Pa. ... 5-11/200. ... Full name: Anthony Drew Dorsett Jr. ... Son of Tony Dorsett, Hall of Fame running back with Dallas Cowboys (1977-87) and Denver Broncos (1988).
HIGH SCHOOL: Richland (Dallas), then J.J. Pearce (Richardson, Texas).
COLLEGE: Pittsburgh.
TRANSACTIONS/CAREER NOTES: Selected by Houston Oilers in sixth round (177th pick overall) of 1996 NFL draft. ... Signed by Oilers (June 21, 1996). ... Assigned by Oilers to Barcelona Dragons in 1997 World League enhancement allocation program (February 19, 1997). ... Oilers franchise moved to Tennessee for 1997 season. ... Oilers franchise renamed Tennessee Titans for 1999 season (December 26, 1998). ... Granted free agency (February 12, 1999). ... Re-signed by Titans (June 15, 1999). ... Granted unconditional free agency (February 11, 2000). ... Signed by Oakland Raiders (March 21, 2000).
PLAYING EXPERIENCE: Houston NFL, 1996; Barcelona W.L., 1997; Tennessee NFL, 1997-1999; Oakland NFL, 2000. ... Games/Games started: 1996 (8/0), W.L. 1997 (games played unavailable),1997 (16/0), 1998 (16/0), 1999 (16/1), 2000 (16/16). Total NFL: 72/17.
CHAMPIONSHIP GAME EXPERIENCE: Played in AFC championship game (1999 and 2000 seasons). ... Played in Super Bowl XXXIV (1999 season).
PRO STATISTICS: 1999—Intercepted one pass for 43 yards. 2000—Credited with one sack.

DOTSON, EARL   OT   PACKERS

PERSONAL: Born December 17, 1970, in Beaumont, Texas. ... 6-4/317. ... Full name: Earl Christopher Dotson.
HIGH SCHOOL: Westbrook (Texas).
JUNIOR COLLEGE: Tyler (Texas) Junior College.
COLLEGE: Texas A&I.
TRANSACTIONS/CAREER NOTES: Selected by Green Bay Packers in third round (81st pick overall) of 1993 NFL draft. ... Signed by Packers (June 14, 1993). ... Released by Packers (February 27, 2001). ... Re-signed by Packers (March 8, 2001).
PLAYING EXPERIENCE: Green Bay NFL, 1993-2000. ... Games/Games started: 1993 (13/0), 1994 (4/0), 1995 (16/16), 1996 (15/15), 1997 (13/13), 1998 (16/16), 1999 (15/15), 2000 (2/2). Total: 94/77.
CHAMPIONSHIP GAME EXPERIENCE: Played in NFC championship game (1995-97 seasons). ... Member of Super Bowl championship team (1996 season). ... Played in Super Bowl XXXII (1997 season).
PRO STATISTICS: 1996—Recovered one fumble. 1997—Recovered one fumble. 2000—Recovered one fumble.

DOTSON, SANTANA   DT   PACKERS

PERSONAL: Born December 19, 1969, in New Orleans. ... 6-5/285. ... Full name: Santana N. Dotson. ... Son of Alphonse Dotson, defensive tackle with Kansas City Chiefs (1965), Miami Dolphins (1966) and Oakland Raiders (1968-70).
HIGH SCHOOL: Jack Yates (Houston).
COLLEGE: Baylor.
TRANSACTIONS/CAREER NOTES: Selected by Tampa Bay Buccaneers in fifth round (132nd pick overall) of 1992 NFL draft. ... Signed by Buccaneers (July 7, 1992). ... Granted free agency (February 17, 1995). ... Re-signed by Buccaneers (June 14, 1995). ... Granted unconditional free agency (February 16, 1996). ... Signed by Green Bay Packers (March 7, 1996). ... Granted unconditional free agency (February 12, 1999). ... Re-signed by Packers (February 19, 1999). ... On injured reserve with knee injury (November 29, 2000-remainder of season).
CHAMPIONSHIP GAME EXPERIENCE: Played in NFC championship game (1996 and 1997 seasons). ... Member of Super Bowl championship team (1996 season). ... Played in Super Bowl XXXII (1997 season).
HONORS: Named defensive lineman on THE SPORTING NEWS college All-America first team (1991). ... Named NFL Rookie of the Year by THE SPORTING NEWS (1992).
PRO STATISTICS: 1992—Recovered two fumbles for 42 yards and one touchdown. 1995—Recovered two fumbles. 1996—Recovered one fumble for eight yards. 1998—Recovered one fumble.

Year	Team	G	GS	SACKS
1992—Tampa Bay NFL		16	16	10.0
1993—Tampa Bay NFL		16	13	5.0
1994—Tampa Bay NFL		16	9	3.0
1995—Tampa Bay NFL		16	8	5.0
1996—Green Bay NFL		16	15	5.5
1997—Green Bay NFL		16	16	5.5
1998—Green Bay NFL		16	16	3.0
1999—Green Bay NFL		12	12	2.5
2000—Green Bay NFL		12	11	6.0
Pro totals (9 years)		136	116	45.5

DOUGLAS, DAMEANE — WR — EAGLES

PERSONAL: Born March 15, 1976, in Hanford, Calif. ... 6-0/195.
HIGH SCHOOL: Hanford (Calif.).
COLLEGE: California.
TRANSACTIONS/CAREER NOTES: Selected by Oakland Raiders in fourth round (102nd pick overall) of 1999 NFL draft. ... Signed by Raiders for 1999 season. ... Claimed on waivers by Philadelphia Eagles (September 7, 1999).
PRO STATISTICS: 2000—Returned two kickoffs for 50 yards.
SINGLE GAME HIGHS (regular season): Receptions—3 (December 5, 1999, vs. Arizona); yards—47 (December 5, 1999, vs. Arizona); and touchdown receptions—1 (December 5, 1999, vs. Arizona).

				RECEIVING				TOTALS		
Year	Team	G	GS	No.	Yds.	Avg.	TD	TD	2pt.	Pts.	Fum.
1999—Philadelphia NFL		14	0	8	79	9.9	1	1	0	6	0
2000—Philadelphia NFL		6	0	1	9	9.0	0	0	0	0	0
Pro totals (2 years)		20	0	9	88	9.8	1	1	0	6	0

DOUGLAS, HUGH — LB/DE — EAGLES

PERSONAL: Born August 23, 1971, in Mansfield, Ohio. ... 6-2/280.
HIGH SCHOOL: Mansfield (Ohio).
COLLEGE: Central State (Ohio).
TRANSACTIONS/CAREER NOTES: Selected after junior season by New York Jets in first round (16th pick overall) of 1995 NFL draft. ... Signed by Jets (June 8, 1995). ... Traded by Jets to Philadelphia Eagles for second- (traded to Pittsburgh) and fifth-round (LB Casey Dailey) picks in 1998 draft (March 13, 1998). ... On injured reserve with bicep injury (October 20, 1999-remainder of season).
HONORS: Named defensive end on THE SPORTING NEWS NFL All-Pro team (2000). ... Played in Pro Bowl (2000 season).
PRO STATISTICS: 1995—Recovered two fumbles. 1996—Recovered three fumbles for 64 yards and one touchdown. 2000—Intercepted one pass for nine yards.

Year	Team	G	GS	SACKS
1995—New York Jets NFL		15	3	10.0
1996—New York Jets NFL		10	10	8.0
1997—New York Jets NFL		15	15	4.0
1998—Philadelphia NFL		15	13	12.5
1999—Philadelphia NFL		4	2	2.0
2000—Philadelphia NFL		16	15	15.0
Pro totals (6 years)		75	58	51.5

DOUGLAS, MARQUES — DE — SAINTS

PERSONAL: Born March 5, 1977, in Greensboro, N.C. ... 6-2/270. ... Full name: Marques Lamont Douglas.
HIGH SCHOOL: Dudley (Greensboro, N.C.).
COLLEGE: Howard.
TRANSACTIONS/CAREER NOTES: Signed by Baltimore Ravens as non-drafted free agent (April 23, 1999). ... Released by Ravens (September 4, 1999). ... Re-signed by Ravens (December 22, 1999). ... Claimed on waivers by New Orleans Saints (August 28, 2000). ... Released by Saints (September 14, 2000). ... Re-signed by Saints (September 20, 2000). ... On injured reserve with knee injury (October 12, 2000-remainder of season).
PLAYING EXPERIENCE: New Orleans NFL, 2000. ... Games/Games started: 2000 (1/0).

DOWNS, GARY — RB — FALCONS

PERSONAL: Born June 6, 1972, in Columbus, Ga. ... 6-1/215. ... Full name: Gary McLinton Downs.
HIGH SCHOOL: William H. Spencer (Columbus, Ga.).
COLLEGE: North Carolina State.
TRANSACTIONS/CAREER NOTES: Selected by New York Giants in third round (95th pick overall) of 1994 NFL draft. ... Signed by Giants (July 19, 1994). ... Released by Giants (August 27, 1995). ... Signed by Denver Broncos (August 28, 1995). ... Released by Broncos (August 28, 1996). ... Signed by Giants (October 31, 1996). ... Granted unconditional free agency (February 14, 1997). ... Signed by Atlanta Falcons (March 17, 1997). ... Granted unconditional free agency (February 13, 1998). ... Re-signed by Falcons (March 13, 1998). ... On injured reserve with knee injury (August 2, 1999-entire season).
CHAMPIONSHIP GAME EXPERIENCE: Played in NFC championship game (1998 season). ... Played in Super Bowl XXXIII (1998 season).
PRO STATISTICS: 1996—Recovered one fumble. 2000—Recovered one fumble.
SINGLE GAME HIGHS (regular season): Attempts—22 (December 21, 1996, vs. New England); yards—52 (December 21, 1996, vs. New England); and rushing touchdowns—0.

D

| | | | RUSHING | | | | RECEIVING | | | | TOTALS | | | |
Year Team	G	GS	Att.	Yds.	Avg.	TD	No.	Yds.	Avg.	TD	TD	2pt.	Pts.	Fum.
1994—New York Giants NFL	14	0	15	51	3.4	0	2	15	7.5	0	0	0	0	1
1995—Denver NFL	1	0	0	0	0.0	0	0	0	0.0	0	0	0	0	0
1996—New York Giants NFL	6	1	29	94	3.2	0	3	20	6.7	0	0	0	0	1
1997—Atlanta NFL	16	0	0	0	0.0	0	0	0	0.0	0	0	0	0	0
1998—Atlanta NFL	16	1	1	4	4.0	0	4	31	7.8	0	0	0	0	0
1999—Atlanta NFL							Did not play.							
2000—Atlanta NFL	16	0	0	0	0.0	0	0	0	0.0	0	0	0	0	0
Pro totals (6 years)	69	2	45	149	3.3	0	9	66	7.3	0	0	0	0	2

DRAFT, CHRIS LB FALCONS

PERSONAL: Born February 26, 1976, in Anaheim. ... 5-11/232.
HIGH SCHOOL: Valencia (Placentia, Calif.).
COLLEGE: Stanford.
TRANSACTIONS/CAREER NOTES: Selected by Chicago Bears in sixth round (157th pick overall) of 1998 NFL draft. ... Signed by Bears (June 16, 1998). ... Released by Bears (August 30, 1998). ... Re-signed by Bears to practice squad (August 31, 1998). ... Activated (December 2, 1998). ... Released by Bears (August 30, 1999). ... Signed by San Francisco 49ers to practice squad (September 29, 1999). ... Activated (November 19, 1999). ... Released by 49ers (February 10, 2000). ... Signed by Atlanta Falcons (February 14, 2000).
PLAYING EXPERIENCE: Chicago NFL, 1998; San Francisco NFL, 1999; Atlanta NFL, 2000. ... Games/Games started: 1998 (1/0), 1999 (7/0), 2000 (13/8). Total: 21/8.
PRO STATISTICS: 2000—Credited with one sack.

DRAGOS, SCOTT FB/TE BEARS

PERSONAL: Born October 28, 1975, in Old Rochester, Mass. ... 6-2/245. ... Name pronounced DRAY-gos.
HIGH SCHOOL: Old Rochester (Mass.) Regional.
COLLEGE: Boston College.
TRANSACTIONS/CAREER NOTES: Signed as non-drafted free agent by New England Patriots (April 19, 1998). ... Released by Patriots (August 19, 1998). ... Signed by New York Giants to practice squad (November 18, 1998). ... Assigned by Giants to Barcelona Dragons in 1999 NFL Europe enhancement allocation program (February 22, 1999). ... Released by Giants (September 5, 1999). ... Signed by Chicago Bears to practice squad (September 28, 1999). ... Released by Bears (August 27, 2000). ... Re-signed by Bears (October 10, 2000).
SINGLE GAME HIGHS (regular season): Receptions—2 (December 10, 2000, vs. New England); yards—14 (December 10, 2000, vs. New England); and touchdown receptions—0

| | | | | RECEIVING | | |
Year Team	G	GS	No.	Yds.	Avg.	TD
1999—Barcelona NFLE	...	...	12	158	13.2	3
2000—Chicago NFL	9	2	4	28	7.0	0
NFL Europe totals (1 year)	...	...	12	158	13.2	3
NFL totals (1 year)	9	2	4	28	7.0	0
Pro totals (2 years)	...	...	16	186	11.6	3

DRAKEFORD, TYRONNE CB

PERSONAL: Born June 21, 1971, in Camden, S.C. ... 5-11/185. ... Full name: Tyronne James Drakeford.
HIGH SCHOOL: North Central (Kershaw, S.C.).
COLLEGE: Virginia Tech (degree in finance).
TRANSACTIONS/CAREER NOTES: Selected by San Francisco 49ers in second round (62nd pick overall) of 1994 NFL draft. ... Signed by 49ers (July 20, 1994). ... Granted free agency (February 14, 1997). ... Re-signed by 49ers (April 8, 1997). ... Granted unconditional free agency (February 13, 1998). ... Signed by New Orleans Saints (February 19, 1998). ... Released by Saints (May 11, 2000). ... Signed by Washington Redskins (June 23, 2000). ... Granted unconditional free agency (March 2, 2001).
CHAMPIONSHIP GAME EXPERIENCE: Played in NFC championship game (1994 and 1997 seasons). ... Member of Super Bowl championship team (1994 season).
PRO STATISTICS: 1995—Credited with one sack, fumbled once and recovered one fumble for 12 yards. 1996—Credited with two sacks and recovered one fumble for eight yards. 1997—Returned one kickoff for 24 yards. 1999—Recovered one fumble for 20 yards.

| | | | | INTERCEPTIONS | | |
Year Team	G	GS	No.	Yds.	Avg.	TD
1994—San Francisco NFL	13	0	1	6	6.0	0
1995—San Francisco NFL	16	2	5	54	10.8	0
1996—San Francisco NFL	16	16	1	11	11.0	0
1997—San Francisco NFL	16	2	5	15	3.0	0
1998—New Orleans NFL	16	15	4	76	19.0	1
1999—New Orleans NFL	10	5	0	0	0.0	0
2000—Washington NFL	9	1	0	0	0.0	0
Pro totals (7 years)	96	41	16	162	10.1	1

DRAYTON, TROY TE

PERSONAL: Born June 29, 1970, in Harrisburg, Pa. ... 6-3/270. ... Full name: Troy Anthony Drayton. ... Cousin of Kevin Mitchell, linebacker, Washington Redskins.
HIGH SCHOOL: Steelton Highspire (Steelton, Pa.).
COLLEGE: Penn State.
TRANSACTIONS/CAREER NOTES: Selected by Los Angeles Rams in second round (39th pick overall) of 1993 NFL draft. ... Signed by Rams (July 20, 1993). ... Rams franchise moved to St. Louis (April 12, 1995). ... Granted free agency (February 16, 1996). ... Re-signed by Rams

(April 17, 1996). ... Traded by Rams to Miami Dolphins for OT Bill Milner (October 1, 1996). ... Released by Dolphins (February 10, 2000). ... Signed by Oakland Raiders (May 31, 2000). ... Released by Raiders (June 5, 2000). ... Signed by Kansas City Chiefs (June 13, 2000). ... Granted unconditional free agency (March 2, 2001).

PRO STATISTICS: 1993—Rushed once for seven yards and returned one kickoff for minus 15 yards. 1994—Rushed once for four yards. 1996—Recovered one fumble.

SINGLE GAME HIGHS (regular season): Receptions—8 (November 19, 1995, vs. Atlanta); yards—106 (September 24, 1995, vs. Chicago); and touchdown receptions—2 (October 12, 1998, vs. Jacksonville).

STATISTICAL PLATEAUS: 100-yard receiving games: 1995 (1).

				RECEIVING				TOTALS		
Year Team	G	GS	No.	Yds.	Avg.	TD	TD	2pt.	Pts.	Fum.
1993—Los Angeles Rams NFL	16	2	27	319	11.8	4	4	0	24	1
1994—Los Angeles Rams NFL	16	16	32	276	8.6	6	6	0	36	0
1995—St. Louis NFL	16	16	47	458	9.7	4	4	0	24	2
1996—St. Louis NFL	3	3	2	11	5.5	0	0	0	0	0
—Miami NFL	10	10	26	320	12.3	0	0	1	2	0
1997—Miami NFL	16	15	39	558	14.3	4	4	0	24	0
1998—Miami NFL	15	15	30	334	11.1	3	3	0	18	0
1999—Miami NFL	14	13	32	299	9.3	1	1	0	6	0
2000—Kansas City NFL	16	1	8	70	8.8	2	2	0	12	0
Pro totals (8 years)	122	91	243	2645	10.9	24	24	1	146	3

DRIVER, DONALD   WR   PACKERS

PERSONAL: Born February 2, 1975, in Houston. ... 6-0/177. ... Full name: Donald Jerome Driver.
HIGH SCHOOL: Milby (Houston).
COLLEGE: Alcorn State (degree in accounting).
TRANSACTIONS/CAREER NOTES: Selected by Green Bay Packers in seventh round (213th pick overall) of 1999 NFL draft. ... Signed by Packers (June 2, 1999).
PRO STATISTICS: 2000—Rushed once for four yards and recovered one fumble.
SINGLE GAME HIGHS (regular season): Receptions—3 (October 1, 2000, vs. Chicago); yards—31 (September 10, 2000, vs. Buffalo); and touchdown receptions—1 (November 27, 2000, vs. Carolina).

				RECEIVING				TOTALS		
Year Team	G	GS	No.	Yds.	Avg.	TD	TD	2pt.	Pts.	Fum.
1999—Green Bay NFL	5	0	3	31	10.3	1	1	0	6	0
2000—Green Bay NFL	16	2	21	322	15.3	1	1	1	8	0
Pro totals (2 years)	21	2	24	353	14.7	2	2	1	14	0

D

DRONETT, SHANE   DT   FALCONS

PERSONAL: Born January 12, 1971, in Orange, Texas. ... 6-6/300.
HIGH SCHOOL: Bridge City (Texas).
COLLEGE: Texas.
TRANSACTIONS/CAREER NOTES: Selected after junior season by Denver Broncos in second round (54th pick overall) of 1992 NFL draft. ... Signed by Broncos (July 15, 1992). ... Granted free agency (February 17, 1995). ... Re-signed by Broncos (May 12, 1995). ... Granted unconditional free agency (February 16, 1996). ... Signed by Atlanta Falcons (April 9, 1996). ... Released by Falcons (October 7, 1996). ... Signed by Detroit Lions (October 9, 1996). ... Granted unconditional free agency (February 14, 1997). ... Signed by Lions for 1997 season. ... Released by Lions (August 24, 1997). ... Signed by Falcons (August 27, 1997). ... Granted unconditional free agency (February 13, 1998). ... Re-signed by Falcons (February 20, 1998). ... On injured reserve with knee injury (September 19, 2000-remainder of season).
CHAMPIONSHIP GAME EXPERIENCE: Played in NFC championship game (1998 season). ... Played in Super Bowl XXXIII (1998 season).
PRO STATISTICS: 1992—Recovered two fumbles for minus five yards. 1993—Intercepted two passes for 13 yards. 1998—Recovered one fumble. 1999—Recovered one fumble for 15 yards.

Year Team	G	GS	SACKS
1992—Denver NFL	16	2	6.5
1993—Denver NFL	16	16	7.0
1994—Denver NFL	16	15	6.0
1995—Denver NFL	13	2	2.0
1996—Atlanta NFL	5	0	0.0
—Detroit NFL	7	0	0.0
1997—Atlanta NFL	16	1	3.0
1998—Atlanta NFL	16	16	6.5
1999—Atlanta NFL	16	16	6.5
2000—Atlanta NFL	3	3	1.0
Pro totals (9 years)	124	71	38.5

DROUGHNS, REUBEN   RB   LIONS

PERSONAL: Born August 21, 1978, in Chicago. ... 5-11/207.
HIGH SCHOOL: Anaheim (Calif.).
JUNIOR COLLEGE: Merced (Calif.) College.
COLLEGE: Oregon.
TRANSACTIONS/CAREER NOTES: Selected by Detroit Lions in third round (81st pick overall) of 2000 NFL draft. ... Signed by Lions (July 15, 2000). ... On injured reserve with shoulder injury (August 22, 2000-entire season).

			RUSHING				RECEIVING				TOTALS		
Year Team	G	GS	Att.	Yds.	Avg.	TD	No.	Yds.	Avg.	TD	TD	2pt.	Pts.	Fum.
2000—Detroit								Did not play.						

DUDLEY, RICKEY   TE   BROWNS

PERSONAL: Born July 15, 1972, in Henderson, Texas. ... 6-6/255.
HIGH SCHOOL: Henderson (Texas).
COLLEGE: Ohio State.
TRANSACTIONS/CAREER NOTES: Selected by Oakland Raiders in first round (ninth pick overall) of 1996 NFL draft. ... Signed by Raiders (July 12, 1996). ... Granted unconditional free agency (March 2, 2001). ... Signed by Cleveland Browns (March 30, 2001).
CHAMPIONSHIP GAME EXPERIENCE: Played in AFC championship game (2000 season).
PRO STATISTICS: 1998—Rushed once for minus two yards. 2000—Rushed once for minus seven yards and recovered one fumble.
SINGLE GAME HIGHS (regular season): Receptions—6 (November 8, 1998, vs. Baltimore); yards—116 (November 9, 1997, vs. New Orleans); and touchdown receptions—2 (December 24, 2000, vs. Carolina).
STATISTICAL PLATEAUS: 100-yard receiving games: 1997 (2), 1998 (1). Total: 3.
MISCELLANEOUS: Member of Ohio State basketball team (1991-92 through 1993-94).

| | | | RECEIVING | | | | TOTALS | | |
Year Team	G	GS	No.	Yds.	Avg.	TD	TD	2pt.	Pts.	Fum.
1996—Oakland NFL	16	15	34	386	11.4	4	4	0	24	1
1997—Oakland NFL	16	16	48	787	16.4	7	7	0	42	0
1998—Oakland NFL	16	15	36	549	15.3	5	5	1	32	1
1999—Oakland NFL	16	16	39	555	14.2	9	9	0	54	0
2000—Oakland NFL	16	16	29	350	12.1	4	4	0	24	1
Pro totals (5 years)	80	78	186	2627	14.1	29	29	1	176	3

DUFFY, ROGER   G/C   STEELERS

PERSONAL: Born July 16, 1967, in Pittsburgh. ... 6-3/299. ... Full name: Roger Thomas Duffy.
HIGH SCHOOL: Canton (Ohio) Central Catholic.
COLLEGE: Penn State (degree in communications, 1990).
TRANSACTIONS/CAREER NOTES: Selected by New York Jets in eighth round (196th pick overall) of 1990 NFL draft. ... Signed by Jets (July 18, 1990). ... Granted free agency (February 1, 1992). ... Re-signed by Jets (May 15, 1992). ... Granted unconditional free agency (February 17, 1994). ... Re-signed by Jets (March 2, 1994). ... Granted unconditional free agency (February 16, 1996). ... Re-signed by Jets (April 1, 1996). ... Granted unconditional free agency (February 13, 1998). ... Signed by Pittsburgh Steelers (March 13, 1998).
PLAYING EXPERIENCE: New York Jets NFL, 1990-1997; Pittsburgh NFL, 1998-2000. ... Games/Games started: 1990 (16/2), 1991 (12/0), 1992 (16/6), 1993 (16/1), 1994 (16/14), 1995 (16/16), 1996 (16/16), 1997 (15/15), 1998 (15/4), 1999 (16/11), 2000 (13/7). Total: 167/92.
PRO STATISTICS: 1991—Returned one kickoff for eight yards. 1992—Returned one kickoff for seven yards and recovered one fumble. 1993—Recovered one fumble. 1995—Recovered two fumbles. 1996—Recovered one fumble. 1997—Fumbled twice and recovered one fumble for minus 22 yards. 2000—Fumbled once for minus 10 yards.

DUGANS, RON   WR   BENGALS

PERSONAL: Born April 27, 1977, in Tallahassee, Fla. ... 6-2/205.
HIGH SCHOOL: Florida A&M University Develop Research (Tallahassee, Fla.).
COLLEGE: Florida State (degree in political science, 1999).
TRANSACTIONS/CAREER NOTES: Selected by Cincinnati Bengals in third round (66th pick overall) of 2000 NFL draft. ... Signed by Bengals (July 25, 2000).
SINGLE GAME HIGHS (regular season): Receptions—3 (October 8, 2000, vs. Tennessee); yards—29 (October 15, 2000, vs. Pittsburgh); and touchdown receptions—1 (September 10, 2000, vs. Cleveland).

| | | | RECEIVING | | | |
Year Team	G	GS	No.	Yds.	Avg.	TD
2000—Cincinnati NFL	14	5	14	125	8.9	1

DUKES, CHAD   RB   PANTHERS

PERSONAL: Born December 29, 1971, in Albany, N.Y. ... 6-0/230.
HIGH SCHOOL: Colonie High (Penn.).
COLLEGE: Pittsburgh.
TRANSACTIONS/CAREER NOTES: Played with Albany Firebirds of Arena League (1998). ... Signed as non-drafted free agent by San Diego Chargers to practice squad (October 22, 1998). ... Released by Chargers (November 24, 1998). ... Signed by Washington Redskins to practice squad (December 1, 1998). ... Released by Redskins (September 4, 1999). ... Signed by Redskins to practioce squad (September 6, 1999). ... Claimed on waivers by Jacksonville Jaguars (September 6, 2000). ... Released by Jaguars (September 19, 2000). ... Signed by Carolina Panthers (April 21, 2001).
PLAYING EXPERIENCE: Washington (1)-Jacksonville (1) NFL, 2000. ... Games/Games started: 2000 (Wash.-1/0; Jack.-1/0; Total: 2/0).
SINGLE GAME HIGHS (regular season): Attempts—2 (September 17, 2000, vs. Cincinnati); yards—2 (September 17, 2000, vs. Cincinnati); and rushing touchdowns—0.

DUMAS, MIKE   S

PERSONAL: Born March 18, 1969, in Grand Rapids, Mich. ... 6-0/202. ... Full name: Michael Dion Dumas.
HIGH SCHOOL: Lowell (Mich.).
COLLEGE: Indiana.
TRANSACTIONS/CAREER NOTES: Selected by Houston Oilers in second round (28th pick overall) of 1991 NFL draft. ... Signed by Oilers (August 12, 1991). ... On injured reserve with Achilles' tendon injury (August 23, 1993-entire season). ... Granted free agency (February 17, 1994). ... Re-signed by Oilers (June 1994). ... Released by Oilers (July 14, 1994). ... Signed by Buffalo Bills (July 25, 1994). ...

Granted unconditional free agency (February 17, 1995). ... Signed by Jacksonville Jaguars (April 24, 1995). ... Released by Jaguars (April 24, 1996). ... Signed by San Diego Chargers (March 4, 1997). ... Granted unconditional free agency (February 13, 1998). ... Re-signed by Chargers (February 20, 1998). ... On injured reserve with knee injury (September 26, 1998-remainder of season). ... Granted unconditional free agency (February 11, 2000). ... Re-signed by Chargers (April 20, 2000). ... Released by Chargers (March 1, 2001).

HONORS: Named defensive back on THE SPORTING NEWS college All-America second team (1990).

PRO STATISTICS: 1991—Recovered three fumbles for 19 yards and one touchdown. 1992—Recovered one fumble. 1994—Recovered two fumbles for 40 yards. 1995—Recovered two fumbles. 1997—Credited with one sack and recovered one fumble. 1998—Credited with one sack. 1999—Credited with two sacks. 2000—Credited with one sack and returned one punt for one yard.

| | | | INTERCEPTIONS | | | |
Year Team	G	GS	No.	Yds.	Avg.	TD
1991—Houston NFL	13	0	1	19	19.0	0
1992—Houston NFL	16	1	1	0	0.0	0
1993—Houston NFL			Did not play.			
1994—Buffalo NFL	14	0	0	0	0.0	0
1995—Jacksonville NFL	14	8	1	0	0.0	0
1996—			Did not play.			
1997—San Diego NFL	16	15	1	0	0.0	0
1998—San Diego NFL	3	3	0	0	0.0	0
1999—San Diego NFL	14	14	2	92	46.0	0
2000—San Diego NFL	12	12	1	56	56.0	1
Pro totals (8 years)	102	53	7	167	23.9	1

DUNCAN, JAMIE LB BUCCANEERS

PERSONAL: Born July 20, 1975, in Wilmington, Del. ... 6-0/242.
HIGH SCHOOL: Christiana (Newark, Del.).
COLLEGE: Vanderbilt (degree in human and organizational development, 1998).
TRANSACTIONS/CAREER NOTES: Selected by Tampa Bay Buccaneers in third round (84th pick overall) of 1998 NFL draft. ... Signed by Buccaneers (July 10, 1998).
PLAYING EXPERIENCE: Tampa Bay NFL, 1998-2000. ... Games/Games started: 1998 (14/6), 1999 (16/0), 2000 (15/15). Total: 45/21.
CHAMPIONSHIP GAME EXPERIENCE: Played in NFC championship game (1999 season).
HONORS: Named inside linebacker on THE SPORTING NEWS college All-America second team (1997).
PRO STATISTICS: 2000—Intercepted four passes for 55 yards and one touchdown and recovered one touchdown.

DUNN, DAMON WR COWBOYS

PERSONAL: Born March 15, 1976, in Fort Worth, Texas ... 5-9/182. ... Full name: Damon Jerrel Dunn.
HIGH SCHOOL: Sam Houston (Arlington, Texas).
COLLEGE: Stanford.
TRANSACTIONS/CAREER NOTES: Signed as non-drafted free agent by Jacksonville Jaguars (April 23, 1998). ... Released by Jaguars (August 25, 1998). ... Re-signed by Jaguars to practice squad (August 31, 1998). ... Released by Jaguars (August 29, 1999). ... Signed by Cleveland Browns to practice squad (November 16, 1999). ... Activated (December 14, 1999). ... Assigned by Browns to Berlin Thunder in 2000 NFL Europe enhancement allocation program (February 11, 2000). ... Released by Browns (August 27, 2000). ... Signed by New York Jets (September 6, 2000). ... Released by Jets (September 19, 2000). ... Re-signed by Browns (October 18, 2000). ... Released by Browns (November 22, 2000). ... Signed by Dallas Cowboys (May 4, 2001).
PRO STATISTICS: NFLE: 2000—Returned one punt for no yards.
SINGLE GAME HIGHS (regular season): Receptions—1 (November 12, 2000, vs. New England); yards—6 (November 12, 2000, vs. New England); and touchdown receptions—0.

| | | | RECEIVING | | | | KICKOFF RETURNS | | | | TOTALS | | | |
Year Team	G	GS	No.	Yds.	Avg.	TD	No.	Yds.	Avg.	TD	TD	2pt.	Pts.	Fum.
1999—Cleveland NFL	1	0	0	0	0.0	0	0	0	0.0	0	0	0	0	0
2000—Berlin NFLE	...	...	41	794	19.4	6	14	227	16.2	0	0	0	0	0
—New York Jets NFL	1	0	0	0	0.0	0	2	35	17.5	0	0	0	0	1
—Cleveland NFL	3	0	1	6	6.0	0	0	0	0.0	0	0	0	0	0
NFL Europe totals (1 year)	...	...	41	794	19.4	6	14	227	16.2	0	0	0	0	0
NFL totals (2 years)	5	0	1	6	6.0	0	2	35	17.5	0	0	0	0	1
Pro totals (3 years)	...	...	42	800	19.0	6	16	262	16.4	0	0	0	0	1

DUNN, DAVID WR RAIDERS

PERSONAL: Born June 10, 1972, in San Diego. ... 6-3/210.
HIGH SCHOOL: Samuel F.B. Morse (San Diego).
JUNIOR COLLEGE: Bakersfield (Calif.) College.
COLLEGE: Fresno State.
TRANSACTIONS/CAREER NOTES: Selected by Cincinnati Bengals in fifth round (139th pick overall) of 1995 NFL draft. ... Signed by Bengals (July 31, 1995). ... Granted free agency (February 13, 1998). ... Re-signed by Bengals (April 23, 1998). ... Released by Bengals (September 9, 1998). ... Signed by Pittsburgh Steelers (October 14, 1998). ... Released by Steelers (August 30, 1999). ... Signed by Cleveland Browns (September 28, 1999). ... Released by Browns (November 9, 1999). ... Signed by Oakland Raiders (February 29, 2000). ... Granted unconditional free agency (March 2, 2001). ... Re-signed by Raiders (March 22, 2001).
CHAMPIONSHIP GAME EXPERIENCE: Played in AFC championship game (2000 season).
HONORS: Named kick returner on THE SPORTING NEWS college All-America second team (1994).
PRO STATISTICS: 1995—Rushed once for minus 13 yards. 1997—Recovered one fumble. 1999—Recovered one fumble.
SINGLE GAME HIGHS (regular season): Receptions—7 (December 15, 1996, vs. Houston); yards—95 (December 15, 1996, vs. Houston); and touchdown receptions—1 (December 14, 1997, vs. Dallas).

Year Team	G	GS	RECEIVING				PUNT RETURNS				KICKOFF RETURNS				TOTALS			
			No.	Yds.	Avg.	TD	No.	Yds.	Avg.	TD	No.	Yds.	Avg.	TD	TD	2pt.	Pts.	Fum.
1995—Cincinnati NFL............	16	0	17	209	12.3	1	0	0	0.0	0	50	1092	21.8	0	1	0	6	2
1996—Cincinnati NFL............	16	0	32	509	15.9	1	7	54	7.7	0	35	782	22.3	▲1	3	0	18	1
1997—Cincinnati NFL............	14	5	27	414	15.3	2	0	0	0.0	0	19	487	25.6	0	2	0	12	1
1998—Cincinnati NFL............	1	0	0	0	0.0	0	0	0	0.0	0	0	0	0.0	0	0	0	0	0
—Pittsburgh NFL......	10	0	9	87	9.7	0	0	0	0.0	0	21	525	25.0	0	0	0	0	1
1999—Cleveland NFL............	6	0	1	4	4.0	0	4	25	6.3	0	9	180	20.0	0	0	0	0	3
2000—Oakland NFL...............	15	0	4	33	8.3	0	8	99	12.4	0	44	1073	24.4	▲1	1	0	6	0
Pro totals (6 years)	78	5	90	1256	14.0	4	19	178	9.4	0	178	4139	23.3	2	7	0	42	8

DUNN, JASON — TE — CHIEFS

PERSONAL: Born November 15, 1973, in Harrodsburg, Ky. ... 6-4/260. ... Full name: Jason Adam Dunn.
HIGH SCHOOL: Harrodsburg (Ky.).
COLLEGE: Eastern Kentucky.
TRANSACTIONS/CAREER NOTES: Selected by Philadelphia Eagles in second round (54th pick overall) of 1996 NFL draft. ... Signed by Eagles (July 17, 1996). ... On injured reserve with knee injury (December 1, 1998-remainder of season). ... Granted free agency (February 12, 1999). ... Re-signed by Eagles for 1999 season. ... Released by Eagles (June 17, 1999). ... Signed by Kansas City Chiefs (July 11, 2000). ... Granted unconditional free agency (March 2, 2001). ... Re-signed by Chiefs (March 26, 2001).
PRO STATISTICS: 1996—Recovered one fumble. 1997—Returned two kickoffs for 32 yards. 1998—Rushed once for minus five yards and recovered one fumble.
SINGLE GAME HIGHS (regular season): Receptions—4 (November 15, 1998, vs. Washington); yards—58 (September 22, 1996, vs. Atlanta); and touchdown receptions—1 (December 21, 1997, vs. Washington).

Year Team	G	GS	RECEIVING				TOTALS			
			No.	Yds.	Avg.	TD	TD	2pt.	Pts.	Fum.
1996—Philadelphia NFL	16	12	15	332	22.1	2	2	0	12	0
1997—Philadelphia NFL	15	4	7	93	13.3	2	2	0	12	0
1998—Philadelphia NFL	10	10	18	132	7.3	0	0	0	0	1
2000—Kansas City NFL	14	2	2	26	13.0	0	0	0	0	0
Pro totals (4 years)	55	28	42	583	13.9	4	4	0	24	1

D

DUNN, WARRICK — RB — BUCCANEERS

PERSONAL: Born January 5, 1975, in Baton Rouge, La. ... 5-8/180. ... Full name: Warrick De'Mon Dunn.
HIGH SCHOOL: Catholic (Baton Rouge, La.).
COLLEGE: Florida State (degree in information studies, 1997).
TRANSACTIONS/CAREER NOTES: Selected by Tampa Bay Buccaneers in first round (12th pick overall) of 1997 NFL draft. ... Signed by Buccaneers (July 24, 1997).
CHAMPIONSHIP GAME EXPERIENCE: Played in NFC championship game (1999 season).
HONORS: Named NFL Rookie of the Year by THE SPORTING NEWS (1997). ... Played in Pro Bowl (1997 and 2000 seasons).
PRO STATISTICS: 1997—Returned five punts for 48 yards and recovered four fumbles. 1998—Recovered one fumble. 1999—Recovered one fumble.
SINGLE GAME HIGHS (regular season): Attempts—28 (December 10, 2000, vs. Miami); yards—210 (December 3, 2000, vs. Dallas); and rushing touchdowns—3 (December 18, 2000, vs. St. Louis).
STATISTICAL PLATEAUS: 100-yard rushing games: 1997 (5), 1998 (2), 2000 (3). Total: 10. ... 100-yard receiving games: 1997 (1), 1999 (1). Total: 2.

Year Team	G	GS	RUSHING				RECEIVING				KICKOFF RETURNS				TOTALS			
			Att.	Yds.	Avg.	TD	No.	Yds.	Avg.	TD	No.	Yds.	Avg.	TD	TD	2pt.	Pts.	Fum.
1997—Tampa Bay NFL..........	16	10	224	978	4.4	4	39	462	11.8	3	6	129	21.5	0	7	0	42	4
1998—Tampa Bay NFL..........	16	14	245	1026	4.2	2	44	344	7.8	0	1	25	25.0	0	2	0	12	1
1999—Tampa Bay NFL..........	15	15	195	616	3.2	0	64	589	9.2	2	8	156	19.5	0	2	0	12	3
2000—Tampa Bay NFL..........	16	14	248	1133	4.6	8	44	422	9.6	1	0	0	0.0	0	9	0	54	1
Pro totals (4 years)	63	53	912	3753	4.1	14	191	1817	9.5	6	15	310	20.7	0	20	0	120	9

DWIGHT, TIM — WR/KR — CHARGERS

PERSONAL: Born July 13, 1975, in Iowa City, Iowa. ... 5-9/180.
HIGH SCHOOL: Iowa City (Iowa) High.
COLLEGE: Iowa.
TRANSACTIONS/CAREER NOTES: Selected by Atlanta Falcons in fourth round (114th pick overall) of 1998 NFL draft. ... Signed by Falcons (June 25, 1998). ... Granted free agency (March 2, 2001). ... Re-signed by Falcons (April 20, 2001). ... Traded by Falcons with first-(RB LaDainian Tomlinson) and third-round (DB Tay Cody) picks in 2001 draft and second-round pick in 2002 draft to San Diego Chargers for first-round pick (QB Michael Vick) in 2001 draft (April 20, 2001).
CHAMPIONSHIP GAME EXPERIENCE: Played in NFC championship game (1998 season). ... Played in Super Bowl XXXIII (1998 season).
HONORS: Named kick returner on THE SPORTING NEWS college All-America second team (1996). ... Named kick returner on THE SPORTING NEWS college All-America first team (1997).
POST SEASON RECORDS: Holds Super Bowl career record for highest kickoff return average (minimum four returns)—42.0. ... Shares Super Bowl single-game record for most touchdowns by kickoff return—1 (January 31, 1999, vs. Denver).
PRO STATISTICS: 1998—Attempted two passes with one completion for 22 yards and fumbled three times. 1999—Fumbled twice. 2000—Fumbled three times and recovered one fumble.
SINGLE GAME HIGHS (regular season): Receptions—7 (January 3, 2000, vs. San Francisco); yards—162 (January 3, 2000, vs. San Francisco); and touchdown receptions—2 (January 3, 2000, vs. San Francisco).
STATISTICAL PLATEAUS: 100-yard receiving games: 1999 (2).

Year	Team	G	GS	RUSHING Att.	Yds.	Avg.	TD	RECEIVING No.	Yds.	Avg.	TD	PUNT RETURNS No.	Yds.	Avg.	TD	KICKOFF RETURNS No.	Yds.	Avg.	TD	TOTALS TD	2pt.	Pts.
1998—Atlanta NFL		12	0	8	19	2.4	0	4	94	23.5	1	31	263	8.5	0	36	973	27.0	1	2	0	12
1999—Atlanta NFL		12	8	5	28	5.6	1	32	669	*20.9	7	20	220	11.0	∞1	44	944	21.5	0	9	0	54
2000—Atlanta NFL		14	1	5	8	1.6	0	26	406	15.6	3	33	309	9.4	1	32	680	21.3	0	4	0	24
Pro totals (3 years)		38	9	18	55	3.1	1	62	1169	18.9	11	84	792	9.4	2	112	2597	23.2	1	15	0	90

DYER, DEON   FB   DOLPHINS

PERSONAL: Born October 2, 1977, in Chesapeake, Va. ... 6-0/255. ... Full name: Deon Joseph Dyer.
HIGH SCHOOL: Deep Creek (Chesapeake, Va.).
COLLEGE: North Carolina.
TRANSACTIONS/CAREER NOTES: Selected by Miami Dolphins in fourth round (117th pick overall) of 2000 NFL draft. ... Signed by Dolphins (June 2, 2000).

Year	Team	G	GS	RUSHING Att.	Yds.	Avg.	TD	RECEIVING No.	Yds.	Avg.	TD	TOTALS TD	2pt.	Pts.	Fum.
2000—Miami NFL		16	1	0	0	0.0	0	2	14	7.0	0	0	0	0	0

DYSON, KEVIN   WR   TITANS

PERSONAL: Born June 23, 1975, in Logan, Utah ... 6-1/201.
HIGH SCHOOL: Clearfield (Utah).
COLLEGE: Utah.
TRANSACTIONS/CAREER NOTES: Selected by Tennessee Oilers in first round (16th pick overall) of 1998 NFL draft. ... Signed by Oilers (July 24, 1998). ... Oilers franchise renamed Tennessee Titans for 1999 season (December 26, 1998). ... On injured reserve with knee injury (September 29, 2000-remainder of season).
CHAMPIONSHIP GAME EXPERIENCE: Played in AFC championship game (1999 season). ... Played in Super Bowl XXXIV (1999 season).
PRO STATISTICS: 1998—Rushed once for four yards. 1999—Rushed once for three yards.
SINGLE GAME HIGHS (regular season): Receptions—9 (September 12, 1999, vs. Cincinnati); yards—162 (September 12, 1999, vs. Cincinnati); and touchdown receptions—2 (September 12, 1999, vs. Cincinnati).
STATISTICAL PLATEAUS: 100-yard receiving games: 1999 (1), 2000 (1). Total: 2.

Year	Team	G	GS	RECEIVING No.	Yds.	Avg.	TD	TOTALS TD	2pt.	Pts.	Fum.
1998—Tennessee NFL		13	9	21	263	12.5	2	2	0	12	0
1999—Tennessee NFL		16	16	54	658	12.2	4	4	0	24	0
2000—Tennessee NFL		2	2	6	104	17.3	1	1	0	6	0
Pro totals (3 years)		31	27	81	1025	12.7	7	7	0	42	0

EATON, CHAD   DT   SEAHAWKS

PERSONAL: Born April 6, 1972, in Exeter, N.H. ... 6-5/300. ... Full name: Chad Everett Eaton.
HIGH SCHOOL: Rogers (Puyallup, Wash.).
COLLEGE: Washington State.
TRANSACTIONS/CAREER NOTES: Selected by Arizona Cardinals in seventh round (241st pick overall) of 1995 NFL draft. ... Signed by Cardinals (July 24, 1995). ... Released by Cardinals (August 14, 1995). ... Signed by New York Jets (August 15, 1995). ... Released by Jets (August 27, 1995). ... Signed by Cleveland Browns to practice squad (September 28, 1995). ... Activated (December 15, 1995); did not play. ... Browns franchise moved to Baltimore and renamed Ravens for 1996 season (March 11, 1996). ... Released by Ravens (August 19, 1996). ... Signed by New England Patriots to practice squad (August 27, 1996). ... Activated (November 28, 1996). ... Granted unconditional free agency (March 2, 2001). ... Signed by Seattle Seahawks (March 9, 2001).
CHAMPIONSHIP GAME EXPERIENCE: Played in AFC championship game (1996 season). ... Played in Super Bowl XXXI (1996 season).
HONORS: Named defensive lineman on THE SPORTING NEWS college All-America second team (1994).
PRO STATISTICS: 1998—Returned one kickoff for 13 yards and recovered one fumble for two yards. 1999—Recovered three fumbles for 53 yards and one touchdown.

Year	Team	G	GS	SACKS
1995—Cleveland NFL		Did not play.		
1996—New England NFL		4	0	1.0
1997—New England NFL		16	1	1.0
1998—New England NFL		15	14	6.0
1999—New England NFL		16	16	3.0
2000—New England NFL		13	12	2.5
Pro totals (5 years)		64	43	13.5

EDINGER, PAUL   K   BEARS

PERSONAL: Born January 17, 1978, in Frankfort, Mich. ... 5-10/162.
HIGH SCHOOL: Kathleen (Lakeland, Fla.).
COLLEGE: Michigan State.
TRANSACTIONS/CAREER NOTES: Selected by Chicago Bears in sixth round (174th pick overall) of 2000 NFL draft. ... Signed by Bears (June 8, 2000).

Year	Team	G	KICKING XPM	XPA	FGM	FGA	Lg.	50+	Pts.
2000—Chicago NFL		16	21	21	21	27	54	2-2	84

EDWARDS, ANTUAN   CB/SS   PACKERS

PERSONAL: Born May 26, 1977, in Starkville, Miss. ... 6-1/205. ... Full name: Antuan Minye' Edwards. ... Name pronounced AN-twan.
HIGH SCHOOL: Starkville (Miss.).
COLLEGE: Clemson.
TRANSACTIONS/CAREER NOTES: Selected by Green Bay Packers in first round (25th pick overall) of 1999 NFL draft. ... Signed by Packers (June 7, 1999).

| | | | INTERCEPTIONS | | | | PUNT RETURNS | | | | TOTALS | |
Year Team	G	GS	No.	Yds.	Avg.	TD	No.	Yds.	Avg.	TD	TD	2pt.	Pts.	Fum.
1999—Green Bay NFL	16	1	4	26	6.5	1	10	90	9.0	0	1	0	6	1
2000—Green Bay NFL	12	3	2	4	2.0	0	0	0	0.0	0	0	0	0	0
Pro totals (2 years)	28	4	6	30	5.0	1	10	90	9.0	0	1	0	6	1

EDWARDS, DONNIE   LB   CHIEFS

PERSONAL: Born April 6, 1973, in San Diego ... 6-2/227. ... Full name: Donnie Lewis Edwards Jr.
HIGH SCHOOL: Chula Vista (San Diego).
COLLEGE: UCLA (degree in political science).
TRANSACTIONS/CAREER NOTES: Selected by Kansas City Chiefs in fourth round (98th pick overall) of 1996 NFL draft. ... Signed by Chiefs (July 24, 1996).
PRO STATISTICS: 1997—Recovered one fumble. 1998—Recovered one fumble. 1999—Recovered two fumbles for 79 yards and one touchdown. 2000—Recovered one fumble for 11 yards.

| | | | INTERCEPTIONS | | | | SACKS |
Year Team	G	GS	No.	Yds.	Avg.	TD	No.
1996—Kansas City NFL	15	1	1	22	22.0	0	0.0
1997—Kansas City NFL	16	16	2	15	7.5	0	2.5
1998—Kansas City NFL	15	15	0	0	0.0	0	6.0
1999—Kansas City NFL	16	16	5	50	10.0	1	3.0
2000—Kansas City NFL	16	16	2	45	22.5	1	1.0
Pro totals (5 years)	78	64	10	132	13.2	2	12.5

EDWARDS, MARC   FB   PATRIOTS

PERSONAL: Born November 17, 1974, in Cincinnati. ... 6-0/240. ... Full name: Marc Alexander Edwards.
HIGH SCHOOL: Norwood (Cincinnati).
COLLEGE: Notre Dame (degree in business management, 1996).
TRANSACTIONS/CAREER NOTES: Selected by San Francisco 49ers in second round (55th pick overall) of 1997 NFL draft. ... Signed by 49ers (July 23, 1997). ... On physically unable to perform list with back injury (July 17-August 10, 1998). ... Traded by 49ers to Cleveland Browns for fourth-round pick (DB Pierson Prioleau) in 1999 draft (April 18, 1999). ... Granted unconditional free agency (March 2, 2001). ... Signed by New England Patriots (March 19, 2001).
CHAMPIONSHIP GAME EXPERIENCE: Played in NFC championship game (1997 season).
PRO STATISTICS: 1997—Returned one kickoff for 30 yards. 2000—Returned one kickoff for 24 yards and recovered one fumble.
SINGLE GAME HIGHS (regular season): Attempts—3 (December 27, 1998, vs. St. Louis); yards—41 (September 27, 1998, vs. Atlanta); and rushing touchdowns—1 (September 27, 1998, vs. Atlanta).

| | | | RUSHING | | | | RECEIVING | | | | TOTALS | |
Year Team	G	GS	Att.	Yds.	Avg.	TD	No.	Yds.	Avg.	TD	TD	2pt.	Pts.	Fum.
1997—San Francisco NFL	15	1	5	17	3.4	0	6	48	8.0	0	0	0	0	0
1998—San Francisco NFL	16	11	22	94	4.3	1	22	218	9.9	2	3	0	18	0
1999—Cleveland NFL	16	14	6	35	5.8	0	27	212	7.9	2	2	0	12	1
2000—Cleveland NFL	16	8	2	9	4.5	0	16	128	8.0	2	2	0	12	2
Pro totals (4 years)	63	34	35	155	4.4	1	71	606	8.5	6	7	0	42	3

EDWARDS, MARIO   CB   COWBOYS

PERSONAL: Born December 1, 1975, in Gautier, Miss. ... 6-0/191.
HIGH SCHOOL: Pascagoula (Miss.).
COLLEGE: Florida State.
TRANSACTIONS/CAREER NOTES: Selected by Dallas Cowboys in sixth round (180th pick overall) of 2000 NFL draft. ... Signed by Cowboys (July 14, 2000).
PLAYING EXPERIENCE: Dallas NFL, 2000. ... Games/Games started: 2000 (11/1).

EDWARDS, ROBERT   RB   PATRIOTS

PERSONAL: Born October 2, 1974, in Tennille, Ga. ... 5-11/220. ... Full name: Robert Lee Edwards III.
HIGH SCHOOL: Washington County (Sandersville, Ga.).
COLLEGE: Georgia.
TRANSACTIONS/CAREER NOTES: Selected by New England Patriots in first round (18th pick overall) of 1998 NFL draft. ... Signed by Patriots (July 17, 1998). ... On non-football injury list with knee injury (August 31, 1999-entire season). ... On non-football injury list with knee injury (August 22, 2000-entire season).
PRO STATISTICS: 1998—Recovered two fumbles.
SINGLE GAME HIGHS (regular season): Attempts—28 (December 6, 1998, vs. Pittsburgh); yards—196 (December 13, 1998, vs. St. Louis); and rushing touchdowns—1 (December 20, 1998, vs. San Francisco).
STATISTICAL PLATEAUS: 100-yard rushing games: 1998 (4).

E

				RUSHING				RECEIVING				TOTALS		
Year	Team	G	GS	Att.	Yds.	Avg.	TD	No.	Yds.	Avg.	TD	TD	2pt.	Pts.	Fum.
1998—New England NFL		16	15	291	1115	3.8	9	35	331	9.5	3	12	0	72	5
1999—New England NFL								Did not play.							
2000—New England NFL								Did not play.							
Pro totals (1 years)		16	15	291	1115	3.8	9	35	331	9.5	3	12	0	72	5

EDWARDS, TROY WR STEELERS

PERSONAL: Born April 7, 1977, in Shreveport, La. ... 5-9/192.
HIGH SCHOOL: Huntington (Shreveport, La.).
COLLEGE: Louisiana Tech.
TRANSACTIONS/CAREER NOTES: Selected by Pittsburgh Steelers in first round (13th pick overall) of 1999 NFL draft. ... Signed by Steelers (July 28, 1999).
HONORS: Fred Biletnikoff Award winner (1998). ... Named wide receiver on THE SPORTING NEWS college All-America second team (1998).
PRO STATISTICS: 1999—Recovered three fumbles.
SINGLE GAME HIGHS (regular season): Receptions—7 (November 28, 1999, vs. Cincinnati); yards—86 (November 28, 1999, vs. Cincinnati); and touchdown receptions—1 (December 18, 1999, vs. Kansas City).

				RECEIVING				PUNT RETURNS				KICKOFF RETURNS				TOTALS		
Year	Team	G	GS	No.	Yds.	Avg.	TD	No.	Yds.	Avg.	TD	No.	Yds.	Avg.	TD	TD	2pt.	Pts.	Fum.
1999—Pittsburgh NFL		16	6	61	714	11.7	5	25	234	9.4	0	13	234	18.0	0	5	0	30	4
2000—Pittsburgh NFL		14	1	18	215	11.9	0	0	0	0.0	0	15	298	19.9	0	0	0	0	1
Pro totals (2 years)		30	7	79	929	11.8	5	25	234	9.4	0	28	532	19.0	0	5	0	30	5

EITZMANN, CHRIS TE PATRIOTS

PERSONAL: Born April 1, 1977, in Belleville, Kan. ... 6-5/255. ... Full name: Chris John Eitzmann.
HIGH SCHOOL: Chester-Hubbell-Byron (Neb.).
COLLEGE: Harvard (degree in psychology).
TRANSACTIONS/CAREER NOTES: Signed as non-drafted free agent by New England Patriots (April 19, 2000). ... Claimed on waivers by Green Bay Packers (August 28, 2000). ... Released by Packers (September 4, 2000). ... Signed by Patriots to practice squad (September 6, 2000). ... Activated (October 21, 2000). ... On injured reserve with rib injury (December 1, 2000-remainder of season).
PLAYING EXPERIENCE: New England NFL, 2000. ... Games/Games started: 2000 (5/1).

EKUBAN, EBENEZER DE COWBOYS

PERSONAL: Born May 29, 1976, in Ghana, Africa. ... 6-3/265. ... Full name: Ebenezer Ekuban Jr. ... Name pronounced ECK-you-bon.
HIGH SCHOOL: Bladensburg (Md.).
COLLEGE: North Carolina.
TRANSACTIONS/CAREER NOTES: Selected by Dallas Cowboys in first round (20th pick overall) of 1999 NFL draft. ... Signed by Cowboys (July 27, 1999).
PRO STATISTICS: 2000—Recovered one fumble.

Year	Team	G	GS	SACKS
1999—Dallas NFL		16	2	2.5
2000—Dallas NFL		12	2	6.5
Pro totals (2 years)		28	4	9.0

ELAM, JASON K BRONCOS

PERSONAL: Born March 8, 1970, in Fort Walton Beach, Fla. ... 5-11/200. ... Name pronounced EE-lum.
HIGH SCHOOL: Brookwood (Snellville, Ga.).
COLLEGE: Hawaii.
TRANSACTIONS/CAREER NOTES: Selected by Denver Broncos in third round (70th pick overall) of 1993 NFL draft. ... Signed by Broncos (July 12, 1993).
CHAMPIONSHIP GAME EXPERIENCE: Played in AFC championship game (1997 and 1998 seasons). ... Member of Super Bowl championship team (1997 and 1998 seasons).
HONORS: Named kicker on THE SPORTING NEWS college All-America second team (1989 and 1991). ... Played in Pro Bowl (1995 and 1998 seasons).
RECORDS: Holds NFL career record for most consecutive PATs made—313 (1993-current). ... Holds NFL career record for highest PAT percentage—99.65. ... Shares NFL career record for longest field goal—63 (October 25, 1998, vs. Jacksonville).
PRO STATISTICS: 1995—Punted once for 17 yards.

					KICKING				
Year	Team	G	XPM	XPA	FGM	FGA	Lg.	50+	Pts.
1993—Denver NFL		16	§41	§42	26	35	54	4-6	119
1994—Denver NFL		16	29	29	30	37	†54	1-3	119
1995—Denver NFL		16	39	39	31	38	§56	5-7	132
1996—Denver NFL		16	§46	§46	21	28	51	1-3	109
1997—Denver NFL		15	§46	§46	26	36	53	3-5	124
1998—Denver NFL		16	§58	§58	23	27	*63	3-4	§127
1999—Denver NFL		16	29	29	29	36	*55	5-8	116
2000—Denver NFL		13	*49	*49	18	24	51	1-1	103
Pro totals (8 years)		124	337	338	204	261	63	23-37	949

ELLIOTT, JUMBO   OT   JETS

PERSONAL: Born April 1, 1965, in Lake Ronkonkoma, N.Y. ... 6-7/308. ... Full name: John Elliott.
HIGH SCHOOL: Sachem (Lake Ronkonkoma, N.Y.).
COLLEGE: Michigan.
TRANSACTIONS/CAREER NOTES: Selected by New York Giants in second round (36th pick overall) of 1988 NFL draft. ... Signed by Giants (July 18, 1988). ... Granted free agency (February 1, 1991). ... Re-signed by Giants (August 22, 1991). ... Designated by Giants as franchise player (February 25, 1993). ... On injured reserve with back injury (January 7, 1994-remainder of playoffs). ... Granted unconditional free agency (February 16, 1996). ... Signed by New York Jets (February 24, 1996). ... On injured reserve with ankle injury (December 1, 1997-remainder of season). ... Announced retirement (March 6, 2000). ... Re-signed by Jets (August 14, 2000). ... On suspended list (August 29-September 4, 2000).
PLAYING EXPERIENCE: New York Giants NFL, 1988-1995; New York Jets NFL, 1996-2000. ... Games/Games started: 1988 (16/5), 1989 (13/11), 1990 (8/8), 1991 (16/16), 1992 (16/16), 1993 (11/11), 1994 (16/15), 1995 (16/16), 1996 (14/14), 1997 (13/13), 1998 (16/16), 1999 (16/15), 2000 (10/0). Total: 181/156.
CHAMPIONSHIP GAME EXPERIENCE: Played in NFC championship game (1990 season). ... Member of Super Bowl championship team (1990 season). ... Played in AFC championship game (1998 season).
HONORS: Played in Pro Bowl (1993 season).
PRO STATISTICS: 1988—Recovered one fumble. 2000—Caught one pass for three yards and one touchdown.

ELLIS, ED   OT   CHARGERS

PERSONAL: Born October 13, 1975, in Hamden, Conn. ... 6-7/325. ... Full name: Edward Key Ellis.
HIGH SCHOOL: Hamden (Conn.).
COLLEGE: Buffalo.
TRANSACTIONS/CAREER NOTES: Selected by New England Patriots in fourth round (125th pick overall) of 1997 NFL draft. ... Signed by Patriots (June 19, 1997). ... Granted free agency (February 11, 2000). ... Assigned by Patriots to Barcelona Dragons in 2000 NFL Europe enhancement allocation program (February 18, 2000). ... Re-signed by Patriots (March 13, 2000). ... Released by Patriots (July 17, 2000). ... Signed by Washington Redskins (July 20, 2000). ... Granted unconditional free agency (March 2, 2001). ... Signed by San Diego Chargers (March 29, 2001).
PLAYING EXPERIENCE: New England NFL, 1997-1999; Washington NFL, 2000. ... Games/Games started: 1997 (1/0), 1998 (7/0), 1999 (1/1), 2000 (12/0). Total: 21/1.

ELLIS, GREG   DE   COWBOYS

PERSONAL: Born August 14, 1975, in Wendell. N.C. ... 6-6/286. ... Full name: Gregory Lemont Ellis.
HIGH SCHOOL: East Wake (Wendell, N.C.).
COLLEGE: North Carolina.
TRANSACTIONS/CAREER NOTES: Selected by Dallas Cowboys in first round (eighth pick overall) of 1998 NFL draft. ... Signed by Cowboys (July 13, 1998). ... On injured reserve with leg injury (December 16, 1999-remainder of season).
HONORS: Named defensive end on The Sporting News college All-America second team (1996 and 1997).
PRO STATISTICS: 1998—Recovered one fumble for two yards. 1999—Intercepted one pass for 87 yards and a touchdown and recovered one fumble for 98 yards and a touchdown. 2000—Recovered two fumbles.

Year Team	G	GS	SACKS
1998—Dallas NFL	16	16	3.0
1999—Dallas NFL	13	13	7.5
2000—Dallas NFL	16	16	3.0
Pro totals (3 years)	45	45	13.5

ELLIS, SHAUN   DE   JETS

PERSONAL: Born June 24, 1977, in Anderson, S.C. ... 6-5/280. ... Full name: MeShaunda Pizarrur Ellis.
HIGH SCHOOL: Westside (Anderson, S.C.).
COLLEGE: Tennessee.
TRANSACTIONS/CAREER NOTES: Selected by New York Jets in first round (12th pick overall) of 2000 NFL draft. ... Signed by Jets (July 10, 2000).
PRO STATISTICS: 2000—Intercepted one pass for one yard and recovered two fumbles for two yards.

Year Team	G	GS	SACKS
2000—New York Jets NFL	16	3	8.5

ELLISS, LUTHER   DT   LIONS

PERSONAL: Born March 22, 1973, in Mancos, Colo. ... 6-5/305.
HIGH SCHOOL: Mancos (Colo.).
COLLEGE: Utah.
TRANSACTIONS/CAREER NOTES: Selected by Detroit Lions in first round (20th pick overall) of 1995 NFL draft. ... Signed by Lions (July 19, 1995).
HONORS: Named defensive lineman on The Sporting News college All-America first team (1994). ... Played in Pro Bowl (1999 and 2000 seasons).
PRO STATISTICS: 1997—Recovered two fumbles. 1998—Recovered one fumble. 1999—Recovered two fumbles for 11 yards and one touchdown. 2000—Recovered two fumbles for three yards.

Year Team	G	GS	SACKS
1995—Detroit NFL	16	16	0.0
1996—Detroit NFL	14	14	6.5
1997—Detroit NFL	16	16	8.5
1998—Detroit NFL	16	16	3.0
1999—Detroit NFL	15	14	3.5
2000—Detroit NFL	16	16	3.0
Pro totals (6 years)	93	92	24.5

ELLSWORTH, PERCY   DB   BROWNS

PERSONAL: Born October 19, 1974, in Drewryville, Va. ... 6-2/225.
HIGH SCHOOL: Southhampton (Courtland, Va.).
COLLEGE: Virginia.
TRANSACTIONS/CAREER NOTES: Signed as non-drafted free agent by New York Giants (April 27, 1996). ... Granted free agency (February 12, 1999). ... Re-signed by Giants (July 19, 1999). ... Granted unconditional free agency (February 11, 2000). ... Signed by Cleveland Browns (February 18, 2000).
PRO STATISTICS: 1996—Recovered one fumble. 1997—Recovered two fumbles for 24 yards. 1999—Recovered one fumble for 15 yards. 2000—Recovered one fumble for 16 yards.

			INTERCEPTIONS			
Year Team	G	GS	No.	Yds.	Avg.	TD
1996—New York Giants NFL	14	4	3	62	20.7	0
1997—New York Giants NFL	16	1	4	40	10.0	0
1998—New York Giants NFL	16	9	5	92	18.4	2
1999—New York Giants NFL	14	14	6	80	13.3	0
2000—Cleveland NFL	16	16	1	33	33.0	1
Pro totals (5 years)	76	44	19	307	16.2	3

EMANUEL, BERT   WR   PATRIOTS

PERSONAL: Born October 26, 1970, in Kansas City, Mo. ... 5-10/185. ... Full name: Bert Tyrone Emanuel.
HIGH SCHOOL: Langham Creek (Houston).
COLLEGE: UCLA, then Rice (degree in business, 1993).
TRANSACTIONS/CAREER NOTES: Selected by Atlanta Falcons in second round (45th pick overall) of 1994 NFL draft. ... Signed by Falcons (July 11, 1994). ... Granted free agency (February 14, 1997). ... Re-signed by Falcons (July 16, 1997). ... Designated by Falcons as transition player (February 13, 1998). ... Tendered offer sheet by Tampa Bay Buccaneers (April 10, 1998). ... Falcons declined to match offer (April 14, 1998). ... Released by Buccaneers (April 12, 2000). ... Signed by Miami Dolphins (May 2, 2000). ... On injured reserve with broken rib (December 20, 2000-remainder of season). ... Granted unconditional free agency (March 2, 2001). ... Signed by New England Patriots (March 30, 2001).
CHAMPIONSHIP GAME EXPERIENCE: Played in NFC championship game (1999 season).
PRO STATISTICS: 1994—Rushed twice for four yards and had only pass attempt intercepted. 1995—Rushed once for no yards. 1997—Recovered two fumbles. 1998—Rushed once for 11 yards. 2000—Rushed three times for minus two yards.
SINGLE GAME HIGHS (regular season): Receptions—9 (December 15, 1996, vs. St. Louis); yards—173 (December 15, 1996, vs. St. Louis); and touchdown receptions—2 (November 2, 1997, vs. St. Louis).
STATISTICAL PLATEAUS: 100-yard receiving games: 1994 (1), 1995 (4), 1996 (3), 1997 (1), 1998 (1). Total: 10.
MISCELLANEOUS: Selected by Toronto Blue Jays organization in 75th round of free-agent baseball draft (June 5, 1989); did not sign. ... Selected by Pittsburgh Pirates organization in 49th round of free-agent baseball draft (June 1, 1992); did not sign.

			RECEIVING				TOTALS			
Year Team	G	GS	No.	Yds.	Avg.	TD	TD	2pt.	Pts.	Fum.
1994—Atlanta NFL	16	16	46	649	14.1	4	4	0	24	0
1995—Atlanta NFL	16	16	74	1039	14.0	5	5	0	30	2
1996—Atlanta NFL	14	13	75	921	12.3	6	6	0	36	0
1997—Atlanta NFL	16	16	65	991	15.2	9	9	0	54	2
1998—Tampa Bay NFL	11	11	41	636	15.5	2	2	0	12	0
1999—Tampa Bay NFL	11	10	22	238	10.8	1	1	0	6	0
2000—Miami NFL	11	0	7	132	18.9	1	1	0	6	1
Pro totals (7 years)	95	82	330	4606	14.0	28	28	0	168	5

EMBRAY, KEITH   DE   TITANS

PERSONAL: Born November 29, 1974, in San Diego. ... 6-4/265.
HIGH SCHOOL: Mount Miguel (San Diego).
COLLEGE: Utah.
TRANSACTIONS/CAREER NOTES: Signed as non-drafted free agent by Tennessee Titans (July 14, 2000).
PLAYING EXPERIENCE: Tennessee NFL, 2000. ... Games/Games started: 2000 (14/0).
PRO STATISTICS: 2000—Credited with 3 1/2 sacks.

EMMONS, CARLOS   LB   EAGLES

PERSONAL: Born September 3, 1973, in Greenwood, Miss. ... 6-5/250. ... Name pronounced EM-mins.
HIGH SCHOOL: Greenwood (Miss.).
COLLEGE: Arkansas State (degree in business management, 1995).
TRANSACTIONS/CAREER NOTES: Selected by Pittsburgh Steelers in seventh round (242nd pick overall) of 1996 NFL draft. ... Signed by Steelers (July 16, 1996). ... Granted free agency (February 12, 1999). ... Re-signed by Steelers (April 23, 1999). ... Granted unconditional free agency (February 11, 2000). ... Signed by Philadelphia Eagles (March 23, 2000).
CHAMPIONSHIP GAME EXPERIENCE: Played in AFC championship game (1997 season).
PRO STATISTICS: 1996—Recovered one fumble. 1998—Intercepted one pass for two yards and recovered one fumble. 1999—Intercepted one pass for 22 yards and recovered three fumbles for two yards. 2000—Intercepted two passes for eight yards and recovered one fumble for two yards.

E

Year	Team	G	GS	SACKS
1996—Pittsburgh NFL		15	0	2.5
1997—Pittsburgh NFL		5	0	0.0
1998—Pittsburgh NFL		15	13	3.5
1999—Pittsburgh NFL		16	16	6.0
2000—Philadelphia NFL		16	13	0.5
Pro totals (5 years)		67	42	12.5

ENGELBERGER, JOHN — DE — 49ERS

PERSONAL: Born October 18, 1976, in Heidelburg, Germany. ... 6-4/260. ... Full name: John Albert Engelberger.

HIGH SCHOOL: Robert E. Lee (Springfield, Va.).

COLLEGE: Virginia Tech.

TRANSACTIONS/CAREER NOTES: Selected by San Francisco 49ers in second round (35th pick overall) of 2000 NFL draft. ... Signed by 49ers (July 18, 2000).

Year	Team	G	GS	SACKS
2000—San Francisco NFL		16	13	3.0

ENGLER, DEREK — C

PERSONAL: Born July 11, 1974, in St. Paul, Minn. ... 6-5/300.

HIGH SCHOOL: Cretin-Derham Hall (St. Paul, Minn.).

COLLEGE: Wisconsin.

TRANSACTIONS/CAREER NOTES: Signed as non-drafted free agent by New York Giants (April 28, 1997). ... Granted free agency (February 11, 2000). ... Re-signed by Giants (April 4, 2000). ... Granted unconditional free agency (March 2, 2001).

PLAYING EXPERIENCE: New York Giants NFL, 1997-2000. ... Games/Games started: 1997 (5/5), 1998 (11/0), 1999 (10/4), 2000 (9/0). Total: 35/9.

CHAMPIONSHIP GAME EXPERIENCE: Played in NFC championship game (2000 season). ... Played in Super Bowl XXXV (2000 season).

PRO STATISTICS: 1997—Fumbled once for minus two yards.

ENGRAM, BOBBY — WR — BEARS

PERSONAL: Born January 7, 1973, in Camden, S.C. ... 5-10/185. ... Full name: Simon Engram III.

HIGH SCHOOL: Camden (S.C.).

COLLEGE: Penn State.

TRANSACTIONS/CAREER NOTES: Selected by Chicago Bears in second round (52nd pick overall) of 1996 NFL draft. ... Signed by Bears (July 17, 1996). ... Granted free agency (February 12, 1999). ... Re-signed by Bears (April 16, 1999). ... Granted unconditional free agency (February 11, 2000). ... Re-signed by Bears (April 26, 2000). ... On injured reserve with knee injury (September 19, 2000-remainder of season).

HONORS: Named wide receiver on THE SPORTING NEWS college All-America second team (1994 and 1995).

PRO STATISTICS: 1997—Recovered one fumble. 1998—Rushed once for three yards. 1999—Rushed twice for 11 yards and recovered two fumbles. 2000—Rushed once for one yard and recovered one fumble.

SINGLE GAME HIGHS (regular season): Receptions—13 (December 26, 1999, vs. St. Louis); yards—143 (December 26, 1999, vs. St. Louis); and touchdown receptions—2 (December 26, 1999, vs. St. Louis).

STATISTICAL PLATEAUS: 100-yard receiving games: 1998 (3), 1999 (2). Total: 5.

				RECEIVING				PUNT RETURNS				KICKOFF RETURNS				TOTALS			
Year	Team	G	GS	No.	Yds.	Avg.	TD	No.	Yds.	Avg.	TD	No.	Yds.	Avg.	TD	TD	2pt.	Pts.	Fum.
1996—Chicago NFL		16	2	33	389	11.8	6	31	282	9.1	0	25	580	23.2	0	6	0	36	2
1997—Chicago NFL		11	11	45	399	8.9	2	1	4	4.0	0	2	27	13.5	0	2	1	14	1
1998—Chicago NFL		16	16	64	987	15.4	5	0	0	0.0	0	0	0	0.0	0	5	0	30	1
1999—Chicago NFL		16	14	88	947	10.8	4	0	0	0.0	0	0	0	0.0	0	4	0	24	2
2000—Chicago NFL		3	3	16	109	6.8	0	0	0	0.0	0	0	0	0.0	0	0	0	0	1
Pro totals (5 years)		62	46	246	2831	11.5	17	32	286	8.9	0	27	607	22.5	0	17	1	104	7

ENIS, CURTIS — RB

PERSONAL: Born June 15, 1976, in Union City, Ohio. ... 6-0/240. ... Full name: Curtis D. Enis.

HIGH SCHOOL: Mississinawa Valley (Union City, Ohio), then Kiski Prep (Saltsburg, Pa.).

COLLEGE: Penn State.

TRANSACTIONS/CAREER NOTES: Selected after junior season by Chicago Bears in first round (fifth pick overall) of 1998 NFL draft. ... Signed by Bears (August 18, 1998). ... On injured reserve with knee injury (November 11, 1998-remainder of season). ... On injured reserve with shoulder and elbow injuries (December 31, 1999-remainder of season). ... Released by Bears (February 27, 2001). ... Signed by Cleveland Browns (March 13, 2001). ... Announced retirement (April 25, 2001).

HONORS: Named running back on THE SPORTING NEWS college All-America second team (1997).

PRO STATISTICS: 1999—Recovered two fumbles. 2000—Returned two kickoffs for 30 yards.

SINGLE GAME HIGHS (regular season): Attempts—27 (October 10, 1999, vs. Minnesota); yards—94 (September 19, 1999, vs. Seattle); and rushing touchdowns—1 (November 5, 2000, vs. Indianapolis).

				RUSHING				RECEIVING				TOTALS			
Year	Team	G	GS	Att.	Yds.	Avg.	TD	No.	Yds.	Avg.	TD	TD	2pt.	Pts.	Fum.
1998—Chicago NFL		9	1	133	497	3.7	0	6	20	3.3	0	0	0	0	1
1999—Chicago NFL		15	12	287	916	3.2	3	45	340	7.6	2	5	0	30	4
2000—Chicago NFL		12	5	36	84	2.3	1	8	68	8.5	0	1	0	6	0
Pro totals (3 years)		36	18	456	1497	3.3	4	59	428	7.3	2	6	0	36	5

EVANS, CHUCK — FB

PERSONAL: Born April 16, 1967, in Augusta, Ga. ... 6-1/245. ... Full name: Charles Evans Jr.
HIGH SCHOOL: Glenn Hills (Augusta, Ga.).
COLLEGE: Clark Atlanta University.
TRANSACTIONS/CAREER NOTES: Selected by Minnesota Vikings in 11th round (295th pick overall) of 1992 NFL draft. ... Signed by Vikings (June 10, 1992). ... Released by Vikings (August 31, 1992). ... Re-signed by Vikings (February 10, 1993). ... On injured reserve with wrist injury (October 11, 1993-remainder of season). ... Granted free agency (February 16, 1996). ... Re-signed by Vikings (May 9, 1996). ... Granted unconditional free agency (February 14, 1997). ... Re-signed by Vikings (April 11, 1997). ... Granted unconditional free agency (February 12, 1999). ... Signed by Baltimore Ravens (February 17, 1999). ... Released by Ravens (August 22, 2000). ... Re-signed by Ravens (November 28, 2000). ... Granted unconditional free agency (March 2, 2001).
CHAMPIONSHIP GAME EXPERIENCE: Played in NFC championship game (1998 season). ... Played in AFC championship game (2000 season). ... Member of Super Bowl championship team (2000 season).
PRO STATISTICS: 1993—Returned one kickoff for 11 yards. 1994—Returned one kickoff for four yards. 1997—Recovered one fumble. 1999—Recovered one fumble.
SINGLE GAME HIGHS (regular season): Attempts—10 (December 9, 1995, vs. Cleveland); yards—50 (November 9, 1997, vs. Chicago); and rushing touchdowns—1 (December 20, 1998, vs. Jacksonville).

			RUSHING				RECEIVING				TOTALS			
Year Team	G	GS	Att.	Yds.	Avg.	TD	No.	Yds.	Avg.	TD	TD	2pt.	Pts.	Fum.
1993—Minnesota NFL	3	0	14	32	2.3	0	4	39	9.8	0	0	0	0	0
1994—Minnesota NFL	14	0	6	20	3.3	0	1	2	2.0	0	0	0	0	0
1995—Minnesota NFL	16	7	19	59	3.1	1	18	119	6.6	1	2	0	12	0
1996—Minnesota NFL	16	6	13	29	2.2	0	22	135	6.1	0	0	0	0	0
1997—Minnesota NFL	16	13	43	157	3.7	2	21	152	7.2	0	2	1	14	0
1998—Minnesota NFL	16	8	23	67	2.9	1	12	84	7.0	0	1	0	6	0
1999—Baltimore NFL	16	10	38	134	3.5	0	32	235	7.3	1	1	†1	8	0
2000—Baltimore NFL	1	0	0	0	0.0	0	0	0	0.0	0	0	0	0	0
Pro totals (8 years)	98	44	156	498	3.2	4	110	766	7.0	2	6	2	40	0

EVANS, DOUG — CB — PANTHERS

PERSONAL: Born May 13, 1970, in Shreveport, La. ... 6-1/190. ... Full name: Douglas Edwards Evans. ... Brother of Bobby Evans, safety with Winnipeg Blue Bombers of the CFL (1990-94).
HIGH SCHOOL: Haynesville (La.).
COLLEGE: Louisiana Tech (degree in finance).
TRANSACTIONS/CAREER NOTES: Selected by Green Bay Packers in sixth round (141st pick overall) of 1993 NFL draft. ... Signed by Packers (July 9, 1993). ... Granted unconditional free agency (February 13, 1998). ... Signed by Carolina Panthers (February 18, 1998). ... On injured reserve with broken collarbone (November 10, 1998-remainder of season).
CHAMPIONSHIP GAME EXPERIENCE: Played in NFC championship game (1995-1997 seasons). ... Member of Super Bowl championship team (1996 season). ... Played in Super Bowl XXXII (1997 season).
PRO STATISTICS: 1993—Recovered two fumbles. 1994—Recovered one fumble for three yards. 1995—Returned one punt for no yards and fumbled once. 1996—Fumbled once and recovered one fumble for two yards. 2000—Recovered five fumbles for minus three yards and one touchdown.

			INTERCEPTIONS				SACKS
Year Team	G	GS	No.	Yds.	Avg.	TD	No.
1993—Green Bay NFL	16	0	1	0	0.0	0	0.0
1994—Green Bay NFL	16	15	1	0	0.0	0	1.0
1995—Green Bay NFL	16	16	2	24	12.0	0	1.0
1996—Green Bay NFL	16	16	5	102	20.4	1	3.0
1997—Green Bay NFL	15	15	3	33	11.0	0	1.0
1998—Carolina NFL	9	7	2	18	9.0	0	0.0
1999—Carolina NFL	16	16	2	1	0.5	0	0.0
2000—Carolina NFL	16	16	2	17	8.5	0	0.0
Pro totals (8 years)	120	101	18	195	10.8	1	6.0

EVANS, JOSH — DT/DE — TITANS

PERSONAL: Born September 6, 1972, in Langdale, Ala. ... 6-2/288. ... Full name: Mijoshki Antwon Evans.
HIGH SCHOOL: Lanett (Ala.).
COLLEGE: Alabama-Birmingham.
TRANSACTIONS/CAREER NOTES: Signed as non-drafted free agent by Dallas Cowboys (April 27, 1995). ... Released by Cowboys (August 22, 1995). ... Signed by Houston Oilers to practice squad (September 1, 1995). ... Activated (November 10, 1995). ... On injured reserve with knee injury (November 29, 1996-remainder of season). ... Oilers franchise moved to Tennessee for 1997 season. ... Granted free agency (February 13, 1998). ... Re-signed by Oilers (July 25, 1998). ... Oilers franchise renamed Tennessee Titans for 1999 season (December 26, 1998). ... On suspended list for violating league substance abuse policy (September 6-October 4, 1999). ... On suspended list for violating league substance abuse policy (March 1, 2000-April 13, 2001).
CHAMPIONSHIP GAME EXPERIENCE: Played in AFC championship game (1999 season). ... Played in Super Bowl XXXIV (1999 season).
PRO STATISTICS: 1997—Recovered one fumble. 1999—Recovered two fumbles.

Year Team	G	GS	SACKS
1995—Houston NFL	7	0	0.0
1996—Houston NFL	8	0	0.0
1997—Tennessee NFL	15	0	2.0
1998—Tennessee NFL	14	11	3.5
1999—Tennessee NFL	11	10	3.5
2000—Tennessee NFL		Did not play.	
Pro totals (5 years)	55	21	9.0

E

EVERITT, STEVE   C

PERSONAL: Born August 21, 1970, in Miami. ... 6-5/310. ... Full name: Steven Michael Everitt.
HIGH SCHOOL: Southridge (Miami).
COLLEGE: Michigan (degree in fine arts, 1993).
TRANSACTIONS/CAREER NOTES: Selected by Cleveland Browns in first round (14th pick overall) of 1993 NFL draft. ... Signed by Browns (July 15, 1993). ... Designated by Browns as transition player (February 15, 1994). ... Browns franchise moved to Baltimore and renamed Ravens for 1996 season (March 11, 1996). ... Free agency status changed by Ravens from transitional to unconditional (February 14, 1997). ... Signed by Philadelphia Eagles (March 6, 1997). ... Released by Eagles (April 25, 2000). ... Signed by St. Louis Rams (June 13, 2000). ... Released by Rams (February 21, 2001).
PLAYING EXPERIENCE: Cleveland NFL, 1993-1995; Baltimore NFL, 1996; Philadelphia NFL, 1997-1999; St. Louis NFL, 2000. ... Games/Games started: 1993 (16/16), 1994 (15/15), 1995 (15/14), 1996 (8/7), 1997 (16/16), 1998 (13/13), 1999 (16/16), 2000 (4/1). Total: 103/98.
HONORS: Named center on THE SPORTING NEWS college All-America second team (1992).
PRO STATISTICS: 1993—Recovered two fumbles. 1995—Recovered one fumble. 1997—Recovered one fumble. 1999—Recovered one fumble.

FABINI, JASON   OT   JETS

PERSONAL: Born August 25, 1974, in Fort Wayne, Ind. ... 6-7/312.
HIGH SCHOOL: Bishop Dwenger (Fort Wayne, Ind.).
COLLEGE: Cincinnati.
TRANSACTIONS/CAREER NOTES: Selected by New York Jets in fourth round (111th pick overall) of 1998 NFL draft. ... Signed by Jets (July 13, 1998). ... On injured reserve with knee injury (November 16, 1999-remainder of season). ... Granted free agency (March 2, 2001). ... Re-signed by Jets (May 30, 2001).
PLAYING EXPERIENCE: New York Jets NFL, 1998-2000. ... Games/Games started: 1998 (16/16), 1999 (9/9), 2000 (16/16). Total: 41/41.
CHAMPIONSHIP GAME EXPERIENCE: Played in AFC championship game (1998 season).

FAIR, TERRY   CB   LIONS

PERSONAL: Born July 20, 1976, in Phoenix. ... 5-9/184. ... Full name: Terrance Delon Fair.
HIGH SCHOOL: South Mountain (Phoenix).
COLLEGE: Tennessee.
TRANSACTIONS/CAREER NOTES: Selected by Detroit Lions in first round (20th pick overall) of 1998 NFL draft. ... Signed by Lions (July 20, 1998). ... On non-football injury list with hand injury (December 14, 1999-remainder of season).
HONORS: Named kick returner on THE SPORTING NEWS NFL All-Pro team (1998).
PRO STATISTICS: 1998—Credited with one sack and recovered one fumble. 1999—Recovered one fumble for 35 yards and a touchdown. 2000—Recovered one fumble for two yards.

			INTERCEPTIONS			PUNT RETURNS			KICKOFF RETURNS				TOTALS		
Year Team	G	GS	No.	Yds.	Avg.	TD	No.	Yds.	Avg.	TD	No.	Yds.	Avg.	TD	TD 2pt. Pts. Fum.
1998—Detroit NFL	14	10	0	0	0.0	0	30	189	6.3	0	51	1428	*28.0	†2	2 0 12 5
1999—Detroit NFL	11	11	3	49	16.3	0	11	97	8.8	0	34	752	22.1	0	2 0 12 2
2000—Detroit NFL	15	15	2	0	0.0	0	2	15	7.5	0	6	149	24.8	0	0 0 0 1
Pro totals (3 years)	40	36	5	49	9.8	1	43	301	7.0	0	91	2329	25.6	2	4 0 24 8

FANECA, ALAN   G   STEELERS

PERSONAL: Born December 7, 1976, in New Orleans. ... 6-4/315. ... Full name: Alan Joseph Faneca Jr.
HIGH SCHOOL: John Curtis Christian (New Orleans), then Lamar (Houston).
COLLEGE: Louisiana State.
TRANSACTIONS/CAREER NOTES: Selected after junior season by Pittsburgh Steelers in first round (26th pick overall) of 1998 NFL draft. ... Signed by Steelers (July 29, 1998).
PLAYING EXPERIENCE: Pittsburgh NFL, 1998-2000. ... Games/Games started: 1998 (16/12), 1999 (15/14), 2000 (16/16). Total: 47/42.
HONORS: Named guard on THE SPORTING NEWS college All-America first team (1997).
PRO STATISTICS: 2000—Recovered one fumble.

FARMER, DANNY   WR   BENGALS

PERSONAL: Born May 21, 1977, in Los Angeles. ... 6-3/217. ... Full name: Daniel Steven Farmer. ... Son of George Farmer, wide receiver with Chicago Bears (1970-75) and Detroit Lions (1975); nephew of Dave Farmer, running back with Tampa Bay Buccaneers (1978).
HIGH SCHOOL: Loyola (Los Angeles).
COLLEGE: UCLA.
TRANSACTIONS/CAREER NOTES: Selected by Pittsburgh Steelers in fourth round (103rd pick overall) of 2000 NFL draft. ... Signed by Steelers (July 7, 2000). ... Claimed on waivers by Cincinnati Bengals (August 28, 2000).
PRO STATISTICS: 2000—Fumbled once.
SINGLE GAME HIGHS (regular season): Receptions—5 (December 24, 2000, vs. Philadelphia); yards—102 (December 17, 2000, vs. Jacksonville); and touchdown receptions—0.
STATISTICAL PLATEAUS: 100-yard receiving games: 2000 (1).

			RECEIVING			
Year Team	G	GS	No.	Yds.	Avg.	TD
2000—Cincinnati NFL	13	2	19	268	14.1	0

FARR, D'MARCO — DT

PERSONAL: Born June 9, 1971, in San Pablo, Calif. ... 6-1/280. ... Full name: D'Marco Marcellus Farr. ... Cousin of Mel Farr Sr., running back with Detroit Lions (1967-73); cousin of Mel Farr Jr., running back with Los Angeles Rams (1989) and Sacramento Surge of World League (1991); and cousin of Mike Farr, wide receiver with Detroit Lions (1990-92).

HIGH SCHOOL: John F. Kennedy (Richmond, Calif.).

COLLEGE: Washington (degree in society and justice, 1993).

TRANSACTIONS/CAREER NOTES: Signed as non-drafted free agent by Los Angeles Rams (May 4, 1994). ... On injured reserve with dislocated left elbow (December 7, 1994-remainder of season). ... Rams franchise moved to St. Louis (April 12, 1995). ... Released by Rams (February 21, 2001).

CHAMPIONSHIP GAME EXPERIENCE: Played in NFC championship game (1999 season). ... Member of Super Bowl championship team (1999 season).

PRO STATISTICS: 1994—Returned one kickoff for 16 yards. 1995—Intercepted one pass for five yards. 1996—Intercepted one pass for five yards. 1997—Intercepted one pass for 22 yards and recovered two fumbles. 1998—Recovered one fumble for 18 yards.

Year Team	G	GS	SACKS
1994—Los Angeles Rams NFL	10	3	1.0
1995—St. Louis NFL	16	16	11.5
1996—St. Louis NFL	16	16	4.5
1997—St. Louis NFL	16	16	3.0
1998—St. Louis NFL	16	16	7.0
1999—St. Louis NFL	16	16	8.5
2000—St. Louis NFL	10	5	1.0
Pro totals (7 years)	**100**	**88**	**36.5**

FARRIOR, JAMES — LB — JETS

PERSONAL: Born January 6, 1975, in Ettrick, Va. ... 6-2/244. ... Full name: James Alfred Farrior.

HIGH SCHOOL: Matoaca (Ettrick, Va.).

COLLEGE: Virginia.

TRANSACTIONS/CAREER NOTES: Selected by New York Jets in first round (eighth pick overall) of 1997 NFL draft. ... Signed by Jets (July 20, 1997).

CHAMPIONSHIP GAME EXPERIENCE: Played in AFC championship game (1998 season).

PRO STATISTICS: 1998—Recovered one fumble. 2000—Intercepted one pass for no yards and recovered one fumble.

Year Team	G	GS	SACKS
1997—New York Jets NFL	16	15	1.5
1998—New York Jets NFL	12	2	0.0
1999—New York Jets NFL	16	4	2.0
2000—New York Jets NFL	16	6	1.0
Pro totals (4 years)	**60**	**27**	**4.5**

FAULK, KEVIN — RB/KR — PATRIOTS

PERSONAL: Born June 15, 1976, in Lafayette, La. ... 5-8/200. ... Full name: Kevin Tony Faulk.

HIGH SCHOOL: Carencro (Lafayette, La.).

COLLEGE: Louisiana State (degree in kinesiology).

TRANSACTIONS/CAREER NOTES: Selected by New England Patriots in second round (46th pick overall) of 1999 NFL draft. ... Signed by Patriots (July 28, 1999). ... On injured reserve with broken ankle (December 15, 1999-remainder of season).

HONORS: Named kick returner on The Sporting News college All-America second team (1998).

PRO STATISTICS: 1999—Fumbled three times for minus nine yards. 2000—Fumbled six times and recovered one fumble.

SINGLE GAME HIGHS (regular season): Attempts—22 (December 4, 2000, vs. Kansas City); yards—82 (September 11, 2000, vs. New York Jets); and rushing touchdowns—1 (December 17, 2000, vs. Buffalo).

			RUSHING				RECEIVING				PUNT RETURNS				KICKOFF RETURNS				TOTALS		
Year Team	G	GS	Att.	Yds.	Avg.	TD	No.	Yds.	Avg.	TD	No.	Yds.	Avg.	TD	No.	Yds.	Avg.	TD	TD	2pt.	Pts.
1999—New England NFL	11	2	67	227	3.4	1	12	98	8.2	1	10	90	9.0	0	39	943	24.2	0	2	0	12
2000—New England NFL	16	9	164	570	3.5	4	51	465	9.1	1	6	58	9.7	0	38	816	21.5	0	5	▲1	32
Pro totals (2 years)	**27**	**11**	**231**	**797**	**3.5**	**5**	**63**	**563**	**8.9**	**2**	**16**	**148**	**9.3**	**0**	**77**	**1759**	**22.8**	**0**	**7**	**1**	**44**

FAULK, MARSHALL — RB — RAMS

PERSONAL: Born February 26, 1973, in New Orleans. ... 5-10/211. ... Full name: Marshall William Faulk.

HIGH SCHOOL: G. W. Carver (New Orleans).

COLLEGE: San Diego State.

TRANSACTIONS/CAREER NOTES: Selected after junior season by Indianapolis Colts in first round (second pick overall) of 1994 NFL draft. ... Signed by Colts (July 24, 1994). ... Traded by Colts to St. Louis Rams for second- (LB Mike Peterson) and fifth-round (DE Brad Scioli) picks in 1999 draft (April 15, 1999).

CHAMPIONSHIP GAME EXPERIENCE: Member of Colts for AFC championship game (1995 season); inactive due to injury. ... Played in NFC championship game (1999 season). ... Member of Super Bowl championship team (1999 season).

HONORS: Named running back on The Sporting News college All-America first team (1991-1993). ... Named NFL Rookie of the Year by The Sporting News (1994). ... Played in Pro Bowl (1994, 1995, 1998 and 1999 seasons). ... Named Outstanding Player of Pro Bowl (1994 season). ... Named running back on The Sporting News NFL All-Pro team (1999 and 2000). ... Named NFL Player of the Year by The Sporting News (2000). ... Named to play in Pro Bowl (2000 season); replaced by Stephen Davis due to injury.

RECORDS: Holds NFL single-season record for most touchdowns—26 (2000).

PRO STATISTICS: 1994—Recovered one fumble. 1995—Recovered one fumble. 1997—Recovered one fumble. 1998—Recovered two fumbles for 13 yards. 1999—Attempted one pass without a completion. 2000—Returned one kickoff for 18 yards and recovered two fumbles.

SINGLE GAME HIGHS (regular season): Attempts—32 (December 24, 2000, vs. New Orleans); yards—200 (December 24, 2000, vs. New Orleans); and rushing touchdowns—4 (December 10, 2000, vs. Minnesota).
STATISTICAL PLATEAUS: 100-yard rushing games: 1994 (4), 1995 (1), 1996 (1), 1997 (4), 1998 (4), 1999 (7), 2000 (4). Total: 25. ... 100-yard receiving games: 1994 (1), 1998 (3), 1999 (1), 2000 (2). Total: 7.

				RUSHING				RECEIVING				TOTALS		
Year Team	G	GS	Att.	Yds.	Avg.	TD	No.	Yds.	Avg.	TD	TD	2pt.	Pts.	Fum.
1994—Indianapolis NFL	16	16	314	1282	4.1	11	52	522	10.0	1	▲12	0	72	5
1995—Indianapolis NFL	16	16	289	1078	3.7	11	56	475	8.5	3	14	0	84	8
1996—Indianapolis NFL	13	13	198	587	3.0	7	56	428	7.6	0	7	0	42	2
1997—Indianapolis NFL	16	16	264	1054	4.0	7	47	471	10.0	1	8	0	48	5
1998—Indianapolis NFL	16	15	324	1319	4.1	6	86	908	10.6	4	10	0	60	3
1999—St. Louis NFL	16	16	253	1381	*5.5	7	87	1048	12.0	5	12	†1	74	2
2000—St. Louis NFL	14	14	253	1359	*5.4	*18	81	830	10.2	8	*26	2	*160	0
Pro totals (7 years)	107	106	1895	8060	4.3	67	465	4682	10.1	22	89	3	540	25

FAURIA, CHRISTIAN   TE   SEAHAWKS

PERSONAL: Born September 22, 1971, in Harbor City, Calif. ... 6-4/245. ... Name pronounced FOUR-ee-ah.
HIGH SCHOOL: Crespi Carmelite (Encino, Calif.).
COLLEGE: Colorado (degree in communications, 1995).
TRANSACTIONS/CAREER NOTES: Selected by Seattle Seahawks in second round (39th pick overall) of 1995 NFL draft. ... Signed by Seahawks (July 17, 1995). ... Granted free agency (February 13, 1998). ... Re-signed by Seahawks (April 20, 1998). ... Granted unconditional free agency (February 12, 1999). ... Re-signed by Seahawks (March 5, 1999).
PRO STATISTICS: 1996—Returned one kickoff for eight yards. 1998—Returned one kickoff for no yards and recovered one fumble. 1999—Returned two kickoffs for 15 yards. 2000—Returned one kickoff for nine yards and recovered one fumble.
SINGLE GAME HIGHS (regular season): Receptions—6 (December 26, 1999, vs. Kansas City); yards—84 (December 26, 1999, vs. Kansas City); and touchdown receptions—1 (November 5, 2000, vs. San Diego).

			RECEIVING				TOTALS		
Year Team	G	GS	No.	Yds.	Avg.	TD	TD	2pt.	Pts.	Fum.
1995—Seattle NFL	14	9	17	181	10.6	1	1	0	6	0
1996—Seattle NFL	10	9	18	214	11.9	1	1	0	6	0
1997—Seattle NFL	16	3	10	110	11.0	0	0	0	0	0
1998—Seattle NFL	16	15	37	377	10.2	2	2	0	12	1
1999—Seattle NFL	16	16	35	376	10.7	0	0	0	0	1
2000—Seattle NFL	15	10	28	237	8.5	2	2	0	12	1
Pro totals (6 years)	87	62	145	1495	10.3	6	6	0	36	3

FAVORS, GREG   LB   TITANS

PERSONAL: Born September 30, 1974, in Atlanta. ... 6-1/244. ... Full name: Gregory Bernard Favors.
HIGH SCHOOL: Southside (Atlanta).
COLLEGE: Mississippi State (degree in correction, 1997).
TRANSACTIONS/CAREER NOTES: Selected by Kansas City Chiefs in fourth round (120th pick overall) of 1998 NFL draft. ... Signed by Chiefs (July 17, 1998). ... Claimed on waivers by Tennessee Titans (September 8, 1999). ... Granted free agency (March 2, 2001).
CHAMPIONSHIP GAME EXPERIENCE: Played in AFC championship game (1999 season). ... Played in Super Bowl XXXIV (1999 season).
PRO STATISTICS: 1998—Recovered one fumble for 41 yards. 1999—Recovered one fumble.

Year Team	G	GS	SACKS
1998—Kansas City NFL	16	4	2.0
1999—Tennessee NFL	15	0	0.0
2000—Tennessee NFL	16	15	5.5
Pro totals (3 years)	47	19	7.5

FAVRE, BRETT   QB   PACKERS

PERSONAL: Born October 10, 1969, in Gulfport, Miss. ... 6-2/225. ... Full name: Brett Lorenzo Favre. ... Name pronounced FARVE.
HIGH SCHOOL: Hancock North Central (Kiln, Miss.).
COLLEGE: Southern Mississippi.
TRANSACTIONS/CAREER NOTES: Selected by Atlanta Falcons in second round (33rd pick overall) of 1991 NFL draft. ... Signed by Falcons (July 18, 1991). ... Traded by Falcons to Green Bay Packers for first-round pick (OT Bob Whitfield) in 1992 draft (February 11, 1992). ... Granted free agency (February 17, 1994). ... Re-signed by Packers (July 14, 1994).
CHAMPIONSHIP GAME EXPERIENCE: Played in NFC championship game (1995-1997 seasons). ... Member of Super Bowl championship team (1996 season). ... Played in Super Bowl XXXII (1997 season).
HONORS: Played in Pro Bowl (1992, 1993, 1995 and 1996 seasons). ... Named NFL Player of the Year by THE SPORTING NEWS (1995 and 1996). ... Named quarterback on THE SPORTING NEWS NFL All-Pro team (1995-97). ... Named to play in Pro Bowl (1997 season); replaced by Chris Chandler due to injury.
RECORDS: Shares NFL record for longest pass completion (to Robert Brooks)—99 yards, touchdown (September 11, 1995, at Chicago).
POST SEASON RECORDS: Holds Super Bowl record for longest pass completion (to Antonio Freeman)—81 yards (January 26, 1997, vs. New England).
PRO STATISTICS: 1992—Caught one pass for minus seven yards, fumbled 12 times and recovered three fumbles for minus 12 yards. 1993—Fumbled 12 times and recovered two fumbles for minus one yard. 1994—Fumbled seven times and recovered one fumble for minus two yards. 1995—Fumbled eight times. 1996—Fumbled 11 times and recovered five fumbles for minus 10 yards. 1997—Fumbled seven times and recovered one fumble for minus 10 yards. 1998—Fumbled eight times and recovered three fumbles for minus nine times and recovered one fumble for minus two yards. 2000—Fumbled nine times and recovered two fumbles for minus 12 yards.
SINGLE GAME HIGHS (regular season): Attempts—61 (October 14, 1996, vs. San Francisco); completions—36 (December 5, 1993, vs. Chicago); yards—402 (December 5, 1993, vs. Chicago); and touchdown passes—5 (September 27, 1998, vs. Carolina).
STATISTICAL PLATEAUS: 300-yard passing games: 1993 (1), 1994 (4), 1995 (7), 1996 (2), 1997 (2), 1998 (4), 1999 (6), 2000 (2). Total: 28.

MISCELLANEOUS: Regular-season record as starting NFL quarterback: 91-50 (.645). ... Postseason record as starting NFL quarterback: 9-5 (.643). ... Active NFL leader in touchdown passes (255). ... Holds Green Bay Packers all-time records for most yards passing (34,706) and most touchdown passes (255).

				PASSING								RUSHING				TOTALS		
Year Team	G	GS	Att.	Cmp.	Pct.	Yds.	TD	Int.	Avg.	Rat.	Att.	Yds.	Avg.	TD	TD	2pt.	Pts.
1991—Atlanta NFL	2	0	5	0	0.0	0	0	2	0.0	0.0	0	0	0.0	0	0	0	0
1992—Green Bay NFL	15	13	471	∞302	64.1	3227	18	13	6.85	85.3	47	198	4.2	1	1	0	6
1993—Green Bay NFL	16	16	‡522	‡318	60.9	3303	19	*24	6.33	72.2	58	216	3.7	1	1	0	6
1994—Green Bay NFL	16	16	582	363	62.4	3882	33	14	6.67	90.7	42	202	4.8	2	2	0	12
1995—Green Bay NFL	16	16	570	359	63.0	*4413	*38	13	‡7.74	‡99.5	39	181	4.6	3	3	0	18
1996—Green Bay NFL	16	16	‡543	‡325	59.9	‡3899	*39	13	7.18	95.8	49	136	2.8	2	2	0	12
1997—Green Bay NFL	16	16	513	‡304	59.3	‡3867	*35	16	7.54	92.6	58	187	3.2	1	1	0	6
1998—Green Bay NFL	16	16	‡551	*347	*63.0	*4212	31	‡23	7.64	87.8	40	133	3.3	1	1	0	6
1999—Green Bay NFL	16	16	*595	341	57.3	4091	22	23	6.88	74.7	28	142	5.1	0	0	0	0
2000—Green Bay NFL	16	16	‡580	338	58.3	3812	20	16	6.57	78.0	27	108	4.0	0	0	0	0
Pro totals (10 years)	145	141	4932	2997	60.8	34706	255	157	7.04	86.0	388	1503	3.9	11	11	0	66

FAZANDE, JERMAINE RB CHARGERS

PERSONAL: Born January 14, 1975, in Marrero, La. ... 6-2/255. ... Full name: Jermaine Keith Fazande. ... Name pronounced FUH-zand.
HIGH SCHOOL: John Ehret (Marrero, La.).
COLLEGE: Oklahoma.
TRANSACTIONS/CAREER NOTES: Selected by San Diego Chargers in second round (60th pick overall) of 1999 NFL draft. ... Signed by Chargers (July 23, 1999).
PRO STATISTICS: 2000—Recovered one fumble.
SINGLE GAME HIGHS (regular season): Attempts—30 (January 2, 2000, vs. Denver); yards—183 (January 2, 2000, vs. Denver); and rushing touchdowns—1 (October 15, 2000, vs. Denver).
STATISTICAL PLATEAUS: 100-yard rushing games: 1999 (1).

			RUSHING				RECEIVING				TOTALS			
Year Team	G	GS	Att.	Yds.	Avg.	TD	No.	Yds.	Avg.	TD	TD	2pt.	Pts.	Fum.
1999—San Diego NFL	7	3	91	365	4.0	2	0	0	0.0	0	2	0	12	2
2000—San Diego NFL	13	7	119	368	3.1	2	16	104	6.5	0	2	0	12	1
Pro totals (2 years)	20	10	210	733	3.5	4	16	104	6.5	0	4	0	24	3

FEAGLES, JEFF P SEAHAWKS

PERSONAL: Born March 7, 1966, in Anaheim ... 6-1/207. ... Full name: Jeffrey Allan Feagles.
HIGH SCHOOL: Gerard Catholic (Phoenix).
JUNIOR COLLEGE: Scottsdale (Ariz.) Community College.
COLLEGE: Miami, Fla (degree in business administration, 1988).
TRANSACTIONS/CAREER NOTES: Signed as non-drafted free agent by New England Patriots (May 1, 1988). ... Claimed on waivers by Philadelphia Eagles (June 5, 1990). ... Granted unconditional free agency (February 1-April 1, 1992). ... Re-signed by Eagles for 1992 season. ... Granted unconditional free agency (February 17, 1994). ... Signed by Phoenix Cardinals (March 2, 1994). ... Cardinals franchise renamed Arizona Cardinals for 1994 season. ... Granted unconditional free agency (February 13, 1998). ... Signed by Seattle Seahawks (March 4, 1998).
HONORS: Played in Pro Bowl (1995 season).
PRO STATISTICS: 1988—Rushed once for no yards and recovered one fumble. 1989—Attempted two passes without a completion, fumbled once and recovered one fumble. 1990—Rushed twice for three yards and attempted one pass without a completion. 1991—Rushed three times for minus one yard, fumbled once and recovered one fumble. 1993—Rushed twice for six yards and recovered one fumble. 1994—Rushed twice for eight yards. 1995—Rushed twice for four yards and fumbled once for minus 22 yards. 1996—Rushed once for no yards and fumbled once for minus seven yards. 1997—Fumbled once and recovered one fumble. 1999—Rushed twice for no yards. 2000—Attempted one pass without a completion.

				PUNTING			
Year Team	G	No.	Yds.	Avg.	Net avg.	In. 20	Blk.
1988—New England NFL	16	▲91	3482	38.3	34.1	24	0
1989—New England NFL	16	63	2392	38.0	31.3	13	1
1990—Philadelphia NFL	16	72	3026	42.0	35.5	20	2
1991—Philadelphia NFL	16	*87	3640	41.8	34.0	*29	1
1992—Philadelphia NFL	16	‡82	‡3459	42.2	36.8	25	0
1993—Philadelphia NFL	16	83	3323	40.0	35.2	*31	0
1994—Arizona NFL	16	*98	‡3997	40.8	36.0	‡33	0
1995—Arizona NFL	16	72	3150	43.8	‡38.2	20	0
1996—Arizona NFL	16	76	3328	43.8	36.3	23	1
1997—Arizona NFL	16	91	4028	44.3	36.8	24	1
1998—Seattle NFL	16	81	3568	44.0	36.5	27	0
1999—Seattle NFL	16	84	3425	40.8	35.2	34	0
2000—Seattle NFL	16	74	2960	40.0	36.9	24	▲1
Pro totals (13 years)	208	1054	43778	41.5	35.6	328	7

FERGUSON, JASON DT JETS

PERSONAL: Born November 28, 1974, in Nettleton, Miss. ... 6-3/305. ... Full name: Jason O. Ferguson. ... Cousin of Terance Mathis, wide receiver, Atlanta Falcons.
HIGH SCHOOL: Nettleton (Miss.).
JUNIOR COLLEGE: Itawamba Community College (Miss.).
COLLEGE: Georgia.
TRANSACTIONS/CAREER NOTES: Selected by New York Jets in seventh round (229th pick overall) of 1997 NFL draft. ... Signed by Jets (April 30, 1997). ... On suspended list for violating league substance abuse policy (November 24-December 22, 1999). ... Granted free agency (February 11, 2000). ... Re-signed by Jets (May 24, 2000). ... Granted unconditional free agency (March 2, 2001). ... Re-signed by Jets (March 11, 2001).

F

CHAMPIONSHIP GAME EXPERIENCE: Played in AFC championship game (1998 season).
PRO STATISTICS: 1997—Returned one kickoff for one yard.

Year Team	G	GS	SACKS
1997—New York Jets NFL	13	1	3.5
1998—New York Jets NFL	16	16	4.0
1999—New York Jets NFL	9	9	1.0
2000—New York Jets NFL	15	11	1.0
Pro totals (4 years)	53	37	9.5

FERGUSON, NICK   CB   JETS

PERSONAL: Born November 27, 1973, in Miami. ... 5-11/201.
HIGH SCHOOL: Jackson (Miami).
COLLEGE: Morris Brown College, then Georgia Tech.
TRANSACTIONS/CAREER NOTES: Signed as non-drafted free agent by Cincinnati Bengals (April 23, 1996). ... Released by Bengals (August 5, 1006). ... Signed by Saskatchewan Roughriders of CFL (September 27, 1996). ... Traded by Roughriders to Winnipeg Blue Bombers (May 9, 1997). ... Signed by Chicago Bears (February 12, 1999). ... Assigned by Bears to Rhein Fire in 1999 NFL Europe enhancement allocation program (February 22, 1999). ... Released by Bears (August 30, 1999). ... Re-signed by Blue Bombers (October 9, 1999). ... Released by Blue Bombers (October 27, 1999). ... Signed by Buffalo Bills (July 6, 2000). ... Released by Bills (August 27, 2000). ... Re-signed by Bills to practice squad (August 28, 2000). ... Signed by New York Jets off Bills practice squad (November 7, 2000).
PRO STATISTICS: 1997—Recovered one fumble. 1998—Recovered one fumble.

Year Team	G	GS	INTERCEPTIONS No.	Yds.	Avg.	TD
1996—Saskatchewan CFL	5	...	0	0	0.0	0
1997—Winnipeg CFL	15	...	2	35	17.5	0
1998—Winnipeg CFL	16	...	1	0	0.0	0
1999—Winnipeg CFL	3	...	0	0	0.0	0
—Rhein NFLE	...	...	0	0	0.0	0
2000—Rhein NFLE	...	...	2	0	0.0	0
—New York Jets NFL	7	0	1	20	20.0	0
NFL Europe totals (2 years)	...	...	2	0	0.0	0
CFL totals (4 years)	39	...	3	35	11.7	0
NFL totals (1 year)	7	0	1	20	20.0	0
Pro totals (7 years)	...	...	6	55	9.2	0

FIALA, JOHN   LB   STEELERS

PERSONAL: Born November 25, 1973, in Fullerton, Calif. ... 6-2/235. ... Full name: John Charles Fiala. ... Name pronounced FEE-ah-lah.
HIGH SCHOOL: Lake Washington (Kirkland, Wash.).
COLLEGE: Washington.
TRANSACTIONS/CAREER NOTES: Selected by Miami Dolphins in sixth round (166th pick overall) of 1997 NFL draft. ... Signed by Dolphins (June 17, 1997). ... Released by Dolphins (July 31, 1997). ... Signed by Pittsburgh Steelers to practice squad (August 26, 1997). ... Granted free agency (March 2, 2001).
PLAYING EXPERIENCE: Pittsburgh NFL, 1998-2000. ... Games/Games started: 1998 (16/0), 1999 (16/0), 2000 (16/0). Total: 48/0.

FIEDLER, JAY   QB   DOLPHINS

F

PERSONAL: Born December 29, 1971, in Oceanside, N.Y. ... 6-2/225. ... Full name: Jay Brian Fiedler.
HIGH SCHOOL: Oceanside (N.Y.).
COLLEGE: Dartmouth (degree in engineering sciences).
TRANSACTIONS/CAREER NOTES: Signed as non-drafted free agent by Philadelphia Eagles (April 29, 1994). ... Inactive for all 16 games (1994). ... Claimed on waivers by Cincinnati Bengals (July 31, 1996). ... Released by Bengals (August 25, 1996). ... Played for Amsterdam Admirals of World League (1997). ... Signed by Minnesota Vikings (April 3, 1998). ... Released by Vikings (August 30, 1998). ... Re-signed by Vikings (September 15, 1998). ... Granted free agency (February 12, 1999). ... Signed by Jacksonville Jaguars (April 16, 1999). ... Granted unconditional free agency (February 11, 2000). ... Signed by Miami Dolphins (February 17, 2000).
CHAMPIONSHIP GAME EXPERIENCE: Member of Vikings for NFC championship game (1998 season); inactive. ... Member of Jaguars for AFC championship game (1999 season); did not play.
PRO STATISTICS: 1999—Fumbled once. 2000—Fumbled twice for minus eight yards.
SINGLE GAME HIGHS (regular season): Attempts—45 (December 24, 2000, vs. New England); completions—30 (December 24, 2000, vs.New England); yards—317 (January 2, 2000, vs.Cincinnati); and touchdown passes—3 (December 3, 2000, vs. Cincinnati).
STATISTICAL PLATEAUS: 300-yard passing games: 1999 (1).
MISCELLANEOUS: Regular-season record as starting NFL quarterback: 11-5 (.688). ... Postseason record as starting NFL quarterback: 1-1 (.500).

Year Team	G	GS	PASSING Att.	Cmp.	Pct.	Yds.	TD	Int.	Avg.	Rat.	RUSHING Att.	Yds.	Avg.	TD	TOTALS TD	2pt.	Pts.
1994—Philadelphia NFL								Did not play.									
1995—Philadelphia NFL								Did not play.									
1996—								Did not play.									
1997—Amsterdam W.L.	...	...	109	46	42.2	678	2	8	6.22	38.7	16	93	5.8	0	0	0	0
1998—Minnesota NFL	5	0	7	3	42.9	41	0	1	5.86	22.6	4	-6	-1.5	0	0	0	0
1999—Jacksonville NFL	7	1	94	61	64.9	656	2	2	6.98	83.5	13	26	2.0	0	0	0	0
2000—Miami NFL	15	15	357	204	57.1	2402	14	14	6.73	74.5	54	267	4.9	1	1	0	6
W.L. totals (1 year)	...	...	109	46	42.2	678	2	8	6.22	38.7	16	93	5.8	0	0	0	0
NFL totals (3 years)	27	16	458	268	58.5	3099	16	17	6.77	75.2	71	287	4.0	1	1	0	6
Pro totals (4 years)	...	...	567	314	55.4	3777	18	25	6.66	68.2	87	380	4.4	1	1	0	6

FIELDS, AARON   DE   COWBOYS

PERSONAL: Born January 9, 1976, in Notasulga, Ala. ... 6-4/243.
HIGH SCHOOL: Notasulga (Ala.).
COLLEGE: Troy State.
TRANSACTIONS/CAREER NOTES: Signed as non-drafted free agent by Dallas Cowboys (April 19, 2000). ... Released by Cowboys (August 27, 2000). ... Signed by Atlanta Falcons to practice squad (August 30, 2000). ... Signed by Cowboys off Falcons practice squad (November 8, 2000).
PLAYING EXPERIENCE: Dallas NFL, 2000. ... Games/Games started: 2000 (3/0).

FIELDS, MARK   LB   RAMS

PERSONAL: Born November 9, 1972, in Los Angeles. ... 6-2/244. ... Full name: Mark Lee Fields.
HIGH SCHOOL: Washington (Cerritos, Calif.).
JUNIOR COLLEGE: Los Angeles Southwest Community College.
COLLEGE: Washington State.
TRANSACTIONS/CAREER NOTES: Selected by New Orleans Saints in first round (13th pick overall) of 1995 NFL draft. ... Signed by Saints (July 20, 1995). ... Released by Saints (March 30, 2001). ... Signed by St. Louis Rams (April 10, 2001).
HONORS: Played in Pro Bowl (2000 season).
PRO STATISTICS: 1996—Recovered one fumble for 20 yards. 1997—Recovered two fumbles for 28 yards and one touchdown. 1998—Recovered one fumble for 36 yards and a touchdown. 1999—Intercepted two passes for no yards and recovered one fumble.

Year Team	G	GS	SACKS
1995—New Orleans NFL	16	3	1.0
1996—New Orleans NFL	16	15	2.0
1997—New Orleans NFL	16	15	8.0
1998—New Orleans NFL	15	15	6.0
1999—New Orleans NFL	14	14	4.0
2000—New Orleans NFL	16	14	2.0
Pro totals (6 years)	93	76	23.0

FINA, JOHN   OT   BILLS

PERSONAL: Born March 11, 1969, in Rochester, Minn. ... 6-5/300. ... Full name: John Joseph Fina. ... Name pronounced FEE-nuh.
HIGH SCHOOL: Salpointe Catholic (Tucson, Ariz.).
COLLEGE: Arizona.
TRANSACTIONS/CAREER NOTES: Selected by Buffalo Bills in first round (27th pick overall) of 1992 NFL draft. ... Signed by Bills (July 21, 1992). ... Designated by Bills as franchise player (February 16, 1996).
PLAYING EXPERIENCE: Buffalo NFL, 1992-2000. ... Games/Games started: 1992 (16/0), 1993 (16/16), 1994 (12/12), 1995 (16/16), 1996 (15/15), 1997 (16/16), 1998 (14/14), 1999 (16/16), 2000 (14/14). Total: 135/119.
CHAMPIONSHIP GAME EXPERIENCE: Played in AFC championship game (1992 and 1993 seasons). ... Played in Super Bowl XXVII (1992 season) and Super Bowl XXVIII (1993 season).
PRO STATISTICS: 1992—Caught one pass for one yard and a touchdown. 1993—Rushed once for minus two yards. 1996—Recovered two fumbles for minus one yard. 1997—Recovered one fumble. 2000—Recovered one fumble.

FINN, JIM   RB   COLTS

PERSONAL: Born December 9, 1976, in Teaneck, N.J. ... 6-0/235.
HIGH SCHOOL: Bergen Catholic (Oradell, N.J.).
COLLEGE: Pennsylvania.
TRANSACTIONS/CAREER NOTES: Selected by Chicago Bears in seventh round (253rd pick overall) of 1999 NFL draft. ... Signed by Bears (June 3, 1999). ... Released by Bears (August 30, 1999). ... Re-signed by Bears to practice squad (September 21, 1999). ... Released by Bears (October 11, 1999). ... Signed by Indianapolis Colts (January 25, 2000).
PLAYING EXPERIENCE: Indianapolis NFL, 2000. ... Games/Games started: 2000 (16/1).
PRO STATISTICS: 2000—Rushed once for one yard, caught four passes for 13 yards and a touchdown and fumbled once.
SINGLE GAME HIGHS (regular season): Attempts—1 (November 12, 2000, vs. New York Jets); yards—1 (November 12, 2000, vs. New York Jets); and rushing touchdowns—0.

FINNERAN, BRIAN   WR   FALCONS

PERSONAL: Born January 31, 1976, in Mission Viejo, Calif. ... 6-5/210.
HIGH SCHOOL: Santa Margarita (Mission Viejo, Calif.).
COLLEGE: Villanova.
TRANSACTIONS/CAREER NOTES: Signed as non-drafted free agent by Seattle Seahawks (April 21, 1998). ... Released by Seahawks (August 24, 1998). ... Selected by Barcelona Dragons in 1999 NFL Europe draft (February 18, 1999). ... Signed by Philadelphia Eagles (July 6, 1999). ... Released by Eagles (October 12, 1999). ... Signed by Atlanta Falcons to practice squad (December 13, 1999).
HONORS: Won Walter Payton Award (1997).
PRO STATISTICS: NFLE: 1999—Returned one kickoff for no yards. 2000—Returned one kickoff for two yards.
SINGLE GAME HIGHS (regular season): Receptions—3 (September 17, 2000, vs. Carolina); yards—25 (October 15, 2000, vs. St. Louis); and touchdown receptions—0.

Year Team	G	GS	RECEIVING No.	Yds.	Avg.	TD	TOTALS TD	2pt.	Pts.	Fum.
1999—Barcelona NFLE	...	...	54	844	15.6	8	8	1	50	0
—Philadelphia NFL	3	0	2	21	10.5	0	0	0	0	0
2000—Atlanta NFL	12	0	7	60	8.6	0	0	0	0	0
NFL Europe totals (1 year)	...	...	54	844	15.6	8	8	1	50	0
NFL totals (2 years)	15	0	9	81	9.0	0	0	0	0	0
Pro totals (3 years)	...	...	63	925	14.7	8	8	1	50	0

F

FIORE, DAVE OT 49ERS

PERSONAL: Born August 10, 1974, in Hackensack, N.J. ... 6-4/290. ... Full name: David Fiore. ... Name pronounced fee-OR-ee.
HIGH SCHOOL: Waldwick (N.J.).
COLLEGE: Hofstra.
TRANSACTIONS/CAREER NOTES: Signed as non-drafted free agent by San Francisco 49ers (April 23, 1996). ... Claimed on waivers by New York Jets (October 14, 1996). ... Active for nine games (1996); did not play. ... Released by Jets (July 31, 1997). ... Signed by 49ers (August 1, 1997). ... On injured reserve with knee injury (August 19, 1997-entire season).
PLAYING EXPERIENCE: San Francisco NFL, 1998-2000. ... Games/Games started: 1998 (9/3), 1999 (16/16), 2000 (15/15). Total: 40/34.

FISCHER, MARK C REDSKINS

PERSONAL: Born July 29, 1974, in Cincinnati. ... 6-3/303. ... Full name: Mark Raymond Fischer. ... Name pronounced fish-er.
HIGH SCHOOL: LaSalle (Cincinnati).
COLLEGE: Purdue.
TRANSACTIONS/CAREER NOTES: Selected by Washington Redskins in fifth round (140th pick overall) of 1998 NFL draft. ... Signed by Redskins (May 26, 1998). ... Active for three games (1999); did not play. ... Granted free agency (March 2, 2001).
PLAYING EXPERIENCE: Washington NFL, 1998 and 2000. ... Games/Games started: 1998 (6/0), 2000 (16/16). Total: 22/16.
PRO STATISTICS: 2000—Fumbled once for minus 18 yards.

FISK, JASON DT TITANS

PERSONAL: Born September 4, 1972, in Davis, Calif. ... 6-3/295.
HIGH SCHOOL: Davis (Calif.).
COLLEGE: Stanford.
TRANSACTIONS/CAREER NOTES: Selected by Minnesota Vikings in seventh round (243rd pick overall) of 1995 NFL draft. ... Signed by Vikings (July 24, 1995). ... Granted unconditional free agency (February 12, 1999). ... Signed by Tennessee Titans (March 3, 1999).
CHAMPIONSHIP GAME EXPERIENCE: Played in NFC championship game (1998 season). ... Played in AFC championship game (1999 season). ... Played in Super Bowl XXXIV (1999 season).
PRO STATISTICS: 1996—Intercepted one pass for no yards and recovered one fumble. 1997—Intercepted one pass for one yard and recovered one fumble. 1998—Recovered one fumble. 1999—Intercepted one pass for 17 yards.

Year Team	G	GS	SACKS
1995—Minnesota NFL	8	0	0.0
1996—Minnesota NFL	16	6	1.0
1997—Minnesota NFL	16	10	3.0
1998—Minnesota NFL	16	0	1.5
1999—Tennessee NFL	16	16	4.0
2000—Tennessee NFL	15	15	2.0
Pro totals (6 years)	87	47	11.5

FLANAGAN, MIKE C PACKERS

PERSONAL: Born November 10, 1973, in Washington, D.C. ... 6-5/297. ... Full name: Michael Christopher Flanagan.
HIGH SCHOOL: Rio Americano (Sacramento).
COLLEGE: UCLA.
TRANSACTIONS/CAREER NOTES: Selected by Green Bay Packers in third round (90th pick overall) of 1996 NFL draft. ... Signed by Packers (July 17, 1996). ... On injured reserve with leg injury (August 19, 1996-entire season). ... On physically unable to perform list with ankle injury (August 19, 1997-entire season). ... Traded by Packers to Carolina Panthers for an undisclosed draft pick (August 31, 1998); trade later voided because Flanagan failed physical (September 1, 1998). ... Granted free agency (February 12, 1999). ... Re-signed by Packers (March 25, 1999).
PLAYING EXPERIENCE: Green Bay NFL, 1998-2000. ... Games/Games started: 1998 (2/0), 1999 (15/0), 2000 (16/2). Total: 33/2.

FLANIGAN, JIM DT PACKERS

PERSONAL: Born August 27, 1971, in Green Bay. ... 6-2/288. ... Full name: James Michael Flanigan. ... Son of Jim Flanigan, linebacker with Green Bay Packers (1967-70) and New Orleans Saints (1971).
HIGH SCHOOL: Southern Door (Brussels, Wis.).
COLLEGE: Notre Dame.
TRANSACTIONS/CAREER NOTES: Selected by Chicago Bears in third round (74th pick overall) of 1994 NFL draft. ... Signed by Bears (July 14, 1994). ... Granted free agency (February 14, 1997). ... Re-signed by Bears (June 1, 1997). ... Granted unconditional free agency (February 13, 1998). ... Re-signed by Bears (February 13, 1998). ... Released by Bears (April 26, 2001). ... Signed by Green Bay Packers (May 29, 2001).
PRO STATISTICS: 1994—Returned two kickoffs for 26 yards. 1995—Rushed once for no yards, caught two passes for six yards and two touchdowns and recovered one fumble. 1996—Caught one pass for one yard and a touchdown. 1997—Recovered three fumbles for three yards and credited with one two-point conversion. 1998—Recovered one fumble. 1999—Intercepted one pass for six yards and recovered one fumble. 2000—Recovered one fumble.

Year Team	G	GS	SACKS
1994—Chicago NFL	14	0	0.0
1995—Chicago NFL	16	12	11.0
1996—Chicago NFL	14	14	5.0
1997—Chicago NFL	16	16	6.0
1998—Chicago NFL	16	16	8.5
1999—Chicago NFL	16	16	6.0
2000—Chicago NFL	16	14	4.0
Pro totals (7 years)	108	88	40.5

F

FLEMISTER, ZERON   TE   REDSKINS

PERSONAL: Born September 8, 1976, in Sioux City, Iowa. ... 6-4/249.
HIGH SCHOOL: West (Iowa).
COLLEGE: Iowa.
TRANSACTIONS/CAREER NOTES: Signed as non-drafted free agent by Washington Redskins (April 18, 2000).
PLAYING EXPERIENCE: Washington NFL, 2000. ... Games/Games started: 2000 (5/0).
PRO STATISTICS: 2000—Caught one pass for eight yards.
SINGLE GAME HIGHS (regular season): Receptions—1 (September 3, 2000, vs. Carolina); yards—8 (September 3, 2000, vs. Carolina); and touchdown receptions—0.

FLETCHER, DERRICK   OT/G   REDSKINS

PERSONAL: Born September 9, 1975, in Houston. ... 6-6/348. ... Full name: Derrick W. Fletcher.
HIGH SCHOOL: Aldine (Houston).
COLLEGE: Baylor.
TRANSACTIONS/CAREER NOTES: Selected by New England Patriots in fifth round (154th pick overall) of 1999 NFL draft. ... Signed by Patriots (July 28, 1999). ... Active for one game (1999); did not play. ... Released by Patriots (September 19, 2000). ... Signed by Washington Redskins (October 3, 2000). ... Released by Redskins (November 9, 2000). ... Re-signed by Redskins to practice squad (November 13, 2000). ... Activated (November 14, 2000).
PLAYING EXPERIENCE: New England (2)-Washington (1) NFL, 2000. ... Games/Games started: 2000 (N.E.-2/2; Wash.-1/0; Total: 3/2).

FLETCHER, LONDON   LB   RAMS

PERSONAL: Born May 19, 1975, in Cleveland. ... 5-10/241. ... Full name: London Levi Fletcher.
HIGH SCHOOL: Villa Angela-St. Joseph (Cleveland).
COLLEGE: John Carroll (degree in sociology).
TRANSACTIONS/CAREER NOTES: Signed as non-drafted free agent by St. Louis Rams (April 28, 1998). ... Granted free agency (March 2, 2001).
PLAYING EXPERIENCE: St. Louis NFL, 1998-2000. ... Games/Games started: 1998 (16/1), 1999 (16/16), 2000 (16/15). Total: 48/32.
CHAMPIONSHIP GAME EXPERIENCE: Played in NFC championship game (1999 season). ... Member of Super Bowl championship team (1999 season).
PRO STATISTICS: 1998—Returned five kickoffs for 72 yards and fumbled once. 1999—Returned two kickoffs for 13 yards, credited with three sacks and credited with a safety. 2000—Intercepted four passes for 33 yards, credited with 5 1/2 sacks, returned one kickoff for 17 yards and credited with a two-point conversion.

FLETCHER, TERRELL   RB   CHARGERS

PERSONAL: Born September 14, 1973, in St. Louis. ... 5-8/196. ... Full name: Terrell Antoine Fletcher.
HIGH SCHOOL: Hazelwood East (St. Louis).
COLLEGE: Wisconsin (degree in English, 1994).
TRANSACTIONS/CAREER NOTES: Selected by San Diego Chargers in second round (51st pick overall) of 1995 NFL draft. ... Signed by Chargers (July 12, 1995). ... On injured reserve with knee injury (December 17, 1997-remainder of season). ... Granted free agency (February 13, 1998). ... Re-signed by Chargers (June 1998).
PRO STATISTICS: 1995—Returned three punts for 12 yards and recovered two fumbles. 1996—Recovered one fumble. 1998—Completed only pass attempt for 23 yards and a touchdown and recovered two fumbles for 21 yards. 1999—Recovered one fumble.
SINGLE GAME HIGHS (regular season): Attempts—34 (December 6, 1998, vs. Washington); yards—127 (December 27, 1998, vs. Arizona); and rushing touchdowns—2 (November 22, 1998, vs. Kansas City).
STATISTICAL PLATEAUS: 100-yard rushing games: 1998 (2).

			RUSHING				RECEIVING				KICKOFF RETURNS				TOTALS			
Year Team	G	GS	Att.	Yds.	Avg.	TD	No.	Yds.	Avg.	TD	No.	Yds.	Avg.	TD	TD	2pt.	Pts.	Fum.
1995—San Diego NFL	16	0	26	140	5.4	1	3	26	8.7	0	4	65	16.3	0	1	0	6	2
1996—San Diego NFL	16	0	77	282	3.7	0	61	476	7.8	2	0	0	0.0	0	2	0	12	1
1997—San Diego NFL	13	1	51	161	3.2	0	39	292	7.5	0	0	0	0.0	0	0	0	0	4
1998—San Diego NFL	12	5	153	543	3.5	5	30	188	6.3	0	3	71	23.7	0	5	0	30	1
1999—San Diego NFL	15	2	48	126	2.6	0	45	360	8.0	0	7	112	16.0	0	0	0	0	1
2000—San Diego NFL	16	6	116	384	3.3	3	48	355	7.4	1	0	0	0.0	0	4	0	24	2
Pro totals (6 years)	88	14	471	1636	3.5	9	226	1697	7.5	3	14	248	17.7	0	12	0	72	11

FLOWERS, ERIK   DE   BILLS

PERSONAL: Born March 1, 1978, in Oceanside, Calif. ... 6-4/270. ... Full name: Erik Mathews Flowers.
HIGH SCHOOL: Theodore Roosevelt (San Antonio, Texas).
JUNIOR COLLEGE: Trinity Valley Community College (Texas).
COLLEGE: Arizona State.
TRANSACTIONS/CAREER NOTES: Selected by Buffalo Bills in first round (26th pick overall) of 2000 NFL draft. ... Signed by Bills (July 23, 2000).
PRO STATISTICS: 2000—Intercepted one pass for no yards.

Year Team	G	GS	SACKS
2000—Buffalo NFL	16	0	2.0

F

FLOWERS, LEE — S — STEELERS

PERSONAL: Born January 14, 1973, in Columbia, S.C. ... 6-0/211. ... Full name: Lethon Flowers III.
HIGH SCHOOL: Spring Valley (Columbia, S.C.).
COLLEGE: Georgia Tech.
TRANSACTIONS/CAREER NOTES: Selected by Pittsburgh Steelers in fifth round (151st pick overall) of 1995 NFL draft. ... Signed by Steelers (July 18, 1995). ... Granted free agency (February 13, 1998). ... Re-signed by Steelers (June 9, 1998). ... Granted unconditional free agency (February 12, 1999). ... Re-signed by Steelers (February 16, 1999).
PLAYING EXPERIENCE: Pittsburgh NFL, 1995-2000. ... Games/Games started: 1995 (10/0), 1996 (16/0), 1997 (10/0), 1998 (16/16), 1999 (15/15), 2000 (14/14). Total: 81/45.
CHAMPIONSHIP GAME EXPERIENCE: Played in AFC championship game (1995 and 1997 seasons). ... Played in Super Bowl XXX (1995 season).
PRO STATISTICS: 1997—Recovered one fumble. 1998—Intercepted one pass for two yards, credited with one sack and recovered two fumbles. 1999—Credited with five sacks. 2000—Intercepted one pass for no yards, credited with one sack and recovered three fumbles.

FLOYD, CHRIS — FB — BROWNS

PERSONAL: Born June 23, 1975, in Detroit. ... 6-2/235. ... Full name: Christopher Michael Floyd.
HIGH SCHOOL: Cooley (Detroit).
COLLEGE: Michigan (degree in sports management and communications).
TRANSACTIONS/CAREER NOTES: Selected by New England Patriots in third round (81st pick overall) of 1998 NFL draft. ... Signed by Patriots (July 15, 1998). ... Released by Patriots (November 28, 2000). ... Signed by Cleveland Browns (December 1, 2000).
SINGLE GAME HIGHS (regular season): Attempts—3 (October 3, 1999, vs. Cleveland); yards—14 (December 20, 1998, vs. San Francisco); and rushing touchdowns—0.

Year Team	G	GS	RUSHING				RECEIVING				TOTALS			
			Att.	Yds.	Avg.	TD	No.	Yds.	Avg.	TD	TD	2pt.	Pts.	Fum.
1998—New England NFL	16	2	6	22	3.7	0	1	6	6.0	0	0	0	0	0
1999—New England NFL	13	0	6	12	2.0	0	2	16	8.0	0	0	0	0	0
2000—New England NFL	11	0	2	-1	-0.5	0	1	21	21.0	0	0	0	0	0
—Cleveland NFL	2	0	0	0	0.0	0	0	0	0.0	0	0	0	0	0
Pro totals (3 years)	42	2	14	33	2.4	0	4	43	10.8	0	0	0	0	0

FLOYD, WILLIAM — FB

PERSONAL: Born February 17, 1972, in St. Petersburg, Fla. ... 6-1/242. ... Full name: William Ali Floyd.
HIGH SCHOOL: Lakewood Senior (St. Petersburg, Fla.).
COLLEGE: Florida State.
TRANSACTIONS/CAREER NOTES: Selected after junior season by San Francisco 49ers in first round (28th pick overall) of 1994 NFL draft. ... Signed by 49ers (July 28, 1994). ... On injured reserve with knee injury (October 31, 1995-remainder of season). ... On physically unable to perform list with knee injury (August 20-October 12, 1996). ... Granted unconditional free agency (February 13, 1998). ... Signed by Carolina Panthers (March 6, 1998). ... On injured reserve with rib injury (December 20, 2000-remainder of season). ... Released by Panthers (February 28, 2001).
CHAMPIONSHIP GAME EXPERIENCE: Played in NFC championship game (1994 and 1997 seasons). ... Member of Super Bowl championship team (1994 season).
POST SEASON RECORDS: Holds postseason single-game record for most touchdowns by rookie—3 (January 7, 1995, vs Chicago).
PRO STATISTICS: 1996—Recovered one fumble. 1998—Had only pass attempt intercepted. 1999—Recovered one fumble.
SINGLE GAME HIGHS (regular season): Attempts—12 (October 1, 1995, vs. New York Giants); yards—61 (December 4, 1994, vs. Atlanta); and rushing touchdowns—2 (November 21, 1999, vs. Cleveland).

Year Team	G	GS	RUSHING				RECEIVING				TOTALS			
			Att.	Yds.	Avg.	TD	No.	Yds.	Avg.	TD	TD	2pt.	Pts.	Fum.
1994—San Francisco NFL	16	11	87	305	3.5	6	19	145	7.6	0	6	0	36	0
1995—San Francisco NFL	8	8	64	237	3.7	2	47	348	7.4	1	3	0	18	1
1996—San Francisco NFL	9	8	47	186	4.0	2	26	197	7.6	1	3	0	18	4
1997—San Francisco NFL	15	15	78	231	3.0	3	37	321	8.7	1	4	0	24	2
1998—Carolina NFL	16	13	28	71	2.5	3	24	123	5.1	1	4	0	24	1
1999—Carolina NFL	16	16	35	78	2.2	3	21	179	8.5	0	3	0	18	1
2000—Carolina NFL	10	8	16	33	2.1	1	17	114	6.7	1	2	0	12	0
Pro totals (7 years)	90	79	355	1141	3.2	20	191	1427	7.5	5	25	0	150	9

FLUTIE, DOUG — QB — CHARGERS

PERSONAL: Born October 23, 1962, in Manchester, Md. ... 5-10/178. ... Full name: Douglas Richard Flutie. ... Brother of Darren Flutie, wide receiver with San Diego Chargers (1998), B.C. Lions of CFL (1991-95), Edmonton Eskimos of CFL (1996 and 1997) and Hamilton Tiger-Cats of CFL (1998).
HIGH SCHOOL: Natick (Mass.).
COLLEGE: Boston College (degrees in computer science and speech communications, 1984).
TRANSACTIONS/CAREER NOTES: Selected by New Jersey Generals in 1985 USFL territorial draft. ... Signed by Generals (February 4, 1985). ... Granted roster exemption (February 4-14, 1985). ... Activated (February 15, 1985). ... On developmental squad for three games with Generals (1985). ... Selected by Los Angeles Rams in 11th round (285th pick overall) of 1985 NFL draft. ... Signed by Rams (June 10, 1995-remainder of season). ... Rights traded by Rams with fourth-round pick in 1987 draft to Chicago Bears for third- and sixth-round picks in 1987 draft (October 14, 1986). ... Signed by Bears (October 21, 1986). ... Granted roster exemption (October 21-November 3, 1986). ... Activated (November 4, 1986). ... Crossed picket line during players strike (October 13, 1987). ... Traded by Bears to New England Patriots for eighth-round pick in 1988 draft (October 13, 1987). ... Released by Patriots after 1989 season. ... Signed by B.C. Lions of CFL (June 1990). ... Granted free agency (February 1992). ... Signed by Calgary Stampeders of CFL (March 1992). ... Rights assigned to Toronto Argonauts of CFL (March 15, 1996). ... Signed by Buffalo Bills (January 16, 1998). ... Released by Bills (March 1, 2001). ... Signed by San Diego Chargers (March 9, 2001).

CHAMPIONSHIP GAME EXPERIENCE: Member of CFL championship team (1992, 1996 and 1997). ... Named Most Valuable Player of Grey Cup, CFL championship game (1992, 1996 and 1997). ... Played in Grey Cup (1993 and 1995).

HONORS: Heisman Trophy winner (1984). ... Named College Football Player of the Year by THE SPORTING NEWS (1984). ... Named quarterback on THE SPORTING NEWS college All-America first team (1984). ... Most Outstanding Player of CFL (1991-1994, 1996 and 1997). ... Played in Pro Bowl (1998 season).

PRO STATISTICS: USFL: 1985—Recovered two fumbles. NFL: 1986—Recovered two fumbles and fumbled three times for minus four yards. 1987—Recovered one fumble. 1988—Fumbled three times. 1989—Fumbled once. CFL: 1990—Fumbled six times. 1991—Fumbled seven times. 1992—Fumbled five times. 1993—Caught one pass for 11 yards and fumbled five times. 1994—Fumbled eight times. 1995—Fumbled twice. 1996—Fumbled once. 1997—Fumbled three times. NFL: 1998—Fumbled three times and recovered four fumbles for minus 13 yards. 1999—Fumbled six times and recovered one fumble for minus five yards. 2000—Fumbled five times and recovered two fumbles for nine yards.

SINGLE GAME HIGHS (regular season): Attempts—50 (October 24, 1999, vs. Seattle); completions—28 (October 22, 2000, vs. Minnesota); yards—366 (December 23, 2000, vs. Seattle); and touchdown passes—4 (October 30, 1988, vs. Chicago).

STATISTICAL PLATEAUS: 300-yard passing games: 1998 (2), 1999 (1), 2000 (1). Total: 4.

MISCELLANEOUS: Regular-season record as starting NFL quarterback: 30-14 (.682). ... Postseason record as starting NFL quarterback: 0-2.

					PASSING							RUSHING				TOTALS		
Year	Team	G	GS	Att.	Cmp.	Pct.	Yds.	TD	Int.	Avg.	Rat.	Att.	Yds.	Avg.	TD	TD	2pt.	Pts.
1985—New Jersey USFL........		15	...	281	134	47.7	2109	13	14	7.51	67.8	65	465	7.2	6	6	0	36
1986—Chicago NFL..............		4	1	46	23	50.0	361	3	2	7.85	80.1	9	36	4.0	1	1	0	6
1987—Chicago NFL..............								Did not play.										
—New England NFL......		1	1	25	15	60.0	199	1	0	7.96	98.6	6	43	7.2	0	0	0	0
1988—New England NFL.......		11	9	179	92	51.4	1150	8	10	6.42	63.3	38	179	4.7	1	1	0	6
1989—New England NFL.......		5	3	91	36	39.6	493	2	4	5.42	46.6	16	87	5.4	0	0	0	0
1990—British Columbia CFL ..		16	...	392	207	52.8	2960	16	19	7.55	71.0	79	662	8.4	3	3	0	18
1991—British Columbia CFL ..		18	...	730	466	63.8	6619	38	24	9.07	96.7	120	610	5.1	14	14	1	86
1992—Calgary CFL..............		18	...	688	396	57.6	5945	32	30	8.64	83.4	96	669	7.0	11	11	0	66
1993—Calgary CFL..............		18	...	703	416	59.2	6092	44	17	8.67	98.3	74	373	5.0	11	11	0	66
1994—Calgary CFL..............		18	...	659	403	61.2	5726	48	19	8.69	101.5	96	760	7.9	8	8	0	48
1995—Calgary CFL..............		12	...	332	223	67.2	2788	16	5	8.40	102.8	46	288	6.3	5	5	0	30
1996—Toronto CFL..............		18	...	677	434	64.1	5720	29	17	8.45	94.5	101	756	7.5	9	9	0	54
1997—Toronto CFL..............		18	18	673	430	63.9	5505	47	24	8.18	97.8	92	542	5.9	9	9	0	54
1998—Buffalo NFL..............		13	10	354	202	57.1	2711	20	11	7.66	87.4	48	248	5.2	1	1	0	6
1999—Buffalo NFL..............		15	15	478	264	55.2	3171	19	16	6.63	75.1	88	476	5.4	1	1	0	6
2000—Buffalo NFL..............		11	5	231	132	57.1	1700	8	3	7.36	86.5	36	161	4.5	1	1	0	6
USFL totals (1 year).............		15	...	281	134	47.7	2109	13	14	7.51	67.8	65	465	7.2	6	6	0	36
CFL totals (8 years).............		136	...	4854	2975	61.3	41355	270	155	8.52	93.9	704	4660	6.6	70	70	1	422
NFL totals (7 years)..............		60	44	1404	764	54.4	9785	61	46	6.97	77.3	241	1230	5.1	5	5	0	30
Pro totals (16 years).............		211	...	6539	3873	59.2	53249	344	215	8.14	89.2	1010	6355	6.3	81	81	1	488

FLYNN, MIKE   OL   RAVENS

PERSONAL: Born June 15, 1974, in Doylestown, Pa. ... 6-3/300. ... Full name: Michael Patrick Flynn.

HIGH SCHOOL: Cathedral (Springfield, Mass.).

COLLEGE: Maine.

TRANSACTIONS/CAREER NOTES: Signed as non-drafted free agent by Baltimore Ravens (April 25, 1997). ... Released by Ravens (August 24, 1997). ... Signed by Tampa Bay Buccaneers to practice squad (August 27, 1997). ... Released by Buccaneers (September 2, 1997). ... Signed by Jacksonville Jaguars to practice squad (November 4, 1997). ... Signed by Ravens off Jaguars practice squad (December 3, 1997). ... Inactive for three games (1997). ... Granted free agency (March 2, 2001). ... Re-signed by Ravens (March 13, 2001).

PLAYING EXPERIENCE: Baltimore NFL, 1998-2000. ... Games/Games started: 1998 (2/0), 1999 (12/0), 2000 (16/16). Total: 30/16.

CHAMPIONSHIP GAME EXPERIENCE: Played in AFC championship game (2000 season). ... Member of Super Bowl championship team (2000 season).

PRO STATISTICS: 2000—Fumbled once and recovered two fumbles for minus 18 yards.

FOLAU, SPENCER   OT

PERSONAL: Born April 5, 1973, in Nuk 'Alofa, Tonga, Samoan Islands. ... 6-5/300. ... Full name: Spencer Sione Folau. ... Name pronounced fah-LOWE.

HIGH SCHOOL: Sequoia (Redwood City, Calif.).

COLLEGE: Idaho.

TRANSACTIONS/CAREER NOTES: Signed as non-drafted free agent by Baltimore Ravens (April 26, 1996). ... Released by Ravens (August 25, 1996). ... Re-signed by Ravens to practice squad (October 29, 1996). ... Assigned by Ravens to Rhein Fire in 1997 World League enhancement allocation program (February 1997). ... Released by Ravens (October 28, 1998). ... Re-signed by Ravens (November 3, 1998). ... Granted free agency (February 11, 2000). ... Tendered offer sheet by New England Patriots (April 10, 2000). ... Offer matched by Ravens (April 12, 2000). ... Released by Ravens (March 1, 2001).

PLAYING EXPERIENCE: Rhein W.L., 1997; Baltimore NFL, 1997-2000. ... Games/Games started: W.L. 1997 (games played unavailable), NFL 1997 (10/0), 1998 (3/3), 1999 (5/1), 2000 (11/4). Total NFL: 29/8.

CHAMPIONSHIP GAME EXPERIENCE: Played in AFC championship game (2000 season). ... Member of Super Bowl championship team (2000 season).

FOLEY, STEVE   LB   BENGALS

PERSONAL: Born September 9, 1975, in Little Rock, Ark. ... 6-3/260.

HIGH SCHOOL: Hall (Little Rock, Ark.).

COLLEGE: Northeast Louisiana.

F

TRANSACTIONS/CAREER NOTES: Selected by Cincinnati Bengals in third round (75th pick overall) of 1998 NFL draft. ... Signed by Bengals (July 19, 1998).
PRO STATISTICS: 1999—Recovered two fumbles. 2000—Intercepted one pass for one yard and recovered one fumble.

Year Team	G	GS	SACKS
1998—Cincinnati NFL	10	1	2.0
1999—Cincinnati NFL	16	16	3.5
2000—Cincinnati NFL	16	16	4.0
Pro totals (3 years)	42	33	9.5

FOLSTON, JAMES   LB   CARDINALS

PERSONAL: Born August 14, 1971, in Cocoa, Fla. ... Full name: James Edward Folston.
HIGH SCHOOL: Cocoa (Fla.).
COLLEGE: Northeast Louisiana.
TRANSACTIONS/CAREER NOTES: Selected by Los Angeles Raiders in second round (52nd pick overall) of 1994 NFL draft. ... Signed by Raiders (July 13, 1994). ... Raiders franchise moved to Oakland (July 21, 1995). ... Granted free agency (February 14, 1997). ... Re-signed by Raiders for 1997 season. ... Released by Raiders (September 4, 1999). ... Signed by Arizona Cardinals (November 17, 1999).
PLAYING EXPERIENCE: Los Angeles Raiders NFL, 1994; Oakland NFL, 1995-1998; Arizona NFL, 1999 and 2000. ... Games/Games started: 1994 (7/0), 1995 (15/0), 1996 (12/0), 1997 (16/7), 1998 (16/5), 1999 (6/0), 2000 (13/3). Total: 85/15.
PRO STATISTICS: 1997—Recovered one fumble. 1998—Caught one pass for minus one yard and credited with one sack. 2000—Credited with two sacks.

FONTENOT, AL   DE   CHARGERS

PERSONAL: Born September 17, 1970, in Houston. ... 6-4/287. ... Full name: Albert Paul Fontenot.
HIGH SCHOOL: Jack Yates (Houston).
JUNIOR COLLEGE: Navarro College (Texas).
COLLEGE: Baylor (degree in communications).
TRANSACTIONS/CAREER NOTES: Selected by Chicago Bears in fourth round (112th pick overall) of 1993 NFL draft. ... Signed by Bears (July 16, 1993). ... Granted free agency (February 16, 1996). ... Re-signed by Bears (April 18, 1996). ... Granted unconditional free agency (February 14, 1997). ... Signed by Indianapolis Colts (April 3, 1997). ... On injured reserve with calf injury (November 25, 1998-remainder of season). ... Released by Colts (April 28, 1999). ... Signed by San Diego Chargers (May 12, 1999). ... Granted unconditional free agency (February 11, 2000). ... Re-signed by Chargers (March 10, 2000). ... Granted unconditional free agency (March 2, 2001). ... Re-signed by Chargers (April 5, 2001).
PRO STATISTICS: 1993—Returned one kickoff for eight yards. 1995—Credited with one safety and recovered one fumble. 1997—Recovered three fumbles for 35 yards and one touchdown. 1998—Recovered one fumble. 1999—Recovered one fumble. 2000—Credited with one safety.

Year Team	G	GS	SACKS
1993—Chicago NFL	16	0	1.0
1994—Chicago NFL	16	8	4.0
1995—Chicago NFL	13	5	2.5
1996—Chicago NFL	16	15	4.5
1997—Indianapolis NFL	16	16	4.5
1998—Indianapolis NFL	7	5	1.0
1999—San Diego NFL	15	15	5.0
2000—San Diego NFL	15	15	4.0
Pro totals (8 years)	114	79	26.5

FONTENOT, JERRY   C   SAINTS

F

PERSONAL: Born November 21, 1966, in Lafayette, La. ... 6-3/300. ... Full name: Jerry Paul Fontenot.
HIGH SCHOOL: Lafayette (La.).
COLLEGE: Texas A&M.
TRANSACTIONS/CAREER NOTES: Selected by Chicago Bears in third round (65th pick overall) of 1989 NFL draft. ... Signed by Bears (July 27, 1989). ... Granted free agency (March 1, 1993). ... Re-signed by Bears (June 16, 1993). ... Granted free agency (February 16, 1996). ... Re-signed by Bears (July 10, 1996). ... Granted unconditional free agency (February 14, 1997). ... Signed by New Orleans Saints (May 28, 1997). ... On injured reserve with knee injury (October 14, 1998-remainder of season). ... Granted unconditional free agency (February 12, 1999). ... Re-signed by Saints (February 15, 1999).
PLAYING EXPERIENCE: Chicago NFL, 1989-1996; New Orleans NFL, 1997-2000. ... Games/Games started: 1989 (16/0), 1990 (16/2), 1991 (16/7), 1992 (16/16), 1993 (16/16), 1994 (16/16), 1995 (16/16), 1996 (16/16), 1997 (16/16), 1998 (4/4), 1999 (16/16), 2000 (16/16). Total: 180/141.
PRO STATISTICS: 1989—Recovered one fumble. 1990—Fumbled once. 1992—Fumbled once for minus two yards. 1993—Recovered one fumble. 1997—Fumbled three times. 1999—Recovered one fumble. 2000—Recovered one fumble.

FORD, HENRY   DT   TITANS

PERSONAL: Born October 30, 1971, in Fort Worth, Texas. ... 6-3/295.
HIGH SCHOOL: Trimble Technical (Fort Worth, Texas).
COLLEGE: Arkansas.
TRANSACTIONS/CAREER NOTES: Selected by Houston Oilers in first round (26th pick overall) of 1994 NFL draft. ... Signed by Oilers (June 16, 1994). ... Oilers franchise moved to Tennessee for 1997 season. ... Granted unconditional free agency (February 13, 1998). ... Re-signed by Oilers (March 2, 1998). ... Oilers franchise renamed Tennessee Titans for 1999 season (December 26, 1998).
CHAMPIONSHIP GAME EXPERIENCE: Played in AFC championship game (1999 season). ... Played in Super Bowl XXXIV (1999 season).
PRO STATISTICS: 1997—Recovered two fumbles for 13 yards. 1998—Recovered one fumble. 1999—Recovered two fumbles. 2000—Recovered one fumble for 30 yards.

Year Team	G	GS	SACKS
1994—Houston NFL	11	0	0.0
1995—Houston NFL	16	16	4.5
1996—Houston NFL	15	14	1.0
1997—Tennessee NFL	16	16	5.0
1998—Tennessee NFL	13	5	1.5
1999—Tennessee NFL	12	9	5.5
2000—Tennessee NFL	14	3	2.0
Pro totals (7 years)	97	63	19.5

FORDHAM, TODD   OT   BRONCOS

PERSONAL: Born October 9, 1973, in Atlanta. ... 6-5/308. ... Full name: Lindsey Todd Fordham.
HIGH SCHOOL: Tift County (Tifton, Ga.).
COLLEGE: Florida State (degree in business, 1996).
TRANSACTIONS/CAREER NOTES: Signed as non-drafted free agent by Jacksonville Jaguars (April 21, 1997). ... Released by Jaguars (August 24, 1997). ... Re-signed by Jaguars to practice squad (August 25, 1997). ... Activated (September 23, 1997). ... On injured reserve with knee injury (August 31, 1999-entire season). ... Granted free agency (February 11, 2000). ... Re-signed by Jaguars (February 24, 2000). ... Granted unconditional free agency (March 2, 2001). ... Signed by Denver Broncos (April 13, 2001).
PLAYING EXPERIENCE: Jacksonville NFL, 1997, 1998 and 2000. ... Games/Games started: 1997 (1/0), 1998 (11/1), 2000 (16/8). Total: 28/9.
PRO STATISTICS: 1998—Returned one kickoff for no yards and recovered one fumble. 2000—Returned one kickoff for no yards and fumbled once.

FOREMAN, JAY   LB   BILLS

PERSONAL: Born February 18, 1976, in Eden Prairie, Minn. ... 6-1/240. ... Full name: Jamal A. Foreman. ... Son of Chuck Foreman, running back with Minnesota Vikings (1973-79) and New England Patriots (1980).
HIGH SCHOOL: Eden Prairie (Minn.).
COLLEGE: Nebraska (degree in business administration).
TRANSACTIONS/CAREER NOTES: Selected by Buffalo Bills in fifth round (156th pick overall) of 1999 NFL draft. ... Signed by Bills (July 27, 1999).
PLAYING EXPERIENCE: Buffalo NFL, 1999 and 2000. ... Games/Games started: 1999 (7/0), 2000 (15/4). Total: 22/4.
PRO STATISTICS: 2000—Returned one kickoff for 19 yards.

FORTIN, ROMAN   C   CHARGERS

PERSONAL: Born February 26, 1967, in Columbus, Ohio. ... 6-5/297. ... Full name: Roman Brian Fortin.
HIGH SCHOOL: Ventura (Calif.).
COLLEGE: Oregon, then San Diego State.
TRANSACTIONS/CAREER NOTES: Selected by Detroit Lions in eighth round (203rd pick overall) of 1990 NFL draft. ... On injured reserve (September 5, 1990-entire season). ... Granted unconditional free agency (February 1, 1992). ... Signed by Atlanta Falcons (March 31, 1992). ... Granted unconditional free agency (February 17, 1994). ... Re-signed by Falcons (February 24, 1994). ... Granted unconditional free agency (February 16, 1996). ... Re-signed by Falcons (February 20, 1996). ... Released by Falcons (February 11, 1998). ... Signed by San Diego Chargers (March 17, 1998). ... Granted unconditional free agency (February 11, 2000). ... Re-signed by Chargers (February 17, 2000).
PLAYING EXPERIENCE: Detroit NFL, 1991; Atlanta NFL, 1992-1997; San Diego NFL, 1998-2000. ... Games/Games started: 1991 (16/2), 1992 (16/1), 1993 (16/1), 1994 (16/16), 1995 (16/16), 1996 (16/16), 1997 (3/3), 1998 (16/16), 1999 (16/16), 2000 (16/16). Total: 147/103.
CHAMPIONSHIP GAME EXPERIENCE: Played in NFC championship game (1991 season).
PRO STATISTICS: 1991—Caught one pass for four yards. 1992—Returned one kickoff for five yards and recovered one fumble. 1995—Fumbled twice for minus six yards. 1996—Recovered two fumbles. 1999—Recovered two fumbles. 2000—Fumbled twice for minus one yard.

FOSTER, LARRY   WR   LIONS

PERSONAL: Born November 7, 1976, in Shreveport, La. ... 5-10/196.
HIGH SCHOOL: West Jefferson (La.).
COLLEGE: Louisiana State.
TRANSACTIONS/CAREER NOTES: Signed as non-drafted free agent by Detroit Lions (April 28, 2000). ... Released by Lions (August 27, 2000). ... Re-signed by Lions to practice squad (August 29, 2000). ... Activated (October 16, 2000).
PLAYING EXPERIENCE: Detroit NFL, 2000. ... Games/Games started: 2000 (10/0).
PRO STATISTICS: 2000—Rushed two times for 31 yards, caught 17 passes for 175 yards and one touchdown, fumbled twice and recovered one fumble.
SINGLE GAME HIGHS (regular season): Receptions—8 (November 30, 2000, vs. Minnesota); yards—106 (November 30, 2000, vs. Minnesota); and touchdown receptions—1 (November 30, 2000, vs. Minnesota).
STATISTICAL PLATEAUS: 100-yard receiving games: 2000 (1).

FRANKS, BUBBA   TE   PACKERS

PERSONAL: Born January 6, 1978, in Riverside, Calif. ... 6-6/260. ... Full name: Daniel Lamont Franks.
HIGH SCHOOL: Big Springs (Texas).
COLLEGE: Miami (Fla.).
TRANSACTIONS/CAREER NOTES: Selected after junior season by Green Bay Packers in first round (14th pick overall) of 2000 NFL draft. ... Signed by Packers (July 19, 2000).
HONORS: Named tight end on THE SPORTING NEWS college All-America first team (1999).
PRO STATISTICS: 2000—Fumbled once.
SINGLE GAME HIGHS (regular season): Receptions—5 (October 1, 2000, vs. Chicago); yards—54 (October 1, 2000, vs. Chicago); and touchdown receptions—1 (November 12, 2000, vs. Tampa Bay).

				RECEIVING		
Year Team	G	GS	No.	Yds.	Avg.	TD
2000—Green Bay NFL	16	13	34	363	10.7	1

F

FRANZ, TODD   CB   BROWNS

PERSONAL: Born April 12, 1976, in Enid, Okla. ... 6-0/194. ... Full name: Stephen Todd Franz.
HIGH SCHOOL: Weatherford (Okla.).
COLLEGE: Tulsa.
TRANSACTIONS/CAREER NOTES: Selected by Detroit Lions in fifth round (145th pick overall) of 2000 NFL draft. ... Signed by Lions (July 15, 2000). ... Claimed on waivers by New Orleans Saints (August 28, 2000). ... Released by Saints (October 10, 2000). ... Signed by Cleveland Browns (November 14, 2000).
PLAYING EXPERIENCE: New Orleans (5)-Cleveland (2) NFL, 2000. ... Games/Games started: 2000 (N.O.-5/0; Cleve.-2/0; Total:7/0).

FREDRICKSON, ROB   LB   CARDINALS

PERSONAL: Born May 13, 1971, in Saint Joseph, Mich. ... 6-4/243. ... Full name: Robert J. Fredrickson.
HIGH SCHOOL: Saint Joseph (Mich.) Senior.
COLLEGE: Michigan State.
TRANSACTIONS/CAREER NOTES: Selected by Los Angeles Raiders in first round (22nd pick overall) of 1994 NFL draft. ... Signed by Raiders (July 19, 1994). ... Raiders franchise moved to Oakland (July 21, 1995). ... On injured reserve with shoulder injury (November 20, 1996-remainder of season). ... Traded by Raiders to Detroit Lions for fourth-round pick (traded to Washington) in 1998 draft (March 25, 1998). ... Granted unconditional free agency (February 12, 1999). ... Signed by Arizona Cardinals (March 26, 1999).
PRO STATISTICS: 1995—Recovered four fumbles for 35 yards and one touchdown. 1999—Recovered one fumble.

			INTERCEPTIONS				SACKS
Year Team	G	GS	No.	Yds.	Avg.	TD	No.
1994—Los Angeles Raiders NFL	16	12	0	0	0.0	0	3.0
1995—Oakland NFL	16	15	1	14	14.0	0	0.0
1996—Oakland NFL	10	10	0	0	0.0	0	0.0
1997—Oakland NFL	16	13	0	0	0.0	0	2.0
1998—Detroit NFL	16	16	1	0	0.0	0	2.5
1999—Arizona NFL	16	16	2	57	28.5	1	2.0
2000—Arizona NFL	13	12	1	8	8.0	0	1.0
Pro totals (7 years)	103	94	5	79	15.8	1	10.5

FREEMAN, ANTONIO   WR   PACKERS

PERSONAL: Born May 27, 1972, in Baltimore. ... 6-1/198. ... Full name: Antonio Michael Freeman.
HIGH SCHOOL: Polytechnic (Baltimore).
COLLEGE: Virginia Tech.
TRANSACTIONS/CAREER NOTES: Selected by Green Bay Packers in third round (90th pick overall) of 1995 NFL draft. ... Signed by Packers (June 22, 1995). ... Granted free agency (February 13, 1998). ... Re-signed by Packers (June 16, 1998). ... Designated by Packers as franchise player (February 12, 1999).
CHAMPIONSHIP GAME EXPERIENCE: Played in NFC championship game (1995-1997 seasons). ... Member of Super Bowl championship team (1996 season). ... Played in Super Bowl XXXII (1997 season).
HONORS: Named wide receiver on THE SPORTING NEWS NFL All-Pro team (1998). ... Played in Pro Bowl (1998 season).
POST SEASON RECORDS: Holds Super Bowl record for longest pass reception (from Brett Favre)—81 yards (January 26, 1997, vs. New England). ... Shares NFL postseason record for most touchdowns by punt return—1 (December 31, 1995, vs. Atlanta).
PRO STATISTICS: 1995—Recovered four fumbles. 1996—Recovered one fumble for 14 yards. 1997—Rushed once for 14 yards. 1998—Rushed three times for five yards. 1999—Rushed once for minus two yards and recovered one fumble. 2000—Rushed twice for five yards.
SINGLE GAME HIGHS (regular season): Receptions—10 (December 14, 1997, vs. Carolina); yards—193 (November 1, 1998, vs. San Francisco); and touchdown receptions—3 (December 20, 1998, vs. Tennessee).
STATISTICAL PLATEAUS: 100-yard receiving games: 1996 (4), 1997 (3), 1998 (6), 1999 (3), 2000 (2). Total: 18.

			RECEIVING				PUNT RETURNS				KICKOFF RETURNS				TOTALS			
Year Team	G	GS	No.	Yds.	Avg.	TD	No.	Yds.	Avg.	TD	No.	Yds.	Avg.	TD	TD	2pt.	Pts.	Fum.
1995—Green Bay NFL	11	0	8	106	13.3	1	37	292	7.9	0	24	556	23.2	0	1	0	6	7
1996—Green Bay NFL	12	12	56	933	16.7	9	0	0	0.0	0	1	16	16.0	0	9	0	54	3
1997—Green Bay NFL	16	16	81	1243	15.3	12	0	0	0.0	0	0	0	0.0	0	12	0	72	1
1998—Green Bay NFL	15	15	84	*1424	17.0	14	0	0	0.0	0	0	0	0.0	0	14	1	86	0
1999—Green Bay NFL	16	16	74	1074	14.5	6	0	0	0.0	0	0	0	0.0	0	6	0	36	1
2000—Green Bay NFL	15	15	62	912	14.7	9	0	0	0.0	0	0	0	0.0	0	9	0	54	1
Pro totals (6 years)	85	74	365	5692	15.6	51	37	292	7.9	0	25	572	22.9	0	51	1	308	13

FREEMAN, ARTURO   S   DOLPHINS

PERSONAL: Born October 27, 1976, in Orangeburg, S.C. ... 6-0/195. ... Full name: Arturo C. Freeman.
HIGH SCHOOL: Orangeburg-Wilkinson (Orangeburg, S.C.).
COLLEGE: South Carolina.
TRANSACTIONS/CAREER NOTES: Selected by Miami Dolphins in fifth round (152nd pick overall) of 2000 NFL draft. ... Signed by Dolphins (July 11, 2000).
PLAYING EXPERIENCE: Miami NFL, 2000. ... Games/Games started: 2000 (8/0).

FREROTTE, GUS   QB   BRONCOS

PERSONAL: Born July 31, 1971, in Kittanning, Pa. ... 6-3/225. ... Full name: Gustave Joseph Frerotte. ... Cousin of Mitch Frerotte, guard with Buffalo Bills (1987 and 1990-92).
HIGH SCHOOL: Ford City (Pa.) Junior-Senior.
COLLEGE: Tulsa.

F

TRANSACTIONS/CAREER NOTES: Selected by Washington Redskins in seventh round (197th pick overall) of 1994 NFL draft. ... Signed by Redskins (July 19, 1994). ... Granted free agency (February 14, 1997). ... Re-signed by Redskins (July 18, 1997). ... On injured reserve with hip injury (December 2, 1997-remainder of season). ... Released by Redskins (February 11, 1999). ... Signed by Detroit Lions (March 3, 1999). ... Granted unconditional free agency (February 11, 2000). ... Signed by Denver Broncos (March 7, 2000). ... Granted unconditional free agency (March 2, 2001). ... Re-signed by Broncos (March 13, 2001).

HONORS: Played in Pro Bowl (1996 season).

PRO STATISTICS: 1994—Fumbled four times and recovered two fumbles for minus four yards. 1995—Fumbled seven times and recovered four fumbles for minus 16 yards. 1996—Fumbled 12 times and recovered one fumble for minus 12 yards. 1997—Fumbled eight times and recovered two fumbles for minus 16 yards. 1999—Fumbled three times and recovered one fumble. 2000—Fumbled five times.

SINGLE GAME HIGHS (regular season): Attempts—58 (November 19, 2000, vs. San Diego); completions—36 (November 19, 2000, vs. San Diego); yards—462 (November 19, 2000, vs. San Diego); and touchdown passes—5 (November 19, 2000, vs. San Diego).

STATISTICAL PLATEAUS: 300-yard passing games: 1995 (1), 1996 (1), 1999 (2), 2000 (1). Total: 5.

MISCELLANEOUS: Regular-season record as starting NFL quarterback: 25-32-1 (.431). ... Postseason record as starting NFL quarterback: 0-1.

Year Team	G	GS	PASSING								RUSHING				TOTALS		
			Att.	Cmp.	Pct.	Yds.	TD	Int.	Avg.	Rat.	Att.	Yds.	Avg.	TD	TD	2pt.	Pts.
1994—Washington NFL	4	4	100	46	46.0	600	5	5	6.00	61.3	4	1	0.3	0	0	0	0
1995—Washington NFL	16	11	396	199	50.3	2751	13	13	6.95	70.2	22	16	0.7	1	1	0	6
1996—Washington NFL	16	16	470	270	57.4	3453	12	11	7.35	79.3	28	16	0.6	0	0	0	0
1997—Washington NFL	13	13	402	204	50.7	2682	17	12	6.67	73.8	24	65	2.7	2	2	0	12
1998—Washington NFL	3	2	54	25	46.3	283	1	3	5.24	45.5	3	20	6.7	0	0	0	0
1999—Detroit NFL	9	6	288	175	60.8	2117	9	7	7.35	83.6	15	33	2.2	0	0	0	0
2000—Denver NFL	10	6	232	138	59.5	1776	9	8	7.66	82.1	22	64	2.9	1	1	0	6
Pro totals (7 years)	71	58	1942	1057	54.4	13662	66	59	7.04	75.4	118	215	1.8	4	4	0	24

FRICKE, BEN   G/C   COWBOYS

PERSONAL: Born November 3, 1975, in Austin, Texas. ... 6-0/295.

HIGH SCHOOL: L.C. Anderson (Austin, Texas).

COLLEGE: Houston.

TRANSACTIONS/CAREER NOTES: Selected by New York Giants in seventh round (213th pick overall) of 1998 NFL draft. ... Signed by Giants (July 20, 1998). ... Released by Giants (August 22, 1998). ... Selected by Amsterdam Admirals in 1999 NFL Europe draft (February 23, 1999). ... Signed by Dallas Cowboys (August 3, 1999). ... Released by Cowboys (September 22, 1999). ... Re-signed by Cowboys (October 5, 1999). ... Released by Cowboys (October 27, 1999). ... Re-signed by Cowboys to practice squad (October 28, 1999). ... Activated (November 19, 1999). ... Assigned by Cowboys to Admirals in 2000 NFL Europe enhancement allocation program (February 18, 2000).

PLAYING EXPERIENCE: Amsterdam Admirals NFLE, 1999 and 2000; Dallas NFL, 1999 and 2000. ... Games/Games started: NFLE 1999 (games played unavailable), NFL 1999 (3/0), NFLE 2000 (-), 2000 (9/5). Total: 12/5.

HONORS: Named center on THE SPORTING NEWS college All-America second team (1997).

PRO STATISTICS: 2000—Fumbled twice.

FRIEDMAN, LENNIE   G   BRONCOS

PERSONAL: Born October 13, 1976, in Livingston, N.J. ... 6-3/285. ... Full name: Leonard Lebrecht Friedman.

HIGH SCHOOL: West Milford (N.J.).

COLLEGE: Duke.

TRANSACTIONS/CAREER NOTES: Selected by Denver Broncos in second round (61st pick overall) of 1999 NFL draft. ... Signed by Broncos (June 14, 1999). ... On injured reserve with knee injury (August 31, 1999-entire season). ... Assigned by Broncos to Barcelona Dragons in 2000 NFL Europe enhancement allocation program (February 18, 2000).

PLAYING EXPERIENCE: Barcelona NFLE, 2000; Denver NFL, 2000. ... Games/Games started: NFLE 2000 (games played unavailable), NFL 2000 (16/8).

PRO STATISTICS: 2000—Recovered two fumbles.

F

FRIESZ, JOHN   QB

PERSONAL: Born May 19, 1967, in Missoula, Mont. ... 6-4/223. ... Full name: John Melvin Friesz. ... Name pronounced FREEZE.

HIGH SCHOOL: Coeur D'Alene (Idaho).

COLLEGE: Idaho.

TRANSACTIONS/CAREER NOTES: Selected by San Diego Chargers in sixth round (138th pick overall) of 1990 NFL draft. ... Signed by Chargers (July 20, 1990). ... On injured reserve with elbow injury (September 4-October 3, 1990). ... On practice squad (October 3-December 28, 1990). ... Granted free agency (February 1, 1992). ... Re-signed by Chargers (July 27, 1992). ... On injured reserve with knee injury (August 25, 1992-entire season). ... Granted unconditional free agency (February 17, 1994). ... Signed by Washington Redskins (April 18, 1994). ... Granted unconditional free agency (February 17, 1995). ... Signed by Seattle Seahawks (March 17, 1995). ... Released by Seahawks (February 10, 1999). ... Signed by New England Patriots (April 22, 1999). ... Released by Patriots (February 22, 2001).

HONORS: Walter Payton Award winner (1989).

PRO STATISTICS: 1991—Fumbled 10 times and recovered two fumbles for minus 21 yards. 1993—Fumbled twice and recovered one fumble for minus three yards. 1994—Fumbled twice and recovered one fumble. 1995—Fumbled twice and recovered one fumble for minus three yards. 1996—Fumbled seven times and recovered two fumbles for minus six yards. 1997—Fumbled once and recovered one fumble for minus two yards.

SINGLE GAME HIGHS (regular season): Attempts—54 (October 20, 1991, vs. Cleveland); completions—33 (October 20, 1991, vs. Cleveland); yards—381 (September 18, 1994, vs. New York Giants); and touchdown passes—4 (September 11, 1994, vs. New Orleans).

STATISTICAL PLATEAUS: 300-yard passing games: 1991 (2), 1994 (1), 1996 (1). Total: 4.

MISCELLANEOUS: Regular-season record as starting NFL quarterback: 13-25 (.342).

				PASSING							RUSHING				TOTALS		
Year Team	G	GS	Att.	Cmp.	Pct.	Yds.	TD	Int.	Avg.	Rat.	Att.	Yds.	Avg.	TD	TD	2pt.	Pts.
1990—San Diego NFL.............	1	1	22	11	50.0	98	1	1	4.45	58.5	1	3	3.0	0	0	0	0
1991—San Diego NFL.............	16	16	487	262	53.8	2896	12	15	5.95	67.1	10	18	1.8	0	0	0	0
1992—San Diego NFL.............						Did not play.											
1993—San Diego NFL.............	12	6	238	128	53.8	1402	6	4	5.89	72.8	10	3	0.3	0	0	0	0
1994—Washington NFL	16	4	180	105	58.3	1266	10	9	7.03	77.7	1	1	1.0	0	0	0	0
1995—Seattle NFL.................	6	3	120	64	53.3	795	6	3	6.63	80.4	11	0	0.0	0	0	0	0
1996—Seattle NFL.................	8	6	211	120	56.9	1629	8	4	7.72	86.4	12	1	0.1	0	0	0	0
1997—Seattle NFL.................	2	1	36	15	41.7	138	0	3	3.83	18.1	1	0	0.0	0	0	0	0
1998—Seattle NFL.................	6	1	49	29	59.2	409	2	2	8.35	82.8	5	5	1.0	0	0	0	0
1999—New England NFL.......	1	0	0	0	0.0	0	0	0	0.0	...	2	-2	-1.0	0	0	0	0
2000—New England NFL.......	1	0	21	11	52.4	66	0	1	3.14	39.0	0	0	0.0	0	0	0	0
Pro totals (10 years).............	69	38	1364	745	54.6	8699	45	42	6.38	72.3	53	29	0.5	0	0	0	0

FROST, SCOTT S JETS

PERSONAL: Born January 4, 1975, in Wood River, Neb. ... 6-3/219.
HIGH SCHOOL: Wood River (Neb.).
COLLEGE: Stanford, then Nebraska (degree in finance, 1997).
TRANSACTIONS/CAREER NOTES: Selected by New York Jets in third round (67th pick overall) of 1998 NFL draft. ... Signed by Jets (July 21, 1998). ... Granted free agency (March 2, 2001).
PLAYING EXPERIENCE: New York Jets NFL, 1998-2000. ... Games/Games started: 1998 (13/0), 1999 (14/0), 2000 (16/1). Total: 43/1.
CHAMPIONSHIP GAME EXPERIENCE: Played in AFC championship game (1998 season).
PRO STATISTICS: 1998—Returned one punt for no yards and fumbled once. 2000—Intercepted one pass for one yard and credited with one sack.

FRYAR, IRVING WR

PERSONAL: Born September 28, 1962, in Mount Holly, N.J. ... 6-0/198. ... Full name: Irving Dale Fryar.
HIGH SCHOOL: Rancocas Valley (Mount Holly, N.J.).
COLLEGE: Nebraska (degree in bible study).
TRANSACTIONS/CAREER NOTES: Selected by Chicago Blitz in first round (third pick overall) of 1984 USFL draft. ... Signed by New England Patriots (April 11, 1984). ... Selected officially by Patriots in first round (first pick overall) of 1984 NFL draft. ... Traded to Miami Dolphins for second-round pick (OL Todd Rucci) in 1993 draft and third-round pick (C Joe Burch) in 1994 draft (April 1, 1993). ... Granted unconditional free agency (February 16, 1996). ... Signed by Philadelphia Eagles (March 19, 1996). ... Announced retirement (December 23, 1998). ... Signed by Washington Redskins (August 19, 1999). ... Released by Redskins (February 21, 2001).
CHAMPIONSHIP GAME EXPERIENCE: Played in Super Bowl XX (1985 season).
HONORS: Named wide receiver on THE SPORTING NEWS college All-America first team (1983). ... Played in Pro Bowl (1985, 1993, 1994, 1996 and 1997 seasons).
PRO STATISTICS: 1984—Fumbled four times and recovered one fumble. 1985—Fumbled four times. 1986—Fumbled four times and recovered one fumble. 1987—Fumbled twice. 1988—Fumbled twice. 1989—Fumbled twice. 1990—Fumbled once and recovered one fumble. 1991—Attempted one pass without a completion and fumbled twice. 1994—Ran two yards with lateral from reception for a touchdown and recovered one fumble for seven yards. 1997—Fumbled once.
SINGLE GAME HIGHS (regular season): Receptions—10 (October 12, 1997, vs. Jacksonville); yards—211 (September 4, 1994, vs. New England); and touchdown receptions—4 (October 20, 1996, vs. Miami).
STATISTICAL PLATEAUS: 100-yard receiving games: 1985 (1), 1986 (2), 1987 (1), 1988 (1), 1989 (1), 1990 (1), 1991 (3), 1992 (2), 1993 (2), 1994 (6), 1995 (2), 1996 (4), 1997 (4). Total: 32.

			RUSHING				RECEIVING				PUNT RETURNS				KICKOFF RETURNS				TOTALS		
Year Team	G	GS	Att.	Yds.	Avg.	TD	No.	Yds.	Avg.	TD	No.	Yds.	Avg.	TD	No.	Yds.	Avg.	TD	TD	2pt.	Pts.
1984—New England NFL	14	2	2	-11	-5.5	0	11	164	14.9	1	36	347	9.6	0	5	95	19.0	0	1	0	6
1985—New England NFL	16	14	7	27	3.9	1	39	670	17.2	7	37	520*14.1		†2	3	39	13.0	0	10	0	60
1986—New England NFL	14	13	4	80	20.0	0	43	737	17.1	6	35	366	10.5	▲1	10	192	19.2	0	7	0	42
1987—New England NFL	12	12	9	52	5.8	0	31	467	15.1	5	18	174	9.7	0	6	119	19.8	0	5	0	30
1988—New England NFL	15	14	6	12	2.0	0	33	490	14.8	5	38	398	10.5	0	1	3	3.0	0	5	0	30
1989—New England NFL	11	5	2	15	7.5	0	29	537	18.5	3	12	107	8.9	0	1	47	47.0	0	3	0	18
1990—New England NFL	16	15	0	0	0.0	0	54	856	15.9	4	28	133	4.8	0	0	0	0.0	0	4	0	24
1991—New England NFL	16	15	2	11	5.5	0	68	1014	14.9	3	2	10	5.0	0	0	0	0.0	0	3	0	18
1992—New England NFL	15	14	1	6	6.0	0	55	791	14.4	4	0	0	0.0	0	0	0	0.0	0	4	0	24
1993—Miami NFL	16	16	3	-4	-1.3	0	64	1010	15.8	5	0	0	0.0	0	1	10	10.0	0	5	0	30
1994—Miami NFL	16	16	0	0	0.0	0	73	1270	17.4	7	0	0	0.0	0	0	0	0.0	0	7	2	46
1995—Miami NFL	16	16	0	0	0.0	0	62	910	14.7	8	0	0	0.0	0	0	0	0.0	0	8	0	48
1996—Philadelphia NFL.	16	16	1	-4	-4.0	0	88	1195	13.6	†11	0	0	0.0	0	0	0	0.0	0	11	0	66
1997—Philadelphia NFL.	16	16	0	0	0.0	0	86	1316	15.3	6	0	0	0.0	0	0	0	0.0	0	6	0	36
1998—Philadelphia NFL.	16	16	3	46	15.3	0	48	556	11.6	2	0	0	0.0	0	0	0	0.0	0	2	0	12
1999—Washington NFL .	16	1	0	0	0.0	0	26	254	9.8	2	0	0	0.0	0	0	0	0.0	0	2	0	12
2000—Washington NFL .	14	5	2	16	8.0	0	41	548	13.4	5	0	0	0.0	0	0	0	0.0	0	5	0	30
Pro totals (17 years)......	255	206	42	246	5.9	1	851	12785	15.0	84	206	2055	10.0	3	27	505	18.7	0	88	2	532

FUAMATU-MA'AFALA, CHRIS RB STEELERS

PERSONAL: Born March 4, 1977, in Honolulu. ... 5-11/252. ... Name pronounced fu-ah-MAH-tu ma-ah-FAH-la.
HIGH SCHOOL: St. Louis (Honolulu).
COLLEGE: Utah.

TRANSACTIONS/CAREER NOTES: Selected after junior season by Pittsburgh Steelers in sixth round (178th pick overall) of 1998 NFL draft. ... Signed by Steelers (July 10, 1998). ... On injured reserve with broken foot (Decemeber 20, 2000-remainder of season). ... Granted free agency (March 2, 2001). ... Tendered offer sheet by New England Patriots (April 14, 2001). ... Offer matched by Steelers (April 19, 2001).
PRO STATISTICS: 1999—Returned one kickoff for nine yards.
SINGLE GAME HIGHS (regular season): Attempts—7 (October 8, 2000, vs. New York Jets); yards—51 (October 1, 2000, vs. Jacksonville); and rushing touchdowns—1 (October 1, 2000, vs. Jacksonville).

			RUSHING				RECEIVING				TOTALS			
Year Team	G	GS	Att.	Yds.	Avg.	TD	No.	Yds.	Avg.	TD	TD	2pt.	Pts.	Fum.
1998—Pittsburgh NFL	12	0	7	30	4.3	2	9	84	9.3	1	3	0	18	0
1999—Pittsburgh NFL	10	0	1	4	4.0	0	0	0	0.0	0	0	0	0	0
2000—Pittsburgh NFL	7	1	21	149	7.1	1	11	107	9.7	0	1	0	6	0
Pro totals (3 years)	29	1	29	183	6.3	3	20	191	9.6	1	4	0	24	0

FULCHER, MONDRIEL   TE   RAIDERS

PERSONAL: Born October 15, 1976, in Coffeyville, Kan. ... 6-3/250. ... Full name: Mondriel DeCarlos A. Fulcher.
HIGH SCHOOL: Field Kindley (Coffeyville, Kan.).
COLLEGE: Miami (Fla.).
TRANSACTIONS/CAREER NOTES: Selected by Oakland Raiders in seventh round (227th pick overall) of 2000 NFL draft. ... Signed by Raiders (July 11, 2000).
PLAYING EXPERIENCE: Oakland NFL, 2000. ... Games/Games started: 2000 (10/0).
CHAMPIONSHIP GAME EXPERIENCE: Member of Raiders for AFC Championship game (2000 season); inactive.

FULLER, COREY   DB   BROWNS

PERSONAL: Born May 1, 1971, in Tallahassee, Fla. ... 5-10/205.
HIGH SCHOOL: James S. Rickards (Tallahassee, Fla.).
COLLEGE: Florida State (degree in criminology and child development, 1994).
TRANSACTIONS/CAREER NOTES: Selected by Minnesota Vikings in second round (55th pick overall) of 1995 NFL draft. ... Signed by Vikings (July 24, 1995). ... Granted unconditional free agency (February 12, 1999). ... Signed by Cleveland Browns (February 18, 1999).
CHAMPIONSHIP GAME EXPERIENCE: Played in NFC championship game (1998 season).
PRO STATISTICS: 1995—Credited with $1/2$ sack and recovered one fumble for 12 yards and a touchdown. 1998—Credited with one sack. 1999—Recovered two fumbles. 2000—Recovered one fumble.

			INTERCEPTIONS			
Year Team	G	GS	No.	Yds.	Avg.	TD
1995—Minnesota NFL	16	11	1	0	0.0	0
1996—Minnesota NFL	16	14	3	3	1.0	0
1997—Minnesota NFL	16	16	2	24	12.0	0
1998—Minnesota NFL	16	16	4	36	9.0	0
1999—Cleveland NFL	16	16	0	0	0.0	0
2000—Cleveland NFL	15	15	3	0	0.0	0
Pro totals (6 years)	95	88	13	63	4.8	0

GADSDEN, ORONDE   WR   DOLPHINS

PERSONAL: Born August 20, 1971, in Charleston, S.C. ... 6-2/215. ... Full name: Oronde Benjamin Gadsden. ... Name pronounced o-RON-day.
HIGH SCHOOL: Burke (Charleston, S.C.).
COLLEGE: Winston-Salem (degree in marketing).
TRANSACTIONS/CAREER NOTES: Signed by Dallas Cowboys as non-drafted free agent (August 1995). ... Released by Cowboys (August 22, 1995). ... Re-signed by Cowboys to practice squad (August 30, 1995). ... Activated (January 8, 1996). ... On injured reserve with left ankle sprain (January 11, 1996-remainder of playoffs). ... Released by Cowboys (August 27, 1996). ... Signed by Pittsburgh Steelers (February 4, 1997). ... Released by Steelers (August 19, 1997). ... Signed by Cowboys (August 21, 1997). ... Released by Cowboys (August 24, 1997). ... Played with Portland Forest Dragons of Arena League (1998). ... Signed by Miami Dolphins (August 3, 1998).
PRO STATISTICS: 2000—Recovered two fumbles.
SINGLE GAME HIGHS (regular season): Receptions—9 (January 2, 2000, vs. Washington); yards—153 (December 27, 1998, vs. Atlanta); and touchdown receptions—2 (October 1, 2000, vs. Cincinnati).
STATISTICAL PLATEAUS: 100-yard receiving games: 1998 (1), 1999 (3), 2000 (1). Total: 5.

			RECEIVING					TOTALS		
Year Team	G	GS	No.	Yds.	Avg.	TD	TD	2pt.	Pts.	Fum.
1995—Dallas NFL						Did not play.				
1996—						Did not play.				
1997—						Did not play.				
1998—Miami NFL	16	12	48	713	14.9	7	7	0	42	2
1999—Miami NFL	16	7	48	803	16.7	6	6	0	36	0
2000—Miami NFL	16	16	56	786	14.0	6	6	0	36	0
Pro totals (3 years)	48	35	152	2302	15.1	19	19	0	114	2

GALLOWAY, JOEY   WR   COWBOYS

PERSONAL: Born November 20, 1971, in Bellaire, Ohio. ... 5-11/188.
HIGH SCHOOL: Bellaire (Ohio).
COLLEGE: Ohio State (degree in business/marketing, 1994).

F

G

TRANSACTIONS/CAREER NOTES: Selected by Seattle Seahawks in first round (eighth pick overall) of 1995 NFL draft. ... Signed by Seahawks (July 20, 1995). ... On did not report list (September 4-November 9, 1999). ... Designated by Seahawks as franchise player (February 11, 2000). ... Traded by Seahawks to Dallas Cowboys for first-round pick (RB Shaun Alexander) in 2000 draft and first round pick (traded to San Francisco) in 2001 draft (February 12, 2000). ... On injured reserve with knee injury (September 8, 2000-remainder of season).

PRO STATISTICS: 1995—Returned two kickoffs for 30 yards. 1997—Recovered one fumble.

SINGLE GAME HIGHS (regular season): Receptions—8 (November 2, 1997, vs. Denver); yards—142 (September 6, 1998, vs. Philadelphia); and touchdown receptions—3 (October 26, 1997, vs. Oakland).

STATISTICAL PLATEAUS: 100-yard receiving games: 1995 (3), 1996 (2), 1997 (3), 1998 (4). Total: 12.

			RUSHING				RECEIVING				PUNT RETURNS				TOTALS			
Year Team	G	GS	Att.	Yds.	Avg.	TD	No.	Yds.	Avg.	TD	No.	Yds.	Avg.	TD	TD	2pt.	Pts.	Fum.
1995—Seattle NFL	16	16	11	154	14.0	1	67	1039	15.5	7	36	360	10.0	†1	9	0	54	1
1996—Seattle NFL	16	16	15	127	8.5	0	57	987	17.3	7	15	158	10.5	▲1	8	0	48	2
1997—Seattle NFL	15	15	9	72	8.0	0	72	1049	14.6 ▲	12	0	0	0.0	0	12	0	72	1
1998—Seattle NFL	16	16	9	26	2.9	0	65	1047	16.1 ▲	10	25	251	10.0	†2	12	0	72	1
1999—Seattle NFL	8	4	1	-1	-1.0	0	22	335	15.2	1	3	54	18.0	0	1	0	6	0
2000—Dallas NFL	1	1	0	0	0.0	0	4	62	15.5	1	1	2	2.0	0	1	0	6	0
Pro totals (6 years)	72	68	45	378	8.4	1	287	4519	15.7	38	80	825	10.3	4	43	0	258	5

GALYON, SCOTT　　　　LB　　　　DOLPHINS

PERSONAL: Born March 23, 1974, in Seymour, Tenn. ... 6-2/245. ... Name pronounced GAL-yun.
HIGH SCHOOL: Seymour (Tenn.).
COLLEGE: Tennessee.
TRANSACTIONS/CAREER NOTES: Selected by New York Giants in sixth round (182nd pick overall) of 1996 NFL draft. ... Signed by Giants (July 17, 1996). ... On injured reserve with knee injury (December 8, 1998-remainder of season). ... Granted free agency (February 12, 1999). ... Re-signed by Giants (May 3, 1999). ... Granted unconditional free agency (February 11, 2000). ... Signed by Miami Dolphins (February 25, 2000). ... On injured reserve with knee injury (October 11, 2000-remainder of season).
PLAYING EXPERIENCE: New York Giants NFL, 1996-1999; Miami NFL, 2000. ... Games/Games started: 1996 (16/0), 1997 (16/0), 1998 (10/1), 1999 (16/0), 2000 (6/1). Total: 64/2.
PRO STATISTICS: 1997—Credited with three sacks. 1998—Credited with one sack and recovered one fumble. 1999—Credited with one sack.

GAMBLE, TRENT　　　　S　　　　DOLPHINS

PERSONAL: Born July 24, 1977, in Denver. ... 5-9/195. ... Full name: Trent Ashford Gamble.
HIGH SCHOOL: Ponderosa (Parker, Colo.).
COLLEGE: Wyoming (degree in finance).
TRANSACTIONS/CAREER NOTES: Signed as non-drafted free agent by Miami Dolphins (April 25, 2000).
PLAYING EXPERIENCE: Miami NFL, 2000. ... Games/Games started: 2000 (16/0).
PRO STATISTICS: 2000—Recovered one fumble.

GAMMON, KENDALL　　　　TE　　　　CHIEFS

PERSONAL: Born October 23, 1968, in Wichita, Kan. ... 6-4/258. ... Full name: Kendall Robert Gammon.
HIGH SCHOOL: Rose Hill (Kan.).
COLLEGE: Pittsburg (Kan.) State (degree in physical education).
TRANSACTIONS/CAREER NOTES: Selected by Pittsburgh Steelers in 11th round (291st pick overall) of 1992 NFL draft. ... Signed by Steelers (July 14, 1992). ... Released by Steelers (August 30, 1993). ... Re-signed by Steelers (August 31, 1993). ... Granted unconditional free agency (February 17, 1995). ... Re-signed by Steelers (May 8, 1995). ... Released by Steelers (August 26, 1996). ... Signed by New Orleans Saints (August 28, 1996). ... Granted unconditional free agency (February 11, 2000). ... Signed by Kansas City Chiefs (February 23, 2000).
PLAYING EXPERIENCE: Pittsburgh NFL, 1992-1995; New Orleans NFL, 1996-1999; Kansas City NFL, 2000. ... Games/Games started: 1992 (16/0), 1993 (16/0), 1994 (16/0), 1995 (16/0), 1996 (16/0), 1997 (16/0), 1998 (16/0), 1999 (16/0), 2000 (16/0). Total: 144/0.
CHAMPIONSHIP GAME EXPERIENCE: Played in AFC championship game (1994 and 1995 seasons). ... Played in Super Bowl XXX (1995 season).
PRO STATISTICS: 1999—Returned one kickoff for nine yards.

GANDY, WAYNE　　　　OT　　　　STEELERS

PERSONAL: Born February 10, 1971, in Haines City, Fla. ... 6-5/310. ... Full name: Wayne Lamar Gandy.
HIGH SCHOOL: Haines City (Fla.).
COLLEGE: Auburn.
TRANSACTIONS/CAREER NOTES: Selected by Los Angeles Rams in first round (15th pick overall) of 1994 NFL draft. ... Signed by Rams (July 23, 1994). ... Rams franchise moved to St. Louis (April 12, 1995). ... Granted unconditional free agency (February 12, 1999). ... Signed by Pittsburgh Steelers (April 6, 1999).
PLAYING EXPERIENCE: Los Angeles Rams NFL, 1994; St. Louis NFL, 1995-1998; Pittsburgh NFL, 1999 and 2000. ... Games/Games started: 1994 (16/9), 1995 (16/16), 1996 (16/16), 1997 (16/16), 1998 (16/16), 1999 (16/16), 2000 (16/16). Total: 112/105.
HONORS: Named offensive lineman on THE SPORTING NEWS college All-America first team (1993).
PRO STATISTICS: 2000—Recovered one fumble.

GANNON, RICH　　　　QB　　　　RAIDERS

PERSONAL: Born December 20, 1965, in Philadelphia. ... 6-3/210. ... Full name: Richard Joseph Gannon.
HIGH SCHOOL: St. Joseph's Prep (Philadelphia).
COLLEGE: Delaware (degree in criminal justice, 1987).

G

TRANSACTIONS/CAREER NOTES: Selected by New England Patriots in fourth round (98th pick overall) of 1987 NFL draft. ... Rights traded by Patriots to Minnesota Vikings for fourth- (WR Sammy Martin) and 11th-round (traded) picks in 1988 draft (May 6, 1987). ... Signed by Vikings (July 30, 1987). ... Active for 13 games (1989); did not play. ... Granted free agency (February 1, 1990). ... Re-signed by Vikings (July 30, 1990). ... Granted free agency (February 1, 1991). ... Re-signed by Vikings (July 25, 1991). ... Granted free agency (February 1, 1992). ... Re-signed by Vikings (August 8, 1992). ... Traded by Vikings to Washington Redskins for conditional draft pick (August 20, 1993). ... Granted unconditional free agency (February 17, 1994). ... Signed by Kansas City Chiefs (March 29, 1995). ... Released by Chiefs (February 15, 1996). ... Re-signed by Chiefs (April 3, 1996). ... Granted unconditional free agency (February 12, 1999). ... Signed by Oakland Raiders (February 16, 1999).
CHAMPIONSHIP GAME EXPERIENCE: Member of Vikings for NFC championship game (1987 season); did not play. ... Played in AFC championship game (2000 season).
HONORS: Played in Pro Bowl (1999 and 2000 seasons). ... Named quarterback on THE SPORTING NEWS NFL All-Pro team (2000). ... Named Outstanding Player of Pro Bowl (2000).
PRO STATISTICS: 1990—Recovered six fumbles for minus three yards. 1991—Caught one pass for no yards. 1993—Recovered one fumble. 1996—Fumbled once. 1997—Fumbled five times. 1998—Fumbled nine times and recovered four fumbles for minus 15 yards. 1999—Caught one pass for minus three yards, fumbled eight times and recovered one fumble for minus five yards. 2000—Fumbled nine times and recovered two fumbles for minus one yard.
SINGLE GAME HIGHS (regular season): Attempts—63 (October 20, 1991, vs. New England); completions—35 (October 20, 1991, vs. New England); yards—382 (November 13, 2000, vs. Denver); and touchdown passes—5 (December 24, 2000, vs. Carolina).
STATISTICAL PLATEAUS: 300-yard passing games: 1991 (1), 1992 (1), 1997 (1), 1998 (1), 1999 (2), 2000 (2). Total: 8.
MISCELLANEOUS: Regular-season record as starting NFL quarterback: 51-39 (.567). ... Postseason record as starting NFL quarterback: 1-1 (.500).

Year Team	G	GS	PASSING								RUSHING				TOTALS		
			Att.	Cmp.	Pct.	Yds.	TD	Int.	Avg.	Rat.	Att.	Yds.	Avg.	TD	TD	2pt.	Pts.
1987—Minnesota NFL	4	0	6	2	33.3	18	0	1	3.00	2.8	0	0	0.0	0	0	0	0
1988—Minnesota NFL	3	0	15	7	46.7	90	0	0	6.00	66.0	4	29	7.3	0	0	0	0
1989—Minnesota NFL								Did not play.									
1990—Minnesota NFL	14	12	349	182	52.1	2278	16	16	6.53	68.9	52	268	5.2	1	1	0	6
1991—Minnesota NFL	15	11	354	211	59.6	2166	12	6	6.12	81.5	43	236	5.5	2	2	0	12
1992—Minnesota NFL	12	12	279	159	57.0	1905	12	13	6.83	72.9	45	187	4.2	0	0	0	0
1993—Washington NFL	8	4	125	74	59.2	704	3	7	5.63	59.6	21	88	4.2	1	1	0	6
1994—								Did not play.									
1995—Kansas City NFL	2	0	11	7	63.6	57	0	0	5.18	76.7	8	25	3.1	1	0	0	0
1996—Kansas City NFL	4	3	90	54	60.0	491	6	1	5.46	92.4	12	81	6.8	0	0	0	0
1997—Kansas City NFL	9	6	175	98	56.0	1144	7	4	6.54	79.8	33	109	3.3	2	2	0	12
1998—Kansas City NFL	12	10	354	206	58.2	2305	10	6	6.51	80.1	44	168	3.8	3	3	0	18
1999—Oakland NFL	16	16	515	304	59.0	3840	24	14	7.46	86.5	46	298	6.5	2	2	0	12
2000—Oakland NFL	16	16	473	284	60.0	3430	28	11	7.25	92.4	89	529	5.9	4	4	▲1	26
Pro totals (12 years)	115	90	2746	1588	57.8	18428	118	79	6.71	80.6	397	2018	5.1	16	15	1	92

GARCIA, FRANK　　　　C　　　　RAMS

PERSONAL: Born January 28, 1972, in Phoenix. ... 6-2/302. ... Full name: Frank Christopher Garcia.
HIGH SCHOOL: Maryvale (Phoenix).
COLLEGE: Washington.
TRANSACTIONS/CAREER NOTES: Selected by Carolina Panthers in fourth round (132nd pick overall) of 1995 NFL draft. ... Signed by Panthers (July 14, 1995). ... Granted free agency (February 13, 1998). ... Re-signed by Panthers (March 16, 1998). ... Granted unconditional free agency (March 2, 2001). ... Signed by St. Louis Rams (April 26, 2001).
PLAYING EXPERIENCE: Carolina NFL, 1995-2000. ... Games/Games started: 1995 (15/14), 1996 (14/8), 1997 (16/16), 1998 (14/14), 1999 (16/16), 2000 (16/16). Total: 91/84.
CHAMPIONSHIP GAME EXPERIENCE: Played in NFC championship game (1996 season).
PRO STATISTICS: 1995—Fumbled once and recovered one fumble for 10 yards. 1996—Recovered two fumbles. 1997—Returned one kickoff for 11 yards. 1998—Recovered two fumbles for two yards. 1999—Recovered two fumbles. 2000—Recovered one fumble.

GARCIA, JEFF　　　　QB　　　　49ERS

PERSONAL: Born February 24, 1970, in Gilroy, Calif. ... 6-1/195.
HIGH SCHOOL: Gilroy (Calif.).
JUNIOR COLLEGE: Gavilan College (Calif.).
COLLEGE: San Jose State.
TRANSACTIONS/CAREER NOTES: Signed by Calgary Stampeders of CFL (1994). ... Granted free agency (February 16, 1997). ... Re-signed by Stampeders (April 30, 1997). ... Signed as non-drafted free agent by San Francisco 49ers (February 16, 1999).
CHAMPIONSHIP GAME EXPERIENCE: Played in Grey Cup (1995). ... Member of CFL Championship team (1998). ... Named Most Valuable Player of Grey Cup, CFL championship game (1998).
HONORS: Played in Pro Bowl (2000 season).
PRO STATISTICS: 1999—Fumbled five times and recovered one fumble for minus one yard. 2000—Fumbled seven times and recovered four fumbles for minus six yards.
SINGLE GAME HIGHS (regular season): Attempts—49 (December 5, 1999, vs. Cincinnati); completions—36 (December 17, 2000, vs. Chicago); passing yards—437 (December 5, 1999, vs. Cincinnati); and touchdown passes—4 (October 15, 2000, vs. Green Bay).
STATISTICAL PLATEAUS: 300-yard passing games: 1999 (3), 2000 (6). Total: 9.
MISCELLANEOUS: Regular-season record as starting NFL quarterback: 8-18 (.308).

G

Year Team	G	GS		Att.	Cmp.	Pct.	PASSING Yds.	TD	Int.	Avg.	Rat.	RUSHING Att.	Yds.	Avg.	TD	TOTALS TD	2pt.	Pts.
1994—Calgary CFL	7	...		3	2	66.7	10	0	0	3.33	71.5	2	3	1.5	0	0	0	0
1995—Calgary CFL	18	...		364	230	63.2	3358	25	7	9.23	108.1	61	396	6.5	5	5	0	30
1996—Calgary CFL	18	...		537	315	58.7	4225	25	16	7.87	86.9	92	657	7.1	6	6	0	36
1998—Calgary CFL	18	...		554	348	62.8	4276	28	15	7.72	92.2	94	575	6.1	6	6	0	36
1999—San Francisco NFL	13	10		375	225	60.0	2544	11	11	6.78	77.9	45	231	5.1	2	2	0	12
2000—San Francisco NFL	16	16		561	‡355	63.3	4278	‡31	10	7.63	97.6	72	414	5.8	4	4	0	24
CFL totals (4 years)	61	...		1458	895	61.4	11869	78	38	8.14	94.1	249	1631	6.6	17	17	0	102
NFL totals (2 years)	29	26		936	580	62.0	6822	42	21	7.29	89.7	117	645	5.5	6	6	0	36
Pro totals (6 years)	90	...		2394	1475	61.6	18691	120	59	7.81	92.4	366	2276	6.2	23	23	0	138

GARDENER, DARYL — DT — DOLPHINS

PERSONAL: Born February 25, 1973, in Baltimore. ... 6-6/315. ... Full name: Daryl Ronald Gardener.
HIGH SCHOOL: Lawton (Okla.).
COLLEGE: Baylor.
TRANSACTIONS/CAREER NOTES: Selected by Miami Dolphins in first round (20th pick overall) of 1996 NFL draft. ... Signed by Dolphins (June 6, 1996).
PRO STATISTICS: 1996—Recovered one fumble. 1997—Recovered one fumble. 1998—Intercepted one pass for minus one yard. 1999—Recovered one fumble for 33 yards.

Year Team	G	GS	SACKS
1996—Miami NFL	16	12	1.0
1997—Miami NFL	16	16	1.5
1998—Miami NFL	16	16	1.0
1999—Miami NFL	16	15	5.0
2000—Miami NFL	10	10	2.5
Pro totals (5 years)	74	69	11.0

GARDNER, BARRY — LB — EAGLES

PERSONAL: Born December 13, 1976, in Harvey, Ill. ... 6-0/248. ... Full name: Barry Allan Gardner.
HIGH SCHOOL: Thornton (Harvey, Ill.).
COLLEGE: Northwestern.
TRANSACTIONS/CAREER NOTES: Selected by Philadelphia Eagles in second round (35th pick overall) of 1999 NFL draft. ... Signed by Eagles (July 25, 1999).
PLAYING EXPERIENCE: Philadelphia NFL, 1999 and 2000. ... Games/Games started: 1999 (16/5), 2000 (16/13). Total: 32/18.
PRO STATISTICS: 1999—Recovered one fumble for 20 yards. 2000—Credited with one sack.

GARDOCKI, CHRIS — P — BROWNS

PERSONAL: Born February 7, 1970, in Stone Mountain, Ga. ... 6-1/200. ... Full name: Christopher Allen Gardocki.
HIGH SCHOOL: Redan (Stone Mountain, Ga.).
COLLEGE: Clemson.
TRANSACTIONS/CAREER NOTES: Selected after junior season by Chicago Bears in third round (78th pick overall) of 1991 NFL draft. ... Signed by Bears (June 24, 1991). ... On injured reserve with groin injury (August 27-November 27, 1991). ... Granted unconditional free agency (February 17, 1995). ... Signed by Indianapolis Colts (February 24, 1995). ... Granted unconditional free agency (February 12, 1999). ... Signed by Cleveland Browns (February 16, 1999).
CHAMPIONSHIP GAME EXPERIENCE: Played in AFC championship game (1995 season).
HONORS: Named kicker on THE SPORTING NEWS college All-America second team (1990). ... Named punter on THE SPORTING NEWS NFL All-Pro team (1996). ... Played in Pro Bowl (1996 season).
RECORDS: Holds NFL career record for most consecutive punts without a block—726.
PRO STATISTICS: 1992—Attempted three passes with one completion for 43 yards and recovered one fumble. 1993—Attempted two passes without a completion, fumbled once and recovered one fumble. 1995—Attempted one pass without a completion.

Year Team	G	PUNTING No.	Yds.	Avg.	Net avg.	In. 20	Blk.
1991—Chicago NFL	4	0	0	0.0	.0	0	0
1992—Chicago NFL	16	79	3393	42.9	36.2	19	0
1993—Chicago NFL	16	80	3080	38.5	36.6	28	0
1994—Chicago NFL	16	76	2871	37.8	32.3	23	0
1995—Indianapolis NFL	16	63	2681	42.6	33.3	16	0
1996—Indianapolis NFL	16	68	3105	45.7	§39.0	23	0
1997—Indianapolis NFL	16	67	3034	45.3	36.2	18	0
1998—Indianapolis NFL	16	79	3583	45.4	37.1	23	0
1999—Cleveland NFL	16	§106	*4645	43.8	34.6	20	0
2000—Cleveland NFL	16	*108	*4919	45.5	37.3	25	0
Pro totals (10 years)	148	726	31311	43.1	35.9	195	0

GARNER, CHARLIE — RB — RAIDERS

PERSONAL: Born February 13, 1972, in Falls Church, Va. ... 5-9/187.
HIGH SCHOOL: Jeb Stuart (Falls Church, Va.).
JUNIOR COLLEGE: Scottsdale (Ariz.) Community College.
COLLEGE: Tennessee.

G

TRANSACTIONS/CAREER NOTES: Selected by Philadelphia Eagles in second round (42nd pick overall) of 1994 NFL draft. ... Signed by Eagles (July 18, 1994). ... Granted free agency (February 14, 1997). ... Re-signed by Eagles (June 16, 1997). ... Granted unconditional free agency (February 13, 1998). ... Re-signed by Eagles (February 23, 1998). ... On injured reserve with rib injury (December 10, 1998-remainder of season). ... Released by Eagles (April 20, 1999). ... Signed by San Francisco 49ers (July 19, 1999). ... Granted unconditional free agency (March 2, 2001). ... Signed by Oakland Raiders (April 13, 2001).

HONORS: Played in Pro Bowl (2000 season).

SINGLE GAME HIGHS (regular season): Attempts—36 (September 24, 2000, vs. Dallas); yards—201 (September 24, 2000, vs. Dallas); and rushing touchdowns—3 (October 8, 1995, vs. Washington).

STATISTICAL PLATEAUS: 100-yard rushing games: 1994 (2), 1995 (1), 1997 (1), 1998 (1), 1999 (3), 2000 (3). Total: 11. ... 100-yard receiving games: 2000 (1).

			RUSHING				RECEIVING				KICKOFF RETURNS				TOTALS		
Year Team	G	GS	Att.	Yds.	Avg.	TD	No.	Yds.	Avg.	TD	No.	Yds.	Avg.	TD	TD 2pt.	Pts.	Fum.
1994—Philadelphia NFL	10	8	109	399	3.7	3	8	74	9.3	0	0	0	0.0	0	3 0	18	3
1995—Philadelphia NFL	15	2	108	588	*5.4	6	10	61	6.1	0	29	590	20.3	0	6 0	36	2
1996—Philadelphia NFL	15	1	66	346	5.2	1	14	92	6.6	0	6	117	19.5	0	1 0	6	1
1997—Philadelphia NFL	16	2	116	547	4.7	3	24	225	9.4	0	0	0	0.0	0	3 0	18	1
1998—Philadelphia NFL	10	3	96	381	4.0	4	19	110	5.8	0	0	0	0.0	0	4 0	24	1
1999—San Francisco NFL	16	15	241	1229	5.1	4	56	535	9.6	2	0	0	0.0	0	6 0	36	4
2000—San Francisco NFL	16	15	258	1142	4.4	7	68	647	9.5	3	0	0	0.0	0	10 0	60	4
Pro totals (7 years)	98	46	994	4632	4.7	28	199	1744	8.8	5	35	707	20.2	0	33 0	198	16

GARNES, SAM   S   GIANTS

PERSONAL: Born July 12, 1974, in Bronx, N.Y. ... 6-3/225. ... Full name: Sam Aaron Garnes.

HIGH SCHOOL: DeWitt Clinton (Bronx, N.Y.).

COLLEGE: Cincinnati.

TRANSACTIONS/CAREER NOTES: Selected by New York Giants in fifth round (136th pick overall) of 1997 NFL draft. ... Signed by Giants for 1997 season. ... Granted free agency (February 11, 2000). ... Re-signed by Giants (February 12, 2000).

PRO STATISTICS: 1999—Credited with one sack. 2000—Credited with one sack.

			INTERCEPTIONS			
Year Team	G	GS	No.	Yds.	Avg.	TD
1997—New York Giants NFL	16	15	1	95	95.0	1
1998—New York Giants NFL	11	11	1	13	13.0	0
1999—New York Giants NFL	16	16	2	7	3.5	0
2000—New York Giants NFL	15	15	1	4	4.0	0
Pro totals (4 years)	58	57	5	119	23.8	1

GARRETT, JASON   QB   GIANTS

PERSONAL: Born March 28, 1966, in Abington, Pa. ... 6-2/200. ... Full name: Jason Calvin Garrett. ... Son of Jim Garrett, scout, Dallas Cowboys; brother of John Garrett, wide receiver with Cincinnati Bengals (1989) and San Antonio Riders of World League (1991); and brother of Judd Garrett, running back with London of World League (1991-92).

HIGH SCHOOL: University (Chargin Falls, Ohio).

COLLEGE: Princeton (degree in history).

TRANSACTIONS/CAREER NOTES: Signed as non-drafted free agent by New Orleans Saints (1989). ... Released by Saints (August 30, 1989). ... Re-signed by Saints to developmental squad (September 6, 1989). ... Released by Saints (December 29, 1989). ... Re-signed by Saints for 1990 season. ... Released by Saints (September 3, 1990). ... Signed by WLAF (January 3, 1991). ... Selected by San Antonio Riders in first round (seventh quarterback) of 1991 WLAF positional draft. ... Signed by Ottawa Rough Riders of CFL (1991). ... Released by San Antonio Riders (March 3, 1992). ... Signed by Dallas Cowboys (March 23, 1992). ... Released by Cowboys (August 31, 1992). ... Re-signed by Cowboys to practice squad (September 1, 1992). ... Granted unconditional free agency (February 16, 1996). ... Re-signed by Cowboys (April 3, 1996). ... Granted unconditional free agency (February 14, 1997). ... Re-signed by Cowboys (April 8, 1997). ... Granted unconditional free agency (February 11, 2000). ... Signed by New York Giants (February 22, 2000).

CHAMPIONSHIP GAME EXPERIENCE: Member of Cowboys for NFC championship game (1993-1995 seasons); inactive. ... Member of Super Bowl championship team (1993 and 1995 seasons). ... Played in NFC championship game (2000 season). ... Member of Giants for Super Bowl XXXV (2000 season); did not play.

PRO STATISTICS: W.L.: 1991—Fumbled twice. CFL: 1991—Fumbled once. NFL: 1993—Fumbled once. 1994—Recovered one fumble. 1998—Fumbled four times for minus 17 yards.

SINGLE GAME HIGHS (regular season): Attempts—33 (September 27, 1998, vs. Oakland); completions—18 (September 27, 1998, vs. Oakland); yards—311 (November 24, 1994, vs. Green Bay); and touchdown passes—2 (November 14, 1999, vs. Green Bay).

STATISTICAL PLATEAUS: 300-yard passing games: 1994 (1).

MISCELLANEOUS: Regular-season record as starting NFL quarterback: 6-3 (.667).

			PASSING								RUSHING				TOTALS		
Year Team	G	GS	Att.	Cmp.	Pct.	Yds.	TD	Int.	Avg.	Rat.	Att.	Yds.	Avg.	TD	TD	2pt.	Pts.
1991—San Antonio W.L.	5	3	113	66	58.4	609	3	3	5.39	71.0	7	7	1.0	0	0	0	0
—Ottawa CFL	13	0	3	2	66.7	28	0	0	9.33	96.5	0	0	0.0	0	0	0	0
1992—Dallas NFL							Did not play.										
1993—Dallas NFL	5	1	19	9	47.4	61	0	0	3.21	54.9	8	-8	-1.0	0	0	0	0
1994—Dallas NFL	2	1	31	16	51.6	315	2	1	10.16	95.5	3	-2	-0.7	0	0	0	0
1995—Dallas NFL	1	0	5	4	80.0	46	1	0	9.20	144.6	1	-1	-1.0	0	0	0	0
1996—Dallas NFL	1	0	3	3	100.0	44	0	0	14.67	118.8	0	0	0.0	0	0	0	0
1997—Dallas NFL	1	0	14	10	71.4	56	0	0	4.00	78.3	0	0	0.0	0	0	0	0
1998—Dallas NFL	8	5	158	91	57.6	1206	5	3	7.63	84.5	11	14	1.3	0	0	0	0
1999—Dallas NFL	9	2	64	32	50.0	314	3	1	4.91	73.3	6	12	2.0	0	0	0	0
2000—N.Y. Giants NFL	2	0	0	0	0.0	0	0	0	0.0	...	4	-4	-1.0	0	0	0	0
W.L. totals (1 year)	5	3	113	66	58.4	609	3	3	5.39	71.0	7	7	1.0	0	0	0	0
CFL totals (1 year)	13	0	3	2	66.7	28	0	0	9.33	96.5	0	0	0.0	0	0	0	0
NFL totals (8 years)	29	9	294	165	56.1	2042	11	5	6.95	83.2	33	11	0.3	0	0	0	0
Pro totals (10 years)	47	12	410	233	56.8	2679	14	8	6.53	79.9	40	18	0.5	0	0	0	0

G

GARY, OLANDIS　　　　RB　　　　BRONCOS

PERSONAL: Born May 18, 1975, in Washington, D.C. ... 5-11/218. ... Full name: Olandis C. Gary.
HIGH SCHOOL: Riverdale Baptist (Upper Marlboro, Md.).
COLLEGE: Marshall, then Georgia.
TRANSACTIONS/CAREER NOTES: Selected by Denver Broncos in fourth round (127th pick overall) of 1999 NFL draft. ... Signed by Broncos (July 20, 1999). ... On injured reserve with knee injury (September 8, 2000-remainder of season).
PRO STATISTICS: 1999—Recovered one fumble.
SINGLE GAME HIGHS (regular season): Attempts—37 (October 17, 1999, vs. Green Bay); yards—185 (December 25, 1999, vs. Detroit); and rushing touchdowns—2 (November 7, 1999, vs. San Diego).
STATISTICAL PLATEAUS: 100-yard rushing games: 1999 (4).

Year　Team	G	GS	RUSHING				RECEIVING				TOTALS			
			Att.	Yds.	Avg.	TD	No.	Yds.	Avg.	TD	TD	2pt.	Pts.	Fum.
1999—Denver NFL	12	12	276	1159	4.2	7	21	159	7.6	0	7	†1	44	2
2000—Denver NFL	1	0	13	80	6.2	0	3	10	3.3	0	0	0	0	0
Pro totals (2 years)	13	12	289	1239	4.3	7	24	169	7.0	0	7	1	44	2

GASH, SAM　　　　FB

PERSONAL: Born March 7, 1969, in Hendersonville, N.C. ... 6-0/235. ... Full name: Samuel Lee Gash Jr. ... Cousin of Thane Gash, safety with Cleveland Browns (1988-90) and San Francisco 49ers (1992).
HIGH SCHOOL: Hendersonville (N.C.).
COLLEGE: Penn State (degree in liberal arts).
TRANSACTIONS/CAREER NOTES: Selected by New England Patriots in eighth round (205th pick overall) of 1992 NFL draft. ... Signed by Patriots (June 10, 1992). ... Granted free agency (February 17, 1995). ... Re-signed by Patriots (May 5, 1995). ... On injured reserve with knee injury (December 10, 1996-remainder of season). ... Granted unconditional free agency (February 13, 1998). ... Signed by Buffalo Bills (March 5, 1998). ... Released by Bills (April 14, 2000). ... Signed by Baltimore Ravens (August 7, 2000). ... Granted unconditional free agency (March 2, 2001).
CHAMPIONSHIP GAME EXPERIENCE: Played in AFC championship game (2000 season). ... Member of Super Bowl championship team (2000 season).
HONORS: Played in Pro Bowl (1998 and 1999 seasons).
PRO STATISTICS: 1992—Recovered two fumbles. 1994—Returned one kickoff for nine yards and recovered one fumble. 1998—Returned three kickoffs for 41 yards. 1999—Returned one kickoff for 13 yards and recovered one fumble.
SINGLE GAME HIGHS (regular season): Attempts—15 (December 18, 1994, vs. Buffalo); yards—56 (December 18, 1994, vs. Buffalo); and rushing touchdowns—1 (September 19, 1993, vs. Seattle).

Year　Team	G	GS	RUSHING				RECEIVING				TOTALS			
			Att.	Yds.	Avg.	TD	No.	Yds.	Avg.	TD	TD	2pt.	Pts.	Fum.
1992—New England NFL	15	0	5	7	1.4	1	0	0	0.0	0	1	0	6	1
1993—New England NFL	15	4	48	149	3.1	1	14	93	6.6	0	1	0	6	1
1994—New England NFL	13	6	30	86	2.9	0	9	61	6.8	0	0	0	0	1
1995—New England NFL	15	12	8	24	3.0	0	26	242	9.3	1	1	0	6	0
1996—New England NFL	14	9	8	15	1.9	0	33	276	8.4	2	2	1	14	0
1997—New England NFL	16	5	6	10	1.7	0	22	154	7.0	3	3	0	18	0
1998—Buffalo NFL	16	13	11	32	2.9	0	19	165	8.7	3	3	0	18	0
1999—Buffalo NFL	15	11	0	0	0.0	0	20	163	8.2	2	2	0	12	0
2000—Baltimore NFL	15	4	2	2	1.0	0	6	30	5.0	1	1	0	6	0
Pro totals (9 years)	134	64	118	325	2.8	2	149	1184	7.9	12	14	1	86	3

GAYLOR, TREVOR　　　　WR　　　　CHARGERS

PERSONAL: Born November 3, 1977, in St. Louis. ... 6-3/195. ... Full name: Trevor Alexander Gaylor.
HIGH SCHOOL: Hazelwood (Mo.) West.
COLLEGE: Miami of Ohio.
TRANSACTIONS/CAREER NOTES: Selected by San Diego Chargers in fourth round (111th pick overall) of 2000 NFL draft. ... Signed by Chargers (July 20, 2000).
PRO STATISTICS: 2000—Recovered one fumble for 13 yards.
SINGLE GAME HIGHS (regular season): Receptions—4 (September 10, 2000, vs. New Orleans); yards—62 (November 1, 2000, vs. St. Louis); and touchdown receptions—1 (November 1, 2000, vs. St. Louis).

Year　Team	G	GS	RECEIVING			
			No.	Yds.	Avg.	TD
2000—San Diego NFL	14	2	13	182	14.0	1

GBAJA-BIAMILA, KABEER　　　　DE　　　　PACKERS

PERSONAL: Born September 24, 1977, in Los Angeles. ... 6-4/245. ... Full name: Muhammed-Kabeer Olarewaja Gbaja-Biamila.
HIGH SCHOOL: Crenshaw (Los Angeles).
COLLEGE: San Diego State.
TRANSACTIONS/CAREER NOTES: Selected by Green Bay Packers in fifth round (149th pick overall) of 2000 NFL draft. ... Signed by Packers (July 17, 2000). ... Released by Packers (August 27, 2000). ... Re-signed by Packers to practice squad (August 28, 2000). ... Activated (October 10, 2000).

Year　Team	G	GS	SACKS
2000—Green Bay NFL	7	0	1.5

G

GEASON, COREY   TE   STEELERS

PERSONAL: Born August 12, 1975, in St. James, La. ... 6-3/255.
HIGH SCHOOL: St. James (La.).
COLLEGE: Tulane.
TRANSACTIONS/CAREER NOTES: Signed as non-drafted free agent by Dallas Cowboys (April 21, 1998). ... Released by Cowboys (August 24, 1998). ... Signed by Tampa Bay Buccaneers (July 14, 1999). ... Released by Buccaneers (September 5, 1999). ... Signed by Pittsburgh Steelers to practice squad (December 21, 1999). ... On injured reserve with knee injury (November 7, 2000-remainder of season).
PLAYING EXPERIENCE: Pittsburgh NFL, 2000. ... Games/Games started: 2000 (9/3).
PRO STATISTICS: 2000—Caught three passes for 66 yards.
SINGLE GAME HIGHS (regular season): Receptions—1 (November 5, 2000, vs. Tennessee); yards—36 (September 24, 2000, vs. Tennessee); and touchdown receptions—0.

GEDNEY, CHRIS   TE

PERSONAL: Born August 9, 1970, in Liverpool, N.Y. ... 6-5/257. ... Full name: Christopher Joseph Gedney.
HIGH SCHOOL: Liverpool (N.Y.).
COLLEGE: Syracuse (degree in speech communications, 1993).
TRANSACTIONS/CAREER NOTES: Selected by Chicago Bears in third round (61st pick overall) of 1993 NFL draft. ... Signed by Bears (June 16, 1994). ... On injured reserve with broken fibula (October 24, 1994-remainder of season). ... Granted free agency (February 16, 1996). ... Re-signed by Bears (March 29, 1996). ... On injured reserve with ankle injury (September 20, 1996-entire season). ... Granted unconditional free agency (February 14, 1997). ... Signed by Arizona Cardinals (February 28, 1997). ... Granted unconditional free agency (February 13, 1998). ... Re-signed by Cardinals (February 24, 1998). ... Released by Cardinals (July 30, 1999). ... Re-signed by Cardinals (February 23, 2000). ... Granted unconditional free agency (March 2, 2001).
HONORS: Named tight end on THE SPORTING NEWS college All-America first team (1992).
PRO STATISTICS: 1997—Rushed once for 15 yards and returned two kickoffs for 26 yards. 1998—Returned two kickoffs for 12 yards.
SINGLE GAME HIGHS (regular season): Receptions—6 (October 25, 1993, vs. Minnesota); yards—69 (October 25, 1993, vs. Minnesota); and touchdown receptions—2 (September 4, 1994, vs. Tampa Bay).

			RECEIVING				TOTALS			
Year Team	G	GS	No.	Yds.	Avg.	TD	TD	2pt.	Pts.	Fum.
1993—Chicago NFL	7	4	10	98	9.8	0	0	0	0	1
1994—Chicago NFL	7	7	13	157	12.1	3	3	0	18	1
1995—Chicago NFL	14	1	5	52	10.4	0	0	0	0	0
1996—Chicago NFL						Did not play.				
1997—Arizona NFL	16	3	23	261	11.3	4	4	0	24	1
1998—Arizona NFL	16	3	22	271	12.3	1	1	0	6	1
2000—Arizona NFL	13	3	10	75	7.5	0	0	0	0	0
Pro totals (6 years)	73	21	83	914	11.0	8	8	0	48	4

GEORGE, EDDIE   RB   TITANS

PERSONAL: Born September 24, 1973, in Philadelphia. ... 6-3/240. ... Full name: Edward Nathan George.
HIGH SCHOOL: Abington (Philadelphia), then Fork Union (Va.) Military Academy.
COLLEGE: Ohio State.
TRANSACTIONS/CAREER NOTES: Selected by Houston Oilers in first round (14th pick overall) of 1996 NFL draft. ... Signed by Oilers (July 20, 1996). ... Oilers franchise moved to Tennessee for 1997 season. ... Oilers franchise renamed Tennessee Titans for 1999 season (December 26, 1998).
CHAMPIONSHIP GAME EXPERIENCE: Played in AFC championship game (1999 season). ... Played in Super Bowl XXXIV (1999 season).
HONORS: Heisman Trophy winner (1995). ... Maxwell Award winner (1995). ... Doak Walker Award winner (1995). ... Named running back on THE SPORTING NEWS college All-America first team (1995). ... Named NFL Rookie of the Year by THE SPORTING NEWS (1996). ... Played in Pro Bowl (1997-2000 seasons).
PRO STATISTICS: 1996—Recovered one fumble. 1998—Recovered five fumbles. 1999—Recovered one fumble. 2000—Recovered two fumbles.
SINGLE GAME HIGHS (regular season): Attempts—36 (November 19, 2000, vs. Cleveland); yards—216 (August 31, 1997, vs. Oakland); and rushing touchdowns—3 (December 17, 2000, vs. Cleveland).
STATISTICAL PLATEAUS: 100-yard rushing games: 1996 (4), 1997 (8), 1998 (6), 1999 (5), 2000 (6). Total: 29. ... 100-yard receiving games: 2000 (1).

			RUSHING				RECEIVING				TOTALS			
Year Team	G	GS	Att.	Yds.	Avg.	TD	No.	Yds.	Avg.	TD	TD	2pt.	Pts.	Fum.
1996—Houston NFL	16	16	335	1368	4.1	8	23	182	7.9	0	8	0	48	3
1997—Tennessee NFL	16	16	357	1399	3.9	6	7	44	6.3	1	7	1	44	4
1998—Tennessee NFL	16	16	348	1294	3.7	5	37	310	8.4	1	6	1	38	7
1999—Tennessee NFL	16	16	320	1304	4.1	9	47	458	9.7	4	13	0	78	5
2000—Tennessee NFL	16	16	*403	1509	3.7	14	50	453	9.1	2	16	0	96	5
Pro totals (5 years)	80	80	1763	6874	3.9	42	164	1447	8.8	8	50	2	304	24

G

GEORGE, JEFF   QB   REDSKINS

PERSONAL: Born December 8, 1967, in Indianapolis. ... 6-4/215. ... Full name: Jeffrey Scott George.
HIGH SCHOOL: Warren Central (Indianapolis).
COLLEGE: Purdue, then Illinois (degree in speech communications, 1991).
TRANSACTIONS/CAREER NOTES: Signed after junior season by Indianapolis Colts (April 20, 1990). ... Selected officially by Colts in first round (first pick overall) of 1990 NFL draft. ... On reserve/did not report list (July 23-August 20, 1993). ... Traded by Colts to Atlanta Falcons for first-(LB Trev Alberts) and third-round (OT Jason Mathews) picks in 1994 draft and a first-round pick (WR Marvin Harrison) in 1996 draft (March 24, 1994). ... Designated by Falcons as transition player (February 16, 1996). ... Released by Falcons (October 22, 1996). ... Signed by Oakland

Raiders (February 15, 1997). ... Granted unconditional free agency (February 12, 1999). ... Signed by Minnesota Vikings (April 6, 1999). ... Granted unconditional free agency (February 11, 2000). ... Signed by Washington Redskins (April 11, 2000).

PRO STATISTICS: 1990—Fumbled four times and recovered two fumbles. 1991—Fumbled eight times and recovered two fumbles for minus four yards. 1992—Fumbled six times and recovered one fumble for minus two yards. 1993—Fumbled four times. 1994—Led league with 12 fumbles and recovered six fumbles for minus 12 yards. 1995—Fumbled six times and recovered two fumbles for minus 15 yards. 1996—Fumbled three times and recovered two fumbles for minus 24 yards. 1997—Fumbled seven times and recovered three fumbles for minus 14 yards. 1998—Fumbled seven times and recovered one fumble for minus six yards. 1999—Fumbled eight times and recovered two fumbles. 2000—Fumbled three times and recovered one fumble for minus three yards.

SINGLE GAME HIGHS (regular season): Attempts—59 (November 7, 1993, vs. Washington); completions—37 (November 7, 1993, vs. Washington); yards—386 (September 17, 1995, vs. New Orleans); and touchdown passes—4 (November 28, 1999, vs. San Diego).

STATISTICAL PLATEAUS: 300-yard passing games: 1991 (2), 1992 (3), 1993 (2), 1994 (2), 1995 (3), 1997 (2), 1998 (1), 1999 (2). Total: 17.

MISCELLANEOUS: Regular-season record as starting NFL quarterback: 46-76 (.378). ... Postseason record as starting NFL quarterback: 1-2 (.333).

Year Team	G	GS	PASSING Att.	Cmp.	Pct.	Yds.	TD	Int.	Avg.	Rat.	RUSHING Att.	Yds.	Avg.	TD	TOTALS TD	2pt.	Pts.
1990—Indianapolis NFL	13	12	334	181	54.2	2152	16	13	6.44	73.8	11	2	0.2	1	1	0	6
1991—Indianapolis NFL	16	16	485	292	60.2	2910	10	12	6.00	73.8	16	36	2.3	0	0	0	0
1992—Indianapolis NFL	10	10	306	167	54.6	1963	7	15	6.42	61.5	14	26	1.9	1	1	0	6
1993—Indianapolis NFL	13	11	407	234	57.5	2526	8	6	6.21	76.3	13	39	3.0	0	0	0	0
1994—Atlanta NFL	16	16	524	322	61.5	3734	23	18	7.13	83.3	30	66	2.2	0	0	0	0
1995—Atlanta NFL	16	16	557	336	60.3	4143	24	11	7.44	89.5	27	17	0.6	0	0	0	0
1996—Atlanta NFL	3	3	99	56	56.6	698	3	3	7.05	76.1	5	10	2.0	0	0	0	0
1997—Oakland NFL	16	16	521	290	55.7	*3917	§29	9	7.52	91.2	17	44	2.6	0	0	0	0
1998—Oakland NFL	8	7	169	93	55.0	1186	4	5	7.02	72.7	8	2	0.3	0	0	0	0
1999—Minnesota NFL	12	10	329	191	58.1	2816	23	12	8.56	94.2	16	41	2.6	0	0	0	0
2000—Washington NFL	7	5	194	113	58.2	1389	7	6	7.16	79.6	7	24	3.4	0	0	0	0
Pro totals (11 years)	130	122	3925	2275	58.0	27434	154	110	6.99	80.9	164	307	1.9	2	2	0	12

GEORGE, RON   LB   CHIEFS

PERSONAL: Born March 20, 1970, in Heidelberg, West Germany. ... 6-2/247. ... Full name: Ronald L. George.

HIGH SCHOOL: Heidelberg (West Germany) American.

COLLEGE: Air Force, then Stanford (degree in economics, 1992).

TRANSACTIONS/CAREER NOTES: Selected by Atlanta Falcons in fifth round (121st pick overall) of 1993 NFL draft. ... Signed by Falcons (June 4, 1993). ... Granted free agency (February 16, 1996). ... Re-signed by Falcons (June 12, 1996). ... Granted unconditional free agency (February 14, 1997). ... Signed by Minnesota Vikings (June 9, 1997). ... Released by Vikings (February 11, 1998). ... Signed by Kansas City Chiefs (April 6, 1998).

PLAYING EXPERIENCE: Atlanta NFL, 1993-1996; Minnesota NFL, 1997; Kansas City NFL, 1998-2000. ... Games/Games started: 1993 (12/4), 1994 (16/9), 1995 (16/0), 1996 (16/15), 1997 (16/0), 1998 (16/0), 1999 (16/0), 2000 (16/0). Total: 124/28.

HONORS: Named linebacker on THE SPORTING NEWS college All-America second team (1992).

PRO STATISTICS: 1993—Credited with one sack. 1994—Recovered one fumble. 1995—Returned three kickoffs for 45 yards. 1996—Credited with two sacks and recovered three fumbles for 14 yards. 1997—Returned one kickoff for 10 yards. 1998—Recovered one fumble.

GEORGE, TONY   S   PATRIOTS

PERSONAL: Born August 10, 1975, in Cincinnati. ... 5-11/205. ... Full name: Houston Antonio George Jr.

HIGH SCHOOL: Winton Woods (Cincinnati).

COLLEGE: Florida.

TRANSACTIONS/CAREER NOTES: Selected by New England Patriots in third round (91st pick overall) of 1999 NFL draft. ... Signed by Patriots (July 28, 1999). ... Assigned by Patriots to Frankfurt Galaxy in 2001 NFL Europe enhancement allocation program (February 19, 2001).

PLAYING EXPERIENCE: New England NFL, 1999 and 2000. ... Games/Games started: 1999 (16/1), 2000 (15/0). Total: 31/1.

PRO STATISTICS: 2000—Recovered two fumbles for 24 yards.

GERMAINE, JOE   QB   RAMS

G

PERSONAL: Born August 11, 1975, in Denver. ... 6-0/220. ... Full name: Joe Berton Germaine.

HIGH SCHOOL: Mountain View (Mesa, Ariz.).

JUNIOR COLLEGE: Scottsdale (Ariz.) Community College.

COLLEGE: Ohio State.

TRANSACTIONS/CAREER NOTES: Selected by St. Louis Rams in fourth round (101st pick overall) of 1999 NFL draft. ... Signed by Rams (July 19, 1999).

CHAMPIONSHIP GAME EXPERIENCE: Member of Rams for NFC championship game (1999 season); inactive. ... Member of Super Bowl championship team (1999 season); inactive

PRO STATISTICS: 1999—Fumbled once.

SINGLE GAME HIGHS (regular season): Attempts—12 (January 2, 2000, vs. Philadelphia); completions—9 (January 2, 2000, vs. Philadelphia); passing yards—136 (January 2, 2000, vs. Philadelphia); and touchdown passes—1 (January 2, 1999, vs. Philadelphia).

MISCELLANEOUS: Selected by Colorado Rockies organization in 25th round of free-agent baseball draft (June 2, 1994); did not sign.

Year Team	G	GS	PASSING Att.	Cmp.	Pct.	Yds.	TD	Int.	Avg.	Rat.	RUSHING Att.	Yds.	Avg.	TD	TOTALS TD	2pt.	Pts.
1999—St. Louis NFL	3	0	16	9	56.3	136	1	2	8.50	65.6	3	0	0.0	0	0	0	0
2000—St. Louis NFL							Did not play.										
Pro totals (1 years)	3	0	16	9	56.3	136	1	2	8.50	65.6	3	0	0.0	0	0	0	0

GERMAN, JAMMI — WR — FALCONS

PERSONAL: Born July 4, 1974, in Fort Myers, Fla. ... 6-1/191. ... Full name: Jammi Darnell German.
HIGH SCHOOL: Fort Myers (Fla.).
COLLEGE: Miami (Fla.).
TRANSACTIONS/CAREER NOTES: Selected by Atlanta Falcons in third round (74th pick overall) of 1998 NFL draft. ... Signed by Falcons (July 8, 1998). ... On injured reserve with knee injury (November 10, 1998-remainder of season). ... Released by Falcons (September 5, 1999). ... Re-signed by Falcons to practice squad (September 7, 1999). ... Activated (September 14, 1999). ... On injured reserve with ankle injury (December 13, 2000-remainder of season). ... Granted free agency (March 2, 2001). ... Re-signed by Falcons (April 5, 2001).
PLAYING EXPERIENCE: Atlanta NFL, 1998-2000. ... Games/Games started: 1998 (6/0), 1999 (14/0), 2000 (9/0). Total: 29/0.
PRO STATISTICS: 1999—Caught 12 passes for 219 yards and three touchdowns and returned one kickoff for one yard. 2000—Caught one pass for 10 yards.
SINGLE GAME HIGHS (regular season): Receptions—3 (December 19, 1999, vs. Seattle); yards—62 (October 10, 1999, vs. New Orleans); and touchdown receptions—2 (December 19, 1999, vs. Tennessee).

GIBSON, AARON — OT — LIONS

PERSONAL: Born September 27, 1977, in Indianapolis. ... 6-4/380.
HIGH SCHOOL: Decatur Central (Indianapolis).
COLLEGE: Wisconsin.
TRANSACTIONS/CAREER NOTES: Selected by Detroit Lions in first round (27th pick overall) of 1999 NFL draft. ... Signed by Lions (July 24, 1999). ... On injured reserve with shoulder injury (August 31, 1999-entire season). ... On injured reserve with shoulder injury (December 4, 2000-remainder of season).
PLAYING EXPERIENCE: Detroit NFL, 2000. ... Games/Games started: 2000 (10/10).
HONORS: Named offensive tackle on THE SPORTING NEWS college All-America second team (1998).

GIBSON, DAVID — S — BUCCANEERS

PERSONAL: Born November 5, 1977, in Santa Ana, Calif. ... 6-1/210.
HIGH SCHOOL: Mater Dei (Santa, Ana, Calif.).
COLLEGE: Southern California.
TRANSACTIONS/CAREER NOTES: Selected by Tampa Bay Buccaneers in sixth round (193rd pick overall) of 2000 NFL draft. ... Signed by Buccaneers (July 10, 2000).
PLAYING EXPERIENCE: Tampa Bay NFL, 2000. ... Games/Games started: 2000 (9/0).

GIBSON, OLIVER — DT — BENGALS

PERSONAL: Born March 15, 1972, in Chicago. ... 6-2/315. ... Full name: Oliver Donnovan Gibson. ... Cousin of Godfrey Myles, linebacker with Dallas Cowboys (1991-96).
HIGH SCHOOL: Romeoville (Ill.).
COLLEGE: Notre Dame (degree in economics, 1994).
TRANSACTIONS/CAREER NOTES: Selected by Pittsburgh Steelers in fourth round (120th pick overall) of 1995 NFL draft. ... Signed by Steelers (July 18, 1995). ... Re-signed by Steelers (June 9, 1998). ... Granted unconditional free agency (February 12, 1999). ... Signed by Cincinnati Bengals (March 9, 1999).
CHAMPIONSHIP GAME EXPERIENCE: Member of Steelers for AFC championship game (1995 season); inactive. ... Played in AFC championship game (1997 season).
HONORS: Earned first-team All-Independent honors from The Sporting News (1994).
PRO STATISTICS: 1995—Returned one kickoff for 10 yards. 1997—Recovered one fumble. 1998—Returned one kickoff for nine yards. 1999—Recovered one fumble.

Year Team	G	GS	SACKS
1995—Pittsburgh NFL	12	0	0.0
1996—Pittsburgh NFL	16	0	2.5
1997—Pittsburgh NFL	16	0	1.0
1998—Pittsburgh NFL	16	0	2.0
1999—Cincinnati NFL	16	16	4.5
2000—Cincinnati NFL	16	16	4.0
Pro totals (6 years)	92	32	14.0

GILBERT, SEAN — DT — PANTHERS

PERSONAL: Born April 10, 1970, in Aliquippa, Pa. ... 6-5/318.
HIGH SCHOOL: Aliquippa (Pa.).
COLLEGE: Pittsburgh.
TRANSACTIONS/CAREER NOTES: Selected after junior season by Los Angeles Rams in first round (third pick overall) of 1992 NFL draft. ... Signed by Rams (July 28, 1992). ... Designated by Rams as transition player (February 25, 1993). ... Rams franchise moved to St. Louis (April 12, 1995). ... Traded by Rams to Washington Redskins for first-round pick (RB Lawrence Phillips) in 1996 draft (April 8, 1996). ... Designated by Redskins as franchise player (February 12, 1997). ... Sat out 1997 season due to contract dispute. ... Designated by Redskins as franchise player (February 11, 1998). ... Tendered offer sheet by Carolina Panthers (March 24, 1998). ... Redskins declined to match offer (April 21, 1998).
HONORS: Played in Pro Bowl (1993 season).
PRO STATISTICS: 1992—Recovered one fumble. 1994—Credited with one safety. 1995—Recovered one fumble. 1999—Intercepted one pass for four yards. 2000—Intercepted one pass for no yards and recovered one fumble.

G

Year	Team	G	GS	SACKS
1992—Los Angeles Rams NFL		16	16	5.0
1993—Los Angeles Rams NFL		16	16	10.5
1994—Los Angeles Rams NFL		14	14	3.0
1995—St. Louis NFL		14	14	5.5
1996—Washington NFL		16	16	3.0
1997—Washington NFL		Did not play.		
1998—Carolina NFL		16	16	6.0
1999—Carolina NFL		16	16	2.5
2000—Carolina NFL		15	15	4.0
Pro totals (8 years)		**123**	**123**	**39.5**

GILDON, JASON   LB   STEELERS

PERSONAL: Born July 31, 1972, in Altus, Okla. ... 6-3/255. ... Full name: Jason Larue Gildon. ... Related to Wendall Gaines, guard with Arizona Cardinals (1995).
HIGH SCHOOL: Altus (Okla.).
COLLEGE: Oklahoma State.
TRANSACTIONS/CAREER NOTES: Selected by Pittsburgh Steelers in third round (88th pick overall) of 1994 NFL draft. ... Signed by Steelers (July 15, 1994). ... Granted free agency (February 14, 1997). ... Re-signed by Steelers (July 21, 1997). ... Granted unconditional free agency (February 13, 1998). ... Re-signed by Steelers (April 7, 1998).
CHAMPIONSHIP GAME EXPERIENCE: Played in AFC championship game (1994, 1995 and 1997 seasons). ... Played in Super Bowl XXX (1995 season).
HONORS: Played in Pro Bowl (2000 season).
PRO STATISTICS: 1995—Recovered one fumble. 1997—Recovered two fumbles for 32 yards and one touchdown. 1998—Recovered one fumble. 2000—Recovered four fumbles for 22 yards and one touchdown.

Year	Team	G	GS	SACKS
1994—Pittsburgh NFL		16	1	2.0
1995—Pittsburgh NFL		16	0	3.0
1996—Pittsburgh NFL		14	13	7.0
1997—Pittsburgh NFL		16	16	5.0
1998—Pittsburgh NFL		16	16	11.0
1999—Pittsburgh NFL		16	16	8.5
2000—Pittsburgh NFL		16	16	13.5
Pro totals (7 years)		**110**	**78**	**50.0**

GILMORE, BRYAN   WR   CARDINALS

PERSONAL: Born July 21, 1978, in Lufkin, Texas. ... 6-0/194.
HIGH SCHOOL: Lufkin (Texas).
COLLEGE: Midwestern State (Texas).
TRANSACTIONS/CAREER NOTES: Signed as non-drafted free agent by Arizona Cardinals (April 17, 2000). ... Released by Cardinals (August 27, 2000). ... Re-signed by Cardinals to practice squad (August 28, 2000). ... Activated (December 15, 2000).
PLAYING EXPERIENCE: Arizona NFL, 2000. ... Games/Games started: 2000 (1/0).

GIVENS, REGGIE   LB

PERSONAL: Born October 3, 1971, in Emporia, Va. ... 6-0/234. ... Full name: Reginald Alonzo Givens.
HIGH SCHOOL: Sussex (Va.) Central.
COLLEGE: Penn State.
TRANSACTIONS/CAREER NOTES: Selected by Dallas Cowboys in eighth round (213rd pick overall) of 1993 NFL draft. ... Signed by Cowboys (July 15, 1993). ... Released by Cowboys (August 30, 1993). ... Signed by Chicago Bears (April 20, 1994). ... Released by Bears (August 18, 1994). ... Signed by Winnipeg Blue Bombers of CFL (October 1994). ... Released by Blue Bombers (July 11, 1995). ... Signed by Baltimore Stallions of CFL (August 9, 1995). ... Transferred to Saskatchewan Roughriders of CFL (May 16, 1996). ... Released by Roughriders (June 3, 1996). ... Signed by Toronto Argonauts of CFL (June 6, 1996). ... Granted free agency (February 16, 1998). ... Signed by San Francisco 49ers (March 12, 1998). ... Granted free agency (February 11, 2000). ... Signed by Washington Redskins (April 7, 2000). ... Released by Redskins (November 9, 2000).
PLAYING EXPERIENCE: Winnipeg CFL, 1994; Winnipeg (1)-Baltimore (4) CFL, 1995; Toronto CFL, 1996 and 1997; San Francisco NFL, 1998 and 1999; Washington NFL, 2000. ... Games/Games started: 1994 (4/games started unavailable), 1995 (Win.-1/-; Bal.-4/-; Total: 5/-), 1996 (18/-), 1997 (18/-), 1998 (16/0), 1999 (16/0), 2000 (9/0). Total CFL: 45/-. Total NFL: 41/0. Total Pro: 86/-.
PRO STATISTICS: CFL: 1994—Intercepted one pass for no yards and credited with two sacks. 1996—Rushed once for one yard, intercepted one pass for no yards, credited with eight sacks, fumbled once and recovered four fumbles. 1997—Intercepted one pass for six yards, credited with six sacks and recovered two fumbles for 182 yards and two touchdowns. 1999—Returned one punt for no yards and fumbled once.

G

GIZZI, CHRIS   LB   PACKERS

PERSONAL: Born March 8, 1975, in Brunswick, Ohio. ... 6-0/235.
HIGH SCHOOL: St. Ignatius (Cleveland).
COLLEGE: Air Force.
TRANSACTIONS/CAREER NOTES: Signed as non-drafted free agent by Denver Broncos (April 23, 1998). ... On military reserved list (June 10, 1998-entire season). ... On military reserved list (August 31, 1999-entire season). ... Claimed on waivers by Green Bay Packers (August 28, 2000). ... Released by Packers (October 3, 2000). ... Re-signed by Packers to practice squad (October 5, 2000). ... Activated (October 9, 2000).
PLAYING EXPERIENCE: Green Bay NFL, 2000. ... Games/Games started: 2000 (11/0).

GLEASON, STEVE   DB   SAINTS

PERSONAL: Born March 19, 1977, in Gonzaga, Calif. ... 5-11/215. ... Full name: Stephen Gleason.
HIGH SCHOOL: Gonzaga Prep (Spokane, Wash.).
COLLEGE: Washington State.
TRANSACTIONS/CAREER NOTES: Signed as non-drafted free agent by Indianapolis Colts (April 16, 2000). ... Released by Colts (August 27, 2000). ... Signed by New Orleans Saints to practice squad (November 21, 2000). ... Activated (December 3, 2000).
PLAYING EXPERIENCE: New Orleans NFL, 2000. ... Games/Games started: 2000 (3/0).

GLENN, AARON   CB/KR   JETS

PERSONAL: Born July 16, 1972, in Humble, Texas. ... 5-9/185. ... Full name: Aaron DeVon Glenn.
HIGH SCHOOL: Nimitz (Irving, Texas).
JUNIOR COLLEGE: Navarro College (Texas).
COLLEGE: Texas A&M.
TRANSACTIONS/CAREER NOTES: Selected by New York Jets in first round (12th pick overall) of 1994 NFL draft. ... Signed by Jets (July 21, 1994).
CHAMPIONSHIP GAME EXPERIENCE: Played in AFC championship game (1998 season).
HONORS: Named defensive back on THE SPORTING NEWS college All-America first team (1993). ... Played in Pro Bowl (1997 season). ... Named to play in Pro Bowl (1998 season); replaced by Charles Woodson due to injury.
PRO STATISTICS: 1994—Recovered one fumble. 1995—Recovered one fumble. 1998—Recovered one fumble and returned a missed field goal attempt 104 yards for a touchdown. 1999—Recovered one fumble.

			INTERCEPTIONS				KICKOFF RETURNS				TOTALS		
Year Team	G	GS	No.	Yds.	Avg.	TD	No.	Yds.	Avg.	TD	TD	2pt.	Pts.	Fum.
1994—New York Jets NFL	15	15	0	0	0.0	0	27	582	21.6	0	0	0	0	2
1995—New York Jets NFL	16	16	1	17	17.0	0	1	12	12.0	0	0	0	0	0
1996—New York Jets NFL	16	16	4	113	28.3	†2	1	6	6.0	0	2	0	12	0
1997—New York Jets NFL	16	16	1	5	5.0	0	28	741	§26.5	▲1	1	0	6	1
1998—New York Jets NFL	13	13	6	23	3.8	0	24	585	24.4	0	1	0	6	1
1999—New York Jets NFL	16	16	3	20	6.7	0	27	601	22.3	0	0	0	0	0
2000—New York Jets NFL	16	16	4	34	8.5	0	3	51	17.0	0	0	0	0	0
Pro totals (7 years)	108	108	19	212	11.2	2	111	2578	23.2	1	4	0	24	4

GLENN, TARIK   OT   COLTS

PERSONAL: Born May 25, 1976, in Cleveland. ... 6-5/332.
HIGH SCHOOL: Bishop O'Dowd (Oakland).
COLLEGE: California.
TRANSACTIONS/CAREER NOTES: Selected by Indianapolis Colts in first round (19th pick overall) of 1997 NFL draft. ... Signed by Colts (August 11, 1997).
PLAYING EXPERIENCE: Indianapolis NFL, 1997-1999. ... Games/Games started: 1997 (16/16), 1998 (16/16), 1999 (16/16), 2000 (16/16). Total: 64/64.
HONORS: Named offensive tackle on THE SPORTING NEWS college All-America second team (1996).
PRO STATISTICS: 1997—Caught one pass for three yards and recovered one fumble.

GLENN, TERRY   WR   •   PATRIOTS

PERSONAL: Born July 23, 1974, in Columbus, Ohio. ... 5-11/195.
HIGH SCHOOL: Brookhaven (Columbus, Ohio).
COLLEGE: Ohio State.
TRANSACTIONS/CAREER NOTES: Selected after junior season by New England Patriots in first round (seventh pick overall) of 1996 NFL draft. ... Signed by Patriots (July 12, 1996). ... On injured reserve with fractured ankle (December 18, 1998-remainder of season).
CHAMPIONSHIP GAME EXPERIENCE: Played in AFC championship game (1996 season). ... Played in Super Bowl XXXI (1996 season).
HONORS: Fred Biletnikoff Award winner (1995). ... Named wide receiver on THE SPORTING NEWS college All-America first team (1995).
RECORDS: Holds NFL single-season record for most receptions by a rookie—90 (1996).
PRO STATISTICS: 1999—Recovered one fumble.
SINGLE GAME HIGHS (regular season): Receptions—13 (October 3, 1999, vs. Cleveland); yards—214 (October 3, 1999, vs. Cleveland); and touchdown receptions—1 (December 24, 2000, vs. Miami).
STATISTICAL PLATEAUS: 100-yard receiving games: 1996 (2), 1997 (1), 1998 (4), 1999 (4), 2000 (1). Total: 12.

			RUSHING				RECEIVING				TOTALS		
Year Team	G	GS	Att.	Yds.	Avg.	TD	No.	Yds.	Avg.	TD	TD	2pt.	Pts.	Fum.
1996—New England NFL	15	15	5	42	8.4	0	90	1132	12.6	6	6	0	36	1
1997—New England NFL	9	9	0	0	0.0	0	27	431	16.0	2	2	0	12	1
1998—New England NFL	10	9	2	-1	-0.5	0	50	792	15.8	3	3	0	18	0
1999—New England NFL	14	13	0	0	0.0	0	69	1147	16.6	4	4	0	24	2
2000—New England NFL	16	16	4	39	9.8	0	79	963	12.2	6	6	0	36	0
Pro totals (5 years)	64	62	11	80	7.3	0	315	4465	14.2	21	21	0	126	4

G

GLOVER, ANDREW   TE

PERSONAL: Born August 12, 1967, in New Orleans. ... 6-6/252. ... Full name: Andrew Lee Glover.
HIGH SCHOOL: East Ascension (Gonzales, La.).
COLLEGE: Grambling State (degree in criminal justice, 1990).
TRANSACTIONS/CAREER NOTES: Selected by Los Angeles Raiders in 10th round (274th pick overall) of 1991 NFL draft. ... Signed by Raiders (1991). ... On injured reserve with knee injury (December 27, 1993-remainder of season). ... Raiders franchise moved to Oakland (July 21, 1995). ... Granted unconditional free agency (February 16, 1996). ... Re-signed by Raiders (May 24, 1996). ... Granted unconditional free agency (February 14, 1997). ... Signed by Minnesota Vikings (July 28, 1997). ... Granted unconditional free agency (February 13, 1998). ... Re-signed by Vikings (February 18, 1998). ... Released by Vikings (February 10, 2000). ... Signed by New Orleans Saints (February 18, 2000). ... Released by Saints (March 1, 2001).
CHAMPIONSHIP GAME EXPERIENCE: Played in NFC championship game (1998 season).
PRO STATISTICS: 1992—Recovered one fumble.
SINGLE GAME HIGHS (regular season): Receptions—9 (November 8, 1998, vs. New Orleans); yards—93 (November 8, 1998, vs. New Orleans); and touchdown receptions—2 (December 20, 1998, vs. Jacksonville).

			RECEIVING				TOTALS			
Year Team	G	GS	No.	Yds.	Avg.	TD	TD	2pt.	Pts.	Fum.
1991—Los Angeles Raiders NFL	16	1	5	45	9.0	3	3	0	18	0
1992—Los Angeles Raiders NFL	16	2	15	178	11.9	1	1	0	6	1
1993—Los Angeles Raiders NFL	15	0	4	55	13.8	1	1	0	6	0
1994—Los Angeles Raiders NFL	16	16	33	371	11.2	2	2	0	12	0
1995—Oakland NFL	16	7	26	220	8.5	3	3	0	18	0
1996—Oakland NFL	14	4	9	101	11.2	1	1	0	6	0
1997—Minnesota NFL	13	11	32	378	11.8	3	3	0	18	0
1998—Minnesota NFL	16	12	35	522	14.9	5	5	0	30	0
1999—Minnesota NFL	16	13	28	327	11.7	1	1	0	6	0
2000—New Orleans NFL	16	15	21	281	13.4	4	4	0	24	0
Pro totals (10 years)	154	81	208	2478	11.9	24	24	0	144	1

GLOVER, La'ROI   DT   SAINTS

PERSONAL: Born July 4, 1974, in San Diego. ... 6-2/285. ... Full name: La'Roi Damon Glover. ... Name pronounced la-ROY.
HIGH SCHOOL: Point Loma (San Diego).
COLLEGE: San Diego State.
TRANSACTIONS/CAREER NOTES: Selected by Oakland Raiders in fifth round (166th pick overall) of 1996 NFL draft. ... Signed by Raiders (July 12, 1996). ... Assigned by Raiders to Barcelona Dragons in 1997 World League enhancement allocation program (February 19, 1997). ... Claimed on waivers by New Orleans Saints (August 25, 1997).
HONORS: Named defensive tackle on THE SPORTING NEWS NFL All-Pro team (2000). ... Played in Pro Bowl (2000 season).
PRO STATISTICS: 1997—Recovered one fumble. 1998—Intercepted one pass for no yards. 1999—Recovered one fumble for two yards. 2000—Recovered one fumble.

Year Team	G	GS	SACKS
1996—Oakland NFL	2	0	0.0
1997—Barcelona W.L.	10	10	6.5
—New Orleans NFL	15	2	6.5
1998—New Orleans NFL	16	15	10.0
1999—New Orleans NFL	16	16	8.5
2000—New Orleans NFL	16	16	*17.0
W.L. totals (1 year)	10	10	6.5
NFL totals (5 years)	65	49	42.0
Pro totals (6 years)	75	59	48.5

GLOVER, PHIL   LB   COLTS

PERSONAL: Born December 17, 1975, in San Fernando Calif. ... 5-11/241. ... Full name: Phil Dwyain Glover.
HIGH SCHOOL: Clark (Las Vegas, Nev.).
COLLEGE: Washington State, then Utah.
TRANSACTIONS/CAREER NOTES: Selected by Tennessee Titans in seventh round (222nd pick overall) of 1999 NFL draft. ... Signed by Titans (July 26, 1999). ... Assigned by Titans to Scottish Claymores in 2000 NFL Europe enhancement allocation program (February 18, 2000). ... Released by Titans (August 26, 2000). ... Signed by Indianapolis Colts to practice squad (September 27, 2000). ... Activated (October 25, 2000).
PLAYING EXPERIENCE: Tennessee NFL, 1999 and 2000; Scottish NFLE, 2000. ... Games/Games started: 1999 (1/0), 2000 NFLE (games played unavailable), NFL 2000 (9/0). Total NFL: 10/0.
CHAMPIONSHIP GAME EXPERIENCE: Member of Titans for AFC championship game (1999 season); inactive. ... Member of Titans for Super Bowl XXXIV (1999 season); inactive.
PRO STATISTICS: NFLE: 2000—Intercepted one pass for 13 yards and credited with three sacks.

GODFREY, RANDALL   LB   TITANS

PERSONAL: Born April 6, 1973, in Valdosta, Ga. ... 6-2/245. ... Full name: Randall Euralentris Godfrey.
HIGH SCHOOL: Lowndes County (Valdosta, Ga.).
COLLEGE: Georgia.
TRANSACTIONS/CAREER NOTES: Selected by Dallas Cowboys in second round (49th pick overall) of 1996 NFL draft. ... Signed by Cowboys (July 17, 1996). ... Granted free agency (February 12, 1999). ... Re-signed by Cowboys (June 25, 1999). ... Granted unconditional free agency (February 11, 2000). ... Signed by Tennessee Titans (February 16, 2000).
PRO STATISTICS: 1997—Recovered one fumble. 1998—Recovered one fumble. 2000—Recovered one fumble.

G

Year	Team	G	GS	INTERCEPTIONS				SACKS
				No.	Yds.	Avg.	TD	No.
1996—Dallas NFL		16	6	0	0	0.0	0	0.0
1997—Dallas NFL		16	16	0	0	0.0	0	1.0
1998—Dallas NFL		16	16	1	0	0.0	0	3.0
1999—Dallas NFL		16	16	1	10	10.0	0	1.0
2000—Tennessee NFL		16	16	2	25	12.5	1	3.0
Pro totals (5 years)		80	80	4	35	8.8	1	8.0

GOFF, MIKE   G   BENGALS

PERSONAL: Born January 6, 1976, in Spring Valley, Ill. ... 6-5/316. ... Full name: Michael J. Goff.
HIGH SCHOOL: Lasalle-Peru (Peru, Ill.).
COLLEGE: Iowa.
TRANSACTIONS/CAREER NOTES: Selected by Cincinnati Bengals in third round (78th pick overall) of 1998 NFL draft. ... Signed by Bengals (July 20, 1998).
PLAYING EXPERIENCE: Cincinnati NFL, 1998-2000. ... Games/Games started: 1998 (10/5), 1999 (12/1), 2000 (16/16). Total: 38/22.
PRO STATISTICS: 1999—Recovered one fumble. 2000—Recovered two fumbles.

GOGAN, KEVIN   G

PERSONAL: Born November 2, 1964, in Pacifica, Calif. ... 6-7/330. ... Full name: Kevin Patrick Gogan.
HIGH SCHOOL: Sacred Heart (San Francisco).
COLLEGE: Washington (degree in sociology, 1987).
TRANSACTIONS/CAREER NOTES: Selected by Dallas Cowboys in eighth round (206th pick overall) of 1987 NFL draft. ... Signed by Cowboys (July 18, 1987). ... On non-football injury list with substance abuse problem (August 5-31, 1988). ... Granted roster exemption (August 31-September 5, 1988). ... Granted unconditional free agency (February 17, 1994). ... Signed by Los Angeles Raiders (April 18, 1994). ... Raiders franchise moved to Oakland (July 21, 1995). ... Granted unconditional free agency (February 14, 1997). ... Signed by San Francisco 49ers (February 25, 1997). ... On physically unable to perform list with hamstring injury (July 21-28, 1998). ... Traded by 49ers to Miami Dolphins for fifth-round pick (RB Terry Jackson) in 1999 draft (March 1, 1999). ... Released by Dolphins (February 25, 2000). ... Signed by San Diego Chargers (June 6, 2000). ... Released by Chargers (February 28, 2001).
PLAYING EXPERIENCE: Dallas NFL, 1987-1993; Los Angeles Raiders NFL, 1994; Oakland NFL, 1995 and 1996; San Francisco NFL, 1997 and 1998; Miami NFL, 1999; San Diego NFL, 2000. ... Games/Games started: 1987 (11/10), 1988 (15/15), 1989 (13/13), 1990 (16/4), 1991 (16/16), 1992 (16/1), 1993 (16/16), 1994 (16/16), 1995 (16/16), 1996 (16/16), 1997 (16/16), 1998 (16/16), 1999 (16/10), 2000 (14/14). Total: 213/179.
CHAMPIONSHIP GAME EXPERIENCE: Played in NFC championship game (1992, 1993 and 1997 seasons). ... Member of Super Bowl championship team (1992 and 1993 seasons).
HONORS: Played in Pro Bowl (1994, 1997 and 1998 seasons).
PRO STATISTICS: 1987—Recovered one fumble. 1990—Recovered one fumble. 1996—Recovered one fumble. 1999—Recovered one fumble.

GOLD, IAN   LB   BRONCOS

PERSONAL: Born August 23, 1978, in Ann Arbor, Mich. ... 6-0/223. ... Full name: Ian Maurice Gold.
HIGH SCHOOL: Belleville (Mich.).
COLLEGE: Michigan.
TRANSACTIONS/CAREER NOTES: Selected by Denver Broncos in second round (40th pick overall) of 2000 NFL draft. ... Signed by Broncos (July 23, 2000).
PRO STATISTICS: 2000—Recovered two fumbles.

Year	Team	G	GS	SACKS
2000—Denver NFL		16	0	2.0

GOLDEN, JACK   LB   GIANTS

PERSONAL: Born January 28, 1977, in Harvey, Ill. ... 6-1/240.
HIGH SCHOOL: Thornton (Harvey, Ill.).
COLLEGE: Oklahoma State.
TRANSACTIONS/CAREER NOTES: Signed as non-drafted free agent by New York Giants (April 20, 2000).
PLAYING EXPERIENCE: New York Giants NFL, 2000. ... Games/Games started: 2000 (16/0).
CHAMPIONSHIP GAME EXPERIENCE: Played in NFC championship game (2000 season). ... Played in Super Bowl XXXV (2000 season).
PRO STATISTICS: 2000—Recovered one fumble.

GONZALEZ, TONY   TE   CHIEFS

PERSONAL: Born February 27, 1976, in Torrance, Calif. ... 6-4/249. ... Full name: Anthony Gonzalez.
HIGH SCHOOL: Huntington Beach (Calif.).
COLLEGE: California.
TRANSACTIONS/CAREER NOTES: Selected by Kansas City Chiefs in first round (13th pick overall) of 1997 NFL draft. ... Signed by Chiefs (July 29, 1997).
HONORS: Named tight end on THE SPORTING NEWS college All-America first team (1996). ... Named tight end on THE SPORTING NEWS NFL All-Pro team (1999 and 2000). ... Played in Pro Bowl (1999 and 2000 seasons).
PRO STATISTICS: 1999—Recovered one fumble. 2000—Recovered one fumble.
SINGLE GAME HIGHS (regular season): Receptions—10 (December 4, 2000, vs. New England); yards—147 (December 4, 2000, vs. New England); and touchdown receptions—2 (November 19, 2000, vs. Buffalo).
STATISTICAL PLATEAUS: 100-yard receiving games: 2000 (6).

G

Year Team	G	GS	RECEIVING				TOTALS			
			No.	Yds.	Avg.	TD	TD	2pt.	Pts.	Fum.
1997—Kansas City NFL	16	0	33	368	11.2	2	2	1	14	0
1998—Kansas City NFL	16	16	59	621	10.5	2	2	0	12	3
1999—Kansas City NFL	15	15	76	849	11.2	11	11	0	66	2
2000—Kansas City NFL	16	16	93	1203	12.9	9	9	0	54	0
Pro totals (4 years)	63	47	261	3041	11.7	24	24	1	146	5

GOOCH, JEFF   LB   BUCCANEERS

PERSONAL: Born October 31, 1974, in Nashville. ... 5-11/225. ... Full name: Jeffery Lance Gooch.
HIGH SCHOOL: Overton (Nashville).
COLLEGE: Austin Peay State.
TRANSACTIONS/CAREER NOTES: Signed as non-drafted free agent by Tampa Bay Buccaneers (April 23, 1996). ... On injured reserve with knee injury (December 17, 1996-remainder of season). ... Granted free agency (February 12, 1999). ... Re-signed by Buccaneers (April 13, 1999). ... Traded by Buccaneers to St. Louis Rams for fifth-round pick in 2001 draft (March 19, 2001); traded voided because Gooch failed physical (March 23, 2001).
PLAYING EXPERIENCE: Tampa Bay NFL, 1996-2000. ... Games/Games started: 1996 (15/0), 1997 (14/5), 1998 (16/16), 1999 (15/0), 2000 (16/0). Total: 76/21.
CHAMPIONSHIP GAME EXPERIENCE: Played in NFC championship game (1999 season).
PRO STATISTICS: 1996—Recovered one fumble. 1998—Credited with one sack and recovered one fumble.

GOODMAN, HERBERT   RB   PACKERS

PERSONAL: Born August 31, 1977, in Miami. ... 5-11/203.
HIGH SCHOOL: Homestead (Fla.).
COLLEGE: Graceland College (Iowa).
TRANSACTIONS/CAREER NOTES: Signed as non-drafted free agent by Green Bay Packers (April 20, 2000). ... Released by Packers (October 27, 2000). ... Re-signed by Packers to practice squad (November 1, 2000). ... Activated (November 29, 2000).
PLAYING EXPERIENCE: Green Bay NFL, 2000. ... Games/Games started: 2000 (5/0).
PRO STATISTICS: 2000—Rushed three times for minus two yards, caught one pass for no yards, returned four kickoffs for 129 yards and fumbled twice.
SINGLE GAME HIGHS (regular season): Attempts—2 (September 24, 2000, vs. Arizona); yards—4 (September 24, 2000, vs. Arizona); and rushing touchdowns—0.

GOODRICH, DWAYNE   CB   COWBOYS

PERSONAL: Born May 29, 1978, in Oak Lawn, Ill. ... 5-11/198. ... Full name: Dwayne Lewis Goodrich.
HIGH SCHOOL: H.L. Richards (Oak Lawn, Ill.).
COLLEGE: Tennessee.
TRANSACTIONS/CAREER NOTES: Selected by Dallas Cowboys in second round (49th pick overall) of 2000 NFL draft. ... Signed by Cowboys (July 17, 2000).
PLAYING EXPERIENCE: Dallas NFL, 2000. ... Games/Games started: 2000 (5/0).
PRO STATISTICS: 2000—Returned one kickoff for 12 yards.

GOODWIN, HUNTER   TE   DOLPHINS

PERSONAL: Born October 10, 1972, in Bellville, Texas. ... 6-5/270. ... Full name: Robert Hunter Goodwin.
HIGH SCHOOL: Bellville (Texas).
COLLEGE: Texas A&M-Kingsville, then Texas A&M.
TRANSACTIONS/CAREER NOTES: Selected by Minnesota Vikings in fourth round (97th pick overall) of 1996 NFL draft. ... Signed by Vikings (July 20, 1996). ... Granted free agency (February 12, 1999). ... Tendered offer sheet by Miami Dolphins (April 8, 1999). ... Vikings declined to match offer (April 9, 1999). ... Released by Dolphins (March 14, 2001). ... Re-signed by Dolphins (March 16, 2001).
CHAMPIONSHIP GAME EXPERIENCE: Played in NFC championship game (1998 season).
PRO STATISTICS: 1998—Recovered one fumble. 2000—Returned two kickoffs for six yards.
SINGLE GAME HIGHS (regular season): Receptions—3 (December 27, 1999, vs. New York Jets); yards—24 (December 1, 1996, vs. Arizona); and touchdown receptions—1 (December 24, 2000, vs. New England).

Year Team	G	GS	RECEIVING				TOTALS			
			No.	Yds.	Avg.	TD	TD	2pt.	Pts.	Fum.
1996—Minnesota NFL	9	6	1	24	24.0	0	0	0	0	0
1997—Minnesota NFL	16	5	7	61	8.7	0	0	0	0	0
1998—Minnesota NFL	15	0	3	16	5.3	0	0	0	0	0
1999—Miami NFL	15	5	8	55	6.9	0	0	0	0	1
2000—Miami NFL	16	16	6	36	6.0	1	1	0	6	0
Pro totals (5 years)	71	32	25	192	7.7	1	1	0	6	1

GORDON, DARRIEN   CB/PR

PERSONAL: Born November 14, 1970, in Shawnee, Okla. ... 5-11/190. ... Full name: Darrien Jamal Gordon.
HIGH SCHOOL: Shawnee (Okla.).
COLLEGE: Stanford.
TRANSACTIONS/CAREER NOTES: Selected by San Diego Chargers in first round (22nd pick overall) of 1993 NFL draft. ... Signed by Chargers (July 16, 1993). ... Inactive for all 16 games due to shoulder injury (1995 season). ... Granted unconditional free agency (February 14, 1997). ... Signed by Denver Broncos (April 30, 1997). ... Granted unconditional free agency (February 12, 1999). ... Signed by Oakland Raiders (June 9, 1999). ... Released by Raiders (February 10, 2000). ... Re-signed by Raiders (February 28, 2000). ... Released by Raiders (March 1, 2001).

G

CHAMPIONSHIP GAME EXPERIENCE: Played in AFC championship game (1994, 1997, 1998 and 2000 seasons). ... Played in Super Bowl XXIX (1994 season). ... Member of Super Bowl championship team (1997 and 1998 seasons).
HONORS: Named punt returner on THE SPORTING NEWS NFL All-Pro team (1997).
RECORDS: Shares NFL single-game records for most touchdowns by punt return—2; and most touchdowns by combined kick return—2 (November 9, 1997, vs. Carolina).
POST SEASON RECORDS: Holds Super Bowl career and single-game records for most interception return yards—108 (January 31, 1999, vs. Atlanta).
PRO STATISTICS: 1993—Recovered two fumbles for minus two yards. 1994—Recovered three fumbles for 15 yards. 1996—Credited with two sacks. 1997—Credited with two sacks and recovered four fumbles. 1998—Recovered one fumble. 1999—Credited with one sack and recovered two fumbles for 40 yards. 2000—Returned one kickoff for 17 yards and recovered one fumble for a touchdown.

			INTERCEPTIONS				PUNT RETURNS				TOTALS			
Year Team	G	GS	No.	Yds.	Avg.	TD	No.	Yds.	Avg.	TD	TD	2pt.	Pts.	Fum.
1993—San Diego NFL	16	7	1	3	3.0	0	31	395	12.7	0	0	0	0	4
1994—San Diego NFL	16	16	4	32	8.0	0	36	475	§13.2	†2	2	0	12	2
1995—San Diego NFL								Did not play.						
1996—San Diego NFL	16	6	2	55	27.5	0	36	537	§14.9	▲1	1	0	6	3
1997—Denver NFL	16	16	4	64	16.0	1	40	543	13.6	†3	4	0	24	3
1998—Denver NFL	16	16	4	125	31.3	1	34	379	11.1	0	1	0	6	1
1999—Oakland NFL	16	2	3	44	14.7	0	42	397	9.5	0	0	0	0	3
2000—Oakland NFL	13	0	0	0	0.0	0	29	258	8.9	0	1	0	6	2
Pro totals (7 years)	109	63	18	323	17.9	2	248	2984	12.0	6	9	0	54	18

GORDON, DWAYNE   LB

PERSONAL: Born November 2, 1969, in White Plains, N.Y. ... 6-1/245. ... Full name: Dwayne K. Gordon.
HIGH SCHOOL: Arlington North (LaGrangeville, N.Y.).
COLLEGE: New Hampshire.
TRANSACTIONS/CAREER NOTES: Selected by Miami Dolphins in eighth round (218th pick overall) of 1993 NFL draft. ... Signed by Dolphins for 1993 season. ... Released by Dolphins (July 12, 1993). ... Signed by Atlanta Falcons (July 19, 1993). ... Released by Falcons (August 27, 1995). ... Signed by San Diego Chargers (August 28, 1995). ... Granted free agency (February 16, 1996). ... Re-signed by Chargers (June 14, 1996). ... Granted unconditional free agency (February 17, 1997). ... Signed by New York Jets (June 4, 1997). ... Granted unconditional free agency (February 12, 1999). ... Re-signed by Jets (March 10, 1999). ... Released by Jets (February 21, 2001).
PLAYING EXPERIENCE: Atlanta NFL, 1993 and 1994; San Diego NFL, 1995 and 1996; New York Jets NFL, 1997-2000. ... Games/Games started: 1993 (5/0), 1994 (16/0), 1995 (16/3), 1996 (13/0), 1997 (16/8), 1998 (16/4), 1999 (16/4), 2000 (15/1). Total: 113/20.
CHAMPIONSHIP GAME EXPERIENCE: Played in AFC championship game (1998 season).
PRO STATISTICS: 1993—Fumbled once. 1995—Credited with one sack and recovered one fumble. 1997—Credited with one sack. 1998—Intercepted one pass for 31 yards and a touchdown. 1999—Credited with one sack.

GORDON, LENNOX   RB   COLTS

PERSONAL: Born April 9, 1978, in Higley, Ariz. ... 6-0/201. ... Full name: Lennox Constantine Gordon.
HIGH SCHOOL: Red Mountain (Mesa, Ariz.).
COLLEGE: New Mexico.
TRANSACTIONS/CAREER NOTES: Signed as non-drafted free agent by Buffalo Bills (April 19, 1999). ... Released by Bills (August 27, 2000). ... Signed by Indianapolis Colts to practice squad (August 29, 2000). ... Released by Colts (September 6, 2000). ... Re-signed by Colts to practice squad (September 13, 2000). ... Activated (September 27, 2000).
PLAYING EXPERIENCE: Buffalo NFL, 1999; Indianapolis NFL 2000. ... Games/Games started: 1999 (8/0), 2000 (9/0). Total: 17/0.
PRO STATISTICS: 1999—Rushed 11 times for 38 yards and returned one kickoff for 11 yards. 2000—Rushed four times for 13 yards.
SINGLE GAME HIGHS (regular season): Attempts—5 (November 14, 1999, vs. Miami); yards—18 (November 28, 1999, vs. New England); and rushing touchdowns—0.

GOWIN, TOBY   P   SAINTS

PERSONAL: Born March 30, 1975, in Jacksonville, Texas. ... 5-10/167. ... Name pronounced GO-in.
HIGH SCHOOL: Jacksonville (Texas).
COLLEGE: North Texas (degree in kinesiology).
TRANSACTIONS/CAREER NOTES: Signed as non-drafted free agent by Dallas Cowboys (April 24, 1997). ... Granted free agency (February 11, 2000). ... Tendered offer sheet by New Orleans Saints (April 6, 2000). ... Cowboys declined to match offer (April 6, 2000).
PRO STATISTICS: 1997—Missed only field-goal attempt. 2000—Rushed once for five yards.

		PUNTING					
Year Team	G	No.	Yds.	Avg.	Net avg.	In. 20	Blk.
1997—Dallas NFL	16	86	3592	41.8	35.4	26	0
1998—Dallas NFL	16	77	3342	43.4	36.6	31	∞1
1999—Dallas NFL	16	81	3500	43.2	35.1	24	0
2000—New Orleans NFL	16	74	3043	41.1	32.3	22	0
Pro totals (4 years)	64	318	13477	42.4	34.9	103	1

G

GRAGG, SCOTT   OT   49ERS

PERSONAL: Born February 28, 1972, in Silverton, Ore. ... 6-8/325.
HIGH SCHOOL: Silverton (Ore.) Union.
COLLEGE: Montana.
TRANSACTIONS/CAREER NOTES: Selected by New York Giants in second round (54th pick overall) of 1995 NFL draft. ... Signed by Giants (July 23, 1995). ... Granted free agency (February 13, 1998). ... Re-signed by Giants (September 4, 1998). ... Released by Giants (March 28,

2000). ... Signed by San Francisco 49ers (July 19, 2000). ... Granted unconditional free agency (March 2, 2001). ... Re-signed by 49ers (April 5, 2001).
PLAYING EXPERIENCE: New York Giants NFL, 1995-1999; San Francisco NFL, 2000. ... Games/Games started: 1995 (13/0), 1996 (16/16), 1997 (16/16), 1998 (16/16), 1999 (16/16), 2000 (16/16). Total: 93/80.
PRO STATISTICS: 1997—Recovered one fumble. 1998—Recovered one fumble. 1999—Recovered one fumble. 2000—Recovered one fumble.

GRAHAM, DEMINGO   G   CHARGERS

PERSONAL: Born September 10, 1973, in Newark, N.J. ... 6-3/310.
HIGH SCHOOL: Newark (N.J.) Central.
COLLEGE: Hofstra.
TRANSACTIONS/CAREER NOTES: Signed as non-drafted free agent by San Diego Chargers (April 20, 1998). ... Inactive for all 16 games (1998). ... Granted free agency (March 2, 2001). ... Re-signed by Chargers (April 19, 2001).
PLAYING EXPERIENCE: San Diego NFL, 1999 and 2000. ... Games/Games started: 1999 (16/10), 2000 (14/1). Total: 30/11.
PRO STATISTICS: 2000—Returned one kickoff for no yards.

GRAHAM, JEFF   WR   CHARGERS

PERSONAL: Born February 14, 1969, in Dayton, Ohio. ... 6-2/206. ... Full name: Jeff Todd Graham.
HIGH SCHOOL: Archbishop Hoban (Akron, Ohio).
COLLEGE: Ohio State.
TRANSACTIONS/CAREER NOTES: Selected by Pittsburgh Steelers in second round (46th pick overall) of 1991 NFL draft. ... Signed by Steelers (August 3, 1991). ... Traded by Steelers to Chicago Bears for fifth-round pick (DB Lethon Flowers) in 1995 draft (April 29, 1994). ... Granted unconditional free agency (February 16, 1996). ... Signed by New York Jets (March 14, 1996). ... Traded by Jets to Philadelphia Eagles for sixth-round pick (DE Eric Ogbogu) in 1998 draft (April 19, 1998). ... Released by Eagles (February 13, 1999). ... Signed by San Diego Chargers (March 19, 1999). ... Granted unconditional free agency (February 11, 2000). ... Re-signed by Chargers (February 21, 2000).
PRO STATISTICS: 1991—Returned three kickoffs for 48 yards. 1994—Recovered one fumble. 1995—Returned one kickoff for 12 yards. 1997—Recovered one fumble.
SINGLE GAME HIGHS (regular season): Receptions—9 (October 15, 2000, vs. Buffalo); yards—192 (December 19, 1993, vs. Houston); and touchdown receptions—3 (November 17, 1996, vs. Indianapolis).
STATISTICAL PLATEAUS: 100-yard receiving games: 1992 (2), 1993 (2), 1994 (2), 1995 (7), 1996 (3), 1997 (1), 1999 (4), 2000 (4). Total: 25.

			RECEIVING				PUNT RETURNS				TOTALS		
Year Team	G	GS	No.	Yds.	Avg.	TD	No.	Yds.	Avg.	TD	TD	2pt.	Pts.	Fum.
1991—Pittsburgh NFL	13	1	2	21	10.5	0	8	46	5.8	0	0	0	0	0
1992—Pittsburgh NFL	14	10	49	711	14.5	1	0	0	0.0	0	1	0	6	0
1993—Pittsburgh NFL	15	12	38	579	15.2	0	0	0	0.0	0	0	0	0	0
1994—Chicago NFL	16	15	68	944	13.9	4	15	140	9.3	1	5	1	32	1
1995—Chicago NFL	16	16	82	1301	15.9	4	23	183	8.0	0	4	0	24	3
1996—New York Jets NFL	11	9	50	788	15.8	6	0	0	0.0	0	6	0	36	0
1997—New York Jets NFL	16	16	42	542	12.9	2	0	0	0.0	0	2	0	12	0
1998—Philadelphia NFL	15	15	47	600	12.8	2	0	0	0.0	0	2	0	12	0
1999—San Diego NFL	16	11	57	968	17.0	2	0	0	0.0	0	2	0	12	0
2000—San Diego NFL	14	13	55	907	16.5	4	3	7	2.3	0	4	0	24	1
Pro totals (10 years)	146	118	490	7361	15.0	25	49	376	7.7	1	26	1	158	5

GRAHAM, KENT   QB   STEELERS

PERSONAL: Born November 1, 1968, in Wheaton, Ill. ... 6-5/245. ... Full name: Kent Douglas Graham.
HIGH SCHOOL: Wheaton (Ill.) North.
COLLEGE: Notre Dame, then Ohio State.
TRANSACTIONS/CAREER NOTES: Selected by New York Giants in eighth round (211th pick overall) of 1992 NFL draft. ... Signed by Giants (July 21, 1992). ... On injured reserve with elbow injury (September 18-October 14, 1992). ... Granted free agency (February 17, 1995). ... Re-signed by Giants (July 1995). ... Released by Giants (August 30, 1995). ... Signed by Detroit Lions (September 5, 1995). ... Granted unconditional free agency (February 16, 1996). ... Signed by Arizona Cardinals (March 7, 1996). ... Granted unconditional free agency (February 13, 1998). ... Signed by New York Giants (February 17, 1998). ... Released by Giants (February 10, 2000). ... Signed by Pittsburgh Steelers (February 28, 2000).
PRO STATISTICS: 1992—Fumbled once and recovered one fumble. 1994—Fumbled twice and recovered one fumble. 1996—Fumbled five times. 1997—Fumbled five times. 1998—Caught one pass for 16 yards and fumbled twice for minus three yards. 1999—Caught one pass for minus one yard, fumbled four times and recovered two fumbles. 2000—Fumbled once.
SINGLE GAME HIGHS (regular season): Attempts—58 (September 29, 1996, vs. St. Louis); completions—37 (September 29, 1996, vs. St. Louis); yards—366 (September 29, 1996, vs. St. Louis); and touchdown passes—4 (September 29, 1996, vs. St. Louis).
STATISTICAL PLATEAUS: 300-yard passing games: 1996 (1), 1997 (1). Total: 2.
MISCELLANEOUS: Regular-season record as starting NFL quarterback: 17-21 (.447).

			PASSING							RUSHING				TOTALS		
Year Team	G	GS	Att.	Cmp.	Pct.	Yds.	TD	Int.	Avg.	Rat.	Att.	Yds.	Avg.	TD	TD	2pt.	Pts.
1992—N.Y. Giants NFL	6	3	97	42	43.3	470	1	4	4.85	44.6	6	36	6.0	0	0	0	0
1993—N.Y. Giants NFL	9	0	22	8	36.4	79	0	0	3.59	47.3	2	-3	-1.5	0	0	0	0
1994—N.Y. Giants NFL	13	1	53	24	45.3	295	3	2	5.57	66.2	2	11	5.5	0	0	0	0
1995—Detroit NFL	2	0	0	0	0.0	0	0	0	0.0	...	0	0	0.0	0	0	0	0
1996—Arizona NFL	10	8	274	146	53.3	1624	12	7	5.93	75.1	21	87	4.1	0	0	0	0
1997—Arizona NFL	8	6	250	130	52.0	1408	4	5	5.63	65.9	13	23	1.8	2	2	0	12
1998—N.Y. Giants NFL	11	6	205	105	51.2	1219	7	5	5.95	70.8	27	138	5.1	2	2	0	12
1999—N.Y. Giants NFL	9	9	271	160	59.0	1697	9	9	6.26	74.6	35	132	3.8	1	1	0	6
2000—Pittsburgh NFL	12	5	148	66	44.6	878	1	1	5.93	63.4	8	7	0.9	0	0	0	0
Pro totals (9 years)	80	38	1320	681	51.6	7670	37	33	5.81	68.2	114	431	3.8	5	5	0	30

G

GRAMATICA, MARTIN　　　　K　　　　BUCCANEERS

PERSONAL: Born November 27, 1975, in Buenos Aires, Argentina. ... 5-8/170. ... Name pronounced mar-TEEN gruh-MAT-ee-ka. ... Brother of Bill Gramatica, kicker, Arizona Cardinals.
HIGH SCHOOL: La Belle (Fla.).
COLLEGE: Kansas State.
TRANSACTIONS/CAREER NOTES: Selected by Tampa Bay Buccaneers in third round (80th pick overall) of 1999 NFL draft. ... Signed by Buccaneers (July 29, 1999).
CHAMPIONSHIP GAME EXPERIENCE: Played in NFC championship game (1999 season).
HONORS: Named kicker on THE SPORTING NEWS college All-America first team (1997). ... Named kicker on THE SPORTING NEWS college All-America second team (1998). ... Won Lou Groza Award (1997). ... Played in Pro Bowl (2000 season).
PRO STATISTICS: 1999—Recovered one fumble.

| | | | | | KICKING | | | |
Year　Team	G	XPM	XPA	FGM	FGA	Lg.	50+	Pts.
1999—Tampa Bay NFL	16	25	25	‡27	∞32	∞53	3-4	106
2000—Tampa Bay NFL	16	42	42	28	34	*55	5-7	126
Pro totals (2 years)	32	67	67	55	66	55	8-11	232

GRANT, ERNEST　　　　DT　　　　DOLPHINS

PERSONAL: Born May 17, 1976, in Atlanta. ... 6-5/310. ... Full name: Ernest Jouoa Grant.
HIGH SCHOOL: Forest (Atlanta).
COLLEGE: Arkansas-Pine Bluff.
TRANSACTIONS/CAREER NOTES: Selected by Miami Dolphins in sixth round (167th pick overall) of 2000 NFL draft. ... Signed by Dolphins (July 17, 2000).
PLAYING EXPERIENCE: Miami NFL, 2000. ... Games/Games started: 2000 (2/0).

GRANT, ORANTES　　　　LB　　　　COWBOYS

PERSONAL: Born March 18, 1978, in Atlanta. ... 6-0/225.
HIGH SCHOOL: Dunwoody (Atlanta).
COLLEGE: Georgia.
TRANSACTIONS/CAREER NOTES: Selected by Dallas Cowboys in seventh round (219th pick overall) of 2000 NFL draft. ... Signed by Cowboys (July 17, 2000).
PLAYING EXPERIENCE: Dallas NFL, 2000. ... Games/Games started: 2000 (13/0).
PRO STATISTICS: 2000—Recovered two fumbles.

GRANVILLE, BILLY　　　　LB

PERSONAL: Born March 11, 1974, in Lawrenceville, N.J. ... 6-3/246.
HIGH SCHOOL: Lawrenceville (N.J.).
COLLEGE: Duke (degree in sociology, 1997).
TRANSACTIONS/CAREER NOTES: Signed as non-drafted free agent by Cincinnati Bengals (April 25, 1997). ... Granted free agency (February 11, 2000). ... Re-signed by Bengals (April 18, 2000). ... Granted unconditional free agency (March 2, 2001).
PLAYING EXPERIENCE: Cincinnati NFL, 1997-2000. ... Games/Games started: 1997 (12/4), 1998 (16/0), 1999 (16/0), 2000 (14/0). Total: 58/4.
PRO STATISTICS: 1998—Recovered one fumble. 2000—Recovered one fumble.

GRASMANIS, PAUL　　　　DT　　　　EAGLES

PERSONAL: Born August 2, 1974, in Grand Rapids, Mich. ... 6-2/298. ... Full name: Paul Ryan Grasmanis.
HIGH SCHOOL: Jenison (Mich.).
COLLEGE: Notre Dame.
TRANSACTIONS/CAREER NOTES: Selected by Chicago Bears in fourth round (116th pick overall) of 1996 NFL draft. ... Signed by Bears (June 13, 1996). ... Granted free agency (February 12, 1999). ... Re-signed by Bears (April 13, 1999). ... Released by Bears (September 5, 1999). ... Signed by St. Louis Rams (September 7, 1999). ... Inactive for one game with Rams (1999). ... Released by Rams (September 13, 1999). ... Signed by Denver Broncos (November 1, 1999). ... Granted unconditional free agency (February 11, 2000). ... Signed by Philadelphia Eagles (March 3, 2000). ... Granted unconditional free agency (March 2, 2001). ... Re-signed by Eagles (April 23, 2001).
PLAYING EXPERIENCE: Chicago NFL, 1996-1998; Denver NFL, 1999; Philadelphia NFL, 2000. ... Games/Games started: 1996 (14/3), 1997 (16/0), 1998 (15/0), 1999 (5/0), 2000 (16/0). Total: 66/3.
PRO STATISTICS: 1997—Credited with 1/2 sack and recovered one fumble. 1998—Credited with one sack. 2000—Credited with 3 1/2 sacks.

G

GRAY, CARLTON　　　　CB

PERSONAL: Born June 26, 1971, in Cincinnati. ... 6-0/202. ... Full name: Carlton Patrick Gray.
HIGH SCHOOL: Forest Park (Cincinnati).
COLLEGE: UCLA.
TRANSACTIONS/CAREER NOTES: Selected by Seattle Seahawks in second round (30th pick overall) of 1993 NFL draft. ... Signed by Seahawks (July 22, 1993). ... On injured reserve with forearm injury (November 23, 1994-remainder of season). ... Granted free agency (February 16, 1996). ... Re-signed by Seahawks (February 16, 1996). ... Granted free agency (February 14, 1997). ... Signed by Indianapolis Colts (March 3, 1997). ... Released by Colts (September 3, 1998). ... Signed by New York Giants (September 9, 1998). ... Released by Giants (February 11, 1999). ... Signed by Kansas City Chiefs (February 26, 1999). ... Released by Chiefs (June 6, 2001).
HONORS: Named defensive back on THE SPORTING NEWS college All-America first team (1992).
PRO STATISTICS: 1993—Credited with one sack. 1995—Fumbled once. 1996—Ran three yards with lateral from interception return and recovered one fumble for 62 yards. 1998—Credited with one sack.

Year Team	G	GS	No.	INTERCEPTIONS Yds.	Avg.	TD
1993—Seattle NFL	10	2	3	33	11.0	0
1994—Seattle NFL	11	11	2	0	0.0	0
1995—Seattle NFL	16	16	4	45	11.3	0
1996—Seattle NFL	16	16	0	3	0.0	0
1997—Indianapolis NFL	15	13	2	0	0.0	0
1998—New York Giants NFL	14	3	1	36	36.0	0
1999—Kansas City NFL	16	0	0	0	0.0	0
2000—Kansas City NFL	4	1	0	0	0.0	0
Pro totals (8 years)	102	62	12	117	9.8	0

GRAY, CHRIS   G/C   SEAHAWKS

PERSONAL: Born June 19, 1970, in Birmingham, Ala. ... 6-4/305. ... Full name: Christopher William Gray.
HIGH SCHOOL: Homewood (Ala.).
COLLEGE: Auburn (degree in marketing, 1992).
TRANSACTIONS/CAREER NOTES: Selected by Miami Dolphins in fifth round (132nd pick overall) of 1993 NFL draft. ... Signed by Dolphins (July 12, 1993). ... On injured reserve with ankle injury (November 15, 1995-remainder of season). ... On injured reserve with broken leg (November 19, 1996-remainder of season). ... Released by Dolphins (August 12, 1997). ... Signed by Chicago Bears (September 9, 1997). ... Granted unconditional free agency (February 13, 1998). ... Signed by Seattle Seahawks (February 20, 1998).
PLAYING EXPERIENCE: Miami NFL, 1993-1996; Chicago NFL, 1997; Seattle NFL, 1998-2000. ... Games/Games started: 1993 (5/0), 1994 (16/2), 1995 (10/10), 1996 (11/11), 1997 (8/2), 1998 (15/8), 1999 (16/10), 2000 (16/16). Total: 97/59.
PRO STATISTICS: 1994—Recovered one fumble. 1999—Recovered one fumble. 2000—Recovered one fumble.

GRBAC, ELVIS   QB   RAVENS

PERSONAL: Born August 13, 1970, in Cleveland. ... 6-5/240. ... Name pronounced ger-BACK.
HIGH SCHOOL: St. Joseph (Cleveland).
COLLEGE: Michigan (degree in graphic design, 1993).
TRANSACTIONS/CAREER NOTES: Selected by San Francisco 49ers in eighth round (219th pick overall) of 1993 NFL draft. ... Signed by 49ers (July 13, 1993). ... Inactive for all 16 games (1993). ... Granted unconditional free agency (February 14, 1997). ... Signed by Kansas City Chiefs (March 17, 1997). ... Released by Chiefs (March 1, 2001). ... Signed by Baltimore Ravens (March 6, 2001).
CHAMPIONSHIP GAME EXPERIENCE: Member of 49ers for NFC championship game (1993 season); inactive. ... Member of 49ers for NFC championship game (1994 season); did not play. ... Member of Super Bowl championship team (1994 season).
HONORS: Played in Pro Bowl (2000 season).
PRO STATISTICS: 1994—Fumbled five times. 1995—Fumbled twice and recovered two fumbles for minus one yard. 1997—Fumbled once. 1998—Fumbled once and recovered one fumble. 1999—Fumbled seven times and recovered one fumble. 2000—Fumbled seven times and recovered two fumbles for minus six yards.
SINGLE GAME HIGHS (regular season): Attempts—53 (November 5, 2000, vs. Oakland); completions—39 (November 5, 2000, vs. Oakland); yards—504 (November 5, 2000, vs. Oakland); and touchdown passes—5 (September 19, 2000, vs. San Diego).
STATISTICAL PLATEAUS: 300-yard passing games: 1995 (3), 1997 (1), 1999 (1), 2000 (5). Total: 10.
MISCELLANEOUS: Regular-season record as starting NFL quarterback: 32-24 (.571). ... Postseason record as starting NFL quarterback: 0-1.

Year Team	G	GS	Att.	Cmp.	Pct.	PASSING Yds.	TD	Int.	Avg.	Rat.	RUSHING Att.	Yds.	Avg.	TD	TOTALS TD	2pt.	Pts.
1993—San Francisco NFL						Did not play.											
1994—San Francisco NFL	11	0	50	35	70.0	393	2	1	7.86	98.2	13	1	0.1	0	0	0	0
1995—San Francisco NFL	16	5	183	127	69.4	1469	8	5	8.03	96.6	20	33	1.7	2	2	0	12
1996—San Francisco NFL	15	4	197	122	61.9	1236	8	10	6.27	72.2	23	21	0.9	2	2	0	12
1997—Kansas City NFL	10	10	314	179	57.0	1943	11	6	6.19	79.1	30	168	5.6	1	1	0	6
1998—Kansas City NFL	8	6	188	98	52.1	1142	5	12	6.07	53.1	7	27	3.9	0	0	0	0
1999—Kansas City NFL	16	16	499	294	58.9	3389	22	15	6.79	81.7	19	10	0.5	0	0	0	0
2000—Kansas City NFL	15	15	547	326	59.6	4169	28	14	7.62	89.9	30	110	3.7	1	1	0	6
Pro totals (7 years)	91	56	1978	1181	59.7	13741	84	63	6.95	81.7	142	370	2.6	6	6	0	36

GREEN, AHMAN   RB   PACKERS

G

PERSONAL: Born February 16, 1977, in Omaha, Neb. ... 6-0/217.
HIGH SCHOOL: North (Omaha, Neb.), then Central Christian (Omaha, Neb.).
COLLEGE: Nebraska.
TRANSACTIONS/CAREER NOTES: Selected after junior season by Seattle Seahawks in third round (76th pick overall) of 1998 NFL draft. ... Signed by Seahawks (July 18, 1998). ... Traded by Seahawks with fifth-round pick (WR/KR Joey Jamison) in 2000 draft to Green Bay Packers for CB Fred Vinson and sixth-round pick (DT Tim Watson) in 2000 draft (April 14, 2000). ... Granted free agency (March 2, 2001). ... Re-signed by Packers (May 5, 2001).
HONORS: Named running back on THE SPORTING NEWS college All-America second team (1997).
PRO STATISTICS: 1998—Recovered one fumble. 1999—Recovered one fumble. 2000—Attempted one pass without a completion and recovered one fumble.
SINGLE GAME HIGHS (regular season): Attempts—27 (December 24, 2000, vs. Tampa Bay); yards—161 (December 17, 2000, vs. Minnesota); and rushing touchdowns—2 (December 24, 2000, vs. Tampa Bay).
STATISTICAL PLATEAUS: 100-yard rushing games: 1998 (1), 2000 (3). Total: 4.

Year Team	G	GS	RUSHING Att.	Yds.	Avg.	TD	RECEIVING No.	Yds.	Avg.	TD	KICKOFF RETURNS No.	Yds.	Avg.	TD	TOTALS TD	2pt.	Pts.	Fum.
1998—Seattle NFL	16	0	35	209	6.0	1	3	2	0.7	0	27	620	23.0	0	1	0	6	1
1999—Seattle NFL	14	0	26	120	4.6	0	0	0	0.0	0	36	818	22.7	0	0	0	0	2
2000—Green Bay NFL	16	11	263	1175	4.5	10	73	559	7.7	3	0	0	0.0	0	13	0	78	6
Pro totals (3 years)	46	11	324	1504	4.6	11	76	561	7.4	3	63	1438	22.8	0	14	0	84	9

GREEN, BARRETT   LB   LIONS

PERSONAL: Born October 29, 1977, in West Palm Beach, Fla. ... 6-0/217. ... Son of Joe Green, defensive back with New York Giants (1970 and 1971).
HIGH SCHOOL: Suncoast (West Palm Beach, Fla.).
COLLEGE: West Virginia.
TRANSACTIONS/CAREER NOTES: Selected by Detroit Lions in second round (50th pick overall) of 2000 NFL draft. ... Signed by Lions (July 15, 2000).
PLAYING EXPERIENCE: Detroit NFL, 2000. ... Games/Games started: 2000 (9/0).
PRO STATISTICS: 2000—Recovered one fumble.

GREEN, DARRELL   CB   REDSKINS

PERSONAL: Born February 15, 1960, in Houston. ... 5-8/184.
HIGH SCHOOL: Jesse H. Jones Senior (Houston).
COLLEGE: Texas A&I.
TRANSACTIONS/CAREER NOTES: Selected by Denver Gold in 10th round (112th pick overall) of 1983 USFL draft. ... Selected by Washington Redskins in first round (28th pick overall) of 1983 NFL draft. ... Signed by Redskins (June 10, 1983). ... On injured reserve with broken hand (December 13, 1988-remainder of season). ... On injured reserve with broken bone in wrist (October 24, 1989-remainder of season). ... Granted free agency (February 1, 1992). ... Re-signed by Redskins (August 25, 1992). ... On injured reserve with broken forearm (September 16-November 23, 1992). ... Granted unconditional free agency (February 17, 1995). ... Re-signed by Redskins (March 10, 1995). ... Granted unconditional free agency (February 14, 1997). ... Re-signed by Redskins (April 25, 1997).
CHAMPIONSHIP GAME EXPERIENCE: Played in NFC championship game (1983, 1986, 1987 and 1991 seasons). ... Played in Super Bowl XVIII (1983 season). ... Member of Super Bowl championship team (1987 and 1991 seasons).
HONORS: Played in Pro Bowl (1984, 1986, 1987, 1990, 1991, 1996 and 1997 seasons). ... Named cornerback on THE SPORTING NEWS NFL All-Pro team (1991).
POST SEASON RECORDS: Shares NFL postseason career record for most touchdowns by punt return—1 (January 10, 1988, at Chicago).
PRO STATISTICS: 1983—Recovered one fumble. 1985—Rushed once for six yards and recovered one fumble. 1986—Recovered one fumble. 1987—Recovered one fumble for 26 yards and a touchdown. 1988—Credited with one sack and recovered one fumble. 1989—Recovered one fumble. 1993—Recovered one fumble for 78 yards and a touchdown. 1996—Recovered one fumble for 15 yards. 1997—Returned one kickoff for nine yards. 1999—Recovered one fumble for four yards.
MISCELLANEOUS: Holds Washington Redskins all-time record for most interceptions (53).

			INTERCEPTIONS				PUNT RETURNS				TOTALS		
Year Team	G	GS	No.	Yds.	Avg.	TD	No.	Yds.	Avg.	TD	TD	2pt.	Pts.	Fum.
1983—Washington NFL	16	16	2	7	3.5	0	4	29	7.3	0	0	0	0	1
1984—Washington NFL	16	16	5	91	18.2	1	2	13	6.5	0	1	0	6	0
1985—Washington NFL	16	16	2	0	0.0	0	16	214	13.4	0	0	0	0	2
1986—Washington NFL	16	15	5	9	1.8	0	12	120	10.0	0	0	0	0	1
1987—Washington NFL	12	12	3	65	21.7	0	5	53	10.6	0	1	0	6	0
1988—Washington NFL	15	15	1	12	12.0	0	9	103	11.4	0	0	0	0	1
1989—Washington NFL	7	7	2	0	0.0	0	1	11	11.0	0	0	0	0	1
1990—Washington NFL	16	16	4	20	5.0	1	1	6	6.0	0	1	0	6	0
1991—Washington NFL	16	16	5	47	9.4	0	0	0	0.0	0	0	0	0	0
1992—Washington NFL	8	7	1	15	15.0	0	0	0	0.0	0	0	0	0	0
1993—Washington NFL	16	16	4	10	2.5	0	1	27	27.0	0	1	0	6	0
1994—Washington NFL	16	16	3	32	10.7	1	0	0	0.0	0	1	0	6	0
1995—Washington NFL	16	16	3	42	14.0	1	0	0	0.0	0	1	0	6	0
1996—Washington NFL	16	16	3	84	28.0	1	0	0	0.0	0	1	0	6	0
1997—Washington NFL	16	16	1	83	83.0	1	0	0	0.0	0	1	0	6	0
1998—Washington NFL	16	16	3	36	12.0	0	0	0	0.0	0	0	0	0	0
1999—Washington NFL	16	16	3	33	11.0	0	0	0	0.0	0	0	0	0	0
2000—Washington NFL	13	2	3	35	11.7	0	0	0	0.0	0	0	0	0	0
Pro totals (18 years)	263	250	53	621	11.7	6	51	576	11.3	0	8	0	48	6

GREEN, E.G.   WR   COLTS

PERSONAL: Born June 28, 1975, in Fort Walton Beach, Fla. ... 5-11/188. ... Full name: Ernie G. Green.
HIGH SCHOOL: Fort Walton Beach (Fla.).
COLLEGE: Florida State.
TRANSACTIONS/CAREER NOTES: Selected by Indianapolis Colts in third round (71st pick overall) of 1998 NFL draft. ... Signed by Colts (July 21, 1998). ... Granted free agency (March 2, 2001). ... Re-signed by Colts (April 21, 2001).
SINGLE GAME HIGHS (regular season): Receptions—6 (November 19, 2000, vs. Green Bay); yards—124 (September 12, 1999, vs. Buffalo); and touchdown receptions—1 (November 19, 2000, vs. Green Bay).
STATISTICAL PLATEAUS: 100-yard receiving games: 1999 (1).

			RECEIVING				TOTALS		
Year Team	G	GS	No.	Yds.	Avg.	TD	TD	2pt.	Pts.	Fum.
1998—Indianapolis NFL	12	0	15	177	11.8	1	1	0	6	0
1999—Indianapolis NFL	11	4	21	287	13.7	0	0	0	0	0
2000—Indianapolis NFL	7	0	18	201	11.2	1	1	0	6	0
Pro totals (3 years)	30	4	54	665	12.3	2	2	0	12	0

GREEN, JACQUEZ   WR   BUCCANEERS

PERSONAL: Born January 15, 1976, in Fort Valley, Ga. ... 5-9/168. ... Full name: D'Tanyian Jacquez Green.
HIGH SCHOOL: Peach County (Fort Valley, Ga.).
COLLEGE: Florida.

G

TRANSACTIONS/CAREER NOTES: Selected after junior season by Tampa Bay Buccaneers in second round (34th pick overall) of 1998 NFL draft. ... Signed by Buccaneers (July 19, 1998).

CHAMPIONSHIP GAME EXPERIENCE: Played in NFC championship game (1999 season).

HONORS: Named wide receiver on THE SPORTING NEWS college All-America second team (1997).

PRO STATISTICS: 1998—Fumbled five times and recovered two fumbles. 1999—Fumbled once.

SINGLE GAME HIGHS (regular season): Receptions—10 (October 9, 2000, vs. Minnesota); yards—164 (November 14, 1999, vs. Kansas City); and touchdown receptions—1 (September 10, 2000, vs. Chicago).

STATISTICAL PLATEAUS: 100-yard receiving games: 1999 (2), 2000 (2). Total: 4.

Year	Team	G	GS	RUSHING				RECEIVING				PUNT RETURNS				KICKOFF RETURNS				TOTALS		
				Att.	Yds.	Avg.	TD	No.	Yds.	Avg.	TD	No.	Yds.	Avg.	TD	No.	Yds.	Avg.	TD	TD	2pt.	Pts.
1998—Tampa Bay NFL...		12	1	3	12	4.0	0	14	251	17.9	2	30	453	15.1	1	10	229	22.9	0	3	0	18
1999—Tampa Bay NFL...		16	10	3	8	2.7	0	56	791	14.1	3	23	204	8.9	0	10	185	18.5	0	3	0	18
2000—Tampa Bay NFL...		16	16	5	13	2.6	0	51	773	15.2	1	2	1	0.5	0	1	11	11.0	0	1	0	6
Pro totals (3 years)........		44	27	11	33	3.0	0	121	1815	15.0	6	55	658	12.0	1	21	425	20.2	0	7	0	42

GREEN, MIKE　　　　S　　　　BEARS

PERSONAL: Born December 6, 1976, in Ruston, La. ... 6-0/176.

HIGH SCHOOL: Ruston (La.).

COLLEGE: Louisiana-Lafayette.

TRANSACTIONS/CAREER NOTES: Selected by Chicago Bears in seventh round (254th pick overall) of 2000 NFL draft. ... Signed by Bears (May 30, 2000).

PLAYING EXPERIENCE: Chicago NFL, 2000. ... Games/Games started: 2000 (7/0).

GREEN, MIKE　　　　RB　　　　TITANS

PERSONAL: Born September 2, 1976, in Houston. ... 6-0/249. ... Full name: Mike Lewayne Green.

HIGH SCHOOL: Klein (Houston).

JUNIOR COLLEGE: Blinn College (Texas).

COLLEGE: Houston.

TRANSACTIONS/CAREER NOTES: Selected by Tennessee Titans in seventh round (213th pick overall) of 2000 NFL draft. ... Signed by Titans (July 10, 2000). ... Assigned by Titans to Barcelona Dragons in 2001 NFL Europe enhancement allocation program (February 19, 2001).

PLAYING EXPERIENCE: Tennessee NFL, 2000. ... Games/Games started: 2000 (1/0).

GREEN, RAY　　　　S　　　　PANTHERS

PERSONAL: Born March 22, 1977, in Queens, New York. ... 6-3/187.

HIGH SCHOOL: Burke (Charleston, S.C.).

COLLEGE: South Carolina.

TRANSACTIONS/CAREER NOTES: Signed as non-drafted free agent by Carolina Panthers (April 17, 2000).

PLAYING EXPERIENCE: Carolina NFL, 2000. ... Games/Games started: 2000 (16/0).

PRO STATISTICS: 2000—Returned one kickoff for one yards.

GREEN, TRENT　　　　QB　　　　CHIEFS

PERSONAL: Born July 9, 1970, in Cedar Rapids, Iowa. ... 6-3/215. ... Full name: Trent Jason Green.

HIGH SCHOOL: Vianney (St. Louis).

COLLEGE: Indiana.

TRANSACTIONS/CAREER NOTES: Selected by San Diego Chargers in eighth round (222nd pick overall) of 1993 NFL draft. ... Signed by Chargers (July 15, 1993). ... Inactive for all 16 games (1993). ... Released by Chargers (August 22, 1994). ... Signed by Washington Redskins (April 5, 1995). ... Inactive for all 16 games (1995). ... Inactive for all 16 games (1996). ... Granted free agency (February 14, 1997). ... Re-signed by Redskins (June 6, 1997). ... Granted unconditional free agency (February 12, 1999). ... Signed by St. Louis Rams (February 16, 1999). ... On injured reserve with knee injury (August 30, 1999-entire season). ... Traded by Rams with fifth-round pick (RB Derrick Blaylock) in 2001 draft to Kansas City Chiefs for first-round pick (DT Damione Lewis) in 2001 draft (April 20, 2001).

PRO STATISTICS: 1998—Caught two passes for minus eight yards, led NFL with 14 fumbles and recovered four fumbles. 2000—Fumbled three times.

SINGLE GAME HIGHS (regular season): Attempts—54 (September 20, 1998, vs. Seattle); completions—30 (November 22, 1998, vs. Arizona); yards—431 (November 5, 2000, vs. Carolina); and touchdown passes—4 (November 11, 2000, vs. New York Giants).

STATISTICAL PLATEAUS: 300-yard passing games: 1998 (2), 2000 (3). Total: 5.

MISCELLANEOUS: Regular-season record as starting NFL quarterback: 8-11 (.421).

Year	Team	G	GS	PASSING								RUSHING				TOTALS		
				Att.	Cmp.	Pct.	Yds.	TD	Int.	Avg.	Rat.	Att.	Yds.	Avg.	TD	TD	2pt.	Pts.
1993—San Diego NFL...........								Did not play.										
1994—								Did not play.										
1995—Washington NFL								Did not play.										
1996—Washington NFL								Did not play.										
1997—Washington NFL		1	0	1	0	0.0	0	0	0	0.0	39.6	0	0	0.0	0	0	0	0
1998—Washington NFL		15	14	509	278	54.6	3441	23	11	6.76	81.8	42	117	2.8	2	2	0	12
1999—St. Louis NFL								Did not play.										
2000—St. Louis NFL.............		8	5	240	145	60.4	2063	16	5	8.60	‡101.8	20	69	3.5	1	1	0	6
Pro totals (3 years)		24	19	750	423	56.4	5504	39	16	7.34	88.1	62	186	3.0	3	3	0	18

G

GREEN, VICTOR   S   JETS

PERSONAL: Born December 8, 1969, in Americus, Ga. ... 5-11/210. ... Full name: Victor Bernard Green. ... Cousin of Tommy Sims, defensive back with Indianapolis Colts (1986).
HIGH SCHOOL: Americus (Ga.).
JUNIOR COLLEGE: Copiah-Lincoln Junior College (Miss.).
COLLEGE: Akron (degree in criminal justice, 1993).
TRANSACTIONS/CAREER NOTES: Signed as non-drafted free agent by New York Jets (April 29, 1993). ... Released by Jets (August 30, 1993). ... Re-signed by Jets to practice squad (September 1, 1993). ... Activated (September 28, 1993).
CHAMPIONSHIP GAME EXPERIENCE: Played in AFC championship game (1998 season).
PRO STATISTICS: 1994—Recovered one fumble. 1995—Recovered one fumble. 1996—Recovered three fumbles. 1998—Recovered one fumble. 1999—Recovered two fumbles for nine yards. 2000—Recovered four fumbles.

			INTERCEPTIONS				SACKS
Year Team	G	GS	No.	Yds.	Avg.	TD	No.
1993—New York Jets NFL	11	0	0	0	0.0	0	0.0
1994—New York Jets NFL	16	0	0	0	0.0	0	1.0
1995—New York Jets NFL	16	12	1	2	2.0	0	2.0
1996—New York Jets NFL	16	16	2	27	13.5	0	2.0
1997—New York Jets NFL	16	16	3	89	29.7	0	1.0
1998—New York Jets NFL	16	16	4	99	24.8	0	1.0
1999—New York Jets NFL	16	16	5	92	18.4	0	0.0
2000—New York Jets NFL	16	16	6	144	24.0	1	0.0
Pro totals (8 years)	123	92	21	453	21.6	1	7.0

GREER, DONOVAN   DB   REDSKINS

PERSONAL: Born September 11, 1974, in Houston. ... 5-9/178.
HIGH SCHOOL: Elsik (Alief, Texas).
COLLEGE: Texas A&M.
TRANSACTIONS/CAREER NOTES: Signed as non-drafted free agent by New Orleans Saints (April 25, 1997). ... Released by Saints (August 24, 1997). ... Signed by Atlanta Falcons (August 26, 1997). ... Released by Falcons (September 3, 1997). ... Signed by Saints to practice squad (September 4, 1997). ... Activated (November 15, 1997). ... Released by Saints (August 24, 1998). ... Signed by Buffalo Bills to practice squad (September 9, 1998). ... Activated (September 30, 1998). ... Granted free agency (February 11, 2000). ... Re-signed by Bills (April 14, 2000). ... Granted unconditional free agency (March 2, 2001). ... Signed by Washington Redskins (April 20, 2001).
PLAYING EXPERIENCE: Atlanta (1)-New Orleans (6) NFL, 1997; Buffalo NFL, 1998-2000. ... Games/Games started: 1997 (Atl.-1/0; N.O.-6/1; Total: 7/1), 1998 (11/2), 1999 (16/0), 2000 (13/1). Total: 47/4.
PRO STATISTICS: 1998—Recovered one fumble for 18 yards. 1999—Intercepted one pass for no yards. 2000—Recovered one fumble.

GREISEN, CHRIS   QB   CARDINALS

PERSONAL: Born July 2, 1976, in Sturgeon Bay, Wis. ... 6-3/227.
HIGH SCHOOL: Sturgeon Bay (Wis.).
COLLEGE: Northwest Missouri State (degree in physical education).
TRANSACTIONS/CAREER NOTES: Selected by Arizona Cardinals in seventh round (239th pick overall) of 1999 NFL draft. ... Signed by Cardinals (June 18, 1999).
PRO STATISTICS: 2000—Fumbled once.
SINGLE GAME HIGHS (regular season): Attempts—7 (December 10, 2000, vs. Jacksonville); completions—4 (December 10, 2000, vs. Jacksonville); passing yards—46 (December 10, 2000, vs. Jacksonville); and touchdown passes—1 (December 10, 2000, vs. Jacksonville).

			PASSING							RUSHING				TOTALS		
Year Team	G	GS	Att.	Cmp.	Pct.	Yds.	TD	Int.	Avg.	Rat.	Att.	Yds.	Avg.	TD	TD	2pt.	Pts.
1999—Arizona NFL	2	0	6	1	16.7	4	0	0	0.67	39.6	0	0	0.0	0	0	0	0
2000—Arizona NFL	3	0	10	6	60.0	65	1	0	6.50	112.5	1	1	1.0	0	0	0	0
Pro totals (2 years)	5	0	16	7	43.8	69	1	0	4.31	77.3	1	1	1.0	0	0	0	0

GRIESE, BRIAN   QB   BRONCOS

PERSONAL: Born March 18, 1975, in Miami. ... 6-3/215. ... Full name: Brian David Griese. ... Son of Bob Griese, Hall of Fame quarterback with Miami Dolphins (1967-80). ... Name pronounced GREE-see.
HIGH SCHOOL: Columbus (Miami).
COLLEGE: Michigan.
TRANSACTIONS/CAREER NOTES: Selected by Denver Broncos in third round (91st pick overall) of 1998 NFL draft. ... Signed by Broncos (July 22, 1998). ... Granted free agency (March 2, 2001). ... Re-signed by Broncos (April 11, 2001).
CHAMPIONSHIP GAME EXPERIENCE: Member of Broncos for AFC championship game (1998 season); inactive. ... Member of Super Bowl championship team (1998 season); inactive.
HONORS: Played in Pro Bowl (2000 season).
PRO STATISTICS: 1998—Fumbled once for minus one yard. 1999—Led league with 16 fumbles and recovered nine fumbles for minus 46 yards. 2000—Fumbled five times and recovered two fumbles for minus eight yards.
SINGLE GAME HIGHS (regular season): Attempts—50 (October 1, 2000, vs. New England); completions—31 (October 1, 2000, vs. New England); yards—365 (October 22, 2000, vs. Cincinnati); and touchdown passes—3 (October 15, 2000, vs. Cleveland).
STATISTICAL PLATEAUS: 300-yard passing games: 1999 (2), 2000 (5). Total: 7.
MISCELLANEOUS: Regular-season record as starting NFL quarterback: 11-12 (.478).

			PASSING							RUSHING				TOTALS		
Year Team	G	GS	Att.	Cmp.	Pct.	Yds.	TD	Int.	Avg.	Rat.	Att.	Yds.	Avg.	TD	TD	2pt.	Pts.
1998—Denver NFL	1	0	3	1	33.3	2	0	1	0.67	2.8	4	-4	-1.0	0	0	0	0
1999—Denver NFL	14	13	452	261	57.7	3032	14	14	6.71	75.6	46	138	3.0	2	2	0	12
2000—Denver NFL	10	10	336	216	§64.3	2688	19	4	§§8.00	*102.9	29	102	3.5	1	1	0	6
Pro totals (3 years)	25	23	791	478	60.4	5722	33	19	7.23	86.5	79	236	3.0	3	3	0	18

G

GRIFFIN, CORNELIUS　　DT　　GIANTS

PERSONAL: Born December 3, 1976, in Brundidge, Ala. ... 6-3/300.
HIGH SCHOOL: Pike County (Brundidge, Ala.).
JUNIOR COLLEGE: Pearl River Community College (Miss.).
COLLEGE: Alabama.
TRANSACTIONS/CAREER NOTES: Selected by New York Giants in second round (42nd pick overall) of 2000 NFL draft. ... Signed by Giants (July 25, 2000).
CHAMPIONSHIP GAME EXPERIENCE: Played in NFC championship game (2000 season). ... Played in Super Bowl XXXV (2000 season).

Year　Team	G	GS	SACKS
2000—New York Giants NFL	15	0	5.0

GRIFFIN, DAMON　　WR/KR　　BENGALS

PERSONAL: Born June 14, 1976, in Los Angeles. ... 5-9/186. ... Full name: Damon Gilbert Griffin.
HIGH SCHOOL: Monrovia (Los Angeles).
COLLEGE: Oregon.
TRANSACTIONS/CAREER NOTES: Signed as non-drafted free agent by San Francisco 49ers (April 23, 1999). ... Claimed on waivers by Cincinnati Bengals (September 6, 1999).
PRO STATISTICS: 1999—Recovered two fumbles.
SINGLE GAME HIGHS (regular season): Receptions—4 (October 17, 1999, vs. Pittsburgh); yards—46 (October 17, 1999, vs. Pittsburgh); and touchdown receptions—0.

Year　Team	G	GS	RECEIVING No.	Yds.	Avg.	TD	PUNT RETURNS No.	Yds.	Avg.	TD	KICKOFF RETURNS No.	Yds.	Avg.	TD	TOTALS TD	2pt.	Pts.	Fum.
1999—Cincinnati NFL	13	0	12	112	9.3	0	23	195	8.5	0	15	296	19.7	0	0	0	0	5
2000—Cincinnati NFL	8	0	2	25	12.5	0	1	9	9.0	0	8	129	16.1	0	0	0	0	0
Pro totals (2 years)	21	0	14	137	9.8	0	24	204	8.5	0	23	425	18.5	0	0	0	0	5

GRIFFITH, HOWARD　　FB　　BRONCOS

PERSONAL: Born November 17, 1967, in Chicago. ... 6-0/240. ... Full name: Howard Thomas Griffith.
HIGH SCHOOL: Percy L. Julian (Chicago).
COLLEGE: Illinois.
TRANSACTIONS/CAREER NOTES: Selected by Indianapolis Colts in ninth round (237th pick overall) of 1991 NFL draft. ... Signed by Colts (July 12, 1991). ... Released by Colts (August 26, 1991). ... Signed by Buffalo Bills to practice squad (September 4, 1991). ... Released by Bills (August 31, 1992). ... Re-signed by Bills to practice squad (September 2, 1992). ... Released by Bills (October 21, 1992). ... Signed by San Diego Chargers to practice squad (October 23, 1992). ... Released by Chargers (October 28, 1992). ... Re-signed by Chargers to practice squad (October 30, 1992). ... Released by Chargers (December 9, 1992). ... Re-signed by Chargers to practice squad (December 14, 1992). ... Released by Chargers (August 30, 1993). ... Signed by Los Angeles Rams (September 2, 1993). ... Selected by Carolina Panthers from Rams in NFL expansion draft (February 15, 1995). ... Granted free agency (February 16, 1996). ... Re-signed by Panthers (July 20, 1996). ... Granted unconditional free agency (February 14, 1997). ... Signed by Denver Broncos (February 18, 1997). ... Granted unconditional free agency (March 2, 2001). ... Re-signed by Broncos (May 1, 2001).
CHAMPIONSHIP GAME EXPERIENCE: Played in NFC championship game (1996 season). ... Played in AFC championship game (1997 and 1998 seasons). ... Member of Super Bowl championship team (1997 and 1998 seasons).
PRO STATISTICS: 1995—Recovered one fumble. 1996—Recovered one fumble. 1997—Recovered one fumble. 1999—Recovered one fumble. 2000—Recovered one fumble.
SINGLE GAME HIGHS (regular season): Attempts—25 (November 19, 1995, vs. Arizona); yards—88 (November 19, 1995, vs. Arizona); and rushing touchdowns—1 (November 22, 1999, vs. Oakland).

Year　Team	G	GS	RUSHING Att.	Yds.	Avg.	TD	RECEIVING No.	Yds.	Avg.	TD	KICKOFF RETURNS No.	Yds.	Avg.	TD	TOTALS TD	2pt.	Pts.	Fum.
1991—Buffalo NFL									Did not play.									
1992—San Diego NFL									Did not play.									
1993—LA Rams NFL	15	0	0	0	0.0	0	0	0	0.0	0	8	169	21.1	0	0	0	0	0
1994—LA Rams NFL	16	10	9	30	3.3	0	16	113	7.1	1	2	35	17.5	0	1	0	6	0
1995—Carolina NFL	15	7	65	197	3.0	1	11	63	5.7	1	0	0	0.0	0	2	0	12	0
1996—Carolina NFL	16	14	12	7	0.6	1	27	223	8.3	1	0	0	0.0	0	2	0	12	1
1997—Denver NFL	15	13	9	34	3.8	0	11	55	5.0	0	0	0	0.0	0	0	0	0	0
1998—Denver NFL	14	13	4	13	3.3	0	15	97	6.5	3	0	0	0.0	0	3	0	18	0
1999—Denver NFL	16	16	17	66	3.9	1	26	192	7.4	1	0	0	0.0	0	2	0	12	0
2000—Denver NFL	14	14	5	4	0.8	0	16	101	6.3	2	0	0	0.0	0	2	0	12	0
Pro totals (8 years)	121	87	121	351	2.9	3	122	844	6.9	9	10	204	20.4	0	12	0	72	2

GRIFFITH, RICH　　TE

PERSONAL: Born July 31, 1969, in Tucson, Ariz. ... 6-5/260. ... Full name: Richard Pope Griffith.
HIGH SCHOOL: Catalina (Tucson, Ariz.).
COLLEGE: Arizona (degree in communications, 1993).
TRANSACTIONS/CAREER NOTES: Selected by New England Patriots in fifth round (138th pick overall) of 1993 NFL draft. ... Signed by Patriots (July 16, 1993). ... Released by Patriots (August 20, 1994). ... Signed by Jacksonville Jaguars (January 6, 1995). ... Granted free agency (February 14, 1997). ... Re-signed by Jaguars (April 15, 1997). ... Granted unconditional free agency (February 13, 1998). ... Re-signed by Jaguars (February 16, 1998). ... On injured reserve with knee injury (October 28, 1998-remainder of season). ... Granted unconditional free agency (February 11, 2000). ... Re-signed by Jaguars (March 21, 2000). ... Released by Jaguars (March 1, 2001).

G

PLAYING EXPERIENCE: New England NFL, 1993; Jacksonville NFL, 1995-2000. ... Games/Games started: 1993 (3/0), 1995 (16/15), 1996 (16/2), 1997 (16/1), 1998 (7/0), 1999 (16/0), 2000 (16/1). Total: 90/19.
CHAMPIONSHIP GAME EXPERIENCE: Played in AFC championship game (1996 and 1999 seasons).
PRO STATISTICS: 1995—Caught 16 passes for 243 yards and returned one kickoff for nine yards. 1996—Caught five passes for 53 yards, returned two kickoffs for 24 yards and recovered one fumble.
SINGLE GAME HIGHS (regular season): Receptions—4 (December 10, 1995, vs. Indianapolis); yards—54 (December 10, 1995, vs. Indianapolis); and touchdown receptions—0.

GRIFFITH, ROBERT　　　S　　　VIKINGS

PERSONAL: Born November 30, 1970, in Landham, Md. ... 5-11/198. ... Full name: Robert Otis Griffith.
HIGH SCHOOL: Mount Miguel (Spring Valley, Calif.).
COLLEGE: San Diego State.
TRANSACTIONS/CAREER NOTES: Signed by Sacramento Gold Miners of CFL to practice squad (August 8, 1993). ... Granted free agency after 1993 season. ... Signed as non-drafted free agent by Minnesota Vikings (April 21, 1994). ... Granted free agency (February 14, 1997). ... Re-signed by Vikings (May 7, 1997).
CHAMPIONSHIP GAME EXPERIENCE: Played in NFC championship game (1998 and 2000 seasons).
HONORS: Named safety on THE SPORTING NEWS NFL All-Pro team (1998). ... Played in Pro Bowl (2000 season).
PRO STATISTICS: 1996—Fumbled once. 2000—Recovered two fumbles.

			INTERCEPTIONS				SACKS
Year　Team	G	GS	No.	Yds.	Avg.	TD	No.
1994—Minnesota NFL	15	0	0	0	0.0	0	0.0
1995—Minnesota NFL	16	0	0	0	0.0	0	0.5
1996—Minnesota NFL	14	14	4	67	16.8	0	2.0
1997—Minnesota NFL	16	16	2	26	13.0	0	0.0
1998—Minnesota NFL	16	16	5	25	5.0	0	0.0
1999—Minnesota NFL	16	16	3	0	0.0	0	4.0
2000—Minnesota NFL	16	16	1	25	25.0	0	1.0
Pro totals (7 years)	109	78	15	143	9.5	0	7.5

GRIMES, REGGIE　　　DE　　　PATRIOTS

PERSONAL: Born November 7, 1976, in Nashville. ... 6-4/290. ... Full name: Reginald Dewayne Grimes.
HIGH SCHOOL: Hunters Lane (Tenn.).
COLLEGE: Alabama.
TRANSACTIONS/CAREER NOTES: Signed as non-drafted free agent by New England Patriots (April 19, 2000).
PLAYING EXPERIENCE: New England NFL, 2000. ... Games/Games started: 2000 (8/0).

GROCE, CLIF　　　FB　　　BENGALS

PERSONAL: Born July 30, 1972, in College Station, Texas. ... 5-11/245. ... Full name: Clifton Allen Groce. ... Name pronounced gross.
HIGH SCHOOL: A&M Consolidated (College Station, Texas).
COLLEGE: Texas A&M.
TRANSACTIONS/CAREER NOTES: Signed as non-drafted free agent by Indianapolis Colts (April 27, 1995). ... Released by Colts (August 22, 1995). ... Re-signed by Colts to practice squad (August 28, 1995). ... Activated (December 7, 1995). ... Released by Colts (August 28, 1998). ... Signed by New England Patriots (December 16, 1998). ... Claimed on waivers by Cincinnati Bengals (December 24, 1998). ... Inactive for two games (1998). ... Released by Bengals (August 30, 1999). ... Re-signed by Bengals (September 2, 1999).
CHAMPIONSHIP GAME EXPERIENCE: Played in AFC championship game (1995 season).
PRO STATISTICS: 1996—Returned one kickoff for 18 yards and recovered one fumble. 1997—Returned one kickoff for 15 yards.
SINGLE GAME HIGHS (regular season): Attempts—11 (October 13, 1996, vs. Baltimore); yards—55 (October 13, 196, vs. Baltimore); and rushing touchdowns—1 (December 12, 1999, vs. Cleveland).

			RUSHING				RECEIVING				TOTALS			
Year　Team	G	GS	Att.	Yds.	Avg.	TD	No.	Yds.	Avg.	TD	TD	2pt.	Pts.	Fum.
1995—Indianapolis NFL	1	0	0	0	0.0	0	0	0	0.0	0	0	0	0	0
1996—Indianapolis NFL	15	8	46	184	4.0	0	13	106	8.2	0	0	0	0	2
1997—Indianapolis NFL	7	0	10	66	6.6	0	0	0	0.0	0	0	0	0	0
1998—Cincinnati NFL							Did not play.							
1999—Cincinnati NFL	16	15	8	22	2.8	1	25	154	6.2	0	1	0	6	0
2000—Cincinnati NFL	8	6	3	4	1.3	0	11	45	4.1	0	0	0	0	0
Pro totals (5 years)	47	29	67	276	4.1	1	49	305	6.2	0	1	0	6	2

GRUNHARD, TIM　　　C

PERSONAL: Born May 17, 1968, in Chicago. ... 6-2/311. ... Full name: Timothy Gerard Grunhard.
HIGH SCHOOL: St. Laurence (Burbank, Ill.).
COLLEGE: Notre Dame (degree in political science).
TRANSACTIONS/CAREER NOTES: Selected by Kansas City Chiefs in second round (40th pick overall) of 1990 NFL draft. ... Signed by Chiefs (July 22, 1990). ... Granted unconditional free agency (March 2, 2001). ... Announced retirement (April 28, 2001).
PLAYING EXPERIENCE: Kansas City NFL, 1990-2000. ... Games/Games started: 1990 (14/9), 1991 (16/16), 1992 (12/12), 1993 (16/16), 1994 (16/16), 1995 (16/16), 1996 (16/16), 1997 (16/16), 1998 (16/16), 1999 (16/16), 2000 (15/15). Total: 169/164.
CHAMPIONSHIP GAME EXPERIENCE: Played in AFC championship game (1993 season).
PRO STATISTICS: 1991—Recovered one fumble. 1992—Recovered two fumbles. 1993—Fumbled once. 1995—Recovered one fumble. 1996—Recovered one fumble. 1997—Recovered one fumble. 1999—Recovered one fumble. 2000—Recovered one fumble.

G

GRUTTADAURIA, MIKE   C   CARDINALS

PERSONAL: Born December 6, 1972, in Fort Lauderdale, Fla. ... 6-3/286. ... Full name: Michael Jason Gruttadauria. ... Name pronounced GRU-da-DOOR-ri-ah.

HIGH SCHOOL: Tarpon Springs (Fla.).

COLLEGE: Central Florida.

TRANSACTIONS/CAREER NOTES: Signed as non-drafted free agent by Dallas Cowboys (April 26, 1995). ... Released by Cowboys (August 22, 1995). ... Signed by St. Louis Rams (February 9, 1996). ... Granted free agency (February 12, 1999). ... Re-signed by Rams (June 8, 1999). ... Granted unconditional free agency (February 11, 2000). ... Signed by Arizona Cardinals (February 19, 2000). ... On injured reserve with neck injury (November 24, 2000-remainder of season).

PLAYING EXPERIENCE: St. Louis NFL, 1996-1999; Arizona NFL, 2000. ... Games/Games started: 1996 (9/3), 1997 (14/14), 1998 (12/3), 1999 (16/16), 2000 (8/8). Total: 59/44.

CHAMPIONSHIP GAME EXPERIENCE: Played in NFC championship game (1999 season). ... Member of Super Bowl championship team (1999 season).

PRO STATISTICS: 1997—Caught one pass for no yards.

GUTIERREZ, BROCK   C

PERSONAL: Born September 25, 1973, in Charlotte, Mich. ... 6-3/304.

HIGH SCHOOL: Charlotte (Mich.).

COLLEGE: Central Michigan.

TRANSACTIONS/CAREER NOTES: Signed as non-drafted free agent by Cincinnati Bengals (April 23, 1996). ... Active for two games (1996). ... Released by Bengals (August 30, 1998). ... Re-signed by Bengals (November 4, 1998). ... Released by Bengals (November 17, 1998). ... Signed by Jacksonville Jaguars to practice squad (November 30, 1998). ... Signed by Bengals off Jaguars practice squad (December 15, 1998). ... Granted free agency (February 11, 2000). ... Re-signed by Bengals (March 17, 2000). ... Granted unconditional free agency (March 2, 2001).

PLAYING EXPERIENCE: Cincinnati NFL, 1997-2000. ... Games/Games started: 1997 (5/0), 1998 (1/0), 1999 (16/0), 2000 (16/7). Total: 38/7.

HAGGANS, CLARK   DE   STEELERS

PERSONAL: Born January 10, 1977, in Torrance, Calif. ... 6-3/250. ... Full name: Clark Cromwell Haggans.

HIGH SCHOOL: Peninsula (Torrance, Calif.).

COLLEGE: Colorado State.

TRANSACTIONS/CAREER NOTES: Selected by Pittsburgh Steelers in fifth round (137th pick overall) of 2000 NFL draft. ... Signed by Steelers (July 7, 2000).

PLAYING EXPERIENCE: Pittsburgh NFL, 2000. ... Games/Games started: 2000 (2/0).

HAKIM, Az-ZAHIR   WR/PR   RAMS

PERSONAL: Born June 3, 1977, in Los Angeles. ... 5-10/182. ... Full name: Az-Zahir Ali Hakim. ... Name pronounced oz-za-HERE ha-KEEM.

HIGH SCHOOL: Fairfax (Los Angeles).

COLLEGE: San Diego State.

TRANSACTIONS/CAREER NOTES: Selected by St. Louis Rams in fourth round (96th pick overall) of 1998 NFL draft. ... Signed by Rams (July 13, 1998). ... Granted free agency (March 2, 2001).

CHAMPIONSHIP GAME EXPERIENCE: Played in NFC championship game (1999 season). ... Member of Super Bowl championship team (1999 season).

HONORS: Named punt returner on THE SPORTING NEWS NFL All-Pro team (2000).

PRO STATISTICS: 1998—Fumbled once. 1999—Fumbled six times and recovered three fumbles. 2000—Fumbled seven times and recovered one fumble.

SINGLE GAME HIGHS (regular season): Receptions—8 (November 5, 2000, vs. Carolina); yards—147 (November 5, 2000, vs. Carolina); and touchdown receptions—3 (October 3, 1999, vs. Cincinnati).

STATISTICAL PLATEAUS: 100-yard receiving games: 1999 (1), 2000 (3). Total: 4.

			RUSHING				RECEIVING				PUNT RETURNS				KICKOFF RETURNS				TOTALS		
Year Team	G	GS	Att.	Yds.	Avg.	TD	No.	Yds.	Avg.	TD	No.	Yds.	Avg.	TD	No.	Yds.	Avg.	TD	TD	2pt.	Pts.
1998—St. Louis NFL	9	4	2	30	15.0	1	20	247	12.4	1	0	0	0.0	0	0	0	0.0	0	2	0	12
1999—St. Louis NFL	15	0	4	44	11.0	0	36	677	18.8	8	∞44	461	10.5	∞1	2	35	17.5	0	9	0	54
2000—St. Louis NFL	16	4	5	19	3.8	0	53	734	13.8	4	32	‡489‡	15.3	1	1	2	2.0	0	5	0	30
Pro totals (3 years)	40	8	11	93	8.5	1	109	1658	15.2	13	76	950	12.5	2	3	37	12.3	0	16	0	96

HALE, RYAN   DT   GIANTS

PERSONAL: Born July 10, 1975, in Rogers, Ark ... 6-4/300.

HIGH SCHOOL: Rogers (Ark.).

COLLEGE: Arkansas.

TRANSACTIONS/CAREER NOTES: Selected by New York Giants in seventh round (225th pick overall) of 1999 NFL draft. ... Signed by Giants (July 29, 1999).

PLAYING EXPERIENCE: New York Giants NFL, 1999 and 2000. ... Games/Games started: 1999 (8/0), 2000 (16/0). Total: 24/0.

CHAMPIONSHIP GAME EXPERIENCE: Played in NFC championship game (2000 season). ... Played in Super Bowl XXXV (2000 season).

G
H

HALEY, JERMAINE — DT — DOLPHINS

PERSONAL: Born February 13, 1973, in Fresno, Calif. ... 6-4/305.
HIGH SCHOOL: Hanford (Calif.).
JUNIOR COLLEGE: Butte Junior College (Calif.).
TRANSACTIONS/CAREER NOTES: Signed by Toronto Argonauts of CFL (May 1998). ... Selected by Miami Dolphins in seventh round (232nd pick overall) of 1999 NFL draft. ... Signed by Dolphins (March 2, 2000).
PRO STATISTICS: 2000—Credited with one safety.

			INTERCEPTIONS				SACKS
Year Team	G	GS	No.	Yds.	Avg.	TD	No.
1998—Toronto CFL	16	...	0	0	0.0	0	7.0
1999—Toronto CFL	...	...	1	0	0.0	0	3.0
2000—Miami NFL	15	4	0	0	0.0	0	1.5
CFL totals (2 years)	...	...	1	0	0.0	0	10.0
NFL totals (1 year)	15	4	0	0	0.0	0	1.5
Pro totals (3 years)	...	...	1	0	0.0	0	11.5

HALL, CORY — S — BENGALS

PERSONAL: Born December 5, 1976, in Bakersfield, Calif. ... 6-0/210.
HIGH SCHOOL: South (Bakersfield, Calif.).
COLLEGE: Fresno State.
TRANSACTIONS/CAREER NOTES: Selected by Cincinnati Bengals in third round (65th pick overall) of 1999 NFL draft. ... Signed by Bengals (May 7, 1999).
PLAYING EXPERIENCE: Cincinnati NFL, 1999 and 2000. ... Games/Games started: 1999 (16/12), 2000 (16/6). Total: 32/18.
PRO STATISTICS: 1999—Intercepted one pass for no yards and recovered one fumble. 2000—Intercepted one pass for 12 yards and credited with four sacks.

HALL, DANTE — WR/KR — CHIEFS

PERSONAL: Born September 1, 1978, in Lufkin, Texas. ... 5-8/193. ... Full name: Damieon Dante Hall.
HIGH SCHOOL: Nimitz (Irving, Texas).
COLLEGE: Texas A&M.
TRANSACTIONS/CAREER NOTES: Selected by Kansas City Chiefs in fifth round (153rd pick overall) of 2000 NFL draft. ... Signed by Chiefs (July 6, 2000). ... Assigned by Chiefs to Scottish Claymores in 2001 NFL Europe enhancement allocation program (February 19, 2001).

			PUNT RETURNS				KICKOFF RETURNS				TOTALS			
Year Team	G	GS	No.	Yds.	Avg.	TD	No.	Yds.	Avg.	TD	TD	2pt.	Pts.	Fum.
2000—Kansas City NFL	5	0	6	37	6.2	0	17	358	21.1	0	0	0	0	1

HALL, JAMES — DE — LIONS

PERSONAL: Born February 4, 1977, in New Orleans. ... 6-2/271.
HIGH SCHOOL: St. Augustine (La.).
COLLEGE: Michigan.
TRANSACTIONS/CAREER NOTES: Signed as non-drafted free agent by Detroit Lions (April 28, 2000).
PLAYING EXPERIENCE: Detroit NFL, 2000. ... Games/Games started: 2000 (5/0).
PRO STATISTICS: 2000—Credited with one sack.

HALL, JEFF — K — SAINTS

PERSONAL: Born July 30, 1976, in Winchester, Tenn. ... 5-11/190. ... Full name: Paul Jeffery Hall.
HIGH SCHOOL: Franklin (Winchester, Tenn.).
COLLEGE: Tennessee.
TRANSACTIONS/CAREER NOTES: Selected by Washington Redskins in sixth round (181st pick overall) of 1999 NFL draft. ... Signed by Redskins (July 8, 1999). ... Released by Redskins (September 4, 1999). ... Signed by St. Louis Rams (January 20, 2000). ... Released by Rams (August 1, 2000). ... Signed by Green Bay Packers (August 4, 2000). ... Released by Packers (August 22, 2000). ... Signed by Rams (November 7, 2000). ... Released by Rams (December 4, 2000). ... Signed by New Orleans Saints (April 1, 2001).

		KICKING						
Year Team	G	XPM	XPA	FGM	FGA	Lg.	50+	Pts.
2000—St. Louis NFL	3	9	9	4	5	50	1-1	21

HALL, JOHN — K — JETS

PERSONAL: Born March 17, 1974, in Port Charlotte, Fla. ... 6-3/228.
HIGH SCHOOL: Port Charlotte (Fla.).
COLLEGE: Wisconsin.
TRANSACTIONS/CAREER NOTES: Signed as non-drafted free agent by New York Jets (April 25, 1997). ... Granted free agency (February 11, 2000). ... Re-signed by Jets (April 13, 2000).
CHAMPIONSHIP GAME EXPERIENCE: Played in AFC championship game (1998 season).
PRO STATISTICS: 1997—Punted three times for 144 yards. 1999—Punted once for 34 yards.

H

Year Team	G	XPM	XPA	FGM	FGA	Lg.	50+	Pts.
				KICKING				
1997—New York Jets NFL	16	36	36	28	†41	†55	4-6	120
1998—New York Jets NFL	16	45	46	25	35	54	1-3	120
1999—New York Jets NFL	16	27	29	27	33	48	0-0	108
2000—New York Jets NFL	15	30	30	21	32	51	1-3	93
Pro totals (4 years)	63	138	141	101	141	55	6-12	441

HALL, LAMONT   TE   SAINTS

PERSONAL: Born November 16, 1974, in York, S.C. ... 6-4/260. ... Full name: James Lamont Hall.
HIGH SCHOOL: Clover (S.C.).
COLLEGE: Clemson (degree in history).
TRANSACTIONS/CAREER NOTES: Signed as non-drafted free agent by Tampa Bay Buccaneers (April 24, 1998). ... Released by Buccaneers (August 25, 1998). ... Re-signed by Buccaneers to practice squad (October 21, 1998). ... Granted free agency following 1998 season. ... Selected by Rhein Fire in 1999 NFL Europe draft (February 18, 1999). ... Signed by Green Bay Packers (July 7, 1999). ... Traded by Packers with QB Aaron Brooks to New Orleans Saints for LB K.D. Williams and third-round pick (traded to San Francisco) in 2001 draft (July 31, 2000).
PRO STATISTICS: NFLE: 1999—Returned one kickoff for 15 yards.
SINGLE GAME HIGHS (regular season): Receptions—2 (October 22, 2000, vs. Atlanta); yards—20 (October 22, 2000, vs. Atlanta); and touchdown receptions—1 (October 29, 2000, vs. Arizona).

Year Team	G	GS	No.	Yds.	Avg.	TD	TD	2pt.	Pts.	Fum.
				RECEIVING				**TOTALS**		
1998—Tampa Bay NFL						Did not play.				
1999—Rhein NFLE	...	...	5	60	12.0	0	0	0	0	0
—Green Bay NFL	14	0	3	33	11.0	0	0	0	0	0
2000—New Orleans NFL	16	5	5	33	6.6	1	1	0	6	0
NFL Europe totals (1 year)	...	...	5	60	12.0	0	0	0	0	0
NFL totals (1 year)	30	5	8	66	8.3	1	1	0	6	0
Pro totals (2 years)	...	...	13	126	9.7	1	1	0	6	0

HALL, LEMANSKI   LB   VIKINGS

PERSONAL: Born November 24, 1970, in Valley, Ala. ... 6-0/235. ... Full name: Lemanski S. Hall.
HIGH SCHOOL: Valley (Ala.).
COLLEGE: Alabama.
TRANSACTIONS/CAREER NOTES: Selected by Houston Oilers in seventh round (220th pick overall) of 1994 NFL draft. ... Signed by Oilers (June 20, 1994). ... Released by Oilers (August 28, 1994). ... Re-signed by Oilers to practice squad (August 30, 1994). ... Activated (December 23, 1994); did not play. ... Assigned by Oilers to Frankfurt Galaxy in 1995 World League enhancement allocation program (February 20, 1995). ... Assigned by Oilers to Amsterdam Admirals in 1996 World League enhancement allocation program (February 19, 1996). ... Oilers franchise moved to Tennessee for 1997 season. ... Granted free agency (February 13, 1998). ... Re-signed by Oilers (May 28, 1998). ... Traded by Oilers to Chicago Bears for seventh-round pick (RB Mike Green) in 2000 draft (September 1, 1998). ... Released by Bears (September 5, 1999). ... Signed by Dallas Cowboys (October 27, 1999). ... Granted unconditional free agency (February 11, 2000). ... Signed by Minnesota Vikings (February 24, 2000).
PLAYING EXPERIENCE: Frankfurt W.L., 1995; Houston NFL, 1995 and 1996; Amsterdam W.L., 1996; Tennessee NFL, 1997; Chicago NFL, 1998; Dallas NFL, 1999; Minnesota NFL, 2000. ... Games/Games started: W.L.1995 (games played unavailable), NFL 1995 (12/0), W.L. 1996 (-), NFL 1996 (3/0), 1997 (16/2), 1998 (15/0), 1999 (10/0), 2000 (15/1). Total: 71/3.
CHAMPIONSHIP GAME EXPERIENCE: Played in NFC championship game (2000 season).
PRO STATISTICS: 1997—Credited with two sacks. 1998—Recovered one fumble for five yards. 2000—Recovered one fumble for one yards.

HALL, TRAVIS   DT   FALCONS

PERSONAL: Born August 3, 1972, in Kenai, Alaska. ... 6-5/295.
HIGH SCHOOL: West Jordan (Utah).
COLLEGE: Brigham Young.
TRANSACTIONS/CAREER NOTES: Selected by Atlanta Falcons in sixth round (181st pick overall) of 1995 NFL draft. ... Signed by Falcons (June 30, 1995).
CHAMPIONSHIP GAME EXPERIENCE: Played in NFC championship game (1998 season). ... Played in Super Bowl XXXIII (1998 season).
PRO STATISTICS: 1996—Recovered one fumble. 1997—Recovered one fumble. 1998—Recovered four fumbles. 1999—Recovered one fumble. 2000—Recovered one fumble.

Year Team	G	GS	SACKS
1995—Atlanta NFL	1	0	0.0
1996—Atlanta NFL	14	13	6.0
1997—Atlanta NFL	16	16	10.5
1998—Atlanta NFL	14	13	4.5
1999—Atlanta NFL	16	15	4.5
2000—Atlanta NFL	16	16	4.5
Pro totals (6 years)	77	73	30.0

HALLEN, BOB   G   FALCONS

PERSONAL: Born March 9, 1975, in Mentor, Ohio. ... 6-4/295. ... Full name: Robert Joseph Hallen.
HIGH SCHOOL: Mentor (Ohio).
COLLEGE: Kent.
TRANSACTIONS/CAREER NOTES: Selected by Atlanta Falcons in second round (53rd pick overall) of 1998 NFL draft. ... Signed by Falcons (June 3, 1998).
PLAYING EXPERIENCE: Atlanta NFL, 1998-2000. ... Games/Games started: 1998 (12/0), 1999 (16/14), 2000 (16/5). Total: 44/19.
CHAMPIONSHIP GAME EXPERIENCE: Played in NFC championship game (1998 season). ... Played in Super Bowl XXXIII (1998 season).

H

HALLOCK, TY — LB

PERSONAL: Born April 30, 1971, in Grand Rapids, Mich. ... 6-2/254. ... Full name: Ty Edward Hallock.
HIGH SCHOOL: Greenville (Mich.).
COLLEGE: Michigan State (degree in employee relations, 1997).
TRANSACTIONS/CAREER NOTES: Selected by Detroit Lions in seventh round (174th pick overall) of 1993 NFL draft. ... Signed by Lions (July 15, 1993). ... Released by Lions (August 30, 1993). ... Re-signed by Lions to practice squad (August 31, 1993). ... Activated (September 3, 1993). ... Traded by Lions to Jacksonville Jaguars for CB Corey Raymond (May 30, 1995). ... On reserve/retired list (July 10, 1995-February 12, 1996). ... Granted free agency (February 14, 1997). ... Re-signed by Jaguars (June 9, 1997). ... Granted unconditional free agency (February 13, 1998). ... Signed by Chicago Bears (February 16, 1998). ... Released by Bears (September 26, 2000).
CHAMPIONSHIP GAME EXPERIENCE: Played in AFC championship game (1996 season).
PRO STATISTICS: 1993—Returned one kickoff for 11 yards. 1997—Returned one kickoff for six yards. 1998—Recovered one fumble. 1999—Returned two kickoffs for 10 yards and recovered one fumble.
SINGLE GAME HIGHS (regular season): Attempts—3 (December 6, 1998, vs. Minnesota); yards—17 (December 6, 1998, vs. Minnesota); and rushing touchdowns—1 (October 25, 1998, vs. Tennessee).
MISCELLANEOUS: Played fullback and tight end (1993-99).

				RUSHING				RECEIVING				TOTALS		
Year Team	G	GS	Att.	Yds.	Avg.	TD	No.	Yds.	Avg.	TD	TD	2pt.	Pts.	Fum.
1993—Detroit NFL	16	4	0	0	0.0	0	8	88	11.0	2	2	0	12	0
1994—Detroit NFL	15	10	0	0	0.0	0	7	75	10.7	0	0	0	0	0
1995—Jacksonville NFL								Did not play.						
1996—Jacksonville NFL	7	0	0	0	0.0	0	1	5	5.0	0	0	0	0	0
1997—Jacksonville NFL	15	8	4	21	5.3	0	18	131	7.3	1	1	0	6	0
1998—Chicago NFL	16	12	13	41	3.2	1	25	166	6.6	0	1	0	6	3
1999—Chicago NFL	15	4	0	0	0.0	0	6	22	3.7	0	0	0	0	0
2000—Chicago NFL	2	0	0	0	0.0	0	0	0	0.0	0	0	0	0	0
Pro totals (7 years)	86	38	17	62	3.6	1	65	487	7.5	3	4	0	24	3

HAM, DERRICK — DE — REDSKINS

PERSONAL: Born March 23, 1975, in Merritt Island, Fla. ... 6-4/257. ... Full name: Derrick Jerome Ham.
HIGH SCHOOL: Merritt Island (Fla.).
COLLEGE: Miami.
TRANSACTIONS/CAREER NOTES: Signed as non-drafted free agent by Washington Redskins (April 21, 1999). ... Released by Redskins (September 4, 1999). ... Re-signed by Redskins to practice squad (September 6, 1999). ... Released by Redskins (September 14, 1999). ... Re-signed by Redskins (February 10, 2000). ... Assigned by Redskins to Rhein Fire in 2000 NFL Europe enhancement allocation program (February 18, 2000).

Year Team	G	GS	SACKS
2000—Rhein NFLE	...	...	9.0
—Washington NFL	1	0	0.0
NFL Europe totals (1 year)	...	...	9.0
NFL totals (1 year)	1	0	0.0
Pro totals (2 years)	...	...	9.0

HAMBRICK, DARREN — LB — COWBOYS

PERSONAL: Born August 30, 1975, in Lacoochee, Fla. ... 6-2/227. ... Nephew of Mudcat Grant, pitcher with seven major league teams (1958-71).
HIGH SCHOOL: Pasco (Dade City, Fla.).
COLLEGE: Florida, then South Carolina.
TRANSACTIONS/CAREER NOTES: Selected by Dallas Cowboys in fifth round (130th pick overall) of 1998 NFL draft. ... Signed by Cowboys (July 14, 1998). ... Granted free agency (March 2, 2001).
PLAYING EXPERIENCE: Dallas NFL, 1998-2000. ... Games/Games started: 1998 (14/0), 1999 (16/12), 2000 (16/16). Total: 46/28.
PRO STATISTICS: 1999—Intercepted two passes for 44 yards, credited with 2^1/$_2$ sacks and credited with a safety. 2000—Credited with one sack.

HAMBRICK, TROY — RB — COWBOYS

PERSONAL: Born November 6, 1976, in Pasco, Fla. ... 6-1/235.
HIGH SCHOOL: Pasco (Fla.).
COLLEGE: Savannah State.
TRANSACTIONS/CAREER NOTES: Signed as non-drafted free agent by Dallas Cowboys (June 1, 2000). ... Released by Cowboys (August 27, 2000). ... Re-signed by Cowboys to practice squad (August 29, 2000). ... Activated (December 8, 2000).
PLAYING EXPERIENCE: Dallas NFL, 2000. ... Games/Games started: 2000 (3/0).
PRO STATISTICS: 2000—Rushed six times for 28 yards.
SINGLE GAME HIGHS (regular season): Attempts—6 (December 25, 2000, vs. Tennessee); yards—28 (December 25, 2000, vs. Tennessee); and rushing touchdowns—0.

HAMILTON, BOBBY — DE — PATRIOTS

PERSONAL: Born January 7, 1971, in Denver. ... 6-5/280.
HIGH SCHOOL: East Marion (Columbia, Miss.).
COLLEGE: Southern Mississippi.
TRANSACTIONS/CAREER NOTES: Signed as non-drafted free agent by Seattle Seahawks (April 19, 1994). ... On injured reserve with knee injury (August 17, 1994-entire season). ... Assigned by Seahawks to Amsterdam Admirals in 1995 World League enhancement allocation draft.

H

... Released by Seahawks (August 15, 1995). ... Signed by New York Jets (June 1996). ... Released by Jets (August 24, 1996). ... Re-signed by Jets to practice squad (August 26, 1996). ... Activated (September 4, 1996). ... Granted unconditional free agency (February 11, 2000). ... Signed by New England Patriots (July 16, 2000).

CHAMPIONSHIP GAME EXPERIENCE: Played in AFC championship game (1998 season).

PRO STATISTICS: 1996—Recovered one fumble for seven yards. 1997—Returned one kickoff for no yards. 2000—Returned one kickoff for no yards and recovered one fumble.

Year Team	G	GS	SACKS
1994—Seattle NFL	Did not play.		
1995—Amsterdam W.L.	10	9	5.0
1996—Amsterdam W.L.	11	9	5.0
—New York Jets NFL	15	11	4.5
1997—New York Jets NFL	16	0	1.0
1998—New York Jets NFL	16	1	0.0
1999—New York Jets NFL	7	0	0.0
2000—New England NFL	16	16	1.5
W.L. totals (2 years)	21	18	10.0
NFL totals (4 years)	70	28	7.0
Pro totals (6 years)	91	46	17.0

HAMILTON, JOE — QB — BUCCANEERS

PERSONAL: Born March 13, 1977, in Alvin, S.C. ... 5-10/190. ... Full name: Joseph Fitzgerald Hamilton.
HIGH SCHOOL: Macedonia (Alvin, S.C.).
COLLEGE: Georgia Tech.
TRANSACTIONS/CAREER NOTES: Selected by Tampa Bay Buccaneers in seventh round (234th pick overall) of 2000 NFL draft. ... Signed by Buccaneers (July 11, 2000).
PLAYING EXPERIENCE: Tampa Bay NFL, 2000. ... Games/Games started: 2000 (1/0).
HONORS: Davey O'Brien Award winner (1999). ... Named quarterback on THE SPORTING NEWS college All-America second team (1999).
PRO STATISTICS: 2000—Rushed once for minus two yards and fumbled once.

HAMILTON, KEITH — DT — GIANTS

PERSONAL: Born May 25, 1971, in Paterson, N.J. ... 6-6/295. ... Full name: Keith Lamarr Hamilton.
HIGH SCHOOL: Heritage (Lynchburg, Va.).
COLLEGE: Pittsburgh.
TRANSACTIONS/CAREER NOTES: Selected after junior season by New York Giants in fourth round (99th pick overall) of 1992 NFL draft. ... Signed by Giants (July 21, 1992).
CHAMPIONSHIP GAME EXPERIENCE: Played in NFC championship game (2000 season). ... Played in Super Bowl XXXV (2000 season).
PRO STATISTICS: 1992—Recovered one fumble for four yards. 1993—Credited with a safety and recovered one fumble for 10 yards. 1994—Recovered three fumbles. 1995—Fumbled once and recovered three fumbles for 87 yards. 1997—Recovered three fumbles. 1998—Recovered one fumble. 1999—Recovered two fumbles.

Year Team	G	GS	SACKS
1992—New York Giants NFL	16	0	3.5
1993—New York Giants NFL	16	16	11.5
1994—New York Giants NFL	15	15	6.5
1995—New York Giants NFL	14	14	2.0
1996—New York Giants NFL	14	14	3.0
1997—New York Giants NFL	16	16	8.0
1998—New York Giants NFL	16	16	7.0
1999—New York Giants NFL	16	16	4.0
2000—New York Giants NFL	16	16	10.0
Pro totals (9 years)	139	123	55.5

HAMILTON, MICHAEL — LB

PERSONAL: Born December 3, 1973, in Greenville, S.C. ... 6-2/245. ... Full name: Michael Antonio Hamilton.
HIGH SCHOOL: Southside (Greenville, S.C.).
COLLEGE: North Carolina A&T.
TRANSACTIONS/CAREER NOTES: Selected by San Diego Chargers in third round (74th pick overall) of 1997 NFL draft. ... Signed by Chargers (June 11, 1997). ... Released by Chargers (September 2, 1997). ... Re-signed by Chargers to practice squad (September 3, 1997). ... Activated (November 4, 1997). ... Granted free agency (February 11, 2000). ... Re-signed by Chargers (June 5, 2000). ... Released by Chargers (August 27, 2000). ... Signed by Miami Dolphins (October 11, 2000). ... Released by Dolphins (October 23, 2000). ... Re-signed by Dolphins (October 25, 2000). ... Released by Dolphins (November 13, 2000). ... Signed by Cleveland Browns (November 28, 2000). ... Granted unconditional free agency (March 2, 2001).
PLAYING EXPERIENCE: San Diego NFL, 1997-1999; Miami (3)-Cleveland (1) NFL, 2000. ... Games/ Games started: 1997 (6/0), 1998 (13/0), 1999 (14/2), 2000 (Miami-3/0; Cleve.-1/0; Total:4/0). Total: 37/2.
PRO STATISTICS: 1998—Recovered one fumble.

HAMITER, UHURU — DE — EAGLES

PERSONAL: Born March 14, 1973, in Kingstree, S.C. ... 6-4/280.
HIGH SCHOOL: Mastbaum Area Vo-Tech (Philadelphia).
COLLEGE: Delaware State.
TRANSACTIONS/CAREER NOTES: Selected by England Monarchs in 1998 NFL Europe draft (February 18, 1998). ... Signed as non-drafted free agent by Philadelphia Eagles (June 19, 1998). ... Claimed on waivers by New Orleans Saints (August 31, 1998). ... Active for one game (1998);

H

did not play. ... Released by Saints (September 28, 1999). ... Re-signed by Saints to practice squad (September 30, 1999). ... Activated (November 19, 1999). ... Released by Saints (August 28, 2000). ... Signed by Eagles to practice squad (September 14, 2000). ... Activated (October 31, 2000).
PLAYING EXPERIENCE: England NFLE, 1998; New Orleans NFL, 1999; Philadelphia NFL, 2000. ... Games/Games started: 1998 (10/games started unavailable), 1999 (5/0), 2000 (7/0). Total NFLE: (10/-). Total NFL: (12/0). Total Pro: (22/-).
PRO STATISTICS: 1998—Credited with seven sacks.

HAND, NORMAN   DT   SAINTS

PERSONAL: Born September 4, 1972, in Queens, N.Y. ... 6-3/310. ... Full name: Norman L. Hand.
HIGH SCHOOL: Walterboro (S.C.).
JUNIOR COLLEGE: Itawamba Community College (Miss.).
COLLEGE: Mississippi.
TRANSACTIONS/CAREER NOTES: Selected by Miami Dolphins in fifth round (158th pick overall) of 1995 NFL draft. ... Signed by Dolphins (May 17, 1995). ... Inactive for all 16 games (1995). ... Claimed on waivers by San Diego Chargers (August 25, 1997). ... Granted free agency (February 13, 1998). ... Re-signed by Chargers (July 14, 1998). ... Designated by Chargers as franchise player (February 11, 2000). ... Free agency status changed from franchise to unconditional (February 16, 2000). ... Signed by New Orleans Saints (February 23, 2000).
PRO STATISTICS: 1998—Intercepted two passes for 47 yards.

Year Team	G	GS	SACKS
1995—Miami NFL	Did not play.		
1996—Miami NFL	9	0	0.5
1997—San Diego NFL	15	1	1.0
1998—San Diego NFL	16	16	6.0
1999—San Diego NFL	14	14	4.0
2000—New Orleans NFL	15	15	3.0
Pro totals (5 years)	69	46	14.5

HANKTON, KARL   WR   PANTHERS

PERSONAL: Born July 24, 1970, in New Orleans ... 6-2/202.
HIGH SCHOOL: De La Salle (New Orleans).
COLLEGE: Louisiana State, then Trinity (Ill.).
TRANSACTIONS/CAREER NOTES: Signed as non-drafted free agent by Washington Redskins (April 1, 1997). ... Released by Redskins (February 25, 1998). ... Signed by Philadelphia Eagles (April 9, 1998). ... Released by Eagles (August 31, 1998). ... Re-signed by Eagles to practice squad (September 2, 1998). ... Released by Eagles (August 31, 1998). ... Re-signed by Eagles to practice squad (September 25, 1998). ... Activated (September 25, 1998). ... Released by Eagles (September 7, 1999). ... Signed by Carolina Panthers (February 29, 2000). ... Granted free agency (March 2, 2001).
PLAYING EXPERIENCE: Philadelphia NFL, 1998; Carolina NFL, 2000. ... Games/Games started: 1998 (10/0), 2000 (16/0). Total: 26/0.
PRO STATISTICS: 1998—Rushed once for minus four yards and returned one kickoff for 18 yards. 2000—Caught four passes for 38 yards and recovered one fumble.
SINGLE GAME HIGHS (regular season): Receptions—2 (November 27, 2000, vs. Green Bay); yards—14 (November 27, 2000, vs. Green Bay); and touchdown receptions—0.

HANSEN, PHIL   DE   BILLS

PERSONAL: Born May 20, 1968, in Ellendale, N.D. ... 6-5/273. ... Full name: Phillip Allen Hansen.
HIGH SCHOOL: Oakes (N.D.).
COLLEGE: North Dakota State (degree in agricultural economics).
TRANSACTIONS/CAREER NOTES: Selected by Buffalo Bills in second round (54th pick overall) of 1991 NFL draft. ... Signed by Bills (July 10, 1991). ... Granted free agency (February 17, 1994). ... Re-signed by Bills (April 29, 1994).
CHAMPIONSHIP GAME EXPERIENCE: Played in AFC championship game (1991-1993 seasons). ... Played in Super Bowl XXVI (1991 season), Super Bowl XXVII (1992 season) and Super Bowl XXVIII (1993 season).
PRO STATISTICS: 1991—Recovered one fumble. 1995—Recovered one fumble. 1996—Recovered two fumbles. 1997—Credited with a safety. 1998—Recovered three fumbles for 13 yards and one touchdown. 1999—Recovered two fumbles for 24 yards. 2000—Recovered one fumble for 29 yards.

Year Team	G	GS	SACKS
1991—Buffalo NFL	14	10	2.0
1992—Buffalo NFL	16	16	8.0
1993—Buffalo NFL	11	9	3.5
1994—Buffalo NFL	16	16	5.5
1995—Buffalo NFL	16	16	10.0
1996—Buffalo NFL	16	16	8.0
1997—Buffalo NFL	16	16	6.0
1998—Buffalo NFL	15	15	7.5
1999—Buffalo NFL	14	14	6.0
2000—Buffalo NFL	10	9	2.0
Pro totals (10 years)	144	137	58.5

HANSON, JASON   K   LIONS

PERSONAL: Born June 17, 1970, in Spokane, Wash. ... 5-11/182. ... Full name: Jason Douglas Hanson.
HIGH SCHOOL: Mead (Spokane, Wash.).
COLLEGE: Washington State (degree in pre-med).
TRANSACTIONS/CAREER NOTES: Selected by Detroit Lions in second round (56th pick overall) of 1992 NFL draft. ... Signed by Lions (July 23, 1992). ... Designated by Lions as transition player (February 15, 1994).
HONORS: Named kicker on THE SPORTING NEWS college All-America first team (1989). ... Named kicker on THE SPORTING NEWS NFL All-Pro team (1993). ... Played in Pro Bowl (1997 and 1999 season).
PRO STATISTICS: 1995—Punted once for 34 yards. 1996—Punted once for 24 yards. 1998—Punted three times for 94 yards.

H

Year Team	G	KICKING						
		XPM	XPA	FGM	FGA	Lg.	50+	Pts.
1992—Detroit NFL	16	30	30	21	26	52	2-5	93
1993—Detroit NFL	16	28	28	‡34	‡43	53	3-7	‡130
1994—Detroit NFL	16	39	40	18	27	49	0-5	93
1995—Detroit NFL	16	*48	†48	28	34	56	1-1	132
1996—Detroit NFL	16	36	36	12	17	51	1-3	72
1997—Detroit NFL	16	39	40	26	29	†55	3-5	117
1998—Detroit NFL	16	27	29	29	33	51	1-3	114
1999—Detroit NFL	16	28	29	26	∞32	52	4-8	106
2000—Detroit NFL	16	29	29	24	30	54	2-2	101
Pro totals (9 years)	144	304	309	218	271	56	17-39	958

HAPE, PATRICK — TE — BRONCOS

PERSONAL: Born June 6, 1974, in Killen, Ala. ... 6-4/262. ... Full name: Patrick Stephen Hape.
HIGH SCHOOL: Brooks (Killen, Ala.).
COLLEGE: Alabama.
TRANSACTIONS/CAREER NOTES: Selected by Tampa Bay Buccaneers in fifth round (137th pick overall) of 1997 NFL draft. ... Signed by Buccaneers (July 20, 1997). ... Granted free agency (February 11, 2000). ... Re-signed by Buccaneers (July 23, 2000). ... Granted unconditional free agency (March 2, 2001). ... Signed by Denver Broncos (March 14, 2001).
CHAMPIONSHIP GAME EXPERIENCE: Played in NFC championship game (1999 season).
PRO STATISTICS: 1997—Rushed once for one yard.
SINGLE GAME HIGHS (regular season): Receptions—2 (October 1, 2000, vs. Washington); yards—13 (September 10, 2000, vs. Chicago); and touchdown receptions—1 (November 28, 1999, vs. Seattle).

Year Team	G	GS	RECEIVING				TOTALS			
			No.	Yds.	Avg.	TD	TD	2pt.	Pts.	Fum.
1997—Tampa Bay NFL	14	3	4	22	5.5	1	1	0	6	1
1998—Tampa Bay NFL	16	2	4	27	6.8	0	0	1	2	1
1999—Tampa Bay NFL	15	1	5	12	2.4	1	1	0	6	0
2000—Tampa Bay NFL	16	2	6	39	6.5	0	0	0	0	0
Pro totals (4 years)	61	8	19	100	5.3	2	2	1	14	2

HARBAUGH, JIM — QB — LIONS

PERSONAL: Born December 23, 1963, in Toledo, Ohio. ... 6-3/215. ... Full name: James Joseph Harbaugh. ... Son of Jack Harbaugh, head coach, Western Kentucky University; and cousin of Mike Gottfried, ESPN college football analyst; and former head coach, Murray State University, University of Cincinnati, University of Kansas and University of Pittsburgh.
HIGH SCHOOL: Pioneer (Ann Arbor, Mich.), then Palo Alto (Calif.).
COLLEGE: Michigan (degree in communications, 1987).
TRANSACTIONS/CAREER NOTES: Selected by Chicago Bears in first round (26th pick overall) of 1987 NFL draft. ... Signed by Bears (August 3, 1987). ... On injured reserve with separated shoulder (December 19, 1990-remainder of season). ... Granted free agency (February 1, 1991). ... Re-signed by Bears (July 22, 1991). ... Granted unconditional free agency (March 1, 1993). ... Re-signed by Bears (March 19, 1993). ... Released by Bears (March 16, 1994). ... Signed by Indianapolis Colts (April 7, 1994). ... Designated by Colts as franchise player (February 16, 1996). ... Traded by Colts with fourth-round pick (traded to Tampa Bay) in 1998 draft to Baltimore Ravens for third- (WR E.G. Green) and fourth-round (traded back to Baltimore) picks in 1998 draft (February 14, 1998). ... Traded by Ravens to San Diego Chargers for fifth-round pick (G Richard Mercier) in 2000 draft (March 15, 1999). ... Granted unconditional free agency (March 2, 2001). ... Signed by Detroit Lions (March 5, 2001).
CHAMPIONSHIP GAME EXPERIENCE: Member of Bears for NFC championship game (1988 season); did not play. ... Played in AFC championship game (1995 season).
HONORS: Played in Pro Bowl (1995 season).
PRO STATISTICS: 1988—Fumbled once. 1989—Fumbled twice. 1990—Fumbled eight times and recovered three fumbles for minus four yards. 1991—Fumbled six times. 1992—Fumbled six times and recovered three fumbles. 1993—Caught one pass for one yard, led league with 15 fumbles and recovered four fumbles for minus one yard. 1994—Fumbled once. 1995—Caught one pass for minus nine yards, fumbled four times and recovered one fumble for minus 20 yards. 1996—Fumbled eight times and recovered four fumbles for minus three yards. 1997—Fumbled four times and recovered one fumble. 1998—Fumbled seven times and recovered three fumbles for minus seven yards. 1999—Fumbled 12 times and recovered four fumbles for minus 20 yards. 2000—Fumbled five times and recovered one fumble for minus five yards.
SINGLE GAME HIGHS (regular season): Attempts—47 (November 28, 1991, vs. Detroit); completions—30 (September 7, 1997, vs. New England); yards—404 (November 28, 1999, vs. Minnesota); and touchdown passes—4 (December 14, 1997, vs. Miami).
STATISTICAL PLATEAUS: 300-yard passing games: 1991 (1), 1992 (1), 1995 (1), 1997 (1), 1999 (2), 2000 (1). Total: 7.
MISCELLANEOUS: Regular-season record as starting NFL quarterback: 66-74 (.471). ... Postseason record as starting NFL quarterback: 2-3 (.400).

Year Team	G	GS	PASSING								RUSHING				TOTALS		
			Att.	Cmp.	Pct.	Yds.	TD	Int.	Avg.	Rat.	Att.	Yds.	Avg.	TD	TD	2pt.	Pts.
1987—Chicago NFL	6	0	11	8	72.7	62	0	0	5.64	86.2	4	15	3.8	0	0	0	0
1988—Chicago NFL	10	2	97	47	48.5	514	0	2	5.30	55.9	19	110	5.8	1	1	0	6
1989—Chicago NFL	12	5	178	111	62.4	1204	5	9	6.76	70.5	45	276	6.1	3	3	0	18
1990—Chicago NFL	14	14	312	180	57.7	2178	10	6	6.98	81.9	51	321	6.3	4	4	0	24
1991—Chicago NFL	16	16	478	275	57.5	3121	15	16	6.53	73.7	70	338	4.8	2	2	0	12
1992—Chicago NFL	16	13	358	202	56.4	2486	13	12	6.94	76.2	47	272	5.8	1	1	0	6
1993—Chicago NFL	15	15	325	200	61.5	2002	7	11	6.16	72.1	60	277	4.6	4	4	0	24
1994—Indianapolis NFL	12	9	202	125	61.9	1440	9	6	7.13	85.8	39	223	5.7	0	0	0	0
1995—Indianapolis NFL	15	12	314	200	63.7	2575	17	5	*8.20	*100.7	52	235	4.5	2	2	0	12
1996—Indianapolis NFL	14	14	405	232	57.3	2630	13	11	6.49	76.3	48	192	4.0	1	1	0	6
1997—Indianapolis NFL	12	11	309	189	§61.2	2060	10	4	6.67	86.2	36	206	5.7	0	0	0	0
1998—Baltimore NFL	14	12	293	164	56.0	1839	12	11	6.28	72.9	40	172	4.3	0	0	0	0
1999—San Diego NFL	14	12	434	249	57.4	2761	10	14	6.36	70.6	34	126	3.7	0	0	0	0
2000—San Diego NFL	7	5	202	123	60.9	1416	8	10	7.01	74.6	16	24	1.5	0	0	0	0
Pro totals (14 years)	177	140	3918	2305	58.8	26288	129	117	6.71	77.6	561	2787	5.0	18	18	0	108

H

HARDY, KEVIN   LB   JAGUARS

PERSONAL: Born July 24, 1973, in Evansville, Ind. ... 6-4/248. ... Full name: Kevin Lamont Hardy.
HIGH SCHOOL: Harrison (Evansville, Ind.).
COLLEGE: Illinois (degree in marketing, 1995).
TRANSACTIONS/CAREER NOTES: Selected by Jacksonville Jaguars in first round (second pick overall) of 1996 NFL draft. ... Signed by Jaguars (July 17, 1996).
CHAMPIONSHIP GAME EXPERIENCE: Played in AFC championship game (1996 and 1999 seasons).
HONORS: Butkus Award winner (1995). ... Named linebacker on THE SPORTING NEWS college All-America first team (1995). ... Named linebacker on THE SPORTING NEWS NFL All-Pro team (1999). ... Played in Pro Bowl (1999 season).
PRO STATISTICS: 1996—Recovered one fumble for 13 yards. 1998—Recovered one fumble. 1999—Recovered one fumble. 2000—Recovered two fumbles for two yards.

| | | | INTERCEPTIONS | | | SACKS |
Year Team	G	GS	No.	Yds.	Avg.	TD	No.
1996—Jacksonville NFL	16	15	2	19	9.5	0	5.5
1997—Jacksonville NFL	13	11	0	0	0.0	0	2.5
1998—Jacksonville NFL	16	16	2	40	20.0	0	1.5
1999—Jacksonville NFL	16	16	0	0	0.0	0	10.5
2000—Jacksonville NFL	16	16	1	0	0.0	0	3.0
Pro totals (5 years)	77	74	5	59	11.8	0	23.0

HARDY, TERRY   TE   CARDINALS

PERSONAL: Born May 31, 1976, in Montgomery, Ala. ... 6-4/270.
HIGH SCHOOL: Carver (Montgomery, Ala.).
COLLEGE: Southern Mississippi (degree in coaching and sports information, 1997).
TRANSACTIONS/CAREER NOTES: Selected by Arizona Cardinals in fifth round (125th pick overall) of 1998 NFL draft. ... Signed by Cardinals (June 15, 1998). ... Granted free agency (March 2, 2001).
SINGLE GAME HIGHS (regular season): Receptions—7 (October 29, 2000, vs. New Orleans); yards—49 (September 12, 1999, vs. Philadelphia); and touchdown receptions—1 (October 29, 2000, vs. New Orleans).

| | | | RECEIVING | | | | TOTALS | | | |
Year Team	G	GS	No.	Yds.	Avg.	TD	TD	2pt.	Pts.	Fum.
1998—Arizona NFL	9	0	0	0	0.0	0	0	0	0	0
1999—Arizona NFL	16	16	30	222	7.4	0	0	0	0	1
2000—Arizona NFL	16	15	27	160	5.9	1	1	0	6	2
Pro totals (3 years)	41	31	57	382	6.7	1	1	0	6	3

HARPER, DEVERON   CB   PANTHERS

PERSONAL: Born November 15, 1977, in Orangeburg, S.C. ... 5-11/187. ... Full name: Deveron Alfredo Harper.
HIGH SCHOOL: Wilkinson (Orangeburg, S.C.).
COLLEGE: Notre Dame.
TRANSACTIONS/CAREER NOTES: Signed as non-drafted free agent by Carolina Panthers (April 17, 2000).
PLAYING EXPERIENCE: Carolina NFL, 2000. ... Games/Games started: 2000 (16/0).

HARRIS, AL   CB   EAGLES

PERSONAL: Born December 7, 1974, in Pompano Beach, Fla. ... 6-1/185. ... Full name: Alshinard Harris.
HIGH SCHOOL: Ely (Pompano Beach, Fla.).
JUNIOR COLLEGE: Trinity Valley Community College (Texas).
COLLEGE: Texas A&M-Kingsville.
TRANSACTIONS/CAREER NOTES: Selected by Tampa Bay Buccaneers in sixth round (169th pick overall) of 1997 NFL draft. ... Signed by Buccaneers (July 1, 1997). ... Released by Buccaneers (August 24, 1997). ... Re-signed by Buccaneers to practice squad (August 26, 1997). ... Claimed on waivers by Philadelphia Eagles (August 31, 1998).
PLAYING EXPERIENCE: Philadelphia NFL, 1998-2000. ... Games/Games started: 1998 (16/7), 1999 (16/6), 2000 (16/4). Total: 48/17.
PRO STATISTICS: 1998—Returned one punt for minus two yards and fumbled once. 1999—Intercepted four passes for 151 yards and one touchdown and fumbled once. 2000—Ran one yard with lateral from interception.

HARRIS, ANTWAN   CB   PATRIOTS

PERSONAL: Born May 29, 1977, in Raleigh, N.C. ... 5-9/190. ... Full name: Melvin Antwan Harris.
HIGH SCHOOL: Ravenscroft (Raleigh, N.C.).
COLLEGE: Virginia.
TRANSACTIONS/CAREER NOTES: Selected by New England Patriots in sixth round (187th pick overall) of 2000 NFL draft. ... Signed by Patriots (July 14, 2000).
PRO STATISTICS: 2000—Recovered one fumble.

| | | | INTERCEPTIONS | | | SACKS |
Year Team	G	GS	No.	Yds.	Avg.	TD	No.
2000—New England NFL	14	0	1	11	11.0	0	1.0

H

HARRIS, BERNARDO — LB — PACKERS

PERSONAL: Born October 15, 1971, in Chapel Hill, N.C. ... 6-2/246. ... Full name: Bernardo Jamaine Harris.
HIGH SCHOOL: Chapel Hill (N.C.).
COLLEGE: North Carolina.
TRANSACTIONS/CAREER NOTES: Signed as non-drafted free agent by Kansas City Chiefs (June 2, 1994). ... Released by Chiefs (August 2, 1994). ... Signed by Green Bay Packers (January 20, 1995).
PLAYING EXPERIENCE: Green Bay NFL, 1995-2000. ... Games/Games started: 1995 (11/0), 1996 (16/0), 1997 (16/16), 1998 (16/16), 1999 (16/15), 2000 (16/16). Total: 91/63.
CHAMPIONSHIP GAME EXPERIENCE: Played in NFC championship game (1995-1997 seasons). ... Member of Super Bowl championship team (1996 season). ... Played in Super Bowl XXXII (1997 season).
PRO STATISTICS: 1997—Intercepted one pass for no yards and credited with one sack. 1998—Credited with two sacks. 1999—Recovered one fumble. 2000—Credited with two sacks.

HARRIS, COREY — CB — SAINTS

PERSONAL: Born November 28, 1976, in Warner Robins, Ga. ... 5-10/191.
HIGH SCHOOL: Northside (Warner Robins, Ga.).
COLLEGE: The Citadel, then North Alabama.
TRANSACTIONS/CAREER NOTES: Signed as non-drafted free agent by New Orleans Saints (May 20, 1999). ... Released by Saints (September 5, 1999). ... Re-signed by Saints to practice squad (September 6, 1999). ... Released by Saints (September 28, 1999). ... Re-signed by Saints to practice squad (October 27, 1999). ... Activated (December 17, 1999). ... Released by Saints (September 20, 2000). ... Re-signed by Saints (February 19, 2001). ... Assigned by Saints to Rhein Fire in 2001 NFL Europe enhancement allocation program (February 19, 2001).
PLAYING EXPERIENCE: New Orleans NFL, 1999 and 2000. ... Games/Games started: 1999 (3/0), 2000 (3/1). Total: 6/1.

HARRIS, COREY — S — RAVENS

PERSONAL: Born October 25, 1969, in Indianapolis. ... 5-11/200. ... Full name: Corey Lamont Harris.
HIGH SCHOOL: Ben Davis (Indianapolis).
COLLEGE: Vanderbilt (degree in human resources).
TRANSACTIONS/CAREER NOTES: Selected by Houston Oilers in third round (77th pick overall) of 1992 NFL draft. ... Signed by Oilers (August 5, 1992). ... Claimed on waivers by Green Bay Packers (October 14, 1992). ... Granted free agency (February 17, 1995). ... Tendered offer sheet by Seattle Seahawks (March 3, 1995). ... Packers declined to match offer (March 10, 1995). ... Granted unconditional free agency (February 14, 1997). ... Signed by Miami Dolphins (March 17, 1997). ... Released by Dolphins (August 3, 1998). ... Signed by Baltimore Ravens (August 17, 1998). ... Granted unconditional free agency (February 12, 1999). ... Re-signed by Ravens (May 17, 1999). ... Granted unconditional free agency (February 11, 2000). ... Re-signed by Ravens (March 21, 2000).
CHAMPIONSHIP GAME EXPERIENCE: Played in AFC championship game (2000 season). ... Member of Super Bowl championship team (2000 season).
PRO STATISTICS: 1992—Rushed twice for 10 yards and returned six punts for 17 yards. 1993—Caught two passes for 11 yards. 1994—Recovered one fumble. 1995—Recovered one fumble for 57 yards and a touchdown. 1996—Credited with one sack and recovered three fumbles for 28 yards. 1998—Credited with one sack and recovered one fumble. 1999—Credited with one sack.
MISCELLANEOUS: Played wide receiver (1992 and 1993).

Year Team	G	GS	INTERCEPTIONS				KICKOFF RETURNS				TOTALS			
			No.	Yds.	Avg.	TD	No.	Yds.	Avg.	TD	TD	2pt.	Pts.	Fum.
1992—Houston NFL	5	0	0	0	0.0	0	0	0	0.0	0	0	0	0	0
—Green Bay NFL	10	0	0	0	0.0	0	33	691	20.9	0	0	0	0	0
1993—Green Bay NFL	11	0	0	0	0.0	0	16	482	30.1	0	0	0	0	0
1994—Green Bay NFL	16	2	0	0	0.0	0	29	618	21.3	0	0	0	0	1
1995—Seattle NFL	16	16	3	-5	-1.7	0	19	397	20.9	0	1	0	6	0
1996—Seattle NFL	16	16	1	25	25.0	0	7	166	23.7	0	0	0	0	0
1997—Miami NFL	16	7	0	0	0.0	0	11	224	20.4	0	0	0	0	0
1998—Baltimore NFL	16	6	0	0	0.0	0	35	965	§27.6	▲1	1	0	6	2
1999—Baltimore NFL	16	0	1	24	24.0	1	38	843	22.2	0	1	0	6	0
2000—Baltimore NFL	16	0	2	44	22.0	0	39	907	23.3	0	0	0	0	1
Pro totals (9 years)	138	47	7	88	12.6	1	227	5293	23.3	1	3	0	18	4

HARRIS, JACKIE — TE — COWBOYS

PERSONAL: Born January 4, 1968, in Pine Bluff, Ark. ... 6-4/250. ... Full name: Jackie Bernard Harris. ... Second cousin of Chris Akins, safety, Green Bay Packers.
HIGH SCHOOL: Dollarway (Pine Bluff, Ark.).
COLLEGE: Northeast Louisiana.
TRANSACTIONS/CAREER NOTES: Selected by Green Bay Packers in fourth round (102nd pick overall) of 1990 NFL draft. ... Signed by Packers (July 22, 1990). ... Granted free agency (February 1, 1992). ... Re-signed by Packers (August 14, 1992). ... Designated by Packers as transition player (February 25, 1993). ... Tendered offer sheet by Tampa Bay Buccaneers (June 15, 1994). ... Packers declined to match offer (June 22, 1994). ... On injured reserve with shoulder injury (November 22, 1994-remainder of season). ... On injured reserve with hernia (January 2, 1998-remainder of 1997 playoffs). ... Granted unconditional free agency (February 13, 1998). ... Signed by Tennessee Oilers (March 11, 1998). ... Oilers franchise renamed Tennessee Titans for 1999 season (December 26, 1998). ... Granted unconditional free agency (February 11, 2000). ... Signed by Dallas Cowboys (March 17, 2000).

CHAMPIONSHIP GAME EXPERIENCE: Played in AFC championship game (1999 season). ... Played in Super Bowl XXXIV (1999 season).
PRO STATISTICS: 1991—Rushed once for one yard and recovered one fumble. 1998—Returned one kickoff for three yards.
SINGLE GAME HIGHS (regular season): Receptions—10 (November 26, 1995, vs. Green Bay); yards—128 (October 10, 1993, vs. Denver); and touchdown receptions—2 (September 24, 2000, vs. San Francisco).
STATISTICAL PLATEAUS: 100-yard receiving games: 1993 (1), 1995 (2). Total: 3.

Year Team	G	GS	RECEIVING				TOTALS			
			No.	Yds.	Avg.	TD	TD	2pt.	Pts.	Fum.
1990—Green Bay NFL	16	3	12	157	13.1	0	0	0	0	0
1991—Green Bay NFL	16	6	24	264	11.0	3	3	0	18	1
1992—Green Bay NFL	16	11	55	595	10.8	2	2	0	12	1
1993—Green Bay NFL	12	12	42	604	14.4	4	4	0	24	0
1994—Tampa Bay NFL	9	9	26	337	13.0	3	3	1	20	1
1995—Tampa Bay NFL	16	16	62	751	12.1	1	1	0	6	2
1996—Tampa Bay NFL	13	12	30	349	11.6	1	1	1	8	1
1997—Tampa Bay NFL	12	11	19	197	10.4	1	1	0	6	0
1998—Tennessee NFL	16	16	43	412	9.6	2	2	0	12	0
1999—Tennessee NFL	12	1	26	297	11.4	1	1	†1	8	0
2000—Dallas NFL	16	7	39	306	7.8	5	5	1	32	0
Pro totals (11 years)	154	104	378	4269	11.3	23	23	4	146	5

HARRIS, JOHNNIE   S   RAIDERS

PERSONAL: Born August 21, 1972, in Chicago. ... 6-2/210.
HIGH SCHOOL: Martin Luther King (Chicago).
JUNIOR COLLEGE: San Bernardino (Calif.) Valley.
COLLEGE: Mississippi State.
TRANSACTIONS/CAREER NOTES: Signed by San Antonio Texans of CFL (October 17, 1995). ... Selected by Edmonton Eskimos in 1996 U.S. Team Dispersal draft. ... Released by Eskimos (June 5, 1996). ... Played with Tampa Bay Storm of Arena League (1996-98). ... Signed by Toronto Argonauts of CFL (October 12, 1996). ... Released by Argonauts (May 15, 1997). ... Re-signed by Argonauts (June 2, 1997). ... Signed as non-drafted free agent by Oakland Raiders (February 28, 1999). ... Released by Raiders (September 5, 1999). ... Re-signed by Raiders to practice squad (September 7, 1999). ... Activated (December 1999).
PLAYING EXPERIENCE: Toronto Argonauts CFL, 1996 and 1997; Oakland NFL, 1999 and 2000. ... Games/Games started: 1996 (4/games started unavailable), 1997 (18/-), 1999 (4/0), 2000 (15/2). Total CFL: 22/-. Total NFL: 19/2. Total Pro: 41/-.
CHAMPIONSHIP GAME EXPERIENCE: Member of CFL championship team (1996). ... Played in AFC championship game (2000 season).
PRO STATISTICS: CFL: 1996—Returned one kickoff for seven yards. 1997—Intercepted five passes for 72 yards.

HARRIS, RAYMONT   RB

PERSONAL: Born December 23, 1970, in Lorain, Ohio. ... 6-0/230. ... Full name: Raymont LeShawn Harris.
HIGH SCHOOL: Lorain (Ohio) Admiral King.
COLLEGE: Ohio State.
TRANSACTIONS/CAREER NOTES: Selected by Chicago Bears in fourth round (114th pick overall) of 1994 NFL draft. ... Signed by Bears (June 21, 1994). ... On injured reserve with broken collarbone (November 29, 1995-remainder of season). ... Granted free agency (February 14, 1997). ... On injured reserve with ankle injury (December 9, 1997-remainder of season). ... Designated by Bears as transition player (February 12, 1998). ... Free agency status changed from transitional to unconditional (April 20, 1998). ... Signed by Green Bay Packers (July 20, 1998). ... Released by Packers (December 8, 1998). ... Signed by New England Patriots (February 14, 2000). ... Released by Patriots (August 27, 2000). ... Signed by Denver Broncos (September 12, 2000). ... Released by Broncos (November 25, 2000). ... Signed by Patriots (December 6, 2000). ... Released by Patriots (December 19, 2000).
PRO STATISTICS: 1994—Returned one kickoff for 18 yards and recovered three fumbles.
SINGLE GAME HIGHS (regular season): Attempts—33 (November 23, 1997, vs. Tampa Bay); yards—122 (September 1, 1997, vs. Green Bay); and rushing touchdowns—2 (September 1, 1997, vs. Green Bay).
STATISTICAL PLATEAUS: 100-yard rushing games: 1996 (3), 1997 (5). Total: 8. ... 100-yard receiving games: 1996 (1).

Year Team	G	GS	RUSHING				RECEIVING				TOTALS			
			Att.	Yds.	Avg.	TD	No.	Yds.	Avg.	TD	TD	2pt.	Pts.	Fum.
1994—Chicago NFL	16	11	123	464	3.8	1	39	236	6.1	0	1	0	6	1
1995—Chicago NFL	2	1	0	0	0.0	0	1	4	4.0	0	0	0	0	0
1996—Chicago NFL	12	10	194	748	3.9	4	32	296	9.3	1	5	0	30	3
1997—Chicago NFL	13	13	275	1033	3.8	10	28	115	4.1	0	10	0	60	1
1998—Green Bay NFL	8	3	79	228	2.9	1	10	68	6.8	0	1	0	6	3
1999—							Did not play.							
2000—Denver NFL	2	0	10	22	2.2	0	2	19	9.5	0	0	0	0	0
—New England NFL	1	0	3	14	4.7	0	2	1	0.5	0	0	0	0	0
Pro totals (6 years)	54	38	684	2509	3.7	16	114	739	6.5	1	17	0	102	8

HARRIS, SEAN   LB   BEARS

PERSONAL: Born February 25, 1972, in Tucson, Ariz. ... 6-3/252. ... Full name: Sean Eugene Harris.
HIGH SCHOOL: Magnet (Tucson, Ariz.).
COLLEGE: Arizona.
TRANSACTIONS/CAREER NOTES: Selected by Chicago Bears in third round (83rd pick overall) of 1995 NFL draft. ... Signed by Bears (July 18, 1995). ... Granted free agency (February 13, 1998). ... Re-signed by Bears (May 12, 1998). ... Granted unconditional free agency (February 12, 1999). ... Re-signed by Bears (March 11, 1999).
PLAYING EXPERIENCE: Chicago NFL, 1995-2000. ... Games/Games started: 1995 (11/0), 1996 (15/0), 1997 (11/1), 1998 (16/14), 1999 (14/10), 2000 (15/13). Total: 82/38.
PRO STATISTICS: 1998—Intercepted one pass for no yards and credited with one sack. 1999—Intercepted one pass for no yards and recovered two fumbles, including one in end zone for a touchdown. 2000—Credited with one sack.

H

HARRIS, WALT   CB   BEARS

PERSONAL: Born August 10, 1974, in La Grange, Ga. ... 5-11/195. ... Full name: Walter Lee Harris.
HIGH SCHOOL: La Grange (Ga.).
COLLEGE: Mississippi State.
TRANSACTIONS/CAREER NOTES: Selected by Chicago Bears in first round (13th pick overall) of 1996 NFL draft. ... Signed by Bears (July 11, 1996). ... On injured reserve with knee injury (December 22, 1998-remainder of season). ... On injured reserve with knee injury (December 22, 2000-remainder of season). ... Granted unconditional free agency (March 2, 2001). ... Re-signed by Bears (April 25, 2001).
PRO STATISTICS: 1996—Recovered two fumbles for eight yards. 1997—Fumbled once and recovered one fumble. 1998—Recovered one fumble. 1999—Credited with one sack and recovered one fumble. 2000—Returned one punt for 14 yards.

			INTERCEPTIONS			
Year Team	G	GS	No.	Yds.	Avg.	TD
1996—Chicago NFL	15	13	2	0	0.0	0
1997—Chicago NFL	16	16	5	30	6.0	0
1998—Chicago NFL	14	14	4	41	10.3	1
1999—Chicago NFL	15	15	1	-1	-1.0	0
2000—Chicago NFL	12	12	2	35	17.5	1
Pro totals (5 years)	72	70	14	105	7.5	2

HARRISON, LLOYD   CB   REDSKINS

PERSONAL: Born June 21, 1977, in Jamaica. ... 5-10/190.
HIGH SCHOOL: Sewanhaka (Floral Park, N.Y.).
COLLEGE: North Carolina State.
TRANSACTIONS/CAREER NOTES: Selected by Washington Redskins in third round (64th pick overall) of 2000 NFL draft. ... Signed by Redskins (July 7, 2000).
PLAYING EXPERIENCE: Washington NFL, 2000. ... Games/Games started: 2000 (2/0).

HARRISON, MARVIN   WR   COLTS

PERSONAL: Born August 25, 1972, in Philadelphia. ... 6-0/178. ... Full name: Marvin Daniel Harrison.
HIGH SCHOOL: Roman Catholic (Philadelphia).
COLLEGE: Syracuse.
TRANSACTIONS/CAREER NOTES: Selected by Indianapolis Colts in first round (19th pick overall) of 1996 NFL draft. ... Signed by Colts (July 8, 1996). ... On injured reserve with shoulder injury (December 2, 1998-remainder of season).
HONORS: Named kick returner on THE SPORTING NEWS All-America first team (1995). ... Named wide receiver on THE SPORTING NEWS NFL All-Pro team (1999 and 2000). ... Played in Pro Bowl (1999 and 2000 seasons).
PRO STATISTICS: 1996—Rushed three times for 15 yards. 1997—Recovered one fumble for five yards. 1999—Rushed once for four yards and recovered one fumble.
SINGLE GAME HIGHS (regular season): Receptions—14 (December 26, 1999, vs. Cleveland); yards—196 (September 26, 1999, vs. San Diego); and touchdown receptions—3 (December 24, 2000, vs. Minnesota).
STATISTICAL PLATEAUS: 100-yard receiving games: 1996 (2), 1998 (2), 1999 (9), 2000 (8). Total: 21.

			RECEIVING				PUNT RETURNS				TOTALS			
Year Team	G	GS	No.	Yds.	Avg.	TD	No.	Yds.	Avg.	TD	TD	2pt.	Pts.	Fum.
1996—Indianapolis NFL	16	15	64	836	13.1	8	18	177	9.8	0	8	0	48	1
1997—Indianapolis NFL	16	15	73	866	11.9	6	0	0	0.0	0	6	2	40	2
1998—Indianapolis NFL	12	12	59	776	13.2	7	0	0	0.0	0	7	1	44	0
1999—Indianapolis NFL	16	16	115	*1663	14.5	§12	0	0	0.0	0	12	†1	74	2
2000—Indianapolis NFL	16	16	†102	1413	13.9	§14	0	0	0.0	0	14	0	84	2
Pro totals (5 years)	76	74	413	5554	13.4	47	18	177	9.8	0	47	4	290	7

HARRISON, NOLAN   DE

PERSONAL: Born January 25, 1969, in Chicago. ... 6-5/291. ... Full name: Nolan Harrison III.
HIGH SCHOOL: Homewood-Flossmoor (Flossmoor, Ill.).
COLLEGE: Indiana (degree in criminal justice, 1991).
TRANSACTIONS/CAREER NOTES: Selected by Los Angeles Raiders in sixth round (146th pick overall) of 1991 NFL draft. ... Signed by Raiders (1991). ... Raiders franchise moved to Oakland (July 21, 1995). ... Granted unconditional free agency (February 16, 1996). ... Signed by Pittsburgh Steelers (May 20, 1997). ... On injured reserve with chest injury (December 15, 1999-remainder of season). ... Granted unconditional free agency (February 11, 2000). ... Signed by Washington Redskins (June 8, 2000). ... Granted unconditional free agency (March 2, 2001).
CHAMPIONSHIP GAME EXPERIENCE: Played in AFC championship game (1997 season).
PRO STATISTICS: 1992—Credited with a safety. 1993—Recovered one fumble for five yards. 1994—Recovered two fumbles. 1999—Recovered one fumble.

Year Team	G	GS	SACKS
1991—Los Angeles Raiders NFL	14	3	1.0
1992—Los Angeles Raiders NFL	14	14	2.5
1993—Los Angeles Raiders NFL	16	14	3.0
1994—Los Angeles Raiders NFL	16	16	5.0
1995—Oakland NFL	7	6	0.0
1996—Oakland NFL	15	2	2.0
1997—Pittsburgh NFL	16	16	4.0
1998—Pittsburgh NFL	9	7	3.5
1999—Pittsburgh NFL	5	3	0.0
2000—Washington NFL	16	2	1.0
Pro totals (10 years)	128	83	22.0

HARRISON, RODNEY   S   CHARGERS

PERSONAL: Born December 15, 1972, in Markham, Ill. ... 6-1/207. ... Full name: Rodney Scott Harrison.
HIGH SCHOOL: Marian Catholic (Chicago Heights, Ill.).
COLLEGE: Western Illinois.
TRANSACTIONS/CAREER NOTES: Selected after junior season by San Diego Chargers in fifth round (145th pick overall) of 1994 NFL draft. ... Signed by Chargers (June 29, 1994).
CHAMPIONSHIP GAME EXPERIENCE: Played in AFC championship game (1994 season). ... Played in Super Bowl XXIX (1994 season).
HONORS: Named safety on THE SPORTING NEWS NFL All-Pro team (1998). ... Played in Pro Bowl (1998 season).
PRO STATISTICS: 1994—Recovered one fumble. 1996—Returned one kickoff for 10 yards, fumbled once and recovered two fumbles for four yards. 1997—Returned one punt for no yards, returned one kickoff for 40 yards and a touchdown and recovered three fumbles, including one in the end zone for a touchdown.

			INTERCEPTIONS			SACKS
Year Team	G	GS	No.	Yds.	Avg.	TD	No.
1994—San Diego NFL	15	0	0	0	0.0	0	0.0
1995—San Diego NFL	11	0	5	22	4.4	0	0.0
1996—San Diego NFL	16	16	5	56	11.2	0	1.0
1997—San Diego NFL	16	16	2	75	37.5	1	4.0
1998—San Diego NFL	16	16	3	42	14.0	0	4.0
1999—San Diego NFL	6	6	1	0	0.0	0	1.0
2000—San Diego NFL	16	16	6	97	16.2	1	6.0
Pro totals (7 years)	96	70	22	292	13.3	2	16.0

HARTINGS, JEFF   G   STEELERS

PERSONAL: Born September 7, 1972, in Henry, Ohio. ... 6-3/295. ... Full name: Jeffrey Allen Hartings.
HIGH SCHOOL: St. Henry (Ohio).
COLLEGE: Penn State.
TRANSACTIONS/CAREER NOTES: Selected by Detroit Lions in first round (23rd pick overall) of 1996 NFL draft. ... Signed by Lions (September 27, 1996). ... Granted unconditional free agency (March 2, 2001). ... Signed by Pittsburgh Steelers (March 8, 2001).
PLAYING EXPERIENCE: Detroit NFL, 1996-2000. ... Games/Games started: 1996 (11/10), 1997 (16/16), 1998 (13/13), 1999 (16/16), 2000 (16/16). Total: 72/71.
HONORS: Named offensive lineman on THE SPORTING NEWS college All-America second team (1994). ... Named offensive lineman on THE SPORTING NEWS college All-America first team (1995).
PRO STATISTICS: 1996—Recovered one fumble. 1999—Recovered two fumbles for one yard. 2000—Recovered one fumble in end zone for touchdown.

HARTSELL, MARK   QB   COLTS

PERSONAL: Born December 7, 1973, in Brockton, Mass. ... 6-4/225.
HIGH SCHOOL: Brockton (Mass.).
COLLEGE: Boston College.
TRANSACTIONS/CAREER NOTES: Signed as non-drafted free agent by Chicago Bears (March 22, 2000). ... Released by Bears (August 27, 2000). ... Re-signed by Bears to practice squad (October 25, 2000). ... Activated (November 15, 2000). ... Claimed on waivers by Indianapolis Colts (May 25, 2001).
PLAYING EXPERIENCE: Chicago NFL, 2000. ... Games/Games started: 2000 (1/0).
PRO STATISTICS: 2000—Attempted one pass without a completion.
SINGLE GAME HIGHS (regular season): Attempts—1 (December 3, 2000, vs. Green Bay); completions—0; yards—0; and touchdown passes—0.

HARVEY, RICHARD   LB

PERSONAL: Born September 11, 1966, in Pascagoula, Miss. ... 6-1/235. ... Full name: Richard Clemont Harvey. ... Son of Richard Harvey Sr., defensive back with Philadelphia Eagles (1970) and New Orleans Saints (1971).
HIGH SCHOOL: Pascagoula (Miss.).
COLLEGE: Tulane.
TRANSACTIONS/CAREER NOTES: Selected by Buffalo Bills in 11th round (305th pick overall) of 1989 NFL draft. ... Signed by Bills for 1989 season. ... On injured reserve with shoulder injury (September 4, 1989-entire season). ... Granted unconditional free agency (February 1, 1990). ... Signed by New England Patriots (March 23, 1990). ... Released by Patriots (September 2, 1991). ... Signed by Bills (February 3, 1992). ... Selected by Ohio Glory in first round of 1992 World League supplemental draft. ... Granted unconditional free agency (February 17, 1994). ... Signed by Denver Broncos (May 9, 1994). ... Granted unconditional free agency (February 17, 1995). ... Signed by New Orleans Saints (April 3, 1995). ... Granted unconditional free agency (February 14, 1997). ... Re-signed by Saints (May 1, 1997). ... On injured reserve with foot injury (December 20, 1997-remainder of season). ... Granted unconditional free agency (February 13, 1998). ... Re-signed by Saints (March 2, 1998). ... Released by Saints (August 24, 1998). ... Signed by Oakland Raiders (August 26, 1998). ... Released by Raiders (February 10, 2000). ... Signed by San Diego Chargers (July 14, 2000). ... Released by Chargers (November 20, 2000).
CHAMPIONSHIP GAME EXPERIENCE: Member of Bills for AFC championship game (1992 season); inactive. ... Member of Bills for Super Bowl XXVII (1992 season); inactive. ... Played in AFC championship game (1993 season). ... Played in Super Bowl XXVIII (1993 season).
PRO STATISTICS: 1992—Recovered one fumble. 1994—Recovered one fumble. 1997—Intercepted one pass for seven yards and recovered one fumble. 1998—Intercepted one pass for two yards.

Year Team	G	GS	SACKS
1989—Buffalo NFL	Did not play.		
1990—New England NFL	16	9	0.0
1991—New England NFL	1	0	0.0
1992—Buffalo NFL	12	0	0.0
1993—Buffalo NFL	15	0	0.0
1994—Denver NFL	16	1	0.0
1995—New Orleans NFL	16	14	2.0
1996—New Orleans NFL	14	7	2.0
1997—New Orleans NFL	14	13	3.0
1998—Oakland NFL	16	16	4.0
1999—Oakland NFL	15	15	2.0
2000—San Diego NFL	7	0	0.0
Pro totals (11 years)	142	75	13.0

H

PERSONAL: Born September 22, 1967, in Amsterdam, Holland. ... 6-6/285. ... Name pronounced HASS-el-back.
HIGH SCHOOL: South Delta (Delta, B.C.).
COLLEGE: Washington.
TRANSACTIONS/CAREER NOTES: Selected by Calgary Stampeders in fifth round (34th pick overall) of 1989 CFL draft. ... Granted free agency after 1993 season. ... Signed as non-drafted free agent by Denver Broncos (April 11, 1994).
CHAMPIONSHIP GAME EXPERIENCE: Played in Grey Cup (1992). ... Played in AFC championship game (1997 and 1998 seasons). ... Member of Super Bowl championship team (1997 and 1998 seasons).
PRO STATISTICS: CFL: 1992—Recovered two fumbles. 1993—Recovered four fumbles for 16 yards, intercepted one pass for no yards and fumbled once. NFL: 1995—Recovered four fumbles.

Year — Team	G	GS	SACKS
1990—Calgary CFL	3	...	0.0
1991—Calgary CFL	11	...	3.0
1992—Calgary CFL	18	...	4.0
1993—Calgary CFL	18	...	7.0
1994—Denver NFL	16	9	2.0
1995—Denver NFL	16	10	4.0
1996—Denver NFL	16	1	2.0
1997—Denver NFL	16	3	1.5
1998—Denver NFL	16	3	3.0
1999—Denver NFL	16	2	2.5
2000—Denver NFL	16	1	2.5
CFL totals (4 years)	50	...	14.0
NFL totals (7 years)	112	29	17.5
Pro totals (11 years)	162	...	31.5

PERSONAL: Born September 25, 1975, in Boulder, Colo. ... 6-4/220. ... Full name: Matthew Michael Hasselbeck. ... Son of Don Hasselbeck, tight end with New England Patriots (1977-85); and brother of Tim Hasselbeck, quarterback, Buffalo Bills.
HIGH SCHOOL: Westwood (Mass.).
COLLEGE: Boston College (degree in marketing and finance, 1997).
TRANSACTIONS/CAREER NOTES: Selected by Green Bay Packers in sixth round (187th pick overall) of 1998 NFL draft. ... Signed by Packers (July 17, 1998). ... Released by Packers (September 3, 1998). ... Re-signed by Packers to practice squad (September 5, 1998). ... Traded by Packers with first-round pick (G Steve Hutchinson) in 2001 draft to Seattle Seahawks for first-round pick (DE Jamal Reynolds) in 2001 draft (March 2, 2001).
PRO STATISTICS: 1999—Fumbled once and recovered one fumble for minus 16 yards.
SINGLE GAME HIGHS (regular season): Attempts—18 (November 12, 2000, vs. Tampa Bay); completions—9 (November 12, 2000, vs. Tampa Bay); passing yards—93 (November 12, 2000, vs. Tampa Bay); and touchdown passes—1 (November 12, 2000, vs. Tampa Bay).

Year Team	G	GS		PASSING								RUSHING				TOTALS	
			Att.	Cmp.	Pct.	Yds.	TD	Int.	Avg.	Rat.	Att.	Yds.	Avg.	TD	TD	2pt.	Pts.
1999—Green Bay NFL	16	0	10	3	30.0	41	1	0	4.10	77.5	6	15	2.5	0	0	0	0
2000—Green Bay NFL	16	0	19	10	52.6	104	1	0	5.47	86.3	4	-5	-1.3	0	0	0	0
Pro totals (2 years)	32	0	29	13	44.8	145	2	0	5.00	83.3	10	10	1.0	0	0	0	0

PERSONAL: Born November 7, 1970, in Atlanta. ... 6-1/190. ... Full name: Andre Orlando Hastings.
HIGH SCHOOL: Morrow (Ga.).
COLLEGE: Georgia.
TRANSACTIONS/CAREER NOTES: Selected after junior season by Pittsburgh Steelers in third round (76th pick overall) of 1993 NFL draft. ... Signed by Steelers (July 18, 1993). ... Granted free agency (February 16, 1996). ... Re-signed by Steelers (August 9, 1996). ... Granted unconditional free agency (February 14, 1997). ... Signed by New Orleans Saints (May 28, 1997). ... Released by Saints (February 10, 1998). ... Re-signed by Saints (March 6, 1998). ... Released by Saints (April 24, 2000). ... Signed by Tampa Bay Buccaneers (August 3, 2000). ... Released by Buccaneers (November 22, 2000).
CHAMPIONSHIP GAME EXPERIENCE: Played in AFC championship game (1994 and 1995 seasons). ... Played in Super Bowl XXX (1995 season).
PRO STATISTICS: 1996—Recovered one fumble. 1998—Recovered one fumble. 2000—Fumbled once.
SINGLE GAME HIGHS (regular season): Receptions—10 (September 18, 1995, vs. Miami); yards—122 (December 6, 1998, vs. Dallas); and touchdown receptions—2 (December 1, 1996, vs. Baltimore).
STATISTICAL PLATEAUS: 100-yard receiving games: 1997 (1), 1998 (1), 1999 (1). Total: 3.

Year Team	G	GS	RUSHING				RECEIVING				PUNT RETURNS				KICKOFF RETURNS				TOTALS		
			Att.	Yds.	Avg.	TD	No.	Yds.	Avg.	TD	No.	Yds.	Avg.	TD	No.	Yds.	Avg.	TD	TD	2pt.	Pts.
1993—Pittsburgh NFL	6	0	0	0	0.0	0	3	44	14.7	0	0	0	0.0	0	12	177	14.8	0	0	0	0
1994—Pittsburgh NFL	16	8	0	0	0.0	0	20	281	14.1	2	2	15	7.5	0	0	0	0.0	0	2	0	12
1995—Pittsburgh NFL	16	0	1	14	14.0	0	48	502	10.5	1	48	474	9.9	†1	0	0	0.0*	0	2	0	12
1996—Pittsburgh NFL	16	10	4	71	17.8	0	72	739	10.3	6	37	242	6.5	0	1	42	42.0	0	6	0	36
1997—New Orleans NFL	16	16	4	35	8.8	0	48	722	15.0	5	1	-2	-2.0	0	0	0	0.0	0	5	1	32
1998—New Orleans NFL	16	12	3	32	10.7	0	35	455	13.0	3	22	307	14.0	0	1	16	16.0	0	3	0	18
1999—New Orleans NFL	15	5	1	4	4.0	0	40	564	14.1	1	0	0	0.0	0	0	0	0.0	0	1	0	6
2000—Tampa Bay NFL	3	0	0	0	0.0	0	0	0	0.0	0	5	50	10.0	0	0	0	0.0	0	0	0	0
Pro totals (8 years)	104	51	13	156	12.0	0	266	3307	12.4	18	115	1086	9.4	1	14	235	16.8	0	19	1	116

HASTY, JAMES   CB

PERSONAL: Born May 23, 1965, in Seattle. ... 6-0/213. ... Full name: James Edward Hasty.
HIGH SCHOOL: Franklin (Seattle).
COLLEGE: Central Washington, then Washington State (degree in communications, 1988).
TRANSACTIONS/CAREER NOTES: Selected by New York Jets in third round (74th pick overall) of 1988 NFL draft. ... Signed by Jets (July 12, 1988). ... Designated by Jets as transition player (February 25, 1993). ... Tendered offer sheet by Cincinnati Bengals (April 29, 1993). ... Offer matched by Jets (May 4, 1993). ... Granted unconditional free agency (February 17, 1995). ... Signed by Kansas City Chiefs (March 29, 1995). ... On reserve/did not report list (July 20-August 3, 1997). ... Granted unconditional free agency (February 13, 1998). ... Re-signed by Chiefs (February 17, 1998). ... Released by Chiefs (February 28, 2001).
HONORS: Played in Pro Bowl (1997 and 1999 seasons).
PRO STATISTICS: 1988—Recovered three fumbles for 35 yards. 1989—Fumbled once and recovered two fumbles for two yards. 1990—Returned one punt for no yards, fumbled once and recovered three fumbles. 1991—Recovered four fumbles for seven yards. 1992—Recovered two fumbles. 1993—Recovered two fumbles for 28 yards. 1994—Recovered two fumbles. 1995—Recovered one fumble for 20 yards. 1996—Recovered one fumble for 80 yards and a touchdown. 1997—Recovered one fumble. 1998—Recovered one fumble. 2000—Recovered two fumbles.

				INTERCEPTIONS			SACKS
Year Team	G	GS	No.	Yds.	Avg.	TD	No.
1988—New York Jets NFL	15	15	5	20	4.0	0	1.0
1989—New York Jets NFL	16	16	5	62	12.4	1	0.0
1990—New York Jets NFL	16	16	2	0	0.0	0	0.0
1991—New York Jets NFL	16	16	3	39	13.0	0	0.0
1992—New York Jets NFL	16	16	2	18	9.0	0	0.0
1993—New York Jets NFL	16	16	2	22	11.0	0	0.0
1994—New York Jets NFL	16	16	5	90	18.0	0	3.0
1995—Kansas City NFL	16	16	3	89	29.7	▲1	0.0
1996—Kansas City NFL	15	14	0	0	0.0	0	1.0
1997—Kansas City NFL	16	15	3	22	7.3	0	2.0
1998—Kansas City NFL	16	14	4	42	10.5	0	1.0
1999—Kansas City NFL	15	15	†7	98	14.0	†2	1.0
2000—Kansas City NFL	16	15	4	53	13.3	0	1.0
Pro totals (13 years)	205	200	45	555	12.3	4	10.0

HATCHER, ARMON   S   CHARGERS

PERSONAL: Born July 15, 1976, in Diamond Bar, Calif. ... 6-0/212. ... Full name: Armon Merrell Hatcher. ... Cousin of Billy Hatcher, outfielder with eight major league baseball teams (1981-95).
HIGH SCHOOL: Diamond Bar (Calif.).
COLLEGE: Oregon State.
TRANSACTIONS/CAREER NOTES: Selected by Buffalo Bills in sixth round (194th pick overall) of 1999 NFL draft. ... Signed by Bills (June 15, 1999). ... Released by Bills (September 6, 1999). ... Selected by Barcelona Dragons in 2000 NFL Europe draft (February 22, 2000). ... Signed by San Diego Chargers to practice squad (October 24, 2000). ... Activated (November 24, 2000). ... Released by Chargers (November 27, 2000). ... Re-signed by Chargers to practice squad (November 29, 2000). ... Activated (December 8, 2000). ... Assigned by Chargers to Amsterdam Admirals in 2001 NFL Europe enhancement allocation program (February 19, 2001).
PLAYING EXPERIENCE: Barcelona NFLE, 2000; San Diego NFL, 2000. ... Games/Games started: NFLE 2000 (games played unavailable), NFL 2000 (4/0).

HATCHETTE, MATTHEW   WR   JETS

PERSONAL: Born May 1, 1974, in Cleveland. ... 6-3/193. ... Full name: Matthew Isaac Hatchette.
HIGH SCHOOL: Jefferson (Delphos, Ohio).
COLLEGE: Mercyhurst College (Pa.), then Langston University (Okla.).
TRANSACTIONS/CAREER NOTES: Selected by Minnesota Vikings in seventh round (235th pick overall) of 1997 NFL draft. ... Signed by Vikings (June 20, 1997). ... Granted free agency (February 11, 2000). ... Re-signed by Vikings (April 11, 2000). ... Granted unconditional free agency (March 2, 2001). ... Signed by New York Jets (March 19, 2001).
CHAMPIONSHIP GAME EXPERIENCE: Played in NFC championship game (1998 and 2000 seasons).
SINGLE GAME HIGHS (regular season): Receptions—6 (December 13, 1998, vs. Baltimore); yards—95 (December 13, 1998, vs. Baltimore); and touchdown receptions—1 (October 15, 2000, vs. Chicago).

			RECEIVING				TOTALS			
Year Team	G	GS	No.	Yds.	Avg.	TD	TD	2pt.	Pts.	Fum.
1997—Minnesota NFL	16	0	3	54	18.0	0	0	0	0	0
1998—Minnesota NFL	5	0	15	216	14.4	0	0	0	0	0
1999—Minnesota NFL	13	0	9	180	20.0	2	2	0	12	0
2000—Minnesota NFL	14	4	16	190	11.9	2	2	0	12	0
Pro totals (4 years)	48	4	43	640	14.9	4	4	0	24	0

HAUCK, TIM   S

PERSONAL: Born December 20, 1966, in Butte, Mont. ... 5-10/187. ... Full name: Timothy Christian Hauck. ... Name pronounced HOWK.
HIGH SCHOOL: Sweet Grass County (Big Timber, Mont.).
COLLEGE: Pacific (Ore.), then Montana.
TRANSACTIONS/CAREER NOTES: Signed as non-drafted free agent by New England Patriots (May 1, 1990). ... Released by Patriots (August 26, 1990). ... Re-signed by Patriots to practice squad (October 1, 1990). ... Activated (October 27, 1990). ... Granted unconditional free agency (February 1, 1991). ... Signed by Green Bay Packers (April 1, 1991). ... Granted unconditional free agency (February 1-April 1, 1992). ... Re-signed by Packers for 1992 season. ... Granted free agency (March 1, 1993). ... Re-signed by Packers (July 13, 1993). ... Granted unconditional free agency (February 17, 1994). ... Re-signed by Packers (July 20, 1994). ... Granted unconditional free agency (February 17, 1995).

H

... Signed by Denver Broncos (March 6, 1995). ... Granted unconditional free agency (February 14, 1997). ... Signed by Seattle Seahawks (June 2, 1997). ... Granted unconditional free agency (February 13, 1998). ... Signed by Indianapolis Colts (July 26, 1998). ... Granted unconditional free agency (February 12, 1999). ... Signed by Philadelphia Eagles (April 20, 1999). ... Granted unconditional free agency (February 11, 2000). ... Re-signed by Eagles (August 24, 2000). ... Granted unconditional free agency (March 2, 2001).

PLAYING EXPERIENCE: New England NFL, 1990; Green Bay NFL, 1991-1994; Denver NFL, 1995 and 1996; Seattle NFL, 1997; Indianapolis NFL, 1998; Philadelphia NFL, 1999 and 2000. ... Games/Games started: 1990 (10/0), 1991 (16/0), 1992 (16/0), 1993 (13/0), 1994 (13/3), 1995 (16/0), 1996 (16/0), 1997 (16/0), 1998 (16/7), 1999 (16/15), 2000 (16/3). Total: 148/25.

PRO STATISTICS: 1991—Recovered one fumble. 1992—Returned one punt for two yards. 1993—Recovered one fumble. 1997—Recovered one fumble for eight yards. 1999—Intercepted one pass for two yards and recovered one fumble. 2000—Recovered one fumble.

HAWKINS, ARTRELL   CB   BENGALS

PERSONAL: Born November 24, 1975, in Johnstown, Pa. ... 5-10/190. ... Cousin of Carlton Haselrig, guard with Pittsburgh Steelers (1990-93) and New York Jets (1995).
HIGH SCHOOL: Bishop McCort (Johnstown, Pa.).
COLLEGE: Cincinnati.
TRANSACTIONS/CAREER NOTES: Selected by Cincinnati Bengals in second round (43rd pick overall) of 1998 NFL draft. ... Signed by Bengals (May 14, 1998). ... Granted free agency (March 2, 2001). ... Re-signed by Bengals (April 4, 2001).
PRO STATISTICS: 1998—Credited with one sack and recovered one fumble for 25 yards. 1999—Recovered one fumble. 2000—Recovered one fumble for 12 yards.

| | | | INTERCEPTIONS | | |
Year Team	G	GS	No.	Yds.	Avg.	TD
1998—Cincinnati NFL	16	16	3	21	7.0	0
1999—Cincinnati NFL	14	13	0	0	0.0	0
2000—Cincinnati NFL	16	6	0	0	0.0	0
Pro totals (3 years)	46	35	3	21	7.0	0

HAWKINS, COURTNEY   WR

PERSONAL: Born December 12, 1969, in Flint, Mich. ... 5-9/190. ... Full name: Courtney Tyrone Hawkins Jr. ... Cousin of Roy Marble, guard/forward with Atlanta Hawks (1989-90) and Denver Nuggets (1993-94) of NBA.
HIGH SCHOOL: Beecher (Flint, Mich.).
COLLEGE: Michigan State.
TRANSACTIONS/CAREER NOTES: Selected by Tampa Bay Buccaneers in second round (44th pick overall) of 1992 NFL draft. ... Signed by Buccaneers (July 16, 1992). ... On injured reserve with knee injury (December 16, 1994-remainder of season). ... Granted free agency (February 17, 1995). ... Re-signed by Buccaneers (July 21, 1995). ... Granted unconditional free agency (February 16, 1996). ... Re-signed by Buccaneers (April 27, 1996). ... Granted free agency (February 14, 1997). ... Signed by Pittsburgh Steelers (June 2, 1997). ... Granted unconditional free agency (February 11, 2000). ... Re-signed by Steelers (July 12, 2000). ... Granted unconditional free agency (March 2, 2001).
CHAMPIONSHIP GAME EXPERIENCE: Played in AFC championship game (1997 season).
PRO STATISTICS: 1992—Returned nine kickoffs for 118 yards and recovered one fumble. 1995—Rushed four times for five yards. 1996—Rushed once for minus 13 yards. 1998—Rushed 10 times for 41 yards and recovered one fumble.
SINGLE GAME HIGHS (regular season): Receptions—14 (November 1, 1998, vs. Tennessee); yards—147 (November 1, 1998, vs. Tennessee); and touchdown receptions—2 (November 20, 1994, vs. Seattle).
STATISTICAL PLATEAUS: 100-yard receiving games: 1992 (1), 1993 (2), 1996 (1), 1998 (1). Total: 5.

| | | | RECEIVING | | | | PUNT RETURNS | | | | TOTALS | | | |
Year Team	G	GS	No.	Yds.	Avg.	TD	No.	Yds.	Avg.	TD	TD	2pt.	Pts.	Fum.
1992—Tampa Bay NFL	16	5	20	336	16.8	2	13	53	4.1	0	2	0	12	2
1993—Tampa Bay NFL	16	12	62	933	15.0	5	15	166	11.1	0	5	0	30	2
1994—Tampa Bay NFL	13	12	37	438	11.8	5	5	28	5.6	0	5	0	30	0
1995—Tampa Bay NFL	16	3	41	493	12.0	0	0	0	0.0	0	0	0	0	1
1996—Tampa Bay NFL	16	16	46	544	11.8	1	1	-1	-1.0	0	1	0	6	1
1997—Pittsburgh NFL	15	3	45	555	12.3	3	4	68	17.0	0	3	0	18	1
1998—Pittsburgh NFL	15	14	66	751	11.4	1	15	175	11.7	0	1	0	6	1
1999—Pittsburgh NFL	11	11	30	285	9.5	0	11	49	4.5	0	0	0	0	0
2000—Pittsburgh NFL	13	5	19	238	12.5	1	4	15	3.8	0	1	0	6	0
Pro totals (9 years)	131	81	366	4573	12.5	18	68	553	8.1	0	18	0	108	8

HAWTHORNE, DUANE   CB   COWBOYS

PERSONAL: Born August 26, 1976, in St. Louis. ... 5-10/175. ... Name pronounced DUH-wann.
HIGH SCHOOL: Ladue (Mo.).
COLLEGE: Northern Illinois.
TRANSACTIONS/CAREER NOTES: Signed as non-drafted free agent by Dallas Cowboys (April 23, 1999). ... Assigned by Cowboys to Scottish Claymores in 2000 NFL Europe enhancement allocation program (February 18, 2000).

| | | | INTERCEPTIONS | | |
Year Team	G	GS	No.	Yds.	Avg.	TD
1999—Dallas NFL	13	0	3	-2	-0.7	0
2000—Scottish NFLE	...	...	4	51	12.8	0
—Dallas NFL	14	0	0	0	0.0	0
NFL Europe totals (1 year)	...	...	4	51	12.8	0
NFL totals (2 years)	27	0	3	-2	-0.7	0
Pro totals (3 years)	...	...	7	49	7.0	0

H

HAWTHORNE, MICHAEL CB SAINTS

PERSONAL: Born January 26, 1977, in Sarasota, Fla. ... 6-3/196. ... Full name: Michael Seneca Hawthorne.
HIGH SCHOOL: Booker (Sarasota, Fla.).
COLLEGE: Purdue.
TRANSACTIONS/CAREER NOTES: Selected by New Orleans Saints in sixth round (195th pick overall) of 2000 NFL draft. ... Signed by Saints (June 23, 2000).
PLAYING EXPERIENCE: New Orleans NFL, 2000. ... Games/Games started: 2000 (11/1).

HAYES, CHRIS S JETS

PERSONAL: Born May 7, 1972, in San Bernardino, Calif. ... 6-0/206.
HIGH SCHOOL: San Gorgonio (San Bernardino, Calif.).
COLLEGE: Washington State.
TRANSACTIONS/CAREER NOTES: Selected by New York Jets in seventh round (210th pick overall) of 1996 NFL draft. ... Signed by Jets (June 26, 1996). ... Released by Jets (August 19, 1996). ... Signed by Washington Redskins to practice squad (September 11, 1996). ... Released by Redskins (October 2, 1996). ... Signed by Green Bay Packers to practice squad (October 4, 1996). ... Activated (December 9, 1996). ... Traded by Packers to Jets for CB Carl Greenwood (June 5, 1997). ... Granted free agency (February 11, 2000). ... Re-signed by Jets (May 8, 2000). ... Granted unconditional free agency (March 2, 2001). ... Re-signed by Jets (March 12, 2001).
PLAYING EXPERIENCE: Green Bay NFL, 1996; New York Jets NFL, 1997-2000. ... Games/Games started: 1996 (2/0), 1997 (16/0), 1998 (15/0), 1999 (15/0), 2000 (16/8). Total: 64/8.
CHAMPIONSHIP GAME EXPERIENCE: Played in NFC championship game (1996 season). ... Member of Super Bowl championship team (1996 season). ... Played in AFC championship game (1998 season).
PRO STATISTICS: 2000—Intercepted one pass for no yards and recovered one fumble.

HAYES, DONALD WR PANTHERS

PERSONAL: Born July 13, 1975, in Madison, Wis. ... 6-4/218. ... Full name: Donald Ross Hayes Jr.
HIGH SCHOOL: Madison East (Wis.).
COLLEGE: Wisconsin.
TRANSACTIONS/CAREER NOTES: Selected by Carolina Panthers in fourth round (106th pick overall) of 1998 NFL draft. ... Signed by Panthers (July 8, 1998). ... Granted free agency (March 2, 2001).
PRO STATISTICS: 2000—Fumbled once.
SINGLE GAME HIGHS (regular season): Receptions—7 (November 12, 2000, vs. New Orleans); yards—133 (November 28, 1999, vs. Atlanta); and touchdown receptions—1 (November 5, 2000, vs. St. Louis).
STATISTICAL PLATEAUS: 100-yard receiving games: 1999 (1), 2000 (1). Total: 2.

				RECEIVING		
Year Team	G	GS	No.	Yds.	Avg.	TD
1998—Carolina NFL	8	0	3	62	20.7	0
1999—Carolina NFL	13	1	11	270	24.5	2
2000—Carolina NFL	15	15	66	926	14.0	3
Pro totals (3 years)	36	16	80	1258	15.7	5

HAYES, WINDRELL WR JETS

PERSONAL: Born December 14, 1976, in Stockton, Calif. ... 5-11/198.
HIGH SCHOOL: St. Mary's (Stockton, Calif.), then Franklin (Stockton, Calif.).
JUNIOR COLLEGE: San Joaquin Delta College, Calif. (did not play football).
COLLEGE: San Jose State, then Southern California.
TRANSACTIONS/CAREER NOTES: Selected by New York Jets in fifth round (143rd pick overall) of 2000 NFL draft. ... Signed by Jets (May 24, 2000).
PLAYING EXPERIENCE: New York Jets NFL, 2000. ... Games/Games started: 2000 (8/1).
PRO STATISTICS: 2000—Caught six passes for 126 yards and rushed once for two yards.
SINGLE GAME HIGHS (regular season): Receptions—4 (December 3, 2000, vs. Indianapolis); yards—84 (December 3, 2000, vs. Indianapolis); and touchdown receptions—0.

HEARD, RONNIE S 49ERS

PERSONAL: Born October 5, 1976, in Bay City, Texas ... 6-2/215.
HIGH SCHOOL: Brazoswood (Clute, Texas) High.
COLLEGE: Mississippi.
TRANSACTIONS/CAREER NOTES: Signed as non-drafted free agent by San Francisco 49ers (April 20, 2000). ... Released by 49ers (August 27, 2000). ... Re-signed by 49ers to practice squad (August 29, 2000). ... Activated (October 16, 2000).
PLAYING EXPERIENCE: San Francisco NFL, 2000. ... Games/Games started: 2000 (13/3).
PRO STATISTICS: 2000—Credited with two sacks.

HEARST, GARRISON RB 49ERS H

PERSONAL: Born January 4, 1971, in Lincolnton, Ga. ... 5-11/215. ... Full name: Gerald Garrison Hearst.
HIGH SCHOOL: Lincoln County (Lincolnton, Ga.).
COLLEGE: Georgia.

TRANSACTIONS/CAREER NOTES: Selected after junior season by Phoenix Cardinals in first round (third pick overall) of 1993 NFL draft. ... Signed by Cardinals (August 28, 1993). ... On injured reserve with knee injury (November 4, 1993-remainder of season). ... Cardinals franchise renamed Arizona Cardinals for 1994 season. ... On physically unable to perform list with knee injury (August 23-October 13, 1994). ... Granted free agency (February 16, 1996). ... Re-signed by Cardinals (May 23, 1996). ... Claimed on waivers by Cincinnati Bengals (August 21, 1996). ... Granted unconditional free agency (February 14, 1997). ... Signed by San Francisco 49ers (March 7, 1997). ... On physically unable to perform list with leg injury (July 30, 1999-entire season). ... On physically unable to perform list with leg injury (August 22-November 21, 2000).

CHAMPIONSHIP GAME EXPERIENCE: Played in NFC championship game (1997 season).

HONORS: Doak Walker Award winner (1992). ... Named running back on THE SPORTING NEWS college All-America first team (1992). ... Named to play in Pro Bowl (1998 season); replaced by Emmitt Smith due to injury.

PRO STATISTICS: 1993—Had only pass attempt intercepted. 1994—Completed only pass attempt for 10 yards and a touchdown. 1995—Attempted two passes with one completion for 16 yards and recovered two fumbles. 1996—Recovered one fumble. 1997—Recovered two fumbles. 1998—Recovered one fumble.

SINGLE GAME HIGHS (regular season): Attempts—28 (September 29, 1997, vs. Carolina); yards—198 (December 14, 1998, vs. Detroit); and rushing touchdowns—2 (September 6, 1998, vs. New York Jets).

STATISTICAL PLATEAUS: 100-yard rushing games: 1995 (3), 1997 (3), 1998 (6). Total: 12. ... 100-yard receiving games: 1998 (2).

Year Team	G	GS	RUSHING				RECEIVING				TOTALS			
			Att.	Yds.	Avg.	TD	No.	Yds.	Avg.	TD	TD	2pt.	Pts.	Fum.
1993—Phoenix NFL	6	5	76	264	3.5	1	6	18	3.0	0	1	0	6	2
1994—Arizona NFL	8	0	37	169	4.6	1	6	49	8.2	0	1	0	6	0
1995—Arizona NFL	16	15	284	1070	3.8	1	29	243	8.4	1	2	0	12	12
1996—Cincinnati NFL	16	12	225	847	3.8	0	12	131	10.9	1	1	1	8	1
1997—San Francisco NFL	13	13	234	1019	4.4	4	21	194	9.2	2	6	0	36	2
1998—San Francisco NFL	16	16	310	1570	‡5.1	7	39	535	13.7	2	9	1	56	4
1999—San Francisco NFL							Did not play.							
2000—San Francisco NFL							Did not play.							
Pro totals (6 years)	75	61	1166	4939	4.2	14	113	1170	10.4	6	20	2	124	21

HEATH, RODNEY   CB   BENGALS

PERSONAL: Born October 29, 1974, in Cincinnati ... 5-10/175. ... Full name: Rodney Larece Heath.

HIGH SCHOOL: Western Hills (Cincinnati).

COLLEGE: Minnesota (degree in sports studies).

TRANSACTIONS/CAREER NOTES: Signed as non-drafted free agent by Cincinnati Bengals (January 27, 1999). ... On injured reserve with shoulder injury (December 4, 2000-remainder of season).

PRO STATISTICS: 1999—Recovered two fumbles for minus four yards. 2000—Returned one kickoff for 22 yards and recovered one fumble.

Year Team	G	GS	INTERCEPTIONS				TOTALS			
			No.	Yds.	Avg.	TD	TD	2pt.	Pts.	Fum.
1999—Cincinnati NFL	16	9	3	72	24.0	1	1	0	6	0
2000—Cincinnati NFL	13	9	0	0	0.0	0	0	0	0	0
Pro totals (2 years)	29	18	3	72	24.0	1	1	0	6	0

HECK, ANDY   OT

PERSONAL: Born January 1, 1967, in Fargo, N.D. ... 6-6/298. ... Full name: Andrew Robert Heck.

HIGH SCHOOL: W.T. Woodson (Fairfax, Va.).

COLLEGE: Notre Dame (degree in American studies, 1989).

TRANSACTIONS/CAREER NOTES: Selected by Seattle Seahawks in first round (15th pick overall) of 1989 NFL draft. ... Signed by Seahawks (July 31, 1989). ... On injured reserve with ankle injury (October 21-November 20, 1992); on practice squad (November 18-20, 1992). ... Designated by Seahawks as transition player (February 25, 1993). ... Tendered offer sheet by Chicago Bears (February 21, 1994). ... Seahawks declined to match offer (March 1, 1994). ... Released by Bears (June 2, 1999). ... Signed by Washington Redskins (June 17, 1999). ... Granted unconditional free agency (February 11, 2000). ... Re-signed by Redskins (March 20, 2000). ... Released by Redskins (February 22, 2001).

PLAYING EXPERIENCE: Seattle NFL, 1989-1993; Chicago NFL, 1994-1998; Washington NFL, 1999 and 2000. ... Games/Games started: 1989 (16/9), 1990 (16/16), 1991 (16/16), 1992 (13/13), 1993 (16/16), 1994 (14/14), 1995 (16/16), 1996 (16/16), 1997 (16/16), 1998 (14/14), 1999 (16/16), 2000 (16/2). Total: 185/164.

HONORS: Named offensive tackle on THE SPORTING NEWS college All-America first team (1988).

PRO STATISTICS: 1989—Recovered one fumble. 1990—Recovered one fumble. 1993—Recovered two fumbles. 2000—Recovered one fumble.

HEFFNER-LIDDIARD, BRODY   TE   DOLPHINS

PERSONAL: Born June 12, 1977, in San Diego. ... 6-4/234. ... Full name: Jon Brody Heffner-Liddiard.

HIGH SCHOOL: Torrey Pines (San Diego).

COLLEGE: Colorado.

TRANSACTIONS/CAREER NOTES: Signed as non-drafted free agent by Minnesota Vikings (April 25, 2000). ... Released by Vikings (August 14, 2000). ... Signed by New York Giants (August 20, 2000). ... Released by Giants (September 4, 2000). ... Re-signed by Giants to practice squad (September 5, 2000). ... Activated (September 9, 2000); did not play. ... Released by Giants (September 12, 2000). ... Signed by Miami Dolphins (November 23, 2000).

PLAYING EXPERIENCE: Miami NFL, 2000. ... Games/Games started: 2000 (5/0).

H   HEGAMIN, GEORGE   OT   BUCCANEERS

PERSONAL: Born February 14, 1973, in Camden, N.J. ... 6-7/331. ... Full name: George Russell Hegamin. ... Name pronounced HEG-a-min.

HIGH SCHOOL: Camden (N.J.).

COLLEGE: North Carolina State.

TRANSACTIONS/CAREER NOTES: Selected after junior season by Dallas Cowboys in third round (102nd pick overall) of 1994 NFL draft. ... Signed by Cowboys (July 15, 1994). ... Active for four games (1995); did not play. ... Assigned by Cowboys to Frankfurt Galaxy in 1996 World League enhancement allocation program (February 19, 1996). ... Granted unconditional free agency (February 13, 1998). ... Signed by Philadelphia Eagles (February 19, 1998). ... Released by Eagles (September 4, 1999). ... Signed by Tampa Bay Buccaneers (November 10, 1999).

PLAYING EXPERIENCE: Dallas NFL, 1994, 1996 and 1997; Frankfurt W.L., 1996, Philadelphia NFL, 1998; Tampa Bay NFL, 1999 and 2000. ... Games/Games started: 1994 (2/0), W.L. 1996 (games played unavailable), NFL 1996 (16/1), 1997 (13/9), 1998 (16/6), 1999 (1/0), 2000 (16/1). Total: 64/17.

CHAMPIONSHIP GAME EXPERIENCE: Member of Cowboys for NFC championship game (1994 season); inactive. ... Member of Cowboys for NFC championship game (1995 season); did not play. ... Member of Super Bowl championship team (1995 season). ... Played in NFC championship game (1999 season).

PRO STATISTICS: 1997—Recovered one fumble.

HEIDEN, STEVE   TE   CHARGERS

PERSONAL: Born September 21, 1976, in Rushford, Minn. ... 6-5/270. ... Full name: Steve Allen Heiden. ... Name pronounced HIGH-den.
HIGH SCHOOL: Rushford-Peterson (Rushford, Minn.).
COLLEGE: South Dakota State.
TRANSACTIONS/CAREER NOTES: Selected by San Diego Chargers in third round (69th pick overall) of 1999 NFL draft. ... Signed by Chargers (July 22, 1999).
PLAYING EXPERIENCE: San Diego NFL, 1999 and 2000. ... Games/Games started: 1999 (11/0), 2000 (15/3). Total: 26/3.
PRO STATISTICS: 2000—Caught six passes for 32 yards and one touchdown and recovered one fumble.
SINGLE GAME HIGHS (regular season): Receptions—2 (September 24, 2000, vs. Seattle); yards—10 (November 19, 2000, vs. Denver); and touchdown receptions—1 (December 17, 2000, vs. Carolina).

HELLESTRAE, DALE   G/C

PERSONAL: Born July 11, 1962, in Phoenix. ... 6-5/291. ... Full name: Dale Robert Hellestrae. ... Name pronounced HELL-uh-stray.
HIGH SCHOOL: Saguaro (Scottsdale, Ariz.).
COLLEGE: Southern Methodist (degree in business administration).
TRANSACTIONS/CAREER NOTES: Selected by Houston Gamblers in 1985 USFL territorial draft. ... Selected by Buffalo Bills in fourth round (112th pick overall) of 1985 NFL draft. ... Signed by Bills (July 19, 1985). ... On injured reserve with broken thumb (October 4, 1985-remainder of season). ... On injured reserve with broken wrist (September 17-November 15, 1986). ... On injured reserve with hip injury (September 1, 1987-entire season). ... Granted unconditional free agency (February 1, 1989). ... Signed by Los Angeles Raiders (February 24, 1989). ... On injured reserve with broken leg (August 29, 1989-entire season). ... Traded by Raiders to Dallas Cowboys for seventh-round pick (traded to Chicago) in 1991 draft (August 20, 1990). ... Granted unconditional free agency (February 1-April 1, 1991). ... Re-signed by Cowboys for 1991 season. ... Granted unconditional free agency (February 1-April 1, 1992). ... Re-signed by Cowboys for 1992 season. ... Released by Cowboys (August 31, 1992). ... Re-signed by Cowboys (September 2, 1992). ... Granted unconditional free agency (March 1, 1993). ... Re-signed by Cowboys (June 2, 1993). ... Released by Cowboys (August 30, 1993). ... Re-signed by Cowboys (August 31, 1993). ... Granted unconditional free agency (February 17, 1994). ... Re-signed by Cowboys (July 14, 1994). ... Granted unconditional free agency (February 16, 1996). ... Re-signed by Cowboys (April 9, 1996). ... Granted unconditional free agency (February 13, 1998). ... Re-signed by Cowboys (April 7, 1998). ... Granted unconditional free agency (February 12, 1999). ... Re-signed by Cowboys (June 23, 1999). ... Granted unconditional free agency (February 11, 2000). ... Re-signed by Cowboys (June 19, 2000). ... Released by Cowboys (March 1, 2001).
PLAYING EXPERIENCE: Buffalo NFL, 1985, 1986 and 1988; Dallas NFL, 1990-2000. ... Games/Games started: 1985 (4/0), 1986 (8/0), 1988 (16/2), 1990 (16/0), 1991 (16/0), 1992 (16/0), 1993 (16/0), 1994 (16/0), 1995 (16/0), 1996 (16/0), 1997 (16/0), 1998 (16/0), 1999 (16/0), 2000 (16/0). Total: 204/2.
CHAMPIONSHIP GAME EXPERIENCE: Played in AFC championship game (1988 season). ... Played in NFC championship game (1992-1995 seasons). ... Member of Super Bowl championship team (1992, 1993 and 1995 seasons).
PRO STATISTICS: 1986—Fumbled once for minus 14 yards.

HENDERSON, WILLIAM   FB   PACKERS

PERSONAL: Born February 19, 1971, in Richmond, Va. ... 6-1/253. ... Full name: William Terrelle Henderson.
HIGH SCHOOL: Thomas Dale (Chester, Va.).
COLLEGE: North Carolina.
TRANSACTIONS/CAREER NOTES: Selected by Green Bay Packers in third round (66th pick overall) of 1995 NFL draft. ... Signed by Packers (July 17, 1995). ... Granted free agency (February 13, 1998). ... Re-signed by Packers (June 15, 1998). ... Granted unconditional free agency (February 12, 1999). ... Re-signed by Packers (April 6, 1999).
CHAMPIONSHIP GAME EXPERIENCE: Played in NFC championship game (1995-1997 seasons). ... Member of Super Bowl championship team (1996 season). ... Played in Super Bowl XXXII (1997 season).
PRO STATISTICS: 1996—Returned two kickoffs for 38 yards. 1997—Recovered two fumbles. 1999—Returned two kickoffs for 23 yards. 2000—Returned five kickoffs for 80 yards and recovered one fumble.
SINGLE GAME HIGHS (regular season): Attempts—6 (September 7, 1997, vs. Philadelphia); yards—40 (September 9, 1996, vs. Philadelphia); and rushing touchdowns—1 (December 12, 1999, vs. Carolina).

			RUSHING				RECEIVING				TOTALS		
Year Team	G	GS	Att.	Yds.	Avg.	TD	No.	Yds.	Avg.	TD	TD	2pt.	Pts.	Fum.
1995—Green Bay NFL	15	2	7	35	5.0	0	3	21	7.0	0	0	0	0	0
1996—Green Bay NFL	16	11	39	130	3.3	0	27	203	7.5	1	1	0	6	1
1997—Green Bay NFL	16	14	31	113	3.6	0	41	367	9.0	1	1	0	6	1
1998—Green Bay NFL	16	10	23	70	3.0	2	37	241	6.5	1	3	0	18	1
1999—Green Bay NFL	16	13	7	29	4.1	2	30	203	6.8	1	3	0	18	1
2000—Green Bay NFL	16	6	2	16	8.0	0	35	234	6.7	1	1	0	6	1
Pro totals (6 years)	95	56	109	393	3.6	4	173	1269	7.3	5	9	0	54	5

H

HENDRICKS, TOMMY   LB   DOLPHINS

PERSONAL: Born October 23, 1978, in Houston. ... 6-2/231. ... Full name: Thomas Emmett Hendricks III.
HIGH SCHOOL: Scarborough (Texas), then Eiserhower (Houston).
COLLEGE: Michigan.
TRANSACTIONS/CAREER NOTES: Signed as non-drafted free agent by Miami Dolphins (April 25, 2000). ... Released by Dolphins (August 27, 2000). ... Re-signed by Dophins (September 26, 2000). ... Released by Dolphins (October 2, 2000). ... Re-signed by Dolphins to practice squad (October 4, 2000). ... Activated (November 10, 2000).
PLAYING EXPERIENCE: Miami NFL, 2000. ... Games/Games started: 2000 (8/0).

HENNINGS, CHAD   DT   COWBOYS

PERSONAL: Born October 20, 1965, in Elberton, Iowa. ... 6-6/291. ... Full name: Chad William Hennings.
HIGH SCHOOL: Benton Community (Van Horne, Iowa).
COLLEGE: Air Force (degree in management).
TRANSACTIONS/CAREER NOTES: Selected by Dallas Cowboys in 11th round (290th pick overall) of 1988 NFL draft. ... Signed by Cowboys (November 22, 1988). ... Served in military (1988-1992). ... Granted unconditional free agency (February 17, 1994). ... Re-signed by Cowboys (September 17, 1994). ... On injured reserve with neck injury (November 8, 2000-remainder of season).
CHAMPIONSHIP GAME EXPERIENCE: Played in NFC championship game (1992, 1994 and 1995 seasons). ... Member of Cowboys for NFC championship game (1993 season); inactive. ... Member of Super Bowl championship team (1992, 1993 and 1995 seasons).
HONORS: Outland Trophy winner (1987). ... Named defensive lineman on THE SPORTING NEWS college All-America first team (1987).
PRO STATISTICS: 1993—Returned one kickoff for seven yards. 1994—Recovered one fumble. 1995—Recovered one fumble. 1996—Recovered one fumble. 1997—Recovered one fumble for four yards and a touchdown. 1998—Recovered one fumble. 2000—Recovered one fumble.

Year Team	G	GS	SACKS
1992—Dallas NFL	8	0	0.0
1993—Dallas NFL	13	0	0.0
1994—Dallas NFL	16	0	7.0
1995—Dallas NFL	16	7	5.5
1996—Dallas NFL	15	15	4.5
1997—Dallas NFL	11	10	4.5
1998—Dallas NFL	16	16	1.0
1999—Dallas NFL	16	16	5.0
2000—Dallas NFL	8	8	0.0
Pro totals (9 years)	119	72	27.5

HENRY, KEVIN   DE   BENGALS

PERSONAL: Born October 23, 1968, in Mound Bayou, Miss. ... 6-4/285. ... Full name: Kevin Lerell Henry. ... Name pronounced KEE-vin.
HIGH SCHOOL: John F. Kennedy (Mound Bayou, Miss.).
COLLEGE: Mississippi State.
TRANSACTIONS/CAREER NOTES: Selected by Pittsburgh Steelers in fourth round (108th pick overall) of 1993 NFL draft. ... Signed by Steelers (July 9, 1993). ... Granted free agency (February 16, 1996). ... Re-signed by Steelers (August 2, 1996). ... Granted unconditional free agency (February 14, 1997). ... Re-signed by Steelers (April 3, 1997). ... Placed on physically unable to perform list with knee injury (July 20-August 21, 2000). ... Released by Steelers (March 1, 2001). ... Signed by Cincinnati Bengals (April 11, 2001).
CHAMPIONSHIP GAME EXPERIENCE: Played in AFC championship game (1994, 1995 and 1997 seasons). ... Played in Super Bowl XXX (1995 season).
PRO STATISTICS: 1993—Intercepted one pass for 10 yards. 1994—Recovered one fumble. 1996—Recovered one fumble for four yards. 1997—Intercepted one pass for 36 yards and recovered two fumbles. 2000—Recovered one fumble.

Year Team	G	GS	SACKS
1993—Pittsburgh NFL	12	1	1.0
1994—Pittsburgh NFL	16	5	0.0
1995—Pittsburgh NFL	13	5	2.0
1996—Pittsburgh NFL	12	10	1.5
1997—Pittsburgh NFL	16	16	4.5
1998—Pittsburgh NFL	16	16	4.0
1999—Pittsburgh NFL	16	13	1.0
2000—Pittsburgh NFL	15	15	0.0
Pro totals (8 years)	116	81	14.0

HENTRICH, CRAIG   P   TITANS

PERSONAL: Born May 18, 1971, in Alton, Ill. ... 6-3/205. ... Full name: Craig Anthony Hentrich. ... Name pronounced HEN-trick.
HIGH SCHOOL: Marquette (Ottawa, Ill.).
COLLEGE: Notre Dame.
TRANSACTIONS/CAREER NOTES: Selected by New York Jets in eighth round (200th pick overall) of 1993 NFL draft. ... Signed by Jets (July 14, 1993). ... Released by Jets (August 24, 1993). ... Signed by Green Bay Packers to practice squad (September 7, 1993). ... Activated (January 14, 1994); did not play. ... Granted unconditional free agency (February 13, 1998). ... Signed by Tennessee Oilers (February 19, 1998). ... Oilers franchise renamed Tennessee Titans for 1999 season (December 26, 1998).
CHAMPIONSHIP GAME EXPERIENCE: Played in NFC championship game (1995-1997 seasons). ... Member of Super Bowl championship team (1996 season). ... Played in Super Bowl XXXII (1997 season) and Super Bowl XXXIV (1999 season). ... Played in AFC championship game (1999 season).
HONORS: Named punter on THE SPORTING NEWS NFL All-Pro team (1998). ... Played in Pro Bowl (1998 season).
PRO STATISTICS: 1996—Attempted one pass without a completion and recovered one fumble. 1998—Rushed once for minus one yard and completed only pass attempt for 13 yards. 1999—Rushed twice for one yard and recovered two fumbles.

H

Year Team	G	PUNTING						KICKING						
		No.	Yds.	Avg.	Net avg.	In. 20	Blk.	XPM	XPA	FGM	FGA	Lg.	50+	Pts.
1993—Green Bay NFL								Did not play.						
1994—Green Bay NFL	16	81	3351	41.4	35.5	24	0	0	0	0	0	0	0-0	0
1995—Green Bay NFL	16	65	2740	42.2	34.6	26	2	5	5	3	5	49	0-0	14
1996—Green Bay NFL	16	68	2886	42.4	36.2	28	0	0	0	0	0	0	0-0	0
1997—Green Bay NFL	16	75	3378	45.0	36.0	26	0	0	0	0	0	0	0-0	0
1998—Tennessee NFL	16	69	3258	*47.2	*39.2	18	0	0	0	0	1	0	0-0	0
1999—Tennessee NFL	16	90	3824	42.5	38.1	35	0	0	0	0	0	0	0-0	0
2000—Tennessee NFL	16	76	3101	40.8	36.3	33	0	0	0	0	1	0	0-1	0
Pro totals (7 years)	112	524	22538	43.0	36.6	190	2	5	5	3	7	49	0-1	14

HEPPNER, KRIS　　K

PERSONAL: Born January 18, 1977, in Great Falls, Mon. ... 5-9/180.
HIGH SCHOOL: Great Falls (Mon.).
COLLEGE: Montana.
TRANSACTIONS/CAREER NOTES: Signed as non-drafted free agent by Seattle Seahawks (April 24, 2000). ... Released by Seahawks (September 26, 2000). ... Signed by Washington Redskins (October 10, 2000). ... Released by Redskins (November 6, 2000).

Year Team	G	KICKING						
		XPM	XPA	FGM	FGA	Lg.	50+	Pts.
2000—Seattle NFL	4	8	8	6	9	45	0-1	26
—Washington NFL	4	9	9	4	6	37	0-1	21
Pro totals (1 years)	8	17	17	10	15	45	0-2	47

HERNDON, JIMMY　　OT　　BEARS

PERSONAL: Born August 30, 1973, in Baytown, Texas. ... 6-8/318.
HIGH SCHOOL: Lee (Baytown, Texas).
COLLEGE: Houston (degree in sociology, 1996).
TRANSACTIONS/CAREER NOTES: Selected by Jacksonville Jaguars in fifth round (146th pick overall) of 1996 NFL draft. ... Signed by Jaguars (May 24, 1996). ... Active for eight games (1996); did not play. ... Traded by Jaguars to Chicago Bears for seventh-round pick (WR Alvis Whitted) in 1998 draft (August 24, 1997). ... On injured reserve with knee injury (August 31, 1999-entire season).
PLAYING EXPERIENCE: Chicago NFL, 1997, 1998 and 2000. ... Games/Games started: 1997 (7/0), 1998 (9/2), 2000 (10/2). Total: 26/4.
CHAMPIONSHIP GAME EXPERIENCE: Member of Jaguars for AFC championship game (1996 season); inactive.

HERRING, KIM　　S　　RAMS

PERSONAL: Born September 10, 1975, in Cleveland. ... 6-0/200. ... Full name: Kimani Masai Herring.
HIGH SCHOOL: Solon (Ohio).
COLLEGE: Penn State.
TRANSACTIONS/CAREER NOTES: Selected by Baltimore Ravens in second round (58th pick overall) of 1997 NFL draft. ... Signed by Ravens (July 18, 1997). ... On injured reserve with shoulder injury (December 2, 1998-remainder of season). ... Granted free agency (February 11, 2000). ... Re-signed by Ravens (April 18, 2000) ... Granted unconditional free agency (March 2, 2001). ... Signed by St. Louis Rams (March 22, 2001).
PLAYING EXPERIENCE: Baltimore NFL, 1997-2000. ... Games/Games started: 1997 (15/4), 1998 (7/7), 1999 (16/16), 2000 (16/16). Total: 54/43.
CHAMPIONSHIP GAME EXPERIENCE: Member of Ravens for AFC Championship game (2000 season); inactive. ... Member of Super Bowl championship team (2000 season).
HONORS: Named free safety on THE SPORTING NEWS college All-America first team (1996).
PRO STATISTICS: 1997—Credited with one sack and recovered one fumble. 1999—Recovered two fumbles. 2000—Intercepted three passes for 74 yards and credited with one sack.

HETHERINGTON, CHRIS　　FB　　PANTHERS

PERSONAL: Born November 27, 1972, in North Branford, Conn. ... 6-3/244. ... Full name: Christopher Raymond Hetherington.
HIGH SCHOOL: Avon (Conn.) Old Farms.
COLLEGE: Yale (degree in psychology).
TRANSACTIONS/CAREER NOTES: Signed as non-drafted free agent by Cincinnati Bengals (April 23, 1996). ... Released by Bengals (August 21, 1996). ... Re-signed by Bengals to practice squad (August 26, 1996). ... Signed by Indianapolis Colts off Bengals practice squad (October 22, 1996). ... Released by Colts (August 24, 1998). ... Re-signed by Colts (August 31, 1998). ... Released by Colts (February 12, 1999). ... Signed by Carolina Panthers (March 5, 1999). ... Granted unconditional free agency (February 11, 2000). ... Re-signed by Panthers (February 23, 2000).
PRO STATISTICS: 1999—Recovered one fumble. 2000—Recovered one fumble.
SINGLE GAME HIGHS (regular season): Attempts—5 (December 10, 2000, vs. Kansas City); yards—29 (December 24, 2000, vs. Oakland); and rushing touchdowns—1 (December 10, 2000, vs. Kansas City).

Year Team	G	GS	RUSHING				RECEIVING				KICKOFF RETURNS				TOTALS			
			Att.	Yds.	Avg.	TD	No.	Yds.	Avg.	TD	No.	Yds.	Avg.	TD	TD	2pt.	Pts.	Fum.
1996—Indianapolis NFL	6	0	0	0	0.0	0	0	0	0.0	0	1	16	16.0	0	0	0	0	0
1997—Indianapolis NFL	16	0	0	0	0.0	0	0	0	0.0	0	2	23	11.5	0	0	0	0	0
1998—Indianapolis NFL	14	1	0	0	0.0	0	0	0	0.0	0	5	71	14.2	0	0	0	0	1
1999—Carolina NFL	14	0	2	7	3.5	0	0	0	0.0	0	1	16	16.0	0	0	0	0	0
2000—Carolina NFL	16	5	23	65	2.8	2	14	116	8.3	1	2	21	10.5	0	3	0	18	0
Pro totals (5 years)	66	6	25	72	2.9	2	14	116	8.3	1	11	147	13.4	0	3	0	18	1

H

HICKS, ERIC　　　　　　　DE　　　　　　　CHIEFS

PERSONAL: Born June 17, 1976, in Erie, Pa. ... 6-6/286. ... Full name: Eric David Hicks.
HIGH SCHOOL: Mercyhurst (Erie, Pa.).
COLLEGE: Maryland.
TRANSACTIONS/CAREER NOTES: Signed as non-drafted free agent by Kansas City Chiefs (April 25, 1998).
PRO STATISTICS: 1998—Recovered one fumble. 1999—Recovered two fumbles for 44 yards and one touchdown. 2000—Recovered one fumble.

Year　Team	G	GS	SACKS
1998—Kansas City NFL	3	0	0.0
1999—Kansas City NFL	16	16	4.0
2000—Kansas City NFL	13	11	14.0
Pro totals (3 years)	32	27	18.0

HICKS, ROBERT　　　　　　　OT　　　　　　　BILLS

PERSONAL: Born November 17, 1974, in Atlanta ... 6-7/330. ... Full name: Robert Otis Hicks Jr.
HIGH SCHOOL: Douglass (Atlanta).
COLLEGE: Mississippi State.
TRANSACTIONS/CAREER NOTES: Selected by Buffalo Bills in third round (68th pick overall) of 1998 NFL draft. ... Signed by Bills (July 20, 1998). ... Granted free agency (March 2, 2001).
PLAYING EXPERIENCE: Buffalo NFL, 1998-2000. ... Games/Games started: 1998 (9/2), 1999 (14/14), 2000 (14/7). Total: 37/23.
PRO STATISTICS: 1999—Rushed once for minus two yards and caught one pass for minus six yards.

HICKS, SKIP　　　　　　　RB　　　　　　　BEARS

PERSONAL: Born October 13, 1974, in Corsicana, Texas. ... 6-0/230. ... Full name: Brian LaVell Hicks.
HIGH SCHOOL: Burkburnett (Texas).
COLLEGE: UCLA.
TRANSACTIONS/CAREER NOTES: Selected by Washington Redskins in third round (69th pick overall) of 1998 NFL draft. ... Signed by Redskins (July 7, 1998). ... Granted free agency (March 2, 2001). ... Signed by Chicago Bears (May 22, 2001).
HONORS: Named running back on THE SPORTING NEWS college All-America first team (1997).
PRO STATISTICS: 2000—Returned one kickoff for 17 yards.
SINGLE GAME HIGHS (regular season): Attempts—26 (November 15, 1998, vs. Philadelphia); yards—94 (November 15, 1998, vs. Philadelphia); and rushing touchdowns—3 (November 15, 1998, vs. Philadelphia).

			RUSHING				RECEIVING				TOTALS			
Year　Team	G	GS	Att.	Yds.	Avg.	TD	No.	Yds.	Avg.	TD	TD	2pt.	Pts.	Fum.
1998—Washington NFL	9	5	122	433	3.5	8	4	23	5.8	0	8	0	48	0
1999—Washington NFL	10	2	78	257	3.3	3	8	72	9.0	0	3	0	18	1
2000—Washington NFL	10	1	29	78	2.7	1	5	43	8.6	0	1	0	6	1
Pro totals (3 years)	29	8	229	768	3.4	12	17	138	8.1	0	12	0	72	2

HILL, JAMES　　　　　　　TE　　　　　　　SEAHAWKS

PERSONAL: Born October 25, 1974, in Dallas. ... 6-4/246.
HIGH SCHOOL: Riverhead (N.Y.).
COLLEGE: Abilene Christian.
TRANSACTIONS/CAREER NOTES: Signed as non-drafted free agent by Seattle Seahawks (February 25, 2000).
PLAYING EXPERIENCE: Seattle NFL, 2000. ... Games/Games started: 2000 (10/0).

HILL, RAION　　　　　　　S　　　　　　　BILLS

PERSONAL: Born September 2, 1976, in Marrero, La. ... 6-0/200. ... Full name: Raion Yance Hill.
HIGH SCHOOL: Brother Martin (New Orleans).
COLLEGE: Louisiana State.
TRANSACTIONS/CAREER NOTES: Signed as non-drafted free agent by Buffalo Bills (April 23, 1999). ... Released by Bills (August 30, 1999). ... Re-signed by Bills to practice squad (October 26, 1999).
PLAYING EXPERIENCE: Buffalo NFL, 2000. ... Games/Games started: 2000 (16/0).

HILL, RAY　　　　　　　CB

PERSONAL: Born August 7, 1975, in Detroit. ... 6-0/192. ... Full name: Raymond Millous Hill.
HIGH SCHOOL: Chadsey (Detroit).
COLLEGE: Michigan State.
TRANSACTIONS/CAREER NOTES: Signed as non-drafted free agent by Buffalo Bills (April 23, 1998). ... Released by Bills (August 30, 1998). ... Re-signed by Bills to practice squad (August 31, 1998). ... Activated (September 9, 1998). ... Claimed on waivers by Miami Dolphins (November 19, 1998). ... Released by Dolphins (October 25, 2000). ... Signed by Bills (November 22, 2000). ... Released by Bills (June 1, 2001).
PLAYING EXPERIENCE: Buffalo (4)-Miami (2) NFL, 1998; Miami NFL, 1999; Miami (3)-Buffalo (5) NFL, 2000. ... Games/Games started: 1998 (Buf.-4/0; Mia.-2/0; Total: 6/0), 1999 (16/0), 2000 (Mia.-3/0; Buf.-5/0; Total: 8/0). Total: 30/0.
PRO STATISTICS: 1999—Recovered one fumble for one yard.

H

HILLIARD, IKE   WR   GIANTS

PERSONAL: Born April 5, 1976, in Patterson, La. ... 5-11/195. ... Full name: Isaac Jason Hilliard. ... Nephew of Dalton Hilliard, running back with New Orleans Saints (1986-93).
HIGH SCHOOL: Patterson (La.).
COLLEGE: Florida.
TRANSACTIONS/CAREER NOTES: Selected by New York Giants in first round (seventh pick overall) of 1997 NFL draft. ... Signed by Giants (July 19, 1997). ... On injured reserve with neck injury (September 30, 1997-remainder of season).
CHAMPIONSHIP GAME EXPERIENCE: Played in NFC championship game (2000 season).
PRO STATISTICS: 1998—Rushed once for four yards. 1999—Rushed three times for 16 yards. 2000—Rushed three times for 19 yards.
SINGLE GAME HIGHS (regular season): Receptions—8 (September 10, 2000, vs. Philadelphia); yards—141 (November 30, 1998, vs. San Francisco); and touchdown receptions—2 (November 12, 2000, vs. St. Louis).
STATISTICAL PLATEAUS: 100-yard receiving games: 1998 (1), 1999 (3), 2000 (1). Total: 5.

				RECEIVING				TOTALS		
Year Team	G	GS	No.	Yds.	Avg.	TD	TD	2pt.	Pts.	Fum.
1997—New York Giants NFL	2	2	2	42	21.0	0	0	0	0	0
1998—New York Giants NFL	16	16	51	715	14.0	2	2	0	12	2
1999—New York Giants NFL	16	16	72	996	13.8	3	3	0	18	0
2000—New York Giants NFL	14	14	55	787	14.3	8	8	0	48	0
Pro totals (4 years)	48	48	180	2540	14.1	13	13	0	78	2

HILLIARD, JOHN   DE   SEAHAWKS

PERSONAL: Born April 16, 1976, in Coushatta, La. ... 6-2/285. ... Full name: John Edward Hilliard.
HIGH SCHOOL: Sterling (Houston).
COLLEGE: Mississippi State.
TRANSACTIONS/CAREER NOTES: Selected by Seattle Seahawks in sixth round (190th pick overall) of 2000 NFL draft. ... Signed by Seahawks (July 13, 2000).
PLAYING EXPERIENCE: Seattle NFL, 2000. ... Games/Games started: 2000 (5/0).

HITCHCOCK, JIMMY   CB   PANTHERS

PERSONAL: Born November 9, 1970, in Concord, N.C. ... 5-10/187. ... Full name: Jimmy Davis Hitchcock Jr.
HIGH SCHOOL: Concord (N.C.).
COLLEGE: North Carolina.
TRANSACTIONS/CAREER NOTES: Selected by New England Patriots in third round (88th pick overall) of 1995 NFL draft. ... Signed by Patriots (July 19, 1995). ... Granted free agency (February 13, 1998). ... Re-signed by Patriots (April 18, 1998). ... Traded by Patriots to Minnesota Vikings for third-round pick (S Tony George) in 1999 draft (April 18, 1998). ... Granted unconditional free agency (February 11, 2000). ... Signed by Carolina Panthers (February 24, 2000).
CHAMPIONSHIP GAME EXPERIENCE: Member of Patriots for AFC championship game (1996 season); inactive. ... Member of Patriots for Super Bowl XXXI (1996 season); inactive. ... Played in NFC championship game (1998 season).
PRO STATISTICS: 1998—Recovered one fumble for one yard. 1999—Credited with two sacks. 2000—Returned one punt for no yards and fumbled once.

			INTERCEPTIONS			
Year Team	G	GS	No.	Yds.	Avg.	TD
1995—New England NFL	8	0	0	0	0.0	0
1996—New England NFL	13	5	2	14	7.0	0
1997—New England NFL	15	15	2	104	52.0	1
1998—Minnesota NFL	16	16	7	*242	‡34.6	*3
1999—Minnesota NFL	16	16	2	0	0.0	0
2000—Carolina NFL	16	2	3	116	38.7	1
Pro totals (6 years)	84	54	16	476	29.8	5

HOBERT, BILLY JOE   QB   COLTS

PERSONAL: Born January 8, 1971, in Puyallup, Wash. ... 6-3/230.
HIGH SCHOOL: Puyallup (Wash.).
COLLEGE: Washington.
TRANSACTIONS/CAREER NOTES: Selected after junior season by Los Angeles Raiders in third round (58th pick overall) of 1993 NFL draft. ... Raiders franchise moved to Oakland (July 21, 1995). ... Traded by Raiders to Buffalo Bills for undisclosed draft pick (February 17, 1997). ... Released by Bills (October 15, 1997). ... Signed by New Orleans Saints (November 19, 1997). ... On injured reserve with Achilles' tendon injury (September 9, 1998-remainder of season). ... Granted unconditional free agency (February 11, 2000). ... Signed by Indianapolis Colts (August 3, 2000). ... Granted unconditional free agency (March 2, 2001). ... Re-signed by Colts (March 2, 2001).
PRO STATISTICS: 1996—Punted nine times for 371 yards (41.2 avg./35.1 net avg.) and fumbled six times. 1997—Fumbled three times and recovered one fumble for minus five yards. 1999—Fumbled twice and recovered one fumble for minus eight yards.
SINGLE GAME HIGHS (regular season): Attempts—42 (December 7, 1997, vs. St. Louis); completions—23 (November 28, 1999, vs. St. Louis); yards—259 (December 7, 1997, vs. St. Louis); and touchdown passes—3 (September 19, 1999, vs. San Francisco).
MISCELLANEOUS: Regular-season record as starting quarterback: 4-13 (.235).

			PASSING							RUSHING				TOTALS		
Year Team	G	GS	Att.	Cmp.	Pct.	Yds.	TD	Int.	Avg.	Rat.	Att.	Yds.	Avg.	TD	TD	2pt.	Pts.
1993—L.A. Raiders NFL							Did not play.										
1994—L.A. Raiders NFL							Did not play.										
1995—Oakland NFL	4	2	80	44	55.0	540	6	4	6.75	80.2	3	5	1.7	0	0	0	0
1996—Oakland NFL	8	3	104	57	54.8	667	4	5	6.41	67.3	2	13	6.5	0	0	0	0

H

Year Team	G	GS	PASSING								RUSHING				TOTALS		
			Att.	Cmp.	Pct.	Yds.	TD	Int.	Avg.	Rat.	Att.	Yds.	Avg.	TD	TD	2pt.	Pts.
1997—Buffalo NFL	2	0	30	17	56.7	133	0	2	4.43	40.0	2	7	3.5	0	0	0	0
—New Orleans NFL	5	4	131	61	46.6	891	6	8	6.80	59.0	12	36	3.0	0	0	0	0
1998—New Orleans NFL	1	1	23	11	47.8	170	1	0	7.39	87.2	2	13	6.5	0	0	0	0
1999—New Orleans NFL	9	7	159	85	53.5	970	6	6	6.10	68.9	12	47	3.9	1	1	0	6
2000—Indianapolis NFL							Did not play.										
Pro totals (5 years)	29	17	527	275	52.2	3371	23	25	6.40	67.0	33	121	3.7	1	1	0	6

HOBGOOD-CHITTICK, NATE   DT   49ERS

PERSONAL: Born November 30, 1974, in New Haven, Conn. ... 6-3/290. ... Full name: Nate Broe Hobgood-Chittick.

HIGH SCHOOL: William Allen (Allentown, Pa.).

COLLEGE: North Carolina.

TRANSACTIONS/CAREER NOTES: Signed as non drafted free agent by New York Giants (April 24, 1998). ... Inactive for four games with Giants (1998). ... Released by Giants (September 30, 1998). ... Re-signed by Giants to practice squad (October 2, 1998). ... Signed by Indianapolis Colts off Giants practice squad (November 25, 1998). ... Inactive for five games with Colts (1998). ... Released by Colts (September 7, 1999). ... Signed by St. Louis Rams (September 13, 1999). ... Released by Rams (October 10, 2000). ... Signed by San Francisco 49ers (October 11, 2000).

PLAYING EXPERIENCE: St. Louis NFL, 1999; St. Louis (5)-San Francisco (5) NFL, 2000. ... Games/Games started: 1999 (10/1), 2000 (St.L-5/0; S.F.-5/0; Total: 10/0). Total: 20/1.

CHAMPIONSHIP GAME EXPERIENCE: Played in NFC championship game (1999 season). ... Member of Super Bowl championship team (1999 season).

PRO STATISTICS: 1999—Credited with ½ sack. 2000—Credited with one sack and recovered one fumble.

HODGE, DAMON   WR   COWBOYS

PERSONAL: Born February 16, 1977, in Thomaston, Ala. ... 6-1/192.

HIGH SCHOOL: Johnson (Thomaston, Ala.).

COLLEGE: Alabama State.

TRANSACTIONS/CAREER NOTES: Signed as non-drafted free agent by Dallas Cowboys (April 19, 2000). ... Released by Cowboys (August 27, 2000). ... Re-signed by Cowboys to practice squad (August 29, 2000). ... Activated (October 11, 2000).

PLAYING EXPERIENCE: Dallas NFL, 2000. ... Games/Games started: 2000 (8/0).

PRO STATISTICS: 2000—Caught four passes for 60 yards.

SINGLE GAME HIGHS (regular season): Receptions—3 (October 15, 2000, vs. New York Giants); yards—52 (October 15, 2000, vs. New York Giants); and touchdown receptions—0.

HODGINS, JAMES   FB   RAMS

PERSONAL: Born April 30, 1977, in San Jose, Calif. ... 6-1/270.

HIGH SCHOOL: Oak Grove (San Jose, Calif.).

COLLEGE: San Jose State.

TRANSACTIONS/CAREER NOTES: Signed as non-drafted free agent by St. Louis Rams (April 20, 1999).

CHAMPIONSHIP GAME EXPERIENCE: Played in NFC championship game (1999 season). ... Member of Super Bowl championship team (1999 season).

PRO STATISTICS: 1999—Returned two kickoffs for four yards. 2000—Recovered one fumble.

SINGLE GAME HIGHS (regular season): Attempts—3 (November 28, 1999, vs. New Orleans); yards—3 (October 1, 2000, vs. San Diego); and rushing touchdowns—1 (November 28, 1999, vs. New Orleans).

Year Team	G	GS	RUSHING				RECEIVING				TOTALS			
			Att.	Yds.	Avg.	TD	No.	Yds.	Avg.	TD	TD	2pt.	Pts.	Fum.
1999—St. Louis NFL....................................	15	0	7	10	1.4	1	6	35	5.8	0	1	0	6	0
2000—St. Louis NFL....................................	15	2	1	3	3.0	0	2	5	2.5	0	0	0	0	0
Pro totals (2 years)...................................	30	2	8	13	1.6	1	8	40	5.0	0	1	0	6	0

HOLCOMB, KELLY   QB   BROWNS

PERSONAL: Born July 9, 1973, in Fayetteville, Tenn. ... 6-2/212. ... Full name: Bryan Kelly Holcomb.

HIGH SCHOOL: Lincoln County (Fayetteville, Tenn.).

COLLEGE: Middle Tennessee State.

TRANSACTIONS/CAREER NOTES: Signed as non-drafted free agent by Tampa Bay Buccaneers (May 1, 1995). ... Released by Buccaneers (August 22, 1995). ... Re-signed by Buccaneers to practice squad (August 29, 1995). ... Released by Buccaneers (September 19, 1995). ... Re-signed by Buccaneers to practice squad (October 4, 1995). ... Released by Buccaneers (October 17, 1995). ... Re-signed by Buccaneers to practice squad (December 19, 1995). ... Played for Barcelona Dragons of World League (1996). ... Released by Buccaneers (August 19, 1996). ... Signed by Indianapolis Colts to practice squad (November 27, 1996). ... Activated (December 12, 1996). ... Active for all 16 games (1998); did not play. ... Granted free agency (February 11, 2000). ... Re-signed by Colts (February 26, 2000). ... Released by Colts (February 28, 2001). ... Signed by Cleveland Browns (March 2, 2001).

PRO STATISTICS: W.L.: 1995—Caught one pass for minus eight yards. 1997—Fumbled four times and recovered one fumble for minus eight yards.

SINGLE GAME HIGHS (regular season): Attempts—32 (November 9, 1997, vs. Cincinnati); completions—19 (November 9, 1997, vs. Cincinnati); yards—236 (November 9, 1997, vs. Cincinnati); touchdown passes—1 (November 9, 1997, vs. Cincinnati).

MISCELLANEOUS: Regular-season record as starting NFL quarterback: 0-1.

H

Year Team	G	GS	Att.	Cmp.	Pct.	PASSING Yds.	TD	Int.	Avg.	Rat.	RUSHING Att.	Yds.	Avg.	TD	TOTALS TD	2pt.	Pts.
1995—Tampa Bay NFL						Did not play.											
1996—Barcelona W.L.	10	10	319	191	59.9	2382	14	16	7.47	76.8	38	111	2.9	2	2	0	12
—Indianapolis NFL.........						Did not play.											
1997—Indianapolis NFL	5	1	73	45	61.6	454	1	8	6.22	44.3	5	5	1.0	0	0	0	0
1998—Indianapolis NFL						Did not play.											
1999—Indianapolis NFL						Did not play.											
2000—Indianapolis NFL	3	0	0	0	0.0	0	0	0	0.0	...	0	0	0.0	0	0	0	0
W.L. totals (1 year)	10	10	319	191	59.9	2382	14	16	7.47	76.8	38	111	2.9	2	2	0	12
NFL totals (2 years)	8	1	73	45	61.6	454	1	8	6.22	44.3	5	5	1.0	0	0	0	0
Pro totals (3 years)	18	11	392	236	60.2	2836	15	24	7.23	69.6	43	116	2.7	2	2	0	12

HOLCOMBE, ROBERT   RB/FB   RAMS

PERSONAL: Born December 11, 1975, in Houston. ... 5-11/225. ... Full name: Robert Wayne Holcombe.
HIGH SCHOOL: Jeff Davis Senior (Houston), then Mesa (Ariz.).
COLLEGE: Illinois.
TRANSACTIONS/CAREER NOTES: Selected by St. Louis Rams in second round (37th pick overall) of 1998 NFL draft. ... Signed by Rams (July 2, 1998).
CHAMPIONSHIP GAME EXPERIENCE: Played in NFC championship game (1999 season). ... Member of Super Bowl championship team (1999 season).
SINGLE GAME HIGHS (regular season): Attempts—21 (September 27, 1998, vs. Arizona); yards—86 (January 2, 2000); and rushing touchdowns—2 (September 27, 1998, vs. Arizona).

Year Team	G	GS	RUSHING Att.	Yds.	Avg.	TD	RECEIVING No.	Yds.	Avg.	TD	TOTALS TD	2pt.	Pts.	Fum.
1998—St. Louis NFL....................................	13	7	98	230	2.3	2	6	34	5.7	0	2	0	12	0
1999—St. Louis NFL....................................	15	7	78	294	3.8	4	14	163	11.6	1	5	0	30	4
2000—St. Louis NFL....................................	14	9	21	70	3.3	3	8	90	11.3	1	4	0	24	0
Pro totals (3 years)..	42	23	197	594	3.0	9	28	287	10.3	2	11	0	66	4

HOLDMAN, WARRICK   LB   BEARS

PERSONAL: Born November 22, 1975, in Alief, Texas. ... 6-1/246. ... Full name: Warrick Donte Holdman.
HIGH SCHOOL: Elsik (Alief, Texas).
COLLEGE: Texas A&M.
TRANSACTIONS/CAREER NOTES: Selected by Chicago Bears in fourth round (106th pick overall) of 1999 NFL draft. ... Signed by Bears (July 25, 1999). ... On injured reserve with knee injury (November 21, 2000-remainder of season).
PRO STATISTICS: 1999—Recovered one fumble for 33 yards.

Year Team	G	GS	SACKS
1999—Chicago NFL	16	5	2.0
2000—Chicago NFL	10	10	0.0
Pro totals (2 years)...	26	15	2.0

HOLECEK, JOHN   LB   BILLS

PERSONAL: Born May 7, 1972, in Steger, Ill. ... 6-2/242. ... Full name: John Francis Holecek. ... Name pronounced HOLL-uh-sek.
HIGH SCHOOL: Marian Catholic (Chicago Heights, Ill.).
COLLEGE: Illinois.
TRANSACTIONS/CAREER NOTES: Selected by Buffalo Bills in fifth round (144th pick overall) of 1995 NFL draft. ... Signed by Bills (June 12, 1995). ... On physically unable to perform list with hamstring injury (August 22-November 21, 1995). ... On injured reserve with knee injury (August 16, 1996-entire season). ... Granted free agency (February 13, 1998). ... Re-signed by Bills (April 27, 1998).
PLAYING EXPERIENCE: Buffalo NFL, 1995 and 1997-2000. ... Games/Games started: 1995 (1/0), 1997 (14/8), 1998 (13/13), 1999 (14/14), 2000 (16/16). Total: 58/51.
PRO STATISTICS: 1997—Credited with 1 1/2 sacks. 1999—Intercepted one pass for 35 yards and credited with one sack. 2000—Intercepted one pass for no yards.

HOLLAND, DARIUS   DT   BROWNS

PERSONAL: Born November 10, 1973, in Petersburg, Va. ... 6-5/330. ... Full name: Darius Jerome Holland.
HIGH SCHOOL: Mayfield (Las Cruces, N.M.).
COLLEGE: Colorado.
TRANSACTIONS/CAREER NOTES: Selected by Green Bay Packers in third round (65th pick overall) of 1995 NFL draft. ... Signed by Packers (July 18, 1995). ... Granted free agency (February 13, 1998). ... Re-signed by Packers (April 10, 1998). ... Traded by Packers to Kansas City Chiefs for DE Vaughn Booker (May 13, 1998). ... Released by Chiefs (October 13, 1998). ... Signed by Detroit Lions (October 19, 1998). ... Granted unconditional free agency (February 12, 1999). ... Signed by Cleveland Browns (April 23, 1999). ... Granted unconditional free agency (February 11, 2000). ... Re-signed by Browns (February 15, 2000).
PLAYING EXPERIENCE: Green Bay NFL, 1995-1997; Kansas City (6)-Detroit (10) NFL, 1998; Cleveland NFL, 1999 and 2000. ... Games/Games started: 1995 (14/4), 1996 (16/0), 1997 (12/1), 1998 (K.C.-6/0; Det.-10/4; Total: 16/4), 1999 (15/11), 2000 (16/1). Total: 89/21.
CHAMPIONSHIP GAME EXPERIENCE: Played in NFC championship game (1995-1997 seasons). ... Member of Super Bowl championship team (1996 season). ... Played in Super Bowl XXXII (1997 season).
PRO STATISTICS: 1995—Credited with 1 1/2 sacks. 1999—Credited with two sacks and recovered one fumble for 14 yards. 2000—Intercepted one pass for no yards and credited with one sack.

H

HOLLIDAY, VONNIE — DE — PACKERS

PERSONAL: Born December 11, 1975, in Camden, S.C. ... 6-5/290. ... Full name: Dimetry Giovonni Holliday. ... Cousin of Corey Holliday, wide receiver with Pittsburgh Steelers (1995-97).
HIGH SCHOOL: Camden (S.C.).
COLLEGE: North Carolina.
TRANSACTIONS/CAREER NOTES: Selected by Green Bay Packers in first round (19th pick overall) of 1998 NFL draft. ... Signed by Packers (June 15, 1998).
PRO STATISTICS: 1998—Recovered two fumbles. 1999—Recovered one fumble. 2000—Intercepted one pass for three yards.

Year Team	G	GS	SACKS
1998—Green Bay NFL	12	12	8.0
1999—Green Bay NFL	16	16	6.0
2000—Green Bay NFL	12	9	5.0
Pro totals (3 years)	40	37	19.0

HOLLIER, DWIGHT — LB

PERSONAL: Born April 21, 1969, in Hampton, Va. ... 6-2/242. ... Full name: Dwight Leon Hollier Jr. ... Name pronounced HALL-yer.
HIGH SCHOOL: Kecoughtan (Hampton, Va.).
COLLEGE: North Carolina (degree in speech communications and psychology).
TRANSACTIONS/CAREER NOTES: Selected by Miami Dolphins in fourth round (97th pick overall) of 1992 NFL draft. ... Signed by Dolphins (July 10, 1992). ... Granted free agency (February 17, 1995). ... Re-signed by Dolphins (May 9, 1995). ... Granted unconditional free agency (February 14, 1997). ... Re-signed by Dolphins (April 17, 1997). ... Granted unconditional free agency (February 11, 2000). ... Signed by Indianapolis Colts (July 14, 2000). ... Granted unconditional free agency (March 2, 2001).
PLAYING EXPERIENCE: Miami NFL, 1992-1999; Indianapolis NFL, 2000. ... Games/Games started: 1992 (16/5), 1993 (16/10), 1994 (11/7), 1995 (16/14), 1996 (16/15), 1997 (16/3), 1998 (16/0), 1999 (15/0), 2000 (16/15). Total: 138/69.
CHAMPIONSHIP GAME EXPERIENCE: Played in AFC championship game (1992 season).
PRO STATISTICS: 1992—Credited with one sack and recovered three fumbles. 1993—Recovered one fumble. 1994—Intercepted one pass for 36 yards. 1995—Recovered one fumble. 1996—Intercepted one pass for 11 yards and credited with one sack. 1997—Returned one kickoff for no yards. 1998—Recovered one fumble. 1999—Recovered one fumble. 2000—Credited with one sack.

HOLLIS, MIKE — K — JAGUARS

PERSONAL: Born May 22, 1972, in Kellogg, Idaho. ... 5-7/174. ... Full name: Michael Shane Hollis.
HIGH SCHOOL: Central Valley (Veradale, Wash.).
COLLEGE: Idaho (degree in sports science, 1996).
TRANSACTIONS/CAREER NOTES: Signed as non-drafted free agent by San Diego Chargers (May 6, 1994). ... Released by Chargers (August 22, 1994). ... Signed by Jacksonville Jaguars (June 5, 1995).
CHAMPIONSHIP GAME EXPERIENCE: Played in AFC championship game (1996 and 1999 seasons).
HONORS: Played in Pro Bowl (1997 season).

Year Team	G	KICKING						
		XPM	XPA	FGM	FGA	Lg.	50+	Pts.
1995—Jacksonville NFL	16	27	28	20	27	53	2-3	87
1996—Jacksonville NFL	16	27	27	30	36	53	2-3	117
1997—Jacksonville NFL	16	41	41	31	36	52	2-2	*134
1998—Jacksonville NFL	16	45	45	21	26	47	0-1	108
1999—Jacksonville NFL	16	37	37	31	38	50	1-1	130
2000—Jacksonville NFL	12	33	33	24	26	51	3-3	105
Pro totals (6 years)	92	210	211	157	189	53	10-13	681

HOLMBERG, ROB — LB — PATRIOTS

PERSONAL: Born May 6, 1971, in McKeesport, Pa. ... 6-3/240. ... Full name: Robert Anthony Holmberg.
HIGH SCHOOL: Mt. Pleasant (Pa.).
COLLEGE: Navy, then Penn State.
TRANSACTIONS/CAREER NOTES: Selected by Los Angeles Raiders in seventh round (217th pick overall) of 1994 NFL draft. ... Signed by Raiders for 1994 season. ... Raiders franchise moved to Oakland (July 21, 1995). ... Released by Raiders (August 30, 1998). ... Signed by Indianapolis Colts (September 9, 1998). ... Released by Colts (September 29, 1998). ... Signed by New York Jets (October 27, 1998). ... Released by Jets (September 5, 1999). ... Signed by Minnesota Vikings (September 6, 1999). ... Released by Vikings (March 31, 2000). ... Signed by New England Patriots (July 23, 2000).
PLAYING EXPERIENCE: Los Angeles Raiders NFL, 1994; Oakland NFL, 1995-1997; Indianapolis (3)-New York Jets (9) NFL, 1998; Minnesota NFL, 1999; New England NFL, 2000. ... Games/Games started: 1994 (16/0), 1995 (16/0), 1996 (13/1), 1997 (16/0), 1998 (Ind.-3/0; NYJ-9/0; Total: 12/0), 1999 (16/0), 2000 (16/5). Total: 105/6.
CHAMPIONSHIP GAME EXPERIENCE: Played in AFC championship game (1998 season).
PRO STATISTICS: 1995—Credited with one sack and recovered one fumble. 1996—Credited with one sack. 1997—Returned one kickoff for 15 yards and recovered one fumble.

HOLMES, EARL — LB — STEELERS

PERSONAL: Born April 28, 1973, in Tallahassee, Fla. ... 6-2/250. ... Full name: Earl L. Holmes.
HIGH SCHOOL: Florida A&M University (Tallahassee, Fla.).
COLLEGE: Florida A&M.
TRANSACTIONS/CAREER NOTES: Selected by Pittsburgh Steelers in fourth round (126th pick overall) of 1996 NFL draft. ... Signed by Steelers (July 16, 1996).

H

CHAMPIONSHIP GAME EXPERIENCE: Played in AFC championship game (1997 season).
PRO STATISTICS: 1997—Recovered one fumble. 1998—Intercepted one pass for 36 yards. 1999—Recovered one fumble. 2000—Recovered one fumble for four yards.

Year Team	G	GS	SACKS
1996—Pittsburgh NFL	3	1	1.0
1997—Pittsburgh NFL	16	16	4.0
1998—Pittsburgh NFL	14	14	1.5
1999—Pittsburgh NFL	16	16	0.0
2000—Pittsburgh NFL	16	16	1.0
Pro totals (5 years)	65	63	7.5

HOLMES, JARET K GIANTS

PERSONAL: Born March 3, 1976, in Clinton, Miss. ... 6-0/203. ... Full name: Jaret D. Holmes.
HIGH SCHOOL: Clinton (Miss.).
JUNIOR COLLEGE: Hinds Community College (Miss.).
COLLEGE: Auburn.
TRANSACTIONS/CAREER NOTES: Signed as non-drafted free agent by Philadelphia Eagles (April 21, 1998). ... Released by Eagles (August 17, 1998). ... Signed by Buffalo Bills (April 23, 1999). ... Released by Bills (August 30, 1999). ... Signed by Chicago Bears to practice squad (November 18, 1999). ... Released by Bears (November 23, 1999). ... Signed by New York Giants to practice squad (December 2, 1999). ... Signed by Bears off Giants practice squad (December 13, 1999). ... Released by Bears (August 27, 2000). ... Signed by Giants (September 30, 2000).
CHAMPIONSHIP GAME EXPERIENCE: Member of Giants for NFC championship game (2000 season); inactive. ... Member of Giants for Super Bowl XXXV (2000 season); inactive.

Year Team	G	XPM	XPA	FGM	FGA	Lg.	50+	Pts.
				KICKING				
1999—Chicago NFL	3	0	0	2	2	39	0-0	6
2000—Berlin NFLE	...	0	0	9	12	0	0-0	27
—New York Giants NFL	4	3	3	2	2	34	0-0	9
NFL Europe totals (1 year)	...	0	0	9	12	0	0-0	27
NFL totals (2 years)	7	3	3	4	4	39	0-0	15
Pro totals (3 years)	...	3	3	13	16	39	0-0	42

HOLMES, KENNY DE GIANTS

PERSONAL: Born October 24, 1973, in Vero Beach, Fla. ... 6-4/270. ... Full name: Kenneth Holmes.
HIGH SCHOOL: Vero Beach (Fla.).
COLLEGE: Miami, Fla. (degree in criminal justice).
TRANSACTIONS/CAREER NOTES: Selected by Houston Oilers in first round (18th pick overall) of 1997 NFL draft. ... Oilers franchise moved to Tennessee for 1997 season. ... Signed by Oilers (July 18, 1997). ... Oilers franchise renamed Tennessee Titans for 1999 season (December 26, 1998). ... Granted unconditional free agency (March 2, 2001). ... Signed by New York Giants (March 14, 2001).
CHAMPIONSHIP GAME EXPERIENCE: Played in AFC championship game (1999 season). ... Played in Super Bowl XXXIV (1999 season).
PRO STATISTICS: 1997—Recovered one fumble. 1999—Intercepted two passes for 17 yards.

Year Team	G	GS	SACKS
1997—Tennessee NFL	16	5	7.0
1998—Tennessee NFL	14	11	2.5
1999—Tennessee NFL	14	7	4.0
2000—Tennessee NFL	14	13	8.0
Pro totals (4 years)	58	36	21.5

HOLMES, LESTER G

PERSONAL: Born September 27, 1969, in Tylertown, Miss. ... 6-5/330.
HIGH SCHOOL: Tylertown (Miss.).
COLLEGE: Jackson State.
TRANSACTIONS/CAREER NOTES: Selected by Philadelphia Eagles in first round (19th pick overall) of 1993 NFL draft. ... Signed by Eagles (August 2, 1993). ... On injured reserve with knee injury (November 28, 1995-remainder of season). ... Granted free agency (February 16, 1996). ... Re-signed by Eagles (July 17, 1996). ... Granted unconditional free agency (February 14, 1997). ... Signed by Oakland Raiders (May 1, 1997). ... Released by Raiders (February 12, 1998). ... Signed by Arizona Cardinals (February 26, 1998). ... Released by Cardinals (March 1, 2001).
PLAYING EXPERIENCE: Philadelphia NFL, 1993-1996; Oakland NFL, 1997; Arizona NFL, 1998-2000. ... Games/Games started: 1993 (12/6), 1994 (16/16), 1995 (2/2), 1996 (16/14), 1997 (15/15), 1998 (16/16), 1999 (13/13), 2000 (12/12). Total: 102/94.
PRO STATISTICS: 1993—Recovered one fumble. 1994—Recovered three fumbles. 1999—Recovered one fumble.

HOLMES, PRIEST RB CHIEFS

PERSONAL: Born October 7, 1973, in Fort Smith, Ark. ... 5-9/205. ... Full name: Priest Anthony Holmes.
HIGH SCHOOL: Marshall (Texas).
COLLEGE: Texas.
TRANSACTIONS/CAREER NOTES: Signed as non-drafted free agent by Baltimore Ravens (April 25, 1997). ... Granted free agency (February 11, 2000). ... Re-signed by Ravens (June 9, 2000). ... Granted unconditional free agency (March 2, 2001). ... Signed by Kansas City Chiefs (April 1, 2001).
CHAMPIONSHIP GAME EXPERIENCE: Played in AFC championship game (2000 season). ... Member of Super Bowl championship team (2000 season).

H

PRO STATISTICS: 1997—Returned one kickoff for 14 yards. 1998—Had only pass attempt intercepted, returned two kickoffs for 30 yards and recovered one fumble for one yard. 1999—Recovered one fumble. 2000—Returned one kickoff for seven yards and recovered one fumble.
SINGLE GAME HIGHS (regular season): Attempts—36 (November 22, 1998, vs. Cincinnati); yards—227 (November 22, 1998, vs. Cincinnati); and rushing touchdowns—2 (November 29, 1998, vs. Indianapolis).
STATISTICAL PLATEAUS: 100-yard rushing games: 1998 (4), 1999 (2), 2000 (1). Total: 7.
MISCELLANEOUS: Holds Baltimore Ravens all-time record for most yards rushing (2,102) and rushing touchdowns (10).

| | | | RUSHING | | | | RECEIVING | | | | TOTALS | | |
Year Team	G	GS	Att.	Yds.	Avg.	TD	No.	Yds.	Avg.	TD	TD	2pt.	Pts.	Fum.
1997—Baltimore NFL	7	0	0	0	0.0	0	0	0	0.0	0	0	0	0	0
1998—Baltimore NFL	16	13	233	1008	4.3	7	43	260	6.0	0	7	0	42	3
1999—Baltimore NFL	9	4	89	506	5.7	1	13	104	8.0	1	2	0	12	0
2000—Baltimore NFL	16	2	137	588	4.3	2	32	221	6.9	0	2	0	12	2
Pro totals (4 years)	48	19	459	2102	4.6	10	88	585	6.6	1	11	0	66	5

HOLSEY, BERNARD — DL — COLTS

PERSONAL: Born December 10, 1973, in Cave Spring, Ga. ... 6-2/286.
HIGH SCHOOL: Coosa (Rome, Ga.).
COLLEGE: Duke.
TRANSACTIONS/CAREER NOTES: Signed as non-drafted free agent by New York Giants (April 26, 1996). ... Granted free agency (February 12, 1999). ... Re-signed by Giants (June 2, 1999). ... Granted unconditional free agency (February 11, 2000). ... Signed by Indianapolis Colts (March 15, 2000).
PLAYING EXPERIENCE: New York Giants NFL, 1996-1999; Indianapolis NFL, 2000. ... Games/Games started: 1996 (16/0), 1997 (16/4), 1998 (16/0), 1999 (16/0), 2000 (16/13). Total: 80/17.
PRO STATISTICS: 1997—Credited with 3 1/2 sacks. 1999—Recovered one fumble. 2000—Returned one kickoff for 10 yards, credited with two sacks and recovered one fumble for 48 yards and one touchdown.

HOLT, TORRY — WR — RAMS

PERSONAL: Born June 5, 1976, in Greensboro, N.C. ... 6-0/190. ... Full name: Torry Jabar Holt.
HIGH SCHOOL: Eastern Guilford (Gibsonville, N.C.).
COLLEGE: North Carolina State.
TRANSACTIONS/CAREER NOTES: Selected by St. Louis Rams in first round (sixth pick overall) of 1999 NFL draft. ... Signed by Rams (June 5, 1999).
CHAMPIONSHIP GAME EXPERIENCE: Played in NFC championship game (1999 season). ... Member of Super Bowl championship team (1999 season).
HONORS: Named wide receiver on THE SPORTING NEWS college All-America first team (1998). ... Played in Pro Bowl (2000 season).
PRO STATISTICS: 1999—Returned three punts for 15 yards and recovered one fumble. 2000—Recovered one fumble.
SINGLE GAME HIGHS (regular season): Receptions—9 (December 18, 2000, vs. Tampa Bay); yards—189 (September 24, 2000, vs. Atlanta); and touchdown receptions—2 (September 24, 2000, vs. Atlanta).
STATISTICAL PLATEAUS: 100-yard receiving games: 1999 (2), 2000 (8). Total: 10.

| | | | RUSHING | | | | RECEIVING | | | | TOTALS | | |
Year Team	G	GS	Att.	Yds.	Avg.	TD	No.	Yds.	Avg.	TD	TD	2pt.	Pts.	Fum.
1999—St. Louis NFL	16	15	3	25	8.3	0	52	788	15.2	6	6	0	36	4
2000—St. Louis NFL	16	15	2	7	3.5	0	82	*1635	*19.9	6	6	0	36	2
Pro totals (2 years)	32	30	5	32	6.4	0	134	2423	18.1	12	12	0	72	6

HOOVER, BRAD — FB — PANTHERS

PERSONAL: Born November 11, 1976, in High Point, N.C. ... 6-2/225. ... Full name: Bradley R. Hoover.
HIGH SCHOOL: Ledford (Thomasville, N.C.).
COLLEGE: Western Carolina.
TRANSACTIONS/CAREER NOTES: Signed as non-drafted free agent by Carolina Panthers (April 17, 2000).
PRO STATISTICS: 2000—Recovered one fumble.
SINGLE GAME HIGHS (regular season): Attempts—24 (November 27, 2000, vs. Green Bay); yards—117 (November 27, 2000, vs. Green Bay); and rushing touchdowns—1 (November 27, 2000, vs. Green Bay).
STATISTICAL PLATEAUS: 100-yard rushing games: 2000 (1).

| | | | RUSHING | | | | RECEIVING | | | | TOTALS | | |
Year Team	G	GS	Att.	Yds.	Avg.	TD	No.	Yds.	Avg.	TD	TD	2pt.	Pts.	Fum.
2000—Carolina NFL	16	4	89	290	3.3	1	15	112	7.5	0	1	0	6	1

HOPKINS, BRAD — OT — TITANS

PERSONAL: Born September 5, 1970, in Columbia, S.C. ... 6-3/305. ... Full name: Bradley D. Hopkins.
HIGH SCHOOL: Moline (Ill.).
COLLEGE: Illinois (degree in speech communications, 1993).
TRANSACTIONS/CAREER NOTES: Selected by Houston Oilers in first round (13th pick overall) of 1993 NFL draft. ... Signed by Oilers (August 10, 1993). ... Granted unconditional free agency (February 14, 1997). ... Re-signed by Oilers (March 10, 1997). ... Oilers franchise moved to Tennessee for 1997 season. ... Oilers franchise renamed Tennessee Titans for 1999 season (December 26, 1998).
PLAYING EXPERIENCE: Houston NFL, 1993-1996; Tennessee NFL, 1997-2000. ... Games/Games started: 1993 (16/11), 1994 (16/15), 1995 (16/16), 1996 (16/16), 1997 (16/16), 1998 (13/13), 1999 (16/16), 2000 (15/15). Total: 124/118.
CHAMPIONSHIP GAME EXPERIENCE: Played in AFC championship game (1999 season). ... Played in Super Bowl XXXIV (1999 season).
HONORS: Played in Pro Bowl (2000 season).
PRO STATISTICS: 1994—Recovered one fumble. 1995—Recovered three fumbles. 1996—Recovered one fumble. 1997—Recovered one fumble.

H

HOPSON, TYRONE　　　　　　G　　　　　　49ERS

PERSONAL: Born May 28, 1976, in Hopkinsville, Ky. ... 6-2/305. ... Full name: Tyrone Hopson Jr.
HIGH SCHOOL: Davies County (Owensboro, Ky.).
COLLEGE: Eastern Kentucky.
TRANSACTIONS/CAREER NOTES: Selected by San Francisco 49ers in fifth round (161st pick overall) of 1999 NFL draft. ... Signed by 49ers (July 26, 1999). ... On injured reserve with shoulder injury (October 20, 1999-remainder of season). ... Released by 49ers (August 27, 2000). ... Re-signed by 49ers to practice squad (August 29, 2000). ... Activated (November 14, 2000).
PLAYING EXPERIENCE: San Francisco NFL, 1999 and 2000. ... Games/Games started: 1999 (1/0), 2000 (3/1). Total: 4/1.

HORN, JOE　　　　　　WR　　　　　　SAINTS

PERSONAL: Born January 16, 1972, in New Haven, Conn. ... 6-1/206. ... Full name: Joseph Horn.
HIGH SCHOOL: Douglas Bird (Fayetteville, N.C.).
JUNIOR COLLEGE: Itawamba Community College (Miss.).
COLLEGE: None.
TRANSACTIONS/CAREER NOTES: Signed by Memphis Mad Dogs of CFL (March 25, 1995). ... Selected by Kansas City Chiefs in fifth round (135th pick overall) of 1996 NFL draft. ... Signed by Chiefs (June 25, 1996). ... Granted free agency (February 12, 1999). ... Re-signed by Chiefs (June 16, 1999). ... Granted unconditional free agency (February 11, 2000). ... Signed by New Orleans Saints (February 13, 2000).
HONORS: Played in Pro Bowl (2000 season).
PRO STATISTICS: 1996—Rushed once for eight yards. 1998—Rushed once for no yards, returned one punt for six yards and recovered three fumbles for minus eight yards. 1999—Rushed twice for 15 yards, returned one punt for 18 yards and recovered one fumble. 2000—Rushed six times for 10 yards and recovered one fumble.
SINGLE GAME HIGHS (regular season): Receptions—12 (September 10, 2000, vs. San Diego); yards—180 (November 5, 2000, vs. San Francisco); and touchdown receptions—2 (October 8, 2000, vs. Chicago).
STATISTICAL PLATEAUS: 100-yard receiving games: 2000 (5).

			RECEIVING				KICKOFF RETURNS				TOTALS		
Year　Team	G	GS	No.	Yds.	Avg.	TD	No.	Yds.	Avg.	TD	TD	2pt.	Pts.	Fum.
1995—Memphis CFL	17	17	71	1415	19.9	5	2	17	8.5	0	5	0	30	0
1996—Kansas City NFL	9	0	2	30	15.0	0	0	0	0.0	0	0	0	0	0
1997—Kansas City NFL	8	0	2	65	32.5	0	0	0	0.0	0	0	0	0	0
1998—Kansas City NFL	16	1	14	198	14.1	1	11	233	21.2	0	1	0	6	2
1999—Kansas City NFL	16	1	35	586	16.7	6	9	165	18.3	0	6	0	36	0
2000—New Orleans NFL	16	16	94	1340	14.3	8	0	0	0.0	0	8	0	48	1
CFL totals (1 year)	17	17	71	1415	19.9	5	2	17	8.5	0	5	0	30	0
NFL totals (5 years)	65	18	147	2219	15.1	15	20	398	19.9	0	15	0	90	3
Pro totals (6 years)	82	35	218	3634	16.7	20	22	415	18.9	0	20	0	120	3

HORNE, TONY　　　　　　WR/KR　　　　　　CHIEFS

PERSONAL: Born March 21, 1976, in Montgomery County, N.C. ... 5-9/173. ... Full name: Tony Tremaine Horne.
HIGH SCHOOL: Richmond City (Rockingham, N.C.).
COLLEGE: Clemson.
TRANSACTIONS/CAREER NOTES: Signed as non-drafted free agent by St. Louis Rams (April 20, 1998). ... On suspended list for violating league substance abuse policy (October 20-November 16, 1999). ... Granted free agency (March 2, 2001). ... Tendered offer sheet by Kansas City Chiefs (April 17, 2001). ... Rams declined to match offer (April 20, 2001).
CHAMPIONSHIP GAME EXPERIENCE: Played in NFC championship game (1999 season). ... Member of Super Bowl championship team (1999 season).
HONORS: Named kick returner on THE SPORTING NEWS NFL All-Pro team (1999).
RECORDS: Holds NFL rookie-season record for most kickoff returns—56 (1998).
PRO STATISTICS: 2000—Rushed twice for six yards, caught four passes for 32 yards and two touchdowns and recovered one fumble.
SINGLE GAME HIGHS (regular season): Receptions—2 (October 15, 2000, vs. Atlanta); yards—18 (September 15, 2000, vs. San Francisco); and touchdown receptions—1 (October 15, 2000, vs. Atlanta).

			PUNT RETURNS				KICKOFF RETURNS				TOTALS		
Year　Team	G	GS	No.	Yds.	Avg.	TD	No.	Yds.	Avg.	TD	TD	2pt.	Pts.	Fum.
1998—St. Louis NFL	16	0	1	0	0.0	0	56	1306	23.3	1	1	0	6	1
1999—St. Louis NFL	12	0	5	22	4.4	0	30	892	*29.7	†2	2	0	12	0
2000—St. Louis NFL	11	0	1	16	16.0	0	57	1379	24.2	1	3	0	18	3
Pro totals (3 years)	39	0	7	38	5.4	0	143	3577	25.0	4	6	0	36	4

HOUSER, KEVIN　　　　　　FB　　　　　　SAINTS

PERSONAL: Born August 23, 1977, in Westlake, Ohio. ... 6-2/250.
HIGH SCHOOL: Westlake (Ohio).
COLLEGE: Ohio State.
TRANSACTIONS/CAREER NOTES: Selected by New Orleans Saints in seventh round (228th pick overall) of 2000 NFL draft. ... Signed by Saints (June 20, 2000).
PLAYING EXPERIENCE: New Orleans NFL, 2000. ... Games/Games started: 2000 (16/0).

H

HOVAN, CHRIS — DT — VIKINGS

PERSONAL: Born May 12, 1978, in Rocky River, Ohio. ... 6-2/294. ... Full name: Christopher James Hovan.
HIGH SCHOOL: St. Ignatius (Rocky River, Ohio).
COLLEGE: Boston College.
TRANSACTIONS/CAREER NOTES: Selected by Minnesota Vikings in first round (25th pick overall) of 2000 NFL draft. ... Signed by Vikings (July 24, 2000).
CHAMPIONSHIP GAME EXPERIENCE: Played in NFC championship game (2000 season).

Year Team	G	GS	SACKS
2000—Minnesota NFL	16	13	2.0

HOWARD, CHRIS — RB — RAIDERS

PERSONAL: Born May 5, 1975, in Kenner, La. ... 5-10/226. ... Full name: Christopher L. Howard.
HIGH SCHOOL: John Curtis (River Ridge, La.).
COLLEGE: Michigan.
TRANSACTIONS/CAREER NOTES: Selected by Denver Broncos in fifth round (153rd pick overall) of 1998 NFL draft. ... Signed by Broncos (July 22, 1998). ... Released by Broncos (August 30, 1998). ... Re-signed by Broncos to practice squad (September 8, 1998). ... Released by Broncos (September 22, 1998). ... Signed by Jacksonville Jaguars (September 22, 1998). ... Released by Jaguars (September 13, 2000). ... Signed by Oakland Raiders (March 13, 2001).
CHAMPIONSHIP GAME EXPERIENCE: Played in AFC championship game (1999 season).
SINGLE GAME HIGHS (regular season): Attempts—13 (September 3, 2000, vs. Cleveland); yards—45 (September 3, 2000, vs. Cleveland); and rushing touchdowns—1 (September 3, 2000, vs. Cleveland).

			RUSHING				RECEIVING				TOTALS			
Year Team	G	GS	Att.	Yds.	Avg.	TD	No.	Yds.	Avg.	TD	TD	2pt.	Pts.	Fum.
1998—Jacksonville NFL	8	0	7	16	2.3	0	1	3	3.0	0	0	0	0	0
1999—Jacksonville NFL	12	0	13	55	4.2	0	1	8	8.0	0	0	0	0	0
2000—Jacksonville NFL	2	1	21	52	2.5	1	3	26	8.7	0	1	0	6	2
Pro totals (3 years)	22	1	41	123	3.0	1	5	37	7.4	0	1	0	6	2

HOWARD, DARREN — DE — SAINTS

PERSONAL: Born November 19, 1976, in St. Petersburg, Fla. ... 6-3/281.
HIGH SCHOOL: Boca Ciega (Fla.).
COLLEGE: Kansas State.
TRANSACTIONS/CAREER NOTES: Selected by New Orleans Saints in second round (33rd pick overall) of 2000 NFL draft. ... Signed by Saints (July 17, 2000).
PRO STATISTICS: 2000—Intercepted one pass for 46 yards, fumbled once and recovered two fumbles.

Year Team	G	GS	SACKS
2000—New Orleans NFL	16	16	11.0

HOWARD, DESMOND — PR/KR — LIONS

PERSONAL: Born May 15, 1970, in Cleveland. ... 5-10/185. ... Full name: Desmond Kevin Howard.
HIGH SCHOOL: St. Joseph (Cleveland) Academy.
COLLEGE: Michigan (degree in communication studies).
TRANSACTIONS/CAREER NOTES: Selected by Washington Redskins in first round (fourth pick overall) of 1992 NFL draft. ... Signed by Redskins (August 25, 1992). ... On injured reserve with separated shoulder (December 29, 1992-remainder of 1992 playoffs). ... Selected by Jacksonville Jaguars from Redskins in NFL expansion draft (February 15, 1995). ... Granted unconditional free agency (February 16, 1996). ... Signed by Green Bay Packers (July 11, 1996). ... Granted unconditional free agency (February 14, 1997). ... Signed by Oakland Raiders (March 4, 1997). ... Released by Raiders (June 9, 1999). ... Signed by Packers (June 29, 1999). ... Released by Packers (November 30, 1999). ... Signed by Detroit Lions (December 4, 1999). ... Granted unconditional free agency (February 11, 2000). ... Re-signed by Lions (July 19, 2000). ... Granted unconditional free agency (March 2, 2001). ... Re-signed by Lions (March 2, 2001).
CHAMPIONSHIP GAME EXPERIENCE: Played in NFC championship game (1996 season). ... Member of Super Bowl championship team (1996 season).
HONORS: Heisman Trophy winner (1991). ... Named College Football Player of the Year by THE SPORTING NEWS (1991). ... Maxwell Award winner (1991). ... Named wide receiver on THE SPORTING NEWS college All-America first team (1991). ... Named punt returner on THE SPORTING NEWS NFL All-Pro team (1996). ... Named Most Valuable Player of Super Bowl XXXI (1996 season). ... Played in Pro Bowl (2000 season).
RECORDS: Holds NFL single-season record for most yards by punt return—875 (1996).
POST SEASON RECORDS: Holds Super Bowl and NFL postseason record for longest kickoff return—99 yards (January 26, 1997, vs. New England). ... Holds Super Bowl single-game record for most yards by punt return—90 (January 26, 1997, vs. New England). ... Shares Super Bowl career and single-game records for most punt returns—6. ... Shares Super Bowl single-game records for most combined yards—244; most combined yards by kick returns—244; most touchdowns by kickoff return—1 (January 26, 1997, vs. New England). ... Shares NFL postseason single-game record for most combined yards —244; most combined kick return yards—244; and most touchdowns by kickoff return—1 (January 26, 1997, vs. New England).
PRO STATISTICS: 1992—Fumbled once. 1996—Fumbled twice and recovered one fumble. 1997—Fumbled twice and recovered two fumbles. 1998—Fumbled four times. 2000—Fumbled twice and recovered one fumble.
SINGLE GAME HIGHS (regular season): Receptions—7 (November 20, 1994, vs. Dallas); yards—130 (December 4, 1994, vs. Tampa Bay); and touchdown receptions—1 (October 1, 1995, vs. Houston).
STATISTICAL PLATEAUS: 100-yard receiving games: 1994 (2).

H

Year Team	G	GS	RUSHING				RECEIVING				PUNT RETURNS				KICKOFF RETURNS				TOTALS		
			Att.	Yds.	Avg.	TD	No.	Yds.	Avg.	TD	No.	Yds.	Avg.	TD	No.	Yds.	Avg.	TD	TD	2pt.	Pts.
1992—Washington NFL .	16	1	3	14	4.7	0	3	20	6.7	0	6	84	14.0	1	22	462	21.0	0	1	0	6
1993—Washington NFL .	16	5	2	17	8.5	0	23	286	12.4	0	4	25	6.3	0	21	405	19.3	0	0	0	0
1994—Washington NFL .	16	15	1	4	4.0	0	40	727	18.2	5	0	0	0.0	0	0	0	0.0	0	5	1	32
1995—Jacksonville NFL .	13	7	1	8	8.0	0	26	276	10.6	1	24	246	10.3	0	10	178	17.8	0	1	0	6
1996—Green Bay NFL	16	0	0	0	0.0	0	13	95	7.3	0	*58	*875	*15.1	*3	22	460	20.9	0	3	0	18
1997—Oakland NFL......	15	0	0	0	0.0	0	4	30	7.5	0	27	210	7.8	0	*61	§1318	21.6	0	0	0	0
1998—Oakland NFL....	15	1	0	0	0.0	0	2	16	8.0	0	§45	541	12.0	†2	§49	1040	21.2	0	2	0	12
1999—Green Bay NFL....	8	0	0	0	0.0	0	0	0	0.0	0	12	93	7.8	0	19	364	19.2	0	0	0	0
—Detroit NFL.......	5	0	0	0	0.0	0	0	0	0.0	0	6	115	19.2	∞1	15	298	19.9	0	1	0	6
2000—Detroit NFL.......	15	0	0	0	0.0	0	2	14	7.0	0	31	457	14.7	1	57	1401	24.6	0	1	0	6
Pro totals (9 years)........	135	29	7	43	6.1	0	113	1464	13.0	6	213	2646	12.4	8	276	5926	21.5	0	14	1	86

HOWARD, REGGIE — CB — PANTHERS

PERSONAL: Born May 17, 1977, in Memphis, Tenn. ... 6-0/190. ... Full name: Reginald Clement Howard.
HIGH SCHOOL: Kirby (Memphis,Tenn.).
COLLEGE: Memphis State.
TRANSACTIONS/CAREER NOTES: Signed as non-drafted free agent by Carolina Panthers (April 17, 2000). ... Released by Panthers (August 29, 2000). ... Signed by New Orleans Saints to practice squad (September 1, 2000). ... Activated (October 22, 2000). ... Claimed on waivers by Panthers (October 25, 2000).
PLAYING EXPERIENCE: New Orleans (1)-Carolina (1) NFL, 2000. ... Games/Games started: 2000 (N.O.-1/0; Caro.-1/0; Total: 2/0).

HOWARD, TY — CB

PERSONAL: Born November 30, 1973, in Columbus, Ohio. ... 5-10/185.
HIGH SCHOOL: Briggs (Columbus, Ohio).
COLLEGE: Ohio State.
TRANSACTIONS/CAREER NOTES: Selected by Arizona Cardinals in third round (84th pick overall) of 1997 NFL draft. ... Signed by Cardinals (June 10, 1997). ... Claimed on waivers by Cincinnati Bengals (September 6, 1999). ... Granted free agency (February 11, 2000). ... Re-signed by Bengals (April 11, 2000). ... Released by Bengals (July 17, 2000). ... Signed by Tennessee Titans (July 31, 2000). ... Released by Titans (September 5, 2000).
PLAYING EXPERIENCE: Arizona NFL, 1997 and 1998; Cincinnati NFL, 1999; Tennessee NFL, 2000. ... Games/Games started: 1997 (15/2), 1998 (9/0), 1999 (12/3), 2000 (1/0). Total: 37/5.
PRO STATISTICS: 1997—Credited with one sack.

HOYING, BOBBY — QB — RAIDERS

PERSONAL: Born September 20, 1972, in St. Henry, Ohio. ... 6-3/220. ... Full name: Robert Carl Hoying.
HIGH SCHOOL: St. Henry (Ohio).
COLLEGE: Ohio State (degree in production and operations management).
TRANSACTIONS/CAREER NOTES: Selected by Philadelphia Eagles in third round (85th pick overall) of 1996 NFL draft. ... Signed by Eagles (July 15, 1996). ... Granted free agency (February 12, 1999). ... Re-signed by Eagles (April 15, 1999). ... Traded by Eagles to Oakland Raiders for sixth-round pick (DE John Frank) in 2000 draft (August 24, 1999).
CHAMPIONSHIP GAME EXPERIENCE: Played in AFC championship game (2000 season).
PRO STATISTICS: 1997—Fumbled seven times and recovered one fumble. 1998—Fumbled six times and recovered two fumbles for minus two yards.
SINGLE GAME HIGHS (regular season): Attempts—42 (November 30, 1997, vs. Cincinnati); completions—26 (November 30, 1997, vs. Cincinnati); yards—313 (November 30, 1997, vs. Cincinnati); and touchdown passes—4 (November 30, 1997, vs. Cincinnati).
STATISTICAL PLATEAUS: 300-yard passing games: 1997 (1).
MISCELLANEOUS: Regular-season record as starting NFL quarterback: 3-9-1 (.269).

Year Team	G	GS	PASSING								RUSHING				TOTALS		
			Att.	Cmp.	Pct.	Yds.	TD	Int.	Avg.	Rat.	Att.	Yds.	Avg.	TD	TD	2pt.	Pts.
1996—Philadelphia NFL	1	0	0	0	0.0	0	0	0	0.0	...	0	0	0.0	0	0	0	0
1997—Philadelphia NFL	7	6	225	128	56.9	1573	11	6	6.99	83.8	16	78	4.9	0	0	0	0
1998—Philadelphia NFL	8	7	224	114	50.9	961	0	9	4.29	45.6	22	84	3.8	0	0	0	0
1999—Oakland NFL.............	2	0	5	2	40.0	10	0	0	2.00	47.9	2	-3	-1.5	0	0	0	0
2000—Oakland NFL.............	4	0	2	0	0.0	0	0	0	0.0	39.6	2	-3	-1.5	0	0	0	0
Pro totals (5 years)	22	13	456	244	53.5	2544	11	15	5.58	64.3	42	156	3.7	0	0	0	0

HUARD, BROCK — QB — SEAHAWKS

PERSONAL: Born April 15, 1976, in Seattle. ... 6-4/228. ... Brother of Damon Huard, quarterback, New England Patriots.
HIGH SCHOOL: Puyallup (Wash.).
COLLEGE: Washington.
TRANSACTIONS/CAREER NOTES: Selected after junior season by Seattle Seahawks in third round (77th pick overall) of 1999 NFL draft. ... Signed by Seahawks (July 29, 1999). ... Inactive for all 16 games (1999).
PRO STATISTICS: 2000—Fumbled twice and recovered one fumble.
SINGLE GAME HIGHS (regular season): Attempts—34 (October 8, 2000, vs. Carolina); completions—19 (October 15, 2000, vs. Indianapolis); yards—226 (October 15, 2000, vs. Indianapolis); and touchdown passes—3 (October 15, 2000, vs. Indianapolis).
MISCELLANEOUS: Regular-season record as starting NFL quarterback: 0-4.

Year Team	G	GS	PASSING								RUSHING				TOTALS		
			Att.	Cmp.	Pct.	Yds.	TD	Int.	Avg.	Rat.	Att.	Yds.	Avg.	TD	TD	2pt.	Pts.
1999—Seattle NFL..................						Did not play.											
2000—Seattle NFL..................	5	4	87	49	56.3	540	3	2	6.21	76.8	5	29	5.8	0	0	0	0
Pro totals (1 years)	5	4	87	49	56.3	540	3	2	6.21	76.8	5	29	5.8	0	0	0	0

HUARD, DAMON — QB — PATRIOTS

PERSONAL: Born July 9, 1973, in Yakima, Wash. ... 6-3/215. ... Brother of Brock Huard, quarterback, Seattle Seahawks.
HIGH SCHOOL: Puyallup (Wash.).
COLLEGE: Washington.
TRANSACTIONS/CAREER NOTES: Signed as non-drafted free agent by Cincinnati Bengals (April 23, 1996). ... Released by Bengals (August 19, 1996). ... Signed by Miami Dolphins (April 24, 1997). ... Released by Dolphins (August 24, 1997). ... Re-signed by Dolphins to practice squad (August 26, 1997). ... Activated (September 6, 1997); did not play. ... Assigned by Dolphins to Frankfurt Galaxy in 1998 NFL Europe enhancement allocation program (February 18, 1998). ... Released by Dolphins (March 19, 2001). ... Signed by New England Patriots (April 2, 2001).
PRO STATISTICS: 1999—Caught one pass for no yards, fumbled three times and recovered one fumble for minus five yards.
SINGLE GAME HIGHS (regular season): Attempts—42 (October 17, 1999, vs. New England); completions—24 (October 17, 1999, vs. New England); yards—240 (October 17, 1999, vs. New England); and touchdown passes—2 (November 21, 1999, vs. New England).
MISCELLANEOUS: Regular-season record as starting NFL quarterback: 5-1 (.833).

					PASSING						RUSHING				TOTALS		
Year Team	G	GS	Att.	Cmp.	Pct.	Yds.	TD	Int.	Avg.	Rat.	Att.	Yds.	Avg.	TD	TD	2pt.	Pts.
1997—Miami NFL							Did not play.										
1998—Frankfurt NFLE	10	10	290	159	54.8	1857	12	7	6.40	78.2	28	65	2.3	1	1	0	6
—Miami NFL	2	0	9	6	66.7	85	0	1	9.44	57.4	0	0	0.0	0	0	0	0
1999—Miami NFL	16	5	216	125	57.9	1288	8	4	5.96	79.8	28	124	4.4	0	0	0	0
2000—Miami NFL	16	1	63	39	61.9	318	1	3	5.05	60.2	0	0	0.0	0	0	0	0
NFL Europe totals (1 year)	10	10	290	159	54.8	1857	12	7	6.40	78.2	28	65	2.3	1	1	0	6
NFL totals (2 years)	34	6	288	170	59.0	1691	9	8	5.87	74.6	28	124	4.4	0	0	0	0
Pro totals (3 years)	44	16	578	329	56.9	3548	21	15	6.14	76.4	56	189	3.4	1	1	0	6

HUDSON, JOHN — C/G

PERSONAL: Born January 29, 1968, in Memphis, Tenn. ... 6-2/270. ... Full name: John Lewis Hudson.
HIGH SCHOOL: Henry County (Paris, Tenn.).
COLLEGE: Auburn.
TRANSACTIONS/CAREER NOTES: Selected by Philadelphia Eagles in 11th round (294th pick overall) of 1990 NFL draft. ... Signed by Eagles (July 31, 1990). ... On physically unable to perform list with knee laceration (August 2, 1990-entire season). ... Granted unconditional free agency (February 1-April 1, 1992). ... Re-signed by Eagles (July 23, 1992). ... On injured reserve with broken hand (September 28, 1992-remainder of season). ... Granted free agency (March 1, 1993). ... Re-signed by Eagles (May 12, 1993). ... Granted unconditional free agency (February 17, 1994). ... Re-signed by Eagles (April 7, 1994). ... Granted unconditional free agency (February 16, 1996). ... Signed by New York Jets (February 26, 1996). ... Granted unconditional free agency (February 11, 2000). ... Re-signed by Jets (August 28, 2000). ... Released by Jets (Augusy 29, 2000). ... Signed by Baltimore Ravens (October 25, 2000). ... Granted unconditional free agency (March 2, 2001).
PLAYING EXPERIENCE: Philadelphia NFL, 1991-1995; New York Jets NFL, 1996-1999; Baltimore NFL, 2000. ... Games/Games started: 1991 (16/0), 1992 (3/0), 1993 (16/0), 1994 (16/0), 1995 (16/0), 1996 (16/0), 1997 (16/0), 1998 (16/0), 1999 (16/0), 2000 (8/0). Total: 139/0.
CHAMPIONSHIP GAME EXPERIENCE: Played in AFC championship game (1998 and 2000 seasons). ... Member of Super Bowl championship team (2000 season).
PRO STATISTICS: 1991—Fumbled once. 1993—Fumbled once.

HUMPHREY, DEON — LB — CHARGERS

PERSONAL: Born May 7, 1976, in Clewiston, Fla. ... 6-3/240. ... Full name: Deon Morie Humphrey.
HIGH SCHOOL: Lake Worth (Fla.).
COLLEGE: Florida State.
TRANSACTIONS/CAREER NOTES: Signed as non-drafted free agent by Green Bay Packers (April 19, 1999). ... Released by Packers (September 5, 1999). ... Re-signed by Packers to practice squad (December 1, 1999). ... Released by Packers (December 12, 1999). ... Selected by Amsterdam Admirals in NFL Europe draft (February 12, 2000). ... Signed by San Diego Chargers (June 28, 2000). ... Claimed on waivers by Carolina Panthers (August 28, 2000). ... Released by Panthers (September 30, 2000). ... Signed by Chargers to practice squad (October 4, 2000). ... Activated (October 24, 2000).
PLAYING EXPERIENCE: Amsterdam Admirals NFLE, 2000; Carolina (3)-San Diego (7) NFL, 2000. ... Games/Games started: NFLE 2000 (games played unavailable), NFL 2000 (Car.-3/0; S.D.-7/0; Total: 10/0).
PRO STATISTICS: NFLE: 2000—Credited with 1/2 sack. NFL: 2000—Recovered one fumble.

HUNT, CLETIDUS — DT — PACKERS

PERSONAL: Born January 2, 1976, in Memphis, Tenn. ... 6-4/299. ... Full name: Cletidus Marquell Hunt.
HIGH SCHOOL: Whitehaven (Memphis, Tenn.).
JUNIOR COLLEGE: Northwest Mississippi Community College.
COLLEGE: Kentucky State.
TRANSACTIONS/CAREER NOTES: Selected by Green Bay Packers in third round (94th pick overall) of NFL draft. ... Signed by Packers (July 26, 1999).
PLAYING EXPERIENCE: Green Bay NFL, 1999 and 2000. ... Games/Games started: 1999 (11/1), 2000 (16/11). Total: 27/12.
PRO STATISTICS: 1999—Credited with 1/2 sack and recovered one fumble. 2000—Credited with five sacks.

HUNTLEY, RICHARD — RB — PANTHERS

PERSONAL: Born September 18, 1972, in Monroe, N.C. ... 5-11/225. ... Full name: Richard Earl Huntley.
HIGH SCHOOL: Monroe (N.C.).
COLLEGE: Winston-Salem (N.C.) State.

TRANSACTIONS/CAREER NOTES: Selected by Atlanta Falcons in fourth round (117th pick overall) of 1996 NFL draft. ... Signed by Falcons for 1996 season. ... Released by Falcons (August 18, 1997). ... Signed by Pittsburgh Steelers (February 13, 1998). ... Granted free agency (February 11, 2000). ... Re-signed by Steelers (March 14, 2000). ... Released by Steelers (June 4, 2001). ... Signed by Carolina Panthers (June 6, 2001).

SINGLE GAME HIGHS (regular season): Attempts—21 (October 18, 1998, vs. Baltimore); yards—85 (October 11, 1998, vs. Cincinnati); and rushing touchdowns—2 (December 16, 2000, vs. Washington).

			RUSHING				RECEIVING				KICKOFF RETURNS				TOTALS			
Year Team	G	GS	Att.	Yds.	Avg.	TD	No.	Yds.	Avg.	TD	No.	Yds.	Avg.	TD	TD	2pt.	Pts.	Fum.
1996—Atlanta NFL	1	0	2	8	4.0	0	1	14	14.0	0	0	0	0.0	0	0	0	0	0
1997—								Did not play.										
1998—Pittsburgh NFL	16	1	55	242	4.4	1	3	18	6.0	0	6	119	19.8	0	1	0	6	5
1999—Pittsburgh NFL	16	2	93	567	6.1	5	27	253	9.4	3	15	336	22.4	0	8	0	48	3
2000—Pittsburgh NFL	13	0	46	215	4.7	3	10	91	9.1	0	0	0	0.0	0	3	▲1	20	1
Pro totals (4 years)	46	3	196	1032	5.3	9	41	376	9.2	3	21	455	21.7	0	12	1	74	9

HUSAK, TODD QB REDSKINS

PERSONAL: Born July 6, 1978, in Long Beach, Calif. ... 6-3/216.
HIGH SCHOOL: St. John Bosco (Bellflower, Calif.).
COLLEGE: Stanford.
TRANSACTIONS/CAREER NOTES: Selected by Washington Redskins in sixth round (202nd pick overall) of 2000 NFL draft. ... Signed by Redskins (July 14, 2000).
PLAYING EXPERIENCE: Washington NFL, 2000. ... Games/Games started: 2000 (1/0).
PRO STATISTICS: 2000—Attempted two passes with two completions for minus two yards and rushed once for minus one yard.
SINGLE GAME HIGHS (regular season): Attempts—2 (December 24, 2000, vs. Arizona); completions—2 (December 24, 2000, vs. Arizona); yards— -2 (December 24, 2000, vs. Arizona); and touchdown passes—0.

HUSTED, MICHAEL K

PERSONAL: Born June 16, 1970, in El Paso, Texas. ... 6-0/195. ... Full name: Michael James Husted.
HIGH SCHOOL: Hampton (Va.).
COLLEGE: Virginia (degree in sociology, 1992).
TRANSACTIONS/CAREER NOTES: Signed as non-drafted free agent by Tampa Bay Buccaneers (May 3, 1993). ... Granted free agency (February 16, 1996). ... Tendered offer sheet by San Francisco 49ers (February 21, 1996). ... Offer matched by Buccaneers (February 28, 1996). ... Released by Buccaneers (February 11, 1999). ... Signed by Oakland Raiders (February 24, 1999). ... Released by Raiders (July 21, 2000). ... Signed by Chicago Bears (July 27, 2000). ... Released by Bears (August 7, 2000). ... Signed by Washington Redskins (September 18, 2000). ... Released by Redskins (October 10, 2000).
PRO STATISTICS: 1994—Punted twice for 53 yards. 1998—Rushed once for 20 yards.

		KICKING						
Year Team	G	XPM	XPA	FGM	FGA	Lg.	50+	Pts.
1993—Tampa Bay NFL	16	27	27	16	22	‡57	3-5	75
1994—Tampa Bay NFL	16	20	20	23	35	53	1-5	89
1995—Tampa Bay NFL	16	25	25	19	26	53	3-3	82
1996—Tampa Bay NFL	16	18	19	25	32	50	1-3	93
1997—Tampa Bay NFL	16	32	35	13	17	54	1-3	71
1998—Tampa Bay NFL	16	29	30	21	28	52	1-1	92
1999—Oakland NFL	13	30	30	20	31	49	0-3	90
2000—Washington NFL	4	8	9	4	8	28	0-0	20
Pro totals (8 years)	113	189	195	141	199	57	10-23	612

HUTSON, TONY G/OT

PERSONAL: Born March 13, 1974, in Houston ... 6-3/317.
HIGH SCHOOL: MacArthur (Houston).
JUNIOR COLLEGE: Kilgore (Texas) College.
COLLEGE: Northeastern Oklahoma State.
TRANSACTIONS/CAREER NOTES: Signed as non-drafted free agent by Dallas Cowboys (April 23, 1996). ... Released by Cowboys (August 25, 1996). ... Re-signed by Cowboys to practice squad (August 27, 1996). ... Activated (January 5, 1997). ... Released by Cowboys (August 24, 1997). ... Re-signed by Cowboys to practice squad (August 26, 1997). ... Activated (November 4, 1997). ... On injured reserve with knee injury (October 5, 1999-remainder of season). ... Granted free agency (February 11, 2000). ... Re-signed by Cowboys (March 14, 2000). ... Released by Cowboys (August 27, 2000). ... Signed by Washington Redskins (October 9, 2000). ... Granted unconditional free agency (March 2, 2001).
PLAYING EXPERIENCE: Dallas NFL, 1997-1999; Washington NFL, 2000. ... Games/Games started: 1997 (5/1), 1998 (9/1), 1999 (2/2), 2000 (3/0). Total: 19/4.

HYDER, GAYLON DT RAMS

PERSONAL: Born October 18, 1974, in Longview, Texas. ... 6-5/317.
HIGH SCHOOL: Longview (Texas).
COLLEGE: Texas Christian.
TRANSACTIONS/CAREER NOTES: Signed as non-drafted free agent by St. Louis Rams (July 30, 1999). ... On injured reserve with back injury (November 19, 1999-remainder of season). ... Released by Rams (August 27, 2000). ... Re-signed by Rams to practice squad (August 29, 2000). ... Activated (October 10, 2000). ... Assigned by Rams to Rhein Fire in 2001 NFL Europe enhancement allocation program (February 19, 2001).
PLAYING EXPERIENCE: St. Louis NFL, 1999 and 2000. ... Games/Games started: 1999 (4/0), 2000 (5/1). Total: 9/1.

H

IRVIN, KEN   CB   BILLS

PERSONAL: Born July 11, 1972, in Rome, Ga. ... 5-11/186. ... Full name: Kenneth Irvin.
HIGH SCHOOL: Pepperell (Lindale, Ga.).
COLLEGE: Memphis (degree in criminal justice, 1998).
TRANSACTIONS/CAREER NOTES: Selected by Buffalo Bills in fourth round (109th pick overall) of 1995 NFL draft. ... Signed by Bills (July 10, 1995). ... Granted free agency (February 13, 1998). ... Re-signed by Bills (April 17, 1998). ... Granted unconditional free agency (February 12, 1999). ... Re-signed by Bills (March 17, 1999). ... On injured reserve with foot injury (December 23, 1999-remainder of season).
PLAYING EXPERIENCE: Buffalo NFL, 1995-2000. ... Games/Games started: 1995 (16/3), 1996 (16/1), 1997 (16/0), 1998 (16/16), 1999 (14/14), 2000 (16/16). Total: 94/50.
PRO STATISTICS: 1995—Returned one kickoff for 12 yards. 1996—Credited with two sacks and recovered one fumble. 1997—Intercepted two passes for 28 yards. 1998—Intercepted one pass for 43 yards. 1999—Intercepted one pass for one yard. 2000—Intercepted two passes for one yard.

IRVIN, SEDRICK   RB   LIONS

PERSONAL: Born March 30, 1978, in Miami. ... 5-11/226. ... Cousin of Michael Irvin, wide receiver with Dallas Cowboys (1988-99).
HIGH SCHOOL: Miami Southridge, then Miami High.
COLLEGE: Michigan State.
TRANSACTIONS/CAREER NOTES: Selected after junior season by Detroit Lions in fourth round (103rd pick overall) of 1999 NFL draft. ... Signed by Lions (July 25, 1999).
PRO STATISTICS: 1999—Fumbled twice. 2000—Fumbled once.
SINGLE GAME HIGHS (regular season): Attempts—8 (November 21, 1999, vs. Green Bay); yards—62 (November 21, 1999, vs. Green Bay); and rushing touchdowns—1 (November 21, 1999, vs. Green Bay).

		RUSHING				RECEIVING				PUNT RETURNS				KICKOFF RETURNS				TOTALS		
Year Team	G	GS	Att.	Yds.	Avg.	TD	No.	Yds.	Avg.	TD	No.	Yds.	Avg.	TD	No.	Yds.	Avg.	TD	TD	2pt. Pts.
1999—Detroit NFL	14	0	36	133	3.7	4	25	233	9.3	0	2	15	7.5	0	3	21	7.0	0	4	0 24
2000—Detroit NFL	6	0	9	49	5.4	0	8	90	11.3	0	0	0	0.0	0	0	0	0.0	0	0	0 0
Pro totals (2 years)	20	0	45	182	4.0	4	33	323	9.8	0	2	15	7.5	0	3	21	7.0	0	4	0 24

IRWIN, HEATH   G   DOLPHINS

PERSONAL: Born June 27, 1973, in Boulder, Colo. ... 6-4/300. ... Nephew of Hale Irwin, professional golfer.
HIGH SCHOOL: Boulder (Colo.).
COLLEGE: Colorado.
TRANSACTIONS/CAREER NOTES: Selected by New England Patriots in fourth round (101st pick overall) of 1996 NFL draft. ... Signed by Patriots (July 17, 1996). ... Inactive for all 16 games (1996). ... Granted free agency (February 12, 1999). ... Re-signed by Patriots (June 24, 1999). ... Granted unconditional free agency (February 11, 2000). ... Signed by Miami Dolphins (February 25, 2000).
PLAYING EXPERIENCE: New England NFL, 1997-1999; Miami NFL, 2000. ... Games/Games started: 1997 (15/1), 1998 (13/3), 1999 (15/13), 2000 (13/0). Total: 56/17.
CHAMPIONSHIP GAME EXPERIENCE: Member of Patriots for AFC championship game (1996 season); inactive. ... Member of Patriots for Super Bowl XXXI (1996 season); inactive.

ISAIA, SALE   G

PERSONAL: Born June 13, 1972, in Honolulu ... 6-5/320. ... Full name: Sale Isaia Jr.. ... Cousin of Junior Seau, linebacker, San Diego Chargers. ... Name pronounced SAH-lay i-ZAY-uh.
HIGH SCHOOL: Oceanside (Calif.).
COLLEGE: UCLA.
TRANSACTIONS/CAREER NOTES: Signed as non-drafted free agent by Cleveland Browns (April 2, 1995). ... On injured reserve with ankle injury (August 27, 1995-entire season). ... Browns franchise moved to Baltimore and renamed Ravens for 1996 season (March 11, 1996). ... On injured reserve with knee injury (August 18, 1997-entire season). ... Granted free agency (February 13, 1998). ... Re-signed by Ravens (April 13, 1998). ... On injured reserve with heel injury (August 25, 1998-entire season). ... Granted unconditional free agency (February 12, 1999). ... Signed by Indianapolis Colts (March 30, 1999). ... Released by Colts (July 20, 1999). ... Signed by Oakland Raiders (February 4, 2000). ... Released by Raiders (August 27, 2000). ... Signed by New England Patriots (August 30, 2000). ... Released by Patriots (May 15, 2001).
PLAYING EXPERIENCE: Baltimore NFL, 1996; New England NFL, 2000. ... Games/Games started: 1996 (9/0), 2000 (16/14). Total: 25/14.
PRO STATISTICS: 1996—Returned one kickoff for two yards, fumbled once and recovered one fumble. 2000—Recovered one fumble.

ISMAIL, QADRY   WR   RAVENS

PERSONAL: Born November 8, 1970, in Newark, N.J. ... 6-0/200. ... Full name: Qadry Rahmadan Ismail. ... Brother of Rocket Ismail, wide receiver, Dallas Cowboys. ... Name pronounced KAH-dree ISS-my-el.
HIGH SCHOOL: Elmer L. Meyers (Wilkes-Barre, Pa.).
COLLEGE: Syracuse (degree in communications).
TRANSACTIONS/CAREER NOTES: Selected by Minnesota Vikings in second round (52nd pick overall) of 1993 NFL draft. ... Signed by Vikings (July 20, 1993). ... Granted unconditional free agency (February 14, 1997). ... Signed by Green Bay Packers (June 2, 1997). ... Traded by Packers to Miami Dolphins for first-round pick in (DT Vonnie Holliday) in 1998 draft (August 24, 1997). ... Granted unconditional free agency (February 13, 1998). ... Signed by New Orleans Saints (February 27, 1998). ... Released by Saints (February 10, 1999). ... Signed by Baltimore Ravens (April 27, 1999). ... Granted unconditional free agency (February 11, 2000). ... Re-signed by Ravens (April 28, 2000).
CHAMPIONSHIP GAME EXPERIENCE: Played in AFC championship game (2000 season). ... Member of Super Bowl championship team (2000 season).

HONORS: Named kick returner on THE SPORTING NEWS college All-America second team (1991).

PRO STATISTICS: 1993—Rushed three times for 14 yards. 1994—Recovered one fumble. 1995—Rushed once for seven yards. 1996—Recovered one fumble. 1999—Rushed once for four yards.

SINGLE GAME HIGHS (regular season): Receptions—9 (October 8, 2000, vs. Jacksonville); yards—258 (December 12, 1999, vs. Pittsburgh); and touchdown receptions—3 (December 12, 1999, vs. Pittsburgh).

STATISTICAL PLATEAUS: 100-yard receiving games: 1994 (2), 1995 (1), 1999 (3), 2000 (1). Total: 7.

Year Team	G	GS	RECEIVING				KICKOFF RETURNS				TOTALS			
			No.	Yds.	Avg.	TD	No.	Yds.	Avg.	TD	TD	2pt.	Pts.	Fum.
1993—Minnesota NFL	15	3	19	212	11.2	1	‡42	902	21.5	0	1	0	6	1
1994—Minnesota NFL	16	3	45	696	15.5	5	35	807	23.1	0	5	0	30	2
1995—Minnesota NFL	16	2	32	597	18.7	3	42	1037	24.7	0	3	0	18	3
1996—Minnesota NFL	16	2	22	351	16.0	3	28	527	18.8	0	3	0	18	2
1997—Miami NFL	3	0	0	0	0.0	0	8	166	20.8	0	0	0	0	0
1998—New Orleans NFL	10	1	0	0	0.0	0	28	590	21.1	0	0	0	0	2
1999—Baltimore NFL	16	16	68	1105	16.3	6	4	55	13.8	0	6	0	36	2
2000—Baltimore NFL	15	13	49	655	13.4	5	2	51	25.5	0	5	0	30	0
Pro totals (8 years)	107	40	235	3616	15.4	23	189	4135	21.9	0	23	0	138	12

ISMAIL, ROCKET WR COWBOYS

PERSONAL: Born November 18, 1969, in Elizabeth, N.J. ... 5-11/190. ... Full name: Raghib Ramadian Ismail. ... Brother of Qadry Ismail, wide receiver, Baltimore Ravens. ... Name pronounced rah-GIBB ISS-my-ell.

HIGH SCHOOL: Elmer L. Meyers (Wilkes-Barre, Pa.).

COLLEGE: Notre Dame (degree in sociology, 1994).

TRANSACTIONS/CAREER NOTES: Signed after junior season by Toronto Argonauts of CFL (April 21, 1991). ... Selected by Los Angeles Raiders in fourth round (100th pick overall) of 1991 NFL draft. ... Granted free agency from Argonauts (February 15, 1993). ... Signed by Raiders (August 30, 1993). ... Raiders franchise moved to Oakland (July 21, 1995). ... Granted free agency (February 16, 1996). ... Re-signed by Raiders (August 25, 1996). ... Traded by Raiders to Carolina Panthers for fifth-round pick (traded to Miami) in 1997 draft (August 25, 1996). ... Granted unconditional free agency (February 14, 1997). ... Re-signed by Panthers (February 26, 1997). ... Granted unconditional free agency (February 13, 1998). ... Re-signed by Panthers (June 2, 1998). ... Granted unconditional free agency (February 12, 1999). ... Signed by Dallas Cowboys (April 15, 1999). ... On injured reserve with knee injury (November 8, 2000-remainder of season).

CHAMPIONSHIP GAME EXPERIENCE: Played in Grey Cup, CFL championship game (1991). ... Played in NFC championship game (1996 season).

HONORS: Named kick returner on THE SPORTING NEWS college All-America first team (1989). ... Named College Football Player of the Year by THE SPORTING NEWS (1990). ... Named wide receiver on THE SPORTING NEWS college All-America first team (1990).

PRO STATISTICS: CFL: 1991—Returned two unsuccessful field-goals for 90 yards, attempted one pass without a completion, fumbled eight times and recovered two fumbles. 1992—Fumbled seven times and recovered two fumbles. NFL: 1993—Recovered one fumble. 1995—Fumbled four times and recovered one fumble. 1998—Fumbled twice and recovered one fumble. 1999—Fumbled once. 2000—Fumbled once.

SINGLE GAME HIGHS (regular season): Receptions—8 (December 5, 1999, vs. New England); yards—149 (September 12, 1999, vs. Washington); and touchdown receptions—2 (October 11, 1998, vs. Dallas).

STATISTICAL PLATEAUS: 100-yard receiving games: 1995 (1), 1996 (1), 1997 (1), 1998 (3), 1999 (3). Total: 9.

Year Team	G	GS	RUSHING				RECEIVING				PUNT RETURNS				KICKOFF RETURNS				TOTALS		
			Att.	Yds.	Avg.	TD	No.	Yds.	Avg.	TD	No.	Yds.	Avg.	TD	No.	Yds.	Avg.	TD	TD	2pt.	Pts.
1991—Toronto CFL	17	17	36	271	7.5	3	64	1300	20.3	9	48	602	12.5	1	31	786	25.4	0	13	0	78
1992—Toronto CFL	16	16	34	154	4.5	3	36	651	18.1	4	59	614	10.4	1	43 *1139	26.5	0	8	0	48
1993—LA Raiders NFL	13	0	4	-5	-1.3	0	26	353	13.6	1	0	0	0.0	0	25	605	§24.2	0	1	0	6
1994—LA Raiders NFL	16	0	4	31	7.8	0	34	513	15.1	5	0	0	0.0	0	43	923	21.5	0	5	0	30
1995—Oakland NFL	16	16	6	29	4.8	0	28	491	17.5	3	0	0	0.0	0	36	706	19.6	0	3	0	18
1996—Carolina NFL	13	5	8	80	10.0	1	12	214	17.8	0	0	0	0.0	0	5	100	20.0	0	1	0	6
1997—Carolina NFL	13	2	4	32	8.0	0	36	419	11.6	2	0	0	0.0	0	0	0	0.0	0	2	0	12
1998—Carolina NFL	16	15	3	42	14.0	0	69	1024	14.8	8	0	0	0.0	0	0	0	0.0	0	8	0	48
1999—Dallas NFL	16	14	13	110	8.5	1	80	1097	13.7	6	0	0	0.0	0	0	0	0.0	0	7	0	42
2000—Dallas NFL	9	9	8	73	9.1	0	25	350	14.0	1	0	0	0.0	0	0	0	0.0	0	1	1	8
CFL totals (2 years)	33	33	70	425	6.1	6	100	1951	19.5	13	107	1216	11.4	2	74	1925	26.0	0	21	0	126
NFL totals (8 years)	112	61	50	392	7.8	2	310	4461	14.4	26	0	0	0.0	0	109	2334	21.4	0	28	1	170
Pro totals (10 years)	145	94	120	817	6.8	8	410	6412	15.6	39	107	1216	11.4	2	183	4259	23.3	0	49	1	296

ISRAEL, STEVE CB SAINTS

PERSONAL: Born March 16, 1969, in Lawnside, N.J. ... 5-11/194. ... Full name: Steven Douglas Israel.

HIGH SCHOOL: Haddon Heights (N.J.).

COLLEGE: Pittsburgh (degree in economics).

TRANSACTIONS/CAREER NOTES: Selected by Los Angeles Rams in second round (30th pick overall) of 1992 NFL draft. ... Signed by Rams (August 23, 1992). ... Granted roster exemption (August 25-September 4, 1992). ... Claimed on waivers by Green Bay Packers (August 7, 1995). ... Released by Packers (August 25, 1995). ... Signed by San Francisco 49ers (October 3, 1995). ... Granted unconditional free agency (February 16, 1996). ... Re-signed by 49ers (March 1, 1996). ... Granted unconditional free agency (February 14, 1997). ... Signed by New England Patriots (March 24, 1997). ... Granted unconditional free agency (February 11, 2000). ... Signed by New Orleans Saints (April 21, 2000). ... On injured reserve with broken leg (August 7, 2000-entire season).

PLAYING EXPERIENCE: Los Angeles Rams NFL, 1992-1994; San Francisco, NFL, 1995 and 1996; New England NFL, 1997-1999. ... Games/Games started: 1992 (16/1), 1993 (16/12), 1994 (10/2), 1995 (8/0), 1996 (14/2), 1997 (5/0), 1998 (11/7), 1999 (13/13). Total: 93/37.

PRO STATISTICS: 1992—Returned one kickoff for minus three yards and recovered one fumble. 1993—Returned five kickoffs for 92 yards. 1996—Intercepted one pass for three yards and recovered one fumble. 1997—Credited with one sack. 1998—Intercepted three passes for 13 yards and credited with two sacks. 1999—Intercepted one pass for no yards, credited with one sack and recovered two fumbles.

ISSA, JABARI   DT/DE   CARDINALS

PERSONAL: Born April 18, 1978, in Foster City, Calif. ... 6-5/302.
HIGH SCHOOL: San Mateo (Calif.).
COLLEGE: Washington.
TRANSACTIONS/CAREER NOTES: Selected by Arizona Cardinals in sixth round (176th pick overall) of 2000 NFL draft. ... Signed by Cardinals (June 13, 2000).

Year Team	G	GS	SACKS
2000—Arizona NFL	10	0	1.0

IZZO, LARRY   LB   PATRIOTS

PERSONAL: Born September 26, 1974, in Fort Belvoir, Va. ... 5-10/228. ... Full name: Lawrence Alexander Izzo.
HIGH SCHOOL: McCullough (Houston).
COLLEGE: Rice.
TRANSACTIONS/CAREER NOTES: Signed as non-drafted free agent by Miami Dolphins (April 25, 1996). ... On injured reserve with foot injury (August 18, 1997-entire season). ... Granted free agency (February 12, 1999). ... Re-signed by Dolphins (March 31, 1999). ... Granted unconditional free agency (March 2, 2001). ... Signed by New England Patriots (March 6, 2001).
PLAYING EXPERIENCE: Miami NFL, 1996, 1998-2000. ... Games/Games started: 1996 (16/0), 1998 (13/0), 1999 (16/0), 2000 (16/0). Total: 61/0.
HONORS: Played in Pro Bowl (2000 season).
PRO STATISTICS: 1996—Rushed once for 26 yards. 1999—Recovered one fumble. 2000—Rushed once for 39 yards and fumbled once.

JACKSON, AL   G   COWBOYS

PERSONAL: Born May 18, 1977, in Moss Point, Miss. ... 6-3/306. ... Full name: Alexander O'Neal Jackson.
HIGH SCHOOL: Moss Point (Miss.).
COLLEGE: Louisiana State.
TRANSACTIONS/CAREER NOTES: Signed as non-drafted free agent by Dallas Cowboys (April 17, 2000).
PLAYING EXPERIENCE: Dallas NFL, 2000. ... Games/Games started: 2000 (3/0).

JACKSON, BRAD   LB   RAVENS

PERSONAL: Born January 11, 1975, in Canton, Ohio. ... 6-0/230. ... Full name: Bradley Michael Jackson.
HIGH SCHOOL: Firestone (Akron, Ohio).
COLLEGE: Cincinnati.
TRANSACTIONS/CAREER NOTES: Selected by Miami Dolphins in third round (79th pick overall) of 1998 NFL draft. ... Signed by Dolphins (July 21, 1998). ... Released by Dolphins (August 25, 1998). ... Signed by Tennessee Oilers to practice squad (September 1, 1998). ... Released by Oilers (September 29, 1998). ... Signed by Baltimore Ravens to practice squad (September 30, 1998). ... Activated (December 17, 1998); did not play.
PLAYING EXPERIENCE: Baltimore NFL, 1999 and 2000. ... Games/Games started: 1999 (13/0), 2000 (10/0). Total: 23/0.
CHAMPIONSHIP GAME EXPERIENCE: Played in AFC championship game (2000 season). ... Member of Super Bowl championship team (2000 season).
HONORS: Named outside linebacker on THE SPORTING NEWS college All-America third team (1997).
PRO STATISTICS: 1999—Recovered one fumble. 2000—Recovered two fumbles.

JACKSON, CHRIS   WR   TITANS

PERSONAL: Born February 26, 1975, in Bristol, Pa. ... 6-2/204.
HIGH SCHOOL: Mater Dei (Santa Ana, Calif.).
COLLEGE: Washington State.
TRANSACTIONS/CAREER NOTES: Signed as non-drafted free agent by Tennessee Titans to practice squad (October 8, 2000). ... Activated (November 4, 2000). ... On injured reserve with back injury (December 1, 2000-remainder of season).
PLAYING EXPERIENCE: Tennessee NFL, 2000. ... Games/Games started: 2000 (1/0).

JACKSON, CURTIS   WR   PATRIOTS

PERSONAL: Born September 22, 1973, in Fort Worth, Texas. ... 5-10/190. ... Full name: Curtis Ray Jackson.
HIGH SCHOOL: Plano (Texas).
COLLEGE: Texas.
TRANSACTIONS/CAREER NOTES: Signed as non-drafted free agent by St. Louis Rams (April 18, 2000). ... Released by Rams (August 27, 2000). ... Re-signed by Rams to practice squad (August 29, 2000). ... Signed by New England Patriots off Rams practice squad (November 15, 2000).
PLAYING EXPERIENCE: New England NFL, 2000. ... Games/Games started: 2000 (5/2).
PRO STATISTICS: 2000—Caught five passes for 44 yards, returned 13 kickoffs for 323 yards and fumbled once.
SINGLE GAME HIGHS (regular season): Receptions—3 (December 10, 2000, vs. Chicago); yards—27 (December 10, 2000, vs. Chicago); and touchdown receptions—0.

JACKSON, DARRELL   WR   SEAHAWKS

PERSONAL: Born December 6, 1978, in Dayton, Ohio. ... 6-0/197. ... Full name: Darrell Lamont Jackson.
HIGH SCHOOL: Tampa Catholic.
COLLEGE: Florida.

TRANSACTIONS/CAREER NOTES: Selected after junior season by Seattle Seahawks in third round (80th pick overall) of 2000 NFL draft. ... Signed by Seahawks (July 19, 2000).
PRO STATISTICS: 2000—Rushed once for minus one yard, fumbled twice and recovered one fumble for 18 yards.
SINGLE GAME HIGHS (regular season): Receptions—6 (October 15, 2000, vs. Indianapolis); yards—98 (September 3, 2000, vs. Atlanta); and touchdown receptions—1 (December 16, 2000, vs. Oakland).

Year Team	G	GS	RECEIVING No.	Yds.	Avg.	TD
2000—Seattle NFL	16	9	53	713	13.5	6

JACKSON, DEXTER   S   BUCCANEERS

PERSONAL: Born July 28, 1977, in Quincy, Fla. ... 6-0/196. ... Full name: Dexter Lamar Jackson.
HIGH SCHOOL: James A. Shanks (Quincy, Fla.).
COLLEGE: Florida State.
TRANSACTIONS/CAREER NOTES: Selected by Tampa Bay Buccaneers in fourth round (113th pick overall) of 1999 NFL draft. ... Signed by Buccaneers (July 29, 1999).
PLAYING EXPERIENCE: Tampa Bay NFL, 1999 and 2000. ... Games/Games started: 1999 (12/0), 2000 (13/0). Total: 25/0.
CHAMPIONSHIP GAME EXPERIENCE: Played in NFC championship game (1999 season).
PRO STATISTICS: 2000—Recovered one fumble.

JACKSON, GRADY   DT   RAIDERS

PERSONAL: Born January 21, 1973, in Greensboro, Ala. ... 6-2/325.
HIGH SCHOOL: Greensboro (Ala.) East.
JUNIOR COLLEGE: Hinds Community College (Miss.).
COLLEGE: Knoxville (Tenn.) College.
TRANSACTIONS/CAREER NOTES: Selected by Oakland Raiders in sixth round (193rd pick overall) of 1997 NFL draft. ... Signed by Raiders (July 18, 1997).
CHAMPIONSHIP GAME EXPERIENCE: Played in AFC championship game (2000 season).
PRO STATISTICS: 1998—Recovered one fumble for two yards. 1999—Recovered one fumble. 2000—Recovered one fumble.

Year Team	G	GS	SACKS
1997—Oakland NFL	5	0	0.0
1998—Oakland NFL	15	1	3.0
1999—Oakland NFL	15	0	4.0
2000—Oakland NFL	16	15	8.0
Pro totals (4 years)	51	16	15.0

JACKSON, GREG   S

PERSONAL: Born August 20, 1966, in Hialeah, Fla. ... 6-1/217. ... Full name: Greg Allen Jackson.
HIGH SCHOOL: American (Hialeah, Fla.).
COLLEGE: Louisiana State.
TRANSACTIONS/CAREER NOTES: Selected by New York Giants in third round (78th pick overall) of 1989 NFL draft. ... Signed by Giants (July 24, 1989). ... Granted free agency (February 1, 1992). ... Re-signed by Giants (August 3, 1992). ... Granted unconditional free agency (February 17, 1994). ... Signed by Philadelphia Eagles (June 30, 1994). ... Granted unconditional free agency (February 16, 1996). ... Signed by New Orleans Saints (June 18, 1996). ... Granted unconditional free agency (February 14, 1997). ... Signed by San Diego Chargers (June 13, 1997). ... On injured reserve with leg injury (December 1, 1997-remainder of season). ... Granted unconditional free agency (February 13, 1998). ... Re-signed by Chargers (May 4, 1998). ... Released by Chargers (August 26, 1998). ... Re-signed by Chargers (August 30, 1998). ... Granted unconditional free agency (February 12, 1999). ... Re-signed by Chargers (August 9, 1999). ... Granted unconditional free agency (February 11, 2000). ... Re-signed by Chargers (April 24, 2000). ... Released by Chargers (August 17, 2000). ... Re-signed by Chargers (September 26, 2000). ... On injured reserve with knee injury (October 18, 2000-remainder of season). ... Granted unconditional free agency (March 2, 2001).
CHAMPIONSHIP GAME EXPERIENCE: Played in NFC championship game (1990 season). ... Member of Super Bowl championship team (1990 season).
PRO STATISTICS: 1989—Recovered one fumble. 1990—Credited with four sacks. 1991—Fumbled once. 1992—Recovered one fumble. 1993—Recovered three fumbles for three yards. 1995—Recovered three fumbles for 45 yards and one touchdown. 1996—Fumbled once. 1997—Returned one punt for no yards and recovered one fumble for 41 yards and a touchdown. 1998—Recovered one fumble. 1999—Recovered one fumble.

Year Team	G	GS	INTERCEPTIONS No.	Yds.	Avg.	TD
1989—New York Giants NFL	16	1	0	0	0.0	0
1990—New York Giants NFL	14	14	5	8	1.6	0
1991—New York Giants NFL	13	12	1	3	3.0	0
1992—New York Giants NFL	16	16	4	71	17.8	0
1993—New York Giants NFL	16	16	4	32	8.0	0
1994—Philadelphia NFL	16	16	6	86	14.3	1
1995—Philadelphia NFL	16	16	1	18	18.0	0
1996—New Orleans NFL	16	15	3	24	8.0	0
1997—San Diego NFL	13	0	2	37	18.5	1
1998—San Diego NFL	16	13	6	50	8.3	0
1999—San Diego NFL	14	9	0	0	0.0	0
2000—San Diego NFL	2	1	0	0	0.0	0
Pro totals (12 years)	168	129	32	329	10.3	2

JACKSON, JARIOUS   QB   BRONCOS

PERSONAL: Born May 3, 1977, in Tupelo, Miss. ... 6-0/228. ... Full name: Jarious K. Jackson.
HIGH SCHOOL: Tupelo (Miss.).
COLLEGE: Notre Dame.
TRANSACTIONS/CAREER NOTES: Selected by Denver Broncos in seventh round (214th pick overall) of 2000 NFL draft. ... Signed by Broncos (July 20, 2000). ... Assigned by Broncos to Bracelona Dragons in 2001 NFL Europe enhancement allocation program (February 19, 2001).
PLAYING EXPERIENCE: Denver NFL, 2000. ... Games/Games started: 2000 (2/0).
PRO STATISTICS: 2000—Attempted one pass without a completion and rushed once for minus one yard.
SINGLE GAME HIGHS (regular season): Attempts—1 (December 17, 2000, vs. Kansas City); completions—0; yards—0; and touchdown passes—0.

JACKSON, JOHN   OT   BENGALS

PERSONAL: Born January 4, 1965, in Camp Kwe, Okinawa, Japan. ... 6-6/297.
HIGH SCHOOL: Woodward (Cincinnati).
COLLEGE: Eastern Kentucky (degree in police administration, 1991).
TRANSACTIONS/CAREER NOTES: Selected by Pittsburgh Steelers in 10th round (252nd pick overall) of 1988 NFL draft. ... Signed by Steelers (May 17, 1988). ... Granted unconditional free agency (February 13, 1998). ... Signed by San Diego Chargers (February 18, 1998). ... Released by Chargers (June 9, 2000). ... Signed by Cincinnati Bengals (July 23, 2000).
PLAYING EXPERIENCE: Pittsburgh NFL, 1988-1997; San Diego NFL, 1998 and 1999; Cincinnati NFL, 2000. ... Games/Games started: 1988 (16/0), 1989 (14/12), 1990 (16/16), 1991 (16/16), 1992 (16/13), 1993 (16/16), 1994 (16/16), 1995 (11/9), 1996 (16/16), 1997 (16/16), 1998 (16/16), 1999 (15/15), 2000 (8/5). Total: 192/166.
CHAMPIONSHIP GAME EXPERIENCE: Played in AFC championship game (1994, 1995 and 1997 seasons). ... Played in Super Bowl XXX (1995 season).
PRO STATISTICS: 1988—Returned one kickoff for 10 yards. 1991—Recovered one fumble. 1993—Recovered one fumble. 1994—Recovered two fumbles. 1996—Recovered one fumble.

JACKSON, LENZIE   WR   BROWNS

PERSONAL: Born June 17, 1977, in Santa Clara, Calif. ... 6-0/184. ... Full name: Lenzie Maurice Jackson.
HIGH SCHOOL: Milpitas (Calif.).
COLLEGE: Arizona State (degree in justice studies).
TRANSACTIONS/CAREER NOTES: Signed as non-drafted free agent by Jacksonville Jaguars (April 22, 1999). ... Released by Jaguars (September 5, 1999). ... Re-signed by Jaguars to practice squad (September 6, 1999). ... Activated (November 10, 1999). ... Released by Jaguars (August 22, 2000). ... Signed by Oakland Raiders to practice squad (August 30, 2000). ... Signed by Cleveland Browns off Raiders practice squad (September 13, 2000). ... On physically unable to perform list with toe injury (November 1, 2000-remainder of season).
PLAYING EXPERIENCE: Jacksonville NFL, 1999; Cleveland NFL, 2000. ... Games/Games started: 1999 (4/0), 2000 (5/0). Total: 9/0.
CHAMPIONSHIP GAME EXPERIENCE: Member of Jaguars for AFC championship game (1999 season); inactive.
PRO STATISTICS: 1999—Returned three kickoffs for 58 yards. 2000—Caught one pass for five yards and returned nine kickoffs for 168 yards.
SINGLE GAME HIGHS (regular season): Receptions—1 (October 22, 2000, vs. Pittsburgh); yards—5 (October 22, 2000, vs. Pittsburgh); touchdown receptions—0.

JACKSON, RAYMOND   DB   BROWNS

PERSONAL: Born February 17, 1973, in East Chicago, Ind. ... 5-10/189. ... Full name: Raymond DeWayne Jackson.
HIGH SCHOOL: Montbello (Denver).
COLLEGE: Colorado State.
TRANSACTIONS/CAREER NOTES: Selected by Buffalo Bills in fifth round (156th pick overall) of 1996 NFL draft. ... Signed by Bills (June 25, 1996). ... Selected by Cleveland Browns from Bills in NFL expansion draft (February 9, 1999). ... Granted free agency (February 12, 1999). ... Re-signed by Browns (April 14, 1999). ... Granted unconditional free agency (February 11, 2000). ... Re-signed by Browns (February 24, 2000).
PRO STATISTICS: 1997—Returned one punt for no yards and fumbled once.

| | | | | INTERCEPTIONS | | |
Year Team	G	GS	No.	Yds.	Avg.	TD
1996—Buffalo NFL	12	0	1	0	0.0	0
1997—Buffalo NFL	9	0	0	0	0.0	0
1998—Buffalo NFL	14	0	2	27	13.5	0
1999—Cleveland NFL	14	0	0	0	0.0	0
2000—Cleveland NFL	9	1	0	0	0.0	0
Pro totals (5 years)	58	1	3	27	9.0	0

JACKSON, SHELDON   TE   BILLS

PERSONAL: Born July 24, 1976, in Diamond Bar, Calif. ... 6-3/250. ... Full name: Sheldon B. Jackson Jr.
HIGH SCHOOL: Damien (La Verne, Calif.).
COLLEGE: Nebraska (degree in psychology).
TRANSACTIONS/CAREER NOTES: Selected by Buffalo Bills in seventh round (230th pick overall) of 1999 NFL draft. ... Signed by Bills (June 22, 1999).
PLAYING EXPERIENCE: Buffalo NFL, 1999 and 2000. ... Games/Games started: 1999 (13/4), 2000 (16/8). Total: 29/12.
PRO STATISTICS: 1999—Caught four passes for 34 yards. 2000—Caught five passes for 36 yards and one touchdown and recovered one fumble.
SINGLE GAME HIGHS (regular season): Receptions—2 (January 2, 2000, vs. Indianapolis); yards—22 (January 2, 2000, vs. Indianapolis); and touchdown receptions—0.

JACKSON, TERRY — RB — 49ERS

PERSONAL: Born January 10, 1976, in Gainesville, Fla. ... 6-0/232. ... Full name: Terrance Bernard Jackson. ... Brother of Willie Jackson Jr., wide receiver, New Orleans Saints.
HIGH SCHOOL: P.K. Yonge (Gainesville, Fla.).
COLLEGE: Florida.
TRANSACTIONS/CAREER NOTES: Selected by San Francisco 49ers in fifth round (157th pick overall) of 1999 NFL draft. ... Signed by 49ers (July 26, 1999).
PRO STATISTICS: 2000—Recovered one fumble.
SINGLE GAME HIGHS (regular season): Attempts—5 (January 3, 2000, vs. Atlanta); yards—35 (January 3, 2000, vs. Atlanta); and rushing touchdowns—1 (September 10, 2000, vs. Carolina).

			RUSHING				RECEIVING				TOTALS			
Year Team	G	GS	Att.	Yds.	Avg.	TD	No.	Yds.	Avg.	TD	TD	2pt.	Pts.	Fum.
1999—San Francisco NFL	16	0	15	75	5.0	0	3	6	2.0	0	0	0	0	1
2000—San Francisco NFL	15	1	5	6	1.2	1	5	48	9.6	1	2	1	14	0
Pro totals (2 years)	31	1	20	81	4.1	1	8	54	6.8	1	2	1	14	1

JACKSON, TYOKA — DL — RAMS

PERSONAL: Born November 22, 1971, in Washington, D.C. ... 6-2/280. ... Name pronounced tie-OH-kah.
HIGH SCHOOL: Bishop McNamara (Forestville, Md.).
COLLEGE: Penn State.
TRANSACTIONS/CAREER NOTES: Signed as non-drafted free agent by Atlanta Falcons (May 2, 1994). ... Released by Falcons (August 29, 1994). ... Re-signed by Falcons to practice squad (August 30, 1994). ... Signed by Miami Dolphins off Falcons practice squad (November 16, 1994). ... Released by Dolphins (August 27, 1995). ... Signed by Tampa Bay Buccaneers (December 27, 1995). ... Granted free agency (February 13, 1998). ... Re-signed by Buccaneers (June 22, 1998). ... Granted unconditional free agency (March 2, 2001). ... Signed by St. Louis Rams (May 1, 2001).
CHAMPIONSHIP GAME EXPERIENCE: Member of Buccaneers for NFC championship game (1999 season); inactive.
PRO STATISTICS: 1994—Recovered one fumble.

Year Team	G	GS	SACKS
1994—Miami NFL	1	0	0.0
1995—	Did not play.		
1996—Tampa Bay NFL	13	2	0.0
1997—Tampa Bay NFL	12	0	2.5
1998—Tampa Bay NFL	16	12	3.0
1999—Tampa Bay NFL	6	0	1.0
2000—Tampa Bay NFL	16	1	2.0
Pro totals (6 years)	64	15	8.5

JACKSON, WAVERLY — G — COLTS

PERSONAL: Born December 19, 1972, in South Hill, Va. ... 6-2/315.
HIGH SCHOOL: Park View (Sterling, Va.).
COLLEGE: Virginia Tech.
TRANSACTIONS/CAREER NOTES: Signed as non-drafted free agent by Carolina Panthers (April 19, 1997). ... Released by Panthers (August 25, 1997). ... Re-signed by Panthers to practice squad (August 26, 1997). ... Granted free agency after 1997 season. ... Signed by Indianapolis Colts (January 12, 1998). ... Granted free agency (March 2, 2001). ... Re-signed by Colts (March 7, 2001).
PLAYING EXPERIENCE: Indianapolis NFL, 1998-2000. ... Games/Games started: 1998 (7/2), 1999 (16/16), 2000 (16/0). Total: 39/18.

JACKSON, WILLIE — WR — SAINTS

PERSONAL: Born August 16, 1971, in Gainesville, Fla. ... 6-1/212. ... Full name: Willie Bernard Jackson Jr. ... Brother of Terry Jackson, running back, San Francisco 49ers.
HIGH SCHOOL: P.K. Yonge (Gainesville, Fla.).
COLLEGE: Florida (degree in telecommunications, 1993).
TRANSACTIONS/CAREER NOTES: Selected by Dallas Cowboys in fourth round (109th pick overall) of 1994 NFL draft. ... Signed by Cowboys (July 16, 1994). ... Inactive for 16 games (1994). ... Selected by Jacksonville Jaguars from Cowboys in NFL expansion draft (February 15, 1995). ... Granted free agency (February 14, 1997). ... Re-signed by Jaguars (March 26, 1997). ... Released by Jaguars (August 30, 1998). ... Signed by Cincinnati Bengals (September 10, 1998). ... Granted unconditional free agency (February 11, 2000). ... Signed by New Orleans Saints (April 28, 2000). ... Granted unconditional free agency (March 2, 2001). ... Re-signed by Saints (April 24, 2001).
CHAMPIONSHIP GAME EXPERIENCE: Member of Cowboys for NFC championship game (1994 season); inactive. ... Played in AFC championship game (1996 season).
PRO STATISTICS: 1995—Returned one punt for minus two yards and recovered one fumble. 1996—Rushed once for two yards. 1997—Rushed three times for 14 yards. 1999—Returned two punts for six yards and recovered one fumble.
SINGLE GAME HIGHS (regular season): Receptions—8 (November 17, 1996, vs. Pittsburgh); yards—113 (December 10, 1995, vs. Indianapolis); and touchdown receptions—2 (November 19, 2000, vs. Oakland).
STATISTICAL PLATEAUS: 100-yard receiving games: 1995 (1), 1996 (1). Total: 2.

			RECEIVING				KICKOFF RETURNS				TOTALS			
Year Team	G	GS	No.	Yds.	Avg.	TD	No.	Yds.	Avg.	TD	TD	2pt.	Pts.	Fum.
1994—Dallas NFL	Did not play.													
1995—Jacksonville NFL	14	10	53	589	11.1	5	19	404	21.3	0	5	1	32	2
1996—Jacksonville NFL	16	2	33	486	14.7	3	7	149	21.3	0	3	1	20	0
1997—Jacksonville NFL	16	1	17	206	12.1	2	32	653	20.4	0	2	1	14	1
1998—Cincinnati NFL	8	0	7	165	23.6	0	0	0	0.0	0	0	0	0	0
1999—Cincinnati NFL	16	2	31	369	11.9	2	6	179	29.8	0	2	†1	14	1
2000—New Orleans NFL	15	7	37	523	14.1	6	0	0	0.0	0	6	0	36	2
Pro totals (6 years)	85	22	178	2338	13.1	18	64	1385	21.6	0	18	4	116	6

JACOX, KENDYL　　C　　CHARGERS

PERSONAL: Born June 10, 1975, in Dallas. ... 6-2/330. ... Full name: Kendyl LaMarc Jacox. ... Name pronounced JAY-cox.
HIGH SCHOOL: Carter (Dallas).
COLLEGE: Kansas State.
TRANSACTIONS/CAREER NOTES: Signed as non-drafted free agent by San Diego Chargers (April 20, 1998). ... On injured reserve with knee injury (December 4, 1999-remainder of season). ... Granted free agency (March 2, 2001). ... Re-signed by Chargers (April 10, 2001).
PLAYING EXPERIENCE: San Diego NFL, 1998-2000. ... Games/Games started: 1998 (16/6), 1999 (10/5), 2000 (16/3). Total: 42/14.
PRO STATISTICS: 1998—Returned one kickoff for no yards. 2000—Returned one kickoff for eight yards.

JACQUET, NATE　　WR　　VIKINGS

PERSONAL: Born September 2, 1975, in Duarte, Calif. ... 6-0/185. ... Full name: Nathaniel Martin Jacquet.
HIGH SCHOOL: Duarte (Calif.).
JUNIOR COLLEGE: Mount San Antonio College (Calif.).
COLLEGE: San Diego State.
TRANSACTIONS/CAREER NOTES: Selected by Indianapolis Colts in fifth round (150th pick overall) of 1997 NFL draft. ... Signed by Colts (June 26, 1997). ... Released by Colts (August 24, 1997). ... Re-signed by Colts to practice squad (August 25, 1997). ... Activated (November 4, 1997). ... Claimed on waivers by Miami Dolphins (August 26, 1998). ... Released by Dolphins (August 30, 1998). ... Re-signed by Dolphins to practice squad (August 31, 1998). ... Activated (September 9, 1998). ... Released by Dolphins (September 5, 1999). ... Re-signed by Dolphins (October 8, 1999). ... Granted free agency (February 11, 2000). ... Re-signed by Dolphins (April 28, 2000). ... Traded by Dolphins to San Diego Chargers for sixth-round pick (OT Brandon Winey) in 2001 (August 22, 2000). ... Released by Chargers (December 12, 2000). ... Signed by Minnesota Vikings (December 13, 2000). ... Granted unconditional free agency (March 2, 2001). ... Re-signed by Vikings (April 1, 2001).
PRO STATISTICS: 1997—Recovered one fumble. 1999—Rushed once for four yards. 2000—Recovered two fumbles.
SINGLE GAME HIGHS (regular season): Receptions—5 (December 13, 1998, vs. New York Jets); yards—68 (December 13, 1998, vs. New York Jets); and touchdown receptions—0.

			RECEIVING			PUNT RETURNS				KICKOFF RETURNS				TOTALS			
Year Team	G	GS	No.	Yds.	Avg.	TD	No.	Yds.	Avg.	TD	No.	Yds.	Avg.	TD	TD	2pt.	Pts. Fum.
1997—Indianapolis NFL	5	0	0	0	0.0	0	13	96	7.4	0	8	156	19.5	0	0	0	0 1
1998—Miami NFL	15	0	8	122	15.3	0	0	0	0.0	0	4	103	25.8	0	0	0	0 0
1999—Miami NFL	13	0	1	18	18.0	0	28	351	12.5	0	1	26	26.0	·0	0	0	0 0
2000—San Diego NFL	11	0	1	25	25.0	0	30	211	7.0	0	0	0	0.0	0	0	0	0 3
—Minnesota NFL	1	0	0	0	0.0	0	0	0	0.0	0	0	0	0.0	0	0	0	0 0
Pro totals (4 years)	45	0	10	165	16.5	0	71	658	9.3	0	13	285	21.9	0	0	0	0 5

JAMES, EDGERRIN　　RB　　COLTS

PERSONAL: Born August 1, 1978, in Immokalee, Fla. ... 6-0/214. ... Full name: Edgerrin Tyree James. ... Name pronounced EDGE-rin.
HIGH SCHOOL: Immokalee (Fla.).
COLLEGE: Miami (Fla.).
TRANSACTIONS/CAREER NOTES: Selected after junior season by Indianapolis Colts in first round (fourth pick overall) of 1999 NFL draft. ... Signed by Colts (August 12, 1999).
HONORS: Named NFL Rookie of the Year by THE SPORTING NEWS (1999). ... Named running back on THE SPORTING NEWS NFL All-Pro team (1999 and 2000). ... Played in Pro Bowl (1999 and 2000 seasons).
PRO STATISTICS: 1999—Recovered two fumbles.
SINGLE GAME HIGHS (regular season): Attempts—38 (October 15, 2000, vs. Seattle); yards—219 (October 15, 2000, vs. Seattle); and rushing touchdowns—3 (December 11, 2000, vs. Buffalo).
STATISTICAL PLATEAUS: 100-yard rushing games: 1999 (10), 2000 (9). Total: 19.

			RUSHING				RECEIVING				TOTALS			
Year Team	G	GS	Att.	Yds.	Avg.	TD	No.	Yds.	Avg.	TD	TD	2pt.	Pts.	Fum.
1999—Indianapolis NFL	16	16	*369	*1553	4.2	▲13	62	586	9.5	4	†17	0	102	8
2000—Indianapolis NFL	16	16	387	*1709	4.4	13	63	594	9.4	5	§18	▲1	110	5
Pro totals (2 years)	32	32	756	3262	4.3	26	125	1180	9.4	9	35	1	212	13

JAMES, JENO　　G　　PANTHERS

PERSONAL: Born January 12, 1977, in Montgomery, Ala. ... 6-3/292. ... Full name: Jenorris James.
HIGH SCHOOL: Sidney Lanier (Montgomery, Ala.).
COLLEGE: Auburn.
TRANSACTIONS/CAREER NOTES: Selected by Carolina Panthers in sixth round (182nd pick overall) of 2000 NFL draft. ... Signed by Panthers (June 19, 2000).
PLAYING EXPERIENCE: Carolina NFL, 2000. ... Games/Games started: 2000 (16/4).

JAMES, TORY　　CB　　RAIDERS

PERSONAL: Born May 18, 1973, in New Orleans. ... 6-2/185. ... Full name: Tory Steven James.
HIGH SCHOOL: Archbishop Shaw (Marrero, La.).
COLLEGE: Louisiana State.
TRANSACTIONS/CAREER NOTES: Selected by Denver Broncos in second round (44th pick overall) of 1996 NFL draft. ... Signed by Broncos (July 22, 1996). ... On injured reserve with knee injury (August 18, 1997-entire season). ... Granted unconditional free agency (February 11, 2000). ... Signed by Oakland Raiders (February 28, 2000).
CHAMPIONSHIP GAME EXPERIENCE: Played in AFC championship game (1998 and 2000 seasons). ... Member of Super Bowl championship team (1998 season).
PRO STATISTICS: 1996—Recovered one fumble for 15 yards. 1998—Recovered one fumble.

Year Team	G	GS	No.	INTERCEPTIONS Yds.	Avg.	TD
1996—Denver NFL	16	2	2	15	7.5	0
1997—Denver NFL				Did not play.		
1998—Denver NFL	16	0	0	0	0.0	0
1999—Denver NFL	16	4	5	59	11.8	0
2000—Oakland NFL	16	1	2	25	12.5	0
Pro totals (4 years)	64	7	9	99	11.0	0

JANIKOWSKI, SEBASTIAN   K   RAIDERS

PERSONAL: Born March 2, 1978, in Poland. ... 6-1/255.
HIGH SCHOOL: Seabreeze (Daytona, Fla.).
COLLEGE: Florida State.
TRANSACTIONS/CAREER NOTES: Selected after junior season by Oakland Raiders in first round (17th pick overall) of 2000 NFL draft. ... Signed by Raiders (July 20, 2000).
CHAMPIONSHIP GAME EXPERIENCE: Played in AFC championship game (2000 season).
HONORS: Named kicker on THE SPORTING NEWS college All-America first team (1998 and 1999). ... Lou Groza Award winner (1998 and 1999).

					KICKING			
Year Team	G	XPM	XPA	FGM	FGA	Lg.	50+	Pts.
2000—Oakland NFL	14	46	46	22	32	▲54	1-4	112

JANSEN, JON   OT   REDSKINS

PERSONAL: Born January 28, 1976, in Clawson, Mich. ... 6-6/302. ... Full name: Jonathan Ward Jansen.
HIGH SCHOOL: Clawson (Mich.).
COLLEGE: Michigan.
TRANSACTIONS/CAREER NOTES: Selected by Washington Redskins in second round (37th pick overall) of 1999 NFL draft. ... Signed by Redskins (July 9, 1999).
PLAYING EXPERIENCE: Washington NFL, 1999 and 2000. ... Games/Games started: 1999 (16/16), 2000 (16/16). Total: 32/32.

JASPER, ED   DT   FALCONS

PERSONAL: Born January 18, 1973, in Tyler, Texas. ... 6-2/293. ... Full name: Edward Vidal Jasper.
HIGH SCHOOL: Troup (Texas).
COLLEGE: Texas A&M.
TRANSACTIONS/CAREER NOTES: Selected by Philadelphia Eagles in sixth round (198th pick overall) of 1997 NFL draft. ... Signed by Eagles (July 16, 1997). ... Released by Eagles (August 30, 1998). ... Re-signed by Eagles (September 17, 1998). ... Released by Eagles (October 23, 1998). ... Re-signed by Eagles (December 9, 1998). ... Released by Eagles (February 12, 1999). ... Signed by Atlanta Falcons (March 5, 1999).
PLAYING EXPERIENCE: Philadelphia NFL, 1997 and 1998; Atlanta NFL, 1999 and 2000. ... Games/Games started: 1997 (9/1), 1998 (7/0), 1999 (13/0), 2000 (15/15). Total: 44/16.
PRO STATISTICS: 2000—Credited with 3$\frac{1}{2}$ sacks.

JEFFERS, PATRICK   WR   PANTHERS

PERSONAL: Born February 2, 1973, in Fort Campbell, Ky. ... 6-3/218. ... Full name: Patrick Christopher Jeffers.
HIGH SCHOOL: Fort Worth (Texas) Country Day.
COLLEGE: Virginia.
TRANSACTIONS/CAREER NOTES: Selected by Denver Broncos in fifth round (159th pick overall) of 1996 NFL draft. ... Signed by Broncos (July 17, 1996). ... Traded by Broncos to Dallas Cowboys for past considerations (August 30, 1998). ... Granted free agency (February 12, 1999). ... Tendered offer sheet by Carolina Panthers (April 12, 1999). ... Cowboys declined to match offer (April 15, 1999). ... On injured reserve with knee injury (August 13, 2000-entire season).
CHAMPIONSHIP GAME EXPERIENCE: Played in AFC championship game (1997 season). ... Member of Super Bowl championship team (1997 season).
PRO STATISTICS: 1996—Returned one kickoff for 18 yards. 1999—Rushed twice for 16 yards and recovered one fumble for three yards.
SINGLE GAME HIGHS (regular season): Receptions—8 (December 18, 1999, vs. San Francisco); yards—165 (January 2, 2000, vs. New Orleans); and touchdown receptions—2 (January 2, 2000, vs. New Orleans).
STATISTICAL PLATEAUS: 100-yard receiving games: 1999 (5).

				RECEIVING				TOTALS		
Year Team	G	GS	No.	Yds.	Avg.	TD	TD	2pt.	Pts.	Fum.
1996—Denver NFL	4	0	0	0	0.0	0	0	0	0	0
1997—Denver NFL	10	0	3	24	8.0	0	0	0	0	0
1998—Dallas NFL	8	1	18	330	18.3	2	2	0	12	0
1999—Carolina NFL	15	10	63	1082	17.2	12	12	0	72	0
2000—Carolina NFL					Did not play.					
Pro totals (4 years)	37	11	84	1436	17.1	14	14	0	84	0

JEFFERSON, GREG   DE/DT   EAGLES

PERSONAL: Born August 31, 1971, in Orlando. ... 6-3/280. ... Full name: Greg Benton Jefferson.
HIGH SCHOOL: Bartow (Fla.).
COLLEGE: Central Florida.

TRANSACTIONS/CAREER NOTES: Selected by Philadelphia Eagles in third round (72nd pick overall) of 1995 NFL draft. ... Signed by Eagles (June 29, 1995). ... On injured reserve with knee injury (September 21, 1995-remainder of season). ... Granted free agency (February 13, 1998). ... Re-signed by Eagles (June 3, 1998). ... On injured reserve with knee injury (August 23, 2000-entire season).

PRO STATISTICS: 1997—Recovered one fumble. 1999—Recovered two fumbles for four yards.

Year	Team	G	GS	SACKS
1995—Philadelphia NFL		3	0	0.0
1996—Philadelphia NFL		11	0	2.5
1997—Philadelphia NFL		12	11	3.0
1998—Philadelphia NFL		15	14	4.0
1999—Philadelphia NFL		16	16	4.0
2000—Philadelphia NFL		Did not play.		
Pro totals (5 years)		**57**	**41**	**13.5**

J

JEFFERSON, SHAWN   WR   FALCONS

PERSONAL: Born February 22, 1969, in Jacksonville. ... 5-11/185. ... Full name: Vanchi LaShawn Jefferson.

HIGH SCHOOL: Raines (Jacksonville).

COLLEGE: Central Florida.

TRANSACTIONS/CAREER NOTES: Selected by Houston Oilers in ninth round (240th pick overall) of 1991 NFL draft. ... Signed by Oilers (July 15, 1991). ... Traded by Oilers with first-round pick (DE Chris Mims) in 1992 draft to San Diego Chargers for DL Lee Williams (August 22, 1991). ... Granted free agency (March 1, 1993). ... Re-signed by Chargers (July 15, 1993). ... Granted free agency (February 17, 1994). ... Re-signed by Chargers (May 2, 1994). ... Released by Chargers (February 29, 1996). ... Signed by New England Patriots (March 14, 1996). ... Granted unconditional free agency (February 11, 2000). ... Signed by Atlanta Falcons (February 12, 2000).

CHAMPIONSHIP GAME EXPERIENCE: Played in AFC championship game (1994 and 1996 seasons). ... Played in Super Bowl XXIX (1994 season) and Super Bowl XXXI (1996 season).

PRO STATISTICS: 1998—Recovered one fumble. 1999—Recovered one fumble.

SINGLE GAME HIGHS (regular season): Receptions—7 (November 26, 2000, vs. Oakland); yards—148 (September 3, 2000, vs. San Francisco); and touchdown receptions—2 (October 31, 1999, vs. Arizona).

STATISTICAL PLATEAUS: 100-yard receiving games: 1995 (1), 1997 (1), 1998 (2), 1999 (1), 2000 (2). Total: 7.

Year	Team	G	GS	Att.	RUSHING Yds.	Avg.	TD	No.	RECEIVING Yds.	Avg.	TD	TD	TOTALS 2pt.	Pts.	Fum.
1991—San Diego NFL		16	3	1	27	27.0	0	12	125	10.4	1	1	0	6	0
1992—San Diego NFL		16	1	0	0	0.0	0	29	377	13.0	2	2	0	12	0
1993—San Diego NFL		16	4	5	53	10.6	0	30	391	13.0	2	2	0	12	0
1994—San Diego NFL		16	16	3	40	13.3	0	43	627	14.6	3	3	0	18	0
1995—San Diego NFL		16	15	2	1	0.5	0	48	621	12.9	2	2	0	12	0
1996—New England NFL		15	15	1	6	6.0	0	50	771	15.4	4	4	0	24	2
1997—New England NFL		16	14	0	0	0.0	0	54	841	15.6	2	2	0	12	2
1998—New England NFL		16	16	1	15	15.0	0	34	771	*22.7	2	2	0	12	0
1999—New England NFL		16	16	0	0	0.0	0	40	698	§17.5	6	6	0	36	0
2000—Atlanta NFL		16	14	1	1	1.0	0	60	822	13.7	2	2	0	12	1
Pro totals (10 years)		**159**	**114**	**14**	**143**	**10.2**	**0**	**400**	**6044**	**15.1**	**26**	**26**	**0**	**156**	**5**

JEFFRIES, GREG   CB

PERSONAL: Born October 16, 1971, in High Point, N.C. ... 5-9/195. ... Full name: Greg Lemont Jeffries.

HIGH SCHOOL: T.W. Andrews (High Point, N.C.).

COLLEGE: Virginia.

TRANSACTIONS/CAREER NOTES: Selected by Detroit Lions in sixth round (147th pick overall) of 1993 NFL draft. ... Signed by Lions (July 17, 1993). ... Granted unconditional free agency (February 14, 1997). ... Re-signed by Lions (February 19, 1997). ... Granted unconditional free agency (February 12, 1999). ... Signed by Miami Dolphins (February 19, 1999). ... On injured reserve with knee injury (November 28, 2000-remainder of season). ... Released by Dolphins (February 28, 2001).

PLAYING EXPERIENCE: Detroit NFL, 1993-1998; Miami NFL, 1999 and 2000. ... Games/Games started: 1993 (7/0), 1994 (16/1), 1995 (14/0), 1996 (16/4), 1997 (15/2), 1998 (15/3), 1999 (16/0), 2000 (11/0). Total: 110/10.

PRO STATISTICS: 1993—Recovered one fumble. 1995—Credited with 1/2 sack. 1996—Intercepted one pass for no yards. 1997—Intercepted one pass for no yards and credited with one sack. 1998—Recovered one fumble. 2000—Intercepted one pass for three yards.

JENKINS, BILLY   S   BRONCOS

PERSONAL: Born July 8, 1974, in Albuquerque, N.M. ... 5-10/205.

HIGH SCHOOL: Albuquerque (N.M.).

COLLEGE: Howard.

TRANSACTIONS/CAREER NOTES: Signed as non-drafted free agent by St. Louis Rams (April 29, 1997). ... Granted free agency (February 11, 2000). ... Re-signed by Rams (March 3, 2000). ... Traded by Rams to Denver Broncos for fifth-round pick (DL Brian Young) in 2000 draft and fifth-round pick (traded to Washington) in 2001 draft (March 7, 2000).

CHAMPIONSHIP GAME EXPERIENCE: Played in NFC championship game (1999 season). ... Member of Super Bowl championship team (1999 season).

PRO STATISTICS: 2000—Fumbled once and recovered one fumble.

Year	Team	G	GS	INTERCEPTIONS No.	Yds.	Avg.	TD	SACKS No.
1997—St. Louis NFL		16	2	0	0	0.0	0	0.0
1998—St. Louis NFL		16	13	2	31	15.5	0	3.0
1999—St. Louis NFL		16	16	2	16	8.0	0	1.0
2000—Denver NFL		16	16	4	61	15.3	1	0.0
Pro totals (4 years)		**64**	**47**	**8**	**108**	**13.5**	**1**	**4.0**

JENKINS, DeRON — CB

PERSONAL: Born November 14, 1973, in St. Louis. ... 5-11/192. ... Full name: DeRon Charles Jenkins.
HIGH SCHOOL: Ritenour (St. Louis).
COLLEGE: Tennessee.
TRANSACTIONS/CAREER NOTES: Selected by Baltimore Ravens in second round (55th pick overall) of 1996 NFL draft. ... Signed by Ravens (July 19, 1996). ... Granted free agency (February 12, 1999). ... Re-signed by Ravens (July 28, 1999). ... Granted unconditional free agency (February 11, 2000). ... Signed by San Diego Chargers (February 21, 2000). ... Released by Chargers (February 28, 2001).
PLAYING EXPERIENCE: Baltimore NFL, 1996-1999; San Diego NFL, 2000. ... Games/Games started: 1996 (15/2), 1997 (16/6), 1998 (16/7), 1999 (16/15), 2000 (15/14). Total: 78/44.
PRO STATISTICS: 1996—Recovered one fumble. 1997—Intercepted one pass for 15 yards and recovered one fumble. 1998—Intercepted one pass for no yards and recovered one fumble. 1999—Credited with one sack. 2000—Intercepted one pass for 16 yards, returned one punt for no yards and fumbled once.

JENKINS, JAMES — TE

J

PERSONAL: Born August 17, 1967, in Staten Island, N.Y. ... 6-2/249.
HIGH SCHOOL: Curtis (Staten Island, N.Y.).
COLLEGE: Rutgers.
TRANSACTIONS/CAREER NOTES: Signed as non-drafted free agent by Washington Redskins (April 25, 1991). ... Released by Redskins (August 26, 1991). ... Re-signed by Redskins to practice squad (August 27, 1991). ... Activated (November 30, 1991). ... Released by Redskins (August 31, 1992). ... Re-signed by Redskins (September 1, 1992). ... On injured reserve with back injury (September-November 28, 1992). ... On injured reserve with shoulder injury (December 28, 1993-remainder of season). ... Granted free agency (February 17, 1995). ... Re-signed by Redskins (July 19, 1995). ... Granted unconditional free agency (February 14, 1997). ... Re-signed by Redskins (July 16, 1997). ... Granted unconditional free agency (February 12, 1999). ... Re-signed by Redskins (May 11, 1999). ... On injured reserve with shoulder injury (December 18, 2000-remainder of season). ... Granted unconditional free agency (March 2, 2001).
CHAMPIONSHIP GAME EXPERIENCE: Played in NFC championship game (1991 season). ... Member of Super Bowl championship team (1991 season).
PRO STATISTICS: 1994—Returned one kickoff for four yards. 1995—Returned one kickoff for 12 yards and recovered one fumble. 1996—Recovered one fumble. 1998—Returned one kickoff for no yards and recovered one fumble. 1999—Returned one kickoff for 10 yards.
SINGLE GAME HIGHS (regular season): Receptions—2 (October 23, 1994, vs. Indianapolis); yards—30 (November 21, 1999, vs. New York Giants); and touchdown receptions—2 (October 23, 1994, vs. Indianapolis).

				RECEIVING				TOTALS		
Year Team	G	GS	No.	Yds.	Avg.	TD	TD	2pt.	Pts.	Fum.
1991—Washington NFL	4	0	0	0	0.0	0	0	0	0	0
1992—Washington NFL	5	1	0	0	0.0	0	0	0	0	0
1993—Washington NFL	15	5	0	0	0.0	0	0	0	0	0
1994—Washington NFL	16	3	8	32	4.0	4	4	0	24	0
1995—Washington NFL	16	5	1	2	2.0	0	0	0	0	0
1996—Washington NFL	16	5	1	7	7.0	0	0	0	0	0
1997—Washington NFL	16	4	4	43	10.8	3	3	0	18	0
1998—Washington NFL	16	4	0	0	0.0	0	0	0	0	0
1999—Washington NFL	16	4	1	30	30.0	0	0	0	0	0
2000—Washington NFL	13	6	0	0	0.0	0	0	0	0	0
Pro totals (10 years)	133	37	15	114	7.6	7	7	0	42	0

JENKINS, KERRY — G/OT

JETS

PERSONAL: Born September 6, 1973, in Tuscaloosa, Ala. ... 6-5/305.
HIGH SCHOOL: Holt (Ala.).
COLLEGE: Louisiana State, then Troy (Ala.) State.
TRANSACTIONS/CAREER NOTES: Signed as non-drafted free agent by Chicago Bears (April 25, 1997). ... Released by Bears (August 24, 1997). ... Re-signed by Bears to practice squad (August 27, 1997). ... Signed by New York Jets off Bears practice squad (December 3, 1997). ... Granted free agency (March 2, 2001). ... Re-signed by Jets (May 30, 2001).
PLAYING EXPERIENCE: New York Jets NFL, 1997-2000. ... Games/Games started: 1997 (2/2), 1998 (16/0), 1999 (16/16), 2000 (16/16). Total: 50/34.
CHAMPIONSHIP GAME EXPERIENCE: Played in AFC championship game (1998 season).
PRO STATISTICS: 1999—Recovered one fumble.

JENKINS, MARTAY — WR/KR

CARDINALS

PERSONAL: Born February 28, 1975, in Waterloo, Iowa ... 6-0/201.
HIGH SCHOOL: Waterloo (Iowa) North.
JUNIOR COLLEGE: North Iowa Area Community College.
COLLEGE: Nebraska-Omaha (degree in sociology).
TRANSACTIONS/CAREER NOTES: Selected by Dallas Cowboys in sixth round (193rd pick overall) of 1999 NFL draft. ... Signed by Cowboys (July 27, 1999). ... Claimed on waivers by Arizona Cardinals (September 6, 1999).
PRO STATISTICS: 2000—Rushed once for minus four yards and returned one punt for one yard.
SINGLE GAME HIGHS (regular season): Receptions—2 (December 24, 2000, vs. Washington); yards—35 (December 3, 2000, vs. Cincinnati); and touchdown receptions—0.

			RECEIVING				KICKOFF RETURNS				TOTALS			
Year Team	G	GS	No.	Yds.	Avg.	TD	No.	Yds.	Avg.	TD	TD	2pt.	Pts.	Fum.
1999—Arizona NFL	3	0	0	0	0.0	0	0	0	0.0	0	0	0	0	0
2000—Arizona NFL	16	2	17	219	12.9	0	*82	*2186	26.7	1	1	0	6	3
Pro totals (2 years)	19	2	17	219	12.9	0	82	2186	26.7	1	1	0	6	3

JENKINS, RONNEY   RB/KR   CHARGERS

PERSONAL: Born May 25, 1977, in Los Angeles. ... 5-11/188. ... Full name: Ronney Gene Jenkins.
HIGH SCHOOL: Point Hueneme (Oxnard, Calif.).
COLLEGE: Northern Arizona.
TRANSACTIONS/CAREER NOTES: Signed as non-drafted free agent by San Diego Chargers (April 17, 2000).
PRO STATISTICS: 2000—Rushed eight times for six yards, caught one pass for one yard and recovered two fumbles.
SINGLE GAME HIGHS (regular season): Attempts—3 (October 29, 2000, vs. Oakland); yards—6 (October 1, 2000, vs. St. Louis); and rushing touchdowns—0.

			KICKOFF RETURNS				TOTALS			
Year Team	G	GS	No.	Yds.	Avg.	TD	TD	2pt.	Pts.	Fum.
2000—San Diego NFL	16	0	§67	1531	22.9	▲1	1	0	6	3

JENNINGS, BRANDON   S   RAIDERS

PERSONAL: Born July 15, 1978, in Houston. ... 6-0/195.
HIGH SCHOOL: Channelview (Houston).
COLLEGE: Texas A&M.
TRANSACTIONS/CAREER NOTES: Signed as non-drafted free agent by Oakland Raiders (April 18, 2000).
PLAYING EXPERIENCE: Oakland NFL, 2000. ... Games/Games started: 2000 (2/0).

JENNINGS, BRIAN   TE   49ERS

PERSONAL: Born October 14, 1976, in Mesa, Ariz. ... 6-5/245. ... Full name: Brian Lewis Jennings.
HIGH SCHOOL: Red Mountain (Mesa, Ariz.).
COLLEGE: Arizona State.
TRANSACTIONS/CAREER NOTES: Selected by San Francisco 49ers in seventh round (230th pick overall) of 2000 NFL draft. ... Signed by 49ers (July 10, 2000).
PLAYING EXPERIENCE: San Francisco NFL, 2000. ... Games/Games started: 2000 (16/0).

JERVEY, TRAVIS   RB   FALCONS

PERSONAL: Born May 5, 1972, in Columbia, S.C. ... 6-0/222. ... Full name: Travis Richard Jervey.
HIGH SCHOOL: Wando (Mount Pleasant, S.C.).
COLLEGE: The Citadel.
TRANSACTIONS/CAREER NOTES: Selected by Green Bay Packers in fifth round (170th pick overall) of 1995 NFL draft. ... Signed by Packers (May 23, 1995). ... Granted free agency (February 13, 1998). ... Re-signed by Packers (June 16, 1998). ... On injured reserve with knee and ankle injuries (November 11, 1998-remainder of season). ... Granted unconditional free agency (February 12, 1999). ... Signed by San Francisco 49ers (March 22, 1999). ... On physically unable to perform list with ankle injury (July 27-August 26, 1999). ... On suspended list for violating league substance abuse policy (October 21-November 26, 1999). ... On injured reserve with broken collarbone (October 30, 2000-remainder of season). ... Released by 49ers (March 19, 2001). ... Signed by Atlanta Falcons (May 1, 2001).
CHAMPIONSHIP GAME EXPERIENCE: Played in NFC championship game (1995-97 seasons). ... Member of Super Bowl championship team (1996 season). ... Played in Super Bowl XXXII (1997 season).
HONORS: Played in Pro Bowl (1997 season).
PRO STATISTICS: 1995—Recovered one fumble. 1996—Recovered one fumble.
SINGLE GAME HIGHS (regular season): Attempts—29 (October 25, 1998, vs. Baltimore); yards—95 (November 1, 1998, vs. San Francisco); and rushing touchdowns—1 (January 3, 2000, vs. Atlanta).

			RUSHING				RECEIVING				KICKOFF RETURNS				TOTALS			
Year Team	G	GS	Att.	Yds.	Avg.	TD	No.	Yds.	Avg.	TD	No.	Yds.	Avg.	TD	TD	2pt.	Pts.	Fum.
1995—Green Bay NFL	16	0	0	0	0.0	0	0	0	0.0	0	8	165	20.6	0	0	0	0	0
1996—Green Bay NFL	16	0	26	106	4.1	0	0	0	0.0	0	1	17	17.0	0	0	0	0	4
1997—Green Bay NFL	16	0	0	0	0.0	0	0	0	0.0	0	0	0	0.0	0	0	0	0	0
1998—Green Bay NFL	8	5	83	325	3.9	1	9	33	3.7	0	0	0	0.0	0	1	0	6	0
1999—San Francisco NFL	8	0	6	49	8.2	1	1	2	2.0	0	8	191	23.9	0	1	0	6	0
2000—San Francisco NFL	8	0	1	0	0.0	0	0	0	0.0	0	8	209	26.1	0	0	0	0	0
Pro totals (6 years)	72	5	116	480	4.1	2	10	35	3.5	0	25	582	23.3	0	2	0	12	4

JETT, JAMES   WR   RAIDERS

PERSONAL: Born December 28, 1970, in Charles Town, W.Va. ... 5-10/170.
HIGH SCHOOL: Jefferson (Shenandoah Junction, W.Va.).
COLLEGE: West Virginia.
TRANSACTIONS/CAREER NOTES: Signed as non-drafted free agent by Los Angeles Raiders (May 1993). ... Raiders franchise moved to Oakland (July 21, 1995). ... Granted unconditional free agency (March 2, 2001). ... Re-signed by Raiders (March 2, 2001).
CHAMPIONSHIP GAME EXPERIENCE: Played in AFC championship game (2000 season).
PRO STATISTICS: 1993—Rushed once for no yards. 1994—Recovered two fumbles for 15 yards. 1997—Recovered one fumble. 1998—Rushed once for three yards and recovered one fumble for four yards.
SINGLE GAME HIGHS (regular season): Receptions—7 (October 13, 1996, vs. Detroit); yards—148 (September 21, 1997, vs. New York Jets); and touchdown receptions—2 (October 26, 1997, vs. Seattle).
STATISTICAL PLATEAUS: 100-yard receiving games: 1993 (2), 1996 (1), 1997 (1), 1998 (2). Total: 6.

Year Team	G	GS	RECEIVING				TOTALS			
			No.	Yds.	Avg.	TD	TD	2pt.	Pts.	Fum.
1993—Los Angeles Raiders NFL	16	1	33	771	*23.4	3	3	0	18	1
1994—Los Angeles Raiders NFL	16	1	15	253	16.9	0	0	0	0	0
1995—Oakland NFL	16	0	13	179	13.8	1	1	0	6	1
1996—Oakland NFL	16	16	43	601	14.0	4	4	0	24	0
1997—Oakland NFL	16	16	46	804	17.5	▲12	12	0	72	2
1998—Oakland NFL	16	16	45	882	19.6	6	6	0	36	0
1999—Oakland NFL	16	11	39	552	14.2	2	2	†1	14	0
2000—Oakland NFL	16	13	20	356	17.8	2	2	0	12	0
Pro totals (8 years)	128	74	254	4398	17.3	30	30	1	182	4

JETT, JOHN   P   LIONS

J

PERSONAL: Born November 11, 1968, in Richmond, Va. ... 6-0/197.

HIGH SCHOOL: Northumberland (Heathsville, Va.).

COLLEGE: East Carolina.

TRANSACTIONS/CAREER NOTES: Signed as non-drafted free agent by Minnesota Vikings (June 22, 1992). ... Released by Vikings (August 25, 1992). ... Signed by Dallas Cowboys (March 10, 1993). ... Granted unconditional free agency (February 16, 1996). ... Re-signed by Cowboys (April 15, 1996). ... Granted unconditional free agency (February 14, 1997). ... Signed by Detroit Lions (March 7, 1997). ... Granted unconditional free agency (February 11, 2000). ... Re-signed by Lions (February 21, 2000).

CHAMPIONSHIP GAME EXPERIENCE: Played in NFC championship game (1993-1995 seasons). ... Member of Super Bowl championship team (1993 and 1995 seasons).

PRO STATISTICS: 1996—Rushed once for minus 23 yards. 1998—Attempted one pass without a completion. 1999—Rushed twice for minus eight yards and fumbled once. 2000—Rushed once for no yards, fumbled once and recovered one fumble for minus 10 yards.

Year Team	G	PUNTING					
		No.	Yds.	Avg.	Net avg.	In. 20	Blk.
1993—Dallas NFL	16	56	2342	41.8	37.7	22	0
1994—Dallas NFL	16	70	2935	41.9	35.3	26	0
1995—Dallas NFL	16	53	2166	40.9	34.5	17	0
1996—Dallas NFL	16	74	3150	42.6	36.7	22	0
1997—Detroit NFL	16	84	3576	42.6	35.6	24	†2
1998—Detroit NFL	14	66	2892	43.8	36.0	17	0
1999—Detroit NFL	16	86	3637	42.3	34.8	27	0
2000—Detroit NFL	16	‡93	‡4044	43.5	34.8	‡33	†2
Pro totals (8 years)	126	582	24742	42.5	35.6	188	4

JOHNSON, ANTHONY   RB

PERSONAL: Born October 25, 1967, in Indianapolis. ... 6-0/225. ... Full name: Anthony Scott Johnson.

HIGH SCHOOL: John Adams (South Bend, Ind.).

COLLEGE: Notre Dame.

TRANSACTIONS/CAREER NOTES: Selected by Indianapolis Colts in second round (36th pick overall) of 1990 NFL draft. ... Signed by Colts (July 27, 1990). ... On injured reserve with eye injury (November 5, 1991-remainder of season). ... Granted unconditional free agency (February 17, 1994). ... Signed by New York Jets (June 21, 1994). ... Granted unconditional free agency (February 17, 1995). ... Signed by Chicago Bears (March 21, 1995). ... Claimed on waivers by Carolina Panthers (November 7, 1995). ... Granted unconditional free agency (February 14, 1997). ... Re-signed by Panthers (February 24, 1997). ... Granted unconditional free agency (February 11, 2000). ... Re-signed by Panthers (April 27, 2000). ... Released by Panthers (August 26, 2000). ... Signed by Jacksonville Jaguars (September 19, 2000). ... Granted unconditional free agency (March 2, 2001).

CHAMPIONSHIP GAME EXPERIENCE: Played in NFC championship game (1996 season).

PRO STATISTICS: 1992—Attempted one pass without a completion and recovered four fumbles. 1993—Had only pass attempt intercepted and recovered two fumbles. 1994—Returned one punt for three yards. 1997—Recovered two fumbles. 1998—Returned two kickoffs for 12 yards and recovered one fumble. 1999—Returned one punt for three yards and returned one kickoff for nine yards.

SINGLE GAME HIGHS (regular season): Attempts—29 (October 20, 1996, vs. New Orleans); yards—134 (August 31, 1997, vs. Washington); and rushing touchdowns—1 (October 16, 2000, vs. Tennessee).

STATISTICAL PLATEAUS: 100-yard rushing games: 1996 (5), 1997 (1). Total: 6. ... 100-yard receiving games: 1991 (1), 1992 (1). Total: 2.

MISCELLANEOUS: Holds Carolina Panthers all-time record for most yards rushing (1,795).

Year Team	G	GS	RUSHING				RECEIVING				TOTALS			
			Att.	Yds.	Avg.	TD	No.	Yds.	Avg.	TD	TD	2pt.	Pts.	Fum.
1990—Indianapolis NFL	16	0	0	0	0.0	0	5	32	6.4	2	2	0	12	0
1991—Indianapolis NFL	9	6	22	94	4.3	0	42	344	8.2	0	0	0	0	2
1992—Indianapolis NFL	15	13	178	592	3.3	0	49	517	10.6	3	3	0	18	6
1993—Indianapolis NFL	13	8	95	331	3.5	1	55	443	8.1	0	1	0	6	5
1994—New York Jets NFL	15	0	5	12	2.4	0	5	31	6.2	0	0	0	0	0
1995—Chicago NFL	8	0	6	30	5.0	0	13	86	6.6	0	0	0	0	2
—Carolina NFL	7	0	24	110	4.6	1	16	121	7.6	0	1	0	6	0
1996—Carolina NFL	16	11	300	1120	3.7	6	26	192	7.4	0	6	0	36	2
1997—Carolina NFL	16	7	97	358	3.7	0	21	158	7.5	1	1	1	8	2
1998—Carolina NFL	16	2	36	135	3.8	0	27	242	9.0	1	1	0	6	3
1999—Carolina NFL	16	0	25	72	2.9	0	13	103	7.9	0	0	0	0	1
2000—Jacksonville NFL	12	3	28	112	4.0	1	12	153	12.8	0	1	0	6	0
Pro totals (11 years)	159	50	816	2966	3.6	9	284	2422	8.5	7	16	1	98	23

PERSONAL: Born September 13, 1968, in Marietta, Ga. ... 6-5/224. ... Full name: James Bradley Johnson.
HIGH SCHOOL: Charles D. Owen (Black Mountain, N.C.).
COLLEGE: Florida State (degree in physical education, 1991).
TRANSACTIONS/CAREER NOTES: Selected by Minnesota Vikings in ninth round (227th pick overall) of 1992 NFL draft. ... Signed by Vikings (July 17, 1992). ... Active for one game (1992); did not play. ... Inactive for all 16 games (1993). ... Granted free agency (February 17, 1995). ... Assigned by Vikings to London Monarchs in 1995 World League enhancement allocation program (February 20, 1995). ... Re-signed by Vikings (March 27, 1995). ... On injured reserve with neck injury (December 5, 1997-remainder of season). ... Traded by Vikings to Washington Redskins for first- (QB Daunte Culpepper) and third-round (traded to Pittsburgh) picks in 1999 draft and second-round pick (DE Michael Boireau) in 2000 draft (February 15, 1999). ... Granted unconditional free agency (March 2, 2001). ... Signed by Tampa Bay Buccaneers (March 5, 2001).
CHAMPIONSHIP GAME EXPERIENCE: Member of Vikings for NFC championship game (1998 season); did not play.
HONORS: Played in Pro Bowl (1999 season).
PRO STATISTICS: 1995—Fumbled twice. 1996—Fumbled five times and recovered three fumbles for minus eight yards. 1997—Caught one pass for three yards and a touchdown, fumbled four times and recovered three fumbles. 1998—Fumbled once. 1999—Tied for NFC lead with 12 fumbles and recovered two fumbles for minus eight yards. 2000—Fumbled five times and recovered two fumbles for minus 14 yards.
SINGLE GAME HIGHS (regular season): Attempts—49 (September 18, 2000, vs. Dallas); completions—33 (September 7, 1997, vs. Chicago); yards—471 (December 26, 1999, vs. San Francisco); and touchdown passes—4 (October 3, 1999, vs. Carolina).
STATISTICAL PLATEAUS: 300-yard passing games: 1997 (2), 1998 (1), 1999 (4). Total: 7.
MISCELLANEOUS: Regular-season record as starting NFL quarterback: 32-18 (.640). ... Postseason record as starting NFL quarterback: 1-2 (.333).

Year Team	G	GS	PASSING								RUSHING				TOTALS		
			Att.	Cmp.	Pct.	Yds.	TD	Int.	Avg.	Rat.	Att.	Yds.	Avg.	TD	TD	2pt.	Pts.
1992—Minnesota NFL..........								Did not play.									
1993—Minnesota NFL..........								Did not play.									
1994—Minnesota NFL..........	4	0	37	22	59.5	150	0	0	4.05	68.5	2	-2	-1.0	0	0	0	0
1995—London W.L.	...	...	328	194	59.1	2227	13	14	6.79	75.1	24	99	4.1	1	1	1	8
—Minnesota NFL	5	0	36	25	69.4	272	0	2	7.56	68.3	9	-9	-1.0	0	0	0	0
1996—Minnesota NFL	12	8	311	195	62.7	2258	17	10	7.26	89.4	34	90	2.6	1	1	0	6
1997—Minnesota NFL	13	13	452	275	60.8	3036	20	12	6.72	84.5	35	139	4.0	0	1	2	10
1998—Minnesota NFL	4	2	101	65	64.4	747	7	5	7.40	89.0	12	15	1.3	0	0	0	0
1999—Washington NFL	16	16	519	316	60.9	4005	24	13	7.72	90.0	26	31	1.2	2	2	0	12
2000—Washington NFL	12	11	365	228	62.5	2505	11	15	6.86	75.7	22	58	2.6	1	1	0	6
W.L. totals (1 year)	...	...	328	194	59.1	2227	13	14	6.79	75.1	24	99	4.1	1	1	1	8
NFL totals (7 years)	66	50	1821	1126	61.8	12973	79	57	7.12	84.7	140	322	2.3	4	5	2	34
Pro totals (8 years)	...	...	2149	1320	61.4	15200	92	71	7.07	83.2	164	421	2.6	5	6	3	42

PERSONAL: Born January 18, 1978, in Pocatello, Idaho. ... 6-1/234.
HIGH SCHOOL: Highland (Pocatello, Idaho).
COLLEGE: Boise State.
TRANSACTIONS/CAREER NOTES: Signed as non-drafted free agent by Washington Redskins (April 18, 2000). ... Released by Redskins (August 27, 2000). ... Re-signed by Redskins to practice squad (August 28, 2000). ... Activated (December 18, 2000).
PLAYING EXPERIENCE: Washington NFL, 2000. ... Games/Games started: 2000 (1/0).

PERSONAL: Born January 3, 1972, in San Bernardino, Calif. ... 6-0/200. ... Full name: Charles Everett Johnson.
HIGH SCHOOL: Cajon (San Bernardino, Calif.).
COLLEGE: Colorado (degree in marketing, 1993).
TRANSACTIONS/CAREER NOTES: Selected by Pittsburgh Steelers in first round (17th pick overall) of 1994 NFL draft. ... Signed by Steelers (July 21, 1994). ... On injured reserve with knee injury (December 23, 1995-remainder of season). ... Granted unconditional free agency (February 12, 1999). ... Signed by Philadelphia Eagles (February 16, 1999). ... On injured reserve with knee injury (December 3, 1999-remainder of season). ... Released by Eagles (April 24, 2001). ... Signed by New England Patriots (May 31, 2001).
CHAMPIONSHIP GAME EXPERIENCE: Played in AFC championship game (1994 and 1997 seasons).
HONORS: Named wide receiver on THE SPORTING NEWS college All-America second team (1993).
RECORDS: Shares NFL single-game record for most two-point converstions—2 (November 1, 1998).
PRO STATISTICS: 1994—Fumbled twice. 1995—Recovered one fumble. 1996—Fumbled once. 1999—Credited with a safety, fumbled twice and recovered one fumble.
SINGLE GAME HIGHS (regular season): Receptions—9 (November 1, 1998, vs. Tennessee); yards—165 (December 24, 1994, vs. San Diego); and touchdown receptions—3 (November 1, 1998, vs. Tennessee).
STATISTICAL PLATEAUS: 100-yard receiving games: 1994 (1), 1996 (4), 1997 (1), 1998 (1). Total: 7.

Year Team	G	GS	RUSHING				RECEIVING				PUNT RETURNS				KICKOFF RETURNS				TOTALS		
			Att.	Yds.	Avg.	TD	No.	Yds.	Avg.	TD	No.	Yds.	Avg.	TD	No.	Yds.	Avg.	TD	TD	2pt.	Pts.
1994—Pittsburgh NFL..	16	9	4	-1	-0.3	0	38	577	15.2	3	15	90	6.0	0	16	345	21.6	0	3	0	18
1995—Pittsburgh NFL..	14	12	1	-10	-10.0	0	38	432	11.4	0	0	0	0.0	0	2	47	23.5	0	0	0	0
1996—Pittsburgh NFL..	16	12	0	0	0.0	0	60	1008	16.8	3	0	0	0.0	0	6	111	18.5	0	3	1	20
1997—Pittsburgh NFL..	13	11	0	0	0.0	0	46	568	12.3	2	0	0	0.0	0	0	0	0.0	0	2	0	12
1998—Pittsburgh NFL..	16	16	1	4	4.0	0	65	815	12.5	7	0	0	0.0	0	0	0	0.0	0	7	†2	46
1999—Philadelphia NFL.	11	11	0	0	0.0	0	34	414	12.2	1	1	0	0.0	0	0	0	0.0	0	1	0	8
2000—Philadelphia NFL.	16	15	5	18	3.6	0	56	642	11.5	7	0	0	0.0	0	0	0	0.0	0	7	0	42
Pro totals (7 years)	102	86	11	11	1.0	0	337	4456	13.2	23	16	90	5.6	0	24	503	21.0	0	23	3	146

JOHNSON, DOUG   QB   FALCONS

PERSONAL: Born October 27, 1977, in Gainesville, Fla. ... 6-2/225.
HIGH SCHOOL: Buchholz (Gainesville, Fla.).
COLLEGE: Florida.
TRANSACTIONS/CAREER NOTES: Signed as non-drafted free agent by Atlanta Falcons (April 17, 2000).
PRO STATISTICS: 2000—Fumbled four times.
SINGLE GAME HIGHS (regular season): Attempts—33 (December 3, 2000, vs. Seattle); completions—17 (December 3, 2000, vs. Seattle); yards—233 (December 3, 2000, vs. Seattle); and touchdown passes—1 (December 3, 2000, vs. Seattle).
MISCELLANEOUS: Regular-season record as starting NFL quarterback: 0-2.

			PASSING							RUSHING				TOTALS		
Year Team	G	GS	Att.	Cmp.	Pct.	Yds.	TD	Int.	Avg.	Rat.	Att.	Yds.	Avg.	TD	TD	2pt.	Pts.
2000—Atlanta NFL	4	2	67	36	53.7	406	2	3	6.06	63.4	3	11	3.7	0	0	0	0

JOHNSON, DWIGHT   DE   EAGLES

PERSONAL: Born January 30, 1977, in Waco, Texas. ... 6-4/285. ... Full name: Dwight O'Neal Johnson.
HIGH SCHOOL: Waco (Texas).
COLLEGE: Baylor.
TRANSACTIONS/CAREER NOTES: Signed as non-drafted free agent by Philadelphia Eagles (April 19, 2000). ... Released by Eagles (October 31, 2000). ... Re-signed by Eagles to practice squad (November 1, 2000).
PLAYING EXPERIENCE: Philadelphia NFL, 2000. ... Games/Games started: 2000 (4/0).

JOHNSON, ELLIS   DT   COLTS

PERSONAL: Born October 30, 1973, in Wildwood, Fla. ... 6-2/288. ... Full name: Ellis Bernard Johnson.
HIGH SCHOOL: Wildwood (Fla.).
COLLEGE: Florida.
TRANSACTIONS/CAREER NOTES: Selected by Indianapolis Colts in first round (15th pick overall) of 1995 NFL draft. ... Signed by Colts (June 7, 1995).
CHAMPIONSHIP GAME EXPERIENCE: Played in AFC championship game (1995 season).
PRO STATISTICS: 1997—Intercepted one pass for 18 yards and recovered two fumbles. 1999—Recovered one fumble. 2000—Intercepted one pass for minus one yard.

Year Team	G	GS	SACKS
1995—Indianapolis NFL	16	2	4.5
1996—Indianapolis NFL	12	6	0.0
1997—Indianapolis NFL	15	15	4.5
1998—Indianapolis NFL	16	16	8.0
1999—Indianapolis NFL	16	16	7.5
2000—Indianapolis NFL	13	13	5.0
Pro totals (6 years)	88	68	29.5

JOHNSON, ERIC   S   RAIDERS

PERSONAL: Born June 30, 1976, in Phoenix, Ariz. ... 6-0/210.
HIGH SCHOOL: Alhambra (Ariz.).
COLLEGE: Nebraska.
TRANSACTIONS/CAREER NOTES: Signed as non-drafted free agent by Oakland Raiders (April 18, 2000).
PLAYING EXPERIENCE: Oakland NFL, 2000. ... Games/Games started: 2000 (16/0).

JOHNSON, GARRETT   NT   PATRIOTS

PERSONAL: Born December 31, 1975, in Delleville, Ill. ... 6-3/295.
HIGH SCHOOL: Delleville East (Ill.).
COLLEGE: Illinois.
TRANSACTIONS/CAREER NOTES: Signed by New England Patriots as non-drafted free agent (April 20, 1999). ... Released by Patriots (September 5, 1999). ... Re-signed by Patriots practice squad (September 7, 1999). ... Released by Patriots (September 29, 1999). ... Re-signed by Patriots practice squad (December 7, 1999). ... Activated (January 5, 2000). ... Allocated to Barcelona Dragons of NFL Europe (February 18, 2000). ... Released by Patriots (August 27, 2000). ... Re-signed by Patriots to practice squad (August 29, 2000). ... Activated (October 14, 2000).
PLAYING EXPERIENCE: New England NFL, 2000. ... Games/Games started: 2000 (8/2).
PRO STATISTICS: 2000—Recovered one fumble.

JOHNSON, J.J.   RB   DOLPHINS

PERSONAL: Born April 20, 1974, in Mobile, Ala. ... 6-1/230. ... Full name: James E. Johnson.
HIGH SCHOOL: Dothan (Ala.), then Davidson (Mobile, Ala.).
JUNIOR COLLEGE: East Mississippi Junior College.
COLLEGE: Mississippi State.
TRANSACTIONS/CAREER NOTES: Selected by Miami Dolphins in second round (39th pick overall) of 1999 NFL draft. ... Signed by Dolphins (July 27, 1999).

HONORS: Named running back on THE SPORTING NEWS college All-America second team (1998).
PRO STATISTICS: 1999—Returned two kickoffs for 26 yards and recovered one fumble. 2000—Returned two kickoffs for 26 yards.
SINGLE GAME HIGHS (regular season): Attempts—31 (November 21, 1999, vs. New England); yards—106 (November 21, 1999, vs. New England); and rushing touchdowns—1 (November 26, 2000, vs. Indianapolis).
STATISTICAL PLATEAUS: 100-yard rushing games: 1999 (1).

				RUSHING				RECEIVING				TOTALS	
Year Team	G	GS	Att.	Yds.	Avg.	TD	No.	Yds.	Avg.	TD	TD	2pt.	Pts. Fum.
1999—Miami NFL	13	4	164	558	3.4	4	15	100	6.7	0	4	0	24	2
2000—Miami NFL	13	1	50	168	3.4	1	10	61	6.1	0	1	0	6	0
Pro totals (2 years)	26	5	214	726	3.4	5	25	161	6.4	0	5	0	30	2

JOHNSON, JOE　　　　　DE　　　　　SAINTS

PERSONAL: Born July 11, 1972, in St. Louis. ... 6-4/270. ... Full name: Joe T. Johnson.
HIGH SCHOOL: Jennings (Mo.).
COLLEGE: Louisville.
TRANSACTIONS/CAREER NOTES: Selected after junior season by New Orleans Saints in first round (13th pick overall) of 1994 NFL draft. ... Signed by Saints (June 7, 1994). ... Designated by Saints as franchise player (February 13, 1998). ... Re-signed by Saints (September 2, 1998). ... On injured reserve with knee injury (August 31, 1999-entire season).
HONORS: Played in Pro Bowl (1998 and 2000 seasons).
PRO STATISTICS: 1994—Recovered one fumble. 1997—Recovered one fumble. 1998—Recovered one fumble for five yards and a touchdown. 2000—Recovered two fumbles.

Year Team	G	GS	SACKS
1994—New Orleans NFL	15	14	1.0
1995—New Orleans NFL	14	14	5.5
1996—New Orleans NFL	13	13	7.5
1997—New Orleans NFL	16	16	8.5
1998—New Orleans NFL	16	16	7.0
1999—New Orleans NFL	Did not play.		
2000—New Orleans NFL	16	15	12.0
Pro totals (6 years)	90	88	41.5

JOHNSON, KEVIN　　　　　WR　　　　　BROWNS

PERSONAL: Born July 15, 1976, in Trenton, N.J. ... 5-11/195. ... Full name: Kevin L. Johnson.
HIGH SCHOOL: Hamilton West (Trenton, N.J.).
COLLEGE: Syracuse.
TRANSACTIONS/CAREER NOTES: Selected by Cleveland Browns in second round (32nd pick overall) of 1999 NFL draft. ... Signed by Browns (July 22, 1999).
PRO STATISTICS: 1999—Attempted one pass without a completion, returned one kickoff for 25 yards and recovered one fumble. 2000—Attempted three passes with one completion for 23 yards and one interception.
SINGLE GAME HIGHS (regular season): Receptions—8 (October 15, 2000, vs. Denver); yards—135 (December 12, 1999, vs. Cincinnati); and touchdown receptions—2 (October 31, 1999, vs. New Orleans).
STATISTICAL PLATEAUS: 100-yard receiving games: 1999 (2), 2000 (1). Total: 3.

			RUSHING				RECEIVING				PUNT RETURNS				TOTALS	
Year Team	G	GS	Att.	Yds.	Avg.	TD	No.	Yds.	Avg.	TD	No.	Yds.	Avg.	TD	TD 2pt.	Pts. Fum.
1999—Cleveland NFL	16	16	1	-6	-6.0	0	66	986	14.9	8	19	128	6.7	0	8	0	48	1
2000—Cleveland NFL	16	16	0	0	0.0	0	57	669	11.7	0	0	0	0.0	0	0	0	0	0
Pro totals (2 years)	32	32	1	-6	-6.0	0	123	1655	13.5	8	19	128	6.7	0	8	0	48	1

JOHNSON, KEYSHAWN　　　　　WR　　　　　BUCCANEERS

PERSONAL: Born July 22, 1972, in Los Angeles. ... 6-4/212. ... Cousin of Chris Miller, wide receiver with Green Bay Packers (1997), Detroit Lions (1997) and Chicago Bears (1998); and cousin of Ed Gray, guard with Atlanta Hawks (1997-98 and 1998-99).
HIGH SCHOOL: Dorsey (Los Angeles).
JUNIOR COLLEGE: West Los Angeles College.
COLLEGE: Southern California (degree in history).
TRANSACTIONS/CAREER NOTES: Selected by New York Jets in first round (first pick overall) of 1996 NFL draft. ... Signed by Jets (August 6, 1996). ... Traded by Jets to Tampa Bay Buccaneers for two first-round picks (LB John Abraham and TE Anthony Becht) in 2000 draft (April 12, 2000).
CHAMPIONSHIP GAME EXPERIENCE: Played in AFC championship game (1998 season).
HONORS: Named wide receiver on THE SPORTING NEWS college All-America first team (1995). ... Played in Pro Bowl (1998 and 1999 seasons). ... Named co-Oustanding Player of Pro Bowl (1998 season).
PRO STATISTICS: 1998—Rushed twice for 60 yards and one touchdown. 1999—Rushed five times for six yards and attempted one pass without a completion. 2000—Rushed twice for five yards.
SINGLE GAME HIGHS (regular season): Receptions—11 (December 12, 1999, vs. Miami); yards—194 (September 12, 1999, vs. New England); and touchdown receptions—2 (December 18, 2000, vs. St. Louis).
STATISTICAL PLATEAUS: 100-yard receiving games: 1997 (1), 1998 (4), 1999 (2), 2000 (2). Total: 9.

			RECEIVING				TOTALS		
Year Team	G	GS	No.	Yds.	Avg.	TD	TD	2pt.	Pts.	Fum.
1996—New York Jets NFL	14	11	63	844	13.4	8	8	1	50	0
1997—New York Jets NFL	16	16	70	963	13.8	5	5	0	30	0
1998—New York Jets NFL	16	16	83	1131	13.6	▲10	11	0	66	0
1999—New York Jets NFL	16	16	89	1170	13.1	8	8	0	48	0
2000—Tampa Bay NFL	16	16	71	874	12.3	8	8	0	48	2
Pro totals (5 years)	78	75	376	4982	13.3	39	40	1	242	2

PERSONAL: Born November 27, 1961, in Dallas. ... 6-2/200.
HIGH SCHOOL: McCullough (The Woodlands, Texas).
COLLEGE: Brigham Young.
TRANSACTIONS/CAREER NOTES: Selected by Houston Gamblers in ninth round (125th pick overall) of 1985 USFL draft. ... Selected by Houston Oilers in fifth round (138th pick overall) of 1985 NFL draft. ... Signed by Oilers (June 25, 1985). ... Crossed picket line during players strike (October 14, 1987). ... Claimed on waivers by Buffalo Bills (December 2, 1987). ... Claimed on waivers by Cleveland Browns (December 10, 1987). ... Claimed on waivers by Cincinnati Bengals (September 23, 1988). ... Granted free agency (February 1, 1991). ... Resigned by Bengals (1991). ... Granted unconditional free agency (March 1, 1993). ... Re-signed by Bengals (May 10, 1993). ... Released by Bengals (December 7, 1998). ... Signed by New England Patriots (February 18, 1999).
CHAMPIONSHIP GAME EXPERIENCE: Played in AFC championship game (1987 and 1988 seasons). ... Played in Super Bowl XXIII (1988 season).
POST SEASON RECORDS: Holds Super Bowl career record for longest punt—63 yards (January 22, 1989, vs. San Francisco).
PRO STATISTICS: 1985—Rushed once for no yards, fumbled twice and recovered one fumble for seven yards. 1987—Had 32.8-yard net punting average. 1988—Had 33.4-yard net punting average. 1989—Rushed once for minus seven yards. 1990—Attempted one pass with a completion for four yards and a touchdown. 1991—Attempted one pass with a completion for three yards, rushed once for minus two yards and fumbled once. 1993—Attempted one pass without a completion. 1994—Attempted one pass with a completion for seven yards and one touchdown. 1995—Attempted one pass with a completion for five yards, rushed once for minus 16 yards and fumbled once. 1997—Rushed once for no yards and recovered two fumbles. 1999—Rushed twice for 13 yards. 2000—Rushed twice for minus one yard, completed only pass attempt for 18 yards, fumbled twice and recovered one fumble for minus 12 yards.

Year Team	G		PUNTING						KICKING					
		No.	Yds.	Avg.	Net avg.	In. 20	Blk.	XPM	XPA	FGM	FGA	Lg.	50+	Pts.
1985—Houston NFL	16	83	3464	41.7	35.7	22	0	0	0	0	0	0	0-0	0
1986—Houston NFL	16	88	3623	41.2	35.7	26	0	0	0	0	0	0	0-0	0
1987—Houston NFL	9	25	1008	40.3	.0	5	1	0	0	0	0	0	0-0	0
—Cleveland NFL	3	9	317	35.2	32.2	3	0	0	0	0	0	0	0-0	0
1988—Cleveland NFL	3	31	1237	39.9	.0	6	0	0	0	1	2	50	1-2	3
—Cincinnati NFL	12	14	594	42.4	.0	4	0	0	0	0	0	0	0-0	0
1989—Cincinnati NFL	16	61	2446	40.1	30.1	14	2	0	1	0	0	0	0-0	0
1990—Cincinnati NFL	16	64	2705	42.3	34.2	12	0	0	0	1	0	0	0-0	0
1991—Cincinnati NFL	16	64	2795	43.7	34.7	15	0	0	0	1	3	53	1-3	3
1992—Cincinnati NFL	16	76	3196	42.1	35.8	15	0	0	0	1	0	0	0-1	0
1993—Cincinnati NFL	16	▲90	3954	43.9	36.6	24	0	0	0	0	0	0	0-0	0
1994—Cincinnati NFL	16	79	3461	43.8	35.2	19	1	0	0	0	0	0	0-0	0
1995—Cincinnati NFL	16	68	2861	42.1	38.6	26	0	0	0	0	0	0	0-0	0
1996—Cincinnati NFL	16	80	3630	45.4	34.3	16	1	0	0	0	0	0	0-0	0
1997—Cincinnati NFL	16	81	3471	42.9	35.9	27	0	0	0	0	0	0	0-0	0
1998—Cincinnati NFL	13	69	3083	44.7	35.6	14	1	0	0	0	0	0	0-0	0
1999—New England NFL	16	90	3735	41.5	34.6	23	0	0	0	0	0	0	0-0	0
2000—New England NFL	16	89	3798	42.7	36.8	31	▲1	0	0	0	0	0	0-0	0
Pro totals (16 years)	248	1161	49378	42.5	33.2	302	7	0	1	2	7	53	2-6	6

PERSONAL: Born July 13, 1974, in Morganton, N.C.. ... 6-0/218. ... Full name: William Leon Johnson.
HIGH SCHOOL: Freedom (Morganton, N.C.).
COLLEGE: North Carolina.
TRANSACTIONS/CAREER NOTES: Selected by New York Jets in fourth round (104th pick overall) of 1997 NFL draft. ... Signed by Jets (July 17, 1997). ... On injured reserve with rib injury (December 16, 1998-remainder of season). ... On injured reserve with knee injury (September 13, 1999-remainder of season). ... Granted free agency (February 11, 2000). ... Re-signed by Jets (May 8, 2000). ... Released by Jets (June 27, 2000). ... Re-signed by Jets (November 28, 2000). ... Released by Jets (February 19, 2001).
PRO STATISTICS: 1997—Attempted two passes without a completion and one interception, fumbled five times and recovered five fumbles. 1998—Fumbled three times and recovered three fumbles. 1999—Fumbled once.
SINGLE GAME HIGHS (regular season): Attempts—13 (October 11, 1998, vs. St. Louis); yards—56 (October 11, 1998, vs. St. Louis); and rushing touchdowns—2 (September 20, 1998, vs Indianapolis).

Year Team	G	GS	RUSHING				RECEIVING				PUNT RETURNS				KICKOFF RETURNS				TOTALS		
			Att.	Yds.	Avg.	TD	No.	Yds.	Avg.	TD	No.	Yds.	Avg.	TD	No.	Yds.	Avg.	TD	TD	2pt.	Pts.
1997—N.Y. Jets NFL	16	1	48	158	3.3	2	16	142	8.9	0	§51	*619	12.1	1	12	319	26.6	▲1	4	0	24
1998—N.Y. Jets NFL	12	2	41	185	4.5	2	13	222	17.1	2	29	203	7.0	0	16	366	22.9	0	4	0	24
1999—N.Y. Jets NFL	1	0	1	2	2.0	0	0	0	0.0	0	1	6	6.0	0	2	31	15.5	0	0	0	0
2000—N.Y. Jets NFL	3	0	0	0	0.0	0	0	0	0.0	0	10	62	6.2	0	6	117	19.5	0	0	0	0
Pro totals (4 years)	32	3	90	345	3.8	4	29	364	12.6	2	91	890	9.8	1	36	833	23.1	1	8	0	48

PERSONAL: Born August 27, 1977, in Washington, D.C. ... 6-5/215. ... Full name: Malcolm Alexander Johnson.
HIGH SCHOOL: Gonzaga (Washington, D.C.).
COLLEGE: Notre Dame (degree in marketing).
TRANSACTIONS/CAREER NOTES: Selected by Pittsburgh Steelers in fifth round (195th pick overall) of 1999 NFL draft. ... Signed by Steelers (July 12, 1999). ... Released by Steelers (November 20, 2000). ... Signed by New York Jets (November 21, 2000). ... Released by Jets (December 5, 2000). ... Re-signed by Jets to practice squad (December 7, 2000). ... Released by Jets (June 1, 2001).
PLAYING EXPERIENCE: Pittsburgh NFL, 1999; Pittsburgh (4)-New York Jets (1) NFL, 2000. ... Games/Games started: 1999 (6/0), 2000 (Pit.-4/0; NYJ-1/0; Total: 5/0). Total: 11/0.
PRO STATISTICS: 1999—Caught two passes for 23 yards.
SINGLE GAME HIGHS (regular season): Receptions—1 (January 2, 2000, vs. Tennessee); yards—18 (December 12, 1999, vs. Baltimore); and touchdown receptions—0.

JOHNSON, OLRICK — LB

PERSONAL: Born August 20, 1977, in Miami. ... 6-0/244. ... Nephew of Cecil Johnson, linebacker with Tampa Bay Buccaneers (1977-85).
HIGH SCHOOL: Northwestern (Miami).
COLLEGE: Florida A&M.
TRANSACTIONS/CAREER NOTES: Signed as non-drafted free agent by New York Jets (April 19, 1999). ... Released by Jets (September 5, 1999). ... Re-signed by Jets to practice squad (September 6, 1999). ... Activated (November 5, 1999). ... Released by Jets (November 23, 1999). ... Signed by Minnesota Vikings (November 27, 1999). ... Released by Vikings (August 19, 2000). ... Signed by New Englad Patriots (August 22, 2000). ... Released by Patriots (August 27, 2000). ... Re-signed by Patriots to practice squad (August 29, 2000). ... Activated (September 20, 2000). ... Released by Patriots (October 14, 2000). ... Re-signed by Patriots to practice squad (October 16, 2000). ... Activated (October 21, 2000). ... Released by Patriots (February 22, 2001).
PLAYING EXPERIENCE: New York Jets (3)-Minnesota (5) NFL, 1999; New England NFL, 2000. ... Games/Games started: 1999 (NYJ-3/0; Min.-5/0; Total: 8/0), 2000 (12/0). Total: 20/0.

JOHNSON, PATRICK — WR — RAVENS

PERSONAL: Born August 10, 1976, in Gainesville, Ga. ... 5-10/180. ... Full name: Patrick Jevon Johnson.
HIGH SCHOOL: Redlands (Calif.).
COLLEGE: Oregon.
TRANSACTIONS/CAREER NOTES: Selected by Baltimore Ravens in second round (42nd pick overall) of 1998 NFL draft. ... Signed by Ravens (June 24, 1998). ... Granted free agency (March 2, 2001).
CHAMPIONSHIP GAME EXPERIENCE: Played in AFC championship game (2000 season). ... Member of Super Bowl championship team (2000 season).
HONORS: Named kick returner on THE SPORTING NEWS college All-America second team (1997).
PRO STATISTICS: 1998—Returned one punt for six yards. 1999—Rushed once for 12 yards and recovered one fumble for 12 yards. 2000—Rushed twice for 21 yards.
SINGLE GAME HIGHS (regular season): Receptions—9 (January 2, 2000, vs. New England); yards—114 (January 2, 2000, vs. New England); and touchdown receptions—1 (November 26, 2000, vs. Cleveland).
STATISTICAL PLATEAUS: 100-yard receiving games: 1999 (1).

Year Team	G	GS	No.	Yds.	Avg.	TD	No.	Yds.	Avg.	TD	TD	2pt.	Pts.	Fum.
				RECEIVING				KICKOFF RETURNS				TOTALS		
1998—Baltimore NFL	13	0	12	159	13.3	1	16	399	24.9	▲1	2	0	12	1
1999—Baltimore NFL	10	6	29	526	18.1	3	0	0	0.0	0	3	0	18	1
2000—Baltimore NFL	12	9	12	156	13.0	2	0	0	0.0	0	2	0	12	0
Pro totals (3 years)	35	15	53	841	15.9	6	16	399	24.9	1	7	0	42	2

JOHNSON, RAYLEE — DE — CHARGERS

PERSONAL: Born June 1, 1970, in Chicago, Ill. ... 6-3/272. ... Full name: Raylee Terrell Johnson.
HIGH SCHOOL: Fordyce (Ark.).
COLLEGE: Arkansas.
TRANSACTIONS/CAREER NOTES: Selected by San Diego Chargers in fourth round (95th pick overall) of 1993 NFL draft. ... Signed by Chargers (July 15, 1993). ... Granted unconditional free agency (February 14, 1997). ... Re-signed by Chargers (March 11, 1997). ... On injured reserve with knee injury (August 22, 2000-entire season).
CHAMPIONSHIP GAME EXPERIENCE: Played in AFC championship game (1994 season). ... Played in Super Bowl XXIX (1994 season).
PRO STATISTICS: 1999—Recovered one fumble.

Year Team	G	GS	SACKS
1993—San Diego NFL	9	0	0.0
1994—San Diego NFL	15	0	1.5
1995—San Diego NFL	16	1	3.0
1996—San Diego NFL	16	1	3.0
1997—San Diego NFL	16	0	2.5
1998—San Diego NFL	16	3	5.5
1999—San Diego NFL	16	16	10.5
2000—San Diego NFL	Did not play.		
Pro totals (7 years)	104	21	26.0

JOHNSON, ROB — QB — BILLS

PERSONAL: Born March 18, 1973, in Newport Beach, Calif. ... 6-4/212. ... Full name: Rob Garland Johnson. ... Brother of Bret Johnson, quarterback with Toronto Argonauts of CFL (1993); and cousin of Bart Johnson, pitcher with Chicago White Sox (1969-74, 1976 and 1977).
HIGH SCHOOL: El Toro (Calif.).
COLLEGE: Southern California.
TRANSACTIONS/CAREER NOTES: Selected by Jacksonville Jaguars in fourth round (99th pick overall) of 1995 NFL draft. ... Signed by Jaguars (June 1, 1995). ... Traded by Jaguars to Buffalo Bills for first- (RB Fred Taylor) and fourth-round (RB Tavian Banks) picks in 1998 draft (February 13, 1998).
CHAMPIONSHIP GAME EXPERIENCE: Member of Jaguars for AFC championship game (1996 season); did not play.
PRO STATISTICS: 1998—Fumbled twice and recovered one fumble for minus one yard. 2000—Fumbled four times, recovered two fumbles and caught one pass for minus six yards.
SINGLE GAME HIGHS (regular season): Attempts—47 (October 15, 2000, vs. San Diego); completions—29 (October 15, 2000, vs. San Diego); yards—321 (October 15, 2000, vs. San Diego); and touchdown passes—3 (September 10, 2000, vs. Green Bay).
STATISTICAL PLATEAUS: 300-yard passing games: 2000 (1).
MISCELLANEOUS: Selected by Minnesota Twins organization in 16th round of free-agent draft (June 4, 1991); did not sign. ... Regular-season record as starting NFL quarterback: 9-10 (.474). ... Postseason record as starting NFL quarterback: 0-1.

| Year Team | G | GS | PASSING | | | | | | | | RUSHING | | | | TOTALS | | |
			Att.	Cmp.	Pct.	Yds.	TD	Int.	Avg.	Rat.	Att.	Yds.	Avg.	TD	TD	2pt.	Pts.
1995—Jacksonville NFL	1	0	7	3	42.9	24	0	1	3.43	12.5	3	17	5.7	0	0	0	0
1996—Jacksonville NFL	2	0	0	0	0.0	0	0	0	0.0	...	0	0	0.0	0	0	0	0
1997—Jacksonville NFL	5	1	28	22	78.6	344	2	2	12.29	111.9	10	34	3.4	1	1	0	6
1998—Buffalo NFL	8	6	107	67	62.6	910	8	3	8.50	102.9	24	123	5.1	1	1	0	6
1999—Buffalo NFL	2	1	34	25	73.5	298	2	0	8.76	119.5	8	61	7.6	0	0	0	0
2000—Buffalo NFL	12	11	306	175	57.2	2125	12	7	6.94	82.2	42	307	7.3	1	1	0	6
Pro totals (6 years)	30	19	482	292	60.6	3701	24	13	7.68	89.9	87	542	6.2	3	3	0	18

JOHNSON, TED — LB — PATRIOTS

PERSONAL: Born December 4, 1972, in Alameda, Calif. ... 6-4/255. ... Full name: Ted Curtis Johnson.
HIGH SCHOOL: Carlsbad (Calif.).
COLLEGE: Colorado.
TRANSACTIONS/CAREER NOTES: Selected by New England Patriots in second round (57th pick overall) of 1995 NFL draft. ... Signed by Patriots (July 18, 1995). ... On injured reserve with bicep injury (December 11, 1998-remainder of season).
CHAMPIONSHIP GAME EXPERIENCE: Played in AFC championship game (1996 season). ... Played in Super Bowl XXXI (1996 season).
HONORS: Named linebacker on THE SPORTING NEWS college All-America second team (1994).
PRO STATISTICS: 1995—Recovered two fumbles. 1996—Intercepted one pass for no yards and recovered one fumble. 2000—Recovered three fumbles.

Year Team	G	GS	SACKS
1995—New England NFL	12	11	0.5
1996—New England NFL	16	16	0.0
1997—New England NFL	16	16	4.0
1998—New England NFL	13	13	2.0
1999—New England NFL	5	5	2.0
2000—New England NFL	13	11	0.5
Pro totals (6 years)	75	72	9.0

JOHNSON, TRE' — G — BROWNS

PERSONAL: Born August 30, 1971, in Manhattan, N.Y. ... 6-2/326. ... Full name: Edward Stanton Johnson III.
HIGH SCHOOL: Peekskill (N.Y.).
COLLEGE: Temple (degree in social administration, 1993).
TRANSACTIONS/CAREER NOTES: Selected by Washington Redskins in second round (31st pick overall) of 1994 NFL draft. ... Signed by Redskins (July 22, 1994). ... On injured reserve with shoulder injury (December 16, 1997-remainder of season). ... Granted unconditional free agency (February 13, 1998). ... Re-signed by Redskins (February 13, 1998). ... On injured reserve with knee injury (November 24, 1998-remainder of season). ... On injured reserve with knee injury (October 9, 2000-remainder of season). ... Released by Redskins (February 21, 2001). ... Signed by Cleveland Browns (May 24, 2001).
PLAYING EXPERIENCE: Washington NFL, 1994-2000. ... Games/Games started: 1994 (14/1), 1995 (10/9), 1996 (15/15), 1997 (11/10), 1998 (10/10), 1999 (16/16), 2000 (4/4). Total: 80/65.
HONORS: Played in Pro Bowl (1999 season).
PRO STATISTICS: 1994—Ran four yards with lateral from kickoff return. 1996—Recovered one fumble. 1999—Recovered three fumbles.

JOHNSTONE, LANCE — DE — VIKINGS

PERSONAL: Born June 11, 1973, in Philadelphia. ... 6-4/253.
HIGH SCHOOL: Germantown (Philadelphia).
COLLEGE: Temple.
TRANSACTIONS/CAREER NOTES: Selected by Oakland Raiders in second round (57th pick overall) of 1996 NFL draft. ... Signed by Raiders for 1996 season. ... Granted unconditional free agency (March 2, 2001). ... Signed by Minnesota Vikings (March 27, 2001).
CHAMPIONSHIP GAME EXPERIENCE: Played in AFC championship game (2000 season).
PRO STATISTICS: 1997—Recovered one fumble for two yards. 1998—Recovered one fumble for 40 yards and a touchdown. 1999—Intercepted one pass for no yards and recovered one fumble for 13 yards and a touchdown.

Year Team	G	GS	SACKS
1996—Oakland NFL	16	10	1.0
1997—Oakland NFL	14	6	3.5
1998—Oakland NFL	16	15	11.0
1999—Oakland NFL	16	16	10.0
2000—Oakland NFL	14	9	3.5
Pro totals (5 years)	76	56	29.0

JONES, CEDRIC — DE — RAMS

PERSONAL: Born April 30, 1974, in Houston. ... 6-4/290.
HIGH SCHOOL: Lamar (Houston).
COLLEGE: Oklahoma.
TRANSACTIONS/CAREER NOTES: Selected by New York Giants in first round (fifth pick overall) of 1996 NFL draft. ... Signed by Giants (July 27, 1996). ... On injured reserve with leg injury (December 11, 1997-remainder of season). ... Released by Giants (March 14, 2001). ... Signed by St. Louis Rams (May 3, 2001).
CHAMPIONSHIP GAME EXPERIENCE: Played in NFC championship game (2000 season). ... Played in Super Bowl XXXV (2000 season).
HONORS: Named defensive lineman on THE SPORTING NEWS college All-America first team (1995).
PRO STATISTICS: 1998—Recovered one fumble.

Year Team	G	GS	SACKS
1996—New York Giants NFL	16	0	0.0
1997—New York Giants NFL	9	2	0.0
1998—New York Giants NFL	16	1	4.0
1999—New York Giants NFL	16	16	7.5
2000—New York Giants NFL	16	16	3.5
Pro totals (5 years)	73	35	15.0

JONES, CLARENCE — OT

PERSONAL: Born May 6, 1968, in Brooklyn, N.Y. ... 6-6/300. ... Full name: Clarence Thomas Jones.
HIGH SCHOOL: Central Islip (N.Y.).
COLLEGE: Maryland.
TRANSACTIONS/CAREER NOTES: Selected by New York Giants in fourth round (111th pick overall) of 1991 NFL draft. ... Signed by Giants for 1991 season. ... On injured reserve with ankle injury (October 1991). ... Activated (November 1991). ... Granted free agency (February 17, 1994). ... Released by Giants (May 6, 1994). ... Signed by Los Angeles Rams (June 1, 1994). ... Rams franchise moved to St. Louis (April 12, 1995). ... Granted unconditional free agency (February 16, 1996). ... Signed by New Orleans Saints (February 20, 1996). ... Granted unconditional free agency (February 12, 1999). ... Signed by Carolina Panthers (March 26, 1999). ... Granted unconditional free agency (March 2, 2001).
PLAYING EXPERIENCE: New York Giants NFL, 1991-1993; Los Angeles Rams NFL, 1994; St. Louis NFL, 1995; New Orleans NFL, 1996-1998; Carolina NFL, 1999 and 2000. ... Games/Games started: 1991 (3/0), 1992 (3/0), 1993 (4/0), 1994 (16/16), 1995 (13/0), 1996 (16/16), 1997 (15/15), 1998 (14/14), 1999 (16/16), 2000 (11/11). Total: 111/88.
PRO STATISTICS: 1997—Recovered two fumbles. 1998—Recovered one fumble.

JONES, DAMON — TE — JAGUARS

PERSONAL: Born September 18, 1974, in Evanston, Ill. ... 6-5/266.
HIGH SCHOOL: Evanston (Ill.).
COLLEGE: Michigan, then Southern Illinois (degree in consumer economics, 1997).
TRANSACTIONS/CAREER NOTES: Selected by Jacksonville Jaguars in fifth round (147th pick overall) of 1997 NFL draft. ... Signed by Jaguars (May 30, 1997). ... Granted free agency (February 11, 2000). ... Re-signed by Jaguars (April 10, 2000). ... On injured reserve with knee injury (September 5, 2000-remainder of season). ... Granted unconditional free agency (March 2, 2001). ... Re-signed by Jaguars (March 2, 2001).
CHAMPIONSHIP GAME EXPERIENCE: Played in AFC championship game (1999 season).
PRO STATISTICS: 1998—Returned two kickoffs for minus one yard.
SINGLE GAME HIGHS (regular season): Receptions—2 (December 26, 1999, vs. Tennessee); yards—34 (November 30, 1997, vs. Baltimore); and touchdown receptions—1 (December 19, 1999, vs. Cleveland).

Year Team	G	GS	RECEIVING				TOTALS			
			No.	Yds.	Avg.	TD	TD	2pt.	Pts.	Fum.
1997—Jacksonville NFL	11	3	5	87	17.4	2	2	0	12	0
1998—Jacksonville NFL	16	7	8	90	11.3	4	4	0	24	1
1999—Jacksonville NFL	15	8	19	221	11.6	4	4	0	24	0
2000—Jacksonville NFL	1	0	1	12	12.0	0	0	0	0	0
Pro totals (4 years)	43	18	33	410	12.4	10	10	0	60	1

JONES, DONTA — LB

PERSONAL: Born August 27, 1972, in Washington, D.C. ... 6-2/235. ... Full name: Markeysia Donta Jones. ... Name pronounced DON-tay.
HIGH SCHOOL: McDonough (Pomfret, Md.).
COLLEGE: Nebraska (degree in accounting and business administration, 1994).
TRANSACTIONS/CAREER NOTES: Selected by Pittsburgh Steelers in fourth round (125th pick overall) of 1995 NFL draft. ... Signed by Steelers (July 19, 1995). ... Granted free agency (February 13, 1998). ... Re-signed by Steelers (June 9, 1998). ... Granted unconditional free agency (February 12, 1999). ... Signed by Carolina Panthers (February 15, 1999). ... Released by Panthers (August 20, 2000). ... Signed by New Orleans Saints (August 22, 2000). ... Granted unconditional free agency (March 2, 2001).
PLAYING EXPERIENCE: Pittsburgh NFL, 1995-1998; Carolina NFL, 1999; New Orleans NFL, 2000. ... Games/Games started: 1995 (16/0), 1996 (15/2), 1997 (16/4), 1998 (16/4), 1999 (16/0), 2000 (12/0). Total: 91/10.
CHAMPIONSHIP GAME EXPERIENCE: Played in AFC championship game (1995 and 1997 seasons). ... Played in Super Bowl XXX (1995 season).
PRO STATISTICS: 1996—Credited with one sack and returned one punt for three yards. 1997—Recovered one fumble for six yards. 1998—Credited with three sacks.

JONES, FRED — LB — BILLS

PERSONAL: Born October 18, 1977, in Subic Bay, The Phillipines. ... 6-2/246. ... Full name: Fred Allen Jones.
HIGH SCHOOL: St. Augustine (San Diego).
COLLEGE: Colorado.
TRANSACTIONS/CAREER NOTES: Signed as non-drafted free agent by Buffalo Bills (April 23, 2000).
PLAYING EXPERIENCE: Buffalo NFL, 2000. ... Games/Games started: 2000 (15/0).
PRO STATISTICS: 2000—Credited with one sack.

JONES, FREDDIE — TE — CHARGERS

PERSONAL: Born September 16, 1974, in Cheverly, Md. ... 6-5/270. ... Full name: Freddie Ray Jones Jr.
HIGH SCHOOL: McKinley (Landover, Md.).

COLLEGE: North Carolina.
TRANSACTIONS/CAREER NOTES: Selected by San Diego Chargers in second round (45th pick overall) of 1997 NFL draft. ... Signed by Chargers (May 21, 1997). ... On injured reserve with leg injury (December 12, 1997-remainder of season). ... Granted free agency (February 11, 2000). ... Re-signed by Chargers (April 29, 2000).
PRO STATISTICS: 2000—Recovered one fumble.
SINGLE GAME HIGHS (regular season): Receptions—10 (October 29, 2000, vs. Oakland); yards—111 (October 29, 2000, vs. Oakland); and touchdown receptions—2 (November 26, 2000, vs. Kansas City).
STATISTICAL PLATEAUS: 100-yard receiving games: 2000 (1).

				RECEIVING				TOTALS		
Year Team	G	GS	No.	Yds.	Avg.	TD	TD	2pt.	Pts.	Fum.
1997—San Diego NFL	13	8	41	505	12.3	2	2	0	12	0
1998—San Diego NFL	16	16	57	602	10.6	3	3	1	20	1
1999—San Diego NFL	16	16	56	670	12.0	2	2	0	12	0
2000—San Diego NFL	16	16	71	766	10.8	5	5	0	30	3
Pro totals (4 years)	61	56	225	2543	11.3	12	12	1	74	4

JONES, GREG   LB   BEARS

PERSONAL: Born May 22, 1974, in Denver. ... 6-4/248. ... Full name: Greg Phillip Jones.
HIGH SCHOOL: John F. Kennedy (Denver).
COLLEGE: Colorado (degree in small business management, 1996).
TRANSACTIONS/CAREER NOTES: Selected by Washington Redskins in second round (51st pick overall) of 1997 NFL draft. ... Signed by Redskins (July 11, 1997). ... Granted unconditional free agency (March 2, 2001). ... Signed by Chicago Bears (May 8, 2001).
PRO STATISTICS: 1997—Returned one kickoff for six yards. 1998—Intercepted one pass for nine yards. 2000—Recovered one fumble.

Year Team	G	GS	SACKS
1997—Washington NFL	16	3	3.5
1998—Washington NFL	16	5	1.0
1999—Washington NFL	15	15	0.5
2000—Washington NFL	16	4	1.0
Pro totals (4 years)	63	27	6.0

JONES, HENRY   S   BILLS

PERSONAL: Born December 29, 1967, in St. Louis. ... 6-0/200.
HIGH SCHOOL: St. Louis University High.
COLLEGE: Illinois (degree in psychology, 1990).
TRANSACTIONS/CAREER NOTES: Selected by Buffalo Bills in first round (26th pick overall) of 1991 NFL draft. ... Signed by Bills (August 30, 1991). ... Activated (September 7, 1991). ... Designated by Bills as transition player (February 15, 1994). ... On injured reserve with broken leg (October 9, 1996-remainder of season).
CHAMPIONSHIP GAME EXPERIENCE: Played in AFC championship game (1991-1993 seasons). ... Played in Super Bowl XXVI (1991 season), Super Bowl XXVII (1992 season) and Super Bowl XXVIII (1993 season).
HONORS: Named strong safety on THE SPORTING NEWS NFL All-Pro team (1992). ... Played in Pro Bowl (1992 season).
RECORDS: Shares NFL single-game record for most touchdowns scored by interception—2 (September 20, 1992, vs. Indianapolis).
PRO STATISTICS: 1991—Recovered one fumble. 1992—Recovered two fumbles. 1993—Credited with a safety and recovered two fumbles. 1994—Recovered one fumble. 1995—Recovered one fumble. 1997—Returned one punt for no yards, fumbled once and recovered one fumble. 1999—Returned one kickoff for 37 yards and a touchdown. 2000—Returned one kickoff for four yards and recovered one fumble for 14 yards.

			INTERCEPTIONS				SACKS
Year Team	G	GS	No.	Yds.	Avg.	TD	No.
1991—Buffalo NFL	15	0	0	0	0.0	0	0.0
1992—Buffalo NFL	16	16	†8	*263	32.9	▲2	0.0
1993—Buffalo NFL	16	16	2	92	46.0	▲1	2.0
1994—Buffalo NFL	16	16	2	45	22.5	0	1.0
1995—Buffalo NFL	13	13	1	10	10.0	0	0.0
1996—Buffalo NFL	5	5	0	0	0.0	0	0.0
1997—Buffalo NFL	15	15	0	0	0.0	0	2.0
1998—Buffalo NFL	16	16	3	0	0.0	0	0.0
1999—Buffalo NFL	16	16	0	0	0.0	0	0.0
2000—Buffalo NFL	16	16	2	45	22.5	1	0.0
Pro totals (10 years)	144	129	18	455	25.3	4	5.0

JONES, ISAAC   WR

PERSONAL: Born December 7, 1975, in Little Rock, Ark. ... 6-0/190. ... Full name: Isaac Douglas Jones.
HIGH SCHOOL: Strath Haven (Wallingford, Pa.).
COLLEGE: Purdue.
TRANSACTIONS/CAREER NOTES: Signed as non-drafted free agent by Indianapolis Colts (April 20, 1999). ... On physically unable to perform list with leg injury (August 26-October 23, 1999). ... Released by Colts (August 27, 2000). ... Re-signed by Colts to practice squad (August 29, 2000). ... Activated (November 24, 2000). ... Released by Colts (December 22, 2000).
PLAYING EXPERIENCE: Indianapolis NFL, 1999 and 2000. ... Games/Games started: 1999 (1/1), 2000 (1/0). Total: 2/1.
PRO STATISTICS: 1999—Caught one pass for eight yards.
SINGLE GAME HIGHS (regular season): Receptions—1 (November 21, 1999, vs. Philadelphia); yards—8 (November 21, 1999, vs. Philadelphia); and touchdown receptions—0.

JONES, JAMES   DT   LIONS

PERSONAL: Born February 6, 1969, in Davenport, Iowa. ... 6-2/295. ... Full name: James Alfie Jones.
HIGH SCHOOL: Davenport (Iowa) Central.
COLLEGE: Northern Iowa (degree in science, 1992).
TRANSACTIONS/CAREER NOTES: Selected by Cleveland Browns in third round (57th pick overall) of 1991 NFL draft. ... Signed by Browns (1991). ... Granted unconditional free agency (February 17, 1995). ... Signed by Denver Broncos (February 24, 1995). ... Released by Broncos (July 17, 1996). ... Signed by Baltimore Ravens (August 21, 1996). ... Granted unconditional free agency (February 12, 1999). ... Signed by Detroit Lions (February 16, 1999).
PRO STATISTICS: 1991—Credited with one safety, intercepted one pass for 20 yards and a touchdown and recovered three fumbles for 15 yards. 1992—Recovered one fumble. 1993—Rushed twice for two yards and one touchdown. 1994—Rushed once for no yards, caught one pass for one yard and recovered two fumbles. 1995—Recovered two fumbles. 1996—Caught one pass for two yards and a touchdown. 1997—Recovered one fumble. 1998—Recovered one fumble. 1999—Recovered one fumble. 2000—Recovered one fumble.

Year Team	G	GS	SACKS
1991—Cleveland NFL	16	16	1.0
1992—Cleveland NFL	16	16	4.0
1993—Cleveland NFL	16	12	5.5
1994—Cleveland NFL	16	5	3.0
1995—Denver NFL	16	16	1.0
1996—Baltimore NFL	16	11	1.0
1997—Baltimore NFL	16	16	6.0
1998—Baltimore NFL	16	16	5.5
1999—Detroit NFL	16	16	7.0
2000—Detroit NFL	16	16	3.0
Pro totals (10 years)	160	140	37.0

JONES, JOHN   TE   RAVENS

PERSONAL: Born April 4, 1975, in Cleveland. ... 6-4/255.
HIGH SCHOOL: Glen Mills (Concordville, Pa.).
COLLEGE: Indiana (Pa.).
TRANSACTIONS/CAREER NOTES: Signed as non-drafted free agent by Baltimore Ravens (April 28, 2000). ... On injured reserve with ankle injury (January 3, 2001-remainder of 2000 playoffs).
PLAYING EXPERIENCE: Baltimore NFL, 2000. ... Games/Games started: 2000 (8/0).

JONES, K.C   C   BRONCOS

PERSONAL: Born March 28, 1974, in Midland, Texas. ... 6-1/275. ... Full name: Kirk Cameron Jones.
HIGH SCHOOL: Robert E. Lee (Midland, Texas).
COLLEGE: Miami (Fla.).
TRANSACTIONS/CAREER NOTES: Signed as non-drafted free agent by Denver Broncos (May 2, 1997). ... On injured reserve with pectoral injury (August 18, 1997-remainder of season). ... Active for four games (1998); did not play. ... Active for one game (1999); did not play. ... Granted free agency (February 11, 2000). ... Re-signed by Broncos (March 22, 2000). ... Granted unconditional free agency (March 2, 2001). ... Re-signed by Broncos (April 10, 2001).
PLAYING EXPERIENCE: Denver NFL, 2000. ... Games/Games started: 2000 (16/0).
CHAMPIONSHIP GAME EXPERIENCE: Member of Broncos for AFC championship game (1998 season); inactive. ... Member of Super Bowl championship team (1998 season); inactive.

JONES, LENOY   LB   BROWNS

PERSONAL: Born September 25, 1974, in Marlin, Texas. ... 6-1/235.
HIGH SCHOOL: Groesbeck (Texas).
COLLEGE: Texas Christian.
TRANSACTIONS/CAREER NOTES: Signed as non-drafted free agent by Houston Oilers (April 23, 1996). ... Released by Oilers (August 20, 1996). ... Re-signed by Oilers to practice squad (August 26, 1996). ... Activated (October 9, 1996). ... Oilers franchise moved to Tennessee for 1997 season. ... Oilers franchise renamed Tennessee Titans for 1999 season (December 26, 1998). ... Selected by Cleveland Browns from Titans in NFL expansion draft (February 9, 1999). ... Granted free agency (February 12, 1999). ... Re-signed by Browns (May 26, 1999). ... Granted unconditional free agency (February 11, 2000). ... Re-signed by Browns (March 6, 2000). ... On injured reserve with knee injury (November 28, 2000-remainder of season).
PLAYING EXPERIENCE: Houston NFL, 1996; Tennessee NFL, 1997 and 1998; Cleveland NFL, 1999 and 2000. ... Games/Games started: 1996 (11/0), 1997 (16/0), 1998 (9/0), 1999 (16/1), 2000 (8/1). Total: 60/2.
PRO STATISTICS: 1996—Recovered one fumble. 1997—Credited with one sack. 1999—Intercepted one pass for three yards and fumbled once. 2000—Credited with 2^1/$_2$ sacks and recovered one fumble.

JONES, MARCUS   DE   BUCCANEERS

PERSONAL: Born August 15, 1973, in Jacksonville, N.C. ... 6-6/278. ... Full name: Marcus Edward Jones.
HIGH SCHOOL: Southwest Onslow (Jacksonville, N.C.).
COLLEGE: North Carolina.
TRANSACTIONS/CAREER NOTES: Selected by Tampa Bay Buccaneers in first round (22nd pick overall) of 1996 NFL draft. ... Signed by Buccaneers (July 21, 1996). ... On injured reserve with ankle injury (December 23, 1997-remainder of season).
CHAMPIONSHIP GAME EXPERIENCE: Played in NFC championship game (1999 season).
HONORS: Named defensive lineman on THE SPORTING NEWS college All-America second team (1995).
PRO STATISTICS: 1997—Recovered one fumble. 1998—Recovered one fumble. 2000—Recovered one fumble.

Year	Team	G	GS	SACKS
1996—Tampa Bay NFL		16	3	1.0
1997—Tampa Bay NFL		7	1	0.0
1998—Tampa Bay NFL		15	0	0.0
1999—Tampa Bay NFL		16	4	7.0
2000—Tampa Bay NFL		16	16	13.0
Pro totals (5 years)		70	24	21.0

JONES, MARVIN　　　LB　　　JETS

PERSONAL: Born June 28, 1972, in Miami. ... 6-2/250. ... Full name: Marvin Maurice Jones.
HIGH SCHOOL: Miami Northwestern.
COLLEGE: Florida State.
TRANSACTIONS/CAREER NOTES: Selected after junior season by New York Jets in first round (fourth pick overall) of 1993 NFL draft. ... Signed by Jets (August 5, 1993). ... On injured reserve with hip injury (November 16, 1993-remainder of season). ... On injured reserve with knee injury (July 29, 1998-entire season).
HONORS: Butkus Award winner (1992). ... Named College Football Player of the Year by THE SPORTING NEWS (1992). ... Named linebacker on THE SPORTING NEWS college All-America first team (1992).
PRO STATISTICS: 1993—Recovered one fumble. 1997—Recovered one fumble. 1999—Intercepted one pass for 15 yards and recovered one fumble. 2000—Recovered one fumble.

Year	Team	G	GS	SACKS
1993—New York Jets NFL		9	0	0.0
1994—New York Jets NFL		15	11	0.5
1995—New York Jets NFL		10	10	1.5
1996—New York Jets NFL		12	12	1.0
1997—New York Jets NFL		16	16	3.0
1998—New York Jets NFL		Did not play.		
1999—New York Jets NFL		16	16	1.0
2000—New York Jets NFL		16	16	1.0
Pro totals (7 years)		94	81	8.0

JONES, MIKE　　　LB　　　STEELERS

PERSONAL: Born April 15, 1969, in Kansas City, Mo. ... 6-1/240. ... Full name: Michael Anthony Jones.
HIGH SCHOOL: Southwest (Kansas City, Mo.).
COLLEGE: Missouri.
TRANSACTIONS/CAREER NOTES: Signed as non-drafted free agent by Los Angeles Raiders (April 1991). ... Assigned by Raiders to Sacramento Surge in 1992 World League enhancement allocation program (February 20, 1992). ... Raiders franchise moved to Oakland (July 21, 1995). ... Granted unconditional free agency (February 14, 1997). ... Signed by St. Louis Rams (March 18, 1997). ... Granted unconditional free agency (March 2, 2001). ... Signed by Pittsburgh Steelers (April 20, 2001).
CHAMPIONSHIP GAME EXPERIENCE: Played in NFC championship game (1999 season). ... Member of Super Bowl championship team (1999 season).
PRO STATISTICS: 1995—Recovered two fumbles for 52 yards and a touchdown. 1999—Fumbled once and recovered two fumbles for 42 yards and one touchdown.

Year	Team	G	GS	INTERCEPTIONS No.	Yds.	Avg.	TD	SACKS No.
1991—Los Angeles Raiders NFL		16	0	0	0	0.0	0	0.0
1992—Sacramento W.L.		7	7	0	0	0.0	0	2.0
—Los Angeles Raiders NFL		16	0	0	0	0.0	0	0.0
1993—Los Angeles Raiders NFL		16	2	0	0	0.0	0	0.0
1994—Los Angeles Raiders NFL		16	1	0	0	0.0	0	0.0
1995—Oakland NFL		16	16	1	23	23.0	0	0.0
1996—Oakland NFL		15	15	0	0	0.0	0	1.0
1997—St. Louis NFL		16	16	1	0	0.0	0	2.0
1998—St. Louis NFL		16	16	2	13	6.5	0	3.0
1999—St. Louis NFL		16	16	4	96	24.0	†2	1.0
2000—St. Louis NFL		16	16	0	0	0.0	0	2.0
W.L. totals (1 year)		7	7	0	0	0.0	0	2.0
NFL totals (10 years)		159	98	8	132	16.5	2	9.0
Pro totals (11 years)		166	105	8	132	16.5	2	11.0

JONES, REGGIE　　　WR　　　CHARGERS

PERSONAL: Born May 8, 1971, in Kansas City, Kan. ... 6-0/195. ... Full name: Reginald Lee Jones.
HIGH SCHOOL: Wyandotte (Kansas City, Kan.).
JUNIOR COLLEGE: Butler County (Kan.) Community College.
COLLEGE: Louisiana State (did not play football) (degree in business management).
TRANSACTIONS/CAREER NOTES: Signed as non-drafted free agent by Washington Redskins (April 27, 1995). ... Released by Redskins (August 22, 1995). ... Signed by Carolina Panthers to practice squad (September 4, 1995). ... Activated (October 21, 1995); did not play. ... Released by Panthers (August 22, 1996). ... Signed by Kansas City Chiefs (April 7, 1997). ... On injured reserve with thigh injury (August 15, 1997- entire season). ... Assigned by Chiefs to England Monarchs in 1998 NFL Europe enhancement allocation program (February 18, 1998). ... Released by Chiefs (August 30, 1998). ... Re-signed by Chiefs to practice squad (September 1, 1998). ... Released by Chiefs (August 30, 1999). ... Signed by Saskatchewan Roughriders of CFL (September 3, 1999). ... Signed by San Diego Chargers (February 28, 2000). ... Granted free agency (March 2, 2001). ... Re-signed by Chargers (April 30, 2001).
PRO STATISTICS: NFLE: 1998—Rushed six time for 49 yards. 2000—Recovered one fumble.
SINGLE GAME HIGHS (regular season): Receptions—7 (October 8, 2000, vs. Denver); yards—101 (October 8, 2000, vs. Denver); and touchdown receptions—0.
STATISTICAL PLATEAUS: 100-yard receiving games: 2000 (1).

Year Team	G	GS	RECEIVING No.	Yds.	Avg.	TD	PUNT RETURNS No.	Yds.	Avg.	TD	KICKOFF RETURNS No.	Yds.	Avg.	TD	TOTALS TD	2pt.	Pts.	Fum.
1995—Carolina NFL	1	0	0	0	0.0	0	0	0	0.0	0	0	0	0.0	0	0	0	0	0
1998—England NFLE...............	...	...	36	649	18.0	7	0	0	0.0	0	0	0	0.0	0	7	0	42	0
1999—Saskatchewan CFL......	...	...	38	625	16.4	3	0	0	0.0	0	0	0	0.0	0	0	0	0	0
2000—San Diego NFL	11	2	22	253	11.5	0	9	53	5.9	0	1	11	11.0	0	0	0	0	1
NFL Europe totals (1 year)	...	...	36	649	18.0	7	0	0	0.0	0	0	0	0.0	0	7	0	42	0
CFL totals (1 year).................	...	...	38	625	16.4	3	0	0	0.0	0	0	0	0.0	0	0	0	0	0
NFL totals (2 years)...............	12	2	22	253	11.5	0	9	53	5.9	0	1	11	11.0	0	0	0	0	1
Pro totals (4 years).................	...	...	96	1527	15.9	10	9	53	5.9	0	1	11	11.0	0	7	0	42	1

J

JONES, ROBERT — LB

PERSONAL: Born September 27, 1969, in Blackstone, Va. ... 6-3/245. ... Full name: Robert Lee Jones.
HIGH SCHOOL: Nottoway (Va.), then Fork Union (Va.) Military Academy.
COLLEGE: East Carolina.
TRANSACTIONS/CAREER NOTES: Selected by Dallas Cowboys in first round (24th pick overall) of 1992 NFL draft. ... Signed by Cowboys (April 26, 1992). ... Granted unconditional free agency (February 16, 1996). ... Signed by St. Louis Rams (March 5, 1996). ... Released by Rams (June 2, 1998). ... Signed by Miami Dolphins (June 10, 1998). ... Granted unconditional free agency (February 12, 1999). ... Re-signed by Dolphins (February 19, 1999). ... Released by Dolphins (March 1, 2001).
PLAYING EXPERIENCE: Dallas NFL, 1992-1995; St. Louis NFL, 1996 and 1997; Miami NFL, 1998-2000. ... Games/Games started: 1992 (15/13), 1993 (13/3), 1994 (16/16), 1995 (12/12), 1996 (16/13), 1997 (16/15), 1998 (16/16), 1999 (16/15), 2000 (16/16). Total: 136/119.
CHAMPIONSHIP GAME EXPERIENCE: Played in NFC championship game (1992-1995 seasons). ... Member of Super Bowl championship team (1992, 1993 and 1995 seasons).
HONORS: Named linebacker on THE SPORTING NEWS college All-America second team (1990). ... Named linebacker on THE SPORTING NEWS college All-America first team (1991).
PRO STATISTICS: 1992—Credited with one sack and recovered one fumble. 1993—Returned one kickoff for 12 yards. 1994—Returned one kickoff for eight yards and recovered one fumble. 1995—Credited with one sack. 1996—Intercepted one pass for no yards. 1997—Credited with one sack. 1998—Intercepted two passes for 14 yards and one touchdown and credited with five sacks. 2000—Recovered one fumble.

JONES, ROD — OT

PERSONAL: Born January 11, 1974, in Detroit. ... 6-4/330. ... Full name: Rodrek E. Jones.
HIGH SCHOOL: Henry Ford (Detroit).
COLLEGE: Kansas (degree in human development/family living).
TRANSACTIONS/CAREER NOTES: Selected by Cincinnati Bengals in seventh round (219th pick overall) of 1996 NFL draft. ... Signed by Bengals (July 15, 1996). ... Granted free agency (February 12, 1999). ... Re-signed by Bengals (April 15, 1999). ... Released by Bengals (May 31, 2001).
PLAYING EXPERIENCE: Cincinnati NFL, 1996-2000. ... Games/Games started: 1996 (6/1), 1997 (13/8), 1998 (7/2), 1999 (16/15), 2000 (16/11). Total: 58/37.

JONES, TEBUCKY — S — PATRIOTS

PERSONAL: Born October 6, 1974, in New Britain, Conn. ... 6-2/220. ... Full name: Tebucky Shermaine Jones.
HIGH SCHOOL: New Britain (Conn.).
COLLEGE: Syracuse.
TRANSACTIONS/CAREER NOTES: Selected by New England Patriots in first round (22nd pick overall) of 1998 NFL draft. ... Signed by Patriots (July 18, 1998). ... On injured reserve with knee injury (December 31, 1999-remainder of season).
PLAYING EXPERIENCE: New England NFL, 1998-2000. ... Games/Games started: 1998 (16/0), 1999 (11/2), 2000 (15/9). Total: 42/11.
PRO STATISTICS: 1998—Recovered one fumble. 1999—Returned five kickoffs for 113 yards. 2000—Intercepted two passes for 20 yards.

JONES, THOMAS — RB — CARDINALS

PERSONAL: Born August 19, 1978, in Big Stone Gap, Va. ... 5-10/211. ... Full name: Thomas Quinn Jones.
HIGH SCHOOL: Powell Valley (Big Stone Gap, Va.).
COLLEGE: Virginia (degree in psychology, 1999).
TRANSACTIONS/CAREER NOTES: Selected by Arizona Cardinals in first round (seventh pick overall) of 2000 NFL draft. ... Signed by Cardinals (July 21, 2000).
HONORS: Named running back on THE SPORTING NEWS college All-America first team (1999).
PRO STATISTICS: 2000—Recovered one fumble.
SINGLE GAME HIGHS (regular season): Attempts—23 (September 10, 2000, vs. Dallas); yards—70 (September 10, 2000, vs. Dallas); and rushing touchdowns—1 (October 8, 2000, vs. Cleveland).

Year Team	G	GS	RUSHING Att.	Yds.	Avg.	TD	RECEIVING No.	Yds.	Avg.	TD	TOTALS TD	2pt.	Pts.	Fum.
2000—Arizona NFL	14	4	112	373	3.3	2	32	208	6.5	0	2	0	12	4

JONES, TONY — OT

PERSONAL: Born May 24, 1966, in Royston, Ga. ... 6-5/291. ... Full name: Tony Edward Jones.
HIGH SCHOOL: Franklin County (Carnesville, Ga.).
COLLEGE: Western Carolina (degree in management, 1989).
TRANSACTIONS/CAREER NOTES: Signed as non-drafted free agent by Cleveland Browns (May 2, 1988). ... On injured reserve with toe injury (August 29-October 22, 1988). ... On injured reserve with toe injury (September 20-November 7, 1989). ... Granted free agency (February 1, 1992). ... Re-signed by Browns (July 29, 1992). ... Browns franchise moved to Baltimore and renamed Ravens for 1996 season (March 11,

1996). ... Traded by Ravens to Denver Broncos for second-round pick (S Kim Herring) in 1997 draft (February 14, 1997). ... On injured reserve with arm injury (December 31, 1999-remainder of season). ... Released by Broncos (February 23, 2001).

PLAYING EXPERIENCE: Cleveland NFL, 1988-1995; Baltimore NFL, 1996; Denver NFL, 1997-2000. ... Games/Games started: 1988 (4/0), 1989 (9/3), 1990 (16/16), 1991 (16/16), 1992 (16/16), 1993 (16/16), 1994 (16/16), 1995 (16/16), 1996 (15/15), 1997 (16/16), 1998 (16/16), 1999 (12/12), 2000 (16/16). Total: 184/174.

CHAMPIONSHIP GAME EXPERIENCE: Played in AFC championship game (1989, 1997 and 1998 seasons). ... Member of Super Bowl championship team (1997 and 1998 seasons).

HONORS: Played in Pro Bowl (1998 season).

PRO STATISTICS: 1989—Recovered one fumble. 1991—Recovered one fumble. 1994—Recovered one fumble. 1995—Recovered one fumble.

JONES, WALTER   OT   SEAHAWKS

PERSONAL: Born January 19, 1974, in Aliceville, Ala. ... 6-5/300.
HIGH SCHOOL: Aliceville (Ala.).
JUNIOR COLLEGE: Holmes Junior College (Miss.).
COLLEGE: Florida State.
TRANSACTIONS/CAREER NOTES: Selected by Seattle Seahawks in first round (sixth pick overall) of 1997 NFL draft. ... Signed by Seahawks (August 6, 1997).
PLAYING EXPERIENCE: Seattle NFL, 1997-2000. ... Games/Games started: 1997 (12/12), 1998 (16/16), 1999 (16/16), 2000 (16/16). Total: 60/60.
HONORS: Played in Pro Bowl (1999 season).
PRO STATISTICS: 1999—Recovered one fumble.

JORDAN, ANDREW   TE   VIKINGS

PERSONAL: Born June 21, 1972, in Charlotte. ... 6-6/263. ... Full name: Andrew Jordan Jr.
HIGH SCHOOL: West Charlotte.
COLLEGE: North Greenville College (S.C.), then Western Carolina (degree in criminal justice, 1993).
TRANSACTIONS/CAREER NOTES: Selected by Minnesota Vikings in sixth round (179th pick overall) of 1994 NFL draft. ... Signed by Vikings (June 17, 1994). ... Released by Vikings (September 23, 1997). ... Signed by Tampa Bay Buccaneers (December 9, 1997). ... Released by Buccaneers (August 25, 1998). ... Signed by Philadelphia Eagles (December 1, 1998). ... Granted unconditional free agency (February 12, 1999). ... Re-signed by Eagles (February 18, 1999). ... Released by Eagles (September 7, 1999). ... Signed by Vikings (October 13, 1999). ... Granted unconditional free agency (March 2, 2001). ... Re-signed by Vikings (March 13, 2001).
CHAMPIONSHIP GAME EXPERIENCE: Played in NFC championship game (2000 season).
PRO STATISTICS: 1994—Returned one kickoff for eight yards and recovered a fumble. 1999—Returned one kickoff for no yards.
SINGLE GAME HIGHS (regular season): Receptions—5 (November 13, 1994, vs. New England); yards—57 (November 13, 1994, vs. New England); and touchdown receptions—1 (October 24, 1999, vs. San Francisco).

				RECEIVING				TOTALS		
Year Team	G	GS	No.	Yds.	Avg.	TD	TD	2pt.	Pts.	Fum.
1994—Minnesota NFL	16	12	35	336	9.6	0	0	1	2	1
1995—Minnesota NFL	13	7	27	185	6.9	2	2	0	12	1
1996—Minnesota NFL	13	9	19	128	6.7	0	0	1	2	0
1997—Minnesota NFL	2	0	0	0	0.0	0	0	0	0	0
—Tampa Bay NFL	2	0	1	0	0.0	0	0	0	0	0
1998—Philadelphia NFL	3	0	2	9	4.5	0	0	0	0	0
1999—Minnesota NFL	11	1	5	40	8.0	1	1	0	6	0
2000—Minnesota NFL	16	4	8	63	7.9	0	0	0	0	0
Pro totals (7 years)	76	33	97	761	7.8	3	3	2	22	2

JORDAN, ANTONY   LB   FALCONS

PERSONAL: Born December 19, 1974, in Sewell, N.J. ... 6-3/235. ... Name pronounced ANT-knee.
HIGH SCHOOL: Washington Township (Sewell, N.J.).
COLLEGE: Vanderbilt.
TRANSACTIONS/CAREER NOTES: Selected by Indianapolis Colts in fifth round (135th pick overall) of 1998 NFL draft. ... Signed by Colts (July 24, 1998). ... Released by Colts (August 16, 1999). ... Signed by Chicago Bears (August 18, 1999). ... Released by Bears (September 5, 1999). ... Signed by Tampa Bay Buccaneers (January 22, 2000). ... Claimed on waivers by Philadelphia Eagles (August 23, 2000). ... Released by Eagles (August 27, 2000). ... Signed by Atlanta Falcons (October 25, 2000).
PLAYING EXPERIENCE: Indianapolis NFL, 1998; Atlanta NFL, 2000. ... Games/Games started: 1998 (15/3), 2000 (8/0). Total: 23/3.

JORDAN, RANDY   RB   RAIDERS

PERSONAL: Born June 6, 1970, in Henderson, N.C. ... 5-11/215. ... Full name: Randy Loment Jordan.
HIGH SCHOOL: Warren County (Warrenton, N.C.).
COLLEGE: North Carolina.
TRANSACTIONS/CAREER NOTES: Signed as non-drafted free agent by Los Angeles Raiders (May 1993). ... Released by Raiders (August 25, 1993). ... Re-signed by Raiders to practice squad (August 31, 1993). ... Activated (October 30, 1993). ... Released by Raiders (August 28, 1994). ... Signed by Jacksonville Jaguars (December 15, 1994). ... Granted free agency (February 14, 1997). ... Re-signed by Jaguars (May 5, 1997). ... Released by Jaguars (August 19, 1997). ... Re-signed by Jaguars (September 24, 1997). ... Granted unconditional free agency (February 13, 1998). ... Signed by Oakland Raiders (June 2, 1998).
CHAMPIONSHIP GAME EXPERIENCE: Played in AFC championship game (1996 and 2000 seasons).
PRO STATISTICS: 1996—Recovered one fumble.
SINGLE GAME HIGHS (regular season): Attempts—24 (December 20, 1998, vs. San Diego); yards—82 (December 20, 1998, vs. San Diego); and rushing touchdowns—2 (December 16, 2000, vs. Seattle).

Year Team	G	GS	RUSHING				RECEIVING				KICKOFF RETURNS				TOTALS			
			Att.	Yds.	Avg.	TD	No.	Yds.	Avg.	TD	No.	Yds.	Avg.	TD	TD	2pt.	Pts.	Fum.
1993—LA Raiders NFL..........	10	2	12	33	2.8	0	4	42	10.5	0	0	0	0.0	0	0	0	0	2
1994—Jacksonville NFL									Did not play.									
1995—Jacksonville NFL	12	2	21	62	3.0	0	5	89	17.8	1	2	41	20.5	0	1	0	6	0
1996—Jacksonville NFL	15	0	0	0	0.0	0	0	0	0.0	0	26	553	21.3	0	0	0	0	1
1997—Jacksonville NFL	7	0	1	2	2.0	0	0	0	0.0	0	0	0	0.0	0	0	0	0	0
1998—Oakland NFL...............	16	0	47	159	3.4	1	3	2	0.7	0	0	0	0.0	0	1	0	6	1
1999—Oakland NFL...............	16	0	9	32	3.6	2	8	82	10.3	0	10	207	20.7	0	2	0	12	2
2000—Oakland NFL...............	16	0	46	213	4.6	3	27	299	11.1	1	0	0	0.0	0	5	0	30	1
Pro totals (7 years)...............	92	4	136	501	3.7	6	47	514	10.9	2	38	801	21.1	0	9	0	54	7

JOSEPH, KERRY S

PERSONAL: Born October 4, 1973, in New Iberia, La. ... 6-2/205.
HIGH SCHOOL: New Iberia (La.).
COLLEGE: McNeese State.
TRANSACTIONS/CAREER NOTES: Signed as non-drafted free agent by Cincinnati Bengals (April 22, 1996). ... Inactive for all 16 games (1996). ... Released by Bengals (May 6, 1997). ... Signed by Washington Redskins (May 16, 1997). ... Released by Redskins (August 25, 1997). ... Selected by Rhein Fire in 1998 NFL Europe draft (February 18, 1998). ... Signed by Seattle Seahawks (June 29, 1998). ... Granted free agency (February 11, 2000). ... Re-signed by Seahawks (April 19, 2000). ... Granted unconditional free agency (March 2, 2001).
PRO STATISTICS: 1999—Recovered one fumble.

Year Team	G	GS	INTERCEPTIONS				PUNT RETURNS				KICKOFF RETURNS				TOTALS			
			No.	Yds.	Avg.	TD	No.	Yds.	Avg.	TD	No.	Yds.	Avg.	TD	TD	2pt.	Pts.	Fum.
1996—Cincinnati NFL............									Did not play.									
1997—									Did not play.									
1998—Rhein NFLE	...	...	4	25	6.3	0	4	43	10.8	0	0	0	0.0	0	0	0	0	0
—Seattle NFL..................	16	0	0	0	0.0	0	15	182	12.1	0	2	49	24.5	0	0	0	0	1
1999—Seattle NFL.................	16	4	3	82	27.3	0	0	0	0.0	0	6	132	22.0	0	0	0	0	0
2000—Seattle NFL.................	16	10	0	0	0.0	0	0	0	0.0	0	3	71	23.7	0	0	0	0	0
NFL Europe totals (1 year)	...	...	4	25	6.3	0	4	43	10.8	0	0	0	0.0	0	0	0	0	0
NFL totals (2 years)	48	14	3	82	27.3	0	15	182	12.1	0	11	252	22.9	0	0	0	0	1
Pro totals (3 years)	...	...	7	107	15.3	0	19	225	11.8	0	11	252	22.9	0	0	0	0	1

JOYCE, MATT G LIONS

PERSONAL: Born March 30, 1972, in La Crosse, Wis. ... 6-7/305.
HIGH SCHOOL: New York Military Academy (Cornwall Hudson, N.Y.).
COLLEGE: Richmond (degree in health science, 1994).
TRANSACTIONS/CAREER NOTES: Signed as non-drafted free agent by Dallas Cowboys (May 2, 1994). ... Claimed on waivers by Cincinnati Bengals (August 28, 1994); released after failing physical. ... Signed by Cowboys to practice squad (September 5, 1994). ... Granted free agency after 1994 season. ... Signed by Seattle Seahawks (March 1, 1995). ... Released by Seahawks (August 25, 1996). ... Signed by Arizona Cardinals (December 3, 1996). ... Assigned by Cardinals to Scottish Claymores in 1997 World League enhancement allocation program (February 19, 1997). ... Granted free agency (February 12, 1999). ... Re-signed by Cardinals (April 1, 1999). ... Granted unconditional free agency (February 11, 2000). ... Re-signed by Cardinals (February 21, 2000). ... Released by Cardinals (March 16, 2001). ... Signed by Detriot Lions (April 26, 2001).
PLAYING EXPERIENCE: Seattle NFL, 1995; Scottish W.L., 1997; Arizona NFL, 1996-2000. ... Games/Games started: 1995 (16/13), 1996 (2/0), W.L. 1997 (games played unavailable), NFL 1997 (9/6), 1998 (11/0), 1999 (15/15), 2000 (13/13). Total NFL: 55/47.
PRO STATISTICS: 1995—Recovered one fumble. 1999—Recovered one fumble.

JUNKIN, TREY TE CARDINALS

PERSONAL: Born January 23, 1961, in Conway, Ark. ... 6-2/247. ... Full name: Abner Kirk Junkin. ... Brother of Mike Junkin, linebacker with Cleveland Browns (1987 and 1988) and Kansas City Chiefs (1989).
HIGH SCHOOL: North Little Rock (Ark.).
COLLEGE: Louisiana Tech.
TRANSACTIONS/CAREER NOTES: Selected by Buffalo Bills in fourth round (93rd pick overall) of 1983 NFL draft. ... Signed by Bills for 1983 season. ... Released by Bills (September 12, 1984). ... Signed by Washington Redskins (September 25, 1984). ... Rights relinquished by Redskins (February 1, 1985). ... Signed by Los Angeles Raiders (March 10, 1985). ... On injured reserve with knee injury (September 24, 1986-remainder of season). ... Released by Raiders (September 3, 1990). ... Signed by Seattle Seahawks (October 3, 1990). ... Granted unconditional free agency (February 1-April 1, 1991). ... Re-signed by Seahawks (July 9, 1991). ... Granted unconditional free agency (February 1-April 1, 1992). ... Re-signed by Seahawks for 1992 season. ... Granted unconditional free agency (March 1, 1993). ... Re-signed by Seahawks (March 11, 1993). ... Released by Seahawks (August 30, 1993). ... Re-signed by Seahawks (August 31, 1993). ... Granted unconditional free agency (February 17, 1994). ... Re-signed by Seahawks (May 31, 1994). ... Granted unconditional free agency (February 17, 1995). ... Re-signed by Seahawks (March 20, 1995). ... Granted unconditional free agency (February 16, 1996). ... Signed by Oakland Raiders (June 10, 1996). ... Claimed on waivers by Arizona Cardinals (October 14, 1996).
PRO STATISTICS: 1983—Recovered one fumble. 1984—Recovered one fumble. 1989—Returned one kickoff for no yards.
SINGLE GAME HIGHS (regular season): Receptions—2 (November 22, 1992, vs. Kansas City); yards—38 (September 21, 1986, vs. New York Giants); and touchdown receptions—1 (September 25, 1994, vs. Pittsburgh).

Year Team	G	GS	RECEIVING				TOTALS			
			No.	Yds.	Avg.	TD	TD	2pt.	Pts.	Fum.
1983—Buffalo NFL	16	0	0	0	0.0	0	0	0	0	0
1984—Buffalo NFL	2	0	0	0	0.0	0	0	0	0	0
—Washington NFL	12	0	0	0	0.0	0	0	0	0	0
1985—Los Angeles Raiders NFL	16	0	2	8	4.0	1	1	0	6	0
1986—Los Angeles Raiders NFL	3	0	2	38	19.0	0	0	0	0	0
1987—Los Angeles Raiders NFL	12	1	2	15	7.5	0	0	0	0	0

Year Team	G	GS	RECEIVING				TOTALS			
			No.	Yds.	Avg.	TD	TD	2pt.	Pts.	Fum.
1988—Los Angeles Raiders NFL	16	1	4	25	6.3	2	2	0	12	0
1989—Los Angeles Raiders NFL	16	0	3	32	10.7	2	2	0	12	0
1990—Seattle NFL	12	0	0	0	0.0	0	0	0	0	0
1991—Seattle NFL	16	0	0	0	0.0	0	0	0	0	0
1992—Seattle NFL	16	1	3	25	8.3	1	1	0	6	0
1993—Seattle NFL	16	1	0	0	0.0	0	0	0	0	0
1994—Seattle NFL	16	0	1	1	1.0	1	1	0	6	0
1995—Seattle NFL	16	0	0	0	0.0	0	0	0	0	0
1996—Oakland NFL	6	0	0	0	0.0	0	0	0	0	0
—Arizona NFL	10	0	0	0	0.0	0	0	0	0	0
1997—Arizona NFL	16	0	0	0	0.0	0	0	0	0	0
1998—Arizona NFL	16	0	0	0 ·	0.0	0	0	0	0	0
1999—Arizona NFL	16	0	0	0	0.0	0	0	0	0	0
2000—Arizona NFL	16	0	0	0	0.0	0	0	0	0	0
Pro totals (18 years)	265	4	17	144	8.5	7	7	0	42	0

JUREVICIUS, JOE — WR — GIANTS

PERSONAL: Born December 23, 1974, in Cleveland. ... 6-5/230. ... Full name: Joe Michael Jurevicius. ... Name pronounced jur-uh-VISH-us.
HIGH SCHOOL: Lake Catholic (Mentor, Ohio).
COLLEGE: Penn State.
TRANSACTIONS/CAREER NOTES: Selected by New York Giants in second round (55th pick overall) of 1998 NFL draft. ... Signed by Giants (July 28, 1998). ... Granted free agency (March 2, 2001).
CHAMPIONSHIP GAME EXPERIENCE: Played in NFC championship game (2000 season). ... Played in Super Bowl XXXV (2000 season).
PRO STATISTICS: 2000—Returned one kickoff for three yards.
SINGLE GAME HIGHS (regular season): Receptions—6 (December 3, 2000, vs. Washington); yards—86 (January 2, 2000, vs. Dallas); and touchdown receptions—1 (November 19, 1999, vs. Detroit).

Year Team	G	GS	RECEIVING				TOTALS			
			No.	Yds.	Avg.	TD	TD	2pt.	Pts.	Fum.
1998—New York Giants NFL	14	1	9	146	16.2	0	0	0	0	0
1999—New York Giants NFL	16	1	18	318	17.7	1	1	0	6	1
2000—New York Giants NFL	14	3	24	272	11.3	1	1	0	6	1
Pro totals (3 years)	44	5	51	736	14.4	2	2	0	12	2

JUSTIN, PAUL — QB — RAMS

PERSONAL: Born May 19, 1968, in Schaumburg, Ill. ... 6-4/211. ... Full name: Paul Donald Justin.
HIGH SCHOOL: Schaumburg (Ill.).
COLLEGE: Arizona State.
TRANSACTIONS/CAREER NOTES: Selected by Chicago Bears in seventh round (190th pick overall) of 1991 NFL draft. ... Signed by Bears for 1991 season. ... Released by Bears (August 27, 1991). ... Re-signed by Bears to practice squad (August 28, 1991). ... Released by Bears (August 31, 1992). ... Signed by Indianapolis Colts (April 11, 1994). ... Released by Colts (August 25, 1994). ... Re-signed by Colts to practice squad (August 29, 1994). ... Assigned by Colts to Frankfurt Galaxy in 1995 World League enhancement allocation program (February 20, 1995). ... On injured reserve with knee injury (December 5, 1997-remainder of season). ... Granted free agency (February 13, 1998). ... Re-signed by Colts (March 26, 1998). ... Traded by Colts to Cincinnati Bengals for fifth-round pick (LB Antony Jordon) in 1998 draft (March 26, 1998). ... Released by Bengals (April 20, 1999). ... Signed by Oakland Raiders (July 1999). ... Traded by Raiders to St. Louis Rams for seventh-round pick (traded to Indianapolis) in 2000 draft (August 29, 1999). ... Granted unconditional free agency (February 11, 2000). ... Signed by Dallas Cowboys (April 7, 2000). ... Released by Cowboys (August 24, 2000). ... Signed by Rams (October 27, 2000). ... Released by Rams (November 28, 2000). ... Re-signed by Rams (May 1, 2001).
CHAMPIONSHIP GAME EXPERIENCE: Member of Colts for AFC championship game (1995 season); inactive. ... Member of Rams for NFC championship game (1999 season); did not play. ... Member of Super Bowl championship team (1999 season); did not play.
PRO STATISTICS: 1995—Fumbled once and recovered one fumble for minus one yard. 1996—Fumbled once and recovered one fumble. 1997—Fumbled once.
SINGLE GAME HIGHS (regular season): Attempts—40 (December 1, 1996, vs. Buffalo); completions—24 (November 16, 1997, vs. Green Bay); yards—340 (November 16, 1997, vs. Green Bay); and touchdown passes—2 (October 26, 1997, vs. San Diego).
STATISTICAL PLATEAUS: 300-yard passing games: 1997 (1).
MISCELLANEOUS: Regular-season record as starting NFL quarterback: 3-7 (.300).

Year Team	G	GS	PASSING								RUSHING				TOTALS		
			Att.	Cmp.	Pct.	Yds.	TD	Int.	Avg.	Rat.	Att.	Yds.	Avg.	TD	TD	2pt.	Pts.
1991—Chicago NFL							Did not play.										
1992—							Did not play.										
1993—							Did not play.										
1994—Indianapolis NFL							Did not play.										
1995—Frankfurt W.L.	...	...	279	172	61.6	2394	17	12	8.58	91.6	14	50	3.6	0	0	0	0
—Indianapolis NFL	3	1	36	20	55.6	212	0	2	5.89	49.8	3	1	0.3	0	0	0	0
1996—Indianapolis NFL	8	2	127	74	58.3	839	2	0	6.61	83.4	2	7	3.5	0	0	0	0
1997—Indianapolis NFL	8	4	140	83	59.3	1046	5	5	7.47	79.6	6	2	0.3	0	0	0	0
1998—Cincinnati NFL	5	3	63	34	54.0	426	1	3	6.76	60.7	1	2	2.0	0	0	1	2
1999—St. Louis NFL	10	0	14	9	64.3	91	0	0	6.50	82.7	5	-1	-0.2	0	0	0	0
2000—							Did not play.										
W.L. totals (1 year)	...	...	279	172	61.6	2394	17	12	8.58	91.6	14	50	3.6	0	0	0	0
NFL totals (4 years)	34	10	380	220	57.9	2614	8	10	6.88	75.0	17	11	0.6	0	0	1	2
Pro totals (5 years)	...	...	659	392	59.5	5008	25	22	7.60	82.1	31	61	2.0	0	0	1	2

KACYVENSKI, ISAIAH LB SEAHAWKS

PERSONAL: Born October 3, 1977, in Endicott, N.Y. ... 6-1/250. ... Name pronounced kaz-uh-VEN-skee.
HIGH SCHOOL: Union Endicott (N.Y.).
COLLEGE: Harvard (degree in pre-med).
TRANSACTIONS/CAREER NOTES: Selected by Seattle Seahawks in fourth round (119th pick overall) of 2000 NFL draft. ... Signed by Seahawks (June 9, 2000).
PRO STATISTICS: 2000—Recovered one fumble.

				INTERCEPTIONS		
Year Team	G	GS	No.	Yds.	Avg.	TD
2000—Seattle NFL	16	0	1	0	0.0	0

KALU, NDUKWE DE EAGLES

PERSONAL: Born August 3, 1975, in Baltimore. ... 6-3/265. ... Full name: Ndukwe Dike Kalu. ... Name pronounced EN-doo-kway ka-LOO.
HIGH SCHOOL: John Marshall (San Antonio).
COLLEGE: Rice.
TRANSACTIONS/CAREER NOTES: Selected by Philadelphia Eagles in fifth round (152nd pick overall) of 1997 NFL draft. ... Signed by Eagles (July 15, 1997). ... Released by Eagles (August 25, 1998). ... Signed by Washington Redskins (August 30, 1998). ... Granted free agency (February 11, 2000). ... Re-signed by Redskins (May 18, 2000). ... Granted unconditional free agency (March 2, 2001). ... Signed by Eagles (March 12, 2001).
PRO STATISTICS: 2000—Recovered one fumble for four yards.

Year Team	G	GS	SACKS
1997—Philadelphia NFL	3	0	0.0
1998—Washington NFL	13	1	3.0
1999—Washington NFL	12	0	3.5
2000—Washington NFL	15	0	1.0
Pro totals (4 years)	43	1	7.5

KANELL, DANNY QB

PERSONAL: Born November 21, 1973, in Fort Lauderdale, Fla. ... 6-3/218. ... Son of Dan Kanell, team physician, Miami Dolphins and spring training physician, New York Yankees. ... Name pronounced KA-nell.
HIGH SCHOOL: Westminster Academy (Fort Lauderdale, Fla.).
COLLEGE: Florida State.
TRANSACTIONS/CAREER NOTES: Selected by New York Giants in fourth round (130th pick overall) of 1996 NFL draft. ... Signed by Giants (July 18, 1996). ... Released by Giants (February 19, 1999). ... Signed by Atlanta Falcons (March 19, 1999). ... On injured reserve with knee injury (December 22, 1999-remainder of season). ... Granted unconditional free agency (March 2, 2001).
PRO STATISTICS: 1996—Fumbled twice for minus one yard. 1997—Fumbled six times for minus 10 yards. 1998—Fumbled six times and recovered one fumble. 2000—Fumbled twice and recovered two fumbles for minus two yards.
SINGLE GAME HIGHS (regular season): Attempts—45 (September 21, 1998, vs. Dallas); completions—26 (November 5, 2000, vs. Tampa Bay); yards—259 (October 18, 1998, vs. Arizona); and touchdown passes—3 (October 18, 1998, vs. Arizona).
MISCELLANEOUS: Selected by Milwaukee Brewers organization in 19th round of free-agent baseball draft (June 1, 1992); did not sign. ... Selected by New York Yankees organization in 25th round of free-agent baseball draft (June 1, 1995); did not sign. ... Regular-season record as starting NFL quarterback: 10-11-1 (.454). ... Postseason record as starting NFL quarterback: 0-1.

			PASSING							RUSHING				TOTALS		
Year Team	G	GS	Att.	Cmp.	Pct.	Yds.	TD	Int.	Avg.	Rat.	Att.	Yds.	Avg.	TD	TD	2pt.	Pts.
1996—N.Y. Giants NFL	4	0	60	23	38.3	227	1	1	3.78	48.4	7	6	0.9	0	0	0	0
1997—N.Y. Giants NFL	16	10	294	156	53.1	1740	11	9	5.92	70.7	15	2	0.1	0	0	0	0
1998—N.Y. Giants NFL	10	10	299	160	53.5	1603	11	10	5.36	67.3	15	36	2.4	0	0	0	0
1999—Atlanta NFL	3	1	84	42	50.0	593	4	4	7.06	69.2	0	0	0.0	0	0	0	0
2000—Atlanta NFL	5	1	116	57	49.1	524	2	5	4.52	49.6	1	0	0.0	0	0	0	0
Pro totals (5 years)	38	22	853	438	51.3	4687	29	29	5.49	64.9	38	44	1.2	0	0	0	0

KATZENMOYER, ANDY LB PATRIOTS

PERSONAL: Born December 2, 1977, in Westerville, Ohio. ... 6-3/255. ... Full name: Andrew Warren Katzenmoyer.
HIGH SCHOOL: Westerville (Ohio) North.
COLLEGE: Ohio State.
TRANSACTIONS/CAREER NOTES: Selected after junior season by New England Patriots in first round (28th pick overall) of 1999 NFL draft. ... Signed by Patriots (July 30, 1999). ... On injured reserve with back injury (November 1, 2000-remainder of season).
HONORS: Butkus Award winner (1997). ... Named inside linebacker on THE SPORTING NEWS college All-America third team (1997).

			INTERCEPTIONS				SACKS
Year Team	G	GS	No.	Yds.	Avg.	TD	No.
1999—New England NFL	16	11	1	57	57.0	1	3.5
2000—New England NFL	8	3	0	0	0.0	0	0.0
Pro totals (2 years)	24	14	1	57	57.0	1	3.5

KAUFMAN, NAPOLEON RB/KR

PERSONAL: Born June 7, 1973, in Kansas City, Mo. ... 5-9/185.
HIGH SCHOOL: Lompoc (Calif.).
COLLEGE: Washington.

TRANSACTIONS/CAREER NOTES: Selected by Los Angeles Raiders in first round (18th pick overall) of 1995 NFL draft. ... Signed by Raiders (May 24, 1995). ... Raiders franchise moved to Oakland (July 21, 1995). ... Announced retirement (April 11, 2001).
CHAMPIONSHIP GAME EXPERIENCE: Member of Raiders for AFC Championship game (2000 season); inactive.
HONORS: Named running back on THE SPORTING NEWS college All-America second team (1994).
PRO STATISTICS: 1997—Attempted one pass without a completion and recovered one fumble. 1998—Recovered one fumble. 1999—Recovered two fumbles.
SINGLE GAME HIGHS (regular season): Attempts—31 (October 25, 1998, vs. Cincinnati); yards—227 (October 19, 1997, vs. Denver); and rushing touchdowns—2 (December 19, 1999, vs. Tampa Bay).
STATISTICAL PLATEAUS: 100-yard rushing games: 1996 (3), 1997 (6), 1998 (4), 1999 (1). Total: 14. ... 100-yard receiving games: 1997 (1).

			RUSHING				RECEIVING				KICKOFF RETURNS				TOTALS			
Year Team	G	GS	Att.	Yds.	Avg.	TD	No.	Yds.	Avg.	TD	No.	Yds.	Avg.	TD	TD	2pt.	Pts.	Fum.
1995—Oakland NFL	16	1	108	490	4.5	1	9	62	6.9	0	22	572	26.0	1	2	0	12	0
1996—Oakland NFL	16	9	150	874	*5.8	1	22	143	6.5	1	25	548	21.9	0	2	0	12	3
1997—Oakland NFL	16	16	272	1294	4.8	6	40	403	10.1	2	0	0	0.0	0	8	0	48	7
1998—Oakland NFL	13	13	217	921	4.2	2	25	191	7.6	0	0	0	0.0	0	2	0	12	2
1999—Oakland NFL	16	5	138	714	§5.2	2	18	181	10.1	1	42	831	19.8	0	3	0	18	3
2000—Oakland NFL	14	2	93	499	5.4	0	13	127	9.8	1	9	198	22.0	0	1	0	6	1
Pro totals (6 years)	91	46	978	4792	4.9	12	127	1107	8.7	5	98	2149	21.9	1	18	0	108	16

KEARSE, JEVON   DE   TITANS

PERSONAL: Born September 3, 1976, in Fort Myers, Fla. ... 6-4/265. ... Name pronounced juh-VAUGHN CURSE.
HIGH SCHOOL: North Fort Myers (Fla.).
COLLEGE: Florida.
TRANSACTIONS/CAREER NOTES: Selected after junior season by Tennessee Titans in first round (16th pick overall) of 1999 NFL draft. ... Signed by Titans (July 27, 1999).
CHAMPIONSHIP GAME EXPERIENCE: Played in AFC championship game (1999 season). ... Played in Super Bowl XXXIV (1999 season).
HONORS: Named outside linebacker on THE SPORTING NEWS college All-America second team (1998). ... Named defensive end on THE SPORTING NEWS NFL All-Pro team (1999). ... Played in Pro Bowl (1999 and 2000 seasons).
RECORDS: Holds NFL rookie-season record for most sacks—14.5 (1999).
PRO STATISTICS: 1999—Recovered one fumble for 14 yards and a touchdown.

Year Team	G	GS	SACKS
1999—Tennessee NFL	16	16	§14.5
2000—Tennessee NFL	16	16	11.5
Pro totals (2 years)	32	32	26.0

KEATON, CURTIS   RB   BENGALS

PERSONAL: Born October 18, 1976, in Columbus, Ohio. ... 5-10/212. ... Full name: Curtis Isaiah Keaton.
HIGH SCHOOL: Beechcroft (Columbus, Ohio).
COLLEGE: West Virginia, then James Madison.
TRANSACTIONS/CAREER NOTES: Selected by Cincinnati Bengals in fourth round (97th pick overall) of 2000 NFL draft. ... Signed by Bengals (June 23, 2000).
PLAYING EXPERIENCE: Cincinnati NFL, 2000. ... Games/Games started: 2000 (6/0).
PRO STATISTICS: 2000—Rushed six times for 24 yards and returned six kickoffs for 100 yards.
SINGLE GAME HIGHS (regular season): Attempts—3 (October 15, 2000, vs. Pittsburgh); yards—12 (October 15, 2000, vs. Pittsburgh); and rushing touchdowns—0.

KEITH, JOHN   S   49ERS

PERSONAL: Born February 4, 1977, in Newman, Ga. ... 6-0/207. ... Full name: John Martin Keith.
HIGH SCHOOL: East Coweta (Ga.).
COLLEGE: Furman.
TRANSACTIONS/CAREER NOTES: Selected by San Francisco 49ers in fourth round (108th pick overall) of 2000 NFL draft. ... Signed by 49ers (July 16, 2000). ... On injured reserve with broken arm (October 10, 2000-remainder of season).

			INTERCEPTIONS				SACKS
Year Team	G	GS	No.	Yds.	Avg.	TD	No.
2000—San Francisco NFL	6	3	1	0	0.0	0	1.0

KELLY, BEN   CB   DOLPHINS

PERSONAL: Born September 15, 1978, in Cleveland. ... 5-9/185. ... Full name: Ben O. Kelly.
HIGH SCHOOL: Mentor Lake (Cleveland).
COLLEGE: Colorado.
TRANSACTIONS/CAREER NOTES: Selected after junior season by Miami Dolphins in third round (84th pick overall) of 2000 NFL draft. ... Signed by Dolphins (July 24, 2000). ... On injured reserve with knee injury (September 26, 2000-remainder of season).
PLAYING EXPERIENCE: Miami NFL, 2000. ... Games/Games started: 2000 (2/0).
PRO STATISTICS: 2000—Returned five punts for 31 yards.

K

KELLY, BRIAN   CB   BUCCANEERS

PERSONAL: Born January 14, 1976, in Las Vegas, Nev. ... 5-11/193.
HIGH SCHOOL: Overland (Aurora, Colo.).
COLLEGE: Southern California.
TRANSACTIONS/CAREER NOTES: Selected by Tampa Bay Buccaneers in second round (45th pick overall) of 1998 NFL draft. ... Signed by Buccaneers (July 19, 1998). ... Granted free agency (March 2, 2001).
PLAYING EXPERIENCE: Tampa Bay NFL, 1998-2000. ... Games/Games started: 1998 (16/3), 1999 (16/3), 2000 (16/3). Total: 48/9.
CHAMPIONSHIP GAME EXPERIENCE: Played in NFC championship game (1999 season).
PRO STATISTICS: 1998—Intercepted one pass for four yards, fumbled once and recovered one fumble for 15 yards. 1999—Intercepted one pass for 26 yards. 2000—Intercepted one pass for nine yards and one touchdown and recovered two fumbles.

KELLY, JEFF   LB   FALCONS

PERSONAL: Born December 13, 1975, in La Grange, Texas. ... 5-11/242.
HIGH SCHOOL: La Grange (Texas).
JUNIOR COLLEGE: Garden City (Kan.) Community College.
COLLEGE: Stephen F. Austin State, then Kansas State.
TRANSACTIONS/CAREER NOTES: Selected by Atlanta Falcons in sixth round (198th pick overall) of 1999 NFL draft. ... Signed by Falcons (June 28, 1999).
PLAYING EXPERIENCE: Atlanta NFL, 1999 and 2000. ... Games/Games started: 1999 (16/1), 2000 (12/6). Total: 28/7.
HONORS: Named inside linebacker on THE SPORTING NEWS college All-America second team (1998).
PRO STATISTICS: 1999—Recovered one fumble.

KELLY, MAURICE   S   SEAHAWKS

PERSONAL: Born October 9, 1972, in Orangebury, S.C. ... 6-2/205.
HIGH SCHOOL: Wilkinson (Orangebury, S.C.).
COLLEGE: East Tennessee State.
TRANSACTIONS/CAREER NOTES: Signed as non-drafted free agent by Seattle Seahawks (April 24, 2000).
PLAYING EXPERIENCE: Seattle NFL, 2000. ... Games/Games started: 2000 (16/0).

KELLY, REGGIE   TE   FALCONS

PERSONAL: Born February 22, 1977, in Aberdeen, Miss. ... 6-3/255. ... Full name: Reginald Kuta Kelly.
HIGH SCHOOL: Aberdeen (Miss.).
COLLEGE: Mississippi State.
TRANSACTIONS/CAREER NOTES: Selected by Atlanta Falcons in second round (42nd pick overall) of 1999 NFL draft. ... Signed by Falcons (June 25, 1999).
PRO STATISTICS: 2000—Fumbled once.
SINGLE GAME HIGHS (regular season): Receptions—4 (December 24, 2000, vs. Kansas City); yards—83 (September 24, 2000, vs. St. Louis); and touchdown receptions—1 (December 3, 2000, vs. Seattle).

				RECEIVING		
Year Team	G	GS	No.	Yds.	Avg.	TD
1999—Atlanta NFL	16	2	8	146	18.3	0
2000—Atlanta NFL	16	16	31	340	11.0	2
Pro totals (2 years)	32	18	39	486	12.5	2

KELLY, ROB   S

PERSONAL: Born June 21, 1974, in Newark, Ohio. ... 6-0/199. ... Full name: Robert James Kelly.
HIGH SCHOOL: Newark Catholic (Ohio).
COLLEGE: Ohio State.
TRANSACTIONS/CAREER NOTES: Selected by New Orleans Saints in second round (33rd pick overall) of 1997 NFL draft. ... Signed by Saints (July 17, 1997). ... Granted free agency (February 11, 2000). ... Re-signed by Saints (April 24, 2000). ... Granted unconditional free agency (March 2, 2001).
PRO STATISTICS: 1999—Recovered one fumble.

				INTERCEPTIONS		
Year Team	G	GS	No.	Yds.	Avg.	TD
1997—New Orleans NFL	16	2	1	15	15.0	0
1998—New Orleans NFL	16	3	2	104	52.0	1
1999—New Orleans NFL	16	7	1	6	6.0	0
2000—New Orleans NFL	12	0	0	0	0.0	0
Pro totals (4 years)	60	12	4	125	31.3	1

KENDALL, PETE   G   CARDINALS

PERSONAL: Born July 9, 1973, in Quincy, Mass. ... 6-5/292. ... Full name: Peter Marcus Kendall.
HIGH SCHOOL: Archbishop Williams (Braintree, Mass.).
COLLEGE: Boston College (degree in marketing, 1995).

TRANSACTIONS/CAREER NOTES: Selected by Seattle Seahawks in first round (21st pick overall) of 1996 NFL draft. ... Signed by Seahawks (July 21, 1996). ... Granted unconditional free agency (March 2, 2001). ... Signed by Arizona Cardinals (March 12, 2001).
PLAYING EXPERIENCE: Seattle NFL, 1996-2000. ... Games/Games started: 1996 (12/11), 1997 (16/16), 1998 (16/16), 1999 (16/16), 2000 (16/16). Total: 76/75.
PRO STATISTICS: 2000—Recovered one fumble.

KENNEDY, CORTEZ   DT

PERSONAL: Born August 23, 1968, in Osceola, Ark. ... 6-3/306.
HIGH SCHOOL: Rivercrest (Wilson, Ark.).
JUNIOR COLLEGE: Northwest Mississippi Community College.
COLLEGE: Miami, Fla. (degree in criminal justice).
TRANSACTIONS/CAREER NOTES: Selected by Seattle Seahawks in first round (third pick overall) of 1990 NFL draft. ... Signed by Seahawks (September 3, 1990). ... Granted roster exemption (September 3-9, 1990). ... On injured reserve with ankle injury (December 10, 1997-remainder of season). ... Released by Seahawks (March 8, 2001).
HONORS: Named defensive tackle on THE SPORTING NEWS college All-America first team (1989). ... Played in Pro Bowl (1991-1996, 1998 and 1999 seasons). ... Named defensive tackle on THE SPORTING NEWS NFL All-Pro team (1992 and 1993).
PRO STATISTICS: 1990—Recovered one fumble. 1991—Recovered one fumble. 1992—Fumbled once and recovered one fumble for 19 yards. 1993—Recovered one fumble. 1994—Recovered one fumble. 1998—Recovered one fumble for 39 yards and a touchdown. 1999—Intercepted two passes for 12 yards. 2000—Intercepted one pass for 14 yards.

Year Team	G	GS	SACKS
1990—Seattle NFL	16	2	1.0
1991—Seattle NFL	16	16	6.5
1992—Seattle NFL	16	16	14.0
1993—Seattle NFL	16	16	6.5
1994—Seattle NFL	16	16	4.0
1995—Seattle NFL	16	16	6.5
1996—Seattle NFL	16	16	8.0
1997—Seattle NFL	8	8	2.0
1998—Seattle NFL	15	15	2.0
1999—Seattle NFL	16	16	6.5
2000—Seattle NFL	16	16	1.0
Pro totals (11 years)	167	153	58.0

K

KENNEDY, KENOY   S   BRONCOS

PERSONAL: Born November 15, 1977, in Dallas. ... 6-1/215. ... Full name: Kenoy Wayne Kennedy.
HIGH SCHOOL: Terrell (Texas).
COLLEGE: Arkansas.
TRANSACTIONS/CAREER NOTES: Selected by Denver Broncos in second round (45th pick overall) of 2000 NFL draft. ... Signed by Broncos (June 1, 2000).

Year Team	G	GS	INTERCEPTIONS No.	Yds.	Avg.	TD
2000—Denver NFL	13	0	1	0	0.0	0

KENNEDY, LINCOLN   OT   RAIDERS

PERSONAL: Born February 12, 1971, in York, Pa. ... 6-6/335. ... Full name: Tamerlane Lincoln Kennedy.
HIGH SCHOOL: Samuel F.B. Morse (San Diego).
COLLEGE: Washington (degree in speech and drama, 1993).
TRANSACTIONS/CAREER NOTES: Selected by Atlanta Falcons in first round (ninth pick overall) of 1993 NFL draft. ... Signed by Falcons (August 2, 1993). ... Granted free agency (February 16, 1996). ... Re-signed by Falcons (May 13, 1996). ... Traded by Falcons to Oakland Raiders for fifth-round pick (traded to Washington) in 1997 draft (May 13, 1996).
PLAYING EXPERIENCE: Atlanta NFL, 1993-1995; Oakland NFL, 1996-2000. ... Games/Games started: 1993 (16/16), 1994 (16/2), 1995 (16/4), 1996 (16/16), 1997 (16/16), 1998 (16/16), 1999 (15/15), 2000 (16/16). Total: 127/101.
CHAMPIONSHIP GAME EXPERIENCE: Played in AFC championship game (2000 season).
HONORS: Named offensive tackle on THE SPORTING NEWS college All-America first team (1992). ... Played in Pro Bowl (2000 season).
PRO STATISTICS: 1993—Recovered one fumble. 1994—Recovered one fumble. 1996—Recovered one fumble. 1998—Recovered one fumble for 27 yards. 2000—Recovered two fumbles.

KENNISON, EDDIE   WR   BRONCOS

PERSONAL: Born January 20, 1973, in Lake Charles, La. ... 6-1/190. ... Full name: Eddie Joseph Kennison III.
HIGH SCHOOL: Washington-Marion (Lake Charles, La.).
COLLEGE: Louisiana State.
TRANSACTIONS/CAREER NOTES: Selected after junior season by St. Louis Rams in first round (18th pick overall) of 1996 NFL draft. ... Signed by Rams (July 27, 1996). ... Traded by Rams to New Orleans Saints for second-round pick (DB Dre' Bly) in 1999 draft (February 18, 1999). ... Traded by Saints to Chicago Bears for fifth-round pick (traded to Indianapolis) in 2000 draft (February 21, 2000). ... Granted unconditional free agency (March 2, 2001). ... Signed by Denver Broncos (April 5, 2001).
PRO STATISTICS: 1996—Fumbled five times. 1997—Fumbled twice. 1998—Fumbled four times and recovered one fumble. 1999—Fumbled six times and recovered four fumbles. 2000—Fumbled once and recovered one fumble.
SINGLE GAME HIGHS (regular season): Receptions—8 (December 10, 2000, vs. New England); yards—226 (December 15, 1996, vs. Atlanta); and touchdown receptions—3 (December 15, 1996, vs. Atlanta).
STATISTICAL PLATEAUS: 100-yard receiving games: 1996 (2), 1999 (1), 2000 (1). Total: 4.

Year—Team	G	GS	RUSHING				RECEIVING				PUNT RETURNS				KICKOFF RETURNS				TOTALS		
			Att.	Yds.	Avg.	TD	No.	Yds.	Avg.	TD	No.	Yds.	Avg.	TD	No.	Yds.	Avg.	TD	TD	2pt.	Pts.
1996—St. Louis NFL	15	14	0	0	0.0	0	54	924	17.1	9	29	423	14.6	2	23	454	19.7	0	11	0	66
1997—St. Louis NFL	14	9	3	13	4.3	0	25	404	16.2	0	34	247	7.3	0	1	14	14.0	0	0	0	0
1998—St. Louis NFL	16	13	2	9	4.5	0	17	234	13.8	1	40	415	10.4	1	0	0	0.0	0	2	0	12
1999—New Orleans NFL	16	16	3	20	6.7	0	61	835	13.7	4	35	258	7.4	0	0	0	0.0	0	4	†1	26
2000—Chicago NFL	16	10	3	72	24.0	0	55	549	10.0	2	0	0	0.0	0	0	0	0.0	0	2	0	12
Pro totals (5 years)	77	62	11	114	10.4	0	212	2946	13.9	16	138	1343	9.7	3	24	468	19.5	0	19	1	116

KERNEY, PATRICK DE FALCONS

PERSONAL: Born December 30, 1976, in Trenton, N.J. ... 6-5/273. ... Full name: Patrick Manning Kerney.
HIGH SCHOOL: Taft Prep (Watertown, Conn.).
COLLEGE: Virginia.
TRANSACTIONS/CAREER NOTES: Selected by Atlanta Falcons in first round (30th pick overall) of 1999 NFL draft. ... Signed by Falcons (June 25, 1999).
HONORS: Named defensive end on THE SPORTING NEWS college All-America second team (1998).
PRO STATISTICS: 2000—Intercepted one pass for eight yards.

Year Team	G	GS	SACKS
1999—Atlanta NFL	16	2	2.5
2000—Atlanta NFL	16	16	2.5
Pro totals (2 years)	32	18	5.0

K

KEUR, JOSH TE COLTS

PERSONAL: Born September 4, 1976, in Muskegon, Mich. ... 6-4/270.
HIGH SCHOOL: Orchard View (Muskegon, Mich.).
COLLEGE: Michigan State.
TRANSACTIONS/CAREER NOTES: Signed as non-drafted free agent by Indianapolis Colts (May 11, 1999). ... Released by Colts (September 5, 1999). ... Re-signed by Colts to practice squad (September 7, 1999). ... Released by Colts (September 8, 1999). ... Re-signed by Colts (January 25, 2000).
PLAYING EXPERIENCE: Indianapolis NFL, 2000. ... Games/Games started: 2000 (1/0).

KIGHT, DANNY K COLTS

PERSONAL: Born August 18, 1971, in Atlanta. ... 6-1/214.
HIGH SCHOOL: Druid Hills (Ga.).
COLLEGE: Augusta (Ga.) State.
TRANSACTIONS/CAREER NOTES: Signed as non-drafted free agent by San Diego Chargers (April 23, 1996). ... Released by Chargers (August 14, 1996). ... Signed by Dallas Cowboys (April 15, 1997). ... Released by Cowboys (August 12, 1997). ... Signed by Washington Redskins (February 11, 1998). ... On non-football injury list with leg injury (July 20-September 22, 1998). ... Released by Redskins (September 22, 1998). ... Signed by Tampa Bay Buccaneers (April 7, 1999). ... Claimed on waivers by Cleveland Browns (April 20, 1999). ... Released by Browns (August 25, 1999). ... Signed by Indianapolis Colts (October 13, 1999).
PLAYING EXPERIENCE: Indianapolis NFL, 1999 and 2000; Rhein Fire NFLE, 2000. ... Games/Games started: 1999 (12/0) NFLE 2000 (games played unavailable), NFL 2000 (16/0). Total NFL: 28/0.
PRO STATISTICS: NFLE: 2000—Attempted five field goals with three made for nine points.

KILLENS, TERRY LB

PERSONAL: Born March 24, 1974, in Cincinnati. ... 6-1/235. ... Full name: Terry Deleon Killens.
HIGH SCHOOL: Purcell (Cincinnati).
COLLEGE: Penn State.
TRANSACTIONS/CAREER NOTES: Selected by Houston Oilers in third round (74th pick overall) of 1996 NFL draft. ... Signed by Oilers (July 20, 1996). ... Oilers franchise moved to Tennessee for 1997 season. ... Oilers franchise renamed Tennessee Titans for 1999 season (December 26, 1998). ... Granted free agency (February 12, 1999). ... Re-signed by Titans (June 2, 1999). ... Granted unconditional free agency (February 11, 2000). ... Re-signed by Titans (May 26, 2000). ... Released by Titans (March 1, 2001).
PLAYING EXPERIENCE: Houston NFL, 1996; Tennessee NFL, 1997-2000. ... Games/Games started: 1996 (14/0), 1997 (16/0), 1998 (16/1), 1999 (16/1), 2000 (16/0). Total: 78/2.
CHAMPIONSHIP GAME EXPERIENCE: Played in AFC championship game (1999 season). ... Played in Super Bowl XXXIV (1999 season).
PRO STATISTICS: 1999—Recovered one fumble. 2000—Credited with one sack.

KILLINGS, CEDRIC DT 49ERS

PERSONAL: Born December 14, 1977, in Miami. ... 6-2/290. ... Full name: Cedric Laquon Killings.
HIGH SCHOOL: Miami Central.
COLLEGE: Carson-Newman College (Tenn.).
TRANSACTIONS/CAREER NOTES: Signed as non-drafted free agent by San Francisco 49ers (April 27, 2000).
PLAYING EXPERIENCE: San Francisco NFL, 2000. ... Games/Games started: 2000 (14/1).
PRO STATISTICS: 2000—Credited with three sacks.

KINCHEN, BRIAN — TE

PERSONAL: Born August 6, 1965, in Baton Rouge, La. ... 6-2/240. ... Full name: Brian Douglas Kinchen. ... Brother of Todd Kinchen, wide receiver/kick returner with four NFL teams (1992-98).
HIGH SCHOOL: University (Baton Rouge, La.).
COLLEGE: Louisiana State.
TRANSACTIONS/CAREER NOTES: Selected by Miami Dolphins in 12th round (320th pick overall) of 1988 NFL draft. ... Signed by Dolphins (June 6, 1988). ... On injured reserve with hamstring injury (October 4, 1990-remainder of season). ... Granted unconditional free agency (February 1, 1991). ... Signed by Green Bay Packers (April 1, 1991). ... Released by Packers (August 26, 1991). ... Signed by Cleveland Browns (September 13, 1991). ... Granted unconditional free agency (February 1-April 1, 1992). ... Re-signed by Browns for 1992 season. ... Granted unconditional free agency (February 17, 1994). ... Re-signed by Browns (March 4, 1994). ... Granted unconditional free agency (February 16, 1996). ... Browns franchise moved to Baltimore and renamed Ravens for 1996 season (March 11, 1996). ... Re-signed by Ravens (April 3, 1996). ... Granted unconditional free agency (February 12, 1999). ... Signed by Carolina Panthers (March 8, 1999). ... Released by Panthers (March 5, 2001).
PRO STATISTICS: 1995—Recovered one fumble. 1999—Recovered one fumble.
SINGLE GAME HIGHS (regular season): Receptions—9 (November 24, 1996, vs. Jacksonville); yards—87 (December 15, 1996, vs. Carolina); and touchdown receptions—1 (December 12, 1999, vs. Green Bay).

				RECEIVING				KICKOFF RETURNS				TOTALS		
Year Team	G	GS	No.	Yds.	Avg.	TD	No.	Yds.	Avg.	TD	TD	2pt.	Pts.	Fum.
1988—Miami NFL	16	0	1	3	3.0	0	0	0	0.0	0	0	0	0	0
1989—Miami NFL	16	0	1	12	12.0	0	2	26	13.0	0	0	0	0	2
1990—Miami NFL	4	0	0	0	0.0	0	1	16	16.0	0	0	0	0	0
1991—Cleveland NFL	14	0	0	0	0.0	0	0	0	0.0	0	0	0	0	1
1992—Cleveland NFL	16	0	0	0	0.0	0	0	0	0.0	0	0	0	0	1
1993—Cleveland NFL	16	15	29	347	12.0	2	1	0	0.0	0	2	0	12	1
1994—Cleveland NFL	16	11	24	232	9.7	1	3	38	12.7	0	1	0	6	1
1995—Cleveland NFL	13	12	20	216	10.8	0	0	0	0.0	0	0	0	0	1
1996—Baltimore NFL	16	16	55	581	10.6	1	1	19	19.0	0	1	0	6	1
1997—Baltimore NFL	16	6	11	95	8.6	1	0	0	0.0	0	1	0	6	0
1998—Baltimore NFL	16	5	13	110	8.5	0	2	33	16.5	0	0	0	0	0
1999—Carolina NFL	16	0	5	45	9.0	2	3	29	9.7	0	2	0	12	0
2000—Carolina NFL	16	0	1	7	7.0	0	0	0	0.0	0	0	0	0	0
Pro totals (13 years)	191	65	160	1648	10.3	7	13	161	12.4	0	7	0	42	7

KING, LAMAR — DE — SEAHAWKS

PERSONAL: Born August 10, 1975, in Boston. ... 6-3/294.
HIGH SCHOOL: Chesapeake (Md.).
JUNIOR COLLEGE: Montgomery College (Md.).
COLLEGE: Saginaw Valley State (Mich.).
TRANSACTIONS/CAREER NOTES: Selected by Seattle Seahawks in first round (22nd pick overall) of 1999 NFL draft. ... Signed by Seahawks (August 12, 1999).

Year Team	G	GS	SACKS
1999—Seattle NFL	14	0	2.0
2000—Seattle NFL	14	14	6.0
Pro totals (2 years)	28	14	8.0

KING, SHAUN — QB — BUCCANEERS

PERSONAL: Born May 29, 1977, in St. Petersburg, Fla. ... 6-0/225. ... Full name: Shaun Earl King.
HIGH SCHOOL: Gibbs (St. Petersburg, Fla.).
COLLEGE: Tulane.
TRANSACTIONS/CAREER NOTES: Selected by Tampa Bay Buccaneers in second round (50th pick overall) of 1999 NFL draft. ... Signed by Buccaneers (August 1, 1999).
CHAMPIONSHIP GAME EXPERIENCE: Played in NFC championship game (1999 season).
PRO STATISTICS: 1999—Fumbled four times and recovered one fumble. 2000—Fumbled four times and recovered three fumbles.
SINGLE GAME HIGHS (regular season): Attempts—42 (December 24, 2000, vs. Green Bay); completions—26 (October 9, 2000, vs. Minnesota); passing yards—297 (December 12, 1999, vs. Detroit); and touchdown passes—4 (October 29, 2000, vs. Minnesota).
MISCELLANEOUS: Regular-season record as starting NFL quarterback: 14-7 (.667). ... Postseason record as starting NFL quarterback: 1-2 (.333).

					PASSING						RUSHING				TOTALS	
Year Team	G	GS	Att.	Cmp.	Pct.	Yds.	TD	Int.	Avg.	Rat.	Att.	Yds.	Avg.	TD	TD	2pt.	Pts.
1999—Tampa Bay NFL	6	5	146	89	61.0	875	7	4	5.99	82.4	18	38	2.1	0	0	0	0
2000—Tampa Bay NFL	16	16	428	233	54.4	2769	18	13	6.47	75.8	73	353	4.8	5	5	1	32
Pro totals (2 years)	22	21	574	322	56.1	3644	25	17	6.35	77.5	91	391	4.3	5	5	1	32

KING, SHAWN — DE — COLTS

PERSONAL: Born June 24, 1972, in West Monroe, La. ... 6-3/275.
HIGH SCHOOL: West Monroe (La.).
COLLEGE: Louisiana State, then Northeast Louisiana.
TRANSACTIONS/CAREER NOTES: Selected by Carolina Panthers in second round (36th pick overall) of 1995 NFL draft. ... Signed by Panthers (July 15, 1995). ... On reserve/suspended list for violating league substance abuse policy (August 24-October 17, 1997). ... On injured reserve with knee injury (December 15, 1997-remainder of season). ... On injured reserve with arm injury (August 24, 1998-entire season). ...

K

Granted unconditional free agency (February 12, 1999). ... Signed by Indianapolis Colts (February 15, 1999). ... On suspended list for violating league substance abuse policy (December 20, 1999-January 17, 2001).

PRO STATISTICS: 1996—Intercepted one pass for one yard and recovered one fumble for 12 yards and a touchdown.

Year Team	G	GS	SACKS
1995—Carolina NFL	13	0	2.0
1996—Carolina NFL	16	0	3.0
1997—Carolina NFL	9	2	2.0
1998—Carolina NFL	Did not play.		
1999—Indianapolis NFL	9	8	1.5
2000—Indianapolis NFL	Did not play.		
Pro totals (4 years)	**47**	**10**	**8.5**

KINNEY, ERRON — TE — TITANS

PERSONAL: Born July 28, 1977, in Ashland, Va. ... 6-5/272. ... Full name: Erron Quincy Kinney.
HIGH SCHOOL: Patrick Henry (Ashland, Va.).
COLLEGE: Florida.
TRANSACTIONS/CAREER NOTES: Selected by Tennessee Titans in third round (68th pick overall) of 2000 NFL draft. ... Signed by Titans (July 17, 2000).
PRO STATISTICS: 2000—Fumbled once and recovered one fumble.
SINGLE GAME HIGHS (regular season): Receptions—5 (October 1, 2000, vs. New York Giants); yards—60 (October 1, 2000, vs. New York Giants); and touchdown receptions—1 (September 24, 2000, vs. Pittsburgh).

			RECEIVING			
Year Team	G	GS	No.	Yds.	Avg.	TD
2000—Tennessee NFL	16	9	19	197	10.4	1

KIRBY, CHARLES — FB — BUCCANEERS

PERSONAL: Born November 27, 1974, in South View, N.C. ... 6-1/249. ... Full name: Charles Edward Kirby Jr.
HIGH SCHOOL: South View (North Carolina).
COLLEGE: Virginia.
TRANSACTIONS/CAREER NOTES: Signed as non-drafted free agent by Indianapolis Colts (April 24, 1998). ... Released by Colts (September 5, 1999). ... Signed by Kansas City Chiefs (November 10, 1999). ... Released by Chiefs (August 21, 2000). ... Signed by Tampa Bay Buccaneers to practice squad (September 12, 2000). ... Activated (October 5, 2000).
PLAYING EXPERIENCE: Tampa Bay NFL, 2000. ... Games/Games started: 2000 (6/2).

KIRBY, TERRY — RB — RAIDERS

PERSONAL: Born January 20, 1970, in Hampton, Va. ... 6-1/213. ... Full name: Terry Gayle Kirby. ... Brother of Wayne Kirby, outfielder with three major league teams (1991-98); and cousin of Chris Slade, linebacker with New England Patriots (1993-2000).
HIGH SCHOOL: Tabb (Va.).
COLLEGE: Virginia (degree in psychology).
TRANSACTIONS/CAREER NOTES: Selected by Miami Dolphins in third round (78th pick overall) of 1993 NFL draft. ... Signed by Dolphins (July 19, 1993). ... On injured reserve with knee injury (September 26, 1994-remainder of season). ... Granted free agency (February 16, 1996). ... Traded by Dolphins to San Francisco 49ers for fourth-round pick (traded to Oakland) in 1997 draft (August 19, 1996). ... Released by 49ers (March 3, 1998). ... Re-signed by 49ers (September 23, 1998). ... Granted unconditional free agency (February 12, 1999). ... Signed by Cleveland Browns (March 9, 1999). ... Released by Browns (August 29, 2000). ... Signed by Oakland Raiders (November 21, 2000).
CHAMPIONSHIP GAME EXPERIENCE: Played in NFC championship game (1997 season). ... Played in AFC championship game (2000 season).
PRO STATISTICS: 1993—Recovered four fumbles. 1995—Completed only pass attempt for 31 yards and a touchdown. 1996—Attempted two passes with one completion for 24 yards and a touchdown and returned one punt for three yards. 1997—Recovered two fumbles. 1998—Completed only pass attempt for 28 yards and a touchdown. 1999—Completed only pass attempt for two yards and recovered two fumbles.
SINGLE GAME HIGHS (regular season): Attempts—22 (October 17, 1999, vs. Jacksonville); yards—105 (December 2, 1996, vs. Atlanta); and rushing touchdowns—2 (December 26, 1999, vs. Indianapolis).
STATISTICAL PLATEAUS: 100-yard rushing games: 1994 (1), 1996 (1). Total: 2. ... 100-yard receiving games: 1993 (2).

			RUSHING				RECEIVING				KICKOFF RETURNS				TOTALS			
Year Team	G	GS	Att.	Yds.	Avg.	TD	No.	Yds.	Avg.	TD	No.	Yds.	Avg.	TD	TD	2pt.	Pts.	Fum.
1993—Miami NFL	16	8	119	390	3.3	3	75	874	11.7	3	4	85	21.3	0	6	0	36	5
1994—Miami NFL	4	4	60	233	3.9	2	14	154	11.0	0	0	0	0.0	0	2	1	14	2
1995—Miami NFL	16	4	108	414	3.8	4	66	618	9.4	3	0	0	0.0	0	7	0	42	2
1996—San Francisco NFL	14	10	134	559	4.2	3	52	439	8.4	1	1	22	22.0	0	4	0	24	1
1997—San Francisco NFL	16	3	125	418	3.3	6	23	279	12.1	1	3	124	41.3	1	8	2	52	3
1998—San Francisco NFL	9	0	48	258	5.4	3	16	134	8.4	0	17	340	20.0	0	3	0	18	0
1999—Cleveland NFL	16	10	130	452	3.5	6	58	528	9.1	3	11	230	20.9	0	9	0	54	4
2000—Oakland NFL	2	0	11	51	4.6	0	3	19	6.3	0	0	0	0.0	0	0	0	0	0
Pro totals (8 years)	**93**	**39**	**735**	**2775**	**3.8**	**27**	**307**	**3045**	**9.9**	**11**	**36**	**801**	**22.3**	**1**	**39**	**3**	**240**	**17**

KIRKLAND, LEVON — LB — SEAHAWKS

PERSONAL: Born February 17, 1969, in Lamar, S.C. ... 6-1/270. ... Full name: Lorenzo Levon Kirkland. ... Name pronounced luh-VON.
HIGH SCHOOL: Lamar (S.C.).
COLLEGE: Clemson.
TRANSACTIONS/CAREER NOTES: Selected by Pittsburgh Steelers in second round (38th pick overall) of 1992 NFL draft. ... Signed by Steelers (July 25, 1992). ... Released by Steelers (March 8, 2001). ... Signed by Seattle Seahawks (April 5, 2001).
CHAMPIONSHIP GAME EXPERIENCE: Played in AFC championship game (1994, 1995 and 1997 seasons). ... Played in Super Bowl XXX (1995 season).

HONORS: Named linebacker on THE SPORTING NEWS college All-America first team (1991). ... Played in Pro Bowl (1996 and 1997 seasons). ... Named inside linebacker on THE SPORTING NEWS NFL All-Pro team (1997).

PRO STATISTICS: 1993—Recovered two fumbles for 24 yards and one touchdown. 1995—Recovered two fumbles. 1997—Recovered one fumble. 1999—Recovered two fumbles. 2000—Recovered one fumble.

				INTERCEPTIONS				SACKS
Year Team		G	GS	No.	Yds.	Avg.	TD	No.
1992—Pittsburgh NFL		16	0	0	0	0.0	0	0.0
1993—Pittsburgh NFL		16	13	0	0	0.0	0	1.0
1994—Pittsburgh NFL		16	15	2	0	0.0	0	3.0
1995—Pittsburgh NFL		16	16	0	0	0.0	0	1.0
1996—Pittsburgh NFL		16	16	4	12	3.0	0	4.0
1997—Pittsburgh NFL		16	16	2	14	7.0	0	5.0
1998—Pittsburgh NFL		16	16	1	1	1.0	0	2.5
1999—Pittsburgh NFL		16	16	1	23	23.0	0	2.0
2000—Pittsburgh NFL		16	16	1	1	1.0	0	0.0
Pro totals (9 years)		144	124	11	51	4.6	0	18.5

KIRSCHKE, TRAVIS DE LIONS

PERSONAL: Born September 6, 1974, in Fullerton, Calif. ... 6-3/287.
HIGH SCHOOL: Esperanza (Anaheim, Calif.).
COLLEGE: UCLA.
TRANSACTIONS/CAREER NOTES: Signed as non-drafted free agent by Detroit Lions (April 24, 1997). ... Inactive for three games (1998). ... On injured reserve with abdominal injury (September 24, 1998-remainder of season). ... Granted free agency (February 11, 2000). ... Re-signed by Lions (April 25, 2000).
PLAYING EXPERIENCE: Detroit NFL, 1997, 1999 and 2000. ... Games/Games started: 1997 (3/0), 1999 (15/7), 2000 (13/0). Total: 31/7.
PRO STATISTICS: 1999—Credited with two sacks and recovered one fumble. 2000—Credited with $1/2$ sack and recovered one fumble.

KITNA, JON QB BENGALS

PERSONAL: Born September 21, 1972, in Tacoma, Wash. ... 6-2/217.
HIGH SCHOOL: Lincoln (Tacoma, Wash.).
COLLEGE: Central Washington (degree in math education, 1995).
TRANSACTIONS/CAREER NOTES: Signed as non-drafted free agent by Seattle Seahawks (April 25, 1996) ... Released by Seahawks (August 19, 1996) ... Re-signed by Seahawks to practice squad (August 20, 1996). ... Assigned by Seahawks to Barcelona Dragons in 1997 World League enhancement allocation program (April 7, 1997). ... Granted free agency (February 11, 2000). ... Re-signed by Seahawks (March 15, 2000). ... Granted unconditional free agency (March 2, 2001). ... Signed by Cincinnati Bengals (March 8, 2001).
PRO STATISTICS: 1997—Fumbled once and recovered one fumble for minus two yards. 1998—Fumbled six times and recovered four fumbles for minus 10 yards. 1999—Fumbled 14 times and recovered six fumbles for minus nine yards. 2000—Led NFL with 17 fumbles and recovered nine fumbles for minus 19 yards.
SINGLE GAME HIGHS (regular season): Attempts—45 (January 2, 2000, vs. New York Jets); completions—26 (December 10, 2000, vs. Denver); yards—298 (December 10, 2000, vs. Denver); and touchdown passes—3 (December 10, 2000, vs. Denver).
MISCELLANEOUS: Regular-season record as starting NFL quarterback: 18-15 (.545). ... Postseason record as starting NFL quarterback: 0-1.

				PASSING							RUSHING				TOTALS		
Year Team	G	GS	Att.	Cmp.	Pct.	Yds.	TD	Int.	Avg.	Rat.	Att.	Yds.	Avg.	TD	TD	2pt.	Pts.
1997—Barcelona W.L.	10	...	317	171	53.9	2448	22	15	7.72	82.6	50	334	6.7	3	3	0	18
—Seattle NFL	3	1	45	31	68.9	371	1	2	8.24	82.7	10	9	0.9	1	1	0	6
1998—Seattle NFL	6	5	172	98	57.0	1177	7	8	6.84	72.3	20	67	3.4	1	1	0	6
1999—Seattle NFL	15	15	495	270	54.5	3346	23	16	6.76	77.7	35	56	1.6	0	0	0	0
2000—Seattle NFL	15	12	418	259	62.0	2658	18	19	6.36	75.6	48	127	2.6	1	1	0	6
W.L. totals (1 year)	10	...	317	171	53.9	2448	22	15	7.72	82.6	50	334	6.7	3	3	0	18
NFL totals (4 years)	39	33	1130	658	58.2	7552	49	45	6.68	76.3	113	259	2.3	3	3	0	18
Pro totals (5 years)	49	...	1447	829	57.3	10000	71	60	6.91	77.7	163	593	3.6	6	6	0	36

KLEINSASSER, JIM FB VIKINGS

PERSONAL: Born January 31, 1977, in Carrington, N.D. ... 6-3/274.
HIGH SCHOOL: Carrington (N.D.).
COLLEGE: North Dakota.
TRANSACTIONS/CAREER NOTES: Selected by Minnesota Vikings in second round (44th pick overall) of 1999 NFL draft. ... Signed by Vikings (August 1, 1999).
PLAYING EXPERIENCE: Minnesota NFL, 1999 and 2000. ... Games/Games started: 1999 (13/7), 2000 (14/8). Total: 27/15.
CHAMPIONSHIP GAME EXPERIENCE: Played in NFC championship game (2000 season).
PRO STATISTICS: 1999—Caught six passes for 13 yards, returned one kickoff for no yards and fumbled twice. 2000—Rushed 12 times for 43 yards and caught 10 passes for 98 yards.
SINGLE GAME HIGHS (regular season): Attempts—2 (November 6, 2000, vs. Green Bay); yards—9 (November 6, 2000, vs. Green Bay); and rushing touchdowns—0.

KLEMM, ADRIAN OT PATRIOTS

PERSONAL: Born May 21, 1977, in Los Angeles. ... 6-3/310. ... Full name: Adrian William Klemm.
HIGH SCHOOL: St. Monica (Santa Monica, Calif.).
COLLEGE: Hawaii.
TRANSACTIONS/CAREER NOTES: Selected by New England Patriots in second round (46th pick overall) of 2000 NFL draft. ... Signed by Patriots (July 12, 2000). ... On non-football injured list with knee injury (August 27-November 1, 2000).
PLAYING EXPERIENCE: New England NFL, 2000. ... Games/Games started: 2000 (5/4).

K

KLINE, ANDREW   G   RAMS

PERSONAL: Born October 5, 1976 ... 6-2/303. ... Full name: Andrew William Kline.
HIGH SCHOOL: Beverly Hills (Calif.).
COLLEGE: San Diego State.
TRANSACTIONS/CAREER NOTES: Selected by St. Louis Rams in seventh round (220th pick overall) of 2000 NFL draft. ... Signed by Rams (July 7, 2000). ... On injured reserve with concussion (August 22, 2000-entire season).

KNIGHT, SAMMY   S   SAINTS

PERSONAL: Born September 10, 1975, in Fontana, Calif. ... 6-0/205.
HIGH SCHOOL: Rubidoux (Riverside, Calif.).
COLLEGE: Southern California.
TRANSACTIONS/CAREER NOTES: Signed as non-drafted free agent by New Orleans Saints (April 25, 1997).
PRO STATISTICS: 1997—Recovered one fumble. 1998—Recovered two fumbles for three yards. 1999—Recovered one fumble. 2000—Credited with two sacks.

			INTERCEPTIONS		
Year Team	G	GS	No.	Yds.	Avg.	TD
1997—New Orleans NFL	16	12	5	75	15.0	0
1998—New Orleans NFL	14	13	6	171	28.5	2
1999—New Orleans NFL	16	16	1	0	0.0	0
2000—New Orleans NFL	16	16	5	68	13.6	‡2
Pro totals (4 years)	62	57	17	314	18.5	4

KNIGHT, TOM   CB   CARDINALS

PERSONAL: Born December 29, 1974, in Marlton, N.J. ... 6-0/196. ... Full name: Thomas Lorenzo Knight.
HIGH SCHOOL: Cherokee (Marlton, N.J.).
COLLEGE: Iowa.
TRANSACTIONS/CAREER NOTES: Selected by Arizona Cardinals in first round (ninth pick overall) of 1997 NFL draft. ... Signed by Cardinals (July 16, 1997).
PLAYING EXPERIENCE: Arizona NFL, 1997-2000. ... Games/Games Started: 1997 (15/14), 1998 (8/5), 1999 (16/11), 2000 (16/15). Total: 55/45.
PRO STATISTICS: 1998—Credited with one sack. 1999—Intercepted two passes for 16 yards and returned three punts for 38 yards. 2000—Credited with one sack.

KNORR, MICAH   P   COWBOYS

PERSONAL: Born January 9, 1975, in Orange, Calif. ... 6-2/193.
HIGH SCHOOL: Orange (Calif.).
COLLEGE: Utah State.
TRANSACTIONS/CAREER NOTES: Signed as non-drafted free agent by Dallas Cowboys (April 19, 2000).

				PUNTING		
Year Team	G	No.	Yds.	Avg.	Net avg.	In. 20	Blk.
2000—Dallas NFL	14	58	2485	42.8	35.7	12	0

KOCH, AARON   G/OT   JAGUARS

PERSONAL: Born February 1, 1978, in Portland, Ore. ... 6-3/300. ... Full name: Aaron Paul Koch.
HIGH SCHOOL: McNary (Kelzer, Ore.).
COLLEGE: Oregon State.
TRANSACTIONS/CAREER NOTES: Signed by Tennessee Titans as non-drafted free agent (April 18, 2000). ... Released by Titans (August 30, 2000). ... Re-signed by Titans to practice squad (September 5, 2000). ... Signed by Jacksonville Jaguars off Titans practice squad (September 27, 2000).
PLAYING EXPERIENCE: Jacksonville NFL, 2000. ... Games/Games started: 2000 (8/0).

KONRAD, ROB   FB   DOLPHINS

PERSONAL: Born November 12, 1976, in Rochester, N.Y. ... 6-3/255. ... Full name: Robert L. Konrad.
HIGH SCHOOL: St. John's (Andover, Mass.).
COLLEGE: Syracuse.
TRANSACTIONS/CAREER NOTES: Selected by Miami Dolphins in second round (43rd pick overall) of 1999 NFL draft. ... Signed by Dolphins (July 27, 1999).
PRO STATISTICS: 1999—Recovered one fumble.
SINGLE GAME HIGHS (regular season): Attempts—7 (September 3, 2000, vs. Seattle); yards—19 (September 3, 2000, vs. Seattle); and rushing touchdowns—0.

			RUSHING				RECEIVING				TOTALS			
Year Team	G	GS	Att.	Yds.	Avg.	TD	No.	Yds.	Avg.	TD	TD	2pt.	Pts.	Fum.
1999—Miami NFL	15	9	9	16	1.8	0	34	251	7.4	1	1	0	6	3
2000—Miami NFL	15	14	15	39	2.6	0	14	83	5.9	0	0	0	0	0
Pro totals (2 years)	30	23	24	55	2.3	0	48	334	7.0	1	1	0	6	3

KOONCE, GEORGE — LB

PERSONAL: Born October 15, 1968, in New Bern, N.C. ... 6-1/245. ... Full name: George Earl Koonce Jr.
HIGH SCHOOL: West Craven (Vanceboro, N.C.).
COLLEGE: Chowan College (N.C.), then East Carolina.
TRANSACTIONS/CAREER NOTES: Signed as non-drafted free agent by Atlanta Falcons (April 30, 1991). ... Released by Falcons (August 26, 1991). ... Selected by Ohio Glory in 13th round (143rd pick overall) of 1992 World League draft. ... Signed by Green Bay Packers (June 2, 1992). ... On injured reserve with shoulder injury (January 3, 1994-entire 1993 playoffs). ... Granted free agency (February 17, 1995). ... Re-signed by Packers (June 2, 1995). ... On injured reserve with knee injury (January 10, 1997-remainder of 1996 playoffs). ... On physically unable to perform list with knee injury (August 19-November 18, 1997). ... Granted unconditional free agency (February 12, 1999). ... Re-signed by Packers (February 18, 1999). ... Released by Packers (June 5, 2000). ... Signed by Seattle Seahawks (June 19, 2000). ... Granted unconditional free agency (March 2, 2001).
CHAMPIONSHIP GAME EXPERIENCE: Played in NFC championship game (1995 and 1997 seasons). ... Member of Packers for NFC championship game (1996); inactive. ... Member of Super Bowl championship team (1996 season); inactive. ... Played in Super Bowl XXXII (1997 season).
PRO STATISTICS: W.L.: 1992—Recovered two fumbles for 35 yards. NFL: 1992—Recovered one fumble. 1993—Recovered one fumble. 1994—Recovered two fumbles. 1996—Recovered one fumble. 1998—Recovered one fumble for four yards. 2000—Recovered one fumble.

| | | | INTERCEPTIONS | | | | SACKS |
Year Team	G	GS	No.	Yds.	Avg.	TD	No.
1992—Ohio W.L.	10	9	0	0	0.0	0	2.5
—Green Bay NFL	16	10	0	0	0.0	0	1.5
1993—Green Bay NFL	15	15	0	0	0.0	0	3.0
1994—Green Bay NFL	16	16	0	0	0.0	0	1.0
1995—Green Bay NFL	16	16	1	12	12.0	0	1.0
1996—Green Bay NFL	16	16	3	84	28.0	1	0.0
1997—Green Bay NFL	4	0	0	0	0.0	0	0.0
1998—Green Bay NFL	14	14	0	0	0.0	0	1.0
1999—Green Bay NFL	15	15	0	0	0.0	0	0.0
2000—Seattle NFL	16	16	1	27	27.0	1	1.5
W.L. totals (1 year)	10	9	0	0	0.0	0	2.5
NFL totals (9 years)	128	118	5	123	24.6	2	9.0
Pro totals (10 years)	138	127	5	123	24.6	2	11.5

KOWALKOWSKI, SCOTT — LB — LIONS

PERSONAL: Born August 23, 1968, in Farmington Hills, Mich. ... 6-2/220. ... Full name: Scott Thomas Kowalkowski. ... Son of Bob Kowalkowski, guard with Detroit Lions (1966-76) and Green Bay Packers (1977). ... Name pronounced ko-wal-KOW-ski.
HIGH SCHOOL: St. Mary's Prep (Orchard Lake, Mich.).
COLLEGE: Notre Dame (degree in American studies).
TRANSACTIONS/CAREER NOTES: Selected by Philadelphia Eagles in eighth round (217th pick overall) of 1991 NFL draft. ... Signed by Eagles (July 10, 1991). ... On injured reserve with ankle injury (August 30-November 23, 1993). ... Released by Eagles (November 23, 1993). ... Signed by Detroit Lions (February 4, 1994). ... Granted unconditional free agency (February 17, 1995). ... Re-signed by Lions (March 24, 1995). ... Granted unconditional free agency (February 16, 1996). ... Re-signed by Lions (February 29,1996). ... Granted unconditional free agency (February 14, 1997). ... Re-signed by Lions (March 18, 1997). ... Granted unconditional free agency (February 11, 2000). ... Re-signed by Lions (April 26, 2000).
PLAYING EXPERIENCE: Philadelphia NFL, 1991 and 1992; Detroit NFL, 1994-2000. ... Games/Games started: 1991 (16/0), 1992 (16/0), 1994 (16/0), 1995 (16/0), 1996 (16/1), 1997 (16/0), 1998 (15/0), 1999 (16/3), 2000 (16/2). Total: 143/6.
PRO STATISTICS: 1991—Recovered one fumble. 1996—Recovered one fumble. 1998—Recovered one fumble. 1999—Intercepted one pass for 29 yards and credited with one sack. 2000—Recovered one fumble for two yards.

KOZLOWSKI, BRIAN — TE — FALCONS

PERSONAL: Born October 4, 1970, in Rochester, N.Y. ... 6-3/250. ... Full name: Brian Scott Kozlowski.
HIGH SCHOOL: Webster (N.Y.).
COLLEGE: Connecticut.
TRANSACTIONS/CAREER NOTES: Signed as non-drafted free agent by New York Giants (May 1, 1993). ... Released by Giants (August 16, 1993). ... Re-signed by Giants to practice squad (December 8, 1993). ... Granted unconditional free agency (February 14, 1997). ... Signed by Atlanta Falcons (March 21, 1997). ... Granted unconditional free agency (February 13, 1998). ... Re-signed by Falcons (March 4, 1998). ... Granted unconditional free agency (March 2, 2001). ... Re-signed by Falcons (April 5, 2001).
CHAMPIONSHIP GAME EXPERIENCE: Played in NFC championship game (1998 season). ... Played in Super Bowl XXXIII (1998 season).
PRO STATISTICS: 1995—Recovered one fumble. 2000—Recovered two fumbles.
SINGLE GAME HIGHS (regular season): Receptions—3 (October 8, 2000, vs. New York Giants); yards—49 (November 7, 1999, vs. Jacksonville); and touchdown receptions—1 (December 24, 2000, vs. Kansas City).

| | | | RECEIVING | | | | KICKOFF RETURNS | | | | TOTALS | | | |
Year Team	G	GS	No.	Yds.	Avg.	TD	No.	Yds.	Avg.	TD	TD	2pt.	Pts.	Fum.
1993—New York Giants NFL								Did not play.						
1994—New York Giants NFL	16	3	1	5	5.0	0	2	21	10.5	0	0	0	0	0
1995—New York Giants NFL	16	0	2	17	8.5	0	5	75	15.0	0	0	0	0	1
1996—New York Giants NFL	5	0	1	4	4.0	1	1	16	16.0	0	1	0	6	0
1997—Atlanta NFL	16	5	7	99	14.1	1	2	49	24.5	0	1	0	6	0
1998—Atlanta NFL	16	4	10	103	10.3	1	1	12	12.0	0	1	0	6	0
1999—Atlanta NFL	16	3	11	122	11.1	2	2	19	9.5	0	2	0	12	1
2000—Atlanta NFL	16	2	15	151	10.1	2	7	77	11.0	0	2	0	12	0
Pro totals (7 years)	101	17	47	501	10.7	7	20	269	13.5	0	7	0	42	2

KREIDER, DAN   FB   STEELERS

PERSONAL: Born March 11, 1977, in Lancaster, Pa. ... 5-11/242.
HIGH SCHOOL: Manheim Central (Pa.).
COLLEGE: New Hampshire.
TRANSACTIONS/CAREER NOTES: Signed as non-drafted free agent by Pittsburgh Steelers (April 21, 2000).
PLAYING EXPERIENCE: Pittsburgh NFL, 2000. ... Games/Games started: 2000 (10/7).
PRO STATISTICS: 2000—Rushed two times for 24 yards, caught five passes for 42 yards and returned one kickoff for no yards.
SINGLE GAME HIGHS (regular season): Attempts—2 (December 3, 2000, vs. Oakland); yards—24 (December 3, 2000, vs. Oakland); and rushing touchdowns—0.

KREUTZ, OLIN   C   BEARS

PERSONAL: Born June 9, 1977, in Honolulu. ... 6-2/285.
HIGH SCHOOL: St. Louis (Honolulu).
COLLEGE: Washington.
TRANSACTIONS/CAREER NOTES: Selected after junior season by Chicago Bears in third round (64th pick overall) of 1998 NFL draft. ... Signed by Bears (July 20, 1998). ... On injured reserve with knee injury (November 21, 2000-remainder of season). ... Granted free agency (March 2, 2001).
PLAYING EXPERIENCE: Chicago NFL, 1998-2000. ... Games/Games started: 1998 (9/0), 1999 (16/16), 2000 (7/7). Total: 32/23.
HONORS: Named center on THE SPORTING NEWS college All-America first team (1997).
PRO STATISTICS: 1999—Fumbled once and recovered two fumbles for minus 17 yards.

KRIEWALDT, CLINT   LB   LIONS

PERSONAL: Born March 17, 1976, in Shiocton, Wis. ... 6-1/236.
HIGH SCHOOL: Shiocton (Wis.).
COLLEGE: Wisconsin-Stevens Point.
TRANSACTIONS/CAREER NOTES: Selected by Detroit Lions in sixth round (177th pick overall) of 1999 NFL draft. ... Signed by Lions (July 22, 1999).
PLAYING EXPERIENCE: Detroit NFL, 1999 and 2000. ... Games/Games started: 1999 (12/0), 2000 (13/1). Total: 25/1.
PRO STATISTICS: 1999—Intercepted one pass for two yards. 2000—Recovered one fumble.

KUEHL, RYAN   DT   BROWNS

PERSONAL: Born January 18, 1972, in Washington, D.C. ... 6-5/290. ... Full name: Ryan Philip Kuehl.
HIGH SCHOOL: Walt Whitman (Bethesda, Md.).
COLLEGE: Virginia (degree in marketing, 1994).
TRANSACTIONS/CAREER NOTES: Signed as non-drafted free agent by San Francisco 49ers (April 26, 1995). ... Released by 49ers (August 19, 1995). ... Re-signed by Redskins to practice squad (August 26, 1995). ... Signed by Washington Redskins (February 16, 1996). ... Released by Redskins (August 25, 1996). ... Re-signed by Redskins to practice squad (August 26, 1996). ... Activated (October 19, 1996). ... Released by Redskins (November 6, 1996). ... Re-signed by Redskins to practice squad (November 7, 1996). ... Activated (November 11, 1996). ... Released by Redskins (August 23, 1997). ... Re-signed by Redskins (September 9, 1997). ... Released by Redskins (August 30, 1998). ... Signed by Cleveland Browns (February 11, 1999).
PLAYING EXPERIENCE: Washington NFL, 1996 and 1997; Cleveland NFL, 1999 and 2000. ... Games/Games started: 1996 (2/0), 1997 (12/5), 1999 (16/0), 2000 (16/0). Total: 46/5.

KYLE, JASON   LB   PANTHERS

PERSONAL: Born May 12, 1972, in Tempe, Ariz. ... 6-3/242. ... Full name: Jason C. Kyle.
HIGH SCHOOL: McClintock (Tempe, Ariz.).
COLLEGE: Arizona State.
TRANSACTIONS/CAREER NOTES: Selected by Seattle Seahawks in fourth round (126th pick overall) of 1995 NFL draft. ... Signed by Seahawks (July 16, 1995). ... On injured reserve with shoulder injury (August 18, 1997-entire season). ... Granted free agency (February 13, 1998). ... Re-signed by Seahawks (April 16, 1998). ... Selected by Cleveland Browns from Seahawks in NFL expansion draft (February 9, 1999). ... On physically unable to perform list with knee injury (August 26, 1999-entire season). ... Released by Browns (August 27, 2000). ... Signed by St. Louis Rams (October 5, 2000). ... Released by Rams (October 16, 2000). ... Re-signed by Rams (October 24, 2000). ... Released by Rams (October 27, 2000). ... Signed by San Francisco 49ers (October 30, 2000). ... Granted unconditional free agency (March 2, 2001). ... Signed by Carolina Panthers (March 5, 2001).
PLAYING EXPERIENCE: Seattle NFL, 1995, 1996 and 1998; San Francisco NFL, 2000. ... Games/Games started: 1995 (16/0), 1996 (16/0), 1998 (16/0), 2000 (2/0). Total: 50/0.

LaBOUNTY, MATT   DT   SEAHAWKS

PERSONAL: Born January 3, 1969, in San Francisco. ... 6-4/275. ... Full name: Matthew James LaBounty.
HIGH SCHOOL: San Marin (Novato, Calif.).
COLLEGE: Oregon.
TRANSACTIONS/CAREER NOTES: Selected by San Francisco 49ers in 12th round (327th pick overall) of 1992 NFL draft. ... Signed by 49ers (July 13, 1992). ... Released by 49ers (August 31, 1992). ... Re-signed by 49ers to practice squad (September 1, 1992). ... Released by 49ers (October 17, 1993). ... Re-signed by 49ers to practice squad (October 20, 1993). ... Activated (December 2, 1993). ... Claimed on waivers by Green Bay Packers (December 8, 1993). ... On injured reserve with back injury (August 23, 1994-entire season). ... Traded by Packers to Seattle Seahawks for S Eugene Robinson (June 27, 1996). ... Granted unconditional free agency (February 13, 1998). ... Re-signed by Seahawks (February 11, 1998).
CHAMPIONSHIP GAME EXPERIENCE: Played in NFC championship game (1995 season).
PRO STATISTICS: 1998—Fumbled once and recovered one fumble for 13 yards.

Year Team	G	GS	SACKS
1992—San Francisco NFL	Did not play.		
1993—San Francisco NFL	6	0	0.0
1994—Green Bay NFL	Did not play.		
1995—Green Bay NFL	14	2	3.0
1996—Seattle NFL	3	0	0.0
1997—Seattle NFL	15	6	3.0
1998—Seattle NFL	16	1	6.0
1999—Seattle NFL	16	1	2.0
2000—Seattle NFL	12	2	0.5
Pro totals (7 years)	82	12	14.5

LACINA, CORBIN   G

PERSONAL: Born November 2, 1970, in Mankato, Minn. ... 6-4/302.
HIGH SCHOOL: Cretin-Derham Hall (St. Paul, Minn.).
COLLEGE: Augustana (S.D.).
TRANSACTIONS/CAREER NOTES: Selected by Buffalo Bills in sixth round (167th pick overall) of 1993 NFL draft. ... Signed by Bills (July 12, 1993). ... Released by Bills (August 30, 1993). ... Re-signed by Bills to practice squad (September 1, 1993). ... Activated (December 30, 1993); did not play. ... On injured reserve with foot injury (December 22, 1994-remainder of season). ... On injured reserve with groin injury (November 30, 1996-remainder of season). ... Granted free agency (February 14, 1997). ... Re-signed by Bills (June 12, 1997). ... Granted unconditional free agency (February 13, 1998). ... Signed by Carolina Panthers (February 26, 1998). ... Released by Panthers (June 16, 1999). ... Signed by Minnesota Vikings (June 18, 1999). ... Granted unconditional free agency (March 2, 2001).
PLAYING EXPERIENCE: Buffalo NFL, 1994-1997; Carolina NFL, 1998; Minnesota NFL, 1999 and 2000. ... Games/Games started: 1994 (11/10), 1995 (16/3), 1996 (12/2), 1997 (16/13), 1998 (10/10), 1999 (14/0), 2000 (15/15). Total: 94/53.
CHAMPIONSHIP GAME EXPERIENCE: Member of Bills for AFC championship game (1993 season); inactive. ... Member of Bills for Super Bowl XXVIII (1993 season); inactive. ... Played in NFC championship game (2000 season).
PRO STATISTICS: 1997—Recovered one fumble. 1998—Recovered one fumble.

LaFLEUR, DAVID   TE   COWBOYS

PERSONAL: Born January 29, 1974, in Lake Charles, La. ... 6-7/272. ... Full name: David Alan LaFleur.
HIGH SCHOOL: Westlake (La.).
COLLEGE: Louisiana State.
TRANSACTIONS/CAREER NOTES: Selected by Dallas Cowboys in first round (22nd pick overall) of 1997 NFL draft. ... Signed by Cowboys (July 17, 1997).
PRO STATISTICS: 1998—Returned one kickoff for 12 yards. 1999—Recovered one fumble. 2000—Returned two kickoffs for 21 yards.
SINGLE GAME HIGHS (regular season): Receptions—6 (November 23, 2000, vs. Minnesota); yards—45 (November 23, 2000, vs. Minnesota); and touchdown receptions—2 (September 12, 1999, vs. Washington).

Year Team	G	GS	RECEIVING No.	Yds.	Avg.	TD	TOTALS TD	2pt.	Pts.	Fum.
1997—Dallas NFL	16	5	18	122	6.8	2	2	0	12	1
1998—Dallas NFL	13	13	20	176	8.8	2	2	0	12	1
1999—Dallas NFL	16	16	35	322	9.2	7	7	0	42	0
2000—Dallas NFL	15	10	12	109	9.1	1	1	0	6	0
Pro totals (4 years)	60	44	85	729	8.6	12	12	0	72	2

LAKE, CARNELL   S   JAGUARS

PERSONAL: Born July 15, 1967, in Salt Lake City. ... 6-1/213. ... Full name: Carnell Augustino Lake.
HIGH SCHOOL: Culver City (Calif.).
COLLEGE: UCLA (degree in political science, 1993).
TRANSACTIONS/CAREER NOTES: Selected by Pittsburgh Steelers in second round (34th pick overall) of 1989 NFL draft. ... Signed by Steelers (July 23, 1989). ... Granted free agency (February 1, 1992). ... Re-signed by Steelers (August 21, 1992). ... Granted roster exemption (August 21-28, 1992). ... Designated by Steelers as franchise player (February 15, 1995). ... Granted unconditional free agency (February 12, 1999). ... Signed by Jacksonville Jaguars (February 13, 1999). ... On injured reserve with foot injury (August 18, 2000-entire season).
CHAMPIONSHIP GAME EXPERIENCE: Played in AFC championship game (1994, 1995, 1997 and 1999 seasons). ... Played in Super Bowl XXX (1995 season).
HONORS: Named linebacker on THE SPORTING NEWS college All-America second team (1987). ... Played in Pro Bowl (1994-1997 and 1999 seasons). ... Named strong safety on THE SPORTING NEWS NFL All-Pro team (1997).
POST SEASON RECORDS: Shares NFL postseason single-game record for most safeties—1 (January 7, 1995, vs. Cleveland).
PRO STATISTICS: 1989—Recovered six fumbles for two yards. 1990—Recovered one fumble. 1992—Recovered one fumble for 12 yards. 1993—Recovered two fumbles. 1994—Recovered one fumble. 1995—Recovered one fumble. 1996—Recovered two fumbles for 85 yards and one touchdown. 1997—Recovered one fumble for 38 yards and a touchdown. 1998—Recovered one fumble for minus two yards.

Year Team	G	GS	INTERCEPTIONS No.	Yds.	Avg.	TD	SACKS No.
1989—Pittsburgh NFL	15	15	1	0	0.0	0	1.0
1990—Pittsburgh NFL	16	16	1	0	0.0	0	1.0
1991—Pittsburgh NFL	16	16	0	0	0.0	0	1.0
1992—Pittsburgh NFL	16	16	0	0	0.0	0	2.0
1993—Pittsburgh NFL	14	14	4	31	7.8	0	5.0
1994—Pittsburgh NFL	16	16	1	2	2.0	0	1.0
1995—Pittsburgh NFL	16	16	1	32	32.0	▲1	1.5
1996—Pittsburgh NFL	13	13	1	47	47.0	1	2.0
1997—Pittsburgh NFL	16	16	3	16	5.3	0	6.0
1998—Pittsburgh NFL	16	16	4	33	8.3	1	1.0
1999—Jacksonville NFL	16	16	0	0	0.0	0	3.5
2000—Jacksonville NFL			Did not play.				
Pro totals (11 years)	170	170	16	161	10.1	3	25.0

LAMONTAGNE, NOEL — OL — BROWNS

PERSONAL: Born March 9, 1977, in Bethlehem, Pa. ... 6-4/301. ... Full name: Noel Michael Lamontagne.
HIGH SCHOOL: Southern Lehigh (Bethlehem, Pa.).
COLLEGE: Virginia.
TRANSACTIONS/CAREER NOTES: Signed as non-drafted free agent by Cleveland Browns (April 17, 2000). ... On non-football injury list with knee injury (August 27-November 1, 2000).
PLAYING EXPERIENCE: Cleveland NFL, 2000. ... Games/Games started: 2000 (2/0).

LANDETA, SEAN — P — EAGLES

PERSONAL: Born January 6, 1962, in Baltimore. ... 6-0/215. ... Full name: Sean Edward Landeta.
HIGH SCHOOL: Loch Raven (Baltimore).
COLLEGE: Towson State.
TRANSACTIONS/CAREER NOTES: Selected by Philadelphia Stars in 14th round (161st pick overall) of 1983 USFL draft. ... Signed by Stars (January 24, 1983). ... Stars franchise moved to Baltimore (November 1, 1984). ... Granted free agency (August 1, 1985). ... Signed by New York Giants (August 5, 1985). ... On injured reserve with back injury (September 7, 1988-remainder of season). ... Granted free agency (February 1, 1990). ... Re-signed by Giants (July 23, 1990). ... On injured reserve with knee injury (November 25, 1992-remainder of season). ... Granted unconditional free agency (March 1, 1993). ... Re-signed by Giants (March 18, 1993). ... Released by Giants (November 9, 1993). ... Signed by Los Angeles Rams (November 12, 1993). ... Granted unconditional free agency (February 17, 1994). ... Re-signed by Rams (May 10, 1994). ... Granted unconditional free agency (February 17, 1995). ... Rams franchise moved to St. Louis (April 12, 1995). ... Re-signed by Rams (May 8, 1995). ... Released by Rams (March 18, 1997). ... Signed by Tampa Bay Buccaneers (October 9, 1997). ... Granted unconditional free agency (February 13, 1998). ... Signed by Green Bay Packers (February 26, 1998). ... Granted unconditional free agency (February 12, 1999). ... Signed by Philadelphia Eagles (February 26, 1999).
CHAMPIONSHIP GAME EXPERIENCE: Played in USFL championship game (1983-1985 seasons). ... Played in NFC championship game (1986 and 1990 seasons). ... Member of Super Bowl championship team (1986 and 1990 seasons).
HONORS: Named punter on THE SPORTING NEWS USFL All-Star team (1983 and 1984). ... Named punter on THE SPORTING NEWS NFL All-Pro team (1986, 1989 and 1990). ... Played in Pro Bowl (1986 and 1990 seasons).
PRO STATISTICS: USFL: 1983—Rushed once for minus five yards, fumbled once and recovered one fumble. 1984—Recovered one fumble. NFL: 1985—Attempted one pass without a completion. 1996—Rushed twice for no yards, fumbled once and recovered one fumble for minus 11 yards. 1999—Fumbled once and recovered one fumble.

				PUNTING			
Year Team	G	No.	Yds.	Avg.	Net avg.	In. 20	Blk.
1983—Philadelphia USFL	18	86	3601	41.9	36.5	31	0
1984—Philadelphia USFL	18	53	2171	41.0	*38.1	18	0
1985—Baltimore USFL	18	65	2718	41.8	33.2	18	0
—New York Giants NFL	16	81	3472	42.9	36.3	20	0
1986—New York Giants NFL	16	79	3539	‡44.8	‡37.1	24	0
1987—New York Giants NFL	12	65	2773	42.7	31.0	13	1
1988—New York Giants NFL	1	6	222	37.0	35.7	1	0
1989—New York Giants NFL	16	70	3019	43.1	*37.7	19	0
1990—New York Giants NFL	16	75	3306	‡44.1	37.2	†24	0
1991—New York Giants NFL	15	64	2768	43.3	35.2	16	0
1992—New York Giants NFL	11	53	2317	43.7	31.5	13	*2
1993—New York Giants NFL	8	33	1390	42.1	35.0	11	1
—Los Angeles Rams NFL	8	42	1825	43.5	32.8	7	0
1994—Los Angeles Rams NFL	16	78	3494	*44.8	34.2	23	0
1995—St. Louis NFL	16	83	3679	‡44.3	36.7	23	0
1996—St. Louis NFL	16	78	3491	44.8	36.1	23	0
1997—Tampa Bay NFL	10	54	2274	42.1	34.1	15	1
1998—Green Bay NFL	16	65	2788	42.9	37.1	30	0
1999—Philadelphia NFL	16	*107	‡4524	42.3	35.1	21	1
2000—Philadelphia NFL	16	86	3635	42.3	36.0	23	0
USFL totals (3 years)	54	204	8490	41.6	35.9	67	0
NFL totals (16 years)	225	1119	48516	43.4	35.4	306	6
Pro totals (19 years)	279	1323	57006	43.1	35.5	373	6

LANE, MAX — G/OT

PERSONAL: Born February 22, 1971, in Norborne, Mo. ... 6-6/320. ... Full name: Max Aaron Lane.
HIGH SCHOOL: Norborne (Mo.), then Naval Academy Preparatory (Newport, R.I.).
COLLEGE: Navy.
TRANSACTIONS/CAREER NOTES: Selected by New England Patriots in sixth round (168th pick overall) of 1994 NFL draft. ... Signed by Patriots (June 1, 1994). ... Granted free agency (February 14, 1997). ... Re-signed by Patriots (June 20, 1997). ... On injured reserve with broken leg (November 13, 2000-remainder of season). ... Released by Patriots (May 4, 2001).
PLAYING EXPERIENCE: New England NFL, 1994-2000. ... Games/Games started: 1994 (14/0), 1995 (16/16), 1996 (16/16), 1997 (16/16), 1998 (16/11), 1999 (16/6), 2000 (6/5). Total: 100/70.
CHAMPIONSHIP GAME EXPERIENCE: Played in AFC championship game (1996 season). ... Played in Super Bowl XXXI (1996 season).
PRO STATISTICS: 1995—Recovered one fumble. 1996—Recovered three fumbles. 1997—Recovered one fumble.

LANG, KENARD — DE — REDSKINS

PERSONAL: Born January 31, 1975, in Orlando. ... 6-4/277. ... Full name: Kenard Dushun Lang.
HIGH SCHOOL: Maynard Evans (Orlando).
COLLEGE: Miami (Fla.).

TRANSACTIONS/CAREER NOTES: Selected by Washington Redskins in first round (17th pick overall) of 1997 NFL draft. ... Signed by Redskins (July 28, 1997).
PRO STATISTICS: 1997—Recovered two fumbles. 1999—Recovered one fumble. 2000—Recovered one fumble.

Year Team	G	GS	SACKS
1997—Washington NFL	12	11	1.5
1998—Washington NFL	16	16	7.0
1999—Washington NFL	16	9	6.0
2000—Washington NFL	16	0	3.0
Pro totals (4 years)	60	36	17.5

LANGFORD, JEVON　　　　DE　　　　BENGALS

PERSONAL: Born February 16, 1974, in Washington, D.C. ... 6-3/290.
HIGH SCHOOL: Bishop Carroll (Washington, D.C.).
COLLEGE: Oklahoma State.
TRANSACTIONS/CAREER NOTES: Selected after junior season by Cincinnati Bengals in fourth round (108th pick overall) of 1996 NFL draft. ... Signed by Bengals (August 5, 1996). ... Granted free agency (February 12, 1999). ... Re-signed by Bengals (May 25, 1999). ... Granted unconditional free agency (February 11, 2000). ... Re-signed by Bengals (May 5, 2000).
PRO STATISTICS: 1996—Recovered one fumble.

Year Team	G	GS	SACKS
1996—Cincinnati NFL	12	3	2.0
1997—Cincinnati NFL	15	0	1.0
1998—Cincinnati NFL	14	1	0.5
1999—Cincinnati NFL	12	7	0.0
2000—Cincinnati NFL	11	3	0.0
Pro totals (5 years)	64	14	3.5

LANGHAM, ANTONIO　　　　CB

PERSONAL: Born July 31, 1972, in Town Creek, Ala. ... 6-0/184. ... Full name: Collie Antonio Langham.
HIGH SCHOOL: Hazelwood (Town Creek, Ala.).
COLLEGE: Alabama.
TRANSACTIONS/CAREER NOTES: Selected by Cleveland Browns in first round (ninth pick overall) of 1994 NFL draft. ... Signed by Browns (August 4, 1994). ... Browns franchise moved to Baltimore and renamed Ravens for 1996 season (March 11, 1996). ... Granted unconditional free agency (February 13, 1998). ... Signed by San Francisco 49ers (March 9, 1998). ... Selected by Browns from 49ers in NFL expansion draft (February 9, 1999). ... Released by Browns (February 9, 2000). ... Signed by New England Patriots (April 25, 2000). ... Released by Patriots (April 26, 2001).
HONORS: Jim Thorpe Award winner (1993). ... Named defensive back on THE SPORTING NEWS college All-America first team (1993).
PRO STATISTICS: 1994—Fumbled once. 1997—Credited with one sack.

Year Team	G	GS	INTERCEPTIONS No.	Yds.	Avg.	TD
1994—Cleveland NFL	16	16	2	2	1.0	0
1995—Cleveland NFL	16	16	2	29	14.5	0
1996—Baltimore NFL	15	14	5	59	11.8	0
1997—Baltimore NFL	16	15	3	40	13.3	1
1998—San Francisco NFL	11	6	1	0	0.0	0
1999—Cleveland NFL	13	2	0	0	0.0	0
2000—New England NFL	15	7	1	24	24.0	0
Pro totals (7 years)	102	76	14	154	11.0	1

LARRIMORE, KAREEM　　　　CB　　　　COWBOYS

PERSONAL: Born April 21, 1976, in Los Angeles. ... 5-11/190. ... Full name: Kareem Maktrel Larrimore.
HIGH SCHOOL: Alain Locke Senior (Los Angeles).
JUNIOR COLLEGE: Cerritos College (Calif.).
COLLEGE: West Texas A&M.
TRANSACTIONS/CAREER NOTES: Selected by Dallas Cowboys in fourth round (109th pick overall) of 2000 NFL draft. ... Signed by Cowboys (July 14, 2000).
PLAYING EXPERIENCE: Dallas NFL, 2000. ... Games/Games started: 2000 (15/4).

LARSEN, LEIF　　　　DT　　　　BILLS

PERSONAL: Born April 3, 1975, in Oslo, Norway. ... 6-4/295. ... Name pronounced LIFE.
HIGH SCHOOL: St. Halluard U.G.S. (Tofte, Norway).
COLLEGE: Texas-El Paso.
TRANSACTIONS/CAREER NOTES: Selected by Buffalo Bills in sixth round (194th pick overall) of 2000 NFL draft. ... Signed by Bills (June 20, 2000).

Year Team	G	GS	SACKS
2000—Buffalo NFL	6	0	1.0

L

LASSITER, KWAMIE S CARDINALS

PERSONAL: Born December 3, 1969, in Hampton, Va. ... 6-0/203.
HIGH SCHOOL: Menchville (Newport News, Va.).
JUNIOR COLLEGE: Butler County Community College (Kan.).
COLLEGE: Kansas.
TRANSACTIONS/CAREER NOTES: Signed as non-drafted free agent by Arizona Cardinals (April 28, 1995). ... On injured reserve with ankle injury (October 5, 1995-remainder of season). ... Granted free agency (February 13, 1998). ... Re-signed by Cardinals (May 21, 1998). ... Granted unconditional free agency (February 12, 1999). ... Re-signed by Cardinals (March 9, 1999).
PRO STATISTICS: 1995—Rushed once for one yard. 1997—Credited with three sacks. 1998—Recovered one fumble. 1999—Returned one kickoff for 13 yards and recovered two fumbles. 2000—Recovered one fumble.

				INTERCEPTIONS		
Year Team	G	GS	No.	Yds.	Avg.	TD
1995—Arizona NFL	5	0	0	0	0.0	0
1996—Arizona NFL	14	0	1	20	20.0	0
1997—Arizona NFL	16	1	1	10	10.0	0
1998—Arizona NFL	16	6	‡8	80	10.0	0
1999—Arizona NFL	16	16	2	110	55.0	1
2000—Arizona NFL	16	16	1	11	11.0	0
Pro totals (6 years)	83	39	13	231	17.8	1

LAW, TY CB PATRIOTS

PERSONAL: Born February 10, 1974, in Aliquippa, Pa. ... 5-11/200. ... Full name: Tajuan Law.
HIGH SCHOOL: Aliquippa (Pa.).
COLLEGE: Michigan.
TRANSACTIONS/CAREER NOTES: Selected after junior season by New England Patriots in first round (23rd pick overall) of 1995 NFL draft. ... Signed by Patriots (July 20, 1995). ... On injured reserve with hand injury (December 29, 1999-remainder of season).
CHAMPIONSHIP GAME EXPERIENCE: Played in AFC championship game (1996 season). ... Played in Super Bowl XXXI (1996 season).
HONORS: Named cornerback on THE SPORTING NEWS NFL All-Pro team (1998). ... Played in Pro Bowl (1998 season). ... Named co-Oustanding Player of Pro Bowl (1998 season).
PRO STATISTICS: 1995—Credited with one sack. 1997—Credited with 1/2 sack, fumbled once and recovered one fumble. 1998—Recovered one fumble for 17 yards. 1999—Credited with 1/2 sack, fumbled once and recovered one fumble.

				INTERCEPTIONS		
Year Team	G	GS	No.	Yds.	Avg.	TD
1995—New England NFL	14	7	3	47	15.7	0
1996—New England NFL	13	12	3	45	15.0	1
1997—New England NFL	16	16	3	70	23.3	0
1998—New England NFL	16	16	*9	133	14.8	1
1999—New England NFL	13	13	2	20	10.0	1
2000—New England NFL	15	15	2	32	16.0	0
Pro totals (6 years)	87	79	22	347	15.8	3

LEACH, MIKE TE TITANS

PERSONAL: Born October 18, 1976, in Lake Hopatcong, N.J. ... 6-4/238.
HIGH SCHOOL: Jefferson Township (N.J.).
COLLEGE: Boston University, then William & Mary.
TRANSACTIONS/CAREER NOTES: Signed as non-drafted free agent by Tennessee Titans (April 20, 2000).
PLAYING EXPERIENCE: Tennessee NFL, 2000. ... Games/Games started: 2000 (15/0).
PRO STATISTICS: 2000—Returned one kickoff for 10 yards.

LEAF, RYAN QB BUCCANEERS

PERSONAL: Born May 15, 1976, in Great Falls, Mont. ... 6-5/235. ... Full name: Ryan David Leaf.
HIGH SCHOOL: Russell (Great Falls, Mont.).
COLLEGE: Washington State.
TRANSACTIONS/CAREER NOTES: Selected after junior season by San Diego Chargers in first round (second pick overall) of 1998 NFL draft. ... Signed by Chargers (July 28, 1998). ... Inactive for 15 games (1999). ... On injured reserve with shoulder injury (December 30, 1999-remainder of season). ... Claimed on waivers by Tampa Bay Buccaneers (March 2, 2001).
HONORS: Named quarterback on THE SPORTING NEWS college All-America first team (1997).
PRO STATISTICS: 1998—Fumbled eight times and recovered two fumbles for minus 18 yards. 2000—Fumbled 12 times and recovered four fumbles for minus 18 yards.
SINGLE GAME HIGHS (regular season): Attempts—52 (October 25, 1998, vs. Seattle); completions—25 (October 25, 1998, vs. Seattle); yards—311 (November 19, 2000, vs. Denver); and touchdown passes—3 (November 19, 2000, vs. Denver).
STATISTICAL PLATEAUS: 300-yard passing games: 2000 (1).
MISCELLANEOUS: Regular-season record as starting NFL quarterback: 4-14 (.222).

			PASSING							RUSHING				TOTALS	
Year Team	G	GS	Att.	Cmp.	Pct.	Yds.	TD	Int.	Avg.	Rat.	Att.	Yds.	Avg.	TD	TD	2pt.	Pts.
1998—San Diego NFL	10	9	245	111	45.3	1289	2	15	5.26	39.0	27	80	3.0	0	0	0	0
1999—San Diego NFL									Did not play.								
2000—San Diego NFL	11	9	322	161	50.0	1883	11	18	5.85	56.2	28	54	1.9	0	0	0	0
Pro totals (2 years)	21	18	567	272	48.0	3172	13	33	5.59	48.8	55	134	2.4	0	0	0	0

LECHLER, SHANE   P   RAIDERS

PERSONAL: Born August 7, 1976, in Sealy, Texas. ... 6-2/230. ... Full name: Edward Shane Lechler.
HIGH SCHOOL: East Bernard (Texas).
COLLEGE: Texas A&M.
TRANSACTIONS/CAREER NOTES: Selected by Oakland Raiders in fifth round (142nd pick overall) of 2000 NFL draft. ... Signed by Raiders (July 22, 2000).
CHAMPIONSHIP GAME EXPERIENCE: Played in AFC championship game (2000 season).
HONORS: Named punter on THE SPORTING NEWS college All-America second team (1997). ... Named punter on THE SPORTING NEWS college All-America first team (1998). ... Named punter on THE SPORTING NEWS NFL All-Pro team (2000).
PRO STATISTICS: 2000—Missed only field-goal attempt and converted seven extra points.

			PUNTING				
Year Team	G	No.	Yds.	Avg.	Net avg.	In. 20	Blk.
2000—Oakland NFL	16	65	2984	45.9	*38.0	24	▲1

LEDFORD, DWAYNE   G   JAGUARS

PERSONAL: Born November 2, 1976, in Morgantown, N.C. ... 6-3/295. ... Full name: Billy Dwayne Ledford.
HIGH SCHOOL: McDowell (N.C.).
COLLEGE: East Carolina.
TRANSACTIONS/CAREER NOTES: Signed as non-drafted free agent by San Francisco 49ers (April 23, 1999). ... Released by 49ers (September 4, 1999). ... Re-signed by 49ers to practice squad (September 7, 1999). ... Activated (December 29, 1999). ... Released by 49ers (September 15, 2000). ... Signed by Jacksonville Jaguars to practice squad (November 15, 2000). ... Activated (December 19, 2000); did not play.
PLAYING EXPERIENCE: San Francisco NFL, 2000. ... Games/Games started: 2000 (1/0).

LEDYARD, COURTNEY   LB   JETS

PERSONAL: Born March 9, 1977, in Shaker Heights, Ohio. ... 6-2/250.
HIGH SCHOOL: Shaker Heights (Ohio).
COLLEGE: Michigan State.
TRANSACTIONS/CAREER NOTES: Signed as non-drafted free agent by New York Jets (April 19, 1999). ... Released by Jets (August 27, 1999). ... Re-signed by Jets (April 20, 2000).
PLAYING EXPERIENCE: New York Jets NFL, 2000. ... Games/Games started: 2000 (4/0).

L

LEE, AMP   RB   LIONS

PERSONAL: Born October 1, 1971, in Chipley, Fla. ... 5-11/200. ... Full name: Anthonia Wayne Lee.
HIGH SCHOOL: Chipley (Fla.).
COLLEGE: Florida State.
TRANSACTIONS/CAREER NOTES: Selected after junior season by San Francisco 49ers in second round (45th pick overall) of 1992 NFL draft. ... Signed by 49ers (July 18, 1992). ... Released by 49ers (May 4, 1994). ... Signed by Minnesota Vikings (May 24, 1994). ... On physically unable to perform list (July 13-20, 1994). ... Granted unconditional free agency (February 14, 1997). ... Signed by St. Louis Rams (August 4, 1997). ... Granted unconditional free agency (February 13, 1998). ... Re-signed by Rams (February 24, 1998). ... Released by Rams (February 29, 2000). ... Signed by Philadelphia Eagles (October 10, 2000). ... Released by Eagles (November 22, 2000). ... Signed by Detroit Lions (March 9, 2001).
CHAMPIONSHIP GAME EXPERIENCE: Played in NFC championship game (1992, 1993 and 1999 seasons). ... Member of Super Bowl championship team (1999 season).
PRO STATISTICS: 1992—Fumbled once and recovered three fumbles. 1993—Fumbled once. 1994—Fumbled once and recovered one fumble. 1995—Fumbled three times and recovered two fumbles. 1996—Fumbled twice and recovered one fumble. 1998—Fumbled three times. 1999—Recovered one fumble.
SINGLE GAME HIGHS (regular season): Attempts—23 (December 13, 1992, vs. Minnesota); yards—134 (December 13, 1992, vs. Minnesota); and rushing touchdowns—2 (October 11, 1998, vs. New York Jets).
STATISTICAL PLATEAUS: 100-yard rushing games: 1992 (1). ... 100-yard receiving games: 1997 (3).

			RUSHING				RECEIVING				PUNT RETURNS				KICKOFF RETURNS				TOTALS		
Year Team	G	GS	Att.	Yds.	Avg.	TD	No.	Yds.	Avg.	TD	No.	Yds.	Avg.	TD	No.	Yds.	Avg.	TD	TD	2pt.	Pts.
1992—San Fran. NFL	16	3	91	362	4.0	2	20	102	5.1	2	0	0	0.0	0	14	276	19.7	0	4	0	24
1993—San Fran. NFL	15	3	72	230	3.2	1	16	115	7.2	2	0	0	0.0	0	10	160	16.0	0	3	0	18
1994—Minnesota NFL	13	0	29	104	3.6	-0	45	368	8.2	2	0	0	0.0	0	3	42	14.0	0	2	0	12
1995—Minnesota NFL	16	3	69	371	5.4	2	71	558	7.9	1	5	50	10.0	0	5	100	20.0	0	3	0	18
1996—Minnesota NFL	16	3	51	161	3.2	0	54	422	7.8	2	10	84	8.4	0	5	85	17.0	0	2	0	12
1997—St. Louis NFL	16	1	28	104	3.7	0	61	825	13.5	3	0	0	0.0	0	4	71	17.8	0	3	0	18
1998—St. Louis NFL	14	1	44	175	4.0	2	64	667	10.4	2	0	0	0.0	0	0	0	0.0	0	4	1	26
1999—St. Louis NFL	7	0	3	3	1.0	0	3	22	7.3	1	0	0	0.0	0	0	0	0.0	0	1	0	6
2000—Philadelphia NFL	3	0	1	2	2.0	0	1	20	20.0	0	0	0	0.0	0	0	0	0.0	0	0	0	0
Pro totals (9 years)	116	14	388	1512	3.9	7	335	3099	9.3	15	15	134	8.9	0	41	734	17.9	0	22	1	134

LEE, CHARLES   WR   PACKERS

PERSONAL: Born November 19, 1977, in Miami. ... 6-2/202. ... Cousin of Harvey Clayton, defensive back with Pittsburgh Steelers (1983-86) and New York Giants (1987).
HIGH SCHOOL: Homestead (Fla.).
COLLEGE: Central Florida (degree in communications).

TRANSACTIONS/CAREER NOTES: Selected by Green Bay Packers in seventh round (242nd pick overall) of 2000 NFL draft. ... Signed by Packers (June 21, 2000).

PRO STATISTICS: 2000—Returned five punts for 52 yards.

SINGLE GAME HIGHS (regular season): Receptions—3 (September 10, 2000, vs. Buffalo); yards—46 (October 8, 2000, vs. Detroit); and touchdown receptions—0.

				RECEIVING		
Year Team	G	GS	No.	Yds.	Avg.	TD
2000—Green Bay NFL	15	1	10	134	13.4	0

LEEUWENBURG, JAY — C/G

PERSONAL: Born June 18, 1969, in St. Louis. ... 6-3/290. ... Full name: Jay Robert Leeuwenburg. ... Son of Richard Leeuwenburg, tackle with Chicago Bears (1965). ... Name pronounced LEW-in-berg.

HIGH SCHOOL: Kirkwood (Mo.).

COLLEGE: Colorado (degree in English).

TRANSACTIONS/CAREER NOTES: Selected by Kansas City Chiefs in ninth round (244th pick overall) of 1992 NFL draft. ... Signed by Chiefs (July 20, 1992). ... Claimed on waivers by Chicago Bears (September 2, 1992). ... Granted free agency (February 17, 1995). ... Re-signed by Bears (April 12, 1995). ... Granted unconditional free agency (February 16, 1996). ... Signed by Indianapolis Colts (February 21, 1996). ... Released by Colts (August 31, 1999). ... Signed by Cincinnati Bengals (September 3, 1999). ... Granted unconditional free agency (February 11, 2000). ... Signed by Washington Redskins (June 13, 2000). ... Granted unconditional free agency (March 2, 2001).

PLAYING EXPERIENCE: Chicago NFL, 1992-1995; Indianapolis NFL, 1996-1998; Cincinnati NFL, 1999; Washington NFL, 2000. ... Games/Games started: 1992 (12/0), 1993 (16/16), 1994 (16/16), 1995 (16/16), 1996 (15/7), 1997 (16/16), 1998 (16/16), 1999 (14/9), 2000 (16/12). Total: 137/108.

HONORS: Named center on THE SPORTING NEWS college All-America first team (1991).

PRO STATISTICS: 1992—Returned one kickoff for 12 yards. 1995—Recovered one fumble. 1997—Fumbled once for minus 20 yards. 1998—Recovered one fumble. 1999—Fumbled once.

LEPSIS, MATT — OT — BRONCOS

PERSONAL: Born January 13, 1974, in Conroe, Texas ... 6-4/290. ... Full name: Matthew Lepsis.

HIGH SCHOOL: Frisco (Texas).

COLLEGE: Colorado.

TRANSACTIONS/CAREER NOTES: Signed as non-drafted free agent by Denver Broncos (April 22, 1997). ... On non-football injury list with knee injury (July 16, 1997-entire season). ... Assigned by Broncos to Barcelona Dragons in 1998 NFL Europe enhancement allocation program (February 18, 1998). ... Granted free agency (March 2, 2001). ... Re-signed by Broncos (March 21, 2001).

PLAYING EXPERIENCE: Barcelona Dragons NFLE, 1998; Denver NFL, 1998-2000. ... Games/Games started: NFLE 1998 (games played unavailable), NFL 1998 (16/0), 1999 (16/16), 2000 (16/16). Total NFL: 48/32.

CHAMPIONSHIP GAME EXPERIENCE: Played in AFC championship game (1998 season). ... Member of Super Bowl championship team (1998 season).

PRO STATISTICS: 2000—Recovered one fumble.

LEROY, EMARLOS — DT — PATRIOTS

PERSONAL: Born July 31, 1975, in Albany, Ga. ... 6-1/304. ... Full name: Emarlos S. Leroy. ... Name pronounced LEE-roy.

HIGH SCHOOL: Monroe (Albany, Ga.).

JUNIOR COLLEGE: Northwest Mississippi Community College.

COLLEGE: Georgia (degree in child and family development).

TRANSACTIONS/CAREER NOTES: Selected by Jacksonville Jaguars in sixth round (182nd pick overall) of 1999 NFL draft. ... Signed by Jaguars (May 26, 1999). ... Claimed on waivers by New England Patriots (May 25, 2001).

PLAYING EXPERIENCE: Jacksonville NFL, 1999 and 2000. ... Games/Games started: 1999 (13/0), 2000 (9/1). Total: 22/1.

CHAMPIONSHIP GAME EXPERIENCE: Played in AFC championship game (1999 season).

PRO STATISTICS: 2000—Returned one kickoff for no yards.

LETT, LEON — DT — BRONCOS

PERSONAL: Born October 12, 1968, in Mobile, Ala. ... 6-6/290. ... Full name: Leon Lett Jr.

HIGH SCHOOL: Fairhope (Ala.).

JUNIOR COLLEGE: Hinds Community College (Miss.).

COLLEGE: Emporia (Kan.) State.

TRANSACTIONS/CAREER NOTES: Selected by Dallas Cowboys in seventh round (173rd pick overall) of 1991 NFL draft. ... Signed by Cowboys (July 14, 1991). ... On injured reserve with back injury (August 27-November 21, 1991). ... On suspended list for violating league substance abuse policy (November 3-24, 1995). ... On suspended list for violating league substance abuse policy (December 3, 1996-December 1, 1997). ... On suspended list for violating league substance abuse policy (June 4-November 9, 1999). ... On injured reserve with knee injury (December 14, 2000-remainder of season). ... Granted unconditional free agency (March 2, 2001). ... Signed by Denver Broncos (March 22, 2001).

CHAMPIONSHIP GAME EXPERIENCE: Played in NFC championship game (1992-1995 seasons). ... Member of Super Bowl championship team (1992, 1993 and 1995 seasons).

HONORS: Played in Pro Bowl (1994 and 1998 seasons).

POST SEASON RECORDS: Holds Super Bowl career record for most yards by fumble recovery—64. ... Holds Super Bowl single-game record for most yards by fumble recovery—64 (January 31, 1993).

PRO STATISTICS: 1992—Recovered one fumble. 1993—Fumbled once. 1995—Recovered two fumbles. 1996—Recovered two fumbles. 1999—Recovered two fumbles.

Year Team	G	GS	SACKS
1991—Dallas NFL	5	0	0.0
1992—Dallas NFL	16	0	3.5
1993—Dallas NFL	11	6	0.0
1994—Dallas NFL	16	16	4.0
1995—Dallas NFL	12	12	3.0
1996—Dallas NFL	13	13	3.5
1997—Dallas NFL	3	3	0.5
1998—Dallas NFL	16	15	4.0
1999—Dallas NFL	8	1	1.5
2000—Dallas NFL	9	7	2.5
Pro totals (10 years)	109	73	22.5

LEVENS, DORSEY RB PACKERS

PERSONAL: Born May 21, 1970, in Syracuse, N.Y. ... 6-1/230. ... Full name: Herbert Dorsey Levens.
HIGH SCHOOL: Nottingham (Syracuse, N.Y.).
COLLEGE: Notre Dame, then Georgia Tech (degree in business management).
TRANSACTIONS/CAREER NOTES: Selected by Green Bay Packers in fifth round (149th pick overall) of 1994 NFL draft. ... Signed by Packers (June 9, 1994). ... Granted free agency (February 14, 1997). ... Re-signed by Packers (June 20, 1997). ... Designated by Packers as franchise player (February 13, 1998). ... Re-signed by Packers (August 30, 1998).
CHAMPIONSHIP GAME EXPERIENCE: Played in NFC championship game (1995-97 seasons). ... Member of Super Bowl championship team (1996 season). ... Played in Super Bowl XXXII (1997 season).
HONORS: Played in Pro Bowl (1997 season).
PRO STATISTICS: 1996—Recovered one fumble. 1997—Recovered one fumble for minus seven yards.
SINGLE GAME HIGHS (regular season): Attempts—33 (November 23, 1997, vs. Dallas); yards—190 (November 23, 1997, vs. Dallas); and rushing touchdowns—4 (January 2, 2000, vs. Arizona).
STATISTICAL PLATEAUS: 100-yard rushing games: 1997 (6), 1998 (1), 1999 (3). Total: 10.

			RUSHING				RECEIVING				KICKOFF RETURNS				TOTALS		
Year Team	G	GS	Att.	Yds.	Avg.	TD	No.	Yds.	Avg.	TD	No.	Yds.	Avg.	TD	TD	2pt.	Pts. Fum.
1994—Green Bay NFL	14	0	5	15	3.0	0	1	9	9.0	0	2	31	15.5	0	0	0	0 0
1995—Green Bay NFL	15	12	36	120	3.3	3	48	434	9.0	4	0	0	0.0	0	7	0	42 0
1996—Green Bay NFL	16	1	121	566	4.7	5	31	226	7.3	5	5	84	16.8	0	10	0	60 2
1997—Green Bay NFL	16	16	329	1435	4.4	7	53	370	7.0	5	0	0	0.0	0	12	1	74 5
1998—Green Bay NFL	7	4	115	378	3.3	1	27	162	6.0	0	0	0	0.0	0	1	0	6 0
1999—Green Bay NFL	14	14	279	1034	3.7	9	71	573	8.1	1	0	0	0.0	0	10	0	60 5
2000—Green Bay NFL	5	5	77	224	2.9	3	16	146	9.1	0	0	0	0.0	0	3	0	18 0
Pro totals (7 years)	87	52	962	3772	3.9	28	247	1920	7.8	15	7	115	16.4	0	43	1	260 12

LEVINGSTON, BASHIR CB

PERSONAL: Born October 2, 1976, in Inglewood, Calif. ... 5-9/180. ... Name pronounced buh-SHEER.
HIGH SCHOOL: Seaside (Calif.).
JUNIOR COLLEGE: Monterey (Calif.) Peninsula College.
COLLEGE: Utah State, then Eastern Washington.
TRANSACTIONS/CAREER NOTES: Signed as non-drafted free agent by New York Giants (April 23, 1999). ... Assigned by Giants to Amsterdam Admirals in 2000 NFL Europe enhancement allocation program (February 18, 2000). ... On physically unable to perform list with ankle injury (July 23-August 27, 2000). ... On non-football injury list with ankle injury (August 27-November 2, 2000). ... Released by Giants (November 20, 2000).

			INTERCEPTIONS				PUNT RETURNS				KICKOFF RETURNS				TOTALS		
Year Team	G	GS	No.	Yds.	Avg.	TD	No.	Yds.	Avg.	TD	No.	Yds.	Avg.	TD	TD	2pt.	Pts. Fum.
1999—New York Giants NFL	12	0	1	34	34.0	0	0	0	0.0	0	22	532	24.2	0	0	0	0 1
2000—Amsterdam NFLE	...	...	3	60	20.0	1	20	266	13.3	0	15	421	28.1	1	2	0	12 0
—New York Giants NFL	3	0	0	0	0.0	0	0	0	0.0	0	7	153	21.9	0	0	0	0 2
NFL Europe totals (1 year)	...	...	3	60	20.0	1	20	266	13.3	0	15	421	28.1	1	2	0	12 0
NFL totals (2 years)	15	0	1	34	34.0	0	0	0	0.0	0	29	685	23.6	0	0	0	0 3
Pro totals (3 years)	...	...	4	94	23.5	1	20	266	13.3	0	44	1106	25.1	1	2	0	12 3

LEWIS, CHAD TE EAGLES

PERSONAL: Born October 5, 1971, in Fort Dix, N.J. ... 6-6/252. ... Full name: Chad Wayne Lewis.
HIGH SCHOOL: Orem (Utah).
COLLEGE: Brigham Young (degrees in communications and Chinese).
TRANSACTIONS/CAREER NOTES: Signed as non-drafted free agent by Philadelphia Eagles (April 23, 1997). ... Released by Eagles (September 15, 1998). ... Signed by St. Louis Rams (December 9, 1998). ... Inactive for three games with Rams (1998). ... Claimed on waivers by Eagles (November 16, 1999). ... Granted free agency (February 11, 2000). ... Re-signed by Eagles (March 17, 2000).
HONORS: Played in Pro Bowl (2000 season).
PRO STATISTICS: 1997—Returned one kickoff for 11 yards.
SINGLE GAME HIGHS (regular season): Receptions—9 (December 24, 2000, vs. Cincinnati); yards—100 (December 10, 2000, vs. Cleveland); and touchdown receptions—1 (October 15, 2000, vs. Arizona).
STATISTICAL PLATEAUS: 100-yard receiving games: 2000 (1).

			RECEIVING				TOTALS		
Year Team	G	GS	No.	Yds.	Avg.	TD	TD	2pt.	Pts. Fum.
1997—Philadelphia NFL	16	3	12	94	7.8	4	4	0	24 0
1998—Philadelphia NFL	2	0	0	0	0.0	0	0	0	0 0
1999—St. Louis NFL	6	0	1	12	12.0	0	0	0	0 0
—Philadelphia NFL	6	4	7	76	10.9	3	3	0	18 0
2000—Philadelphia NFL	16	16	69	735	10.7	3	3	0	18 0
Pro totals (4 years)	46	23	89	917	10.3	10	10	0	60 0

L

LEWIS, DARRYLL   CB   BRONCOS

PERSONAL: Born December 16, 1968, in West Covina, Calif. ... 5-9/188. ... Full name: Darryll Lamont Lewis.

HIGH SCHOOL: Nogales (La Puente, Calif.).

COLLEGE: Arizona.

TRANSACTIONS/CAREER NOTES: Selected by Houston Oilers in second round (38th pick overall) of 1991 NFL draft. ... Signed by Oilers (July 19, 1991). ... On injured reserve with knee injury (October 25, 1993-remainder of season). ... Granted free agency (February 17, 1994). ... Re-signed by Oilers (July 17, 1994). ... Granted unconditional free agency (February 17, 1995). ... Re-signed by Oilers (March 9, 1995). ... Oilers franchise moved to Tennessee for 1997 season. ... Oilers franchise renamed Tennessee Titans for 1999 season (December 26, 1998). ... Released by Titans (September 5, 1999). ... Signed by San Diego Chargers (September 6, 1999). ... Granted unconditional free agency (February 11, 2000). ... Re-signed by Chargers (March 6, 2000). ... Released by Chargers (February 28, 2001). ... Signed by Denver Broncos (April 20, 2001).

HONORS: Jim Thorpe Award winner (1990). ... Named defensive back on THE SPORTING NEWS college All-America first team (1990). ... Played in Pro Bowl (1995 season).

PRO STATISTICS: 1991—Recovered one fumble. 1992—Returned eight kickoffs for 171 yards and recovered one fumble. 1997—Recovered three fumbles for 68 yards and fumbled once. 1999—Recovered blocked punt in end zone for a touchdown and recovered two fumbles for 42 yards and one touchdown. 2000—Recovered one fumble for 29 yards.

				INTERCEPTIONS			SACKS
Year Team	G	GS	No.	Yds.	Avg.	TD	No.
1991—Houston NFL	16	1	1	33	33.0	1	1.0
1992—Houston NFL	13	0	0	0	0.0	0	1.0
1993—Houston NFL	4	4	1	47	47.0	▲1	0.0
1994—Houston NFL	16	15	5	57	11.4	0	0.0
1995—Houston NFL	16	15	6	§145	24.2	▲1	1.0
1996—Houston NFL	16	16	5	103	20.6	1	0.0
1997—Tennessee NFL	16	14	5	115	23.0	1	0.0
1998—Tennessee NFL	16	15	4	40	10.0	0	1.0
1999—San Diego NFL	13	8	4	9	2.3	0	0.0
2000—San Diego NFL	15	7	1	6	6.0	0	1.0
Pro totals (10 years)	141	95	32	555	17.3	5	5.0

LEWIS, JAMAL   RB   RAVENS

PERSONAL: Born August 28, 1979, in Atlanta. ... 5-11/231. ... Full name: Jamal Lafitte Lewis.

HIGH SCHOOL: Douglass (Atlanta).

COLLEGE: Tennessee.

TRANSACTIONS/CAREER NOTES: Selected after junior season by Baltimore Ravens in first round (fifth pick overall) of 2000 NFL draft. ... Signed by Ravens (July 24, 2000).

CHAMPIONSHIP GAME EXPERIENCE: Played in AFC championship game (2000 season). ... Member of Super Bowl championship team (2000 season).

HONORS: Named College Football Freshman of the Year by THE SPORTING NEWS (1997).

PRO STATISTICS: 2000—Recovered three fumbles.

SINGLE GAME HIGHS (regular season): Attempts—30 (November 26, 2000, vs. Cleveland); yards—187 (November 19, 2000, vs. Dallas); and rushing touchdowns—2 (November 26, 2000, vs. Cleveland).

STATISTICAL PLATEAUS: 100-yard rushing games: 2000 (5).

			RUSHING				RECEIVING				TOTALS			
Year Team	G	GS	Att.	Yds.	Avg.	TD	No.	Yds.	Avg.	TD	TD	2pt.	Pts.	Fum.
2000—Baltimore NFL	16	13	309	1364	4.4	6	27	296	11.0	0	6	▲1	38	6

LEWIS, JEFF   QB   PANTHERS

PERSONAL: Born April 17, 1973, in Columbus, Ohio. ... 6-2/211. ... Full name: Jeffery Scott Lewis.

HIGH SCHOOL: Horizon (Scottsdale, Ariz.).

COLLEGE: Northern Arizona.

TRANSACTIONS/CAREER NOTES: Selected by Denver Broncos in fourth round (100th pick overall) of 1996 NFL draft. ... Signed by Broncos (July 19, 1996). ... On physically unable to perform list with knee injury (July 24-August 24, 1998). ... On non-football injury list with knee injury (August 25, 1998-entire season). ... Traded by Broncos to Carolina Panthers for third-round pick (CB Chris Watson) and fourth-round pick (OT Cooper Carlisle) in 2000 draft (March 1, 1999).

CHAMPIONSHIP GAME EXPERIENCE: Member of Broncos for AFC championship game (1997 season); inactive. ... Member of Super Bowl championship team (1997 season); inactive.

PRO STATISTICS: 2000—Fumbled once.

SINGLE GAME HIGHS (regular season): Attempts—16 (December 24, 2000, vs. Oakland); completions—10 (December 24, 2000, vs. Oakland); yards—79 (December 24, 2000, vs. Oakland); and touchdown passes—0.

			PASSING								RUSHING				TOTALS		
Year Team	G	GS	Att.	Cmp.	Pct.	Yds.	TD	Int.	Avg.	Rat.	Att.	Yds.	Avg.	TD	TD	2pt.	Pts.
1996—Denver NFL	2	0	17	9	52.9	58	0	1	3.41	35.9	4	39	9.8	0	0	0	0
1997—Denver NFL	3	0	2	1	50.0	21	0	0	10.50	87.5	5	2	0.4	0	0	0	0
1998—Denver NFL									Did not play.								
1999—Carolina NFL	2	0	3	2	66.7	11	0	0	3.67	72.9	4	1	0.3	0	0	0	0
2000—Carolina NFL	5	0	32	16	50.0	120	0	1	3.75	46.4	8	36	4.5	0	0	0	0
Pro totals (4 years)	12	0	54	28	51.9	210	0	2	3.89	46.1	21	78	3.7	0	0	0	0

LEWIS, JERMAINE — WR/PR — RAVENS

PERSONAL: Born October 16, 1974, in Lanham, Md. ... 5-7/180. ... Full name: Jermaine Edward Lewis.
HIGH SCHOOL: Eleanor Roosevelt (Greenbelt, Md.).
COLLEGE: Maryland.
TRANSACTIONS/CAREER NOTES: Selected by Baltimore Ravens in fifth round (153rd pick overall) of 1996 NFL draft. ... Signed by Ravens (July 18, 1996).
CHAMPIONSHIP GAME EXPERIENCE: Played in AFC championship game (2000 season). ... Member of Super Bowl championship team (2000 season).
HONORS: Named punt returner on THE SPORTING NEWS NFL All-Pro team (1998). ... Played in Pro Bowl (1998 season).
RECORDS: Shares NFL single-game records for most touchdowns by punt returns—2; and most touchdowns by combined kick return—2 (December 7, 1997, vs. Seattle).
PRO STATISTICS: 1996—Fumbled four times and recovered one fumble. 1997—Fumbled three times and recovered two fumbles. 1998—Fumbled three times and recovered three fumbles. 1999—Fumbled once and recovered one fumble. 2000—Attempted one pass with a completion for three yards.
SINGLE GAME HIGHS (regular season): Receptions—8 (September 21, 1997, vs. Tennessee); yards—124 (September 21, 1997, vs. Tennessee); and touchdown receptions—2 (December 5, 1999, vs. Tennessee).
STATISTICAL PLATEAUS: 100-yard receiving games: 1997 (2), 1998 (2). Total: 4.
MISCELLANEOUS: Holds Baltimore Ravens all-time record for most touchdowns (22).

				RUSHING				RECEIVING				PUNT RETURNS				KICKOFF RETURNS				TOTALS		
Year	Team	G	GS	Att.	Yds.	Avg.	TD	No.	Yds.	Avg.	TD	No.	Yds.	Avg.	TD	No.	Yds.	Avg.	TD	TD	2pt.	Pts.
1996—Baltimore NFL		16	1	1	-3	-3.0	0	5	78	15.6	1	36	339	9.4	0	41	883	21.5	0	1	0	6
1997—Baltimore NFL		14	7	3	35	11.7	0	42	648	15.4	6	28	437*	15.6	2	41	905	22.1	0	8	0	48
1998—Baltimore NFL		13	13	5	20	4.0	0	41	784	19.1	6	32	405	12.7	†2	6	145	24.2	0	8	0	48
1999—Baltimore NFL		15	6	5	11	2.2	0	25	281	11.2	2	*57	452	7.9	0	8	158	19.8	0	2	0	12
2000—Baltimore NFL		15	1	3	38	12.7	0	19	161	8.5	1	36	578*	16.1	†2	1	23	23.0	0	3	0	18
Pro totals (5 years)		73	28	17	101	5.9	0	132	1952	14.8	16	189	2211	11.7	6	97	2114	21.8	0	22	0	132

LEWIS, JONAS — RB — 49ERS

PERSONAL: Born December 27, 1976, in Riverside, Calif. ... 5-9/210. ... Full name: Jonas W. Allen Lewis.
HIGH SCHOOL: Beaumont (Calif.).
COLLEGE: San Diego State.
TRANSACTIONS/CAREER NOTES: Signed by San Francisco 49ers as non-drafted free agent (April 24, 2000).
PLAYING EXPERIENCE: San Francisco NFL, 2000. ... Games/Games started: 2000 (10/0).
PRO STATISTICS: 2000—Rushed once for six yards, returned nine kickoffs for 168 yards and recovered one fumble.
SINGLE GAME HIGHS (regular season): Attempts—1 (September 24, 2000, vs. Dallas); yards—6 (September 24, 2000, vs. Dallas); and rushing touchdowns—0.

LEWIS, KEVIN — LB — GIANTS

PERSONAL: Born October 6, 1978, in Orlando, Fla. ... 6-1/230.
HIGH SCHOOL: Jones (Orlando, Fla.).
COLLEGE: Duke.
TRANSACTIONS/CAREER NOTES: Signed by New York Giants as non-drafted free agent (April 20, 2000).
PLAYING EXPERIENCE: New York Giants NFL, 2000. ... Games/Games started: 2000 (7/0).
CHAMPIONSHIP GAME EXPERIENCE: Member of Giants for NFL Championship game (2000 season); inactive. ... Member of Giants for Super Bowl XXXV (2000 season); inactive.

LEWIS, MO — LB — JETS

PERSONAL: Born October 21, 1969, in Atlanta. ... 6-3/258. ... Full name: Morris C. Lewis.
HIGH SCHOOL: J.C. Murphy (Atlanta).
COLLEGE: Georgia.
TRANSACTIONS/CAREER NOTES: Selected by New York Jets in third round (62nd pick overall) of 1991 NFL draft. ... Signed by Jets (July 18, 1991). ... Designated by Jets as franchise player (February 11, 2000).
CHAMPIONSHIP GAME EXPERIENCE: Played in AFC championship game (1998 season).
HONORS: Played in Pro Bowl (1998-2000 seasons).
PRO STATISTICS: 1991—Recovered one fumble. 1992—Recovered four fumbles for 22 yards. 1994—Recovered one fumble for 11 yards. 1997—Recovered one fumble for 26 yards. 1998—Fumbled once and recovered one fumble. 1999—Recovered one fumble. 2000—Rushed once for three yards and recovered two fumbles.

				INTERCEPTIONS				SACKS
Year	Team	G	GS	No.	Yds.	Avg.	TD	No.
1991—New York Jets NFL		16	16	0	0	0.0	0	2.0
1992—New York Jets NFL		16	16	1	1	1.0	0	2.0
1993—New York Jets NFL		16	16	2	4	2.0	0	4.0
1994—New York Jets NFL		16	16	4	106	26.5	2	6.0
1995—New York Jets NFL		16	16	2	22	11.0	▲1	5.0
1996—New York Jets NFL		9	9	0	0	0.0	0	0.5
1997—New York Jets NFL		16	16	1	43	43.0	1	8.0
1998—New York Jets NFL		16	16	1	11	11.0	0	7.0
1999—New York Jets NFL		16	16	0	0	0.0	0	5.5
2000—New York Jets NFL		16	16	1	23	23.0	0	10.0
Pro totals (10 years)		153	153	12	210	17.5	4	50.0

L

LEWIS, RAY — LB — RAVENS

PERSONAL: Born May 15, 1975, in Bartow, Fla. ... 6-1/245. ... Full name: Ray Anthony Lewis.
HIGH SCHOOL: Kathleen (Lakeland, Fla.).
COLLEGE: Miami (Fla.).
TRANSACTIONS/CAREER NOTES: Selected after junior season by Baltimore Ravens in first round (26th pick overall) of 1996 NFL draft. ... Signed by Ravens (July 15, 1996).
CHAMPIONSHIP GAME EXPERIENCE: Played in AFC championship game (2000 season). ... Member of Super Bowl championship team (2000 season).
HONORS: Named linebacker on THE SPORTING NEWS college All-America second team (1995). ... Played in Pro Bowl (1997, 1998 and 2000 seasons). ... Named linebacker on THE SPORTING NEWS NFL All-Pro team (1998-2000). ... Named to play in Pro Bowl (1999 season); replaced by Junior Seau due to personal reasons. ... Named Most Valuable Player of Super Bowl XXXV (2000 season).
PRO STATISTICS: 1997—Recovered one fumble. 1999—Credited with a safety and fumbled once. 2000—Recovered three fumbles.

Year Team	G	GS	INTERCEPTIONS No.	Yds.	Avg.	TD	SACKS No.
1996—Baltimore NFL	14	13	1	0	0.0	0	2.5
1997—Baltimore NFL	16	16	1	18	18.0	0	4.0
1998—Baltimore NFL	14	14	2	25	12.5	0	3.0
1999—Baltimore NFL	16	16	3	97	32.3	0	3.5
2000—Baltimore NFL	16	16	2	1	0.5	0	3.0
Pro totals (5 years)	76	75	9	141	15.7	0	16.0

LINCOLN, JEREMY — CB

PERSONAL: Born April 7, 1969, in Toledo, Ohio. ... 5-10/182. ... Full name: Jeremy Arlo Lincoln.
HIGH SCHOOL: DeVilbiss (Toledo, Ohio).
COLLEGE: Tennessee.
TRANSACTIONS/CAREER NOTES: Selected by Chicago Bears in third round (80th pick overall) of 1992 NFL draft. ... Signed by Bears (July 23, 1992). ... On injured reserve with knee injury (September 1, 1992-entire season). ... Granted free agency (February 17, 1995). ... Re-signed by Bears (July 17, 1995). ... Released by Bears (August 20, 1996). ... Signed by St. Louis Rams (September 5, 1996). ... Released by Rams (February 24, 1997). ... Signed by Seattle Seahawks (June 4, 1997). ... Granted unconditional free agency (February 13, 1998). ... Signed by New York Giants (June 15, 1998). ... Granted unconditional free agency (February 12, 1999). ... Re-signed by Giants (June 14, 1999). ... Granted unconditional free agency (February 11, 2000). ... Signed by Denver Broncos (February 16, 2000). ... Released by Broncos (July 19, 2000). ... Signed by Green Bay Packers (August 1, 2000). ... Released by Packers (August 23, 2000). ... Signed by Detroit Lions (December 4, 2000). ... Granted unconditional free agency (March 2, 2001).
PRO STATISTICS: 1995—Credited with one sack. 1996—Recovered one fumble. 1997—Recovered one fumble. 2000—Recovered one fumble.

Year Team	G	GS	INTERCEPTIONS No.	Yds.	Avg.	TD
1992—Chicago NFL					Did not play.	
1993—Chicago NFL	16	7	3	109	‡36.3	1
1994—Chicago NFL	15	14	1	5	5.0	0
1995—Chicago NFL	16	14	1	32	32.0	0
1996—St. Louis NFL	13	1	1	3	3.0	0
1997—Seattle NFL	13	3	0	0	0.0	0
1998—New York Giants NFL	16	1	1	0	0.0	0
1999—New York Giants NFL	15	7	1	0	0.0	0
2000—Detroit NFL	3	0	0	0	0.0	0
Pro totals (8 years)	107	47	8	149	18.6	1

LINDELL, RIAN — K — SEAHAWKS

PERSONAL: Born January 20, 1977, in Vancouver, Wash. ... 6-3/241. ... Full name: Rian David Lindell.
HIGH SCHOOL: Mountain View (Vancouver, Wash.).
COLLEGE: Washington State.
TRANSACTIONS/CAREER NOTES: Signed as non-drafted free agent by Dallas Cowboys (April 20, 2000). ... Released by Cowboys (August 15, 2000). ... Signed by Seattle Seahawks (September 26, 2000).

Year Team	G	KICKING XPM	XPA	FGM	FGA	Lg.	50+	Pts.
2000—Seattle NFL	12	25	25	15	17	52	3-3	70

LINDSAY, EVERETT — OL — BROWNS

PERSONAL: Born September 18, 1970, in Burlington, Iowa. ... 6-4/302. ... Full name: Everett Eric Lindsay.
HIGH SCHOOL: Millbrook (Raleigh, N.C.).
COLLEGE: Mississippi (degree in general business, 1992).
TRANSACTIONS/CAREER NOTES: Selected by Minnesota Vikings in fifth round (133rd pick overall) of 1993 NFL draft. ... Signed by Vikings (July 14, 1993). ... On injured reserve with shoulder injury (December 22, 1993-remainder of season). ... On injured reserve with shoulder injury (August 23, 1994-entire season). ... On physically unable to perform list with knee injury (July 22-August 20, 1996). ... On non-football injury list with knee injury (August 20, 1996-entire season). ... Assigned to Barcelona Dragons in 1997 World League enhancement allocation program (February 19, 1997). ... Granted unconditional free agency (February 13, 1998). ... Re-signed by Vikings (February 17, 1998). ... Traded by Vikings to Baltimore Ravens for sixth-round pick (DE Talance Sawyer) in 1999 draft (April 17, 1999). ... Granted free agency (February 11, 2000). ... Signed by Cleveland Browns (February 15, 2000).
PLAYING EXPERIENCE: Minnesota NFL, 1993, 1995, 1997 and 1998; Baltimore NFL, 1999; Cleveland NFL, 2000. ... Games/Games started: 1993 (12/12), 1995 (16/0), 1997 (16/3), 1998 (16/3), 1999 (16/16), 2000 (16/16). Total: 92/50.
CHAMPIONSHIP GAME EXPERIENCE: Played in NFC championship game (1998 season).
HONORS: Named offensive tackle on THE SPORTING NEWS college All-America second team (1992).
PRO STATISTICS: 2000—Recovered one fumble.

LINDSEY, STEVE K BRONCOS

PERSONAL: Born November 25, 1974, in Hattiesburg, Miss. ... 6-1/185. ... Full name: Steve Kendall Lindsey.
HIGH SCHOOL: North Forrest (Hattiesburg, Miss.).
COLLEGE: Mississippi.
TRANSACTIONS/CAREER NOTES: Signed as non-drafted free agent by San Francisco 49ers (April 24, 1998). ... Released by 49ers (July 15, 1998). ... Signed by Jacksonville Jaguars (January 6, 1999). ... Released by Jaguars (November 15, 2000). ... Signed by Denver Broncos (November 16, 2000).
CHAMPIONSHIP GAME EXPERIENCE: Played in AFC championship game (1999 season).

		PUNTING						KICKING					
Year Team	G	No.	Yds.	Avg.	Net avg.	In. 20	Blk.	XPM	XPA	FGM	FGA	Lg.	50+	Pts.
1999—Jacksonville NFL	16	0	0	0.0	0	0	0	0	0	0	0	0	0-0	0
2000—Jacksonville NFL	10	3	117	39.0	32.3	0	0	5	5	5	7	49	0-0	20
—Denver NFL	6	0	0	0.0	0	0	0	0	0	0	0	0	0-0	0
Pro totals (2 years)	32	3	117	39.0	32.3	0	0	5	5	5	7	49	0-0	20

LINTON, JONATHAN FB

PERSONAL: Born November 7, 1974, in Allentown, Pa ... 6-1/234. ... Full name: Jonathan C. Linton.
HIGH SCHOOL: Catasauqua (Pa).
COLLEGE: North Carolina.
TRANSACTIONS/CAREER NOTES: Selected by Buffalo Bills in fifth round (131st pick overall) of 1998 NFL draft. ... Signed by Bills (June 8, 1998). ... Granted free agency (March 2, 2001).
PRO STATISTICS: 1998—Recovered one fumble. 1999—Recovered one fumble. 2000—Returned three kickoffs for 40 yards and recovered one fumble.
SINGLE GAME HIGHS (regular season): Attempts—24 (November 7, 1999, vs. Washington); yards—96 (November 7, 1999, vs. Washington); rushing touchdowns—1 (January 2, 2000, vs. Indianapolis).

			RUSHING				RECEIVING				TOTALS		
Year Team	G	GS	Att.	Yds.	Avg.	TD	No.	Yds.	Avg.	TD	TD	2pt.	Pts.	Fum.
1998—Buffalo NFL	14	0	45	195	4.3	1	1	10	10.0	0	1	0	6	0
1999—Buffalo NFL	16	2	205	695	3.4	5	29	228	7.9	1	6	†1	38	4
2000—Buffalo NFL	14	2	38	112	2.9	0	3	8	2.7	1	1	0	6	3
Pro totals (3 years)	44	4	288	1002	3.5	6	33	246	7.5	2	8	1	50	7

L

LITTLE, EARL DB BROWNS

PERSONAL: Born March 10, 1973, in Miami. ... 6-0/198. ... Full name: Earl Jerome Little.
HIGH SCHOOL: North Miami.
COLLEGE: Michigan, then Miami (Fla.).
TRANSACTIONS/CAREER NOTES: Signed as non-drafted free agent by Miami Dolphins (April 24, 1997). ... Released by Dolphins (August 24, 1997). ... Re-signed by Dolphins to practice squad (August 26, 1997). ... Released by Dolphins (August 29, 1997). ... Signed by New Orleans Saints to practice squad (October 1, 1997). ... Claimed on waivers by Cleveland Browns (October 25, 1999).
PLAYING EXPERIENCE: New Orleans NFL, 1998; New Orleans (1)-Cleveland (9) NFL, 1999; Cleveland NFL, 2000. ... Games/Games started: 1998 (16/0), 1999 (N.O.- 1/0; Cle.-9/0; Total: 10/0), 2000 (16/0). Total: 42/0.
PRO STATISTICS: 1998—Returned four kickoffs for 64 yards. 1999—Intercepted one pass for no yards, returned two kickoffs for 34 yards and fumbled once. 2000—Intercepted one pass for seven yards, returned two kickoffs for 20 yards, fumbled once and recovered one fumble.

LITTLE, LEONARD DE RAMS

PERSONAL: Born October 19, 1974, in Asheville, N.C. ... 6-3/257. ... Full name: Leonard Antonio Little.
HIGH SCHOOL: Asheville (N.C.).
JUNIOR COLLEGE: Coffeyville (Kan.) Community College..
COLLEGE: Tennessee (degree in psychology, 1997).
TRANSACTIONS/CAREER NOTES: Selected by St. Louis Rams in third round (65th pick overall) of 1998 NFL draft. ... Signed by Rams (July 2, 1998). ... On non-football injury list for personal reasons (November 17, 1998-November 9, 1999). ... On suspended list for violating league substance abuse policy (July 16-November 9, 1999). ... Granted free agency (March 2, 2001).
PLAYING EXPERIENCE: St. Louis NFL, 1998-2000. ... Games/Games started: 1998 (6/0), 1999 (6/0), 2000 (14/0). Total: 26/0.
CHAMPIONSHIP GAME EXPERIENCE: Played in NFC championship game (1999 season). ... Member of Super Bowl championship team (1999 season).
PRO STATISTICS: 1998—Credited with $1/2$ sack. 2000—Credited with five sacks.

LIWIENSKI, CHRIS G VIKINGS

PERSONAL: Born August 2, 1975, in Sterling Heights, Mich. ... 6-5/321. ... Name pronounced Loo-win-ski.
HIGH SCHOOL: Stevenson (Sterling Heights, Mich.).
COLLEGE: Indiana.
TRANSACTIONS/CAREER NOTES: Selected by Detroit Lions in seventh round (207th pick overall) of 1998 NFL draft. ... Signed by Lions (July 15, 1998). ... Released by Lions (August 24, 1998). ... Signed by Minnesota Vikings to practice squad (August 31, 1998). ... Activated (November 18, 1998). ... Released by Vikings (September 9, 1999). ... Re-signed by Vikings to practice squad (September 10, 1999). ... Activated (December 10, 1999); did not play.
PLAYING EXPERIENCE: Minnesota NFL, 1998 and 2000. ... Games/Games started: 1998 (1/0), 2000 (14/1). Total: 15/1.
CHAMPIONSHIP GAME EXPERIENCE: Member of Vikings for NFC championship game (1998 season); inactive. ... Played in NFC championship game (2000 season).

LOCKETT, KEVIN　　　　WR　　　　REDSKINS

PERSONAL: Born September 8, 1974, in Tulsa, Okla. ... 6-0/187.
HIGH SCHOOL: Washington (Okla.).
COLLEGE: Kansas State (degree in accounting).
TRANSACTIONS/CAREER NOTES: Selected by Kansas City Chiefs in second round (47th pick overall) of 1997 NFL draft. ... Signed by Chiefs (July 25, 1997). ... Granted free agency (February 11, 2000). ... Re-signed by Chiefs (May 3, 2000) ... Granted unconditional free agency (March 2, 2001). ... Signed by Washington Redskins (April 9, 2001).
PRO STATISTICS: 1998—Recovered two fumbles. 2000—Returned one kickoff for 25 yards and recovered one fumble.
SINGLE GAME HIGHS (regular season): Receptions—7 (November 5, 2000, vs. Oakland); yards—77 (October 29, 2000, vs. Seattle); and touchdown receptions—1 (December 4, 2000, vs. New England).

| | | | RECEIVING | | | | PUNT RETURNS | | | | TOTALS | | |
Year　Team	G	GS	No.	Yds.	Avg.	TD	No.	Yds.	Avg.	TD	TD	2pt.	Pts.	Fum.
1997—Kansas City NFL	9	0	1	35	35.0	0	0	0	0.0	0	0	0	0	0
1998—Kansas City NFL	13	3	19	281	14.8	0	7	36	5.1	0	0	0	0	2
1999—Kansas City NFL	16	1	34	426	12.5	2	1	10	10.0	0	2	0	12	0
2000—Kansas City NFL	16	2	33	422	12.8	2	26	208	8.0	0	2	0	12	3
Pro totals (4 years)	**54**	**6**	**87**	**1164**	**13.4**	**4**	**34**	**254**	**7.5**	**0**	**4**	**0**	**24**	**5**

LODISH, MIKE　　　　DT

PERSONAL: Born August 11, 1967, in Detroit. ... 6-3/270. ... Full name: Michael Timothy Lodish.
HIGH SCHOOL: Brother Rice (Birmingham, Mich.).
COLLEGE: UCLA (degree in history and business administration, 1990).
TRANSACTIONS/CAREER NOTES: Selected by Buffalo Bills in 10th round (265th pick overall) of 1990 NFL draft. ... Signed by Bills (July 26, 1990). ... Granted free agency (February 1, 1992). ... Re-signed by Bills (July 23, 1992). ... Granted unconditional free agency (February 17, 1995). ... Signed by Denver Broncos (April 4, 1995). ... Granted unconditional free agency (February 14, 1997). ... Re-signed by Broncos (August 6, 1997). ... Granted unconditional free agency (February 11, 2000). ... Re-signed by Broncos (March 23, 2000). ... Granted unconditional free agency (March 2, 2001).
CHAMPIONSHIP GAME EXPERIENCE: Played in AFC championship game (1990-1993, 1997 and 1998 seasons). ... Played in Super Bowl XXV (1990 season), Super Bowl XXVI (1991 season), Super Bowl XXVII (1992 season) and Super Bowl XXVIII (1993 season). ... Member of Super Bowl championship team (1997 and 1998 seasons).
POST SEASON RECORDS: Holds Super Bowl career record for most games—6.
PRO STATISTICS: 1992—Recovered one fumble for 18 yards and a touchdown. 1993—Recovered one fumble. 1994—Recovered one fumble in end zone for a touchdown. 1997—Recovered one fumble.

Year　Team	G	GS	SACKS
1990—Buffalo NFL	12	0	2.0
1991—Buffalo NFL	16	6	1.5
1992—Buffalo NFL	16	0	0.0
1993—Buffalo NFL	15	1	0.5
1994—Buffalo NFL	15	5	0.0
1995—Denver NFL	16	0	0.0
1996—Denver NFL	16	16	1.5
1997—Denver NFL	16	0	1.0
1998—Denver NFL	15	1	2.0
1999—Denver NFL	13	2	0.0
2000—Denver NFL	16	0	0.0
Pro totals (11 years)	**166**	**31**	**8.5**

LOGAN, ERNIE　　　　DT/DE

PERSONAL: Born May 18, 1968, in Fort Bragg, N.C. ... 6-3/290. ... Full name: Ernest Edward Logan.
HIGH SCHOOL: Pine Forest (Fayetteville, N.C.).
COLLEGE: East Carolina.
TRANSACTIONS/CAREER NOTES: Selected by Atlanta Falcons in ninth round (226th pick overall) of 1991 NFL draft. ... Released by Falcons (August 19, 1991). ... Signed by Cleveland Browns (August 21, 1991). ... Released by Browns (September 8, 1993). ... Signed by Falcons (October 7, 1993). ... Granted free agency (February 17, 1994). ... Re-signed by Falcons (April 28, 1994). ... Released by Falcons (August 22, 1994). ... Signed by Jacksonville Jaguars (December 15, 1994). ... Granted unconditional free agency (February 14, 1997). ... Signed by New York Jets (March 20, 1997). ... On injured reserve with leg injury (December 15, 1997-remainder of season). ... Released by Jets (September 11, 1999). ... Re-signed by Jets (September 13, 1999). ... Released by Jets (February 21, 2001).
CHAMPIONSHIP GAME EXPERIENCE: Member of Jaguars for AFC championship game (1996 season); inactive. ... Played in AFC championship game (1998 season).
PRO STATISTICS: 1991—Recovered one fumble.

Year　Team	G	GS	SACKS
1991—Cleveland NFL	15	5	0.5
1992—Cleveland NFL	16	0	1.0
1993—Atlanta NFL	8	1	1.0
1994—	Did not play.		
1995—Jacksonville NFL	15	1	3.0
1996—Jacksonville NFL	4	0	0.0
1997—New York Jets NFL	15	14	0.0
1998—New York Jets NFL	16	12	2.5
1999—New York Jets NFL	14	7	3.0
2000—New York Jets NFL	16	5	0.0
Pro totals (9 years)	**119**	**45**	**11.0**

LOGAN, JAMES — LB

PERSONAL: Born December 6, 1972, in Opp, Ala. ... 6-2/225.
HIGH SCHOOL: Opp (Ala.).
JUNIOR COLLEGE: Jones County Junior College (Miss.).
COLLEGE: Memphis State.
TRANSACTIONS/CAREER NOTES: Signed as non-drafted free agent by Houston Oilers (May 3, 1995). ... Released by Oilers (August 27, 1995). ... Re-signed by Oilers to practice squad (August 30, 1995). ... Activated (September 15, 1995). ... Claimed on waivers by Cincinnati Bengals (October 18, 1995). ... Claimed on waivers by Seattle Seahawks (October 31, 1995). ... Assigned by Seahawks to Scottish Claymores in 1997 World League enhancement allocation program (February 19, 1997). ... On injured reserve with fractured leg (September 30, 1998-remainder of season). ... Granted unconditional free agency (February 12, 1999). ... Re-signed by Seahawks (March 23, 1999). ... Granted unconditional free agency (March 2, 2001).
PLAYING EXPERIENCE: Houston (3)-Cincinnati (1)-Seattle (6) NFL, 1995; Seattle NFL, 1996-2000; Scottish W.L., 1997. ... Games/Games started: 1995 (Hou.-3/0; Cin.-1/0; Sea.-6/0; Total: 10/0), 1996 (6/0), W.L. 1997 (games played unavailable), NFL 1997 (14/1), 1998 (4/1), 1999 (16/2), 2000 (16/0). Total NFL: 66/4.
PRO STATISTICS: W.L.: 1997—Intercepted one pass for no yards, NFL: 1997—Recovered one fumble. 1998—Credited with one sack.

LOGAN, MIKE — DB — STEELERS

PERSONAL: Born September 15, 1974, in Pittsburgh. ... 6-0/209. ... Full name: Michael V. Logan.
HIGH SCHOOL: McKeesport (Pa.).
COLLEGE: West Virginia.
TRANSACTIONS/CAREER NOTES: Selected by Jacksonville Jaguars in second round (50th pick overall) of 1997 NFL draft. ... Signed by Jaguars (May 23, 1997). ... On injured reserve with ankle injury (September 20, 1999-remainder of season). ... Granted free agency (February 11, 2000). ... Re-signed by Jaguars (March 10, 2000). ... Granted unconditional free agency (March 2, 2001). ... Signed by Pittsburgh Steelers (March 24, 2001).
PRO STATISTICS: 1998—Recovered one fumble for two yards. 2000—Intercepted two passes for 14 yards and recovered one fumble for three yards.

			PUNT RETURNS				KICKOFF RETURNS				TOTALS			
Year Team	G	GS	No.	Yds.	Avg.	TD	No.	Yds.	Avg.	TD	TD	2pt.	Pts.	Fum.
1997—Jacksonville NFL	11	0	0	0	0.0	0	10	236	23.6	0	0	0	0	0
1998—Jacksonville NFL	15	0	2	26	13.0	0	18	414	23.0	0	0	0	0	1
1999—Jacksonville NFL	2	0	1	7	7.0	0	1	25	25.0	0	0	0	0	0
2000—Jacksonville NFL	15	11	0	0	0.0	0	0	0	0.0	0	0	0	0	0
Pro totals (4 years)	43	11	3	33	11.0	0	29	675	23.3	0	0	0	0	1

LONG, KEVIN — C — TITANS

PERSONAL: Born May 2, 1975, in Summerville, S.C. ... 6-5/295. ... Full name: Kevin Dale Long.
HIGH SCHOOL: Summerville (S.C.).
COLLEGE: Florida State.
TRANSACTIONS/CAREER NOTES: Selected by Tennessee Oilers in seventh round (229th pick overall) of 1998 NFL draft. ... Signed by Oilers (July 2, 1998). ... Oilers franchise renamed Tennessee Titans for 1999 season (December 26, 1998). ... Granted free agency (March 2, 2001).
PLAYING EXPERIENCE: Tennessee NFL, 1998-2000. ... Games/Games started: 1998 (16/2), 1999 (16/12), 2000 (16/16). Total: 48/30.
CHAMPIONSHIP GAME EXPERIENCE: Played in AFC championship game (1999 season). ... Played in Super Bowl XXXIV (1999 season).
PRO STATISTICS: 1999—Fumbled once for minus 10 yards. 2000—Recovered one fumble.

LONGWELL, RYAN — K — PACKERS

PERSONAL: Born August 16, 1974, in Seattle. ... 6-0/198. ... Full name: Ryan Walker Longwell.
HIGH SCHOOL: Bend (Ore.).
COLLEGE: California (degree in English).
TRANSACTIONS/CAREER NOTES: Signed as non-drafted free agent by San Francisco 49ers (April 28, 1997). ... Claimed on waivers by Green Bay Packers (July 10, 1997).
CHAMPIONSHIP GAME EXPERIENCE: Played in NFC championship game (1997 season). ... Played in Super Bowl XXXII (1997 season).
RECORDS: Holds NFL career record for highest field-goal percentage—84.73.
PRO STATISTICS: 1999—Punted once for 19 yards. 2000—Punted once for 30 yards.

		KICKING							
Year Team	G	XPM	XPA	FGM	FGA	Lg.	50+	Pts.
1997—Green Bay NFL	16	*48	*48	24	30	50	1-1	120
1998—Green Bay NFL	16	41	43	29	33	45	0-1	128
1999—Green Bay NFL	16	38	38	25	30	50	1-2	113
2000—Green Bay NFL	16	32	32	‡33	‡38	52	3-5	131
Pro totals (4 years)	64	159	161	111	131	52	5-9	492

LOVE, CLARENCE — CB — RAVENS

PERSONAL: Born June 16, 1976, in Jackson, Mich. ... 5-10/181. ... Full name: Clarence Eugene Love.
HIGH SCHOOL: Jackson (Mich.).
COLLEGE: Toledo.
TRANSACTIONS/CAREER NOTES: Selected by Philadelphia Eagles in fourth round (116th pick overall) of 1998 NFL draft. ... Signed by Eagles (July 14, 1998). ... Assigned by Eagles to Frankfurt Galaxy in 1999 NFL Europe enhancement allocation program (February 22, 1999). ... Released by Eagles (September 5, 1999). ... Signed by Jacksonville Jaguars to practice squad (September 21, 1999). ... Released by Jaguars (November 23, 1999). ... Signed by Baltimore Ravens to practice squad (December 15, 1999). ... Activated (December 31, 1999); did not play.
PLAYING EXPERIENCE: Philadelphia NFL, 1998; Baltimore NFL, 2000. ... Games/Games started: 1998 (6/0); 2000 (1/0). Total: 7/0.
CHAMPIONSHIP GAME EXPERIENCE: Member of Ravens for AFC Championship game (2000 season); inactive. ... Member of Super Bowl championship team (2000 season); inactive.

L

LOVERNE, DAVID   G   JETS

PERSONAL: Born May 22, 1976, in San Ramon, Calif. ... 6-3/299. ... Name pronounced LAH-vern.
HIGH SCHOOL: De La Salle (Concord, Calif.).
COLLEGE: Idaho, then San Jose State.
TRANSACTIONS/CAREER NOTES: Selected by New York Jets in third round (90th pick overall) of 1999 NFL draft. ... Signed by Jets (July 1, 1999). ... Inactive for all 16 games (1999).
PLAYING EXPERIENCE: New York Jets NFL, 2000. ... Games/Games started: 2000 (16/0).
PRO STATISTICS: 2000—Recovered one fumble.

LUCAS, ALBERT   DT   PANTHERS

PERSONAL: Born September 1, 1978, in Macon, Ga. ... 6-1/294.
HIGH SCHOOL: Northeast (Macon, Ga.).
COLLEGE: Troy State.
TRANSACTIONS/CAREER NOTES: Signed as non-drafted free agent by Pittsburgh Steelers (April 21, 2000). ... Released by Steelers (August 27, 2000). ... Signed by Carolina Panthers to practice squad (September 20, 2000). ... Activated (September 30, 2000).
PLAYING EXPERIENCE: Carolina NFL, 2000. ... Games/Games started: 2000 (13/0).
PRO STATISTICS: 2000—Recovered one fumble.

LUCAS, JUSTIN   DB   CARDINALS

PERSONAL: Born July 15, 1976, in Victoria, Texas. ... 5-10/197.
HIGH SCHOOL: Stroman (Victoria, Texas).
COLLEGE: Texas A&M, then Abilene Christian (degree in industrial technology).
TRANSACTIONS/CAREER NOTES: Signed as non-drafted free agent by Arizona Cardinals (April 23, 1999). ... Released by Cardinals (September 5, 1999). ... Re-signed by Cardinals to practice squad (September 7, 1999). ... Activated (October 17, 1999). ... Released by Cardinals (October 19, 1999). ... Re-signed by Cardinals to practice squad (October 20, 1999). ... Activated (December 31, 1999).
PLAYING EXPERIENCE: Arizona NFL, 1999 and 2000. ... Games/Games started: 1999 (2/0), 2000 (16/0). Total: 18/0.

LUCAS, RAY   QB   DOLPHINS

PERSONAL: Born August 6, 1972, in Harrison, N.J. ... 6-3/215.
HIGH SCHOOL: Harrison (N.J.).
COLLEGE: Rutgers.
TRANSACTIONS/CAREER NOTES: Signed as non-drafted free agent by New England Patriots (May 1, 1996). ... Released by Patriots (August 25, 1996). ... Re-signed by Patriots to practice squad (August 27, 1996). ... Activated (December 12, 1996). ... Claimed on waivers by New York Jets (August 19, 1997). ... Released by Jets (August 24, 1997). ... Re-signed by Jets to practice squad (August 26, 1997). ... Activated (November 22, 1997). ... Granted free agency (March 2, 2001). ... Tendered offer sheet by Miami Dolphins (March 9, 2001). ... Jets declined to match offer (March 16, 2001).
CHAMPIONSHIP GAME EXPERIENCE: Played in AFC championship game (1996 season). ... Played in Super Bowl XXXI (1996 season). ... Member of Jets for AFC championship game (1998 season); did not play.
PRO STATISTICS: 1999—Fumbled eight times and recovered four fumbles for minus 28 yards. 2000—Fumbled twice and recovered one fumble.
SINGLE GAME HIGHS (regular season): Attempts—48 (December 5, 1999, vs. New York Giants); completions—31 (December 5, 1999, vs. New York Giants); yards—284 (December 5, 1999, vs. New York Giants); and touchdown passes—4 (December 5, 1999, vs. New York Giants).
MISCELLANEOUS: Regular-season record as starting NFL quarterback: 6-3 (.667).

Year Team	G	GS	PASSING								RUSHING				TOTALS		
			Att.	Cmp.	Pct.	Yds.	TD	Int.	Avg.	Rat.	Att.	Yds.	Avg.	TD	TD	2pt.	Pts.
1996—New England NFL........	2	0	0	0	0.0	0	0	0	0.00	...	0	0	0.0	0	0	0	0
1997—New York Jets NFL......	5	0	4	3	75.0	28	0	1	7.00	54.2	6	55	9.2	0	0	0	0
1998—New York Jets NFL......	15	0	3	1	33.3	27	0	0	9.00	67.4	5	23	4.6	0	0	0	0
1999—New York Jets NFL......	9	9	272	161	59.2	1678	14	6	6.17	85.1	41	144	3.5	1	1	0	6
2000—New York Jets NFL......	7	0	41	21	51.2	206	0	4	5.02	26.1	6	42	7.0	0	0	0	0
Pro totals (5 years)	38	9	320	186	58.1	1939	14	11	6.06	76.0	58	264	4.6	1	1	0	6

LYGHT, TODD   CB   LIONS

PERSONAL: Born February 9, 1969, in Kwajalein, Marshall Islands. ... 6-0/190. ... Full name: Todd William Lyght.
HIGH SCHOOL: Luke M. Powers Catholic (Flint, Mich.).
COLLEGE: Notre Dame.
TRANSACTIONS/CAREER NOTES: Selected by Los Angeles Rams in first round (fifth pick overall) of 1991 NFL draft. ... Signed by Rams (August 16, 1991). ... On injured reserve with shoulder injury (September 22-October 22, 1992). ... On injured reserve with knee injury (November 23, 1993-remainder of season). ... Designated by Rams as transition player (February 15, 1994). ... Rams franchise moved to St. Louis (April 12, 1995). ... Tendered offer sheet by Jacksonville Jaguars (April 12, 1996). ... Offer matched by Rams (April 15, 1996). ... Designated by Rams as transition player (February 11, 2000). ... Granted unconditional free agency (March 2, 2001). ... Signed by Detroit Lions (April 12, 2001).
CHAMPIONSHIP GAME EXPERIENCE: Played in NFC championship game (1999 season). ... Member of Super Bowl championship team (1999 season).
HONORS: Named defensive back on THE SPORTING NEWS college All-America first team (1989). ... Named defensive back on THE SPORTING NEWS college All-America second team (1990). ... Played in Pro Bowl (1999 season).
PRO STATISTICS: 1991—Fumbled once and recovered one fumble. 1993—Recovered one fumble for 13 yards. 1994—Returned one punt for 29 yards and recovered one fumble for 74 yards and a touchdown. 1995—Ran 16 yards with lateral from punt return. 1996—Fumbled once. 1997—Recovered two fumbles. 2000—Ran 16 yards with lateral from punt return.

				INTERCEPTIONS			SACKS
Year Team	G	GS	No.	Yds.	Avg.	TD	No.
1991—Los Angeles Rams NFL	12	8	1	0	0.0	0	0.0
1992—Los Angeles Rams NFL	12	12	3	80	26.7	0	0.0
1993—Los Angeles Rams NFL	9	9	2	0	0.0	0	0.0
1994—Los Angeles Rams NFL	16	16	1	14	14.0	0	0.0
1995—St. Louis NFL	16	16	4	34	8.5	1	0.0
1996—St. Louis NFL	16	16	5	43	8.6	1	0.0
1997—St. Louis NFL	16	16	4	25	6.3	0	1.0
1998—St. Louis NFL	16	16	3	30	10.0	0	1.5
1999—St. Louis NFL	16	16	6	112	18.7	0	2.5
2000—St. Louis NFL	14	12	2	21	10.5	0	1.0
Pro totals (10 years)	143	137	31	359	11.6	3	6.0

LYLE, KEITH   S

PERSONAL: Born April 17, 1972, in Washington, D.C. ... 6-2/210. ... Full name: Keith Allen Lyle. ... Son of Garry Lyle, free safety/running back with Chicago Bears (1968-74).
HIGH SCHOOL: Mendon (N.Y.), then George C. Marshall (Falls Church, Va.).
COLLEGE: Virginia (degree in psychology, 1993).
TRANSACTIONS/CAREER NOTES: Selected by Los Angeles Rams in third round (71st pick overall) of 1994 NFL draft. ... Signed by Rams (July 8, 1994). ... Rams franchise moved to St. Louis (April 12, 1995). ... Granted free agency (February 14, 1997). ... Re-signed by Rams (April 15, 1997). ... Released by Rams (March 22, 2001).
CHAMPIONSHIP GAME EXPERIENCE: Played in NFC championship game (1999 season). ... Member of Super Bowl championship team (1999 season).
PRO STATISTICS: 1995—Rushed once for four yards. 1996—Rushed three times for 39 yards and fumbled once. 2000—Rushed once for four yards and recovered one fumble for 94 yards and a touchdown.

				INTERCEPTIONS			SACKS
Year Team	G	GS	No.	Yds.	Avg.	TD	No.
1994—Los Angeles Rams NFL	16	0	2	1	0.5	0	0.0
1995—St. Louis NFL	16	16	3	42	14.0	0	0.0
1996—St. Louis NFL	16	16	†9	‡152	16.9	0	0.0
1997—St. Louis NFL	16	16	8	102	12.8	0	2.0
1998—St. Louis NFL	16	16	3	20	6.7	0	1.0
1999—St. Louis NFL	9	9	2	10	5.0	0	1.0
2000—St. Louis NFL	16	16	1	9	9.0	0	0.0
Pro totals (7 years)	105	89	28	336	12.0	0	4.0

LYLE, RICK   DE/DT   JETS

PERSONAL: Born February 26, 1971, in Monroe, La. ... 6-5/290. ... Full name: Rick James Earl Lyle.
HIGH SCHOOL: Hickman Mills (Kansas City, Mo.).
COLLEGE: Missouri (degree in parks, recreation and tourism).
TRANSACTIONS/CAREER NOTES: Signed as non-drafted free agent by Cleveland Browns (May 2, 1994). ... On injured reserve with back injury (September 2, 1995-entire season). ... Browns franchise moved to Baltimore and renamed Ravens for 1996 season (March 11, 1996). ... Granted unconditional free agency (February 14, 1997). ... Signed by New York Jets (March 24, 1997). ... Granted unconditional free agency (March 2, 2001). ... Re-signed by Jets (May 14, 2001).
PLAYING EXPERIENCE: Cleveland NFL, 1994; Baltimore NFL, 1996; New York Jets NFL, 1997-2000. ... Games/Games started: 1994 (3/0), 1996 (11/3), 1997 (16/16), 1998 (16/16), 1999 (16/16), 2000 (14/14). Total: 76/65.
CHAMPIONSHIP GAME EXPERIENCE: Played in AFC championship game (1998 season).
PRO STATISTICS: 1997—Credited with three sacks and recovered one fumble for two yards. 1998—Credited with 1$^1/_2$ sacks. 1999—Credited with one sack. 2000—Credited with one sack.

LYMAN, DUSTIN   TE   BEARS

PERSONAL: Born August 5, 1976, in Boulder, Colo. ... 6-4/250.
HIGH SCHOOL: Fairview (Boulder, Colo.).
COLLEGE: Wake Forest.
TRANSACTIONS/CAREER NOTES: Selected by Chicago Bears in third round (87th pick overall) of 2000 NFL draft. ... Signed by Bears (June 15, 2000).
PLAYING EXPERIENCE: Chicago NFL, 2000. ... Games/Games started: 2000 (14/7).
PRO STATISTICS: 2000—Caught one pass for four yards.
SINGLE GAME HIGHS (regular season): Receptions—1 (December 17, 2000, vs. San Francisco); yards—4 (December 17, 2000, vs. San Francisco); and touchdown receptions—0.

LYNCH, BEN   C   49ERS

PERSONAL: Born November 18, 1972, in Santa Rosa, Calif. ... 6-4/295. ... Full name: Benjamin John Lynch.
HIGH SCHOOL: Analy (Sebastopol, Calif.).
COLLEGE: California.
TRANSACTIONS/CAREER NOTES: Selected by Kansas City Chiefs in seventh round (211th pick overall) of 1996 NFL draft. ... Signed by Chiefs (July 24, 1996). ... Released by Chiefs (August 20, 1996). ... Signed by Minnesota Vikings (February 10, 1997). ... Released by Vikings (August 18, 1997). ... Re-signed by Vikings to practice squad (December 11, 1997). ... Activated (December 30, 1997); did not play. ... Granted free agency (February 13, 1998). ... Selected by Frankfurt Galaxy in 1998 NFL Europe draft (February 18, 1998). ... Signed by Chicago Bears (July 1, 1998). ... On injured reserve with ankle injury (August 5-12, 1998). ... Released by Bears (August 12, 1998). ... Signed by San Francisco 49ers (May 4, 1999).
PLAYING EXPERIENCE: Frankfurt NFLE, 1998; San Francisco NFL, 1999 and 2000. ... Games/Games started: 1998 (games played unavailable), 1999 (16/1), 2000 (9/0). Total: 25/1.
PRO STATISTICS: 1999—Returned one kickoff for four yards.

LYNCH, JOHN   S   BUCCANEERS

PERSONAL: Born September 25, 1971, in Hinsdale, Ill. ... 6-2/220. ... Full name: John Terrence Lynch. ... Son of John Lynch, linebacker with Pittsburgh Steelers (1969); brother-in-law of John Allred, tight end, Chicago Bears; and brother of Ryan Lynch, pitcher in Baltimore Orioles organization.
HIGH SCHOOL: Torrey Pines (Encinitas, Calif.).
COLLEGE: Stanford.
TRANSACTIONS/CAREER NOTES: Selected by Tampa Bay Buccaneers in third round (82nd pick overall) of 1993 NFL draft. ... Signed by Buccaneers (June 1, 1993). ... On injured reserve with knee injury (December 12, 1995-remainder of season). ... Granted free agency (February 16, 1996). ... Re-signed by Buccaneers (July 13, 1996).
CHAMPIONSHIP GAME EXPERIENCE: Played in NFC championship game (1999 season).
HONORS: Played in Pro Bowl (1997, 1999 and 2000 seasons). ... Named safety on THE SPORTING NEWS NFL All-Pro team (1999 and 2000).
PRO STATISTICS: 1996—Rushed once for 40 yards, credited with one sack, fumbled once and recovered one fumble. 1997—Recovered two fumbles. 1998—Credited with two sacks and recovered one fumble. 1999—Credited with $1/2$ sack. 2000—Credited with one sack and recovered two fumbles for eight yards.

| | | | INTERCEPTIONS | | | |
Year Team	G	GS	No.	Yds.	Avg.	TD
1993—Tampa Bay NFL	15	4	0	0	0.0	0
1994—Tampa Bay NFL	16	0	0	0	0.0	0
1995—Tampa Bay NFL	9	6	3	3	1.0	0
1996—Tampa Bay NFL	16	14	3	26	8.7	0
1997—Tampa Bay NFL	16	16	2	28	14.0	0
1998—Tampa Bay NFL	15	15	2	29	14.5	0
1999—Tampa Bay NFL	16	16	2	32	16.0	0
2000—Tampa Bay NFL	16	16	3	43	14.3	0
Pro totals (8 years)	119	87	15	161	10.7	0

RECORD AS BASEBALL PLAYER
TRANSACTIONS/CAREER NOTES: Threw right, batted right. ... Selected by Florida Marlins organization in second round (66th pick overall) of free-agent draft (June 1, 1992).

PITCHING TOTALS

Year Team (League)	W	L	Pct.	ERA	G	GS	CG	ShO	Sv.	IP	H	R	ER	BB	SO
1992— Erie (N.Y.-Penn.)	0	3	.000	2.15	7	7	0	0	0	29 $1/3$	24	15	7	17	16
1993— Kane County (Midwest)	1	0	1.000	3.00	2	2	0	0	0	9	4	4	3	12	3

LYON, BILLY   DE/DT   PACKERS

PERSONAL: Born December 10, 1973, in Ashland, Ky. ... 6-5/295. ... Full name: William Morton Lyon.
HIGH SCHOOL: Lloyd (Erlanger, Ky.).
COLLEGE: Marshall (degree in occupational safety).
TRANSACTIONS/CAREER NOTES: Signed as non-drafted free agent by Kansas City Chiefs (April 28, 1997). ... Released by Chiefs (August 15, 1997). ... Signed by Green Bay Packers to practice squad (November 20, 1997)
PLAYING EXPERIENCE: Green Bay NFL, 1998-2000. ... Games/Games started: 1998 (4/0), 1999 (16/4), 2000 (11/1). Total: 31/5.
PRO STATISTICS: 1998—Credited with one sack. 1999—Intercepted one pass for no yards and credited with two sacks. 2000—Credited with one sack.

LYTLE, MATT   QB   PANTHERS

PERSONAL: Born September 4, 1975, in Wyomissing, Pa. ... 6-4/225.
HIGH SCHOOL: Wyomissing (Pa.).
COLLEGE: Pittsburgh.
TRANSACTIONS/CAREER NOTES: Signed as non-drafted free agent by Seattle Seahawks (August 28, 2000). ... Released by Seahawks (November 21, 2000). ... Re-signed by Seahawks to practice sqaud (November 23, 2000). ... Signed by Carolina Panthers off Seahawks practice squad (December 3, 2000).
PLAYING EXPERIENCE: Seattle NFL, 2000. ... Games/Games started: 2000 (2/0).

MACHADO, J.P.   C/G   JETS

PERSONAL: Born January 6, 1976, in Monmouth, Ill. ... 6-4/300.
HIGH SCHOOL: Monmouth (Ill.).
COLLEGE: Illinois.
TRANSACTIONS/CAREER NOTES: Selected by New York Jets in sixth round (197th pick overall) of 1999 NFL draft. ... Signed by Jets (July 27, 1999).
PLAYING EXPERIENCE: New York Jets NFL, 1999 and 2000. ... Games/Games started: 1999 (5/0), 2000 (16/0). Total: 21/0.
PRO STATISTICS: 1999—Recovered one fumble.

MACK, STACEY   FB   JAGUARS

PERSONAL: Born June 26, 1975, in Orlando, Fla. ... 6-1/237. ... Full name: Stacey Lamar Mack.
HIGH SCHOOL: Boone (Orlando, Fla.).
JUNIOR COLLEGE: Southwest Mississippi College.
COLLEGE: Temple.

TRANSACTIONS/CAREER NOTES: Signed as non-drafted free agent by Jacksonville Jaguars (April 22, 1999). ... On injured reserve with finger injury (October 12, 2000-remainder of season).
CHAMPIONSHIP GAME EXPERIENCE: Member of Jaguars for AFC championship game (1999 season); inactive.
PRO STATISTICS: 1999—Returned six kickoffs for 112 yards. 2000—Returned six kickoffs for 104 yards, fumbled three times and recovered one fumble.
SINGLE GAME HIGHS (regular season): Attempts—23 (September 3, 2000, vs. Cleveland); yards—74 (September 3, 2000, vs. Cleveland); and rushing touchdowns—1 (September 3, 2000, vs. Cleveland).

			RUSHING				TOTALS			
Year Team	G	GS	Att.	Yds.	Avg.	TD	TD	2pt.	Pts.	Fum.
1999—Jacksonville NFL	12	0	7	40	5.7	0	0	0	0	0
2000—Jacksonville NFL	6	2	54	145	2.7	1	1	0	6	3
Pro totals (2 years)	18	2	61	185	3.0	1	1	0	6	3

MACK, TREMAIN   S/KR   BENGALS

PERSONAL: Born November 21, 1974, in Tyler, Texas. ... 6-0/193. ... Nephew of Phillip Epps, wide receiver with Green Bay Packers (1982-88) and New York Jets (1989).
HIGH SCHOOL: Chapel Hill (Tyler, Texas).
COLLEGE: Miami (Fla.).
TRANSACTIONS/CAREER NOTES: Selected by Cincinnati Bengals in fourth round (111th pick overall) of 1997 NFL draft. ... Signed by Bengals (June 5, 1997). ... On non-football injury list with illness (November 5-December 1, 1997). ... On exempt/left squad list (December 3, 1998-remainder of season). ... On suspended list for violating league substance abuse policy (September 5-October 3, 1999).
HONORS: Played in Pro Bowl (1999 season).
PRO STATISTICS: 1997—Intercepted one pass for 29 yards. 1998—Recovered one fumble. 1999—Recovered one fumble. 2000—Recovered one fumble.

			KICKOFF RETURNS				TOTALS			
Year Team	G	GS	No.	Yds.	Avg.	TD	TD	2pt.	Pts.	Fum.
1997—Cincinnati NFL	4	4	0	0	0.0	0	0	0	0	0
1998—Cincinnati NFL	12	0	45	1165	25.9	▲1	1	0	6	2
1999—Cincinnati NFL	12	0	51	1382	§27.1	▲1	1	0	6	3
2000—Cincinnati NFL	16	0	50	1036	20.7	0	0	0	0	3
Pro totals (4 years)	44	4	146	3583	24.5	2	2	0	12	8

MACKLIN, DAVID   DB   COLTS

PERSONAL: Born July 14, 1978, in Newport News, Va. ... 5-9/193. ... Full name: David Thurman Macklin.
HIGH SCHOOL: Menchville (Newport News, Va.).
COLLEGE: Penn State.
TRANSACTIONS/CAREER NOTES: Selected by Indianapolis Colts in third round (91st pick overall) of 2000 NFL draft. ... Signed by Colts (July 13, 2000).
PRO STATISTICS: 2000—Returned one kickoff for no yards.

			INTERCEPTIONS		
Year Team	G	GS	No.	Yds.	Avg.	TD
2000—Indianapolis NFL	16	2	2	35	17.5	0

MADDOX, MARK   LB

PERSONAL: Born March 23, 1968, in Milwaukee. ... 6-1/238. ... Full name: Mark Anthony Maddox.
HIGH SCHOOL: James Madison Memorial (Madison, Wis.).
COLLEGE: Northern Michigan.
TRANSACTIONS/CAREER NOTES: Selected by Buffalo Bills in ninth round (249th pick overall) of 1991 NFL draft. ... Signed by Bills (June 18, 1991). ... On injured reserve with knee injury (August 27, 1991-entire season). ... On injured reserve with knee injury (October 10, 1995-remainder of season). ... Granted unconditional free agency (February 16, 1996). ... Re-signed by Bills (March 4, 1996). ... Released by Bills (June 2, 1997). ... Re-signed by Bills (July 2, 1997). ... Released by Bills (August 12, 1997). ... Re-signed by Bills (October 28, 1997). ... Granted unconditional free agency (February 13, 1998). ... Signed by Arizona Cardinals (March 19, 1998). ... Granted unconditional free agency (February 12, 1999). ... Re-signed by Cardinals (April 2, 1999). ... Granted unconditional free agency (February 11, 2000). ... Re-signed by Cardinals (March 28, 2000). ... Released by Cardinals (January 9, 2001).
PLAYING EXPERIENCE: Buffalo NFL, 1992-1997; Arizona NFL, 1998-2000. ... Games/Games started: 1992 (15/1), 1993 (11/8), 1994 (15/14), 1995 (4/4), 1996 (14/14), 1997 (8/1), 1998 (14/3), 1999 (16/2), 2000 (14/0). Total: 111/47.
CHAMPIONSHIP GAME EXPERIENCE: Played in AFC championship game (1992 and 1993 season). ... Played in Super Bowl XXVII (1992 season) and Super Bowl XXVIII (1993 season).
PRO STATISTICS: 1993—Recovered two fumbles. 1994—Intercepted one pass for 11 yards and recovered one fumble. 1997—Intercepted one pass for 25 yards. 1998—Credited with one sack and recovered one fumble. 2000—Credited with 1$\frac{1}{2}$ sacks and recovered one fumble for minus two yards.

MADISON, SAM   CB   DOLPHINS

PERSONAL: Born April 23, 1974, in Thomasville, Ga. ... 5-11/185. ... Full name: Samuel A. Madison Jr.
HIGH SCHOOL: Florida A&M High (Monticello, Fla.).
COLLEGE: Louisville.
TRANSACTIONS/CAREER NOTES: Selected by Miami Dolphins in second round (44th pick overall) of 1997 NFL draft. ... Signed by Dolphins (June 16, 1997).
HONORS: Named cornerback on THE SPORTING NEWS NFL All-Pro team (1999 and 2000). ... Played in Pro Bowl (1999 and 2000 seasons).
PRO STATISTICS: 1998—Credited with one sack. 1999—Credited with a safety. 2000—Recovered two fumbles for 20 yards and a touchdown.

M

Year Team	G	GS	No.	Yds.	Avg.	TD	TD	2pt.	Pts.	Fum.
				INTERCEPTIONS				TOTALS		
1997—Miami NFL	14	3	1	21	21.0	0	0	0	0	0
1998—Miami NFL	16	16	8	114	14.3	0	0	0	0	0
1999—Miami NFL	16	16	†7	164	23.4	1	1	0	8	0
2000—Miami NFL	16	16	5	80	16.0	0	1	0	6	1
Pro totals (4 years)	62	51	21	379	18.0	1	2	0	14	1

MAKOVICKA, JOEL — FB — CARDINALS

PERSONAL: Born October 6, 1975, in Brainard, Neb. ... 5-11/246. ... Name pronounced mack-oh-VIK-uh.
HIGH SCHOOL: East Butler (Brainard, Neb.).
COLLEGE: Nebraska.
TRANSACTIONS/CAREER NOTES: Selected by Arizona Cardinals in fourth round (116th pick overall) of 1999 NFL draft. ... Signed by Cardinals (June 18, 1999).
PRO STATISTICS: 1999—Returned one kickoff for 10 yards and recovered one fumble.
SINGLE GAME HIGHS (regular season): Attempts—2 (October 31, 1999, vs. New England); yards—7 (October 8, 2000, vs. Cleveland); and rushing touchdowns—0.

Year Team	G	GS	Att.	Yds.	Avg.	TD	No.	Yds.	Avg.	TD	TD	2pt.	Pts.	Fum.
			RUSHING				RECEIVING				TOTALS			
1999—Arizona NFL	16	10	8	7	0.9	0	10	70	7.0	1	1	0	6	1
2000—Arizona NFL	14	10	3	8	2.7	0	6	18	3.0	0	0	0	0	0
Pro totals (2 years)	30	20	11	15	1.4	0	16	88	5.5	1	1	0	6	1

MALBROUGH, ANTHONY — DB — BROWNS

PERSONAL: Born December 9, 1976, in Beaumont, Texas. ... 5-10/185. ... Half brother of Jerry Ball, defensive tackle with five NFL teams (1987-99).
HIGH SCHOOL: Westbrook (Texas).
COLLEGE: Texas Tech.
TRANSACTIONS/CAREER NOTES: Selected by Cleveland Browns in fifth round (130th pick overall) of 2000 NFL draft. ... Signed by Browns (June 16, 2000). ... Assigned by Browns to Barcelona Dragons in 2001 NFL Europe enhancement allocation program (February 19, 2001).
PLAYING EXPERIENCE: Cleveland NFL, 2000. ... Games/Games started: 2000 (9/1).

MAMULA, MIKE — LB/DE

M

PERSONAL: Born August 14, 1973, in Lackawanna, N.Y. ... 6-4/252. ... Full name: Michael David Mamula. ... Name pronounced muh-MOO-la.
HIGH SCHOOL: Lackawanna (N.Y.) Secondary.
COLLEGE: Boston College (degree in sociology, 1994).
TRANSACTIONS/CAREER NOTES: Selected after junior season by Philadelphia Eagles in first round (seventh pick overall) of 1995 NFL draft. ... Signed by Eagles (July 19, 1995). ... On injured reserve with knee injury (August 18, 1998-entire season). ... Granted unconditional free agency (February 12, 1999). ... Re-signed by Eagles (February 12, 1999). ... Released by Eagles (April 23, 2000).
PRO STATISTICS: 1995—Recovered one fumble for 25 yards. 1996—Recovered three fumbles for four yards and a touchdown. 1999—Intercepted one pass for 41 yards and a touchdown and recovered two fumbles.

Year Team	G	GS	SACKS
1995—Philadelphia NFL	14	13	5.5
1996—Philadelphia NFL	16	16	8.0
1997—Philadelphia NFL	16	16	4.0
1998—Philadelphia NFL	Did not play.		
1999—Philadelphia NFL	16	13	8.5
2000—Philadelphia NFL	15	6	5.5
Pro totals (5 years)	77	64	31.5

MANGUM, KRIS — TE — PANTHERS

PERSONAL: Born August 15, 1973, in Magee, Miss. ... 6-4/249. ... Full name: Kris Thomas Mangum. ... Son of John Mangum, defensive tackle with Boston Patriots (1966 and 1967) of AFL; and brother of John Mangum, cornerback with Chicago Bears (1990-98).
HIGH SCHOOL: Magee (Miss.).
COLLEGE: Mississippi.
TRANSACTIONS/CAREER NOTES: Selected by Carolina Panthers in seventh round (228th pick overall) of 1997 NFL draft. ... Signed by Panthers (May 20, 1997). ... Released by Panthers (September 2, 1997). ... Re-signed by Panthers to practice squad (September 4, 1997). ... Activated (December 5, 1997).
PRO STATISTICS: 1999—Returned two kickoffs for 20 yards.
SINGLE GAME HIGHS (regular season): Receptions—4 (November 19, 2000, vs. Minnesota); yards—56 (December 20, 1997, vs. St. Louis); and touchdown receptions—1 (December 10, 2000, vs. Kansas City).

Year Team	G	GS	No.	Yds.	Avg.	TD	TD	2pt.	Pts.	Fum.
			RECEIVING				TOTALS			
1997—Carolina NFL	2	1	4	56	14.0	0	0	0	0	0
1998—Carolina NFL	6	0	1	5	5.0	0	0	0	0	0
1999—Carolina NFL	11	0	1	6	6.0	0	0	0	0	0
2000—Carolina NFL	15	7	19	215	11.3	1	1	0	6	0
Pro totals (4 years)	34	8	25	282	11.3	1	1	0	6	0

MANNELLY, PATRICK OT BEARS

PERSONAL: Born April 18, 1975, in Atlanta. ... 6-5/270. ... Full name: James Patrick Mannelly.
HIGH SCHOOL: Marist (Atlanta).
COLLEGE: Duke.
TRANSACTIONS/CAREER NOTES: Selected by Chicago Bears in sixth round (189th pick overall) of 1998 NFL draft. ... Signed by Bears (June 11, 1998).
PLAYING EXPERIENCE: Chicago NFL, 1998-2000. ... Games/Games started: 1998 (16/0), 1999 (16/0), 2000 (16/0). Total: 48/0.

MANNING, PEYTON QB COLTS

PERSONAL: Born March 24, 1976, in New Orleans. ... 6-5/225. ... Full name: Peyton Williams Manning. ... Son of Archie Manning, quarterback with New Orleans Saints (1971-82), Houston Oilers (1982-83) and Minnesota Vikings (1983-84).
HIGH SCHOOL: Isidore Newman (New Orleans).
COLLEGE: Tennessee (degree in speech communication).
TRANSACTIONS/CAREER NOTES: Selected by Indianapolis Colts in first round (first pick overall) of 1998 NFL draft. ... Signed by Colts (July 28, 1998).
HONORS: Davey O'Brien Award winner (1997). ... Named College Player of the Year by THE SPORTING NEWS (1997). ... Named quarterback on THE SPORTING NEWS college All-America second team (1997). ... Played in Pro Bowl (1999 and 2000 seasons).
RECORDS: Holds NFL rookie-season records for most passes attempted—575 (1998); most passes completed—326 (1998); and most yards passing—3,739.
PRO STATISTICS: 1998—Fumbled three times. 1999—Fumbled six times and recovered two fumbles for minus five yards. 2000—Fumbled five times and recovered one fumble for minus three yards.
SINGLE GAME HIGHS (regular season): Attempts—54 (October 8, 2000, vs. New England); completions—33 (September 10, 2000, vs. Oakland); yards—440 (September 25, 2000, vs. Jacksonville); and touchdown passes—4 (December 24, 2000, vs. Minnesota).
STATISTICAL PLATEAUS: 300-yard passing games: 1998 (4), 1999 (2), 2000 (5). Total: 11.
MISCELLANEOUS: Regular-season record as starting NFL quarterback: 26-22 (.542). ... Postseason record as starting NFL quarterback: 0-2.

			PASSING								RUSHING				TOTALS		
Year Team	G	GS	Att.	Cmp.	Pct.	Yds.	TD	Int.	Avg.	Rat.	Att.	Yds.	Avg.	TD	TD	2pt.	Pts.
1998—Indianapolis NFL	16	16	*575	§326	56.7	§3739	26	*28	6.50	71.2	15	62	4.1	0	0	0	0
1999—Indianapolis NFL	16	16	533	§331	§62.1	§4135	§26	15	§7.76	§90.7	35	73	2.1	2	2	0	12
2000—Indianapolis NFL	16	16	571	*357	62.5	4413	*33	15	7.73	94.7	37	116	3.1	1	1	0	6
Pro totals (3 years)	48	48	1679	1014	60.4	12287	85	58	7.32	85.4	87	251	2.9	3	3	0	18

MARE, OLINDO K DOLPHINS

PERSONAL: Born June 6, 1973, in Hollywood, Fla. ... 5-10/195. ... Full name: Olindo Franco Mare. ... Name pronounced o-LEND-o MAR-ray.
HIGH SCHOOL: Cooper City (Fla.).
JUNIOR COLLEGE: Valencia Community College (Fla.).
COLLEGE: Syracuse.
TRANSACTIONS/CAREER NOTES: Signed as non-drafted free agent by New York Giants (May 2, 1996). ... Released by Giants (August 25, 1996). ... Re-signed by Giants to practice squad (August 27, 1996). ... Granted free agency after 1996 season. ... Signed by Miami Dolphins (February 27, 1997). ... Granted free agency (February 11, 2000). ... Re-signed by Dolphins (June 15, 2000). ... Granted unconditional free agency (March 2, 2001). ... Re-signed by Dolphins (March 2, 2001).
HONORS: Named kicker on THE SPORTING NEWS NFL All-Pro team (1999). ... Played in Pro Bowl (1999 season).
RECORDS: Holds NFL single-season record for most field goals made—39 (1999).

		PUNTING						KICKING						
Year Team	G	No.	Yds.	Avg.	Net avg.	In. 20	Blk.	XPM	XPA	FGM	FGA	Lg.	50+	Pts.
1996—New York Giants NFL					Did not play.									
1997—Miami NFL	16	5	235	47.0	46.2	2	0	33	33	28	36	50	1-3	117
1998—Miami NFL	16	3	115	38.3	31.7	1	0	33	34	22	27	48	0-2	99
1999—Miami NFL	16	1	36	36.0	30.0	0	0	27	27	*39	*46	54	3-5	144
2000—Miami NFL	16	0	0	0.0	0	0	0	33	34	28	31	49	0-0	117
Pro totals (4 years)	64	9	386	42.9	39.6	3	0	126	128	117	140	54	4-10	477

MARION, BROCK S

PERSONAL: Born June 11, 1970, in Bakersfield, Calif. ... 5-11/205. ... Full name: Brock Elliot Marion. ... Son of Jerry Marion, wide receiver with Pittsburgh Steelers (1967); and nephew of Brent McClanahan, running back with Minnesota Vikings (1973-79).
HIGH SCHOOL: West (Bakersfield, Calif.).
COLLEGE: Nevada.
TRANSACTIONS/CAREER NOTES: Selected by Dallas Cowboys in seventh round (196th overall) of 1993 NFL draft. ... Signed by Cowboys (July 14, 1993). ... Granted free agency (February 16, 1996). ... Re-signed by Cowboys (May 2, 1996). ... Granted unconditional free agency (February 14, 1997). ... Re-signed by Cowboys (April 7, 1997). ... Granted unconditional free agency (February 13, 1998). ... Signed by Miami Dolphins (March 3, 1998). ... Granted unconditional free agency (March 2, 2001).
CHAMPIONSHIP GAME EXPERIENCE: Played in NFC championship game (1993-1995 seasons). ... Member of Super Bowl championship team (1993 and 1995 seasons).
HONORS: Played in Pro Bowl (2000 season).
PRO STATISTICS: 1993—Recovered one fumble. 1994—Credited with one sack and returned two kickoffs for 39 yards. 1996—Fumbled once and recovered one fumble for 45 yards. 1997—Recovered one fumble for 13 yards. 1998—Recovered one fumble for two yards. 1999—Credited with one sack and recovered one fumble. 2000—Recovered one fumble.

Year Team	G	GS	INTERCEPTIONS				KICKOFF RETURNS				TOTALS			
			No.	Yds.	Avg.	TD	No.	Yds.	Avg.	TD	TD	2pt.	Pts.	Fum.
1993—Dallas NFL	15	0	1	2	2.0	0	0	0	0.0	0	0	0	0	0
1994—Dallas NFL	14	1	1	11	11.0	0	2	39	19.5	0	0	0	0	0
1995—Dallas NFL	16	16	6	40	6.7	1	1	16	16.0	0	1	0	6	0
1996—Dallas NFL	10	10	0	0	0.0	0	3	68	22.7	0	0	0	0	1
1997—Dallas NFL	16	16	0	0	0.0	0	10	311	31.1	0	0	0	0	0
1998—Miami NFL	16	16	0	0	0.0	0	6	109	18.2	0	0	0	0	0
1999—Miami NFL	16	16	2	30	15.0	0	*62	*1524	24.6	0	0	0	0	2
2000—Miami NFL	16	16	5	72	14.4	0	22	513	23.3	0	0	0	0	0
Pro totals (8 years)	119	91	15	155	10.3	1	106	2580	24.3	0	1	0	6	3

MARTIN, CECIL   FB   EAGLES

PERSONAL: Born July 8, 1975, in Chicago. ... 6-0/235.
HIGH SCHOOL: Evanston (Ill.).
COLLEGE: Wisconsin.
TRANSACTIONS/CAREER NOTES: Selected by Philadelphia Eagles in sixth round (172nd pick overall) of 1999 NFL draft. ... Signed by Eagles (July 25, 1999).
SINGLE GAME HIGHS (regular season): Attempts—3 (November 19, 2000, vs. Arizona); yards—28 (December 24, 2000, vs. Cincinnati); and rushing touchdowns—0.

Year Team	G	GS	RUSHING				RECEIVING				TOTALS			
			Att.	Yds.	Avg.	TD	No.	Yds.	Avg.	TD	TD	2pt.	Pts.	Fum.
1999—Philadelphia NFL	12	5	3	3	1.0	0	11	22	2.0	0	0	0	0	0
2000—Philadelphia NFL	16	9	13	77	5.9	0	31	219	7.1	0	0	0	0	1
Pro totals (2 years)	28	14	16	80	5.0	0	42	241	5.7	0	0	0	0	1

MARTIN, CURTIS   RB   JETS

PERSONAL: Born May 1, 1973, in Pittsburgh. ... 5-11/210.
HIGH SCHOOL: Taylor-Allderdice (Pittsburgh).
COLLEGE: Pittsburgh.
TRANSACTIONS/CAREER NOTES: Selected after junior season by New England Patriots in third round (74th pick overall) of 1995 NFL draft. ... Signed by Patriots (July 18, 1995). ... Granted free agency (February 13, 1998). ... Tendered offer sheet by New York Jets (March 20, 1998). ... Patriots declined to match offer (March 25, 1998).
CHAMPIONSHIP GAME EXPERIENCE: Played in AFC championship game (1996 and 1998 seasons). ... Played in Super Bowl XXXI (1996 season).
HONORS: Named NFL Rookie of the Year by THE SPORTING NEWS (1995). ... Played in Pro Bowl (1995, 1996 and 1998 seasons).
PRO STATISTICS: 1995—Recovered three fumbles. 1996—Recovered one fumble. 1998—Recovered one fumble. 1999—Recovered two fumbles. 2000—Completed only pass attempt for 18 yards and a touchdown.
SINGLE GAME HIGHS (regular season): Attempts—40 (September 14, 1997, vs. New York Jets); yards—203 (December 3, 2000, vs. Indianapolis); and rushing touchdowns—3 (October 15, 2000, vs. New England).
STATISTICAL PLATEAUS: 100-yard rushing games: 1995 (9), 1996 (2), 1997 (3), 1998 (8), 1999 (6), 2000 (3). Total: 31.

Year Team	G	GS	RUSHING				RECEIVING				TOTALS			
			Att.	Yds.	Avg.	TD	No.	Yds.	Avg.	TD	TD	2pt.	Pts.	Fum.
1995—New England NFL	16	15	§368	§1487	4.0	14	30	261	8.7	1	15	1	92	5
1996—New England NFL	16	15	316	1152	3.6	§14	46	333	7.2	3	§17	1	104	4
1997—New England NFL	13	13	274	1160	4.2	4	41	296	7.2	1	5	0	30	3
1998—New York Jets NFL	15	15	369	1287	3.5	8	43	365	8.5	1	9	0	54	5
1999—New York Jets NFL	16	16	367	1464	4.0	5	45	259	5.8	0	5	0	30	2
2000—New York Jets NFL	16	16	316	1204	3.8	9	70	508	7.3	2	11	0	66	2
Pro totals (6 years)	92	90	2010	7754	3.9	54	275	2022	7.4	8	62	2	376	21

MARTIN, JAMIE   QB   JAGUARS

PERSONAL: Born February 8, 1970, in Orange, Calif. ... 6-2/208. ... Full name: Jamie Blane Martin.
HIGH SCHOOL: Arroyo Grande (Calif.).
COLLEGE: Weber State.
TRANSACTIONS/CAREER NOTES: Signed as non-drafted free agent by Los Angeles Rams (May 3, 1993). ... Released by Rams (August 24, 1993). ... Re-signed by Rams to practice squad (August 31, 1993). ... Activated (November 23, 1993). ... Inactive for five games (1993). ... Released by Rams (August 27, 1994). ... Re-signed by Rams (October 4, 1994). ... Released by Rams (October 12, 1994). ... Re-signed by Rams (November 15, 1994). ... Active for one game (1994); did not play. ... Assigned by Rams to Amsterdam Admirals of World Football League (1995). ... Rams franchise moved to St. Louis (April 12, 1995). ... On physically unable to perform list with broken collarbone (June 3, 1995-entire season). ... Released by Rams (August 17, 1997). ... Signed by Washington Redskins (December 2, 1997). ... Granted free agency (February 13, 1998). ... Signed by Jacksonville Jaguars (March 6, 1998). ... On injured reserve with knee injury (December 15, 1998-remainder of season). ... Granted unconditional free agency (February 12, 1999). ... Signed by Cleveland Browns (August 25, 1999). ... Granted unconditional free agency (February 11, 2000). ... Signed by Jaguars (February 22, 2000). ... Released by Jaguars (March 1, 2001). ... Re-signed by Jaguars (April 2, 2001).
HONORS: Walter Payton Award winner (1991).
PRO STATISTICS: 1996—Fumbled twice and recovered one fumble for minus two yards.
SINGLE GAME HIGHS (regular season): Attempts—23 (December 6, 1998, vs. Detroit); completions—15 (December 6, 1998, vs. Detroit); yards—228 (December 6, 1998, vs. Detroit); and touchdown passes—2 (December 6, 1998, vs. Detroit).
MISCELLANEOUS: Regular-season record as starting NFL quarterback: 0-1.

Year Team	G	GS	PASSING Att.	Cmp.	Pct.	Yds.	TD	Int.	Avg.	Rat.	RUSHING Att.	Yds.	Avg.	TD	TOTALS TD	2pt.	Pts.
1993—L.A. Rams NFL............								Did not play.									
1994—L.A. Rams NFL............								Did not play.									
1995—Amsterdam W.L.	9	9	219	126	57.5	1433	11	6	6.54	82.6	0	0	0.0	0	0	0	0
—St. Louis NFL.................								Did not play.									
1996—St. Louis NFL..............	6	0	34	23	67.6	241	3	2	7.09	92.9	7	14	2.0	0	0	0	0
1997—Washington NFL								Did not play.									
1998—Jacksonville NFL	4	1	45	27	60.0	355	2	0	7.89	99.8	5	8	1.6	0	0	0	0
1999—Cleveland NFL								Did not play.									
2000—Jacksonville NFL	5	0	33	22	66.7	307	2	1	9.30	104.0	7	-6	-0.9	0	0	0	0
W.L. totals (1 year)	9	9	219	126	57.5	1433	11	6	6.54	82.6	0	0	0.0	0	0	0	0
NFL totals (3 years)..............	17	1	112	72	64.3	903	7	3	8.06	98.9	19	16	0.8	0	0	0	0
Pro totals (4 years).............	26	10	331	198	59.8	2336	18	9	7.06	88.1	19	16	0.8	0	0	0	0

MARTIN, STEVE   DT   CHIEFS

PERSONAL: Born May 31, 1974, in St. Paul, Minn. ... 6-4/312. ... Full name: Steven Albert Martin.
HIGH SCHOOL: Jefferson City (Mo.).
COLLEGE: Missouri.
TRANSACTIONS/CAREER NOTES: Selected by Indianapolis Colts in fifth round (151st pick overall) of 1996 NFL draft. ... Signed by Colts (July 5, 1996). ... Claimed on waivers by Philadelphia Eagles (October 23, 1998). ... Granted free agency (February 12, 1999). ... Re-signed by Eagles (April 9, 1999). ... Granted unconditional free agency (February 11, 2000). ... Signed by Kansas City Chiefs (February 24, 2000).
PRO STATISTICS: 1996—Recovered one fumble. 1999—Recovered one fumble.

Year Team	G	GS	SACKS
1996—Indianapolis NFL..	14	5	1.0
1997—Indianapolis NFL..	12	0	0.0
1998—Indianapolis NFL..	4	0	0.0
—Philadelphia NFL..	9	3	1.0
1999—Philadelphia NFL..	16	15	2.0
2000—Kansas City NFL..	16	0	0.0
Pro totals (5 years)..	71	23	4.0

MARTIN, TEE   QB   STEELERS

PERSONAL: Born July 25, 1978, in Mobile, Ala. ... 6-1/221. ... Full name: Tamaurice Nigel Martin.
HIGH SCHOOL: Williamson (Mobile, Ala.).
COLLEGE: Tennessee.
TRANSACTIONS/CAREER NOTES: Selected by Pittsburgh Steelers in fifth round (163rd pick overall) of 2000 NFL draft. ... Signed by Steelers (July 16, 2000).
PLAYING EXPERIENCE: Pittsburgh NFL, 2000. ... Games/Games started: 2000 (2/0).

MARTIN, TONY   WR

M

PERSONAL: Born September 5, 1965, in Miami. ... 6-1/175. ... Full name: Tony Derrick Martin.
HIGH SCHOOL: Miami Northwestern.
COLLEGE: Bishop (Texas), then Mesa State College (Colo.).
TRANSACTIONS/CAREER NOTES: Selected by New York Jets in fifth round (126th pick overall) of 1989 NFL draft. ... Signed by New York Jets for 1989 season. ... Released by Jets (September 4, 1989). ... Signed by Miami Dolphins to developmental squad (September 5, 1989). ... Activated (December 23, 1989); did not play. ... Granted free agency (February 1, 1992). ... Re-signed by Dolphins (March 10, 1992). ... Traded by Dolphins to San Diego Chargers for fourth-round pick (traded to Arizona) in 1994 draft (March 24, 1994). ... Designated by Chargers as franchise player (February 13, 1997). ... Re-signed by Chargers (May 1, 1997). ... Traded by Chargers to Atlanta Falcons for second-round pick (RB Jermaine Fazande) in 1999 draft (June 3, 1998). ... Released by Falcons (February 26, 1999). ... Signed by Dolphins (April 9, 1999). ... Released by Dolphins (February 22, 2001).
CHAMPIONSHIP GAME EXPERIENCE: Played in AFC championship game (1992 and 1994 seasons). ... Played in Super Bowl XXIX (1994 season) and Super Bowl XXXIII (1998 season). ... Played in NFC championship game (1998 season).
HONORS: Played in Pro Bowl (1996 season).
RECORDS: Shares NFL record for longest pass reception (from Stan Humphries)—99 yards, touchdown (September 18, 1994, at Seattle).
PRO STATISTICS: 1990—Recovered two fumbles. 1992—Attempted one pass without a completion and recovered one fumble. 1994—Attempted one pass without a completion and returned eight kickoffs for 167 yards. 1995—Attempted one pass without a completion. 1998—Attempted one pass without a completion.
SINGLE GAME HIGHS (regular season): Receptions—13 (September 10, 1995, vs. Seattle); yards—172 (December 11, 1994, vs. San Francisco); and touchdown receptions—3 (September 28, 1997, vs. Baltimore).
STATISTICAL PLATEAUS: 100-yard receiving games: 1991 (2), 1993 (1), 1994 (2), 1995 (4), 1996 (4), 1997 (2), 1998 (5), 1999 (5), 2000 (1). Total: 26.

Year Team	G	GS	RUSHING Att.	Yds.	Avg.	TD	RECEIVING No.	Yds.	Avg.	TD	PUNT RETURNS No.	Yds.	Avg.	TD	TOTALS TD	2pt.	Pts.	Fum.
1990—Miami NFL	16	5	1	8	8.0	0	29	388	13.4	2	26	140	5.4	0	2	0	12	4
1991—Miami NFL	16	0	0	0	0.0	0	27	434	16.1	2	1	10	10.0	0	2	0	12	2
1992—Miami NFL	16	3	1	-2	-2.0	0	33	553	16.8	2	1	0	0.0	0	2	0	12	2
1993—Miami NFL	12	0	1	6	6.0	0	20	347	17.4	3	0	0	0.0	0	3	0	18	1
1994—San Diego NFL............	16	1	2	-9	-4.5	0	50	885	17.7	7	0	0	0.0	0	7	0	42	2
1995—San Diego NFL............	16	16	0	0	0.0	0	90	1224	13.6	6	0	0	0.0	0	6	0	36	3
1996—San Diego NFL............	16	16	0	0	0.0	0	85	1171	13.8	†14	0	0	0.0	0	14	0	84	0
1997—San Diego NFL............	16	16	0	0	0.0	0	63	904	14.3	6	0	0	0.0	0	6	0	36	0
1998—Atlanta NFL	16	16	0	0	0.0	0	66	1181	17.9	6	0	0	0.0	0	6	0	36	0
1999—Miami NFL	16	13	1	-6	-6.0	0	67	1037	15.5	5	0	0	0.0	0	5	0	30	0
2000—Miami NFL	10	5	0	0	0.0	0	26	393	15.1	0	0	0	0.0	0	0	0	0	0
Pro totals (11 years)	166	91	6	-3	-0.5	0	556	8517	15.3	53	28	150	5.4	0	53	0	318	14

MARTS, LONNIE　　　LB

PERSONAL: Born November 10, 1968, in New Orleans. ... 6-2/250. ... Full name: Lonnie Marts Jr.
HIGH SCHOOL: St. Augustine (New Orleans).
COLLEGE: Tulane (degree in sociology).
TRANSACTIONS/CAREER NOTES: Signed as non-drafted free agent by Kansas City Chiefs (May 1, 1990). ... On injured reserve with ankle injury (September 8, 1990-entire season). ... Granted unconditional free agency (February 17, 1994). ... Signed by Tampa Bay Buccaneers (March 21, 1994). ... Granted unconditional free agency (February 14, 1997). ... Signed by Houston Oilers (April 3, 1997). ... Oilers franchise moved to Tennessee for 1997 season. ... Oilers franchise renamed Tennessee Titans for 1999 season (December 26, 1998). ... Released by Titans (July 28, 1999). ... Signed by Jacksonville Jaguars (July 30, 1999). ... Granted unconditional free agency (February 11, 2000). ... Re-signed by Jaguars (February 11, 2000). ... On injured reserve with groin injury (December 5, 2000-remainder of season). ... Released by Jaguars (June 4, 2001).
CHAMPIONSHIP GAME EXPERIENCE: Played in AFC championship game (1993 and 1999 seasons).
PRO STATISTICS: 1991—Recovered one fumble. 1992—Recovered one fumble for two yards. 1993—Returned one kickoff for no yards and recovered one fumble. 1994—Recovered two fumbles. 1995—Recovered one fumble. 1996—Recovered two fumbles. 1997—Recovered one fumble. 1999—Recovered two fumbles for three yards. 2000—Recovered one fumble for three yards.

Year　Team	G	GS	INTERCEPTIONS No.	Yds.	Avg.	TD	SACKS No.
1990—Kansas City NFL			Did not play.				
1991—Kansas City NFL	16	2	0	0	0.0	0	1.0
1992—Kansas City NFL	15	3	1	36	36.0	1	0.0
1993—Kansas City NFL	16	15	1	20	20.0	0	2.0
1994—Tampa Bay NFL	16	14	0	0	0.0	0	0.0
1995—Tampa Bay NFL	15	13	1	8	8.0	0	0.0
1996—Tampa Bay NFL	16	13	0	0	0.0	0	7.0
1997—Tennessee NFL	14	14	0	0	0.0	0	1.0
1998—Tennessee NFL	16	15	1	27	27.0	1	4.0
1999—Jacksonville NFL	16	16	1	10	10.0	0	2.0
2000—Jacksonville NFL	7	3	0	0	0.0	0	0.0
Pro totals (10 years)	147	108	5	101	20.2	2	17.0

MARYLAND, RUSSELL　　　DT　　　PACKERS

PERSONAL: Born March 22, 1969, in Chicago. ... 6-1/308.
HIGH SCHOOL: Whitney-Young (Chicago).
COLLEGE: Miami, Fla. (degree in psychology, 1990).
TRANSACTIONS/CAREER NOTES: Selected by Dallas Cowboys in first round (first pick overall) of 1991 NFL draft. ... Signed by Cowboys (April 22, 1991). ... Granted unconditional free agency (February 16, 1996). ... Signed by Oakland Raiders (February 22, 1996). ... Released by Raiders (April 1, 2000). ... Signed by Green Bay Packers (April 20, 2000).
CHAMPIONSHIP GAME EXPERIENCE: Played in NFC championship game (1992-1995 seasons). ... Member of Super Bowl championship team (1992, 1993 and 1995 seasons).
HONORS: Named defensive tackle on THE SPORTING NEWS college All-America second team (1989). ... Outland Trophy winner (1990). ... Named defensive lineman on THE SPORTING NEWS college All-America first team (1990). ... Played in Pro Bowl (1993 season).
PRO STATISTICS: 1992—Recovered two fumbles for 26 yards and a touchdown. 1993—Recovered two fumbles. 1994—Recovered one fumble. 1999—Intercepted one pass for two yards and recovered one fumble. 2000—Credited with a safety.

Year　Team	G	GS	SACKS
1991—Dallas NFL	16	7	4.5
1992—Dallas NFL	14	13	2.5
1993—Dallas NFL	16	12	2.5
1994—Dallas NFL	16	16	3.0
1995—Dallas NFL	13	13	2.0
1996—Oakland NFL	16	16	2.0
1997—Oakland NFL	16	16	4.5
1998—Oakland NFL	15	15	2.0
1999—Oakland NFL	16	16	1.5
2000—Green Bay NFL	16	16	0.0
Pro totals (10 years)	154	140	24.5

MASLOWSKI, MIKE　　　LB　　　CHIEFS

PERSONAL: Born July 11, 1974, in Thorp, Wis. ... 6-1/251. ... Full name: Michael John Maslowski.
HIGH SCHOOL: Thorp (Wis.).
COLLEGE: Wisconsin-La Crosse.
TRANSACTIONS/CAREER NOTES: Signed as non-drafted free agent by San Diego Chargers (April 21, 1997). ... Released by Chargers (August 1997). ... Played for San Jose Sabercats of Arena League (1998). ... Signed by Kansas City Chiefs (January 12, 1999). ... Assigned by Chiefs to Barcelona Dragons in 1999 NFL Europe enhancement allocation program (February 22, 1999).
PLAYING EXPERIENCE: Barcelona NFLE, 1999; Kansas City NFL, 1999 and 2000. ... Games/Games started: NFLE 1999 (games played unavailable); NFL 1999 (15/0), 2000 (16/5). Total NFL: 31/5.
PRO STATISTICS: NFLE: 1999—Intercepted four passes for 56 yards and one touchdown and credited with two sacks. 2000—Credited with two sacks and recovered one fumble.

MASON, DERRICK　　　WR/KR/PR　　　TITANS

PERSONAL: Born January 17, 1974, in Detroit. ... 5-10/188. ... Full name: Derrick James Mason.
HIGH SCHOOL: Mumford (Detroit).
COLLEGE: Michigan State.

TRANSACTIONS/CAREER NOTES: Selected by Houston Oilers in fourth round (98th pick overall) of 1997 NFL draft. ... Oilers franchise moved to Tennessee for 1997 season. ... Signed by Oilers (July 19, 1997). ... Oilers franchise renamed Tennessee Titans for 1999 season (December 26, 1998). ... Granted free agency (February 11, 2000). ... Re-signed by Titans (June 1, 2000). ... Granted unconditional free agency (March 2, 2001). ... Re-signed by Titans (March 2, 2001).

CHAMPIONSHIP GAME EXPERIENCE: Played in AFC championship game (1999 season). ... Played in Super Bowl XXXIV (1999 season).

HONORS: Named kick returner on THE SPORTING NEWS NFL All-Pro team (2000). ... Played in Pro Bowl (2000 season).

PRO STATISTICS: 1997—Rushed once for minus seven yards. 1998—Recovered one fumble. 2000—Rushed once for one yard and recovered one fumble.

SINGLE GAME HIGHS (regular season): Receptions—8 (November 5, 2000, vs. Pittsburgh); yards—103 (October 1, 2000, vs. New York Giants); and touchdown receptions—2 (December 20, 1998, vs. Green Bay).

STATISTICAL PLATEAUS: 100-yard receiving games: 2000 (1).

			RECEIVING				PUNT RETURNS				KICKOFF RETURNS				TOTALS			
Year Team	G	GS	No.	Yds.	Avg.	TD	No.	Yds.	Avg.	TD	No.	Yds.	Avg.	TD	TD	2pt.	Pts.	Fum.
1997—Tennessee NFL............	16	2	14	186	13.3	0	13	95	7.3	0	26	551	21.2	0	0	0	0	5
1998—Tennessee NFL............	16	0	25	333	13.3	0	31	228	7.4	0	8	154	19.3	0	3	0	18	1
1999—Tennessee NFL............	13	0	8	89	11.1	0	26	225	8.7	1	41	805	19.6	0	1	0	6	0
2000—Tennessee NFL............	16	10	63	895	14.2	5	*51	*662	13.0	1	42	1132	§27.0	0	6	0	36	1
Pro totals (4 years)................	61	12	110	1503	13.7	8	121	1210	10.0	2	117	2642	22.6	0	10	0	60	7

MASON, EDDIE   LB   REDSKINS

PERSONAL: Born January 9, 1972, in Siler City, N.C. ... 6-0/236. ... Full name: Eddie Lee Mason.

HIGH SCHOOL: Jordan-Matthews (Siler City, N.C.).

COLLEGE: North Carolina.

TRANSACTIONS/CAREER NOTES: Selected by New York Jets in sixth round (178th pick overall) of 1995 NFL draft. ... Signed by Jets (June 14, 1995). ... On injured reserve with knee injury (August 20, 1996-entire season). ... Granted unconditional free agency (February 14, 1997). ... Signed by Tampa Bay Buccaneers (April 21, 1997). ... Released by Buccaneers (August 17, 1997). ... Signed by Carolina Panthers (March 1, 1998). ... Released by Panthers (August 24, 1998). ... Signed by Jacksonville Jaguars (December 2, 1998). ... Released by Jaguars (September 5, 1999). ... Signed by Washington Redskins (September 21, 1999). ... Granted free agency (February 11, 2000). ... Re-signed by Redskins (April 10, 2000).

PLAYING EXPERIENCE: New York Jets NFL, 1995; Jacksonville NFL, 1998; Washington NFL, 1999 and 2000. ... Games/Games started: 1995 (15/0), 1998 (4/0), 1999 (14/0), 2000 (16/2). Total: 49/2.

PRO STATISTICS: 2000—Credited with two sacks.

MATHEWS, JASON   OT   TITANS

PERSONAL: Born February 9, 1971, in Orange, Texas. ... 6-5/304. ... Full name: Samuel Jason Mathews.

HIGH SCHOOL: Bridge City (Texas).

COLLEGE: Brigham Young, then Texas A&M.

TRANSACTIONS/CAREER NOTES: Selected by Indianapolis Colts in third round (67th pick overall) of 1994 NFL draft. ... Signed by Colts (July 23, 1994). ... Granted free agency (February 14, 1997). ... Re-signed by Colts (April 30, 1997). ... Granted unconditional free agency (February 13, 1998). ... Signed by Tampa Bay Buccaneers (May 7, 1998). ... Released by Buccaneers (August 30, 1998). ... Signed by Tennessee Oilers (September 1, 1998). ... Oilers franchise renamed Tennessee Titans for 1999 season (December 26, 1998).

PLAYING EXPERIENCE: Indianapolis NFL, 1994-1997; Tennessee NFL, 1998-2000. ... Games/Games started: 1994 (10/0), 1995 (16/16), 1996 (16/15), 1997 (16/0), 1998 (3/0), 1999 (5/0), 2000 (16/1). Total: 82/32.

CHAMPIONSHIP GAME EXPERIENCE: Played in AFC championship game (1995 and 1999 seasons). ... Member of Titans for Super Bowl XXXIV (1999 season); did not play.

PRO STATISTICS: 1996—Recovered one fumble.

MATHIS, KEVIN   CB   SAINTS

PERSONAL: Born April 29, 1974, in Gainesville, Texas ... 5-9/181.

HIGH SCHOOL: Gainesville (Texas).

COLLEGE: East Texas State.

TRANSACTIONS/CAREER NOTES: Signed as non-drafted free agent by Dallas Cowboys (April 24, 1997). ... Granted free agency (February 11, 2000). ... Re-signed by Cowboys (April 26, 2000). ... Traded by Cowboys to New Orleans Saints for LB Chris Bordano (April 26, 2000). ... Granted unconditional free agency (March 2, 2001). ... Re-signed by Saints (March 2, 2001).

PRO STATISTICS: 1997—Recovered two fumbles. 1998—Recovered four fumbles for six yards. 1999—Recovered one fumble. 2000—Intercepted one pass for no yards.

			PUNT RETURNS				KICKOFF RETURNS				TOTALS			
Year Team	G	GS	No.	Yds.	Avg.	TD	No.	Yds.	Avg.	TD	TD	2pt.	Pts.	Fum.
1997—Dallas NFL	16	3	11	91	8.3	0	0	0	0.0	0	0	0	0	2
1998—Dallas NFL	13	4	2	3	1.5	0	25	621	24.8	0	0	0	0	2
1999—Dallas NFL	8	4	0	0	0.0	0	18	408	22.7	0	0	0	0	1
2000—New Orleans NFL	16	16	1	5	5.0	0	8	187	23.4	0	0	0	0	1
Pro totals (4 years).............................	53	27	14	99	7.1	0	51	1216	23.8	0	0	0	0	6

MATHIS, TERANCE   WR   FALCONS

PERSONAL: Born June 7, 1967, in Detroit. ... 5-10/185. ... Cousin of Jason Ferguson, defensive tackle, New York Jets.

HIGH SCHOOL: Redan (Stone Mountain, Ga.).

COLLEGE: New Mexico.

M

TRANSACTIONS/CAREER NOTES: Selected by New York Jets in sixth round (140th pick overall) of 1990 NFL draft. ... Signed by Jets (July 12, 1990). ... Granted unconditional free agency (February 17, 1994). ... Signed by Atlanta Falcons (May 3, 1994). ... Granted unconditional free agency (February 16, 1996). ... Re-signed by Falcons (April 30, 1996).
CHAMPIONSHIP GAME EXPERIENCE: Played in NFC championship game (1998 season). ... Played in Super Bowl XXXIII (1998 season).
HONORS: Named wide receiver on THE SPORTING NEWS college All-America first team (1989). ... Played in Pro Bowl (1994 season).
RECORDS: Holds NFL career record for most two-point conversions—6.
PRO STATISTICS: 1990—Fumbled once. 1991—Fumbled four times and recovered one fumble. 1992—Fumbled twice and recovered one fumble. 1993—Fumbled five times and recovered one fumble. 1994—Recovered one fumble. 1995—Fumbled once. 1996—Recovered one fumble. 2000—Recovered two fumbles.
SINGLE GAME HIGHS (regular season): Receptions—13 (September 18, 1994, vs. Kansas City); yards—198 (December 13, 1998, vs. New Orleans); and touchdown receptions—3 (November 19, 1995, vs. St. Louis).
STATISTICAL PLATEAUS: 100-yard receiving games: 1992 (1), 1994 (5), 1995 (2), 1996 (2), 1997 (1), 1998 (3), 1999 (1). Total: 15.
MISCELLANEOUS: Holds Atlanta Falcons all-time records for most receptions (522) and yards receiving (6,785).

			RUSHING				RECEIVING				PUNT RETURNS				KICKOFF RETURNS				TOTALS		
Year Team	G	GS	Att.	Yds.	Avg.	TD	No.	Yds.	Avg.	TD	No.	Yds.	Avg.	TD	No.	Yds.	Avg.	TD	TD	2pt.	Pts.
1990—N.Y. Jets NFL	16	1	2	9	4.5	0	19	245	12.9	0	11	165	15.0	†1	43	787	18.3	0	1	0	6
1991—N.Y. Jets NFL	16	0	1	19	19.0	0	28	329	11.8	1	23	157	6.8	0	29	599	20.7	0	1	0	6
1992—N.Y. Jets NFL	16	1	3	25	8.3	1	22	316	14.4	3	2	24	12.0	0	28	492	17.6	0	4	0	24
1993—N.Y. Jets NFL	16	3	2	20	10.0	1	24	352	14.7	0	14	99	7.1	0	7	102	14.6	0	1	0	6
1994—Atlanta NFL	16	16	0	0	0.0	0	111	1342	12.1	11	0	0	0.0	0	0	0	0.0	0	11	∞2	70
1995—Atlanta NFL	14	12	0	0	0.0	0	78	1039	13.3	9	0	0	0.0	0	0	0	0.0	0	9	*3	60
1996—Atlanta NFL	16	16	0	0	0.0	0	69	771	11.2	7	3	19	6.3	0	0	0	0.0	0	7	1	44
1997—Atlanta NFL	16	16	3	35	11.7	0	62	802	12.9	6	0	0	0.0	0	0	0	0.0	0	6	0	36
1998—Atlanta NFL	16	16	1	-6	-6.0	0	64	1136	17.8	11	1	0	0.0	0	0	0	0.0	0	11	0	66
1999—Atlanta NFL	16	16	1	0	0.0	0	81	1016	12.5	6	0	0	0.0	0	0	0	0.0	0	6	0	36
2000—Atlanta NFL	16	16	1	-5	-5.0	0	57	679	11.9	5	0	0	0.0	0	0	0	0.0	0	5	0	30
Pro totals (11 years)	174	113	14	97	6.9	2	615	8027	13.1	59	54	464	8.6	1	107	1980	18.5	0	62	6	384

MATTHEWS, BRUCE　　　　G/C　　　　TITANS

PERSONAL: Born August 8, 1961, in Raleigh, N.C. ... 6-5/305. ... Full name: Bruce Rankin Matthews. ... Son of Clay Matthews Sr., defensive end/tackle with San Francisco 49ers (1950 and 1953-55); and brother of Clay Matthews Jr., linebacker with Cleveland Browns (1978-93) and Atlanta Falcons (1994-96).
HIGH SCHOOL: Arcadia (Calif.).
COLLEGE: Southern California (degree in industrial engineering, 1983).
TRANSACTIONS/CAREER NOTES: Selected by Los Angeles Express in 1983 USFL territorial draft. ... Selected by Houston Oilers in first round (ninth pick overall) of 1983 NFL draft. ... Signed by Oilers (July 24, 1983). ... Granted free agency (February 1, 1987). ... On reserve/unsigned list (August 31-November 3, 1987). ... Re-signed by Oilers (November 4, 1987). ... Granted roster exemption (November 4-7, 1987). ... Granted unconditional free agency (February 17, 1995). ... Re-signed by Oilers (August 8, 1995). ... Oilers franchise moved to Tennessee for 1997 season. ... Oilers franchise renamed Tennessee Titans for 1999 season (December 26, 1998). ... Granted unconditional free agency (February 12, 1999). ... Re-signed by Titans (May 13, 1999).
PLAYING EXPERIENCE: Houston NFL, 1983-1996; Tennessee NFL, 1997-2000. ... Games/Games started: 1983 (16/15), 1984 (16/16), 1985 (16/16), 1986 (16/16), 1987 (8/5), 1988 (16/16), 1989 (16/16), 1990 (16/16), 1991 (16/16), 1992 (16/16), 1993 (16/16), 1994 (16/16), 1995 (16/16), 1996 (16/16), 1997 (16/16), 1998 (16/16), 1999 (16/16), 2000 (16/16). Total: 280/276.
CHAMPIONSHIP GAME EXPERIENCE: Played in AFC championship game (1999 season). ... Played in Super Bowl XXXIV (1999 season).
HONORS: Named guard on THE SPORTING NEWS college All-America first team (1982). ... Named guard on THE SPORTING NEWS NFL All-Pro team (1988-1990, 1992, 1998 and 2000). ... Played in Pro Bowl (1988-1994, 1996, 1997 and 1999 seasons). ... Named center on THE SPORTING NEWS NFL All-Pro team (1993). ... Named to play in Pro Bowl (1995 season); replaced by Will Shields due to injury. ... Named to play in Pro Bowl (1998 season); replaced by Mark Schlereth due to injury. ... Named to play in Pro Bowl (2000 season); replaced by Will Shields due to injury.
PRO STATISTICS: 1985—Recovered three fumbles. 1986—Recovered one fumble for seven yards. 1989—Fumbled twice and recovered one fumble for minus 29 yards. 1990—Recovered one fumble. 1991—Fumbled once and recovered one fumble for minus three yards. 1994—Fumbled twice. 1997—Recovered two fumbles. 1998—Recovered one fumble.

MATTHEWS, SHANE　　　　QB　　　　BEARS

PERSONAL: Born June 1, 1970, in Pascagoula, Miss. ... 6-3/196. ... Full name: Michael Shane Matthews.
HIGH SCHOOL: Pascagoula (Miss.).
COLLEGE: Florida.
TRANSACTIONS/CAREER NOTES: Signed as non-drafted free agent by Chicago Bears (April 29, 1993). ... Released by Bears (August 30, 1993). ... Re-signed by Bears to practice squad (September 1, 1993). ... Activated (October 8, 1993); did not play. ... Active for two games (1994); did not play. ... Released by Bears (September 15, 1995). ... Re-signed by Bears (February 12, 1996). ... Released by Bears (June 7, 1996). ... Re-signed by Bears (October 9, 1996). ... Granted unconditional free agency (February 14, 1997). ... Assigned by Bears to Rhein Fire in 1997 World League enhancement allocation program (February 19, 1997). ... Signed by Carolina Panthers (August 25, 1997). ... Released by Panthers (September 17, 1997). ... Re-signed by Panthers (October 16, 1997). ... Active for two games (1997); did not play. ... Granted unconditional free agency (February 13, 1998). ... Re-signed by Panthers (March 19, 1998). ... Active for 12 games (1998); did not play. ... Granted unconditional free agency (February 12, 1999). ... Signed by Bears (April 3, 1999). ... Granted unconditional free agency (February 11, 2000). ... Re-signed by Bears (July 18, 2000). ... Granted unconditional free agency (March 2, 2001). ... Re-signed by Bears (March 13, 2001).
PRO STATISTICS: 1999—Fumbled seven times and recovered two fumbles for minus 14 yards. 2000—Fumbled twice and recovered one fumble.
SINGLE GAME HIGHS (regular season): Attempts—43 (December 3, 2000, vs. Green Bay); completions—25 (October 3, 1999, vs. New Orleans); yards—266 (December 26, 1999, vs. St. Louis); and touchdown passes—2 (December 10, 2000, vs. New England).
MISCELLANEOUS: Regular-season record as starting NFL quarterback: 6-6 (.500).

M

Year Team	G	GS	Att.	Cmp.	Pct.	Yds.	TD	Int.	Avg.	Rat.	Att.	Yds.	Avg.	TD	TD	2pt.	Pts.
						PASSING						RUSHING				TOTALS	
1993—Chicago NFL...............						Did not play.											
1994—Chicago NFL...............						Did not play.											
1995—						Did not play.											
1996—Chicago NFL...............	2	0	17	13	76.5	158	1	0	9.29	124.1	1	2	2.0	1	0	0	0
1997—Carolina NFL						Did not play.											
1998—Carolina NFL						Did not play.											
1999—Chicago NFL...............	8	7	275	167	60.7	1645	10	6	5.98	80.6	14	31	2.2	0	0	0	0
2000—Chicago NFL...............	6	5	178	102	57.3	964	3	6	5.42	64.0	10	35	3.5	0	0	0	0
Pro totals (3 years)	16	12	470	282	60.0	2767	14	12	5.89	75.9	25	68	2.7	1	0	0	0

MAWAE, KEVIN — C — JETS

PERSONAL: Born January 23, 1971, in Savannah, Ga. ... 6-4/305. ... Full name: Kevin James Mawae. ... Name pronounced ma-WHY.
HIGH SCHOOL: Leesville (La.).
COLLEGE: Louisiana State (degree in general studies).
TRANSACTIONS/CAREER NOTES: Selected by Seattle Seahawks in second round (36th pick overall) of 1994 NFL draft. ... Signed by Seahawks (July 21, 1994). ... Granted free agency (February 14, 1997). ... Re-signed by Seahawks (May 5, 1997). ... Granted unconditional free agency (February 13, 1998). ... Signed by New York Jets (February 19, 1998).
PLAYING EXPERIENCE: Seattle NFL, 1994-1997; New York Jets NFL, 1998-2000. ... Games/Games started: 1994 (14/11), 1995 (16/16), 1996 (16/16), 1997 (16/16), 1998 (16/16), 1999 (16/16), 2000 (16/16). Total: 110/107.
CHAMPIONSHIP GAME EXPERIENCE: Played in AFC championship game (1998 season).
HONORS: Named center on THE SPORTING NEWS NFL All-Pro team (1999). ... Played in Pro Bowl (1999 and 2000 seasons).
PRO STATISTICS: 1994—Recovered one fumble. 1996—Recovered two fumbles. 1997—Recovered two fumbles.

MAYBERRY, JERMANE — G/OT — EAGLES

PERSONAL: Born August 29, 1973, in Floresville, Texas. ... 6-4/325. ... Full name: Jermane Timothy Mayberry.
HIGH SCHOOL: Floresville (Texas).
JUNIOR COLLEGE: Navarro College (Texas).
COLLEGE: Texas A&M-Kingsville.
TRANSACTIONS/CAREER NOTES: Selected by Philadelphia Eagles in first round (25th pick overall) of 1996 NFL draft. ... Signed by Eagles (June 13, 1996).
PLAYING EXPERIENCE: Philadelphia NFL, 1996-2000. ... Games/Games started: 1996 (3/1), 1997 (16/16), 1998 (15/10), 1999 (13/5), 2000 (16/16). Total: 63/48.
PRO STATISTICS: 1997—Recovered one fumble.

MAYES, ALONZO — TE — DOLPHINS

M

PERSONAL: Born June 4, 1975, in Oklahoma City. ... 6-4/265.
HIGH SCHOOL: Douglass (Oklahoma City).
JUNIOR COLLEGE: Rose State College (Okla.); did not play football.
COLLEGE: Oklahoma State.
TRANSACTIONS/CAREER NOTES: Selected by Chicago Bears in fourth round (94th pick overall) of 1998 NFL draft. ... Signed by Bears (August 2, 1998). ... Traded by Bears to Miami Dolphins for undisclosed draft pick (October 2, 2000). ... Granted free agency (March 2, 2001). ... Re-signed by Dolphins (March 15, 2001).
HONORS: Named tight end on THE SPORTING NEWS college All-America first team (1997).
SINGLE GAME HIGHS (regular season): Receptions—4 (October 18, 1998, vs. Dallas); yards—57 (October 18, 1998, vs. Dallas); and touchdown receptions—1 (November 25, 1999, vs. Detroit).

Year Team	G	GS	No.	Yds.	Avg.	TD	TD	2pt.	Pts.	Fum.
			RECEIVING					TOTALS		
1998—Chicago NFL..	16	16	21	217	10.3	0	0	0	0	2
1999—Chicago NFL..	16	9	8	82	10.3	1	1	0	6	0
2000—Chicago NFL..	5	3	4	40	10.0	0	0	0	0	0
Pro totals (3 years)	37	28	33	339	10.3	1	1	0	6	2

MAYES, DERRICK — WR

PERSONAL: Born January 28, 1974, in Indianapolis. ... 6-0/205. ... Full name: Derrick Binet Mayes.
HIGH SCHOOL: North Central (Indianapolis).
COLLEGE: Notre Dame (degree in communications).
TRANSACTIONS/CAREER NOTES: Selected by Green Bay Packers in second round (56th pick overall) of 1996 NFL draft. ... Signed by Packers (July 17, 1996). ... Granted free agency (February 12, 1999). ... Re-signed by Packers (June 21, 1999). ... Traded by Packers to Seattle Seahawks for seventh-round pick (DT Ron Moore) pick in 2000 draft (August 30, 1999). ... Granted unconditional free agency (February 11, 2000). ... Re-signed by Seahawks (February 25, 2000). ... Released by Seahawks (March 1, 2001).
CHAMPIONSHIP GAME EXPERIENCE: Member of Packers for NFC championship game (1996 season); inactive. ... Member of Super Bowl championship team (1996 season); inactive. ... Played in NFC championship game (1997 season). ... Played in Super Bowl XXXII (1997 season).
PRO STATISTICS: 1997—Returned 14 punts for 141 yards. 1998—Returned one punt for nine yards.
SINGLE GAME HIGHS (regular season): Receptions—7 (September 19, 1999, vs. Chicago); yards—137 (September 19, 1999, vs. Chicago); and touchdown receptions—3 (September 27, 1998, vs. Carolina).
STATISTICAL PLATEAUS: 100-yard receiving games: 1997 (1), 1999 (2). Total: 3.

Year Team	G	GS	RECEIVING No.	Yds.	Avg.	TD	TOTALS TD	2pt.	Pts.	Fum.
1996—Green Bay NFL	7	0	6	46	7.7	2	2	0	12	0
1997—Green Bay NFL	12	3	18	290	16.1	0	0	0	0	0
1998—Green Bay NFL	10	6	30	394	13.1	3	3	0	18	1
1999—Seattle NFL	16	15	62	829	13.4	10	10	0	60	1
2000—Seattle NFL	13	8	29	264	9.1	1	1	0	6	0
Pro totals (5 years)	58	32	145	1823	12.6	16	16	0	96	2

MAYNARD, BRAD   P   BEARS

PERSONAL: Born February 9, 1974, in Tipton, Ind. ... 6-1/190. ... Full name: Bradley Alan Maynard.
HIGH SCHOOL: Sheridan (Ind.).
COLLEGE: Ball State.
TRANSACTIONS/CAREER NOTES: Selected by New York Giants in third round (95th pick overall) of 1997 NFL draft. ... Signed by Giants (July 19, 1997). ... Granted free agency (February 11, 2000). ... Re-signed by Giants (June 8, 2000). ... Granted unconditional free agency (March 2, 2001). ... Signed by Chicago Bears (March 3, 2001).
CHAMPIONSHIP GAME EXPERIENCE: Played in NFC championship game (2000 season). ... Played in Super Bowl XXXV (2000 season).
HONORS: Named punter on THE SPORTING NEWS college All-America second team (1996).
PRO STATISTICS: 1998—Rushed once for minus five yards and attempted one pass without a completion.

Year Team	G	PUNTING No.	Yds.	Avg.	Net avg.	In. 20	Blk.
1997—New York Giants NFL	16	*111	*4531	40.8	34.6	*33	1
1998—New York Giants NFL	16	101	*4566	45.2	37.8	∞33	0
1999—New York Giants NFL	16	89	3651	41.0	35.1	‡31	0
2000—New York Giants NFL	16	79	3210	40.6	33.7	26	1
Pro totals (4 years)	64	380	15958	42.0	35.4	123	2

McAFEE, FRED   RB   SAINTS

PERSONAL: Born June 20, 1968, in Philadelphia, Miss. ... 5-10/198. ... Full name: Fred Lee McAfee.
HIGH SCHOOL: Philadelphia (Miss.).
COLLEGE: Mississippi College (degree in mass communications, 1990).
TRANSACTIONS/CAREER NOTES: Selected by New Orleans Saints in sixth round (154th pick overall) of 1991 NFL draft. ... Signed by Saints (July 14, 1991). ... Released by Saints (August 26, 1991). ... Re-signed by Saints to practice squad (August 28, 1991). ... Activated (October 18, 1991). ... On injured reserve with shoulder injury (December 15, 1992-remainder of season). ... Granted free agency (February 17, 1994). ... Signed by Arizona Cardinals (August 2, 1994). ... Released by Cardinals (October 31, 1994). ... Signed by Pittsburgh Steelers (November 9, 1994). ... Granted unconditional free agency (February 16, 1996). ... Re-signed by Steelers (April 12, 1996). ... Granted unconditional free agency (February 12, 1999). ... Signed by Kansas City Chiefs (July 30, 1999). ... Released by Chiefs (August 31, 1999). ... Signed by Tampa Bay Buccaneers (December 28, 1999). ... Granted unconditional free agency (February 11, 2000). ... Signed by Saints (October 2, 2000). ... Granted unconditional free agency (March 2, 2001). ... Re-signed by Saints (June 5, 2001).
CHAMPIONSHIP GAME EXPERIENCE: Played in AFC championship game (1994, 1995 and 1997 seasons). ... Played in Super Bowl XXX (1995 season). ... Played in NFC championship game (1999 season).
PRO STATISTICS: 1995—Recovered one fumble. 1998—Recovered a blocked punt in end zone for a touchdown. 2000—Recovered one fumble.
SINGLE GAME HIGHS (regular season): Attempts—28 (November 24, 1991, vs. Atlanta); yards—138 (November 24, 1991, vs. Atlanta); and rushing touchdowns—1 (September 10, 1995, vs. Houston).
STATISTICAL PLATEAUS: 100-yard rushing games: 1991 (1).

Year Team	G	GS	RUSHING Att.	Yds.	Avg.	TD	RECEIVING No.	Yds.	Avg.	TD	KICKOFF RETURNS No.	Yds.	Avg.	TD	TOTALS TD	2pt.	Pts.	Fum.
1991—New Orleans NFL	9	0	109	494	4.5	2	1	8	8.0	0	1	14	14.0	0	2	0	12	2
1992—New Orleans NFL	14	1	39	114	2.9	1	1	16	16.0	0	19	393	20.7	0	1	0	6	0
1993—New Orleans NFL	15	4	51	160	3.1	1	1	3	3.0	0	28	580	20.7	0	1	0	6	3
1994—Arizona NFL	7	0	2	-5	-2.5	1	1	4	4.0	0	7	113	16.1	0	1	0	6	1
—Pittsburgh NFL	6	0	16	56	3.5	1	0	0	0.0	0	0	0	0.0	0	1	0	6	0
1995—Pittsburgh NFL	16	1	39	156	4.0	1	15	88	5.9	0	5	56	11.2	0	1	0	6	0
1996—Pittsburgh NFL	14	0	7	17	2.4	0	5	21	4.2	0	0	0	0.0	0	0	0	0	0
1997—Pittsburgh NFL	14	0	13	41	3.2	0	2	44	22.0	0	0	0	0.0	0	0	0	0	1
1998—Pittsburgh NFL	14	0	18	111	6.2	0	9	27	3.0	0	1	10	10.0	0	1	0	6	0
1999—Tampa Bay NFL	1	0	0	0	0.0	0	0	0	0.0	0	0	0	0.0	0	0	0	0	0
2000—New Orleans NFL	12	0	2	37	18.5	0	0	0	0.0	0	10	251	25.1	0	0	0	0	0
Pro totals (10 years)	122	6	296	1181	4.0	7	35	211	6.0	0	71	1417	20.0	0	8	0	48	7

McALISTER, CHRIS   CB   RAVENS

PERSONAL: Born June 14, 1977, in Pasedena, Calif. ... 6-1/206. ... Full name: Christopher James McAlister. ... Son of James McAlister, running back with Philadelphia Eagles (1975 and 1976) and New England Patriots (1978).
HIGH SCHOOL: Pasadena (Calif.).
JUNIOR COLLEGE: Mount San Antonio College (Calif.).
COLLEGE: Arizona.
TRANSACTIONS/CAREER NOTES: Selected by Baltimore Ravens in first round (10th pick overall) of 1999 NFL draft. ... Signed by Ravens (July 23, 1999).
CHAMPIONSHIP GAME EXPERIENCE: Played in AFC championship game (2000 season). ... Member of Super Bowl championship team (2000 season).
HONORS: Named cornerback on THE SPORTING NEWS college All-America third team (1997). ... Named cornerback on THE SPORTING NEWS college All-America first team (1998).
PRO STATISTICS: 1999—Returned one kickoff for 12 yards. 2000—Recovered one fumble.

Year Team	G	GS	No.	Yds.	Avg.	TD
1999—Baltimore NFL	16	12	5	28	5.6	0
2000—Baltimore NFL	16	16	4	*165	41.3	1
Pro totals (2 years)	32	28	9	193	21.4	1

The header spanning "No. Yds. Avg. TD" is **INTERCEPTIONS**.

McBRIDE, TOD   S   PACKERS

PERSONAL: Born January 26, 1976, in Los Angeles. ... 6-1/207. ... Full name: Tod Anthony McBride.
HIGH SCHOOL: Walnut (Calif.).
COLLEGE: UCLA.
TRANSACTIONS/CAREER NOTES: Signed as non-drafted free agent by Seattle Seahawks (April 23, 1999). ... Claimed on waivers by Green Bay Packers (June 23, 1999).
PLAYING EXPERIENCE: Green Bay NFL, 1999 and 2000. ... Games/Games started: 1999 (15/0), 2000 (15/6). Total: 30/6.
PRO STATISTICS: 1999—Recovered two fumbles. 2000—Intercepted two passes for 43 yards.

McBURROWS, GERALD   S   FALCONS

PERSONAL: Born October 7, 1973, in Detroit. ... 5-11/208. ... Full name: Gerald Lance McBurrows.
HIGH SCHOOL: Martin Luther King (Detroit).
COLLEGE: Kansas.
TRANSACTIONS/CAREER NOTES: Selected by St. Louis Rams in seventh round (214th pick overall) of 1995 NFL draft. ... Signed by Rams (June 16, 1995). ... On injured reserve with knee injury (October 29, 1997-remainder of season). ... Granted free agency (February 13, 1998). ... Re-signed by Rams (April 24, 1998). ... On injured reserve with knee injury (November 17, 1998-remainder of season). ... Granted unconditional free agency (February 12, 1999). ... Signed by Atlanta Falcons (March 2, 1999). ... Granted unconditional free agency (March 2, 2001). ... Re-signed by Falcons (March 21, 2001).
PLAYING EXPERIENCE: St. Louis NFL, 1995-1998; Atlanta NFL, 1999 and 2000. ... Games/Games started: 1995 (14/3), 1996 (16/7), 1997 (8/3), 1998 (10/0), 1999 (16/4), 2000 (16/4). Total: 80/21.
PRO STATISTICS: 1995—Credited with one sack. 1996—Intercepted one pass for three yards. 1998—Recovered one fumble. 1999—Intercepted two passes for 64 yards, credited with one sack and recovered one fumble. 2000—Credited with two sacks and recovered two fumbles.

McCAFFREY, ED   WR   BRONCOS

PERSONAL: Born August 17, 1968, in Waynesboro, Pa. ... 6-5/215. ... Full name: Edward McCaffrey.
HIGH SCHOOL: Allentown (Pa.) Central Catholic.
COLLEGE: Stanford.
TRANSACTIONS/CAREER NOTES: Selected by New York Giants in third round (83rd pick overall) of 1991 NFL draft. ... Signed by Giants (July 23, 1991). ... Granted free agency (February 17, 1994). ... Signed by San Francisco 49ers (July 24, 1994). ... Granted unconditional free agency (February 17, 1995). ... Signed by Denver Broncos (March 7, 1995).
CHAMPIONSHIP GAME EXPERIENCE: Played in NFC championship game (1994 season). ... Member of Super Bowl championship team (1994, 1997 and 1998 seasons). ... Played in AFC championship game (1997 and 1998 seasons).
HONORS: Named wide receiver on THE SPORTING NEWS college All-America second team (1990). ... Played in Pro Bowl (1998 season).
PRO STATISTICS: 1995—Rushed once for minus one yard. 1997—Recovered two fumbles.
SINGLE GAME HIGHS (regular season): Receptions—10 (November 19, 2000, vs. San Diego); yards—148 (November 19, 2000, vs. San Diego); and touchdown receptions—3 (September 13, 1999, vs. Miami).
STATISTICAL PLATEAUS: 100-yard receiving games: 1992 (1), 1997 (1), 1998 (1), 1999 (4), 2000 (5). Total: 15.

Year Team	G	GS	No.	Yds.	Avg.	TD	TD	2pt.	Pts.	Fum.
1991—New York Giants NFL	16	0	16	146	9.1	0	0	0	0	0
1992—New York Giants NFL	16	3	49	610	12.4	5	5	0	30	2
1993—New York Giants NFL	16	1	27	335	12.4	2	2	0	12	0
1994—San Francisco NFL	16	0	11	131	11.9	2	2	0	12	0
1995—Denver NFL	16	5	39	477	12.2	2	2	1	14	1
1996—Denver NFL	15	15	48	553	11.5	7	7	0	42	0
1997—Denver NFL	15	15	45	590	13.1	8	8	0	48	0
1998—Denver NFL	15	15	64	1053	16.5	▲10	10	1	62	1
1999—Denver NFL	15	15	71	1018	14.3	7	7	0	42	0
2000—Denver NFL	16	16	101	1317	13.0	9	9	▲1	56	0
Pro totals (10 years)	156	85	471	6230	13.2	52	52	3	318	4

The No./Yds./Avg./TD group is under **RECEIVING**; the TD/2pt./Pts./Fum. group is under **TOTALS**.

McCARDELL, KEENAN   WR   JAGUARS

PERSONAL: Born January 6, 1970, in Houston. ... 6-1/190. ... Full name: Keenan Wayne McCardell. ... Name pronounced mc-CAR-dell.
HIGH SCHOOL: Waltrip (Houston).
COLLEGE: UNLV (degree in business management, 1991).
TRANSACTIONS/CAREER NOTES: Selected by Washington Redskins in 12th round (326th pick overall) of 1991 NFL draft. ... Signed by Redskins for 1991 season. ... On injured reserve with knee injury (August 20, 1991-entire season). ... Granted unconditional free agency (February 1, 1992). ... Signed by Cleveland Browns (March 24, 1992). ... Released by Browns (September 1, 1992). ... Re-signed by Browns to practice squad (September 3, 1992). ... Activated (October 6, 1992). ... Released by Browns (October 13, 1992). ... Re-signed by Browns to practice squad (October 14, 1992). ... Activated (November 14, 1992). ... Released by Browns (November 19, 1992). ... Re-signed by Browns to practice squad (November 20, 1992). ... Activated (December 26, 1992). ... Released by Browns (September 22, 1993). ... Signed by Chicago Bears to practice squad (November 2, 1993). ... Signed by Browns off Bears practice squad (November 24, 1993). ... Granted free

agency (February 17, 1994). ... Re-signed by Browns (March 4, 1994). ... Granted unconditional free agency (February 16, 1996). ... Signed by Jacksonville Jaguars (March 2, 1996).

CHAMPIONSHIP GAME EXPERIENCE: Played in AFC championship game (1996 and 1999 seasons).

HONORS: Played in Pro Bowl (1996 season).

PRO STATISTICS: 1995—Returned 13 punts for 93 yards and returned nine kickoffs for 161 yards. 1996—Returned one punt for two yards and recovered three fumbles. 1998—Returned one kickoff for 15 yards. 1999—Returned six punts for 41 yards, returned two kickoffs for 19 yards and recovered one fumble. 2000—Returned three kickoffs for 25 yards and recovered one fumble for four yards.

SINGLE GAME HIGHS (regular season): Receptions—16 (October 20, 1996, vs. St. Louis); yards—232 (October 20, 1996, vs. St. Louis); and touchdown receptions—2 (November 29, 1998, vs. Cincinnati).

STATISTICAL PLATEAUS: 100-yard receiving games: 1995 (1), 1996 (3), 1997 (4), 1998 (2), 1999 (3), 2000 (5). Total: 18.

			RECEIVING				TOTALS			
Year Team	G	GS	No.	Yds.	Avg.	TD	TD	2pt.	Pts.	Fum.
1991—Washington NFL						Did not play.				
1992—Cleveland NFL	2	0	1	8	8.0	0	0	0	0	0
1993—Cleveland NFL	6	3	13	234	18.0	4	4	0	24	0
1994—Cleveland NFL	13	3	10	182	18.2	0	0	0	0	0
1995—Cleveland NFL	16	5	56	709	12.7	4	4	0	24	0
1996—Jacksonville NFL	16	15	85	1129	13.3	3	3	2	22	1
1997—Jacksonville NFL	16	16	85	1164	13.7	5	5	0	30	0
1998—Jacksonville NFL	15	15	64	892	13.9	6	6	1	38	0
1999—Jacksonville NFL	16	15	78	891	11.4	5	5	†1	32	1
2000—Jacksonville NFL	16	16	94	1207	12.8	5	5	0	30	3
Pro totals (9 years)	116	88	486	6416	13.2	32	32	4	200	5

McCASLIN, EUGENE   LB   PACKERS

PERSONAL: Born July 12, 1977, in Tampa. ... 6-1/226. ... Full name: Eugene William McCaslin Jr.

HIGH SCHOOL: Chamberlain (Tampa).

COLLEGE: Florida.

TRANSACTIONS/CAREER NOTES: Selected by Green Bay Packers in seventh round (249th pick overall) of 2000 NFL draft. ... Signed by Packers (July 10, 2000). ... Released by Packers (August 27, 2000). ... Re-signed by Packers to practice squad (August 28, 2000). ... Activated (December 15, 2000).

PLAYING EXPERIENCE: Green Bay NFL, 2000. ... Games/Games started: 2000 (1/0).

McCLEARY, NORRIS   DT   CHIEFS

PERSONAL: Born May 10, 1977, in Shelby, N.C. ... 6-4/305. ... Full name: Norris Ellington McCleary.

HIGH SCHOOL: Bessemer (N.C.).

COLLEGE: East Carolina.

TRANSACTIONS/CAREER NOTES: Signed as non-drafted free agent by Kansas City Chiefs (June 6, 2000). ... Released by Chiefs (August 27, 2000). ... Re-signed by Chiefs to practice squad (August 30, 2000). ... Acitvated (November 24, 2000).

PLAYING EXPERIENCE: Kansas City NFL, 2000. ... Games/Games started: 2000 (3/0).

McCLEON, DEXTER   CB   RAMS

PERSONAL: Born October 9, 1973, in Meridian, Miss. ... 5-10/195. ... Full name: Dexter Keith McCleon.

HIGH SCHOOL: Meridian (Miss.).

COLLEGE: Clemson (degree in management, 1996).

TRANSACTIONS/CAREER NOTES: Selected by St. Louis Rams in second round (40th pick overall) of 1997 NFL draft. ... Signed by Rams (July 3, 1997). ... Granted free agency (February 11, 2000). ... Re-signed by Rams (June 13, 2000).

CHAMPIONSHIP GAME EXPERIENCE: Played in NFC championship game (1999 season). ... Member of Super Bowl championship team (1999 season).

PRO STATISTICS: 1997—Credited with one sack. 1999—Credited with 1½ sacks. 2000—Credited with two sacks, returned one punt for no yards, fumbled once and recovered one fumble for 21 yards.

MISCELLANEOUS: Selected by Minnesota Twins organization in 13th round of free-agent baseball draft (June 3, 1993); did not sign.

			INTERCEPTIONS			
Year Team	G	GS	No.	Yds.	Avg.	TD
1997—St. Louis NFL	16	1	1	0	0.0	0
1998—St. Louis NFL	15	6	2	29	14.5	0
1999—St. Louis NFL	15	15	4	17	4.3	0
2000—St. Louis NFL	16	16	8	28	3.5	0
Pro totals (4 years)	62	38	15	74	4.9	0

McCLURE, TODD   C   FALCONS

PERSONAL: Born February 16, 1977, in Baton Rouge, La. ... 6-1/288.

HIGH SCHOOL: Central (Baton Rouge, La.).

COLLEGE: Louisiana State.

TRANSACTIONS/CAREER NOTES: Selected by Atlanta Falcons in seventh round (237th pick overall) of 1999 NFL draft. ... Signed by Falcons (June 25, 1999). ... On injured reserve with knee injury (August 30, 1999-entire season).

PLAYING EXPERIENCE: Atlanta NFL, 2000. ... Games/Games started: 2000 (10/7).

McCOLLUM, ANDY   G   RAMS

PERSONAL: Born June 2, 1970, in Akron, Ohio. ... 6-4/295. ... Full name: Andrew Jon McCollum. ... Name pronounced Mc-COL-umn.
HIGH SCHOOL: Revere (Richfield, Ohio).
COLLEGE: Toledo.
TRANSACTIONS/CAREER NOTES: Played with Milwaukee Mustangs of Arena League (1994). ... Signed as non-drafted free agent by Cleveland Browns (June 1994). ... Released by Browns (August 28, 1994). ... Re-signed by Browns to practice squad (August 30, 1994). ... Signed by New Orleans Saints off Browns practice squad (November 15, 1994). ... Inactive for five games (1994). ... Assigned by Saints to Barcelona Dragons in 1995 World League enhancement allocation program (February 20, 1995). ... Granted unconditional free agency (February 12, 1999). ... Signed by St. Louis Rams (April 13, 1999). ... Granted unconditional free agency (February 11, 2000). ... Re-signed by Rams (February 22, 2000).
PLAYING EXPERIENCE: Barcelona W.L., 1995; New Orleans NFL, 1995-1998; St. Louis NFL, 1999 and 2000. ... Games/Games started: W.L. 1995 (games played unavailable), NFL 1995 (11/9), 1996 (16/16), 1997 (16/16), 1998 (16/5), 1999 (16/2), 2000 (16/16). Total NFL: 91/64.
CHAMPIONSHIP GAME EXPERIENCE: Played in NFC championship game (1999 season). ... Member of Super Bowl championship team (1999 season).
PRO STATISTICS: 1996—Recovered one fumble. 1998—Recovered one fumble. 1999—Returned one kickoff for three yards. 2000—Fumbled once for minus four yards.

McCOY, TONY   DT

PERSONAL: Born June 10, 1969, in Orlando. ... 6-1/285. ... Full name: Anthony Bernard McCoy.
HIGH SCHOOL: Maynard Evans (Orlando).
COLLEGE: Florida.
TRANSACTIONS/CAREER NOTES: Selected by Indianapolis Colts in fourth round (105th pick overall) of 1992 NFL draft. ... Signed by Colts (July 17, 1992). ... Granted free agency (February 17, 1995). ... Re-signed by Colts (June 7, 1995). ... Released by Colts (June 2, 2000). ... Signed by Arizona Cardinals (June 9, 2000). ... On injured reserve with knee injury (November 6, 2000-remainder of season). ... Released by Cardinals (March 1, 2001).
CHAMPIONSHIP GAME EXPERIENCE: Played in AFC championship game (1995 season).
PRO STATISTICS: 1992—Recovered one fumble. 1994—Recovered one fumble. 1996—Recovered one fumble.

Year—Team	G	GS	SACKS
1992—Indianapolis NFL	16	3	1.0
1993—Indianapolis NFL	6	0	0.0
1994—Indianapolis NFL	15	15	6.0
1995—Indianapolis NFL	16	16	2.5
1996—Indianapolis NFL	15	15	5.0
1997—Indianapolis NFL	16	11	2.5
1998—Indianapolis NFL	14	13	6.0
1999—Indianapolis NFL	10	0	0.0
2000—Arizona NFL	6	6	0.0
Pro totals (9 years)	114	79	23.0

McCRARY, FRED   FB   CHARGERS

M

PERSONAL: Born September 19, 1972, in Naples, Fla. ... 6-0/235. ... Full name: Freddy Demetrius McCrary.
HIGH SCHOOL: Naples (Fla.).
COLLEGE: Mississippi State.
TRANSACTIONS/CAREER NOTES: Selected by Philadelphia Eagles in sixth round (208th pick overall) of 1995 NFL draft. ... Signed by Eagles (June 27, 1995). ... Released by Eagles (August 25, 1996). ... Signed by New Orleans Saints (March 5, 1997). ... Released by Saints (August 24, 1998). ... Signed by San Diego Chargers (March 26, 1999). ... Granted free agency (February 11, 2000). ... Re-signed by Chargers (May 12, 2000).
PRO STATISTICS: 1995—Returned one kickoff for one yard. 1997—Returned two kickoffs for 26 yards. 1999—Returned one kickoff for four yards.
SINGLE GAME HIGHS (regular season): Attempts—5 (September 24, 2000, vs. Seattle); yards—13 (November 23, 1997, vs. Atlanta); and rushing touchdowns—1 (September 10, 1995, vs. Arizona).

			RUSHING				RECEIVING				TOTALS			
Year—Team	G	GS	Att.	Yds.	Avg.	TD	No.	Yds.	Avg.	TD	TD	2pt.	Pts.	Fum.
1995—Philadelphia NFL	13	5	3	1	0.3	1	9	60	6.7	0	1	0	6	0
1996—							Did not play.							
1997—New Orleans NFL	7	0	8	15	1.9	0	4	17	4.3	0	0	0	0	0
1999—San Diego NFL	16	14	0	0	0.0	0	37	201	5.4	1	1	0	6	0
2000—San Diego NFL	15	12	7	8	1.1	0	18	141	7.8	2	2	0	12	1
Pro totals (4 years)	51	31	18	24	1.3	1	68	419	6.2	3	4	0	24	1

McCRARY, MICHAEL   DE   RAVENS

PERSONAL: Born July 7, 1970, in Vienna, Va. ... 6-4/260. ... Full name: Michael Curtis McCrary.
HIGH SCHOOL: George C. Marshall (Falls Church, Va.).
COLLEGE: Wake Forest.
TRANSACTIONS/CAREER NOTES: Selected by Seattle Seahawks in seventh round (170th pick overall) of 1993 NFL draft. ... Signed by Seahawks (July 13, 1993). ... Granted free agency (February 16, 1996). ... Re-signed by Seahawks (June 6, 1996). ... Granted unconditional free agency (February 14, 1997). ... Signed by Baltimore Ravens (April 7, 1997).
CHAMPIONSHIP GAME EXPERIENCE: Played in AFC championship game (2000 season). ... Member of Super Bowl championship team (2000 season).

HONORS: Named defensive end on THE SPORTING NEWS NFL All-Pro team (1998). ... Played in Pro Bowl (1998 and 1999 seasons).
PRO STATISTICS: 1996—Recovered one fumble. 1997—Recovered two fumbles. 1999—Recovered one fumble. 2000—Credited with a safety and recovered three fumbles.
MISCELLANEOUS: Holds Baltimore Ravens all-time record for most sacks (41.5).

Year Team	G	GS	SACKS
1993—Seattle NFL	15	0	4.0
1994—Seattle NFL	16	0	1.5
1995—Seattle NFL	11	0	1.0
1996—Seattle NFL	16	13	▲13.5
1997—Baltimore NFL	15	15	9.0
1998—Baltimore NFL	16	16	14.5
1999—Baltimore NFL	16	16	11.5
2000—Baltimore NFL	16	16	6.5
Pro totals (8 years)	121	76	61.5

McCULLOUGH, GEORGE   CB   CHIEFS

PERSONAL: Born February 18, 1975, in Galveston, Texas. ... 5-10/187. ... Full name: George Wayne McCullough Jr.
HIGH SCHOOL: Ball (Galveston, Texas).
COLLEGE: Baylor.
TRANSACTIONS/CAREER NOTES: Selected by Houston Oilers in fifth round (143rd pick overall) of 1997 NFL draft. ... Oilers franchise moved to Tennessee for 1997 season. ... Signed by Oilers (July 19, 1997). ... Released by Oilers (August 25, 1997). ... Re-signed by Oilers to practice squad (August 26, 1997). ... Activated (December 5, 1997). ... Assigned by Oilers to Barcelona Dragons in 1998 NFL Europe enhancement allocation program (February 18, 1998). ... Oilers franchise renamed Tennessee Titans for 1999 season (December 26, 1998). ... Granted free agency (March 2, 2001). ... Signed by Kansas City Chiefs (May 10, 2001).
PLAYING EXPERIENCE: Tennessee NFL, 1997-2000; Barcelona Dragons NFLE, 1998. ... Games/Games started: 1997 (2/0), NFLE 1998 (games played unavailable), NFL 1998 (6/0), 1999 (5/0), 2000 (11/0). Total NFL: 24/0.
CHAMPIONSHIP GAME EXPERIENCE: Member of Titans for AFC championship game (1999 season); inactive. ... Played in Super Bowl XXXIV (1999 season).
PRO STATISTICS: NFLE: 1998—Intercepted three passes for 89 yards and one touchdown and credited with two sacks.

McCUTCHEON, DAYLON   CB   BROWNS

PERSONAL: Born December 9, 1976, in Walnut, Calif. ... 5-10/180. ... Son of Lawrence McCutcheon, Director of Scouting, St. Louis Rams, and former running back with four NFL teams (1972-81). ... Name pronounced mc-CUTCH-in.
HIGH SCHOOL: Bishop Amat (La Puente, Calif.).
COLLEGE: Southern California.
TRANSACTIONS/CAREER NOTES: Selected by Cleveland Browns in third round (62nd pick overall) of 1999 NFL draft. ... Signed by Browns (July 22, 1999).
HONORS: Named cornerback on THE SPORTING NEWS college All-America second team (1998).

Year Team	G	GS	INTERCEPTIONS No.	Yds.	Avg.	TD	SACKS No.
1999—Cleveland NFL	16	15	1	12	12.0	0	1.0
2000—Cleveland NFL	15	15	1	20	20.0	0	4.0
Pro totals (2 years)	31	30	2	32	16.0	0	5.0

McDANIEL, ED   LB   VIKINGS

PERSONAL: Born February 23, 1969, in Battesburg, S.C. ... 5-11/234.
HIGH SCHOOL: Battesburg (S.C.)-Leesville.
COLLEGE: Clemson (degree in human resource and development, 1991).
TRANSACTIONS/CAREER NOTES: Selected by Minnesota Vikings in fifth round (125th pick overall) of 1992 NFL draft. ... Signed by Vikings (July 20, 1992). ... Released by Vikings (August 31, 1992). ... Re-signed by Vikings to practice squad (September 1, 1992). ... Activated (November 5, 1992). ... On injured reserve with knee injury (August 25, 1996-entire season). ... Granted unconditional free agency (February 12, 1999). ... Re-signed by Vikings (February 18, 1999). ... On physically unable to perform list with knee injury (August 1-10, 1999).
CHAMPIONSHIP GAME EXPERIENCE: Played in NFC championship game (1998 and 2000 seasons).
HONORS: Named to play in Pro Bowl (1998 season); replaced by Hardy Nickerson due to injury.
PRO STATISTICS: 1995—Recovered one fumble. 1998—Recovered two fumbles for five yards. 1999—Recovered two fumbles.

Year Team	G	GS	INTERCEPTIONS No.	Yds.	Avg.	TD	SACKS No.
1992—Minnesota NFL	8	0	0	0	0.0	0	0.0
1993—Minnesota NFL	7	1	0	0	0.0	0	0.0
1994—Minnesota NFL	16	16	1	0	0.0	0	1.5
1995—Minnesota NFL	16	16	1	3	3.0	0	4.5
1996—Minnesota NFL					Did not play.		
1997—Minnesota NFL	16	16	1	18	18.0	0	1.5
1998—Minnesota NFL	16	16	0	0	0.0	0	7.0
1999—Minnesota NFL	16	16	0	0	0.0	0	2.0
2000—Minnesota NFL	16	15	0	0	0.0	0	2.0
Pro totals (8 years)	111	96	3	21	7.0	0	18.5

McDANIEL, EMMANUEL — CB — GIANTS

PERSONAL: Born July 27, 1972, in Griffin, Ga. ... 5-9/180.
HIGH SCHOOL: Jonesboro (Ga.).
COLLEGE: East Carolina.
TRANSACTIONS/CAREER NOTES: Selected by Carolina Panthers in fourth round (111th pick overall) of 1996 NFL draft. ... Signed by Panthers (July 20, 1996). ... Released by Panthers (August 26, 1997). ... Signed by Indianapolis Colts (November 27, 1997). ... Released by Colts (August 24, 1998). ... Re-signed by Colts (September 3, 1998). ... Inactive for one game with Colts (1998). ... Released by Colts (September 9, 1998). ... Signed by Miami Dolphins (October 8, 1998). ... Inactive for one game with Dolphins (1998). ... Released by Dolphins (October 14, 1998). ... Re-signed by Dolphins to practice squad (October 15, 1998). ... Activated (January 7, 1999). ... Claimed on waivers by New York Giants (September 1, 1999). ... Released by Giants (September 5, 1999). ... Re-signed by Giants to practice squad (September 6, 1999). ... Activated (November 15, 1999). ... Granted free agency (March 2, 2001).
PLAYING EXPERIENCE: Carolina NFL, 1996; Indianapolis NFL, 1997; New York Giants NFL, 1999 and 2000. ... Games/Games started: 1996 (2/0), 1997 (3/0), 2000 (16/3). Total: 28/5.
CHAMPIONSHIP GAME EXPERIENCE: Member of Panthers for NFC championship game (1996 season); inactive. ... Played in NFC championship game (2000 season). ... Played in Super Bowl XXXV (2000 season).
PRO STATISTICS: 2000—Intercepted six passes for 30 yards, credited with one sack and recovered one fumble.

McDANIEL, JEREMY — WR — BILLS

PERSONAL: Born May 2, 1976, in New Bern, N.C. ... 6-0/197. ... Full name: Jeremy Dwayne McDaniel.
HIGH SCHOOL: New Bern (N.C.).
JUNIOR COLLEGE: Fort Scott (Kan.) Community College.
COLLEGE: Arizona.
TRANSACTIONS/CAREER NOTES: Signed as non-drafted free agent by Buffalo Bills (April 23, 1999). ... Released by Bills (September 4, 1999). ... Re-signed by Bills to practice squad (September 7, 1999). ... Activated (December 23, 1999).
SINGLE GAME HIGHS (regular season): Receptions—5 (October 22, 2000, vs. Minnesota); yards—93 (September 17, 2000, vs. New York Jets); and touchdown receptions—1 (September 17, 2000, vs. New York Jets).

				RECEIVING		
Year Team	G	GS	No.	Yds.	Avg.	TD
1999—Buffalo NFL	1	0	0	0	0.0	0
2000—Buffalo NFL	16	5	43	697	16.2	2
Pro totals (2 years)	17	5	43	697	16.2	2

McDANIEL, RANDALL — G — BUCCANEERS

PERSONAL: Born December 19, 1964, in Phoenix. ... 6-3/287. ... Full name: Randall Cornell McDaniel.
HIGH SCHOOL: Agua Fria Union (Avondale, Ariz.).
COLLEGE: Arizona State (degree in physical education, 1988).
TRANSACTIONS/CAREER NOTES: Selected by Minnesota Vikings in first round (19th pick overall) of 1988 NFL draft. ... Signed by Vikings (July 22, 1988). ... Granted free agency (February 1, 1991). ... Re-signed by Vikings (July 22, 1991). ... Designated by Vikings as transition player (February 25, 1993). ... Free agency status changed by Vikings from transitional to unconditional (February 17, 1994). ... Re-signed by Vikings (April 21, 1994). ... Designated by Vikings as franchise player (February 13, 1997). ... Re-signed by Vikings (February 21, 1997). ... Released by Vikings (February 10, 2000). ... Signed by Tampa Bay Buccaneers (March 1, 2000).
PLAYING EXPERIENCE: Minnesota NFL, 1988-1999; Tampa Bay NFL, 2000. ... Games/Games started: 1988 (16/15), 1989 (14/13), 1990 (16/16), 1991 (16/16), 1992 (16/16), 1993 (16/16), 1994 (16/16), 1995 (16/16), 1996 (16/16), 1997 (16/16), 1998 (16/16), 1999 (16/16), 2000 (16/16). Total: 206/204.
CHAMPIONSHIP GAME EXPERIENCE: Played in NFC championship game (1998 season).
HONORS: Named guard on THE SPORTING NEWS college All-America second team (1987). ... Played in Pro Bowl (1989-2000 seasons). ... Named guard on THE SPORTING NEWS NFL All-Pro team (1991-1994 and 1996-1998).
PRO STATISTICS: 1991—Recovered one fumble. 1994—Recovered one fumble. 1996—Rushed twice for one yard. 2000—Caught one pass for two yards and a touchdown.

M

McDONALD, RAMOS — CB — RAIDERS

PERSONAL: Born April 30, 1976, in Dallas. ... 5-11/194.
HIGH SCHOOL: Liberty Eylau (Texarkana, Texas).
JUNIOR COLLEGE: Navarro College (Texas).
COLLEGE: New Mexico.
TRANSACTIONS/CAREER NOTES: Selected by Minnesota Vikings in third round (80th pick overall) of 1998 NFL draft. ... Signed by Vikings (July 25, 1998). ... Claimed on waivers by San Francisco 49ers (October 26, 1999). ... Claimed on waivers by New York Giants (August 25, 2000). ... Released by Giants (August 30, 2000). ... Re-signed by Giants (September 5, 2000). ... Released by Giants (September 9, 2000). ... Re-signed by Giants (September 11, 2000). ... Released by Giants (February 19, 2001). ... Signed by Oakland Raiders (April 1, 2001).
PLAYING EXPERIENCE: Minnesota NFL, 1998; Minnesota (5)-San Francisco (9) NFL, 1999; New York Giants NFL, 2000. ... Games/Games started: 1998 (15/0), 1999 (Min.-5/5; S.F.-9/7; Total: 14/12), 2000 (3/0). Total: 32/12.
CHAMPIONSHIP GAME EXPERIENCE: Played in NFC championship game (1998 and 2000 season). ... Played in Super Bowl XXXV (2000 season).
PRO STATISTICS: 1999—Intercepted one pass for four yards.

McDOUGAL, KEVIN — RB — COLTS

PERSONAL: Born May 18, 1977, in Denver, Colo. ... 5-11/203. ... Full name: Kevin John McDougal.
HIGH SCHOOL: Arvada West (Colorado).
COLLEGE: Colorado State.
TRANSACTIONS/CAREER NOTES: Signed by Indianapolis Colts as non-drafted free agent (April 20, 2000). ... On injured reserve with neck injury (November 28, 2000-remainder of season).
PLAYING EXPERIENCE: Indianapolis NFL, 2000. ... Games/Games started: 2000 (6/0).

McDOUGLE, STOCKAR — OT — LIONS

PERSONAL: Born January 11, 1977, in Deerfield Beach, Fla. ... 6-6/350.
HIGH SCHOOL: Deerfield Beach (Fla.).
JUNIOR COLLEGE: Navarro College (Texas).
COLLEGE: Oklahoma.
TRANSACTIONS/CAREER NOTES: Selected by Detroit Lions in first round (20th pick overall) of 2000 NFL draft. ... Signed by Lions (July 15, 2000).
PLAYING EXPERIENCE: Detroit NFL, 2000. ... Games/Games started: 2000 (8/8).

McDUFFIE, O.J. — WR — DOLPHINS

PERSONAL: Born December 2, 1969, in Marion, Ohio. ... 5-10/195. ... Full name: Otis James McDuffie.
HIGH SCHOOL: Hawken (Gates Mills, Ohio).
COLLEGE: Penn State (degree in labor and industrial relations).
TRANSACTIONS/CAREER NOTES: Selected by Miami Dolphins in first round (25th pick overall) of 1993 NFL draft. ... Signed by Dolphins (July 18, 1993). ... On physically unable to perform list with toe injury (August 22-October 23, 2000).
HONORS: Named wide receiver on THE SPORTING NEWS college All-America second team (1992).
POST SEASON RECORDS: Shares NFL postseason career and single-game records for most two-point conversions—1 (December 30, 1995, vs. Buffalo). ... (December 30, 1995, vs. Buffalo).
PRO STATISTICS: 1993—Fumbled four times and recovered one fumble. 1994—Fumbled three times. 1995—Fumbled four times and recovered two fumbles. 1996—Fumbled six times and recovered three fumbles. 1997—Recovered two fumbles for three yards. 1999—Fumbled twice.
SINGLE GAME HIGHS (regular season): Receptions—11 (December 13, 1998, vs. New York Jets); yards—137 (October 27, 1997, vs. Chicago); and touchdown receptions—3 (November 29, 1998, vs. New Orleans).
STATISTICAL PLATEAUS: 100-yard receiving games: 1994 (1), 1996 (2), 1997 (3), 1998 (3). Total: 9.

			RUSHING				RECEIVING				PUNT RETURNS				KICKOFF RETURNS				TOTALS		
Year Team	G	GS	Att.	Yds.	Avg.	TD	No.	Yds.	Avg.	TD	No.	Yds.	Avg.	TD	No.	Yds.	Avg.	TD	TD	2pt.	Pts.
1993—Miami NFL	16	0	1	-4	-4.0	0	19	197	10.4	0	28	317	11.3	†2	32	755	23.6	0	2	0	12
1994—Miami NFL	15	3	5	32	6.4	0	37	488	13.2	3	32	228	7.1	0	36	767	21.3	0	3	0	18
1995—Miami NFL	16	16	3	6	2.0	0	62	819	13.2	8	24	163	6.8	0	23	564	24.5	0	8	1	50
1996—Miami NFL	16	16	2	7	3.5	0	74	918	12.4	8	22	212	9.6	0	0	0	0.0	0	8	0	48
1997—Miami NFL	16	16	0	0	0.0	0	76	943	12.4	1	2	4	2.0	0	0	0	0.0	0	1	0	6
1998—Miami NFL	16	16	3	11	3.7	0	*90	1050	11.7	7	12	141	11.8	0	0	0	0.0	0	7	0	42
1999—Miami NFL	12	10	0	0	0.0	0	43	516	12.0	2	7	62	8.9	0	1	17	17.0	0	2	0	12
2000—Miami NFL	9	1	1	-3	-3.0	0	14	143	10.2	0	0	0	0.0	0	0	0	0.0	0	0	0	0
Pro totals (8 years)	116	78	15	49	3.3	0	415	5074	12.2	29	127	1127	8.9	2	92	2103	22.9	0	31	1	188

McELROY, RAY — CB — BEARS

PERSONAL: Born July 31, 1972, in Bellwood, Ill. ... 5-11/207. ... Full name: Raymond Edward McElroy. ... Name pronounced Mc-ELL-roy.
HIGH SCHOOL: Proviso West (Hillside, Ill.).
COLLEGE: Eastern Illinois.
TRANSACTIONS/CAREER NOTES: Selected by Indianapolis Colts in fourth round (114th pick overall) of 1995 NFL draft. ... Signed by Colts (July 12, 1995). ... Granted free agency (February 13, 1998). ... Re-signed by Colts (February 24, 1998). ... Released by Colts (August 24, 1998). ... Re-signed by Colts (August 28, 1998). ... Granted unconditional free agency (February 12, 1999). ... Re-signed by Colts (May 3, 1999). ... Released by Colts (August 9, 1999). ... Signed by Carolina Panthers (August 11, 1999). ... Released by Panthers (September 4, 1999). ... Signed by Chicago Bears (April 17, 2000). ... Released by Bears (August 27, 2000). ... Re-signed by Bears (September 19, 2000).
PLAYING EXPERIENCE: Indianapolis NFL, 1995-1998; Chicago NFL, 2000. ... Games/Games started: 1995 (16/0), 1996 (16/5), 1997 (16/4), 1998 (16/0), 2000 (13/0). Total: 77/9.
CHAMPIONSHIP GAME EXPERIENCE: Played in AFC championship game (1995 season).
PRO STATISTICS: 1997—Returned blocked field goal attempt 42 yards for a touchdown. 2000—Recovered one fumble.

McFARLAND, ANTHONY — DT — BUCCANEERS

PERSONAL: Born December 18, 1977, in Winnsboro, La. ... 6-0/300. ... Full name: Anthony Darelle McFarland.
HIGH SCHOOL: Winnsboro (La.).
COLLEGE: Louisiana State.
TRANSACTIONS/CAREER NOTES: Selected by Tampa Bay Buccaneers in first round (15th pick overall) of 1999 NFL draft. ... Signed by Buccaneers (August 3, 1999).
PLAYING EXPERIENCE: Tampa Bay NFL, 1999 and 2000. ... Games/Games started: 1999 (14/0), 2000 (16/16). Total: 30/16.
CHAMPIONSHIP GAME EXPERIENCE: Played in NFC championship game (1999 season).
HONORS: Named defensive tackle on THE SPORTING NEWS college All-America second team (1998).
PRO STATISTICS: 1999—Credited with one sack. 2000—Credited with 6$\frac{1}{2}$ sacks and recovered one fumble.

McGARITY, WANE — WR — COWBOYS

PERSONAL: Born September 30, 1976, in San Antonio. ... 5-8/197. ... Full name: Wane Keith McGarity.
HIGH SCHOOL: Clark (San Antonio).
COLLEGE: Texas.
TRANSACTIONS/CAREER NOTES: Selected by Dallas Cowboys in fourth round (118th pick overall) of 1999 NFL draft. ... Signed by Cowboys (July 26, 1999). ... On injured reserve with finger injury (December 10, 1999-remainder of season).
PRO STATISTICS: 2000—Rushed six times for 49 yards and one touchdown and recovered two fumbles.
SINGLE GAME HIGHS (regular season): Receptions—6 (November 19, 2000, vs. Baltimore); yards—59 (December 3, 2000, vs. Tampa Bay); and touchdown receptions—0.

					RECEIVING			PUNT RETURNS				TOTALS		
Year	Team	G	GS	No.	Yds.	Avg.	TD	No.	Yds.	Avg.	TD	TD	2pt.	Pts.	Fum.
1999—Dallas NFL		5	1	7	70	10.0	0	3	16	5.3	0	0	0	0	0
2000—Dallas NFL		14	0	25	250	10.0	0	30	353	11.8	†2	3	0	18	2
Pro totals (2 years)		19	1	32	320	10.0	0	33	369	11.2	2	3	0	18	2

McGARRAHAN, SCOTT   S   PACKERS

PERSONAL: Born February 12, 1974, in Arlington, Texas. ... 6-1/198. ... Full name: John Scott McGarrahan. ... Name pronounced ma-GAIR-a-han.
HIGH SCHOOL: Lamar (Arlington, Texas).
COLLEGE: New Mexico.
TRANSACTIONS/CAREER NOTES: Selected by Green Bay Packers in sixth round (156th pick overall) of 1998 NFL draft. ... Signed by Packers (July 17, 1998). ... On injured reserve with hamstring injury (December 29, 1999-remainder of season). ... Granted free agency (March 2, 2001).
PLAYING EXPERIENCE: Green Bay NFL, 1998-2000. ... Games/Games started: 1998 (15/0), 1999 (13/0), 2000 (16/0). Total: 44/0.
PRO STATISTICS: 1999—Recovered one fumble. 2000—Credited with 1/2 sack.

McGEE, TONY   TE   BENGALS

PERSONAL: Born April 21, 1971, in Terre Haute, Ind. ... 6-3/248.
HIGH SCHOOL: Terre Haute (Ind.) South.
COLLEGE: Michigan (degree in communications).
TRANSACTIONS/CAREER NOTES: Selected by Cincinnati Bengals in second round (37th pick overall) of 1993 NFL draft. ... Signed by Bengals (July 20, 1993). ... Granted free agency (February 16, 1996). ... Re-signed by Bengals for 1996 season. ... On injured reserve with broken ankle (December 14, 2000-remainder of season).
PRO STATISTICS: 1994—Returned one kickoff for four yards.
SINGLE GAME HIGHS (regular season): Receptions—8 (December 22, 1996, vs. Indianapolis); yards—118 (September 3, 1995, vs. Indianapolis); and touchdown receptions—2 (November 9, 1997, vs. Indianapolis).
STATISTICAL PLATEAUS: 100-yard receiving games: 1993 (1), 1995 (1). Total: 2.

				RECEIVING				TOTALS			
Year	Team	G	GS	No.	Yds.	Avg.	TD	TD	2pt.	Pts.	Fum.
1993—Cincinnati NFL		15	15	44	525	11.9	0	0	0	0	1
1994—Cincinnati NFL		16	16	40	492	12.3	1	1	0	6	0
1995—Cincinnati NFL		16	16	55	754	13.7	4	4	0	24	2
1996—Cincinnati NFL		16	16	38	446	11.7	4	4	0	24	0
1997—Cincinnati NFL		16	16	34	414	12.2	6	6	1	38	0
1998—Cincinnati NFL		16	16	22	363	16.5	1	1	0	6	0
1999—Cincinnati NFL		16	16	26	344	13.2	2	2	0	12	0
2000—Cincinnati NFL		14	14	26	309	11.9	1	1	0	6	0
Pro totals (8 years)		125	125	285	3647	12.8	19	19	1	116	3

McGINEST, WILLIE   DE   PATRIOTS

M

PERSONAL: Born December 11, 1971, in Long Beach, Calif. ... 6-5/270. ... Full name: William Lee McGinest Jr.
HIGH SCHOOL: Polytechnic (Pasadena, Calif.).
COLLEGE: Southern California.
TRANSACTIONS/CAREER NOTES: Selected by New England Patriots in first round (fourth pick overall) of 1994 NFL draft. ... Signed by Patriots (May 17, 1994). ... Granted unconditional free agency (February 13, 1998). ... Re-signed by Patriots (February 12, 1998).
CHAMPIONSHIP GAME EXPERIENCE: Played in AFC championship game (1996 season). ... Played in Super Bowl XXXI (1996 season).
PRO STATISTICS: 1994—Recovered two fumbles. 1996—Intercepted one pass for 46 yards and a touchdown and recovered two fumbles, including one in end zone for a touchdown. 1997—Recovered three fumbles. 1999—Recovered two fumbles for two yards and one touchdown. 2000—Recovered two fumbles.

Year	Team	G	GS	SACKS
1994—New England NFL		16	7	4.5
1995—New England NFL		16	16	11.0
1996—New England NFL		16	16	9.5
1997—New England NFL		11	11	2.0
1998—New England NFL		9	8	3.5
1999—New England NFL		16	16	9.0
2000—New England NFL		14	14	6.0
Pro totals (7 years)		98	88	45.5

McGLOCKTON, CHESTER   DT   BRONCOS

PERSONAL: Born September 16, 1969, in Whiteville, N.C. ... 6-4/334.
HIGH SCHOOL: Whiteville (N.C.).
COLLEGE: Clemson.
TRANSACTIONS/CAREER NOTES: Selected after junior season by Los Angeles Raiders in first round (16th pick overall) of 1992 NFL draft. ... Signed by Raiders for 1992 season. ... On injured reserve (January 11, 1994-remainder of 1993 playoffs). ... Raiders franchise moved to Oakland (July 21, 1995). ... Designated by Raiders as franchise player (February 12, 1998). ... Tendered offer sheet by Kansas City Chiefs (April 10, 1998). ... Raiders declined to match offer (April 17, 1998). ... Released by Chiefs (February 28, 2001). ... Signed by Denver Broncos (April 10, 2001).
HONORS: Named defensive tackle ON THE SPORTING NEWS NFL All-Pro team (1994). ... Played in Pro Bowl (1994-1997 seasons).

PRO STATISTICS: 1993—Intercepted one pass for 19 yards. 1994—Recovered one fumble. 1995—Recovered two fumbles. 1997—Recovered one fumble. 1998—Recovered one fumble. 1999—Intercepted one pass for 30 yards, fumbled once and recovered one fumble for minus two yards. 2000—Recovered one fumble.

Year Team	G	GS	SACKS
1992—Los Angeles Raiders NFL	10	0	3.0
1993—Los Angeles Raiders NFL	16	16	7.0
1994—Los Angeles Raiders NFL	16	16	9.5
1995—Oakland NFL	16	16	7.5
1996—Oakland NFL	16	16	8.0
1997—Oakland NFL	16	16	4.5
1998—Kansas City NFL	10	9	1.0
1999—Kansas City NFL	16	16	1.5
2000—Kansas City NFL	15	15	4.5
Pro totals (9 years)	131	120	46.5

McGREW, REGGIE   DT   49ERS

PERSONAL: Born December 16, 1976, in Mayo, Fla. ... 6-1/301. ... Full name: Reginald Gerard McGrew.
HIGH SCHOOL: Lafayette (Mayo, Fla.).
COLLEGE: Florida.
TRANSACTIONS/CAREER NOTES: Selected after junior season by San Francisco 49ers in first round (24th pick overall) of 1999 NFL draft. ... Signed by 49ers (July 26, 1999). ... Inactive for four games (1999). ... On injured reserve with triceps injury (October 4, 1999-remainder of season).

Year Team	G	GS	SACKS
1999—San Francisco NFL	Did not play.		
2000—San Francisco NFL	10	0	0.0
Pro totals (1 years)	10	0	0.0

McGRIFF, TRAVIS   WR   BRONCOS

PERSONAL: Born June 24, 1976, in Gainesville, Fla. ... 5-8/185. ... Full name: William Travis McGriff.
HIGH SCHOOL: P.K. Yonge (Gainesville, Fla.).
COLLEGE: Florida.
TRANSACTIONS/CAREER NOTES: Selected by Denver Broncos in third round (93rd pick overall) of 1999 NFL draft. ... Signed by Broncos (July 22, 1999).
PRO STATISTICS: 1999—Recovered one fumble.
SINGLE GAME HIGHS (regular season): Receptions—1 (November 5, 2000, vs. New York Jets); yards—43 (October 1, 2000, vs. New England); and touchdown receptions—1 (October 1, 2000, vs. New England).

			RECEIVING			PUNT RETURNS			TOTALS			
Year Team	G	GS	No.	Yds.	Avg.	TD	No.	Yds.	Avg.	TD	TD	2pt.	Pts.	Fum.
1999—Denver NFL	14	0	3	37	12.3	0	7	50	7.1	0	0	0	0	1
2000—Denver NFL	15	0	2	51	25.5	1	0	0	0.0	0	1	0	6	0
Pro totals (2 years)	29	0	5	88	17.6	1	7	50	7.1	0	1	0	6	1

M

McINTOSH, CHRIS   OT   SEAHAWKS

PERSONAL: Born February 20, 1977, in Pewaukee, Wis. ... 6-6/315.
HIGH SCHOOL: Pewaukee (Wis.).
COLLEGE: Wisconsin.
TRANSACTIONS/CAREER NOTES: Selected by Seattle Seahawks in first round (22nd pick overall) of 2000 NFL draft. ... Signed by Seahawks (August 26, 2000).
PLAYING EXPERIENCE: Seattle NFL, 2000. ... Games/Games started: 2000 (14/10).
HONORS: Named offensive tackle on THE SPORTING NEWS college All-America first team (1999).

McINTOSH, DAMION   OT   CHARGERS

PERSONAL: Born March 25, 1977, in Kingston, Jamaica. ... 6-4/325. ... Full name: Damion Alexis McIntosh.
HIGH SCHOOL: McArthur (Hollywood, Fla.).
COLLEGE: Kansas State.
TRANSACTIONS/CAREER NOTES: Selected by San Diego Chargers in third round (83rd pick overall) of 2000 NFL draft. ... Signed by Chargers (July 20, 2000).
PLAYING EXPERIENCE: San Diego NFL, 2000. ... Games/Games started: 2000 (3/0).

McKENZIE, KEITH   DL   BROWNS

PERSONAL: Born October 17, 1973, in Detroit. ... 6-3/273. ... Full name: Keith Derrick McKenzie.
HIGH SCHOOL: Highland Park (Mich.).
COLLEGE: Ball State (degree in history).
TRANSACTIONS/CAREER NOTES: Selected by Green Bay Packers in seventh round (252nd pick overall) of 1996 NFL draft. ... Signed by Packers (July 15, 1996). ... Granted free agency (February 12, 1999). ... Re-signed by Packers (June 1, 1999). ... Granted unconditional free agency (February 11, 2000). ... Signed by Cleveland Browns (February 24, 2000).
CHAMPIONSHIP GAME EXPERIENCE: Member of Super Bowl championship team (1996 season). ... Played in NFC championship game (1996 and 1997 seasons). ... Played in Super Bowl XXXII (1997 season).
PRO STATISTICS: 1998—Intercepted one pass for 33 yards and a touchdown, returned one kickoff for 17 yards and recovered three fumbles for 88 yards and one touchdown. 1999—Recovered four fumbles for 63 yards and two touchdowns. 2000—Recovered one fumble for 29 yards.

Year Team	G	GS	SACKS
1996—Green Bay NFL	10	0	1.0
1997—Green Bay NFL	16	0	1.5
1998—Green Bay NFL	16	0	8.0
1999—Green Bay NFL	16	2	8.0
2000—Cleveland NFL	16	16	8.0
Pro totals (5 years)	74	18	26.5

McKENZIE, MIKE — CB — PACKERS

PERSONAL: Born April 26, 1976, in Miami. ... 6-0/190. ... Full name: Michael Terrance McKenzie.
HIGH SCHOOL: Norland (Miami).
COLLEGE: Memphis.
TRANSACTIONS/CAREER NOTES: Selected after junior season by Green Bay Packers in third round (87th pick overall) of 1999 NFL draft. ... Signed by Packers (July 8, 1999).
PRO STATISTICS: 2000—Returned one punt for no yards and fumbled once.

			INTERCEPTIONS			
Year Team	G	GS	No.	Yds.	Avg.	TD
1999—Green Bay NFL	16	16	6	4	0.7	0
2000—Green Bay NFL	10	8	1	26	26.0	0
Pro totals (2 years)	26	24	7	30	4.3	0

McKENZIE, RALEIGH — G

PERSONAL: Born February 8, 1963, in Knoxville, Tenn. ... 6-2/290. ... Twin brother of Reggie McKenzie, linebacker with Los Angeles Raiders (1985-88), Montreal Machine of World League (1990) and San Francisco 49ers (1992).
HIGH SCHOOL: Austin-East (Knoxville, Tenn.).
COLLEGE: Tennessee.
TRANSACTIONS/CAREER NOTES: Selected by Washington Redskins in 11th round (290th pick overall) of 1985 NFL draft. ... Signed by Redskins (June 20, 1985). ... Granted free agency (February 1, 1992). ... Re-signed by Redskins for 1992 season. ... Granted unconditional free agency (February 17, 1995). ... Signed by Philadelphia Eagles (March 28, 1995). ... Granted unconditional free agency (February 14, 1997). ... Signed by San Diego Chargers (February 20, 1997). ... Granted unconditional free agency (February 12, 1999). ... Signed by Green Bay Packers (February 25, 1999). ... Released by Packers (August 22, 2000). ... Re-signed by Packers (September 22, 2000). ... Released by Packers (October 16, 2000).
PLAYING EXPERIENCE: Washington NFL, 1985-1994; Philadelphia NFL, 1995 and 1996; San Diego NFL, 1997 and 1998; Green Bay NFL, 1999 and 2000. ... Games/Games started: 1985 (6/0), 1986 (15/5), 1987 (12/12), 1988 (16/14), 1989 (15/8), 1990 (16/12), 1991 (16/14), 1992 (16/16), 1993 (16/16), 1994 (16/16), 1995 (16/16), 1996 (16/16), 1997 (16/16), 1998 (16/16), 1999 (16/7), 2000 (2/0). Total: 226/184.
CHAMPIONSHIP GAME EXPERIENCE: Played in NFC championship game (1986, 1987 and 1991 seasons). ... Member of Super Bowl championship team (1987 and 1991 seasons).
PRO STATISTICS: 1994—Recovered one fumble. 1995—Recovered one fumble. 1997—Recovered one fumble. 1999—Returned one kickoff for 13 yards. 2000—Recovered one fumble.

McKINLEY, ALVIN — DT — PANTHERS

M

PERSONAL: Born June 9, 1978, in Kosciusko, Miss. ... 6-3/292. ... Full name: Alvin Jerome McKinley.
HIGH SCHOOL: Weir (Miss.).
JUNIOR COLLEGE: Holmes Junior College (Miss.).
COLLEGE: Mississippi State.
TRANSACTIONS/CAREER NOTES: Selected by Carolina Panthers in fourth round (120th pick overall) of 2000 NFL draft. ... Signed by Panthers (June 21, 2000).
PLAYING EXPERIENCE: Carolina NFL, 2000, ... Games/Games started: 2000 (7/0).

McKINLEY, DENNIS — FB — CARDINALS

PERSONAL: Born November 3, 1976, in Kosciusko, Miss. ... 6-2/250. ... Full name: Dennis L. McKinley.
HIGH SCHOOL: Weir (Miss.) Attendance Center.
COLLEGE: Mississippi State (degree in educational psychology).
TRANSACTIONS/CAREER NOTES: Selected by Arizona Cardinals in sixth round (206th pick overall) of 1999 NFL draft. ... Signed by Cardinals for 1999 season.
PLAYING EXPERIENCE: Arizona NFL, 1999 and 2000. ... Games/Games started: 1999 (16/0), 2000 (16/0). Total: 32/0.
PRO STATISTICS: 1999—Caught one pass for four yards and recovered two fumbles. 2000—Caught two passes for 13 yards and returned one kickoff for 20 yards.

McKINNEY, STEVE — G — COLTS

PERSONAL: Born October 15, 1975, in Houston. ... 6-4/295. ... Full name: Stephen Michael McKinney.
HIGH SCHOOL: Clear Lake (Houston).
COLLEGE: Texas A&M.
TRANSACTIONS/CAREER NOTES: Selected by Indianapolis Colts in fourth round (93rd pick overall) of 1998 NFL draft. ... Signed by Colts (July 23, 1998). ... Granted free agency (March 2, 2001).
PLAYING EXPERIENCE: Indianapolis NFL, 1998-2000. ... Games/Games started: 1998 (16/16), 1999 (15/14), 2000 (16/16). Total: 47/46.
PRO STATISTICS: 2000—Recovered one fumble.

McKINNON, RONALD   LB   CARDINALS

PERSONAL: Born September 20, 1973, in Fort Rucker Army Base, Ala. ... 6-0/255.
HIGH SCHOOL: Elba (Ala.).
COLLEGE: North Alabama.
TRANSACTIONS/CAREER NOTES: Signed as non-drafted free agent by Arizona Cardinals (April 23, 1996). ... Granted free agency (February 12, 1999). ... Re-signed by Cardinals (June 14, 1999). ... Granted unconditional free agency (February 11, 2000). ... Re-signed by Cardinals (February 24, 2000).
HONORS: Harlon Hill Trophy winner (1995).
PRO STATISTICS: 1996—Rushed once for minus four yards. 1997—Rushed once for three yards. 1998—Fumbled once and recovered two fumbles. 1999—Recovered one fumble. 2000—Recovered one fumble.

| | | | INTERCEPTIONS | | | SACKS |
Year Team	G	GS	No.	Yds.	Avg.	TD	No.
1996—Arizona NFL	16	0	0	0	0.0	0	0.0
1997—Arizona NFL	16	16	3	40	13.3	0	1.0
1998—Arizona NFL	13	13	5	25	5.0	0	2.0
1999—Arizona NFL	16	16	1	0	0.0	0	1.0
2000—Arizona NFL	16	16	0	0	0.0	0	4.0
Pro totals (5 years)	77	61	9	65	7.2	0	8.0

McKNIGHT, JAMES   WR   DOLPHINS

PERSONAL: Born June 17, 1972, in Orlando. ... 6-1/200.
HIGH SCHOOL: Apopka (Fla.).
COLLEGE: Liberty (Va.).
TRANSACTIONS/CAREER NOTES: Signed as non-drafted free agent by Seattle Seahawks (April 29, 1994). ... Released by Seahawks (August 28, 1994). ... Re-signed by Seahawks to practice squad (August 29, 1994). ... Activated (November 19, 1994). ... Granted unconditional free agency (February 13, 1998). ... Re-signed by Seahawks (February 17, 1998). ... Traded by Seahawks to Dallas Cowboys for third-round pick (WR Darrell Jackson) in 2000 draft (June 24, 1999). ... On injured reserve with knee injury (August 27, 1999-entire season). ... Granted unconditional free agency (March 2, 2001). ... Signed by Miami Dolphins (March 16, 2001).
PRO STATISTICS: 1995—Returned one kickoff for four yards and recovered one fumble. 1996—Returned three kickoffs for 86 yards and recovered one fumble. 1997—Returned one kickoff for 14 yards.
SINGLE GAME HIGHS (regular season): Receptions—8 (November 12, 2000, vs. Cincinnati); yards—164 (November 12, 2000, vs. Cincinnati); and touchdown receptions—1 (November 12, 2000, vs. Cincinnati).
STATISTICAL PLATEAUS: 100-yard receiving games: 1997 (1), 1998 (1), 2000 (3). Total: 5.

| | | | RECEIVING | | | | TOTALS | | | |
Year Team	G	GS	No.	Yds.	Avg.	TD	TD	2pt.	Pts.	Fum.
1994—Seattle NFL	2	0	1	25	25.0	1	1	0	6	0
1995—Seattle NFL	16	0	6	91	15.2	0	0	0	0	1
1996—Seattle NFL	16	0	1	73	73.0	0	0	0	0	1
1997—Seattle NFL	12	5	34	637	*18.7	6	6	0	36	0
1998—Seattle NFL	14	2	21	346	16.5	2	2	0	12	0
1999—Dallas NFL						Did not play.				
2000—Dallas NFL	16	15	52	926	17.8	2	2	0	12	1
Pro totals (6 years)	76	22	115	2098	18.2	11	11	0	66	3

McLAUGHLIN, JOHN   DE   BUCCANEERS

PERSONAL: Born November 13, 1975, in Cleveland. ... 6-4/247. ... Full name: John Raymond McLaughlin.
HIGH SCHOOL: Hart (Newall, Calif.).
COLLEGE: Notre Dame, then California.
TRANSACTIONS/CAREER NOTES: Selected by Tampa Bay Buccaneers in fifth round (150th pick overall) of 1999 NFL draft. ... Signed by Buccaneers (July 26, 1999).
PLAYING EXPERIENCE: Tampa Bay NFL, 1999 and 2000. ... Games/Games started: 1999 (12/0), 2000 (6/0). Total: 18/0.
CHAMPIONSHIP GAME EXPERIENCE: Played in NFC championship game (1999 season).

McMILLON, TODD   CB   BEARS

PERSONAL: Born September 9, 1973, in Bellflower, Calif. ... 5-10/183.
HIGH SCHOOL: Cerritus (Bellflower, Calif.).
COLLEGE: Northern Arizona.
TRANSACTIONS/CAREER NOTES: Signed as non-drafted free agent by Chicago Bears (February 16, 2000). ... Released by Bears (August 22, 2000). ... Re-signed by Bears to practice squad (August 29, 2000). ... Activated (November 15, 2000).
PLAYING EXPERIENCE: Chicago NFL, 2000. ... Games/Games started: 2000 (3/0).

McNABB, DONOVAN   QB   EAGLES

PERSONAL: Born November 25, 1976, in Chicago. ... 6-2/226. ... Full name: Donovan Jamal McNabb.
HIGH SCHOOL: Mount Carmel (Ill.).
COLLEGE: Syracuse (degree in speech communications).
TRANSACTIONS/CAREER NOTES: Selected by Philadelphia Eagles in first round (second pick overall) of 1999 NFL draft. ... Signed by Eagles (July 30, 1999).
HONORS: Played in Pro Bowl (2000 season).

PRO STATISTICS: 1999—Fumbled eight times for minus three yards. 2000—Fumbled seven times, recovered two fumbles for minus five yards and caught two passes for five yards.
SINGLE GAME HIGHS (regular season): Attempts—55 (November 12, 2000, vs. Pittsburgh); completions—30 (October 1, 2000, vs. Atlanta); passing yards—390 (December 10, 2000, vs. Cleveland); and touchdown passes—4 (December 10, 2000, vs. Cleveland).
STATISTICAL PLATEAUS: 300-yard passing games: 2000 (2). ... 100-yard rushing games: 2000 (1).
MISCELLANEOUS: Regular-season record as starting NFL quarterback: 13-9 (.542). ... Postseason record as starting NFL quarterback: 1-1 (.500).

				PASSING							RUSHING				TOTALS		
Year Team	G	GS	Att.	Cmp.	Pct.	Yds.	TD	Int.	Avg.	Rat.	Att.	Yds.	Avg.	TD	TD	2pt.	Pts.
1999—Philadelphia NFL	12	6	216	106	49.1	948	8	7	4.39	60.1	47	313	6.7	0	0	†1	2
2000—Philadelphia NFL	16	16	569	330	58.0	3365	21	13	5.91	77.8	86	629	7.3	6	6	0	36
Pro totals (2 years)	28	22	785	436	55.5	4313	29	20	5.49	73.0	133	942	7.1	6	6	1	38

McNAIR, STEVE   QB   TITANS

PERSONAL: Born February 14, 1973, in Mount Olive, Miss. ... 6-2/225. ... Full name: Steve LaTreal McNair. ... Brother of Fred McNair, quarterback with Florida Bobcats of Arena League.
HIGH SCHOOL: Mount Olive (Miss.).
COLLEGE: Alcorn State.
TRANSACTIONS/CAREER NOTES: Selected by Houston Oilers in first round (third pick overall) of 1995 NFL draft. ... Signed by Oilers (July 25, 1995). ... Oilers franchise moved to Tennessee for 1997 season. ... Oilers franchise renamed Tennessee Titans for 1999 season (December 26, 1998).
CHAMPIONSHIP GAME EXPERIENCE: Played in AFC championship game (1999 season). ... Played in Super Bowl XXXIV (1999 season).
HONORS: Walter Payton Award winner (1994). ... Named to play in Pro Bowl (2000 season); replaced by Elvis Grbac due to injury.
PRO STATISTICS: 1995—Fumbled three times and recovered two fumbles for minus two yards. 1996—Fumbled seven times and recovered four fumbles. 1997—Led NFL with 16 fumbles and recovered seven fumbles for minus two yards. 1998—Fumbled five times and recovered three fumbles seven yards. 1999—Fumbled three times and recovered one fumble. 2000—Fumbled 12 times and recovered three fumbles for minus 31 yards.
SINGLE GAME HIGHS (regular season): Attempts—49 (December 20, 1998, vs. Green Bay); completions—29 (December 20, 1998, vs. Green Bay); yards—341 (September 12, 1999, vs. Cincinnati); and touchdown passes—5 (December 26, 1999, vs. Jacksonville).
STATISTICAL PLATEAUS: 300-yard passing games: 1996 (1), 1999 (1). Total: 2.
MISCELLANEOUS: Regular-season record as starting NFL quarterback: 41-23 (.641). ... Postseason record as starting NFL quarterback: 3-2 (.600).

				PASSING							RUSHING				TOTALS		
Year Team	G	GS	Att.	Cmp.	Pct.	Yds.	TD	Int.	Avg.	Rat.	Att.	Yds.	Avg.	TD	TD	2pt.	Pts.
1995—Houston NFL	6	2	80	41	51.3	569	3	1	7.11	81.7	11	38	3.5	0	0	0	0
1996—Houston NFL	9	4	143	88	61.5	1197	6	4	8.37	90.6	31	169	5.5	2	2	0	12
1997—Tennessee NFL	16	16	415	216	52.0	2665	14	13	6.42	70.4	101	674	*6.7	8	8	0	48
1998—Tennessee NFL	16	16	492	289	58.7	3228	15	10	6.56	80.1	77	559	7.3	4	4	0	24
1999—Tennessee NFL	11	11	331	187	56.5	2179	12	8	6.58	78.6	72	337	4.7	8	8	0	48
2000—Tennessee NFL	16	15	396	248	62.6	2847	15	13	7.19	83.2	72	403	5.6	0	0	0	0
Pro totals (6 years)	74	64	1857	1069	57.6	12685	65	49	6.83	79.2	364	2180	6.0	22	22	0	132

McNEIL, RYAN   CB   CHARGERS

PERSONAL: Born October 4, 1970, in Fort Pierce, Fla. ... 6-2/192. ... Full name: Ryan Darrell McNeil.
HIGH SCHOOL: Westwood Christian (Miami).
COLLEGE: Miami, Fla. (degree in psychology, 1992).
TRANSACTIONS/CAREER NOTES: Selected by Detroit Lions in second round (33rd pick overall) of 1993 NFL draft. ... Signed by Lions (August 25, 1993). ... Granted unconditional free agency (February 14, 1997). ... Signed by St. Louis Rams (July 7, 1997). ... Designated by Rams as franchise player (February 13, 1998). ... Re-signed by Rams (August 31, 1998). ... Granted unconditional free agency (February 12, 1999). ... Signed by Cleveland Browns (August 1, 1999). ... Granted unconditional free agency (February 11, 2000). ... Signed by Dallas Cowboys (March 2, 2000). ... Released by Cowboys (February 28, 2001). ... Signed by San Diego Chargers (March 3, 2001).
HONORS: Named defensive back on THE SPORTING NEWS college All-America second team (1992).
PRO STATISTICS: 1995—Recovered two fumbles. 1996—Recovered two fumbles. 1997—Fumbled once and recovered one fumble. 1998—Recovered one fumble. 1999—Credited with one sack and recovered four fumbles.

			INTERCEPTIONS			
Year Team	G	GS	No.	Yds.	Avg.	TD
1993—Detroit NFL	16	2	2	19	9.5	0
1994—Detroit NFL	14	13	1	14	14.0	0
1995—Detroit NFL	16	16	2	26	13.0	0
1996—Detroit NFL	16	16	5	14	2.8	0
1997—St. Louis NFL	16	16	*9	127	14.1	1
1998—St. Louis NFL	16	12	1	37	37.0	1
1999—Cleveland NFL	16	14	0	0	0.0	0
2000—Dallas NFL	16	16	2	4	2.0	0
Pro totals (8 years)	126	105	22	241	11.0	2

McNOWN, CADE   QB   BEARS

PERSONAL: Born January 12, 1977, in Portland, Ore. ... 6-1/208. ... Full name: Cade B. McNown.
HIGH SCHOOL: San Benito (Hollister, Calif.), then West Linn (Ore.).
COLLEGE: UCLA.
TRANSACTIONS/CAREER NOTES: Selected by Chicago Bears in first round (12th pick overall) of 1999 NFL draft. ... Signed by Bears (August 2, 1999).

HONORS: Named quarterback on THE SPORTING NEWS college All-America third team (1997). ... Named quarterback on THE SPORTING NEWS college All-America second team (1998).
PRO STATISTICS: 1999—Fumbled six times and recovered two fumbles for minus two yards. 2000—Fumbled eight times and recovered four fumbles for minus 17 yards.
SINGLE GAME HIGHS (regular season): Attempts—42 (January 2, 2000, vs. Tampa Bay); completions—27 (September 3, 2000, vs. Minnesota); passing yards—301 (December 19, 1999, vs. Detroit); and touchdown passes—4 (December 19, 1999, vs. Detroit).
STATISTICAL PLATEAUS: 300-yard passing games: 1999 (1).
MISCELLANEOUS: Regular-season record as starting NFL quarterback: 3-12 (.200).

				PASSING							RUSHING			TOTALS		
Year Team	G	GS	Att.	Cmp.	Pct.	Yds.	TD	Int.	Avg.	Rat.	Att.	Yds.	Avg.	TD	TD	2pt.	Pts.
1999—Chicago NFL............	15	6	235	127	54.0	1465	8	10	6.23	66.7	32	160	5.0	0	0	†1	2
2000—Chicago NFL............	10	9	280	154	55.0	1646	8	9	5.88	68.5	50	326	6.5	3	3	0	18
Pro totals (2 years)..............	25	15	515	281	54.6	3111	16	19	6.04	67.7	82	486	5.9	3	3	1	20

McQUARTERS, R.W.   CB   BEARS

PERSONAL: Born December 21, 1976, in Tulsa, Okla. ... 5-9/198. ... Full name: Robert William McQuarters II.
HIGH SCHOOL: Washington (Okla.).
COLLEGE: Oklahoma State.
TRANSACTIONS/CAREER NOTES: Selected after junior season by San Francisco 49ers in first round (28th pick overall) of 1998 NFL draft. ... Signed by 49ers (July 28, 1998). ... On injured reserve with shoulder injury (November 30, 1999-remainder of season). ... Traded by 49ers to Chicago Bears for sixth-round pick (WR Cedrick Wilson) in 2001 draft (June 5, 2000).
PRO STATISTICS: 1998—Recovered two fumbles. 2000—Credited with one sack.

			INTERCEPTIONS				PUNT RETURNS				KICKOFF RETURNS				TOTALS			
Year Team	G	GS	No.	Yds.	Avg.	TD	No.	Yds.	Avg.	TD	No.	Yds.	Avg.	TD	TD	2pt.	Pts.	Fum.
1998—San Francisco NFL	16	7	0	0	0.0	0	*47	406	8.6	1	17	339	19.9	0	1	0	6	4
1999—San Francisco NFL	11	4	1	25	25.0	0	18	90	5.0	0	26	568	21.8	0	0	0	0	1
2000—Chicago NFL..............	15	2	1	61	61.0	1	0	0	0.0	0	0	0	0.0	0	1	0	6	0
Pro totals (3 years)..............	42	13	2	86	43.0	1	65	496	7.6	1	43	907	21.1	0	2	0	12	5

McWILLIAMS, JOHNNY   TE   PATRIOTS

PERSONAL: Born December 14, 1972, in Ontario, Calif. ... 6-4/271.
HIGH SCHOOL: Pomona (Calif.).
COLLEGE: Southern California.
TRANSACTIONS/CAREER NOTES: Selected by Arizona Cardinals in third round (64th pick overall) of 1996 NFL draft. ... Signed by Cardinals (August 28, 1996). ... On reserve/did not report list (August 25-September 9, 1996). ... Granted free agency (February 12, 1999). ... Re-signed by Cardinals (June 17, 1999). ... Granted unconditional free agency (February 11, 2000). ... Signed by Minnesota Vikings (July 28, 2000). ... Granted unconditional free agency (March 2, 2001). ... Signed by New England Patriots (May 25, 2001).
CHAMPIONSHIP GAME EXPERIENCE: Played in NFC championship game (2000 season).
PRO STATISTICS: 1999—Recovered one fumble.
SINGLE GAME HIGHS (regular season): Receptions—5 (December 10, 2000, vs. St. Louis); yards—54 (November 10, 1996, vs. Washington); and touchdown receptions—1 (December 17, 2000, vs. Green Bay).

			RECEIVING				TOTALS			
Year Team	G	GS	No.	Yds.	Avg.	TD	TD	2pt.	Pts.	Fum.
1996—Arizona NFL...	12	0	7	80	11.4	1	1	0	6	0
1997—Arizona NFL...	16	7	7	75	10.7	0	0	0	0	0
1998—Arizona NFL...	16	15	26	284	10.9	4	4	0	24	0
1999—Arizona NFL...	15	4	11	71	6.5	1	1	0	6	1
2000—Minnesota NFL..	15	7	22	180	8.2	3	3	0	18	0
Pro totals (5 years)	74	33	73	690	9.5	9	9	0	54	1

MEADOWS, ADAM   OT   COLTS

PERSONAL: Born January 25, 1974, in Powder Springs, Ga. ... 6-5/295. ... Full name: Adam Jonathon Meadows.
HIGH SCHOOL: McEachern (Powder Springs, Ga.).
COLLEGE: Georgia.
TRANSACTIONS/CAREER NOTES: Selected by Indianapolis Colts in second round (48th pick overall) of 1997 NFL draft. ... Signed by Colts (July 8, 1997). ... Granted free agency (February 11, 2000). ... Re-signed by Colts (March 1, 2000).
PLAYING EXPERIENCE: Indianapolis NFL, 1997-2000. ... Games/Games started: 1997 (16/16), 1998 (14/14), 1999 (16/16), 2000 (16/16). Total: 62/62.

MEANS, NATRONE   RB

PERSONAL: Born April 26, 1972, in Harrisburg, N.C. ... 5-10/245. ... Full name: Natrone Jermaine Means. ... Name pronounced NAY-tron.
HIGH SCHOOL: Central Cabarrus (Concord, N.C.).
COLLEGE: North Carolina.
TRANSACTIONS/CAREER NOTES: Selected after junior season by San Diego Chargers in second round (41st pick overall) of 1993 NFL draft. ... Signed by Chargers (July 18, 1993). ... Claimed on waivers by Jacksonville Jaguars (March 11, 1996). ... Granted unconditional free agency (February 13, 1998). ... Signed by Chargers (March 4, 1998). ... On injured reserve with foot injury (November 16, 1998-remainder of season). ... Released by Chargers (March 6, 2000). ... Signed by Carolina Panthers (April 17, 2000). ... Released by Panthers (October 25, 2000).
CHAMPIONSHIP GAME EXPERIENCE: Played in AFC championship game (1994 and 1996 seasons). ... Played in Super Bowl XXIX (1994 season).
HONORS: Played in Pro Bowl (1994 season).

M

PRO STATISTICS: 1993—Attempted one pass without a completion, returned two kickoffs for 22 yards and recovered one fumble. 1994—Attempted one pass without a completion. 1996—Recovered one fumble. 1998—Recovered one fumble.
SINGLE GAME HIGHS (regular season): Attempts—37 (October 11, 1998, vs. Oakland); yards—165 (September 20, 1998, vs. Kansas City); and rushing touchdowns—3 (October 16, 1994, vs. New Orleans).
STATISTICAL PLATEAUS: 100-yard rushing games: 1993 (2), 1994 (6), 1995 (3), 1996 (1), 1998 (4). Total: 16.

				RUSHING				RECEIVING				TOTALS		
Year Team	G	GS	Att.	Yds.	Avg.	TD	No.	Yds.	Avg.	TD	TD	2pt.	Pts.	Fum.
1993—San Diego NFL	16	0	160	645	4.0	8	10	59	5.9	0	8	0	48	1
1994—San Diego NFL	16	16	§343	1350	3.9	§12	39	235	6.0	0	▲12	0	72	5
1995—San Diego NFL	10	9	186	730	3.9	5	7	46	6.6	0	5	0	30	2
1996—Jacksonville NFL	14	4	152	507	3.3	2	7	45	6.4	1	3	0	18	3
1997—Jacksonville NFL	14	11	244	823	3.4	9	15	104	6.9	0	9	0	54	5
1998—San Diego NFL	10	10	212	883	4.2	5	16	91	5.7	0	5	0	30	2
1999—San Diego NFL	7	5	112	277	2.5	4	9	51	5.7	1	5	0	30	0
2000—Carolina NFL	1	0	0	0	0.0	0	0	0	0.0	0	0	0	0	0
Pro totals (8 years)	88	55	1409	5215	3.7	45	103	631	6.1	2	47	0	282	18

MEESTER, BRAD   G/C   JAGUARS

PERSONAL: Born March 23, 1977, in Iowa Falls, Iowa. ... 6-3/300. ... Full name: Brad Ley Meester.
HIGH SCHOOL: Aplington-Parkersburg (Aplington, Iowa).
COLLEGE: Northern Iowa (degree in business management, 1999).
TRANSACTIONS/CAREER NOTES: Selected by Jacksonville Jaguars in second round (60th pick overall) of 2000 NFL draft. ... Signed by Jaguars (May 16, 2000).
PLAYING EXPERIENCE: Jacksonville NFL, 2000. ... Games/Games started: 2000 (16/16).
PRO STATISTICS: 2000—Recovered one fumble.

MEGNA, MARC   LB

PERSONAL: Born July 30, 1976, in Fall River, Mass. ... 6-2/245.
HIGH SCHOOL: Durfee (Fall River, Mass.).
COLLEGE: Richmond.
TRANSACTIONS/CAREER NOTES: Selected by New York Jets in sixth round (183rd pick overall) of 1999 NFL draft. ... Signed by Jets (June 8, 1999). ... Released by Jets (August 30, 1999). ... Signed by New England Patriots to practice squad (September 7, 1999). ... Activated (December 15, 1999); did not play. ... Assigned by Patriots to Barcelona Dragons in 2000 NFL Europe enhancement allocation program (February 18, 2000). ... Released by Patriots (August 27, 2000). ... Signed by Cincinnati Bengals to practice squad (September 13, 2000). ... Activated (November 9, 2000). ... Claimed on waivers by Patriots (December 1, 2000). ... Assigned by Patriots to Berlin Thunder in 2001 NFL Europe enhancement allocation program (February 19, 2001). ... Released by Patriots (February 22, 2001).
PLAYING EXPERIENCE: Barcelona NFLE, 2000; Cincinnati (2)-New England (4) NFL, 2000. ... Games/Games started: NFLE 2000 (games played unavailable), NFL 2000 (Cin.-2/0; N.E.-4/0; Total: 6/0).
PRO STATISTICS: NFLE: 2000—Credited with five sacks.

MEIER, ROB   DE   JAGUARS

PERSONAL: Born August 29, 1977, in Vancouver, B.C. ... 6-5/270. ... Full name: Robert Jack Daniel Meier.
HIGH SCHOOL: Sentinel (West Vancouver, B.C.).
COLLEGE: Washington State (degree in business).
TRANSACTIONS/CAREER NOTES: Selected by Jacksonville Jaguars in seventh round (241st pick overall) of 2000 NFL draft. ... Signed by Jaguars (May 17, 2000).
PLAYING EXPERIENCE: Jacksonville NFL, 2000. ... Games/Games started: 2000 (16/0).
PRO STATISTICS: 2000—Credited with $1/2$ sack.

MERCIER, RICHARD   G   PACKERS

PERSONAL: Born May 13, 1975, in Montreal. ... 6-3/300. ... Full name: Richard Marc Mercier.
HIGH SCHOOL: Vanier (Quebec).
COLLEGE: Miami (Fla.).
TRANSACTIONS/CAREER NOTES: Selected by Baltimore Ravens in fifth round (148th pick overall) of 2000 NFL draft. ... Signed by Ravens (July 15, 2000). ... Released by Ravens (August 27, 2000). ... Re-signed by Ravens to practice squad (August 28, 2000). ... Released by Ravens (November 15, 2000). ... Signed by Denver Broncos (November 16, 2000); did not play. ... Claimed on waivers by Green Bay Packers (December 22, 2000); did not play.
HONORS: Named guard on THE SPORTING NEWS college All-America first team (1999).

METCALF, ERIC   WR/PR   RAIDERS

PERSONAL: Born January 23, 1968, in Seattle. ... 5-10/188. ... Full name: Eric Quinn Metcalf. ... Son of Terry Metcalf, running back with St. Louis Cardinals (1973-77), Toronto Argonauts of CFL (1978-80) and Washington Redskins (1981); and cousin of Ray Hall, defensive tackle with Jacksonville Jaguars (1995).
HIGH SCHOOL: Bishop Denis J. O'Connell (Arlington, Va.).
COLLEGE: Texas (degree in liberal arts, 1990).
TRANSACTIONS/CAREER NOTES: Selected by Cleveland Browns in first round (13th pick overall) of 1989 NFL draft. ... Signed by Browns (August 20, 1989). ... Granted free agency (February 1, 1991). ... Re-signed by Browns for 1991 season. ... On injured reserve with shoulder injury (November 2, 1991-remainder of season). ... Granted free agency (February 1, 1992). ... Re-signed by Browns (August 30, 1992). ...

M

Granted roster exemption (August 30-September 5, 1992). ... Traded by Browns with first-round pick (DB Devin Bush) in 1995 draft to Atlanta Falcons for first-round pick (traded to San Francisco) in 1995 draft (March 25, 1995). ... Granted unconditional free agency (February 14, 1997). ... Signed by San Diego Chargers (May 8, 1997). ... Traded by Chargers with first- (DE Andre Wadsworth) and second-round (CB Corey Chavous) picks in 1998 draft, first-round pick (WR David Boston) in 1999 draft and LB Patrick Sapp to Arizona Cardinals for first-round pick (QB Ryan Leaf) in 1998 draft (March 12, 1998). ... Granted unconditional free agency (February 12, 1999). ... Signed by Baltimore Ravens (July 2, 1999). ... Released by Ravens (September 5, 1999). ... Signed by Carolina Panthers (September 7, 1999). ... Granted unconditional free agency (February 11, 2000). ... Signed by Oakland Raiders (February 15, 2001).

CHAMPIONSHIP GAME EXPERIENCE: Played in AFC championship game (1989 season).

HONORS: Named all-purpose player on THE SPORTING NEWS college All-America second team (1987). ... Named punt returner on THE SPORTING NEWS NFL All-Pro team (1993 and 1994). ... Played in Pro Bowl (1993, 1994 and 1997 seasons).

RECORDS: Holds NFL career record for most touchdowns by punt return—9. ... Shares NFL single-game records for most touchdowns by punt return—2; most touchdowns by combined kick return—2 (October 24, 1993, vs. Pittsburgh and November 2, 1997, vs. Cincinnati); and most touchdowns by combined kick return—11.

POST SEASON RECORDS: Shares NFL postseason career record for most touchdowns by kickoff return—1 (January 6, 1990, vs. Buffalo).

PRO STATISTICS: 1989—Attempted two passes with one completion for 32 yards and a touchdown and fumbled five times. 1990—Fumbled eight times and recovered one fumble. 1991—Fumbled once. 1992—Attempted one pass without a completion, fumbled six times and recovered two fumbles. 1993—Fumbled five times. 1994—Attempted one pass without a completion and fumbled six times. 1995—Attempted one pass without a completion, fumbled four times and recovered two fumbles. 1996—Fumbled three times. 1997—Fumbled four times and recovered two fumbles. 1998—Fumbled five times and recovered two fumbles. 1999—Fumbled twice.

SINGLE GAME HIGHS (regular season): Receptions—11 (September 17, 1995, vs. New Orleans); yards—177 (September 20, 1992, vs. Los Angeles Raiders); and touchdown receptions—3 (September 20, 1992, vs. Los Angeles Raiders).

STATISTICAL PLATEAUS: 100-yard receiving games: 1992 (1), 1993 (1), 1995 (2), 1996 (1), 1997 (1). Total: 6.

				RUSHING				RECEIVING				PUNT RETURNS				KICKOFF RETURNS				TOTALS		
Year Team	G	GS	Att.	Yds.	Avg.	TD	No.	Yds.	Avg.	TD	No.	Yds.	Avg.	TD	No.	Yds.	Avg.	TD	TD	2pt.	Pts.
1989—Cleveland NFL	16	11	187	633	3.4	6	54	397	7.4	4	0	0	0.0	0	31	718	23.2	0	10	0	60
1990—Cleveland NFL	16	9	80	248	3.1	1	57	452	7.9	1	0	0	0.0	0	*52	*1052	20.2	*2	4	0	24
1991—Cleveland NFL	8	3	30	107	3.6	0	29	294	10.1	0	12	100	8.3	0	23	351	15.3	0	0	0	0
1992—Cleveland NFL	16	5	73	301	4.1	1	47	614	13.1	5	*44	§429	9.8	1	9	157	17.4	0	7	0	42
1993—Cleveland NFL	16	9	129	611	4.7	1	63	539	8.6	2	36	464	§12.9	†2	15	318	21.2	0	5	0	30
1994—Cleveland NFL	16	8	93	329	3.5	2	47	436	9.3	3	35	348	9.9	†2	9	210	23.3	0	7	0	42
1995—Atlanta NFL	16	14	28	133	4.8	1	104	1189	11.4	8	39	383	9.8	†1	12	278	23.2	0	10	0	60
1996—Atlanta NFL	16	11	3	8	2.7	0	54	599	11.1	6	27	296	11.0	0	49	1034	21.1	0	6	0	36
1997—San Diego NFL	16	1	3	-5	-1.7	0	40	576	14.4	2	45	489	10.9	†3	16	355	22.2	0	5	0	30
1998—Arizona NFL	16	3	0	0	0.0	0	31	324	10.5	0	43	295	6.9	0	57	1218	21.4	0	0	0	0
1999—Carolina NFL	16	1	2	20	10.0	0	11	133	12.1	0	34	238	7.0	0	4	56	14.0	0	0	0	0
2000—									Did not play.												
Pro totals (11 years)	168	75	628	2385	3.8	12	537	5553	10.3	31	315	3042	9.7	9	277	5747	20.7	2	54	0	324

MICKELL, DARREN — DE

PERSONAL: Born August 3, 1970, in Miami. ... 6-5/285.

HIGH SCHOOL: Miami Senior.

COLLEGE: Florida.

TRANSACTIONS/CAREER NOTES: Selected by Kansas City Chiefs in second round of 1992 NFL supplemental draft (second of two supplemental drafts in 1992). ... Signed by Chiefs (September 16, 1992). ... Granted roster exemption (September 16-29, 1992). ... On injured reserve with knee injury (September 30-November 11, 1992). ... On practice squad (November 11-December 26, 1992). ... Granted unconditional free agency (February 16, 1996). ... Signed by New Orleans Saints (March 12, 1996). ... On reserve did not report list (July 14-August 12, 1996). ... On physically unable to perform list (August 12-19, 1996). ... On suspended list for violating league substance abuse policy (October 4-November 10, 1996). ... Announced retirement (February 23, 1998). ... Activated from roster exempt list (September 28, 1999). ... Released by Saints (November 10, 1999). ... Signed by San Diego Chargers (February 28, 2000). ... Granted unconditional free agency (March 2, 2001).

CHAMPIONSHIP GAME EXPERIENCE: Played in AFC championship game (1993 season).

PRO STATISTICS: 1993—Recovered one fumble. 1994—Recovered one fumble. 1995—Recovered one fumble. 1997—Recovered one fumble for 11 yards.

Year Team	G	GS	SACKS
1992—Kansas City NFL	1	0	0.0
1993—Kansas City NFL	16	1	1.0
1994—Kansas City NFL	16	13	7.0
1995—Kansas City NFL	12	6	5.5
1996—New Orleans NFL	12	12	3.0
1997—New Orleans NFL	14	13	3.5
1998—		Did not play.	
1999—New Orleans NFL	1	0	0.0
2000—San Diego NFL	16	16	6.0
Pro totals (8 years)	88	61	26.0

MICKENS, RAY — CB — JETS

PERSONAL: Born January 4, 1973, in Frankfurt, West Germany. ... 5-8/184.

HIGH SCHOOL: Andress (El Paso, Texas).

COLLEGE: Texas A&M.

TRANSACTIONS/CAREER NOTES: Selected by New York Jets in third round (62nd pick overall) of 1996 NFL draft. ... Signed by Jets (July 13, 1996). ... Granted free agency (February 12, 1999). ... Re-signed by Jets (April 9, 1999).

CHAMPIONSHIP GAME EXPERIENCE: Played in AFC championship game (1998 season).

HONORS: Named defensive back on THE SPORTING NEWS college All-America second team (1995).

PRO STATISTICS: 1997—Credited with one sack and returned blocked field-goal attempt 72 yards for a touchdown. 1998—Recovered one fumble. 1999—Credited with two sacks.

Year Team	G	GS	INTERCEPTIONS No.	Yds.	Avg.	TD
1996—New York Jets NFL	15	10	0	0	0.0	0
1997—New York Jets NFL	16	0	4	2	0.5	0
1998—New York Jets NFL	16	3	3	10	3.3	0
1999—New York Jets NFL	15	5	2	2	1.0	0
2000—New York Jets NFL	16	0	0	0	0.0	0
Pro totals (5 years)	78	18	9	14	1.6	0

MIDDLETON, FRANK G RAIDERS

PERSONAL: Born October 25, 1974, in Beaumont, Texas. ... 6-3/334. ... Full name: Frank Middleton Jr.
HIGH SCHOOL: West Brook (Beaumont, Texas).
JUNIOR COLLEGE: Fort Scott (Kan.) Community College.
COLLEGE: Arizona.
TRANSACTIONS/CAREER NOTES: Selected by Tampa Bay Buccaneers in third round (63rd pick overall) of 1997 NFL draft. ... Signed by Buccaneers (July 20, 1997). ... Granted free agency (February 11, 2000). ... Re-signed by Buccanners (May 2, 2000). ... Granted unconditional free agency (March 2, 2001). ... Signed by Oakland Raiders (April 27, 2001).
PLAYING EXPERIENCE: Tampa Bay NFL, 1997-2000. ... Games/Games started: 1997 (15/2), 1998 (16/16), 1999 (16/16), 2000 (16/16). Total: 63/50.
CHAMPIONSHIP GAME EXPERIENCE: Played in NFC championship game (1999 season).

MILBURN, GLYN RB/KR BEARS

PERSONAL: Born February 19, 1971, in Santa Monica, Calif. ... 5-8/176. ... Full name: Glyn Curt Milburn. ... Cousin of Rod Milburn, gold medalist in 110-meter high hurdles in 1972 Summer Olympics.
HIGH SCHOOL: Santa Monica (Calif.).
COLLEGE: Oklahoma, then Stanford (degree in public policy).
TRANSACTIONS/CAREER NOTES: Selected by Denver Broncos in second round (43rd pick overall) of 1993 NFL draft. ... Signed by Broncos (July 15, 1993). ... Traded by Broncos to Detroit Lions for second- (traded to Baltimore) and seventh-round (P Brian Gragert) picks in 1996 NFL draft (April 12, 1996). ... Traded by Lions to Green Bay Packers for seventh-round pick (traded to Miami) in 1999 draft (April 21, 1998). ... Traded by Packers to Chicago Bears for seventh-round pick (WR Donald Driver) in 1999 draft (August 30, 1998).
HONORS: Named kick returner on THE SPORTING NEWS NFL All-Pro team (1995). ... Played in Pro Bowl (1995 and 1999 seasons). ... Named punt returner on THE SPORTING NEWS NFL All-Pro team (1999).
RECORDS: Holds NFL single-season record for most combined kick returns—102. ... Holds NFL single-game record for most combined net yards gained—404 (December 10, 1995).
PRO STATISTICS: 1993—Fumbled nine times and recovered one fumble. 1994—Fumbled four times and recovered one fumble. 1995—Fumbled twice. 1997—Fumbled three times and recovered two fumbles. 1998—Fumbled once. 1999—Fumbled four times and recovered two fumbles. 2000—Fumbled four times and recovered three fumbles.
SINGLE GAME HIGHS (regular season): Attempts—18 (December 10, 1995, vs. Seattle); yards—131 (December 10, 1995, vs. Seattle); and rushing touchdowns—1 (November 7, 1999, vs. Green Bay). Receptions—9 (September 18, 1994 vs. Los Angeles Raiders); yards—85 (September 18, 1994 vs. Los Angeles Raiders); and touchdown receptions—1 (November 6, 1994 vs. Los Angeles Rams).
STATISTICAL PLATEAUS: 100-yard rushing games: 1995 (1).

Year Team	G	GS	RUSHING Att.	Yds.	Avg.	TD	RECEIVING No.	Yds.	Avg.	TD	PUNT RETURNS No.	Yds.	Avg.	TD	KICKOFF RETURNS No.	Yds.	Avg.	TD	TOTALS TD	2pt.	Pts.
1993—Denver NFL	16	2	52	231	4.4	0	38	300	7.9	3	40	425	10.6	0	12	188	15.7	0	3	0	18
1994—Denver NFL	16	3	58	201	3.5	1	77	549	7.1	3	41	379	9.2	0	37	793	21.4	0	4	0	24
1995—Denver NFL	16	1	49	266	5.4	0	22	191	8.7	0	31	354	11.4	0	47	1269	27.0	0	0	0	0
1996—Detroit NFL	16	0	0	0	0.0	0	0	0	0.0	0	34	284	8.4	0	64	1627	25.4	0	0	0	0
1997—Detroit NFL	16	1	0	0	0.0	0	5	77	15.4	0	47	433	9.2	0	55	1315	23.9	0	0	0	0
1998—Chicago NFL	16	0	4	8	2.0	0	4	37	9.3	0	25	291	11.6	1	*62	*1550	25.0	†2	3	0	18
1999—Chicago NFL	16	1	16	102	6.4	1	20	151	7.6	0	30	346	11.5	0	‡61	‡1426	23.4	0	1	0	6
2000—Chicago NFL	16	0	1	6	6.0	0	1	8	8.0	0	35	300	8.6	0	63	1468	23.3	0	0	0	0
Pro totals (8 years)	128	8	180	814	4.5	2	167	1313	7.9	6	283	2812	9.9	1	401	9636	24.0	2	11	0	66

MILEM, JOHN DE 49ERS

PERSONAL: Born June 9, 1975, in Concord, N.C. ... 6-7/290.
HIGH SCHOOL: Rowan (Salisbury, N.C.).
COLLEGE: Lenoir-Rhyne College (N.C.).
TRANSACTIONS/CAREER NOTES: Selected by San Francisco 49ers in fifth round (150th pick overall) of 2000 NFL draft. ... Signed by 49ers (July 16, 2000).
PLAYING EXPERIENCE: San Francisco NFL, 2000. ... Games/Games started: 2000 (16/0).
PRO STATISTICS: 2000—Returned one kickoff for 13 yards.

MILI, ITULA TE SEAHAWKS

PERSONAL: Born April 20, 1973, in Kahuku, Hawaii. ... 6-4/265. ... Name pronounced EE-too-la MEE-lee.
HIGH SCHOOL: Kahuku (Hawaii).
COLLEGE: Brigham Young.
TRANSACTIONS/CAREER NOTES: Selected by Seattle Seahawks in sixth round (174th pick overall) of 1997 NFL draft. ... Signed by Seahawks (June 11, 1997). ... On physically unable to perform list with knee injury (August 18, 1997-entire season). ... On injured reserve with knee injury (December 25, 1998-remainder of season). ... Granted free agency (March 2, 2001).
PRO STATISTICS: 2000—Returned one kickoff for 19 yards.
SINGLE GAME HIGHS (regular season): Receptions—5 (October 22, 2000, vs. Oakland); yards—52 (September 10, 2000, vs. St. Louis); and touchdown receptions—1 (October 15, 2000, vs. Indianapolis).

M

Year Team	G	GS	RECEIVING				TOTALS			
			No.	Yds.	Avg.	TD	TD	2pt.	Pts.	Fum.
1997—Seattle NFL						Did not play.				
1998—Seattle NFL	7	0	1	20	20.0	0	0	0	0	0
1999—Seattle NFL	16	1	5	28	5.6	1	1	0	6	1
2000—Seattle NFL	16	6	28	288	10.3	3	3	0	18	1
Pro totals (3 years)	39	7	34	336	9.9	4	4	0	24	2

MILLER, ARNOLD — DE — BROWNS

PERSONAL: Born January 3, 1975, in New Orleans. ... 6-3/239.
HIGH SCHOOL: George Washington Carver (New Orleans).
COLLEGE: Louisiana State.
TRANSACTIONS/CAREER NOTES: Signed as non-drafted free agent by Cleveland Browns (April 23, 1999).
PLAYING EXPERIENCE: Cleveland NFL, 1999 and 2000. ... Games/Games started: 1999 (9/0), 2000 (12/0). Total: 21/0.
PRO STATISTICS: 1999—Credited with one sack. 2000—Credited with 1$\frac{1}{2}$ sacks.

MILLER, BILLY — TE — BRONCOS

PERSONAL: Born April 24, 1977, in Los Angeles. ... 6-3/230. ... Full name: Billy RoShawn Miller.
HIGH SCHOOL: Westlake (Westlake Village, Calif.).
COLLEGE: Southern California.
TRANSACTIONS/CAREER NOTES: Selected by Denver Broncos in seventh round (218th pick overall) of 1999 NFL draft. ... Signed by Broncos (July 20, 1999). ... Released by Broncos (September 5, 1999). ... Re-signed by Broncos to practice squad (September 6, 1999). ... Activated (October 19, 1999).
PLAYING EXPERIENCE: Denver NFL, 1999 and 2000. ... Games/Games started: 1999 (10/0), 2000 (12/0). Total: 22/0.
PRO STATISTICS: 1999—Caught five passes for 59 yards and returned four kickoffs for 79 yards. 2000—Caught one pass for seven yards and returned one kickoff for 13 yards.
SINGLE GAME HIGHS (regular season): Receptions—2 (November 7, 1999, vs. San Diego); yards—36 (November 7, 1999, vs. San Diego); and touchdown receptions—0.

MILLER, BUBBA — C/G — EAGLES

PERSONAL: Born January 24, 1973, in Nashville. ... 6-1/305. ... Full name: Stephen DeJuan Miller.
HIGH SCHOOL: Brentwood Academy (Franklin, Tenn.).
COLLEGE: Tennessee.
TRANSACTIONS/CAREER NOTES: Signed as non-drafted free agent by Philadelphia Eagles (April 26, 1996). ... Inactive for all 16 games (1996). ... Granted free agency (February 12, 1999). ... Re-signed by Eagles (April 22, 1999). ... Granted unconditional free agency (February 11, 2000). ... Re-signed by Eagles (March 1, 2000).
PLAYING EXPERIENCE: Philadelphia NFL, 1997-2000. ... Games/Games started: 1997 (13/3), 1998 (15/4), 1999 (14/0), 2000 (16/16). Total: 58/23.
PRO STATISTICS: 1998—Caught one pass for 11 yards. 2000—Caught one pass for nine yards.

MILLER, CRAIG — S — JAGUARS

PERSONAL: Born October 4, 1977, in Bakersfield, Calif. ... 5-11/199.
HIGH SCHOOL: Bakersfield (Calif.).
COLLEGE: Utah State.
TRANSACTIONS/CAREER NOTES: Signed by Indianapolis Colts (January 24, 2000). ... Released by Colts (August 27, 2000). ... Re-signed by Colts to practice squad (August 29, 2000). ... Signed by Jacksonville Jaguars off Colts practice squad (September 27, 2000). ... Released by Jaguars (October 28, 2000). ... Re-signed by Jaguars to practice squad (November 29, 2000).
PLAYING EXPERIENCE: Jacksonville NFL, 2000. ... Games/Games started: 2000 (4/2).

MILLER, FRED — OT — TITANS

PERSONAL: Born February 6, 1973, in Houston. ... 6-7/315. ... Full name: Fred Miller Jr.
HIGH SCHOOL: Aldine Eisenhower (Houston).
COLLEGE: Baylor (degree in sociology, 1995).
TRANSACTIONS/CAREER NOTES: Selected by St. Louis Rams in fifth round (141st pick overall) of 1996 NFL draft. ... Signed by Rams (July 15, 1996). ... Granted free agency (February 12, 1999). ... Re-signed by Rams (May 24, 1999). ... Granted unconditional free agency (February 11, 2000). ... Signed by Tennessee Titans (February 16, 2000).
PLAYING EXPERIENCE: St. Louis NFL, 1996-1999; Tennessee NFL, 2000. ... Games/Games started: 1996 (14/0), 1997 (15/7), 1998 (15/15), 1999 (16/16), 2000 (16/16). Total: 76/54.
CHAMPIONSHIP GAME EXPERIENCE: Played in NFC championship game (1999 season). ... Member of Super Bowl championship team (1999 season).
PRO STATISTICS: 2000—Recovered two fumbles.

MILLER, JAMIR — LB — BROWNS

PERSONAL: Born November 19, 1973, in Philadelphia. ... 6-5/266. ... Full name: Jamir Malik Miller. ... Cousin of Mark Gunn, defensive lineman with New York Jets (1991-94 and 1996) and Philadelphia Eagles (1995 and 1996). ... Name pronounced JA-meer.
HIGH SCHOOL: El Cerrito (Calif.).
COLLEGE: UCLA.

TRANSACTIONS/CAREER NOTES: Selected after junior season by Arizona Cardinals in first round (10th pick overall) of 1994 NFL draft. ... Signed by Cardinals (August 12, 1994). ... On suspended list for violating league substance abuse policy (September 4-October 3, 1995). ... Granted unconditional free agency (February 12, 1999). ... Signed by Cleveland Browns (May 13, 1999).

HONORS: Named linebacker on THE SPORTING NEWS college All-America first team (1993).

PRO STATISTICS: 1995—Fumbled once and recovered two fumbles for 26 yards. 1996—Recovered one fumble for 26 yards and a touchdown. 1998—Recovered two fumbles. 2000—Intercepted one pass for no yards.

Year Team	G	GS	SACKS
1994—Arizona NFL	16	0	3.0
1995—Arizona NFL	11	8	1.0
1996—Arizona NFL	16	16	1.0
1997—Arizona NFL	16	16	5.5
1998—Arizona NFL	16	16	3.0
1999—Cleveland NFL	15	15	4.5
2000—Cleveland NFL	16	16	5.0
Pro totals (7 years)	**106**	**87**	**23.0**

MILLER, JIM　　　　　　QB　　　　　　BEARS

PERSONAL: Born February 9, 1971, in Grosse Pointe, Mich. ... 6-2/215. ... Full name: James Donald Miller.
HIGH SCHOOL: Kettering (Detroit).
COLLEGE: Michigan State (degree in financial administration).
TRANSACTIONS/CAREER NOTES: Selected by Pittsburgh Steelers in sixth round (178th pick overall) of 1994 NFL draft. ... Signed by Steelers (May 12, 1994). ... Inactive for all 16 games (1994). ... Assigned by Steelers to Frankfurt Galaxy in 1995 World League enhancement allocation program (February 20, 1995). ... Released by Steelers (August 23, 1997). ... Signed by Jacksonville Jaguars (September 2, 1997). ... Released by Jaguars (September 23, 1997). ... Signed by Atlanta Falcons (October 27, 1997). ... Granted unconditional free agency (February 13, 1998). ... Signed by Detroit Lions (March 2, 1998). ... Released by Lions (August 24, 1998). ... Signed by Dallas Cowboys (September 8, 1998). ... Released by Cowboys (October 1998). ... Signed by Chicago Bears (December 1, 1998). ... Active for four games (1998); did not play. ... On suspended list for violating league substance abuse policy (December 1, 1999-remainder of season). ... Granted unconditional free agency (February 11, 2000). ... Re-signed by Bears (February 17, 2000). ... On injured reserve with torn Achilles' tendon (November 13, 2000-remainder of season).
CHAMPIONSHIP GAME EXPERIENCE: Member of Steelers for AFC championship game (1994 and 1995 seasons); inactive. ... Member of Steelers for Super Bowl XXX (1995 season); inactive.
PRO STATISTICS: 1995—Fumbled once. 1996—Fumbled once for minus four yards. 1999—Fumbled four times and recovered three fumbles for minus 19 yards. 2000—Fumbled once.
SINGLE GAME HIGHS (regular season): Attempts—48 (November 14, 1999, vs. Minnesota); completions—34 (November 14, 1999, vs. Minnesota); yards—422 (November 14, 1999, vs. Minnesota); and touchdown passes—3 (November 14, 1999, vs. Minnesota).
STATISTICAL PLATEAUS: 300-yard passing games: 1999 (2).
MISCELLANEOUS: Regular-season record as starting NFL quarterback: 2-4 (.333).

Year Team	G	GS	PASSING Att.	Cmp.	Pct.	Yds.	TD	Int.	Avg.	Rat.	RUSHING Att.	Yds.	Avg.	TD	TOTALS TD	2pt.	Pts.
1994—Pittsburgh NFL						Did not play.											
1995—Frankfurt W.L.	...	...	43	23	53.5	236	1	1	5.49	67.6	3	-2	-0.7	0	0	0	0
—Pittsburgh NFL	4	0	56	32	57.1	397	2	5	7.09	53.9	1	2	2.0	0	0	0	0
1996—Pittsburgh NFL	2	1	25	13	52.0	123	0	0	4.92	65.9	2	-4	-2.0	0	0	0	0
1997—Atlanta NFL						Did not play.											
—Jacksonville NFL						Did not play.											
1998—Chicago NFL						Did not play.											
1999—Chicago NFL	5	3	174	110	63.2	1242	7	6	7.14	83.5	3	9	3.0	0	0	0	0
2000—Chicago NFL	3	2	82	47	57.3	382	1	1	4.66	68.2	7	5	0.7	0	0	0	0
W.L. totals (1 year)	...	...	43	23	53.5	236	1	1	5.49	67.6	3	-2	-0.7	0	0	0	0
NFL totals (3 years)	14	6	337	202	59.9	2144	10	12	6.36	73.6	13	12	0.9	0	0	0	0
Pro totals (4 years)	...	...	380	225	59.2	2380	11	13	6.26	72.9	16	10	0.6	0	0	0	0

MILLER, JOSH　　　　　　P　　　　　　STEELERS

PERSONAL: Born July 14, 1970, in Rockway, N.Y. ... 6-3/219.
HIGH SCHOOL: East Brunswick (N.J.).
JUNIOR COLLEGE: Scottsdale (Ariz.) Community College.
COLLEGE: Arizona (degree in communications, 1993).
TRANSACTIONS/CAREER NOTES: Signed as non-drafted free agent by Green Bay Packers (April 1993). ... Released by Packers before 1993 season. ... Signed by Baltimore Stallions of CFL (June 1994). ... Signed by Seattle Seahawks (May 29, 1996). ... Released by Seahawks (August 13, 1996). ... Signed by Pittsburgh Steelers (August 15, 1996).
CHAMPIONSHIP GAME EXPERIENCE: Played in Grey Cup, CFL championship game (1994). ... Played in AFC championship game (1997 season).
HONORS: Named punter on the Sporting News college All-America first team (1992).
PRO STATISTICS: CFL: 1994—Fumbled once. NFL: 1997—Rushed once for minus seven yards. 1999—Rushed twice for minus nine yards and fumbled once for minus 11 yards. 2000—Rushed once for no yards, fumbled once and recovered one fumbled for minus 18 yards.

Year Team	G	PUNTING No.	Yds.	Avg.	Net avg.	In. 20	Blk.
1994—Baltimore CFL	18	117	5024	42.9	36.9	0	0
1995—Baltimore CFL	18	118	5629	47.7	42.2	0	0
1996—Pittsburgh NFL	12	55	2256	41.0	33.6	18	0
1997—Pittsburgh NFL	16	64	2729	42.6	35.0	17	0
1998—Pittsburgh NFL	16	81	3530	43.6	36.8	*34	0
1999—Pittsburgh NFL	16	84	3795	45.2	38.1	27	0
2000—Pittsburgh NFL	16	90	3944	43.8	37.5	*34	▲1
CFL totals (2 years)	36	235	10653	45.3	39.6	0	0
NFL totals (5 years)	76	374	16254	43.5	36.5	130	1
Pro totals (7 years)	112	609	26907	44.2	37.7	130	1

MILLER, KEITH — LB — RAMS

PERSONAL: Born July 9, 1976, in San Diego. ... 6-1/238.
HIGH SCHOOL: Mt. Carmel (San Diego).
COLLEGE: California.
TRANSACTIONS/CAREER NOTES: Signed as non-drafted free agent by St. Louis Rams (April 18, 2000). ... Assigned by Rams to Scottish Claymores in 2001 NFL Europe enhancement allocation program (February 19, 2001).
PLAYING EXPERIENCE: St. Louis NFL, 2000. ... Games/Games started: 2000 (16/0).
PRO STATISTICS: 2000—Recovered one fumble.

MILLOY, LAWYER — S — PATRIOTS

PERSONAL: Born November 14, 1973, in St. Louis. ... 6-0/210.
HIGH SCHOOL: Lincoln (Tacoma, Wash.).
COLLEGE: Washington.
TRANSACTIONS/CAREER NOTES: Selected after junior season by New England Patriots in second round (36th pick overall) of 1996 NFL draft. ... Signed by Patriots (June 5, 1996).
CHAMPIONSHIP GAME EXPERIENCE: Played in AFC championship game (1996 season). ... Played in Super Bowl XXXI (1996 season).
HONORS: Named defensive back on THE SPORTING NEWS college All-America first team (1995). ... Played in Pro Bowl (1998 and 1999 seasons). ... Named safety on THE SPORTING NEWS NFL All-Pro team (1999).
PRO STATISTICS: 1996—Recovered one fumble. 1997—Recovered two fumbles. 1998—Recovered one fumble. 1999—Recovered two fumbles.

| | | | INTERCEPTIONS | | | SACKS |
Year Team	G	GS	No.	Yds.	Avg.	TD	No.
1996—New England NFL	16	10	2	14	7.0	0	1.0
1997—New England NFL	16	16	3	15	5.0	0	0.0
1998—New England NFL	16	16	6	54	9.0	1	1.0
1999—New England NFL	16	16	4	17	4.3	0	2.0
2000—New England NFL	16	16	2	2	1.0	0	0.0
Pro totals (5 years)	80	74	17	102	6.0	1	4.0

MILNE, BRIAN — FB

PERSONAL: Born January 7, 1973, in Waterford, Pa. ... 6-3/254. ... Full name: Brian Fitzsimons Milne.
HIGH SCHOOL: Fort Le Boeuf (Waterford, Pa.).
COLLEGE: Penn State (degree in labor and industrial relations).
TRANSACTIONS/CAREER NOTES: Selected by Indianapolis Colts in fourth round (115th pick overall) of 1996 NFL draft. ... Signed by Colts (July 5, 1996). ... Claimed on waivers by Cincinnati Bengals (August 21, 1996). ... Granted free agency (February 12, 1999). ... Re-signed by Bengals (May 20, 1999). ... Released by Bengals (September 29, 1999). ... Signed by Seattle Seahawks (October 27, 1999). ... Granted unconditional free agency (February 11, 2000). ... Signed by New Orleans Saints (August 2, 2000). ... Granted unconditional free agency (March 2, 2001). ...
PRO STATISTICS: 1998—Recovered one fumble.
SINGLE GAME HIGHS (regular season): Attempts—3 (September 12, 1999, vs. Tennessee); yards—30 (September 12, 1999, vs. Tennessee); and rushing touchdowns—1 (November 29, 1998, vs. Jacksonville).
MISCELLANEOUS: Won NCAA discus championship (1993).

| | | | RUSHING | | | | RECEIVING | | | | TOTALS | | | |
Year Team	G	GS	Att.	Yds.	Avg.	TD	No.	Yds.	Avg.	TD	TD	2pt.	Pts.	Fum.
1996—Cincinnati NFL	6	5	8	22	2.8	1	3	29	9.7	0	1	0	6	0
1997—Cincinnati NFL	16	16	13	32	2.5	2	23	138	6.0	0	2	0	12	0
1998—Cincinnati NFL	14	14	10	41	4.1	1	26	124	4.8	0	1	0	6	0
1999—Cincinnati NFL	1	1	3	30	10.0	1	0	0	0.0	0	1	0	6	0
—Seattle NFL	10	0	0	0	0.0	0	0	0	0.0	0	0	†1	2	0
2000—New Orleans NFL	16	2	2	1	0.5	0	5	33	6.6	1	1	0	6	0
Pro totals (5 years)	63	38	36	126	3.5	4	57	324	5.7	1	5	1	32	0

MINOR, KORY — LB — PANTHERS

PERSONAL: Born December 14, 1976, in Inglewood, Calif. ... 6-1/247. ... Full name: Kory DeShaun Minor.
HIGH SCHOOL: Bishop Amat (La Puente, Calif.).
COLLEGE: Notre Dame.
TRANSACTIONS/CAREER NOTES: Selected by San Francisco 49ers in seventh round (234th pick overall) of 1999 NFL draft. ... Signed by 49ers (July 26, 1999). ... Released by 49ers (September 5, 1999). ... Signed by Carolina Panthers to practice squad (September 14, 1999). ... Activated (December 28, 1999); did not play. ... On injured reserve with knee injury (December 19, 2000-remainder of season).
PLAYING EXPERIENCE: Carolina NFL, 2000. ... Games/Games started: 2000 (15/0).

MINTER, BARRY — LB — BEARS

PERSONAL: Born January 28, 1970, in Mount Pleasant, Texas. ... 6-2/250. ... Full name: Barry Antoine Minter.
HIGH SCHOOL: Mount Pleasant (Texas).
COLLEGE: Tulsa.
TRANSACTIONS/CAREER NOTES: Selected by Dallas Cowboys in sixth round (168th pick overall) of 1993 NFL draft. ... Signed by Cowboys (July 14, 1993). ... Traded by Cowboys with LB Vinson Smith and sixth-round pick (DE Carl Reeves) in 1995 draft to Chicago Bears for TE

M

Kelly Blackwell, S Markus Paul and LB John Roper (August 17, 1993). ... Granted free agency (February 16, 1996). ... Re-signed by Bears (February 26, 1996). ... Granted unconditional free agency (February 13, 1998). ... Re-signed by Bears (February 20, 1998).

PRO STATISTICS: 1994—Recovered one fumble. 1997—Recovered three fumbles. 1998—Recovered one fumble for 11 yards. 1999—Recovered one fumble.

			INTERCEPTIONS				SACKS
Year Team	G	GS	No.	Yds.	Avg.	TD	No.
1993—Chicago NFL	2	0	0	0	0.0	0	0.0
1994—Chicago NFL	13	1	0	0	0.0	0	0.0
1995—Chicago NFL	16	3	1	2	2.0	1	0.0
1996—Chicago NFL	16	7	1	5	5.0	0	1.5
1997—Chicago NFL	16	16	0	0	0.0	0	6.0
1998—Chicago NFL	16	16	1	17	17.0	0	1.0
1999—Chicago NFL	16	16	2	66	33.0	1	3.0
2000—Chicago NFL	15	2	0	0	0.0	0	0.0
Pro totals (8 years)	110	61	5	90	18.0	2	11.5

MINTER, MIKE   S   PANTHERS

PERSONAL: Born January 15, 1974, in Cleveland. ... 5-10/188. ... Full name: Michael Christopher Minter.

HIGH SCHOOL: Lawton (Okla.).

COLLEGE: Nebraska (degree in engineering, 1996).

TRANSACTIONS/CAREER NOTES: Selected by Carolina Panthers in second round (56th pick overall) of 1997 NFL draft. ... Signed by Panthers (June 12, 1997). ... Granted unconditional free agency (March 2, 2001). ... Re-signed by Panthers (March 3, 2001).

PRO STATISTICS: 1997—Recovered two fumbles. 1999—Recovered two fumbles for 30 yards. 2000—Recovered one fumble.

			INTERCEPTIONS				SACKS
Year Team	G	GS	No.	Yds.	Avg.	TD	No.
1997—Carolina NFL	16	11	0	0	0.0	0	3.5
1998—Carolina NFL	6	4	1	7	7.0	0	0.0
1999—Carolina NFL	16	16	3	69	23.0	0	1.0
2000—Carolina NFL	16	16	2	38	19.0	1	2.0
Pro totals (4 years)	54	47	6	114	19.0	1	6.5

MIRANDA, PAUL   CB   SEAHAWKS

PERSONAL: Born May 2, 1976, in Thomasville, Ga. ... 5-10/182. ... Full name: Paul Nathaniel Miranda.

HIGH SCHOOL: Thomas County Central (Thomasville, Ga.).

JUNIOR COLLEGE: Holmes Junior College (Miss.).

COLLEGE: Central Florida (degree in health services administration).

TRANSACTIONS/CAREER NOTES: Selected by Indianapolis Colts in fourth round (96th pick overall) of 1999 NFL draft. ... Signed by Colts (July 22, 1999). ... Released by Colts (August 31, 2000). ... Signed by Seattle Seahawks (September 1, 2000). ... Released by Seahawks (September 19, 2000). ... Signed by San Francisco 49ers to practice squad (September 21, 2000). ... Signed by Seahawks off 49ers practice squad (November 29, 2000).

PLAYING EXPERIENCE: Indianapolis NFL, 1999; Seattle NFL, 2000. ... Games/Games started: 1999 (5/0), 2000 (3/0). Total: 8/0.

MIRER, RICK   QB   49ERS

PERSONAL: Born March 19, 1970, in Goshen, Ind. ... 6-3/212. ... Full name: Rick F. Mirer.

HIGH SCHOOL: Goshen (Ind.).

COLLEGE: Notre Dame.

TRANSACTIONS/CAREER NOTES: Selected by Seattle Seahawks in first round (second pick overall) of 1993 NFL draft. ... Signed by Seahawks (August 2, 1993). ... On injured reserve with thumb injury (December 20, 1994-remainder of season). ... Traded by Seahawks with fourth-round pick (RB Darnell Autry) in 1997 draft to Chicago Bears for first-round pick (traded to Atlanta) in 1997 draft (February 18, 1997). ... Released by Bears (August 30, 1998). ... Signed by Green Bay Packers (September 2, 1998). ... Active for four games (1998); did not play. ... Traded by Packers to New York Jets for fourth-round pick (traded to San Francisco) in 2000 draft (August 20, 1999). ... Released by Jets (February 2, 2000). ... Signed by San Francisco 49ers (June 13, 2000). ... Granted unconditional free agency (March 2, 2001). ... Re-signed by 49ers (June 5, 2001).

PRO STATISTICS: 1993—Fumbled 13 times and recovered five fumbles for minus 14 yards. 1994—Fumbled twice and recovered one fumble for minus seven yards. 1995—Fumbled five times and recovered one fumble for minus one yard. 1996—Fumbled four times. 1997—Fumbled four times and recovered one fumble for minus four yards. 1999—Fumbled three times and recovered two fumbles for minus one yard.

SINGLE GAME HIGHS (regular season): Attempts—43 (October 24, 1993, vs. New England); completions—25 (October 3, 1993, vs. San Diego); yards—287 (December 5, 1993, vs. Kansas City); and touchdown passes—3 (September 11, 1994, vs. Los Angeles Raiders).

MISCELLANEOUS: Regular-season record as starting NFL quarterback: 22-38 (.367).

			PASSING								RUSHING				TOTALS	
Year Team	G	GS	Att.	Cmp.	Pct.	Yds.	TD	Int.	Avg.	Rat.	Att.	Yds.	Avg.	TD	TD	2pt.	Pts.
1993—Seattle NFL	16	16	486	274	56.4	2833	12	17	5.83	67.0	68	343	5.0	3	3	0	18
1994—Seattle NFL	13	13	381	195	51.2	2151	11	7	5.65	70.2	34	153	4.5	0	0	0	0
1995—Seattle NFL	15	13	391	209	53.5	2564	13	§20	6.56	63.7	43	193	4.5	1	1	0	6
1996—Seattle NFL	11	9	265	136	51.3	1546	5	12	5.83	56.6	33	191	5.8	2	2	0	12
1997—Chicago NFL	7	3	103	53	51.5	420	0	6	4.08	37.7	20	78	3.9	1	1	1	8
1998—Green Bay NFL							Did not play.										
1999—New York Jets NFL	8	6	176	95	54.0	1062	5	9	6.03	60.4	21	89	4.2	1	1	0	6
2000—San Francisco NFL	1	0	20	10	50.0	126	1	0	6.30	86.7	3	0	0.0	0	0	0	0
Pro totals (7 years)	71	60	1822	972	53.3	10702	47	71	5.87	63.4	222	1047	4.7	8	8	1	50

MITCHELL, ANTHONY　　　　S　　　　RAVENS

PERSONAL: Born December 13, 1974, in Youngstown, Ohio. ... 6-1/211. ... Full name: Anthony Maurice Mitchell.
HIGH SCHOOL: West Lake (Atlanta, Ga.).
COLLEGE: Tuskegee.
TRANSACTIONS/CAREER NOTES: Signed as non-drafted free agent by Jacksonville Jaguars (April 26, 1999). ... Released by Jaguars (September 1, 1999). ... Signed by Baltimore Ravens to practice squad (September 7, 1999). ... Activated (December 7, 1999). ... Assigned by Ravens to Rhein Fire in 2000 NFL Europe enhancement allocation program (February 22, 2000).
PLAYING EXPERIENCE: Rhein NFLE, 2000; Baltimore NFL, 2000. ... Games/Games started: NFLE 2000 (games played unavailable), NFL 2000 (16/0).
CHAMPIONSHIP GAME EXPERIENCE: Member of Super Bowl championship team (2000 season).
PRO STATISTICS: 2000—Recovered one fumble.

MITCHELL, BASIL　　　　RB　　　　BRONCOS

PERSONAL: Born September 7, 1975, in Pittsburgh, Texas. ... 5-10/200. ... Full name: Basil Mucktar Mitchell.
HIGH SCHOOL: Mount Pleasant (Texas).
COLLEGE: Texas Christian (degree in psychology).
TRANSACTIONS/CAREER NOTES: Signed as non-drafted free agent by Green Bay Packers (April 26, 1999). ... Released by Packers (September 29, 2000). ... Signed by Denver Broncos (May 17, 2001).
PRO STATISTICS: 1999—Returned two punts for no yards and recovered two fumbles. 2000—Recovered one fumble.
SINGLE GAME HIGHS (regular season): Attempts—12 (December 12, 1999, vs. Carolina); yards—49 (December 12, 1999, vs. Carolina); and rushing touchdowns—0.

			RUSHING				RECEIVING				KICKOFF RETURNS				TOTALS			
Year Team	G	GS	Att.	Yds.	Avg.	TD	No.	Yds.	Avg.	TD	No.	Yds.	Avg.	TD	TD	2pt.	Pts.	Fum.
1999—Green Bay NFL...........	16	2	29	117	4.0	0	6	48	8.0	0	21	464	22.1	1	1	0	6	2
2000—Green Bay NFL...........	1	0	2	8	4.0	0	0	0	0.0	0	1	26	26.0	0	0	0	0	1
Pro totals (2 years)	17	2	31	125	4.0	0	6	48	8.0	0	22	490	22.3	1	1	0	6	3

MITCHELL, BRANDON　　　　DE　　　　PATRIOTS

PERSONAL: Born June 19, 1975, in Abbeville, La. ... 6-3/285. ... Full name: Brandon Pete Mitchell.
HIGH SCHOOL: Abbeville (La.).
COLLEGE: Texas A&M.
TRANSACTIONS/CAREER NOTES: Selected by New England Patriots in second round (59th pick overall) of 1997 NFL draft. ... Signed by Patriots (June 6, 1997). ... On injured reserve with ankle injury (October 30, 1998-remainder of season). ... Granted free agency (February 11, 2000). ... Re-signed by Patriots (July 16, 2000). ... On injured reserve with leg injury (December 6, 2000-remainder of season). ... Granted unconditional free agency (March 2, 2001). ... Re-signed by Patriots (April 16, 2001).
PLAYING EXPERIENCE: New England NFL, 1997-2000. ... Games/Games started: 1997 (11/0), 1998 (7/1), 1999 (16/16), 2000 (11/9). Total: 45/26.
PRO STATISTICS: 1998—Credited with two sacks. 1999—Credited with three sacks and recovered one fumble.

MITCHELL, BRIAN　　　　RB/KR　　　　EAGLES

PERSONAL: Born August 18, 1968, in Fort Polk, La. ... 5-10/221. ... Full name: Brian Keith Mitchell.
HIGH SCHOOL: Plaquemine (La.).
COLLEGE: Southwestern Louisiana.
TRANSACTIONS/CAREER NOTES: Selected by Washington Redskins in fifth round (130th pick overall) of 1990 NFL draft. ... Signed by Redskins (July 22, 1990). ... Granted free agency (February 1, 1992). ... Re-signed by Redskins for 1992 season. ... Granted unconditional free agency (February 17, 1994). ... Re-signed by Redskins (May 24, 1994). ... Granted free agency (February 17, 1995). ... Re-signed by Redskins (March 27, 1995). ... Granted unconditional free agency (February 13, 1998). ... Re-signed by Redskins (February 12, 1998). ... Released by Redskins (June 1, 2000). ... Signed by Philadelphia Eagles (June 9, 2000).
CHAMPIONSHIP GAME EXPERIENCE: Played in NFC championship game (1991 season). ... Member of Super Bowl championship team (1991 season).
HONORS: Named punt returner on THE SPORTING NEWS NFL All-Pro team (1995). ... Played in Pro Bowl (1995 season).
RECORDS: Holds NFL career record for most combined kick returns—797; most yards by combined kick returns—14,521; most yards gained by punt return—3,811; most kickoff returns—468; and most yards gained by kick return—10,710. ... Holds NFL single-season record for most yards by combined kick return—1,930 (1994). ... Shares NFL career records for most punt returns—349; and most touchdowns by combined kick returns—11.
PRO STATISTICS: 1990—Attempted six passes with three completions for 40 yards and fumbled twice. 1991—Fumbled eight times and recovered one fumble. 1992—Attempted one pass without a completion, fumbled four times and recovered two fumbles. 1993—Attempted two passes with one completion for 50 yards and an interception, fumbled three times and recovered one fumble. 1994—Had only pass attempt intercepted and fumbled four times. 1995—Fumbled twice and recovered one fumble. 1996—Attempted one pass without a completion, fumbled once and recovered two fumbles. 1997—Fumbled three times. 1998—Attempted two passes with one completion for no yards and fumbled three times. 1999—Fumbled twice and recovered two fumbles for five yards. 2000—Attempted four passes with one completion for 21 yards, fumbled three times and recovered one fumble.
SINGLE GAME HIGHS (regular season): Attempts—21 (September 6, 1993, vs. Dallas); yards—116 (September 6, 1993, vs. Dallas); and rushing touchdowns—2 (September 6, 1993, vs. Dallas).
STATISTICAL PLATEAUS: 100-yard rushing games: 1993 (1), 2000 (1). Total: 2.

Year	Team	G	GS	RUSHING				RECEIVING				PUNT RETURNS				KICKOFF RETURNS				TOTALS		
				Att.	Yds.	Avg.	TD	No.	Yds.	Avg.	TD	No.	Yds.	Avg.	TD	No.	Yds.	Avg.	TD	TD	2pt.	Pts.
1990—Washington NFL		15	0	15	81	5.4	1	2	5	2.5	0	12	107	8.9	0	18	365	20.3	0	1	0	6
1991—Washington NFL		16	0	3	14	4.7	0	0	0	0.0	0	45	*600	13.3	*2	29	583	20.1	0	2	0	12
1992—Washington NFL		16	0	6	70	11.7	0	3	30	10.0	0	29	271	9.3	1	23	492	21.4	0	1	0	6
1993—Washington NFL		16	4	63	246	3.9	3	20	157	7.9	0	29	193	6.7	0	33	678	20.5	0	3	0	18
1994—Washington NFL		16	7	78	311	4.0	0	26	236	9.1	1	32	‡452	*14.1	†2	58	1478	25.5	0	3	1	20
1995—Washington NFL		16	1	46	301	6.5	1	38	324	8.5	1	25	315	12.6	†1	55	1408	‡25.6	0	3	0	18
1996—Washington NFL		16	2	39	193	4.9	0	32	286	8.9	0	23	258	11.2	0	56	1258	22.5	0	0	0	0
1997—Washington NFL		16	1	23	107	4.7	1	36	438	12.2	1	38	442	11.6	∞1	47	1094	23.3	1	4	0	24
1998—Washington NFL		16	0	39	208	5.3	2	44	306	7.0	0	44	‡506	11.5	0	59	1337	22.7	1	3	0	18
1999—Washington NFL		16	0	40	220	5.5	1	31	305	9.8	0	40	332	8.3	0	43	893	20.8	0	1	0	6
2000—Philadelphia NFL		16	1	25	187	7.5	2	13	89	6.8	1	32	335	10.5	1	47	1124	23.9	1	5	0	30
Pro totals (11 years)		175	16	377	1938	5.1	11	245	2176	8.9	4	349	3811	10.9	8	468	10710	22.9	3	26	1	158

MITCHELL, JEFF C PANTHERS

PERSONAL: Born January 29, 1974, in Dallas ... 6-4/300. ... Full name: Jeffrey Clay Mitchell.
HIGH SCHOOL: Countryside (Clearwater, Fla.).
COLLEGE: Florida.
TRANSACTIONS/CAREER NOTES: Selected by Baltimore Ravens in fifth round (134th pick overall) of 1997 NFL draft. ... Signed by Ravens (July 10, 1997). ... On injured reserve with knee injury (August 18, 1997-entire season). ... Granted free agency (February 11, 2000). ... Re-signed by Ravens (April 17, 2000) ... Granted unconditional free agency (March 2, 2001). ... Signed by Carolina Panthers (March 12, 2001).
PLAYING EXPERIENCE: Baltimore NFL, 1998-2000. ... Games/Games started: 1998 (11/10), 1999 (16/16), 2000 (14/14). Total: 41/40.
CHAMPIONSHIP GAME EXPERIENCE: Played in AFC championship game (2000 season). ... Member of Super Bowl championship team (2000 season).
PRO STATISTICS: 1998—Fumbled once for minus 11 yards. 1999—Fumbled twice for minus 36 yards.

MITCHELL, KEITH LB SAINTS

PERSONAL: Born July 24, 1974, in Garland, Texas ... 6-2/245. ... Full name: Clarence Marquis Mitchell.
HIGH SCHOOL: Lakeview (Garland, Texas).
COLLEGE: Texas A&M.
TRANSACTIONS/CAREER NOTES: Signed as non-drafted free agent by New Orleans Saints (April 25, 1997).
HONORS: Named outside linebacker on THE SPORTING NEWS college All-America second team (1996). ... Played in Pro Bowl (2000 season).
PRO STATISTICS: 1998—Recovered three fumbles for 63 yards and one touchdown. 1999—Intercepted three passes for 22 yards and recovered one fumble. 2000—Intercepted one pass for 40 yards and one touchdown and recovered four fumbles for 90 yards and one touchdown.

Year	Team	G	GS	SACKS
1997—New Orleans NFL		16	2	4.0
1998—New Orleans NFL		16	15	2.5
1999—New Orleans NFL		16	16	3.5
2000—New Orleans NFL		16	14	6.5
Pro totals (4 years)		64	47	16.5

MITCHELL, KEVIN LB REDSKINS

PERSONAL: Born January 1, 1971, in Harrisburg, Pa. ... 6-1/254. ... Full name: Kevin Danyelle Mitchell. ... Cousin of Troy Drayton, tight end with Los Angeles/St. Louis Rams (1993-96), Miami Dolphins (1996-99) and Kansas City Chiefs (2000).
HIGH SCHOOL: Harrisburg (Pa.).
COLLEGE: Syracuse (degree in sociology).
TRANSACTIONS/CAREER NOTES: Selected by San Francisco 49ers in second round (53rd pick overall) of 1994 NFL draft. ... Signed by 49ers (July 20, 1994). ... Granted free agency (February 14, 1997). ... Re-signed by 49ers (April 24, 1997). ... Granted free agency (February 13, 1998). ... Signed by New Orleans Saints (February 19, 1998). ... Granted unconditional free agency (February 11, 2000). ... Signed by Washington Redskins (February 29, 2000). ... Granted unconditional free agency (March 2, 2001). ... Re-signed by Redskins (March 29, 2001).
PLAYING EXPERIENCE: San Francisco NFL, 1994-1997; New Orleans NFL, 1998 and 1999; Washington NFL, 2000. ... Games/Games started: 1994 (16/0), 1995 (15/0), 1996 (12/3), 1997 (16/0), 1998 (8/8), 1999 (16/1), 2000 (16/0). Total: 99/12.
CHAMPIONSHIP GAME EXPERIENCE: Played in NFC championship game (1994 and 1997 seasons). ... Member of Super Bowl championship team (1994 season).
HONORS: Named defensive lineman on THE SPORTING NEWS college All-America second team (1992 and 1993).
PRO STATISTICS: 1996—Credited with one sack and recovered one fumble. 1998—Credited with $2\frac{1}{2}$ sacks. 2000—Intercepted one pass for no yards and credited with one sack.

MITCHELL, PETE TE LIONS

PERSONAL: Born October 9, 1971, in Royal Oak, Mich. ... 6-2/248. ... Full name: Peter Clark Mitchell.
HIGH SCHOOL: Brother Rice (Bloomfield Hills, Mich.).
COLLEGE: Boston College (degree in communications, 1994).
TRANSACTIONS/CAREER NOTES: Selected by Miami Dolphins in fourth round (122nd pick overall) of 1995 NFL draft. ... Signed by Dolphins (July 14, 1995). ... Traded by Dolphins to Jacksonville Jaguars for WR Mike Williams (August 27, 1995). ... Granted free agency (February 13, 1998). ... Re-signed by Jaguars (April 13, 1998). ... Designated by Jaguars as transition player (February 12, 1999). ... Free agency status changed from transition to unconditional (February 18, 1999). ... Signed by New York Giants (March 23, 1999). ... Granted unconditional free agency (March 2, 2001). ... Signed by Detroit Lions (April 26, 2000).

M

CHAMPIONSHIP GAME EXPERIENCE: Played in AFC championship game (1996 season). ... Played in NFC championship game (2000 season). ... Played in Super Bowl XXXV (2000 season).

HONORS: Named tight end on THE SPORTING NEWS college All-America first team (1993 and 1994).

PRO STATISTICS: 1997—Returned two kickoffs for 17 yards and recovered one fumble. 1998—Returned two kickoffs for 27 yards and recovered one fumble. 2000—Fumbled once and recovered one fumble.

SINGLE GAME HIGHS (regular season): Receptions—10 (November 19, 1995, vs. Tampa Bay); yards—161 (November 19, 1995, vs. Tampa Bay); and touchdown receptions—1 (October 15, 2000, vs. Dallas).

STATISTICAL PLATEAUS: 100-yard receiving games: 1995 (1).

				RECEIVING				TOTALS		
Year Team	G	GS	No.	Yds.	Avg.	TD	TD	2pt.	Pts.	Fum.
1995—Jacksonville NFL	16	4	41	527	12.9	2	2	0	12	0
1996—Jacksonville NFL	16	7	52	575	11.1	1	1	0	6	1
1997—Jacksonville NFL	16	12	35	380	10.9	4	4	0	24	0
1998—Jacksonville NFL	16	16	38	363	9.6	2	2	0	12	0
1999—New York Giants NFL	15	6	58	520	9.0	3	3	0	18	1
2000—New York Giants NFL	14	5	25	245	9.8	1	1	0	6	1
Pro totals (6 years)	**93**	**50**	**249**	**2610**	**10.5**	**13**	**13**	**0**	**78**	**3**

MITCHELL, SCOTT   QB   BENGALS

PERSONAL: Born January 2, 1968, in Salt Lake City. ... 6-6/240. ... Full name: William Scott Mitchell.

HIGH SCHOOL: Springville (Utah).

COLLEGE: Utah.

TRANSACTIONS/CAREER NOTES: Selected after junior season by Miami Dolphins in fourth round (93rd pick overall) of 1990 NFL draft. ... Signed by Dolphins (July 20, 1990). ... Inactive for 16 games (1990). ... Granted free agency (February 1, 1992). ... Assigned by Dolphins to Orlando Thunder in 1992 World League enhancement allocation program (February 20, 1992). ... Re-signed by Dolphins (February 21, 1992). ... Granted unconditional free agency (February 17, 1994). ... Signed by Detroit Lions (March 6, 1994). ... On injured reserve with wrist injury (November 8, 1994-remainder of season). ... Traded by Lions to Baltimore Ravens for third-round pick (traded to Miami) in 1999 draft and fifth-round pick (traded to St. Louis) in 2000 draft (March 16, 1999). ... Granted unconditional free agency (February 11, 2000). ... Signed by Cincinnati Bengals (March 9, 2000). ... Granted unconditional free agency (March 2, 2001). ... Re-signed by Bengals (April 22, 2001).

CHAMPIONSHIP GAME EXPERIENCE: Played in AFC championship game (1992 season).

PRO STATISTICS: W.L.: 1992—Fumbled six times and recovered two fumbles for minus 19 yards. NFL: 1993—Fumbled once and recovered one fumble for minus four yards. 1994—Fumbled eight times and recovered two fumbles for minus five yards. 1995—Fumbled eight times and recovered one fumble. 1996—Fumbled nine times and recovered five fumbles for minus three yards. 1997—Tied for NFC lead with 15 fumbles and recovered four fumbles for minus 15 yards. 1998—Fumbled once for minus nine yards. 1999—Fumbled once. 2000—Fumbled four times for minus six yards.

SINGLE GAME HIGHS (regular season): Attempts—50 (September 7, 1997, vs. Tampa Bay); completions—31 (October 13, 1996, vs. Oakland); yards—410 (November 23, 1995, vs. Minnesota); and touchdown passes—4 (September 22, 1996, vs. Chicago).

STATISTICAL PLATEAUS: 300-yard passing games: 1993 (1), 1995 (5), 1996 (2), 1997 (1). Total: 9.

MISCELLANEOUS: Regular-season record as starting NFL quarterback: 32-39 (.451). ... Postseason record as starting NFL quarterback: 0-2.

					PASSING						RUSHING				TOTALS		
Year Team	G	GS	Att.	Cmp.	Pct.	Yds.	TD	Int.	Avg.	Rat.	Att.	Yds.	Avg.	TD	TD	2pt.	Pts.
1990—Miami NFL								Did not play.									
1991—Miami NFL	2	0	0	0	0.0	0	0	0	0.0	...	0	0	0.0	0	0	0	0
1992—Orlando W.L.	10	10	*361	*201	55.7	2213	12	7	6.13	77.0	21	45	2.1	1	1	0	6
—Miami NFL	16	0	8	2	25.0	32	0	1	4.00	4.2	8	10	1.3	0	0	0	0
1993—Miami NFL	13	7	233	133	57.1	1773	12	8	7.61	84.2	21	89	4.2	0	0	0	0
1994—Detroit NFL	9	9	246	119	48.4	1456	10	11	5.92	62.0	15	24	1.6	1	1	0	6
1995—Detroit NFL	16	16	583	346	59.3	4338	32	12	7.44	92.3	36	104	2.9	4	4	0	24
1996—Detroit NFL	14	14	437	253	57.9	2917	17	17	6.68	74.9	37	83	2.2	4	4	0	24
1997—Detroit NFL	16	16	509	293	57.6	3484	19	14	6.84	79.6	37	83	2.2	1	1	0	6
1998—Detroit NFL	2	2	75	38	50.7	452	1	3	6.03	57.2	7	30	4.3	0	0	0	0
1999—Baltimore NFL	2	2	56	24	42.9	236	1	4	4.21	31.5	1	1	1.0	0	0	0	0
2000—Cincinnati NFL	8	5	187	89	47.6	966	3	8	5.17	50.8	10	61	6.1	1	1	0	6
W.L. totals (1 year)	10	10	361	201	55.7	2213	12	7	6.13	77.0	21	45	2.1	1	1	0	6
NFL totals (10 years)	98	71	2334	1297	55.6	15654	95	78	6.71	76.0	172	485	2.8	11	·11	0	66
Pro totals (11 years)	108	81	2695	1498	55.6	17867	107	85	6.63	76.1	193	530	2.7	12	12	0	72

MITCHELL, TYWAN   WR   CARDINALS

PERSONAL: Born December 10, 1975, in Crete, Ill. ... 6-5/245.

HIGH SCHOOL: Crete-Monee (Ill.).

COLLEGE: Minnesota State - Mankato.

TRANSACTIONS/CAREER NOTES: Signed as non-drafted free agent by Arizona Cardinals (April 23, 1999). ... Released by Cardinals (September 5, 1999). ... Re-signed by Cardinals to practice squad (September 7, 1999). ... Assigned by Cardinals to Berlin Thunder in 2000 NFL Europe enhancement allocation program (February 22, 2000). ... Released by Cardinals (September 8, 2000). ... Re-signed by Cardinals (September 11, 2000).

PLAYING EXPERIENCE: Berlin NFLE, 2000; Arizona NFL, 2000. ... Games/Games started: NFLE 2000 (games played unavailable), NFL 2000 (10/1).

PRO STATISTICS: NFLE: 2000—Caught 17 passes for 170 yards and two touchdowns. NFL: 2000—Caught five passes for 80 yards.

SINGLE GAME HIGHS (regular season): Receptions—2 (December 24, 2000, vs. Washington); yards—53 (December 24, 2000, vs. Washington); and touchdown receptions—0.

MIXON, KENNY   DE   DOLPHINS

PERSONAL: Born May 31, 1975, in Sun Valley, Calif. ... 6-4/285. ... Full name: Kenneth Jermaine Mixon.
HIGH SCHOOL: Pineville (La.).
COLLEGE: Louisiana State.
TRANSACTIONS/CAREER NOTES: Selected by Miami Dolphins in second round (49th pick overall) of 1998 NFL draft. ... Signed by Dolphins (July 21, 1998).
PLAYING EXPERIENCE: Miami NFL, 1998-2000. ... Games/Games started: 1998 (16/16), 1999 (11/2), 2000 (16/16). Total: 43/34.
PRO STATISTICS: 1998—Credited with two sacks. 2000—Credited with 2$^1/_2$ sacks and recovered one fumble.

MOBLEY, JOHN   LB   BRONCOS

PERSONAL: Born October 10, 1973, in Chester, Pa. ... 6-1/236. ... Full name: John Ulysses Mobley.
HIGH SCHOOL: Chichester (Marcus Hook, Pa.).
COLLEGE: Kutztown (Pa.) University.
TRANSACTIONS/CAREER NOTES: Selected by Denver Broncos in first round (15th pick overall) of 1996 NFL draft. ... Signed by Broncos (July 23, 1996). ... On injured reserve with knee injury (September 22, 1999-remainder of season). ... Granted unconditional free agency (March 2, 2001). ... Re-signed by Broncos (March 2, 2001).
CHAMPIONSHIP GAME EXPERIENCE: Played in AFC championship game (1997 and 1998 seasons). ... Member of Super Bowl championship team (1997 and 1998 seasons).
HONORS: Named outside linebacker on THE SPORTING NEWS NFL All-Pro team (1997).
PRO STATISTICS: 1997—Recovered one fumble. 1998—Recovered one fumble.

			INTERCEPTIONS				SACKS
Year Team	G	GS	No.	Yds.	Avg.	TD	No.
1996—Denver NFL	16	16	1	8	8.0	0	1.5
1997—Denver NFL	16	16	1	13	13.0	1	4.0
1998—Denver NFL	16	15	1	-2	-2.0	0	1.0
1999—Denver NFL	2	2	0	0	0.0	0	0.0
2000—Denver NFL	15	14	1	9	9.0	0	2.0
Pro totals (5 years)	65	63	4	28	7.0	1	8.5

MOHR, CHRIS   P   FALCONS

PERSONAL: Born May 11, 1966, in Atlanta. ... 6-5/215. ... Full name: Christopher Garrett Mohr.
HIGH SCHOOL: Briarwood Academy (Warrenton, Ga.).
COLLEGE: Alabama (degree in criminal justice).
TRANSACTIONS/CAREER NOTES: Selected by Tampa Bay Buccaneers in sixth round (146th pick overall) of 1989 NFL draft. ... Signed by Buccaneers (July 15, 1989). ... Released by Buccaneers (September 2, 1990). ... Signed by WLAF (January 31, 1991). ... Selected by Montreal Machine in first round (eighth punter) of 1991 WLAF positional draft. ... Signed by Buffalo Bills (June 6, 1991). ... Granted unconditional free agency (February 17, 1994). ... Re-signed by Bills (March 3, 1994). ... Granted unconditional free agency (February 14, 1997). ... Re-signed by Bills (March 4, 1997). ... Released by Bills (February 22, 2001). ... Signed by Atlanta Falcons (March 13, 2001).
CHAMPIONSHIP GAME EXPERIENCE: Played in AFC championship game (1991-1993 seasons). ... Played in Super Bowl XXVI (1991 season), Super Bowl XXVII (1992 season) and Super Bowl XXVIII (1993 season).
HONORS: Named punter on All-World League team (1991).
PRO STATISTICS: NFL: 1989—Converted one extra point. W.L.: 1991—Had only pass attempt intercepted and rushed three times for minus four yards. 1991—Completed only pass attempt for minus nine yards. 1992—Rushed once for 11 yards and recovered one fumble. 1993—Fumbled once and recovered one fumble. 1994—Rushed once for minus nine yards. 1997—Rushed once for no yards, attempted one pass with a completion for 29 yards, fumbled once and recovered one fumble for minus 10 yards. 1999—Rushed once for no yards. 2000—Completed only pass attempt for 44 yards.

		PUNTING					
Year Team	G	No.	Yds.	Avg.	Net avg.	In. 20	Blk.
1989—Tampa Bay NFL	16	∞84	3311	39.4	32.1	10	2
1990—			Did not play.				
1991—Montreal W.L.	10	57	2436	*42.7	34.0	13	2
—Buffalo NFL	16	54	2085	38.6	36.1	12	0
1992—Buffalo NFL	15	60	2531	42.2	36.7	12	0
1993—Buffalo NFL	16	74	2991	40.4	36.0	19	0
1994—Buffalo NFL	16	67	2799	41.8	36.0	13	0
1995—Buffalo NFL	16	86	3473	40.4	36.2	23	0
1996—Buffalo NFL	16	§101	§4194	41.5	36.5	§27	0
1997—Buffalo NFL	16	90	3764	41.8	36.0	24	1
1998—Buffalo NFL	16	69	2882	41.8	33.2	18	0
1999—Buffalo NFL	16	73	2840	38.9	33.9	20	0
2000—Buffalo NFL	16	95	3661	38.5	31.4	19	▲1
W.L. totals (1 year)	10	57	2436	42.7	34.0	13	2
NFL totals (11 years)	175	853	34531	40.5	34.8	197	4
Pro totals (12 years)	185	910	36967	40.6	34.8	210	6

MOHRING, MICHAEL   DT/DE   CHARGERS

PERSONAL: Born March 22, 1974, in Glen Cove, N.Y. ... 6-5/295. ... Full name: Michael Joseph Mohring. ... Cousin of John Mohring, linebacker with Detroit Lions (1980) and Cleveland Browns (1980). ... Name pronounced MORE-ing.
HIGH SCHOOL: West Chester (Pa.) East.
COLLEGE: Pittsburgh.

MOLDEN, ALEX   CB   CHARGERS

PERSONAL: Born August 4, 1973, in Detroit. ... 5-10/190. ... Full name: Alex M. Molden.
HIGH SCHOOL: Sierra (Colorado Springs, Colo.).
COLLEGE: Oregon.
TRANSACTIONS/CAREER NOTES: Selected by New Orleans Saints in first round (11th pick overall) of 1996 NFL draft. ... Signed by Saints (July 21, 1996). ... Granted unconditional free agency (March 2, 2001). ... Signed by San Diego Chargers (March 6, 2001).
HONORS: Named defensive back on THE SPORTING NEWS college All-America second team (1995).
PRO STATISTICS: 1997—Recovered two fumbles.

| | | | INTERCEPTIONS | | | | SACKS |
Year Team	G	GS	No.	Yds.	Avg.	TD	No.
1996—New Orleans NFL	14	2	2	2	1.0	0	2.0
1997—New Orleans NFL	16	15	0	0	0.0	0	4.0
1998—New Orleans NFL	16	15	2	35	17.5	0	0.0
1999—New Orleans NFL	13	0	1	2	2.0	0	0.0
2000—New Orleans NFL	15	6	3	24	8.0	0	0.0
Pro totals (5 years)	74	38	8	63	7.9	0	6.0

MONTGOMERY, JOE   RB   GIANTS

PERSONAL: Born June 8, 1976, in Robbins, Ill. ... 5-10/230.
HIGH SCHOOL: Richards (Oak Lawn, Ill.).
COLLEGE: Ohio State.
TRANSACTIONS/CAREER NOTES: Selected by New York Giants in second round (49th pick overall) of 1999 NFL draft. ... Signed by Giants (July 29, 1999).
CHAMPIONSHIP GAME EXPERIENCE: Played in NFC championship game (2000 season). ... Played in Super Bowl XXXV (2000 season).
SINGLE GAME HIGHS (regular season): Attempts—38 (December 5, 1999, vs. New York Jets); yards—111 (December 5, 1999, vs. New York Jets); and rushing touchdowns—1 (October 29, 2000, vs. Philadelphia).
STATISTICAL PLATEAUS: 100-yard rushing games: 1999 (1).

| | | | RUSHING | | | | TOTALS | | | |
Year Team	G	GS	Att.	Yds.	Avg.	TD	TD	2pt.	Pts.	Fum.
1999—New York Giants NFL	7	5	115	348	3.0	3	3	†1	20	2
2000—New York Giants NFL	3	0	1	4	4.0	1	1	0	6	0
Pro totals (2 years)	10	5	116	352	3.0	4	4	1	26	2

MONTGOMERY, MONTY   CB   EAGLES

PERSONAL: Born December 8, 1973, in Dallas. ... 5-11/197. ... Full name: Delmonico Montgomery.
HIGH SCHOOL: Gladewater (Texas).
COLLEGE: Houston.
TRANSACTIONS/CAREER NOTES: Selected by Indianapolis Colts in fourth round (117th pick overall) of 1997 NFL draft. ... Signed by Colts (July 7, 1997). ... Released by Colts (September 15, 1999). ... Re-signed by Colts (September 17, 1999). ... Released by Colts (September 29, 1999). ... Signed by San Francisco 49ers (October 4, 1999). ... On injured reserve with broken arm (December 8, 1999-remainder of season). ... Granted unconditional free agency (March 2, 2001). ... Signed by Philadelphia Eagles (May 10, 2001).
PRO STATISTICS: 1998—Intercepted one pass for 22 yards and recovered two fumbles for 14 yards. 2000—Intercepted three passes for 68 yards and a touchdown.

Year Team	G	GS	SACKS
1997—Indianapolis NFL	16	3	1.0
1998—Indianapolis NFL	16	5	2.0
1999—Indianapolis NFL	3	0	0.0
—San Francisco NFL	4	2	0.0
2000—San Francisco NFL	15	9	0.5
Pro totals (4 years)	54	19	3.5

MONTGOMERY, SCOTTIE   WR   BRONCOS

PERSONAL: Born May 26, 1978, in Shelby, N.C. ... 6-1/195. ... Full name: Scottie Austin Montgomery.
HIGH SCHOOL: Burns (Cherryville, N.C.).
COLLEGE: Duke.
TRANSACTIONS/CAREER NOTES: Signed as non-drafted free agent by Carolina Panthers (April 27, 2000). ... Released by Panthers (August 27, 2000). ... Signed by Denver Broncos to practice squad (September 13, 2000). ... Activated (October 21, 2000).
PLAYING EXPERIENCE: Denver NFL, 2000. ... Games/Games started: 2000 (4/0).
PRO STATISTICS: 2000—Caught one pass for 10 yards.
SINGLE GAME HIGHS (regular season): Receptions—1 (December 23, 2000, vs. San Francisco); yards—10 (December 23, 2000, vs. San Francisco); and touchdown receptions—0.

MONTY, PETE   LB

PERSONAL: Born July 3, 1974, in Fort Collins, Colo. ... 6-2/250. ... Full name: Peter Monty.
HIGH SCHOOL: Fort Collins (Colo.).
COLLEGE: Wisconsin.
TRANSACTIONS/CAREER NOTES: Selected by New York Giants in fourth round (103rd pick overall) of 1997 NFL draft. ... Signed by Giants (July 19, 1997). ... On injured reserve with knee injury (September 30, 1997-remainder of season). ... Granted free agency (February 11, 2000). ... Re-signed by Giants (April 13, 2000). ... Granted unconditional free agency (March 2, 2001).
PLAYING EXPERIENCE: New York Giants NFL, 1997-2000. ... Games/Games started: 1997 (3/0), 1998 (11/0), 1999 (16/3), 2000 (16/1). Total: 46/4.
CHAMPIONSHIP GAME EXPERIENCE: Played in NFC championship game (2000 season). ... Played in Super Bowl XXXV (2000 season).
PRO STATISTICS: 2000—Credited with two sacks and recovered one fumble.

MOON, WARREN   QB

PERSONAL: Born November 18, 1956, in Los Angeles. ... 6-3/218. ... Full name: Harold Warren Moon.
HIGH SCHOOL: Hamilton (Los Angeles).
JUNIOR COLLEGE: West Los Angeles Junior College.
COLLEGE: Washington.
TRANSACTIONS/CAREER NOTES: Signed by Edmonton Eskimos of CFL (March 1978). ... USFL rights traded by Memphis Showboats to Los Angeles Express for future draft pick (August 30, 1983). ... Granted free agency (March 1, 1984). ... Signed by Houston Oilers (March 1, 1984). ... On injured reserve with fractured scapula (September 5-October 15, 1988). ... Traded by Oilers to Minnesota Vikings for third-round pick (WR Malcolm Seabron) in 1994 draft and third-round pick (RB Rodney Thomas) in 1995 draft (April 14, 1994). ... Released by Vikings (February 21, 1997). ... Signed by Seattle Seahawks (March 7, 1997). ... Released by Seahawks (February 11, 1999). ... Signed by Kansas City Chiefs (April 27, 1999). ... Announced retirement (February 22, 2001).
CHAMPIONSHIP GAME EXPERIENCE: Played in Grey Cup, CFL championship game (1978-1982 seasons).
HONORS: Played in Pro Bowl (1988-1995 and 1997 seasons). ... Named quarterback on THE SPORTING NEWS NFL All-Pro team (1990). ... Named Outstanding Player of Pro Bowl (1997 season).
RECORDS: Holds NFL career records for most fumbles—160; most own and opponents' fumbles recovered—55; and most own fumbles recovered—55. ... Holds NFL single-season record for most passes completed—404 (1991). ... Shares NFL single-season record for most games with 300 or more yards passing—9 (1990). ... Shares NFL single-game record for most times sacked—12 (September 29, 1985, vs. Dallas).
POST SEASON RECORDS: Holds NFL postseason career records for most fumbles—16; and most own fumbles recovered—8. ... Holds NFL postseason single-game records for most passes completed—36 (January 3, 1993, OT, at Buffalo); and most fumbles—5 (January 16, 1994, vs. Kansas City).
PRO STATISTICS: CFL: 1978—Fumbled once. 1979—Fumbled once. 1981—Fumbled once. 1982—Fumbled once and recovered one fumble. 1983—Fumbled seven times. NFL: 1984—Led league with 17 fumbles and recovered seven fumbles for minus one yard. 1985—Fumbled 12 times and recovered five fumbles for minus eight yards. 1986—Fumbled 11 times and recovered three fumbles for minus four yards. 1987—Fumbled eight times and recovered six fumbles for minus seven yards. 1988—Fumbled eight times and recovered four fumbles for minus five yards. 1989—Fumbled 11 times and recovered six fumbles for minus 13 yards. 1990—Led league with 18 fumbles and recovered four fumbles. 1991—Fumbled 11 times and recovered four fumbles for minus four yards. 1992—Fumbled seven times. 1993—Fumbled 13 times and recovered five fumbles for minus seven yards. 1994—Fumbled nine times and recovered two fumbles for minus five yards. 1995—Fumbled 13 times and recovered five fumbles for minus 12 yards. 1996—Fumbled seven times and recovered two fumbles. 1997—Fumbled seven times and recovered one fumble for minus two yards. 1998—Fumbled eight times and recovered one fumble for minus 12 yards. 2000—Fumbled once and recovered one fumble.
SINGLE GAME HIGHS (regular season): Attempts—57 (November 6, 1994, vs. New Orleans); completions—41 (November 10, 1991, vs. Dallas); yards—527 (December 16, 1990, vs. Kansas City); and touchdown passes—5 (October 26, 1997, vs. Oakland).
STATISTICAL PLATEAUS: 300-yard passing games: 1984 (4), 1985 (3), 1986 (3), 1987 (2), 1989 (4), 1990 (9), 1991 (6), 1992 (4), 1993 (3), 1994 (6), 1995 (4), 1997 (1). Total: 49.
MISCELLANEOUS: Regular-season record as starting NFL quarterback: 102-101 (.502). ... Postseason record as starting NFL quarterback: 3-7 (.300). ... Holds Oilers franchise all-time records for most yards passing (33,685) and most touchdown passes (196).

			PASSING								RUSHING				TOTALS		
Year Team	G	GS	Att.	Cmp.	Pct.	Yds.	TD	Int.	Avg.	Rat.	Att.	Yds.	Avg.	TD	TD	2pt.	Pts.
1978—Edmonton CFL	16	...	173	89	51.4	1112	5	7	6.43	64.5	30	114	3.8	1	1	0	6
1979—Edmonton CFL	16	...	274	149	54.4	2382	20	12	8.69	89.7	56	150	2.7	2	2	0	12
1980—Edmonton CFL	16	...	331	181	54.7	3127	25	11	9.45	98.3	55	352	6.4	3	3	0	18
1981—Edmonton CFL	15	9	378	237	62.7	3959	27	12	10.47	108.6	50	298	6.0	3	3	0	18
1982—Edmonton CFL	16	16	562	333	59.3	5000	36	16	8.90	98.0	54	259	4.8	4	4	0	24
1983—Edmonton CFL	16	16	664	380	57.2	5648	31	19	8.51	88.9	85	527	6.2	3	3	0	18
1984—Houston NFL	16	16	450	259	57.6	3338	12	14	7.42	76.9	58	211	3.6	1	1	0	6
1985—Houston NFL	14	14	377	200	53.1	2709	15	19	7.19	68.5	39	130	3.3	0	0	0	0
1986—Houston NFL	15	15	488	256	52.5	3489	13	*26	7.15	62.3	42	157	3.7	2	2	0	12
1987—Houston NFL	12	12	368	184	50.0	2806	21	18	7.63	74.2	34	112	3.3	3	3	0	18
1988—Houston NFL	11	11	294	160	54.4	2327	17	8	7.91	88.4	33	88	2.7	5	5	0	30
1989—Houston NFL	16	16	464	280	60.3	3631	23	14	7.83	88.9	70	268	3.8	4	4	0	24
1990—Houston NFL	15	15	*584	*362	62.0	*4689	*33	13	8.03	96.8	55	215	3.9	2	2	0	12
1991—Houston NFL	16	16	*655	*404	61.7	*4690	23	*21	7.16	81.7	33	68	2.1	2	2	0	12
1992—Houston NFL	11	10	346	224	64.7	2521	18	12	7.29	§89.3	27	147	5.4	1	1	0	6
1993—Houston NFL	15	14	520	303	58.3	3485	21	§21	6.70	75.2	48	145	3.0	1	1	0	6
1994—Minnesota NFL	15	15	‡601	‡371	61.7	‡4264	18	‡19	7.09	79.9	27	55	2.0	0	0	0	0
1995—Minnesota NFL	16	16	‡606	‡377	62.2	4228	33	14	6.98	91.5	33	82	2.5	0	0	0	0
1996—Minnesota NFL	8	8	247	134	54.3	1610	7	9	6.52	68.7	9	6	0.7	0	0	0	0
1997—Seattle NFL	15	14	528	313	59.3	3678	25	16	6.97	83.7	17	40	2.4	1	1	0	6
1998—Seattle NFL	10	10	258	145	56.2	1632	11	8	6.33	76.6	16	10	0.6	0	0	0	0
1999—Kansas City NFL	1	0	3	1	33.3	20	0	0	6.67	57.6	0	0	0.0	0	0	0	0
2000—Kansas City NFL	2	1	34	15	44.1	208	1	1	6.12	61.9	2	2	1.0	0	0	0	0
CFL totals (6 years)	95	...	2382	1369	57.5	21228	144	77	8.91	93.8	330	1700	5.2	16	16	0	96
NFL totals (17 years)	208	203	6823	3988	58.4	49325	291	233	7.23	80.9	543	1736	3.2	22	22	0	132
Pro totals (23 years)	303	...	9205	5357	58.2	70553	435	310	7.66	84.2	873	3436	3.9	38	38	0	228

M

MOORE, COREY — LB — BILLS

PERSONAL: Born March 20, 1977, in Brownsville, Tenn. ... 5-11/225. ... Full name: Corey Antonio Moore.
HIGH SCHOOL: Haywood (Brownsville, Tenn.).
JUNIOR COLLEGE: Holmes Junior College (Miss.).
COLLEGE: Virginia Tech.
TRANSACTIONS/CAREER NOTES: Selected by Buffalo Bills in third round (89th pick overall) of 2000 NFL draft. ... Signed by Bills (July 17, 2000).
PLAYING EXPERIENCE: Buffalo NFL, 2000. ... Games/Games started: 2000 (9/4).
HONORS: Named defensive end on THE SPORTING NEWS college All-America second team (1998). ... Lombardi Award winner (1999). ... Bronko Nagurski Award winner (1999). ... Named defensive end on THE SPORTING NEWS college All-America first team (1999).
PRO STATISTICS: 2000—Credited with one sack and recovered one fumble.

MOORE, DAMON — S — EAGLES

PERSONAL: Born September 15, 1976, in Fostoria, Ohio. ... 5-11/215.
HIGH SCHOOL: Fostoria (Ohio).
COLLEGE: Ohio State.
TRANSACTIONS/CAREER NOTES: Selected by Philadelphia Eagles in fourth round (128th pick overall) of 1999 NFL draft. ... Signed by Eagles (July 28, 1999).
PLAYING EXPERIENCE: Philadelphia NFL, 1999 and 2000. ... Games/Games started: 1999 (16/1), 2000 (16/16). Total: 32/17.
HONORS: Named strong safety on THE SPORTING NEWS college All-America first team (1998).
PRO STATISTICS: 1999—Intercepted one pass for 28 yards and recovered one fumble. 2000—Intercepted two passes for 24 yards and fumbled once.

MOORE, DAVE — TE — BUCCANEERS

PERSONAL: Born November 11, 1969, in Morristown, N.J. ... 6-2/258. ... Full name: David Edward Moore.
HIGH SCHOOL: Roxbury (Succasunna, N.J.).
COLLEGE: Pittsburgh (degree in justice administration, 1991).
TRANSACTIONS/CAREER NOTES: Selected by Miami Dolphins in seventh round (191st pick overall) of 1992 NFL draft. ... Signed by Dolphins (July 15, 1992). ... Released by Dolphins (August 31, 1992). ... Re-signed by Dolphins to practice squad (September 1, 1992). ... Released by Dolphins (September 16, 1992). ... Re-signed by Dolphins to practice squad (October 21, 1992). ... Activated (October 24, 1992). ... Released by Dolphins (October 28, 1992). ... Re-signed by Dolphins to practice squad (October 28, 1992). ... Released by Dolphins (November 18, 1992). ... Signed by Tampa Bay Buccaneers to practice squad (November 24, 1992). ... Activated (December 4, 1992). ... Granted free agency (February 16, 1996). ... Re-signed by Buccaneers (May 31, 1996). ... Granted unconditional free agency (February 14, 1997). ... Re-signed by Buccaneers (February 18, 1997). ... Granted unconditional free agency (February 11, 2000). ... Re-signed by Buccaneers (March 20, 2000).
CHAMPIONSHIP GAME EXPERIENCE: Played in NFC championship game (1999 season).
PRO STATISTICS: 1993—Attempted one pass without a completion and recovered one fumble. 1995—Rushed once for four yards.
SINGLE GAME HIGHS (regular season): Receptions—6 (November 2, 1997, vs. Indianapolis); yards—62 (November 3, 1996, vs. Chicago); and touchdown receptions—1 (November 5, 2000, vs. Atlanta).

| | | | RECEIVING | | | | TOTALS | | | |
Year Team	G	GS	No.	Yds.	Avg.	TD	TD	2pt.	Pts.	Fum.
1992—Miami NFL	1	0	0	0	0.0	0	0	0	0	0
—Tampa Bay NFL	4	2	1	10	10.0	0	0	0	0	0
1993—Tampa Bay NFL	15	1	4	47	11.8	1	1	0	6	0
1994—Tampa Bay NFL	15	5	4	57	14.3	0	0	0	0	0
1995—Tampa Bay NFL	16	9	13	102	7.8	0	0	0	0	0
1996—Tampa Bay NFL	16	8	27	237	8.8	3	3	0	18	0
1997—Tampa Bay NFL	16	7	19	217	11.4	4	4	0	24	0
1998—Tampa Bay NFL	16	16	24	255	10.6	4	4	0	24	1
1999—Tampa Bay NFL	16	16	23	276	12.0	5	5	0	30	0
2000—Tampa Bay NFL	16	16	29	288	9.9	3	3	0	18	0
Pro totals (9 years)	131	80	144	1489	10.3	20	20	0	120	1

MOORE, HERMAN — WR — LIONS

PERSONAL: Born October 20, 1969, in Danville, Va. ... 6-4/224. ... Full name: Herman Joseph Moore.
HIGH SCHOOL: George Washington (Danville, Va.).
COLLEGE: Virginia (degree in rhetoric and communication studies, 1991).
TRANSACTIONS/CAREER NOTES: Selected after junior season by Detroit Lions in first round (10th pick overall) of 1991 NFL draft. ... Signed by Lions (July 19, 1991). ... On injured reserve with quadricep injury (September 11-October 9, 1992). ... On practice squad (October 9-14, 1992). ... Designated by Lions as transition player (February 25, 1993).
CHAMPIONSHIP GAME EXPERIENCE: Played in NFC championship game (1991 season).
HONORS: Named wide receiver on THE SPORTING NEWS college All-America first team (1990). ... Played in Pro Bowl (1994-1997 seasons). ... Named wide receiver on THE SPORTING NEWS NFL All-Pro team (1995-1997).
RECORDS: Holds NFL single-season record for most pass receptions—123 (1995).
POST SEASON RECORDS: Shares NFL postseason career record for most two-point conversions—1.
SINGLE GAME HIGHS (regular season): Receptions—14 (December 4, 1995, vs. Chicago); yards—183 (December 4, 1995, vs. Chicago); and touchdown receptions—3 (October 29, 1995, vs. Green Bay).
STATISTICAL PLATEAUS: 100-yard receiving games: 1992 (3), 1993 (3), 1994 (3), 1995 (10), 1996 (5), 1997 (6), 1998 (4). Total: 34.
MISCELLANEOUS: Holds Detroit Lions all-time records for most yards receiving (9,098), most receptions (666), and most touchdown receptions (62).

Year Team	G	GS	No.	RECEIVING Yds.	Avg.	TD	TD	2pt.	TOTALS Pts.	Fum.
1991—Detroit NFL	13	1	11	135	12.3	0	0	0	0	0
1992—Detroit NFL	12	11	51	966	‡18.9	4	4	0	24	0
1993—Detroit NFL	15	15	61	935	15.3	6	6	0	36	2
1994—Detroit NFL	16	16	72	1173	16.3	11	11	0	66	1
1995—Detroit NFL	16	16	*123	1686	13.7	14	14	0	84	2
1996—Detroit NFL	16	16	106	1296	12.2	9	9	1	56	0
1997—Detroit NFL	16	16	†104	1293	12.4	8	8	1	50	0
1998—Detroit NFL	15	15	82	983	12.0	5	5	0	30	0
1999—Detroit NFL	8	4	16	197	12.3	2	2	0	12	0
2000—Detroit NFL	15	11	40	434	10.9	3	3	0	18	0
Pro totals (10 years)	142	121	666	9098	13.7	62	62	2	376	5

MOORE, JASON   S

PERSONAL: Born January 15, 1976, in San Bernardino, Calif. ... 5-10/191. ... Full name: Jason Dwayne Moore.
HIGH SCHOOL: Pacific (San Bernardino, Calif.).
COLLEGE: San Diego State.
TRANSACTIONS/CAREER NOTES: Signed as non-drafted free agent by Cincinnati Bengals (April 19, 1998). ... Released by Bengals (August 24, 1998). ... Signed by Denver Broncos (March 12, 1999). ... Released by Broncos (August 31, 1999). ... Re-signed by Broncos to practice squad (September 14, 1999). ... Activated (November 18, 1999). ... Released by Broncos (August 27, 2000). ... Signed by Green Bay Packers to practice squad (September 6, 2000). ... Activated (September 16, 2000). ... Released by Packers (September 30, 2000). ... Re-signed by Packers to practice squad (October 3, 2000). ... Activated (October 5, 2000). ... Released by Packers (October 9, 2000). ... Signed by 49ers (October 10, 2000). ... Released by 49ers (November 14, 2000). ... Re-signed by 49ers to practice squad (November 15, 2000). ... Activated (December 21, 2000). ... Released by 49ers (March 21, 2001).
PLAYING EXPERIENCE: Denver NFL, 1999; Green Bay (3)-San Francisco (5) NFL, 2000. ... Games/Games started: 1999 (6/0), 2000 (G.B.-3/0; S.F. 5/0; Total: 8/0). Total: 14/0.

MOORE, JERALD   RB

PERSONAL: Born November 20, 1974, in Houston. ... 5-9/230. ... Full name: Jerald Christopher Moore.
HIGH SCHOOL: Jack Yates (Houston).
COLLEGE: Oklahoma.
TRANSACTIONS/CAREER NOTES: Selected after junior season by St. Louis Rams in third round (83rd pick overall) of 1996 NFL draft. ... Signed by Rams (July 15, 1996). ... Granted free agency (February 12, 1999). ... Signed by Oakland Raiders (March 14, 2000). ... Claimed on waivers by New Orleans Saints (August 28, 2000). ... Released by Saints (December 10, 2000). ... Re-signed by Saints (December 12, 2000). ... Granted unconditional free agency (March 2, 2001).
PRO STATISTICS: 1997—Recovered two fumbles. 1998—Recovered two fumbles.
SINGLE GAME HIGHS (regular season): Attempts—27 (December 20, 1997, vs. Carolina); yards—113 (December 20, 1997, vs. Carolina); and rushing touchdowns—1 (November 26, 2000, vs. St. Louis).
STATISTICAL PLATEAUS: 100-yard rushing games: 1997 (1).

Year Team	G	GS	RUSHING Att.	Yds.	Avg.	TD	No.	RECEIVING Yds.	Avg.	TD	TD	2pt.	TOTALS Pts.	Fum.
1996—St. Louis NFL	11	4	11	32	2.9	0	3	13	4.3	0	0	0	0	0
1997—St. Louis NFL	9	5	104	380	3.7	3	8	69	8.6	0	3	0	18	4
1998—St. Louis NFL	11	4	55	137	2.5	2	9	60	6.7	0	2	0	12	3
1999—							Did not play.							
2000—New Orleans NFL	11	1	37	156	4.2	1	0	0	0.0	0	1	0	6	0
NFL totals (4 years)	42	14	207	705	3.4	6	20	142	7.1	0	6	0	36	7

M

MOORE, LARRY   G   COLTS

PERSONAL: Born June 1, 1975, in San Diego. ... 6-2/296.
HIGH SCHOOL: Monte Vista (Spring Valley, Calif.).
JUNIOR COLLEGE: Grossmont College (Calif.).
COLLEGE: Brigham Young.
TRANSACTIONS/CAREER NOTES: Signed as non-drafted free agent by Seattle Seahawks (April 25, 1997). ... Released by Seahawks (August 17, 1997). ... Signed by Washington Redskins to practice squad (August 26, 1997). ... Released by Redskins (September 3, 1997). ... Signed by Indianapolis Colts (January 29, 1998). ... Granted free agency (March 2, 2001). ... Re-signed by Colts (April 21, 2001).
PLAYING EXPERIENCE: Indianapolis NFL, 1998-2000. ... Games/Games started: 1998 (6/5), 1999 (16/16), 2000 (16/16). Total: 38/37.
PRO STATISTICS: 1999—Fumbled twice for minus 25 yards. 2000—Recovered one fumble.

MOORE, MARTY   LB   BROWNS

PERSONAL: Born March 19, 1971, in Phoenix. ... 6-1/245. ... Full name: Martin Neff Moore.
HIGH SCHOOL: Highlands (Fort Thomas, Ky.).
COLLEGE: Kentucky.
TRANSACTIONS/CAREER NOTES: Selected by New England Patriots in seventh round (222nd pick overall) of 1994 NFL draft. ... Signed by Patriots (June 1, 1994). ... Granted free agency (February 14, 1997). ... Re-signed by Patriots (June 6, 1997). ... Granted unconditional free agency (February 13, 1998). ... Re-signed by Patriots (April 3, 1998). ... Granted unconditional free agency (February 11, 2000). ... Signed by Cleveland Browns (March 2, 2000).
PLAYING EXPERIENCE: New England NFL, 1994-1999; Cleveland NFL, 2000. ... Games/Games started: 1994 (16/4), 1995 (16/3), 1996 (16/0), 1997 (16/0), 1998 (14/2), 1999 (15/2), 2000 (16/9). Total: 109/20.
CHAMPIONSHIP GAME EXPERIENCE: Played in AFC championship game (1996 season). ... Played in Super Bowl XXXI (1996 season).
PRO STATISTICS: 1997—Intercepted two passes for seven yards. 1998—Recovered one fumble. 2000—Intercepted one pass for three yards and credited with one sack.

MOORE, MICHAEL   G   REDSKINS

PERSONAL: Born November 1, 1976, in Fayette, Ark. ... 6-3/320.
HIGH SCHOOL: Fayette (Ark.) County.
COLLEGE: Alabama, then Troy (Ala.) State.
TRANSACTIONS/CAREER NOTES: Selected by Washington Redskins in fourth round (129th pick overall) of 2000 NFL draft. ... Signed by Redskins (June 5, 2000).
PLAYING EXPERIENCE: Washington NFL, 2000. ... Games/Games started: 2000 (5/1).

MORABITO, TIM   DT   PANTHERS

PERSONAL: Born October 12, 1973, in Garnerville, N.Y. ... 6-3/296. ... Full name: Timothy Robert Morabito. ... Name pronounced more-ah-BEE-toe.
HIGH SCHOOL: St. Joseph's Regional (Garnerville, N.Y.).
COLLEGE: Boston College (degree in sociology).
TRANSACTIONS/CAREER NOTES: Signed as non-drafted free agent by Cincinnati Bengals (April 23, 1996). ... Released by Bengals (September 11, 1996). ... Re-signed by Bengals to practice squad (September 12, 1996). ... Activated (November 5, 1996). ... Claimed on waivers by Carolina Panthers (August 26, 1997). ... Granted free agency (February 12, 1999). ... Re-signed by Panthers (June 4, 1999). ... Granted unconditional free agency (February 11, 2000). ... Re-signed by Panthers (March 22, 2000).
PLAYING EXPERIENCE: Cincinnati NFL, 1996; Carolina NFL, 1997-2000. ... Games/Games started: 1996 (7/1), 1997 (8/0), 1998 (8/8), 1999 (16/16), 2000 (16/13). Total: 55/38.
PRO STATISTICS: 1997—Recovered one fumble. 2000—Credited with two sacks and recovered one fumble.

MORAN, SEAN   DE   RAMS

PERSONAL: Born June 5, 1973, in Denver. ... 6-3/280. ... Full name: Sean Farrell Moran.
HIGH SCHOOL: Overland (Aurora, Colo.).
COLLEGE: Colorado State.
TRANSACTIONS/CAREER NOTES: Selected by Buffalo Bills in fourth round (120th pick overall) of 1996 NFL draft. ... Signed by Bills (July 9, 1996). ... Granted free agency (February 12, 1999). ... Re-signed by Bills (April 1, 1999). ... Granted unconditional free agency (February 11, 2000). ... Signed by St. Louis Rams (March 15, 2000).
PLAYING EXPERIENCE: Buffalo NFL, 1996-1999; St. Louis NFL, 2000. ... Games/Games started: 1996 (16/0), 1997 (16/7), 1998 (10/2), 1999 (16/0), 2000 (15/3). Total: 73/12.
PRO STATISTICS: 1997—Intercepted two passes for 12 yards, credited with 4$^{1}/_{2}$ sacks and recovered one fumble. 1999—Credited with $^{1}/_{2}$ sack. 2000—Credited with two sacks and returned one kickoff for 17 yards.

M

MOREAU, FRANK   RB   CHIEFS

PERSONAL: Born September 9, 1976, in Elizabethtown, Ky. ... 6-0/223. ... Full name: Franklin H. Moreau.
HIGH SCHOOL: Central Hardin (Elizabethtown, Ky.).
COLLEGE: Louisville (degree in justice administration).
TRANSACTIONS/CAREER NOTES: Selected by Kansas City Chiefs in fourth round (115th pick overall) of 2000 NFL draft. ... Signed by Chiefs (June 6, 2000).
SINGLE GAME HIGHS (regular season): Attempts—18 (September 17, 2000, vs. San Diego); yards—59 (December 17, 2000, vs. Denver); and rushing touchdowns—1 (December 24, 2000, vs. Atlanta).

				RUSHING				TOTALS		
Year Team	G	GS	Att.	Yds.	Avg.	TD	TD	2pt.	Pts.	Fum.
2000—Kansas City NFL	11	0	67	179	2.7	4	4	0	24	2

MORELAND, EARTHWIND   CB   JETS

PERSONAL: Born June 13, 1977, in Atlanta. ... 5-11/185. ... Full name: Earthwind C. Moreland.
HIGH SCHOOL: Grady (Atlanta).
COLLEGE: Georgia Southern.
TRANSACTIONS/CAREER NOTES: Signed as non-drafted free agent by Tampa Bay Buccaneers (April 16, 2000). ... Released by Buccaneers (August 27, 2000). ... Signed by New York Jets (August 29, 2000).
PLAYING EXPERIENCE: New York Jets NFL, 2000. ... Games/Games started: 2000 (1/0).

MORELAND, JAKE   FB/TE   JETS

PERSONAL: Born January 18, 1977, in Milwaukee. ... 6-3/255.
HIGH SCHOOL: Marquette (Milwaukee).
COLLEGE: Western Michigan.
TRANSACTIONS/CAREER NOTES: Signed as non-drafted free agent by New York Jets (April 20, 2000). ... Released by Jets (September 4, 2000). ... Re-signed by Jets to practice squad (September 6, 2000). ... Activated (October 22, 2000).
PLAYING EXPERIENCE: New York Jets NFL, 2000. ... Games/Games started: 2000 (7/1).

MORENO, MOSES   QB

PERSONAL: Born September 5, 1975, in Chula Vista, Calif. ... 6-1/205. ... Full name: Moses Nathaniel Moreno. ... Name pronounced mo-REH-no.
HIGH SCHOOL: Castle Park (Chula Vista, Calif.).
COLLEGE: Colorado State.
TRANSACTIONS/CAREER NOTES: Selected by Chicago Bears in seventh round (232nd pick overall) of 1998 NFL draft. ... Signed by Bears (June 20, 1998). ... On injured reserve with ankle injury (December 15, 1998-remainder of season). ... Released by Bears (August 30, 1999). ... Signed by San Diego Chargers to practice squad (September 14, 1999). ... Activated (November 20, 1999). ... Granted free agency (March 2, 2001). ... Re-signed by Chargers (April 18, 2001). ... Released by Chargers (May 18, 2001).
PRO STATISTICS: 1998—Fumbled twice for minus four yards. 2000—Fumbled three times and recovered one fumble for minus one yard.
SINGLE GAME HIGHS (regular season): Attempts—41 (November 29, 1998, vs. Tampa Bay); completions—18 (November 29, 1998, vs. Tampa Bay); yards—153 (November 29, 1998, vs. Tampa Bay); and touchdown passes—1 (November 29, 1998, vs. Tampa Bay).
MISCELLANEOUS: Regular-season record as starting NFL quarterback: 0-3.

			PASSING							RUSHING				TOTALS		
Year Team	G	GS	Att.	Cmp.	Pct.	Yds.	TD	Int.	Avg.	Rat.	Att.	Yds.	Avg.	TD	TD	2pt.	Pts.
1998—Chicago NFL	2	1	43	19	44.2	166	1	0	3.86	62.7	4	9	2.3	0	0	0	0
1999—San Diego NFL	1	0	7	5	71.4	78	0	0	11.14	108.0	0	0	0.0	0	0	0	0
2000—San Diego NFL	6	2	53	27	50.9	241	0	2	4.55	47.8	5	20	4.0	0	0	0	0
Pro totals (3 years)	9	3	103	51	49.5	485	1	2	4.71	58.1	9	29	3.2	0	0	0	0

MORGAN, DON   S   VIKINGS

PERSONAL: Born September 18, 1975, in Stockton, Calif. ... 5-11/202.
HIGH SCHOOL: Manteca (Calif.).
COLLEGE: Nevada-Reno.
TRANSACTIONS/CAREER NOTES: Signed as non-drafted free agent by Minnesota Vikings (April 19, 1999). ... Released by Vikings (September 5, 1999). ... Re-signed by Vikings to practice squad (September 6, 1999). ... Activated (December 23, 1999). ... Released by Vikings (August 27, 2000). ... Re-signed by Vikings to practice squad (August 28, 2000). ... Activated (December 5, 2000). ... Released by Vikings (December 19, 2000). ... Re-signed by Vikings to practice squad (December 20, 2000). ... Activated (January 10, 2001).
PLAYING EXPERIENCE: Minnesota NFL, 1999 and 2000. ... Games/Games started: 1999 (2/0), 2000 (2/0). Total: 4/0.
CHAMPIONSHIP GAME EXPERIENCE: Played in NFC championship game (2000 season).

MORRIS, ARIC   S   TITANS

PERSONAL: Born July 22, 1977, in Winston-Salem, N.C. ... 5-10/208.
HIGH SCHOOL: Berkley (Mich.).
COLLEGE: Michigan State.
TRANSACTIONS/CAREER NOTES: Selected by Tennessee Titans in fifth round (135th pick overall) of 2000 NFL draft. ... Signed by Titans (July 5, 2000).
PLAYING EXPERIENCE: Tennessee NFL, 2000. ... Games/Games started: 2000 (15/0).
PRO STATISTICS: 2000—Recovered one fumble.

MORRIS, ROB   LB   COLTS

PERSONAL: Born January 18, 1975, in Nampa, Idaho. ... 6-2/238. ... Full name: Robert Samuel Morris.
HIGH SCHOOL: Nampa (Idaho).
COLLEGE: Brigham Young.
TRANSACTIONS/CAREER NOTES: Selected by Indianapolis Colts in first round (28th pick overall) of 2000 NFL draft. ... Signed by Colts (July 26, 2000). ... On injured reserve with knee injury (October 25, 2000-remainder of season).
PLAYING EXPERIENCE: Indianapolis NFL, 2000. ... Games/Games started: 2000 (7/0).
HONORS: Named linebacker on THE SPORTING NEWS college All-America second team (1999).

Year Team	G	GS	SACKS
2000—Indianapolis NFL	7	0	0.0

MORRIS, SAMMY   RB   BILLS

PERSONAL: Born March 23, 1977, in San Antonio. ... 6-0/228. ... Full name: Samuel Morris III.
HIGH SCHOOL: John Jay (San Antonio).
COLLEGE: Texas Tech.
TRANSACTIONS/CAREER NOTES: Selected by Buffalo Bills in fifth round (156th pick overall) of 2000 NFL draft. ... Signed by Bills (June 21, 2000).
PRO STATISTICS: 2000—Returned one kickoff for 17 yards and recovered one fumble.
SINGLE GAME HIGHS (regular season): Attempts—19 (October 29, 2000, vs. New York Jets); yards—60 (October 15, 2000, vs. San Diego); and rushing touchdowns—1 (December 11, 2000, vs. Indianapolis).

			RUSHING				RECEIVING				TOTALS			
Year Team	G	GS	Att.	Yds.	Avg.	TD	No.	Yds.	Avg.	TD	TD	2pt.	Pts.	Fum.
2000—Buffalo NFL	12	9	93	341	3.7	5	37	268	7.2	1	6	0	36	2

M

MORRIS, SYLVESTER   WR   CHIEFS

PERSONAL: Born October 6, 1977, in New Orleans. ... 6-3/206.
HIGH SCHOOL: McDonogh 35 (New Orleans).
COLLEGE: Jackson State.
TRANSACTIONS/CAREER NOTES: Selected by Kansas City Chiefs in first round (21st pick overall) of 2000 NFL draft. ... Signed by Chiefs (August 9, 2000).
PRO STATISTICS: 2000—Completed only pass attempt for 31 yards and fumbled three times.
SINGLE GAME HIGHS (regular season): Receptions—6 (November 5, 2000, vs. Oakland); yards—112 (September 17, 2000, vs. San Diego); and touchdown receptions—3 (September 17, 2000, vs. San Diego).
STATISTICAL PLATEAUS: 100-yard receiving games: 2000 (2).

				RECEIVING		
Year Team	G	GS	No.	Yds.	Avg.	TD
2000—Kansas City NFL	15	14	48	678	14.1	3

MORROW, HAROLD   FB   VIKINGS

PERSONAL: Born February 24, 1973, in Maplesville, Ala. ... 5-11/232. ... Full name: Harold Morrow Jr. ... Cousin of Tommie Agee, fullback with Seattle Seahawks (1988), Kansas City Chiefs (1989) and Dallas Cowboys (1990-94).
HIGH SCHOOL: Maplesville (Ala.).
COLLEGE: Auburn.
TRANSACTIONS/CAREER NOTES: Signed as non-drafted free agent by Dallas Cowboys (April 25, 1996). ... Claimed on waivers by Minnesota Vikings (August 26, 1996). ... Granted free agency (February 12, 1999). ... Re-signed by Vikings (April 23, 1999). ... Granted unconditional free agency (February 11, 2000). ... Re-signed by Vikings (March 7, 2000).
PLAYING EXPERIENCE: Minnesota NFL, 1996-2000. ... Games/Games started: 1996 (8/0), 1997 (16/0), 1998 (11/0), 1999 (16/0), 2000 (16/0). Total: 67/0.
CHAMPIONSHIP GAME EXPERIENCE: Played in NFC championship game (1998 and 2000 seasons).
PRO STATISTICS: 1996—Returned six kickoffs for 117 yards. 1997—Returned five kickoffs for 99 yards. 1998—Rushed three times for seven yards and recovered one fumble. 1999—Rushed twice for one yard, returned one kickoff for 20 yards and recovered one fumble. 2000—Rushed once for two yards, returned one kickoff for 17 yards and recovered one fumble.
SINGLE GAME HIGHS (regular season): Attempts—3 (December 20, 1998, vs. Jacksonville); yards—7 (December 20, 1998, vs. Jacksonville); and rushing touchdowns—0.

MORTON, CHAD   RB/PR/KR   SAINTS

PERSONAL: Born April 4, 1977, in Torrance, Calif. ... 5-8/186. ... Brother of Johnnie Morton, wide receiver, Detroit Lions; and half brother of Michael Morton, running back with Tampa Bay Buccaneers (1982-84), Washington Redskins (1985) and Seattle Seahawks (1987).
HIGH SCHOOL: South Torrance (Calif.).
COLLEGE: Southern California.
TRANSACTIONS/CAREER NOTES: Selected by New Orleans Saints in fifth round (166th pick overall) of 2000 NFL draft. ... Signed by Saints (July 11, 2000).
PRO STATISTICS: 2000—Fumbled twice and recovered one fumble.
SINGLE GAME HIGHS (regular season): Attempts—12 (November 26, 2000, vs. St. Louis); yards—45 (November 19, 2000, vs. Oakland); and rushing touchdowns—0.

			RUSHING				RECEIVING				PUNT RETURNS				KICKOFF RETURNS				TOTALS		
Year Team	G	GS	Att.	Yds.	Avg.	TD	No.	Yds.	Avg.	TD	No.	Yds.	Avg.	TD	No.	Yds.	Avg.	TD	TD	2pt.	Pts.
2000—New Orleans NFL	16	3	36	136	3.8	0	30	213	7.1	0	30	278	9.3	0	44	1029	23.4	0	0	0	0

MORTON, JOHNNIE   WR   LIONS

PERSONAL: Born October 7, 1971, in Inglewood, Calif. ... 6-0/190. ... Full name: Johnnie James Morton. ... Brother of Chad Morton, running back, New Orleans Saints; half brother of Michael Morton, running back with Tampa Bay Buccaneers (1982-84), Washington Redskins (1985) and Seattle Seahawks (1987).
HIGH SCHOOL: South Torrance (Calif.).
COLLEGE: Southern California (degree in communications).
TRANSACTIONS/CAREER NOTES: Selected by Detroit Lions in first round (21st pick overall) of 1994 NFL draft. ... Signed by Lions (July 18, 1994).
HONORS: Named wide receiver on THE SPORTING NEWS college All-America first team (1993).
PRO STATISTICS: 1994—Recovered one fumble. 1995—Returned seven punts for 48 yards.
SINGLE GAME HIGHS (regular season): Receptions—10 (January 2, 2000, vs. Minnesota); yards—174 (September 22, 1996, vs. Chicago); and touchdown receptions—2 (January 2, 2000, vs. Minnesota).
STATISTICAL PLATEAUS: 100-yard receiving games: 1995 (1), 1996 (2), 1997 (3), 1998 (3), 1999 (5). Total: 14.

			RUSHING				RECEIVING				KICKOFF RETURNS				TOTALS			
Year Team	G	GS	Att.	Yds.	Avg.	TD	No.	Yds.	Avg.	TD	No.	Yds.	Avg.	TD	TD	2pt.	Pts.	Fum.
1994—Detroit NFL	14	0	0	0	0.0	0	3	39	13.0	1	4	143	35.8	1	2	0	12	1
1995—Detroit NFL	16	14	3	33	11.0	0	44	590	13.4	8	18	390	21.7	0	8	0	48	1
1996—Detroit NFL	16	15	9	35	3.9	0	55	714	13.0	6	0	0	0.0	0	6	0	36	1
1997—Detroit NFL	16	16	3	33	11.0	0	80	1057	13.2	6	0	0	0.0	0	6	0	36	2
1998—Detroit NFL	16	16	1	11	11.0	0	69	1028	14.9	2	0	0	0.0	0	2	0	12	0
1999—Detroit NFL	16	12	0	0	0.0	0	80	1129	14.1	5	1	22	22.0	0	5	0	30	0
2000—Detroit NFL	16	16	4	25	6.3	0	61	788	12.9	3	0	0	0.0	0	3	1	20	1
Pro totals (7 years)	110	89	20	137	6.9	0	392	5345	13.6	31	23	555	24.1	1	32	1	194	6

MORTON, MIKE   LB

PERSONAL: Born March 28, 1972, in Kannapolis, N.C. ... 6-4/235. ... Full name: Michael Anthony Morton Jr.
HIGH SCHOOL: A.L. Brown (Kannapolis, N.C.).
COLLEGE: North Carolina.
TRANSACTIONS/CAREER NOTES: Selected by Los Angeles Raiders in fourth round (118th pick overall) of 1995 NFL draft. ... Signed by Raiders (July 21, 1995). ... Raiders' franchise moved to Oakland (July 21, 1995). ... Granted unconditional free agency (February 12, 1999). ... Signed by Green Bay Packers (April 30, 1999). ... Traded by Packers to St. Louis Rams for seventh-round pick (traded to San Francisco) in 2001 draft (July 23, 1999). ... Granted unconditional free agency (February 11, 2000). ... Signed by Packers (May 5, 2000). ... Granted unconditional free agency (March 2, 2001).
PLAYING EXPERIENCE: Oakland NFL, 1995-1998; St. Louis NFL, 1999; Green Bay NFL, 2000. ... Games/Games started: 1995 (12/0), 1996 (16/6), 1997 (11/11), 1998 (16/0), 1999 (16/0), 2000 (16/0). Total: 87/17.
CHAMPIONSHIP GAME EXPERIENCE: Played in NFC championship game (1999 season). ... Member of Super Bowl championship team (1999 season).
PRO STATISTICS: 1995—Recovered one fumble. 1996—Intercepted two passes for 13 yards and credited with one sack. 1997—Returned one kickoff for 14 yards and recovered one fumble. 1998—Returned one kickoff for three yards and recovered two fumbles. 2000—Returned one kickoff for 13 yards.

MOSS, RANDY   WR   VIKINGS

PERSONAL: Born February 13, 1977, in Rand, W.Va. ... 6-4/204. ... Half brother of Eric Moss, offensive lineman with Minnesota Vikings (1997-99).
HIGH SCHOOL: DuPont (Belle, W.Va.).
COLLEGE: Florida State (did not play), then Marshall.
TRANSACTIONS/CAREER NOTES: Selected after sophomore season by Minnesota Vikings in first round (21st pick overall) of 1998 NFL draft. ... Signed by Minnesota Vikings (July 26, 1998).
CHAMPIONSHIP GAME EXPERIENCE: Played in NFC championship game (1998 and 2000 seasons).
HONORS: Fred Biletnikoff Award winner (1997). ... Named wide receiver on THE SPORTING NEWS college All-America first team (1997). ... Named NFL Rookie of the Year by THE SPORTING NEWS (1998). ... Named wide receiver on THE SPORTING NEWS NFL All-Pro team (1998 and 2000). ... Played in Pro Bowl (1998 and 1999 seasons). ... Named Outstanding Player of Pro Bowl (1999). ... Named to play in Pro Bowl (2000 season); replaced by Joe Horn due to injury.
RECORDS: Holds NFL rookie-season record for most touchdowns—17 (1998).
PRO STATISTICS: 1998—Rushed once for four yards. 1999—Rushed four times for 43 yards and completed only pass attempt for 27 yards and a touchdown. 2000—Rushed three times for five yards.
SINGLE GAME HIGHS (regular season): Receptions—12 (November 14, 1999, vs. Chicago); yards—204 (November 14, 1999, vs. Chicago); and touchdown receptions—3 (October 1, 2000, vs. Detroit).
STATISTICAL PLATEAUS: 100-yard receiving games: 1998 (4), 1999 (7), 2000 (8). Total: 19.

			RECEIVING				PUNT RETURNS				TOTALS			
Year Team	G	GS	No.	Yds.	Avg.	TD	No.	Yds.	Avg.	TD	TD	2pt.	Pts.	Fum.
1998—Minnesota NFL	16	11	69	1313	‡19.0	*17	1	0	0.0	0	‡17	†2	106	2
1999—Minnesota NFL	16	16	80	‡1413	17.7	11	17	162	9.5	∞1	12	0	72	3
2000—Minnesota NFL	16	16	77	1437	18.7	*15	0	0	0.0	0	15	1	92	2
Pro totals (3 years)	48	43	226	4163	18.4	43	18	162	9.0	1	44	3	270	7

MOULDS, ERIC   WR   BILLS

PERSONAL: Born July 17, 1973, in Lucedale, Miss. ... 6-2/204. ... Full name: Eric Shannon Moulds.
HIGH SCHOOL: George County (Lucedale, Miss.).
COLLEGE: Mississippi State.
TRANSACTIONS/CAREER NOTES: Selected by Buffalo Bills in first round (24th pick overall) of 1996 NFL draft. ... Signed by Bills (July 16, 1996).
HONORS: Played in Pro Bowl (1998 and 2000 seasons).
POST SEASON RECORDS: Holds NFL postseason single-game record for most yards receiving—240 (January 2, 1999, vs. Miami).
PRO STATISTICS: 1997—Returned two punts for 20 yards and recovered one fumble. 2000—Recovered one fumble.
SINGLE GAME HIGHS (regular season): Receptions—12 (October 22, 2000, vs. Minnesota); yards—196 (December 6, 1998, vs. Cincinnati); and touchdown receptions—2 (December 6, 1998, vs. Cincinnati).
STATISTICAL PLATEAUS: 100-yard receiving games: 1998 (4), 1999 (3), 2000 (7). Total: 14.

			RUSHING				RECEIVING				KICKOFF RETURNS				TOTALS		
Year Team	G	GS	Att.	Yds.	Avg.	TD	No.	Yds.	Avg.	TD	No.	Yds.	Avg.	TD	TD	2pt.	Pts. Fum.
1996—Buffalo NFL	16	5	12	44	3.7	0	20	279	14.0	2	52	1205	23.2	▲1	3	0	18 1
1997—Buffalo NFL	16	8	4	59	14.8	0	29	294	10.1	0	43	921	21.4	0	0	1	2 3
1998—Buffalo NFL	16	15	0	0	0.0	0	67	§1368	20.4	9	0	0	0.0	0	9	0	54 0
1999—Buffalo NFL	14	14	1	1	1.0	0	65	994	15.3	7	0	0	0.0	0	7	0	42 1
2000—Buffalo NFL	16	16	2	24	12.0	0	94	1326	14.1	5	0	0	0.0	0	5	0	30 1
Pro totals (5 years)	78	58	19	128	6.7	0	275	4261	15.5	23	95	2126	22.4	1	24	1	146 6

MUHAMMAD, MUHSIN   WR   PANTHERS

PERSONAL: Born May 5, 1973, in Lansing, Mich. ... 6-2/217. ... Full name: Muhsin Muhammad II. ... Name pronounced moo-SIN moo-HAH-med.
HIGH SCHOOL: Waverly (Lansing, Mich.).
COLLEGE: Michigan State.
TRANSACTIONS/CAREER NOTES: Selected by Carolina Panthers in second round (43rd pick overall) of 1996 NFL draft. ... Signed by Panthers (July 23, 1996).
CHAMPIONSHIP GAME EXPERIENCE: Played in NFC championship game (1996 season).
HONORS: Played in Pro Bowl (1999 season).

M

PRO STATISTICS: 1996—Rushed once for minus one yard. 1998—Recovered one fumble. 2000—Rushed twice for 12 yards, fumbled once and recovered one fumble.
SINGLE GAME HIGHS (regular season): Receptions—11 (November 27, 2000, vs. Green Bay); yards—192 (September 13, 1998, vs. New Orleans); and touchdown receptions—3 (December 18, 1999, vs. San Francisco).
STATISTICAL PLATEAUS: 100-yard receiving games: 1998 (3), 1999 (5), 2000 (5). Total: 13.
MISCELLANEOUS: Holds Carolina Panthers all-time records for most receiving yards (4,101) and receptions (318).

				RECEIVING				TOTALS		
Year Team	G	GS	No.	Yds.	Avg.	TD	TD	2pt.	Pts.	Fum.
1996—Carolina NFL	9	5	25	407	16.3	1	1	0	6	0
1997—Carolina NFL	13	5	27	317	11.7	0	0	1	2	0
1998—Carolina NFL	16	16	68	941	13.8	6	6	1	38	2
1999—Carolina NFL	15	15	‡96	1253	13.1	8	8	0	48	1
2000—Carolina NFL	16	16	†102	1183	11.6	6	6	0	36	1
Pro totals (5 years)	69	57	318	4101	12.9	21	21	2	130	4

MUHAMMAD, MUSTAFAH   DB   COLTS

PERSONAL: Born October 19, 1973, in Los Angeles. ... 5-9/180. ... Full name: Mustafah Jaleel Muhammad. ... Formerly known as Steve Wilson.
HIGH SCHOOL: Moreno Valley (Calif.).
JUNIOR COLLEGE: Shasta College (Calif.), then Chaffey College (Calif.).
COLLEGE: Fresno State.
TRANSACTIONS/CAREER NOTES: Signed by B.C. Lions of CFL (March 11, 1998). ... Signed as non-drafted free agent by Indianapolis Colts (February 2, 1999). ... On suspended list for violating league personal conduct policy (September 20-October 1, 2000).
HONORS: Named CFL Most Outstanding Rookie (1998).
PRO STATISTICS: CFL: 1998—Recovered three fumbles for 60 yards and one touchdown.

			INTERCEPTIONS				PUNT RETURNS				KICKOFF RETURNS				TOTALS			
Year Team	G	GS	No.	Yds.	Avg.	TD	No.	Yds.	Avg.	TD	No.	Yds.	Avg.	TD	TD	2pt.	Pts.	Fum.
1998—British Columbia CFL	17	...	10	165	16.5	0	6	51	8.5	0	1	56	56.0	0	1	0	6	1
1999—Indianapolis NFL	11	1	0	0	0.0	0	0	0	0.0	0	2	41	20.5	0	0	0	0	0
2000—Indianapolis NFL	13	3	1	40	40.0	1	2	4	2.0	0	2	45	22.5	0	1	0	6	1
CFL totals (1 year)	17	...	10	165	16.5	0	6	51	8.5	0	1	56	56.0	0	1	0	6	1
NFL totals (2 years)	24	4	1	40	40.0	1	2	4	2.0	0	4	86	21.5	0	1	0	6	1
Pro totals (3 years)	41	...	11	205	18.6	1	8	55	6.9	0	5	142	28.4	0	2	0	12	2

MULITALO, EDWIN   G   RAVENS

PERSONAL: Born September 1, 1974, in Daly City, Calif. ... 6-3/340. ... Full name: Edwin Moliki Mulitalo. ... Name pronounced moo-lih-TAHL-oh.
HIGH SCHOOL: Jefferson (Daly City, Calif.).
JUNIOR COLLEGE: Ricks College (Idaho).
COLLEGE: Arizona.
TRANSACTIONS/CAREER NOTES: Selected by Baltimore Ravens in fourth round (129th pick overall) of 1999 NFL draft. ... Signed by Ravens (July 29, 1999).
PLAYING EXPERIENCE: Baltimore NFL, 1999 and 2000. ... Games/Games started: 1999 (10/8), 2000 (16/16). Total: 26/24.
CHAMPIONSHIP GAME EXPERIENCE: Played in AFC championship game (2000 season). ... Member of Super Bowl championship team (2000 season).
PRO STATISTICS: 2000—Recovered two fumbles.

M

MURPHY, FRANK   WR   BUCCANEERS

PERSONAL: Born February 11, 1977, in Callahan, Fla. ... 6-0/206.
HIGH SCHOOL: West Nassau (Callahan, Fla.).
JUNIOR COLLEGE: Itawamba Community College (Miss.), then Garden City (Kan.) Commmunity College.
COLLEGE: Kansas State.
TRANSACTIONS/CAREER NOTES: Selected by Chicago Bears in sixth round (170th pick overall) of 2000 NFL draft. ... Signed by Bears (May 31, 2000). ... Released by Bears (August 27, 2000). ... Signed by Tampa Bay Buccaneers to practice squad (August 28, 2000). ... Activated (November 22, 2000).
PLAYING EXPERIENCE: Tampa Bay NFL, 2000. ... Games/Games started: 2000 (1/0).
PRO STATISTICS: 2000—Returned two kickoffs for 24 yards.

MURRAY, EDDIE   K

PERSONAL: Born August 29, 1956, in Halifax, Nova Scotia. ... 5-11/195. ... Full name: Edward Peter Murray. ... Cousin of Mike Rogers, center with Edmonton Oilers, New England/Hartford Whalers and New York Rangers of World Hockey Association and NHL (1974-75 through 1985-86).
HIGH SCHOOL: Spectrum (Victoria, B.C.).
COLLEGE: Tulane (degree in education, 1980).
TRANSACTIONS/CAREER NOTES: Selected by Detroit Lions in seventh round (166th pick overall) of 1980 NFL draft. ... Signed by Lions for 1980 season. ... On suspended list (September 10-November 20, 1982). ... On injured reserve with hip injury (October 12-November 20, 1990). ... Granted unconditional free agency (February 1-April 1, 1991). ... Re-signed by Lions for 1991 season. ... Granted unconditional free agency (February 1-April 1, 1992). ... Rights relinquished by Lions (April 29, 1992). ... Signed by Kansas City Chiefs (October 24, 1992). ... Released by Chiefs (October 28, 1992). ... Signed by Tampa Bay Buccaneers (November 10, 1992). ... Granted unconditional free agency (March 1, 1993). ... Re-signed by Buccaneers for 1993 season. ... Released by Buccaneers (August 23, 1993). ... Signed by Dallas Cowboys (September 14, 1993). ... Granted unconditional free agency (February 17, 1994). ... Signed by Philadelphia Eagles (March 22, 1994). ...

Released by Eagles (July 23, 1995). ... Signed by Washington Redskins (August 8, 1995). ... Granted unconditional free agency (February 16, 1996). ... Re-signed by Redskins (May 15, 1996). ... Released by Redskins (August 25, 1996). ... Signed by Minnesota Vikings (September 24, 1997). ... Granted unconditional free agency (February 13, 1998). ... Signed by Detroit Lions (June 2, 1999). ... Announced retirement (June 3, 1999). ... Signed by Cowboys (December 8, 1999). ... Granted unconditional free agency (February 11, 2000). ... Signed by Washington Redskins (November 9, 2000). ... Granted unconditional free agency (March 2, 2001).

CHAMPIONSHIP GAME EXPERIENCE: Played in NFC championship game (1991 and 1993 seasons). ... Member of Super Bowl championship team (1993 season).

HONORS: Played in Pro Bowl (1980 and 1989 seasons). ... Named Outstanding Player of Pro Bowl (1980 season).

PRO STATISTICS: 1986—Punted once for 37 yards. 1987—Punted four times for 155 yards (38.8-yard average).

				KICKING				
Year Team	G	XPM	XPA	FGM	FGA	Lg.	50+	Pts.
1980—Detroit NFL	16	35	36	*27	*42	52	1-4	‡116
1981—Detroit NFL	16	46	46	25	35	53	3-4	†121
1982—Detroit NFL	7	16	16	11	12	49	0-0	49
1983—Detroit NFL	16	38	38	25	32	54	3-4	113
1984—Detroit NFL	16	31	31	20	27	52	1-4	91
1985—Detroit NFL	16	31	33	26	31	51	2-3	109
1986—Detroit NFL	16	31	32	18	25	52	2-5	85
1987—Detroit NFL	12	21	21	20	32	53	1-2	81
1988—Detroit NFL	16	22	23	20	21	48	0-1	82
1989—Detroit NFL	16	36	36	20	21	50	1-1	96
1990—Detroit NFL	11	34	34	13	19	47	0-2	73
1991—Detroit NFL	16	40	40	19	28	50	2-4	97
1992—Kansas City NFL	1	0	0	1	1	52	1-1	3
—Tampa Bay NFL	7	13	13	4	8	47	0-0	25
1993—Dallas NFL	14	38	38	28	33	52	3-5	122
1994—Philadelphia NFL	16	33	33	21	25	42	0-0	96
1995—Washington NFL	16	33	33	27	36	52	1-2	114
1996—				Did not play.				
1997—Minnesota NFL	12	23	24	12	17	49	0-1	59
1998—				Did not play.				
1999—Dallas NFL	4	10	10	7	9	40	0-0	31
2000—Washington NFL	6	7	8	8	12	47	0-0	31
Pro totals (19 years)	250	538	545	352	466	54	21-43	1594

MURRELL, ADRIAN   RB   PANTHERS

PERSONAL: Born October 16, 1970, in Fayetteville, N.C. ... 5-11/210. ... Full name: Adrian Bryan Murrell.
HIGH SCHOOL: Leilehua (Wahiawa, Hawaii).
COLLEGE: West Virginia.
TRANSACTIONS/CAREER NOTES: Selected by New York Jets in fifth round (120th pick overall) of 1993 NFL draft. ... Signed by Jets (July 22, 1993). ... Granted free agency (February 16, 1996). ... Re-signed by Jets (April 21, 1996). ... Traded by Jets with seventh-round pick (DE Jomo Cousins) in 1998 draft to Arizona Cardinals for third-round pick (traded to St. Louis) in 1998 draft (April 7, 1998). ... Granted unconditional free agency (February 11, 2000). ... Signed by Washington Redskins (March 22, 2000). ... Granted unconditional free agency (March 2, 2001). ... Signed by Carolina Panthers (May 3, 2001).
PRO STATISTICS: 1993—Recovered two fumbles. 1995—Recovered two fumbles. 1996—Recovered two fumbles for minus 16 yards. 1997—Recovered two fumbles. 1998—Recovered one fumble.
SINGLE GAME HIGHS (regular season): Attempts—40 (September 28, 1997, vs. Cincinnati); yards—199 (October 27, 1996, vs. Arizona); and rushing touchdowns—2 (November 10, 1996, vs. New England).
STATISTICAL PLATEAUS: 100-yard rushing games: 1995 (1), 1996 (5), 1997 (3), 1998 (3). Total: 12.

			RUSHING				RECEIVING				KICKOFF RETURNS				TOTALS		
Year Team	G	GS	Att.	Yds.	Avg.	TD	No.	Yds.	Avg.	TD	No.	Yds.	Avg.	TD	TD	2pt.	Pts. Fum.
1993—New York Jets NFL	16	0	34	157	4.6	1	5	12	2.4	0	23	342	14.9	0	1	0	6 4
1994—New York Jets NFL	10	1	33	160	4.8	0	7	76	10.9	0	14	268	19.1	0	0	0	0 1
1995—New York Jets NFL	15	9	192	795	4.1	1	71	465	6.5	2	1	5	5.0	0	3	0	18 2
1996—New York Jets NFL	16	16	301	1249	4.1	6	17	81	4.8	1	0	0	0.0	0	7	0	42 6
1997—New York Jets NFL	16	15	300	1086	3.6	7	27	106	3.9	0	0	0	0.0	0	7	0	42 4
1998—Arizona NFL	15	14	274	1042	3.8	8	18	169	9.4	2	0	0	0.0	0	10	0	60 6
1999—Arizona NFL	16	12	193	553	2.9	0	49	335	6.8	0	0	0	0.0	0	0	0	0 4
2000—Washington NFL	15	0	20	50	2.5	0	16	93	5.8	0	12	214	17.8	0	0	0	0 1
Pro totals (8 years)	119	67	1347	5092	3.8	23	210	1337	6.4	5	50	829	16.6	0	28	0	168 28

MYERS, BOBBY   S   TITANS

PERSONAL: Born October 11, 1976, in New Haven, Conn. ... 6-1/189. ... Full name: Bobby Jermaine Myers.
HIGH SCHOOL: Hamden (Conn.).
COLLEGE: Wisconsin.
TRANSACTIONS/CAREER NOTES: Selected by Tennessee Titans in fourth round (124th pick overall) of 2000 NFL draft. ... Signed by Titans (July 7, 2000).
PLAYING EXPERIENCE: Tennessee NFL, 2000. ... Games/Games started: 2000 (16/1).

MYERS, GREG   S

PERSONAL: Born September 30, 1972, in Tampa. ... 6-1/202. ... Full name: Gregory Jay Myers.
HIGH SCHOOL: Windsor (Colo.).
COLLEGE: Colorado State.

M

TRANSACTIONS/CAREER NOTES: Selected by Cincinnati Bengals in fifth round (144th pick overall) of 1996 NFL draft. ... Signed by Bengals (July 2, 1996). ... Granted free agency (February 12, 1999). ... Re-signed by Bengals (May 6, 1999). ... Granted unconditional free agency (February 11, 2000). ... Re-signed by Bengals (April 3, 2000). ... Released by Bengals (August 18, 2000). ... Signed by Dallas Cowboys (November 8, 2000). ... On injured reserve with knee injury (December 19, 2000-remainder of season). ... Granted unconditional free agency (March 2, 2001).

HONORS: Named defensive back on The Sporting News college All-America first team (1994 and 1995). ... Jim Thorpe Award winner (1995).

PRO STATISTICS: 1996—Fumbled once. 1997—Recovered two fumbles. 1998—Recovered one fumble. 1999—Recovered one fumble for 21 yards.

				INTERCEPTIONS				PUNT RETURNS				TOTALS		
Year Team	G	GS	No.	Yds.	Avg.	TD	No.	Yds.	Avg.	TD	TD	2pt.	Pts.	Fum.
1996—Cincinnati NFL	14	0	2	10	5.0	0	9	51	5.7	0	0	0	0	1
1997—Cincinnati NFL	16	14	1	25	25.0	0	26	201	7.7	0	0	0	0	3
1998—Cincinnati NFL	16	16	0	0	0.0	0	0	0	0.0	0	0	0	0	0
1999—Cincinnati NFL	12	4	1	0	0.0	0	0	0	0.0	0	0	0	0	0
2000—Dallas NFL	6	4	0	0	0.0	0	0	0	0.0	0	0	0	0	0
Pro totals (5 years)	64	38	4	35	8.8	0	35	252	7.2	0	0	0	0	4

MYERS, MICHAEL　　　　DL　　　　COWBOYS

PERSONAL: Born January 20, 1976, in Vicksburg, Miss. ... 6-2/288.
HIGH SCHOOL: Vicksburg (Miss.).
JUNIOR COLLEGE: Hinds Community College (Miss.).
COLLEGE: Alabama.
TRANSACTIONS/CAREER NOTES: Selected by Dallas Cowboys in fourth round (100th pick overall) of 1998 NFL draft. ... Signed by Cowboys (July 10, 1998). ... Granted free agency (March 2, 2001).
HONORS: Named defensive tackle on The Sporting News college All-America first team (1996).
PRO STATISTICS: 2000—Recovered one fumble.

Year Team	G	GS	SACKS
1998—Dallas NFL	16	1	3.0
1999—Dallas NFL	6	0	0.0
2000—Dallas NFL	13	7	0.0
Pro totals (3 years)	35	8	3.0

MYSLINSKI, TOM　　　　G　　　　STEELERS

PERSONAL: Born December 7, 1968, in Rome, N.Y. ... 6-3/293. ... Full name: Thomas Joseph Myslinski.
HIGH SCHOOL: Free Academy (Owego, N.Y.).
COLLEGE: Tennessee (degree in exercise physiology).
TRANSACTIONS/CAREER NOTES: Selected by Dallas Cowboys in fourth round (109th pick overall) of 1992 NFL draft. ... Signed by Cowboys (July 15, 1992). ... Released by Cowboys (August 31, 1992). ... Re-signed by Cowboys to practice squad (September 1, 1992). ... Signed by Cleveland Browns off Cowboys practice squad (September 8, 1992). ... Inactive for three games with Browns (1992). ... Released by Browns (October 9, 1992). ... Re-signed by Browns to practice squad (October 14, 1992). ... Released by Browns (October 17, 1992). ... Signed by Washington Redskins to practice squad (October 21, 1992). ... Activated (November 11, 1992). ... Released by Redskins (November 28, 1992). ... Signed by Buffalo Bills (April 6, 1993). ... Released by Bills (August 30, 1993). ... Re-signed by Bills (August 31, 1993). ... Released by Bills (November 15, 1993). ... Signed by Chicago Bears (November 30, 1993). ... Selected by Jacksonville Jaguars from Bears in NFL expansion draft (February 15, 1995). ... Granted free agency (February 17, 1995). ... Re-signed by Jaguars (April 19, 1995). ... Granted free agency (February 16, 1996). ... Signed by Pittsburgh Steelers (April 24, 1996). ... Released by Steelers (August 24, 1996). ... Re-signed by Steelers (August 27, 1996). ... Granted unconditional free agency (February 13, 1998). ... Signed by Indianapolis Colts (February 19, 1998). ... Released by Colts (July 21, 1999). ... Signed by Cowboys (September 22, 1999). ... Granted unconditional free agency (February 11, 2000). ... Signed by Steelers (April 10, 2000).
PLAYING EXPERIENCE: Washington NFL, 1992; Buffalo (1)-Chicago (1) NFL, 1993; Chicago NFL, 1994; Jacksonville NFL, 1995; Pittsburgh NFL, 1996, 1997 and 2000; Indianapolis NFL, 1998; Dallas NFL, 1999. ... Games/Games started: 1992 (1/0), 1993 (Buf.-1/0; Chi.-1/0; Total: 2/0), 1994 (4/0), 1995 (9/9), 1996 (8/6), 1997 (16/7), 1998 (1/0), 1999 (10/2), 2000 (6/0). Total: 57/24.
CHAMPIONSHIP GAME EXPERIENCE: Played in AFC championship game (1997 season).
PRO STATISTICS: 2000—Recovered one fumble.

NAEOLE, CHRIS　　　　G　　　　SAINTS

PERSONAL: Born December 25, 1974, in Kailua, Hawaii. ... 6-3/313. ... Full name: Chris Kealoha Naeole. ... Name pronounced NAY-oh-lee.
HIGH SCHOOL: Kahuka (Kaaava, Hawaii).
COLLEGE: Colorado.
TRANSACTIONS/CAREER NOTES: Selected by New Orleans Saints in first round (10th pick overall) of 1997 NFL draft. ... Signed by Saints (July 17, 1997). ... On injured reserve with ankle injury (October 17, 1997-remainder of season).
PLAYING EXPERIENCE: New Orleans NFL, 1997-2000. ... Games/Games started: 1997 (4/0), 1998 (16/16), 1999 (15/15), 2000 (16/16). Total: 51/47.
HONORS: Named guard on The Sporting News college All-America second team (1996).
PRO STATISTICS: 1998—Recovered one fumble.

NAILS, JAMIE　　　　OT

PERSONAL: Born June 3, 1975, in Baxley, Ga. ... 6-6/354. ... Full name: Jamie Marcellus Nails.
HIGH SCHOOL: Appling County (Baxley, Ga.).
COLLEGE: Florida A&M.

TRANSACTIONS/CAREER NOTES: Selected by Buffalo Bills in fourth round (120th pick overall) of 1997 NFL draft. ... Signed by Bills (July 2, 1997). ... Granted free agency (February 11, 2000). ... Re-signed by Bills (April 28, 2000) ... Granted unconditional free agency (March 2, 2001).
PLAYING EXPERIENCE: Buffalo NFL, 1997-2000. ... Games/Games started: 1997 (2/0), 1998 (15/3), 1999 (16/3), 2000 (16/16). Total: 49/22.
PRO STATISTICS: 2000—Recovered one fumble.

NALEN, TOM   C   BRONCOS

PERSONAL: Born May 13, 1971, in Foxboro, Mass. ... 6-3/286. ... Full name: Thomas Andrew Nalen.
HIGH SCHOOL: Foxboro (Mass.).
COLLEGE: Boston College.
TRANSACTIONS/CAREER NOTES: Selected by Denver Broncos in seventh round (218th pick overall) of 1994 NFL draft. ... Signed by Broncos July 15, 1994). ... Released by Broncos (September 2, 1994). ... Re-signed by Broncos to practice squad (September 6, 1994). ... Activated October 7, 1994).
PLAYING EXPERIENCE: Denver NFL, 1994-2000. ... Games/Games started: 1994 (7/1), 1995 (15/15), 1996 (16/16), 1997 (16/16), 1998 (16/16), 1999 (16/16), 2000 (16/16). Total: 102/96.
CHAMPIONSHIP GAME EXPERIENCE: Played in AFC championship game (1997 and 1998 seasons). ... Member of Super Bowl championship team (1997 and 1998 seasons).
HONORS: Played in Pro Bowl (1997-1999 seasons). ... Named center on THE SPORTING NEWS NFL All-Pro team (1999 and 2000). ... Named to play in Pro Bowl (2000 season); replaced by Tim Ruddy due to injury.
PRO STATISTICS: 1997—Caught one pass for minus one yard. 2000—Fumbled once for minus two yards.

NAVIES, HANNIBAL   LB   PANTHERS

PERSONAL: Born July 19, 1977, in Chicago. ... 6-2/240. ... Full name: Hannibal Carter Navies. ... Name pronounced NAY-vees.
HIGH SCHOOL: St. Patrick (Chicago), then Berkeley (Oakland).
COLLEGE: Colorado.
TRANSACTIONS/CAREER NOTES: Selected by Carolina Panthers in fourth round (100th pick overall) of 1999 NFL draft. ... Signed by Panthers July 21, 1999).
PLAYING EXPERIENCE: Carolina NFL, 1999 and 2000. ... Games/Games started: 1999 (9/0), 2000 (13/1). Total: 22/1.
PRO STATISTICS: 2000—Intercepted one pass for no yards and credited with two sacks.

NEAL, LORENZO   FB   BENGALS

PERSONAL: Born December 27, 1970, in Hanford, Calif. ... 5-11/240. ... Full name: Lorenzo LaVonne Neal.
HIGH SCHOOL: Lemoore (Calif.).
COLLEGE: Fresno State.
TRANSACTIONS/CAREER NOTES: Selected by New Orleans Saints in fourth round (89th pick overall) of 1993 NFL draft. ... Signed by Saints July 15, 1993). ... On injured reserve with ankle injury (September 15, 1993-remainder of season). ... Granted free agency (February 16, 1996). ... Re-signed by Saints (July 1, 1996). ... Granted unconditional free agency (February 14, 1997). ... Signed by New York Jets (March 1, 1997). ... Traded by Jets to Tampa Bay Buccaneers for fifth-round pick (TE Blake Spence) in 1998 draft (March 12, 1998). ... Released by Buccaneers (February 11, 1999). ... Signed by Tennessee Titans (March 2, 1999). ... Released by Titans (March 1, 2001). ... Signed by Cincinnati Bengals (May 7, 2001).
CHAMPIONSHIP GAME EXPERIENCE: Played in AFC championship game (1999 season). ... Played in Super Bowl XXXIV (1999 season).
PRO STATISTICS: 1994—Returned one kickoff for 17 yards. 1995—Returned two kickoffs for 28 yards. 1996—Recovered two fumbles. 1997—Returned two kickoffs for 22 yards. 1999—Returned two kickoffs for 15 yards. 2000—Returned one kickoff for 15 yards.
SINGLE GAME HIGHS (regular season): Attempts—14 (October 9, 1994, vs. Chicago); yards—89 (September 5, 1993, vs. Houston); and rushing touchdowns—1 (October 10, 1999, vs. Baltimore).

			RUSHING				RECEIVING				TOTALS			
Year Team	G	GS	Att.	Yds.	Avg.	TD	No.	Yds.	Avg.	TD	TD	2pt.	Pts.	Fum.
1993—New Orleans NFL	2	2	21	175	8.3	1	0	0	0.0	0	1	0	6	1
1994—New Orleans NFL	16	7	30	90	3.0	1	2	9	4.5	0	1	0	6	1
1995—New Orleans NFL	16	7	5	3	0.6	0	12	123	10.3	1	1	0	6	2
1996—New Orleans NFL	16	11	21	58	2.8	1	31	194	6.3	1	2	0	12	1
1997—New York Jets NFL	16	3	10	28	2.8	0	8	40	5.0	1	1	0	6	0
1998—Tampa Bay NFL	16	1	5	25	5.0	0	5	14	2.8	1	1	0	6	0
1999—Tennessee NFL	16	14	2	1	0.5	1	7	27	3.9	2	3	0	18	0
2000—Tennessee NFL	16	6	1	-2	-2.0	0	9	31	3.4	2	2	0	12	0
Pro totals (8 years)	114	51	95	378	4.0	4	74	438	5.9	8	12	0	72	5

NEDNEY, JOE   K   TITANS

PERSONAL: Born March 22, 1973, in San Jose, Calif. ... 6-5/220. ... Full name: Joseph Thomas Nedney. ... Name pronounced NED-nee.
HIGH SCHOOL: Santa Teresa (San Jose, Calif.).
COLLEGE: San Jose State (degree in recreation administration, 1998).
TRANSACTIONS/CAREER NOTES: Signed as non-drafted free agent by Green Bay Packers (April 1995). ... Released by Packers (August 27, 1995). ... Signed by Oakland Raiders to practice squad (August 29, 1995). ... Released by Raiders (September 6, 1995). ... Signed by Miami Dolphins to practice squad (September 21, 1995). ... Claimed on waivers by New York Jets (August 12, 1997). ... Released by Jets (August 15, 1997). ... Signed by Dolphins (October 3, 1997). ... Released by Dolphins (October 6, 1997). ... Signed by Arizona Cardinals (October 15, 1997). ... On injured reserve with knee injury (December 1, 1998-remainder of season). ... Released by Cardinals (February 12, 1999). ... Re-signed by Cardinals (March 31, 1999). ... Claimed on waivers by Baltimore Ravens (October 6, 1999). ... Inactive for four games with Ravens (1999). ... Released by Ravens (November 13, 1999). ... Signed by Raiders (December 14, 1999). ... Released by Raiders (August 27, 2000). ... Signed by Denver Broncos (September 12, 2000). ... Released by Broncos (October 2, 2000). ... Signed by Carolina Panthers (October 3, 2000). ... Granted unconditional free agency (March 2, 2001). ... Signed by Tennessee Titans (March 7, 2001).

Year Team	G	KICKING						
		XPM	XPA	FGM	FGA	Lg.	50+	Pts.
1995—Miami NFL		Did not play.						
1996—Miami NFL	16	35	36	18	29	44	0-2	89
1997—Arizona NFL	10	19	19	11	17	45	0-2	52
1998—Arizona NFL	12	30	30	13	19	53	1-4	69
1999—Arizona NFL	1	0	0	0	0	0	0-0	0
—Oakland NFL	3	13	13	5	7	52	1-2	28
2000—Denver NFL	3	4	4	8	10	43	0-1	28
—Carolina NFL	12	20	20	26	28	52	2-2	98
Pro totals (5 years)	57	121	122	81	110	53	4-13	364

NEIL, DALLAS TE FALCONS

PERSONAL: Born September 30, 1976, in Great Falls, Mon. ... 6-1/235.
HIGH SCHOOL: Great Falls (Mon.).
COLLEGE: Montana.
TRANSACTIONS/CAREER NOTES: Signed as non-drafted free agent by Atlanta Falcons (April 17, 2000).
PLAYING EXPERIENCE: Atlanta NFL, 2000. ... Games/Games started: 2000 (6/0).

NEIL, DAN G BRONCOS

PERSONAL: Born October 21, 1973, in Houston. ... 6-2/285. ... Full name: Daniel Neil.
HIGH SCHOOL: Cypress Creek (Houston).
COLLEGE: Texas.
TRANSACTIONS/CAREER NOTES: Selected by Denver Broncos in third round (67th pick overall) of 1997 NFL draft. ... Signed by Broncos (July 17, 1997). ... Granted free agency (February 11, 2000). ... Re-signed by Broncos (April 28, 2000) ... Granted unconditional free agency (March 2, 2001). ... Re-signed by Broncos (March 2, 2001).
PLAYING EXPERIENCE: Denver NFL, 1997-2000. ... Games/Games started: 1997 (3/0), 1998 (16/16), 1999 (15/15), 2000 (16/16). Total: 50/47.
CHAMPIONSHIP GAME EXPERIENCE: Member of Broncos for AFC championship game (1997 season); inactive. ... Member of Super Bowl championship team (1997 season); inactive. ... Played in AFC championship game (1998 season). ... Member of Super Bowl championship team (1998 season).
HONORS: Named guard on THE SPORTING NEWS college All-America first team (1996).

NELSON, JIM LB VIKINGS

PERSONAL: Born April 16, 1975, in Riverside, Calif. ... 6-1/234. ... Full name: James Robert Nelson.
HIGH SCHOOL: McDonough (Waldorf, Md.).
COLLEGE: Penn State (degree in criminal justice).
TRANSACTIONS/CAREER NOTES: Signed as non-drafted free agent by San Francisco 49ers (April 24, 1998). ... Claimed on waivers by Green Bay Packers (July 20, 1998). ... Released by Packers (August 25, 1998). ... Re-signed by Packers to practice squad (September 14, 1998). ... Activated (December 29, 1998). ... Claimed on waivers by Minnesota Vikings (August 28, 2000).
PLAYING EXPERIENCE: Green Bay NFL, 1999; Minnesota NFL, 2000. ... Games/Games started: 1999 (16/0), 2000 (16/0). Total: 32/0.
CHAMPIONSHIP GAME EXPERIENCE: Played in NFC championship game (2000 season).
PRO STATISTICS: 1999—Intercepted one pass for no yards and recovered one fumble.

N

NELSON, REGGIE OT JAGUARS

PERSONAL: Born June 23, 1976, in Alexandria, La. ... 6-3/321. ... Full name: Reginald DeWayne Nelson.
HIGH SCHOOL: Alexandria (La.).
COLLEGE: McNeese State (degree in psychology).
TRANSACTIONS/CAREER NOTES: Selected by San Diego Chargers in fifth round (141st pick overall) of 1999 NFL draft. ... Signed by Chargers (July 22, 1999). ... Released by Chargers (September 4, 1999). ... Re-signed by Chargers to practice squad (September 6, 1999). ... Released by Chargers (September 20, 1999). ... Re-signed by Chargers (September 21, 1999). ... Released by Chargers (October 22, 1999). ... Re-signed by Chargers to practice squad (October 27, 1999). ... Activated (December 30, 1999). ... Released by Chargers (August 21, 2000). ... Signed by Minnesota Vikings to practice squad (September 7, 2000). ... Released by Vikings (September 25, 2000). ... Signed by Jacksonville Jaguars to practice squad (September 27, 2000). ... Activated (October 25, 2000). ... Released by Jaguars (November 11, 2000). ... Re-signed by Jaguars to practice squad (November 14, 2000). ... Activated (November 15, 2000). ... Assigned by Jaguars to Frankfurt Galaxy in 2001 NFL Europe enhancement allocation program (February 19, 2001).
PLAYING EXPERIENCE: San Diego NFL, 1999; Jacksonville NFL, 2000. ... Games/Games started: 1999 (2/0), 2000 (1/0). Total: 3/0.

NESBIT, JAMAR C PANTHERS

PERSONAL: Born December 17, 1976, in Summerville, S.C. ... 6-4/330. ... Full name: Jamar Kendric Nesbit.
HIGH SCHOOL: Summerville (S.C.).
COLLEGE: South Carolina.
TRANSACTIONS/CAREER NOTES: Signed as non-drafted free agent by Carolina Panthers (April 18, 1999).
PLAYING EXPERIENCE: Carolina NFL, 1999 and 2000. ... Games/Games started: 1999 (7/0), 2000 (16/16). Total: 23/16.

NEUFELD, RYAN   TE   JAGUARS

PERSONAL: Born November 22, 1975, in Morgan Hill, Calif. ... 6-4/240. ... Full name: Ryan Matthew Neufeld.
HIGH SCHOOL: Live Oak (Morgan Hill, Calif.).
COLLEGE: UCLA.
TRANSACTIONS/CAREER NOTES: Signed as non-drafted free agent by Dallas Cowboys (April 23, 1999). ... Released by Cowboys (September 5, 1999). ... Re-signed by Cowboys to practice squad (September 6, 1999). ... Activated (October 27, 1999). ... Assigned by Cowboys to Rhein Fire in 2000 NFL Europe enhancement allocation program (February 18, 2000). ... Released by Cowboys (August 27, 2000). ... Signed by Miami Dolphins to practice squad (August 30, 2000). ... Released by Dolphins (September 5, 2000). ... Signed by Jacksonville Jaguars to practice squad (September 13, 2000). ... Activated (October 12, 2000). ... Released by Jaguars (October 21, 2000). ... Re-signed by Jaguars (October 24, 2000).
PLAYING EXPERIENCE: Dallas NFL, 1999; Rhein NFLE, 2000; Jacksonville NFL, 2000. ... Games/Games started: 1999 (6/0), NFLE 2000 (games played unavailable), NFL 2000 (3/0). Total NFL: 9/0.
PRO STATISTICS: NFLE: 2000—Caught eight passes for 75 yards and a touchdown.

NEUJAHR, QUENTIN   C   BRONCOS

PERSONAL: Born January 30, 1971, in Seward, Neb. ... 6-4/302. ... Full name: Quentin Troy Neujahr.
HIGH SCHOOL: Centennial (Utica, Neb.).
COLLEGE: Kansas State.
TRANSACTIONS/CAREER NOTES: Signed as non-drafted free agent by Los Angeles Raiders (May 3, 1994). ... Released by Raiders (August 23, 1994). ... Signed by Cleveland Browns to practice squad (December 27, 1994). ... Active for one game (1995); did not play. ... Browns franchise moved to Baltimore and renamed Ravens for 1996 season (March 11, 1996). ... Granted free agency (February 13, 1998). ... Tendered offer sheet by Jacksonville Jaguars (February 24, 1998). ... Ravens declined to match offer (March 3, 1998). ... Released by Jaguars (February 27, 2001). ... Signed by Denver Broncos (April 3, 2001).
PLAYING EXPERIENCE: Baltimore NFL, 1996 and 1997; Jacksonville NFL, 1998-2000. ... Games/Games started: 1996 (5/0), 1997 (9/7), 1998 (16/16), 1999 (16/0), 2000 (16/2). Total: 62/25.
CHAMPIONSHIP GAME EXPERIENCE: Played in AFC championship game (1999 season).
PRO STATISTICS: 1996—Recovered one fumble.

NEWBERRY, JEREMY   G   49ERS

PERSONAL: Born March 23, 1976, in Antioch, Calif. ... 6-5/315. ... Full name: Jeremy David Newberry.
HIGH SCHOOL: Antioch (Calif.).
COLLEGE: California.
TRANSACTIONS/CAREER NOTES: Selected by after junior season San Francisco 49ers in second round (58th pick overall) of 1998 NFL draft. ... Signed by San Francisco 49ers (July 18, 1998). ... On physically unable to perform list with knee injury (July 17-November 7, 1998). ... Active for one game (1998); did not play.
PLAYING EXPERIENCE: San Francisco NFL, 1999 and 2000. ... Games/Games started: 1999 (16/16), 2000 (16/16). Total: 32/32.

NEWKIRK, ROBERT   DT   BEARS

PERSONAL: Born March 6, 1977, in Belle Glade, Fla. ... 6-3/290.
HIGH SCHOOL: Glade Central (Belle Glade, Fla.).
COLLEGE: Michigan State.
TRANSACTIONS/CAREER NOTES: Signed as non-drafted free agent by Dallas Cowboys (April 23, 1999). ... Released by Cowboys (September 5, 1999). ... Re-signed by Cowboys to practice squad (September 6, 1999). ... Signed by New Orleans Saints off Cowboys practice squad (December 1, 1999). ... Released by Saints (August 28, 2000). ... Signed by Chicago Bears to practice squad (September 7, 2000). ... Activated (September 27, 2000). ... On injured reserve with wrist injury (November 13, 2000-remainder of season).
PLAYING EXPERIENCE: New Orleans NFL, 1999; Chicago NFL, 2000. ... Games/Games started: 1999 (5/0), 2000 (5/0). Total: 10/0.

NEWMAN, KEITH   LB   BILLS

PERSONAL: Born January 19, 1977, in Tampa. ... 6-2/245. ... Full name: Keith Anthony Newman.
HIGH SCHOOL: Thomas Jefferson (Tampa).
COLLEGE: North Carolina.
TRANSACTIONS/CAREER NOTES: Selected by Buffalo Bills in fourth round (119th pick overall) of 1999 NFL draft. ... Signed by Bills (July 27, 1999).
PLAYING EXPERIENCE: Buffalo NFL, 1999 and 2000. ... Games/Games started: 1999 (3/0), 2000 (16/16). Total: 19/16.
PRO STATISTICS: 2000—Credited with eight sacks, fumbled once and recovered one fumble for 25 yards.

NGUYEN, DAT   LB   COWBOYS

PERSONAL: Born September 25, 1975, in Fulton, Texas. ... 5-11/231. ... Name pronounced WIN.
HIGH SCHOOL: Rockport-Fulton (Rockport, Texas).
COLLEGE: Texas A&M (degree in agricultural development).
TRANSACTIONS/CAREER NOTES: Selected by Dallas Cowboys in third round (85th pick overall) of 1999 NFL draft. ... Signed by Cowboys (July 26, 1999).
PLAYING EXPERIENCE: Dallas NFL, 1999 and 2000. ... Games/Games started: 1999 (16/0), 2000 (10/5). Total: 26/5.
HONORS: Lombardi Award winner (1998). ... Chuck Bednarik Award winner (1998). ... Named inside linebacker on THE SPORTING NEWS college All-America first team (1998).
PRO STATISTICS: 1999—Intercepted one pass for six yards and credited with one sack. 2000—Intercepted two passes for 31 yards and recovered one fumble.

N

NICKERSON, HARDY　　　　LB　　　　JAGUARS

PERSONAL: Born September 1, 1965, in Compton, Calif. ... 6-2/235. ... Full name: Hardy Otto Nickerson.
HIGH SCHOOL: Verbum Dei (Los Angeles).
COLLEGE: California (degree in sociology, 1986).
TRANSACTIONS/CAREER NOTES: Selected by Pittsburgh Steelers in fifth round (122nd pick overall) of 1987 NFL draft. ... Signed by Steelers (July 26, 1987). ... On injured reserve with ankle and knee injuries (November 3-December 16, 1989). ... Granted free agency (February 1, 1992). ... Re-signed by Steelers (June 15, 1992). ... Granted unconditional free agency (March 1, 1993). ... Signed by Tampa Bay Buccaneers (March 18, 1993). ... Granted unconditional free agency (February 16, 1996). ... Re-signed by Buccaneers (February 22, 1996). ... On injured reserve with heart problems (November 25, 1998-remainder of season). ... Granted unconditional free agency (February 11, 2000). ... Signed by Jacksonville Jaguars (February 22, 2000). ... On injured reserve with knee injury (December 5, 2000-remainder of season).
CHAMPIONSHIP GAME EXPERIENCE: Played in NFC championship game (1999 season).
HONORS: Named linebacker on THE SPORTING NEWS college All-America second team (1985). ... Named inside linebacker on THE SPORTING NEWS NFL All-Pro team (1993). ... Played in Pro Bowl (1993 and 1996-1999 seasons).
PRO STATISTICS: 1987—Recovered one fumble. 1988—Intercepted one pass for no yards and recovered one fumble. 1992—Recovered two fumbles for 44 yards. 1993—Intercepted one pass for six yards and recovered one fumble. 1994—Intercepted two passes for nine yards. 1995—Recovered three fumbles. 1996—Intercepted two passes for 24 yards and recovered two fumbles. 1997—Recovered two fumbles. 1998—Recovered one fumble. 1999—Intercepted two passes for 18 yards. 2000—Intercepted one pass for 10 yards.

Year　Team	G	GS	SACKS
1987—Pittsburgh NFL	12	0	0.0
1988—Pittsburgh NFL	15	10	3.5
1989—Pittsburgh NFL	10	8	1.0
1990—Pittsburgh NFL	16	14	2.0
1991—Pittsburgh NFL	16	14	1.0
1992—Pittsburgh NFL	15	15	2.0
1993—Tampa Bay NFL	16	16	1.0
1994—Tampa Bay NFL	14	14	1.0
1995—Tampa Bay NFL	16	16	1.5
1996—Tampa Bay NFL	16	16	3.0
1997—Tampa Bay NFL	16	16	1.0
1998—Tampa Bay NFL	10	10	1.0
1999—Tampa Bay NFL	16	16	0.5
2000—Jacksonville NFL	6	6	1.0
Pro totals (14 years)	**194**	**171**	**19.5**

NOA, KAULANA　　　　OT　　　　RAMS

PERSONAL: Born December 29, 1976, in Honokaa, Hawaii. ... 6-3/307.
HIGH SCHOOL: Honokaa (Hawaii).
COLLEGE: Hawaii.
TRANSACTIONS/CAREER NOTES: Selected by St. Louis Rams in fourth round (104th pick overall) of 2000 NFL draft. ... Signed by Rams (July 12, 2000). ... On injured reserve with wrist injury (August 16, 2000-entire season).

NOBLE, BRANDON　　　　DT　　　　COWBOYS

PERSONAL: Born April 10, 1974, in San Rafael, Calif. ... 6-2/285. ... Full name: Brandon Patrick Noble.
HIGH SCHOOL: First Colonial (Virginia Beach, Va.).
COLLEGE: Penn State.
TRANSACTIONS/CAREER NOTES: Signed as non-drafted free agent by San Francisco 49ers (April 29, 1997). ... Released by 49ers (August 19, 1997). ... Re-signed by 49ers to practice squad (November 12, 1997). ... Released by 49ers (November 19, 1997). ... Re-signed by 49ers (January 13, 1998). ... Assigned by 49ers to Barcelona Dragons in 1998 NFL Europe enhancement allocation program (February 18, 1998). ... Released by 49ers (August 25, 1998). ... Re-signed by 49ers to practice squad (December 3, 1998). ... Granted free agency after 1998 season. ... Signed by Dallas Cowboys (February 2, 1999). ... Assigned by Cowboys to Barcelona Dragons in 1999 NFL Europe enhancement allocation program (February 22, 1999).
PRO STATISTICS: NFLE: 1998—Intercepted one pass for no yards, returned one kickoff for 12 yards and recovered one fumble for a touchdown. 1999—Returned one kickoff for 17 yards and recovered one fumble. 2000—Returned one kickoff for eight yards.

Year　Team	G	GS	SACKS
1998—Barcelona NFLE	...	...	2.0
1999—Barcelona NFLE	...	...	5.0
—Dallas NFL	16	0	3.0
2000—Dallas NFL	16	9	1.0
NFL Europe totals (2 years)	...	...	**7.0**
NFL totals (2 years)	**32**	**9**	**4.0**
Pro totals (4 years)			**11.0**

NORTHCUTT, DENNIS　　　　WR　　　　BROWNS

PERSONAL: Born December 22, 1977, in Los Angeles. ... 5-10/175.
HIGH SCHOOL: Dorsey (Los Angeles).
COLLEGE: Arizona.
TRANSACTIONS/CAREER NOTES: Selected by Cleveland Browns in second round (32nd pick overall) of 2000 NFL draft. ... Signed by Browns (July 19, 2000).
HONORS: Named wide receiver on THE SPORTING NEWS college All-America second team (1999).
PRO STATISTICS: 2000—Rushed nine times for 33 yards.
SINGLE GAME HIGHS (regular season): Receptions—5 (December 10, 2000, vs. Philadelphia); yards—80 (October 15, 2000, vs. Denver); and touchdown receptions—0.

			RECEIVING				PUNT RETURNS				TOTALS			
Year　Team	G	GS	No.	Yds.	Avg.	TD	No.	Yds.	Avg.	TD	TD	2pt.	Pts.	Fum.
2000—Cleveland NFL	15	8	39	422	10.8	0	27	289	10.7	0	0	0	0	1

NORTHERN, GABE LB VIKINGS

PERSONAL: Born June 8, 1974, in Baton Rouge, La. ... 6-3/241. ... Full name: Gabriel O'Kara Northern.
HIGH SCHOOL: Southern University Lab (Baton Rouge, La.), then Glen Oaks (Baton Rouge, La.).
COLLEGE: Louisiana State.
TRANSACTIONS/CAREER NOTES: Selected by Buffalo Bills in second round (53rd pick overall) of 1996 NFL draft. ... Signed by Bills (July 17, 1996). ... Granted unconditional free agency (February 11, 2000). ... Signed by Pittsburgh Steelers (June 26, 2000). ... Released by Steelers (August 27, 2000). ... Signed by Minnesota Vikings (September 5, 2000).
CHAMPIONSHIP GAME EXPERIENCE: Member of Vikings for NFC championship game (2000 season); inactive.
PRO STATISTICS: 1996—Returned blocked punt 18 yards for a touchdown. 1998—Intercepted one pass for 40 yards and a touchdown. 1999—Recovered one fumble for 59 yards and a touchdown.

Year Team	G	GS	SACKS
1996—Buffalo NFL	16	2	5.0
1997—Buffalo NFL	16	1	0.0
1998—Buffalo NFL	16	16	2.0
1999—Buffalo NFL	16	16	3.5
2000—Minnesota NFL	9	2	0.0
Pro totals (5 years)	73	37	10.5

NORTON, KEN LB

PERSONAL: Born September 29, 1966, in Lincoln, Ill. ... 6-2/254. ... Full name: Kenneth Howard Norton Jr. ... Son of Ken Norton Sr., former world heavyweight boxing champion.
HIGH SCHOOL: Westchester (Los Angeles).
COLLEGE: UCLA (degree in sociology, 1998).
TRANSACTIONS/CAREER NOTES: Selected by Dallas Cowboys in second round (41st pick overall) of 1988 NFL draft. ... Signed by Cowboys (July 13, 1988). ... On injured reserve with broken arm (August 23-December 3, 1988). ... On injured reserve with knee injury (December 24, 1990-remainder of season). ... Granted free agency (February 1, 1992). ... Re-signed by Cowboys (August 12, 1992). ... Granted unconditional free agency (February 17, 1994). ... Signed by San Francisco 49ers (April 20, 1994). ... Released by 49ers (February 28, 2001).
CHAMPIONSHIP GAME EXPERIENCE: Played in NFC championship game (1992-1994 and 1997 seasons). ... Member of Super Bowl championship team (1992-1994 seasons).
HONORS: Named linebacker on THE SPORTING NEWS college All-America first team (1987). ... Played in Pro Bowl (1993, 1995 and 1997 seasons).
POST SEASON RECORDS: Shares Super Bowl career record for most touchdowns by fumble recovery—1 (January 31, 1993, vs. Buffalo).
PRO STATISTICS: 1988—Recovered one fumble. 1990—Recovered two fumbles. 1992—Recovered two fumbles. 1993—Recovered one fumble for three yards. 1996—Recovered one fumble for 21 yards. 1997—Recovered two fumbles. 1998—Recovered three fumbles for 12 yards. 2000—Recovered one fumble.

Year Team	G	GS	INTERCEPTIONS				SACKS
			No.	Yds.	Avg.	TD	No.
1988—Dallas NFL	3	0	0	0	0.0	0	0.0
1989—Dallas NFL	13	13	0	0	0.0	0	2.5
1990—Dallas NFL	15	15	0	0	0.0	0	2.5
1991—Dallas NFL	16	16	0	0	0.0	0	0.0
1992—Dallas NFL	16	16	0	0	0.0	0	0.0
1993—Dallas NFL	16	16	1	25	25.0	0	2.0
1994—San Francisco NFL	16	16	1	0	0.0	0	0.0
1995—San Francisco NFL	16	16	3	102	‡34.0	†2	1.0
1996—San Francisco NFL	16	16	0	0	0.0	0	0.0
1997—San Francisco NFL	16	16	0	0	0.0	0	1.5
1998—San Francisco NFL	16	16	0	0	0.0	0	2.0
1999—San Francisco NFL	16	16	0	0	0.0	0	1.0
2000—San Francisco NFL	16	16	0	0	0.0	0	0.0
Pro totals (13 years)	191	188	5	127	25.4	2	12.5

NUGENT, DAVID DE PATRIOTS

PERSONAL: Born October 27, 1977, in Cincinnati. ... 6-4/300. ... Full name: David Michael Nugent.
HIGH SCHOOL: Houston (Germantown, Tenn.).
COLLEGE: Purdue.
TRANSACTIONS/CAREER NOTES: Selected by New England Patriots in sixth round (201st pick overall) of 2000 NFL draft. ... Signed by Patriots (July 12, 2000).
PLAYING EXPERIENCE: New England NFL, 2000. ... Games/Games started: 2000 (6/0).

NUTTEN, TOM G RAMS

PERSONAL: Born June 8, 1971, in Magog, Quebec. ... 6-5/304. ... Full name: Thomas Nutten. ... Name pronounced NEW-ton.
HIGH SCHOOL: Champlain Regional (Lennoxville, Quebec).
COLLEGE: Western Michigan (degree in marketing, 1994).
TRANSACTIONS/CAREER NOTES: Selected by Hamilton Tiger-Cats in first round (first pick overall) of 1995 CFL draft. ... Selected by Buffalo Bills in seventh round (221st pick overall) of 1995 NFL draft. ... Signed by Bills (June 12, 1995). ... Released by Bills (August 27, 1995). ... Re-signed by Bills to practice squad (August 29, 1995). ... Activated (October 10, 1995). ... Waived by Bills (August 26, 1996). ... Signed by Denver Broncos (January 14, 1997). ... Released by Broncos (July 16, 1997). ... Signed by Hamilton Tiger-Cats of CFL (July 28, 1997). ... Signed by St. Louis Rams (January 16, 1998). ... Assigned by Rams to Amsterdam Admirals in 1998 NFL Europe enhancement allocation program (February 18, 1998). ... On injured reserve with neck injury (November 17, 1998-remainder of season). ... Granted free agency (February 11, 2000). ... Re-signed by Rams (February 12, 2000).

N

PLAYING EXPERIENCE: Buffalo NFL, 1995; Hamilton CFL, 1997; Amsterdam Admirals NFLE, 1998; St. Louis NFL, 1998-2000. ... Games/Games started: 1995 (1/0), 1997 (13/games started unavailable), NFLE 1998 (games played unavailable), NFL 1998 (4/2), 1999 (14/14), 2000 (16/16). Total NFL: 35/32. Total CFL: 13/-.

CHAMPIONSHIP GAME EXPERIENCE: Played in NFC championship game (1999 season). ... Member of Super Bowl championship team (1999 season).

PRO STATISTICS: 1997—Recovered one fumble. 1999—Recovered one fumble. 2000—Recovered one fumble.

NWOKORIE, CHUKIE   DE   COLTS

PERSONAL: Born July 10, 1975, in Tuskegee, Ala. ... 6-3/280. ... Full name: Chijioke O. Nwkorie. ... Name pronounced CHEW-key wuh-CORE-e.

HIGH SCHOOL: Lafayette-Jefferson (Lafayette, Ind.).

COLLEGE: Purdue.

TRANSACTIONS/CAREER NOTES: Signed as non-drafted free agent by Indianapolis Colts (April 20, 1999). ... Released by Colts (October 25, 2000). ... Re-signed by Colts to practice squad (October 26, 2000). ... Activated (December 22, 2000).

PLAYING EXPERIENCE: Indianapolis NFL, 1999 and 2000. ... Games/Games started: 1999 (1/0), 2000 (1/0). Total: 2/0.

OBEN, ROMAN   OT   BROWNS

PERSONAL: Born October 9, 1972, in Cameroon, West Africa. ... 6-4/305. ... Name pronounced OH-bin.

HIGH SCHOOL: Gonzaga (Washington, D.C.), then Fork Union (Va.) Military Academy.

COLLEGE: Louisville (degree in economics).

TRANSACTIONS/CAREER NOTES: Selected by New York Giants in third round (66th pick overall) of 1996 NFL draft. ... Signed by Giants (July 20, 1996). ... Granted free agency (February 12, 1999). ... Re-signed by Giants (July 28, 1999). ... Granted unconditional free agency (February 11, 2000). ... Signed by Cleveland Browns (March 9, 2000).

PLAYING EXPERIENCE: New York Giants NFL, 1996-1999; Cleveland NFL, 2000. ... Games/Games started: 1996 (2/0), 1997 (16/16), 1998 (16/16), 1999 (16/16), 2000 (16/16). Total: 66/64.

PRO STATISTICS: 1999—Recovered two fumbles.

ODOM, JASON   OT   BUCCANEERS

PERSONAL: Born March 31, 1974, in Winter Haven, Fla. ... 6-5/312. ... Full name: Jason Brian Odom.

HIGH SCHOOL: Bartow (Fla.).

COLLEGE: Florida (degree in sports management, 1995).

TRANSACTIONS/CAREER NOTES: Selected by Tampa Bay Buccaneers in fourth round (96th pick overall) of 1996 NFL draft. ... Signed by Buccaneers (July 16, 1996). ... Granted free agency (February 12, 1999). ... Re-signed by Buccaneers (June 2, 1999). ... On injured reserve with back injury (November 24, 1999-remainder of season). ... Granted unconditional free agency (February 11, 2000). ... Re-signed by Buccaneers (March 1, 2000). ... On injured reserve with back injury (August 27, 2000-entire season).

PLAYING EXPERIENCE: Tampa Bay NFL, 1996-1999. ... Games/Games started: 1996 (12/7), 1997 (16/16), 1998 (15/15), 1999 (3/3). Total: 46/41.

HONORS: Named offensive lineman on THE SPORTING NEWS college All-America first team (1995).

PRO STATISTICS: 1996—Recovered one fumble.

O'DONNELL, NEIL   QB   TITANS

PERSONAL: Born July 3, 1966, in Morristown, N.J. ... 6-3/228. ... Full name: Neil Kennedy O'Donnell.

HIGH SCHOOL: Madison-Boro (Madison, N.J.).

COLLEGE: Maryland (degree in economics, 1990).

TRANSACTIONS/CAREER NOTES: Selected by Pittsburgh Steelers in third round (70th pick overall) of 1990 NFL draft. ... Signed by Steelers (August 8, 1990). ... Active for three games (1990); did not play. ... Granted free agency (March 1, 1993). ... Tendered offer sheet by Tampa Bay Buccaneers (April 2, 1993). ... Offer matched by Steelers (April 12, 1993). ... Granted unconditional free agency (February 16, 1996). ... Signed by New York Jets (February 29, 1996). ... Released by Jets (June 24, 1998). ... Signed by Cincinnati Bengals (July 7, 1998). ... On injured reserve with hand injury (December 9, 1998-remainder of season). ... Released by Bengals (April 19, 1999). ... Signed by Tennessee Titans (July 23, 1999). ... Granted unconditional free agency (February 11, 2000). ... Re-signed by Titans (April 25, 2000).

CHAMPIONSHIP GAME EXPERIENCE: Played in AFC championship game (1994, 1995 and 1999 seasons). ... Played in Super Bowl XXX (1995 season). ... Member of Titans for Super Bowl XXXIV (1999 season); did not play.

HONORS: Played in Pro Bowl (1992 season).

RECORDS: Holds NFL career record for lowest interception percentage—2.08.

POST SEASON RECORDS: Holds NFL postseason single-game record for most passes attempted without an interception—54 (January 15, 1995, vs. San Diego).

PRO STATISTICS: 1991—Fumbled 11 times and recovered two fumbles for minus three yards. 1992—Fumbled six times and recovered four fumbles for minus 20 yards. 1993—Fumbled five times. 1994—Fumbled four times and recovered one fumble. 1995—Fumbled twice and recovered one fumble. 1996—Fumbled twice. 1997—Fumbled nine times and recovered two fumbles for minus one yard. 1998—Fumbled six times and recovered one fumble for minus two yards. 1999—Fumbled five times and recovered three fumbles for minus 14 yards.

SINGLE GAME HIGHS (regular season): Attempts—55 (December 24, 1995, vs. Green Bay); completions—34 (November 5, 1995, vs. Chicago); yards—377 (November 19, 1995, vs. Cincinnati); and touchdown passes—5 (August 31, 1997, vs. Seattle).

STATISTICAL PLATEAUS: 300-yard passing games: 1991 (1), 1993 (1), 1995 (4), 1996 (2), 1997 (1), 1998 (1), 1999 (2). Total: 12.

MISCELLANEOUS: Regular-season record as starting NFL quarterback: 54-44 (.551). ... Postseason record as starting NFL quarterback: 3-4 (.429). ... Active AFC leader in touchdown passes (116).

Year	Team	G	GS	PASSING								RUSHING				TOTALS		
				Att.	Cmp.	Pct.	Yds.	TD	Int.	Avg.	Rat.	Att.	Yds.	Avg.	TD	TD	2pt.	Pts.
1990—Pittsburgh NFL...........							Did not play.											
1991—Pittsburgh NFL...........		12	8	286	156	54.5	1963	11	7	6.86	78.8	18	82	4.6	1	1	0	6
1992—Pittsburgh NFL...........		12	12	313	185	59.1	2283	13	9	7.29	83.6	27	5	0.2	1	1	0	6
1993—Pittsburgh NFL...........		16	15	486	270	55.6	3208	14	7	6.60	79.5	26	111	4.3	0	0	0	0
1994—Pittsburgh NFL...........		14	14	370	212	57.3	2443	13	9	6.60	78.9	31	80	2.6	1	1	0	6
1995—Pittsburgh NFL...........		12	12	416	246	59.1	2970	17	7	7.14	87.7	24	45	1.9	0	0	0	0
1996—New York Jets NFL......		6	6	188	110	58.5	1147	4	7	6.10	67.8	6	30	5.0	0	0	0	0
1997—New York Jets NFL......		15	14	460	259	56.3	2796	17	7	6.08	80.3	32	36	1.1	1	1	0	6
1998—Cincinnati NFL..........		13	11	343	212	§61.8	2216	15	4	6.46	90.2	13	34	2.6	0	0	0	0
1999—Tennessee NFL..........		8	5	195	116	59.5	1382	10	5	7.09	87.6	19	1	0.1	0	0	0	0
2000—Tennessee NFL..........		7	1	64	36	56.3	530	2	3	8.28	74.3	9	-2	-0.2	0	0	0	0
Pro totals (10 years)		115	98	3121	1802	57.7	20938	116	65	6.71	81.9	205	422	2.1	4	4	0	24

O'DWYER, MATT　　　　　G　　　　　BENGALS

PERSONAL: Born September 1, 1972, in Lincolnshire, Ill. ... 6-5/308. ... Full name: Matthew Phillip O'Dwyer.
HIGH SCHOOL: Adlai E. Stevenson (Prairie View, Ill.).
COLLEGE: Northwestern.
TRANSACTIONS/CAREER NOTES: Selected by New York Jets in second round (33rd pick overall) of 1995 NFL draft. ... Signed by Jets (July 20, 1995). ... Granted unconditional free agency (February 12, 1999). ... Signed by Cincinnati Bengals (June 19, 1999). ... Suspended two games by NFL for involvement in bar fight (March 14, 2000). ... On injured reserve with broken ankle (November 20, 2000-remainder of season). ... Granted unconditional free agency (March 2, 2001). ... Re-signed by Bengals (March 2, 2001).
PLAYING EXPERIENCE: New York Jets NFL, 1995-1998; Cincinnati NFL, 1999 and 2000. ... Games/Games started: 1995 (12/2), 1996 (16/16), 1997 (16/16), 1998 (16/16), 1999 (16/16), 2000 (10/10). Total: 86/76.
CHAMPIONSHIP GAME EXPERIENCE: Played in AFC championship game (1998 season).

OGBOGU, ERIC　　　　　DE　　　　　JETS

PERSONAL: Born July 18, 1975, in Irvington, N.Y. ... 6-4/285. ... Name pronounced oh-BOG-u.
HIGH SCHOOL: Archbishop Stepinac (White Plains, N.Y.).
COLLEGE: Maryland.
TRANSACTIONS/CAREER NOTES: Selected by New York Jets in sixth round (163rd pick overall) of 1998 NFL draft. ... Signed by Jets (July 2, 1998). ... On injured reserve with shoulder injury (August 7, 2000-entire season).
PLAYING EXPERIENCE: New York Jets NFL, 1998 and 1999. ... Games/Games started: 1998 (12/0), 1999 (14/0). Total: 26/0.
CHAMPIONSHIP GAME EXPERIENCE: Played in AFC championship game (1998 season).
PRO STATISTICS: 1999—Credited with one sack and recovered two fumbles, including one in end zone for a touchdown.

OGDEN, JEFF　　　　　WR　　　　　DOLPHINS

PERSONAL: Born February 22, 1975, in Snohomish, Wash. ... 6-0/190. ... Full name: Jeffery Ogden.
HIGH SCHOOL: Snohomish (Wash.).
COLLEGE: Eastern Washington.
TRANSACTIONS/CAREER NOTES: Signed as non-drafted free agent by Dallas Cowboys (April 21, 1998). ... Assigned by Cowboys to Rhein Fire in 2000 NFL Europe enhancement allocation program (February 18, 2000). ... Traded by Cowboys to Miami Dolphins for future seventh-round pick (August 22, 2000). ... Granted free agency (March 2, 2001). ... Re-signed by Dolphins (April 20, 2001).
PRO STATISTICS: 1998—Rushed once for 12 yards and returned three kickoffs for 65 yards. 1999—Returned four punts for 28 yards and returned 12 kickoffs for 252 yards. NFLE: 2000—Attempted one pass without a completion, returned four punts for 28 yards and returned four kickoffs for 141 yards. NFL: 2000—Returned 19 punts for 323 yards and a touchdown.
SINGLE GAME HIGHS (regular season): Receptions—4 (November 22, 1998, vs. Seattle); yards—28 (January 2, 2000, vs. New York Giants); and touchdown receptions—0.

Year	Team	G	GS	RECEIVING				TOTALS			
				No.	Yds.	Avg.	TD	TD	2pt.	Pts.	Fum.
1998—Dallas NFL................		16	0	8	63	7.9	0	0	0	0	1
1999—Dallas NFL................		16	0	12	144	12.0	0	0	0	0	0
2000—Rhein NFLE...............		...	...	44	635	14.4	7	0	0	0	0
—Miami NFL....................		16	0	2	24	12.0	0	1	0	6	1
NFL Europe totals (1 year).........		...	...	44	635	14.4	7	0	0	0	0
NFL totals (3 years)		48	0	22	231	10.5	0	1	0	6	2
Pro totals (4 years)		...	...	66	866	13.1	7	1	0	6	2

OGDEN, JONATHAN　　　　　OT　　　　　RAVENS

PERSONAL: Born July 31, 1974, in Washington, D.C. ... 6-8/340. ... Full name: Jonathan Phillip Ogden.
HIGH SCHOOL: St. Alban's (Washington, D.C.).
COLLEGE: UCLA.
TRANSACTIONS/CAREER NOTES: Selected by Baltimore Ravens in first round (fourth pick overall) of 1996 NFL draft. ... Signed by Ravens (July 15, 1996).
PLAYING EXPERIENCE: Baltimore NFL, 1996-2000. ... Games/Games started: 1996 (16/16), 1997 (16/16), 1998 (13/13), 1999 (16/16), 2000 (15/15). Total: 76/76.
CHAMPIONSHIP GAME EXPERIENCE: Played in AFC championship game (2000 season). ... Member of Super Bowl championship team (2000 season).
HONORS: Outland Trophy winner (1995). ... Named offensive lineman on THE SPORTING NEWS college All-America first team (1995). ... Named offensive tackle on THE SPORTING NEWS NFL All-Pro team (1997 and 2000). ... Played in Pro Bowl (1997-2000 seasons).
PRO STATISTICS: 1996—Caught one pass for one yard and a touchdown. 1999—Recovered two fumbles for two yards. 2000—Recovered two fumbles.

O'HARA, SHAUN　　　　C　　　　BROWNS

PERSONAL: Born June 23, 1977, in Hillsborough, N.J. ... 6-3/287.
HIGH SCHOOL: Hillsborough (N.J.).
COLLEGE: Rutgers.
TRANSACTIONS/CAREER NOTES: Signed as non-drafted free agent by Cleveland Browns (April 17, 2000).
PLAYING EXPERIENCE: Cleveland NFL, 2000. ... Games/Games started: 2000 (8/4).
PRO STATISTICS: 2000—Fumbled once for minus seven yards.

OKEAFOR, CHIKE　　　　DE　　　　49ERS

PERSONAL: Born March 27, 1976, in West Lafayette, Ind. ... 6-4/248. ... Full name: Chikeze Russell Okeafor. ... Name pronounced chee-KAY oh-KEY-fer.
HIGH SCHOOL: West Lafayette (Ind.).
COLLEGE: Purdue.
TRANSACTIONS/CAREER NOTES: Selected by San Francisco 49ers in third round (89th pick overall) of 1999 NFL draft. ... Signed by 49ers (July 27, 1999). ... On non-football injury list with back injury (July 27-September 5, 1999).
PLAYING EXPERIENCE: San Francisco NFL, 1999 and 2000. ... Games/Games started: 1999 (12/0), 2000 (15/0). Total: 27/0.
PRO STATISTICS: 1999—Credited with one sack. 2000—Credited with two sacks and returned one kickoff for 17 yards.

OLDHAM, CHRIS　　　　DB　　　　SAINTS

PERSONAL: Born October 26, 1968, in Sacramento. ... 5-9/200. ... Full name: Christopher Martin Oldham. ... Name pronounced OLD-um.
HIGH SCHOOL: O. Perry Walker (New Orleans).
COLLEGE: Oregon (degree in communications).
TRANSACTIONS/CAREER NOTES: Selected by Detroit Lions in fourth round (105th pick overall) of 1990 NFL draft. ... Signed by Lions (July 19, 1990). ... Released by Lions (August 26, 1991). ... Signed by Buffalo Bills (September 25, 1991). ... Released by Bills (October 8, 1991). ... Signed by Phoenix Cardinals (October 15, 1991). ... Released by Cardinals (November 13, 1991). ... Signed by San Diego Chargers (February 15, 1992). ... Assigned to Chargers to San Antonio Riders in 1992 World League enhancement allocation program (February 20, 1992). ... Released by Chargers (August 25, 1992). ... Signed by Cardinals (December 22, 1992). ... Granted unconditional free agency (February 17, 1994). ... Cardinals franchise renamed Arizona Cardinals for 1994 season. ... Re-signed by Cardinals (June 7, 1994). ... Granted unconditional free agency (February 17, 1995). ... Signed by Pittsburgh Steelers (April 12, 1995). ... Granted unconditional free agency (February 11, 2000). ... Signed by New Orleans Saints (February 14, 2000).
CHAMPIONSHIP GAME EXPERIENCE: Played in AFC championship game (1995 and 1997 seasons). ... Played in Super Bowl XXX (1995 season).
PRO STATISTICS: NFL: 1990—Returned 13 kickoffs for 234 yards and fumbled twice. W.L.: 1992—Returned one kickoff for 11 yards and recovered one fumble. 1995—Recovered one fumble for 23 yards and a touchdown. 1998—Recovered five fumbles for 79 yards and one touchdown. 1999—Recovered one fumble. 2000—Recovered two fumbles for two yards.

| | | | INTERCEPTIONS | | | | SACKS |
Year　Team	G	GS	No.	Yds.	Avg.	TD	No.
1990—Detroit NFL	16	0	1	28	28.0	0	0.0
1991—Buffalo NFL	2	0	0	0	0.0	0	0.0
—Phoenix NFL	2	0	0	0	0.0	0	0.0
1992—San Antonio W.L.	9	9	3	52	17.3	*1	1.0
—Phoenix NFL	1	0	0	0	0.0	0	0.0
1993—Phoenix NFL	16	6	1	0	0.0	0	1.0
1994—Arizona NFL	11	1	0	0	0.0	0	0.0
1995—Pittsburgh NFL	15	0	1	12	12.0	0	0.0
1996—Pittsburgh NFL	16	0	0	0	0.0	0	2.0
1997—Pittsburgh NFL	16	0	2	16	8.0	0	4.0
1998—Pittsburgh NFL	16	1	1	14	14.0	0	0.5
1999—Pittsburgh NFL	15	0	1	9	9.0	0	3.0
2000—New Orleans NFL	13	1	2	0	0.0	0	2.0
W.L. totals (1 year)	9	9	3	52	17.3	1	1.0
NFL totals (11 years)	139	9	9	79	8.8	0	12.5
Pro totals (12 years)	148	18	12	131	10.9	1	13.5

OLIVER, WINSLOW　　　　RB/PR

PERSONAL: Born March 3, 1973, in Houston. ... 5-7/200. ... Full name: Winslow Paul Oliver.
HIGH SCHOOL: Clements (Sugar Land, Texas), then Kempner (Sugar Land, Texas).
COLLEGE: New Mexico.
TRANSACTIONS/CAREER NOTES: Selected by Carolina Panthers in third round (73rd pick overall) of 1996 NFL draft. ... Signed by Panthers (July 20, 1996). ... Released by Panthers (September 7, 1999). ... Signed by Atlanta Falcons (September 22, 1999). ... Granted unconditional free agency (February 11, 2000). ... Re-signed by Falcons (March 8, 2000). ... Released by Falcons (February 27, 2000).
CHAMPIONSHIP GAME EXPERIENCE: Played in NFC championship game (1996 season).
PRO STATISTICS: 1996—Fumbled four times. 1997—Fumbled twice. 1998—Fumbled once. 1999—Fumbled twice. 2000—Fumbled once.
SINGLE GAME HIGHS (regular season): Attempts—8 (November 10, 1996, vs. New York Giants); yards—37 (September 1, 1996, vs. Atlanta); and rushing touchdowns—0.

| | | | RUSHING | | | | RECEIVING | | | | PUNT RETURNS | | | | KICKOFF RETURNS | | | | TOTALS | | |
Year　Team	G	GS	Att.	Yds.	Avg.	TD	No.	Yds.	Avg.	TD	No.	Yds.	Avg.	TD	No.	Yds.	Avg.	TD	TD	2pt.	Pts.
1996—Carolina NFL	16	0	47	183	3.9	0	15	144	9.6	0	52	598	11.5	1	7	160	22.9	0	1	0	6
1997—Carolina NFL	6	0	1	0	0.0	0	6	47	7.8	0	14	111	7.9	0	0	0	0.0	0	0	0	0
1998—Carolina NFL	16	0	0	0	0.0	0	0	0	0.0	0	44	464	10.5	0	2	43	21.5	0	0	0	0
1999—Atlanta NFL	14	0	8	32	4.0	0	8	74	9.3	0	12	152	12.7	∞1	24	441	18.4	0	1	0	6
2000—Atlanta NFL	12	0	0	0	0.0	0	0	0	0.0	0	4	39	9.8	0	2	15	7.5	0	0	0	0
Pro totals (5 years)	64	0	56	215	3.8	0	29	265	9.1	0	126	1364	10.8	2	35	659	18.8	0	2	0	12

OLIVO, BROCK   FB   LIONS

PERSONAL: Born June 24, 1976, in St. Louis. ... 6-0/232. ... Name pronounced o-LEEV-o.
HIGH SCHOOL: St. Francis Borgia (Washington, Mo.).
COLLEGE: Missouri.
TRANSACTIONS/CAREER NOTES: Signed as non-drafted free agent by San Francisco 49ers (April 24, 1998). ... Released by 49ers (August 30, 1998). ... Re-signed by 49ers to practice squad (September 1, 1998). ... Signed by Detroit Lions off 49ers practice squad (September 23, 1998). ... Released by Lions (December 8, 1998). ... Re-signed by Lions to practice squad (December 9, 1998). ... On injured reserve with knee injury (December 22, 1999-remainder of season).
PRO STATISTICS: 1999—Recovered one fumble.
SINGLE GAME HIGHS (regular season): Attempts—1 (December 12, 1999, vs. Tampa Bay); yards—1 (December 12, 1999, vs. Tampa Bay); and rushing touchdowns—0.

			RUSHING				RECEIVING				KICKOFF RETURNS				TOTALS		
Year Team	G	GS	Att.	Yds.	Avg.	TD	No.	Yds.	Avg.	TD	No.	Yds.	Avg.	TD	TD	2pt.	Pts. Fum.
1998—Detroit NFL	1	0	0	0	0.0	0	0	0	0.0	0	0	0	0.0	0	0	0	0 0
1999—Detroit NFL	14	0	1	1	1.0	0	4	24	6.0	0	11	198	18.0	0	0	0	0 0
2000—Detroit NFL	13	0	0	0	0.0	0	3	50	16.7	0	3	25	8.3	0	0	0	0 0
Pro totals (3 years)	28	0	1	1	1.0	0	7	74	10.6	0	14	223	15.9	0	0	0	0 0

OLSON, BENJI   G   TITANS

PERSONAL: Born June 5, 1975, in Bremerton, Wash. ... 6-3/315. ... Full name: Benji Dempsey Olson.
HIGH SCHOOL: South Kitsap (Port Orchard, Wash.).
COLLEGE: Washington.
TRANSACTIONS/CAREER NOTES: Selected after junior season by Tennessee Oilers in fifth round (139th pick overall) of 1998 NFL draft. ... Signed by Oilers (June 29, 1998). ... Oilers franchise renamed Tennessee Titans for 1999 season (December 26, 1998). ... Granted free agency (March 2, 2001).
PLAYING EXPERIENCE: Tennessee NFL, 1998-2000. ... Games/Games started: 1998 (13/1), 1999 (16/16), 2000 (16/16). Total: 45/33.
CHAMPIONSHIP GAME EXPERIENCE: Played in AFC championship game (1999 season). ... Played in Super Bowl XXXIV (1999 season).
HONORS: Named guard on The Sporting News college All-America first team (1996).
PRO STATISTICS: 1999—Recovered one fumble.

OLSON, ERIK   S   JAGUARS

PERSONAL: Born January 4, 1977, in Ventura, Calif. ... 6-1/210. ... Full name: Erik James Olson.
HIGH SCHOOL: Ventura (Calif.).
COLLEGE: Colorado State.
TRANSACTIONS/CAREER NOTES: Selected by Jacksonville Jaguars in seventh round (236th pick overall) of 2000 NFL draft. ... Signed by Jaguars (May 19, 2000).

			INTERCEPTIONS				SACKS
Year Team	G	GS	No.	Yds.	Avg.	TD	No.
2000—Jacksonville NFL	14	0	0	0	0.0	0	0.0

O'NEAL, ANDRE   LB   CHIEFS

PERSONAL: Born December 12, 1975, in Decatur, Ga. ... 6-1/235. ... Full name: Andre T. O'Neal.
HIGH SCHOOL: Cedar Grove (Decatur, Ga.).
COLLEGE: Marshall (degree in adult fitness).
TRANSACTIONS/CAREER NOTES: Signed as non-drafted free agent by Kansas City Chiefs (April 27, 2000).
PLAYING EXPERIENCE: Kansas City NFL, 2000. ... Games/Games started: 2000 (10/0).

O'NEAL, DELTHA   CB   BRONCOS

PERSONAL: Born January 30, 1977, in Palo Alto, Calif. ... 5-10/196. ... Full name: Deltha Lee O'Neal III.
HIGH SCHOOL: West (Milpitas, Calif.).
COLLEGE: California.
TRANSACTIONS/CAREER NOTES: Selected by Denver Broncos in first round (15th pick overall) of 2000 NFL draft. ... Signed by Broncos (July 21, 2000).
HONORS: Named kick returner on The Sporting News college All-America first team (1999). ... Named cornerback on The Sporting News college All-America second team (1999).
PRO STATISTICS: 2000—Recovered three fumbles for six yards.

			INTERCEPTIONS				PUNT RETURNS				KICKOFF RETURNS				TOTALS		
Year Team	G	GS	No.	Yds.	Avg.	TD	No.	Yds.	Avg.	TD	No.	Yds.	Avg.	TD	TD	2pt.	Pts. Fum.
2000—Denver NFL	16	0	0	0	0.0	0	34	354	10.4	0	46	1102	24.0	▲1	1	0	6 6

O'NEILL, KEVIN   LB

PERSONAL: Born April 14, 1975, in Twinsburg, Ohio ... 6-2/249.
HIGH SCHOOL: Walsh Jesuit (Cuyahoga Falls, Ohio).
COLLEGE: Bowling Green State.
TRANSACTIONS/CAREER NOTES: Signed as non-drafted free agent by Detroit Lions (April 24, 1998). ... On physically unable to perform list with knee injury (August 30-November 17, 1999). ... Released by Lions (February 19, 2001).
PLAYING EXPERIENCE: Detroit NFL, 1998-2000. ... Games/Games started: 1998 (11/0), 1999 (4/0), 2000 (11/0). Total: 26/0.

O

OSTROSKI, JERRY   G   BILLS

PERSONAL: Born July 12, 1970, in Collegeville, Pa. ... 6-3/327. ... Full name: Gerald Ostroski Jr.
HIGH SCHOOL: Owen J. Roberts (Pottstown, Pa.).
COLLEGE: Tulsa.
TRANSACTIONS/CAREER NOTES: Selected by Kansas City Chiefs in 10th round (271st pick overall) of 1992 NFL draft. ... Signed by Chiefs (July 21, 1992). ... Released by Chiefs (August 25, 1992). ... Signed by Atlanta Falcons (May 7, 1993). ... Released by Falcons (August 24, 1993). ... Signed by Buffalo Bills to practice squad (November 18, 1993). ... Released by Bills (August 28, 1994). ... Re-signed by Bills to practice squad (August 29, 1994). ... Activated (November 30, 1994). ... Granted free agency (February 13, 1998). ... Re-signed by Bills (April 8, 1998). ... Granted unconditional free agency (February 12, 1999). ... Re-signed by Bills (February 17, 1999).
PLAYING EXPERIENCE: Buffalo NFL, 1994-2000. ... Games/Games started: 1994 (4/3), 1995 (16/13), 1996 (16/16), 1997 (16/16), 1998 (16/16), 1999 (15/15), 2000 (16/16). Total: 99/95.
PRO STATISTICS: 1997—Recovered three fumbles. 1999—Fumbled once for minus two yards. 2000—Fumbled once for minus 12 yards and recovered one fumble in end zone for touchdown.

OSTROWSKI, PHIL   G   BRONCOS

PERSONAL: Born September 23, 1975, in Wilkes-Barre, Pa. ... 6-4/291. ... Full name: Phillip Lucas Ostrowski. ... Name pronounced oh-STROW-ski.
HIGH SCHOOL: E.L. Meyers (Wilkes-Barre, Pa.).
COLLEGE: Penn State.
TRANSACTIONS/CAREER NOTES: Selected by San Francisco 49ers in fifth round (151st pick overall) of 1998 NFL draft. ... Signed by 49ers (July 18, 1998). ... Inactive for 16 games (1998). ... Released by 49ers (February 19, 2001). ... Signed by Denver Broncos (April 6, 2001).
PLAYING EXPERIENCE: San Francisco NFL, 1999 and 2000. ... Games/Games started: 1999 (15/0), 2000 (13/0). Total: 28/0.

OTTIS, BRAD   DE   CARDINALS

PERSONAL: Born August 2, 1972, in Wahoo, Neb. ... 6-5/290. ... Full name: Brad Allen Ottis. ... Name pronounced AH-tis.
HIGH SCHOOL: Bergan (Fremont, Neb.).
COLLEGE: Wayne State (Neb.).
TRANSACTIONS/CAREER NOTES: Selected by Los Angeles Rams in second round (56th pick overall) of 1994 NFL draft. ... Signed by Rams (June 23, 1994). ... Rams franchise moved to St. Louis (April 12, 1995). ... Released by Rams (August 20, 1996). ... Signed by Arizona Cardinals (October 1, 1996). ... Granted free agency (February 14, 1997). ... Re-signed by Cardinals for 1997 season. ... Granted unconditional free agency (February 13, 1998). ... Re-signed by Cardinals (February 18, 1998). ... On injured reserve with foot injury (August 30, 1998-entire season). ... Granted unconditional free agency (February 11, 2000). ... Re-signed by Cardinals (March 29, 2000).
PLAYING EXPERIENCE: Los Angeles Rams NFL, 1994; St. Louis NFL, 1995; Arizona NFL, 1996, 1997, 1999 and 2000. ... Games/Games started: 1994 (13/0), 1995 (12/0), 1996 (11/1), 1997 (16/4), 1999 (14/7), 2000 (15/11). Total: 71/23.
PRO STATISTICS: 1994—Credited with one sack. 1996—Credited with one sack. 1999—Credited with one sack. 2000—Credited with one sack.

OWENS, RICH   DE   CHIEFS

PERSONAL: Born May 22, 1972, in Philadelphia. ... 6-6/275.
HIGH SCHOOL: Lincoln (Philadelphia).
COLLEGE: Lehigh.
TRANSACTIONS/CAREER NOTES: Selected by Washington Redskins in fifth round (152nd pick overall) of 1995 NFL draft. ... Signed by Redskins (May 23, 1995). ... Granted free agency (February 13, 1998). ... Re-signed by Redskins (May 7, 1998). ... On injured reserve with knee injury (August 25, 1998-entire season). ... Granted unconditional free agency (February 12, 1999). ... Signed by Miami Dolphins (March 16, 1999). ... Granted unconditional free agency (March 2, 2001). ... Signed by Kansas City Chiefs (April 6, 2001).
PRO STATISTICS: 1997—Recovered one fumble. 1999—Recovered one fumble.

Year Team	G	GS	SACKS
1995—Washington NFL	10	3	3.0
1996—Washington NFL	16	16	11.0
1997—Washington NFL	16	15	2.5
1998—Washington NFL	Did not play.		
1999—Miami NFL	16	14	8.5
2000—Miami NFL	12	3	0.5
Pro totals (5 years)	70	51	25.5

OWENS, TERRELL   WR   49ERS

PERSONAL: Born December 7, 1973, in Alexander City, Ala. ... 6-3/217. ... Full name: Terrell Eldorado Owens. ... Name pronounced TARE-el.
HIGH SCHOOL: Benjamin Russell (Alexander City, Ala.).
COLLEGE: Tennessee-Chattanooga.
TRANSACTIONS/CAREER NOTES: Selected by San Francisco 49ers in third round (89th pick overall) of 1996 NFL draft. ... Signed by 49ers (July 18, 1996). ... On physically unable to perform list with foot injury (July 17-August 11, 1997). ... Designated by 49ers as franchise player (February 12, 1999). ... Re-signed by 49ers (June 4, 1999).
CHAMPIONSHIP GAME EXPERIENCE: Played in NFC championship game (1997 season).
HONORS: Played in Pro Bowl (2000 season).
PRO STATISTICS: 1996—Returned three kickoffs for 47 yards. 1997—Returned two kickoffs for 31 yards and recovered one fumble. 1998—Rushed four times for 53 yards and one touchdown and recovered one fumble for 13 yards. 2000—Rushed three times for 11 yards.
SINGLE GAME HIGHS (regular season): Receptions—20 (December 17, 2000, vs. Chicago); yards—283 (December 17, 2000, vs. Chicago); and touchdown receptions—2 (October 29, 2000, vs. St. Louis).
STATISTICAL PLATEAUS: 100-yard receiving games: 1996 (1), 1998 (2), 1999 (2), 2000 (5). Total: 10.

			RECEIVING				TOTALS			
Year Team	G	GS	No.	Yds.	Avg.	TD	TD	2pt.	Pts.	Fum.
1996—San Francisco NFL	16	10	35	520	14.9	4	4	0	24	1
1997—San Francisco NFL	16	15	60	936	15.6	8	8	0	48	1
1998—San Francisco NFL	16	8	67	1097	16.4	14	15	1	92	1
1999—San Francisco NFL	14	14	60	754	12.6	4	4	0	24	1
2000—San Francisco NFL	14	13	97	1451	15.0	13	13	1	80	3
Pro totals (5 years)	76	60	319	4758	14.9	43	44	2	268	7

PACE, ORLANDO   OT   RAMS

PERSONAL: Born November 4, 1975, in Sandusky, Ohio. ... 6-7/325. ... Full name: Orlando Lamar Pace.
HIGH SCHOOL: Sandusky (Ohio).
COLLEGE: Ohio State.
TRANSACTIONS/CAREER NOTES: Selected after junior season by St. Louis Rams in first round (first pick overall) of 1997 NFL draft. ... Signed by Rams (August 16, 1997).
PLAYING EXPERIENCE: St. Louis NFL, 1997-2000. ... Games/Games started: 1997 (13/9), 1998 (16/16), 1999 (16/16), 2000 (16/16). Total: 61/57.
CHAMPIONSHIP GAME EXPERIENCE: Played in NFC championship game (1999 season). ... Member of Super Bowl championship team (1999 season).
HONORS: Lombardi Award winner (1995 and 1996). ... Named offensive tackle on THE SPORTING NEWS college All-America first team (1995 and 1996). ... Outland Trophy winner (1996). ... Named offensive tackle on THE SPORTING NEWS NFL All-Pro team (1999 and 2000). ... Played in Pro Bowl (1999 and 2000 seasons).
PRO STATISTICS: 1997—Recovered one fumble. 1998—Recovered one fumble.

PAGE, CRAIG   C   COWBOYS

PERSONAL: Born January 17, 1976, in Jupiter, Fla. ... 6-3/303. ... Full name: Warren Craig Page.
HIGH SCHOOL: Jupiter (Fla.).
COLLEGE: Georgia Tech.
TRANSACTIONS/CAREER NOTES: Signed as non-drafted free agent by Tennessee Titans (April 21, 1999). ... Released by Titans (September 5, 1999). ... Re-signed by Titans to practice squad (September 7, 1999). ... Activated (January 14, 2000); did not play. ... Released by Titans (August 26, 2000). ... Re-signed by Titans to practice squad (August 29, 2000). ... Signed by Dallas Cowboys off Titans practice squad (November 22, 2000).
PLAYING EXPERIENCE: Dallas NFL, 2000. ... Games/Games started: 2000 (2/0).

PAGE, SOLOMON   G   COWBOYS

PERSONAL: Born February 27, 1976, in Pittsburgh. ... 6-4/321.
HIGH SCHOOL: Brashear (Pittsburgh).
COLLEGE: West Virginia.
TRANSACTIONS/CAREER NOTES: Selected after junior season by Dallas Cowboys in second round (55th pick overall) of 1999 NFL draft. ... Signed by Cowboys (July 28, 1999).
PLAYING EXPERIENCE: Dallas NFL, 1999 and 2000. ... Games/Games started: 1999 (14/6), 2000 (16/16). Total: 30/22.

PALMER, DAVID   RB/KR

PERSONAL: Born November 19, 1972, in Birmingham, Ala. ... 5-8/172. ... Full name: David L. Palmer.
HIGH SCHOOL: Jackson-Olin (Birmingham, Ala.).
COLLEGE: Alabama.
TRANSACTIONS/CAREER NOTES: Selected after junior season by Minnesota Vikings in second round (40th pick overall) of 1994 NFL draft. ... Signed by Vikings (July 19, 1994). ... Granted free agency (February 14, 1997). ... Re-signed by Vikings (May 7, 1997). ... Granted unconditional free agency (February 12, 1999). ... Re-signed by Vikings (February 22, 1999). ... On injured reserve with knee injury (November 27, 1999-remainder of season). ... Granted unconditional free agency (March 2, 2001).
CHAMPIONSHIP GAME EXPERIENCE: Played in NFC championship game (1998 season). ... Member of Vikings for NFC championship game (2000 season); inactive.
HONORS: Named kick returner on THE SPORTING NEWS college All-America first team (1993).
PRO STATISTICS: 1994—Fumbled twice. 1995—Fumbled once. 1996—Fumbled three times and recovered one fumble. 1997—Fumbled twice. 1998—Fumbled twice and recovered one fumble. 1999—Fumbled once. 2000—Fumbled once.
SINGLE GAME HIGHS (regular season): Attempts—4 (November 16, 1997, vs. Detroit); yards—15 (September 20, 1998, vs. Detroit); and rushing touchdowns—1 (November 9, 1997, vs. Chicago).

			RUSHING				RECEIVING				PUNT RETURNS				KICKOFF RETURNS				TOTALS		
Year Team	G	GS	Att.	Yds.	Avg.	TD	No.	Yds.	Avg.	TD	No.	Yds.	Avg.	TD	No.	Yds.	Avg.	TD	TD	2pt.	Pts.
1994—Minnesota NFL	13	1	1	1	1.0	0	6	90	15.0	0	30	193	6.4	0	0	0	0.0	0	0	0	0
1995—Minnesota NFL	14	0	7	15	2.1	0	12	100	8.3	0	26	342*13.2		†1	17	354	20.8	0	1	0	6
1996—Minnesota NFL	11	1	2	9	4.5	0	6	40	6.7	0	22	216	9.8	1	13	292	22.5	0	1	0	6
1997—Minnesota NFL	16	0	11	36	3.3	1	26	193	7.4	1	34	444‡13.1		0	32	711	22.2	0	2	0	12
1998—Minnesota NFL	16	0	10	52	5.2	0	18	185	10.3	0	28	289	10.3	0	50	1176	23.5	1	1	0	6
1999—Minnesota NFL	8	2	3	12	4.0	0	4	25	6.3	0	12	93	7.8	0	27	621	23.0	0	0	0	0
2000—Minnesota NFL	6	0	0	0	0.0	0	1	-2	-2.0	0	10	33	3.3	0	6	120	20.0	0	0	0	0
Pro totals (7 years)	84	4	34	125	3.7	1	73	631	8.6	1	162	1610	9.9	2	145	3274	22.6	1	5	0	30

O
P

PALMER, MITCH — LB — VIKINGS

PERSONAL: Born September 2, 1973, in San Diego. ... 6-4/257. ... Full name: Richard Mitchell Palmer.
HIGH SCHOOL: Poway (Calif.).
COLLEGE: Colorado State.
TRANSACTIONS/CAREER NOTES: Signed as non-drafted free agent by Carolina Panthers (April 28, 1997). ... Released by Panthers (August 17, 1997). ... Signed by Tampa Bay Buccaneers (April 28, 1998). ... On injured reserve with knee injury (October 5, 1999-remainder of season). ... Released by Buccaneers (July 23, 2000). ... Signed by Minnesota Vikings (August 8, 2000).
PLAYING EXPERIENCE: Tampa Bay NFL, 1998 and 1999; Minnesota NFL, 2000. ... Games/Games started: 1998 (16/0), 1999 (4/0), 2000 (16/0). Total: 36/0.
CHAMPIONSHIP GAME EXPERIENCE: Played in NFC championship game (2000 season).

PANOS, JOE — G — PATRIOTS

PERSONAL: Born January 24, 1971, in Brookfield, Wis. ... 6-3/300. ... Full name: Zois Panagiotopoulos.
HIGH SCHOOL: Brookfield (Wis.) East.
COLLEGE: Wisconsin.
TRANSACTIONS/CAREER NOTES: Selected by Philadelphia Eagles in third round (77th pick overall) of 1994 NFL draft. ... Signed by Eagles (July 11, 1994). ... On injured reserve with shoulder injury (November 12, 1995-remainder of season). ... Granted free agency (February 14, 1997). ... Re-signed by Eagles (July 19, 1997). ... Granted unconditional free agency (February 13, 1998). ... Signed by Buffalo Bills (February 20, 1998). ... Inactive for entire 1999 season due to neck injury. ... Released by Bills (February 22, 2001). ... Signed by New England Patriots (March 20, 2001).
PLAYING EXPERIENCE: Philadelphia NFL, 1994-1997; Buffalo NFL, 1998 and 2000. ... Games/Games started: 1994 (16/2), 1995 (9/9), 1996 (16/16), 1997 (13/13), 1998 (16/16), 2000 (13/0). Total: 83/56.
PRO STATISTICS: 1997—Recovered one fumble.

PARKER, ANTHONY — CB — 49ERS

PERSONAL: Born December 4, 1975, in Denver. ... 6-1/200. ... Full name: Anthony E. Parker.
HIGH SCHOOL: Thornton (Colo.).
JUNIOR COLLEGE: Mesa State College (Colo.).
COLLEGE: Weber State.
TRANSACTIONS/CAREER NOTES: Selected by San Francisco 49ers in fourth round (99th pick overall) of 1999 NFL draft. ... Signed by 49ers (July 26, 1999). ... On injured reserve with knee injury (August 31, 1999-entire season).
PLAYING EXPERIENCE: San Francisco NFL, 2000. ... Games/Games started: 2000 (16/0).

PARKER, De'MOND — RB — PACKERS

PERSONAL: Born December 24, 1976, in Tulsa, Okla. ... 5-10/185. ... Full name: De'Mond Keith Parker. ... Nephew of Patrick Collins, running back with Green Bay Packers (1988). ... Name pronounced de-MOND.
HIGH SCHOOL: Booker T. Washington (Tulsa, Okla.).
COLLEGE: Oklahoma.
TRANSACTIONS/CAREER NOTES: Selected after junior season by Green Bay Packers in fifth round (159th pick overall) of 1999 NFL draft. ... Signed by Packers (July 12, 1999). ... On injured reserve with knee injury (December 28, 1999-remainder of season). ... On physically unable to perform list with knee injury (August 22-October 31, 2000).
PRO STATISTICS: 1999—Recovered two fumbles.
SINGLE GAME HIGHS (regular season): Attempts—19 (December 5, 1999, vs. Chicago); yards—113 (December 5, 1999, vs. Chicago); and rushing touchdowns—2 (December 5, 1999, vs. Chicago).
STATISTICAL PLATEAUS: 100-yard rushing games: 1999 (1).

			RUSHING				RECEIVING				KICKOFF RETURNS				TOTALS			
Year Team	G	GS	Att.	Yds.	Avg.	TD	No.	Yds.	Avg.	TD	No.	Yds.	Avg.	TD	TD	2pt.	Pts.	Fum.
1999—Green Bay NFL	11	0	36	184	5.1	2	4	15	3.8	0	15	268	17.9	0	2	0	12	1
2000—Green Bay NFL	8	0	18	85	4.7	0	9	50	5.6	0	0	0	0.0	0	0	0	0	0
Pro totals (2 years)	19	0	54	269	5.0	2	13	65	5.0	0	15	268	17.9	0	2	0	12	1

PARKER, GLENN — G — GIANTS

PERSONAL: Born April 22, 1966, in Westminster, Calif. ... 6-5/312. ... Full name: Glenn Andrew Parker.
HIGH SCHOOL: Edison (Huntington Beach, Calif.).
JUNIOR COLLEGE: Golden West Junior College (Calif.).
COLLEGE: Arizona.
TRANSACTIONS/CAREER NOTES: Selected by Buffalo Bills in third round (69th pick overall) of 1990 NFL draft. ... Signed by Bills (July 26, 1990). ... Granted free agency (March 1, 1993). ... Re-signed by Bills (March 11, 1993). ... Released by Bills (August 24, 1997). ... Signed by Kansas City Chiefs (August 28, 1997). ... Granted unconditional free agency (February 11, 2000). ... Signed by New York Giants (March 26, 2000).
PLAYING EXPERIENCE: Buffalo NFL, 1990-1996; Kansas City NFL, 1997-2000. ... Games/Games started: 1990 (16/3), 1991 (16/5), 1992 (13/13), 1993 (16/9), 1994 (16/16), 1995 (13/13), 1996 (14/13), 1997 (15/15), 1998 (15/15), 1999 (12/11), 2000 (13/13). Total: 159/126.
CHAMPIONSHIP GAME EXPERIENCE: Played in AFC championship game (1990, 1992 and 1993 seasons). ... Member of Bills for AFC championship game (1991 season); inactive. ... Played in Super Bowl XXV (1990 season), Super Bowl XXVI (1991 season), Super Bowl XXVII (1992 season), Super Bowl XXVIII (1993 season) and Super Bowl XXXV (2000 season) ... Played in NFC championship game (2000 season).
PRO STATISTICS: 1992—Recovered one fumble. 1995—Recovered one fumble. 1996—Recovered two fumbles. 1998—Recovered one fumble.

P

PARKER, JEREMIAH　　　　DE

PERSONAL: Born November 15, 1977, in Franklin, La. ... 6-5/250.
HIGH SCHOOL: DeAnza (Richmond, Va.).
COLLEGE: California.
TRANSACTIONS/CAREER NOTES: Selected by New York Giants in seventh round (217th pick overall) of 2000 NFL draft. ... Signed by Giants (July 11, 2000). ... Released by Giants (June 1, 2001).
PLAYING EXPERIENCE: New York Giants NFL, 2000. ... Games/Games started: 2000 (4/0).
CHAMPIONSHIP GAME EXPERIENCE: Member of Giants for NFC championship game (2000 season); inactive. ... Member of Giants for Super Bowl XXXV (2000 season); inactive.

PARKER, LARRY　　　　WR　　　　CHIEFS

PERSONAL: Born July 14, 1976, in Bakersfield, Calif. ... 6-1/205.
HIGH SCHOOL: Bakersfield (Calif.).
COLLEGE: Southern California.
TRANSACTIONS/CAREER NOTES: Selected by Kansas City Chiefs in fourth round (108th pick overall) of 1999 NFL draft. ... Signed by Chiefs (July 29, 1999).
PRO STATISTICS: 2000—Rushed once for minus seven yards and caught three passes for 41 yards.
SINGLE GAME HIGHS (regular season): Receptions—2 (November 19, 2000, vs. Buffalo); yards—33 (November 19, 2000, vs. Buffalo); and touchdown receptions—0.

			PUNT RETURNS				KICKOFF RETURNS				TOTALS		
Year Team	G	GS	No.	Yds.	Avg.	TD	No.	Yds.	Avg.	TD	TD	2pt.	Pts.	Fum.
1999—Kansas City NFL	10	0	5	51	10.2	0	1	24	24.0	0	0	0	0	1
2000—Kansas City NFL	16	0	5	50	10.0	0	14	279	19.9	0	0	0	0	1
Pro totals (2 years)	26	0	10	101	10.1	0	15	303	20.2	0	0	0	0	2

PARKER, RIDDICK　　　　DT　　　　PATRIOTS

PERSONAL: Born November 20, 1972, in Emporia, Va. ... 6-3/274.
HIGH SCHOOL: Southampton (Courtland, Va.).
COLLEGE: North Carolina.
TRANSACTIONS/CAREER NOTES: Signed as non-drafted free agent by San Diego Chargers (April 28, 1995). ... Released by Chargers (August 22, 1995). ... Signed by Seattle Seahawks (July 8, 1996). ... Released by Seahawks (August 24, 1996). ... Re-signed by Seahawks to practice squad (August 26, 1996). ... Granted free agency (February 11, 2000). ... Re-signed by Seahawks (May 12, 2000). ... Granted unconditional free agency (March 2, 2001). ... Signed by New England Patriots (June 5, 2001).
PLAYING EXPERIENCE: Seattle NFL, 1997-2000. ... Games/Games started: 1997 (11/0), 1998 (8/0), 1999 (16/3), 2000 (16/16). Total: 51/19.
PRO STATISTICS: 1998—Credited with one sack. 1999—Credited with two sacks.

PARKER, SIRR　　　　WR

PERSONAL: Born October 31, 1977, in Los Angeles. ... 5-11/196. ... Full name: Sirr Eluan Parker.
HIGH SCHOOL: Locke (Los Angeles).
COLLEGE: Texas A&M.
TRANSACTIONS/CAREER NOTES: Signed as non-drafted free agent by San Diego Chargers (April 20, 1999). ... Released by Chargers (August 26, 1999). ... Signed by Carolina Panthers to practice squad (September 8, 1999). ... Claimed on waivers by Cincinnati Bengals (July 26, 2000). ... Released by Bengals (August 27, 2000). ... Re-signed by Bengals to practice squad (August 28, 2000). ... Released by Bengals (September 13, 2000). ... Re-signed by Bengals to practice squad (October 3, 2000). ... Activated (December 4, 2000). ... Released by Bengals (May 7, 2001).
PLAYING EXPERIENCE: Cincinnati NFL, 2000. ... Games/Games started: 2000 (2/0).

PARKER, VAUGHN　　　　OT　　　　CHARGERS

PERSONAL: Born June 5, 1971, in Buffalo. ... 6-3/300. ... Full name: Vaughn Antoine Parker.
HIGH SCHOOL: Saint Joseph's Collegiate Institute (Buffalo).
COLLEGE: UCLA.
TRANSACTIONS/CAREER NOTES: Selected by San Diego Chargers in second round (63rd pick overall) of 1994 NFL draft. ... Signed by Chargers (July 12, 1994). ... Granted free agency (February 14, 1997). ... Re-signed by Chargers (June 6, 1997). ... On injured reserve with leg injury (December 12, 1998-remainder of season). ... Granted unconditional free agency (February 11, 2000). ... Re-signed by Chargers (February 11, 2000).
PLAYING EXPERIENCE: San Diego NFL, 1994-2000. ... Games/Games started: 1994 (6/0), 1995 (14/7), 1996 (16/16), 1997 (16/16), 1998 (6/6), 1999 (15/15), 2000 (16/16). Total: 89/76.
CHAMPIONSHIP GAME EXPERIENCE: Played in AFC championship game (1994 season). ... Played in Super Bowl XXIX (1994 season).
PRO STATISTICS: 1994—Returned one kickoff for one yard. 1996—Recovered one fumble. 1997—Recovered two fumbles. 1999—Recovered one fumble.

PARMALEE, BERNIE　　　　RB

PERSONAL: Born September 16, 1967, in Jersey City, N.J. ... 5-11/210. ... Full name: Bernard Parmalee. ... Name pronounced PARM-uh-lee.
HIGH SCHOOL: Lincoln (Jersey City, N.J.).
COLLEGE: Ball State (degree in business administration).

P

TRANSACTIONS/CAREER NOTES: Signed as non-drafted free agent by Miami Dolphins (May 1, 1992). ... Released by Dolphins (August 31, 1992). ... Re-signed by Dolphins to practice squad (September 1, 1992). ... Activated (October 21, 1992). ... Deactivated for remainder of 1992 playoffs (January 16, 1993). ... Granted free agency (February 17, 1995). ... Re-signed by Dolphins (March 31, 1995). ... Granted unconditional free agency (February 14, 1997). ... Re-signed by Dolphins (April 17, 1997). ... Granted unconditional free agency (February 13, 1998). ... Re-signed by Dolphins (March 2, 1998). ... Released by Dolphins (September 5, 1999). ... Signed by New York Jets (September 7, 1999). ... Released by Jets (February 21, 2001).

PRO STATISTICS: 1994—Recovered three fumbles for 20 yards. 1998—Recovered two fumbles. 2000—Recovered one fumble.

SINGLE GAME HIGHS (regular season): Attempts—30 (October 16, 1994, vs. Los Angeles Raiders); yards—150 (October 16, 1994, vs. Los Angeles Raiders); and rushing touchdowns—3 (December 25, 1994, vs. Detroit).

STATISTICAL PLATEAUS: 100-yard rushing games: 1994 (3), 1995 (3). Total: 6.

			RUSHING				RECEIVING				KICKOFF RETURNS				TOTALS			
Year Team	G	GS	Att.	Yds.	Avg.	TD	No.	Yds.	Avg.	TD	No.	Yds.	Avg.	TD	TD	2pt.	Pts.	Fum.
1992—Miami NFL	10	0	6	38	6.3	0	0	0	0.0	0	14	289	20.6	0	0	0	0	3
1993—Miami NFL	16	0	4	16	4.0	0	1	1	1.0	0	0	0	0.0	0	0	0	0	0
1994—Miami NFL	15	10	216	868	4.0	6	34	249	7.3	1	2	0	0.0	0	7	1	44	5
1995—Miami NFL	16	12	236	878	3.7	9	39	345	8.8	1	0	0	0.0	0	10	0	60	5
1996—Miami NFL	16	0	25	80	3.2	0	21	189	9.0	0	0	0	0.0	0	0	0	0	1
1997—Miami NFL	16	4	18	59	3.3	0	28	301	10.8	1	0	0	0.0	0	1	0	6	1
1998—Miami NFL	15	0	8	20	2.5	0	21	221	10.5	0	0	0	0.0	0	0	0	0	2
1999—New York Jets NFL	16	0	27	133	4.9	0	15	113	7.5	0	0	0	0.0	0	0	0	0	0
2000—New York Jets NFL	14	0	27	87	3.2	2	9	66	7.3	0	0	0	0.0	0	2	0	12	0
Pro totals (9 years)	134	26	567	2179	3.8	17	168	1485	8.8	3	16	289	18.1	0	20	1	122	17

PARRELLA, JOHN   DT   CHARGERS

PERSONAL: Born November 22, 1969, in Topeka, Kan. ... 6-3/300. ... Full name: John Lorin Parrella.

HIGH SCHOOL: Grand Island (Neb.) Central Catholic.

COLLEGE: Nebraska.

TRANSACTIONS/CAREER NOTES: Selected by Buffalo Bills in second round (55th pick overall) of 1993 NFL draft. ... Signed by Bills (July 12, 1993). ... Released by Bills (August 28, 1994). ... Signed by San Diego Chargers (September 12, 1994). ... Granted free agency (February 16, 1996). ... Re-signed by Chargers (June 14, 1996).

CHAMPIONSHIP GAME EXPERIENCE: Member of Bills for AFC championship game (1993 season); inactive. ... Member of Bills for Super Bowl XXVIII (1993 season); inactive. ... Played in AFC championship game (1994 season). ... Played in Super Bowl XXIX (1994 season).

PRO STATISTICS: 1997—Recovered one fumble. 1998—Recovered one fumble.

Year Team	G	GS	SACKS
1993—Buffalo NFL	10	0	1.0
1994—San Diego NFL	13	1	1.0
1995—San Diego NFL	16	1	2.0
1996—San Diego NFL	16	9	2.0
1997—San Diego NFL	16	16	3.5
1998—San Diego NFL	16	16	1.5
1999—San Diego NFL	16	16	5.5
2000—San Diego NFL	16	16	7.0
Pro totals (8 years)	119	75	23.5

PARRISH, TONY   S   BEARS

PERSONAL: Born November 23, 1975, in Huntington Beach, Calif. ... 5-10/211.

HIGH SCHOOL: Marina (Huntington Beach, Calif.).

COLLEGE: Washington.

TRANSACTIONS/CAREER NOTES: Selected by Chicago Bears in second round (35th pick overall) of 1998 NFL draft. ... Signed by Bears (July 20, 1998).

PRO STATISTICS: 1998—Credited with one sack, fumbled once and recovered two fumbles for minus two yards. 2000—Credited with two sacks.

			INTERCEPTIONS			
Year Team	G	GS	No.	Yds.	Avg.	TD
1998—Chicago NFL	16	16	1	8	8.0	0
1999—Chicago NFL	16	16	1	41	41.0	0
2000—Chicago NFL	16	16	3	81	27.0	1
Pro totals (3 years)	48	48	5	130	26.0	1

PARTEN, TY   DE

PERSONAL: Born October 13, 1969, in Washington, D.C. ... 6-5/290. ... Full name: Ty Daniel Parten.

HIGH SCHOOL: Horizon (Scottsdale, Ariz.).

COLLEGE: Arizona.

TRANSACTIONS/CAREER NOTES: Selected by Cincinnati Bengals in third round (63rd pick overall) of 1993 draft. ... Signed by Bengals (July 19, 1993). ... On injured reserve with left thumb injury (November 29, 1993-remainder of season). ... Released by Bengals (September 20, 1995). ... Selected by Scottish Claymores in 1996 World League draft (February 22, 1996). ... Signed by St. Louis Rams (April 2, 1997). ... Released by Rams (August 24, 1997). ... Signed by Kansas City Chiefs (December 10, 1997). ... Granted free agency (February 12, 1999). ... Re-signed by Chiefs (June 16, 1999). ... Granted unconditional free agency (February 11, 2000). ... Re-signed by Chiefs (July 20, 2000). ... On injured reserve with knee injury (September 27, 2000-remainder of season). ... Granted unconditional free agency (March 2, 2001).

PLAYING EXPERIENCE: Cincinnati NFL, 1993-1995; Scottish NFLE, 1996; Kansas City NFL, 1997-2000. ... Games/Games started: 1993 (11/1), 1994 (14/4), 1995 (1/1), 1996 (games played unavailable), 1997 (2/0), 1998 (16/6), 1999 (16/0), 2000 (2/0). Total NFL: 62/12.

PRO STATISTICS: NFLE: 1996—Credited with two sacks. 1998—Returned two kickoffs for 22 yards and recovered one fumble. 1999—Returned one kickoff for 11 yards.

PASS, PATRICK   RB   PATRIOTS

PERSONAL: Born December 31, 1977, in Atlanta. ... 5-10/215.
HIGH SCHOOL: Tucker (Ga.).
COLLEGE: Georgia.
TRANSACTIONS/CAREER NOTES: Selected by New England Patriots in seventh round (239th pick overall) of 2000 NFL draft. ... Signed by Patriots (June 29, 2000). ... Released by Patriots (August 27, 2000). ... Re-signed by Patriots to practice squad (August 29, 2000). ... Activated (September 16, 2000).
PRO STATISTICS: 2000—Recovered one fumble.
SINGLE GAME HIGHS (regular season): Attempts—12 (November 19, 2000, vs. Cincinnati); yards—39 (November 19, 2000, vs. Cincinnati); and rushing touchdowns—0.

			RUSHING				RECEIVING				TOTALS		
Year Team	G	GS	Att.	Yds.	Avg.	TD	No.	Yds.	Avg.	TD	TD	2pt.	Pts.	Fum.
2000—New England NFL	5	2	18	58	3.2	0	4	17	4.3	0	0	0	0	0

RECORD AS BASEBALL PLAYER

TRANSACTIONS/CAREER NOTES: Selected by Florida Marlins organization in 44th round of free-agent draft (June 4, 1996).

						BATTING								FIELDING		
Year Team (League)	Pos.	G	AB	R	H	2B	3B	HR	RBI	Avg.	BB	SO	SB	PO	A	E	Avg.
1996—GC Marlins (GCL)	OF	29	90	14	22	4	0	0	8	.244	15	27	5	27	0	2	.931

PATHON, JEROME   WR   COLTS

PERSONAL: Born December 16, 1975, in Capetown, South Africa. ... 6-0/182. ... Name pronounced PAY-thin.
HIGH SCHOOL: Carson Graham Secondary School (North Vancouver).
COLLEGE: Acadia (Nova Scotia), then Washington.
TRANSACTIONS/CAREER NOTES: Selected by Indianapolis Colts in second round (32nd pick overall) of 1998 NFL draft. ... Signed by Colts (July 26, 1998).
HONORS: Named wide receiver on THE SPORTING NEWS college All-America second team (1997).
PRO STATISTICS: 1998—Rushed three times for minus two yards. 1999—Returned six kickoffs for 123 yards. 2000—Rushed once for three yards and returned 26 kickoffs for 583 yards.
SINGLE GAME HIGHS (regular season): Receptions—7 (November 1, 1998, vs. New England); yards—73 (December 3, 2000, vs. New York Jets); and touchdown receptions—1 (November 19, 2000, vs. Green Bay).

			RECEIVING				TOTALS			
Year Team	G	GS	No.	Yds.	Avg.	TD	TD	2pt.	Pts.	Fum.
1998—Indianapolis NFL	16	15	50	511	10.2	1	1	0	6	0
1999—Indianapolis NFL	10	2	14	163	11.6	0	0	0	0	0
2000—Indianapolis NFL	16	10	50	646	12.9	3	3	0	18	0
Pro totals (3 years)	42	27	114	1320	11.6	4	4	0	24	0

PATTEN, DAVID   WR/KR   PATRIOTS

PERSONAL: Born August 19, 1974, in Hopkins, S.C. ... 5-10/195.
HIGH SCHOOL: Lower Richland (Hopkins, S.C.).
COLLEGE: Western Carolina.
TRANSACTIONS/CAREER NOTES: Played for Albany Firebirds of Arena League (1996). ... Signed as non-drafted free agent by New York Giants (March 24, 1997). ... Released by Giants (August 24, 1997). ... Re-signed by Giants to practice squad (August 25, 1997). ... Activated (August 27, 1997). ... On injured reserve with knee injury (December 16, 1998-remainder of season). ... Granted free agency (February 11, 2000). ... Signed by Cleveland Browns (March 16, 2000). ... Granted unconditional free agency (March 2, 2001). ... Signed by New England Patriots (April 2, 2001).
PRO STATISTICS: 1997—Rushed once for two yards and recovered one fumble. 1999—Rushed once for 27 yards.
SINGLE GAME HIGHS (regular season): Receptions—7 (December 10, 2000, vs. Philadelphia); yards—113 (October 1, 2000, vs. Baltimore); and touchdown receptions—1 (December 10, 2000, vs. Philadelphia).
STATISTICAL PLATEAUS: 100-yard receiving games: 2000 (2).

			RECEIVING				KICKOFF RETURNS				TOTALS		
Year Team	G	GS	No.	Yds.	Avg.	TD	No.	Yds.	Avg.	TD	TD	2pt.	Pts.	Fum.
1997—New York Giants NFL	16	3	13	226	17.4	2	8	123	15.4	0	2	0	12	2
1998—New York Giants NFL	12	0	11	119	10.8	1	43	928	21.6	1	2	0	12	0
1999—New York Giants NFL	16	0	9	115	12.8	0	33	673	20.4	0	0	0	0	0
2000—Cleveland NFL	14	11	38	546	14.4	1	22	469	21.3	0	1	0	6	2
Pro totals (4 years)	58	14	71	1006	14.2	4	106	2193	20.7	1	5	0	30	4

PATTON, MARVCUS   LB   CHIEFS

PERSONAL: Born May 1, 1967, in Los Angeles. ... 6-2/237. ... Full name: Marvcus Raymond Patton.
HIGH SCHOOL: Leuzinger (Lawndale, Calif.).
COLLEGE: UCLA (degree in political science, 1990).
TRANSACTIONS/CAREER NOTES: Selected by Buffalo Bills in eighth round (208th pick overall) of 1990 NFL draft. ... Signed by Bills (July 27, 1990). ... On injured reserve with broken leg (January 26, 1991-remainder of 1990 playoffs). ... Granted free agency (February 1, 1992). ... Re-signed by Bills (July 23, 1992). ... Granted unconditional free agency (February 17, 1995). ... Signed by Washington Redskins (February 22, 1995). ... Granted unconditional free agency (February 12, 1999). ... Signed by Kansas City Chiefs (April 27, 1999).
CHAMPIONSHIP GAME EXPERIENCE: Played in AFC championship game (1991-1993 seasons). ... Played in Super Bowl XXVI (1991 season), Super Bowl XXVII (1992 season) and Super Bowl XXVIII (1993 season).
PRO STATISTICS: 1993—Recovered three fumbles for five yards. 1994—Recovered one fumble and fumbled once. 1995—Recovered one fumble. 1997—Returned one kickoff for 10 yards and recovered one fumble. 1999—Recovered three fumbles. 2000—Recovered one fumble.

P

| Year Team | G | GS | INTERCEPTIONS | | | | SACKS |
			No.	Yds.	Avg.	TD	No.
1990—Buffalo NFL	16	0	0	0	0.0	0	0.5
1991—Buffalo NFL	16	2	0	0	0.0	0	0.0
1992—Buffalo NFL	16	4	0	0	0.0	0	2.0
1993—Buffalo NFL	16	16	2	0	0.0	0	1.0
1994—Buffalo NFL	16	16	2	8	4.0	0	0.0
1995—Washington NFL	16	16	2	7	3.5	0	2.0
1996—Washington NFL	16	16	2	26	13.0	0	2.0
1997—Washington NFL	16	16	2	5	2.5	0	4.5
1998—Washington NFL	16	16	0	0	0.0	0	3.0
1999—Kansas City NFL	16	16	1	0	0.0	0	6.5
2000—Kansas City NFL	16	15	2	39	19.5	0	1.0
Pro totals (11 years)	176	133	13	85	6.5	1	22.5

PAULK, JEFF — FB — PATRIOTS

PERSONAL: Born April 26, 1976, in Phoenix. ... 6-0/240. ... Full name: Jeffery Howard Paulk.
HIGH SCHOOL: Corona Del Sol (Tempe, Ariz.).
COLLEGE: Arizona State.
TRANSACTIONS/CAREER NOTES: Selected by Atlanta Falcons in third round (92nd pick overall) of 1999 NFL draft. ... Signed by Falcons (June 16, 1999). ... Released by Falcons (August 19, 2000). ... Signed by New England Patriots to practice squad (December 7, 2000). ... Activated (December 20, 2000).
PLAYING EXPERIENCE: Atlanta NFL, 1999; New England NFL, 2000. ... Games/Games started: 1999 (1/0), 2000 (1/0). Total: 2/0.

PAUP, BRYCE — LB

PERSONAL: Born February 29, 1968, in Jefferson, Iowa. ... 6-5/250. ... Full name: Bryce Eric Paup.
HIGH SCHOOL: Scranton (Iowa).
COLLEGE: Northern Iowa (degree in business).
TRANSACTIONS/CAREER NOTES: Selected by Green Bay Packers in sixth round (159th pick overall) of 1990 NFL draft. ... Signed by Packers (July 22, 1990). ... On injured reserve with hand injury (September 4-November 17, 1990). ... On injured reserve with calf injury (December 12, 1991-remainder of season). ... Granted free agency (February 1, 1992). ... Re-signed by Packers (August 13, 1992). ... Granted unconditional free agency (February 17, 1995). ... Signed by Buffalo Bills (March 9, 1995). ... Granted unconditional free agency (February 13, 1998). ... Signed by Jacksonville Jaguars (February 16, 1998). ... Released by Jaguars (June 2, 2000). ... Signed by Minnesota Vikings (June 6, 2000). ... Granted unconditional free agency (March 2, 2001).
CHAMPIONSHIP GAME EXPERIENCE: Played in AFC championship game (1999 season). ... Played in NFC championship game (2000 season).
HONORS: Played in Pro Bowl (1994-1997 seasons). ... Named linebacker on THE SPORTING NEWS NFL All-Pro team (1995).
PRO STATISTICS: 1991—Credited with a safety. 1992—Recovered two fumbles. 1994—Recovered two fumbles. 1995—Recovered one fumble. 1997—Recovered one fumble.

| Year Team | G | GS | INTERCEPTIONS | | | | SACKS |
			No.	Yds.	Avg.	TD	No.
1990—Green Bay NFL	5	0	0	0	0.0	0	0.0
1991—Green Bay NFL	12	1	0	0	0.0	0	7.5
1992—Green Bay NFL	16	10	0	0	0.0	0	6.5
1993—Green Bay NFL	15	14	1	8	8.0	0	11.0
1994—Green Bay NFL	16	16	3	47	15.7	1	7.5
1995—Buffalo NFL	15	15	2	0	0.0	0	*17.5
1996—Buffalo NFL	12	11	0	0	0.0	0	6.0
1997—Buffalo NFL	16	16	0	0	0.0	0	9.5
1998—Jacksonville NFL	16	16	0	0	0.0	0	6.5
1999—Jacksonville NFL	15	14	0	0	0.0	0	1.0
2000—Minnesota NFL	10	0	0	0	0.0	0	2.0
Pro totals (11 years)	148	113	6	55	9.2	1	75.0

PAXTON, LONIE — TE — PATRIOTS

PERSONAL: Born March 13, 1978, in Orange, Calif. ... 6-2/260. ... Full name: Leonidas E. Paxton.
HIGH SCHOOL: Centennial (Carona, Calif.).
COLLEGE: Sacramento State.
TRANSACTIONS/CAREER NOTES: Signed as non-drafted free agent by New England Patriots (April 19, 2000).
PLAYING EXPERIENCE: New England NFL, 2000. ... Games/Games started: 2000 (16/0).

PAYNE, SETH — DT — JAGUARS

PERSONAL: Born February 12, 1975, in Clifton Springs, N.Y. ... 6-4/290. ... Full name: Seth Copeland Payne.
HIGH SCHOOL: Victor (N.Y.) Central.
COLLEGE: Cornell.
TRANSACTIONS/CAREER NOTES: Selected by Jacksonville Jaguars in fourth round (114th pick overall) of 1997 NFL draft. ... Signed by Jaguars (May 23, 1997). ... On injured reserve with shoulder injury (November 17, 1998-remainder of season).
PLAYING EXPERIENCE: Jacksonville NFL, 1997-2000. ... Games/Games started: 1997 (12/5), 1998 (6/1), 1999 (16/16), 2000 (16/14). Total: 50/36.
CHAMPIONSHIP GAME EXPERIENCE: Played in AFC championship game (1999 season).
PRO STATISTICS: 1999—Credited with 1 1/2 sacks. 2000—Credited with two sacks.

P

PEDERSON, DOUG   QB   PACKERS

PERSONAL: Born January 31, 1968, in Bellingham, Wash. ... 6-3/220. ... Full name: Douglas Irvin Pederson.
HIGH SCHOOL: Ferndale (Wash.).
COLLEGE: Northeast Louisiana (degree in business management).
TRANSACTIONS/CAREER NOTES: Signed as non-drafted free agent by Miami Dolphins (April 30, 1991). ... Released by Dolphins (August 16, 1991). ... Selected by New York/New Jersey Knights in fifth round (49th pick overall) of 1992 World League draft. ... Re-signed by Dolphins (June 1, 1992). ... Released by Dolphins (August 31, 1992). ... Re-signed by Dolphins to practice squad (September 1, 1992). ... Released by Dolphins (October 7, 1992). ... Re-signed by Dolphins (March 3, 1993). ... Released by Dolphins (August 30, 1993). ... Re-signed by Dolphins to practice squad (August 31, 1993). ... Activated (October 22, 1993). ... Released by Dolphins (December 15, 1993). ... Re-signed by Dolphins (April 15, 1994). ... Inactive for all 16 games (1994). ... Selected by Carolina Panthers from Dolphins in NFL expansion draft (February 15, 1995). ... Released by Panthers (May 22, 1995). ... Signed by Dolphins (July 11, 1995). ... Released by Dolphins (August 21, 1995). ... Re-signed by Dolphins (October 10, 1995). ... Inactive for two games with Dolphins (1995). ... Released by Dolphins (October 25, 1995). ... Signed by Green Bay Packers (November 22, 1995). ... Inactive for five games with Packers (1995). ... Granted unconditional free agency (February 14, 1997). ... Re-signed by Packers (February 20, 1997). ... Granted unconditional free agency (February 12, 1999). ... Signed by Philadelphia Eagles (February 17, 1999). ... Released by Eagles (August 27, 2000). ... Signed by Cleveland Browns (September 1, 2000). ... Released by Browns (February 22, 2001). ... Signed by Packers (March 14, 2001).
CHAMPIONSHIP GAME EXPERIENCE: Member of Packers for NFC championship game (1995-97 seasons); inactive. ... Member of Super Bowl championship team (1996 season); inactive. ... Member of Packers for Super Bowl XXXII (1997 season); inactive.
PRO STATISTICS: 1993—Recovered one fumble for minus one yard. 1998—Fumbled once for minus two yards. 1999—Fumbled seven times. 2000—Fumbled four times and recovered three fumbles.
SINGLE GAME HIGHS (regular season): Attempts—40 (December 10, 2000, vs. Philadelphia); completions—29 (December 10, 2000, vs. Philadelphia); yards—309 (December 10, 2000, vs. Philadelphia); and touchdown passes—2 (October 17, 1999, vs. Chicago).
STATISTICAL PLATEAUS: 300-yard passing games: 2000 (1).
MISCELLANEOUS: Regular-season record as starting NFL quarterback: 3-14 (.176).

			PASSING								RUSHING				TOTALS		
Year Team	G	GS	Att.	Cmp.	Pct.	Yds.	TD	Int.	Avg.	Rat.	Att.	Yds.	Avg.	TD	TD	2pt.	Pts.
1992—NY/New Jersey W.L. ...	7	1	128	70	54.7	1077	8	3	8.41	93.8	15	46	3.1	0	0	0	0
1993—Miami NFL	7	0	8	4	50.0	41	0	0	5.13	65.1	2	-1	-0.5	0	0	0	0
1994—Miami NFL							Did not play.										
1995—Miami NFL							Did not play.										
—Green Bay NFL							Did not play.										
1996—Green Bay NFL............	1	0	0	0	0.0	0	0	0	0.0	...	0	0	0.0	0	0	0	0
1997—Green Bay NFL............	1	0	0	0	0.0	0	0	0	0.0	...	3	-4	-1.3	0	0	0	0
1998—Green Bay NFL............	12	0	24	14	58.3	128	2	0	5.33	100.7	8	-4	-0.5	0	0	0	0
1999—Philadelphia NFL...........	16	9	227	119	52.4	1276	7	9	5.62	62.9	20	33	1.7	0	0	0	0
2000—Cleveland NFL	11	8	210	117	55.7	1047	2	8	4.99	56.6	18	68	3.8	0	0	0	0
W.L. totals (1 year)	7	1	128	70	54.7	1077	8	3	8.41	93.8	15	46	3.1	0	0	0	0
NFL totals (6 years)	48	17	469	254	54.2	2492	11	17	5.31	62.1	51	92	1.8	0	0	0	0
Pro totals (7 years)	55	18	597	324	54.3	3569	19	20	5.98	68.9	66	138	2.1	0	0	0	0

PEETE, RODNEY   QB   RAIDERS

PERSONAL: Born March 16, 1966, in Mesa, Ariz. ... 6-0/225. ... Son of Willie Peete, former running backs coach and scout with Chicago Bears; cousin of Calvin Peete, professional golfer.
HIGH SCHOOL: Sahuaro (Tucson, Ariz.), then Shawnee Mission South (Overland Park, Kan.).
COLLEGE: Southern California (degree in communications, 1989).
TRANSACTIONS/CAREER NOTES: Selected by Detroit Lions in sixth round (141st pick overall) of 1989 NFL draft. ... Signed by Lions (July 13, 1989). ... On injured reserve with Achilles' tendon injury (October 30, 1991-remainder of season). ... Granted free agency (February 1, 1992). ... Re-signed by Lions (July 30, 1992). ... Granted unconditional free agency (February 17, 1994). ... Signed by Dallas Cowboys (May 4, 1994). ... Granted unconditional free agency (February 17, 1995). ... Signed by Philadelphia Eagles (April 22, 1995). ... Granted unconditional free agency (February 16, 1996). ... Re-signed by Eagles (March 14, 1996). ... On injured reserve with knee injury (October 3, 1996-remainder of season). ... Granted unconditional free agency (February 14, 1997). ... Re-signed by Eagles (April 1, 1997). ... Traded by Eagles to Washington Redskins for sixth-round pick (C John Romero) in 2000 draft (April 28, 1999). ... Released by Redskins (April 18, 2000). ... Signed by Oakland Raiders (July 13, 2000).
CHAMPIONSHIP GAME EXPERIENCE: Member of Cowboys for NFC championship game (1994 season); did not play. ... Member of Raiders for AFC Championship game (2000 season); inactive.
HONORS: Named quarterback on THE SPORTING NEWS college All-America second team (1988).
PRO STATISTICS: 1989—Fumbled nine times and recovered three fumbles. 1990—Fumbled nine times and recovered one fumble. 1991—Fumbled twice and recovered one fumble for minus one yard. 1992—Fumbled six times and recovered two fumbles for minus seven yards. 1993—Fumbled 11 times and recovered four fumbles for minus eight yards. 1994—Fumbled three times and recovered two fumbles for minus one yard. 1995—Fumbled 13 times and recovered five fumbles. 1996—Fumbled twice and recovered one fumble. 1997—Fumbled five times and recovered two fumbles for minus two yards. 1998—Fumbled once.
SINGLE GAME HIGHS (regular season): Attempts—45 (October 8, 1995, vs. Washington); completions—30 (October 8, 1995, vs. Washington); yards—323 (September 27, 1992, vs. Tampa Bay); and touchdown passes—4 (December 16, 1990, vs. Chicago).
STATISTICAL PLATEAUS: 300-yard passing games: 1990 (1), 1992 (1). Total: 2.
MISCELLANEOUS: Selected by Toronto Blue Jays organization in 30th round of free-agent baseball draft (June 4, 1984); did not sign. ... Selected by Oakland Athletics organization in 14th round of free-agent baseball draft (June 1, 1988); did not sign. ... Selected by Athletics organization in 13th round of free-agent baseball draft (June 5, 1989); did not sign. ... Regular-season record as starting NFL quarterback: 37-35 (.514). ... Postseason record as starting NFL quarterback: 1-1 (.500).

			PASSING								RUSHING				TOTALS		
Year Team	G	GS	Att.	Cmp.	Pct.	Yds.	TD	Int.	Avg.	Rat.	Att.	Yds.	Avg.	TD	TD	2pt.	Pts.
1989—Detroit NFL.................	8	8	195	103	52.8	1479	5	9	7.58	67.0	33	148	4.5	4	4	0	24
1990—Detroit NFL.................	11	11	271	142	52.4	1974	13	8	7.28	79.8	47	363	7.7	6	6	0	36
1991—Detroit NFL.................	8	8	194	116	59.8	1339	5	9	6.90	69.9	25	125	5.0	2	2	0	12
1992—Detroit NFL.................	10	10	213	123	57.7	1702	9	9	7.99	80.0	21	83	4.0	0	0	0	0
1993—Detroit NFL.................	10	10	252	157	62.3	1670	6	14	6.63	66.4	45	165	3.7	1	1	0	6
1994—Dallas NFL.................	7	1	56	33	58.9	470	4	1	8.39	102.5	9	-2	-0.2	0	0	0	0

P

Year Team	G	GS	PASSING Att.	Cmp.	Pct.	Yds.	TD	Int.	Avg.	Rat.	RUSHING Att.	Yds.	Avg.	TD	TOTALS TD	2pt.	Pts.
1995—Philadelphia NFL	15	12	375	215	57.3	2326	8	14	6.20	67.3	32	147	4.6	1	1	0	6
1996—Philadelphia NFL	5	5	134	80	59.7	992	3	5	7.40	74.6	20	31	1.6	1	1	0	6
1997—Philadelphia NFL	5	3	118	68	57.6	869	4	4	7.36	78.0	8	37	4.6	0	0	0	0
1998—Philadelphia NFL	5	4	129	71	55.0	758	2	4	5.88	64.7	5	30	6.0	1	1	0	6
1999—Washington NFL	3	0	17	8	47.1	107	2	1	6.29	82.2	2	-1	-0.5	0	0	0	0
Pro totals (11 years)	87	72	1954	1116	57.1	13686	61	78	7.00	72.6	247	1126	4.6	16	16	0	96

PELSHAK, TROY   LB   JAGUARS

PERSONAL: Born March 6, 1977, in Charlotte, N.C. ... 6-2/242. ... Full name: Zenret Pelshak.
HIGH SCHOOL: Garringer (Charlotte, N.C.).
COLLEGE: North Carolina A&T.
TRANSACTIONS/CAREER NOTES: Signed as non-drafted free agent by St. Louis Rams (April 20, 1999). ... Released by Rams (August 22, 2000). ... Claimed on waivers by Minnesota Vikings (August 23, 2000). ... Released by Vikings (August 27, 2000). ... Re-signed by Rams (September 5, 2000). ... Released by Rams (October 5, 2000). ... Signed by Jacksonville Jaguars (December 6, 2000). ... Assigned by Jaguars to Barcelona Dragons in 2001 NFL Europe enhancement allocation program (February 19, 2001).
PLAYING EXPERIENCE: St. Louis NFL, 1999; St. Louis (3)-Jacksonville (1) NFL, 2000. ... Games/Games started: 1999 (9/0), 2000 (StL-3/0; Jax.-1/0; Total: 4/0). Total: 13/0.
CHAMPIONSHIP GAME EXPERIENCE: Member of Rams for NFC championship game (1999 season); inactive. ... Member of Super Bowl championship team (1999 season); inactive.

PENNINGTON, CHAD   QB   JETS

PERSONAL: Born June 26, 1976, in Knoxville, Tenn. ... 6-3/225. ... Full name: James Chad Pennington.
HIGH SCHOOL: Webb (Knoxville, Tenn.).
COLLEGE: Marshall.
TRANSACTIONS/CAREER NOTES: Selected by New York Jets in first round (18th pick overall) of 2000 NFL draft. ... Signed by Jets (July 13, 2000).
PLAYING EXPERIENCE: New York Jets NFL, 2000. ... Games/Games started: (1/0).
PRO STATISTICS: 2000—Attempted five passes with two completions for 67 yards and one touchdown and rushed once for no yards.
SINGLE GAME HIGHS (regular season): Attempts—5 (December 10, 2000, vs. Oakland); completions—2 (December 10, 2000, vs. Oakland); yards—67 (December 10, 2000, vs. Oakland); and touchdown passes—1 (December 10, 2000, vs. Oakland).

PERRY, DARREN   S

PERSONAL: Born December 29, 1968, in Chesapeake, Va. ... 5-11/200.
HIGH SCHOOL: Deep Creek (Chesapeake, Va.).
COLLEGE: Penn State (degree in business administration/management, 1991).
TRANSACTIONS/CAREER NOTES: Selected by Pittsburgh Steelers in eighth round (203rd pick overall) of 1992 NFL draft. ... Signed by Steelers (July 16, 1992). ... Granted free agency (February 17, 1995). ... Re-signed by Steelers (June 15, 1995). ... Granted unconditional free agency (February 12, 1999). ... Signed by San Diego Chargers (March 12, 1999). ... Announced retirement (July 31, 1999). ... Signed by Baltimore Ravens (November 9, 1999). ... Announced retirement (November 11, 1999) ... Signed by New Orleans Saints (April 27, 2000). ... Granted unconditional free agency (March 2, 2001).
CHAMPIONSHIP GAME EXPERIENCE: Played in AFC championship game (1994, 1995 and 1997 seasons). ... Played in Super Bowl XXX (1995 season).
HONORS: Named defensive back on THE SPORTING NEWS college All-America second team (1991).
PRO STATISTICS: 1992—Recovered one fumble. 1994—Recovered two fumbles. 1995—Fumbled once and recovered two fumbles. 1996—Returned one kickoff for eight yards, fumbled once and recovered two fumbles. 1997—Credited with one sack. 1998—Credited with $1/2$ sack, fumbled once and recovered one fumble.

Year Team	G	GS	INTERCEPTIONS No.	Yds.	Avg.	TD
1992—Pittsburgh NFL	16	16	6	69	11.5	0
1993—Pittsburgh NFL	16	16	4	61	15.3	0
1994—Pittsburgh NFL	16	16	7	112	16.0	0
1995—Pittsburgh NFL	16	16	4	71	17.8	0
1996—Pittsburgh NFL	16	16	5	115	23.0	1
1997—Pittsburgh NFL	16	16	4	77	19.3	0
1998—Pittsburgh NFL	14	14	2	69	34.5	0
1999—			Did not play.			
2000—New Orleans NFL	16	16	3	3	1.0	0
Pro totals (8 years)	126	126	35	577	16.5	1

PERRY, ED   TE   DOLPHINS

PERSONAL: Born September 1, 1974, in Richmond, Va. ... 6-4/270. ... Full name: Edward Lewis Perry.
HIGH SCHOOL: Highlands Springs (Va.).
COLLEGE: James Madison.
TRANSACTIONS/CAREER NOTES: Selected by Miami Dolphins in sixth round (177th pick overall) of 1997 NFL draft. ... Signed by Dolphins (June 13, 1997). ... Granted free agency (February 11, 2000). ... Re-signed by Dolphins (April 28, 2000). ... On injured reserve with shoulder injury (November 23, 2000-remainder of season). ... Granted unconditional free agency (March 2, 2001). ... Re-signed by Dolphins (March 16, 2001).
PRO STATISTICS: 1997—Returned one kickoff for seven yards and recovered one fumble.
SINGLE GAME HIGHS (regular season): Receptions—4 (September 13, 1998, vs. Buffalo); yards—59 (November 23, 1998, vs. New England); and touchdown receptions—1 (December 27, 1999, vs. New York Jets).

P

Year Team	G	GS	RECEIVING				TOTALS			
			No.	Yds.	Avg.	TD	TD	2pt.	Pts.	Fum.
1997—Miami NFL	16	4	11	45	4.1	1	1	0	6	0
1998—Miami NFL	14	5	25	255	10.2	0	0	0	0	0
1999—Miami NFL	16	1	3	8	2.7	1	1	0	6	0
2000—Miami NFL	9	0	0	0	0.0	0	0	0	0	0
Pro totals (4 years)	55	10	39	308	7.9	2	2	0	12	0

PERRY, JASON S CHARGERS

PERSONAL: Born August 1, 1976, in Passaic, N.J. ... 6-0/200. ... Full name: Jason Robert Perry.
HIGH SCHOOL: Paterson (N.J.) Catholic.
COLLEGE: North Carolina State.
TRANSACTIONS/CAREER NOTES: Selected by San Diego Chargers in fourth round (104th pick overall) of 1999 NFL draft. ... Signed by Chargers (July 22, 1999). ... On injured reserve with knee injury (September 26, 2000-remainder of season).
PLAYING EXPERIENCE: San Diego NFL, 1999 and 2000. ... Games/Games started: 1999 (16/5), 2000 (1/0). Total: 17/5.
PRO STATISTICS: 1999—Recovered one fumble.

PERRY, TODD G DOLPHINS

PERSONAL: Born November 28, 1970, in Elizabethtown, Ky. ... 6-5/308. ... Full name: Todd Joseph Perry.
HIGH SCHOOL: North Hardin (Radcliff, Ky.).
COLLEGE: Kentucky.
TRANSACTIONS/CAREER NOTES: Selected by Chicago Bears in fourth round (97th pick overall) of 1993 NFL draft. ... Signed by Bears (June 16, 1993). ... On injured reserve with back injury (December 19, 1997-remainder of season). ... Granted unconditional free agency (February 11, 2000). ... Re-signed by Bears (May 4, 2000). ... Granted unconditional free agency (March 2, 2001). ... Signed by Miami Dolphins (March 3, 2001).
PLAYING EXPERIENCE: Chicago NFL, 1993-2000. ... Games/Games started: 1993 (13/3), 1994 (15/4), 1995 (15/15), 1996 (16/16), 1997 (11/11), 1998 (16/16), 1999 (16/16), 2000 (16/16). Total: 118/97.
PRO STATISTICS: 1996—Recovered one fumble. 1999—Recovered one fumble.

PETER, CHRISTIAN DT COLTS

PERSONAL: Born October 5, 1972, in Locust, N.J. ... 6-3/292. ... Brother of Jason Peter, defensive end, Carolina Panthers.
HIGH SCHOOL: Middletown South (Middleton, N.J.), then Milford (Conn.) Academy.
COLLEGE: Nebraska.
TRANSACTIONS/CAREER NOTES: Selected by New England Patriots in fifth round (149th pick overall) of 1996 NFL draft. ... Patriots released rights (April 24, 1996). ... Signed by New York Giants (January 22, 1997). ... Granted free agency (February 11, 2000). ... Re-signed by Giants (April 12, 2000). ... Granted unconditional free agency (March 2, 2001). ... Signed by Indianapolis Colts (April 21, 2001).
CHAMPIONSHIP GAME EXPERIENCE: Played in NFC championship game (2000 season). ... Played in Super Bowl XXXV (2000 season).
PRO STATISTICS: 1999—Recovered one fumble for 38 yards and a touchdown.

Year Team	G	GS	SACKS
1997—New York Giants NFL	7	0	0.5
1998—New York Giants NFL	16	6	1.0
1999—New York Giants NFL	16	10	0.0
2000—New York Giants NFL	16	15	1.0
Pro totals (4 years)	55	31	2.5

PETER, JASON DE PANTHERS

PERSONAL: Born September 13, 1974, in Locust, N.J. ... 6-4/295. ... Full name: Jason Michael Peter. ... Brother of Christian Peter, defensive tackle, Indianapolis Colts.
HIGH SCHOOL: Middletown South (Middleton, N.J.), then Milford (Conn.) Academy.
COLLEGE: Nebraska (degree in communication studies, 1997).
TRANSACTIONS/CAREER NOTES: Selected by Carolina Panthers in first round (14th pick overall) of 1998 NFL draft. ... Signed by Panthers (August 31, 1998). ... On injured reserve with neck injury (December 5, 2000-remainder of season).
HONORS: Named defensive tackle on THE SPORTING NEWS college All-America first team (1997).
PRO STATISTICS: 1998—Recovered one fumble.

Year Team	G	GS	SACKS
1998—Carolina NFL	14	11	1.0
1999—Carolina NFL	9	9	4.5
2000—Carolina NFL	9	0	2.0
Pro totals (3 years)	32	20	7.5

PETERSON, JULIAN LB 49ERS

PERSONAL: Born July 28, 1978, in Hillcrest Heights, Md. ... 6-3/235.
HIGH SCHOOL: Crossland (Temple Hills, Md.).
JUNIOR COLLEGE: Valley Forge Junior College (Pa.).
COLLEGE: Michigan State.
TRANSACTIONS/CAREER NOTES: Selected by San Francisco 49ers in first round (16th pick overall) of 2000 NFL draft. ... Signed by 49ers (July 27, 2000).
PRO STATISTICS: 2000—Intercepted two passes for 33 yards.

Year Team	G	GS	SACKS
2000—San Francisco NFL	13	7	4.0

P

PETERSON, MIKE   LB   COLTS

PERSONAL: Born June 17, 1976, in Gainesville, Fla. ... 6-1/232. ... Full name: Porter Michael Peterson. ... Couson of Freddie Solomon, wide receiver with Philadelphia Eagles (1995-98).
HIGH SCHOOL: Santa Fe (Alachua, Fla.).
COLLEGE: Florida.
TRANSACTIONS/CAREER NOTES: Selected by Indianapolis Colts in second round (36th pick overall) of 1999 NFL draft. ... Signed by Colts (July 28, 1999).
HONORS: Named outside linebacker on THE SPORTING NEWS college All-America first team (1998).
PRO STATISTICS: 1999—Recovered one fumble. 2000—Intercepted two passes for eight yards.

Year Team	G	GS	SACKS
1999—Indianapolis NFL	16	13	3.0
2000—Indianapolis NFL	16	16	0.0
Pro totals (2 years)	32	29	3.0

PETERSON, TODD   K   CHIEFS

PERSONAL: Born February 4, 1970, in Washington, D.C. ... 5-10/177. ... Full name: Joseph Todd Peterson.
HIGH SCHOOL: Valdosta (Ga.) State.
COLLEGE: Navy, then Georgia (degree in finance, 1992).
TRANSACTIONS/CAREER NOTES: Selected by New York Giants in seventh round (177th pick overall) of 1993 NFL draft. ... Signed by Giants (July 19, 1993). ... Released by Giants (August 24, 1993). ... Signed by New England Patriots to practice squad (November 30, 1993). ... Released by Patriots (December 6, 1993). ... Signed by Atlanta Falcons (May 3, 1994). ... Released by Falcons (August 29, 1994). ... Signed by Arizona Cardinals (October 12, 1994). ... Released by Cardinals (October 24, 1994). ... Signed by Seattle Seahawks (January 17, 1995). ... Granted free agency (February 13, 1998). ... Re-signed by Seahawks for 1998 season. ... Granted unconditional free agency (February 12, 1999). ... Re-signed by Seahawks (March 2, 1999). ... Released by Seahawks (August 27, 2000). ... Signed by Kansas City Chiefs (October 11, 2000).

					KICKING			
Year Team	G	XPM	XPA	FGM	FGA	Lg.	50+	Pts.
1993—New England NFL				Did not play.				
1994—Arizona NFL	2	4	4	2	4	35	0-0	10
1995—Seattle NFL	16	§40	§40	23	28	49	0-2	109
1996—Seattle NFL	16	27	27	28	34	54	2-3	111
1997—Seattle NFL	16	37	37	22	28	52	1-2	103
1998—Seattle NFL	16	41	41	19	24	51	3-7	98
1999—Seattle NFL	16	32	32	34	40	51	1-2	134
2000—Kansas City NFL	11	25	25	15	20	42	0-0	70
Pro totals (7 years)	93	206	206	143	178	54	7-16	635

PETITGOUT, LUKE   OT   GIANTS

PERSONAL: Born June 16, 1976, in Milford, Del. ... 6-6/310. ... Full name: Lucas George Petitgout. ... Name pronounced pet-ee-GOO.
HIGH SCHOOL: Sussex Central (Georgetown, Del.).
COLLEGE: Notre Dame.
TRANSACTIONS/CAREER NOTES: Selected by New York Giants in first round (19th pick overall) of 1999 NFL draft. ... Signed by Giants (July 29, 1999).
PLAYING EXPERIENCE: New York Giants NFL, 1999 and 2000. ... Games/Games started: 1999 (15/8), 2000 (16/16). Total: 31/24.
CHAMPIONSHIP GAME EXPERIENCE: Played in NFC championship game (2000 season). ... Played in Super Bowl XXXV (2000 season).
PRO STATISTICS: 2000—Recovered one fumble.

PHENIX, PERRY   S   TITANS

PERSONAL: Born November 14, 1974, in Dallas. ... 5-11/210.
HIGH SCHOOL: Hillcrest (Dallas).
JUNIOR COLLEGE: Trinity Valley Community College (Texas).
COLLEGE: Southern Mississippi.
TRANSACTIONS/CAREER NOTES: Signed as non-drafted free agent by Tennessee Oilers (April 20, 1998). ... Granted free agency (March 2, 2001).
PLAYING EXPERIENCE: Tennessee NFL, 1998-2000. ... Games/Games started: 1998 (15/3), 1999 (16/1), 2000 (16/0). Total: 47/4.
CHAMPIONSHIP GAME EXPERIENCE: Played in AFC championship game (1999 season). ... Played in Super Bowl XXXIV (1999 season).
PRO STATISTICS: 1998—Recovered one fumble for 18 yards. 2000—Intercepted one pass for 87 yards and a touchdown and recovered one fumble.

PHIFER, ROMAN   LB

PERSONAL: Born March 5, 1968, in Plattsburgh, N.Y. ... 6-2/248. ... Full name: Roman Zubinsky Phifer.
HIGH SCHOOL: South Mecklenburg (Charlotte).
COLLEGE: UCLA.
TRANSACTIONS/CAREER NOTES: Selected by Los Angeles Rams in second round (31st pick overall) of 1991 NFL draft. ... Signed by Rams (July 19, 1991). ... On injured reserve with broken leg (November 26, 1991-remainder of season). ... Granted unconditional free agency (February 17, 1995). ... Re-signed by Rams (March 22, 1995). ... Rams franchise moved to St. Louis (April 12, 1995). ... Granted unconditional free agency (February 12, 1999). ... Signed by New York Jets (March 9, 1999). ... Released by Jets (February 21, 2001).
PRO STATISTICS: 1992—Recovered two fumbles. 1993—Recovered two fumbles for 10 yards. 1995—Fumbled once. 1998—Fumbled once.

P

				INTERCEPTIONS				SACKS
Year Team	G	GS	No.	Yds.	Avg.	TD	No.
1991—Los Angeles Rams NFL	12	5	0	0	0.0	0	2.0
1992—Los Angeles Rams NFL	16	14	1	3	3.0	0	0.0
1993—Los Angeles Rams NFL	16	16	0	0	0.0	0	0.0
1994—Los Angeles Rams NFL	16	15	2	7	3.5	0	1.5
1995—St. Louis NFL	16	16	3	52	17.3	0	3.0
1996—St. Louis NFL	15	15	0	0	0.0	0	1.5
1997—St. Louis NFL	16	15	0	0	0.0	0	2.0
1998—St. Louis NFL	13	13	1	41	41.0	0	6.5
1999—New York Jets NFL	16	12	2	20	10.0	0	4.5
2000—New York Jets NFL	16	10	0	0	0.0	0	4.0
Pro totals (10 years)	152	131	9	123	13.7	0	25.0

PHILLIPS, RYAN — LB — RAIDERS

PERSONAL: Born February 7, 1974, in Renton, Wash. ... 6-4/252.
HIGH SCHOOL: Auburn (Wash.).
COLLEGE: Idaho.
TRANSACTIONS/CAREER NOTES: Selected by New York Giants in third round (68th pick overall) of 1997 NFL draft. ... Signed by Giants (July 19, 1997). ... Granted free agency (February 11, 2000). ... Re-signed by Giants (April 12, 2000). ... Granted unconditional free agency (March 2, 2001). ... Signed by Oakland Raiders (April 27, 2001).
PLAYING EXPERIENCE: New York Giants NFL, 1997-2000. ... Games/Games started: 1997 (10/0), 1998 (16/3), 1999 (16/16), 2000 (16/15). Total: 58/34.
CHAMPIONSHIP GAME EXPERIENCE: Played in NFC championship game (2000 season). ... Played in Super Bowl XXXV (2000 season).
PRO STATISTICS: 1997—Credited with one sack. 1999—Intercepted one pass for no yards. 2000—Intercepted two passes for 22 yards and credited with 1$^1/_2$ sacks.

PHILYAW, MARENO — WR — FALCONS

PERSONAL: Born December 19, 1977, in Atlanta. ... 6-2/208.
HIGH SCHOOL: North Clayton (College Park, Ga.).
COLLEGE: Troy (Ala.) State.
TRANSACTIONS/CAREER NOTES: Selected by Atlanta Falcons in sixth round (172nd pick overall) of 2000 NFL draft. ... Signed by Falcons (May 23, 2000). ... Released by Falcons (August 27, 2000). ... Re-signed by Falcons to practice squad (October 11, 2000). ... Activated (December 15, 2000). ... Assigned by Falcons to Barcelona Dragons in 2001 NFL Europe enhancement allocation program (February 19, 2001).
PLAYING EXPERIENCE: Atlanta NFL, 2000. ... Games/Games started: 2000 (1/0).

PICKENS, CARL — WR

PERSONAL: Born March 23, 1970, in Murphy, N.C. ... 6-2/206. ... Full name: Carl McNally Pickens.
HIGH SCHOOL: Murphy (N.C.).
COLLEGE: Tennessee.
TRANSACTIONS/CAREER NOTES: Selected after junior season by Cincinnati Bengals in second round (31st pick overall) of 1992 NFL draft. ... Signed by Bengals (August 4, 1992). ... Granted free agency (February 17, 1995). ... Tendered offer sheet by Arizona Cardinals (March 17, 1995). ... Offer matched by Bengals (March 24, 1995). ... On injured reserve with groin injury (December 15, 1997-remainder of season). ... Designated by Bengals as franchise player (February 12, 1999). ... Released by Bengals (July 20, 2000). ... Signed by Tennessee Titans (July 26, 2000). ... Released by Titans (March 1, 2001). ... Signed by Dallas Cowboys (April 5, 2001). ... Announced retirement (May 30, 2001).
HONORS: Named wide receiver on THE SPORTING NEWS college All-America first team (1991). ... Played in Pro Bowl (1995 and 1996 seasons).
PRO STATISTICS: 1992—Recovered two fumbles. 1993—Attempted one pass without a completion. 1994—Recovered one fumble. 1995—Rushed once for six yards. 1996—Rushed twice for two yards and attempted one pass with a completion for 12 yards. 1998—Rushed twice for four yards. 1999—Completed only pass attempt for six yards.
SINGLE GAME HIGHS (regular season): Receptions—13 (October 11, 1998, vs. Pittsburgh); yards—204 (October 11, 1998, vs. Pittsburgh); and touchdown receptions—3 (December 1, 1996, vs. Jacksonville).
STATISTICAL PLATEAUS: 100-yard receiving games: 1993 (1), 1994 (5), 1995 (5), 1996 (2), 1997 (1), 1998 (2), 1999 (2), 2000 (1). Total: 19.
MISCELLANEOUS: Holds Cincinnati Bengals all-time records for most receptions (530) and touchdown receptions (63).

			RECEIVING				PUNT RETURNS				TOTALS			
Year Team	G	GS	No.	Yds.	Avg.	TD	No.	Yds.	Avg.	TD	TD	2pt.	Pts.	Fum.
1992—Cincinnati NFL	16	10	26	326	12.5	1	18	229	12.7	1	2	0	12	3
1993—Cincinnati NFL	13	12	43	565	13.1	6	4	16	4.0	0	6	0	36	1
1994—Cincinnati NFL	15	15	71	1127	15.9	§11	9	62	6.9	0	11	0	66	1
1995—Cincinnati NFL	16	15	§99	1234	12.5	†17	5	-2	-0.4	0	§17	0	102	1
1996—Cincinnati NFL	16	16	§100	1180	11.8	12	1	2	2.0	0	12	1	74	0
1997—Cincinnati NFL	12	12	52	695	13.4	5	0	0	0.0	0	5	0	30	1
1998—Cincinnati NFL	16	16	82	1023	12.5	5	0	0	0.0	0	5	1	32	2
1999—Cincinnati NFL	16	14	57	737	12.9	6	0	0	0.0	0	6	0	36	1
2000—Tennessee NFL	9	6	10	242	24.2	0	0	0	0.0	0	0	0	0	0
Pro totals (9 years)	129	116	540	7129	13.2	63	37	307	8.3	1	64	2	388	10

PIERSON, PETE — OT — BUCCANEERS

PERSONAL: Born February 4, 1971, in Portland, Ore. ... 6-5/315. ... Full name: Peter Samuel Pierson.
HIGH SCHOOL: David Douglas (Portland, Ore.).
COLLEGE: Washington (degree in political science, 1994).

TRANSACTIONS/CAREER NOTES: Selected by Tampa Bay Buccaneers in fifth round (136th pick overall) of 1994 NFL draft. ... Signed by Buccaneers (July 6, 1994). ... Released by Buccaneers (August 28, 1994). ... Re-signed by Buccaneers to practice squad (September 2, 1994). ... Activated (November 22, 1994). ... Released by Buccaneers (August 18, 1996). ... Re-signed by Buccaneers (September 10, 1996). ... Granted free agency (February 13, 1998). ... Re-signed by Buccaneers (June 11, 1998).
PLAYING EXPERIENCE: Tampa Bay NFL, 1995-2000. ... Games/Games started: 1995 (12/4), 1996 (11/2), 1997 (15/0), 1998 (16/0), 1999 (15/0), 2000 (15/15). Total: 84/21.
CHAMPIONSHIP GAME EXPERIENCE: Played in NFC championship game (1999 season).
PRO STATISTICS: 1995—Recovered one fumble.

PILGRIM, EVAN — G

PERSONAL: Born August 14, 1972, in Pittsburgh, Calif. ... 6-4/305.
HIGH SCHOOL: Antioch (Calif.).
COLLEGE: Brigham Young.
TRANSACTIONS/CAREER NOTES: Selected by Chicago Bears in third round (87th pick overall) of 1995 NFL draft. ... Signed by Bears (July 19, 1995). ... Inactive for all 16 games (1995). ... Released by Bears (December 9, 1997). ... Signed by Tennessee Oilers (May 14, 1998). ... Released by Oilers (August 30, 1998). ... Re-signed by Oilers (September 9, 1998). ... Released by Oilers (November 4, 1998). ... Re-signed by Oilers (December 16, 1998). ... Oilers franchise renamed Tennessee Titans for 1999 season (December 26, 1998). ... Released by Titans (September 5, 1999). ... Signed by Denver Broncos (October 6, 1999). ... Inactive for two games with Broncos (1999). ... Released by Broncos (October 19, 1999). ... Signed by Atlanta Falcons (November 2, 1999). ... Released by Falcons (August 28, 2000). ... Re-signed by Falcons (October 10, 2000). ... Granted unconditional free agency (March 2, 2001).
PLAYING EXPERIENCE: Chicago NFL, 1996 and 1997; Tennessee NFL, 1998; Atlanta NFL, 1999 and 2000. ... Games/Games started: 1996 (6/0), 1997 (13/6), 1998 (2/0), 1999 (3/1), 2000 (7/1). Total: 31/8.
PRO STATISTICS: 1997—Recovered one fumble.

PILLER, ZACH — G — TITANS

PERSONAL: Born May 2, 1976, in St. Petersburg, Fla. ... 6-5/330. ... Full name: Zachary Paul Piller.
HIGH SCHOOL: Lincoln (Tallahassee, Fla.).
COLLEGE: Georgia Tech, then Florida.
TRANSACTIONS/CAREER NOTES: Selected by Tennessee Titans in third round (81st pick overall) of 1999 NFL draft. ... Signed by Titans (July 22, 1999).
PLAYING EXPERIENCE: Tennessee NFL, 1999 and 2000. ... Games/Games started: 1999 (8/0), 2000 (16/0). Total: 24/0.
CHAMPIONSHIP GAME EXPERIENCE: Member of Titans for AFC championship game (1999 season); inactive. ... Member of Titans for Super Bowl XXXIV (1999 season); inactive.

PINKSTON, TODD — WR — EAGLES

PERSONAL: Born April 23, 1977, in Forest, Miss. ... 6-2/170.
HIGH SCHOOL: Forest (Miss.).
COLLEGE: Southern Mississippi.
TRANSACTIONS/CAREER NOTES: Selected by Philadelphia Eagles in second round (36th pick overall) of 2000 NFL draft. ... Signed by Eagles (July 16, 2000).
SINGLE GAME HIGHS (regular season): Receptions—3 (September 3, 2000, vs. Dallas); yards—56 (December 10, 2000, vs. Cleveland); and touchdown receptions—0.

				RECEIVING		
Year Team	G	GS	No.	Yds.	Avg.	TD
2000—Philadelphia NFL	16	1	10	181	18.1	0

PITTMAN, KAVIKA — DE — BRONCOS

PERSONAL: Born October 9, 1974, in Frankfurt, West Germany. ... 6-6/273. ... Name pronounced kuh-VEE-kuh.
HIGH SCHOOL: Leesville (La.).
COLLEGE: McNeese State.
TRANSACTIONS/CAREER NOTES: Selected by Dallas Cowboys in second round (37th pick overall) of 1996 NFL draft. ... Signed by Cowboys (July 16, 1996). ... Granted unconditional free agency (February 11, 2000). ... Signed by Denver Broncos (February 22, 2000).
PRO STATISTICS: 1997—Returned one kickoff for no yards. 1998—Recovered two fumbles for seven yards. 1999—Recovered two fumbles. 2000—Recovered one fumble.

Year Team	G	GS	SACKS
1996—Dallas NFL	15	0	0.0
1997—Dallas NFL	15	0	1.0
1998—Dallas NFL	15	15	6.0
1999—Dallas NFL	16	16	3.0
2000—Denver NFL	15	15	7.0
Pro totals (5 years)	76	46	17.0

PITTMAN, MICHAEL — RB — CARDINALS

PERSONAL: Born August 14, 1975, in New Orleans. ... 6-0/216.
HIGH SCHOOL: Mira Mesa (San Diego).
COLLEGE: Fresno State.
TRANSACTIONS/CAREER NOTES: Selected by Arizona Cardinals in fourth round (95th pick overall) of 1998 NFL draft. ... Signed by Cardinals (May 20, 1998). ... Granted free agency (March 2, 2001).

P

PRO STATISTICS: 1998—Fumbled once and recovered one fumble. 1999—Completed only pass attempt for 26 yards, fumbled three times and recovered one fumble. 2000—Fumbled five times.

SINGLE GAME HIGHS (regular season): Attempts—23 (November 14, 1999, vs. Detroit); yards—133 (November 14, 1999, vs. Detroit); and rushing touchdowns—1 (November 12, 2000, vs. Minnesota).

STATISTICAL PLATEAUS: 100-yard rushing games: 1999 (1), 2000 (1). Total: 2.

				RUSHING				RECEIVING				PUNT RETURNS				KICKOFF RETURNS				TOTALS	
Year	Team	G	GS	Att.	Yds.	Avg.	TD	No.	Yds.	Avg.	TD	No.	Yds.	Avg.	TD	No.	Yds.	Avg.	TD	TD	2pt.	Pts.
1998—Arizona NFL		15	0	29	91	3.1	0	0	0	0.0	0	0	0	0.0	0	4	84	21.0	0	0	0	0
1999—Arizona NFL		10	2	64	289	4.5	2	16	196	12.3	0	4	16	4.0	0	2	31	15.5	0	2	0	12
2000—Arizona NFL		16	12	184	719	3.9	4	73	579	7.9	2	0	0	0.0	0	0	0	0.0	0	6	0	36
Pro totals (3 years)		41	14	277	1099	4.0	6	89	775	8.7	2	4	16	4.0	0	6	115	19.2	0	8	0	48

PLAYER, SCOTT   P   CARDINALS

PERSONAL: Born December 17, 1969, in St. Augustine, Fla. ... 6-1/217.

HIGH SCHOOL: St. Augustine (Fla.).

JUNIOR COLLEGE: Florida Community College.

COLLEGE: Flagler College (Fla.), then Florida State (degree in education).

TRANSACTIONS/CAREER NOTES: Played with Birmingham Barracudas of CFL (1995). ... Granted free agency (March 7, 1996). ... Signed as non-drafted free agent by Arizona Cardinals (April 23, 1996). ... Released by Cardinals (August 19, 1996). ... Signed by New York Giants (February 14, 1997). ... Assigned by Giants to Frankfurt Galaxy in 1997 World League enhancement allocation program (February 18, 1997). ... Released by Giants (August 24, 1997). ... Signed by New York Jets to practice squad (August 26, 1997). ... Released by Jets (August 28, 1997). ... Re-signed by Cardinals (March 3, 1998). ... Granted free agency (March 2, 2001).

HONORS: Played in Pro Bowl (2000 season).

PRO STATISTICS: CFL: 1995—Attempted two passes with one completion for 52 yards. 1999—Rushed once for minus 18 yards. 2000—Rushed once for minus 11 yards.

					PUNTING			
Year	Team	G	No.	Yds.	Avg.	Net avg.	In. 20	Blk.
1995—Birmingham CFL	18	143	6247	43.7	36.5	0	0
1996—				Did not play.			
1997—Frankfurt W.L.	...	60	2617	43.6	34.3	17	1
1998—Arizona NFL	16	81	3378	41.7	35.9	12	∞1
1999—Arizona NFL	16	94	3948	42.0	36.7	18	0
2000—Arizona NFL	16	65	2871	44.2	37.3	17	0
W.L. totals (1 year)	...	60	2617	43.6	34.3	17	1
CFL totals (1 year)	18	143	6247	43.7	36.5	0	0
NFL totals (3 years)	48	240	10197	42.5	36.6	47	1
Pro totals (5 years)	...	443	19061	43.0	36.3	64	2

PLEASANT, ANTHONY   DE   PATRIOTS

PERSONAL: Born January 27, 1968, in Century, Fla. ... 6-5/280. ... Full name: Anthony Devon Pleasant.

HIGH SCHOOL: Century (Fla.).

COLLEGE: Tennessee State.

TRANSACTIONS/CAREER NOTES: Selected by Cleveland Browns in third round (73rd pick overall) of 1990 NFL draft. ... Signed by Browns (July 22, 1990). ... Browns franchise moved to Baltimore and renamed Ravens for 1996 season (March 11, 1996). ... Granted unconditional free agency (February 14, 1997). ... Signed by Atlanta Falcons (June 21, 1997). ... Released by Falcons (February 11, 1998). ... Signed by New York Jets (March 12, 1998). ... Granted unconditional free agency (February 11, 2000). ... Signed by San Francisco 49ers (July 19, 2000). ... Granted unconditional free agency (March 2, 2001). ... Signed by New England Patriots (March 22, 2001).

CHAMPIONSHIP GAME EXPERIENCE: Played in AFC championship game (1998 season).

PRO STATISTICS: 1991—Recovered one fumble for four yards. 1993—Credited with a safety. 1996—Recovered one fumble for 36 yards.

Year	Team	G	GS	SACKS
1990—Cleveland NFL	16	7	3.5
1991—Cleveland NFL	16	7	2.5
1992—Cleveland NFL	16	14	4.0
1993—Cleveland NFL	16	13	11.0
1994—Cleveland NFL	14	14	4.5
1995—Cleveland NFL	16	16	8.0
1996—Baltimore NFL	12	12	4.0
1997—Atlanta NFL	11	0	0.5
1998—New York Jets NFL	16	15	6.0
1999—New York Jets NFL	16	16	2.0
2000—San Francisco NFL	16	16	2.0
Pro totals (11 years)	165	130	48.0

PLUMMER, AHMED   CB   49ERS

PERSONAL: Born March 26, 1976, in Wyoming, Ohio. ... 5-11/191. ... Full name: Ahmed Kamil Plummer.

HIGH SCHOOL: Wyoming (Ohio).

COLLEGE: Ohio State.

TRANSACTIONS/CAREER NOTES: Selected by San Francisco 49ers in first round (24th pick overall) of 2000 NFL draft. ... Signed by 49ers (July 15, 2000).

PLAYING EXPERIENCE: San Francisco NFL, 2000. ... Games/Games started: 2000 (16/14).

PRO STATISTICS: 2000—Returned one kickoff for no yards.

P

PLUMMER, CHAD · WR BENGALS

PERSONAL: Born November 30, 1975, in Delray Beach, Fla. ... 6-2/223.
HIGH SCHOOL: Godby (Tallahassee, Fla.).
COLLEGE: Cincinnati (degree in communications).
TRANSACTIONS/CAREER NOTES: Selected by Denver Broncos in sixth round (204th pick overall) of 1999 NFL draft. ... Signed by Broncos (July 20, 1999). ... Released by Broncos (August 27, 1999). ... Signed by Indianapolis Colts to practice squad (September 7, 1999). ... Activated (November 20, 1999). ... Released by Colts (October 12, 2000). ... Re-signed by Colts to practice squad (October 13, 2000). ... Released by Colts (December 4, 2000). ... Signed by Cincinnati Bengals to practice squad (December 7, 2000).
PLAYING EXPERIENCE: Indianapolis NFL, 1999 and 2000. ... Games/Games started: 1999 (1/0), 2000 (3/0). Total: 4/0.

PLUMMER, JAKE QB CARDINALS

PERSONAL: Born December 19, 1974, in Boise, Idaho. ... 6-2/198. ... Full name: Jason Steven Plummer.
HIGH SCHOOL: Capital (Boise, Idaho).
COLLEGE: Arizona State.
TRANSACTIONS/CAREER NOTES: Selected by Arizona Cardinals in second round (42nd pick overall) of 1997 NFL draft. ... Signed by Cardinals (July 14, 1997).
HONORS: Named quarterback on THE SPORTING NEWS college All-America second team (1996).
PRO STATISTICS: 1997—Caught one pass for two yards, fumbled six times and recovered one fumble for minus one yard. 1998—Fumbled 12 times and recovered three fumbles for minus two yards. 1999—Fumbled seven times and recovered five fumbles for minus four yards. 2000—Fumbled eight times and recovered four fumbles for minus one yard.
SINGLE GAME HIGHS (regular season): Attempts—57 (January 2, 2000, vs. Green Bay); completions—35 (January 2, 2000, vs. Green Bay); yards—465 (November 15, 1998, vs. Dallas); and touchdown passes—4 (December 7, 1997, vs. Washington).
STATISTICAL PLATEAUS: 300-yard passing games: 1997 (2), 1998 (2), 1999 (1), 2000 (1). Total: 6.
MISCELLANEOUS: Regular-season record as starting NFL quarterback: 18-32 (.360). ... Postseason record as starting NFL quarterback: 1-1 (.500).

					PASSING						RUSHING				TOTALS		
Year Team	G	GS	Att.	Cmp.	Pct.	Yds.	TD	Int.	Avg.	Rat.	Att.	Yds.	Avg.	TD	TD	2pt.	Pts.
1997—Arizona NFL	10	9	296	157	53.0	2203	15	15	7.44	73.1	39	216	5.5	2	2	1	14
1998—Arizona NFL	16	16	547	324	59.2	3737	17	20	6.83	75.0	51	217	4.3	4	4	0	24
1999—Arizona NFL	12	11	381	201	52.8	2111	9	*24	5.54	50.8	39	121	3.1	2	2	0	12
2000—Arizona NFL	14	14	475	270	56.8	2946	13	21	6.20	66.0	37	183	4.9	0	0	0	0
Pro totals (4 years)	52	50	1699	952	56.0	10997	54	80	6.47	66.7	166	737	4.4	8	8	1	50

POINDEXTER, ANTHONY S RAVENS

PERSONAL: Born July 28, 1976, in Lynchburg, Va. ... 6-0/220. ... Full name: Anthony Scott Poindexter.
HIGH SCHOOL: Jefferson Forest (Forest, Va.).
COLLEGE: Virginia.
TRANSACTIONS/CAREER NOTES: Selected by Baltimore Ravens in seventh round (216th pick overall) of 1999 NFL draft. ... Signed by Ravens (July 31, 1999). ... On non-football injury list with knee injury (August 31-November 9, 1999). ... Inactive for four games (1999). ... On injured reserve with knee injury (December 8, 1999-remainder of season).
CHAMPIONSHIP GAME EXPERIENCE: Played in AFC championship game (2000 season). ... Member of Super Bowl championship team (2000 season); inactive.
HONORS: Named free safety on THE SPORTING NEWS college All-America first team (1997 and 1998).
MISCELLANEOUS: Selected by Florida Marlins organization in 70th round of free-agent baseball draft (June 2, 1994); did not sign.

			INTERCEPTIONS				SACKS	PUNT RETURNS				TOTALS			
Year Team	G	GS	No.	Yds.	Avg.	TD	No.	No.	Yds.	Avg.	TD	TD	2pt.	Pts.	Fum.
2000—Baltimore NFL	10	0	0	0	0.0	0	0.0	0	0	0.0	0	0	0	0	0

POLK, DASHON LB BILLS

PERSONAL: Born March 13, 1977, in Pacoima, Calif. ... 6-2/235. ... Full name: DaShon Lamor Polk.
HIGH SCHOOL: Taft (Calif.).
COLLEGE: Arizona.
TRANSACTIONS/CAREER NOTES: Selected by Buffalo Bills in seventh round (251st pick overall) of 2000 NFL draft. ... Signed by Bills (June 22, 2000).
PLAYING EXPERIENCE: Buffalo NFL, 2000. ... Games/Games started: 2000 (5/0).

POLLARD, MARCUS TE COLTS

PERSONAL: Born February 8, 1972, in Valley, Ala. ... 6-4/252. ... Full name: Marcus LaJuan Pollard.
HIGH SCHOOL: Valley (Ala.).
JUNIOR COLLEGE: Seward County Community College, Kan. (did not play football).
COLLEGE: Bradley (did not play football).
TRANSACTIONS/CAREER NOTES: Signed as non-drafted free agent by Indianapolis Colts (January 24, 1995). ... Released by Colts (August 22, 1995). ... Re-signed by Colts to practice squad (August 28, 1995). ... Activated (October 10, 1995). ... Granted free agency (February 13, 1998). ... Tendered offer sheet by Philadelphia Eagles (March 4, 1998). ... Offer matched by Colts (March 9, 1998). ... Designated by Colts as franchise player (February 22, 2001).
CHAMPIONSHIP GAME EXPERIENCE: Played in AFC championship game (1995 season).
PRO STATISTICS: 1996—Recovered one fumble. 1998—Returned one kickoff for four yards.

P

SINGLE GAME HIGHS (regular season): Receptions—6 (September 13, 1998, vs. New England); yards—74 (December 17, 2000, vs. Miami); and touchdown receptions—2 (October 10, 1999, vs. Miami).
MISCELLANEOUS: Played basketball during college.

			RECEIVING				TOTALS			
Year Team	G	GS	No.	Yds.	Avg.	TD	TD	2pt.	Pts.	Fum.
1995—Indianapolis NFL	8	0	0	0	0.0	0	0	0	0	0
1996—Indianapolis NFL	16	4	6	86	14.3	1	1	0	6	0
1997—Indianapolis NFL	16	5	10	116	11.6	0	0	1	2	0
1998—Indianapolis NFL	16	11	24	309	12.9	4	4	†2	28	0
1999—Indianapolis NFL	16	12	34	374	11.0	4	4	0	24	2
2000—Indianapolis NFL	16	14	30	439	14.6	3	3	▲1	20	0
Pro totals (6 years)	88	46	104	1324	12.7	12	12	4	80	2

POOLE, KEITH — WR

PERSONAL: Born June 18, 1974, in San Jose, Calif. ... 6-0/193. ... Full name: Keith Robert Strohmaier Poole.
HIGH SCHOOL: Clovis (Calif.).
COLLEGE: Arizona State.
TRANSACTIONS/CAREER NOTES: Selected by New Orleans Saints in fourth round (116th pick overall) of 1997 NFL draft. ... Signed by Saints (June 10, 1997). ... Released by Saints (June 4, 2001).
PRO STATISTICS: 1999—Rushed once for 14 yards. 2000—Recovered one fumble.
SINGLE GAME HIGHS (regular season): Receptions—6 (January 2, 2000, vs. Carolina); yards—154 (October 18, 1998, vs. Atlanta); and touchdown receptions—2 (October 18, 1998, vs. Atlanta).
STATISTICAL PLATEAUS: 100-yard receiving games: 1998 (1), 1999 (1). Total: 2.

			RECEIVING				TOTALS			
Year Team	G	GS	No.	Yds.	Avg.	TD	TD	2pt.	Pts.	Fum.
1997—New Orleans NFL	3	0	4	98	24.5	2	2	0	12	0
1998—New Orleans NFL	15	4	24	509	21.2	2	2	0	12	0
1999—New Orleans NFL	15	15	42	796	19.0	6	6	0	36	0
2000—New Orleans NFL	15	4	21	293	14.0	1	1	0	6	1
Pro totals (4 years)	48	23	91	1696	18.6	11	11	0	66	1

POOLE, TYRONE — DB — BRONCOS

PERSONAL: Born February 3, 1972, in La Grange, Ga. ... 5-8/188.
HIGH SCHOOL: La Grange (Ga.).
COLLEGE: Fort Valley (Ga.) State.
TRANSACTIONS/CAREER NOTES: Selected by Carolina Panthers in first round (22nd pick overall) of 1995 NFL draft. ... Signed by Panthers (July 15, 1995). ... Traded by Panthers to Indianapolis Colts for second-round pick (OT Chris Terry) in 1999 draft (July 22, 1998). ... Released by Colts (March 1, 2001). ... Signed by Denver Broncos (May 22, 2001).
CHAMPIONSHIP GAME EXPERIENCE: Played in NFC championship game (1996 season).
PRO STATISTICS: 1996—Recovered one fumble. 1997—Returned one kickoff for five yards and recovered three fumbles for 11 yards. 2000—Recovered one fumble for eight yards.

			INTERCEPTIONS				SACKS	PUNT RETURNS				TOTALS			
Year Team	G	GS	No.	Yds.	Avg.	TD	No.	No.	Yds.	Avg.	TD	TD	2pt.	Pts.	Fum.
1995—Carolina NFL	16	13	2	8	4.0	0	2.0	0	0	0.0	0	0	0	0	0
1996—Carolina NFL	15	15	1	35	35.0	0	0.0	3	26	8.7	0	0	0	0	0
1997—Carolina NFL	16	16	2	0	0.0	0	1.0	26	191	7.3	0	0	0	0	3
1998—Indianapolis NFL	15	15	1	0	0.0	0	0.0	12	107	8.9	0	0	0	0	0
1999—Indianapolis NFL	15	14	3	85	28.3	0	1.0	0	0	0.0	0	0	0	0	0
2000—Indianapolis NFL	15	12	1	1	1.0	0	0.0	0	0	0.0	0	0	0	0	0
Pro totals (6 years)	92	85	10	129	12.9	0	4.0	41	324	7.9	0	0	0	0	3

POPE, DANIEL — P — BENGALS

PERSONAL: Born March 28, 1975, in Alpharetta, Ga. ... 5-10/203.
HIGH SCHOOL: Milton (Alpharetta, Ga.).
COLLEGE: Alabama.
TRANSACTIONS/CAREER NOTES: Signed as non-drafted free agent by Detroit Lions (April 23, 1999). ... Released by Lions (August 26, 1999). ... Signed by Kansas City Chiefs (August 27, 1999). ... Claimed on waivers by Cincinnati Bengals (July 20, 2000).
PRO STATISTICS: 1999—Rushed once for no yards, fumbled once and recovered one fumble for minus 11 yards. 2000—Rushed twice for 22 yards, fumbled once and recovered one fumble for minus 19 yards.

		PUNTING					
Year Team	G	No.	Yds.	Avg.	Net avg.	In. 20	Blk.
1999—Kansas City NFL	16	101	4218	41.8	35.1	20	†2
2000—Cincinnati NFL	16	94	3775	40.2	33.1	18	0
Pro totals (2 years)	32	195	7993	41.0	34.1	38	2

POPE, MARQUEZ — DB — RAIDERS

PERSONAL: Born October 29, 1970, in Nashville. ... 5-11/193. ... Full name: Marquez Phillips Pope. ... Name pronounced MAR-kez.
HIGH SCHOOL: Long Beach (Calif.) Polytechnic.
COLLEGE: Fresno State (degree in speech and mass communication, 1998).
TRANSACTIONS/CAREER NOTES: Selected by San Diego Chargers in second round (33rd pick overall) of 1992 NFL draft. ... Signed by Chargers (July 16, 1992). ... On non-football illness list with virus (September 1-28, 1992). ... On practice squad (September 28-November 7, 1992). ...

P

Traded by Chargers to Los Angeles Rams for sixth-round pick (G Troy Sienkiewicz) in 1995 draft (April 11, 1994). ... Granted free agency (February 17, 1995). ... Tendered offer sheet by San Francisco 49ers (April 9, 1995). ... Rams declined to match offer (April 12, 1995); received second-round pick (OL Jesse James) in 1995 draft as compensation. ... Granted unconditional free agency (February 12, 1999). ... Signed by Cleveland Browns (March 8, 1999). ... Released by Browns (February 18, 2000). ... Signed by Oakland Raiders (May 22, 2000).
CHAMPIONSHIP GAME EXPERIENCE: Played in NFC championship game (1997 season). ... Played in AFC championship game (2000 season).
PRO STATISTICS: 1993—Credited with $1/2$ sack. 1996—Recovered one fumble for four yards. 2000—Credited with one sack and recovered five fumbles for minus two yards.

			INTERCEPTIONS			
Year Team	G	GS	No.	Yds.	Avg.	TD
1992—San Diego NFL	7	0	0	0	0.0	0
1993—San Diego NFL	16	1	2	14	7.0	0
1994—Los Angeles Rams NFL	16	16	3	66	22.0	0
1995—San Francisco NFL	16	16	1	-7	-7.0	0
1996—San Francisco NFL	16	16	6	98	16.3	1
1997—San Francisco NFL	5	5	1	7	7.0	0
1998—San Francisco NFL	6	3	1	0	0.0	0
1999—Cleveland NFL	16	15	2	15	7.5	0
2000—Oakland NFL	15	14	2	25	12.5	0
Pro totals (9 years)	113	86	18	218	12.1	1

PORCHER, ROBERT   DE   LIONS

PERSONAL: Born July 30, 1969, in Wando, S.C. ... 6-3/282. ... Full name: Robert Porcher III. ... Name pronounced por-SHAY.
HIGH SCHOOL: Cainhoy (Huger, S.C.).
COLLEGE: Tennessee State, then South Carolina State (degree in criminal justice).
TRANSACTIONS/CAREER NOTES: Selected by Detroit Lions in first round (26th pick overall) of 1992 NFL draft. ... Signed by Lions (July 25, 1992). ... Granted unconditional free agency (February 16, 1996). ... Re-signed by Lions (March 29, 1996). ... Granted unconditional free agency (February 14, 1997). ... Re-signed by Lions (March 4, 1997). ... Designated by Lions as franchise player (February 10, 2000).
HONORS: Played in Pro Bowl (1999 season).
PRO STATISTICS: 1994—Recovered one fumble. 1996—Recovered two fumbles. 2000—Recovered one fumble.

Year Team	G	GS	SACKS
1992—Detroit NFL	16	1	1.0
1993—Detroit NFL	16	4	8.5
1994—Detroit NFL	15	15	3.0
1995—Detroit NFL	16	16	5.0
1996—Detroit NFL	16	16	10.0
1997—Detroit NFL	16	15	12.5
1998—Detroit NFL	16	16	11.5
1999—Detroit NFL	15	14	15.0
2000—Detroit NFL	16	16	8.0
Pro totals (9 years)	142	113	74.5

PORTER, DARYL   CB   DOLPHINS

PERSONAL: Born January 16, 1974, in Fort Lauderdale, Fla. ... 5-9/190. ... Full name: Daryl Maurice Porter. ... Cousin of Bennie Blades, safety with Detroit Lions (1988-96) and Seattle Seahawks (1997); and cousin of Brian Blades, wide receiver with Seattle Seahawks (1988-98).
HIGH SCHOOL: St. Thomas Aquinas (Fort Lauderdale, Fla.).
COLLEGE: Boston College.
TRANSACTIONS/CAREER NOTES: Selected by Pittsburgh Steelers in sixth round (186th pick overall) of 1997 NFL draft. ... Signed by Steelers (June 6, 1997). ... Released by Steelers (August 19, 1997). ... Re-signed by Steelers to practice squad (August 26, 1997). ... Released by Steelers (October 20, 1997). ... Signed by Detroit Lions (October 21, 1997). ... Released by Lions (August 24, 1998). ... Signed by Steelers to practice squad (September 1, 1998). ... Signed by Buffalo Bills off Steelers practice squad (December 16, 1998). ... Granted free agency (March 2, 2001). ... Signed by Miami Dolphins (March 15, 2001).
PLAYING EXPERIENCE: Detroit NFL, 1997; Buffalo NFL, 1998-2000. ... Games/Games started: 1997 (7/0), 1998 (2/0), 1999 (16/0), 2000 (16/0). Total: 41/0.
PRO STATISTICS: 1999—Returned two kickoffs for 41 yards. 2000—Caught one pass for 44 yards, intercepted one pass for no yards and recovered two fumbles for 54 yards and one touchdown.

PORTER, JERRY ·   WR   RAIDERS

PERSONAL: Born July 14, 1978, in Washington, D.C. ... 6-2/225.
HIGH SCHOOL: Coolidge (Washington, D.C.).
COLLEGE: West Virginia.
TRANSACTIONS/CAREER NOTES: Selected by Oakland Raiders in second round (47th pick overall) of 2000 NFL draft. ... Signed by Raiders (July 22, 2000).
PLAYING EXPERIENCE: Oakland NFL, 2000. ... Games/Games started: 2000 (12/0).
CHAMPIONSHIP GAME EXPERIENCE: Played in AFC championship game (2000 season).
PRO STATISTICS: 2000—Caught one pass for six yards.
SINGLE GAME HIGHS (regular season): Receptions—1 (September 3, 2000, vs. San Diego); yards—6 (September 3, 2000); and touchdown receptions—0.

PORTER, JOEY   LB   STEELERS

PERSONAL: Born March 22, 1977, in Kansas City, Mo. ... 6-2/240. ... Full name: Joey Eugene Porter.
HIGH SCHOOL: Foothills (Calif.).
COLLEGE: Colorado State.
TRANSACTIONS/CAREER NOTES: Selected by Pittsburgh Steelers in third round (73rd pick overall) of 1999 NFL draft. ... Signed by Steelers (July 30, 1999).

PRO STATISTICS: 1999—Recovered two fumbles for 50 yards and one touchdown. 2000—Intercepted one pass, recovered one fumble for 32 yards and one touchdown and credited with a safety.

Year Team	G	GS	SACKS
1999—Pittsburgh NFL	16	0	2.0
2000—Pittsburgh NFL	16	16	10.5
Pro totals (2 years)	32	16	12.5

POSEY, JEFF　　　DE

PERSONAL: Born August 14, 1975, in Bassfield, Miss. ... 6-4/240.
HIGH SCHOOL: Greenville (Miss.).
JUNIOR COLLEGE: Pearl River Community College (Miss.).
COLLEGE: Southern Mississippi.
TRANSACTIONS/CAREER NOTES: Signed as non-drafted free agent by San Francisco 49ers (May 2, 1997) ... Released by 49ers (August 19, 1997). ... Re-signed by 49ers to practice squad (August 25, 1997). ... Granted free agency (March 2, 2001).
PLAYING EXPERIENCE: San Francisco NFL, 1998-2000. ... Games/Games started: 1998 (16/0), 1999 (16/6), 2000 (16/8). Total: 48/14.
PRO STATISTICS: 1998—Credited with $1/2$ sack. 1999—Credited with two sacks. 2000—Credited with $1/2$ sack and recovered one fumble.

POTEAT, HANK　　CB/KR/PR　　STEELERS

PERSONAL: Born August 30, 1977, in Harrisburg, Pa. ... 5-10/190. ... Full name: Henry Major Poteat II.
HIGH SCHOOL: Harrisburg (Pa.).
COLLEGE: Pittsburgh.
TRANSACTIONS/CAREER NOTES: Selected by Pittsburgh Steelers in third round (77th pick overall) of 2000 NFL draft. ... Signed by Steelers (July 21, 2000).

			INTERCEPTIONS				PUNT RETURNS				KICKOFF RETURNS				TOTALS			
Year Team	G	GS	No.	Yds.	Avg.	TD	No.	Yds.	Avg.	TD	No.	Yds.	Avg.	TD	TD	2pt.	Pts.	Fum.
2000—Pittsburgh NFL	15	0	0	0	0.0	0	36	467	13.0	1	24	465	19.4	0	1	0	6	3

POUNDS, DARRYL　　CB　　BRONCOS

PERSONAL: Born July 21, 1972, in Fort Worth, Texas. ... 5-10/189.
HIGH SCHOOL: South Pike (Magnolia, Miss.).
COLLEGE: Nicholls State.
TRANSACTIONS/CAREER NOTES: Selected by Washington Redskins in third round (68th pick overall) of 1995 NFL draft. ... Signed by Redskins (May 26, 1995). ... On physically unable to perform list with back injury (August 22-October 17, 1995). ... Granted free agency (February 13, 1998). ... Re-signed by Redskins (April 9, 1998). ... Granted unconditional free agency (February 11, 2000). ... Signed by Denver Broncos (March 3, 2000). ... On injured reserve with elbow injury (November 15, 2000-remainder of season).
PRO STATISTICS: 1995—Fumbled once. 1996—Recovered one fumble. 1997—Credited with two sacks and recovered three fumbles for 18 yards and one touchdown. 1998—Credited with $1/2$ sack and recovered one fumble. 1999—Returned one punt for no yards, credited with one sack, fumbled once and recovered one fumble for two yards.

			INTERCEPTIONS			
Year Team	G	GS	No.	Yds.	Avg.	TD
1995—Washington NFL	9	0	1	26	26.0	0
1996—Washington NFL	12	1	2	11	5.5	0
1997—Washington NFL	16	0	3	42	14.0	1
1998—Washington NFL	16	3	0	0	0.0	0
1999—Washington NFL	16	0	3	37	12.3	0
2000—Denver NFL	9	0	0	0	0.0	0
Pro totals (6 years)	78	4	9	116	12.9	1

POURDANESH, SHAR　　OL

PERSONAL: Born July 19, 1972, in Tehran, Iran. ... 6-6/312. ... Full name: Shahriar Pourdanesh. ... Name pronounced shar-E-are poor-DON-esh.
HIGH SCHOOL: University (Irvine, Calif.).
COLLEGE: Nevada-Reno.
TRANSACTIONS/CAREER NOTES: Signed as non-drafted free agent by Cleveland Browns (April 1993). ... Released by Browns before 1993 season. ... Signed by Baltimore of CFL (1994). ... Signed by Washington Redskins (March 20, 1995). ... Traded by Redskins to Pittsburgh Steelers for seventh-round pick (DT Delbert Cowsette) in 2000 draft (August 13, 1999). ... Granted unconditional free agency (March 2, 2001).
PLAYING EXPERIENCE: Baltimore CFL, 1994 and 1995; Washington NFL, 1996-1998; Pittsburgh NFL, 1999 and 2000. ... Games/Games started: 1994 (18/18), 1995 (14/14), 1996 (16/8), 1997 (16/14), 1998 (16/15), 1999 (4/2), 2000 (5/2). Total CFL: 32/32. Total NFL: 57/41. Total Pro: 89/73.
CHAMPIONSHIP GAME EXPERIENCE: Played in Grey Cup, CFL championship game (1994).
HONORS: Named tackle on CFL All-Star team (1994). ... Named CFL Most Outstanding Offensive Lineman (1994).
PRO STATISTICS: 1998—Fumbled once and recovered one fumble for minus four yards.

POWELL, CARL　　DT　　BEARS

PERSONAL: Born January 4, 1974, in Detroit. ... 6-2/264. ... Full name: Carl Demetris Powell.
HIGH SCHOOL: Northern (Detroit).
JUNIOR COLLEGE: Grand Rapids (Mich.) Community College.
COLLEGE: Louisville.
TRANSACTIONS/CAREER NOTES: Selected by Indianapolis Colts in fifth round (156th pick overall) of 1997 NFL draft. ... Signed by Colts (July 3, 1997). ... Released by Colts (August 28, 1998). ... Selected by Barcelona Dragons in 2000 NFL Europe draft (February 18, 2000). ... Signed by Baltimore Ravens (July 21, 2000). ... Released by Ravens (November 13, 2000). ... Signed by Chicago Bears (March 8, 2001).
PLAYING EXPERIENCE: Indianapolis NFL, 1997; Barcelona NFLE, 2000; Baltimore NFL, 2000. ... Games/Games started: 1997 (11/0), NFLE 2000 (games played unavailable), NFL 2000 (2/0). Total NFL: 13/0.
PRO STATISTICS: NFLE: 2000—Credited with one sack.

P

PRENTICE, TRAVIS — RB — BROWNS

PERSONAL: Born December 8, 1976, in Louisville, Ky. ... 5-11/221. ... Full name: Travis Jason Prentice.
HIGH SCHOOL: Manual (Louisville, Ky.).
COLLEGE: Miami of Ohio.
TRANSACTIONS/CAREER NOTES: Selected by Cleveland Browns in third round (63rd pick overall) of 2000 NFL draft. ... Signed by Browns (July 16, 2000).
HONORS: Named running back on THE SPORTING NEWS college All-America second team (1998 and 1999).
SINGLE GAME HIGHS (regular season): Attempts—28 (Ocotober 8, 2000, vs. Arizona); yards—97 (October 8, 2000, vs. Arizona); and rushing touchdowns—3 (October 8, 2000, vs. Arizona).

				RUSHING				RECEIVING				TOTALS		
Year	Team	G	GS	Att.	Yds.	Avg.	TD	No.	Yds.	Avg.	TD	TD	2pt.	Pts.	Fum.
2000—Cleveland NFL		16	11	173	512	3.0	7	37	191	5.2	1	8	0	48	2

PRICE, MARCUS — OT — SAINTS

PERSONAL: Born March 3, 1972, in Port Arthur, Texas. ... 6-6/321. ... Full name: Marcus Raymond Price.
HIGH SCHOOL: Lincoln (Port Arthur, Texas).
COLLEGE: Louisiana State.
TRANSACTIONS/CAREER NOTES: Selected by Jacksonville Jaguars in sixth round (172nd pick overall) of 1995 NFL draft. ... Signed by Jaguars (June 1, 1995). ... On injured reserve with ankle injury (August 19, 1995-entire season). ... Released by Jaguars (August 25, 1996). ... Signed by Denver Broncos to practice squad (December 3, 1996). ... Released by Broncos (December 30, 1996). ... Signed by Jaguars (January 31, 1997). ... Released by Jaguars (August 19, 1997). ... Re-signed by Jaguars to practice squad (October 28, 1997). ... Signed by San Diego Chargers off Jaguars practice squad (November 26, 1997). ... Released by Chargers (September 21, 1999). ... Signed by New Orleans Saints (March 23, 2000). ... Released by Saints (December 3, 2000). ... Re-signed by Saints (December 5, 2000).
PLAYING EXPERIENCE: San Diego NFL, 1997 and 1998; New Orleans NFL, 2000. ... Games/Games started: 1997 (2/0), 1998 (10/0), 2000 (7/0). Total: 19/0.

PRICE, PEERLESS — WR — BILLS

PERSONAL: Born October 27, 1976, in Dayton, Ohio. ... 6-0/190. ... Full name: Peerless LeCross Price.
HIGH SCHOOL: Meadowdale (Dayton, Ohio).
COLLEGE: Tennessee.
TRANSACTIONS/CAREER NOTES: Selected by Buffalo Bills in second round (53rd pick overall) of 1999 NFL draft. ... Signed by Bills (July 30, 1999).
PRO STATISTICS: 2000—Fumbled four times and recovered one fumble.
SINGLE GAME HIGHS (regular season): Receptions—8 (December 23, 2000, vs. Seattle); yards—132 (December 23, 2000, vs. Seattle); and touchdown receptions—1 (December 23, 2000, vs. Seattle).
STATISTICAL PLATEAUS: 100-yard receiving games: 1999 (1), 2000 (1). Total: 2.

				RUSHING				RECEIVING				PUNT RETURNS				KICKOFF RETURNS				TOTALS		
Year	Team	G	GS	Att.	Yds.	Avg.	TD	No.	Yds.	Avg.	TD	No.	Yds.	Avg.	TD	No.	Yds.	Avg.	TD	TD	2pt.	Pts.
1999—Buffalo NFL		16	4	1	-7	-7.0	0	31	393	12.7	3	1	16	16.0	0	1	27	27.0	0	3	0	18
2000—Buffalo NFL		16	16	2	32	16.0	0	52	762	14.7	3	5	27	5.4	0	0	0	0.0	0	3	0	18
Pro totals (2 years)		32	20	3	25	8.3	0	83	1155	13.9	6	6	43	7.2	0	1	27	27.0	0	6	0	36

PRICE, SHAWN — DE

PERSONAL: Born March 28, 1970, in Van Nuys, Calif. ... 6-4/290. ... Full name: Shawn Sterling Price.
HIGH SCHOOL: North Tahoe (Nev.).
JUNIOR COLLEGE: Sierra College (Calif.).
COLLEGE: Pacific.
TRANSACTIONS/CAREER NOTES: Signed as non-drafted free agent by Tampa Bay Buccaneers (April 29, 1993). ... Released by Buccaneers (August 30, 1993). ... Re-signed by Buccaneers to practice squad (August 31, 1993). ... Activated (November 5, 1993). ... Selected by Carolina Panthers from Buccaneers in NFL expansion draft (February 15, 1995). ... Granted unconditional free agency (February 16, 1996). ... Signed by Buffalo Bills (April 12, 1996). ... Granted unconditional free agency (February 13, 1998). ... Re-signed by Bills (March 9, 1998). ... Granted unconditional free agency (March 2, 2001).

Year	Team	G	GS	SACKS
1993—Tampa Bay NFL		9	6	3.0
1994—Tampa Bay NFL		6	0	0.0
1995—Carolina NFL		16	0	1.0
1996—Buffalo NFL		15	0	0.0
1997—Buffalo NFL		10	0	0.0
1998—Buffalo NFL		14	2	5.0
1999—Buffalo NFL		15	1	2.5
2000—Buffalo NFL		13	6	1.0
Pro totals (8 years)		98	15	12.5

PRINGLEY, MIKE — DE — CHARGERS

PERSONAL: Born May 22, 1976, in Linden, N.J. ... 6-4/277. ... Full name: Michael Charles Pringley.
HIGH SCHOOL: Linden (N.J.).
COLLEGE: North Carolina.
TRANSACTIONS/CAREER NOTES: Selected by Detroit Lions in seventh round (215th pick overall) of 1999 NFL draft. ... Signed by Lions (July 22, 1999). ... Released by Lions (September 19, 2000). ... Signed by San Diego Chagers (December 13, 2000).
PLAYING EXPERIENCE: Detroit NFL, 1999; San Diego NFL, 2000. ... Games/Games started: 1999 (9/0), 2000 (2/0). Total: 11/0.
PRO STATISTICS: 1999—Credited with 1 1/2 sacks.

P

PRIOLEAU, PIERSON　　　CB　　　49ERS

PERSONAL: Born August 6, 1977, in Charleston, S.C. ... 5-10/191. ... Full name: Pierson Olin Prioleau. ... Name pronounced pray-LOW.
HIGH SCHOOL: Macedonia (Saint Stephens, S.C.).
COLLEGE: Virginia Tech.
TRANSACTIONS/CAREER NOTES: Selected by San Francisco 49ers in fourth round (110th pick overall) of 1999 NFL draft. ... Signed by 49ers (July 27, 1999).
PLAYING EXPERIENCE: San Francisco NFL, 1999 and 2000. ... Games/Games started: 1999 (14/5), 2000 (14/6). Total: 28/11.
HONORS: Named strong safety on THE SPORTING NEWS college All-America third team (1997).
PRO STATISTICS: 1999—Returned three kickoffs for 73 yards. 2000—Intercepted one pass for 13 yards.

PRITCHETT, KELVIN　　　DT

PERSONAL: Born October 24, 1969, in Atlanta. ... 6-3/319. ... Full name: Kelvin Bratodd Pritchett.
HIGH SCHOOL: Therrell (Atlanta).
COLLEGE: Mississippi.
TRANSACTIONS/CAREER NOTES: Selected by Dallas Cowboys in first round (20th pick overall) of 1991 NFL draft. ... Rights traded by Cowboys to Detroit Lions for second- (LB Dixon Edwards), third- (G James Richards) and fourth-round (DE Tony Hill) picks in 1991 draft (April 21, 1991). ... Granted free agency (February 17, 1994). ... Re-signed by Lions (August 12, 1994). ... Granted unconditional free agency (February 17, 1995). ... Signed by Jacksonville Jaguars (March 11, 1995). ... On injured reserve with knee injury (November 4, 1997-remainder of season). ... Granted unconditional free agency (February 12, 1999). ... Signed by Lions (April 22, 1999). ... Granted unconditional free agency (February 11, 2000). ... Re-signed by Lions (May 12, 2000). ... Granted unconditional free agency (March 2, 2001).
CHAMPIONSHIP GAME EXPERIENCE: Played in NFC championship game (1991 season). ... Played in AFC championship game (1996 season).
PRO STATISTICS: 1994—Recovered one fumble. 1996—Recovered two fumbles. 1997—Recovered one fumble. 2000—Intercepted one pass for 78 yards.

Year　Team	G	GS	SACKS
1991—Detroit NFL	16	0	1.5
1992—Detroit NFL	16	15	6.5
1993—Detroit NFL	16	5	4.0
1994—Detroit NFL	16	15	5.5
1995—Jacksonville NFL	16	16	1.5
1996—Jacksonville NFL	13	4	2.0
1997—Jacksonville NFL	8	5	3.0
1998—Jacksonville NFL	15	9	3.0
1999—Detroit NFL	16	2	1.0
2000—Detroit NFL	15	0	2.5
Pro totals (10 years)	147	71	30.5

PRITCHETT, STANLEY　　　RB　　　EAGLES

PERSONAL: Born December 22, 1973, in Atlanta. ... 6-1/240. ... Full name: Stanley Jerome Pritchett.
HIGH SCHOOL: Frederick Douglass (College Park, Ga.).
COLLEGE: South Carolina.
TRANSACTIONS/CAREER NOTES: Selected by Miami Dolphins in fourth round (118th pick overall) of 1996 NFL draft. ... Signed by Dolphins (July 10, 1996). ... Granted free agency (February 12, 1999). ... Re-signed by Dolphins (April 13, 1999). ... Granted unconditional free agency (February 11, 2000). ... Signed by Philadelphia Eagles (March 9, 2000).
PRO STATISTICS: 1996—Recovered one fumble. 1998—Recovered one fumble. 2000—Returned one kickoff for 15 yards.
SINGLE GAME HIGHS (regular season): Attempts—17 (December 12, 1999, vs. New York Jets); yards—68 (December 12, 1999, vs. New York Jets); and rushing touchdowns—1 (October 15, 2000, vs. Arizona).

Year　Team	G	GS	RUSHING				RECEIVING				TOTALS			
			Att.	Yds.	Avg.	TD	No.	Yds.	Avg.	TD	TD	2pt.	Pts.	Fum.
1996—Miami NFL	16	16	7	27	3.9	0	33	354	10.7	2	2	0	12	3
1997—Miami NFL	6	5	3	7	2.3	0	5	35	7.0	0	0	0	0	0
1998—Miami NFL	16	12	6	19	3.2	1	17	97	5.7	0	1	0	6	0
1999—Miami NFL	14	7	47	158	3.4	1	43	312	7.3	4	5	0	30	0
2000—Philadelphia NFL	16	2	58	225	3.9	1	25	193	7.7	0	1	0	6	1
Pro totals (5 years)	68	42	121	436	3.6	3	123	991	8.1	6	9	0	54	4

PROEHL, RICKY　　　WR　　　RAMS

PERSONAL: Born March 7, 1968, in Bronx, N.Y. ... 6-0/190. ... Full name: Richard Scott Proehl.
HIGH SCHOOL: Hillsborough (Belle Mead, N.J.).
COLLEGE: Wake Forest.
TRANSACTIONS/CAREER NOTES: Selected by Phoenix Cardinals in third round (58th pick overall) of 1990 NFL draft. ... Signed by Cardinals (July 23, 1990). ... Granted free agency (March 1, 1993). ... Tendered offer sheet by New England Patriots (April 13, 1993). ... Offer matched by Cardinals (April 19, 1993). ... Cardinals franchise renamed Arizona Cardinals for 1994 season. ... Traded by Cardinals to Seattle Seahawks for fourth-round pick (traded to New York Jets) in 1995 draft (April 3, 1995). ... Released by Seahawks (March 7, 1997). ... Signed by Chicago Bears (April 10, 1997). ... Granted unconditional free agency (February 13, 1998). ... Signed by St. Louis Rams (February 25, 1998).
CHAMPIONSHIP GAME EXPERIENCE: Played in NFC championship game (1999 season). ... Member of Super Bowl championship team (1999 season).
PRO STATISTICS: 1990—Returned one punt for two yards and returned four kickoffs for 53 yards. 1991—Returned four punts for 26 yards and recovered one fumble. 1992—Had only pass attempt intercepted and fumbled five times. 1993—Fumbled once. 1994—Fumbled twice and recovered two fumbles. 1997—Returned eight punts for 59 yards. 2000—Returned one kickoff for two yards.
SINGLE GAME HIGHS (regular season): Receptions—11 (November 16, 1997, vs. New York Jets); yards—164 (November 27, 1997, vs. Detroit); and touchdown receptions—2 (December 27, 1998, vs. San Francisco).
STATISTICAL PLATEAUS: 100-yard receiving games: 1990 (2), 1991 (1), 1992 (3), 1993 (1), 1997 (3), 1998 (1). Total: 11.

P

Year Team	G	GS	RUSHING				RECEIVING				TOTALS			
			Att.	Yds.	Avg.	TD	No.	Yds.	Avg.	TD	TD	2pt.	Pts.	Fum.
1990—Phoenix NFL	16	2	1	4	4.0	0	56	802	14.3	4	4	0	24	0
1991—Phoenix NFL	16	16	3	21	7.0	0	55	766	13.9	2	2	0	12	0
1992—Phoenix NFL	16	15	3	23	7.7	0	60	744	12.4	3	3	0	18	5
1993—Phoenix NFL	16	16	8	47	5.9	0	65	877	13.5	7	7	0	42	1
1994—Arizona NFL	16	16	0	0	0.0	0	51	651	12.8	5	5	0	30	2
1995—Seattle NFL	8	0	0	0	0.0	0	5	29	5.8	0	0	0	0	0
1996—Seattle NFL	16	7	0	0	0.0	0	23	309	13.4	2	2	0	12	0
1997—Chicago NFL	15	10	0	0	0.0	0	58	753	13.0	7	7	1	44	2
1998—St. Louis NFL	16	10	1	14	14.0	0	60	771	12.9	3	3	1	20	0
1999—St. Louis NFL	15	2	0	0	0.0	0	33	349	10.6	0	0	0	0	0
2000—St. Louis NFL	12	4	0	0	0.0	0	31	441	14.2	4	4	0	24	0
Pro totals (11 years)	162	98	16	109	6.8	0	497	6492	13.1	37	37	2	226	10

PRYCE, TREVOR — DT — BRONCOS

PERSONAL: Born August 3, 1975, in Brooklyn, N.Y. ... 6-5/295.
HIGH SCHOOL: Lake Howell (Casselberry, Fla.).
COLLEGE: Clemson.
TRANSACTIONS/CAREER NOTES: Selected by Denver Broncos in first round (28th pick overall) of 1997 NFL draft. ... Signed by Broncos (July 24, 1997).
CHAMPIONSHIP GAME EXPERIENCE: Played in AFC championship game (1997 and 1998 seasons). ... Member of Super Bowl championship team (1997 and 1998 seasons).
HONORS: Played in Pro Bowl (1999 and 2000 seasons).
PRO STATISTICS: 1998—Intercepted one pass for one yard. 1999—Intercepted one pass for no yards, credited with a safety and recovered one fumble. 2000—Recovered one fumble for 28 yards and a touchdown.

Year Team	G	GS	SACKS
1997—Denver NFL	8	3	2.0
1998—Denver NFL	16	15	8.5
1999—Denver NFL	15	15	13.0
2000—Denver NFL	16	16	12.0
Pro totals (4 years)	55	49	35.5

PUPUNU, AL — TE

PERSONAL: Born October 17, 1969, in Tonga. ... 6-2/260. ... Full name: Alfred Sione Pupunu. ... Name pronounced Puh-POO-new.
HIGH SCHOOL: Salt Lake City South.
JUNIOR COLLEGE: Dixie College (Utah).
COLLEGE: Weber State.
TRANSACTIONS/CAREER NOTES: Signed as non-drafted free agent by Kansas City Chiefs (May 2, 1992). ... Claimed on waivers by San Diego Chargers (September 1, 1992). ... Granted unconditional free agency (February 16, 1996). ... Re-signed by Chargers (March 5, 1996). ... Released by Chargers (November 4, 1997). ... Signed by Chiefs (November 11, 1997). ... Released by Chiefs (November 25, 1997). ... Signed by New York Giants (December 22, 1997). ... On injured reserve with knee injury (November 17, 1998-remainder of season). ... Granted unconditional free agency (February 12, 1999). ... Signed by Chargers (April 7, 1999). ... Released by Chargers (November 20, 1999). ... Signed by Detroit Lions (August 14, 2000). ... Released by Lions (December 12, 2000).
CHAMPIONSHIP GAME EXPERIENCE: Played in AFC championship game (1994 season). ... Played in Super Bowl XXIX (1994 season).
POST SEASON RECORDS: Shares Super Bowl and NFL postseason career and single-game records for most two-point conversions—1 (January 29, 1995, vs. San Francisco).
PRO STATISTICS: 1993—Recovered one fumble. 1995—Fumbled once. 1996—Returned one kickoff for 15 yards and recovered two fumbles. 1997—Recovered one fumble.
SINGLE GAME HIGHS (regular season): Receptions—6 (December 19, 1993, vs. Kansas City); yards—83 (September 29, 1996, vs. Kansas City); and touchdown receptions—1 (November 11, 1996, vs. Detroit).

Year Team	G	GS	RECEIVING				TOTALS			
			No.	Yds.	Avg.	TD	TD	2pt.	Pts.	Fum.
1992—San Diego NFL	15	2	0	0	0.0	0	0	0	0	0
1993—San Diego NFL	16	7	13	142	10.9	0	0	0	0	0
1994—San Diego NFL	13	10	21	214	10.2	2	2	0	12	0
1995—San Diego NFL	15	14	35	315	9.0	0	0	0	0	1
1996—San Diego NFL	9	8	24	271	11.3	1	1	0	6	1
1997—San Diego NFL	8	1	1	7	7.0	0	0	0	0	0
—Kansas City NFL	1	0	0	0	0.0	0	0	0	0	0
1998—New York Giants NFL	9	0	1	2	2.0	0	0	0	0	0
1999—San Diego NFL	8	0	4	17	4.3	0	0	0	0	0
2000—Detroit NFL	9	0	3	32	10.7	0	0	0	0	0
Pro totals (9 years)	103	42	102	1000	9.8	3	3	0	18	2

PYNE, JIM — OL — BROWNS

PERSONAL: Born November 23, 1971, in Milford, Conn. ... 6-2/297. ... Full name: James M. Pyne. ... Son of George Pyne III, tackle with Boston Patriots of AFL (1965); and grandson of George Pyne Jr., tackle with Providence Steamrollers of NFL (1931).
HIGH SCHOOL: Choate Prep (Wallingford, Conn.), then Milford (Mass.).
COLLEGE: Virginia Tech.
TRANSACTIONS/CAREER NOTES: Selected by Tampa Bay Buccaneers in seventh round (200th pick overall) of 1994 NFL draft. ... Signed by Buccaneers (July 14, 1994). ... On injured reserve with broken leg (December 17, 1996-remainder of season). ... Granted free agency (February 14, 1997). ... Re-signed by Buccaneers (April 18, 1997). ... Granted unconditional free agency (February 13, 1998). ... Signed by Detroit Lions (February 21, 1998). ... Selected by Cleveland Browns from Lions in NFL expansion draft (February 9, 1999). ... On injured reserve with knee injury (September 11, 2000-remainder of season).

PLAYING EXPERIENCE: Tampa Bay NFL, 1995-1997; Detroit NFL, 1998; Cleveland NFL, 1999 and 2000. ... Games/Games started: 1995 (15/13), 1996 (12/11), 1997 (15/14), 1998 (16/16), 1999 (16/16), 2000 (2/2). Total: 76/72.
HONORS: Named offensive lineman on The Sporting News college All-America first team (1993).
PRO STATISTICS: 1995—Recovered one fumble. 1997—Fumbled once for minus five yards.

QUARLES, SHELTON   LB   BUCCANEERS

PERSONAL: Born September 11, 1971, in Nashville. ... 6-1/230. ... Full name: Shelton Eugene Quarles.
HIGH SCHOOL: Whites Creek (Tenn.).
COLLEGE: Vanderbilt (degree in human and organized development).
TRANSACTIONS/CAREER NOTES: Signed as non-drafted free agent by Miami Dolphins (April 29, 1994). ... Released by Dolphins (August 15, 1994). ... Signed by B.C. Lions of CFL (December 1, 1994). ... Granted free agency (February 16, 1997). ... Signed by Tampa Bay Buccaneers (March 21, 1997).
PLAYING EXPERIENCE: B.C. CFL, 1995 and 1996; Tampa Bay NFL, 1997-2000. ... Games/Games started: 1995 (16/games started unavailable), 1996 (16/-), 1997 (16/0), 1998 (16/0), 1999 (16/14), 2000 (14/13). Total CFL: 32/-. Total NFL: 62/27. Total Pro: 94/-.
CHAMPIONSHIP GAME EXPERIENCE: Played in NFC championship game (1999 season).
PRO STATISTICS: 1995—Intercepted one pass for no yards and recovered one fumble for 14 yards. 1996—Credited with 10 sacks and intercepted one pass for 22 yards. 1997—Recovered two fumbles. 1998—Credited with one sack. 1999—Recovered one fumble. 2000—Intercepted one pass for five yards, credited with two sacks and recovered two fumbles for five yards.

QUINN, JONATHON   QB   JAGUARS

PERSONAL: Born February 27, 1975, in Turlock, Calif. ... 6-6/239. ... Full name: Jonathon Ryan Quinn.
HIGH SCHOOL: McGavock (Nashville).
COLLEGE: Tulane, then Middle Tennessee State (degree in business administration, 1997).
TRANSACTIONS/CAREER NOTES: Selected by Jacksonville Jaguars in third round (86th pick overall) of 1998 NFL draft. ... Signed by Jaguars (May 19, 1998). ... Active for one game (1999); did not play. ... Assigned by Jaguars to Berlin Thunder in 2001 NFL Europe enhancement allocation program (February 19, 2001).
CHAMPIONSHIP GAME EXPERIENCE: Member of Jaguars for AFC championship game (1999 season); inactive.
PRO STATISTICS: 1998—Fumbled three times.
SINGLE GAME HIGHS (regular season): Attempts—27 (December 20, 1998, vs. Minnesota); completions—12 (December 20, 1998, vs. Minnesota); yards—192 (December 28, 1998, vs. Pittsburgh); and touchdown passes—1 (December 28, 1998, vs. Pittsburgh).
MISCELLANEOUS: Regular-season record as starting NFL quarterback: 1-1 (.500).

			PASSING							RUSHING				TOTALS		
Year—Team	G	GS	Att.	Cmp.	Pct.	Yds.	TD	Int.	Avg.	Rat.	Att.	Yds.	Avg.	TD	TD	2pt.	Pts.
1998—Jacksonville NFL	4	2	64	34	53.1	387	2	3	6.05	62.4	11	77	7.0	1	1	0	6
1999—Jacksonville NFL									Did not play.								
2000—Jacksonville NFL	1	0	0	0	0.0	0	0	0	0.0	...	2	-2	-1.0	0	0	0	0
Pro totals (2 years)	5	2	64	34	53.1	387	2	3	6.05	62.4	13	75	5.8	1	1	0	6

QUINN, MIKE   QB   DOLPHINS

PERSONAL: Born April 15, 1974, in Houston. ... 6-4/215. ... Full name: Michael Patrick Quinn.
HIGH SCHOOL: Robert E. Lee (Houston).
COLLEGE: Stephen F. Austin State.
TRANSACTIONS/CAREER NOTES: Signed as non-drafted free agent by Pittsburgh Steelers (April 21, 1997). ... Assigned by Steelers to Rhein Fire in 1998 NFL Europe enhancement allocation program (February 18, 1998). ... Claimed on waivers by Indianapolis Colts (August 31, 1998). ... Inactive for one game with Colts (1998). ... Claimed on waivers by Dallas Cowboys (September 9, 1998). ... Active for two games (1998); did not play. ... Granted free agency (February 11, 2000). ... Resigned by Cowboys (April 11, 2000) ... Released by Cowboys (May 4, 2000). ... Signed by Miami Dolphins (May 23, 2000). ... Released by Dolphins (November 10, 2000). ... Re-signed by Dolphins (November 13, 2000). ... Granted unconditional free agency (March 2, 2001). ... Re-signed by Dolphins (March 14, 2001).
CHAMPIONSHIP GAME EXPERIENCE: Member of Steelers for AFC championship game (1997 season); inactive.
SINGLE GAME HIGHS (regular season): Attempts—2 (November 9, 1997, vs. Baltimore); completions—1 (November 2, 1998, vs. Philadelphia); yards—10 (November 2, 1998, vs. Philadelphia); and touchdown passes—0.

			PASSING							RUSHING				TOTALS		
Year—Team	G	GS	Att.	Cmp.	Pct.	Yds.	TD	Int.	Avg.	Rat.	Att.	Yds.	Avg.	TD	TD	2pt.	Pts.
1997—Pittsburgh NFL	1	0	2	1	50.0	10	0	0	5.00	64.6	0	0	0.0	0	0	0	0
1998—Rhein NFLE	...	...	264	133	50.4	1997	13	3	7.56	87.3	29	122	4.2	0	0	0	0
—Dallas NFL	3	0	1	1	100.0	10	0	0	10.00	108.3	5	-6	-1.2	0	0	0	0
1999—Dallas NFL									Did not play.								
2000—Miami NFL	1	0	0	0	0.0	0	0	0	0.0	...	0	0	0.0	0	0	0	0
NFL Europe totals (1 year)	...	...	264	133	50.4	1997	13	3	7.56	87.3	29	122	4.2	0	0	0	0
NFL totals (3 years)	5	0	3	2	66.7	20	0	0	6.67	85.4	5	-6	-1.2	0	0	0	0
Pro totals (4 years)	...	...	267	135	50.6	2017	13	3	7.55	87.2	34	116	3.4	0	0	0	0

RACKERS, NEIL   K   BENGALS

PERSONAL: Born August 16, 1976, in Florissant, Mo. ... 6-0/205.
HIGH SCHOOL: Aquinas-Mercy (Florissant, Mo.).
COLLEGE: Illinois.
TRANSACTIONS/CAREER NOTES: Selected by Cincinnati Bengals in sixth round (169th pick overall) of 2000 NFL draft. ... Signed by Bengals (July 21, 2000).
PRO STATISTICS: 2000—Rushed once for minus five yards.

		KICKING						
Year—Team	G	XPM	XPA	FGM	FGA	Lg.	50+	Pts.
2000—Cincinnati NFL	16	21	21	12	21	45	0-0	57

RACKLEY, DEREK　　TE　　FALCONS

PERSONAL: Born July 18, 1977, in Apple Valley, Minn. ... 6-4/250.
HIGH SCHOOL: Apple Valley (Minn.).
COLLEGE: Minnesota.
TRANSACTIONS/CAREER NOTES: Signed as non-drafted free agent by Atlanta Falcons (April 17, 2000).
PLAYING EXPERIENCE: Atlanta NFL, 2000. ... Games/Games started: 2000 (16/0).

RAINER, WALI　　LB　　BROWNS

PERSONAL: Born April 19, 1977, in Rockingham, N.C. ... 6-2/245. ... Full name: Wali Rashid Rainer.
HIGH SCHOOL: West Charlotte (N.C.).
COLLEGE: Virginia.
TRANSACTIONS/CAREER NOTES: Selected by Cleveland Browns in fourth round (124th pick overall) of 1999 NFL draft. ... Signed by Browns (July 22, 1999).
PLAYING EXPERIENCE: Cleveland NFL, 1999 and 2000. ... Games/Games started: 1999 (16/15), 2000 (16/16). Total: 32/31.
PRO STATISTICS: 1999—Credited with one sack. 2000—Credited with one sack, intercepted one pass for five yards and recovered one fumble.

RANDLE, JOHN　　DT　　SEAHAWKS

PERSONAL: Born December 12, 1967, in Hearne, Texas. ... 6-1/287. ... Brother of Ervin Randle, linebacker with Tampa Bay Buccaneers (1985-90) and Kansas City Chiefs (1991 and 1992).
HIGH SCHOOL: Hearne (Texas).
JUNIOR COLLEGE: Trinity Valley Community College (Texas).
COLLEGE: Texas A&I.
TRANSACTIONS/CAREER NOTES: Signed as non-drafted free agent by Minnesota Vikings (May 4, 1990). ... Designated by Vikings as transition player (January 15, 1994). ... Designated by Vikings as transition player (February 13, 1998). ... Tendered offer sheet by Miami Dolphins (February 16, 1998). ... Offer matched by Vikings (February 18, 1998). ... Released by Vikings (March 1, 2001). ... Signed by Seattle Seahawks (March 3, 2001).
CHAMPIONSHIP GAME EXPERIENCE: Played in NFC championship game (1998 and 2000 seasons).
HONORS: Played in Pro Bowl (1993-1998 seasons). ... Named defensive tackle on THE SPORTING NEWS NFL All-Pro team (1994-1998).
PRO STATISTICS: 1992—Recovered one fumble. 1994—Recovered two fumbles. 1997—Recovered two fumbles for five yards. 1998—Recovered one fumble. 1999—Intercepted one pass for one yard and recovered three fumbles.

Year　Team	G	GS	SACKS
1990—Minnesota NFL	16	0	1.0
1991—Minnesota NFL	16	8	9.5
1992—Minnesota NFL	16	14	11.5
1993—Minnesota NFL	16	16	12.5
1994—Minnesota NFL	16	16	∞13.5
1995—Minnesota NFL	16	16	10.5
1996—Minnesota NFL	16	16	11.5
1997—Minnesota NFL	16	16	*15.5
1998—Minnesota NFL	16	16	10.5
1999—Minnesota NFL	16	16	10.0
2000—Minnesota NFL	16	16	8.0
Pro totals (11 years)	176	150	114.0

RANSOM, DERRICK　　DT　　CHIEFS

PERSONAL: Born September 13, 1976, in Indianapolis. ... 6-3/310. ... Full name: Derrick Wayne Ransom Jr.
HIGH SCHOOL: Lawrence Central (Indianapolis).
COLLEGE: Cincinnati (degree in finance).
TRANSACTIONS/CAREER NOTES: Selected by Kansas City Chiefs in sixth round (181st pick overall) of 1998 NFL draft. ... Signed by Chiefs (June 3, 1998). ... Granted free agency (March 2, 2001).
PLAYING EXPERIENCE: Kansas City NFL, 1998-2000. ... Games/Games started: 1998 (7/0), 1999 (10/0), 2000 (10/0). Total: 27/0.
PRO STATISTICS: 1998—Returned one kickoff for no yards. 1999—Credited with one sack.

RASBY, WALTER　　TE　　REDSKINS

PERSONAL: Born September 7, 1972, in Washington, D.C. ... 6-3/251. ... Full name: Walter Herbert Rasby.
HIGH SCHOOL: Washington (N.C.).
COLLEGE: Wake Forest.
TRANSACTIONS/CAREER NOTES: Signed as non-drafted free agent by Pittsburgh Steelers (April 29, 1994). ... Released by Steelers (August 27, 1995). ... Signed by Carolina Panthers (October 17, 1995). ... Granted free agency (February 14, 1997). ... Re-signed by Panthers (June 3, 1997). ... On injured reserve with knee injury (December 10, 1997-remainder of season). ... Granted unconditional free agency (February 13, 1998). ... Signed by Detroit Lions (April 13, 1998). ... Granted unconditional free agency (March 2, 2001). ... Signed by Washington Redskins (April 10, 2001).
CHAMPIONSHIP GAME EXPERIENCE: Played in AFC championship game (1994 season). ... Played in NFC championship game (1996 season).
PRO STATISTICS: 1996—Recovered one fumble. 1997—Returned three kickoffs for 32 yards. 2000—Recovered one fumble.
SINGLE GAME HIGHS (regular season): Receptions—5 (October 4, 1998, vs. Chicago); yards—39 (October 4, 1998, vs. Chicago); and touchdown receptions—1 (November 19, 2000, vs. New York Giants).

Year Team	G	GS	RECEIVING				TOTALS			
			No.	Yds.	Avg.	TD	TD	2pt.	Pts.	Fum.
994—Pittsburgh NFL	2	0	0	0	0.0	0	0	0	0	0
995—Carolina NFL	9	2	5	47	9.4	0	0	1	2	0
996—Carolina NFL	16	1	0	0	0.0	0	0	0	0	0
997—Carolina NFL	14	2	1	1	1.0	0	0	0	0	0
998—Detroit NFL	16	16	15	119	7.9	1	1	0	6	0
999—Detroit NFL	16	6	3	19	6.3	1	1	0	6	0
000—Detroit NFL	16	8	10	78	7.8	1	1	0	6	0
Pro totals (7 years)	89	35	34	264	7.8	3	3	1	20	0

RATTAY, TIM　　　　QB　　　　49ERS

PERSONAL: Born March 15, 1977, in Elyria, Ohio. ... 6-0/215.
HIGH SCHOOL: Phoenix (Ariz.) Christian.
JUNIOR COLLEGE: Scottsdale (Ariz.) Community College.
COLLEGE: Louisiana Tech.
TRANSACTIONS/CAREER NOTES: Selected by San Francisco 49ers in seventh round (212th pick overall) of 2000 NFL draft. ... Signed by 49ers July 16, 2000).
PLAYING EXPERIENCE: San Francisco NFL, 2000. ... Games/Games started: 2000 (1/0).
PRO STATISTICS: 2000—Completed only pass attempt for minus four yards and rushed twice for minus one yard.
SINGLE GAME HIGHS (regular season): Attempts—1 (December 3, 2000, vs. San Diego); completions—1 (December 3, 2000, vs. San Diego); yards— -4 (December 3, 2000, vs. San Diego); and touchdown passes—0.

RAYMER, CORY　　　　C　　　　REDSKINS

PERSONAL: Born March 3, 1973, in Fond du Lac, Wis. ... 6-2/289.
HIGH SCHOOL: Goodrich (Fond du Lac, Wis.).
COLLEGE: Wisconsin.
TRANSACTIONS/CAREER NOTES: Selected by Washington Redskins in second round (37th pick overall) of 1995 NFL draft. ... Signed by Redskins (July 24, 1995). ... On injured reserve with back injury (November 25, 1996-remainder of season). ... Granted unconditional free agency (February 12, 1999). ... Re-signed by Redskins (March 16, 1999). ... Granted unconditional free agency (February 11, 2000). ... Re-signed by Redskins (February 26, 2000). ... On injured reserve with knee injury (September 28, 2000-remainder of season).
PLAYING EXPERIENCE: Washington NFL, 1995-1999. ... Games/Games started: 1995 (3/2), 1996 (6/5), 1997 (6/3), 1998 (16/16), 1999 (16/16). Total: 47/42.
HONORS: Named offensive lineman on THE SPORTING NEWS college All-America first team (1994).
PRO STATISTICS: 1996—Recovered one fumble. 1998—Recovered one fumble. 1999—Recovered one fumble.

REAGOR, MONTAE　　　　DE　　　　BRONCOS

PERSONAL: Born June 29, 1977, in Waxahachie, Texas. ... 6-2/280. ... Full name: Willie Montae Reagor. ... Name pronounced MON-tay RAY-ger.
HIGH SCHOOL: Waxahachie (Texas).
COLLEGE: Texas Tech (degree in exercise and sports sciences).
TRANSACTIONS/CAREER NOTES: Selected by Denver Broncos in second round (58th pick overall) of 1999 NFL draft. ... Signed by Broncos July 13, 1999).
PLAYING EXPERIENCE: Denver NFL, 1999 and 2000. ... Games/Games started: 1999 (9/0), 2000 (13/0). Total: 22/0.
HONORS: Named defensive end on THE SPORTING NEWS college All-America second team (1997). ... Named defensive end on THE SPORTING NEWS college All-America first team (1998).
PRO STATISTICS: 2000—Credited with two sacks.

REDMAN, CHRIS　　　　QB　　　　RAVENS

PERSONAL: Born July 7, 1977, in Louisville, Ky. ... 6-3/223.
HIGH SCHOOL: Male (Louisville, Ky.).
COLLEGE: Louisville.
TRANSACTIONS/CAREER NOTES: Selected by Baltimore Ravens in third round (75th pick overall) of 2000 NFL draft. ... Signed by Ravens July 24, 2000).
PLAYING EXPERIENCE: Baltimore NFL, 2000. ... Games/Games started: 2000 (3/0).
CHAMPIONSHIP GAME EXPERIENCE: Member of Ravens for AFC Championship game (2000 season); inactive. ... Member of Super Bowl championship team (2000 season); inactive.
PRO STATISTICS: 2000—Attempted three passes with two completions for 19 yards and rushed once for no yards.
SINGLE GAME HIGHS (regular season): Attempts—3 (September 24, 2000, vs. Cincinnati); completions—2 (September 24, 2000, vs. Cincinnati); yards—19 (September 24, 2000, vs. Cincinnati); and touchdown passes—0.

REDMON, ANTHONY　　　　G　　　　FALCONS

PERSONAL: Born April 9, 1971, in Brewton, Ala. ... 6-5/305. ... Full name: Kendrick Anthony Redmon.
HIGH SCHOOL: T. R. Miller (Brewton, Ala.).
COLLEGE: Auburn.
TRANSACTIONS/CAREER NOTES: Selected by Arizona Cardinals in fifth round (139th pick overall) of 1994 NFL draft. ... Signed by Cardinals June 13, 1994). ... Granted free agency (February 14, 1997). ... Re-signed by Cardinals (June 13, 1997). ... Granted unconditional free agency February 13, 1998). ... Signed by Miami Dolphins (July 24, 1998). ... Released by Dolphins (August 30, 1998). ... Signed by Carolina Panthers October 14, 1998). ... Granted unconditional free agency (February 12, 1999). ... Re-signed Panthers (February 12, 1999). ... Released by Panthers (February 16, 2000). ... Signed by Atlanta Falcons (March 22, 2000).
PLAYING EXPERIENCE: Arizona NFL, 1994-1997; Carolina NFL, 1998 and 1999; Atlanta NFL, 2000. ... Games/Games started: 1994 (6/5), 1995 12/9), 1996 (16/16), 1997 (16/16), 1998 (10/4), 1999 (15/15), 2000 (4/4). Total: 79/69.
PRO STATISTICS: 1996—Recovered one fumble. 2000—Recovered one fumble.

REDMOND, J.R.   RB   PATRIOTS

PERSONAL: Born September 28, 1977, in Los Angeles. ... 5-11/210. ... Full name: Joseph Robert Redmond.
HIGH SCHOOL: Carson (Calif.).
COLLEGE: Arizona State.
TRANSACTIONS/CAREER NOTES: Selected by New England Patriots in third round (76th pick overall) of 2000 NFL draft. ... Signed by Patriots (July 23, 2000).
PRO STATISTICS: 2000—Returned one kickoff for 25 yards.
SINGLE GAME HIGHS (regular season): Attempts—24 (November 5, 2000, vs. Buffalo); yards—97 (October 22, 2000, vs. Indianapolis); and rushing touchdowns—1 (November 5, 2000 vs. Buffalo).

			RUSHING				RECEIVING				TOTALS			
Year Team	G	GS	Att.	Yds.	Avg.	TD	No.	Yds.	Avg.	TD	TD	2pt.	Pts.	Fum.
2000—New England NFL	12	5	125	406	3.2	1	20	126	6.3	2	3	0	18	2

REED, ANDRE   WR

PERSONAL: Born January 29, 1964, in Allentown, Pa. ... 6-2/190. ... Full name: Andre Darnell Reed.
HIGH SCHOOL: Louis E. Dieruff (Allentown, Pa.).
COLLEGE: Kutztown (Pa.) University.
TRANSACTIONS/CAREER NOTES: Selected by Orlando Renegades in third round (39th pick overall) of 1985 USFL draft. ... Selected by Buffalo Bills in fourth round (86th pick overall) of 1985 NFL draft. ... Signed by Bills (July 19, 1985). ... Granted unconditional free agency (February 16, 1996). ... Re-signed by Bills (May 7, 1996). ... On injured reserve with shoulder injury (December 18, 1997-remainder of season). ... Released by Bills (February 9, 2000). ... Signed by Denver Broncos (July 20, 2000). ... Released by Broncos (September 1, 2000). ... Signed by Washington Redskins (September 12, 2000). ... On injured reserve with hamstring injury (December 18, 2000-remainder of season). ... Granted unconditional free agency (March 2, 2001).
CHAMPIONSHIP GAME EXPERIENCE: Played in AFC championship game (1988 and 1990-1993 seasons). ... Played in Super Bowl XXV (1990 season), Super Bowl XXVI (1991 season), Super Bowl XXVII (1992 season) and Super Bowl XXVIII (1993 season).
HONORS: Played in Pro Bowl (1988-1990, 1992 and 1994 seasons). ... Member of Pro Bowl squad (1991 season); did not play. ... Named to play in Pro Bowl (1993 season); replaced by Haywood Jeffires due to injury.
RECORDS: Shares NFL record for most seasons with 50 or more receptions—13.
POST SEASON RECORDS: Shares NFL postseason single-game record for most touchdown receptions—3 (January 3, 1993, OT, vs. Houston).
PRO STATISTICS: 1985—Returned five punts for 12 yards and recovered two fumbles. 1986—Recovered two fumbles for two yards. 1990—Recovered one fumble. 1994—Completed only pass attempt for 32 yards and recovered two fumbles. 1999—Recovered one fumble.
SINGLE GAME HIGHS (regular season): Receptions—15 (November 20, 1994, vs. Green Bay); yards—191 (November 20, 1994, vs. Green Bay); and touchdown receptions—3 (September 5, 1993, vs. New England).
STATISTICAL PLATEAUS: 100-yard receiving games: 1985 (1), 1987 (2), 1988 (3), 1989 (6), 1990 (2), 1991 (4), 1992 (2), 1993 (2), 1994 (5), 1996 (5), 1997 (2), 1998 (1). Total: 35.
MISCELLANEOUS: Holds Buffalo Bills all-time record for most receptions (941), most yards receiving (13,095) and most touchdown receptions (86). ... Shares Buffalo Bills all-time record for most touchdowns (87).

			RUSHING				RECEIVING				TOTALS			
Year Team	G	GS	Att.	Yds.	Avg.	TD	No.	Yds.	Avg.	TD	TD	2pt.	Pts.	Fum.
1985—Buffalo NFL	16	15	3	-1	-0.3	1	48	637	13.3	4	5	0	30	1
1986—Buffalo NFL	15	15	3	-8	-2.7	0	53	739	13.9	7	7	0	42	2
1987—Buffalo NFL	12	12	1	1	1.0	0	57	752	13.2	5	5	0	30	0
1988—Buffalo NFL	15	14	6	64	10.7	0	71	968	13.6	6	6	0	36	1
1989—Buffalo NFL	16	16	2	31	15.5	0	§88	§1312	14.9	9	9	0	54	4
1990—Buffalo NFL	16	16	3	23	7.7	0	71	945	13.3	8	8	0	48	1
1991—Buffalo NFL	16	16	12	136	11.3	0	81	1113	13.7	10	10	0	60	1
1992—Buffalo NFL	16	16	8	65	8.1	0	65	913	14.0	3	3	0	18	4
1993—Buffalo NFL	15	15	9	21	2.3	0	52	854	16.4	6	6	0	36	3
1994—Buffalo NFL	16	16	10	87	8.7	0	90	1303	14.5	8	8	0	48	3
1995—Buffalo NFL	6	6	7	48	6.9	0	24	312	13.0	3	3	0	18	2
1996—Buffalo NFL	16	16	8	22	2.8	0	66	1036	15.7	6	6	0	36	1
1997—Buffalo NFL	15	15	3	11	3.7	0	60	880	14.7	5	5	0	30	1
1998—Buffalo NFL	15	13	0	0	0.0	0	63	795	12.6	5	5	0	30	0
1999—Buffalo NFL	16	16	0	0	0.0	0	52	536	10.3	1	1	0	6	0
2000—Washington NFL	13	0	0	0	0.0	0	10	103	10.3	1	1	0	6	0
Pro totals (16 years)	234	217	75	500	6.7	1	951	13198	13.9	87	88	0	528	24

REED, JAKE   WR   VIKINGS

PERSONAL: Born September 28, 1967, in Covington, Ga. ... 6-3/213. ... Full name: Willis Reed. ... Brother of Dale Carter, cornerback, Denver Broncos.
HIGH SCHOOL: Newton County (Covington, Ga.).
COLLEGE: Grambling State (degree in criminal justice, 1990).
TRANSACTIONS/CAREER NOTES: Selected by Minnesota Vikings in third round (68th pick overall) of 1991 NFL draft. ... Signed by Vikings (July 22, 1991). ... On injured reserve with ankle injury (November 2, 1991-remainder of season). ... Granted free agency (February 17, 1994). ... Re-signed by Vikings (May 6, 1994). ... Granted unconditional free agency (February 17, 1995). ... Re-signed by Vikings (February 28, 1995). ... Released by Vikings (February 10, 2000). ... Signed by New Orleans Saints (February 21, 2000). ... Released by Saints (March 1, 2001). ... Signed by Vikings (March 23, 2001).
CHAMPIONSHIP GAME EXPERIENCE: Member of Vikings for NFC championship game (1998 season); inactive.
PRO STATISTICS: 1992—Returned one kickoff for one yard. 1995—Recovered one fumble.
SINGLE GAME HIGHS (regular season): Receptions—12 (September 7, 1997, vs. Chicago); yards—157 (November 6, 1994, vs. New Orleans); and touchdown receptions—2 (November 1, 1998, vs. Tampa Bay).
STATISTICAL PLATEAUS: 100-yard receiving games: 1994 (3), 1995 (3), 1996 (3), 1997 (5), 1998 (1), 1999 (2). Total: 17.

Year Team	G	GS	RECEIVING				TOTALS			
			No.	Yds.	Avg.	TD	TD	2pt.	Pts.	Fum.
1991—Minnesota NFL	1	0	0	0	0.0	0	0	0	0	0
1992—Minnesota NFL	16	0	6	142	23.7	0	0	0	0	0
1993—Minnesota NFL	10	1	5	65	13.0	0	0	0	0	0
1994—Minnesota NFL	16	16	85	1175	13.8	4	4	0	24	3
1995—Minnesota NFL	16	16	72	1167	16.2	9	9	0	54	1
1996—Minnesota NFL	16	15	72	1320	18.3	7	7	0	42	0
1997—Minnesota NFL	16	16	68	1138	16.7	6	6	0	36	0
1998—Minnesota NFL	11	11	34	474	13.9	4	4	0	24	0
1999—Minnesota NFL	16	8	44	643	14.6	2	2	0	12	0
2000—New Orleans NFL	7	6	16	206	12.9	0	0	0	0	0
Pro totals (10 years)	125	89	402	6330	15.7	32	32	0	192	4

REESE, IKE LB EAGLES

R

PERSONAL: Born October 16, 1973, in Jacksonville, N.C. ... 6-2/222. ... Full name: Isaiah Reese.
HIGH SCHOOL: Woodward (Cincinnati), then Aiken (Cincinnati).
COLLEGE: Michigan State.
TRANSACTIONS/CAREER NOTES: Selected by Philadelphia Eagles in fifth round (142nd pick overall) of 1998 NFL draft. ... Signed by Eagles (July 14, 1998). ... Granted free agency (March 2, 2001). ... Re-signed by Eagles (March 20, 2001).
PLAYING EXPERIENCE: Philadelphia NFL, 1998-2000. ... Games/Games started: 1998 (16/0), 1999 (16/0), 2000 (16/0). Total: 48/0.
PRO STATISTICS: 1999—Credited with three sacks.

REESE, IZELL S COWBOYS

PERSONAL: Born May 7, 1974, in Dothan, Ala. ... 6-2/190.
HIGH SCHOOL: Northview (Dothan, Ala.).
COLLEGE: Alabama-Birmingham.
TRANSACTIONS/CAREER NOTES: Selected by Dallas Cowboys in sixth round (188th pick overall) of 1998 NFL draft. ... Signed by Cowboys (July 15, 1998). ... On injured reserve with neck injury (November 19, 1999-remainder of season). ... Granted free agency (March 2, 2001).
PRO STATISTICS: 2000—Credited with one safety.

Year Team	G	GS	INTERCEPTIONS			
			No.	Yds.	Avg.	TD
1998—Dallas NFL	16	0	1	6	6.0	0
1999—Dallas NFL	8	4	3	28	9.3	0
2000—Dallas NFL	16	7	2	60	30.0	0
Pro totals (3 years)	40	11	6	94	15.7	0

REEVES, JOHN LB PANTHERS

PERSONAL: Born February 23, 1975, in Bradenton, Fla. ... 6-3/245. ... Full name: John Edwin Reeves Jr.
HIGH SCHOOL: Southeast (Bradenton, Fla.).
COLLEGE: Purdue.
TRANSACTIONS/CAREER NOTES: Signed as non-drafted free agent by San Diego Chargers (April 20, 1999). ... Released by Chargers (September 4, 1999). ... Re-signed by Chargers to practice squad (September 6, 1999). ... Activated (November 23, 1999). ... Released by Chargers (March 1, 2001). ... Signed by Carolina Panthers (March 12, 2001).
PLAYING EXPERIENCE: San Diego NFL, 1999 and 2000. ... Games/Games started: 1999 (5/0), 2000 (9/0). Total: 14/0.

REHBERG, SCOTT G BENGALS

PERSONAL: Born November 17, 1973, in Kalamazoo, Mich. ... 6-8/330. ... Full name: Scott Joseph Rehberg. ... Name pronounced RAY-berg.
HIGH SCHOOL: Central (Kalamazoo, Mich.).
COLLEGE: Central Michigan.
TRANSACTIONS/CAREER NOTES: Selected by New England Patriots in seventh round (230th pick overall) of 1997 NFL draft. ... Signed by Patriots (June 19, 1997). ... Selected by Cleveland Browns from Patriots in NFL expansion draft (February 9, 1999). ... Granted free agency (February 11, 2000). ... Signed by Cincinnati Bengals (March 2, 2000).
PLAYING EXPERIENCE: New England NFL, 1997 and 1998; Cleveland NFL, 1999; Cincinnati NFL, 2000. ... Games/Games started: 1997 (6/0), 1998 (2/0), 1999 (15/13), 2000 (10/6). Total: 33/19.
PRO STATISTICS: 1999—Recovered one fumble.

RHETT, ERRICT RB BROWNS

PERSONAL: Born December 11, 1970, in Pembroke Pines, Fla. ... 5-11/211. ... Full name: Errict Undra Rhett.
HIGH SCHOOL: McArthur (Hollywood, Fla.).
COLLEGE: Florida (degree in commercial management).
TRANSACTIONS/CAREER NOTES: Selected by Tampa Bay Buccaneers in second round (34th pick overall) of 1994 NFL draft. ... Signed by Buccaneers (August 9, 1994). ... Granted free agency (February 13, 1998). ... Re-signed by Buccaneers (February 18, 1998). ... Traded by Buccaneers to Baltimore Ravens for third-round pick (traded back to Baltimore) in 1999 draft (February 18, 1998). ... Granted unconditional free agency (February 12, 1999). ... Re-signed by Ravens (April 26, 1999). ... Granted unconditional free agency (February 11, 2000). ... Signed by Cleveland Browns (February 28, 2000). ... On injured reserve with foot injury (October 3, 2000-remainder of season).
HONORS: Named running back on THE SPORTING NEWS college All-America second team (1993).

PRO STATISTICS: 1994—Recovered one fumble. 1995—Recovered one fumble. 1996—Recovered one fumble. 1997—Returned one kickoff for 16 yards.
SINGLE GAME HIGHS (regular season): Attempts—40 (December 4, 1994, vs. Washington); yards—192 (December 4, 1994, vs. Washington); and rushing touchdowns—2 (November 7, 1999, vs. Cleveland).
STATISTICAL PLATEAUS: 100-yard rushing games: 1994 (4), 1995 (4), 1999 (4). Total: 12.

Year Team	G	GS	RUSHING				RECEIVING				TOTALS			
			Att.	Yds.	Avg.	TD	No.	Yds.	Avg.	TD	TD	2pt.	Pts.	Fum.
1994—Tampa Bay NFL	16	8	284	1011	3.6	7	22	119	5.4	0	7	1	44	2
1995—Tampa Bay NFL	16	16	332	1207	3.6	11	14	110	7.9	0	11	0	66	2
1996—Tampa Bay NFL	9	7	176	539	3.1	3	4	11	2.8	1	4	0	24	3
1997—Tampa Bay NFL	11	0	31	96	3.1	3	0	0	0.0	0	3	0	18	0
1998—Baltimore NFL	13	1	44	180	4.1	0	11	65	5.9	0	0	0	0	0
1999—Baltimore NFL	16	10	236	852	3.6	5	24	169	7.0	2	7	0	42	0
2000—Cleveland NFL	5	4	71	258	3.6	0	14	78	5.6	0	0	0	0	0
Pro totals (7 years)	86	46	1174	4143	3.5	29	89	552	6.2	3	32	1	194	7

RICE, JERRY   WR   RAIDERS

PERSONAL: Born October 13, 1962, in Starkville, Miss. ... 6-2/196. ... Full name: Jerry Lee Rice.
HIGH SCHOOL: Crawford MS Moor (Crawford, Miss.).
COLLEGE: Mississippi Valley State.
TRANSACTIONS/CAREER NOTES: Selected by Birmingham Stallions in first round (first pick overall) of 1985 USFL draft. ... Selected by San Francisco 49ers in first round (16th pick overall) of 1985 NFL draft. ... Signed by 49ers (July 23, 1985). ... Granted free agency (February 1, 1992). ... Re-signed by 49ers (August 25, 1992). ... On injured reserve with knee injury (December 23, 1997-remainder of season). ... Released by 49ers (June 4, 2001). ... Signed by Oakland Raiders (June 5, 2001).
CHAMPIONSHIP GAME EXPERIENCE: Played in NFC championship game (1988-1990 and 1992-1994 seasons). ... Member of Super Bowl championship team (1988, 1989 and 1994 seasons).
HONORS: Named wide receiver on THE SPORTING NEWS college All-America first team (1984). ... Named wide receiver on THE SPORTING NEWS NFL All-Pro team (1986-1996). ... Played in Pro Bowl (1986, 1987, 1989-1993, 1995 and 1998 seasons). ... Named NFL Player of the Year by THE SPORTING NEWS (1987 and 1990). ... Named Most Valuable Player of Super Bowl XXIII (1988 season). ... Named to play in Pro Bowl (1988 season); replaced by J.T. Smith due to injury. ... Named to play in Pro Bowl (1994 season); replaced by Herman Moore due to injury. ... Named Outstanding Player of Pro Bowl (1995 season). ... Named to play in Pro Bowl (1996 season); replaced by Irving Fryar due to injury.
RECORDS: Holds NFL career records for most touchdowns—187; most touchdown receptions—176; most receiving yards—19,247; most pass receptions—1,281; most seasons with 1,000 or more yards receiving—12; most games with 100 or more yards receiving—66; most consecutive games with one or more reception—209 (December 9, 1985-present); most consecutive games with one or more touchdown reception—13 (December 19, 1986-December 27, 1987); and most seasons with 50 or more receptions—14. ... Holds NFL single-season record for most yards receiving—1,848 (1995); and most touchdown receptions—22 (1987). ... Shares NFL single-game record for most touchdown receptions—5 (October 14, 1990, at Atlanta).
POST SEASON RECORDS: Holds Super Bowl career records for most points—42; most touchdowns—7; most touchdown receptions—7; most receptions—28; most combined yards—527; and most yards receiving—512. ... Holds Super Bowl single-game records for most touchdowns receptions—3 (January 28, 1990, vs. Denver and January 29, 1995, vs. San Diego); and most yards receiving—215 (January 22, 1989, vs. Cincinnati). ... Shares Super Bowl single-game records for most points—18; most touchdowns—3 (January 28, 1990, vs. Denver and January 29, 1995, vs. San Diego); and most receptions—11 (January 22, 1989, vs. Cincinnati). ... Holds NFL postseason career records for most touchdowns—19; most touchdown receptions—19; most receptions—124; most yards receiving—1,811; and most games with 100 or more yards receiving—7. ... Holds NFL postseason record for most consecutive games with one or more receptions—23 (1985-present). ... Shares NFL postseason career record for most consecutive games with 100 or more yards receiving—3 (1988-89). ... Shares NFL postseason single-game record for most touchdown receptions—3 (January 28, 1990, vs. Denver; January 1, 1989, vs. Minnesota; and January 29, 1995, vs. San Diego).
PRO STATISTICS: 1985—Returned one kickoff for six yards. 1986—Attempted two passes with one completion for 16 yards and recovered three fumbles. 1987—Recovered one fumble. 1988—Attempted three passes with one completion for 14 yards and one interception and recovered one fumble. 1993—Recovered one fumble. 1995—Completed only pass attempt for 41 yards and a touchdown and recovered one fumble in end zone for a touchdown. 1996—Attempted one pass without a completion. 1999—Attempted one pass without a completion. 2000—Attempted one pass without a completion and recovered one fumble.
SINGLE GAME HIGHS (regular season): Receptions—16 (November 20, 1994, vs. Los Angeles Rams); yards—289 (December 18, 1995, vs. Minnesota); and touchdown receptions—5 (October 14, 1990, vs. Atlanta).
STATISTICAL PLATEAUS: 100-yard receiving games: 1985 (2), 1986 (6), 1987 (4), 1988 (5), 1989 (8), 1990 (7), 1991 (4), 1992 (3), 1993 (5), 1994 (5), 1995 (9), 1996 (3), 1998 (3), 1999 (2). Total: 66.
MISCELLANEOUS: Active NFL leader for career receptions (1,281), receiving yards (19,247), touchdown receptions (176) and touchdowns (187). ... Holds San Francisco 49ers all-time records for most yards receiving (19,247), most touchdowns (187), most receptions (1,281), and most touchdown receptions (176).

Year Team	G	GS	RUSHING				RECEIVING				TOTALS			
			Att.	Yds.	Avg.	TD	No.	Yds.	Avg.	TD	TD	2pt.	Pts.	Fum.
1985—San Francisco NFL	16	4	6	26	4.3	1	49	927	18.9	3	4	0	24	1
1986—San Francisco NFL	16	15	10	72	7.2	1	‡86	*1570	18.3	*15	16	0	96	2
1987—San Francisco NFL	12	12	8	51	6.4	1	65	1078	16.6	*22	*23	0	*138	2
1988—San Francisco NFL	16	16	13	107	8.2	1	64	1306	20.4	9	10	0	60	2
1989—San Francisco NFL	16	16	5	33	6.6	0	82	*1483	18.1	*17	17	0	102	0
1990—San Francisco NFL	16	16	2	0	0.0	0	*100	*1502	15.0	*13	13	0	78	1
1991—San Francisco NFL	16	16	1	2	2.0	0	80	1206	15.1	*14	14	0	84	1
1992—San Francisco NFL	16	16	9	58	6.4	1	84	1201	14.3	10	11	0	66	2
1993—San Francisco NFL	16	16	3	69	23.0	0	98	*1503	15.3	†15	*16	0	96	3
1994—San Francisco NFL	16	16	7	93	13.3	2	112	*1499	13.4	13	15	1	92	1
1995—San Francisco NFL	16	16	5	36	7.2	1	122	*1848	15.1	15	17	1	104	3
1996—San Francisco NFL	16	16	11	77	7.0	1	*108	1254	11.6	8	9	0	54	0
1997—San Francisco NFL	2	1	1	-10	-10.0	0	7	78	11.1	1	1	0	6	0
1998—San Francisco NFL	16	16	0	0	0.0	0	82	1157	14.1	9	9	†2	58	2
1999—San Francisco NFL	16	16	2	13	6.5	0	67	830	12.4	5	5	0	30	0
2000—San Francisco NFL	16	16	1	-2	-2.0	0	75	805	10.7	7	7	0	42	3
Pro totals (16 years)	238	224	84	625	7.4	10	1281	19247	15.0	176	187	4	1130	23

RICE, RON   S   LIONS

PERSONAL: Born November 9, 1972, in Detroit. ... 6-1/217. ... Full name: Ronald Wilson Rice.
HIGH SCHOOL: University of Detroit Jesuit.
COLLEGE: Eastern Michigan (degree in criminal justice).
TRANSACTIONS/CAREER NOTES: Signed as non-drafted free agent by Detroit Lions (April 24, 1995). ... Released by Lions (August 18, 1995). ... Re-signed by Lions to practice squad (August 29, 1995). ... Activated (November 1, 1995); did not play. ... Granted free agency (February 13, 1998). ... Re-signed by Lions (June 25, 1998).
PRO STATISTICS: 1999—Recovered one fumble. 2000—Recovered one fumble for six yards.

				INTERCEPTIONS			SACKS
Year Team	G	GS	No.	Yds.	Avg.	TD	No.
1995—Detroit NFL				Did not play.			
1996—Detroit NFL	13	2	0	0	0.0	0	0.0
1997—Detroit NFL	12	8	1	18	18.0	0	1.0
1998—Detroit NFL	16	16	3	25	8.3	0	3.5
1999—Detroit NFL	16	16	5	82	16.4	0	1.0
2000—Detroit NFL	14	14	1	7	7.0	0	0.0
Pro totals (5 years)	71	56	10	132	13.2	0	5.5

RICE, SIMEON   DE   BUCCANEERS

PERSONAL: Born February 24, 1974, in Chicago. ... 6-5/268. ... Name pronounced simm-ee-ON.
HIGH SCHOOL: Mount Carmel (Chicago).
COLLEGE: Illinois (degree in speech communications, 1996).
TRANSACTIONS/CAREER NOTES: Selected by Arizona Cardinals in first round (third pick overall) of 1996 NFL draft. ... Signed by Cardinals (August 19, 1996). ... Designated by Cardinals as franchise player (February 11, 2000). ... Re-signed by Cardinals (September 7, 2000). ... Granted unconditional free agency (March 2, 2001). ... Signed by Tampa Bay Buccaneers (March 23, 2001).
HONORS: Played in Pro Bowl (1999 season). ... Named linebacker on THE SPORTING NEWS college All-America second team (1995).
PRO STATISTICS: 1996—Recovered one fumble. 1997—Intercepted one pass for no yards. 1998—Recovered four fumbles for 39 yards. 1999—Recovered one fumble. 2000—Recovered one fumble.

Year Team	G	GS	SACKS
1996—Arizona NFL	16	15	12.5
1997—Arizona NFL	16	15	5.0
1998—Arizona NFL	16	16	10.0
1999—Arizona NFL	16	16	16.5
2000—Arizona NFL	15	11	7.5
Pro totals (5 years)	79	73	51.5

RICHARDSON, DAMIEN   S   PANTHERS

PERSONAL: Born April 3, 1976, in Los Angeles. ... 6-1/210. ... Full name: Damien A. Richardson.
HIGH SCHOOL: Clovis West (Fresno, Calif.).
COLLEGE: Arizona State.
TRANSACTIONS/CAREER NOTES: Selected by Carolina Panthers in sixth round (165th pick overall) of 1998 NFL draft. ... Signed by Panthers (July 24, 1998). ... Granted free agency (March 2, 2001).
PLAYING EXPERIENCE: Carolina NFL, 1998-2000. ... Games/Games started: 1998 (14/7), 1999 (15/0), 2000 (16/1). Total: 45/8.
PRO STATISTICS: 1998—Recovered one fumble. 1999—Intercepted one pass for 27 yards and credited with one sack.

RICHARDSON, KYLE   P   RAVENS

PERSONAL: Born March 2, 1973, in Farmington, Mo. ... 6-2/210. ... Full name: Kyle Davis Richardson.
HIGH SCHOOL: Farmington (Mo.).
COLLEGE: Arkansas State.
TRANSACTIONS/CAREER NOTES: Played for Rhein Fire of World League (1996). ... Signed as non-drafted free agent by Miami Dolphins (September 3, 1997). ... Released by Dolphins (September 8, 1997). ... Re-signed by Dolphins (September 18, 1997). ... Released by Dolphins (October 7, 1997). ... Signed by Seattle Seahawks (November 12, 1997). ... Released by Seahawks (November 25, 1997). ... Signed by Baltimore Ravens (March 25, 1998). ... Granted free agency (March 2, 2001).
CHAMPIONSHIP GAME EXPERIENCE: Played in AFC championship game (2000 season). ... Member of Super Bowl championship team (2000 season).
PRO STATISTICS: 1997—Rushed once for no yards and fumbled once for minus 13 yards. 1998—Rushed once for no yards and recovered one fumble.

				PUNTING			
Year Team	G	No.	Yds.	Avg.	Net avg.	In. 20	Blk.
1996—Rhein W.L.				Statistics unavailable.			
1997—Miami NFL	3	11	480	43.6	33.1	0	0
—Seattle NFL	2	8	324	40.5	23.8	2	†2
1998—Baltimore NFL	16	90	3948	43.9	38.3	25	*2
1999—Baltimore NFL	16	103	4355	42.3	35.5	*39	1
2000—Baltimore NFL	16	86	3457	40.2	33.9	35	0
NFL totals (4 years)	53	298	12564	42.2	35.5	101	5

RICHARDSON, TONY   FB   CHIEFS

PERSONAL: Born December 17, 1971, in Frankfurt, West Germany. ... 6-1/233. ... Full name: Antonio Richardson.
HIGH SCHOOL: Daleville (Ala.).
COLLEGE: Auburn.
TRANSACTIONS/CAREER NOTES: Signed as non-drafted free agent by Dallas Cowboys (April 28, 1994). ... Released by Cowboys (August 28, 1994). ... Re-signed by Cowboys to practice squad (August 30, 1994). ... Granted free agency after 1994 season. ... Signed by Kansas City Chiefs (February 28, 1995). ... On injured reserve with wrist injury (December 11, 1996-remainder of season).
PRO STATISTICS: 1996—Recovered one fumble. 1998—Returned one kickoff for no yards and recovered one fumble.
SINGLE GAME HIGHS (regular season): Attempts—23 (December 17, 2000, vs. Denver); yards—156 (December 17, 2000, vs. Denver); and rushing touchdowns—1 (December 17, 2000, vs. Denver).
STATISTICAL PLATEAUS: 100-yard rushing games: 2000 (1).

			RUSHING				RECEIVING				TOTALS			
Year Team	G	GS	Att.	Yds.	Avg.	TD	No.	Yds.	Avg.	TD	TD	2pt.	Pts.	Fum.
1995—Kansas City NFL	14	1	8	18	2.3	0	0	0	0.0	0	0	0	0	0
1996—Kansas City NFL	13	0	4	10	2.5	0	2	18	9.0	1	1	0	6	0
1997—Kansas City NFL	14	0	2	11	5.5	0	3	6	2.0	3	3	0	18	0
1998—Kansas City NFL	14	1	20	45	2.3	2	2	13	6.5	0	2	0	12	0
1999—Kansas City NFL	16	15	84	387	4.6	1	24	141	5.9	0	1	0	6	1
2000—Kansas City NFL	16	16	147	697	4.7	3	58	468	8.1	3	6	0	36	3
Pro totals (6 years)	87	33	265	1168	4.4	6	89	646	7.3	7	13	0	78	4

RICHEY, WADE   K   CHARGERS

PERSONAL: Born May 19, 1976, in Lafayette, La. ... 6-3/205. ... Full name: Wade Edward Richey.
HIGH SCHOOL: Carencro (Lafayette, La.).
COLLEGE: Louisiana State.
TRANSACTIONS/CAREER NOTES: Signed as non-drafted free agent by Seattle Seahawks (April 21, 1998). ... Claimed on waivers by San Francisco 49ers (August 26, 1998). ... Granted free agency (March 2, 2001). ... Tendered offer sheet by San Diego Chargers (April 13, 2001). ... 49ers declined to match offer (April 18, 2001).
PRO STATISTICS: 1999—Punted four times for 146 yards.

		KICKING						
Year Team	G	XPM	XPA	FGM	FGA	Lg.	50+	Pts.
1998—San Francisco NFL	16	49	51	18	27	46	0-0	103
1999—San Francisco NFL	16	30	31	21	23	52	1-1	93
2000—San Francisco NFL	16	43	45	15	22	47	0-1	88
Pro totals (3 years)	48	122	127	54	72	52	1-2	284

RICHIE, DAVID   DT

PERSONAL: Born September 26, 1973, in Orange, Calif. ... 6-4/280.
HIGH SCHOOL: Kelso (Wash.).
COLLEGE: Washington.
TRANSACTIONS/CAREER NOTES: Signed as non-drafted free agent by Denver Broncos (April 28, 1997). ... Traded by Broncos with C Steve Gordon to San Francisco 49ers for past considerations (August 25, 1998). ... Released by 49ers (November 7, 1998). ... Re-signed by 49ers to practice squad (November 17, 1998). ... Activated (December 2, 1998). ... Released by 49ers (September 21, 1999). ... Re-signed by 49ers (December 8, 1999). ... Granted free agency (February 11, 2000). ... Signed by Jacksonville Jaguars (July 22, 2000). ... Released by Jaguars (August 27, 2000). ... Re-signed by Jaguars (August 30, 2000). ... Released by Jaguars (September 27, 2000). ... Signed by Green Bay Packers (December 6, 2000). ... Released by Packers (December 12, 2000).
PLAYING EXPERIENCE: Denver NFL, 1997; San Francisco NFL, 1998 and 1999; Jacksonville NFL, 2000. ... Games/Games started: 1997 (2/0), 1998 (8/0), 1999 (1/0), 2000 (1/0). Total: 12/0.
CHAMPIONSHIP GAME EXPERIENCE: Member of Broncos for AFC championship game (1997 season); inactive. ... Member of Super Bowl championship team (1997 season); inactive.
PRO STATISTICS: 1997—Credited with 1/2 sack. 1998—Returned one kickoff for 11 yards.

RICKS, MIKHAEL   WR   CHIEFS

PERSONAL: Born November 14, 1974, in Galveston, Texas. ... 6-5/237. ... Full name: Mikhael Roy Ricks. ... Name pronounced Michael.
HIGH SCHOOL: Anahuac (Texas).
COLLEGE: Stephen F. Austin State.
TRANSACTIONS/CAREER NOTES: Selected by San Diego Chargers in second round (59th pick overall) of 1998 NFL draft. ... Signed by Chargers (July 23, 1998). ... Released by Chargers (October 3, 2000). ... Signed by Kansas City Chiefs (October 11, 2000).
PRO STATISTICS: 1999—Rushed twice for 11 yards and attempted one pass without a completion.
SINGLE GAME HIGHS (regular season): Receptions—6 (October 24, 1999,vs. Green Bay); yards—86 (September 19, 1999, vs. Cincinnati); and touchdown receptions—1 (December 20, 1998, vs. Oakland).

			RECEIVING				TOTALS			
Year Team	G	GS	No.	Yds.	Avg.	TD	TD	2pt.	Pts.	Fum.
1998—San Diego NFL	16	9	30	450	15.0	2	2	0	12	1
1999—San Diego NFL	16	15	40	429	10.7	0	0	†1	2	0
2000—San Diego NFL	3	1	3	35	11.7	0	0	0	0	0
—Kansas City NFL	1	0	0	0	0.0	0	0	0	0	0
Pro totals (3 years)	36	25	73	914	12.5	2	2	1	14	1

RIEMERSMA, JAY   TE   BILLS

PERSONAL: Born May 17, 1973, in Evansville, Ind. ... 6-5/254. ... Full name: Allen Jay Riemersma. ... Name pronounced REEM-urz-muh.
HIGH SCHOOL: Zeeland (Mich.).
COLLEGE: Michigan.
TRANSACTIONS/CAREER NOTES: Selected by Buffalo Bills in seventh round (244th pick overall) of 1996 NFL draft. ... Signed by Bills (July 9, 1996). ... Released by Bills (August 25, 1996). ... Re-signed by Bills to practice squad (August 26, 1996). ... Activated (October 15, 1996); did not play. ... Granted free agency (February 12, 1999). ... Re-signed by Bills (April 26, 1999). ... Granted unconditional free agency (February 11, 2000). ... Re-signed by Bills (February 15, 2000).
PRO STATISTICS: 1998—Returned one kickoff for nine yards and recovered one fumble.
SINGLE GAME HIGHS (regular season): Receptions—6 (November 5, 2000, vs. New England); yards—86 (November 7, 1999, vs. Washington); and touchdown receptions—2 (September 10, 2000, vs. Green Bay).

				RECEIVING				TOTALS		
Year Team	G	GS	No.	Yds.	Avg.	TD	TD	2pt.	Pts.	Fum.
1996—Buffalo NFL							Did not play.			
1997—Buffalo NFL	16	8	26	208	8.0	2	2	1	14	1
1998—Buffalo NFL	16	3	25	288	11.5	6	6	0	36	0
1999—Buffalo NFL	14	11	37	496	13.4	4	4	0	24	0
2000—Buffalo NFL	12	12	31	372	12.0	5	5	0	30	1
Pro totals (4 years)	58	34	119	1364	11.5	17	17	1	104	2

RILEY, VICTOR   OT   CHIEFS

PERSONAL: Born November 4, 1974, in Swansea, S.C. ... 6-5/328. ... Full name: Victor Allan Riley.
HIGH SCHOOL: Swansea (S.C.).
COLLEGE: Auburn.
TRANSACTIONS/CAREER NOTES: Selected by Kansas City Chiefs in first round (27th pick overall) of 1998 NFL draft. ... Signed by Chiefs (July 2, 1998).
PLAYING EXPERIENCE: Kansas City NFL, 1998-2000. ... Games/Games started: 1998 (16/15), 1999 (16/16), 2000 (16/16). Total: 48/47.
PRO STATISTICS: 1998—Recovered one fumble.

RISON, ANDRE   WR

PERSONAL: Born March 18, 1967, in Flint, Mich. ... 6-1/199. ... Full name: Andre Previn Rison. ... Name pronounced RYE-zun.
HIGH SCHOOL: Northwestern (Flint, Mich.).
COLLEGE: Michigan State.
TRANSACTIONS/CAREER NOTES: Selected by Indianapolis Colts in first round (22nd pick overall) of 1989 NFL draft. ... Signed by Colts (May 2, 1989). ... Traded by Colts with OT Chris Hinton, fifth-round pick (OT Reggie Redding) in 1990 draft and first-round pick (WR Mike Pritchard) in 1991 draft to Atlanta Falcons for first (QB Jeff George) and fourth-round (WR Stacey Simmons) picks in 1990 draft (April 20, 1990). ... Granted roster exemption for one game (September 1992). ... Designated by Falcons as transition player (February 25, 1993). ... On reserve/did not report list (July 23-August 20, 1993). ... Granted roster exemption (August 20-26, 1993). ... On suspended list (November 21-22, 1994). ... Free agency status changed by Falcons from transitional to unconditional (February 17, 1995). ... Signed by Cleveland Browns (March 24, 1995). ... Browns franchise moved to Baltimore and renamed Ravens for 1996 season (March 11, 1996). ... Released by Ravens (July 9, 1996). ... Signed by Jacksonville Jaguars (July 17, 1996). ... Released by Jaguars (November 18, 1996). ... Claimed on waivers by Green Bay Packers (November 19, 1996). ... Released by Packers (March 25, 1997). ... Signed by Kansas City Chiefs (June 18, 1997). ... Released by Chiefs (August 14, 2000). ... Signed by Oakland Raiders (August 21, 2000). ... Granted unconditional free agency (March 2, 2001).
CHAMPIONSHIP GAME EXPERIENCE: Played in NFC championship game (1996 season). ... Member of Super Bowl championship team (1996 season). ... Played in AFC championship game (2000 season).
HONORS: Named wide receiver on THE SPORTING NEWS NFL All-Pro team (1990). ... Played in Pro Bowl (1990-1993 and 1997 seasons). ... Named Outstanding Player of Pro Bowl (1993 season).
PRO STATISTICS: 1989—Rushed three times for 18 yards and returned two punts for 20 yards. 1990—Returned two punts for 10 yards. 1991—Rushed once for minus nine yards. 1995—Rushed twice for no yards and recovered one fumble. 1997—Rushed once for two yards. 1998—Rushed twice for 12 yards and recovered one fumble.
SINGLE GAME HIGHS (regular season): Receptions—14 (September 4, 1994, vs. Detroit); yards—193 (September 4, 1994, vs. Detroit); and touchdown receptions—3 (September 19, 1993, vs. San Francisco).
STATISTICAL PLATEAUS: 100-yard receiving games: 1989 (3), 1990 (5), 1991 (1), 1992 (2), 1993 (4), 1994 (3), 1995 (2), 1996 (1), 1997 (2), 2000 (1). Total: 24.
MISCELLANEOUS: Holds Atlanta Falcons all-time records for most touchdowns (56) and most touchdown receptions (56).

				RECEIVING				KICKOFF RETURNS				TOTALS			
Year Team	G	GS	No.	Yds.	Avg.	TD	No.	Yds.	Avg.	TD	TD	2pt.	Pts.	Fum.
1989—Indianapolis NFL	16	13	52	820	15.8	4	8	150	18.8	0	4	0	24	1
1990—Atlanta NFL	16	15	82	1208	14.7	10	0	0	0.0	0	10	0	60	2
1991—Atlanta NFL	16	15	81	976	12.0	12	0	0	0.0	0	12	0	72	1
1992—Atlanta NFL	15	13	93	1119	12.0	11	0	0	0.0	0	11	0	66	2
1993—Atlanta NFL	16	16	86	1242	14.4	†15	0	0	0.0	0	15	0	90	2
1994—Atlanta NFL	15	14	81	1088	13.4	8	0	0	0.0	0	8	1	50	1
1995—Cleveland NFL	16	14	47	701	14.9	3	0	0	0.0	0	3	0	18	1
1996—Jacksonville NFL	10	9	34	458	13.5	2	0	0	0.0	0	2	0	12	0
—Green Bay NFL	5	4	13	135	10.4	1	0	0	0.0	0	1	0	6	1
1997—Kansas City NFL	16	16	72	1092	15.2	7	0	0	0.0	0	7	0	42	0
1998—Kansas City NFL	14	13	40	542	13.6	5	0	0	0.0	0	5	0	30	1
1999—Kansas City NFL	15	14	21	218	10.4	0	0	0	0.0	0	0	0	0	0
2000—Oakland NFL	16	0	41	606	14.8	6	0	0	0.0	0	6	0	36	0
Pro totals (12 years)	186	156	743	10205	13.7	84	8	150	18.8	0	84	1	506	12

RITCHIE, JON   RB   RAIDERS

PERSONAL: Born September 4, 1974, in Mechanicsburgh, Pa. ... 6-1/250.
HIGH SCHOOL: Cumberland Valley (Mechanicsburg, Pa.).
COLLEGE: Michigan, then Stanford.
TRANSACTIONS/CAREER NOTES: Selected by Oakland Raiders in third round (63rd pick overall) of 1998 NFL draft. ... Signed by Raiders (July 18, 1998).
CHAMPIONSHIP GAME EXPERIENCE: Played in AFC championship game (2000 season).
SINGLE GAME HIGHS (regular season): Attempts—2 (September 12, 1999, vs. Green Bay); yards—14 (November 15, 1998, vs. Seattle); and rushing touchdowns—0.

			RUSHING				RECEIVING				TOTALS		
Year Team	G	GS	Att.	Yds.	Avg.	TD	No.	Yds.	Avg.	TD	TD	2pt.	Pts.	Fum.
1998—Oakland NFL	15	10	9	23	2.6	0	29	225	7.8	0	0	0	0	2
1999—Oakland NFL	16	14	5	12	2.4	0	45	408	9.1	1	1	0	6	0
2000—Oakland NFL	13	12	0	0	0.0	0	26	173	6.7	0	0	0	0	0
Pro totals (3 years)	44	36	14	35	2.5	0	100	806	8.1	1	1	0	6	2

RIVERA, MARCO   G   PACKERS

PERSONAL: Born April 26, 1972, in Brooklyn, N.Y. ... 6-4/310. ... Full name: Marco Anthony Rivera.
HIGH SCHOOL: Elmont (N.Y.) Memorial.
COLLEGE: Penn State (degree in administration of justice).
TRANSACTIONS/CAREER NOTES: Selected by Green Bay Packers in sixth round (208th pick overall) of 1996 NFL draft. ... Signed by Packers (July 15, 1996). ... Inactive for all 16 games (1996). ... Assigned by Packers to Scottish Claymores in 1997 World League enhancement allocation program (February 19, 1997). ... Granted free agency (February 12, 1999). ... Re-signed by Packers (March 24, 1999).
PLAYING EXPERIENCE: Scottish W.L., 1997, Green Bay NFL, 1997-2000. ... Games/Games started: W.L. 1997 (10/10), NFL 1997 (14/0), 1998 (15/15), 1999 (16/16), 2000 (16/16). Total W.L.:10/10. Total NFL: 61/47. Total Pro: 71/57.
CHAMPIONSHIP GAME EXPERIENCE: Member of Packers for NFC championship game (1996 season); inactive. ... Member of Super Bowl championship team (1996 season); inactive. ... Played in NFC championship game (1997 season). ... Played in Super Bowl XXXII (1997 season).
PRO STATISTICS: 1999—Recovered one fumble.

RIVERS, RON   RB   STEELERS

PERSONAL: Born November 13, 1971, in Elizabeth City, N.J. ... 5-8/205. ... Full name: Ronald Leroy Rivers.
HIGH SCHOOL: San Gorgonio (San Bernardino, Calif.).
COLLEGE: Fresno State.
TRANSACTIONS/CAREER NOTES: Signed as non-drafted free agent by San Diego Chargers (April 28, 1994). ... Released by Chargers (August 29, 1994). ... Signed by Detroit Lions to practice squad (September 21, 1994). ... Activated (December 22, 1994); did not play. ... Granted free agency (February 13, 1998). ... Re-signed by Lions (April 29, 1998). ... Released by Lions (February 4, 2000). ... Signed by Atlanta Falcons (June 30, 2000). ... Granted unconditional free agency (March 2, 2001). ... Signed by Pittsburgh Steelers (May 24, 2001).
POST SEASON RECORDS: Shares NFL postseason career and single-game records for most two-point conversions—1 (December 30, 1995, vs. Philadelphia).
PRO STATISTICS: 1995—Caught one pass for five yards and recovered one fumble. 1997—Recovered one fumble.
SINGLE GAME HIGHS (regular season): Attempts—17 (September 19, 1999, vs. Green Bay); yards—96 (September 12, 1999, vs. Seattle); and rushing touchdowns—1 (November 22, 1998, vs. Tampa Bay).

			RUSHING				RECEIVING				KICKOFF RETURNS				TOTALS		
Year Team	G	GS	Att.	Yds.	Avg.	TD	No.	Yds.	Avg.	TD	No.	Yds.	Avg.	TD	TD	2pt.	Pts.	Fum.
1994—Detroit NFL								Did not play.										
1995—Detroit NFL	16	0	18	73	4.1	1	1	5	5.0	0	19	420	22.1	0	1	0	6	2
1996—Detroit NFL	15	0	19	86	4.5	0	2	28	14.0	0	1	8	8.0	0	0	0	0	0
1997—Detroit NFL	16	0	29	166	5.7	0	0	0	0.0	0	2	34	17.0	0	1	0	6	0
1998—Detroit NFL	15	0	19	102	5.4	1	3	58	19.3	0	2	15	7.5	0	1	0	6	0
1999—Detroit NFL	7	6	82	295	3.6	0	22	173	7.9	1	0	0	0.0	0	1	0	6	0
2000—Atlanta NFL	6	0	8	27	3.4	0	0	0	0.0	0	0	0	0.0	0	0	0	0	0
Pro totals (6 years)	75	6	175	749	4.3	3	28	264	9.4	1	24	477	19.9	0	4	0	24	2

ROAF, WILLIE   OT   SAINTS

PERSONAL: Born April 18, 1970, in Pine Bluff, Ark. ... 6-5/312. ... Full name: William Layton Roaf.
HIGH SCHOOL: Pine Bluff (Ark.).
COLLEGE: Louisiana Tech.
TRANSACTIONS/CAREER NOTES: Selected by New Orleans Saints in first round (eighth pick overall) of 1993 NFL draft. ... Signed by Saints (July 15, 1993). ... Designated by Saints as transition player (February 15, 1994).
PLAYING EXPERIENCE: New Orleans NFL, 1993-2000. ... Games/Games started: 1993 (16/16), 1994 (16/16), 1995 (16/16), 1996 (13/13), 1997 (16/16), 1998 (15/15), 1999 (16/16), 2000 (16/16). Total: 124/124.
HONORS: Named offensive tackle on THE SPORTING NEWS college All-America second team (1992). ... Named offensive tackle on THE SPORTING NEWS NFL All-Pro team (1994-1996). ... Played in Pro Bowl (1994-1997, 1999 and 2000 seasons). ... Named to play in Pro Bowl (1998 season); replaced by Bob Whitfield due to injury.
PRO STATISTICS: 1994—Recovered one fumble. 1996—Recovered one fumble. 1999—Recovered one fumble.

ROAN, MICHAEL   TE

PERSONAL: Born August 29, 1972, in Iowa City, Iowa. ... 6-3/250. ... Full name: Michael Phillip Roan.
HIGH SCHOOL: Iowa City (Iowa) High.
COLLEGE: Wisconsin.
TRANSACTIONS/CAREER NOTES: Selected by Houston Oilers in fourth round (101st pick overall) of 1995 NFL draft. ... Signed by Oilers (July 10, 1995). ... Oilers franchise moved to Tennessee for 1997 season. ... Oilers franchise renamed Tennessee Titans for 1999 season (December 26, 1998). ... On injured reserve with neck injury (January 14, 2000-remainder of 1999 playoffs). ... On injured reserve with leg injury (September 8, 2000-remainder of season). ... Released by Titans (March 1, 2001).
PRO STATISTICS: 1995—Recovered one fumble. 1996—Returned one kickoff for 13 yards. 1997—Returned two kickoffs for 20 yards. 1998—Returned one kickoff for four yards and recovered one fumble in end zone for a touchdown.
SINGLE GAME HIGHS (regular season): Receptions—4 (December 6, 1998, vs. Baltimore); yards—51 (November 2, 1997, vs. Jacksonville); and touchdown receptions—1 (January 2, 2000, vs. Pittsburgh).

| | | | RECEIVING | | | | TOTALS | | |
Year Team	G	GS	No.	Yds.	Avg.	TD	TD	2pt.	Pts.	Fum.
1995—Houston NFL	5	2	8	46	5.8	0	0	0	0	1
1996—Houston NFL	15	1	0	0	0.0	0	0	0	0	0
1997—Tennessee NFL	14	13	12	159	13.3	0	0	0	0	0
1998—Tennessee NFL	16	1	13	93	7.2	0	1	0	6	1
1999—Tennessee NFL	11	1	9	93	10.3	3	3	0	18	0
2000—Tennessee NFL	1	1	3	12	4.0	0	0	0	0	0
Pro totals (6 years)	62	19	45	403	9.0	3	4	0	24	2

ROBBINS, AUSTIN   DT

PERSONAL: Born March 1, 1971, in Washington, D.C. ... 6-6/290. ... Full name: Austin Dion Robbins.
HIGH SCHOOL: Howard D. Woodson (Washington, D.C.).
COLLEGE: North Carolina. •
TRANSACTIONS/CAREER NOTES: Selected by Los Angeles Raiders in fourth round (120th pick overall) of 1994 NFL draft. ... Signed by Raiders (July 14, 1994). ... Raiders franchise moved to Oakland (July 21, 1995). ... Traded by Raiders to New Orleans Saints for undisclosed pick in 1997 draft (August 25, 1996). ... Granted free agency (February 14, 1997). ... Re-signed by Saints (June 7, 1997). ... Granted unconditional free agency (February 13, 1998). ... Re-signed by Saints (March 6, 1998). ... Granted unconditional free agency (February 11, 2000). ... Signed by Raiders (April 18, 2000). ... Released by Raiders (November 11, 2000). ... Signed by Green Bay Packers (December 12, 2000). ... Granted unconditional free agency (March 2, 2001).
PRO STATISTICS: 1995—Recovered two fumbles for six yards and one touchdown. 1998—Recovered one fumble in end zone for a touchdown. 1999—Recovered one fumble.

Year Team	G	GS	SACKS
1994—Los Angeles Raiders NFL	2	0	0.0
1995—Oakland NFL	16	0	2.0
1996—New Orleans NFL	15	7	1.0
1997—New Orleans NFL	12	0	0.0
1998—New Orleans NFL	16	1	1.0
1999—New Orleans NFL	14	3	2.0
2000—Oakland NFL	3	0	0.0
—Green Bay NFL	2	0	0.0
Pro totals (7 years)	80	11	6.0

ROBBINS, BARRET   C   RAIDERS

PERSONAL: Born August 26, 1973, in Houston. ... 6-3/320.
HIGH SCHOOL: Sharpstown (Houston).
COLLEGE: Texas Christian.
TRANSACTIONS/CAREER NOTES: Selected by Los Angeles Raiders in second round (49th pick overall) of 1995 NFL draft. ... Signed by Raiders (June 20, 1995). ... Raiders franchise moved to Oakland (July 21, 1995).
PLAYING EXPERIENCE: Oakland NFL, 1995-2000. ... Games/Games started: 1995 (16/0), 1996 (14/14), 1997 (16/16), 1998 (16/16), 1999 (16/16), 2000 (16/16). Total: 94/78.
CHAMPIONSHIP GAME EXPERIENCE: Played in AFC championship game (2000 season).
PRO STATISTICS: 1996—Recovered one fumble.

ROBBINS, FRED   DT   VIKINGS

PERSONAL: Born March 25, 1977, in Pensacola, Fla. ... 6-4/312. ... Full name: Fredrick Robbins.
HIGH SCHOOL: Gonzalez (Pensacola, Fla.).
COLLEGE: Wake Forest.
TRANSACTIONS/CAREER NOTES: Selected by Minnesota Vikings in second round (55th pick overall) of 2000 NFL draft. ... Signed by Vikings (July 21, 2000).
CHAMPIONSHIP GAME EXPERIENCE: Member of Vikings for NFC championship game (2000 season); inactive.

Year Team	G	GS	SACKS
2000—Minnesota NFL	8	0	1.0

ROBERTS, RAY   OT   LIONS

PERSONAL: Born June 3, 1969, in Asheville, N.C. ... 6-6/320. ... Full name: Richard Ray Roberts Jr.
HIGH SCHOOL: Asheville (N.C.).
COLLEGE: Virginia (degree in communication studies, 1991).
TRANSACTIONS/CAREER NOTES: Selected by Seattle Seahawks in first round (10th pick overall) of 1992 NFL draft. ... Signed by Seahawks (August 1, 1992). ... Designated by Seahawks as transition player (February 15, 1994). ... On injured reserve with ankle injury (December 11, 1994-remainder of season). ... Free agency status changed by Seahawks from transitional to unconditional (February 16, 1996). ... Signed by Detroit Lions (March 11, 1996). ... Granted unconditional free agency (February 13, 1998). ... Re-signed by Lions (February 19, 1998). ... On injured reserve with knee injury (December 22, 1999-remainder of season). ... Released by Lions (March 14, 2001). ... Re-signed by Lions (May 24, 2001).
PLAYING EXPERIENCE: Seattle NFL, 1992-1995; Detroit NFL, 1996-2000. ... Games/Games started: 1992 (16/16), 1993 (16/16), 1994 (14/14), 1995 (11/0), 1996 (16/16), 1997 (14/14), 1998 (16/16), 1999 (14/14), 2000 (10/10). Total: 127/116.
HONORS: Named offensive tackle on THE SPORTING NEWS college All-America second team (1991).
PRO STATISTICS: 1993—Caught one pass for four yards. 1996—Ran five yards with lateral from reception and recovered two fumbles. 1997—Recovered two fumbles for four yards. 1999—Recovered one fumble.

ROBERTSON, MARCUS   S   SEAHAWKS

PERSONAL: Born October 2, 1969, in Pasadena, Calif. ... 5-11/205. ... Full name: Marcus Aaron Robertson.
HIGH SCHOOL: John Muir (Pasadena, Calif.).
COLLEGE: Iowa State.
TRANSACTIONS/CAREER NOTES: Selected by Houston Oilers in fourth round (102nd pick overall) of 1991 NFL draft. ... Signed by Oilers (July 16, 1991). ... On injured reserve with knee injury (December 30, 1993-remainder of season). ... Granted free agency (February 17, 1994). ... Re-signed by Oilers (July 11, 1994). ... On injured reserve with knee injury (November 30, 1995-remainder of season). ... Oilers franchise moved to Tennessee for 1997 season. ... Oilers franchise renamed Tennessee Titans for 1999 season (December 26, 1998). ... Granted unconditional free agency (February 11, 2000). ... Re-signed by Titans (February 22, 2000). ... Released by Titans (March 1, 2001). ... Signed by Seattle Seahawks (April 11, 2001).
CHAMPIONSHIP GAME EXPERIENCE: Played in AFC championship game (1999 season). ... Member of Titans for Super Bowl XXXIV (1999 season); inactive.
HONORS: Named free safety on THE SPORTING NEWS NFL All-Pro team (1993).
PRO STATISTICS: 1991—Credited with one sack, returned one punt for no yards and fumbled once. 1993—Recovered three fumbles for 107 yards and one touchdown. 1994—Returned one punt for no yards, fumbled once and recovered one fumble. 1996—Recovered one fumble for five yards. 1997—Returned one punt for no yards and recovered three fumbles for 67 yards and two touchdowns. 1999—Credited with $1/2$ sack. 2000—Recovered one fumble.

			INTERCEPTIONS			
Year Team	G	GS	No.	Yds.	Avg.	TD
1991—Houston NFL	16	0	0	0	0.0	0
1992—Houston NFL	16	14	1	27	27.0	0
1993—Houston NFL	13	13	7	137	19.6	0
1994—Houston NFL	16	16	3	90	30.0	0
1995—Houston NFL	2	2	0	0	0.0	0
1996—Houston NFL	16	16	4	44	11.0	0
1997—Tennessee NFL	14	14	5	127	25.4	0
1998—Tennessee NFL	12	12	1	0	0.0	0
1999—Tennessee NFL	15	15	1	3	3.0	0
2000—Tennessee NFL	15	15	0	0	0.0	0
Pro totals (10 years)	135	117	22	428	19.5	0

ROBINSON, BRYAN   DL   BEARS

PERSONAL: Born June 22, 1974, in Toledo, Ohio. ... 6-4/300. ... Full name: Bryan Keith Robinson.
HIGH SCHOOL: Woodward (Cincinnati).
JUNIOR COLLEGE: College of the Desert (Palm Desert, Calif.).
COLLEGE: Fresno State.
TRANSACTIONS/CAREER NOTES: Signed as non-drafted free agent by St. Louis Rams (April 29, 1997). ... Claimed on waivers by Chicago Bears (August 31, 1998). ... Granted free agency (February 11, 2000). ... Re-signed by Bears (April 19, 2000). ... Designated by Bears as transition player (February 22, 2001).

Year Team	G	GS	SACKS
1997—St. Louis NFL	11	0	1.0
1998—Chicago NFL	10	5	0.5
1999—Chicago NFL	16	16	5.0
2000—Chicago NFL	16	16	4.5
Pro totals (4 years)	53	37	11.0

ROBINSON, DAMIEN   S   JETS

PERSONAL: Born December 22, 1973, in Dallas. ... 6-2/214. ... Full name: Damien Dion Robinson.
HIGH SCHOOL: Hillcrest (Dallas).
COLLEGE: Iowa.
TRANSACTIONS/CAREER NOTES: Selected by Philadelphia Eagles in fourth round (119th pick overall) of 1997 NFL draft. ... Signed by Eagles (June 4, 1997). ... Released by Eagles (August 25, 1997). ... Re-signed by Eagles to practice squad (August 27, 1997). ... Signed by Tampa Bay Buccaneers off Eagles practice squad (September 17, 1997). ... Inactive for 13 games (1997). ... On injured reserve with arm injury (October 27, 1998-remainder of season). ... Granted free agency (February 11, 2000). ... Re-signed by Buccaneers (May 15, 2000). ... Granted unconditional free agency (March 2, 2001). ... Signed by New York Jets (April 25, 2001).
PLAYING EXPERIENCE: Tampa Bay NFL, 1998-2000. ... Games/Games started: 1998 (7/0), 1999 (16/16), 2000 (16/16). Total: 39/32.
CHAMPIONSHIP GAME EXPERIENCE: Played in NFC championship game (1999 season).
PRO STATISTICS: 1999—Caught one pass for 17 yards, intercepted two passes for 36 yards, credited with $1/2$ sack and recovered two fumbles. 2000—Caught one pass for 36 yards, intercepted six passes for one yard and recovered three fumbles for five yards.

ROBINSON, EDDIE   LB   TITANS

PERSONAL: Born April 13, 1970, in New Orleans. ... 6-1/243. ... Full name: Eddie Joseph Robinson Jr.
HIGH SCHOOL: Brother Martin (New Orleans).
COLLEGE: Alabama State (degree in chemistry, 1993).
TRANSACTIONS/CAREER NOTES: Selected by Houston Oilers in second round (50th pick overall) of 1992 NFL draft. ... Signed by Oilers (July 16, 1992). ... Granted free agency (February 17, 1995). ... Re-signed by Oilers (July 1995). ... Granted unconditional free agency (February 16, 1996). ... Signed by Jacksonville Jaguars (March 1, 1996). ... Released by Jaguars (August 30, 1998). ... Signed by Tennessee Oilers (September 1, 1998). ... Oilers franchise renamed Tennessee Titans for 1999 season (December 26, 1998). ... Granted unconditional free agency (February 12, 1999). ... Re-signed by Titans (March 1, 1999).
CHAMPIONSHIP GAME EXPERIENCE: Played in AFC championship game (1996 and 1999 seasons). ... Played in Super Bowl XXXIV (1999 season).
PRO STATISTICS: 1995—Intercepted one pass for 49 yards and a touchdown and recovered one fumble. 1996—Recovered one fumble. 1997—Intercepted one pass for no yards and recovered two fumbles. 1998—Intercepted one pass for 11 yards. 1999—Recovered three fumbles for one yard. 2000—Recovered three fumbles.

Year Team	G	GS	SACKS
1992—Houston NFL	16	11	1.0
1993—Houston NFL	16	15	1.0
1994—Houston NFL	15	15	0.0
1995—Houston NFL	16	16	3.5
1996—Jacksonville NFL	16	15	1.0
1997—Jacksonville NFL	16	14	2.0
1998—Tennessee NFL	16	16	3.5
1999—Tennessee NFL	16	16	6.0
2000—Tennessee NFL	16	16	4.0
Pro totals (9 years)	143	134	22.0

ROBINSON, EUGENE   S

PERSONAL: Born May 28, 1963, in Hartford, Conn. ... 6-1/200. ... Full name: Eugene Keefe Robinson.
HIGH SCHOOL: Weaver (Hartford, Conn.).
COLLEGE: Colgate.
TRANSACTIONS/CAREER NOTES: Selected by New Jersey Generals in 1985 USFL territorial draft. ... Signed as non-drafted free agent by Seattle Seahawks (May 15, 1985). ... On injured reserve with Achilles' tendon injury (December 11, 1994-remainder of season). ... Traded by Seahawks to Green Bay Packers for LB Matt LaBounty (June 27, 1996). ... Granted unconditional free agency (February 13, 1998). ... Signed by Atlanta Falcons (March 6, 1998). ... Granted unconditional free agency (February 11, 2000). ... Signed by Carolina Panthers (August 13, 2000). ... Granted unconditional free agency (March 2, 2001).
CHAMPIONSHIP GAME EXPERIENCE: Played in NFC championship game (1996-1998 seasons). ... Member of Super Bowl championship team (1996 season). ... Played in Super Bowl XXXII (1997 season) and Super Bowl XXXIII (1998 season).
HONORS: Played in Pro Bowl (1992, 1993 and 1998 seasons).
PRO STATISTICS: 1985—Returned one kickoff for 10 yards. 1986—Recovered three fumbles for six yards. 1987—Returned blocked punt eight yards for a touchdown and recovered one fumble. 1989—Fumbled once and recovered one fumble. 1990—Recovered four fumbles for 16 yards and a touchdown. 1991—Recovered one fumble. 1992—Recovered one fumble. 1993—Recovered two fumbles for seven yards. 1994—Recovered one fumble. 1995—Returned one punt for one yard and recovered one fumble. 1997—Fumbled once and recovered two fumbles. 1998—Recovered two fumbles for 16 yards. 2000—Recovered three fumbles for 26 yards.
MISCELLANEOUS: Active NFL leader for career interceptions (57).

			INTERCEPTIONS				SACKS
Year Team	G	GS	No.	Yds.	Avg.	TD	No.
1985—Seattle NFL	16	0	2	47	23.5	0	0.0
1986—Seattle NFL	16	16	3	39	13.0	0	0.0
1987—Seattle NFL	12	12	3	75	25.0	0	0.0
1988—Seattle NFL	16	16	1	0	0.0	0	1.0
1989—Seattle NFL	16	14	5	24	4.8	0	0.0
1990—Seattle NFL	16	16	3	89	29.7	0	0.0
1991—Seattle NFL	16	16	5	56	11.2	0	1.0
1992—Seattle NFL	16	16	7	126	18.0	0	0.0
1993—Seattle NFL	16	16	†9	80	8.9	0	2.0
1994—Seattle NFL	14	14	3	18	6.0	0	1.0
1995—Seattle NFL	16	16	1	32	32.0	0	0.0
1996—Green Bay NFL	16	16	6	107	17.8	0	0.0
1997—Green Bay NFL	16	16	1	26	26.0	0	2.5
1998—Atlanta NFL	16	16	4	36	9.0	1	0.0
1999—Atlanta NFL	16	16	3	7	2.3	0	0.0
2000—Carolina NFL	16	16	1	0	0.0	0	0.0
Pro totals (16 years)	250	232	57	762	13.4	1	7.5

ROBINSON, JEFF   TE   RAMS

PERSONAL: Born February 20, 1970, in Kennewick, Wash. ... 6-4/275. ... Full name: Jeffrey William Robinson.
HIGH SCHOOL: Joel E. Ferris (Spokane, Wash.).
COLLEGE: Idaho (degree in finance, 1992).
TRANSACTIONS/CAREER NOTES: Selected by Denver Broncos in fourth round (98th pick overall) of 1993 NFL draft. ... Signed by Broncos (July 13, 1993). ... Granted free agency (February 16, 1996). ... Re-signed by Broncos (March 28, 1996). ... Granted unconditional free agency (February 14, 1997). ... Signed by St. Louis Rams (March 14, 1997).
CHAMPIONSHIP GAME EXPERIENCE: Played in NFC championship game (1999 season). ... Member of Super Bowl championship team (1999 season).

PRO STATISTICS: 1993—Recovered one fumble for minus 10 yards. 1995—Returned one kickoff for 14 yards and recovered one fumble. 1996—Recovered one fumble. 1998—Caught one pass for four yards and a touchdown. 1999—Caught six passes for 76 yards and two touchdowns. 2000—Caught five passes for 52 yards and recovered one fumble.

SINGLE GAME HIGHS (regular season): Receptions—2 (December 10, 2000, vs. Minnesota); yards—34 (December 10, 2000, vs. Minnesota); and touchdown receptions—1 (November 7, 1999, vs. Detroit).

MISCELLANEOUS: Played defensive line (1993-98).

Year Team	G	GS	SACKS
1993—Denver NFL	16	0	3.5
1994—Denver NFL	16	0	1.0
1995—Denver NFL	16	0	1.0
1996—Denver NFL	16	0	0.5
1997—St. Louis NFL	16	0	0.5
1998—St. Louis NFL	16	0	0.0
1999—St. Louis NFL	16	9	0.0
2000—St. Louis NFL	16	2	0.0
Pro totals (8 years)	128	11	6.5

ROBINSON, MARCUS   WR   BEARS

PERSONAL: Born February 27, 1975, in Fort Valley, Ga. ... 6-3/215.
HIGH SCHOOL: Peach County (Fort Valley, Ga.).
COLLEGE: South Carolina.
TRANSACTIONS/CAREER NOTES: Selected by Chicago Bears in fourth round (108th pick overall) of 1997 NFL draft. ... Signed by Bears (July 11, 1997). ... Inactive for four games (1997). ... On injured reserve with thumb injury (September 24, 1997-remainder of season). ... Assigned by Bears to Rhein Fire in 1998 NFL Europe enhancement allocation program (February 18, 1998). ... On injured reserve with back injury (December 4, 2000-remainder of season).
PRO STATISTICS: 2000—Rushed once for nine yards.
SINGLE GAME HIGHS (regular season): Receptions—11 (December 19, 1999, vs. Detroit); yards—170 (December 19, 1999, vs. Detroit); and touchdown receptions—3 (December 19, 1999, vs. Detroit).
STATISTICAL PLATEAUS: 100-yard receiving games: 1999 (5), 2000 (1). Total: 6.

Year Team	G	GS	RECEIVING No.	Yds.	Avg.	TD	TOTALS TD	2pt.	Pts.	Fum.
1997—Chicago NFL						Did not play.				
1998—Rhein NFLE	...	...	39	811	20.8	5	5	0	30	0
—Chicago NFL	3	0	4	44	11.0	1	1	0	6	0
1999—Chicago NFL	16	11	84	1400	16.7	9	9	0	54	0
2000—Chicago NFL	11	11	55	738	13.4	5	5	0	30	1
NFL Europe totals (1 year)	...	...	39	811	20.8	5	5	0	30	0
NFL totals (2 years)	30	22	143	2182	15.3	15	15	0	90	1
Pro totals (3 years)	...	...	182	2993	16.4	20	20	0	120	1

ROBINSON-RANDALL, GREG   OT   PATRIOTS

PERSONAL: Born June 23, 1978, in Galveston, Texas. ... 6-5/315.
HIGH SCHOOL: La Marque (Texas).
JUNIOR COLLEGE: Coffeyville (Kan.) Community College.
COLLEGE: Michigan State.
TRANSACTIONS/CAREER NOTES: Selected by New England Patriots in fourth round (127th pick overall) of 2000 NFL draft. ... Signed by Patriots (July 12, 2000).
PLAYING EXPERIENCE: New England NFL, 2000. ... Games/Games started: 2000 (12/3).

RODGERS, DERRICK   LB   DOLPHINS

PERSONAL: Born October 14, 1971, in Memphis, Tenn. ... 6-1/230. ... Full name: Derrick Andre Rodgers.
HIGH SCHOOL: St. Augustine (New Orleans).
JUNIOR COLLEGE: Riverside (Calif.) Community College.
COLLEGE: Arizona State.
TRANSACTIONS/CAREER NOTES: Selected by Miami Dolphins in third round (92nd pick overall) of 1997 NFL draft. ... Signed by Dolphins (July 8, 1997). ... Granted free agency (February 11, 2000). ... Re-signed by Dolphins (April 28, 2000). ... Granted unconditional free agency (March 2, 2001). ... Re-signed by Dolphins (March 3, 2001).
PRO STATISTICS: 1997—Recovered one fumble. 1999—Intercepted one pass for five yards and recovered two fumbles.

Year Team	G	GS	SACKS
1997—Miami NFL	15	14	5.0
1998—Miami NFL	16	16	2.5
1999—Miami NFL	16	15	0.0
2000—Miami NFL	16	14	0.5
Pro totals (4 years)	63	59	8.0

ROGERS, CHARLIE   KR/PR   SEAHAWKS

PERSONAL: Born June 19, 1976, in Cliffwood, N.J. ... 5-9/179. ... Full name: John Edward Rogers.
HIGH SCHOOL: Matawan Regional (Aberdeen, N.J.).
COLLEGE: Georgia Tech.
TRANSACTIONS/CAREER NOTES: Selected by Seattle Seahawks in fifth round (152nd pick overall) of 1999 NFL draft. ... Signed by Seahawks (July 29, 1999).
PRO STATISTICS: 2000—Recovered one fumble.

Year	Team	G	GS	No.	Yds.	Avg.	TD	No.	Yds.	Avg.	TD	TD	2pt.	Pts.	Fum.
				PUNT RETURNS				**KICKOFF RETURNS**				**TOTALS**			
1999—Seattle NFL		12	0	22	318	*14.5	1	18	465	25.8	0	1	0	6	3
2000—Seattle NFL		15	0	26	363	14.0	0	66	§1629	24.7	▲1	1	0	6	5
Pro totals (2 years)		27	0	48	681	14.2	1	84	2094	24.9	1	2	0	12	8

ROGERS, SAM LB CHARGERS

PERSONAL: Born May 30, 1970, in Pontiac, Mich. ... 6-3/245. ... Full name: Sammy Lee Rogers.
HIGH SCHOOL: Saint Mary's Preparatory (Orchard Lake, Mich.).
JUNIOR COLLEGE: West Hills College (Calif.), then West Los Angeles College.
COLLEGE: Colorado.
TRANSACTIONS/CAREER NOTES: Selected by Buffalo Bills in second round (64th pick overall) of 1994 NFL draft. ... Signed by Bills (July 12, 1994). ... Granted free agency (February 14, 1997). ... Re-signed by Bills (June 12, 1997). ... Granted unconditional free agency (February 13, 1998). ... Re-signed by Bills (February 15, 1998). ... Released by Bills (March 1, 2001). ... Signed by San Diego Chargers (May 18, 2001).
PRO STATISTICS: 1995—Recovered one fumble. 1996—Recovered two fumbles. 1999—Intercepted one pass for 24 yards and recovered two fumbles for seven yards. 2000—Intercepted one pass for 10 yards and recovered one fumble.

Year	Team	G	GS	SACKS
1994—Buffalo NFL		14	0	0.0
1995—Buffalo NFL		16	8	2.0
1996—Buffalo NFL		14	14	3.5
1997—Buffalo NFL		15	15	3.5
1998—Buffalo NFL		15	15	4.5
1999—Buffalo NFL		16	16	3.0
2000—Buffalo NFL		11	11	5.0
Pro totals (7 years)		101	79	21.5

ROGERS, TYRONE DE BROWNS

PERSONAL: Born October 11, 1976, in Montgomery, Ala. ... 6-5/236.
HIGH SCHOOL: Robert E. Lee (Montgomery, Ala.).
COLLEGE: Alabama State.
TRANSACTIONS/CAREER NOTES: Signed as non-drafted free agent by Cleveland Browns (April 23, 1999). ... Released by Browns (September 5, 1999). ... Re-signed by Browns to practice squad (September 6, 1999). ... Activated (November 23, 1999).
PLAYING EXPERIENCE: Cleveland NFL, 1999 and 2000. ... Games/Games started: 1999 (3/0), 2000 (16/0). Total: 19/0.
PRO STATISTICS: 2000—Credited with two sacks and recovered three fumbles.

ROLLE, SAMARI CB TITANS

PERSONAL: Born August 10, 1976, in Miami. ... 6-0/175. ... Name pronounced suh-MARI ROLL.
HIGH SCHOOL: Miami Beach.
COLLEGE: Florida State.
TRANSACTIONS/CAREER NOTES: Selected by Tennessee Oilers in second round (46th pick overall) of 1998 NFL draft. ... Signed by Oilers (July 24, 1998). ... Oilers franchise renamed Tennessee Titans for 1999 season (December 26, 1998). ... Granted free agency (March 2, 2001).
CHAMPIONSHIP GAME EXPERIENCE: Played in AFC championship game (1999 season). ... Played in Super Bowl XXXIV (1999 season).
HONORS: Named cornerback on THE SPORTING NEWS NFL All-Pro team (2000). ... Played in Pro Bowl (2000 season).
PRO STATISTICS: 1999—Returned one punt for 23 yards, fumbled once and recovered one fumble for three yards. 2000—Recovered one fumble.

Year	Team	G	GS	No.	Yds.	Avg.	TD	No.
				INTERCEPTIONS				**SACKS**
1998—Tennessee NFL		15	1	0	0	0.0	0	2.0
1999—Tennessee NFL		16	16	4	65	16.3	0	3.0
2000—Tennessee NFL		15	15	▲7	140	20.0	1	1.5
Pro totals (3 years)		46	32	11	205	18.6	1	6.5

ROMAN, MARK CB BENGALS

PERSONAL: Born March 26, 1977, in New Iberia, La. ... 5-11/188. ... Full name: Mark Emery Roman.
HIGH SCHOOL: New Iberia (La.).
COLLEGE: Louisiana State.
TRANSACTIONS/CAREER NOTES: Selected by Cincinnati Bengals in second round (34th pick overall) of 2000 NFL draft. ... Signed by Bengals (August 7, 2000).
PLAYING EXPERIENCE: Cincinnati NFL, 2000. ... Games/Games started: 2000 (8/2).
PRO STATISTICS: 2000—Recovered two fumbles.

ROMANOWSKI, BILL LB BRONCOS

PERSONAL: Born April 2, 1966, in Vernon, Conn. ... 6-4/245. ... Full name: William Thomas Romanowski.
HIGH SCHOOL: Rockville (Vernon, Conn.).
COLLEGE: Boston College (degree in general management, 1988).
TRANSACTIONS/CAREER NOTES: Selected by San Francisco 49ers in third round (80th pick overall) of 1988 NFL draft. ... Signed by 49ers (July 15, 1988). ... Granted free agency (February 1, 1991). ... Re-signed by 49ers (July 17, 1991). ... Granted unconditional free agency (March 1, 1993). ... Re-signed by 49ers (March 23, 1993). ... Traded by 49ers to Philadelphia Eagles for third-(traded to Los Angeles Rams)

and sixth-round (traded to Green Bay) picks in 1994 draft (April 24, 1994). ... Granted unconditional free agency (February 16, 1996). ... Signed by Denver Broncos (February 23, 1996).

CHAMPIONSHIP GAME EXPERIENCE: Played in NFC championship game (1988-1990, 1992 and 1993 seasons). ... Member of Super Bowl championship team (1988, 1989, 1997 and 1998 seasons). ... Played in AFC championship game (1997 and 1998 seasons).

HONORS: Played in Pro Bowl (1996 and 1998 seasons).

PRO STATISTICS: 1988—Recovered one fumble. 1989—Returned one punt for no yards, fumbled once and recovered two fumbles. 1991—Recovered two fumbles. 1992—Recovered one fumble. 1993—Recovered one fumble. 1994—Recovered one fumble. 1995—Recovered one fumble. 1996—Recovered three fumbles. 1998—Recovered three fumbles. 1999—Fumbled once and recovered one fumble. 2000—Recovered two fumbles.

			INTERCEPTIONS				SACKS
Year Team	G	GS	No.	Yds.	Avg.	TD	No.
1988—San Francisco NFL	16	8	0	0	0.0	0	0.0
1989—San Francisco NFL	16	4	1	13	13.0	∞1	1.0
1990—San Francisco NFL	16	16	0	0	0.0	0	1.0
1991—San Francisco NFL	16	16	1	7	7.0	0	1.0
1992—San Francisco NFL	16	16	0	0	0.0	0	1.0
1993—San Francisco NFL	16	16	0	0	0.0	0	3.0
1994—Philadelphia NFL	16	15	2	8	4.0	0	2.5
1995—Philadelphia NFL	16	16	2	5	2.5	0	1.0
1996—Denver NFL	16	16	3	1	0.3	0	3.0
1997—Denver NFL	16	16	1	7	7.0	0	2.0
1998—Denver NFL	16	16	2	22	11.0	0	7.5
1999—Denver NFL	16	16	3	35	11.7	1	0.0
2000—Denver NFL	16	16	2	0	0.0	0	3.5
Pro totals (13 years)	208	187	17	98	5.8	2	26.5

ROSENTHAL, MIKE   G   GIANTS

PERSONAL: Born June 10, 1977, in Pittsburgh. ... 6-7/315. ... Full name: Michael Paul Rosenthal.

HIGH SCHOOL: Penn (Mishawaka, Ind.).

COLLEGE: Notre Dame.

TRANSACTIONS/CAREER NOTES: Selected by New York Giants in fifth round (149th pick overall) of 1999 NFL draft. ... Signed by Giants (July 26, 1999).

PLAYING EXPERIENCE: New York Giants NFL, 1999 and 2000. ... Games/Games started: 1999 (9/7), 2000 (8/2). Total: 17/9.

CHAMPIONSHIP GAME EXPERIENCE: Played in NFC championship game (2000 season). ... Played in Super Bowl XXXV (2000 season).

ROSS, ADRIAN   LB   BENGALS

PERSONAL: Born February 19, 1975, in Santa Clara, Calif. ... 6-2/250. ... Full name: Adrian Lamont Ross.

HIGH SCHOOL: Elk Grove (Calif.).

COLLEGE: Colorado State.

TRANSACTIONS/CAREER NOTES: Signed as non-drafted free agent by Cincinnati Bengals (April 21, 1998). ... Granted free agency (March 2, 2001). ... Re-signed by Bengals (May 1, 2001).

PLAYING EXPERIENCE: Cincinnati NFL, 1998-2000. ... Games/Games started: 1998 (14/1), 1999 (16/10), 2000 (13/4). Total: 43/15.

PRO STATISTICS: 1998—Intercepted one pass for 11 yards. 1999—Credited with one sack. 2000—Credited with one sack.

ROSSUM, ALLEN   CB/KR   PACKERS

PERSONAL: Born October 22, 1975, in Dallas. ... 5-8/178.

HIGH SCHOOL: Skyline (Dallas).

COLLEGE: Notre Dame.

TRANSACTIONS/CAREER NOTES: Granted free agency (March 2, 2001).

PRO STATISTICS: 2000—Rushed once for 16 yards and recovered five fumbles.

			PUNT RETURNS				KICKOFF RETURNS				TOTALS			
Year Team	G	GS	No.	Yds.	Avg.	TD	No.	Yds.	Avg.	TD	TD	2pt.	Pts.	Fum.
2000—Green Bay NFL	16	0	29	248	8.6	0	50	1288	25.8	1	1	0	6	4

ROUEN, TOM   P   BRONCOS

PERSONAL: Born June 9, 1968, in Hinsdale, Ill. ... 6-3/225. ... Full name: Thomas Francis Rouen Jr. ... Name pronounced RUIN.

HIGH SCHOOL: Heritage (Littleton, Colo.).

COLLEGE: Colorado State, then Colorado.

TRANSACTIONS/CAREER NOTES: Signed as non-drafted free agent by New York Giants (April 29, 1991). ... Released by Giants (August 19, 1991). ... Selected by Ohio Glory in fourth round (44th pick overall) of 1992 World League draft. ... Signed by Los Angeles Rams (July 1992). ... Released by Rams (August 24, 1992). ... Signed by Denver Broncos (April 29, 1993). ... Granted unconditional free agency (February 14, 1997). ... Re-signed by Broncos (March 6, 1997). ... Granted unconditional free agency (February 11, 2000). ... Re-signed by Broncos (February 24, 2000).

CHAMPIONSHIP GAME EXPERIENCE: Played in AFC championship game (1997 and 1998 seasons). ... Member of Super Bowl championship team (1997 and 1998 seasons).

HONORS: Named punter on THE SPORTING NEWS college All-America second team (1989).

PRO STATISTICS: 1993—Rushed once for no yards. 1998—Rushed once for no yards, missed one extra-point attempt and fumbled once for minus 15 yards. 1999—Rushed once for no yards and recovered one fumble 2000—Rushed once for minus 11 yards.

Year Team	G	No.	Yds.	Avg.	Net avg.	In. 20	Blk.
			PUNTING				
1992—Ohio W.L.	10	48	1992	41.5	36.1	14	1
1993—Denver NFL	16	67	3017	45.0	37.1	17	1
1994—Denver NFL	16	76	3258	42.9	*37.1	23	0
1995—Denver NFL	16	52	2192	42.2	37.6	22	1
1996—Denver NFL	16	65	2714	41.8	36.2	16	0
1997—Denver NFL	16	60	2598	43.3	38.1	22	0
1998—Denver NFL	16	66	3097	46.9	37.6	14	1
1999—Denver NFL	16	84	3908	*46.5	35.6	19	0
2000—Denver NFL	16	61	2455	40.2	32.3	18	▲1
W.L. totals (1 year)	10	48	1992	41.5	36.1	14	1
NFL totals (8 years)	128	531	23239	43.8	36.4	151	4
Pro totals (9 years)	138	579	25231	43.6	36.4	165	5

ROUNDTREE, RALEIGH   G/OT   CHARGERS

PERSONAL: Born August 31, 1975, in Augusta, Ga. ... 6-4/295. ... Full name: Raleigh Cito Roundtree.
HIGH SCHOOL: Josey (Augusta, Ga.).
COLLEGE: South Carolina State.
TRANSACTIONS/CAREER NOTES: Selected by San Diego Chargers in fourth round (109th pick overall) of 1997 NFL draft. ... Signed by Chargers (July 14, 1997). ... Inactive for all 16 games (1997). ... Granted free agency (February 11, 2000). ... Re-signed by Chargers (May 30, 2000). ... Granted unconditional free agency (March 2, 2001). ... Re-signed by Chargers (May 3, 2001).
PLAYING EXPERIENCE: San Diego NFL, 1998-2000. ... Games/Games started: 1998 (15/5), 1999 (15/5), 2000 (16/15). Total: 46/25.
PRO STATISTICS: 1998—Recovered one fumble. 2000—Recovered one fumble.

ROYALS, MARK   P   BUCCANEERS

PERSONAL: Born June 22, 1965, in Hampton, Va. ... 6-5/215. ... Full name: Mark Alan Royals.
HIGH SCHOOL: Mathews (Va.).
JUNIOR COLLEGE: Chowan College (N.C.).
COLLEGE: Appalachian State (degree in political science).
TRANSACTIONS/CAREER NOTES: Signed as non-drafted free agent by Dallas Cowboys (June 6, 1986). ... Released by Cowboys (August 8, 1986). ... Signed as replacement player by St. Louis Cardinals (September 30, 1987). ... Released by Cardinals (October 7, 1987). ... Signed as replacement player by Philadelphia Eagles (October 14, 1987). ... Released by Eagles (November 1987). ... Signed by Cardinals (December 12, 1987). ... Released by Cardinals (July 27, 1988). ... Signed by Miami Dolphins (May 2, 1989). ... Released by Dolphins (August 28, 1989). ... Signed by Tampa Bay Buccaneers (April 24, 1990). ... Granted unconditional free agency (February 1, 1992). ... Signed by Pittsburgh Steelers (March 15, 1992). ... Granted unconditional free agency (February 17, 1995). ... Signed by Detroit Lions (April 26, 1995). ... Granted free agency (February 16, 1996). ... Re-signed by Lions (June 19, 1996). ... Granted unconditional free agency (February 14, 1997). ... Signed by New Orleans Saints (April 25, 1997). ... Released by Saints (June 29, 1999). ... Signed by Buccaneers (August 4, 1999). ... Granted unconditional free agency (February 11, 2000). ... Re-signed by Buccaneers (March 24, 2000).
CHAMPIONSHIP GAME EXPERIENCE: Played in AFC championship game (1994 season). ... Played in NFC championship game (1999 season).
PRO STATISTICS: 1987—Had 23.3-yard net punting average. 1992—Completed only pass attempt for 44 yards. 1994—Rushed once for minus 13 yards. 1995—Rushed once for minus seven yards. 1996—Completed only pass attempt for minus eight yards and recovered one fumble. 1999—Attempted two passes with one completion for 17 yards. 2000—Completed only pass attempt for 36 yards.

Year Team	G	No.	Yds.	Avg.	Net avg.	In. 20	Blk.
			PUNTING				
1987—St. Louis NFL	1	6	222	37.0	.0	2	0
—Philadelphia NFL	1	5	209	41.8	.0	1	0
1988—			Did not play.				
1989—			Did not play.				
1990—Tampa Bay NFL	16	72	2902	40.3	34.0	8	0
1991—Tampa Bay NFL	16	84	3389	40.3	32.2	22	0
1992—Pittsburgh NFL	16	73	3119	42.7	35.6	22	1
1993—Pittsburgh NFL	16	89	3781	42.5	34.2	§28	0
1994—Pittsburgh NFL	16	§97	3849	39.7	35.7	†35	0
1995—Detroit NFL	16	57	2393	42.0	31.0	15	2
1996—Detroit NFL	16	69	3020	43.8	33.3	11	1
1997—New Orleans NFL	16	88	4038	*45.9	34.9	21	0
1998—New Orleans NFL	16	88	4017	‡45.6	36.0	26	0
1999—Tampa Bay NFL	16	90	3882	43.1	37.4	23	0
2000—Tampa Bay NFL	16	85	3551	41.8	35.1	17	0
Pro totals (12 years)	178	903	38372	42.5	34.2	231	4

ROYE, ORPHEUS   DL   BROWNS

PERSONAL: Born January 21, 1974, in Miami. ... 6-4/288. ... Full name: Orpheus Michael Roye. ... Name pronounced OR-fee-us ROY.
HIGH SCHOOL: Miami Springs.
JUNIOR COLLEGE: Jones County Junior College (Miss.).
COLLEGE: Florida State.
TRANSACTIONS/CAREER NOTES: Selected by Pittsburgh Steelers in sixth round (200th pick overall) of 1996 NFL draft. ... Signed by Steelers (July 16, 1996). ... Granted free agency (February 12, 1999). ... Re-signed by Steelers (April 23, 1999). ... Granted unconditional free agency (February 11, 2000). ... Signed by Cleveland Browns (February 12, 2000).
CHAMPIONSHIP GAME EXPERIENCE: Played in AFC championship game (1997 season).
PRO STATISTICS: 1996—Recovered one fumble. 1998—Returned one kickoff for no yards. 1999—Intercepted one pass for two yards and recovered one fumble. 2000—Recovered one fumble for eight yards.

Year Team	G	GS	SACKS
1996—Pittsburgh NFL	13	1	0.0
1997—Pittsburgh NFL	16	0	1.0
1998—Pittsburgh NFL	16	9	3.5
1999—Pittsburgh NFL	16	16	4.5
2000—Cleveland NFL	16	16	2.0
Pro totals (5 years)	77	42	11.0

RUCKER, MICHAEL   DE   PANTHERS

PERSONAL: Born February 28, 1975, in St. Joseph, Mo. ... 6-5/258. ... Full name: Michael Dean Rucker.
HIGH SCHOOL: Benton (St. Joseph, Mo.).
COLLEGE: Nebraska (degree in sociology).
TRANSACTIONS/CAREER NOTES: Selected by Carolina Panthers in second round (38th pick overall) of 1999 NFL draft. ... Signed by Panthers (July 13, 1999).

Year Team	G	GS	SACKS
1999—Carolina NFL	16	0	3.0
2000—Carolina NFL	16	1	2.5
Pro totals (2 years)	32	1	5.5

RUDD, DWAYNE   LB   BROWNS

PERSONAL: Born February 3, 1976, in Batesville, Miss. ... 6-2/237. ... Full name: Dwayne Dupree Rudd.
HIGH SCHOOL: South Panola (Batesville, Miss.).
COLLEGE: Alabama.
TRANSACTIONS/CAREER NOTES: Selected by Minnesota Vikings in first round (20th pick overall) of 1997 NFL draft. ... Signed by Vikings (July 18, 1997). ... Granted unconditional free agency (March 2, 2001). ... Signed by Cleveland Browns (March 3, 2001).
CHAMPIONSHIP GAME EXPERIENCE: Played in NFC championship game (1998 and 2000 seasons).
RECORDS: Shares NFL single-season records for most touchdowns by fumble recovery—2 (1998); most touchdowns by recovery of opponents' fumbles—2 (1998).
PRO STATISTICS: 1998—Recovered three fumbles for 157 yards and two touchdowns. 1999—Recovered one fumble.

Year Team	G	GS	SACKS
1997—Minnesota NFL	16	2	5.0
1998—Minnesota NFL	15	15	2.0
1999—Minnesota NFL	16	16	3.0
2000—Minnesota NFL	14	13	0.0
Pro totals (4 years)	61	46	10.0

RUDDY, TIM   C   DOLPHINS

PERSONAL: Born April 27, 1972, in Scranton, Pa. ... 6-3/305. ... Full name: Timothy Daniel Ruddy.
HIGH SCHOOL: Dunmore (Pa.).
COLLEGE: Notre Dame (degree in mechanical engineering).
TRANSACTIONS/CAREER NOTES: Selected by Miami Dolphins in second round (65th pick overall) of 1994 NFL draft. ... Signed by Dolphins (July 18, 1994). ... Granted unconditional free agency (February 11, 2000). ... Re-signed by Dolphins (February 24, 2000).
PLAYING EXPERIENCE: Miami NFL, 1994-2000. ... Games/Games started: 1994 (16/0), 1995 (16/16), 1996 (16/16), 1997 (15/15), 1998 (16/16), 1999 (16/16), 2000 (16/16). Total: 111/95.
HONORS: Played in Pro Bowl (2000 season).
PRO STATISTICS: 1995—Fumbled once. 1996—Fumbled once for minus 14 yards. 1998—Fumbled once for minus three yards.

RUEGAMER, GREY   G   PATRIOTS

PERSONAL: Born June 1, 1976, in Las Vegas, Nev. ... 6-5/310. ... Full name: Christopher Grey Ruegamer.
HIGH SCHOOL: Bishop Gorman (Las Vegas, Nev.).
COLLEGE: Arizona State.
TRANSACTIONS/CAREER NOTES: Selected by Miami Dolphins in third round (72nd pick overall) of 1999 NFL draft. ... Signed by Dolphins (July 27, 1999). ... Active for one game (1999); did not play. ... Released by Dolphins (August 27, 2000). ... Signed by Pittsburgh Steelers to practice squad (August 29, 2000). ... Signed by New England Patriots off Steelers practice squad (November 16, 2000).
PLAYING EXPERIENCE: New England NFL, 2000. ... Games/Games started: 2000 (6/0).

RUFF, ORLANDO   LB   CHARGERS

PERSONAL: Born September 28, 1976, in Charleston, S.C. ... 6-3/247. ... Full name: Orlando Bernarda Ruff.
HIGH SCHOOL: Fairfield Central (Winnsboro, S.C.).
COLLEGE: Furman.
TRANSACTIONS/CAREER NOTES: Signed as non-drafted free agent by San Diego Chargers (April 20, 1999).
PLAYING EXPERIENCE: San Diego NFL, 1999 and 2000. ... Games/Games started: 1999 (14/0), 2000 (16/14). Total: 30/14.
PRO STATISTICS: 2000—Intercepted one pass for 18 yards and recovered one fumble.

RUNYAN, JON   OT   EAGLES

PERSONAL: Born November 27, 1973, in Flint, Mich. ... 6-7/330. ... Full name: Jon Daniel Runyan.
HIGH SCHOOL: Carman-Ainsworth (Flint, Mich.).
COLLEGE: Michigan.
TRANSACTIONS/CAREER NOTES: Selected after junior season by Houston Oilers in fourth round (109th pick overall) of 1996 NFL draft. ... Signed by Oilers (July 20, 1996). ... Oilers franchise moved to Tennessee for 1997 season. ... Oilers franchise renamed Tennessee Titans for 1999 season (December 26, 1998). ... Granted free agency (February 12, 1999). ... Re-signed by Titans (June 23, 1999). ... Granted unconditional free agency (February 11, 2000). ... Signed by Philadelphia Eagles (February 14, 2000).
PLAYING EXPERIENCE: Houston NFL, 1996; Tennessee NFL, 1997-1999; Philadelphia NFL, 2000. ... Games/Games started: 1996 (10/0), 1997 (16/16), 1998 (16/16), 1999 (16/16), 2000 (16/16). Total: 74/64.
CHAMPIONSHIP GAME EXPERIENCE: Played in AFC championship game (1999 season). ... Played in Super Bowl XXXIV (1999 season).
HONORS: Named offensive lineman on THE SPORTING NEWS college All-America second team (1995).
PRO STATISTICS: 2000—Recovered one fumble.

R

RUSK, REGGIE   S   CHARGERS

PERSONAL: Born December 19, 1972, in Texas City, Texas. ... 5-10/190. ... Full name: Reggie Leon Rusk.
HIGH SCHOOL: Texas City (Texas).
JUNIOR COLLEGE: City College of San Francisco.
COLLEGE: Kentucky.
TRANSACTIONS/CAREER NOTES: Selected by Tampa Bay Buccaneers in seventh round (221st pick overall) of 1996 NFL draft. ... Signed by Buccaneers (July 12, 1996). ... Released by Buccaneers (August 18, 1996). ... Re-signed by Buccaneers to practice squad (August 27, 1996). ... Activated (September 28, 1996). ... Released by Buccaneers (October 2, 1996). ... Re-signed by Buccaneers to practice squad (October 3, 1996). ... Assigned by Buccaneers to Scottish Claymores in 1997 World League enhancement allocation program (February 19, 1997). ... Released by Buccaneers (September 27, 1997). ... Re-signed by Buccaneers to practice squad (September 29, 1997). ... Signed by Seattle Seahawks off Buccaneers practice squad (December 5, 1997). ... Released by Seahawks (September 9, 1998). ... Signed by San Diego Chargers (December 22, 1998). ... Inactive for two games (1998). ... Released by Chargers (September 4, 1999). ... Re-signed by Chargers (November 3, 1999). ... On injured reserve with knee injury (November 10, 2000-remainder of season).
PLAYING EXPERIENCE: Tampa Bay NFL, 1996; Tampa Bay (4)-Seattle (2) NFL, 1997; San Diego NFL, 1999 and 2000. ... Games/Games started: 1996 (1/0), 1997 (T.B.-4/0; Sea.-2/0; Total: 6/0), 1999 (9/0), 2000 (7/0). Total: 23/0.
PRO STATISTICS: 2000—Credited with one sack and recovered one fumble for 17 yards.

RUSS, STEVE   LB

PERSONAL: Born September 16, 1972, in Stetsonville, Wis. ... 6-4/245.
HIGH SCHOOL: Stetsonville (Wis.).
COLLEGE: Air Force (degree in management).
TRANSACTIONS/CAREER NOTES: Selected by Denver Broncos in seventh round (218th pick overall) of 1995 NFL draft. ... Signed by Broncos for 1995 season. ... On reserved/military list entire 1995 season. ... On reserved/military list (August 13, 1996-entire season). ... On injured reserve with broken leg (August 11, 1998-entire season). ... Released by Broncos (September 5, 1999). ... Re-signed by Broncos (November 2, 1999). ... Released by Broncos (September 19, 2000).
PLAYING EXPERIENCE: Denver NFL, 1997, 1999 and 2000. ... Games/Games started: 1997 (14/0), 1999 (8/0), 2000 (2/0). Total: 24/0.
CHAMPIONSHIP GAME EXPERIENCE: Member of Broncos for AFC championship game (1997 season); inactive. ... Member of Super Bowl championship team (1997 season); inactive.

RUSSELL, DARRELL   DT   RAIDERS

PERSONAL: Born May 27, 1976, in Pensacola, Fla. ... 6-5/325.
HIGH SCHOOL: St. Augustine (San Diego).
COLLEGE: Southern California.
TRANSACTIONS/CAREER NOTES: Selected by Oakland Raiders in first round (second pick overall) of 1997 NFL draft. ... Signed by Raiders (July 23, 1997).
HONORS: Played in Pro Bowl (1998 and 1999 seasons). ... Named defensive tackle on THE SPORTING NEWS NFL All-Pro team (1999).
PRO STATISTICS: 1998—Recovered one fumble. 1999—Recovered one fumble. 2000—Recovered one fumble and credited with one safety.

Year Team	G	GS	SACKS
1997—Oakland NFL	16	10	3.5
1998—Oakland NFL	16	16	10.0
1999—Oakland NFL	16	16	9.5
2000—Oakland NFL	16	16	3.0
Pro totals (4 years)	64	58	26.0

RUSSELL, TWAN   LB   DOLPHINS

PERSONAL: Born April 25, 1974, in Fort Lauderdale, Fla. ... 6-1/228. ... Full name: Twan Sanchez Russell.
HIGH SCHOOL: St. Thomas Aquinas (Fort Lauderdale, Fla.).
COLLEGE: Miami, Fla. (degree in broadcasting, 1996).
TRANSACTIONS/CAREER NOTES: Selected by Washington Redskins in fifth round (148th pick overall) of 1997 NFL draft. ... Signed by Redskins (May 9, 1997). ... On injured reserve with foot and knee injuries (September 23, 1998-remainder of season). ... On injured reserve with knee injury (November 16, 1999-remainder of season). ... Granted free agency (February 11, 2000). ... Signed by Miami Dolphins (March 23, 2000). ... Granted unconditional free agency (March 2, 2001). ... Re-signed by Dolphins (March 6, 2001).
PLAYING EXPERIENCE: Washington NFL, 1997-1999; Miami NFL, 2000. ... Games/Games started: 1997 (14/0), 1998 (3/0), 1999 (9/0), 2000 (16/2). Total: 42/2.
PRO STATISTICS: 2000—Recovered one fumble.

RUTLEDGE, JOHNNY   LB   CARDINALS

PERSONAL: Born January 4, 1977, in Belle Glade, Fla. ... 6-3/243. ... Full name: Johnny Boykins Rutledge III.
HIGH SCHOOL: Glades Central (Belle Glade, Fla.).
COLLEGE: Florida.
TRANSACTIONS/CAREER NOTES: Selected by Arizona Cardinals in second round (51st pick overall) of 1999 NFL draft. ... Signed by Cardinals (July 29, 1999).
PLAYING EXPERIENCE: Arizona NFL, 1999 and 2000. ... Games/Games started: 1999 (6/0), 2000 (11/3). Total: 17/3.
PRO STATISTICS: 2000—Recovered one fumble.

RUTLEDGE, ROD   TE   PATRIOTS

PERSONAL: Born August 12, 1975, in Birmingham, Ala. ... 6-5/270. ... Full name: Rodrick Almar Rutledge.
HIGH SCHOOL: Erwin (Birmingham, Ala.).
COLLEGE: Alabama.
TRANSACTIONS/CAREER NOTES: Selected by New England Patriots in second round (54th pick overall) of 1998 NFL draft. ... Signed by Patriots (June 15, 1998).
PLAYING EXPERIENCE: New England NFL, 1998-2000. ... Games/Games started: 1998 (16/4), 1999 (16/2), 2000 (16/11). Total: 48/17.
PRO STATISTICS: 1999—Caught seven passes for 66 yards and fumbled once. 2000—Caught 15 passes for 103 yards and a touchdown and recovered one fumble.
SINGLE GAME HIGHS (regular season): Receptions—4 (November 23, 2000, vs. Detroit); yards—27 (December 4, 2000, vs. Kansas City); and touchdown receptions—1 (November 12, 2000, vs. Cleveland).

SALAAM, EPHRAIM   OT   FALCONS

PERSONAL: Born June 19, 1976, in Chicago. ... 6-7/300. ... Full name: Ephraim Mateen Salaam. ... Name pronounced EFF-rum sah-LAHM.
HIGH SCHOOL: Florin (Sacramento).
COLLEGE: San Diego State.
TRANSACTIONS/CAREER NOTES: Selected by Atlanta Falcons in seventh round (199th pick overall) of 1998 NFL draft. ... Signed by Falcons (June 3, 1998). ... Granted free agency (March 2, 2001). ... Re-signed by Falcons (April 6, 2001).
PLAYING EXPERIENCE: Atlanta NFL, 1998-2000. ... Games/Games started: 1998 (16/16), 1999 (16/16), 2000 (14/10). Total: 46/42.
CHAMPIONSHIP GAME EXPERIENCE: Played in NFC championship game (1998 season). ... Played in Super Bowl XXXIII (1998 season).

SALAVE'A, JOE   DT   TITANS

PERSONAL: Born March 23, 1975, in Leone, American Samoa. ... 6-3/290. ... Full name: Joe Fagaone Salave'a. ... Name pronounced sala-VAY-uh.
HIGH SCHOOL: Oceanside (Calif.).
COLLEGE: Arizona (degree in sociology, 1997).
TRANSACTIONS/CAREER NOTES: Selected by Tennessee Oilers in fourth round (107th pick overall) of 1998 NFL draft. ... Signed by Oilers (June 30, 1998). ... Oilers franchise renamed Tennessee Titans for 1999 season (December 26, 1998). ... Granted free agency (March 2, 2001).
PLAYING EXPERIENCE: Tennessee NFL, 1998-2000. ... Games/Games started: 1998 (13/0), 1999 (10/0), 2000 (15/1). Total: 38/1.
CHAMPIONSHIP GAME EXPERIENCE: Played in AFC championship game (1999 season). ... Played in Super Bowl XXXIV (1999 season).
HONORS: Named defensive tackle on THE SPORTING NEWS college All-America third team (1997).
PRO STATISTICS: 1998—Credited with one sack. 2000—Credited with four sacks.

SALEH, TAREK   LB   BROWNS

PERSONAL: Born November 7, 1974, in Woodbridge, Conn. ... 6-0/240. ... Full name: Tarek Muhammad Saleh. ... Name pronounced TAR-ick sa-LAY.
HIGH SCHOOL: Notre Dame (West Haven, Conn.).
COLLEGE: Wisconsin.
TRANSACTIONS/CAREER NOTES: Selected by Carolina Panthers in fourth round (122nd pick overall) of 1997 NFL draft. ... Signed by Panthers for 1997 season. ... Selected by Cleveland Browns from Panthers in NFL expansion draft (February 9, 1999). ... Granted free agency (February 11, 2000). ... Re-signed by Browns (April 12, 2000) ... Granted unconditional free agency (March 2, 2001). ... Re-signed by Browns (March 5, 2001).
PLAYING EXPERIENCE: Carolina NFL, 1997 and 1998; Cleveland NFL, 1999 and 2000. ... Games/Games started: 1997 (3/0), 1998 (11/1), 1999 (16/0), 2000 (16/0). Total: 46/1.
PRO STATISTICS: 1997—Credited with one sack. 1998—Returned one kickoff for eight yards. 1999—Returned five kickoffs for 43 yards and recovered one fumble. 2000—Caught one pass for 22 yards, returned four kickoffs for 46 yards and recovered one fumble.

SAMUEL, KHARI   LB   BEARS

PERSONAL: Born October 14, 1976, in New York. ... 6-3/240. ... Full name: Khari Iman Mitchell Samuel. ... Name pronounced CAR-ee.
HIGH SCHOOL: Framingham (Mass.).
COLLEGE: Massachusetts.
TRANSACTIONS/CAREER NOTES: Selected by Chicago Bears in fifth round (144th pick overall) of 1999 NFL draft. ... Signed by Bears (May 26, 1999).
PLAYING EXPERIENCE: Chicago NFL, 1999 and 2000. ... Games/Games started: 1999 (13/1), 2000 (16/0). Total: 29/1.
PRO STATISTICS: 1999—Recovered one fumble.

R
S

SAMUELS, CHRIS — OT — REDSKINS

PERSONAL: Born July 28, 1977, in Mobile, Ala. ... 6-5/325.
HIGH SCHOOL: Shaw (Mobile, Ala.).
COLLEGE: Alabama.
TRANSACTIONS/CAREER NOTES: Selected by Washington Redskins in first round (third pick overall) of 2000 NFL draft. ... Signed by Redskins (July 18, 2000).
PLAYING EXPERIENCE: Washington NFL, 2000. ... Games/Games started: 2000 (16/16).
HONORS: Outland Trophy winner (1999). ... Named offensive tackle on THE SPORTING NEWS college All-America first team (1999).

SANDERS, CHRIS — WR — TITANS

PERSONAL: Born May 8, 1972, in Denver. ... 6-1/188. ... Full name: Christopher Dwayne Sanders.
HIGH SCHOOL: Montbello (Denver).
COLLEGE: Ohio State.
TRANSACTIONS/CAREER NOTES: Selected by Houston Oilers in third round (67th pick overall) of 1995 NFL draft. ... Signed by Oilers (July 20, 1995). ... Oilers franchise moved to Tennessee for 1997 season. ... Oilers franchise renamed Tennessee Titans for 1999 season (December 26, 1998).
CHAMPIONSHIP GAME EXPERIENCE: Played in AFC championship game (1999 season). ... Played in Super Bowl XXXIV (1999 season).
PRO STATISTICS: 1995—Rushed twice for minus 19 yards. 1997—Rushed once for minus eight yards. 1998—Rushed once for minus nine yards.
SINGLE GAME HIGHS (regular season): Receptions—7 (December 14, 1997, vs. Baltimore); yards—147 (November 26, 1995, vs. Denver); and touchdown receptions—2 (October 26, 1997, vs. Arizona).
STATISTICAL PLATEAUS: 100-yard receiving games: 1995 (1), 1996 (3), 1997 (1), 1998 (1), 1999 (1). Total: 7.

			RECEIVING				TOTALS		
Year Team	G	GS	No.	Yds.	Avg.	TD	TD	2pt.	Pts.	Fum.
1995—Houston NFL	16	10	35	823	*23.5	9	9	0	54	0
1996—Houston NFL	16	15	48	882	§18.4	4	4	0	24	0
1997—Tennessee NFL	15	14	31	498	16.1	3	3	0	18	1
1998—Tennessee NFL	14	1	5	136	27.2	0	0	0	0	1
1999—Tennessee NFL	16	0	20	336	16.8	1	1	0	6	0
2000—Tennessee NFL	16	14	33	536	16.2	0	0	0	0	1
Pro totals (6 years)	93	54	172	3211	18.7	17	17	0	102	3

SANDERS, DEION — CB — REDSKINS

PERSONAL: Born August 9, 1967, in Fort Myers, Fla. ... 6-1/198. ... Full name: Deion Luwynn Sanders. ... Nickname: Prime Time.
HIGH SCHOOL: North Fort Myers (Fla.).
COLLEGE: Florida State.
TRANSACTIONS/CAREER NOTES: Selected by Atlanta Falcons in first round (fifth pick overall) of 1989 NFL draft. ... Signed by Falcons (September 7, 1989). ... On reserve/did not report list (July 27-August 13, 1990). ... Granted roster exemption for one game (September 1992). ... On reserve/did not report list (July 23-October 14, 1993). ... Designated by Falcons as transition player (February 15, 1994). ... Free agency status changed by Falcons from transitional to unconditional (April 28, 1994). ... Signed by San Francisco 49ers (September 15, 1994). ... Granted unconditional free agency (February 17, 1995). ... Signed by Dallas Cowboys (September 9, 1995). ... On reserve/did not report list (July 16-August 29, 1997). ... Released by Cowboys (June 2, 2000). ... Signed by Washington Redskins (June 5, 2000).
CHAMPIONSHIP GAME EXPERIENCE: Played in NFC championship game (1994 and 1995 seasons). ... Member of Super Bowl championship team (1994 and 1995 seasons).
HONORS: Named defensive back on THE SPORTING NEWS college All-America first team (1986-1988). ... Jim Thorpe Award winner (1988). ... Named cornerback on THE SPORTING NEWS NFL All-Pro team (1991-1999). ... Played in Pro Bowl (1991-1994 and 1998 seasons). ... Named kick returner on THE SPORTING NEWS NFL All-Pro team (1992). ... Named to play in Pro Bowl (1996 season); replaced by Darrell Green due to injury. ... Named to play in Pro Bowl (1997 season); replaced by Cris Dishman due to injury. ... Named to play in Pro Bowl (1999 season); replaced by Troy Vincent due to injury.
PRO STATISTICS: 1989—Fumbled twice and recovered one fumble. 1990—Fumbled four times and recovered two fumbles. 1991—Credited with a sack, fumbled once and recovered one fumble. 1992—Rushed once for minus four yards, fumbled three times and recovered two fumbles. 1993—Attempted one pass without a completion. 1994—Recovered one fumble. 1995—Rushed twice for nine yards. 1996—Rushed three times for two yards, fumbled twice and recovered three fumbles for 15 yards and one touchdown. 1997—Rushed once for minus 11 yards and fumbled once. 1998—Fumbled once and recovered one fumble. 1999—Attempted one pass without a completion and fumbled once. 2000—Recovered two fumbles.
MISCELLANEOUS: Only person in history to play in both the World Series (1992) and Super Bowl (1994 and 1995 seasons).

			INTERCEPTIONS				RECEIVING				PUNT RETURNS				KICKOFF RETURNS				TOTALS		
Year Team	G	GS	No.	Yds.	Avg.	TD	No.	Yds.	Avg.	TD	No.	Yds.	Avg.	TD	No.	Yds.	Avg.	TD	TD	2pt.	Pts.
1989—Atlanta NFL	15	10	5	52	10.4	0	1	-8	-8.0	0	28	307	11.0	†1	35	725	20.7	0	1	0	6
1990—Atlanta NFL	16	16	3	153	*51.0	2	0	0	0.0	0	29	250	8.6	†1	39	851	21.8	0	3	0	18
1991—Atlanta NFL	15	15	∞6	119	19.8	∞1	1	17	17.0	0	21	170	8.1	0	26	576	22.2	†1	2	0	12
1992—Atlanta NFL	13	12	3	105	‡35.0	0	3	45	15.0	1	13	41	3.2	0	40	*1067	‡26.7	*2	3	0	18
1993—Atlanta NFL	11	10	‡7	91	13.0	0	6	106	17.7	1	2	21	10.5	0	7	169	24.1	0	1	0	6
1994—San Fran. NFL	14	12	6	*303	*50.5	†3	0	0	0.0	0	0	0	0.0	0	0	0	0.0	0	3	0	18
1995—Dallas NFL	9	9	2	34	17.0	0	2	25	12.5	0	1	54	54.0	0	1	15	15.0	0	0	0	0
1996—Dallas NFL	16	15	2	3	1.5	0	36	475	13.2	1	1	4	4.0	0	0	0	0.0	0	2	0	12
1997—Dallas NFL	13	12	2	81	40.5	1	0	0	0.0	0	33	407	12.3	∞1	1	18	18.0	0	2	0	12
1998—Dallas NFL	11	11	5	153	30.6	1	7	100	14.3	0	24	375	*15.6	†2	1	16	16.0	0	3	0	18
1999—Dallas NFL	14	14	3	2	0.7	0	4	24	6.0	0	30	344	11.5	∞1	4	87	21.8	0	1	0	6
2000—Washington NFL	16	15	4	91	22.8	0	0	0	0.0	0	25	185	7.4	0	1	-1	-1.0	0	0	0	0
Pro totals (12 years)	163	151	48	1187	24.7	8	60	784	13.1	3	207	2158	10.4	6	155	3523	22.7	3	21	0	126

S

RECORD AS BASEBALL PLAYER

TRANSACTIONS/CAREER NOTES: Selected by Kansas City Royals organization in sixth round of free-agent draft (June 3, 1985); did not sign. ... Selected by New York Yankees organization in 30th round of free-agent draft (June 1, 1988). ... On disqualified list (August 1-September 24, 1990). ... Released by Yankees organization (September 24, 1990). ... Signed by Atlanta Braves (January 29, 1991). ... Placed on Richmond temporarily inactive list (August 1, 1991). ... On disqualified list (April 29-May 21, 1993). ... On disabled list (August 22-September 6, 1993). ... Traded by Braves to Cincinnati Reds for OF Roberto Kelly and P Roger Etheridge (May 29, 1994). ... On Cincinnati disabled list (June 1-July 16, 1995); included rehabilitation assignment to Chattanooga (July 12-14). ... Traded by Reds with P John Roper, P Ricky Pickett, P Scott Service and IF Dave McCarty to San Francisco Giants for OF Darren Lewis, P Mark Portugal and P Dave Burba (July 21, 1995). ... Granted free agency (December 21, 1995). ... Did not play baseball during 1996 season. ... Granted free agency (November 5, 1996). ... Re-signed by Reds (February 17, 1997). ... Granted free agency after 1997 season. ... Re-signed by Reds organization (January 8, 1998). ... Did not play baseball during 1998 and 1999 season.

STATISTICAL NOTES: Led N.L. in caught stealing with 16 in 1994.

Year Team (League)	Pos.	G	AB	R	H	2B	3B	HR	RBI	Avg.	BB	SO	SB	PO	A	E	Avg.
1988— GC Yankees (GCL)......	OF	17	75	7	21	4	2	0	6	.280	2	10	11	33	1	2	.944
—Fort Lauderdale (FSL)	OF	6	21	5	9	2	0	0	2	.429	1	3	2	22	2	0	1.000
—Columbus (Int'l)	OF	5	20	3	3	1	0	0	0	.150	1	4	1	13	0	0	1.000
1989— Alb./Colon. (Eastern)..	OF	33	119	28	34	2	2	1	6	.286	11	20	17	79	3	0	1.000
—New York (A.L.).........	OF	14	47	7	11	2	0	2	7	.234	3	8	1	30	1	1	.969
—Columbus (Int'l)........	OF	70	259	38	72	12	7	5	30	.278	22	46	16	165	0	4	.976
1990—New York (A.L.).........	OF-DH	57	133	24	21	2	2	3	9	.158	13	27	8	69	2	2	.973
—Columbus (Int'l)........	OF	22	84	21	27	7	1	2	10	.321	17	15	9	49	1	0	1.000
1991—Atlanta (N.L.)■.........	OF	54	110	16	21	1	2	4	13	.191	12	23	11	57	3	3	.952
—Richmond (Int'l)........	OF	29	130	20	34	6	3	5	16	.262	10	28	12	73	1	1	.987
1992—Atlanta (N.L.).........	OF	97	303	54	92	6	*14	8	28	.304	18	52	26	174	4	3	.983
1993—Atlanta (N.L.).........	OF	95	272	42	75	18	6	6	28	.276	16	42	19	137	1	2	.986
1994—Atlanta (N.L.).........	OF	46	191	32	55	10	0	4	21	.288	16	28	19	99	0	2	.980
—Cincinnati (N.L.)■......	OF	46	184	26	51	7	4	0	7	.277	16	35	19	110	2	0	1.000
1995—Cincinnati (N.L.)........	OF	33	129	19	31	2	3	1	10	.240	9	18	16	88	2	3	.968
—Chattanooga (Sou.)....	OF	2	7	1	4	0	0	1	2	.571	0	1	1	3	1	0	1.000
—San Fran. (N.L.)■......	OF	52	214	29	61	9	5	5	18	.285	18	42	8	127	0	2	.984
1996—							Did not play.										
1997—Cincinnati (N.L.)■......	OF	115	465	53	127	13	7	5	23	.273	34	67	56	236	3	4	.984
1998—Cincinnati (N.L.)........							Did not play.										
American League totals (2 years)		71	180	31	32	4	2	5	16	.178	16	35	9	99	3	3	.971
National League totals (6 years)		538	1868	271	513	66	41	33	148	.275	139	307	174	1028	15	19	.982
Major league totals (8 years)		609	2048	302	545	70	43	38	164	.266	155	342	183	1127	18	22	.981

CHAMPIONSHIP SERIES RECORD

Year Team (League)	Pos.	G	AB	R	H	2B	3B	HR	RBI	Avg.	BB	SO	SB	PO	A	E	Avg.
1992—Atlanta (N.L.)..............	OF-PH	4	5	0	0	0	0	0	0	.000	0	3	0	1	0	0	1.000
1993—Atlanta (N.L.)..............	PH-OF-PR	5	3	0	0	0	0	0	0	.000	0	1	0	0	0	0	...
Championship series totals (2 years)		9	8	0	0	0	0	0	0	.000	0	4	0	1	0	0	1.000

WORLD SERIES RECORD

Year Team (League)	Pos.	G	AB	R	H	2B	3B	HR	RBI	Avg.	BB	SO	SB	PO	A	E	Avg.
1992—Atlanta (N.L.)..............	OF	4	15	4	8	2	0	0	1	.533	2	1	5	5	1	0	1.000

SANDERS, FRANK   WR   CARDINALS

PERSONAL: Born February 17, 1973, in Fort Lauderdale, Fla. ... 6-2/200. ... Full name: Frank Vondel Sanders.

HIGH SCHOOL: Dillard (Fort Lauderdale, Fla.).

COLLEGE: Auburn.

TRANSACTIONS/CAREER NOTES: Selected by Arizona Cardinals in second round (47th pick overall) of 1995 NFL draft. ... Signed by Cardinals (July 17, 1995). ... Granted free agency (February 13, 1998). ... Re-signed by Cardinals (March 13, 1998).

HONORS: Named wide receiver on THE SPORTING NEWS college All-America second team (1994).

PRO STATISTICS: 1995—Rushed once for one yard. 1996—Rushed twice for minus four yards and recovered one fumble. 1997—Attempted one pass with a completion for 26 yards and rushed once for five yards. 1998—Rushed four times for no yards and recovered two fumbles. 1999—Attempted one pass without a completion and recovered one fumble.

SINGLE GAME HIGHS (regular season): Receptions—13 (January 2, 2000, vs. Green Bay); yards—190 (November 15, 1998, vs. Dallas); and touchdown receptions—2 (October 8, 2000, vs. Cleveland).

STATISTICAL PLATEAUS: 100-yard receiving games: 1995 (2), 1997 (2), 1998 (5), 1999 (2). Total: 11.

Year Team		G	GS	No.	Yds.	Avg.	TD	TD	2pt.	Pts.	Fum.
				RECEIVING				TOTALS			
1995—Arizona NFL...................................		16	15	52	883	17.0	2	2	2	16	0
1996—Arizona NFL...................................		16	16	69	813	11.8	4	4	0	24	1
1997—Arizona NFL...................................		16	16	75	1017	13.6	4	4	1	26	3
1998—Arizona NFL...................................		16	16	‡89	1145	12.9	3	3	0	18	3
1999—Arizona NFL...................................		16	16	79	954	12.1	1	1	0	6	2
2000—Arizona NFL...................................		16	16	54	749	13.9	6	6	0	36	0
Pro totals (6 years)		96	95	418	5561	13.3	20	20	3	126	9

SANDERS, LEWIS   DB   BROWNS

PERSONAL: Born June 22, 1978, in Staten Island, N.Y. ... 6-0/200. ... Full name: Lewis Lindell Sanders.
HIGH SCHOOL: St. Peter's (Staten Island, N.Y.).
COLLEGE: Maryland.
TRANSACTIONS/CAREER NOTES: Selected after junior season by Cleveland Browns in fourth round (95th pick overall) of 2000 NFL draft. ... Signed by Browns (June 3, 2000).

			INTERCEPTIONS			
Year Team	G	GS	No.	Yds.	Avg.	TD
2000—Cleveland NFL	11	2	1	0	0.0	0

SANDERSON, SCOTT   G/OT

PERSONAL: Born July 25, 1974, in Walnut Creek, Calif. ... 6-6/295. ... Full name: Scott Michael Sanderson.
HIGH SCHOOL: Clayton Valley (Concord, Calif.).
COLLEGE: Washington State.
TRANSACTIONS/CAREER NOTES: Selected by Houston Oilers in third round (81st pick overall) of 1997 NFL draft. ... Oilers franchise moved to Tennessee for 1997 season. ... Signed by Oilers (July 17, 1997). ... Oilers franchise renamed Tennessee Titans for 1999 season (December 26, 1998). ... On injured reserve with back injury (October 9, 1999-remainder of season). ... Granted free agency (February 11, 2000). ... Re-signed by Titans (March 24, 2000). ... Granted unconditional free agency (March 2, 2001).
PLAYING EXPERIENCE: Tennessee NFL, 1997-2000. ... Games/Games started: 1997 (10/0), 1998 (15/3), 1999 (3/3), 2000 (8/0). Total: 36/6.
HONORS: Named offensive tackle on THE SPORTING NEWS college All-America first team (1996).

SANTIAGO, O.J.   TE   BROWNS

PERSONAL: Born April 4, 1974, in Whitby, Ont. ... 6-7/264. ... Full name: Otis Jason Santiago.
HIGH SCHOOL: St. Michael's (Toronto).
COLLEGE: Kent.
TRANSACTIONS/CAREER NOTES: Selected by Atlanta Falcons in third round (70th pick overall) of 1997 NFL draft. ... Signed by Falcons (July 11, 1997). ... On injured reserve with leg injury (November 20, 1997-remainder of season). ... Granted free agency (February 11, 2000). ... Re-signed by Falcons (June 5, 2000). ... Traded by Falcons to Dallas Cowboys for fourth round pick (LB Matt Stewart) in 2001 draft and seventh-round pick in 2002 draft (August 27, 2000). ... Claimed on waivers by Cleveland Browns (November 22, 2000). ... Inactive for four games with Cleveland (2000). ... Granted unconditional free agency (March 2, 2001). ... Re-signed by Browns (March 26, 2001).
CHAMPIONSHIP GAME EXPERIENCE: Played in NFC championship game (1998 season). ... Played in Super Bowl XXXIII (1998 season).
PRO STATISTICS: 1998—Recovered one fumble. 2000—Returned one kickoff for 13 yards.
SINGLE GAME HIGHS (regular season): Receptions—5 (September 14, 1997, vs. Oakland); yards—65 (December 27, 1998, vs. Miami); and touchdown receptions—2 (December 27, 1998, vs. Miami).

			RECEIVING				TOTALS			
Year Team	G	GS	No.	Yds.	Avg.	TD	TD	2pt.	Pts.	Fum.
1997—Atlanta NFL	11	11	17	217	12.8	2	2	0	12	1
1998—Atlanta NFL	16	16	27	428	15.9	5	5	0	30	1
1999—Atlanta NFL	14	14	15	174	11.6	0	0	0	0	0
2000—Dallas NFL	11	0	0	0	0.0	0	0	0	0	0
Pro totals (4 years)	52	41	59	819	13.9	7	7	0	42	2

SANYIKA, SEKOU   LB   CARDINALS

PERSONAL: Born March 17, 1978, in New Orleans. ... 6-3/240.
HIGH SCHOOL: R.L. Stevenson (Hercules, Calif.).
COLLEGE: California.
TRANSACTIONS/CAREER NOTES: Selected by Arizona Cardinals in seventh round (215th pick overall) of 2000 NFL draft. ... Signed by Cardinals (June 19, 2000).
PLAYING EXPERIENCE: Arizona NFL, 2000. ... Games/Games started: 2000 (16/0).

SAPP, WARREN   DT   BUCCANEERS

PERSONAL: Born December 19, 1972, in Orlando. ... 6-2/303. ... Full name: Warren Carlos Sapp.
HIGH SCHOOL: Apopka (Fla.).
COLLEGE: Miami (Fla.).
TRANSACTIONS/CAREER NOTES: Selected after junior season by Tampa Bay Buccaneers in first round (12th pick overall) of 1995 NFL draft. ... Signed by Buccaneers (April 27, 1995).
CHAMPIONSHIP GAME EXPERIENCE: Played in NFC championship game (1999 season).
HONORS: Lombardi Award winner (1994). ... Named defensive lineman on THE SPORTING NEWS college All-America first team (1994). ... Played in Pro Bowl (1997-2000 seasons). ... Named defensive tackle on THE SPORTING NEWS NFL All-Pro team (1999 and 2000).
PRO STATISTICS: 1995—Intercepted one pass for five yards and a touchdown. 1996—Recovered one fumble. 1997—Recovered one fumble for 23 yards. 1998—Recovered one fumble. 1999—Recovered two fumbles. 2000—Recovered one fumble.

Year Team	G	GS	SACKS
1995—Tampa Bay NFL	16	8	3.0
1996—Tampa Bay NFL	15	14	9.0
1997—Tampa Bay NFL	15	15	10.5
1998—Tampa Bay NFL	16	16	7.0
1999—Tampa Bay NFL	15	15	12.5
2000—Tampa Bay NFL	16	15	16.5
Pro totals (6 years)	93	83	58.5

S

SATURDAY, JEFF   C   COLTS

PERSONAL: Born June 8, 1975, in Tucker, Ga. ... 6-2/293. ... Full name: Jeffrey Bryant Saturday.
HIGH SCHOOL: Shamrock (Tucker, Ga.).
COLLEGE: North Carolina.
TRANSACTIONS/CAREER NOTES: Signed as non-drafted free agent by Baltimore Ravens (April 27, 1998). ... Released by Ravens (June 12, 1998). ... Signed by Indianapolis Colts (January 7, 1999).
PLAYING EXPERIENCE: Indianapolis NFL, 1999 and 2000. ... Games/Games started: 1999 (11/2), 2000 (16/16). Total: 27/18.
PRO STATISTICS: 2000—Fumbled once.

SAUER, CRAIG   LB   VIKINGS

PERSONAL: Born December 13, 1972, in Sartell, Minn. ... 6-1/241.
HIGH SCHOOL: Sartell (Minn.).
COLLEGE: Minnesota.
TRANSACTIONS/CAREER NOTES: Selected by Atlanta Falcons in sixth round (188th pick overall) of 1996 NFL draft. ... Signed by Falcons (June 6, 1996). ... Granted unconditional free agency (February 11, 2000). ... Signed by Minnesota Vikings (February 23, 2000). ... On injured reserve with foot injury (November 14, 2000-remainder of season).
PLAYING EXPERIENCE: Atlanta NFL, 1996-1999; Minnesota NFL, 2000. ... Games/Games started: 1996 (16/1), 1997 (16/1), 1998 (16/6), 1999 (16/3), 2000 (9/0). Total: 73/11.
CHAMPIONSHIP GAME EXPERIENCE: Played in NFC championship game (1998 season). ... Played in Super Bowl XXXIII (1998 season).
PRO STATISTICS: 1997—Recovered one fumble. 1998—Intercepted one pass for no yards. 1999—Credited with one sack.

SAUERBRUN, TODD   P   PANTHERS

PERSONAL: Born January 4, 1973, in Setauket, N.Y. ... 5-10/204. ... Name pronounced SOUR-brun.
HIGH SCHOOL: Ward Melville (Setauket, N.Y.).
COLLEGE: West Virginia.
TRANSACTIONS/CAREER NOTES: Selected by Chicago Bears in second round (56th pick overall) of 1995 NFL draft. ... Signed by Bears (July 20, 1995). ... Granted free agency (February 13, 1998). ... Re-signed by Bears (May 19, 1998). ... On injured reserve with knee injury (September 23, 1998-remainder of season). ... Granted unconditional free agency (February 11, 2000). ... Signed by Kansas City Chiefs (March 27, 2000). ... Released by Chiefs (March 13, 2001). ... Signed by Carolina Panthers (April 24, 2001).
HONORS: Named punter on THE SPORTING NEWS college All-America first team (1994).
PRO STATISTICS: 1996—Rushed once for three yards, attempted two passes with two completions for 63 yards. 1997—Rushed twice for eight yards and fumbled once for minus nine yards. 1999—Rushed once for minus two yards and fumbled once.

				PUNTING				
Year Team	G	No.	Yds.	Avg.	Net avg.	In. 20	Blk.	
1995—Chicago NFL	15	55	2080	37.8	31.1	16	0	
1996—Chicago NFL	16	78	3491	44.8	34.8	15	0	
1997—Chicago NFL	16	95	4059	42.7	32.8	26	0	
1998—Chicago NFL	3	15	741	49.4	42.1	6	0	
1999—Chicago NFL	16	85	3478	40.9	35.4	20	0	
2000—Kansas City NFL	16	82	3656	44.6	35.8	28	0	
Pro totals (6 years)	82	410	17505	42.7	34.4	111	0	

SAWYER, TALANCE   DE   VIKINGS

PERSONAL: Born June 14, 1976, in Bastrop, La. ... 6-2/270.
HIGH SCHOOL: Bastrop (La.).
COLLEGE: UNLV.
TRANSACTIONS/CAREER NOTES: Selected by Minnesota Vikings in sixth round (185th pick overall) of 1999 NFL draft. ... Signed by Vikings (June 4, 1999).
PLAYING EXPERIENCE: Minnesota NFL, 1999 and 2000. ... Games/Games started: 1999 (2/0), 2000 (16/16). Total: 18/16.
CHAMPIONSHIP GAME EXPERIENCE: Played in NFC championship game (2000 season).
PRO STATISTICS: 2000—Credited with six sacks and recovered two fumbles.

SCARLETT, NOEL   DT   COWBOYS

PERSONAL: Born January 21, 1974, in Atlanta. ... 6-3/320.
HIGH SCHOOL: Elbert County (Elberton, Ga.).
COLLEGE: Langston University (Okla.).
TRANSACTIONS/CAREER NOTES: Selected by Minnesota Vikings in seventh round (236th pick overall) of 1999 NFL draft. ... Signed by Vikings (June 8, 1999). ... Released by Vikings (September 5, 1999). ... Signed by New England Patriots to practice squad (December 22, 1999). ... Released by Patriots (December 29, 1999). ... Re-signed by Patriots (January 5, 2000). ... Selected by Scottish Claymores in NFL Europe draft (February 18, 2000). ... Released by Patriots (August 1, 2000). ... Signed by Miami Dolphins (August 3, 2000). ... Released by Dolphins (August 14, 2000). ... Signed by Kansas City Chiefs to practice squad (October 25, 2000). ... Signed by Dallas Cowboys off Chiefs practice squad (December 15, 2000).
PLAYING EXPERIENCE: Scottish NFLE, 2000; Dallas NFL, 2000. ... Games/Games started: NFLE 2000 (games played unavailable), NFL 2000 (1/0).
PRO STATISTICS: NFLE: 2000—Credited with 2$\frac{1}{2}$ sacks.

SCHAU, RYAN   OT/G   EAGLES

PERSONAL: Born December 30, 1975, in Hammond, Ind. ... 6-6/300. ... Twin brother of Thomas Schau, center, Green Bay Packers.
HIGH SCHOOL: Bloomington (Ill.).
COLLEGE: Illinois.
TRANSACTIONS/CAREER NOTES: Signed as non-drafted free agent by Philadelphia Eagles (April 19, 1999).
PLAYING EXPERIENCE: Philadelphia NFL, 1999 and 2000. ... Games/Games started: 1999 (1/0), 2000 (10/0). Total: 11/0.

SCHLERETH, MARK   G

PERSONAL: Born January 25, 1966, in Anchorage, Alaska. ... 6-3/287. ... Name pronounced SHLARE-eth.
HIGH SCHOOL: Robert Service (Anchorage, Alaska).
COLLEGE: Idaho.
TRANSACTIONS/CAREER NOTES: Selected by Washington Redskins in 10th round (263rd pick overall) of 1989 NFL draft. ... Signed by Redskins (July 23, 1989). ... On injured reserve with knee injury (September 5-November 11, 1989). ... On injured reserve with a nerve condition known as Guillain-Barre Syndrome (November 16, 1993-remainder of season). ... Released by Redskins (September 2, 1994). ... Re-signed by Redskins (September 3, 1994). ... Granted unconditional free agency (February 17, 1995). ... Signed by Denver Broncos (March 27, 1995). ... Released by Broncos (February 14, 1997). ... Re-signed by Broncos (April 11, 1997). ... Granted unconditional free agency (February 13, 1998). ... Re-signed by Broncos (February 24, 1998). ... On injured reserve with knee injury (November 15, 2000-remainder of season). ... Granted unconditional free agency (March 2, 2001). ... Announced retirement (April 18, 2001).
PLAYING EXPERIENCE: Washington NFL, 1989-1994; Denver NFL, 1995-2000. ... Games/Games started: 1989 (6/6), 1990 (12/7), 1991 (16/16), 1992 (16/16), 1993 (9/8), 1994 (16/6), 1995 (16/16), 1996 (14/14), 1997 (11/11), 1998 (16/16), 1999 (16/16), 2000 (8/8). Total: 156/140.
CHAMPIONSHIP GAME EXPERIENCE: Played in NFC championship game (1991 season). ... Member of Super Bowl championship team (1991, 1997 and 1998 seasons). ... Played in AFC championship game (1997 and 1998 seasons).
HONORS: Played in Pro Bowl (1991 and 1998 seasons).
PRO STATISTICS: 1989—Recovered one fumble. 1993—Recovered one fumble. 1997—Recovered one fumble.

SCHLESINGER, CORY   FB   LIONS

PERSONAL: Born June 23, 1972, in Columbus, Neb. ... 6-0/246.
HIGH SCHOOL: Columbus (Neb.).
COLLEGE: Nebraska (degree in indusrial technology education).
TRANSACTIONS/CAREER NOTES: Selected by Detroit Lions in sixth round (192nd pick overall) of 1995 NFL draft. ... Signed by Lions (July 19, 1995). ... Granted unconditional free agency (March 2, 2001). ... Re-signed by Lions (March 2, 2001).
PRO STATISTICS: 1995—Recovered one fumble for 11 yards. 1999—Returned two kickoffs for 33 yards and recovered one fumble. 2000—Returned two kickoffs for 25 yards.
SINGLE GAME HIGHS (regular season): Attempts—10 (September 12, 1999, vs. Seattle); yards—50 (September 12, 1999, vs. Seattle); and rushing touchdowns—0.

			RUSHING				RECEIVING				TOTALS			
Year Team	G	GS	Att.	Yds.	Avg.	TD	No.	Yds.	Avg.	TD	TD	2pt.	Pts.	Fum.
1995—Detroit NFL	16	1	1	1	1.0	0	1	2	2.0	0	0	0	0	0
1996—Detroit NFL	16	1	0	0	0.0	0	0	0	0.0	0	0	0	0	0
1997—Detroit NFL	16	2	7	11	1.6	0	5	69	13.8	1	1	0	6	0
1998—Detroit NFL	15	2	5	17	3.4	0	3	16	5.3	1	1	0	6	0
1999—Detroit NFL	16	11	43	124	2.9	0	21	151	7.2	1	1	0	6	4
2000—Detroit NFL	16	8	1	3	3.0	0	12	73	6.1	0	0	0	0	0
Pro totals (6 years)	95	25	57	156	2.7	0	42	311	7.4	3	3	0	18	4

SCHNECK, MIKE   C   STEELERS

PERSONAL: Born August 4, 1977, in Whitefish Bay, Wis. ... 6-0/242.
HIGH SCHOOL: Whitefish Bay (Wisc.).
COLLEGE: Wisconsin.
TRANSACTIONS/CAREER NOTES: Signed as non-drafted free agent by Pittsburgh Steelers (April 23, 1999); contract voided by NFL because he did not meet eligibility requirements. ... Re-signed by Steelers (July 12, 1999).
PLAYING EXPERIENCE: Pittsburgh NFL, 1999 and 2000. ... Games/Games started: 1999 (16/0), 2000 (16/0). Total: 32/0.

SCHROEDER, BILL   WR   PACKERS

PERSONAL: Born January 9, 1971, in Eau Claire, Wis. ... 6-3/205. ... Full name: William Fredrich Schroeder. ... Name pronounced SHRAY-der.
HIGH SCHOOL: Sheboygan (Wis.) South.
COLLEGE: Wisconsin-La Crosse (degree in physical education/teaching).
TRANSACTIONS/CAREER NOTES: Selected by Green Bay Packers in sixth (181st pick overall) of 1994 NFL draft. ... Signed by Packers (May 10, 1994). ... Released by Packers (August 28, 1994). ... Re-signed by Packers to practice squad (August 30, 1994). ... Activated (December 29, 1994). ... Traded by Packers with TE Jeff Wilner to New England Patriots for C Mike Arthur (August 11, 1995). ... On injured reserve with foot injury (August 27, 1995-entire season). ... Released by Patriots (August 14, 1996). ... Signed by Packers to practice squad (August 28, 1996). ... Assigned by Packers to Rhein Fire in 1997 World League enhancement allocation program (February 19, 1997). ... On injured reserve with broken collarbone (December 9, 1998-remainder of season).
CHAMPIONSHIP GAME EXPERIENCE: Member of Packers for NFC championship game (1997 season); inactive. ... Member of Packers for Super Bowl XXXII (1997 season); inactive.
PRO STATISTICS: W.L.: 1997—Rushed twice of 18 yards. NFL: 1997—Recovered one fumble. 2000—Rushed twice for 11 yards.
SINGLE GAME HIGHS (regular season): Receptions—8 (December 17, 2000, vs. Minnesota); yards—158 (October 10, 1999, vs. Tampa Bay); and touchdown receptions—2 (October 1, 2000, vs. Chicago).
STATISTICAL PLATEAUS: 100-yard receiving games: 1998 (1), 1999 (1), 2000 (3). Total: 5.

Year Team	G	GS	RECEIVING				PUNT RETURNS				KICKOFF RETURNS				TOTALS			
			No.	Yds.	Avg.	TD	No.	Yds.	Avg.	TD	No.	Yds.	Avg.	TD	TD	2pt.	Pts.	Fum.
1994—Green Bay NFL............									Did not play.									
1995—New England NFL.......									Did not play.									
1996—Green Bay NFL............									Did not play.									
1997—Rhein W.L.	...	...	43	702	16.3	6	0	0	0.0	0	1	20	20.0	0	6	0	36	0
—Green Bay NFL............	15	1	2	15	7.5	1	33	342	10.4	0	24	562	23.4	0	1	0	6	4
1998—Green Bay NFL............	13	3	31	452	14.6	1	2	5	2.5	0	0	0	0.0	0	1	0	6	1
1999—Green Bay NFL............	16	16	74	1051	14.2	5	0	0	0.0	0	1	10	10.0	0	5	0	30	3
2000—Green Bay NFL............	16	16	65	999	15.4	4	0	0	0.0	0	0	0	0.0	0	4	0	24	1
W.L. totals (1 year)	...	...	43	702	16.3	6	0	0	0.0	0	1	20	20.0	0	6	0	36	0
NFL totals (3 years)...............	60	36	172	2517	14.6	11	35	347	9.9	0	25	572	22.9	0	11	0	66	9
Pro totals (4 years)................	...	...	215	3219	15.0	17	35	347	9.9	0	26	592	22.8	0	17	0	102	9

SCHULTERS, LANCE — S — 49ERS

PERSONAL: Born May 27, 1975, in Brooklyn, N.Y. ... 6-2/195.
HIGH SCHOOL: Canarsie (Brooklyn, N.Y.).
JUNIOR COLLEGE: Nassau Community College (N.Y.).
COLLEGE: Hofstra.
TRANSACTIONS/CAREER NOTES: Selected by San Francisco 49ers in fourth round (119th pick overall) of 1998 NFL draft. ... Signed by 49ers (July 18, 1998). ... On injured reserve with knee injury (December 21, 2000-remainder of season). ... Granted free agency (March 2, 2001).
HONORS: Played in Pro Bowl (1999 season).
PRO STATISTICS: 2000—Credited with 1/2 sack and recovered one fumble for 16 yards.

Year Team	G	GS	INTERCEPTIONS			
			No.	Yds.	Avg.	TD
1998—San Francisco NFL.......................................	15	0	0	0	0.0	0
1999—San Francisco NFL.......................................	13	13	6	127	21.2	1
2000—San Francisco NFL.......................................	12	12	0	0	0.0	0
Pro totals (3 years)	40	25	6	127	21.2	1

SCHULZ, KURT — S — LIONS

PERSONAL: Born December 12, 1968, in Wenatchee, Wash. ... 6-1/208. ... Full name: Kurt Erich Schulz.
HIGH SCHOOL: Eisenhower (Yakima, Wash.).
COLLEGE: Eastern Washington.
TRANSACTIONS/CAREER NOTES: Selected by Buffalo Bills in seventh round (195th pick overall) of 1992 NFL draft. ... Signed by Bills (July 22, 1992). ... On injured reserve with knee injury (October 26-December 19, 1992). ... Granted unconditional free agency (February 11, 2000). ... Signed by Detroit Lions (February 18, 2000).
CHAMPIONSHIP GAME EXPERIENCE: Played in AFC championship game (1993 season). ... Member of Bills for Super Bowl XXVII (1992 season); inactive. ... Played in Super Bowl XXVIII (1993 season).
PRO STATISTICS: 1992—Recovered two fumbles. 1998—Recovered one fumble for nine yards. 1999—Recovered one fumble.

Year Team	G	GS	INTERCEPTIONS			
			No.	Yds.	Avg.	TD
1992—Buffalo NFL	8	1	0	0	0.0	0
1993—Buffalo NFL	12	0	0	0	0.0	0
1994—Buffalo NFL	16	0	0	0	0.0	0
1995—Buffalo NFL	13	13	6	48	8.0	▲1
1996—Buffalo NFL	15	15	4	24	6.0	0
1997—Buffalo NFL	15	14	2	23	11.5	0
1998—Buffalo NFL	12	12	6	48	8.0	0
1999—Buffalo NFL...	16	16	3	26	8.7	0
2000—Detroit NFL...	11	11	7	53	7.6	0
Pro totals (9 years)	118	82	28	222	7.9	1

SCIOLI, BRAD — DE — COLTS

PERSONAL: Born September 6, 1976, in Bridgeport, Pa. ... 6-3/274. ... Full name: Brad Elliott Scioli. ... Name pronounced SHE-o-lee.
HIGH SCHOOL: Upper Merion (King of Prussia, Pa.).
COLLEGE: Penn State.
TRANSACTIONS/CAREER NOTES: Selected by Indianapolis Colts in fifth round (138th pick overall) of 1999 NFL draft. ... Signed by Colts (July 22, 1999).
PLAYING EXPERIENCE: Indianapolis NFL, 1999 and 2000. ... Games/Games started: 1999 (10/0), 2000 (16/2). Total: 26/2.
PRO STATISTICS: 2000—Credited with two sacks.

SCOTT, CHAD — DB — STEELERS

PERSONAL: Born September 6, 1974, in Washington, D.C. ... 6-1/192. ... Full name: Chad Oliver Scott.
HIGH SCHOOL: Suitland (Forestville, Md.).
COLLEGE: Towson State, then Maryland.
TRANSACTIONS/CAREER NOTES: Selected by Pittsburgh Steelers in first round (24th pick overall) of 1997 NFL draft. ... Signed by Steelers (July 16, 1997). ... On injured reserve with knee injury (July 20, 1998-entire season).
CHAMPIONSHIP GAME EXPERIENCE: Played in AFC championship game (1997 season).
PRO STATISTICS: 2000—Recovered two fumbles for six yards.

Year—Team	G	GS	No.	Yds.	Avg.	TD
			INTERCEPTIONS			
1997—Pittsburgh NFL	13	9	2	-4	-2.0	0
1998—Pittsburgh NFL			Did not play.			
1999—Pittsburgh NFL	13	12	1	16	16.0	0
2000—Pittsburgh NFL	16	16	5	49	9.8	0
Pro totals (3 years)	42	37	8	61	7.6	0

SCOTT, DARNAY   WR   BENGALS

PERSONAL: Born July 7, 1972, in St. Louis. ... 6-1/205.
HIGH SCHOOL: Kearny (San Diego).
COLLEGE: San Diego State.
TRANSACTIONS/CAREER NOTES: Selected after junior season by Cincinnati Bengals in second round (30th pick overall) of 1994 NFL draft. ... Signed by Bengals (July 18, 1994). ... Granted free agency (February 14, 1997). ... Re-signed by Bengals (June 16, 1997). ... On injured reserve with broken leg (August 2, 2000-entire season).
PRO STATISTICS: 1994—Completed only pass attempt for 53 yards.
SINGLE GAME HIGHS (regular season): Receptions—8 (October 10, 1999, vs. Cleveland); yards—157 (November 6, 1994, vs. Seattle); and touchdown receptions—2 (November 21, 1999, vs. Baltimore).
STATISTICAL PLATEAUS: 100-yard receiving games: 1994 (2), 1995 (1), 1996 (1), 1997 (2), 1998 (2), 1999 (2). Total: 10.

Year—Team	G	GS	Att.	Yds.	Avg.	TD	No.	Yds.	Avg.	TD	No.	Yds.	Avg.	TD	TD	2pt.	Pts.	Fum.
			RUSHING				**RECEIVING**				**KICKOFF RETURNS**				**TOTALS**			
1994—Cincinnati NFL	16	12	10	106	10.6	0	46	866	§18.8	5	15	342	22.8	0	5	0	30	0
1995—Cincinnati NFL	16	16	5	11	2.2	0	52	821	15.8	5	0	0	0.0	0	5	0	30	0
1996—Cincinnati NFL	16	16	3	4	1.3	0	58	833	14.4	5	0	0	0.0	0	5	0	30	0
1997—Cincinnati NFL	16	15	1	6	6.0	0	54	797	14.8	5	0	0	0.0	0	5	0	30	0
1998—Cincinnati NFL	13	13	2	10	5.0	0	51	817	16.0	7	0	0	0.0	0	7	0	42	0
1999—Cincinnati NFL	16	16	0	0	0.0	0	68	1022	15.0	7	0	0	0.0	0	7	0	42	0
2000—Cincinnati NFL							Did not play.											
Pro totals (6 years)	93	88	21	137	6.5	0	329	5156	15.7	34	15	342	22.8	0	34	0	204	0

SCOTT, GARI   WR   EAGLES

PERSONAL: Born June 2, 1978, in West Palm Beach, Fla. ... 6-0/191.
HIGH SCHOOL: Suncoast (Riviera Beach, Fla.).
COLLEGE: Michigan State.
TRANSACTIONS/CAREER NOTES: Selected by Philadelphia Eagles in fourth round (99th pick overall) of 2000 NFL draft. ... Signed by Eagles (June 16, 2000). ... Active for one game (2000); did not play.

Year—Team	G	GS	No.	Yds.	Avg.	TD	No.	Yds.	Avg.	TD	No.	Yds.	Avg.	TD	TD	2pt.	Pts.	Fum.
			RECEIVING				**PUNT RETURNS**				**KICKOFF RETURNS**				**TOTALS**			
2000—Philadelphia NFL							Did not play.											

SCOTT, LANCE   C/G   PATRIOTS

PERSONAL: Born February 15, 1972, in Salt Lake City. ... 6-3/295.
HIGH SCHOOL: Taylorsville (Salt Lake City).
COLLEGE: Utah (degree in exercise and sports science).
TRANSACTIONS/CAREER NOTES: Selected by Arizona Cardinals in fifth round (165th pick overall) of 1995 NFL draft. ... Signed by Cardinals (July 24, 1995). ... Released by Cardinals (August 27, 1995). ... Re-signed by Cardinals to practice squad (October 2, 1995). ... Activated (November 14, 1995); did not play. ... Inactive for one game (1996). ... On injured reserve with shoulder injury (October 16, 1996-remainder of season). ... Released by Cardinals (August 19, 1997). ... Signed by New York Giants (August 25, 1997). ... Granted free agency (February 13, 1998). ... Re-signed by Giants (April 8, 1998). ... Granted unconditional free agency (February 12, 1999). ... Re-signed by Giants (May 11, 1999). ... On injured reserve with knee injury (September 6, 1999-entire season). ... Released by Giants (February 10, 2000). ... Signed by New England Patriots (April 10, 2000). ... On injured reserve with knee injury (August 27, 2000-entire season).
PLAYING EXPERIENCE: New York Giants NFL, 1997 and 1998. ... Games/Games started: 1997 (16/11), 1998 (16/16). Total: 32/27.
PRO STATISTICS: 1998—Fumbled once and recovered one fumble for minus one yard.

SCOTT, TONY   CB   JETS

PERSONAL: Born October 3, 1976, in Lawndale, N.C. ... 5-10/193.
HIGH SCHOOL: Lawndale (N.C.).
COLLEGE: North Carolina State.
TRANSACTIONS/CAREER NOTES: Selected by New York Jets in sixth round (179th pick overall) of 2000 NFL draft. ... Signed by Jets (May 9, 2000).
PRO STATISTICS: 2000—Returned one kickoff for no yards and recovered one fumble.

Year—Team	G	GS	No.	Yds.	Avg.	TD
			INTERCEPTIONS			
2000—New York Jets NFL	16	0	1	0	0.0	0

SCOTT, YUSUF   G   CARDINALS

PERSONAL: Born November 30, 1976, in LaPorte, Texas ... 6-3/348. ... Full name: Yusuf Jamall Scott.
HIGH SCHOOL: La Porte (Texas).
COLLEGE: Arizona (degree in sociology).
TRANSACTIONS/CAREER NOTES: Selected after junior season by Arizona Cardinals in fifth round (168th pick overall) of 1999 NFL draft. ... Signed by Cardinals (June 18, 1999).
PLAYING EXPERIENCE: Arizona NFL, 1999 and 2000. ... Games/Games started: 1999 (10/0), 2000 (9/0). Total: 19/0.

S

SCROGGINS, TRACY — DE — LIONS

PERSONAL: Born September 11, 1969, in Checotah, Okla. ... 6-3/273.
HIGH SCHOOL: Checotah (Okla.).
JUNIOR COLLEGE: Coffeyville (Kan.) Community College.
COLLEGE: Tulsa.
TRANSACTIONS/CAREER NOTES: Selected by Detroit Lions in second round (53rd pick overall) of 1992 NFL draft. ... Signed by Lions (July 23, 1992). ... Granted free agency (February 17, 1995). ... Re-signed by Lions (May 17, 1995). ... Granted unconditional free agency (March 2, 2001). ... Re-signed by Lions (May 3, 2001).
PRO STATISTICS: 1993—Intercepted one pass for no yards and recovered one fumble. 1994—Recovered one fumble. 1995—Recovered one fumble for 81 yards and a touchdown. 1996—Recovered one fumble. 1997—Recovered one fumble for 17 yards and a touchdown and credited with a safety. 1999—Recovered two fumbles for four yards.

Year Team	G	GS	SACKS
1992—Detroit NFL	16	7	7.5
1993—Detroit NFL	16	0	8.0
1994—Detroit NFL	16	9	2.5
1995—Detroit NFL	16	16	9.5
1996—Detroit NFL	6	6	2.0
1997—Detroit NFL	15	6	7.5
1998—Detroit NFL	11	3	6.5
1999—Detroit NFL	14	11	8.5
2000—Detroit NFL	16	15	6.5
Pro totals (9 years)	126	73	58.5

SEARCY, LEON — OT — RAVENS

PERSONAL: Born December 21, 1969, in Washington, D.C. ... 6-4/320. ... Full name: Leon Searcy Jr.
HIGH SCHOOL: Maynard Evans (Orlando).
COLLEGE: Miami, Fla. (degree in sociology, 1992).
TRANSACTIONS/CAREER NOTES: Selected by Pittsburgh Steelers in first round (11th pick overall) of 1992 NFL draft. ... Signed by Steelers (August 3, 1992). ... Granted unconditional free agency (February 16, 1996). ... Signed by Jacksonville Jaguars (February 18, 1996). ... Inactive for 12 games (2000). ... On injured reserve with leg injury (November 29, 2000-remainder of season). ... Released by Jaguars (March 1, 2001). ... Signed by Baltimore Ravens (March 12, 2001).
PLAYING EXPERIENCE: Pittsburgh NFL, 1992-1995; Jacksonville NFL, 1996-1999. ... Games/Games started: 1992 (15/0), 1993 (16/16), 1994 (16/16), 1995 (16/16), 1996 (16/16), 1997 (16/16), 1998 (15/15), 1999 (16/16). Total: 126/111.
CHAMPIONSHIP GAME EXPERIENCE: Played in AFC championship game (1994-1996 and 1999 seasons). ... Played in Super Bowl XXX (1995 season).
HONORS: Named offensive tackle on THE SPORTING NEWS college All-America second team (1991). ... Played in Pro Bowl (1999 season).
PRO STATISTICS: 1993—Recovered one fumble. 1995—Recovered one fumble. 1996—Recovered one fumble.

SEARS, COREY — DT

PERSONAL: Born April 15, 1973, in San Antonio. ... 6-3/300. ... Full name: Corey Alexander Sears.
HIGH SCHOOL: Judson (Converse, Texas).
JUNIOR COLLEGE: Navarro College (Texas).
COLLEGE: Mississippi State.
TRANSACTIONS/CAREER NOTES: Signed as non-drafted free agent by Baltimore Ravens (April 29, 1996). ... On injured reserve with knee injury (August 20-November 6, 1996). ... Released by Ravens (November 6, 1996). ... Signed by St. Louis Rams (April 24, 1998). ... Claimed on waivers by San Francisco 49ers (August 26, 1998). ... Released by 49ers (August 28, 1998). ... Signed by Rams to practice squad (September 1, 1998). ... Activated (November 30, 1998). ... Claimed on waivers by Arizona Cardinals (September 6, 1999). ... Released by Cardinals (February 19, 2001).
PLAYING EXPERIENCE: St. Louis NFL, 1998; Arizona NFL, 1999 and 2000. ... Games/Games started: 1998 (4/0), 1999 (9/1), 2000 (8/2). Total: 21/3.
PRO STATISTICS: 2000—Recovered one fumble.

SEAU, JUNIOR — LB — CHARGERS

PERSONAL: Born January 19, 1969, in San Diego. ... 6-3/250. ... Full name: Tiaina Seau Jr. ... Name pronounced SAY-ow.
HIGH SCHOOL: Oceanside (Calif.).
COLLEGE: Southern California.
TRANSACTIONS/CAREER NOTES: Selected after junior season by San Diego Chargers in first round (fifth pick overall) of 1990 NFL draft. ... Signed by Chargers (August 27, 1990).
CHAMPIONSHIP GAME EXPERIENCE: Played in AFC championship game (1994 season). ... Played in Super Bowl XXIX (1994 season).
HONORS: Named linebacker on THE SPORTING NEWS college All-America first team (1989). ... Played in Pro Bowl (1991-2000 seasons). ... Named inside linebacker on THE SPORTING NEWS NFL All-Pro team (1992-1996, 1998 and 2000).
PRO STATISTICS: 1992—Recovered one fumble for 10 yards. 1993—Recovered one fumble for 21 yards. 1994—Recovered three fumbles. 1995—Recovered three fumbles for 30 yards and one touchdown. 1996—Recovered three fumbles. 1997—Fumbled once and recovered two fumbles for five yards. 1998—Recovered two fumbles. 1999—Caught two passes for eight yards and recovered one fumble.

Year Team	G	GS	INTERCEPTIONS No.	Yds.	Avg.	TD	SACKS No.
1990—San Diego NFL	16	15	0	0	0.0	0	1.0
1991—San Diego NFL	16	16	0	0	0.0	0	7.0
1992—San Diego NFL	15	15	2	51	25.5	0	4.5
1993—San Diego NFL	16	16	2	58	29.0	0	0.0
1994—San Diego NFL	16	16	0	0	0.0	0	5.5
1995—San Diego NFL	16	16	2	5	2.5	0	2.0

Year	Team	G	GS	No.	Yds.	Avg.	TD	No.
				INTERCEPTIONS				SACKS
1996—San Diego NFL		15	15	2	18	9.0	0	7.0
1997—San Diego NFL		15	15	2	33	16.5	0	7.0
1998—San Diego NFL		16	16	0	0	0.0	0	3.5
1999—San Diego NFL		14	14	1	16	16.0	0	3.5
2000—San Diego NFL		16	16	2	2	1.0	0	3.5
Pro totals (11 years)		171	170	13	183	14.1	0	44.5

SEDER, TIM   K   COWBOYS

PERSONAL: Born September 17, 1974, in Ashland, Ohio. ... 5-9/180.
HIGH SCHOOL: Lucas (Ashland, Ohio).
COLLEGE: Ashland University.
TRANSACTIONS/CAREER NOTES: Signed as non-drafted free agent by Dallas Cowboys (April 6, 2000).
PRO STATISTICS: 2000—Rushed once for one yard and a touchdown.

					KICKING				
Year	Team	G	XPM	XPA	FGM	FGA	Lg.	50+	Pts.
2000—Dallas NFL		15	27	27	25	33	48	0-1	108

SEHORN, JASON   CB   GIANTS

PERSONAL: Born April 15, 1971, in Sacramento. ... 6-2/215.
HIGH SCHOOL: Mt. Shasta (Calif.).
JUNIOR COLLEGE: Shasta College (Calif.).
COLLEGE: Southern California.
TRANSACTIONS/CAREER NOTES: Selected by New York Giants in second round (59th pick overall) of 1994 NFL draft. ... Signed by Giants (July 17, 1994). ... Granted free agency (February 14, 1997). ... Re-signed by Giants (August 9, 1997). ... On injured reserve with knee injury (August 25, 1998-entire season). ... Granted unconditional free agency (March 2, 2001). ... Re-signed by Giants (March 2, 2001).
CHAMPIONSHIP GAME EXPERIENCE: Played in NFC championship game (2000 season). ... Played in Super Bowl XXXV (2000 season).
PRO STATISTICS: 1996—Credited with three sacks, returned one punt for no yards, fumbled once and recovered one fumble. 1997—Credited with 1¹/₂ sacks and recovered one fumble for two yards. 1999—Fumbled once for minus one yard. 2000—Returned two kickoffs for 31 yards and one touchdown and recovered one fumble for eight yards.

				INTERCEPTIONS			
Year	Team	G	GS	No.	Yds.	Avg.	TD
1994—New York Giants NFL		8	0	0	0	0.0	0
1995—New York Giants NFL		14	0	0	0	0.0	0
1996—New York Giants NFL		16	15	5	61	12.2	1
1997—New York Giants NFL		16	16	6	74	12.3	1
1998—New York Giants NFL				Did not play.			
1999—New York Giants NFL		10	10	1	-4	-4.0	0
2000—New York Giants NFL		14	14	2	32	16.0	0
Pro totals (6 years)		78	55	14	163	11.6	2

RECORD AS BASEBALL PLAYER

TRANSACTIONS/CAREER NOTES: Threw right, batted right. ... Signed as non-drafted free agent by Chicago Cubs organization (July 24, 1989). ... Released by Cubs (April 4, 1991).

									BATTING						FIELDING		
Year	Team (League)	Pos.	G	AB	R	H	2B	3B	HR	RBI	Avg.	BB	SO	SB	PO	A	E	Avg.
1990—Huntington (Appal.)....		OF	49	125	21	23	3	1	1	10	.184	8	52	9	82	3	5	.944

SELLERS, MIKE   FB   BROWNS

PERSONAL: Born July 21, 1975, in Frankfurt, West Germany. ... 6-3/260.
HIGH SCHOOL: North Thurston (Lacey, Wash.).
JUNIOR COLLEGE: Walla Walla (Wash.) Community College.
COLLEGE: None.
TRANSACTIONS/CAREER NOTES: Signed by Edmonton Eskimos of CFL (March 21, 1995). ... Tranferred by Eskimos to reserve list (August 23, 1995). ... Transferred by Eskimos to injured list (October 12, 1995). ... Transferred by Eskimos to active roster (December 18, 1995). ... Signed as non-drafted free agent by Washington Redskins (February 11, 1998). ... Granted free agency (March 2, 2001). ... Signed by Cleveland Browns (March 15, 2001).
PRO STATISTICS: CFL: 1997—Rushed 40 times for 133 yards, returned one kickoff for 14 yards and recovered one fumble for 43 yards. 1998—Returned two kickoffs for 33 yards and recovered one fumble. 1999—Returned three kickoffs for 32 yards. 2000—Rushed once for two yards and returned three kickoffs for 32 yards.
SINGLE GAME HIGHS (regular season): Attempts—1 (September 24, 2000, vs. New York Giants); yards—2 (September 24, 2000, vs. New York Giants); and rushing touchdowns—0; receptions—3 (December 27, 1998, vs. Dallas); yards—18 (December 27, 1998, vs. Dallas); and touchdown receptions—0.

				RECEIVING				TOTALS			
Year	Team	G	GS	No.	Yds.	Avg.	TD	TD	2pt.	Pts.	Fum.
1996—Edmonton CFL		17	...	0	0	0.0	0	0	0	0	0
1997—Edmonton CFL		16	...	0	0	0.0	0	0	0	0	0
1998—Washington NFL		14	1	3	18	6.0	0	0	0	0	0
1999—Washington NFL		16	2	7	105	15.0	2	2	0	12	1
2000—Washington NFL		15	7	8	78	9.8	2	2	0	12	0
CFL totals (2 years)		33	...	0	0	0.0	0	0	0	0	0
NFL totals (3 years)		45	10	18	201	11.2	4	4	0	24	1
Pro totals (5 years)		78	...	18	201	11.2	4	4	0	24	1

SEMPLE, TONY — G

PERSONAL: Born December 20, 1970, in Springfield, Ill. ... 6-5/303. ... Full name: Anthony Lee Semple.
HIGH SCHOOL: Lincoln (Ill.) Community.
COLLEGE: Memphis State (degree in sports administration).
TRANSACTIONS/CAREER NOTES: Selected by Detroit Lions in fifth round (154th pick overall) of 1994 NFL draft. ... Signed by Lions (July 21, 1994). ... On injured reserve with knee injury (August 19, 1994-entire season). ... Granted free agency (February 14, 1997). ... Re-signed by Lions (June 13, 1997). ... Granted unconditional free agency (February 13, 1998). ... Re-signed by Lions (February 21, 1998). ... Granted unconditional free agency (March 2, 2001).
PLAYING EXPERIENCE: Detroit NFL, 1995-2000. ... Games/Games started: 1995 (16/0), 1996 (15/1), 1997 (16/1), 1998 (16/3), 1999 (12/12), 2000 (11/8). Total: 86/25.

SERWANGA, KATO — CB — PATRIOTS

PERSONAL: Born July 23, 1976, in Kampala, Uganda, Africa. ... 6-0/198. ... Twin brother of Wasswa Serwanga, cornerback, Minnesota Vikings. ... Name pronounced kah-TOE ser-WAN-guh.
HIGH SCHOOL: Sacramento (Calif.).
COLLEGE: Sacramento State, then Pacific, then California.
TRANSACTIONS/CAREER NOTES: Signed as non-drafted free agent by New England Patriots (April 24, 1998). ... Released by Patriots (August 30, 1998). ... Re-signed by Patriots to practice squad (August 31, 1998). ... Activated (December 12, 1998); did not play. ... Assigned by Patriots to Scottish Claymores in 2001 NFL Europe enhancement allocation program (February 19, 2001).
PRO STATISTICS: 1999—Credited with one sack and recovered one fumble. 2000—Credited with two sacks and recovered two fumbles.

			INTERCEPTIONS			
Year Team	G	GS	No.	Yds.	Avg.	TD
1998—New England NFL			Did not play.			
1999—New England NFL	16	3	3	2	0.7	0
2000—New England NFL	15	0	0	0	0.0	0
Pro totals (2 years)	31	3	3	2	0.7	0

SERWANGA, WASSWA — CB — VIKINGS

PERSONAL: Born July 23, 1976, in Kampala, Uganda, Africa. ... 5-11/203. ... Full name: Wasswa Kenneth Serwanga. ... Twin brother of Kato Serwanga, cornerback, New England Patriots. ... Name pronounced ser-WAN-guh.
HIGH SCHOOL: Sacramento (Calif.).
COLLEGE: Sacramento State, then Pacific, then UCLA.
TRANSACTIONS/CAREER NOTES: Signed as non-drafted free agent by Chicago Bears (April 21, 1998). ... Released by Bears (August 21, 1998). ... Signed by San Francisco 49ers (April 23, 1999). ... Released by 49ers (September 5, 1999). ... Re-signed by 49ers to practice squad (September 7, 1999). ... Activated (October 12, 1999). ... Granted free agency (February 11, 2000). ... Selected by Amsterdam Admirals in 2000 NFL Europe draft (February 22, 2000). ... Signed by Kansas City Chiefs (April 24, 2000). ... Released by Chiefs (August 22, 2000). ... Signed by Minnesota Vikings (August 23, 2000).
PLAYING EXPERIENCE: San Francisco NFL, 1999; Minnesota NFL, 2000. ... Games/Games started: 1999 (9/0), 2000 (7/2). Total: 16/2.
CHAMPIONSHIP GAME EXPERIENCE: Played in NFC championship game (2000 season).

SHADE, SAM — S — REDSKINS

PERSONAL: Born June 14, 1973, in Birmingham, Ala. ... 6-1/201.
HIGH SCHOOL: Wenonah (Birmingham, Ala.).
COLLEGE: Alabama.
TRANSACTIONS/CAREER NOTES: Selected by Cincinnati Bengals in fourth round (102nd pick overall) of 1995 NFL draft. ... Signed by Bengals (July 18, 1995). ... Granted free agency (February 13, 1998). ... Re-signed by Bengals (June 15, 1998). ... Granted unconditional free agency (February 12, 1999). ... Signed by Washington Redskins (February 18, 1999).
PRO STATISTICS: 1997—Fumbled once and recovered one fumble. 1998—Recovered two fumbles for 55 yards and one touchdown. 1999—Recovered one fumble. 2000—Recovered four fumbles for one yard.

			INTERCEPTIONS				SACKS
Year Team	G	GS	No.	Yds.	Avg.	TD	No.
1995—Cincinnati NFL	16	2	0	0	0.0	0	0.0
1996—Cincinnati NFL	12	0	0	0	0.0	0	0.0
1997—Cincinnati NFL	16	12	1	21	21.0	0	4.0
1998—Cincinnati NFL	16	14	3	33	11.0	0	1.0
1999—Washington NFL	16	16	2	7	3.5	0	1.5
2000—Washington NFL	16	14	2	15	7.5	0	1.0
Pro totals (6 years)	92	58	8	76	9.5	0	7.5

SHARPE, SHANNON — TE — RAVENS

PERSONAL: Born June 26, 1968, in Chicago. ... 6-2/232. ... Brother of Sterling Sharpe, wide receiver with Green Bay Packers (1988-94).
HIGH SCHOOL: Glennville (Ga.).
COLLEGE: Savannah (Ga.) State.
TRANSACTIONS/CAREER NOTES: Selected by Denver Broncos in seventh round (192nd pick overall) of 1990 NFL draft. ... Signed by Broncos (July 1990). ... Granted free agency (February 1, 1992). ... Re-signed by Broncos (July 31, 1992). ... Designated by Broncos as transition player (February 15, 1994). ... On injured reserve with broken collarbone (November 30, 1999-remainder of season). ... Granted unconditional free agency (February 11, 2000). ... Signed by Baltimore Ravens (February 16, 2000).

S

CHAMPIONSHIP GAME EXPERIENCE: Played in AFC championship game (1991, 1997, 1998 and 2000 seasons). ... Member of Super Bowl championship team (1997, 1998 and 2000 seasons).

HONORS: Played in Pro Bowl (1992, 1993 and 1995-1997 seasons). ... Named tight end on THE SPORTING NEWS NFL All-Pro team (1993 and 1996-1998). ... Named to play in Pro Bowl (1994 season); replaced by Eric Green due to injury. ... Named to play in Pro Bowl (1998 season); replaced by Frank Wycheck due to injury.

POST SEASON RECORDS: Shares NFL postseason single-game record for most receptions—13 (January 9, 1994, vs. Los Angeles Raiders).

PRO STATISTICS: 1991—Rushed once for 15 yards and recovered one fumble. 1992—Rushed twice for minus six yards. 1993—Returned one kickoff for no yards. 1995—Recovered one fumble.

SINGLE GAME HIGHS (regular season): Receptions—13 (October 6, 1996, vs. San Diego); yards—180 (September 3, 1995, vs. Buffalo); and touchdown receptions—3 (October 6, 1996, vs. San Diego).

STATISTICAL PLATEAUS: 100-yard receiving games: 1992 (2), 1993 (2), 1994 (1), 1995 (2), 1996 (3), 1997 (4), 2000 (2). Total: 16.

MISCELLANEOUS: Holds Denver Broncos all-time records for most receiving yards (6,983) and most receptions (552). ... Shares Denver Broncos all-time record most touchdown receptions (44).

Year Team	G	GS	RECEIVING No.	Yds.	Avg.	TD	TOTALS TD	2pt.	Pts.	Fum.
1990—Denver NFL	16	2	7	99	14.1	1	1	0	6	1
1991—Denver NFL	16	9	22	322	14.6	1	1	0	6	0
1992—Denver NFL	16	11	53	640	12.1	2	2	0	12	1
1993—Denver NFL	16	12	81	995	12.3	§9	9	0	54	1
1994—Denver NFL	15	13	87	1010	11.6	4	4	2	28	1
1995—Denver NFL	13	12	63	756	12.0	4	4	0	24	1
1996—Denver NFL	15	15	80	1062	13.3	10	10	0	60	1
1997—Denver NFL	16	16	72	1107	15.4	3	3	1	20	1
1998—Denver NFL	16	16	64	768	12.0	▲10	10	0	60	0
1999—Denver NFL	5	5	23	224	9.7	0	0	0	0	0
2000—Baltimore NFL	16	15	67	810	12.1	5	5	0	30	0
Pro totals (11 years)	160	126	619	7793	12.6	49	49	3	300	7

SHARPER, DARREN S PACKERS

PERSONAL: Born November 3, 1975, in Richmond, Va. ... 6-2/205. ... Full name: Darren Mallory Sharper. ... Brother of Jamie Sharper, linebacker, Baltimore Ravens.

HIGH SCHOOL: Hermitage (Richmond, Va.).

COLLEGE: William & Mary.

TRANSACTIONS/CAREER NOTES: Selected by Green Bay Packers in second round (60th pick overall) of 1997 NFL draft. ... Signed by Packers (July 11, 1997).

CHAMPIONSHIP GAME EXPERIENCE: Played in NFC championship game (1997 season). ... Played in Super Bowl XXXII (1997 season).

HONORS: Named safety on THE SPORTING NEWS NFL All-Pro team (2000). ... Played in Pro Bowl (2000 season).

PRO STATISTICS: 1997—Returned one kickoff for three yards and recovered one fumble for 34 yards and a touchdown. 1999—Returned one kickoff for four yards, credited with one sack and recovered one fumble for nine yards. 2000—Credited with one sack.

Year Team	G	GS	INTERCEPTIONS No.	Yds.	Avg.	TD	PUNT RETURNS No.	Yds.	Avg.	TD	TOTALS TD	2pt.	Pts.	Fum.
1997—Green Bay NFL	14	0	2	70	35.0	∞2	7	32	4.6	0	3	0	18	1
1998—Green Bay NFL	16	16	0	0	0.0	0	0	0	0.0	0	0	0	0	0
1999—Green Bay NFL	16	16	3	12	4.0	0	0	0	0.0	0	0	0	0	0
2000—Green Bay NFL	16	16	*9	109	12.1	0	0	0	0.0	0	0	0	0	0
Pro totals (4 years)	62	48	14	191	13.6	2	7	32	4.6	0	3	0	18	1

SHARPER, JAMIE LB RAVENS

PERSONAL: Born November 23, 1974, in Richmond, Va. ... 6-3/240. ... Full name: Harry Jamie Sharper Jr. ... Brother of Darren Sharper, safety, Green Bay Packers.

HIGH SCHOOL: Hermitage (Glen Allen, Va.).

COLLEGE: Virginia (degree in psychology, 1996).

TRANSACTIONS/CAREER NOTES: Selected by Baltimore Ravens in second round (34th pick overall) of 1997 NFL draft. ... Signed by Ravens (July 23, 1997). ... Granted free agency (February 11, 2000). ... Re-signed by Ravens (June 16, 2000). ... Granted unconditional free agency (March 2, 2001). ... Re-signed by Ravens (April 3, 2001).

CHAMPIONSHIP GAME EXPERIENCE: Played in AFC championship game (2000 season). ... Member of Super Bowl championship team (2000 season).

PRO STATISTICS: 1997—Intercepted one pass for four yards and fumbled once. 2000—Intercepted one pass for 45 yards and recovered two fumbles.

Year Team	G	GS	SACKS
1997—Baltimore NFL	16	15	3.0
1998—Baltimore NFL	16	16	1.0
1999—Baltimore NFL	16	16	4.0
2000—Baltimore NFL	16	16	0.0
Pro totals (4 years)	64	63	8.0

SHAW, BOBBY WR STEELERS

PERSONAL: Born April 23, 1975, in San Francisco. ... 6-0/186.

HIGH SCHOOL: Galileo (San Francisco).

COLLEGE: California.

TRANSACTIONS/CAREER NOTES: Selected by Seattle Seahawks in sixth round (169th pick overall) of 1998 NFL draft. ... Signed by Seahawks (June 5, 1998). ... Released by Seahawks (August 30, 1998). ... Re-signed by Seahawks to practice squad (August 31, 1998). ... Activated (November 4, 1998). ... Released by Seahawks (November 18, 1998). ... Signed by Pittsburgh Steelers (November 20, 1998). ... Granted free agency (March 2, 2001).

HONORS: Named wide receiver on THE SPORTING NEWS college All-America first team (1997).
PRO STATISTICS: 2000—Ran minus eight yards with lateral.
SINGLE GAME HIGHS (regular season): Receptions—7 (January 2, 2000, vs. Tennessee); yards—131 (January 2, 2000, vs. Tennessee); and touchdown receptions—1 (December 10, 2000, vs. New York Giants).
STATISTICAL PLATEAUS: 100-yard receiving games: 1999 (1).

			RECEIVING				PUNT RETURNS				TOTALS		
Year Team	G	GS	No.	Yds.	Avg.	TD	No.	Yds.	Avg.	TD	TD	2pt.	Pts.	Fum.
1998—Seattle NFL	1	1	0	0	0.0	0	0	0	0.0	0	0	0	0	0
1999—Pittsburgh NFL	15	1	28	387	13.8	3	4	53	13.3	0	3	0	18	0
2000—Pittsburgh NFL	16	0	40	672	16.8	4	2	17	8.5	0	4	0	24	2
Pro totals (3 years)	32	2	68	1059	15.6	7	6	70	11.7	0	7	0	42	2

SHAW, HAROLD   FB

PERSONAL: Born September 3, 1974, in Magee, Miss. ... 6-0/228. ... Full name: Harold Lamar Shaw.
HIGH SCHOOL: Magee (Miss.).
COLLEGE: Southern Mississippi.
TRANSACTIONS/CAREER NOTES: Selected by New England Patriots in sixth round (176th pick overall) of 1998 NFL draft. ... Signed by Patriots (July 16, 1998). ... Granted free agency (March 2, 2001).
PLAYING EXPERIENCE: New England NFL, 1998-2000. ... Games/Games started: 1998 (11/0), 1999 (8/0), 2000 (16/0). Total: 35/0.
PRO STATISTICS: 1999—Rushed nine times for 23 yards and caught two passes for 31 yards. 2000—Rushed nine times for 12 yards and caught two passes for 11 yards.
SINGLE GAME HIGHS (regular season): Attempts—5 (January 2, 2000, vs. Baltimore); yards—17 (January 2, 2000, vs. Baltimore); and rushing touchdowns—0.

SHAW, TERRANCE   CB   PATRIOTS

PERSONAL: Born November 11, 1973, in Marshall, Texas. ... 5-11/190. ... Full name: Terrance Bernard Shaw.
HIGH SCHOOL: Marshall (Texas).
COLLEGE: Stephen F. Austin State.
TRANSACTIONS/CAREER NOTES: Selected by San Diego Chargers in second round (34th pick overall) of 1995 NFL draft. ... Signed by Chargers (June 15, 1995). ... Released by Chargers (March 21, 2000). ... Signed by Miami Dolphins (June 13, 2000). ... Granted unconditional free agency (March 2, 2001). ... Signed by New England Patriots (March 22, 2001).
PRO STATISTICS: 1997—Recovered one fumble.

			INTERCEPTIONS		
Year Team	G	GS	No.	Yds.	Avg.	TD
1995—San Diego NFL	16	14	1	31	31.0	0
1996—San Diego NFL	16	16	3	78	26.0	0
1997—San Diego NFL	16	16	1	11	11.0	0
1998—San Diego NFL	13	13	2	0	0.0	0
1999—San Diego NFL	8	8	0	0	0.0	0
2000—Miami NFL	11	3	1	0	0.0	0
Pro totals (6 years)	80	70	8	120	15.0	0

SHEA, AARON   TE/FB   BROWNS

PERSONAL: Born December 5, 1976, in Ottawa, Ill. ... 6-3/244.
HIGH SCHOOL: Ottawa (Ill.).
COLLEGE: Michigan.
TRANSACTIONS/CAREER NOTES: Selected by Cleveland Browns in fourth round (110th pick overall) of 2000 NFL draft. ... Signed by Browns (July 13, 2000).
SINGLE GAME HIGHS (regular season): Receptions—6 (October 15, 2000, vs. Denver); yards—76 (October 15, 2000, vs. Denver); and touchdown receptions—1 (November 12, 2000, vs. New England).

			RECEIVING				TOTALS		
Year Team	G	GS	No.	Yds.	Avg.	TD	TD	2pt.	Pts.	Fum.
2000—Cleveland NFL	15	8	30	302	10.1	2	2	0	12	1

SHEDD, KENNY   WR

PERSONAL: Born February 14, 1971, in Davenport, Iowa. ... 5-10/165.
HIGH SCHOOL: Davenport (Iowa) West.
COLLEGE: Northern Iowa.
TRANSACTIONS/CAREER NOTES: Selected by New York Jets in fifth round (129th pick overall) of 1993 NFL draft. ... Signed by Jets (July 13, 1993). ... Released by Jets (August 24, 1993). ... Re-signed by Jets to practice squad (September 1, 1993). ... Activated (December 31, 1993); did not play. ... Released by Jets (September 17, 1994). ... Re-signed by Jets to practice squad (September 21, 1994). ... Signed by Chicago Bears off Jets practice squad (October 25, 1994). ... Inactive for nine games (1994). ... Released by Bears (August 27, 1995). ... Selected by London Monarchs in 1996 World League draft (February 22, 1996). ... Signed by Barcelona Dragons of World League (May 23, 1996). ... Signed by Oakland Raiders (June 1996). ... Released by Raiders (August 27, 2000). ... Signed by Washington Redskins (November 9, 2000). ... Granted unconditional free agency (March 2, 2001).
PRO STATISTICS: NFL: 1996—Credited with a safety and returned three kickoffs for 51 yards. 1997—Returned two kickoffs for 38 yards and recovered two fumbles for 25 yards and one touchdown. 1998—Returned two kickoffs for 32 yards and recovered two fumbles for four yards. 1999—Returned a blocked punt 20 yards for a touchdown.
SINGLE GAME HIGHS (regular season): Receptions—3 (September 21, 1997, vs. New York Jets); yards—51 (December 22, 1996, vs. Seattle); and touchdown receptions—1 (September 22, 1996, vs. San Diego).

Year Team	G	GS	RECEIVING No.	Yds.	Avg.	TD	TOTALS TD	2pt.	Pts.	Fum.
1993—New York Jets NFL						Did not play.				
1994—Chicago NFL						Did not play.				
—New York Jets NFL						Did not play.				
1995—						Did not play.				
1996—Barcelona W.L.	...	...	14	328	23.4	1	1	0	6	0
—Oakland NFL	16	1	3	87	29.0	1	1	0	8	0
1997—Oakland NFL	16	0	10	115	11.5	0	1	0	6	0
1998—Oakland NFL	15	0	3	50	16.7	0	0	0	0	0
1999—Oakland NFL	12	0	0	0	0.0	0	1	0	6	0
2000—Washington NFL	1	0	0	0	0.0	0	0	0	0	0
W.L. totals (1 year)	...	...	14	328	23.4	1	1	0	6	0
NFL totals (4 years)	60	1	16	252	15.8	1	3	0	20	0
Pro totals (5 years)	...	...	30	580	19.3	2	4	0	26	0

SHELTON, DAIMON   FB   BEARS

PERSONAL: Born September 15, 1972, in Duarte, Calif. ... 6-0/254.
HIGH SCHOOL: Duarte (Calif.).
JUNIOR COLLEGE: Fresno (Calif.) City College.
COLLEGE: Cal State Sacramento.
TRANSACTIONS/CAREER NOTES: Selected by Jacksonville Jaguars in sixth round (184th pick overall) of 1997 NFL draft. ... Signed by Jaguars (May 23, 1997). ... Granted free agency (February 11, 2000). ... Re-signed by Jaguars (March 21, 2000). ... Granted unconditional free agency (March 2, 2001). ... Signed by Chicago Bears (May 16, 2001).
CHAMPIONSHIP GAME EXPERIENCE: Played in AFC championship game (1999 season).
PRO STATISTICS: 1999—Returned one kickoff for no yards and recovered one fumble. 2000—Recovered two fumbles.
SINGLE GAME HIGHS (regular season): Attempts—13 (October 18, 1998, vs. Buffalo); yards —44 (October 18, 1998, vs. Buffalo); and rushing touchdowns—1 (November 1, 1998, vs. Baltimore).

Year Team	G	GS	RUSHING Att.	Yds.	Avg.	TD	RECEIVING No.	Yds.	Avg.	TD	TOTALS TD	2pt.	Pts.	Fum.
1997—Jacksonville NFL	13	0	6	4	0.7	0	0	0	0.0	0	0	0	0	1
1998—Jacksonville NFL	14	8	30	95	3.2	1	10	79	7.9	0	1	0	6	0
1999—Jacksonville NFL	16	9	1	2	2.0	0	12	87	7.3	0	0	0	0	0
2000—Jacksonville NFL	16	9	2	3	1.5	0	4	48	12.0	0	0	0	0	0
Pro totals (4 years)	59	26	39	104	2.7	1	26	214	8.2	0	1	0	6	1

SHELTON, L.J.   OT   CARDINALS

PERSONAL: Born March 21, 1976, in Monrovia, Calif. ... 6-6/360. ... Full name: Lonnie Jewel Shelton. ... Son of Lonnie Shelton, forward with New York Knicks (1976-77 and 1977-78), Seattle SuperSonics (1978-79 through 1982-83) and Cleveland Cavaliers (1983-84 through 1985-86).
HIGH SCHOOL: Rochester (Rochester Hills, Mich.).
COLLEGE: Eastern Michigan.
TRANSACTIONS/CAREER NOTES: Selected by Arizona Cardinals in first round (21st pick overall) of 1999 NFL draft. ... Signed by Cardinals (September 24, 1999).
PLAYING EXPERIENCE: Arizona NFL, 1999 and 2000. ... Games/Games started: 1999 (9/7), 2000 (14/14). Total: 23/21.
PRO STATISTICS: 2000—Recovered one fumble.

SHEPHERD, JACOBY   CB   RAMS

PERSONAL: Born August 31, 1979, in Lufkin, Texas. ... 6-1/195. ... Full name: Jacoby Lamar Shepherd.
HIGH SCHOOL: Lufkin (Texas).
JUNIOR COLLEGE: Tyler (Texas) Junior College, then Cloud County Community College, Kan. (did not play football).
COLLEGE: Oklahoma State.
TRANSACTIONS/CAREER NOTES: Selected after junior season by St. Louis Rams in second round (62nd pick overall) of 2000 NFL draft. ... Signed by Rams (July 17, 2000).

Year Team	G	GS	INTERCEPTIONS No.	Yds.	Avg.	TD
2000—St. Louis NFL	15	1	1	0	0.0	0

SHEPHERD, LESLIE   WR

PERSONAL: Born November 3, 1969, in Washington, D.C. ... 5-11/186. ... Full name: Leslie Glenard Shepherd.
HIGH SCHOOL: Forestville (Md.).
COLLEGE: Temple.
TRANSACTIONS/CAREER NOTES: Signed as non-drafted free agent by Tampa Bay Buccaneers (May 2, 1992). ... Released by Buccaneers (August 31, 1992). ... Signed by Pittsburgh Steelers (March 17, 1993). ... Released by Steelers (August 24, 1993). ... Re-signed by Steelers to practice squad (August 31, 1993). ... Claimed on waivers by Washington Redskins (September 4, 1994). ... Released by Redskins (September 16, 1994). ... Re-signed by Redskins to practice squad (September 20, 1994). ... Activated (December 2, 1994). ... On injured reserve with elbow and wrist injuries (November 19, 1997-remainder of season). ... Granted unconditional free agency (February 12, 1999). ... Signed by Cleveland Browns (April 7, 1999). ... On injured reserve with knee injury (December 6, 1999-remainder of season). ... Granted unconditional free agency (February 11, 2000). ... Signed by Miami Dolphins (June 19, 2000). ... Granted unconditional free agency (March 2, 2001).

PRO STATISTICS: 1995—Returned three kickoffs for 85 yards and recovered one fumble. 1996—Recovered one fumble. 2000—Returned 15 punts for 164 yards and returned one kickoff for 14 yards.

SINGLE GAME HIGHS (regular season): Receptions—7 (November 26, 2000, vs. Indianapolis); yards—135 (October 29, 1995, vs. New York Giants); and touchdown receptions—2 (November 23, 2000, vs. New York Jets).

STATISTICAL PLATEAUS: 100-yard receiving games: 1995 (1), 1998 (1). Total: 2.

			RUSHING				RECEIVING				TOTALS			
Year Team	G	GS	Att.	Yds.	Avg.	TD	No.	Yds.	Avg.	TD	TD	2pt.	Pts.	Fum.
1994—Washington NFL	3	0	0	0	0.0	0	1	8	8.0	0	0	0	0	0
1995—Washington NFL	14	4	7	63	9.0	1	29	486	16.8	2	3	0	18	0
1996—Washington NFL	12	6	6	96	16.0	2	23	344	15.0	3	5	0	30	0
1997—Washington NFL	11	9	4	27	6.8	0	29	562	19.4	5	5	0	30	0
1998—Washington NFL	16	16	6	91	15.2	1	43	712	16.6	8	9	1	56	0
1999—Cleveland NFL	9	8	1	5	5.0	0	23	274	11.9	0	0	0	0	0
2000—Miami NFL	13	11	4	3	0.8	0	35	446	12.7	4	4	0	24	0
Pro totals (7 years)	78	54	28	285	10.2	4	183	2832	15.5	22	26	1	158	0

SHIELDS, PAUL   RB   CARDINALS

PERSONAL: Born January 31, 1976, in Mesa, Ariz. ... 6-1/238. ... Full name: Paul L. Shields Jr.

HIGH SCHOOL: Camelback (Scottsdale, Ariz.).

JUNIOR COLLEGE: Scottsdale (Ariz.) Community College.

COLLEGE: Arizona.

TRANSACTIONS/CAREER NOTES: Signed as non-drafted free agent by Indianapolis Colts (April 22, 1999). ... Released by Colts (September 6, 1999). ... Re-signed by Colts to practice squad (September 7, 1999). ... Released by Colts (September 15, 1999). ... Re-signed by Colts (September 29, 1999). ... Released by Colts (August 27, 2000). ... Re-signed by Colts (October 3, 2000). ... Released by Colts (October 7, 2000). ... Re-signed by Colts (October 9, 2000). ... Granted free agency (March 2, 2001). ... Signed by Arizona Cardinals (May 22, 2001).

PLAYING EXPERIENCE: Indianapolis NFL, 1999 and 2000. ... Games/Games started: 1999 (13/3), 2000 (7/0). Total: 20/3.

PRO STATISTICS: 1999—Caught four passes for 37 yards and returned one kickoff for three yards.

SHIELDS, SCOTT   S

PERSONAL: Born March 29, 1976, in San Diego. ... 6-4/228. ... Full name: Scott Paul Shields.

HIGH SCHOOL: Bonita Vista (Chula Vista, Calif.).

COLLEGE: Weber State.

TRANSACTIONS/CAREER NOTES: Selected by Pittsburgh Steelers in second round (59th pick overall) of 1999 NFL draft. ... Signed by Steelers (August 2, 1999). ... On injured reserve with broken thumb (November 18, 2000-remainder of season). ... Released by Steelers (June 4, 2001).

PRO STATISTICS: 2000—Fumbled once and recovered two fumbles for minus five yards.

			INTERCEPTIONS				SACKS
Year Team	G	GS	No.	Yds.	Avg.	TD	No.
1999—Pittsburgh NFL	16	1	4	75	18.8	0	1.0
2000—Pittsburgh NFL	10	1	0	0	0.0	0	0.0
Pro totals (2 years)	26	2	4	75	18.8	0	1.0

SHIELDS, WILL   G   CHIEFS

PERSONAL: Born September 15, 1971, in Fort Riley, Kan. ... 6-3/311. ... Full name: Will Herthie Shields.

HIGH SCHOOL: Lawton (Okla.).

COLLEGE: Nebraska (degree in communications).

TRANSACTIONS/CAREER NOTES: Selected by Kansas City Chiefs in the third round (74th pick overall) of 1993 NFL draft. ... Signed by Chiefs (May 3, 1993). ... Designated by Chiefs as franchise player (February 11, 2000).

PLAYING EXPERIENCE: Kansas City NFL, 1993-2000. ... Games/Games started: 1993 (16/15), 1994 (16/16), 1995 (16/16), 1996 (16/16), 1997 (16/16), 1998 (16/16), 1999 (16/16), 2000 (16/16). Total: 128/127.

CHAMPIONSHIP GAME EXPERIENCE: Played in AFC championship game (1993 season).

HONORS: Named guard on THE SPORTING NEWS college All-America second team (1991). ... Named guard on THE SPORTING NEWS college All-America first team (1992). ... Named guard on THE SPORTING NEWS NFL All-Pro team (1999). ... Played in Pro Bowl (1995-2000 seasons).

PRO STATISTICS: 1993—Recovered two fumbles. 1994—Recovered one fumble. 1995—Recovered one fumble. 1998—Caught one pass for four yards and recovered one fumble. 1999—Recovered one fumble. 2000—Recovered one fumble.

SHIVERS, WES   OT   FALCONS

PERSONAL: Born March 8, 1977, in Jackson, Miss. ... 6-5/298. ... Full name: Wesley Davis Shivers.

HIGH SCHOOL: Brandon (Miss.), then Benton (Miss.) Academy.

JUNIOR COLLEGE: Hinds Community College (Miss.).

COLLEGE: Mississippi State.

TRANSACTIONS/CAREER NOTES: Selected by Tennessee Titans in seventh round (238th pick overall) of 2000 NFL draft. ... Signed by Titans (July 5, 2000). ... Released by Titans (August 26, 2000). ... Signed by Atlanta Falcons to practice squad (August 30, 2000). ... Activated (November 14, 2000).

PLAYING EXPERIENCE: Atlanta NFL, 2000. ... Games/Games started: 2000 (3/0).

SHORT, BRANDON   LB   GIANTS

PERSONAL: Born July 11, 1977, in McKeesport, Pa. ... 6-3/255. ... Full name: Brandon Darnell Short.
HIGH SCHOOL: McKeesport (Pa.).
COLLEGE: Penn State (degree in marketing, 1999).
TRANSACTIONS/CAREER NOTES: Selected by New York Giants in fourth round (105th pick overall) of 2000 NFL draft. ... Signed by Giants (July 25, 2000).
PLAYING EXPERIENCE: New York Giants NFL, 2000. ... Games/Games started: 2000 (11/0).
CHAMPIONSHIP GAME EXPERIENCE: Played in NFC championship game (2000 season). ... Played in Super Bowl XXXV (2000 season).
HONORS: Named linebacker on THE SPORTING NEWS college All-America second team (1999).

SIDNEY, DAINON   CB   TITANS

PERSONAL: Born May 30, 1975, in Atlanta. ... 6-0/188. ... Full name: Dainon Tarquinius Sidney. ... Name pronounced DAY-nun.
HIGH SCHOOL: Riverdale (Ga.).
COLLEGE: East Tennessee State, then Alabama-Birmingham.
TRANSACTIONS/CAREER NOTES: Selected by Tennessee Oilers in third round (77th pick overall) of 1998 NFL draft. ... Signed by Oilers (July 21, 1998). ... Oilers franchise renamed Tennessee Titans for 1999 season (December 26, 1998). ... Granted free agency (March 2, 2001).
PLAYING EXPERIENCE: Tennessee NFL, 1998-2000. ... Games/Games started: 1998 (16/1), 1999 (16/2), 2000 (11/2). Total: 43/5.
CHAMPIONSHIP GAME EXPERIENCE: Played in AFC championship game (1999 season). ... Played in Super Bowl XXXIV (1999 season).
PRO STATISTICS: 1999—Intercepted three passes for 12 yards and returned one punt for four yards. 2000—Intercepted three passes for 19 yards and recovered two fumbles.

SIMMONS, ANTHONY   LB   SEAHAWKS

PERSONAL: Born June 20, 1976, in Spartanburg, S.C. ... 6-0/230.
HIGH SCHOOL: Spartanburg (S.C.).
COLLEGE: Clemson (degree in marketing, 1998).
TRANSACTIONS/CAREER NOTES: Selected after junior season by Seattle Seahawks in first round (15th pick overall) of 1998 NFL draft. ... Signed by Seahawks (July 18, 1998).
PLAYING EXPERIENCE: Seattle NFL, 1998-2000. ... Games/Games started: 1998 (11/4), 1999 (16/16), 2000 (16/16). Total: 43/36.
HONORS: Named inside linebacker on THE SPORTING NEWS college All-America first team (1996 and 1997).
PRO STATISTICS: 1998—Intercepted one pass for 36 yards and a touchdown. 2000—Intercepted two passes for 15 yards and credited with four sacks.

SIMMONS, BRIAN   LB   BENGALS

PERSONAL: Born June 21, 1975, in New Bern, N.C. ... 6-3/248. ... Full name: Brian Eugene Simmons.
HIGH SCHOOL: New Bern (N.C.).
COLLEGE: North Carolina.
TRANSACTIONS/CAREER NOTES: Selected by Cincinnati Bengals in first round (17th pick overall) of 1998 NFL draft. ... Signed by Bengals (July 27, 1998). ... On injured reserve with knee injury (November 9, 2000-remainder of season).
HONORS: Named outside linebacker on THE SPORTING NEWS college All-America second team (1996). ... Named outside linebacker on THE SPORTING NEWS college All-America third team (1997).
PRO STATISTICS: 1998—Intercepted one pass for 18 yards and recovered one fumble for 22 yards. 1999—Recovered one fumble.

Year Team	G	GS	SACKS
1998—Cincinnati NFL	14	12	3.0
1999—Cincinnati NFL	16	16	3.0
2000—Cincinnati NFL	1	1	1.0
Pro totals (3 years)	31	29	7.0

SIMMONS, CLYDE   DE   BEARS

PERSONAL: Born August 4, 1964, in Lanes, S.C. ... 6-5/292. ... Full name: Clyde Simmons Jr.
HIGH SCHOOL: New Hanover (Wilmington, N.C.).
COLLEGE: Western Carolina (degree in industrial distribution).
TRANSACTIONS/CAREER NOTES: Selected by Philadelphia Eagles in ninth round (233rd pick overall) of 1986 NFL draft. ... Signed by Eagles (July 3, 1986). ... Granted free agency (February 1, 1991). ... Re-signed by Eagles (August 28, 1991). ... Designated by Eagles as transition player (February 15, 1994). ... Signed by Phoenix Cardinals (March 17, 1994); Eagles received second-round pick (DB Brian Dawkins) in 1996 draft as compensation. ... Cardinals franchise renamed Arizona Cardinals for 1994 season. ... Released by Cardinals (August 19, 1996). ... Signed by Jacksonville Jaguars (August 23, 1996). ... Released by Jaguars (March 6, 1998). ... Signed by Cincinnati Bengals (May 13, 1998). ... Granted unconditional free agency (February 12, 1999). ... Signed by Chicago Bears (February 17, 1999). ... Granted unconditional free agency (March 2, 2001). ... Re-signed by Bears (May 15, 2001).
CHAMPIONSHIP GAME EXPERIENCE: Played in AFC championship game (1996 season).
HONORS: Played in Pro Bowl (1991 and 1992 seasons). ... Named defensive end on THE SPORTING NEWS NFL All-Pro team (1991).
PRO STATISTICS: 1986—Returned one kickoff for no yards. 1987—Recovered one fumble. 1988—Credited with one safety, ran 15 yards with blocked field-goal attempt and recovered three fumbles. 1989—Intercepted one pass for 60 yards and a touchdown. 1990—Recovered two fumbles for 28 yards and one touchdown. 1991—Recovered three fumbles (including one in end zone for a touchdown). 1992—Recovered one fumble. 1993—Intercepted one pass for no yards. 1995—Intercepted one pass for 25 yards and a touchdown and recovered one fumble. 1996—Recovered one fumble. 1999—Recovered one fumble. 2000—Recovered one fumble.

Year	Team	G	GS	SACKS
1986—Philadelphia NFL		16	0	2.0
1987—Philadelphia NFL		12	12	6.0
1988—Philadelphia NFL		16	16	8.0
1989—Philadelphia NFL		16	16	15.5
1990—Philadelphia NFL		16	16	7.5
1991—Philadelphia NFL		16	16	13.0
1992—Philadelphia NFL		16	16	*19.0
1993—Philadelphia NFL		16	16	5.0
1994—Arizona NFL		16	16	6.0
1995—Arizona NFL		16	16	11.0
1996—Jacksonville NFL		16	14	7.5
1997—Jacksonville NFL		16	13	8.5
1998—Cincinnati NFL		16	16	5.0
1999—Chicago NFL		16	0	7.0
2000—Chicago NFL		16	2	0.5
Pro totals (15 years)		236	185	121.5

SIMMONS, JASON   CB   STEELERS

PERSONAL: Born March 30, 1976, in Inglewood, Calif. ... 5-8/186. ... Full name: Jason Lawrence Simmons.
HIGH SCHOOL: Leuzinger (Lawndale, Calif.).
COLLEGE: Arizona State.
TRANSACTIONS/CAREER NOTES: Selected by Pittsburgh Steelers in fifth round (137th pick overall) of 1998 NFL draft. ... Signed by Steeler (July 14, 1998). ... Granted free agency (March 2, 2001). ... Re-signed by Steelers (April 26, 2001).
PLAYING EXPERIENCE: Pittsburgh NFL, 1998-2000. ... Games/Games started: 1998 (6/0), 1999 (16/0), 2000 (15/0). Total: 37/0.
PRO STATISTICS: 1999—Recovered one fumble.

SIMMONS, TONY   WR   PATRIOTS

PERSONAL: Born December 8, 1974, in Galliopolis, Ohio. ... 6-1/210. ... Full name: Tony Angelo Simmons.
HIGH SCHOOL: St. Rita (Chicago).
COLLEGE: Wisconsin (degree in construction administration).
TRANSACTIONS/CAREER NOTES: Selected by New England Patriots in second round (52nd pick overall) of 1998 NFL draft. ... Signed b Patriots (July 18, 1998). ... Assigned by Patriots to Barcelona Dragons in 2001 NFL Europe enhancement allocation program (February 19 2001).
PRO STATISTICS: 1999—Returned six kickoffs for 132 yards. 2000—Returned six kickoffs for 82 yards.
SINGLE GAME HIGHS (regular season): Receptions—7 (October 10, 1999, vs. Kansas City); yards—109 (November 1, 1998, vs Indianapolis); and touchdown receptions—1 (October 8, 2000, vs. Indianapolis).
STATISTICAL PLATEAUS: 100-yard receiving games: 1998 (1), 1999 (1). Total: 2.

				RECEIVING				TOTALS		
Year	Team	G	GS	No.	Yds.	Avg.	TD	TD	2pt.	Pts.	Fum.
1998—New England NFL		11	6	23	474	20.6	3	3	0	18	0
1999—New England NFL		15	1	19	276	14.5	2	2	0	12	1
2000—New England NFL		12	2	14	231	16.5	1	1	0	6	0
Pro totals (3 years)		38	9	56	981	17.5	6	6	0	36	1

SIMON, COREY   DT   EAGLES

PERSONAL: Born March 2, 1977, in Boynton Beach, Fla. ... 6-2/293.
HIGH SCHOOL: Ely (Pompano Beach, Fla.).
COLLEGE: Florida State.
TRANSACTIONS/CAREER NOTES: Selected by Philadelphia Eagles in first round (sixth pick overall) of 2000 NFL draft. ... Signed by Eagle (July 28, 2000).
HONORS: Named defensive tackle on THE SPORTING NEWS college All-America first team (1999).
PRO STATISTICS: 2000—Recovered one fumble for five yards.

Year	Team	G	GS	SACKS
2000—Philadelphia NFL		16	16	9.5

SIMONEAU, MARK   LB   FALCONS

PERSONAL: Born January 16, 1977, in Phillipsburg, Kan. ... 6-0/234.
HIGH SCHOOL: Smith Center (Kan.).
COLLEGE: Kansas State.
TRANSACTIONS/CAREER NOTES: Selected by Atlanta Falcons in third round (67th pick overall) of 2000 NFL draft. ... Signed by Falcons (May 17, 2000).

Year	Team	G	GS	SACKS
2000—Atlanta NFL		14	4	0.5

SIMPSON, ANTOINE   DT

PERSONAL: Born December 7, 1976, in Gary, Ind. ... 6-2/310. ... Full name: Antoine Lagree Simpson.
HIGH SCHOOL: La Porte (Texas).
JUNIOR COLLEGE: Fort Scott (Kan.) Community College.
COLLEGE: Houston.

TRANSACTIONS/CAREER NOTES: Signed as non-drafted free agent by Miami Dolphins (April 23, 1998). ... Released Dolphins (August 25, 1998). ... Re-signed by Dolphins to practice squad (September 1, 1998). ... Released by Dolphins (September 8, 1998). ... Re-signed by Dolphins (February 3, 1999). ... Released by Dolphins (August 16, 2000). ... Signed by San Diego Chargers to practice squad (October 18, 2000). ... Activated (November 10, 2000). ... Released by Chargers (March 29, 2001).
PLAYING EXPERIENCE: Miami NFL, 1999; San Diego NFL, 2000. ... Games/Games started: 1999 (3/0), 2000 (7/0). Total: 10/0.
PRO STATISTICS: 2000—Recovered one fumble.

SIMS, BARRY　　　　　G/OT　　　　　RAIDERS

PERSONAL: Born December 1, 1974, in Park City, Utah. ... 6-5/295.
HIGH SCHOOL: Park City (Utah).
JUNIOR COLLEGE: Dixie College (Utah).
COLLEGE: Utah.
TRANSACTIONS/CAREER NOTES: Selected by Scottish Claymores in 1999 NFL Europe draft (February 23, 1999). ... Signed as non-drafted free agent by Oakland Raiders (July 1999).
PLAYING EXPERIENCE: Scottish NFLE, 1999; Oakland NFL, 1999 and 2000. ... Games/Games started: NFLE 1999 (games played unavailable), NFL 1999 (16/10), 2000 (16/8). Total NFL: 32/18.
CHAMPIONSHIP GAME EXPERIENCE: Played in AFC championship game (2000 season).
PRO STATISTICS: 2000—Recovered one fumble.

SIMS, KEITH　　　　　　G

PERSONAL: Born June 17, 1967, in Baltimore. ... 6-3/318. ... Full name: Keith Alexander Sims.
HIGH SCHOOL: Watchung Hills Regional (Warren, N.J.).
COLLEGE: Iowa State (degree in industrial technology, 1989).
TRANSACTIONS/CAREER NOTES: Selected by Miami Dolphins in second round (39th pick overall) of 1990 NFL draft. ... Signed by Dolphins (July 30, 1990). ... On injured reserve with knee injury (October 12-November 18, 1991). ... Granted free agency (March 1, 1993). ... Re-signed by Dolphins (July 16, 1993). ... Granted unconditional free agency (February 16, 1996). ... Re-signed by Dolphins (March 8, 1996). ... Released by Dolphins (December 9, 1997). ... Signed by Washington Redskins (December 11, 1997). ... Inactive for two games with Redskins (1997). ... Granted unconditional free agency (February 13, 1998). ... Signed by Philadelphia Eagles (March 2, 1998). ... Released by Eagles (August 30, 1998). ... Signed by Washington Redskins (November 24, 1998). ... Granted unconditional free agency (February 12, 1999). ... Re-signed by Redskins (March 16, 1999). ... Granted unconditional free agency (February 11, 2000). ... Re-signed by Redskins (February 23, 2000). ... On injured reserve with Achilles' tendon injury (December 12, 2000-remainder of season). ... Released by Redskins (February 21, 2001).
PLAYING EXPERIENCE: Miami NFL, 1990-1997; Washington NFL, 1998-2000. ... Games/Games started: 1990 (14/13), 1991 (12/12), 1992 (16/16), 1993 (16/16), 1994 (16/16), 1995 (16/16), 1996 (15/15), 1997 (8/4), 1998 (4/0), 1999 (12/12), 2000 (13/13). Total: 142/133.
CHAMPIONSHIP GAME EXPERIENCE: Played in AFC championship game (1992 season).
HONORS: Played in Pro Bowl (1993-1995 seasons).
PRO STATISTICS: 1990—Returned one kickoff for nine yards and recovered one fumble. 1991—Caught one pass for nine yards. 1993—Recovered one fumble. 1994—Recovered two fumbles. 1995—Recovered one fumble. 2000—Recovered one fumble.

SINCENO, KASEEM　　　　　TE　　　　　BEARS

PERSONAL: Born March 26, 1976, in Bronx, N.Y. ... 6-4/255. ... Name pronounced sin-SEE-no.
HIGH SCHOOL: Liberty (N.Y.).
COLLEGE: Syracuse.
TRANSACTIONS/CAREER NOTES: Signed as non-drafted free agent by Phiadelphia Eagles (April 21, 1998). ... Released by Eagles (August 30, 1998). ... Re-signed by Eagles to practice squad (September 1, 1998). ... Activated (September 17, 1998). ... On injured reserve with ankle injury (December 1, 1998-remainder of season). ... On injured reserve with foot injury (September 5, 1999-entire season). ... Traded by Eagles to Green Bay Packers for TE Jeff Thomason (March 16, 2000). ... Released by Packers (August 27, 2000). ... Re-signed by Packers (September 5, 2000). ... Released by Packers (September 22, 2000). ... Signed by Chicago Bears (October 2, 2000). ... Granted free agency (March 2, 2001). ... Re-signed by Bears (April 25, 2001).
PLAYING EXPERIENCE: Philadelphia NFL, 1998; Chicago NFL, 2000. ... Games/Games started: 1998 (10/0), 2000 (11/11). Total: 21/11.
PRO STATISTICS: 1998—Caught three passes for 42 yards and one touchdown and fumbled once. 2000—Caught 23 passes for 206 yards and returned one kickoff for 12 yards.
SINGLE GAME HIGHS (regular season): Receptions—4 (December 3, 2000, vs. Green Bay); yards—47 (December 3, 2000, vs. Green Bay); and touchdown receptions—1 (October 11, 1998, vs. Washington).

SINCLAIR, MICHAEL　　　　　DE　　　　　SEAHAWKS

PERSONAL: Born January 31, 1968, in Galveston, Texas. ... 6-4/275. ... Full name: Michael Glenn Sinclair.
HIGH SCHOOL: Charlton-Pollard (Beaumont, Texas).
COLLEGE: Eastern New Mexico (degree in physical education).
TRANSACTIONS/CAREER NOTES: Selected by Seattle Seahawks in sixth round (155th pick overall) of 1991 NFL draft. ... Signed by Seahawks (July 18, 1991). ... Released by Seahawks (August 26, 1991). ... Re-signed by Seahawks to practice squad (August 28, 1991). ... Activated (November 30, 1991). ... On injured reserve with back injury (December 14, 1991-remainder of season). ... Active for two games (1991); did not play. ... Assigned by Seahawks to Sacramento Surge in 1992 World League enhancement allocation program (February 20, 1992). ... On injured reserve with ankle injury (September 1-October 3, 1992). ... On injured reserve with thumb injury (November 10, 1993-remainder of season). ... Granted free agency (February 17, 1995). ... Re-signed by Seahawks (May 24, 1995). ... Granted unconditional free agency (February 16, 1996). ... Re-signed by Seahawks (February 17, 1996).
HONORS: Named defensive end on All-World League team (1992). ... Played in Pro Bowl (1996-1998 seasons).
PRO STATISTICS: W.L.: 1992—Recovered one fumble. NFL: 1995—Recovered two fumbles. 1997—Recovered one fumble in end zone for a touchdown. 1999—Recovered one fumble for 13 yards. 2000—Recovered four fumbles for 69 yards and a touchdown.

Year Team	G	GS	SACKS
1991—Seattle NFL	Did not play.		
1992—Sacramento W.L.	10	10	10.0
—Seattle NFL	12	1	1.0
1993—Seattle NFL	9	1	8.0
1994—Seattle NFL	12	2	4.5
1995—Seattle NFL	16	15	5.5
1996—Seattle NFL	16	16	13.0
1997—Seattle NFL	16	16	12.0
1998—Seattle NFL	16	16	*16.5
1999—Seattle NFL	15	15	6.0
2000—Seattle NFL	16	16	3.5
W.L. totals (1 year)	10	10	10.0
NFL totals (8 years)	128	98	70.0
Pro totals (9 years)	138	108	80.0

SINGLETON, ALSHERMOND — LB — BUCCANEERS

PERSONAL: Born August 7, 1975, in Newark, N.J. ... 6-2/228. ... Full name: Alshermond Glendale Singleton.
HIGH SCHOOL: Irvington (N.J.).
COLLEGE: Temple (degree in sports recreation management).
TRANSACTIONS/CAREER NOTES: Selected by Tampa Bay Buccaneers in fourth round (128th pick overall) of 1997 NFL draft. ... Signed by Buccaneers (July 17, 1997).
PLAYING EXPERIENCE: Tampa Bay NFL, 1997-2000. ... Games/Games started: 1997 (12/0), 1998 (15/0), 1999 (15/0), 2000 (13/1). Total: 55/1.
CHAMPIONSHIP GAME EXPERIENCE: Member of Buccaneers for NFC championship game (1999 season); inactive.
PRO STATISTICS: 1997—Returned blocked punt 28 yards for a touchdown. 1999—Intercepted one pass for seven yards and credited with $1/2$ sack.

SIRAGUSA, TONY — DT — RAVENS

PERSONAL: Born May 14, 1967, in Kenilworth, N.J. ... 6-3/340. ... Full name: Anthony Siragusa.
HIGH SCHOOL: David Brearley Regional (Kenilworth, N.J.).
COLLEGE: Pittsburgh.
TRANSACTIONS/CAREER NOTES: Signed as non-drafted free agent by Indianapolis Colts (April 30, 1990). ... Granted unconditional free agency (February 14, 1997). ... Signed by Baltimore Ravens (April 24, 1997).
CHAMPIONSHIP GAME EXPERIENCE: Played in AFC championship game (1995 and 2000 seasons). ... Member of Super Bowl championship team (2000 season).
PRO STATISTICS: 1990—Recovered one fumble. 1991—Recovered one fumble for five yards. 1992—Recovered one fumble. 1994—Recovered one fumble. 1996—Recovered one fumble. 1997—Recovered one fumble for seven yards. 1998—Recovered one fumble. 1999—Recovered one fumble. 2000—Recovered one fumble.

Year Team	G	GS	SACKS
1990—Indianapolis NFL	13	6	1.0
1991—Indianapolis NFL	13	6	2.0
1992—Indianapolis NFL	16	12	3.0
1993—Indianapolis NFL	14	14	1.5
1994—Indianapolis NFL	16	16	5.0
1995—Indianapolis NFL	14	14	2.0
1996—Indianapolis NFL	10	10	2.0
1997—Baltimore NFL	14	13	0.0
1998—Baltimore NFL	15	15	0.0
1999—Baltimore NFL	14	14	3.5
2000—Baltimore NFL	15	15	0.0
Pro totals (11 years)	154	135	20.0

SIRMON, PETER — LB — TITANS

PERSONAL: Born February 18, 1977, in Wenatchee, Wash. ... 6-2/246. ... Full name: Peter Anton Sirmon.
HIGH SCHOOL: Walla Walla (Wash.).
COLLEGE: Oregon.
TRANSACTIONS/CAREER NOTES: Selected by Tennessee Titans in fourth round (128th pick overall) of 2000 NFL draft. ... Signed by Titans (July 11, 2000).
PLAYING EXPERIENCE: Tennessee NFL, 2000. ... Games/Games started: 2000 (5/0).

SLADE, CHRIS — LB

PERSONAL: Born January 30, 1971, in Newport News, Va. ... 6-5/245. ... Full name: Christopher Carroll Slade. ... Cousin of Terry Kirby, running back, Oakland Raiders; and cousin of Wayne Kirby, outfielder, Baltimore Orioles organization.
HIGH SCHOOL: Tabb (Va.).
COLLEGE: Virginia.
TRANSACTIONS/CAREER NOTES: Selected by New England Patriots in second round (31st pick overall) of 1993 NFL draft. ... Signed by Patriots (July 24, 1993). ... Granted free agency (February 16, 1996). ... Re-signed by Patriots (May 28, 1996). ... Released by Patriots (February 27, 2001).

CHAMPIONSHIP GAME EXPERIENCE: Played in AFC championship game (1996 season). ... Played in Super Bowl XXXI (1996 season).
HONORS: Named defensive lineman on THE SPORTING NEWS college All-America first team (1992). ... Played in Pro Bowl (1997 season).
PRO STATISTICS: 1993—Recovered one fumble. 1995—Recovered two fumbles for 38 yards and one touchdown. 1996—Intercepted one pass for two yards and fumbled once. 1997—Intercepted one pass for one yard and a touchdown. 1999—Intercepted one pass for no yards.

Year Team	G	GS	SACKS
1993—New England NFL	16	5	9.0
1994—New England NFL	16	16	9.5
1995—New England NFL	16	16	4.0
1996—New England NFL	16	9	7.0
1997—New England NFL	16	16	9.0
1998—New England NFL	15	15	4.0
1999—New England NFL	16	16	4.5
2000—New England NFL	16	15	4.0
Pro totals (8 years)	**127**	**108**	**51.0**

SLAUGHTER, T.J.　　　　LB　　　　JAGUARS

PERSONAL: Born February 20, 1977, in Birmingham, Ala. ... 6-0/239. ... Full name: Tavaris Jermell Slaughter.
HIGH SCHOOL: John Carroll (Birmingham, Ala.).
COLLEGE: Southern Mississippi.
TRANSACTIONS/CAREER NOTES: Selected by Jacksonville Jaguars in third round (92nd pick overall) of 2000 NFL draft. ... Signed by Jaguars (May 16, 2000).
PLAYING EXPERIENCE: Jacksonville NFL, 2000. ... Games/Games started: 2000 (16/7).

SLOAN, DAVID　　　　TE　　　　LIONS

PERSONAL: Born June 8, 1972, in Fresno, Calif. ... 6-6/260. ... Full name: David Lyle Sloan.
HIGH SCHOOL: Sierra Joint Union (Tollhouse, Calif.).
JUNIOR COLLEGE: Fresno (Calif.) City College.
COLLEGE: New Mexico.
TRANSACTIONS/CAREER NOTES: Selected by Detroit Lions in third round (70th pick overall) of 1995 NFL draft. ... Signed by Lions (July 20, 1995). ... Granted free agency (February 13, 1998). ... Re-signed by Lions (June 10, 1998). ... On physically unable to perform list with knee injury (August 25-October 23, 1998). ... Granted unconditional free agency (February 12, 1999). ... Re-signed by Lions (March 24, 1999).
HONORS: Played in Pro Bowl (1999 season).
PRO STATISTICS: 1995—Returned one kickoff for 14 yards. 1996—Recovered one fumble.
SINGLE GAME HIGHS (regular season): Receptions—7 (November 14, 1999, vs. Arizona); yards—88 (November 14, 1999, vs. Arizona); and touchdown receptions—1 (December 24, 2000, vs. Chicago).

Year Team	G	GS	RECEIVING No.	Yds.	Avg.	TD	TOTALS TD	2pt.	Pts.	Fum.
1995—Detroit NFL	16	8	17	184	10.8	1	1	0	6	0
1996—Detroit NFL	4	4	7	51	7.3	0	0	0	0	0
1997—Detroit NFL	14	12	29	264	9.1	0	0	0	0	0
1998—Detroit NFL	10	2	11	146	13.3	1	1	0	6	0
1999—Detroit NFL	16	15	47	591	12.6	4	4	0	24	0
2000—Detroit NFL	15	10	32	379	11.8	2	2	0	12	0
Pro totals (6 years)	**75**	**51**	**143**	**1615**	**11.3**	**8**	**8**	**0**	**48**	**0**

SMALL, TORRANCE　　　　WR　　　　PATRIOTS

PERSONAL: Born September 4, 1970, in Tampa. ... 6-3/209. ... Full name: Torrance Ramon Small.
HIGH SCHOOL: Thomas Jefferson (Tampa).
COLLEGE: Alcorn State.
TRANSACTIONS/CAREER NOTES: Selected by New Orleans Saints in fifth round (138th pick overall) of 1992 NFL draft. ... Signed by Saints (July 15, 1992). ... Released by Saints (September 3, 1992). ... Re-signed by Saints to practice squad (September 4, 1992). ... Activated (September 19, 1992). ... Granted free agency (February 17, 1995). ... Tendered offer sheet by Seattle Seahawks (March 8, 1995). ... Offer matched by Saints (March 15, 1995). ... Released by Saints (May 28, 1997). ... Signed by St. Louis Rams (June 7, 1997). ... Granted unconditional free agency (February 13, 1998). ... Signed by Indianapolis Colts (April 15, 1998). ... Granted unconditional free agency (February 12, 1999). ... Signed by Philadelphia Eagles (February 16, 1999). ... Released by Eagles (March 1, 2001). ... Signed by New England Patriots (May 31, 2001).
PRO STATISTICS: 1994—Recovered one fumble. 1995—Rushed six times for 75 yards and one touchdown and recovered one fumble. 1996—Rushed four times for 51 yards and one touchdown. 1998—Rushed once for two yards and attempted one pass without a completion. 1999—Attempted two passes without a completion. 2000—Had only pass attempt intercepted and rushed once for no yards.
SINGLE GAME HIGHS (regular season): Receptions—9 (November 29, 1998, vs. Baltimore); yards—200 (December 24, 1994, vs. Denver); and touchdown receptions—2 (December 10, 2000, vs. Cleveland).
STATISTICAL PLATEAUS: 100-yard receiving games: 1994 (1), 1998 (2), 1999 (1), 2000 (1). Total: 5.

Year Team	G	GS	RECEIVING No.	Yds.	Avg.	TD	TOTALS TD	2pt.	Pts.	Fum.
1992—New Orleans NFL	13	2	23	278	12.1	3	3	0	18	0
1993—New Orleans NFL	11	0	16	164	10.3	1	1	0	6	0
1994—New Orleans NFL	16	0	49	719	14.7	5	5	1	32	0
1995—New Orleans NFL	16	1	38	461	12.1	5	6	0	36	0
1996—New Orleans NFL	16	13	50	558	11.2	2	3	0	18	1
1997—St. Louis NFL	13	7	32	488	15.3	1	1	0	6	0
1998—Indianapolis NFL	16	4	45	681	15.1	7	7	0	42	0
1999—Philadelphia NFL	15	15	49	655	13.4	4	4	0	24	0
2000—Philadelphia NFL	14	14	40	569	14.2	3	3	1	20	0
Pro totals (9 years)	**130**	**56**	**342**	**4573**	**13.4**	**31**	**33**	**2**	**202**	**1**

S

SMEENGE, JOEL — DE — BEARS

PERSONAL: Born April 1, 1968, in Holland, Mich. ... 6-6/265. ... Full name: Joel Andrew Smeenge. ... Name pronounced SMEN-ghee.
HIGH SCHOOL: Hudsonville (Mich.).
COLLEGE: Western Michigan.
TRANSACTIONS/CAREER NOTES: Selected by New Orleans Saints in third round (70th pick overall) of 1990 NFL draft. ... Signed by Saints (July 17, 1990). ... Granted free agency (March 1, 1993). ... Re-signed by Saints (July 9, 1993). ... Granted unconditional free agency (February 17, 1995). ... Signed by Jacksonville Jaguars (February 28, 1995). ... On injured reserve with broken jaw (November 12, 1996-remainder of season). ... Released by Jaguars (February 27, 2001). ... Signed by Chicago Bears (May 11, 2001).
CHAMPIONSHIP GAME EXPERIENCE: Played in AFC championship game (1999 season).
PRO STATISTICS: 1991—Recovered one fumble. 1992—Recovered one fumble. 1995—Intercepted one pass for 12 yards and fumbled once. 1997—Recovered two fumbles for one yard. 1998—Recovered one fumble. 1999—Credited with a safety.

Year—Team	G	GS	SACKS
1990—New Orleans NFL	15	0	0.0
1991—New Orleans NFL	14	0	0.0
1992—New Orleans NFL	11	0	0.5
1993—New Orleans NFL	16	2	1.0
1994—New Orleans NFL	16	2	0.0
1995—Jacksonville NFL	15	15	4.0
1996—Jacksonville NFL	10	10	5.0
1997—Jacksonville NFL	16	0	6.5
1998—Jacksonville NFL	16	14	7.5
1999—Jacksonville NFL	15	7	5.0
2000—Jacksonville NFL	12	1	6.0
Pro totals (11 years)	**156**	**51**	**35.5**

SMITH, AARON — DE — STEELERS

PERSONAL: Born April 9, 1976, in Colorado Springs, Colo. ... 6-5/281. ... Full name: Aaron Douglas Smith.
HIGH SCHOOL: Sierra (Colorado Springs, Colo.).
COLLEGE: Northern Colorado.
TRANSACTIONS/CAREER NOTES: Selected by Pittsburgh Steelers in fourth round (109th pick overall) of 1999 NFL draft. ... Signed by Steelers (August 3, 1999).
PLAYING EXPERIENCE: Pittsburgh NFL, 1999 and 2000. ... Games/Games started: 1999 (6/0), 2000 (16/15). Total: 22/15.
PRO STATISTICS: 2000—Credited with four sacks.

SMITH, AKILI — QB — BENGALS

PERSONAL: Born August 21, 1975, in San Diego. ... 6-3/220. ... Full name: Kabisa Akili Maradu Smith. ... Cousin of Marquis Smith, defensive back, Cleveland Browns. ... Name pronounced uh-KEE-lee.
HIGH SCHOOL: Lincoln (San Diego).
JUNIOR COLLEGE: Grossmont College (Calif.).
COLLEGE: Oregon.
TRANSACTIONS/CAREER NOTES: Selected by Cincinnati Bengals in first round (third pick overall) of 1999 NFL draft. ... Signed by Bengals (August 24, 1999).
PRO STATISTICS: 1999—Caught one pass for six yards, fumbled four times and recovered one fumble for minus three yards. 2000—Fumbled 14 times and recovered two fumbles for minus 14 yards.
SINGLE GAME HIGHS (regular season): Attempts—43 (September 10, 2000, vs. Cleveland); completions—25 (October 10, 1999, vs. Cleveland); passing yards—250 (September 10, 2000, vs. Cleveland); and touchdown passes—2 (October 10, 1999, vs. Cleveland).
MISCELLANEOUS: Regular-season record as starting NFL quarterback: 3-12 (.200).

Year—Team	G	GS	Att.	Cmp.	Pct.	Yds.	TD	Int.	Avg.	Rat.	Att.	Yds.	Avg.	TD	TD	2pt.	Pts.
					PASSING							RUSHING				TOTALS	
1999—Cincinnati NFL	7	4	153	80	52.3	805	2	6	5.26	55.6	19	114	6.0	1	1	0	6
2000—Cincinnati NFL	12	11	267	118	44.2	1253	3	6	4.69	52.8	41	232	5.7	0	0	0	0
Pro totals (2 years)	**19**	**15**	**420**	**198**	**47.1**	**2058**	**5**	**12**	**4.90**	**53.8**	**60**	**346**	**5.8**	**1**	**1**	**0**	**6**

RECORD AS BASEBALL PLAYER

TRANSACTIONS/CAREER NOTES: Threw right, batted right. ... Selected by Pittsburgh Pirates organizaiton in seventh round of free-agent draft (June 3, 1993).

Year—Team (League)	Pos.	G	AB	R	H	2B	3B	HR	RBI	Avg.	BB	SO	SB	PO	A	E	Avg.
					BATTING										FIELDING		
1993—GC Pirates (GCL)	OF	29	95	13	19	3	2	1	9	.200	10	18	1	31	2	4	.892
1994—GC Pirates (GCL)	OF	19	69	10	12	3	0	2	10	.173	2	18	0	18	1	0	1.000
1995—Erie (NY-Penn)	OF	14	40	6	5	0	0	1	1	.125	4	13	0	27	5	5	.864

SMITH, ANTOWAIN — RB — BILLS

PERSONAL: Born March 14, 1972, in Montgomery, Ala. ... 6-2/228. ... Full name: Antowain Drurell Smith. ... Name pronounced AN-twan.
HIGH SCHOOL: Elmore (Ala.).
JUNIOR COLLEGE: East Mississippi Junior College.
COLLEGE: Houston.
TRANSACTIONS/CAREER NOTES: Selected by Buffalo Bills in first round (23rd pick overall) of 1997 NFL draft. ... Signed by Bills (July 10, 1997).
PRO STATISTICS: 1998—Recovered two fumbles. 2000—Returned one kickoff for no yards.
SINGLE GAME HIGHS (regular season): Attempts—31 (October 11, 1998, vs. Indianapolis); yards—147 (December 23, 2000, vs. Seattle); and rushing touchdowns—3 (December 23, 2000, vs. Seattle).

STATISTICAL PLATEAUS: 100-yard rushing games: 1997 (1), 1998 (3), 1999 (2), 2000 (1). Total: 7.

Year Team	G	GS	RUSHING Att.	Yds.	Avg.	TD	RECEIVING No.	Yds.	Avg.	TD	TOTALS TD	2pt.	Pts.	Fum.
1997—Buffalo NFL	16	0	194	840	4.3	8	28	177	6.3	0	8	0	48	4
1998—Buffalo NFL	16	14	300	1124	3.7	8	5	11	2.2	0	8	0	48	5
1999—Buffalo NFL	14	11	165	614	3.7	6	2	32	16.0	0	6	0	36	4
2000—Buffalo NFL	11	3	101	354	3.5	4	3	20	6.7	0	4	0	24	1
Pro totals (4 years)	57	28	760	2932	3.9	26	38	240	6.3	0	26	0	156	14

SMITH, BRADY — DE — FALCONS

PERSONAL: Born June 5, 1973, in Royal Oak, Mich. ... 6-5/274. ... Full name: Brady McKay Smith. ... Son of Steve Smith, offensive tackle with four NFL teams (1966-74).
HIGH SCHOOL: Barrington (Ill.).
COLLEGE: Colorado State (degree in liberal arts).
TRANSACTIONS/CAREER NOTES: Selected by New Orleans Saints in third round (70th pick overall) of 1996 NFL draft. ... Signed by Saints (July 12, 1996). ... Granted free agency (February 12, 1999). ... Re-signed by Saints (April 14, 1999). ... Granted unconditional free agency (February 11, 2000). ... Signed by Atlanta Falcons (February 19, 2000).
PRO STATISTICS: 1996—Returned two kickoffs for 14 yards. 1999—Recovered two fumbles.

Year Team	G	GS	SACKS
1996—New Orleans NFL	16	4	2.0
1997—New Orleans NFL	16	2	5.0
1998—New Orleans NFL	14	5	0.0
1999—New Orleans NFL	16	16	6.0
2000—Atlanta NFL	15	14	4.5
Pro totals (5 years)	77	41	17.5

S

SMITH, BRENT — OT — DOLPHINS

PERSONAL: Born November 21, 1973, in Dallas. ... 6-5/315. ... Full name: Gary Brent Smith.
HIGH SCHOOL: Pontotoc (Miss.).
COLLEGE: Mississippi State.
TRANSACTIONS/CAREER NOTES: Selected by Miami Dolphins in third round (96th pick overall) of 1997 NFL draft. ... Signed by Dolphins (July 8, 1997). ... Active for two games (1997); did not play. ... Granted free agency (February 11, 2000).
PLAYING EXPERIENCE: Miami NFL, 1998-2000. ... Games/Games started: 1998 (8/7), 1999 (13/4), 2000 (16/2). Total: 37/13.

SMITH, BRUCE — DE — REDSKINS

PERSONAL: Born June 18, 1963, in Norfolk, Va. ... 6-4/279. ... Full name: Bruce Bernard Smith.
HIGH SCHOOL: Booker T. Washington (Norfolk, Va.).
COLLEGE: Virginia Tech.
TRANSACTIONS/CAREER NOTES: Selected by Baltimore Stars in 1985 USFL territorial draft. ... Signed by Buffalo Bills (February 28, 1985). ... Selected officially by Bills in first round (first pick overall) of 1985 NFL draft. ... On non-football injury list with substance abuse problem (September 2-28, 1988). ... Granted free agency (February 1, 1989). ... Tendered offer sheet by Denver Broncos (March 23, 1989). ... Offer matched by Bills (March 29, 1989). ... On injured reserve with knee injury (October 12-November 30, 1991). ... Released by Bills (February 10, 2000). ... Signed by Washington Redskins (February 14, 2000).
CHAMPIONSHIP GAME EXPERIENCE: Played in AFC championship game (1988 and 1990-1993 seasons). ... Played in Super Bowl XXV (1990 season), Super Bowl XXVI (1991 season), Super Bowl XXVII (1992 season) and Super Bowl XXVIII (1993 season).
HONORS: Named defensive lineman on THE SPORTING NEWS college All-America second team (1983 and 1984). ... Outland Trophy winner (1984). ... Named defensive end on THE SPORTING NEWS NFL All-Pro team (1987, 1988, 1990 and 1992-1997). ... Played in Pro Bowl (1987-1990, 1994, 1995, 1997 and 1998 seasons). ... Named Outstanding Player of Pro Bowl (1987 season). ... Named to play in Pro Bowl (1992 season); replaced by Howie Long due to injury. ... Named to play in Pro Bowl (1993 season); replaced by Sean Jones due to injury. ... Named to play in Pro Bowl (1996 season); replaced by Willie McGinest due to injury.
POST SEASON RECORDS: Shares Super Bowl single-game record for most safeties—1 (January 27, 1991, vs. New York Giants). ... Shares NFL postseason career record for most sacks—12. ... Shares NFL postseason single-game record for most safeties—1 (January 27, 1991, vs. New York Giants).
PRO STATISTICS: 1985—Rushed once for no yards and recovered four fumbles. 1987—Recovered two fumbles for 15 yards and one touchdown. 1988—Credited with one safety. 1993—Intercepted one pass for no yards and recovered one fumble. 1994—Intercepted one pass for no yards and recovered two fumbles. 1995—Recovered one fumble. 1996—Recovered one fumble. 1998—Recovered two fumbles for 18 yards. 1999—Recovered one fumble. 2000—Credited with one safety.
MISCELLANEOUS: Holds Buffalo Bills all-time record for most sacks (171).

Year Team	G	GS	SACKS
1985—Buffalo NFL	16	13	6.5
1986—Buffalo NFL	16	15	15.0
1987—Buffalo NFL	12	12	12.0
1988—Buffalo NFL	12	12	11.0
1989—Buffalo NFL	16	16	13.0
1990—Buffalo NFL	16	16	19.0
1991—Buffalo NFL	5	5	1.5
1992—Buffalo NFL	15	15	14.0
1993—Buffalo NFL	16	16	14.0
1994—Buffalo NFL	15	15	10.0
1995—Buffalo NFL	15	15	10.5
1996—Buffalo NFL	16	16	▲13.5
1997—Buffalo NFL	16	16	§14.0
1998—Buffalo NFL	15	15	10.0
1999—Buffalo NFL	16	16	7.0
2000—Washington NFL	16	16	10.0
Pro totals (16 years)	233	229	181.0

SMITH, CHUCK   DE   PANTHERS

PERSONAL: Born December 21, 1969, in Athens, Ga. ... 6-2/262. ... Full name: Charles Henry Smith III.
HIGH SCHOOL: Clarke Central (Athens, Ga.).
COLLEGE: Northeastern Oklahoma A&M, then Tennessee.
TRANSACTIONS/CAREER NOTES: Selected by Atlanta Falcons in second round (51st pick overall) of 1992 NFL draft. ... Signed by Falcons (July 27, 1992). ... On suspended list (July 25-August 15, 1994). ... On injured reserve with knee injury (December 21, 1994-remainder of season). ... Granted free agency (February 17, 1995). ... Re-signed by Falcons (July 14, 1995). ... Granted unconditional free agency (February 16, 1996). ... Re-signed by Falcons (February 27, 1996). ... Granted unconditional free agency (February 11, 2000). ... Signed by Carolina Panthers (February 22, 2000). ... On injured reserve with knee injury (October 23, 2000-remainder of season).
CHAMPIONSHIP GAME EXPERIENCE: Played in NFC championship game (1998 season). ... Played in Super Bowl XXXIII (1998 season).
PRO STATISTICS: 1993—Recovered two fumbles. 1994—Intercepted one pass for 36 yards and a touchdown and recovered two fumbles. 1995—Recovered two fumbles. 1996—Intercepted one pass for 21 yards and recovered one fumble. 1997—Intercepted one pass for four yards. 1998—Recovered four fumbles for 71 yards and one touchdown. 1999—Recovered one fumble for 18 yards.

Year Team	G	GS	SACKS
1992—Atlanta NFL	16	0	2.0
1993—Atlanta NFL	15	1	3.5
1994—Atlanta NFL	15	10	11.0
1995—Atlanta NFL	14	13	5.5
1996—Atlanta NFL	15	15	6.0
1997—Atlanta NFL	16	15	12.0
1998—Atlanta NFL	16	16	8.5
1999—Atlanta NFL	16	16	10.0
2000—Carolina NFL	2	2	0.0
Pro totals (9 years)	125	88	58.5

SMITH, DARRIN   LB   SAINTS

PERSONAL: Born April 15, 1970, in Miami. ... 6-1/230. ... Full name: Darrin Andrew Smith.
HIGH SCHOOL: Miami Norland.
COLLEGE: Miam, Fla. (degree in business management, 1991; master's degree in business administration, 1993).
TRANSACTIONS/CAREER NOTES: Selected by Dallas Cowboys in second round (54th pick overall) of 1993 NFL draft. ... Signed by Cowboys (July 21, 1993). ... On reserve/did not report list (July 20-October 14, 1995). ... Granted free agency (February 16, 1996). ... Re-signed by Cowboys (June 17, 1996). ... Granted unconditional free agency (February 14, 1997). ... Signed by Philadelphia Eagles (April 19, 1997). ... On injured reserve with ankle injury (November 19, 1997-remainder of season). ... Granted unconditional free agency (February 13, 1998). ... Signed by Seattle Seahawks (February 19, 1998). ... Released by Seahawks (February 10, 2000). ... Signed by New Orleans Saints (July 16, 2000). ... Granted unconditional free agency (March 2, 2001). ... Re-signed by Saints (March 30, 2001).
CHAMPIONSHIP GAME EXPERIENCE: Played in NFC championship game (1993 and 1995 seasons). ... Member of Super Bowl championship team (1993 and 1995 seasons).
PRO STATISTICS: 1993—Recovered one fumble. 1994—Recovered two fumbles for 11 yards. 1995—Recovered one fumble for 63 yards. 1997—Recovered one fumble. 1998—Recovered two fumbles.

Year Team	G	GS	INTERCEPTIONS No.	Yds.	Avg.	TD	SACKS No.
1993—Dallas NFL	16	13	0	0	0.0	0	1.0
1994—Dallas NFL	16	16	2	13	6.5	1	4.0
1995—Dallas NFL	9	9	0	0	0.0	0	3.0
1996—Dallas NFL	16	16	0	0	0.0	0	1.0
1997—Philadelphia NFL	7	7	0	0	0.0	0	1.0
1998—Seattle NFL	13	12	3	56	18.7	▲2	5.0
1999—Seattle NFL	15	15	1	0	0.0	0	1.0
2000—New Orleans NFL	16	11	2	56	28.0	1	2.0
Pro totals (8 years)	108	99	8	125	15.6	4	18.0

SMITH, DEREK   LB   49ERS

PERSONAL: Born January 18, 1975, in American Fork, Utah. ... 6-2/239. ... Full name: Derek Mecham Smith.
HIGH SCHOOL: American Fork (Utah).
JUNIOR COLLEGE: Snow College (Utah).
COLLEGE: Arizona State.
TRANSACTIONS/CAREER NOTES: Selected by Washington Redskins in third round (80th pick overall) of 1997 NFL draft. ... Signed by Redskins (July 11, 1997). ... Granted free agency (February 11, 2000). ... Re-signed by Redskins (April 11, 2000). ... Granted unconditional free agency (March 2, 2001). ... Signed by San Francisco 49ers (March 23, 2001).
PRO STATISTICS: 1997—Recovered two fumbles for five yards. 1998—Recovered one fumble. 1999—Intercepted one pass for no yards and recovered one fumble. 2000—Recovered one fumble.

Year Team	G	GS	SACKS
1997—Washington NFL	16	16	2.0
1998—Washington NFL	16	15	0.5
1999—Washington NFL	16	16	1.0
2000—Washington NFL	16	14	1.0
Pro totals (4 years)	64	61	4.5

SMITH, DETRON   FB   BRONCOS

PERSONAL: Born February 25, 1974, in Dallas. ... 5-10/230. ... Full name: Detron Negil Smith. ... Name pronounced DEE-tron.
HIGH SCHOOL: Lake Highlands (Dallas).
COLLEGE: Texas A&M.

S

TRANSACTIONS/CAREER NOTES: Selected by Denver Broncos in third round (65th pick overall) of 1996 NFL draft. ... Signed by Broncos (July 20, 1996).
PLAYING EXPERIENCE: Denver NFL, 1996-2000. ... Games/Games started: 1996 (13/0), 1997 (16/0), 1998 (15/2), 1999 (16/0), 2000 (16/0). Total: 76/2.
CHAMPIONSHIP GAME EXPERIENCE: Played in AFC championship game (1997 and 1998 seasons). ... Member of Super Bowl championship team (1997 and 1998 seasons).
HONORS: Played in Pro Bowl (1999 season).
PRO STATISTICS: 1997—Rushed four times for 10 yards, caught four passes for 41 yards and one touchdown and returned one kickoff for no yards. 1998—Caught three passes for 24 yards and returned three kickoffs for 51 yards. 1999—Rushed once for seven yards, caught four passes for 23 yards, returned one kickoff for 12 yards and recovered one fumble. 2000—Caught one pass for one yard and a touchdown and returned five kickoffs for 73 yards.
SINGLE GAME HIGHS (regular season): Attempts—2 (December 21, 1997, vs. San Diego); yards—11 (December 21, 1997, vs. San Diego); and rushing touchdowns—0.

SMITH, EMANUEL　　　WR　　　JAGUARS

PERSONAL: Born February 3, 1976, in Jackson, Miss. ... 6-1/210. ... Full name: Emanuel Smith Jr.
HIGH SCHOOL: Clinton (Miss.).
COLLEGE: Arkansas.
TRANSACTIONS/CAREER NOTES: Selected by Jacksonville Jaguars in sixth round (196th pick overall) of 2000 NFL draft. ... Signed by Jaguars (June 1, 2000). ... Released by Jaguars (August 27, 2000). ... Re-signed by Jaguars to practice squad (August 28, 2000). ... Activated (December 13, 2000).
PLAYING EXPERIENCE: Jacksonville NFL, 2000. ... Games/Games started: 2000 (1/0).

S

SMITH, EMMITT　　　RB　　　COWBOYS

PERSONAL: Born May 15, 1969, in Pensacola, Fla. ... 5-9/209. ... Full name: Emmitt J. Smith III.
HIGH SCHOOL: Escambia (Pensacola, Fla.).
COLLEGE: Florida (degree in public recreation, 1996).
TRANSACTIONS/CAREER NOTES: Selected after junior season by Dallas Cowboys in first round (17th pick overall) of 1990 NFL draft. ... Signed by Cowboys (September 4, 1990). ... Granted roster exemption (September 4-8, 1990). ... Granted free agency (March 1, 1993). ... Re-signed by Cowboys (September 16, 1993).
CHAMPIONSHIP GAME EXPERIENCE: Played in NFC championship game (1992-1995 seasons). ... Member of Super Bowl championship team (1992, 1993 and 1995 seasons).
HONORS: Named running back on THE SPORTING NEWS college All-America first team (1989). ... Played in Pro Bowl (1990-1992, 1995, 1998 and 1999 seasons). ... Named running back on THE SPORTING NEWS NFL All-Pro team (1992-1995). ... Named NFL Player of the Year by THE SPORTING NEWS (1993). ... Named Most Valuable Player of Super Bowl XXVIII (1993 season). ... Named to play in Pro Bowl (1993 season); replaced by Rodney Hampton due to injury. ... Named Sportsman of the Year by THE SPORTING NEWS (1994). ... Named to play in Pro Bowl (1994 season); replaced by Ricky Watters due to injury.
RECORDS: Holds NFL career record for most rushing touchdowns—145. ... Shares NFL record for most consecutive seasons with 1,000 or more yards rushing—10 (1991-2000); and most seasons with 1,000 or more yards rushing—10 (1991-2000).
POST SEASON RECORDS: Holds Super Bowl career record for most rushing touchdowns—5. ... Holds NFL postseason career record for most rushing touchdowns—18. ... Holds NFL postseason career record for most yards rushing—1,586. ... Shares NFL postseason career record for most games with 100 or more yards rushing—7. ... Shares NFL postseason career records for most points scored—126; and most touchdowns—21.
PRO STATISTICS: 1991—Recovered one fumble. 1992—Recovered one fumble. 1993—Recovered three fumbles. 1996—Recovered one fumble. 1997—Recovered one fumble. 1998—Recovered one fumble. 1999—Recovered one fumble. 2000—Recovered one fumble.
SINGLE GAME HIGHS (regular season): Attempts—35 (November 7, 1994, vs. New York Giants); yards—237 (October 31, 1993, vs. Philadelphia); and rushing touchdowns—4 (September 4, 1995, vs. New York Giants).
STATISTICAL PLATEAUS: 100-yard rushing games: 1990 (3), 1991 (8), 1992 (7), 1993 (7), 1994 (6), 1995 (11), 1996 (4), 1997 (2), 1998 (7), 1999 (9), 2000 (6). Total: 70. ... 100-yard receiving games: 1990 (1), 1993 (1). Total: 2.
MISCELLANEOUS: Active NFL leader for career rushing yards (13,963) and rushing touchdowns (136). ... Holds Dallas Cowboys all-time records for most yards rushing (15,166), most touchdowns (156) and most rushing touchdowns (145).

Year　Team	G	GS	RUSHING				RECEIVING				TOTALS			
			Att.	Yds.	Avg.	TD	No.	Yds.	Avg.	TD	TD	2pt.	Pts.	Fum.
1990—Dallas NFL	16	15	241	937	3.9	11	24	228	9.5	0	11	0	66	7
1991—Dallas NFL	16	16	*365	*1563	4.3	12	49	258	5.3	1	13	0	78	8
1992—Dallas NFL	16	16	‡373	*1713	4.6	*18	59	335	5.7	1	*19	0	114	4
1993—Dallas NFL	14	13	283	*1486	*5.3	9	57	414	7.3	1	10	0	60	4
1994—Dallas NFL	15	15	*368	1484	4.0	*21	50	341	6.8	1	*22	0	132	1
1995—Dallas NFL	16	16	*377	*1773	4.7	*25	62	375	6.0	0	*25	0	*150	7
1996—Dallas NFL	15	15	327	1204	3.7	12	47	249	5.3	3	15	0	90	5
1997—Dallas NFL	16	16	261	1074	4.1	4	40	234	5.9	0	4	1	26	1
1998—Dallas NFL	16	16	319	1332	4.2	13	27	175	6.5	2	15	0	90	3
1999—Dallas NFL	15	15	‡329	1397	4.2	11	27	119	4.4	2	13	0	78	5
2000—Dallas NFL	16	16	294	1203	4.1	9	11	79	7.2	0	9	0	54	6
Pro totals (11 years)	171	169	3537	15166	4.3	145	453	2807	6.2	11	156	1	938	51

SMITH, FERNANDO　　　DE　　　VIKINGS

PERSONAL: Born August 2, 1971, in Flint, Mich. ... 6-6/284. ... Full name: Fernando Dewitt Smith. ... Brother of Robaire Smith, defensive end, Tennessee Titans.
HIGH SCHOOL: Northwestern Community (Flint, Mich.).
COLLEGE: Jackson State.
TRANSACTIONS/CAREER NOTES: Selected by Minnesota Vikings in second round (55th pick overall) of 1994 NFL draft. ... Signed by Vikings (July 15, 1994). ... Granted free agency (February 14, 1997). ... Re-signed by Vikings (February 20, 1997). ... Released by Vikings (July 28, 1998).

... Signed by Jacksonville Jaguars (August 13, 1998). ... Granted unconditional free agency (February 12, 1999). ... Signed by Baltimore Ravens (March 19, 1999). ... Granted unconditional free agency (February 11, 2000). ... Signed by Vikings (March 10, 2000). ... Released by Vikings (August 27, 2000). ... Signed by St. Louis Rams (October 10, 2000). ... Released by Rams (October 24, 2000). ... Re-signed by Vikings (December 20, 2000). ... Granted unconditional free agency (March 2, 2001). ... Re-signed by Vikings (March 27, 2001).

CHAMPIONSHIP GAME EXPERIENCE: Played in NFC championship game (2000 season).

PRO STATISTICS: 1996—Recovered two fumbles for four yards. 1997—Recovered one fumble for six yards. 1998—Recovered one fumble. 1999—Recovered three fumbles.

Year Team	G	GS	SACKS
1994—Minnesota NFL	7	0	0.0
1995—Minnesota NFL	12	1	2.5
1996—Minnesota NFL	16	16	9.5
1997—Minnesota NFL	12	11	4.0
1998—Jacksonville NFL	14	0	2.0
1999—Baltimore NFL	15	0	2.0
2000—Minnesota NFL	1	0	0.0
—St. Louis NFL	2	0	0.0
Pro totals (7 years)	**79**	**28**	**20.0**

SMITH, FRANKIE　　　S　　　BEARS

PERSONAL: Born October 8, 1968, in Groesbeck, Texas. ... 5-9/182. ... Full name: Frankie L. Smith.
HIGH SCHOOL: Groesbeck (Texas).
COLLEGE: Baylor.
TRANSACTIONS/CAREER NOTES: Selected by Atlanta Falcons in fourth round (104th pick overall) of 1992 NFL draft. ... Signed by Falcons (July 7, 1992). ... Released by Falcons (August 25, 1992). ... Signed by Miami Dolphins (March 17, 1993). ... Released by Dolphins (October 22, 1993). ... Re-signed by Dolphins to practice squad (October 23, 1993). ... Activated (November 29, 1993). ... Claimed on waivers by New England Patriots (February 27, 1996). ... Released by Patriots (August 17, 1996). ... Signed by San Francisco 49ers (September 12, 1996). ... Granted unconditional free agency (February 14, 1997). ... Re-signed by 49ers (March 26, 1997). ... Granted unconditional free agency (February 13, 1998). ... Signed by Chicago Bears (August 5, 1998). ... Granted unconditional free agency (February 12, 1999). ... Re-signed by Bears (March 26, 1999). ... Granted unconditional free agency (March 2, 2001). ... Re-signed by Bears (May 8, 2001).
PLAYING EXPERIENCE: Miami NFL, 1993-1995; San Francisco NFL, 1996 and 1997; Chicago NFL, 1998-2000. ... Games/Games started: 1993 (5/1), 1994 (13/2), 1995 (11/1), 1996 (14/0), 1997 (16/0), 1998 (15/0), 1999 (15/0), 2000 (14/0). Total: 103/4.
CHAMPIONSHIP GAME EXPERIENCE: Played in NFC championship game (1997 season).
PRO STATISTICS: 1994—Credited with one sack. 1997—Recovered one fumble. 1999—Credited with one sack and recovered one fumble. 2000—Credited with one sack.

SMITH, HUNTER　　　P　　　COLTS

PERSONAL: Born August 9, 1977, in Sherman, Texas. ... 6-2/212. ... Full name: Hunter Dwight Smith.
HIGH SCHOOL: Sherman (Texas).
COLLEGE: Notre Dame.
TRANSACTIONS/CAREER NOTES: Selected by Indianapolis Colts in seventh round (210th pick overall) of 1999 NFL draft. ... Signed by Colts (July 22, 1999).
PRO STATISTICS: 2000—Rushed once for 11 yards.

Year Team	G	No.	Yds.	Avg.	Net avg.	In. 20	Blk.
				PUNTING			
1999—Indianapolis NFL	16	58	2467	42.5	30.6	16	†2
2000—Indianapolis NFL	16	65	2906	44.7	36.4	20	0
Pro totals (2 years)	**32**	**123**	**5373**	**43.7**	**33.7**	**36**	**2**

SMITH, JEFF　　　C/G　　　JAGUARS

PERSONAL: Born May 25, 1973, in Decatur, Tenn. ... 6-3/316. ... Full name: Jeffery Lee Smith.
HIGH SCHOOL: Meigs County (Decatur, Tenn.).
COLLEGE: Tennessee.
TRANSACTIONS/CAREER NOTES: Selected by Kansas City Chiefs in seventh round (241st pick overall) of 1996 NFL draft. ... Signed by Chiefs (July 24, 1996). ... Active for one game (1996); did not play. ... Assigned by Chiefs to Scottish Claymores in 1997 World League enhancement allocation program (February 19, 1997). ... Granted free agency (February 12, 1999). ... Re-signed by Chiefs (June 16, 1999). ... Granted unconditional free agency (February 11, 2000). ... Re-signed by Chiefs (March 21, 2000). ... Released by Chiefs (August 27, 2000). ... Signed by Jacksonville Jaguars (August 29, 2000). ... Granted unconditional free agency (March 2, 2001). ... Re-signed by Jaguars (April 17, 2001).
PLAYING EXPERIENCE: Scottish W.L., 1997; Kansas City NFL, 1997-1999; Jacksonville NFL, 2000. ... Games/Games started: W.L. 1997 (10/games started unavailable), NFL 1997 (3/0), 1998 (11/3), 1999 (15/2), 2000 (14/12). Total: NFL 43/17.
PRO STATISTICS: 2000—Fumbled once.

SMITH, JIMMY　　　WR　　　JAGUARS

PERSONAL: Born February 9, 1969, in Detroit. ... 6-1/204. ... Full name: Jimmy Lee Smith Jr.
HIGH SCHOOL: Callaway (Jackson, Miss.).
COLLEGE: Jackson State (degree in business management, 1992).
TRANSACTIONS/CAREER NOTES: Selected by Dallas Cowboys in second round (36th pick overall) of 1992 NFL draft. ... Signed by Cowboys (April 26, 1992). ... On injured reserve with fibula injury (September 2-October 7, 1992); on practice squad (September 28-October 7, 1992). ... On non-football injury list with appendicitis (September 2, 1993-entire season). ... Released by Cowboys (July 11, 1994). ... Signed by Philadelphia Eagles (July 19, 1994). ... Released by Eagles (August 29, 1994). ... Signed by Jacksonville Jaguars (February 28, 1995). ... Granted free agency (February 16, 1996). ... Re-signed by Jaguars (May 28, 1996).
CHAMPIONSHIP GAME EXPERIENCE: Played in NFC championship game (1992 season). ... Member of Super Bowl championship team (1992 season). ... Played in AFC championship game (1996 and 1999 seasons).

HONORS: Played in Pro Bowl (1997-2000 seasons).
PRO STATISTICS: 1995—Recovered blocked punt in end zone for a touchdown and recovered one fumble. 1997—Recovered one fumble. 1998—Recovered two fumbles.
SINGLE GAME HIGHS (regular season): Receptions—15 (September 10, 2000, vs. Baltimore); yards—291 (September 10, 2000, vs. Baltimore); and touchdown receptions—3 (September 10, 2000, vs. Baltimore).
STATISTICAL PLATEAUS: 100-yard receiving games: 1996 (4), 1997 (6), 1998 (5), 1999 (9), 2000 (5). Total: 29.
MISCELLANEOUS: Holds Jacksonville Jaguars all-time record for most receptions (472), most yards receiving (6,887) and most touchdown receptions (36). ... Shares Jacksonville Jaguars all-time record for touchdowns (38).

			RECEIVING				KICKOFF RETURNS				TOTALS			
Year Team	G	GS	No.	Yds.	Avg.	TD	No.	Yds.	Avg.	TD	TD	2pt.	Pts.	Fum.
1992—Dallas NFL	7	0	0	0	0.0	0	0	0	0.0	0	0	0	0	0
1993—Dallas NFL								Did not play.						
1994—								Did not play.						
1995—Jacksonville NFL	16	4	22	288	13.1	3	24	540	22.5	1	5	0	30	2
1996—Jacksonville NFL	16	9	83	§1244	15.0	7	2	49	24.5	0	7	0	42	1
1997—Jacksonville NFL	16	16	82	1324	16.1	4	0	0	0.0	0	4	0	24	1
1998—Jacksonville NFL	16	15	78	1182	15.2	8	0	0	0.0	0	8	0	48	2
1999—Jacksonville NFL	16	16	*116	1636	14.1	6	0	0	0.0	0	6	†1	38	1
2000—Jacksonville NFL	15	14	91	1213	13.3	8	0	0	0.0	0	8	0	48	1
Pro totals (7 years)	102	74	472	6887	14.6	36	26	589	22.7	1	38	1	230	8

SMITH, LAMAR   RB   DOLPHINS

PERSONAL: Born November 29, 1970, in Fort Wayne, Ind. ... 5-11/229.
HIGH SCHOOL: South Side (Fort Wayne, Ind.).
COLLEGE: Houston.
TRANSACTIONS/CAREER NOTES: Selected by Seattle Seahawks in third round (73rd pick overall) of 1994 NFL draft. ... Signed by Seahawks (July 19, 1994). ... On non-football injury list with back injury (December 13, 1994-remainder of season). ... Granted free agency (February 14, 1997). ... Re-signed by Seahawks (February 1997). ... Granted unconditional free agency (February 13, 1998). ... Signed by New Orleans Saints (February 28, 1998). ... Released by Saints (February 24, 2000). ... Signed by Miami Dolphins (March 15, 2000).
PRO STATISTICS: 1995—Returned one kickoff for 20 yards. 1996—Recovered one fumble. 1997—Returned one kickoff for 14 yards. 1998—Attempted two passes with one completion for 20 yards and a touchdown. 1999—Attempted one pass without a completion. 2000—Attempted one pass without a completion.
SINGLE GAME HIGHS (regular season): Attempts—33 (November 17, 1996, vs. Detroit); yards—157 (September 27, 1998, vs. Indianapolis); and rushing touchdowns—2 (December 24, 2000, vs. New England).
STATISTICAL PLATEAUS: 100-yard rushing games: 1996 (1), 1998 (1), 2000 (4). Total: 6.

			RUSHING				RECEIVING				TOTALS			
Year Team	G	GS	Att.	Yds.	Avg.	TD	No.	Yds.	Avg.	TD	TD	2pt.	Pts.	Fum.
1994—Seattle NFL	2	0	2	-1	-0.5	0	0	0	0.0	0	0	0	0	0
1995—Seattle NFL	13	0	36	215	6.0	0	1	10	10.0	0	0	0	0	1
1996—Seattle NFL	16	2	153	680	4.4	8	9	58	6.4	0	8	*3	54	4
1997—Seattle NFL	12	2	91	392	4.3	2	23	183	8.0	0	2	1	14	0
1998—New Orleans NFL	14	9	138	457	3.3	1	24	249	10.4	2	3	0	18	4
1999—New Orleans NFL	13	2	60	205	3.4	0	20	151	7.6	1	1	0	6	1
2000—Miami NFL	15	15	309	1139	3.7	14	31	201	6.5	2	16	0	96	3
Pro totals (7 years)	85	30	789	3087	3.9	25	108	852	7.9	5	30	4	188	13

SMITH, LARRY   DT   JAGUARS

PERSONAL: Born December 4, 1974, in Kingsland, Ga. ... 6-5/284. ... Full name: Larry Smith Jr.
HIGH SCHOOL: Charlton County (Folkston, Ga.), then Valley Forge (Pa.).
COLLEGE: Florida State.
TRANSACTIONS/CAREER NOTES: Selected after junior season by Jacksonville Jaguars in second round (56th pick overall) of 1999 NFL draft. ... Signed by Jaguars (April 26, 1999).
CHAMPIONSHIP GAME EXPERIENCE: Played in AFC championship game (1999 season).
PRO STATISTICS: 2000—Recovered three fumbles for one yard.

Year Team	G	GS	SACKS
1999—Jacksonville NFL	15	0	3.0
2000—Jacksonville NFL	14	4	0.0
Pro totals (2 years)	29	4	3.0

SMITH, MARK   DT   BROWNS

PERSONAL: Born August 28, 1974, in Vicksburg, Miss. ... 6-4/294. ... Full name: Mark Anthony Smith.
HIGH SCHOOL: Vicksburg (Miss.).
JUNIOR COLLEGE: Navarro College (Texas), then Hinds Community College (Miss.).
COLLEGE: Auburn.
TRANSACTIONS/CAREER NOTES: Selected by Arizona Cardinals in seventh round (212th pick overall) of 1997 NFL draft. ... Signed by Cardinals (May 5, 1997). ... On injured reserve with knee injury (November 1, 1999-remainder of season). ... Granted free agency (February 11, 2000). ... Re-signed by Cardinals (June 27, 2000). ... Granted unconditional free agency (March 2, 2001). ... Signed by Cleveland Browns (March 13, 2001).
PRO STATISTICS: 1998—Recovered one fumble.

Year Team	G	GS	SACKS
1997—Arizona NFL	16	4	6.0
1998—Arizona NFL	14	13	9.0
1999—Arizona NFL	2	0	0.0
2000—Arizona NFL	14	7	3.0
Pro totals (4 years)	46	24	18.0

SMITH, MARQUIS   DB   BROWNS

PERSONAL: Born January 13, 1975, in San Diego. ... 6-2/213. ... Cousin of Akili Smith, quarterback, Cincinnati Bengals. ... Name pronounced mar-KEYS.
HIGH SCHOOL: Patrick Henry (San Diego).
COLLEGE: California.
TRANSACTIONS/CAREER NOTES: Selected by Cleveland Browns in third round (76th pick overall) of 1999 NFL draft. ... Signed by Browns (July 15, 1999).
PLAYING EXPERIENCE: Cleveland NFL, 1999 and 2000. ... Games/Games started: 1999 (16/2), 2000 (16/16). Total: 32/18.
PRO STATISTICS: 2000—Credited with one sack.

SMITH, MARVEL   OT   STEELERS

PERSONAL: Born August 6, 1978, in Oakland. ... 6-5/320. ... Full name: Marvel Amos Smith.
HIGH SCHOOL: Skyline (Oakland).
COLLEGE: Arizona State.
TRANSACTIONS/CAREER NOTES: Selected after junior season by Pittsburgh Steelers in second round (38th pick overall) of 2000 NFL draft. ... Signed by Steelers (July 16, 2000).
PLAYING EXPERIENCE: Pittsburgh NFL, 2000. ... Games/Games started: 2000 (12/9).

SMITH, MAURICE   RB   FALCONS

S

PERSONAL: Born September 7, 1976, in Palmyra, North Carolina. ... 6-0/235.
HIGH SCHOOL: S.E. Halifax (N.C.).
COLLEGE: North Carolina A & T.
TRANSACTIONS/CAREER NOTES: Signed as non-drafted free agent by Atlanta Falcons (April 17, 2000).
PLAYING EXPERIENCE: Atlanta NFL, 2000. ... Games/Games started: 2000 (11/0).
PRO STATISTICS: 2000—Rushed 19 times for 69 yards and caught one pass for five yards.
SINGLE GAME HIGHS (regular season): Attempts—9 (December 3, 2000, vs. Seattle); yards—42 (December 3, 2000, vs. Seattle); and rushing touchdowns—0.

SMITH, NEIL   DE

PERSONAL: Born April 10, 1966, in New Orleans. ... 6-4/270.
HIGH SCHOOL: McDonogh 35 (New Orleans).
COLLEGE: Nebraska.
TRANSACTIONS/CAREER NOTES: Selected by Kansas City Chiefs in first round (second pick overall) of 1988 NFL draft. ... Signed by Chiefs (July 19, 1988). ... Designated by Chiefs as franchise player (February 25, 1993). ... Granted unconditional free agency (February 14, 1997). ... Signed by Denver Broncos (April 14, 1997). ... Granted unconditional free agency (February 13, 1998). ... Re-signed by Broncos (March 11, 1998). ... Granted unconditional free agency (February 10, 2000). ... Signed by San Diego Chargers (September 5, 2000). ... Released by Broncos (February 10, 2000). ... Granted unconditional free agency (March 2, 2001).
CHAMPIONSHIP GAME EXPERIENCE: Played in AFC championship game (1993, 1997 and 1998 seasons). ... Member of Super Bowl championship team (1997 and 1998 season).
HONORS: Named defensive lineman on THE SPORTING NEWS college All-America first team (1987). ... Played in Pro Bowl (1991-1993, 1995 and 1997 seasons). ... Named to play in Pro Bowl (1994 season); replaced by Rob Burnett due to injury.
PRO STATISTICS: 1989—Recovered two fumbles for three yards and one touchdown. 1990—Recovered one fumble. 1991—Recovered two fumbles for 10 yards. 1992—Intercepted one pass for 22 yards and a touchdown and recovered two fumbles. 1993—Intercepted one pass for three yards and recovered three fumbles. 1994—Intercepted one pass for 41 yards and recovered one fumble for six yards. 1995—Recovered one fumble. 1998—Intercepted one pass for two yards.

Year Team	G	GS	SACKS
1988—Kansas City NFL	13	7	2.5
1989—Kansas City NFL	15	15	6.5
1990—Kansas City NFL	16	15	9.5
1991—Kansas City NFL	16	16	8.0
1992—Kansas City NFL	16	16	14.5
1993—Kansas City NFL	16	15	*15.0
1994—Kansas City NFL	14	13	11.5
1995—Kansas City NFL	16	16	12.0
1996—Kansas City NFL	16	16	6.0
1997—Denver NFL	14	13	8.5
1998—Denver NFL	14	14	4.0
1999—Denver NFL	15	8	6.5
2000—San Diego NFL	10	0	0.0
Pro totals (13 years)	191	162	104.5

SMITH, OTIS   CB   PATRIOTS

PERSONAL: Born October 22, 1965, in New Orleans. ... 5-11/195. ... Full name: Otis Smith III.
HIGH SCHOOL: East Jefferson (Metairie, La.).
JUNIOR COLLEGE: Taft (Calif.) College.
COLLEGE: Missouri.
TRANSACTIONS/CAREER NOTES: Signed as non-drafted free agent by Philadelphia Eagles (April 25, 1990). ... On physically unable to perform list with appendectomy (August 2, 1990-entire season). ... Granted free agency (February 1, 1992). ... Re-signed by Eagles (August 11, 1992). ... Granted unconditional free agency (February 17, 1994). ... Re-signed by Eagles (April 25, 1994). ... Released by Eagles (March 22, 1995). ... Signed by New York Jets (April 13, 1995). ... Released by Jets (September 24, 1996). ... Signed by New England Patriots (October 9, 1996). ...

Granted unconditional free agency (February 14, 1997). ... Re-signed by Jets (May 20, 1997). ... Granted unconditional free agency (February 13, 1998). ... Re-signed by Jets (April 9, 1998). ... On injured reserve with broken collarbone (October 5, 1999-remainder of season). ... Released by Jets (August 20, 2000). ... Signed by New England Patriots (August 23, 2000).

CHAMPIONSHIP GAME EXPERIENCE: Played in AFC championship game (1996 season). ... Played in Super Bowl XXXI (1996 season).

PRO STATISTICS: 1991—Recovered one fumble. 1994—Credited with one sack and returned one kickoff for 14 yards. 1995—Returned one kickoff for six yards. 1996—Credited with one sack. 1997—Recovered two fumbles for 40 yards. 2000—Recovered one fumble for 12 yards.

				INTERCEPTIONS			
Year Team	G	GS	No.	Yds.	Avg.	TD
1990—Philadelphia NFL				Did not play.		
1991—Philadelphia NFL	15	1	2	74	37.0	∞1
1992—Philadelphia NFL	16	1	1	0	0.0	0
1993—Philadelphia NFL	15	0	1	0	0.0	0
1994—Philadelphia NFL	16	2	0	0	0.0	0
1995—New York Jets NFL	11	10	6	101	16.8	▲1
1996—New York Jets NFL	2	0	0	0	0.0	0
—New England NFL	11	6	2	20	10.0	0
1997—New York Jets NFL	16	16	6	158	26.3	†3
1998—New York Jets NFL	16	16	2	34	17.0	0
1999—New York Jets NFL	1	0	0	0	0.0	0
2000—New England NFL	16	14	1	56	56.0	0
Pro totals (10 years)	135	67	21	443	21.1	5

SMITH, PAUL　　　　RB　　　　49ERS

S

PERSONAL: Born January 31, 1978, in El Paso, Texas. ... 5-11/234.
HIGH SCHOOL: Andress (El Paso, Texas).
COLLEGE: Texas-El Paso.
TRANSACTIONS/CAREER NOTES: Selected by San Francisco 49ers in fifth round (132nd pick overall) of 2000 NFL draft. ... Signed by 49ers (July 21, 2000).
PRO STATISTICS: 2000—Returned nine kickoffs for 167 yards and recovered two fumbles.
SINGLE GAME HIGHS (regular season): Attempts—5 (December 3, 2000, vs. San Diego); yards—20 (October 22, 2000, vs. Carolina); and rushing touchdowns—0.

			RUSHING				RECEIVING				TOTALS			
Year Team	G	GS	Att.	Yds.	Avg.	TD	No.	Yds.	Avg.	TD	TD	2pt.	Pts.	Fum.
2000—San Francisco NFL	10	0	18	72	4.0	0	2	55	27.5	0	0	0	0	2

SMITH, ROBAIRE　　　　DE/DT　　　　TITANS

PERSONAL: Born November 15, 1977, in Flint, Mich. ... 6-4/271. ... Full name: Robaire Freddick Smith. ... Brother of Fernando Smith, defensive end, Minnesota Vikings.
HIGH SCHOOL: Flint (Mich.).
COLLEGE: Michigan State.
TRANSACTIONS/CAREER NOTES: Selected by Tennessee Titans in sixth round (197th pick overall) of 2000 NFL draft. ... Signed by Titans (July 5, 2000).
HONORS: Named defensive end on THE SPORTING NEWS college All-America second team (1999).

Year Team	G	GS	SACKS
2000—Tennessee NFL	7	0	2.5

SMITH, ROBERT　　　　RB

PERSONAL: Born March 4, 1972, in Euclid, Ohio. ... 6-2/210. ... Full name: Robert Scott Smith.
HIGH SCHOOL: Euclid (Ohio).
COLLEGE: Ohio State.
TRANSACTIONS/CAREER NOTES: Selected after sophomore season by Minnesota Vikings in first round (21st pick overall) of 1993 NFL draft. ... Signed by Vikings (July 16, 1993). ... On injured reserve with knee injury (December 7, 1993-remainder of season). ... On physically unable to perform list with knee injury (July 13-19, 1994). ... Granted free agency (February 16, 1996). ... Re-signed by Vikings (August 10, 1996). ... On injured reserve with knee injury (November 15, 1996-remainder of season). ... Granted unconditional free agency (February 14, 1997). ... Re-signed by Vikings (April 18, 1997). ... Designated by Vikings as franchise player (February 13, 1998). ... Free agency status changed from franchise to transitional (February 25, 1998). ... Re-signed by Vikings (March 4, 1998). ... Announced retirement (February 8, 2001).
CHAMPIONSHIP GAME EXPERIENCE: Played in NFC championship game (1998 and 2000 seasons).
HONORS: Named to play in Pro Bowl (2000 season); replaced by Warrick Dunn due to injury.
PRO STATISTICS: 1993—Returned one punt for four yards. 1996—Recovered one fumble. 1997—Recovered one fumble. 2000—Recovered three fumbles.
SINGLE GAME HIGHS (regular season): Attempts—30 (September 8, 1996, vs. Atlanta); yards—179 (September 13, 1998, vs. St. Louis); and rushing touchdowns—2 (November 30, 2000, vs. Detroit).
STATISTICAL PLATEAUS: 100-yard rushing games: 1993 (1), 1995 (2), 1996 (3), 1997 (6), 1998 (5), 1999 (4), 2000 (8). Total: 29.
MISCELLANEOUS: Holds Minnesota Vikings all-time record for most yards rushing (6,818).

			RUSHING				RECEIVING				KICKOFF RETURNS				TOTALS			
Year Team	G	GS	Att.	Yds.	Avg.	TD	No.	Yds.	Avg.	TD	No.	Yds.	Avg.	TD	TD	2pt.	Pts.	Fum.
1993—Minnesota NFL	10	2	82	399	4.9	2	24	111	4.6	0	3	41	13.7	0	2	0	12	0
1994—Minnesota NFL	14	0	31	106	3.4	1	15	105	7.0	0	16	419	26.2	0	1	0	6	0
1995—Minnesota NFL	9	7	139	632	4.5	5	7	35	5.0	0	0	0	0.0	0	5	1	32	1
1996—Minnesota NFL	8	7	162	692	4.3	3	7	39	5.6	0	0	0	0.0	0	3	0	18	2
1997—Minnesota NFL	14	14	232	1266	5.5	6	37	197	5.3	1	0	0	0.0	0	7	0	42	0
1998—Minnesota NFL	14	14	249	1187	4.8	6	28	291	10.4	2	0	0	0.0	0	8	0	48	1
1999—Minnesota NFL	13	12	221	1015	4.6	2	24	166	6.9	0	0	0	0.0	0	2	0	12	1
2000—Minnesota NFL	16	16	295	‡1521	5.2	7	36	348	9.7	3	0	0	0.0	0	10	0	60	4
Pro totals (8 years)	98	72	1411	6818	4.8	32	178	1292	7.3	6	19	460	24.2	0	38	1	230	9

SMITH, ROD   WR   BRONCOS

PERSONAL: Born May 15, 1970, in Texarkana, Ark. ... 6-0/200.
HIGH SCHOOL: Arkansas (Texarkana, Ark.).
COLLEGE: Missouri Southern.
TRANSACTIONS/CAREER NOTES: Signed as non-drafted free agent by Denver Broncos (March 23, 1995).
CHAMPIONSHIP GAME EXPERIENCE: Played in AFC championship game (1997 and 1998 seasons). ... Member of Super Bowl championship team (1997 and 1998 seasons).
HONORS: Played in Pro Bowl (2000 season).
PRO STATISTICS: 1996—Rushed once for one yard. 1997—Rushed five times for 16 yards and recovered one fumble. 1998—Rushed six times for 63 yards, completed only pass attempt for 14 yards and recovered two fumbles for 11 yards and one touchdown. 1999—Attempted one pass without a completion. 2000—Rushed six times for 99 yards and a touchdown.
SINGLE GAME HIGHS (regular season): Receptions—13 (October 1, 2000, vs. New England); yards—187 (November 19, 2000, vs. San Diego); and touchdown receptions—3 (October 15, 2000, vs. Cleveland).
STATISTICAL PLATEAUS: 100-yard receiving games: 1997 (6), 1998 (4), 1999 (3), 2000 (8). Total: 21.

			RECEIVING				PUNT RETURNS				KICKOFF RETURNS				TOTALS			
Year Team	G	GS	No.	Yds.	Avg.	TD	No.	Yds.	Avg.	TD	No.	Yds.	Avg.	TD	TD	2pt.	Pts.	Fum.
1995—Denver NFL	16	1	6	152	25.3	1	0	0	0.0	0	4	54	13.5	0	1	0	6	0
1996—Denver NFL	10	1	16	237	14.8	2	23	283	12.3	0	1	29	29.0	0	2	0	12	1
1997—Denver NFL	16	16	70	1180	16.9▲	12	1	12	12.0	0	0	0	0.0	0	12	0	72	3
1998—Denver NFL	16	16	86	1222	14.2	6	0	0	0.0	0	0	0	0.0	0	7	0	42	0
1999—Denver NFL	15	15	79	1020	12.9	4	0	0	0.0	0	1	10	10.0	0	4	0	24	1
2000—Denver NFL	16	16	100	§1602	16.0	8	0	0	0.0	0	0	0	0.0	0	9	0	54	1
Pro totals (6 years)	89	65	357	5413	15.2	33	24	295	12.3	0	6	93	15.5	0	35	0	210	6

SMITH, TERRELLE   FB   SAINTS

PERSONAL: Born March 12, 1978, in West Covina, Calif. ... 6-0/246.
HIGH SCHOOL: Canyon Springs (Moreno Valley, Calif.).
COLLEGE: Arizona State.
TRANSACTIONS/CAREER NOTES: Selected by New Orleans Saints in fourth round (96th pick overall) of 2000 NFL draft. ... Signed by Saints (July 11, 2000).
SINGLE GAME HIGHS (regular season): Attempts—6 (December 10, 2000, vs. San Francisco); yards—42 (November 19, 2000, vs. Oakland); and rushing touchdowns—0.

			RUSHING				RECEIVING				TOTALS			
Year Team	G	GS	Att.	Yds.	Avg.	TD	No.	Yds.	Avg.	TD	TD	2pt.	Pts.	Fum.
2000—New Orleans NFL	14	9	29	131	4.5	0	12	65	5.4	0	0	0	0	1

SMITH, THOMAS   CB   BEARS

PERSONAL: Born December 5, 1970, in Gates, N.C. ... 5-11/190. ... Full name: Thomas Lee Smith Jr. ... Cousin of Sam Perkins, forward/center, Indiana Pacers.
HIGH SCHOOL: Gates County (Gatesville, N.C.).
COLLEGE: North Carolina.
TRANSACTIONS/CAREER NOTES: Selected by Buffalo Bills in first round (28th pick overall) of 1993 NFL draft. ... Signed by Bills (July 16, 1993). ... Granted free agency (February 16, 1996). ... Re-signed by Bills (February 27, 1996). ... Granted unconditional free agency (February 11, 2000). ... Signed by Chicago Bears (February 12, 2000).
PRO STATISTICS: 1993—Recovered one fumble. 1997—Fumbled once and recovered one fumble for one yard. 1998—Recovered one fumble. 1999—Recovered one fumble. 2000—Recovered one fumble.

			INTERCEPTIONS			
Year Team	G	GS	No.	Yds.	Avg.	TD
1993—Buffalo NFL	16	1	0	0	0.0	0
1994—Buffalo NFL	16	16	1	4	4.0	0
1995—Buffalo NFL	16	16	2	23	11.5	0
1996—Buffalo NFL	16	16	1	0	0.0	0
1997—Buffalo NFL	16	16	0	0	0.0	0
1998—Buffalo NFL	14	14	1	0	0.0	0
1999—Buffalo NFL	16	16	1	29	29.0	0
2000—Chicago NFL	16	16	0	0	0.0	0
Pro totals (8 years)	126	111	6	56	9.3	0

SMITH, TRAVIAN   LB   RAIDERS

PERSONAL: Born August 26, 1975, in Good Shepard, Texas. ... 6-4/240.
HIGH SCHOOL: Tatum (Texas).
COLLEGE: Oklahoma.
TRANSACTIONS/CAREER NOTES: Selected by Oakland Raiders in fifth round (152nd pick overall) of 1998 NFL draft. ... Signed by Raiders (July 6, 1998). ... Released by Raiders (August 26, 1998). ... Re-signed by Raiders to practice squad (August 31, 1998). ... Activated (December 15, 1998).
PLAYING EXPERIENCE: Oakland NFL, 1998-2000. ... Games/Games started: 1998 (2/0), 1999 (16/1), 2000 (16/0). Total: 34/1.
CHAMPIONSHIP GAME EXPERIENCE: Played in AFC championship game (2000 season).
PRO STATISTICS: 1999—Recovered one fumble for one yard.

SNIDER, MATT   FB   PACKERS

PERSONAL: Born January 26, 1976, in Des Moines, Iowa. ... 6-2/240. ... Full name: Matthew Kale Snider.
HIGH SCHOOL: Lower Merion (Wynnewood, Pa.).
COLLEGE: Richmond.
TRANSACTIONS/CAREER NOTES: Signed as non-drafted free agent by Carolina Panthers (April 27, 1999). ... Claimed on waivers by Green Bay Packers (July 1, 1999).
PLAYING EXPERIENCE: Green Bay NFL, 1999 and 2000. ... Games/Games started: 1999 (8/0), 2000 (16/0). Total: 24/0.

SNOW, JUSTIN   TE   COLTS

PERSONAL: Born December 21, 1976, in Abilene, Texas. ... 6-3/234.
HIGH SCHOOL: Cooper (Abilene, Texas.).
COLLEGE: Baylor.
TRANSACTIONS/CAREER NOTES: Signed as non-drafted free agent by Indianapolis Colts (April 20, 2000).
PLAYING EXPERIENCE: Indianapolis NFL, 2000. ... Games/Games started: (16/0).

SOWARD, R. JAY   WR   JAGUARS

PERSONAL: Born January 16, 1978, in Pomona, Calif. ... 5-11/178. ... Full name: Rodney Jay Soward.
HIGH SCHOOL: Eisenhower (Rialto, Calif.), then Fontana (Calif.).
COLLEGE: Southern California.
TRANSACTIONS/CAREER NOTES: Selected by Jacksonville Jaguars in first round (29th pick overall) of 2000 NFL draft. ... Signed by Jaguars (July 14, 2000). ... On non-football injury list with illness (December 20, 2000-remainder of season).
PRO STATISTICS: 2000—Rushed three times for 28 yards and recovered one fumble.
SINGLE GAME HIGHS (regular season): Receptions—3 (October 16, 2000, vs. Tennessee); yards—45 (November 26, 2000, vs. Tennessee); and touchdown receptions—1 (October 22, 2000, vs. Washington).

			RECEIVING				PUNT RETURNS				KICKOFF RETURNS				TOTALS			
Year Team	G	GS	No.	Yds.	Avg.	TD	No.	Yds.	Avg.	TD	No.	Yds.	Avg.	TD	TD	2pt.	Pts.	Fum.
2000—Jacksonville NFL	13	2	14	154	11.0	1	14	108	7.7	0	4	93	23.3	0	1	0	6	3

SOWELL, JERALD   FB   JETS

PERSONAL: Born January 21, 1974, in Baton Rouge, La. ... 6-0/245. ... Full name: Jerald Monye Sowell.
HIGH SCHOOL: Baker (La.).
COLLEGE: Tulane (degree in exercise science/kinesiology).
TRANSACTIONS/CAREER NOTES: Selected by Green Bay Packers in seventh round (231st pick overall) of 1997 NFL draft. ... Signed by Packers (July 10, 1997). ... Claimed on waivers by New York Jets (August 25, 1997). ... Granted free agency (February 11, 2000). ... Re-signed by Jets (April 25, 2000).
CHAMPIONSHIP GAME EXPERIENCE: Member of Jets for AFC championship game (1998 season); inactive.
PRO STATISTICS: 1999—Attempted one pass without a completion. 2000—Returned one kickoff for nine yards.
SINGLE GAME HIGHS (regular season): Attempts—14 (November 8, 1998, vs. Buffalo); yards—82 (September 20, 1998, vs. Indianapolis); and rushing touchdowns—0.

			RUSHING				RECEIVING				TOTALS			
Year Team	G	GS	Att.	Yds.	Avg.	TD	No.	Yds.	Avg.	TD	TD	2pt.	Pts.	Fum.
1997—New York Jets NFL	9	0	7	35	5.0	0	1	8	8.0	0	0	0	0	0
1998—New York Jets NFL	16	2	40	164	4.1	0	10	59	5.9	0	0	0	0	2
1999—New York Jets NFL	16	0	3	5	1.7	0	0	0	0.0	0	0	0	0	0
2000—New York Jets NFL	16	0	2	0	0.0	0	6	84	14.0	0	0	0	0	0
Pro totals (4 years)	57	2	52	204	3.9	0	17	151	8.9	0	0	0	0	2

SPARKS, PHILLIPPI   CB   COWBOYS

PERSONAL: Born April 15, 1969, in Oklahoma City. ... 5-11/195. ... Full name: Phillippi Dwaine Sparks. ... Name pronounced fuh-LEEP-ee.
HIGH SCHOOL: Maryvale (Phoenix).
JUNIOR COLLEGE: Glendale (Ariz.) Community College.
COLLEGE: Arizona State.
TRANSACTIONS/CAREER NOTES: Selected by New York Giants in second round (41st pick overall) of 1992 NFL draft. ... Signed by Giants (July 21, 1992). ... Granted free agency (February 17, 1995). ... Re-signed by Giants (May 8, 1995). ... Granted unconditional free agency (February 11, 2000). ... Signed by Dallas Cowboys (August 28, 2000).
PRO STATISTICS: 1992—Returned two kickoffs for 23 yards. 1997—Returned one kickoff for eight yards and credited with one sack. 1999—Recovered one fumble.

			INTERCEPTIONS			
Year Team	G	GS	No.	Yds.	Avg.	TD
1992—New York Giants NFL	16	2	1	0	0.0	0
1993—New York Giants NFL	5	3	0	0	0.0	0
1994—New York Giants NFL	11	11	3	4	1.3	0
1995—New York Giants NFL	16	16	5	11	2.2	0
1996—New York Giants NFL	14	14	3	23	7.7	0
1997—New York Giants NFL	13	13	5	72	14.4	0
1998—New York Giants NFL	13	13	4	25	6.3	0
1999—New York Giants NFL	11	11	1	28	28.0	0
2000—Dallas NFL	16	12	5	59	11.8	0
Pro totals (9 years)	115	95	27	222	8.2	0

S

SPEARMAN, ARMEGIS   LB   BENGALS

PERSONAL: Born April 5, 1978, in Bruce, Miss. ... 6-1/254.
HIGH SCHOOL: Bruce (Miss.).
COLLEGE: Mississippi.
TRANSACTIONS/CAREER NOTES: Signed by Cincinnati Bengals as non-drafted free agent (April 27, 2000).
PLAYING EXPERIENCE: Cincinnati NFL, 2000. ... Games/Games started: 2000 (15/11).
PRO STATISTICS: 2000—Credited with one sack.

SPEARS, MARCUS   G/OT   CHIEFS

PERSONAL: Born September 28, 1971, in Baton Rouge, La. ... 6-4/312. ... Full name: Marcus DeWayne Spears.
HIGH SCHOOL: Belaire (Baton Rouge, La.).
COLLEGE: Northwestern State (La.).
TRANSACTIONS/CAREER NOTES: Selected by Chicago Bears in second round (39th pick overall) of 1994 NFL draft. ... Signed by Bears (July 16, 1994). ... Inactive for all 16 games (1994). ... Active for five games (1995); did not play. ... Assigned by Bears to Amsterdam Admirals in 1996 World League enhancement allocation program (February 19, 1996). ... Granted unconditional free agency (February 14, 1997). ... Signed by Green Bay Packers (March 12, 1997). ... Released by Packers (August 19, 1997). ... Signed by Kansas City Chiefs (September 16, 1997). ... On injured reserve with hand injury (December 9, 1998-remainder of season). ... Granted unconditional free agency (February 12, 1999). ... Re-signed by Chiefs (February 16, 1999). ... On injured reserve with arm injury (December 15, 2000-remainder of season).
PLAYING EXPERIENCE: Amsterdam W.L., 1996; Chicago NFL, 1996; Kansas City NFL, 1997-2000. ... Games/Games started: W.L. 1996 (games played unavailable), NFL 1996 (9/0), 1997 (3/0), 1998 (12/0), 1999 (10/2), 2000 (13/0). Total NFL: 47/2.
HONORS: Named offensive lineman on THE SPORTING NEWS college All-America second team (1993).
PRO STATISTICS: 1996—Caught one pass for one yard and a touchdown. 1999—Recovered one fumble. 2000—Returned one kickoff for 11 yards.

SPELLMAN, ALONZO   DL

PERSONAL: Born September 27, 1971, in Mount Holly, N.J. ... 6-4/292. ... Full name: Alonzo Robert Spellman.
HIGH SCHOOL: Rancocas Valley Regional (Mount Holly, N.J.).
COLLEGE: Ohio State.
TRANSACTIONS/CAREER NOTES: Selected after junior season by Chicago Bears in first round (22nd pick overall) of 1992 NFL draft. ... Signed by Bears (July 13, 1992). ... Designated by Bears as transition player (February 16, 1996). ... Tendered offer sheet by Jacksonville Jaguars (February 17, 1996). ... Offer matched by Bears (February 23, 1996). ... Released by Bears (June 12, 1998). ... Signed by Dallas Cowboys (July 29, 1999). ... Granted unconditional free agency (February 11, 2000). ... Re-signed by Cowboys (March 21, 2000). ... Granted unconditional free agency (March 2, 2001).
PRO STATISTICS: 1994—Intercepted one pass for 31 yards. 1995—Recovered one fumble. 1999—Recovered one fumble.

Year Team	G	GS	SACKS
1992—Chicago NFL	15	0	4.0
1993—Chicago NFL	16	0	2.5
1994—Chicago NFL	16	16	7.0
1995—Chicago NFL	16	16	8.5
1996—Chicago NFL	16	15	8.0
1997—Chicago NFL	7	5	2.0
1998—	Did not play.		
1999—Dallas NFL	16	16	5.0
2000—Dallas NFL	16	15	5.0
Pro totals (8 years)	118	83	42.0

SPENCE, BLAKE   FB

PERSONAL: Born June 20, 1975, in Garden Grove, Calif. ... 6-4/249. ... Full name: Blake Andrew Spence.
HIGH SCHOOL: Capistrano Valley (San Juan Capistrano, Calif.).
COLLEGE: Oregon.
TRANSACTIONS/CAREER NOTES: Selected by New York Jets in fifth round (146th pick overall) of 1998 NFL draft. ... Signed by Jets (June 23, 1998). ... Claimed on waivers by Tampa Bay Buccaneers (August 22, 2000). ... On injured reserve with knee injury (September 26, 2000-remainder of season).
PLAYING EXPERIENCE: New York Jets NFL, 1998 and 1999; Tampa Bay NFL, 2000. ... Games/Games started: 1998 (5/0), 1999 (10/0), 2000 (3/0). Total: 18/0.
CHAMPIONSHIP GAME EXPERIENCE: Played in AFC championship game (1998 season).
PRO STATISTICS: 1998—Caught one pass for five yards. 1999—Caught three passes for 15 yards and one touchdown.

SPENCER, JIMMY   CB   BRONCOS

PERSONAL: Born March 29, 1969, in Manning, S.C. ... 5-9/180. ... Full name: James Arthur Spencer Jr.
HIGH SCHOOL: Glades Central (Belle Glade, Fla.).
COLLEGE: Florida.
TRANSACTIONS/CAREER NOTES: Selected by Washington Redskins in eighth round (215th pick overall) of 1991 NFL draft. ... Signed by Redskins for 1991 season. ... Released by Redskins (August 26, 1991). ... Signed by New Orleans Saints (April 2, 1992). ... Granted unconditional free agency (February 16, 1996). ... Signed by Cincinnati Bengals (March 21, 1996). ... Released by Bengals (August 25, 1998). ... Signed by San Diego Chargers (September 1, 1998). ... Granted unconditional free agency (February 12, 1999). ... Re-signed by Chargers (April 7, 1999). ... On injured reserve with broken arm (December 20, 1999-remainder of season). ... Released by Chargers (February 10, 2000). ... Signed by Denver Broncos (March 6, 2000).

PRO STATISTICS: 1992—Recovered one fumble. 1993—Recovered three fumbles for 53 yards. 1994—Recovered one fumble. 1996—Recovered one fumble for 59 yards. 2000—Credited with one sack and recovered one fumble.

| | | | | INTERCEPTIONS | | |
Year Team	G	GS	No.	Yds.	Avg.	TD
1992—New Orleans NFL	16	4	0	0	0.0	0
1993—New Orleans NFL	16	3	0	0	0.0	0
1994—New Orleans NFL	16	16	5	24	4.8	0
1995—New Orleans NFL	16	15	4	11	2.8	0
1996—Cincinnati NFL	15	14	5	48	9.6	0
1997—Cincinnati NFL	16	9	1	-2	-2.0	0
1998—San Diego NFL	15	4	1	0	0.0	0
1999—San Diego NFL	14	7	4	1	0.3	0
2000—Denver NFL	16	6	3	102	34.0	2
Pro totals (9 years)	140	78	23	184	8.0	2

SPICER, PAUL — DE — JAGUARS

PERSONAL: Born August 18, 1975, in Indianapolis. ... 6-4/271.
HIGH SCHOOL: Northwestern (Indianapolis).
COLLEGE: College of DuPage (Ill.), then Saginaw Valley State (Mich.).
TRANSACTIONS/CAREER NOTES: Signed as non-drafted free agent by Seattle Seahawks (April 20, 1998). ... Released by Seahawks (August 24, 1998). ... Signed by Sasketchawan Roughriders of CFL (September 26, 1998). ... Signed by Detroit Lions (February 24, 1999). ... Released by Lions (September 5, 1999). ... Re-signed by Lions to practice squad (September 7, 1999). ... Activated (October 8, 1999). ... Released by Lions (November 6, 1999). ... Re-signed by Lions to practice squad (November 10, 1999). ... Released by Lions (August 22, 2000). ... Signed by Jacksonville Jaguars to practice squad (August 30, 2000). ... Activated (October 4, 2000). ... Assigned by Jaguars to Frankfurt Galaxy in 2001 NFL Europe enhancement allocation program (February 19, 2001).
PLAYING EXPERIENCE: Saskatchewan Roughriders CFL, 1998; Detroit NFL, 1999; Jacksonville NFL, 2000. ... Games/Games started: 1998 (7/games started unavailable), 1999 (2/0), 2000 (3/0). Total NFL: 5/0. Total Pro: 12/-.
PRO STATISTICS: 2000—Credited with one sack.

SPIKES, CAMERON — G — RAMS

PERSONAL: Born November 6, 1976, in Madisonville, Texas. ... 6-2/323. ... Full name: Cameron Wade Spikes.
HIGH SCHOOL: Bryan (Texas).
COLLEGE: Texas A&M.
TRANSACTIONS/CAREER NOTES: Selected by St. Louis Rams in fifth round (145th pick overall) of 1999 NFL draft. ... Signed by Rams (July 19, 1999).
PLAYING EXPERIENCE: St. Louis NFL, 1999 and 2000. ... Games/Games started: 1999 (5/0), 2000 (9/0). Total: 14/0.
CHAMPIONSHIP GAME EXPERIENCE: Member of Rams for NFC championship game (1999 season); inactive. ... Member of Super Bowl championship team (1999 season); inactive.

SPIKES, TAKEO — LB — BENGALS

PERSONAL: Born December 17, 1976, in Sandersville, Ga. ... 6-2/243. ... Full name: Takeo Gerard Spikes. ... Name pronounced tuh-KEE-oh.
HIGH SCHOOL: Washington County (Sandersville, Ga.).
COLLEGE: Auburn.
TRANSACTIONS/CAREER NOTES: Selected after junior season by Cincinnati Bengals in first round (13th pick overall) of 1998 NFL draft. ... Signed by Bengals (July 25, 1998).
HONORS: Named inside linebacker on THE SPORTING NEWS college All-America first team (1997).
PRO STATISTICS: 1999—Intercepted two passes for seven yards and recovered four fumbles. 2000—Intercepted two passes for 12 yards and recovered three fumbles.

Year Team	G	GS	SACKS
1998—Cincinnati NFL	16	16	2.0
1999—Cincinnati NFL	16	16	3.0
2000—Cincinnati NFL	16	16	2.0
Pro totals (3 years)	48	48	7.0

SPIRES, GREG — DE — PATRIOTS

PERSONAL: Born August 12, 1974, in Mariana, Fla. ... 6-1/265. ... Full name: Greg Tyrone Spires.
HIGH SCHOOL: Mariner (Cape Coral, Fla.).
COLLEGE: Florida State.
TRANSACTIONS/CAREER NOTES: Selected by New England Patriots in third round (83rd pick overall) of 1998 NFL draft. ... Signed by Patriots (July 16, 1998). ... On injured reserve with knee injury (December 15, 1999-remainder of season). ... Granted free agency (March 2, 2001). ... Re-signed by Patriots (April 30, 2001).
PRO STATISTICS: 2000—Recovered one fumble.

Year Team	G	GS	SACKS
1998—New England NFL	15	1	3.0
1999—New England NFL	11	0	0.5
2000—New England NFL	16	2	6.0
Pro totals (3 years)	42	3	9.5

SPRIGGS, MARCUS   DT   BROWNS

PERSONAL: Born July 26, 1976, in Washington, D.C. ... 6-4/314.
HIGH SCHOOL: Woodson (Washington, D.C.).
COLLEGE: Ohio State, then Troy (Ala.) State.
TRANSACTIONS/CAREER NOTES: Selected by Cleveland Browns in sixth round (174th pick overall) of 1999 NFL draft. ... Signed by Browns (July 22, 1999). ... On injured reserve with shoulder injury (November 23, 1999-remainder of season).
PLAYING EXPERIENCE: Cleveland NFL, 1999 and 2000. ... Games/Games started: 1999 (10/0), 2000 (8/0). Total: 18/0.
PRO STATISTICS: 2000—Credited with two sacks and recovered one fumble.

SPRIGGS, MARCUS   OT   DOLPHINS

PERSONAL: Born May 17, 1974, in Hattiesburg, Miss. ... 6-3/315. ... Full name: Thomas Marcus Spriggs.
HIGH SCHOOL: Byram (Jackson, Miss.).
JUNIOR COLLEGE: Hinds Community College (Miss.).
COLLEGE: Houston.
TRANSACTIONS/CAREER NOTES: Selected by Buffalo Bills in sixth round (185th pick overall) of 1997 NFL draft. ... Signed by Bills (June 13, 1997). ... Granted free agency (February 11, 2000). ... Re-signed by Bills (April 10, 2000). ... Granted unconditional free agency (March 2, 2001). ... Signed by Miami Dolphins (April 19, 2001).
PLAYING EXPERIENCE: Buffalo NFL, 1997-2000. ... Games/Games started: 1997 (2/0), 1998 (1/0), 1999 (11/2), 2000 (16/11). Total: 30/13.

SPRINGS, SHAWN   CB   SEAHAWKS

PERSONAL: Born March 11, 1975, in Williamsburg, W.Va. ... 6-0/195. ... Son of Ron Springs, running back with Dallas Cowboys (1979-84) and Tampa Bay Buccaneers (1985 and 1986).
HIGH SCHOOL: Springbrook (Silver Spring, Md.).
COLLEGE: Ohio State.
TRANSACTIONS/CAREER NOTES: Selected by Seattle Seahawks in first round (third pick overall) of 1997 NFL draft. ... Signed by Seahawks (August 4, 1997).
HONORS: Named cornerback on THE SPORTING NEWS college All-America second team (1996). ... Played in Pro Bowl (1998 season).
PRO STATISTICS: 1998—Recovered two fumbles for 14 yards and one touchdown. 1999—Returned one kickoff for 15 yards, returned blocked field goal 61 yards for a touchdown and recovered one fumble.

			INTERCEPTIONS				TOTALS		
Year Team	G	GS	No.	Yds.	Avg.	TD	TD	2pt.	Pts.	Fum.
1997—Seattle NFL	10	10	1	0	0.0	0	0	0	0	0
1998—Seattle NFL	16	16	7	142	20.3	▲2	3	0	18	0
1999—Seattle NFL	16	16	5	77	15.4	0	1	0	6	0
2000—Seattle NFL	16	16	2	8	4.0	0	0	0	0	0
Pro totals (4 years)	58	58	15	227	15.1	2	4	0	24	0

ST. CLAIR, JOHN   OT   RAMS

PERSONAL: Born July 15, 1977, in Roanoke, Va. ... 6-4/315. ... Full name: John Bradley St. Clair.
HIGH SCHOOL: William Fleming (Roanoke, Va.).
COLLEGE: Virginia.
TRANSACTIONS/CAREER NOTES: Selected by St. Louis Rams in third round (94th pick overall) of 2000 NFL draft. ... Signed by Rams (July 20, 2000). ... Inactive for all 16 games (2000).

ST. LOUIS, BRAD   TE   BENGALS

PERSONAL: Born August 19, 1976, in Waverly, Mo. ... 6-3/246. ... Full name: Brad Allen St. Louis.
HIGH SCHOOL: Belton (Mo.).
COLLEGE: Southwest Missouri State.
TRANSACTIONS/CAREER NOTES: Selected by Cincinnati Bengals in seventh round (210th pick overall) of 2000 NFL draft. ... Signed by Bengals (July 20, 2000).
PLAYING EXPERIENCE: Cincinnati NFL, 2000. ... Games/Games started: 2000 (16/0).

STAAT, JEREMY   DE   SEAHAWKS

PERSONAL: Born October 10, 1976, in Bakersfield, Calif. ... 6-5/300. ... Full name: Jeremy Ray Staat. ... Name pronounced STOHT.
HIGH SCHOOL: Bakersfield (Calif.).
JUNIOR COLLEGE: Bakersfield (Calif.) College.
COLLEGE: Arizona State.
TRANSACTIONS/CAREER NOTES: Selected by Pittsburgh Steelers in second round (41st pick overall) of 1998 NFL draft. ... Signed by Steelers (June 19, 1998). ... On injured reserve with shoulder injury (December 13, 2000-remainder of season). ... Released by Steelers (February 19, 2001). ... Signed by Seattle Seqhawks (April 1, 2001).
PLAYING EXPERIENCE: Pittsburgh NFL, 1998-2000. ... Games/Games started: 1998 (5/0), 1999 (16/2), 2000 (7/0). Total: 28/2.
HONORS: Named defensive tackle on THE SPORTING NEWS college All-America second team (1997).

STABLEIN, BRIAN — WR

PERSONAL: Born April 14, 1970, in Erie, Pa. ... 6-1/194. ... Full name: Brian Patrick Stablein. ... Name pronounced STABE-line.
HIGH SCHOOL: McDowell (Erie, Pa.).
COLLEGE: Ohio State.
TRANSACTIONS/CAREER NOTES: Selected by Denver Broncos in eighth round (210nd pick overall) of 1993 NFL draft. ... Signed by Broncos (June 7, 1993). ... Released by Broncos (August 24, 1993). ... Signed by Indianapolis Colts to practice squad (September 7, 1993). ... Active for two games (1994); did not play. ... Granted free agency (February 14, 1997). ... Re-signed by Colts (June 10, 1997). ... Granted unconditional free agency (February 13, 1998). ... Signed by New England Patriots (March 19, 1998). ... Released by Patriots (August 30, 1998). ... Signed by Detroit Lions (September 1, 1998). ... Granted unconditional free agency (February 12, 1999). ... Re-signed by Lions (April 6, 1999). ... Granted unconditional free agency (March 2, 2001).
CHAMPIONSHIP GAME EXPERIENCE: Played in AFC championship game (1995 season).
PRO STATISTICS: 1999—Recovered one fumble.
SINGLE GAME HIGHS (regular season): Receptions—5 (November 24, 1996, vs. New England); yards—48 (November 7, 1999, vs. St. Louis); and touchdown receptions—1 (October 24, 1999, vs. Carolina).

				RECEIVING				PUNT RETURNS				TOTALS		
Year Team	G	GS	No.	Yds.	Avg.	TD	No.	Yds.	Avg.	TD	TD	2pt.	Pts.	Fum.
1993—Indianapolis NFL								Did not play.						
1994—Indianapolis NFL								Did not play.						
1995—Indianapolis NFL	15	0	8	95	11.9	0	0	0	0.0	0	0	0	0	0
1996—Indianapolis NFL	16	0	18	192	10.7	1	6	56	9.3	0	1	0	6	0
1997—Indianapolis NFL	16	0	25	253	10.1	1	17	133	7.8	0	1	1	8	0
1998—Detroit NFL	10	0	7	80	11.4	0	0	0	0.0	0	0	0	0	0
1999—Detroit NFL	16	2	11	119	10.8	1	1	9	9.0	0	1	†1	8	1
2000—Detroit NFL	14	5	8	53	6.6	0	0	0	0.0	0	0	0	0	1
Pro totals (6 years)	87	7	77	792	10.3	3	24	198	8.3	0	3	2	22	2

STACHELSKI, DAVE — TE — SAINTS

PERSONAL: Born March 1, 1977, in Chicago. ... 6-3/250.
HIGH SCHOOL: Marysville-Pilchuck (Marysville, Wash.).
COLLEGE: Boise State.
TRANSACTIONS/CAREER NOTES: Selected by New England Patriots in fifth round (141st pick overall) of 2000 NFL draft. ... Signed by Patriots (July 14, 2000). ... Released by Patriots (August 14, 2000). ... Signed by New Orleans Saints (August 15, 2000). ... Released by Saints (August 27, 2000). ... Re-signed by Saints to practice squad (August 29, 2000). ... Activated (September 14, 2000).
PLAYING EXPERIENCE: New Orleans NFL, 2000. ... Games/Games started: 2000 (4/0).
PRO STATISTICS: 2000—Recovered one fumble.

STAI, BRENDEN — G — LIONS

PERSONAL: Born March 30, 1972, in Phoenix. ... 6-4/312. ... Full name: Brenden Michael Stai. ... Name pronounced STY.
HIGH SCHOOL: Anaheim High.
COLLEGE: Nebraska.
TRANSACTIONS/CAREER NOTES: Selected by Pittsburgh Steelers in third round (91st pick overall) of 1995 NFL draft. ... Signed by Steelers (July 18, 1995). ... Granted free agency (February 13, 1998). ... Re-signed by Steelers (June 9, 1998). ... Released by Steelers (March 14, 2000). ... Signed by Kansas City Chiefs (May 4, 2000). ... Traded by Chiefs to Jacksonville Jaguars for fourth-round pick (RB George Layne) in 2001 draft (August 16, 2000). ... Released by Jaguars (March 1, 2001). ... Signed by Detroit Lions (March 12, 2001).
PLAYING EXPERIENCE: Pittsburgh NFL, 1995-1999; Jacksonville NFL, 2000. ... Games/Games started: 1995 (16/9), 1996 (9/9), 1997 (10/9), 1998 (16/16), 1999 (16/16), 2000 (16/16). Total: 83/75.
CHAMPIONSHIP GAME EXPERIENCE: Played in AFC championship game (1995 and 1997 seasons). ... Played in Super Bowl XXX (1995 season).
HONORS: Named offensive lineman on THE SPORTING NEWS college All-America second team (1994).

STALEY, DUCE — RB — EAGLES

PERSONAL: Born February 27, 1975, in Columbia, S.C. ... 5-11/220. ... Name pronounced DEUCE.
HIGH SCHOOL: Airport (Columbia, S.C.).
JUNIOR COLLEGE: Itawamba Community College (Miss.).
COLLEGE: South Carolina.
TRANSACTIONS/CAREER NOTES: Selected by Philadelphia Eagles in third round (71st pick overall) of 1997 NFL draft. ... Signed by Eagles (June 12, 1997). ... On injured reserve with foot injury (October 10, 2000-remainder of season).
PRO STATISTICS: 1997—Recovered one fumble. 1998—Recovered two fumbles. 1999—Recovered two fumbles. 2000—Recovered one fumble.
SINGLE GAME HIGHS (regular season): Attempts—30 (December 13, 1998, vs. Arizona); yards—201 (September 3, 2000, vs. Dallas); and rushing touchdowns—2 (September 27, 1998, vs. Kansas City).
STATISTICAL PLATEAUS: 100-yard rushing games: 1998 (1), 1999 (5), 2000 (1). Total: 7.

			RUSHING				RECEIVING				KICKOFF RETURNS				TOTALS		
Year Team	G	GS	Att.	Yds.	Avg.	TD	No.	Yds.	Avg.	TD	No.	Yds.	Avg.	TD	TD 2pt.	Pts.	Fum.
1997—Philadelphia NFL	16	0	7	29	4.1	0	2	22	11.0	0	47	1139	24.2	0	0 0	0	0
1998—Philadelphia NFL	16	13	258	1065	4.1	5	57	432	7.6	1	1	19	19.0	0	6 0	36	2
1999—Philadelphia NFL	16	16	325	1273	3.9	4	41	294	7.2	2	0	0	0.0	0	6 0	36	5
2000—Philadelphia NFL	5	5	79	344	4.4	1	25	201	8.0	0	0	0	0.0	0	1 0	6	3
Pro totals (4 years)	53	34	669	2711	4.1	10	125	949	7.6	3	48	1158	24.1	0	13 0	78	10

STANLEY, CHAD   P   49ERS

PERSONAL: Born January 29, 1976, in Ore City, Texas. ... 6-3/205. ... Full name: Benjamin Chadwick Stanley.
HIGH SCHOOL: Ore City (Texas).
COLLEGE: Stephen F. Austin State.
TRANSACTIONS/CAREER NOTES: Signed as non-drafted free agent by San Francisco 49ers (April 23, 1999).
PRO STATISTICS: 1999—Rushed once for no yards and recovered one fumble.

				PUNTING			
Year Team	G	No.	Yds.	Avg.	Net avg.	In. 20	Blk.
1999—San Francisco NFL	16	69	2737	39.7	30.7	20	†2
2000—San Francisco NFL	16	69	2727	39.5	32.2	15	1
Pro totals (2 years)	32	138	5464	39.6	31.5	35	3

STARKEY, JASON   C   CARDINALS

PERSONAL: Born July 15, 1977, in Barboursville, W. Va. ... 6-5/270.
HIGH SCHOOL: Cabell-Midland (W. Va.).
COLLEGE: Marshall.
TRANSACTIONS/CAREER NOTES: Signed as non-drafted free agent by Arizona Cardinals (June 1, 2000). ... Released by Cardinals (August 27, 2000). ... Re-signed by Cardinals to practice squad (August 28, 2000). ... Activated (September 8, 2000). ... Released by Cardinals (September 11, 2000). ... Re-signed by Cardinals to practice squad (September 13, 2000).
PLAYING EXPERIENCE: Arizona NFL, 2000. ... Games/Games started: 2000 (2/0).

STARKS, DUANE   CB   RAVENS

PERSONAL: Born May 23, 1974, in Miami. ... 5-10/170. ... Full name: Duane Lonell Starks.
HIGH SCHOOL: Miami Beach Senior.
JUNIOR COLLEGE: Holmes Junior College (Miss.).
COLLEGE: Miami (Fla.).
TRANSACTIONS/CAREER NOTES: Selected by Baltimore Ravens in first round (10th pick overall) of 1998 NFL draft. ... Signed by Ravens (August 5, 1998).
CHAMPIONSHIP GAME EXPERIENCE: Played in AFC championship game (2000 season). ... Member of Super Bowl championship team (2000 season).
PRO STATISTICS: 2000—Returned nine punts for 135 yards, fumbled once and recovered two fumbles.

			INTERCEPTIONS			
Year Team	G	GS	No.	Yds.	Avg.	TD
1998—Baltimore NFL	16	8	5	3	0.6	0
1999—Baltimore NFL	16	5	5	59	11.8	1
2000—Baltimore NFL	15	15	6	125	20.8	0
Pro totals (3 years)	47	28	16	187	11.7	1

STECKER, AARON   RB   BUCCANEERS

PERSONAL: Born November 13, 1975, in Green Bay. ... 5-10/205.
HIGH SCHOOL: Ashwaubenon (Green Bay).
COLLEGE: Western Illinois.
TRANSACTIONS/CAREER NOTES: Signed as non-drafted free agent by Chicago Bears (April 18, 1999). ... Released by Bears (August 30, 1999). ... Signed by Tampa Bay Buccaneers to practice squad (October 20, 1999).
PLAYING EXPERIENCE: Tampa Bay NFL, 2000. ... Games/Games started: 2000 (10/0).
PRO STATISTICS: 2000—Rushed 12 times for 31 yards, caught one pass for 15 yards, returned 29 kickoffs for 663 yards and fumbled once.
SINGLE GAME HIGHS (regular season): Attempts—5 (September 10, 2000, vs. Chicago); yards—26 (September 10, 2000, vs. Chicago); and rushing touchdowns—0.

STEELE, GLEN   DE   BENGALS

PERSONAL: Born October 4, 1974, in Ligonier, Ind. ... 6-4/295. ... Full name: James Lendale Steele Jr.
HIGH SCHOOL: West Noble (Ligonier, Ind.).
COLLEGE: Michigan.
TRANSACTIONS/CAREER NOTES: Selected by Cincinnati Bengals in fourth round (105th pick overall) of 1998 NFL draft. ... Signed by Bengals (July 14, 1998). ... On injured reserve with ankle injury (December 15, 1998-remainder of season).
PLAYING EXPERIENCE: Cincinnati NFL, 1998-2000. ... Games/Games started: 1998 (10/0), 1999 (16/1), 2000 (16/1). Total: 42/2.
PRO STATISTICS: 2000—Credited with two sacks.

STEPHENS, JAMAIN   OT   BENGALS

PERSONAL: Born January 9, 1974, in Lumberton, N.C. ... 6-6/335.
HIGH SCHOOL: Lumberton (N.C.).
COLLEGE: North Carolina A&T.
TRANSACTIONS/CAREER NOTES: Selected by Pittsburgh Steelers in first round (29th pick overall) of 1996 NFL draft. ... Signed by Steelers (July 17, 1996). ... Inactive for all 16 games (1996). ... Claimed on waivers by Cincinnati Bengals (August 3, 1999). ... On reserve/suspended list (September 5-October 11, 1999).
PLAYING EXPERIENCE: Pittsburgh NFL, 1997 and 1998; Cincinnati NFL, 1999 and 2000. ... Games/Games started: 1997 (7/1), 1998 (11/10), 1999 (7/2), 2000 (5/0). Total: 30/13.
CHAMPIONSHIP GAME EXPERIENCE: Member of Steelers for AFC championship game (1997 season); inactive.

STEPHENS, REGGIE — CB

PERSONAL: Born February 21, 1975, in Dallas. ... 5-9/200.
HIGH SCHOOL: Santa Cruz (Calif.).
JUNIOR COLLEGE: Cabrillo College (Calif.).
COLLEGE: Rutgers.
TRANSACTIONS/CAREER NOTES: Signed as non-drafted free agent by New York Giants (April 27, 1999). ... Released by Giants (September 5, 1999). ... Re-signed by Giants to practice squad (November 16, 1999). ... Activated (December 10, 1999). ... Released by Giants (December 14, 1999). ... Re-signed by Giants to practice squad (December 15, 1999). ... Released by Giants (May 15, 2001).
PLAYING EXPERIENCE: New York Giants NFL, 1999 and 2000. ... Games/Games started: 1999 (1/0), 2000 (15/0). Total: 16/0.
CHAMPIONSHIP GAME EXPERIENCE: Member of Giants for NFC championship game (2000 season); inactive. ... Member of Giants for Super Bowl XXXV (2000 season); inactive.
PRO STATISTICS: 2000—Intercepted three passes for four yards and returned three kickoffs for 69 yards.

STEPNOSKI, MARK — C — COWBOYS

PERSONAL: Born January 20, 1967, in Erie, Pa. ... 6-2/265. ... Full name: Mark Matthew Stepnoski.
HIGH SCHOOL: Cathedral Prep (Erie, Pa.).
COLLEGE: Pittsburgh (degree in communications).
TRANSACTIONS/CAREER NOTES: Selected by Dallas Cowboys in third round (57th pick overall) of 1989 NFL draft. ... Signed by Cowboys (July 23, 1989). ... Granted free agency (February 1, 1992). ... Re-signed by Cowboys (September 5, 1992). ... Granted roster exemption (September 5-14, 1992). ... On injured reserve with knee injury (December 22, 1993-remainder of season). ... Granted unconditional free agency (February 17, 1994). ... Re-signed by Cowboys (June 29, 1994). ... Granted unconditional free agency (February 17, 1995). ... Signed by Houston Oilers (March 11, 1995). ... Oilers franchise moved to Tennessee for 1997 season. ... Granted unconditional free agency (February 12, 1999). ... Signed by Cowboys (April 13, 1999). ... On injured reserve with knee injury (December 12, 2000-remainder of season).
PLAYING EXPERIENCE: Dallas NFL, 1989-1994, 1999 and 2000; Houston NFL, 1995 and 1996; Tennessee NFL, 1997 and 1998. ... Games/Games started: 1989 (16/4), 1990 (16/16), 1991 (16/16), 1992 (14/14), 1993 (13/13), 1994 (16/16), 1995 (16/16), 1996 (16/16), 1997 (16/16), 1998 (13/13), 1999 (15/15), 2000 (11/11). Total: 178/166.
CHAMPIONSHIP GAME EXPERIENCE: Played in NFC championship game (1992 and 1994 seasons). ... Member of Super Bowl championship team (1992 season).
HONORS: Named guard on THE SPORTING NEWS college All-America first team (1988). ... Played in Pro Bowl (1992 and 1994-1996 seasons).
PRO STATISTICS: 1989—Recovered three fumbles. 1990—Returned one kickoff for 15 yards. 1992—Recovered one fumble. 1993—Fumbled once. 1994—Fumbled four times for minus three yards. 1997—Fumbled twice and recovered one fumble for minus seven yards. 1998—Rushed once for no yards, fumbled twice and recovered one fumble for minus six yards. 1999—Fumbled once and recovered one fumble for minus 26 yards. 2000—Fumbled once.

STEUSSIE, TODD — OT — PANTHERS

PERSONAL: Born December 1, 1970, in Canoga Park, Calif. ... 6-6/308. ... Full name: Todd Edward Steussie. ... Name pronounced STEW-see.
HIGH SCHOOL: Agoura (Calif.).
COLLEGE: California.
TRANSACTIONS/CAREER NOTES: Selected by Minnesota Vikings in first round (19th pick overall) of 1994 NFL draft. ... Signed by Vikings (July 13, 1994). ... Released by Vikings (March 14, 2001). ... Signed by Carolina Panthers (March 29, 2001).
PLAYING EXPERIENCE: Minnesota NFL, 1994-2000. ... Games/Games started: 1994 (16/16), 1995 (16/16), 1996 (16/16), 1997 (16/16), 1998 (15/15), 1999 (16/16), 2000 (16/16). Total: 111/111.
CHAMPIONSHIP GAME EXPERIENCE: Played in NFC championship game (1998 and 2000 seasons).
HONORS: Named offensive lineman on THE SPORTING NEWS college All-America second team (1993). ... Played in Pro Bowl (1997 and 1998 seasons).
PRO STATISTICS: 1994—Recovered one fumble. 1996—Recovered one fumble. 1999—Recovered one fumble.

STEVENS, MATT — S — PATRIOTS

PERSONAL: Born June 15, 1973, in Chapel Hill, N.C. ... 6-0/206. ... Full name: Matthew Brian Stevens.
HIGH SCHOOL: Chapel Hill (N.C.).
COLLEGE: Appalachian State.
TRANSACTIONS/CAREER NOTES: Selected by Buffalo Bills in third round (87th pick overall) of 1996 NFL draft. ... Signed by Bills (July 15, 1996). ... Claimed on waivers by Philadelphia Eagles (August 25, 1997). ... On suspended list for anabolic steroid use (August 27-September 29, 1997). ... Claimed on waivers by Washington Redskins (December 8, 1998). ... Granted free agency (February 12, 1999). ... Re-signed by Redskins (April 23, 1999). ... Granted unconditional free agency (February 11, 2000). ... Re-signed by Redskins (May 12, 2000). ... Claimed on waivers by New England Patriots (December 20, 2000). ... Granted unconditional free agency (March 2, 2001). ... Re-signed by Patriots (March 16, 2001).
PRO STATISTICS: 1996—Recovered one fumble. 1997—Recovered one fumble. 1999—Credited with one sack and recovered one fumble. 2000—Recovered one fumble for one yard.

			INTERCEPTIONS			
Year Team	G	GS	No.	Yds.	Avg.	TD
1996—Buffalo NFL	13	11	2	0	0.0	0
1997—Philadelphia NFL	11	0	1	0	0.0	0
1998—Philadelphia NFL	7	1	0	0	0.0	0
—Washington NFL	3	0	0	0	0.0	0
1999—Washington NFL	15	1	6	61	10.2	0
2000—Washington NFL	15	4	1	0	0.0	0
—New England NFL	1	0	0	0	0.0	0
Pro totals (5 years)	65	17	10	61	6.1	0

PERSONAL: Born December 27, 1971, in Morristown, Tenn. ... 6-1/226. ... Full name: James Ottis Stewart III.
HIGH SCHOOL: Morristown-Hamblen West (Morristown, Tenn.).
COLLEGE: Tennessee.
TRANSACTIONS/CAREER NOTES: Selected by Jacksonville Jaguars in first round (19th pick overall) of 1995 NFL draft. ... Signed by Jaguars (June 1, 1995). ... On injured reserve with knee injury (September 22, 1998-remainder of season). ... Granted unconditional free agency (February 11, 2000). ... Signed by Detroit Lions (February 14, 2000).
CHAMPIONSHIP GAME EXPERIENCE: Played in AFC championship game (1996 and 1999 seasons).
PRO STATISTICS: 1996—Recovered one fumble. 1999—Recovered one fumble. 2000—Recovered one fumble.
SINGLE GAME HIGHS (regular season): Attempts—37 (December 17, 2000, vs. New York Jets); yards—164 (December 17, 2000, vs. New York Jets); and rushing touchdowns—5 (October 12, 1997, vs. Philadelphia).
STATISTICAL PLATEAUS: 100-yard rushing games: 1996 (1), 1997 (1), 1998 (2), 1999 (2), 2000 (3). Total: 9.
MISCELLANEOUS: Holds Jacksonville Jaguars all-time record for most rushing touchdowns (33). ... Shares Jacksonville Jaguars all-time record for touchdowns (38).

Year Team	G	GS	RUSHING				RECEIVING				TOTALS			
			Att.	Yds.	Avg.	TD	No.	Yds.	Avg.	TD	TD	2pt.	Pts.	Fum.
1995—Jacksonville NFL	14	7	137	525	3.8	2	21	190	9.0	1	3	0	18	1
1996—Jacksonville NFL	13	11	190	723	3.8	8	30	177	5.9	2	10	0	60	2
1997—Jacksonville NFL	16	5	136	555	4.1	8	41	336	8.2	1	9	0	54	0
1998—Jacksonville NFL	3	3	53	217	4.1	2	6	42	7.0	1	3	0	18	2
1999—Jacksonville NFL	14	7	249	931	3.7	▲13	21	108	5.1	0	13	0	78	4
2000—Detroit NFL	16	16	‡339	1184	3.5	10	32	287	9.0	1	11	*3	72	4
Pro totals (6 years)	76	49	1104	4135	3.7	43	151	1140	7.5	6	49	3	300	13

PERSONAL: Born October 16, 1972, in New Orleans. ... 6-1/211.
HIGH SCHOOL: John Ehret (Marrero, La.).
COLLEGE: Colorado.
TRANSACTIONS/CAREER NOTES: Selected by Pittsburgh Steelers in second round (60th pick overall) of 1995 NFL draft. ... Signed by Steelers (July 17, 1995).
CHAMPIONSHIP GAME EXPERIENCE: Played in AFC championship game (1995 and 1997 seasons). ... Played in Super Bowl XXX (1995 season).
PRO STATISTICS: 1995—Compiled a quarterback rating of 136.9. 1996—Compiled a quarterback rating of 18.8 and fumbled once. 1997—Compiled a quarterback rating of 75.2, fumbled six times and recovered one fumble for minus one yard. 1998—Compiled a quarterback rating of 62.9, punted once for 35 yards, fumbled three times and recovered two fumbles. 1999—Compiled a quarterback rating of 64.9, fumbled four times and recovered one fumble. 2000—Compiled a quarterback rating of 73.6 and recovered three fumbles for minus one yard.
SINGLE GAME HIGHS (regular season): Attempts—48 (December 13, 1997, vs. New England); completions—26 (December 13, 1997, vs. New England); yards—317 (October 26, 1997, vs. Jacksonville); and touchdown passes—3 (November 26, 2000, vs. Denver).
STATISTICAL PLATEAUS: 300-yard passing games: 1997 (2). ... 100-yard rushing games: 1996 (1), 1998 (1). Total: 2.
MISCELLANEOUS: Regular-season record as starting NFL quarterback: 30-24 (.556). ... Postseason record as starting NFL quarterback: 1-1 (.500). ... Started two games at wide receiver (1995). ... Started two games at wide receiver (1996). ... Started one game at wide receiver (1999).

Year Team	G	GS	PASSING							RUSHING				RECEIVING				TOTALS		
			Att.	Cmp.	Pct.	Yds.	TD	Int.	Avg.	Att.	Yds.	Avg.	TD	No.	Yds.	Avg.	TD	TD	2pt.	Pts.
1995—Pittsburgh NFL	10	2	7	5	71.4	60	1	0	8.57	15	86	5.7	1	14	235	16.8	1	2	0	12
1996—Pittsburgh NFL	16	2	30	11	36.7	100	0	2	3.33	39	171	4.4	5	17	293	17.2	3	8	0	48
1997—Pittsburgh NFL	16	16	440	236	53.6	3020	21	§17	6.86	88	476	5.4	11	0	0	0.0	0	11	0	66
1998—Pittsburgh NFL	16	16	458	252	55.0	2560	11	18	5.59	81	406	5.0	2	1	17	17.0	0	2	0	12
1999—Pittsburgh NFL	16	12	275	160	58.2	1464	6	10	5.32	56	258	4.6	2	9	113	12.6	1	3	0	18
2000—Pittsburgh NFL	16	11	289	151	52.2	1860	11	8	6.44	78	436	5.6	7	0	0	0.0	0	7	0	42
Pro totals (6 years)	90	59	1499	815	54.4	9064	50	55	6.05	357	1833	5.1	28	41	658	16.0	5	33	0	198

PERSONAL: Born June 18, 1973, in Oklahoma City. ... 5-10/198. ... Full name: Rayna Cottrell Stewart II. ... Name pronounced ruh-NAY.
HIGH SCHOOL: Chatsworth (Calif.).
COLLEGE: Northern Arizona (degree in advertising, 1995).
TRANSACTIONS/CAREER NOTES: Selected by Houston Oilers in fifth round (143rd pick overall) of 1996 NFL draft. ... Signed by Oilers (June 27, 1996). ... Oilers franchise moved to Tennessee for 1997 season. ... Released by Oilers (August 30, 1998). ... Signed by Miami Dolphins (September 15, 1998). ... Released by Dolphins (September 7, 1999). ... Signed by Jacksonville Jaguars (September 20, 1999). ... Granted unconditional free agency (February 11, 2000). ... Re-signed by Jaguars (February 25, 2000). ... Released by Jaguars (February 27, 2001).
PLAYING EXPERIENCE: Houston NFL, 1996; Tennessee NFL, 1997; Miami NFL, 1998; Jacksonville NFL, 1999 and 2000. ... Games/Games started: 1996 (15/0), 1997 (16/5), 1998 (14/0), 1999 (14/0), 2000 (12/10). Total: 71/15.
CHAMPIONSHIP GAME EXPERIENCE: Played in AFC championship game (1999 season).
PRO STATISTICS: 1997—Credited with $^{1}/_{2}$ sack and recovered one fumble. 1999—Recovered one fumble. 2000—Intercepted two passes for 37 yards and recovered two fumbles for two yards.

PERSONAL: Born September 30, 1973, in Moncks Corner, S.C. ... 6-1/206.
HIGH SCHOOL: Berkeley (Moncks Corner, S.C.).
COLLEGE: Georgia Tech (degree in business management).
TRANSACTIONS/CAREER NOTES: Selected by Detroit Lions in third round (76th pick overall) of 1996 NFL draft. ... Signed by Lions (July 21, 1996). ... Released by Lions (August 24, 1997). ... Re-signed by Lions (October 30, 1997). ... Granted free agency (February 12, 1999). ... Re-signed by Lions (April 26, 1999). ... On injured reserve with groin injury (October 30, 1999-remainder of season). ... Granted unconditional

S

free agency (February 11, 2000). ... Re-signed by Lions (April 26, 2000). ... Released by Lions (August 21, 2000). ... Re-signed by Lions (December 12, 2000). ... Granted unconditional free agency (March 2, 2001).
PLAYING EXPERIENCE: Detroit NFL, 1996-2000. ... Games/Games started: 1996 (14/2), 1997 (8/0), 1998 (16/0), 1999 (2/0), 2000 (1/0). Total: 41/2.
PRO STATISTICS: 1996—Intercepted one pass for 14 yards. 1999—Credited with one sack.

STILLS, GARY LB CHIEFS

PERSONAL: Born July 11, 1974, in Trenton, N.J. ... 6-2/235.
HIGH SCHOOL: Valley Forge (Pa.) Military Academy.
COLLEGE: West Virginia.
TRANSACTIONS/CAREER NOTES: Selected by Kansas City Chiefs in third round (75th pick overall) of 1999 NFL draft. ... Signed by Chiefs (July 26, 1999). ... Assigned by Chiefs to Frankfurt Galaxy in 2001 NFL Europe enhancement allocation program (February 19, 2001).
PLAYING EXPERIENCE: Kansas City NFL, 1999 and 2000. ... Games/Games started: 1999 (2/0), 2000 (12/0).
PRO STATISTICS: 2000—Recovered one fumble.

STINCHCOMB, MATT OT RAIDERS

PERSONAL: Born June 3, 1977, in Lilburn, Ga. ... 6-6/310. ... Full name: Matthew Douglass Stinchcomb.
HIGH SCHOOL: Parkview (Lilburn, Ga.).
COLLEGE: Georgia.
TRANSACTIONS/CAREER NOTES: Selected by Oakland Raiders in first round (18th pick overall) of 1999 NFL draft. ... Signed by Raiders (July 22, 1999). ... Inactive for three games (1999). ... On injured reserve with shoulder injury (October 1, 1999-remainder of season).
PLAYING EXPERIENCE: Oakland NFL, 2000. ... Games/Games started: 2000 (13/9).
CHAMPIONSHIP GAME EXPERIENCE: Member of Raiders for AFC Championship game (2000 season); did not play.
HONORS: Named offensive tackle on THE SPORTING NEWS college All-America second team (1997 and 1998).

STITH, SHYRONE RB JAGUARS

PERSONAL: Born April 2, 1978, in Portsmouth, Va. ... 5-7/206. ... Full name: Shyrone Orenthal Stith.
HIGH SCHOOL: Western Branch (Chesapeake, Va.).
COLLEGE: Virginia Tech.
TRANSACTIONS/CAREER NOTES: Selected after junior season by Jacksonville Jaguars in seventh round (243rd pick overall) of 2000 NFL draft. ... Signed by Jaguars (May 17, 2000).
SINGLE GAME HIGHS (regular season): Attempts—11 (December 3, 2000, vs. Cleveland); yards—27 (December 3, 2000, vs. Cleveland); and rushing touchdowns—1 (December 3, 2000, vs. Cleveland).

			RUSHING				KICKOFF RETURNS				TOTALS			
Year Team	G	GS	Att.	Yds.	Avg.	TD	No.	Yds.	Avg.	TD	TD	2pt.	Pts.	Fum.
2000—Jacksonville NFL	14	0	20	55	2.8	1	33	785	23.8	0	1	0	6	1

STOERNER, CLINT QB COWBOYS

PERSONAL: Born December 29, 1977, in Baytown, Texas. ... 6-2/210.
HIGH SCHOOL: Lee (Baytown, Texas).
COLLEGE: Arkansas.
TRANSACTIONS/CAREER NOTES: Signed as non-drafted free agent by Dallas Cowboys (May 5, 2000). ... Released by Cowboys (August 27, 2000). ... Re-signed by Cowboys to practice squad (August 29, 2000). ... Activated (September 8, 2000). ... Released by Cowboys (October 10, 2000). ... Re-signed by Cowboys to practice squad (October 11, 2000). ... Activated (November 1, 2000). ... Released by Cowboys (November 21, 2000). ... Re-signed by Cowboys to practice squad (November 27, 2000). ... Activated (December 13, 2000). ... Assigned by Cowboys to Scottish Claymores in 2001 NFL Europe enhancement allocation program (February 19, 2001).
PLAYING EXPERIENCE: Dallas NFL, 2000. ... Games/Games started: 2000 (1/0).
PRO STATISTICS: 2000—Attempted five passes with three completions for 53 yards and a touchdown.
SINGLE GAME HIGHS (regular season): Attempts—5 (September 24, 2000, vs. San Francisco); completions—3 (September 24, 2000, vs. San Francisco); passing yards—53 (September 24, 2000, vs. San Francisco); and touchdown passes—1 (September 24, 2000, vs. San Francisco).

STOKES, BARRY OT/G PACKERS

PERSONAL: Born December 20, 1973, in Flint, Mich. ... 6-4/310. ... Full name: Barry Wade Stokes.
HIGH SCHOOL: Davison (Mich.).
COLLEGE: Eastern Michigan.
TRANSACTIONS/CAREER NOTES: Signed as non-drafted free agent by Detroit Lions (April 26, 1996). ... Released by Lions (August 14, 1996). ... Signed by Jacksonville Jaguars to practice squad (October 23, 1996). ... Granted free agency after 1996 season. ... Signed by Atlanta Falcons (January 30, 1997). ... Released by Falcons (August 1997). ... Signed by St. Louis Rams to practice squad (August 26, 1997). ... Released by Rams (October 6, 1997). ... Signed by Miami Dolphins to practice squad (November 26, 1997). ... Assigned by Dolphins to Scottish Claymores in 1998 NFL Europe enhancement allocation program (February 18, 1998). ... Released by Dolphins (August 25, 1998). ... Re-signed by Dolphins (November 4, 1998). ... Assigned by Dolphins to Scottish Claymores in 1999 NFL Europe enhancement allocation program (February 22, 1999). ... Released by Dolphins (September 4, 1999). ... Signed by Green Bay Packers (September 8, 1999). ... Released by Packers (September 21, 1999). ... Re-signed by Packers (October 20, 1999). ... Inactive for five games (1999). ... Released by Packers (November 9, 1999). ... Signed by Oakland Raiders (January 2, 2000). ... Released by Raiders (July 21, 2000). ... Signed by Packers (July 22, 2000). ... Released by Packers (September 27, 2000). ... Re-signed by Packers (October 23, 2000).
PLAYING EXPERIENCE: Scottish NFLE, 1998; Miami NFL, 1998; Green Bay NFL, 2000. ... Games/Games started: NFLE 1998 (10/10), NFL 1998 (3/0), 2000 (8/0). Total NFL: 11/0. Total Pro: 21/10.

STOKES, J.J.　　　WR　　　49ERS

PERSONAL: Born October 6, 1972, in San Diego. ... 6-4/217. ... Full name: Jerel Jamal Stokes.
HIGH SCHOOL: Point Loma (San Diego).
COLLEGE: UCLA (degree in sociology, 1994).
TRANSACTIONS/CAREER NOTES: Selected by San Francisco 49ers in first round (10th pick overall) of 1995 NFL draft. ... Signed by 49ers (July 27, 1995). ... On injured reserve with wrist injury (October 26, 1996-remainder of season). ... Granted unconditional free agency (February 12, 1999). ... Re-signed by 49ers (March 8, 1999).
CHAMPIONSHIP GAME EXPERIENCE: Played in NFC championship game (1997 season).
HONORS: Named wide receiver on THE SPORTING NEWS college All-America first team (1993).
PRO STATISTICS: 1997—Recovered two fumbles. 1999—Recovered one fumble. 2000—Rushed once for six yards.
SINGLE GAME HIGHS (regular season): Receptions—9 (October 18, 1998, vs. Indianapolis); yards—130 (January 3, 2000, vs. Atlanta); and touchdown receptions—2 (December 6, 1998, vs. Carolina).
STATISTICAL PLATEAUS: 100-yard receiving games: 1995 (1), 1998 (2), 1999 (1). Total: 4.

| | | | | RECEIVING | | | | TOTALS | | |
Year Team	G	GS	No.	Yds.	Avg.	TD	TD	2pt.	Pts.	Fum.
1995—San Francisco NFL	12	2	38	517	13.6	4	4	0	24	0
1996—San Francisco NFL	6	6	18	249	13.8	0	0	0	0	0
1997—San Francisco NFL	16	16	58	733	12.6	4	4	0	24	1
1998—San Francisco NFL	16	13	63	770	12.2	8	8	0	48	0
1999—San Francisco NFL	16	7	34	429	12.6	3	3	†1	20	1
2000—San Francisco NFL	16	3	30	524	17.5	3	3	1	20	0
Pro totals (6 years)	82	47	241	3222	13.4	22	22	2	136	2

STOKLEY, BRANDON　　　WR　　　RAVENS

PERSONAL: Born June 23, 1976, in Blacksburg, Va. ... 5-11/197.
HIGH SCHOOL: Comeaux (Lafayette, La.).
COLLEGE: Southwestern Louisiana.
TRANSACTIONS/CAREER NOTES: Selected by Baltimore Ravens in fourth round (105th pick overall) of 1999 NFL draft. ... Signed by Ravens (July 28, 1999). ... On injured reserve with shoulder injury (October 25, 1999-remainder of season).
PLAYING EXPERIENCE: Baltimore NFL, 1999 and 2000. ... Games/Games started: 1999 (2/0), 2000 (7/1). Total: 9/1.
CHAMPIONSHIP GAME EXPERIENCE: Played in AFC championship game (2000 season). ... Member of Super Bowl championship team (2000 season).
PRO STATISTICS: 1999—Caught one pass for 28 yards and a touchdown. 2000—Rushed once for six yards and caught 11 passes for 184 yards and two touchdowns.
SINGLE GAME HIGHS (regular season): Receptions—4 (December 10, 2000, vs. San Diego); yards—68 (November 26, 2000, vs. Cleveland); and touchdown receptions—1 (December 10, 2000, vs. San Diego).

STOLTENBERG, BRYAN　　　C　　　PANTHERS

PERSONAL: Born August 25, 1972, in Kearney, Neb. ... 6-1/300. ... Full name: Bryan Douglas Stoltenberg. ... Name pronounced STOLL-ten-burg.
HIGH SCHOOL: Clements (Sugar Land, Texas).
COLLEGE: Colorado (degree in marketing).
TRANSACTIONS/CAREER NOTES: Selected by San Diego Chargers in sixth round (192nd pick overall) of 1996 NFL draft. ... Signed by Chargers (July 2, 1996). ... Released by Chargers (August 25, 1996). ... Re-signed by Chargers to practice squad (August 26, 1996). ... Activated (October 9, 1996). ... Released by Chargers (August 18, 1997). ... Signed by New York Giants (September 30, 1997). ... Granted free agency (February 13, 1998). ... Re-signed by Giants (May 4, 1998). ... Released by Giants (August 30, 1998). ... Signed by Carolina Panthers (September 2, 1998). ... Granted free agency (February 12, 1999). ... Re-signed by Panthers (April 7, 1999). ... On injured reserve with knee injury (December 5, 2000-remainder of season).
PLAYING EXPERIENCE: San Diego NFL, 1996; New York Giants NFL, 1997; Carolina NFL, 1998-2000. ... Games/Games started: 1996 (9/0), 1997 (3/0), 1998 (14/10), 1999 (16/7), 2000 (8/1). Total: 50/18.
HONORS: Named offensive lineman on THE SPORTING NEWS college All-America second team (1995).
PRO STATISTICS: 1997—Fumbled once.

STONE, DWIGHT　　　WR/KR

PERSONAL: Born January 28, 1964, in Florala, Ala. ... 6-0/195.
HIGH SCHOOL: Florala (Ala.).
JUNIOR COLLEGE: Marion (Ala.) Military Academy.
COLLEGE: Middle Tennessee State (degree in social work).
TRANSACTIONS/CAREER NOTES: Signed as non-drafted free agent by Pittsburgh Steelers (May 19, 1987). ... Crossed picket line during players strike (October 7, 1987). ... Granted free agency (February 1, 1992). ... Re-signed by Steelers (May 15, 1992). ... Released by Steelers (August 30, 1993). ... Re-signed by Steelers (August 31, 1993). ... Granted unconditional free agency (February 17, 1995). ... Signed by Carolina Panthers (May 16, 1995). ... Granted unconditional free agency (February 16, 1996). ... Re-signed by Panthers (March 19, 1996). ... Granted unconditional free agency (February 14, 1997). ... Re-signed by Panthers (July 17, 1997). ... Granted unconditional free agency (February 13, 1998). ... Re-signed by Panthers (March 24, 1998). ... Granted unconditional free agency (February 12, 1999). ... Signed by New York Jets (August 7, 1999). ... Granted unconditional free agency (February 11, 2000). ... Re-signed by Jets (May 25, 2000). ... Released by Jets (August 29, 2000). ... Re-signed by Jets (September 19, 2000). ... Granted unconditional free agency (March 2, 2001).
CHAMPIONSHIP GAME EXPERIENCE: Played in AFC championship game (1994 season). ... Played in NFC championship game (1996 season).
PRO STATISTICS: 1987—Recovered one fumble. 1989—Recovered one fumble. 1990—Recovered two fumbles. 1993—Recovered one fumble. 1997—Recovered one fumble and credited with a safety. 1998—Recovered a blocked punt in the end zone for a touchdown. 1999—Recovered two fumbles. 2000—Recovered one fumble.

SINGLE GAME HIGHS (regular season): Receptions—6 (October 19, 1992, vs. Cincinnati); yards—124 (September 1, 1991, vs. San Diego); and touchdown receptions—2 (October 19, 1992, vs. Cincinnati).

STATISTICAL PLATEAUS: 100-yard receiving games: 1991 (1), 1992 (1), 1993 (1). Total: 3.

Year Team	G	GS	RUSHING				RECEIVING				KICKOFF RETURNS				TOTALS			
			Att.	Yds.	Avg.	TD	No.	Yds.	Avg.	TD	No.	Yds.	Avg.	TD	TD	2pt.	Pts.	Fum.
1987—Pittsburgh NFL	14	0	17	135	7.9	0	1	22	22.0	0	28	568	20.3	0	0	0	0	0
1988—Pittsburgh NFL	16	6	40	127	3.2	0	11	196	17.8	1	29	610	21.0	†1	2	0	12	5
1989—Pittsburgh NFL	16	8	10	53	5.3	0	7	92	13.1	0	7	173	24.7	0	0	0	0	2
1990—Pittsburgh NFL	16	2	2	-6	-3.0	0	19	332	17.5	1	5	91	18.2	0	1	0	6	1
1991—Pittsburgh NFL	16	8	1	2	2.0	0	32	649	§20.3	5	6	75	12.5	0	5	0	30	0
1992—Pittsburgh NFL	15	12	12	118	9.8	0	34	501	14.7	3	12	219	18.3	0	3	0	18	0
1993—Pittsburgh NFL	16	15	12	121	10.1	1	41	587	14.3	2	11	168	15.3	0	3	0	18	2
1994—Pittsburgh NFL	15	1	2	7	3.5	0	7	81	11.6	0	11	182	16.5	0	0	1	2	0
1995—Carolina NFL	16	0	1	3	3.0	0	0	0	0.0	0	12	269	22.4	0	0	0	0	0
1996—Carolina NFL	16	0	1	6	6.0	0	1	11	11.0	0	0	0	0.0	0	0	0	0	0
1997—Carolina NFL	16	0	0	0	0.0	0	0	0	0.0	0	3	76	25.3	0	0	0	2	0
1998—Carolina NFL	16	0	0	0	0.0	0	1	7	7.0	0	9	252	28.0	0	1	0	6	0
1999—New York Jets NFL	16	0	2	27	13.5	0	0	0	0.0	0	28	689	24.6	0	0	0	0	3
2000—New York Jets NFL	12	0	3	3	1.0	0	0	0	0.0	0	25	555	22.2	0	0	0	0	1
Pro totals (14 years)	216	52	103	596	5.8	1	154	2478	16.1	12	186	3927	21.1	1	15	1	94	14

STONE, RON G GIANTS

PERSONAL: Born July 20, 1971, in West Roxbury, Mass. ... 6-5/320.
HIGH SCHOOL: West Roxbury (Mass.).
COLLEGE: Boston College.
TRANSACTIONS/CAREER NOTES: Selected by Dallas Cowboys in fourth round (96th pick overall) of 1993 NFL draft. ... Signed by Cowboys (July 16, 1993). ... Active for four games with Cowboys (1993); did not play. ... Granted free agency (February 16, 1996). ... Tendered offer sheet by New York Giants (March 1, 1996). ... Cowboys declined to match offer (March 7, 1996).
PLAYING EXPERIENCE: Dallas NFL, 1994 and 1995; New York Giants NFL, 1996-2000. ... Games/Games started: 1994 (16/0), 1995 (16/1), 1996 (16/16), 1997 (16/16), 1998 (14/14), 1999 (16/16), 2000 (15/15). Total: 109/78.
CHAMPIONSHIP GAME EXPERIENCE: Member of Cowboys for NFC championship game (1993 season); inactive. ... Member of Super Bowl championship team (1993 and 1995 seasons). ... Played in NFC championship game (1994, 1995 and 2000 seasons). ... Played in Super Bowl XXXV (2000 season).
HONORS: Played in Pro Bowl (2000 season).
PRO STATISTICS: 1994—Recovered one fumble. 1997—Recovered one fumble.

STORZ, ERIK LB

PERSONAL: Born June 24, 1975, in Rockaway, N.J. ... 6-2/240. ... Full name: Erik Erwin Storz.
HIGH SCHOOL: Morris Catholic (Denville, N.J.).
COLLEGE: Boston College (degree in marketing).
TRANSACTIONS/CAREER NOTES: Signed as non-drafted free agent by Cincinnati Bengals (April 21, 1998). ... Released by Bengals (July 25, 1998). ... Signed by Jacksonville Jaguars (August 19, 1998). ... Released by Jaguars (August 25, 1998). ... Re-signed by Jaguars to practice squad (November 25, 1998). ... Activated (December 25, 1998). ... On injured reserve with knee injury (November 2, 1999-remainder of season). ... Released by Jaguars (August 27, 2000). ... Re-signed by Jaguars to practice squad (August 28, 2000). ... Activated (September 13, 2000). ... On injured reserve with thumb injury (December 13, 2000-remainder of season). ... Released by Jaguars (March 1, 2001).
PLAYING EXPERIENCE: Jacksonville NFL, 1998-2000. ... Games/Games started: 1998 (1/0), 1999 (7/0), 2000 (10/2). Total: 18/2.
PRO STATISTICS: 2000—Recovered one fumble.

STOUTMIRE, OMAR S GIANTS

PERSONAL: Born July 9, 1974, in Pensacola, Fla. ... 5-11/198.
HIGH SCHOOL: Polytechnic (Pasadena, Calif.).
COLLEGE: Fresno State.
TRANSACTIONS/CAREER NOTES: Selected by Dallas Cowboys in seventh round (224th pick overall) of 1997 NFL draft. ... Signed by Cowboys (July 14, 1997). ... Claimed on waivers by Cleveland Browns (September 6, 1999). ... Inactive for two games with Browns (1999). ... Released by Browns (September 21, 1999). ... Signed by New York Jets (October 6, 1999). ... Granted free agency (February 11, 2000). ... Re-signed by Jets (April 18, 2000). ... Released by Jets (August 27, 2000). ... Signed by New York Giants (August 30, 2000). ... Granted unconditional free agency (March 2, 2001). ... Re-signed by Giants (May 15, 2001).
CHAMPIONSHIP GAME EXPERIENCE: Played in NFC championship game (2000 season). ... Played in Super Bowl XXXV (2000 season).
PRO STATISTICS: 1997—Recovered one fumble. 1998—Recovered one fumble. 1999—Recovered one fumble. 2000—Returned six kickoffs for 140 yards.

Year Team	G	GS	INTERCEPTIONS				SACKS
			No.	Yds.	Avg.	TD	No.
1997—Dallas NFL	16	2	2	8	4.0	0	2.0
1998—Dallas NFL	16	12	0	0	0.0	0	1.0
1999—New York Jets NFL	12	5	2	97	48.5	1	1.0
2000—New York Giants NFL	16	0	0	0	0.0	0	0.0
Pro totals (4 years)	60	19	4	105	26.3	1	4.0

PERSONAL: Born January 27, 1968, in Dallas. ... 5-11/178. ... Full name: John Matthew Stover.
HIGH SCHOOL: Lake Highlands (Dallas).
COLLEGE: Louisiana Tech (degree in marketing, 1991).
TRANSACTIONS/CAREER NOTES: Selected by New York Giants in 12th round (329th pick overall) of 1990 NFL draft. ... Signed by Giants (July 23, 1990). ... On injured reserve with leg injury (September 4, 1990-entire season). ... Granted unconditional free agency (February 1, 1991). ... Signed by Cleveland Browns (March 15, 1991). ... Granted free agency (March 1, 1993). ... Re-signed by Browns (July 24, 1993). ... Released by Browns (August 30, 1993). ... Re-signed by Browns (August 31, 1993). ... Granted unconditional free agency (February 17, 1994). ... Re-signed by Browns (March 4, 1994). ... Browns franchise moved to Baltimore and renamed Ravens for 1996 season (March 11, 1996).
CHAMPIONSHIP GAME EXPERIENCE: Played in AFC championship game (2000 season). ... Member of Super Bowl championship team (2000 season).
HONORS: Named kicker on THE SPORTING NEWS NFL All-Pro team (2000). ... Played in Pro Bowl (2000 season).
PRO STATISTICS: 1992—Had only pass attempt intercepted.

Year　Team	G	XPM	XPA	FGM	FGA	Lg.	50+	Pts.
				KICKING				
1990—New York Giants NFL				Did not play.				
1991—Cleveland NFL	16	33	34	16	22	§55	2-2	81
1992—Cleveland NFL	16	29	30	21	29	51	1-3	92
1993—Cleveland NFL	16	36	36	16	22	53	1-4	84
1994—Cleveland NFL	16	32	32	26	28	45	0-1	110
1995—Cleveland NFL	16	26	26	29	33	47	0-1	113
1996—Baltimore NFL	16	34	35	19	25	50	1-1	91
1997—Baltimore NFL	16	32	32	26	34	49	0-2	110
1998—Baltimore NFL	16	24	24	21	28	48	0-0	87
1999—Baltimore NFL	16	32	32	28	33	50	2-5	116
2000—Baltimore NFL	16	30	30	*35	*39	51	2-3	135
Pro totals (10 years)	160	308	311	237	293	55	9-22	1019

PERSONAL: Born April 28, 1967, in Dearborn Heights, Mich. ... 5-11/194. ... Full name: Peter Stoyanovich. ... Name pronounced sto-YON-ovich.
HIGH SCHOOL: Crestwood (Dearborn Heights, Mich.).
COLLEGE: Indiana (degree in public affairs, 1989).
TRANSACTIONS/CAREER NOTES: Selected by Miami Dolphins in eighth round (203rd pick overall) of 1989 NFL draft. ... Signed by Dolphins (July 27, 1989). ... Granted free agency (February 1, 1991). ... Re-signed by Dolphins (September 6, 1991). ... Activated (September 13, 1991). ... Granted unconditional free agency (February 17, 1994). ... Re-signed by Dolphins (February 21, 1994). ... Traded by Dolphins to Kansas City Chiefs for fifth-round pick (DT Barron Tanner) in 1997 draft (August 21, 1996). ... Released by Chiefs (October 11, 2000). ... Signed by St. Louis Rams (October 17, 2000). ... Released by Rams (October 31, 2000).
CHAMPIONSHIP GAME EXPERIENCE: Played in AFC championship game (1992 season).
HONORS: Named kicker on THE SPORTING NEWS college All-America second team (1988). ... Named kicker on THE SPORTING NEWS NFL All-Pro team (1992).
POST SEASON RECORDS: Holds NFL postseason record for longest field goal—58 yards (January 5, 1991, vs. Kansas City).

Year　Team	G	No.	Yds.	Avg.	Net avg.	In. 20	Blk.	XPM	XPA	FGM	FGA	Lg.	50+	Pts.
			PUNTING							KICKING				
1989—Miami NFL	16	0	0	0.0	0	0	0	38	39	19	26	*59	1-3	95
1990—Miami NFL	16	0	0	0.0	0	0	0	37	37	21	25	53	2-3	100
1991—Miami NFL	14	2	85	42.5	38.5	1	0	28	29	*31	▲37	53	3-5	§121
1992—Miami NFL	16	2	90	45.0	45.0	0	0	34	36	†30	§37	53	3-8	*124
1993—Miami NFL	16	0	0	0.0	0	0	0	37	37	24	32	52	2-2	109
1994—Miami NFL	16	0	0	0.0	0	0	0	35	35	24	31	50	1-2	107
1995—Miami NFL	16	0	0	0.0	0	0	0	37	37	27	34	51	2-5	118
1996—Kansas City NFL	16	0	0	0.0	0	0	0	34	34	17	24	45	0-1	85
1997—Kansas City NFL	16	1	24	24.0	24.0	1	0	35	36	26	27	54	2-2	113
1998—Kansas City NFL	16	1	29	29.0	29.0	1	0	34	34	27	32	53	2-2	115
1999—Kansas City NFL	16	1	35	35.0	35.0	1	0	§45	§45	21	28	51	1-1	108
2000—Kansas City NFL	5	0	0	0.0	.0	0	0	15	15	2	4	42	0-0	21
—St. Louis NFL	3	0	0	0.0	.0	0	0	11	11	3	5	48	0-1	20
Pro totals (12 years)	182	7	263	37.6	36.4	4	0	420	425	272	342	59	19-35	1236

PERSONAL: Born November 21, 1971, in Houston. ... 6-5/275. ... Full name: Michael Anthony Strahan. ... Nephew of Art Strahan, defensive tackle with Atlanta Falcons (1968). ... Name pronounced STRAY-han.
HIGH SCHOOL: Westbury (Houston), then Mannheim (West Germany) American.
COLLEGE: Texas Southern.
TRANSACTIONS/CAREER NOTES: Selected by New York Giants in second round (40th pick overall) of 1993 NFL draft. ... Signed by Giants (July 25, 1993). ... On injured reserve with foot injury (January 13, 1994-remainder of playoffs). ... Granted free agency (February 16, 1996). ... Re-signed by Giants (July 8, 1996).
CHAMPIONSHIP GAME EXPERIENCE: Played in NFC championship game (2000 season). ... Played in Super Bowl XXXV (2000 season).
HONORS: Named defensive end on THE SPORTING NEWS NFL All-Pro team (1997). ... Played in Pro Bowl (1997-1999 seasons).
PRO STATISTICS: 1995—Intercepted two passes for 56 yards. 1997—Recovered one fumble. 1998—Intercepted one pass for 24 yards and a touchdown. 1999—Intercepted one pass for 44 yards and a touchdown and recovered two fumbles. 2000—Recovered four fumbles.

S

Year	Team	G	GS	SACKS
1993—New York Giants NFL		9	0	1.0
1994—New York Giants NFL		15	15	4.5
1995—New York Giants NFL		15	15	7.5
1996—New York Giants NFL		16	16	5.0
1997—New York Giants NFL		16	16	14.0
1998—New York Giants NFL		16	15	15.0
1999—New York Giants NFL		16	16	5.5
2000—New York Giants NFL		16	16	9.5
Pro totals (8 years)		119	109	62.0

STREETS, TAI — WR — 49ERS

PERSONAL: Born April 20, 1977, in Matteson, Ill. ... 6-1/193.
HIGH SCHOOL: Thornton Township (Harvey, Ill.).
COLLEGE: Michigan.
TRANSACTIONS/CAREER NOTES: Selected by San Francisco 49ers in sixth round (171st pick overall) of 1999 NFL draft. ... Signed by 49ers (July 30, 1999). ... On non-football injury list with Achilles' tendon injury (July 30-November 30, 1999).
PRO STATISTICS: 2000—Rushed once for no yards, returned eight kickoffs for 180 yards and fumbled once.
SINGLE GAME HIGHS (regular season): Receptions—4 (November 19, 2000, vs. Atlanta); yards—73 (November 19, 2000, vs. Atlanta); and touchdown receptions—0.

				RECEIVING			
Year	Team	G	GS	No.	Yds.	Avg.	TD
1999—San Francisco NFL		2	0	2	25	12.5	0
2000—San Francisco NFL		15	1	19	287	15.1	0
Pro totals (2 years)		17	1	21	312	14.9	0

STRINGER, KOREY — OT — VIKINGS

PERSONAL: Born May 8, 1974, in Warren, Ohio. ... 6-4/335.
HIGH SCHOOL: Harding (Warren, Ohio).
COLLEGE: Ohio State.
TRANSACTIONS/CAREER NOTES: Selected after junior season by Minnesota Vikings in first round (24th pick overall) of 1995 NFL draft. ... Signed by Vikings (July 22, 1995).
PLAYING EXPERIENCE: Minnesota NFL, 1995-2000. ... Games/Games started: 1995 (16/15), 1996 (16/15), 1997 (15/15), 1998 (14/14), 1999 (16/16), 2000 (16/16). Total: 94/91.
CHAMPIONSHIP GAME EXPERIENCE: Played in NFC championship game (1998 and 2000 seasons).
HONORS: Named offensive lineman on THE SPORTING NEWS college All-America second team (1993). ... Named offensive lineman on THE SPORTING NEWS college All-America first team (1994). ... Played in Pro Bowl (2000 season).
PRO STATISTICS: 1995—Caught one pass for minus one yard and recovered two fumbles.

STRONG, MACK — FB — SEAHAWKS

PERSONAL: Born September 11, 1971, in Fort Benning, Ga. ... 6-0/235.
HIGH SCHOOL: Brookstone (Columbus, Ga.).
COLLEGE: Georgia.
TRANSACTIONS/CAREER NOTES: Signed as non-drafted free agent by Seattle Seahawks (April 28, 1993). ... Released by Seahawks (September 4, 1993). ... Re-signed by Seahawks to practice squad (September 6, 1993). ... Released by Seahawks (February 10, 2000). ... Re-signed by Seahawks (February 14, 2000).
PRO STATISTICS: 1995—Returned four kickoffs for 65 yards and recovered one fumble. 1996—Recovered one fumble. 1997—Returned one kickoff for 16 yards and recovered one fumble. 1998—Recovered one fumble. 2000—Returned one kickoff for 26 yards.
SINGLE GAME HIGHS (regular season): Attempts—10 (December 11, 1994, vs. Houston); yards—44 (December 11, 1994, vs. Houston); rushing touchdowns—1 (November 12, 1995, vs. Jacksonville).

				RUSHING				RECEIVING				TOTALS			
Year	Team	G	GS	Att.	Yds.	Avg.	TD	No.	Yds.	Avg.	TD	TD	2pt.	Pts.	Fum.
1993—Seattle NFL							Did not play.								
1994—Seattle NFL		8	1	27	114	4.2	2	3	3	1.0	0	2	0	12	1
1995—Seattle NFL		16	1	8	23	2.9	1	12	117	9.8	3	4	0	24	2
1996—Seattle NFL		14	8	5	8	1.6	0	9	78	8.7	0	0	0	0	0
1997—Seattle NFL		16	10	4	8	2.0	0	13	91	7.0	2	2	0	12	0
1998—Seattle NFL		16	5	15	47	3.1	0	8	48	6.0	2	2	0	12	2
1999—Seattle NFL		14	1	1	0	0.0	0	1	5	5.0	0	0	0	0	0
2000—Seattle NFL		16	13	3	9	3.0	0	23	141	6.1	1	1	0	6	0
Pro totals (7 years)		100	39	63	209	3.3	3	69	483	7.0	8	11	0	66	5

STRYZINSKI, DAN — P — CHIEFS

PERSONAL: Born May 15, 1965, in Indianapolis. ... 6-2/200. ... Full name: Daniel Thomas Stryzinski. ... Name pronounced stra-ZIN-ski.
HIGH SCHOOL: Lincoln (Vincennes, Ind.).
COLLEGE: Indiana (bachelor of science degree in public finance and management, 1988).
TRANSACTIONS/CAREER NOTES: Signed as non-drafted free agent by Indianapolis Colts (July 1988). ... Released by Colts (August 23, 1988). ... Signed by Cleveland Browns (August 25, 1988). ... Released by Browns (August 30, 1988). ... Re-signed by Browns for 1989 season. ... Released by Browns (August 30, 1989). ... Signed by New Orleans Saints to developmental squad (October 11, 1989). ... Granted free agency following 1989 season. ... Signed by Pittsburgh Steelers (March 14, 1990). ... Granted unconditional free agency (February 1, 1992). ... Signed

by Tampa Bay Buccaneers (February 21, 1992). ... Granted unconditional free agency (February 17, 1995). ... Signed by Atlanta Falcons (February 20, 1995). ... Granted unconditional free agency (March 2, 2001). ... Signed by Kansas City Chiefs (March 9, 2001).
CHAMPIONSHIP GAME EXPERIENCE: Played in NFC championship game (1998 season). ... Played in Super Bowl XXXIII (1998 season).
PRO STATISTICS: 1990—Rushed three times for 17 yards and recovered one fumble. 1991—Rushed four times for minus 11 yards, fumbled once and recovered two fumbles. 1992—Attempted two passes with two completions for 14 yards and rushed once for seven yards. 1994—Completed only pass attempt for 21 yards. 1995—Rushed once for no yards.

Year Team	G		No.	Yds.	Avg.	Net avg.	In. 20	Blk.
					PUNTING			
1990—Pittsburgh NFL	16		65	2454	37.8	34.1	18	1
1991—Pittsburgh NFL	16		74	2996	40.5	36.2	10	1
1992—Tampa Bay NFL	16		74	3015	40.7	36.2	15	0
1993—Tampa Bay NFL	16		*93	3772	40.6	35.2	24	1
1994—Tampa Bay NFL	16		72	2800	38.9	35.8	20	0
1995—Atlanta NFL	16		67	2759	41.2	36.2	21	0
1996—Atlanta NFL	16		75	3152	42.0	35.5	22	0
1997—Atlanta NFL	16		89	3498	39.3	36.7	20	0
1998—Atlanta NFL	16		74	2963	40.0	36.6	25	0
1999—Atlanta NFL	16		80	3163	39.5	37.1	27	0
2000—Atlanta NFL	16		84	3447	41.0	‡37.9	27	1
Pro totals (11 years)	176		847	34019	40.2	36.2	229	4

STUBBLEFIELD, DANA   DT   49ERS

PERSONAL: Born November 14, 1970, in Cleves, Ohio. ... 6-2/315. ... Full name: Dana William Stubblefield.
HIGH SCHOOL: Taylor (North Bend, Ohio).
COLLEGE: Kansas.
TRANSACTIONS/CAREER NOTES: Selected by San Francisco 49ers in first round (26th pick overall) of 1993 NFL draft. ... Signed by 49ers (July 14, 1993). ... Granted unconditional free agency (February 13, 1998). ... Signed by Washington Redskins (February 23, 1998). ... Released by Redskins (March 1, 2001). ... Signed by 49ers (April 26, 2001).
CHAMPIONSHIP GAME EXPERIENCE: Played in NFC championship game (1993, 1994 and 1997 seasons). ... Member of Super Bowl championship team (1994 season).
HONORS: Played in Pro Bowl (1994, 1995 and 1997 seasons). ... Named defensive tackle on THE SPORTING NEWS NFL All-Pro team (1997).
PRO STATISTICS: 1995—Intercepted one pass for 12 yards. 1996—Intercepted one pass for 15 yards and recovered one fumble. 1999—Recovered one fumble. 2000—Recovered one fumble.

Year Team	G	GS	SACKS
1993—San Francisco NFL	16	14	10.5
1994—San Francisco NFL	14	14	8.5
1995—San Francisco NFL	16	16	4.5
1996—San Francisco NFL	15	15	1.0
1997—San Francisco NFL	16	16	15.0
1998—Washington NFL	7	7	1.5
1999—Washington NFL	16	16	3.0
2000—Washington NFL	15	14	2.5
Pro totals (8 years)	115	112	46.5

STYLES, LORENZO   LB

PERSONAL: Born January 31, 1974, in Sharon, Pa., ... 6-1/245.
HIGH SCHOOL: Independence (Columbus, Ohio), then Farrell (Pa.).
COLLEGE: Ohio State.
TRANSACTIONS/CAREER NOTES: Selected after junior season by Atlanta Falcons in third round (77th pick overall) of 1995 NFL draft. ... Signed by Falcons (July 21, 1995). ... Released by Falcons (August 26, 1997). ... Signed by St. Louis Rams (November 4, 1997). ... On injured reserve with shoulder injury (December 9, 1997-remainder of season). ... Granted free agency (February 13, 1998). ... Re-signed by Rams (March 25, 1998). ... On injured reserve with shoulder injury (November 30, 1998-remainder of season). ... Released by Rams (May 4, 2000). ... Re-signed by Rams (June 5, 2000). ... Granted unconditional free agency (March 2, 2001).
PLAYING EXPERIENCE: Atlanta NFL, 1995 and 1996; St. Louis NFL, 1997-2000. ... Games/Games started: 1995 (12/0), 1996 (16/0), 1997 (3/0), 1998 (7/3), 1999 (16/0), 2000 (16/5). Total: 70/8.
CHAMPIONSHIP GAME EXPERIENCE: Played in NFC championship game (1999 season). ... Member of Super Bowl championship team (1999 season).
PRO STATISTICS: 1996—Returned one kickoff for 12 yards. 1999—Recovered one fumble. 2000—Credited with one sack.

SULLIVAN, CHRIS   DL   STEELERS

PERSONAL: Born March 14, 1973, in North Attleboro, Mass. ... 6-4/285. ... Full name: Christopher Patrick Sullivan.
HIGH SCHOOL: North Attleboro (Mass.).
COLLEGE: Boston College (degree in sociology, 1995).
TRANSACTIONS/CAREER NOTES: Selected by New England Patriots in fourth round (119th pick overall) of 1996 NFL draft. ... Signd by Patriots (July 12, 1996). ... Granted free agency (February 12, 1999). ... Re-signed by Patriots (June 1, 1999). ... Granted unconditional free agency (February 11, 2000). ... Signed by Pittsburgh Steelers (February 19, 2000).
PLAYING EXPERIENCE: New England NFL, 1996-1999; Pittsburgh NFL, 2000. ... Games/Games started: 1996 (16/0), 1997 (16/10), 1998 (15/10), 1999 (16/0), 2000 (15/2). Total: 78/22.
CHAMPIONSHIP GAME EXPERIENCE: Played in AFC championship game (1996 season). ... Played in Super Bowl XXXI (1996 season).
PRO STATISTICS: 1996—Recovered one fumble. 1998—Returned two kickoffs for 14 yards and credited with two sacks. 1999—Returned one kickoff for one yard and credited with one sack. 2000—Recovered two fumbles.

SUPERNAW, KYWIN   S   LIONS

PERSONAL: Born June 2, 1975, in Claremore, Okla. ... 6-1/207.
HIGH SCHOOL: Skiatook (Okla.).
COLLEGE: Northeastern Oklahoma A&M, then Indiana.
TRANSACTIONS/CAREER NOTES: Signed as non-drafted free agent by Detroit Lions (April 24, 1998). ... Released by Lions (August 30, 1998). ... Re-signed by Lions to practice squad (September 1, 1998). ... Activated (December 1, 1998). ... On injured reserve with ankle injury (October 14, 1999-remainder of season).
PLAYING EXPERIENCE: Detroit NFL, 1998-2000. ... Games/Games started: 1998 (2/0), 1999 (2/0), 2000 (13/3). Total: 17/3.

SURTAIN, PATRICK   CB   DOLPHINS

PERSONAL: Born June 19, 1976, in New Orleans. ... 5-11/192. ... Full name: Patrick Frank Surtain. ... Name pronounced sir-TANE.
HIGH SCHOOL: Edna Karr (New Orleans).
COLLEGE: Southern Mississippi.
TRANSACTIONS/CAREER NOTES: Selected by Miami Dolphins in second round (44th pick overall) of 1998 NFL draft. ... Signed by Dolphins (July 21, 1998).
HONORS: Named cornerback on THE SPORTING NEWS college All-America second team (1997).
PRO STATISTICS: 1999—Credited with two sacks. 2000—Credited with one sack and recovered one fumble.

| | | | INTERCEPTIONS | | | |
Year Team	G	GS	No.	Yds.	Avg.	TD
1998—Miami NFL	16	0	2	1	0.5	0
1999—Miami NFL	16	6	2	28	14.0	0
2000—Miami NFL	16	16	5	55	11.0	0
Pro totals (3 years)	48	22	9	84	9.3	0

SUTTLE, JASON   CB   BRONCOS

PERSONAL: Born December 2, 1974, in Minneapolis. ... 5-10/182. ... Full name: Jason John Suttle.
HIGH SCHOOL: Burnsville (Minn.).
COLLEGE: Wisconsin (degree in sociology).
TRANSACTIONS/CAREER NOTES: Signed as non-drafted free agent by San Diego Chargers (April 24, 1998). ... Released by Chargers (July 23, 1998). ... Signed by New England Patriots (August 4, 1998). ... Released by Patriots (August 24, 1998). ... Signed by Denver Broncos (March 9, 1999). ... Released by Broncos (September 5, 1999). ... Re-signed by Broncos to practice squad (September 6, 1999). ... Activated (September 18, 1999). ... Released by Broncos (November 9, 1999). ... Re-signed by Broncos to practice squad (November 10, 1999). ... Activated (December 31, 1999). ... Claimed on waivers by Green Bay Packers (August 23, 2000). ... Released by Packers (August 27, 2000). ... Signed by Broncos to practice squad (August 29, 2000). ... Activated (November 25, 2000).
PLAYING EXPERIENCE: Denver NFL, 1999 and 2000. ... Games/Games started: 1999 (5/0), 2000 (5/0). Total: 10/0.
PRO STATISTICS: 2000—Recovered one fumble in end zone for a touchdown.

SWANN, ERIC   DT

PERSONAL: Born August 16, 1970, in Pinehurst, N.C. ... 6-5/317. ... Full name: Eric Jerrod Swann.
HIGH SCHOOL: Western Harnett (Lillington, N.C.).
COLLEGE: Wake Technical College, N.C. (did not play football).
TRANSACTIONS/CAREER NOTES: Played with Bay State Titans of Minor League Football System (1990). ... Selected by Phoenix Cardinals in first round (sixth pick overall) of 1991 NFL draft. ... Signed by Cardinals (April 24, 1991). ... On injured reserve with knee injury (August 27-September 27, 1991). ... On injured reserve with knee injury (November 17, 1993-remainder of season). ... Cardinals franchise renamed Arizona Cardinals for 1994 season. ... Designated by Cardinals as franchise player (February 16, 1996). ... On injured reserve with dislocated finger (December 17, 1997-remainder of season). ... On injured reserve with knee injury (December 10, 1998-remainder of season). ... Released by Cardinals (July 11, 2000). ... Signed by Carolina Panthers (July 24, 2000). ... Granted unconditional free agency (March 2, 2001). ... Announced retirement (May 1, 2001).
HONORS: Named defensive tackle on THE SPORTING NEWS NFL All-Pro team (1995). ... Played in Pro Bowl (1995 and 1996 seasons).
PRO STATISTICS: 1992—Credited with one safety. 1993—Credited with one safety and recovered one fumble. 1994—Credited with one safety and recovered one fumble for 10 yards. 1995—Recovered two fumbles. 1996—Recovered three fumbles for 11 yards. 1997—Rushed once for no yards, fumbled once and recovered one fumble. 1999—Intercepted one pass for 42 yards and a touchdown.

Year Team	G	GS	SACKS
1991—Phoenix NFL	12	3	4.0
1992—Phoenix NFL	16	11	2.0
1993—Phoenix NFL	9	9	3.5
1994—Arizona NFL	16	16	7.0
1995—Arizona NFL	13	12	8.5
1996—Arizona NFL	16	15	5.0
1997—Arizona NFL	13	13	7.5
1998—Arizona NFL	7	5	4.0
1999—Arizona NFL	9	4	4.0
2000—Carolina NFL	16	3	1.0
Pro totals (10 years)	127	87	46.5

SWANSON, PETE   G   RAMS

PERSONAL: Born March 26, 1974, in Hollister, Calif. ... 6-5/315. ... Full name: Peter C. Swanson.
HIGH SCHOOL: San Benito (Calif.).
COLLEGE: Stanford.
TRANSACTIONS/CAREER NOTES: Signed as non-drafted free agent by Kansas City Chiefs (April 26, 1997). ... Released by Chiefs (August 24, 1997). ... Re-signed by Chiefs to practice squad (August 26, 1997). ... Inactive for 14 games (1998). ... Active for two games (1998); did not play. ... Selected by Cleveland Browns from Chiefs in NFL expansion draft (February 9, 1999). ... Released by Browns (August 30, 1999). ... Signed by San Francisco 49ers to practice squad (September 7, 1999). ... Released by 49ers (September 14, 1999). ... Signed by San Diego Chargers (January 8, 2000). ... Assigned by Chargers to Rhein Fire in 2000 NFL Europe enhancement allocation program (February 18, 2000). ... Released by Chargers (July 24, 2000). ... Signed by St. Louis Rams (August 8, 2000).
PLAYING EXPERIENCE: Rhein NFLE, 2000; St. Louis NFL, 2000. ... Games/Games started: NFLE 2000 (games played unavailable), NFL 2000 (3/0).

SWAYDA, SHAWN   DT   FALCONS

PERSONAL: Born September 4, 1974, in Phoenix. ... 6-5/294. ... Full name: Shawn Gerald Swayda.
HIGH SCHOOL: Brophy Prep (Phoenix).
COLLEGE: Arizona State.
TRANSACTIONS/CAREER NOTES: Selected by Chicago Bears in sixth round (196th pick overall) of 1997 NFL draft. ... Signed by Bears (July 10, 1997). ... Released by Bears (August 18, 1997). ... Signed by Dallas Cowboys to practice squad (October 9, 1997). ... Released by Cowboys (November 4, 1997). ... Signed by Detroit Lions to practice squad (November 24, 1997). ... Granted free agency after 1997 season. ... Signed by Atlanta Falcons (March 24, 1998). ... Released by Falcons (September 14, 1999). ... Re-signed by Falcons (September 28, 1999). ... Granted free agency (March 2, 2001).
PLAYING EXPERIENCE: Atlanta NFL, 1998-2000. ... Games/Games started: 1998 (5/0), 1999 (4/0), 2000 (16/0). Total: 25/0.
CHAMPIONSHIP GAME EXPERIENCE: Member of Falcons for NFC championship game (1998 season); inactive. ... Member of Falcons for Super Bowl XXXIII (1998 season); inactive.
PRO STATISTICS: 2000—Credited with 1¹/₂ sacks.

SWAYNE, HARRY   OT   RAVENS

PERSONAL: Born February 2, 1965, in Philadelphia. ... 6-5/300. ... Full name: Harry Vonray Swayne.
HIGH SCHOOL: Cardinal Dougherty (Philadelphia).
COLLEGE: Rutgers.
TRANSACTIONS/CAREER NOTES: Selected by Tampa Bay Buccaneers in seventh round (190th pick overall) of 1987 NFL draft. ... Signed by Buccaneers (July 18, 1987). ... On injured reserve with fractured hand (September 8-October 31, 1987). ... On injured reserve with neck injury (November 18, 1988-remainder of season). ... Granted free agency (February 1, 1990). ... Re-signed by Buccaneers (July 19, 1990). ... Granted unconditional free agency (February 1, 1991). ... Signed by San Diego Chargers (April 1, 1991). ... On injured reserve with fractured leg (November 26, 1991-remainder of season). ... Designated by Chargers as transition player (February 25, 1993). ... Tendered offer sheet by Phoenix Cardinals (April 9, 1993). ... Offer matched by Chargers (April 15, 1993). ... On physically unable to perform list (July 24-August 21, 1995). ... Free agency status changed by Chargers from transitional to unconditional (February 16, 1996). ... Re-signed by Chargers (July 24, 1996). ... Granted unconditional free agency (February 14, 1997). ... Signed by Denver Broncos (April 17, 1997). ... Granted unconditional free agency (February 12, 1999). ... Signed by Baltimore Ravens (February 26, 1999). ... On injured reserve with foot injury (November 10, 1999-remainder of season).
PLAYING EXPERIENCE: Tampa Bay NFL, 1987-1990; San Diego NFL, 1991-1996; Denver NFL, 1997 and 1998; Baltimore NFL, 1999 and 2000. ... Games/Games started: 1987 (8/2), 1988 (10/1), 1989 (16/0), 1990 (10/0), 1991 (12/12), 1992 (16/16), 1993 (11/11), 1994 (16/16), 1995 (16/16), 1996 (16/3), 1997 (7/0), 1998 (16/16), 1999 (6/6), 2000 (13/13). Total: 173/112.
CHAMPIONSHIP GAME EXPERIENCE: Played in AFC championship game (1994, 1997, 1998 and 2000 seasons). ... Played in Super Bowl XXIX (1994 season). ... Member of Super Bowl championship team (1997, 1998 and 2000 seasons).
PRO STATISTICS: 1998—Recovered one fumble. 2000—Recovered one fumble.

SWIFT, JUSTIN   TE   49ERS

PERSONAL: Born August 14, 1975, in Kansas City, Kan. ... 6-3/265. ... Full name: Justin Charles Swift.
HIGH SCHOOL: Blue Valley (Overland Park, Kan.).
COLLEGE: Kansas State.
TRANSACTIONS/CAREER NOTES: Selected by Denver Broncos in seventh round (238th pick overall) of 1999 NFL draft. ... Signed by Broncos (July 20, 1999). ... Released by Broncos (August 27, 1999). ... Signed by Philadelphia Eagles (September 14, 1999). ... Released by Eagles (September 28, 1999). ... Signed by Broncos to practice squad (October 19, 1999). ... Released by Broncos (November 2, 1999). ... Signed by San Francisco 49ers to practice squad (November 15, 1999). ... Released by 49ers (February 10, 2000). ... Assigned by 49ers to Frankfurt Galaxy in 2000 NFL Europe enhancement allocation program (February 18, 2000). ... Re-signed by 49ers (February 18, 2000).
PLAYING EXPERIENCE: Philadelphia NFL, 1999; Frankfurt NFLE, 2000; San Francisco NFL, 2000. ... Games/Games started: 1999 (1/0); 2000 NFLE (games played unavailable), 2000 NFL (16/1). Total NFL: 17/1.
PRO STATISTICS: NFLE: 2000—Caught 27 passes for 260 yards and two touchdowns. NFL: 2000—Caught one pass for eight yards.
SINGLE GAME HIGHS (regular season): Receptions—1 (October 22, 2000, vs. Carolina); yards—8 (October 22, 2000, vs. Carolina); and touchdown receptions—0.

SWIFT, MICHAEL   CB

PERSONAL: Born February 28, 1974, in Dyersburg, Tenn. ... 5-10/165. ... Full name: Michael Aaron Swift.
HIGH SCHOOL: Lake County (Tiptonville, Tenn.).
COLLEGE: Austin Peay.
TRANSACTIONS/CAREER NOTES: Signed as non-drafted free agent by San Diego Chargers (April 26, 1996). ... Released by Chargers (August 25, 1996). ... Re-signed by Chargers to practice squad (October 14, 1996). ... Released by Chargers (November 24, 1996). ... Re-signed by Chargers to practice squad (November 27, 1996). ... Assigned by Chargers to Rhein Fire in 1997 World League enhancement allocation program (February 19, 1997). ... Released by Chargers (August 18, 1997). ... Re-signed by Chargers to practice squad (August 25, 1997). ...

Activated (September 26, 1997). ... Granted free agency (February 13, 1998). ... Signed by Carolina Panthers (June 2, 1998). ... Inactive for four games (1998). ... On injured reserve with leg injury (October 7, 1998-remainder of season). ... On injured reserve with leg injury (December 28, 1999-remainder of season). ... Granted free agency (February 11, 2000). ... Signed by Jacksonville Jaguars (July 23, 2000). ... Released by Jaguars (September 6, 2000).

PLAYING EXPERIENCE: Rhein W.L., 1997; San Diego NFL, 1997; Carolina NFL, 1999; Jacksonville NFL, 2000. ... Games/Games started: W.L. 1997 (games played unavailable), NFL 1997 (12/1), 1999 (15/0), 2000 (1/0). Total NFL: 28/1.

PRO STATISTICS: W.L.: 1997—Intercepted one pass for eight yards. NFL: 1997—Recovered one fumble for six yards. 1999—Recovered one fumble.

SWORD, SAM   LB   COLTS

PERSONAL: Born December 9, 1974, in Saginaw, Mich. ... 6-1/245.
HIGH SCHOOL: Arthur Hill (Saginaw, Mich.).
COLLEGE: Michigan.
TRANSACTIONS/CAREER NOTES: Signed as non-drafted free agent by Oakland Raiders (April 22, 1999). ... Released by Raiders (August 27, 2000). ... Signed by Indianapolis Colts (October 25, 2000). ... Released by Colts (November 24, 2000). ... Re-signed by Colts (November 30, 2000).
PLAYING EXPERIENCE: Oakland NFL, 1999; Indianapolis NFL, 2000. ... Games/Games started: 1999 (10/5), 2000 (3/0). Total: 13/5.
PRO STATISTICS: 1999—Credited with one sack.

SYMONETTE, JOSH   S   REDSKINS

PERSONAL: Born May 8, 1978, in Miami. ... 5-10/180.
HIGH SCHOOL: Stone Mountain (Ga.).
COLLEGE: Tennessee Tech.
TRANSACTIONS/CAREER NOTES: Signed as non-drafted free agent by Washington Redskins (April 19, 2000). ... Released by Redskins (September 11, 2000). ... Re-signed by Redskins to practice squad (September 12, 2000). ... Activated (December 12, 2000).
PLAYING EXPERIENCE: Washington NFL, 2000. ... Games/Games started: 2000 (3/0).

SZOTT, DAVE   G

PERSONAL: Born December 12, 1967, in Passaic, N.J. ... 6-4/289. ... Full name: David Andrew Szott. ... Name pronounced ZOT.
HIGH SCHOOL: Clifton (N.J.).
COLLEGE: Penn State (degree in political science).
TRANSACTIONS/CAREER NOTES: Selected by Kansas City Chiefs in seventh round (180th pick overall) of 1990 NFL draft. ... Signed by Chiefs (July 25, 1990). ... Granted free agency (March 1, 1993). ... Re-signed by Chiefs for 1993 season. ... On injured reserve with arm injury (December 2, 1998-remainder of season). ... On injured reserve with arm injury (October 11, 2000-remainder of season). ... Granted unconditional free agency (March 2, 2001).
PLAYING EXPERIENCE: Kansas City NFL, 1990-2000. ... Games/Games started: 1990 (16/11), 1991 (16/16), 1992 (16/16), 1993 (14/13), 1994 (16/16), 1995 (16/16), 1996 (16/16), 1997 (16/16), 1998 (1/1), 1999 (14/14), 2000 (1/1). Total: 142/136.
CHAMPIONSHIP GAME EXPERIENCE: Played in AFC championship game (1993 season).
PRO STATISTICS: 1990—Recovered one fumble. 1991—Recovered one fumble. 1997—Recovered one fumble. 1999—Recovered one fumble.

TAIT, JOHN   OT   CHIEFS

PERSONAL: Born January 26, 1975, in Phoenix. ... 6-6/305.
HIGH SCHOOL: McClintock (Tempe, Ariz.).
COLLEGE: Brigham Young (degree in communications).
TRANSACTIONS/CAREER NOTES: Selected after junior season by Kansas City Chiefs in first round (14th pick overall) of 1999 NFL draft. ... Signed by Chiefs (September 9, 1999).
PLAYING EXPERIENCE: Kansas City NFL, 1999 and 2000. ... Games/Games started: 1999 (12/3), 2000 (15/15). Total: 27/18.
PRO STATISTICS: 2000—Recovered one fumble.

TANNER, BARRON   DT   CARDINALS

PERSONAL: Born September 14, 1973, in Athens, Texas. ... 6-3/320. ... Full name: Barron Keith Tanner.
HIGH SCHOOL: Athens (Texas).
COLLEGE: Oklahoma.
TRANSACTIONS/CAREER NOTES: Selected by Miami Dolphins in fifth round (149th pick overall) of 1997 NFL draft. ... Signed by Dolphins (July 8, 1997). ... Traded by Dolphins to Washington Redskins for seventh-round pick (traded to San Francisco) in 2001 draft (September 4, 1999). ... Inactive for all 16 games (1999). ... Granted free agency (February 11, 2000). ... Re-signed by Redskins (June 6, 2000). ... Released by Redskins (August 27, 2000). ... Signed by Arizona Cardinals (November 6, 2000).
PLAYING EXPERIENCE: Miami NFL, 1997 and 1998; Arizona NFL, 2000. ... Games/ Games started: 1997 (16/0), 1998 (13/0), 2000 (4/0). Total: 33/0.

TANT, JAY   TE   CARDINALS

PERSONAL: Born December 4, 1977, in Kettering, Ohio. ... 6-3/254. ... Full name: Jay William Tant.
HIGH SCHOOL: Alter (Kettering, Ohio).
COLLEGE: Northwestern.
TRANSACTIONS/CAREER NOTES: Selected by Arizona Cardinals in fifth round (164th pick overall) of 2000 NFL draft. ... Signed by Cardinals (June 15, 2000). ... On injured reserve with knee injury (November 8, 2000-remainder of season).
PLAYING EXPERIENCE: Arizona NFL, 2000. ... Games/Games started: 2000 (5/0).
PRO STATISTICS: 2000—Caught one pass for four yards.

S
T

TANUVASA, MAA   DT   BRONCOS

PERSONAL: Born November 6, 1970, in America Samoa. ... 6-2/270. ... Full name: Maa Junior Tanuvasa. ... Name pronounced MAH-ah TAH-noo-VA-suh.

HIGH SCHOOL: Mililani (Wahiawa, Hawaii).

COLLEGE: Hawaii.

TRANSACTIONS/CAREER NOTES: Selected by Los Angeles Rams in eighth round (209th pick overall) of 1993 NFL draft. ... Signed by Rams for 1993 season. ... On injured reserve with knee injury (August 21, 1993-entire season). ... Released by Rams (August 23, 1994). ... Signed by Steelers to practice squad (December 1, 1994). ... Granted free agency after 1994 season. ... Signed by Denver Broncos (February 22, 1995). ... Released by Broncos (August 27, 1995). ... Re-signed by Broncos to practice squad (August 28, 1995). ... Activated (October 24, 1995). ... Granted free agency (February 14, 1997). ... Re-signed by Broncos (February 14, 1997).

CHAMPIONSHIP GAME EXPERIENCE: Played in AFC championship game (1997 and 1998 seasons). ... Member of Super Bowl championship team (1997 and 1998 seasons).

PRO STATISTICS: 1996—Recovered one fumble. 1998—Returned one kickoff for 13 yards and recovered two fumbles for minus one yard. 2000—Recovered four fumbles for 38 yards.

Year Team	G	GS	SACKS
1993—Los Angeles Rams NFL	Did not play.		
1994—Pittsburgh NFL	Did not play.		
1995—Denver NFL	1	0	0.0
1996—Denver NFL	16	1	5.0
1997—Denver NFL	15	5	8.5
1998—Denver NFL	16	16	8.5
1999—Denver NFL	16	16	7.0
2000—Denver NFL	16	16	4.0
Pro totals (6 years)	**80**	**54**	**33.0**

TARLE, JIM   K   JAGUARS

PERSONAL: Born December 27, 1972, in Jacksonville. ... 6-0/221.

HIGH SCHOOL: Bishop Kenny (Jacksonville).

COLLEGE: South Carolina, then Arkansas State.

TRANSACTIONS/CAREER NOTES: Signed as non-drafted free agent by Jacksonville Jaguars (November 15, 2000).

PLAYING EXPERIENCE: Jacksonville NFL, 2000. ... Games/Games started: 2000 (6/0).

TATE, ROBERT   CB/KR   VIKINGS

PERSONAL: Born October 19, 1973, in Harrisburg, Pa. ... 5-10/193.

HIGH SCHOOL: John Harris (Harrisburg, Pa.), then Milford (Conn.) Academy.

COLLEGE: Cincinnati.

TRANSACTIONS/CAREER NOTES: Selected by Minnesota Vikings in sixth round (183rd pick overall) of 1997 NFL draft. ... Signed by Vikings (June 17, 1997). ... On injured reserve with ankle injury (October 8, 1997-remainder of season).

CHAMPIONSHIP GAME EXPERIENCE: Member of Vikings for NFC championship game (1998 season); inactive. ... Played in NFC championship game (2000 season).

PRO STATISTICS: 1998—Caught one pass for 17 yards. 1999—Rushed once for four yards, caught one pass for three yards and intercepted one pass for 18 yards. 2000—Intercepted two passes for 12 yards and recovered one fumble.

SINGLE GAME HIGHS (regular season): Receptions—1 (November 22, 1998, vs. Green Bay); yards—17 (November 22, 1998, vs Green Bay); and touchdown receptions—0.

Year Team	G	GS	KICKOFF RETURNS				TOTALS			
			No.	Yds.	Avg.	TD	TD	2pt.	Pts.	Fum.
1997—Minnesota NFL	4	0	10	196	19.6	0	0	0	0	0
1998—Minnesota NFL	15	1	2	43	21.5	0	0	0	0	0
1999—Minnesota NFL	16	1	25	627	25.1	1	1	0	6	1
2000—Minnesota NFL	16	16	0	0	0.0	0	0	0	0	0
Pro totals (4 years)	**51**	**18**	**37**	**866**	**23.4**	**1**	**1**	**0**	**6**	**1**

TAUSCHER, MARK   OT   PACKERS

PERSONAL: Born June 17, 1977, in Marshfield, Wis. ... 6-3/313. ... Full name: Mark Gerald Tauscher.

HIGH SCHOOL: Auburndale (Wis.).

COLLEGE: Wisconsin.

TRANSACTIONS/CAREER NOTES: Selected by Green Bay Packers in seventh round (224th pick overall) of 2000 NFL draft. ... Signed by Packers (June 21, 2000).

PLAYING EXPERIENCE: Green Bay NFL, 2000. ... Games/Games started: 2000 (16/14).

TAVES, JOSH   DE   RAIDERS

PERSONAL: Born May 13, 1972, in Truro, Mass. ... 6-7/280. ... Full name: Josh Heinrich-Taves.

HIGH SCHOOL: Dennis-Yarmouth Regional (South Yarmouth, Mass.), then New Hampton Prep.

COLLEGE: Northeastern.

TRANSACTIONS/CAREER NOTES: Signed as non-drafted free agent by Detroit Lions (May 3, 1995). ... Released by Lions (August 28, 1995). ... Re-signed by Lions (August 30, 1995). ... Activated (December 21, 1995); did not play. ... Assigned by Lions to Barcelona Dragons in 1996 World League enhancement allocation program (February 1996). ... Released by Lions (August 21, 1996). ... Signed by Jacksonville Jaguars (November 13, 1996); did not play. ... Released by Jaguars (December 4, 1996). ... Signed by New England Patriots to practice squad (December 31, 1996). ... On injured reserve with ankle injury (August 21-September 22, 1997). ... Released by Patriots (September 22, 1997). ... Signed by Miami Dolphins (June 22, 1998). ... Claimed on waivers by New Orleans Saints (August 18, 1998). ... Released by Saints (September 5, 1998). ... Signed by Oakland Raiders (March 10, 1999). ... Released by Raiders (September 4, 1999). ... Re-signed by Raiders (February 17, 2000).

LAYING EXPERIENCE: Barcelona W.L., 1996; Barcelona NFLE, 1998; Oakland NFL, 2000. ... Games/Games started: 1996 (games played navailable), 1998 (10/10), 2000 (16/0).
HAMPIONSHIP GAME EXPERIENCE: Played in AFC championship game (2000 season).
RO STATISTICS: W.L.: 1996—Credited with six sacks. NFLE: 1998—Tied for league lead with nine sacks. 2000—Intercepted one pass for 4 yards and credited with three sacks.

TAYLOR, BOBBY　　　　CB　　　　EAGLES

ERSONAL: Born December 28, 1973, in Houston. ... 6-3/216. ... Full name: Robert Taylor. ... Son of Robert Taylor, silver medalist in 100-neter dash and member of gold-medal winning 400-meter relay team at 1972 Summer Olympics.
IGH SCHOOL: Longview (Texas).
OLLEGE: Notre Dame.
RANSACTIONS/CAREER NOTES: Selected after junior season by Philadelphia Eagles in second round (49th pick overall) of 1995 NFL draft. . Signed by Eagles (July 19, 1995). ... On injured reserve with knee injury (October 17, 1997-remainder of season). ... Granted free agency February 13, 1998). ... Re-signed by Eagles (June 11, 1998). ... On injured reserve with fractured jaw (December 28, 1999-remainder of season).
ONORS: Named defensive back on THE SPORTING NEWS college All-America first team (1993 and 1994).
RO STATISTICS: 1996—Credited with one sack, fumbled once and recovered two fumbles for nine yards. 1997—Credited with two sacks. 999—Recovered three fumbles. 2000—Recovered one fumble.

			INTERCEPTIONS			
ear　Team	G	GS	No.	Yds.	Avg.	TD
995—Philadelphia NFL	16	12	2	52	26.0	0
996—Philadelphia NFL	16	16	3	-1	-0.3	0
997—Philadelphia NFL	6	5	0	0	0.0	0
998—Philadelphia NFL	11	10	0	0	0.0	0
999—Philadelphia NFL	15	14	4	59	14.8	1
000—Philadelphia NFL	16	15	3	64	21.3	0
ro totals (6 years)	80	72	12	174	14.5	1

TAYLOR, FRED　　　　RB　　　　JAGUARS

ERSONAL: Born January 27, 1976, in Pahokee, Fla. ... 6-1/200. ... Full name: Frederick Antwon Taylor.
IGH SCHOOL: Glades Central (Belle Glade, Fla.).
OLLEGE: Florida.
RANSACTIONS/CAREER NOTES: Selected by Jacksonville Jaguars in first round (ninth pick overall) of 1998 NFL draft. ... Signed by Jaguars July 6, 1998).
HAMPIONSHIP GAME EXPERIENCE: Played in AFC championship game (1999 season).
ONORS: Named running back on THE SPORTING NEWS college All-America third team (1997).
RO STATISTICS: 1998—Recovered one fumble for nine yards. 2000—Recovered two fumbles for minus one yard.
INGLE GAME HIGHS (regular season): Attempts—32 (December 17, 2000, vs. Cincinnati); yards—234 (November 19, 2000, vs. ittsburgh); and rushing touchdowns—3 (December 3, 2000, vs. Cleveland).
TATISTICAL PLATEAUS: 100-yard rushing games: 1998 (6), 1999 (3), 2000 (9). Total: 18.
MISCELLANEOUS: Holds Jacksonville Jaguars all-time record for most yards rushing (3,354).

			RUSHING				RECEIVING				TOTALS			
ear　Team	G	GS	Att.	Yds.	Avg.	TD	No.	Yds.	Avg.	TD	TD	2pt.	Pts.	Fum.
998—Jacksonville NFL	15	12	264	1223	4.6	14	44	421	9.6	3	17	0	102	3
999—Jacksonville NFL	10	9	159	732	4.6	6	10	83	8.3	0	6	0	36	0
000—Jacksonville NFL	13	13	292	1399	4.8	12	36	240	6.7	2	14	0	84	4
ro totals (3 years)	38	34	715	3354	4.7	32	90	744	8.3	5	37	0	222	7

TAYLOR, HENRY　　　　DT

ERSONAL: Born November 29, 1975, in Broward County, Fla. ... 6-2/303.
IGH SCHOOL: Barnwell (S.C.).
OLLEGE: South Carolina.
RANSACTIONS/CAREER NOTES: Signed as non-drafted free agent by San Diego Chargers (April 20, 1998). ... Released by Chargers (July 3, 1998). ... Re-signed by Chargers (July 31, 1998). ... Released by Chargers (August 25, 1998). ... Signed by Detroit Lions to practice squad September 2, 1998). ... Activated (October 8, 1998); did not play. ... Released by Lions (October 19, 1998). ... Re-signed by Lions to prac- ce squad (October 21, 1998). ... Activated (November 23, 1998). ... On injured reserve with groin injury (December 19, 1998-remainder of eason). ... Assigned by Lions to Amsterdam Admirals in 1999 NFL Europe enhancement allocation program (February 22, 1999). ... Released y Lions (September 5, 1999). ... Re-signed by Lions to practice squad (September 7, 1999). ... Assigned by Lions to Frankfurt Galaxy in 2000 FL Europe enhancement allocation program (February 18, 2000). ... Released by Lions (August 27, 2000). ... Signed by Atlanta Falcons November 1, 2000).
LAYING EXPERIENCE: Detroit NFL, 1998; Amsterdam, NFLE, 1999; Frankfurt NFLE, 2000; Atlanta NFL, 2000. ... Games/Games started: 1998 1/0), NFLE 1999 (games played unavailable), NFLE 2000 (-), NFL 2000 (5/0). Total NFL: 6/0.
RO STATISTICS: NFLE: 2000—Credited with six sacks.

TAYLOR, JASON　　　　DE　　　　DOLPHINS

ERSONAL: Born September 1, 1974, in Pittsburgh. ... 6-6/260. ... Full name: Jason Paul Taylor.
IGH SCHOOL: Woodland Hills (Pittsburgh).
OLLEGE: Akron.
RANSACTIONS/CAREER NOTES: Selected by Miami Dolphins in third round (73rd pick overall) of 1997 NFL draft. ... Signed by Dolphins July 9, 1997). ... On injured reserve with broken collarbone (December 29, 1998-remainder of playoffs). ... Granted free agency (February 1, 2000). ... Re-signed by Dolphins (April 13, 2000). ... Designated by Dolphins as franchise player (February 22, 2001).
ONORS: Named defensive end on THE SPORTING NEWS NFL All-Pro team (2000). ... Played in Pro Bowl (2000 season).

PRO STATISTICS: 1997—Recovered two fumbles. 1999—Intercepted one pass for no yards and recovered two fumbles for four yards and one touchdown. 2000—Intercepted one pass for two yards and recovered four fumbles for 29 yards and one touchdown.

Year Team	G	GS	SACKS
1997—Miami NFL	13	11	5.0
1998—Miami NFL	16	15	9.0
1999—Miami NFL	15	15	2.5
2000—Miami NFL	16	16	14.5
Pro totals (4 years)	60	57	31.0

TAYLOR, RYAN — LB — RAIDERS

PERSONAL: Born December 11, 1976, in Dublin, Ga. ... 6-2/230.
HIGH SCHOOL: Dublin (Ga.).
COLLEGE: Auburn.
TRANSACTIONS/CAREER NOTES: Signed as non-drafted free agent by Cleveland Browns (April 23, 1999). ... Assigned by Browns to Scottish Claymores in 2000 NFL Europe enhancement allocation program (February 18, 2000). ... Released by Browns (August 27, 2000). ... Re-signed by Browns to practice squad (August 30, 2000). ... Activated (October 13, 2000). ... On injured reserve with broken arm (November 7, 2000-remainder of season). ... Released by Browns (February 19, 2000). ... Signed by Oakland Raiders (April 1, 2001).
PLAYING EXPERIENCE: Scottish NFLE, 2000; Cleveland NFL, 2000. ... Games/Games started: NFLE 2000 (games played unavailable), NFL 2000 (4/0).

TAYLOR, SHANNON — LB — CHARGERS

PERSONAL: Born February 16, 1975, in Roanoke, Va. ... 6-3/247. ... Full name: Shannon Andre Taylor.
HIGH SCHOOL: Patrick Henry (Roanoke, Va.).
COLLEGE: Virginia.
TRANSACTIONS/CAREER NOTES: Selected by San Diego Chargers in sixth round (184th pick overall) of 2000 NFL draft. ... Signed by Chargers (June 21, 2000). ... Released by Chargers (August 27, 2000). ... Re-signed by Chargers to practice squad (August 29, 2000). ... Activated (October 4, 2000).
PLAYING EXPERIENCE: San Diego NFL, 2000. ... Games/Games started: 2000 (11/0).

TAYLOR, TRAVIS — WR — RAVENS

PERSONAL: Born March 30, 1979, in Fernadina Beach, Fla. ... 6-1/200. ... Full name: Travis Lamont Taylor.
HIGH SCHOOL: Camden County (Ga.), then Jean Ribault (Jacksonville).
COLLEGE: Florida.
TRANSACTIONS/CAREER NOTES: Selected after junior season by Baltimore Ravens in first round (10th pick overall) of 2000 NFL draft. ... Signed by Ravens (August 1, 2000). ... On injured reserve with broken clavicle (November 8, 2000-remainder of season).
PRO STATISTICS: 2000—Rushed twice for 11 yards and fumbled once.
SINGLE GAME HIGHS (regular season): Receptions—5 (October 1, 2000, vs. Cleveland); yards—80 (September 10, 2000, vs. Jacksonville) and touchdown receptions—2 (September 10, 2000, vs. Jacksonville).

			RECEIVING			
Year Team	G	GS	No.	Yds.	Avg.	TD
2000—Baltimore NFL	9	8	28	276	9.9	3

TEAGUE, GEORGE — S — COWBOYS

PERSONAL: Born February 18, 1971, in Lansing, Mich. ... 6-1/196. ... Full name: George Theo Teague. ... Name pronounced TEEG.
HIGH SCHOOL: Jefferson Davis (Montgomery, Ala.).
COLLEGE: Alabama.
TRANSACTIONS/CAREER NOTES: Selected by Green Bay Packers in first round (29th pick overall) of 1993 NFL draft. ... Signed by Packers (July 9, 1993). ... Granted free agency (February 16, 1996). ... Re-signed by Packers (April 12, 1996). ... Traded by Packers to Atlanta Falcons for conditional draft pick (July 16, 1996). ... Released by Falcons (August 17, 1996). ... Signed by Dallas Cowboys (August 23, 1996). ... Granted unconditional free agency (February 14, 1997). ... Signed by Miami Dolphins (March 20, 1997). ... Traded by Dolphins to Cowboys (May 6, 1998), as compensation for Dolphins signing free agent S Brock Marion (March 3, 1998). ... Granted unconditional free agency (February 11, 2000). ... Re-signed by Cowboys (March 13, 2000). ... On injured reserve with broken foot (November 15, 2000-remainder of season).
CHAMPIONSHIP GAME EXPERIENCE: Played in NFC championship game (1995 season).
POST SEASON RECORDS: Holds NFL postseason single-game record for longest interception return—101 yards, touchdown (January 8, 1994, at Detroit).
PRO STATISTICS: 1993—Returned one punt for minus one yard and recovered two fumbles. 1995—Recovered one fumble for four yards. 1998—Credited with two sacks. 1999—Recovered one fumble.

			INTERCEPTIONS			
Year Team	G	GS	No.	Yds.	Avg.	TD
1993—Green Bay NFL	16	12	1	22	22.0	0
1994—Green Bay NFL	16	16	3	33	11.0	0
1995—Green Bay NFL	15	15	2	100	50.0	0
1996—Dallas NFL	16	8	4	47	11.8	0
1997—Miami NFL	15	6	2	25	12.5	0
1998—Dallas NFL	16	5	0	0	0.0	0
1999—Dallas NFL	14	14	3	127	*42.3	†2
2000—Dallas NFL	9	9	0	0	0.0	0
Pro totals (8 years)	117	85	15	354	23.6	2

TEAGUE, TREY — OT — BRONCOS

PERSONAL: Born December 27, 1974, in Jackson, Tenn. ... 6-5/292. ... Full name: Fred Everette Teague III. ... Name pronounced TEEG.
HIGH SCHOOL: University (Jackson, Tenn).
COLLEGE: Tennessee.
TRANSACTIONS/CAREER NOTES: Selected by Denver Broncos in seventh round (200th pick overall) of 1998 NFL draft. ... Signed by Broncos (July 23, 1998). ... Inactive for all 16 games (1998). ... On injured reserve with knee injury (September 12, 2000-remainder of season). ... Granted free agency (March 2, 2001).
PLAYING EXPERIENCE: Denver NFL, 1999 and 2000. ... Games/Games started: 1999 (16/4), 2000 (2/0). Total: 18/4.
CHAMPIONSHIP GAME EXPERIENCE: Member of Broncos for AFC championship game (1998 season); inactive. ... Member of Super Bowl championship team (1998 season); inactive.
PRO STATISTICS: 1999—Fumbled once for minus nine yards.

TERRELL, DARYL — OT — SAINTS

PERSONAL: Born January 25, 1975, in Vossburg, Miss. ... 6-5/296.
HIGH SCHOOL: Heidelberg (Miss.).
JUNIOR COLLEGE: Jones County Community College (Miss.).
COLLEGE: Southern Mississippi.
TRANSACTIONS/CAREER NOTES: Signed as non-drafted free agent by Baltimore Ravens (June 3, 1997). ... Released by Ravens (July 8, 1997). ... Signed by New Orleans Saints (April 27, 1998). ... Released by Saints (August 24, 1998). ... Re-signed by Saints to practice squad (September 2, 1998). ... Assigned by Saints to Amsterdam Admirals in 1999 NFL Europe enhancement allocation program (February 22, 1999).
PLAYING EXPERIENCE: Amsterdam Admirals NFLE, 1999; New Orleans NFL, 1999 and 2000. ... Games/Games started: NFLE 1999 (games played unavailable), NFL 1999 (12/1), 2000 (16/0). Total NFL: 28/1.

TERRELL, DAVID — CB — REDSKINS

PERSONAL: Born July 8, 1975, in Floyada, Texas. ... 6-1/188.
HIGH SCHOOL: Sweetwater (Texas).
COLLEGE: Texas-El Paso.
TRANSACTIONS/CAREER NOTES: Selected by Washington Redskins in seventh round (191st pick overall) of 1998 NFL draft. ... Signed by Redskins (May 13, 1998). ... Released by Redskins (August 25, 1998). ... Selected by Rhein Fire in 1999 NFL Europe draft (February 23, 1999). ... Released by Redskins (September 4, 1999). ... Re-signed by Redskins to practice squad (September 14, 1999).
PLAYING EXPERIENCE: Washington NFL, 2000. ... Games/Games started: 2000 (16/0).
PRO STATISTICS: 2000—Recovered two fumbles.

TERRY, CHRIS — OT — PANTHERS

PERSONAL: Born August 8, 1975, in Jacksonville. ... 6-5/295. ... Full name: Christopher Alexander Terry.
HIGH SCHOOL: Jean Ribault (Jacksonville).
COLLEGE: Georgia.
TRANSACTIONS/CAREER NOTES: Selected by Carolina Panthers in second round (34th pick overall) of 1999 NFL draft. ... Signed by Panthers (May 24, 1999).
PLAYING EXPERIENCE: Carolina NFL, 1999 and 2000. ... Games/Games started: 1999 (16/16), 2000 (16/16). Total: 32/32.
PRO STATISTICS: 1999—Recovered two fumbles.

TERRY, COREY — LB — SAINTS

PERSONAL: Born March 6, 1976, in Warrenton, N.C. ... 6-3/246. ... Full name: Corey TeWana Terry.
HIGH SCHOOL: Warren County (Warrenton, N.C.).
JUNIOR COLLEGE: Garden City (Kan.) Community College.
COLLEGE: Tennessee.
TRANSACTIONS/CAREER NOTES: Selected by Indianapolis Colts in seventh round (250th pick overall) of 1999 NFL draft. ... Signed by Colts (July 22, 1999). ... Released by Colts (August 30, 1999). ... Signed by Pittsburgh Steelers to practice squad (September 6, 1999). ... Signed by Jacksonville Jaguars off Steelers practice squad (November 2, 1999). ... Released by Jaguars (August 27, 2000). ... Signed by Oakland Raiders to practice squad (August 30, 2000). ... Signed by New Orleans Saints off Raiders practice squad (October 12, 2000). ... On injured reserve with knee injury (December 1, 2000-remainder of season).
PLAYING EXPERIENCE: Jacksonville NFL, 1999; New Orleans NFL, 2000. ... Games/Games started: 1999 (8/0), 2000 (7/0). Total: 15/0.
CHAMPIONSHIP GAME EXPERIENCE: Played in AFC championship game (1999 season).

TERRY, TIM — LB — SEAHAWKS

PERSONAL: Born July 26, 1974, in Hempstead, N.Y. ... 6-2/239.
HIGH SCHOOL: Hempstead (N.Y.).
COLLEGE: Temple.
TRANSACTIONS/CAREER NOTES: Signed as non-drafted free agent by Cincinnati Bengals (April 25, 1997). ... Released by Bengals (August 24, 1997). ... Re-signed by Bengals to practice squad (August 26, 1997). ... Activated (September 27, 1997). ... On injured reserve with knee injury (December 8, 1997-remainder of season). ... Released by Bengals (August 19, 1998). ... Re-signed by Bengals to practice squad (December 16, 1998). ... Claimed on waivers by Kansas City Chiefs (August 10, 1999). ... Released by Chiefs (August 31, 1999). ... Re-signed by Chiefs (March 6, 2000). ... Released by Chiefs (August 27, 2000). ... Signed by Seattle Seahawks to practice squad (August 30, 2000). ... Activated (November 10, 2000).
PLAYING EXPERIENCE: Cincinnati NFL, 1997; Seattle NFL, 2000. ... Games/Games started: 1997 (5/0), 2000 (6/0). Total: 11/0.

T

TESTAVERDE, VINNY   QB   JETS

PERSONAL: Born November 13, 1963, in Brooklyn, N.Y. ... 6-5/235. ... Full name: Vincent Frank Testaverde. ... Name pronounced TESS-tuh-VER-dee.

HIGH SCHOOL: Sewanhaka (Floral Park, N.Y.), then Fork Union (Va.) Military Academy.

COLLEGE: Miami (Fla.).

TRANSACTIONS/CAREER NOTES: Signed by Tampa Bay Buccaneers (April 3, 1987). ... Selected officially by Buccaneers in first round (first pick overall) of 1987 NFL draft. ... On injured reserve with ankle injury (December 20, 1989-remainder of season). ... Granted unconditional free agency (March 1, 1993). ... Signed by Cleveland Browns (March 31, 1993). ... Browns franchise moved to Baltimore and renamed Ravens for 1996 season (March 11, 1996). ... Released by Ravens (June 2, 1998). ... Signed by New York Jets (June 24, 1998). ... Granted free agency (February 12, 1999). ... Re-signed by Jets (March 1, 1999). ... On injured reserve with Achilles' tendon injury (September 13, 1999-remainder of season).

CHAMPIONSHIP GAME EXPERIENCE: Played in AFC championship game (1998 season).

HONORS: Named quarterback on THE SPORTING NEWS college All-America second team (1985). ... Heisman Trophy winner (1986). ... Named College Football Player of the Year by THE SPORTING NEWS (1986). ... Maxwell Award winner (1986). ... Davey O'Brien Award winner (1986). ... Named quarterback on THE SPORTING NEWS college All-America first team (1986). ... Played in Pro Bowl (1996 and 1998 seasons).

PRO STATISTICS: 1987—Fumbled seven times and recovered four fumbles for minus three yards. 1988—Fumbled eight times and recovered two fumbles. 1989—Fumbled four times and recovered two fumbles. 1990—Caught one pass for three yards, fumbled 10 times and recovered three fumbles. 1991—Fumbled five times and recovered three fumbles. 1992—Fumbled four times and recovered four fumbles for minus eight yards. 1993—Fumbled four times. 1994—Fumbled three times and recovered two fumbles for two yards. 1995—Caught one pass for seven yards and fumbled four times for minus four yards. 1996—Fumbled nine times for minus 11 yards. 1997—Caught one pass for minus four yards, fumbled 11 times and recovered five fumbles for minus nine yards. 1998—Fumbled seven times and recovered three fumbles for minus six yards. 2000—Fumbled seven times for minus five yards.

SINGLE GAME HIGHS (regular season): Attempts—69 (December 24, 2000, vs. Baltimore); completions—42 (December 6, 1998, vs. Seattle); yards—481 (December 24, 2000, vs. Baltimore); and touchdown passes—5 (October, 23, 2000, vs. Miami).

STATISTICAL PLATEAUS: 300-yard passing games: 1987 (1), 1988 (4), 1989 (4), 1991 (1), 1992 (1), 1993 (1), 1995 (2), 1996 (5), 1997 (3), 1998 (1), 2000 (2). Total: 25. ... 100-yard rushing games: 1990 (1).

MISCELLANEOUS: Regular-season record as starting NFL quarterback: 69-92-1 (.426). ... Postseason record as starting NFL quarterback: 2-2 (.500). ... Holds Tampa Bay Buccaneers all-time records for most yards passing (14,820) and most touchdown passes (77). ... Holds Baltimore Ravens all-time records for most yards passing (7,148) and most touchdown passes (51).

				PASSING							RUSHING				TOTALS	
Year—Team	G	GS	Att.	Cmp.	Pct.	Yds.	TD	Int.	Avg.	Rat.	Att.	Yds.	Avg.	TD	TD	2pt.	Pts.
1987—Tampa Bay NFL	6	4	165	71	43.0	1081	5	6	6.55	60.2	13	50	3.8	1	1	0	6
1988—Tampa Bay NFL	15	15	466	222	47.6	3240	13	*35	6.95	48.8	28	138	4.9	1	1	0	6
1989—Tampa Bay NFL	14	14	480	258	53.8	3133	20	†22	6.53	68.9	25	139	5.6	0	0	0	0
1990—Tampa Bay NFL	14	13	365	203	55.6	2818	17	∞18	‡7.72	75.6	38	280	7.4	1	1	0	6
1991—Tampa Bay NFL	13	12	326	166	50.9	1994	8	15	6.12	59.0	32	101	3.2	0	0	0	0
1992—Tampa Bay NFL	14	14	358	206	57.5	2554	14	16	7.13	74.2	36	197	5.5	2	2	0	12
1993—Cleveland NFL	10	6	230	130	56.5	1797	14	9	‡7.81	85.7	18	74	4.1	0	0	0	0
1994—Cleveland NFL	14	13	376	207	55.1	2575	16	18	6.85	70.7	21	37	1.8	2	2	0	12
1995—Cleveland NFL	13	12	392	241	61.5	2883	17	10	7.35	87.8	18	62	3.4	2	2	0	12
1996—Baltimore NFL	16	16	549	325	59.2	4177	§33	19	7.61	88.7	34	188	5.5	2	2	1	14
1997—Baltimore NFL	13	13	470	271	57.7	2971	18	15	6.32	75.9	34	138	4.1	0	0	0	0
1998—New York Jets NFL	14	13	421	259	61.5	3256	§29	7	7.73	§101.6	24	104	4.3	1	1	0	6
1999—New York Jets NFL	1	1	15	10	66.7	96	1	1	6.40	78.8	0	0	0.0	0	0	0	0
2000—New York Jets NFL	16	16	*590	328	55.6	3732	21	25	6.33	69.0	25	32	1.3	0	0	0	0
Pro totals (14 years)	173	162	5203	2897	55.7	36307	226	216	6.98	74.7	346	1540	4.5	12	12	1	74

THARPE, LARRY   OT   STEELERS

PERSONAL: Born November 19, 1970, in Macon, Ga. ... 6-4/305.

HIGH SCHOOL: Southwest (Macon, Ga.).

COLLEGE: Tennessee State.

TRANSACTIONS/CAREER NOTES: Selected by Detroit Lions in sixth round (145th pick overall) of 1992 NFL draft. ... Signed by Lions (July 23, 1992). ... On injured reserve with back and knee injuries (September 4-October 14, 1992). ... Inactive for 15 games (1994). ... Granted free agency (February 17, 1995). ... Signed by Arizona Cardinals (March 25, 1995); Lions received sixth-round pick (TE Kevin Hickman) in 1995 draft as compensation. ... Granted unconditional free agency (February 16, 1996). ... Signed by New England Patriots (April 29, 1996). ... Active for one game with Patriots (1996); did not play. ... Released by Patriots (October 23, 1996). ... Signed by Lions (February 21, 1997). ... Granted unconditional free agency (February 13, 1998). ... Re-signed by Lions (June 10, 1998). ... Granted unconditional free agency (February 12, 1999). ... Signed by Pittsburgh Steelers (April 4, 2000).

PLAYING EXPERIENCE: Detroit NFL, 1992, 1993, 1997 and 1998; Arizona NFL, 1995; Pittsburgh NFL, 2000. ... Games/Games started: 1992 (11/0), 1993 (5/3), 1995 (16/16), 1997 (16/15), 1998 (16/9), 2000 (12/5). Total: 76/48.

THIBODEAUX, KEITH   CB

PERSONAL: Born May 16, 1974, in Opelousan, La. ... 5-11/189. ... Full name: Keith Trevis Thibodeaux. ... Name pronounced TEE-bo-do.

HIGH SCHOOL: Beau Chene (Opelousas, La.).

COLLEGE: Northwestern (La.) State.

TRANSACTIONS/CAREER NOTES: Selected by Washington Redskins in fifth round (140th pick overall) of 1997 NFL draft. ... Signed by Redskins (May 28, 1997). ... Released by Redskins (August 25, 1998). ... Signed by Atlanta Falcons (February 5, 1999). ... Released by Falcons (November 2, 1999). ... Signed by Minnesota Vikings (November 4, 1999). ... On injured reserve with shoulder injury (December 23, 1999-remainder of season). ... Released by Vikings (February 19, 2001).

PLAYING EXPERIENCE: Washington NFL, 1997; Atlanta (8)-Minnesota (3) NFL, 1999; Minnesota NFL, 2000. ... Games/Games started: 1997 (15/0), 1999 (Atl.-8/0; Min.-3/0; Total: 11/0), 2000 (16/0). Total: 42/0.

CHAMPIONSHIP GAME EXPERIENCE: Played in NFC championship game (2000 season).

PRO STATISTICS: 2000—Intercepted one pass for no yards.

THIERRY, JOHN   DE   PACKERS

PERSONAL: Born September 4, 1971, in Opelousas, La. ... 6-4/262. ... Full name: John Fitzgerald Thierry. ... Name pronounced Theory.
HIGH SCHOOL: Plaisance (Opelousas, La.).
COLLEGE: Alcorn State.
TRANSACTIONS/CAREER NOTES: Selected by Chicago Bears in first round (11th pick overall) of 1994 NFL draft. ... Signed by Bears (June 21, 1994). ... On injured reserve with knee injury (November 5, 1997-remainder of season). ... Granted unconditional free agency (February 12, 1999). ... Signed by Cleveland Browns (February 26, 1999). ... Granted unconditional free agency (February 11, 2000). ... Signed by Green Bay Packers (February 17, 2000).
PRO STATISTICS: 1994—Returned one kickoff for no yards. 1995—Recovered four fumbles. 1998—Intercepted one pass for 14 yards and credited with a safety. 1999—Intercepted one pass for eight yards.

Year Team	G	GS	SACKS
1994—Chicago NFL	16	1	0.0
1995—Chicago NFL	16	7	4.0
1996—Chicago NFL	16	2	2.0
1997—Chicago NFL	9	9	3.0
1998—Chicago NFL	16	9	3.5
1999—Cleveland NFL	16	10	7.0
2000—Green Bay NFL	16	16	6.5
Pro totals (7 years)	105	54	26.0

THIGPEN, YANCEY   WR

PERSONAL: Born August 15, 1969, in Tarboro, N.C. ... 6-1/203. ... Full name: Yancey Dirk Thigpen.
HIGH SCHOOL: Southwest Edgecombe (Tarboro, N.C.).
COLLEGE: Winston-Salem (N.C.) State.
TRANSACTIONS/CAREER NOTES: Selected by San Diego Chargers in fourth round (90th pick overall) of 1991 NFL draft. ... Signed by Chargers (July 15, 1991). ... Released by Chargers (August 26, 1991). ... Re-signed by Chargers to practice squad (August 28, 1991). ... Activated (September 20, 1991). ... Released by Chargers (September 26, 1991). ... Re-signed by Chargers to practice squad (September 28, 1991). ... Activated (December 7, 1991). ... Released by Chargers (August 31, 1992). ... Signed by Pittsburgh Steelers (October 5, 1992). ... On injured reserve with foot injury (January 3, 1997-remainder of playoffs). ... Granted unconditional free agency (February 13, 1998). ... Signed by Tennessee Oilers (February 14, 1998). ... Oilers franchise renamed Tennessee Titans for 1999 season (December 26, 1998). ... Released by Titans (March 1, 2001).
CHAMPIONSHIP GAME EXPERIENCE: Played in AFC championship game (1994, 1995, 1997 and 1999 seasons). ... Played in Super Bowl XXX (1995 season). ... Member of Titans for Super Bowl XXXIV (1999 season); inactive.
HONORS: Played in Pro Bowl (1995 and 1997 seasons).
PRO STATISTICS: 1995—Rushed once for one yard. 1997—Rushed once for three yards and recovered one fumble. 1999—Returned one punt for 21 yards. 2000—Returned one punt for nine yards.
SINGLE GAME HIGHS (regular season): Receptions—11 (October 26, 1997, vs. Jacksonville); yards—196 (October 26, 1997, vs. Jacksonville); and touchdown receptions—3 (December 7, 1997, vs. Denver).
STATISTICAL PLATEAUS: 100-yard receiving games: 1995 (4), 1997 (6), 1998 (1), 1999 (1). Total: 12.

Year Team	G	GS	RECEIVING				KICKOFF RETURNS				TOTALS			
			No.	Yds.	Avg.	TD	No.	Yds.	Avg.	TD	TD	2pt.	Pts.	Fum.
1991—San Diego NFL	4	1	0	0	0.0	0	0	0	0.0	0	0	0	0	0
1992—Pittsburgh NFL	12	0	1	2	2.0	0	2	44	22.0	0	0	0	0	0
1993—Pittsburgh NFL	12	0	9	154	17.1	3	1	23	23.0	0	3	0	18	0
1994—Pittsburgh NFL	15	6	36	546	15.2	4	5	121	24.2	0	4	0	24	0
1995—Pittsburgh NFL	16	15	85	1307	15.4	5	0	0	0.0	0	5	0	30	1
1996—Pittsburgh NFL	6	2	12	244	20.3	2	0	0	0.0	0	2	0	12	0
1997—Pittsburgh NFL	16	15	79	1398	17.7	7	0	0	0.0	0	7	1	44	1
1998—Tennessee NFL	9	8	38	493	13.0	3	0	0	0.0	0	3	0	18	0
1999—Tennessee NFL	10	10	38	648	17.1	4	0	0	0.0	0	4	0	24	1
2000—Tennessee NFL	12	0	15	289	19.3	2	0	0	0.0	0	2	0	12	0
Pro totals (10 years)	112	57	313	5081	16.2	30	8	188	23.5	0	30	1	182	3

THOMAS, ADALIUS   DE   RAVENS

PERSONAL: Born August 18, 1977, in Equality, Ala. ... 6-2/270. ... Full name: Adalius Donquail Thomas.
HIGH SCHOOL: Central Coosa (Equality, Ala.).
COLLEGE: Southern Mississippi.
TRANSACTIONS/CAREER NOTES: Selected by Baltimore Ravens in sixth round (186th pick overall) of 2000 NFL draft. ... Signed by Ravens (July 6, 2000).
PLAYING EXPERIENCE: Baltimore NFL, 2000. ... Games/Games started: 2000 (3/0).
CHAMPIONSHIP GAME EXPERIENCE: Played in AFC championship game (2000 season). ... Member of Super Bowl championship team (2000 season); inactive.
HONORS: Named defensive end on THE SPORTING NEWS college All-America second team (1999).

THOMAS, CHRIS   WR   CHIEFS

PERSONAL: Born July 16, 1971, in Ventura, Calif. ... 6-2/190. ... Full name: Chris Eric Thomas.
HIGH SCHOOL: Ventura (Calif.).
COLLEGE: Cal Poly-SLO (degree in English, 1994).
TRANSACTIONS/CAREER NOTES: Signed as non-drafted free agent by San Diego Chargers (May 6, 1993). ... Released by Chargers (August 30, 1993). ... Re-signed by Chargers to practice squad (September 1, 1993). ... Granted free agency after 1993 season. ... Signed by San Francisco 49ers (May 16, 1995). ... Released by 49ers (February 15, 1996). ... Re-signed by 49ers (May 15, 1996). ... Released by 49ers (August 20, 1996).

... Selected by Rhein Fire in 1997 World League draft (February 17, 1997). ... Signed by Washington Redskins (February 25, 1997). ... Released by Redskins (August 19, 1997). ... Re-signed by Redskins (August 21, 1997). ... Released by Redskins (August 23, 1997). ... Re-signed by Redskins (September 22, 1997). ... Granted free agency (February 12, 1999). ... Re-signed by Redskins (April 23, 1999). ... Released by Redskins (September 21, 1999). ... Signed by St. Louis Rams (October 20, 1999). ... Granted unconditional free agency (February 11, 2000). ... Signed by Minnesota Vikings (February 29, 2000). ... Released by Vikings (August 19, 2000). ... Signed by Rams (August 21, 2000). ... Granted unconditional free agency (March 2, 2001). ... Signed by Kansas City Chiefs (April 1, 2001).

CHAMPIONSHIP GAME EXPERIENCE: Member of Rams for NFC championship game (1999 season); inactive. ... Member of Super Bowl championship team (1999 season); inactive.

PRO STATISTICS: 1995—Returned one punt for 25 yards and returned three kickoffs for 49 yards. 1998—Recovered one fumble. 2000—Recovered one fumble.

SINGLE GAME HIGHS (regular season): Receptions—4 (December 6, 1998, vs. San Diego); yards—62 (December 6, 1998, vs. San Diego); and touchdown receptions—0.

				RECEIVING			TOTALS			
Year Team	G	GS	No.	Yds.	Avg.	TD	TD	2pt.	Pts.	Fum.
1993—San Diego NFL						Did not play.				
1994—						Did not play.				
1995—San Francisco NFL	14	0	6	73	12.2	0	0	0	0	0
1996—						Did not play.				
1997—Washington NFL	13	0	11	93	8.5	0	0	0	0	0
1998—Washington NFL	14	0	14	173	12.4	0	0	0	0	0
1999—Washington NFL	2	0	0	0	0.0	0	0	0	0	0
—St. Louis NFL	6	0	1	6	6.0	0	0	0	0	0
2000—St. Louis NFL	16	0	0	0	0.0	0	0	0	0	0
Pro totals (5 years)	**65**	**0**	**32**	**345**	**10.8**	**0**	**0**	**0**	**0**	**0**

THOMAS, DAVE   CB   GIANTS

PERSONAL: Born August 25, 1968, in Miami. ... 6-3/218. ... Full name: Dave G. Thomas.

HIGH SCHOOL: Miami Beach.

JUNIOR COLLEGE: Butler County Community College (Kan.).

COLLEGE: Tennessee.

TRANSACTIONS/CAREER NOTES: Selected by Dallas Cowboys in eighth round (203rd pick overall) of 1993 NFL draft. ... Signed by Cowboys (July 15, 1993). ... Selected by Jacksonville Jaguars from Cowboys in NFL expansion draft (February 15, 1995). ... Granted free agency (February 16, 1996). ... Re-signed by Jaguars (June 3, 1996). ... On injured reserve with broken leg (October 29, 1996-remainder of season). ... Granted unconditional free agency (February 14, 1997). ... Re-signed by Jaguars (March 3, 1997). ... Granted unconditional free agency (February 11, 2000). ... Signed by New York Giants (April 10, 2000).

CHAMPIONSHIP GAME EXPERIENCE: Played in NFC championship game (1993, 1994 and 2000 seasons). ... Member of Super Bowl championship team (1993 season). ... Played in AFC championship game (1999 season). ... Played in Super Bowl XXXV (2000 season).

PRO STATISTICS: 1995—Recovered one fumble. 1996—Returned one punt for one yard and fumbled once. 1997—Recovered one fumble. 1998—Recovered one fumble.

			INTERCEPTIONS			
Year Team	G	GS	No.	Yds.	Avg.	TD
1993—Dallas NFL	12	0	0	0	0.0	0
1994—Dallas NFL	16	0	0	0	0.0	0
1995—Jacksonville NFL	15	2	0	0	0.0	0
1996—Jacksonville NFL	9	5	2	7	3.5	0
1997—Jacksonville NFL	16	15	2	34	17.0	0
1998—Jacksonville NFL	14	13	1	0	0.0	0
1999—Jacksonville NFL	15	0	2	36	18.0	0
2000—New York Giants NFL	16	16	1	0	0.0	0
Pro totals (8 years)	**113**	**51**	**8**	**77**	**9.6**	**0**

THOMAS, EDWARD   LB   JAGUARS

PERSONAL: Born September 27, 1974, in Thomasville, Ga. ... 6-0/235. ... Full name: Edward Tervin Thomas.

HIGH SCHOOL: C.L. Harper (Atlanta).

COLLEGE: Georgia Southern.

TRANSACTIONS/CAREER NOTES: Signed by Montreal Alouettes of CFL (May 9, 1997). ... Released by Alouettes (June 20, 1997). ... Re-signed by Alouettes (July 14, 1997). ... Signed as non-drafted free agent by San Francisco 49ers (June 7, 2000). ... Released by 49ers (September 19, 2000). ... Re-signed by 49ers to practice squad (September 21, 2001). ... Activated (October 14, 2000). ... Released by 49ers (November 2, 2000). ... Re-signed by 49ers to practice squad (November 7, 2000). ... Released by 49ers (November 14, 2000). ... Signed by Jacksonville Jaguars to practice squad (November 21, 2000). ... Activated (November 29, 2000).

PRO STATISTICS: CFL 1997—Recovered one fumble for three yards.

			INTERCEPTIONS				SACKS
Year Team	G	GS	No.	Yds.	Avg.	TD	No.
1997—Montreal CFL	7	...	1	0	0.0	0	1.0
1998—Montreal CFL	3	...	0	0	0.0	0	0.0
1999—Montreal CFL	12	...	0	0	0.0	0	2.0
2000—San Francisco NFL	4	0	0	0	0.0	0	0.0
—Jacksonville NFL	4	0	0	0	0.0	0	0.0
CFL totals (3 years)	**22**	**...**	**1**	**0**	**0.0**	**0**	**3.0**
NFL totals (1 year)	**8**	**0**	**0**	**0**	**0.0**	**0**	**0.0**
Pro totals (4 years)	**30**	**...**	**1**	**0**	**0.0**	**0**	**3.0**

THOMAS, FRED CB SAINTS

PERSONAL: Born September 11, 1973, in Bruce, Miss. ... 5-9/172.
HIGH SCHOOL: Bruce (Miss.).
JUNIOR COLLEGE: Northwest Mississippi Community College.
COLLEGE: Mississippi Valley State (did not play football), then Mississippi, then Tennessee-Martin.
TRANSACTIONS/CAREER NOTES: Selected by Seattle Seahawks in second round (47th pick overall) of 1996 NFL draft. ... Signed by Seahawks (July 19, 1996). ... Granted free agency (February 12, 1999). ... Re-signed by Seahawks (May 27, 1999). ... On injured reserve with broken leg (September 17, 1999-remainder of season). ... Granted unconditional free agency (February 11, 2000). ... Signed by New Orleans Saints (February 14, 2000).
PLAYING EXPERIENCE: Seattle NFL, 1996-1999; New Orleans NFL, 2000. ... Games/Games started: 1996 (15/0), 1997 (16/3), 1998 (15/2), 1999 (1/0), 2000 (11/0). Total: 58/5.
PRO STATISTICS: 1998—Recovered one fumble.

THOMAS, HENRY DT

PERSONAL: Born January 12, 1965, in Houston. ... 6-2/277. ... Full name: Henry Lee Thomas Jr.
HIGH SCHOOL: Dwight D. Eisenhower (Houston).
COLLEGE: Louisiana Tech.
TRANSACTIONS/CAREER NOTES: Selected by Minnesota Vikings in third round (72nd pick overall) of 1987 NFL draft. ... Signed by Vikings (July 14, 1987). ... Designated by Vikings as transition player (February 25, 1993). ... Designated by Vikings as franchise player (February 15, 1994). ... Free agency status changed by Vikings from franchise to unconditional (February 15, 1995). ... Signed by Detroit Lions (February 27, 1995). ... Released by Lions (April 23, 1997). ... Signed by New England Patriots (June 12, 1997). ... Granted unconditional free agency (February 12, 1999). ... Re-signed by Patriots (February 16, 1999). ... Released by Patriots (March 13, 2001).
CHAMPIONSHIP GAME EXPERIENCE: Played in NFC championship game (1987 season).
HONORS: Named defensive lineman on THE SPORTING NEWS college All-America second team (1986). ... Played in Pro Bowl (1991 and 1992 seasons).
PRO STATISTICS: 1987—Intercepted one pass for no yards and recovered one fumble. 1988—Intercepted one pass for seven yards and recovered one fumble for two yards and a touchdown. 1989—Recovered three fumbles for 37 yards and one touchdown. 1990—Recovered one fumble. 1991—Recovered one fumble. 1993—Credited with one safety. 1994—Recovered one fumble. 1995—Recovered two fumbles. 1996—Recovered one fumble. 1997—Recovered one fumble. 1998—Intercepted one pass for 24 yards and a touchdown and recovered one fumble. 2000—Intercepted one pass for 16 yards and recovered one fumble.

Year Team	G	GS	SACKS
1987—Minnesota NFL	12	12	2.5
1988—Minnesota NFL	15	15	6.0
1989—Minnesota NFL	14	14	9.0
1990—Minnesota NFL	16	16	8.5
1991—Minnesota NFL	16	15	8.0
1992—Minnesota NFL	16	16	6.0
1993—Minnesota NFL	13	13	9.0
1994—Minnesota NFL	16	16	7.0
1995—Detroit NFL	16	16	10.5
1996—Detroit NFL	15	15	6.0
1997—New England NFL	16	16	7.0
1998—New England NFL	16	15	6.5
1999—New England NFL	16	16	3.0
2000—New England NFL	16	7	4.5
Pro totals (14 years)	213	202	93.5

THOMAS, HOLLIS DT EAGLES

PERSONAL: Born January 10, 1974, in Abilene, Texas. ... 6-0/306.
HIGH SCHOOL: Sumner (St. Louis).
COLLEGE: Northern Illinois.
TRANSACTIONS/CAREER NOTES: Signed as non-drafted free agent by Philadelphia Eagles (April 26, 1996). ... On injured reserve with arm/shoulder injury (December 2, 1998-remainder of season).
PRO STATISTICS: 1997—Recovered one fumble. 1998—Recovered one fumble. 1999—Recovered one fumble for two yards. 2000—Recovered one fumble.

Year Team	G	GS	SACKS
1996—Philadelphia NFL	16	5	1.0
1997—Philadelphia NFL	16	16	2.5
1998—Philadelphia NFL	12	12	5.0
1999—Philadelphia NFL	16	16	1.0
2000—Philadelphia NFL	16	16	4.0
Pro totals (5 years)	76	65	13.5

THOMAS, KIWAUKEE CB JAGUARS

PERSONAL: Born June 19, 1977, in Warner Robins, Ga. ... 5-11/182. ... Full name: Kiwaukee Sanchez Thomas. ... Name pronounced kee-WA-kee.
HIGH SCHOOL: Perry (Ga.).
COLLEGE: Georgia Southern.
TRANSACTIONS/CAREER NOTES: Selected by Jacksonville Jaguars in fifth round (159th pick overall) of 2000 NFL draft. ... Signed by Jaguars (May 25, 2000).
PLAYING EXPERIENCE: Jacksonville NFL, 2000. ... Games/Games started: 2000 (16/3).
PRO STATISTICS: 2000—Recovered one fumble.

T

THOMAS, LAMAR   WR   DOLPHINS

PERSONAL: Born February 12, 1970, in Ocala, Fla. ... 6-1/170. ... Full name: Lamar Nathaniel Thomas.
HIGH SCHOOL: Buchholz (Gainesville, Fla.).
COLLEGE: Miami, Fla. (degree in sociology).
TRANSACTIONS/CAREER NOTES: Selected by Tampa Bay Buccaneers in third round (60th pick overall) of 1993 NFL draft. ... Signed by Buccaneers (July 14, 1993). ... Granted free agency (February 16, 1996). ... Re-signed by Buccaneers (May 16, 1996). ... Released by Buccaneers (July 17, 1996). ... Signed by Miami Dolphins (July 27, 1996). ... Granted unconditional free agency (February 14, 1997). ... Re-signed by Dolphins (March 11, 1997). ... On injured reserve with shoulder injury (September 5, 1999-entire season). ... On injured reserve with hip injury (August 22, 2000-entire season).
HONORS: Named wide receiver on THE SPORTING NEWS college All-America second team (1992).
PRO STATISTICS: 1995—Rushed once for five yards.
SINGLE GAME HIGHS (regular season): Receptions—6 (December 21, 1998, vs. Denver); yards—136 (December 21, 1998, vs. Denver); and touchdown receptions—3 (December 21, 1998, vs. Denver).
STATISTICAL PLATEAUS: 100-yard receiving games: 1998 (1).

			RECEIVING				TOTALS			
Year Team	G	GS	No.	Yds.	Avg.	TD	TD	2pt.	Pts.	Fum.
1993—Tampa Bay NFL	14	2	8	186	23.3	2	2	0	12	0
1994—Tampa Bay NFL	11	0	7	94	13.4	0	0	0	0	0
1995—Tampa Bay NFL	11	0	10	107	10.7	0	0	0	0	0
1996—Miami NFL	9	3	10	166	16.6	1	1	0	6	0
1997—Miami NFL	12	6	28	402	14.4	2	2	0	12	1
1998—Miami NFL	16	2	43	603	14.0	5	5	0	30	0
1999—Miami NFL						Did not play.				
2000—Miami NFL						Did not play.				
Pro totals (6 years)	73	13	106	1558	14.7	10	10	0	60	1

THOMAS, MARK   DE   COLTS

PERSONAL: Born May 6, 1969, in Lilburn, Ga. ... 6-5/265. ... Full name: Mark Andrew Thomas.
HIGH SCHOOL: Lilburn (Ga.).
COLLEGE: North Carolina State.
TRANSACTIONS/CAREER NOTES: Selected by San Francisco 49ers in fourth round (89th pick overall) of 1992 NFL draft. ... Signed by 49ers (July 16, 1992). ... On injured reserve with ankle injury (September 1-October 7, 1992). ... On practice squad (October 7-November 11, 1992). ... On injured reserve (November 11, 1992-remainder of season). ... Selected by Carolina Panthers from 49ers in NFL expansion draft (February 15, 1995). ... Granted free agency (February 17, 1995). ... On injured reserve with thumb injury (November 27, 1995-remainder of season). ... Granted unconditional free agency (February 16, 1996). ... Re-signed by Panthers (February 20, 1996). ... Granted unconditional free agency (February 14, 1997). ... Signed by Chicago Bears (March 30, 1997). ... Claimed on waivers by Indianapolis Colts (December 2, 1998). ... Granted unconditional free agency (February 12, 1999). ... Re-signed by Colts (February 12, 1999).
CHAMPIONSHIP GAME EXPERIENCE: Member of 49ers for NFC championship game (1993 and 1994 seasons); inactive. ... Member of Super Bowl championship team (1994 season). ... Played in NFC championship game (1996 season).
PRO STATISTICS: 1993—Recovered one fumble. 1996—Recovered one fumble for 18 yards. 1997—Recovered one fumble. 1999—Recovered one fumble.

Year Team	G	GS	SACKS
1992—San Francisco NFL		Did not play.	
1993—San Francisco NFL	11	1	0.5
1994—San Francisco NFL	9	0	1.0
1995—Carolina NFL	10	0	2.0
1996—Carolina NFL	12	0	4.0
1997—Chicago NFL	16	7	4.5
1998—Chicago NFL	10	4	4.5
—Indianapolis NFL	4	1	1.0
1999—Indianapolis NFL	15	2	3.0
2000—Indianapolis NFL	14	1	5.0
Pro totals (8 years)	101	16	25.5

THOMAS, ORLANDO   S   VIKINGS

PERSONAL: Born October 21, 1972, in Crowley, La. ... 6-1/225.
HIGH SCHOOL: Crowley (La.).
COLLEGE: Southwestern Louisiana.
TRANSACTIONS/CAREER NOTES: Selected by Minnesota Vikings in second round (42nd pick overall) of 1995 NFL draft. ... Signed by Vikings (July 25, 1995). ... Granted unconditional free agency (February 12, 1999). ... Re-signed by Vikings (February 24, 1999). ... On injured reserve with shoulder injury (December 22, 1999-remainder of season). ... On injured reserve with leg injury (January 10, 2001-remainder of 2000 playoffs).
CHAMPIONSHIP GAME EXPERIENCE: Played in NFC championship game (1998 season).
PRO STATISTICS: 1995—Fumbled once and recovered four fumbles for 19 yards and one touchdown. 1996—Recovered one fumble. 1997—Fumbled once and recovered two fumbles for 26 yards and one touchdown. 1998—Credited with 1/2 sack. 1999—Recovered one fumble. 2000—Returned one kickoff for 15 yards, credited with one sack and recovered two fumbles.

			INTERCEPTIONS				TOTALS			
Year Team	G	GS	No.	Yds.	Avg.	TD	TD	2pt.	Pts.	Fum.
1995—Minnesota NFL	16	11	*9	108	12.0	1	2	0	12	1
1996—Minnesota NFL	16	16	5	57	11.4	0	0	0	0	0
1997—Minnesota NFL	15	13	2	1	0.5	0	1	0	6	1
1998—Minnesota NFL	16	16	2	27	13.5	0	0	0	0	0
1999—Minnesota NFL	13	12	2	32	16.0	1	1	0	6	0
2000—Minnesota NFL	9	9	1	0	0.0	0	0	0	0	0
Pro totals (6 years)	85	77	21	225	10.7	2	4	0	24	2

THOMAS, RANDY　　　　　　　G　　　　　　　JETS

PERSONAL: Born January 19, 1976, in East Point, Ga. ... 6-4/301.
HIGH SCHOOL: Tri-Cities (East Point, Ga.).
JUNIOR COLLEGE: Copiah-Lincoln Junior College (Miss.).
COLLEGE: Mississippi State.
TRANSACTIONS/CAREER NOTES: Selected by New York Jets in second round (57th pick overall) of 1999 NFL draft. ... Signed by Jets (July 20, 1999).
PLAYING EXPERIENCE: New York Jets NFL, 1999 and 2000. ... Games/Games started: 1999 (16/16), 2000 (16/16). Total: 32/32.
HONORS: Named offensive guard on THE SPORTING NEWS college All-America second team (1998).

THOMAS, RATCLIFF　　　　　LB　　　　　　COLTS

PERSONAL: Born January 2, 1974, in Alexandria, Va. ... 6-0/240.
HIGH SCHOOL: T.C. Williams (Alexandria, Va.).
COLLEGE: Maryland.
TRANSACTIONS/CAREER NOTES: Selected by Amsterdam Admirals in 1998 NFL Europe draft (February 18, 1998). ... Signed as non-drafted free agent by Indianapolis Colts (August 5, 1998). ... Released by Colts (September 9, 1998). ... Re-signed by Colts (September 29, 1998). ... Released by Colts (October 5, 1998). ... Re-signed by Colts (October 6, 1998). ... Released by Colts (November 25, 1998). ... Re-signed by Colts (January 19, 1999).
PLAYING EXPERIENCE: Indianapolis NFL, 1998-2000. ... Games/Games started: 1998 (5/0), 1999 (16/0), 2000 (12/0). Total: 33/0.
PRO STATISTICS: 1999—Intercepted one pass for no yards.

THOMAS, ROBERT　　　　　　FB　　　　　COWBOYS

PERSONAL: Born December 1, 1974, in Jacksonville, Ark. ... 6-1/252.
HIGH SCHOOL: Jacksonville (Ark.).
COLLEGE: Henderson State (Ark.).
TRANSACTIONS/CAREER NOTES: Signed as non-drafted free agent by Dallas Cowboys (February 24, 1998). ... Assigned by Cowboys to Rhein Fire in 1999 NFL Europe enhancement allocation program (February 22, 1999). ... Granted free agency (March 2, 2001). ... Re-signed by Cowboys (March 21, 2001).
PLAYING EXPERIENCE: Dallas NFL, 1998-2000; Rhein NFLE, 1999. ... Games/Games started: 1998 (16/0), NFLE 1999 (games played unavailable), NFL 1999 (16/7), 2000 (16/15). Total NFL: 48/22.
PRO STATISTICS: NFLE: 1999—Intercepted one pass for 13 yards. NFL: 1999—Rushed eight times for 35 yards and caught 10 passes for 64 yards. 2000—Rushed 15 times for 51 yards, caught 23 passes for 117 yards and two touchdowns, fumbled twice and recovered one fumble.
SINGLE GAME HIGHS (regular season): Attempts—4 (December 19, 1999, vs. New York Jets); yards—22 (December 19, 1999, vs. New York Jets); and rushing touchdowns—0.
MISCELLANEOUS: Played linebacker (1998 and 1999).

THOMAS, RODNEY　　　　　　RB　　　　　FALCONS

PERSONAL: Born March 30, 1973, in Trinity, Texas. ... 5-10/210. ... Full name: Rodney Dejuane Thomas.
HIGH SCHOOL: Groveton (Texas).
COLLEGE: Texas A&M.
TRANSACTIONS/CAREER NOTES: Selected by Houston Oilers in third round (89th pick overall) of 1995 NFL draft. ... Signed by Oilers (August 1, 1995). ... Oilers franchise moved to Tennessee for 1997 season. ... Granted free agency (February 13, 1998). ... Re-signed by Oilers (June 2, 1998). ... Oilers franchise renamed Tennessee Titans for 1999 season (December 26, 1998). ... Released by Titans (March 1, 2001). ... Signed by Atlanta Falcons (May 1, 2001).
CHAMPIONSHIP GAME EXPERIENCE: Played in AFC championship game (1999 season). ... Played in Super Bowl XXXIV (1999 season).
PRO STATISTICS: 2000—Recovered one fumble.
SINGLE GAME HIGHS (regular season): Attempts—25 (November 19, 1995 vs. Kansas City); yards—108 (November 5, 1995, vs. Cleveland); and rushing touchdowns—2 (December 24, 1995, vs. Buffalo).
STATISTICAL PLATEAUS: 100-yard rushing games: 1995 (2).

			RUSHING				RECEIVING				KICKOFF RETURNS				TOTALS			
Year　Team	G	GS	Att.	Yds.	Avg.	TD	No.	Yds.	Avg.	TD	No.	Yds.	Avg.	TD	TD	2pt.	Pts.	Fum.
1995—Houston NFL	16	10	251	947	3.8	5	39	204	5.2	2	3	48	16.0	0	7	1	44	8
1996—Houston NFL	16	0	49	151	3.1	1	13	128	9.8	0	5	80	16.0	0	1	0	6	0
1997—Tennessee NFL	16	1	67	310	4.6	3	14	111	7.9	0	17	346	20.4	0	3	0	18	1
1998—Tennessee NFL	11	0	24	100	4.2	2	6	55	9.2	0	3	64	21.3	0	2	0	12	0
1999—Tennessee NFL	16	0	43	164	3.8	1	9	72	8.0	0	0	0	0.0	0	1	0	6	0
2000—Tennessee NFL	16	0	61	175	2.9	0	8	35	4.4	1	0	0	0.0	0	1	0	6	1
Pro totals (6 years)	91	11	495	1847	3.7	12	89	605	6.8	3	28	538	19.2	0	15	1	92	10

THOMAS, THURMAN　　　　　RB

PERSONAL: Born May 16, 1966, in Houston. ... 5-10/200. ... Full name: Thurman Lee Thomas.
HIGH SCHOOL: Willow Ridge (Sugar Land, Texas).
COLLEGE: Oklahoma State.
TRANSACTIONS/CAREER NOTES: Selected by Buffalo Bills in second round (40th pick overall) of 1988 NFL draft. ... Signed by Bills (July 14, 1988). ... Released by Bills (February 10, 2000). ... Signed by Miami Dolphins (March 6, 2000). ... On injured reserve with knee injury (November 13, 2000-remainder of season). ... Released by Dolphins (February 22, 2001). ... Signed by Buffalo Bills (February 27, 2001). ... Announced retirement (February 27, 2001).

CHAMPIONSHIP GAME EXPERIENCE: Played in AFC championship game (1988 and 1990-1993 seasons). ... Played in Super Bowl XXV (1990 season), Super Bowl XXVI (1991 season), Super Bowl XXVII (1992 season) and Super Bowl XXVIII (1993 season).
HONORS: Named running back on The Sporting News college All-America second team (1985). ... Played in Pro Bowl (1989-1991 and 1993 seasons). ... Named to play in Pro Bowl (1992 season); replaced by Ronnie Harmon due to injury. ... Named running back on The Sporting News NFL All-Pro team (1990 and 1991). ... Named NFL Player of the Year by The Sporting News (1991).
POST SEASON RECORDS: Holds NFL postseason career record for most yards gained—2,114. ... Holds NFL postseason record for most consecutive games with one or more touchdowns—9 (1992-1998). ... Shares NFL postseason single-game record for most receptions—13 (January 6, 1990, at Cleveland). ... Shares NFL postseason career records for most points scored—126; and most touchdowns—21.
PRO STATISTICS: 1988—Recovered one fumble. 1989—Recovered two fumbles. 1990—Recovered two fumbles. 1992—Recovered one fumble. 1993—Attempted one pass without a completion and recovered one fumble. 1994—Recovered two fumbles. 1996—Recovered one fumble.
SINGLE GAME HIGHS (regular season): Attempts—37 (November 8, 1992, vs. Pittsburgh); yards—214 (September 24, 1990, vs. New York Jets); and rushing touchdowns—3 (September 6, 1992, vs. Los Angeles Raiders).
STATISTICAL PLATEAUS: 100-yard rushing games: 1988 (2), 1989 (5), 1990 (5), 1991 (8), 1992 (9), 1993 (7), 1994 (4), 1995 (3), 1996 (2), 1997 (1). Total: 46. ... 100-yard receiving games: 1991 (2), 1996 (1). Total: 3.
MISCELLANEOUS: Holds Buffalo Bills all-time record for most yards rushing (11,938) and most rushing touchdowns (65). ... Shares Buffalo Bills all-time record for most touchdowns (87).

				RUSHING				RECEIVING				TOTALS		
Year Team	G	GS	Att.	Yds.	Avg.	TD	No.	Yds.	Avg.	TD	TD	2pt.	Pts.	Fum.
1988—Buffalo NFL	15	15	207	881	4.3	2	18	208	11.6	0	2	0	12	9
1989—Buffalo NFL	16	16	298	1244	4.2	6	60	669	11.2	6	▲12	0	72	7
1990—Buffalo NFL	16	16	271	§1297	4.8	11	49	532	10.9	2	13	0	78	6
1991—Buffalo NFL	15	15	§288	§1407	*4.9	7	62	631	10.2	5	▲12	0	72	5
1992—Buffalo NFL	16	16	312	1487	§4.8	9	58	626	10.8	3	§12	0	72	6
1993—Buffalo NFL	16	16	*355	§1315	3.7	6	48	387	8.1	0	6	0	36	6
1994—Buffalo NFL	15	15	287	1093	3.8	7	50	349	7.0	2	9	0	54	1
1995—Buffalo NFL	14	14	267	1005	3.8	6	26	220	8.5	2	8	0	48	6
1996—Buffalo NFL	15	15	281	1033	3.7	8	26	254	9.8	0	8	0	48	1
1997—Buffalo NFL	16	16	154	643	4.2	1	30	208	6.9	0	1	0	6	2
1998—Buffalo NFL	14	3	93	381	4.1	2	26	220	8.5	1	3	0	18	0
1999—Buffalo NFL	5	3	36	152	4.2	0	3	37	12.3	1	1	0	6	0
2000—Miami NFL	9	0	28	136	4.9	0	16	117	7.3	1	1	0	6	1
Pro totals (13 years)	182	160	2877	12074	4.2	65	472	4458	9.4	23	88	0	528	50

THOMAS, TRA   OT   EAGLES

PERSONAL: Born November 20, 1974, in De Land, Fla. ... 6-7/349. ... Full name: William Thomas III. ... Name pronounced TRAY.
HIGH SCHOOL: De Land (Fla.).
COLLEGE: Florida State.
TRANSACTIONS/CAREER NOTES: Selected by Philadelphia Eagles in first round (11th pick overall) of 1998 NFL draft. ... Signed by Eagles (June 19, 1998).
PLAYING EXPERIENCE: Philadelphia NFL, 1998-2000. ... Games/Games started: 1998 (16/16), 1999 (16/15), 2000 (16/16). Total: 48/47.
PRO STATISTICS: 1998—Recovered one fumble. 1999—Recovered one fumble.

THOMAS, WILLIAM   LB   RAIDERS

PERSONAL: Born August 13, 1968, in Amarillo, Texas. ... 6-2/223. ... Full name: William Harrison Thomas Jr.
HIGH SCHOOL: Palo Duro (Amarillo, Texas).
COLLEGE: Texas A&M.
TRANSACTIONS/CAREER NOTES: Selected by Philadelphia Eagles in fourth round (105th pick overall) of 1991 NFL draft. ... Signed by Eagles (July 17, 1991). ... Granted free agency (February 17, 1994). ... Re-signed by Eagles (July 23, 1994). ... Released by Eagles (March 23, 2000). ... Signed by Raiders (July 21, 2000). ... Granted unconditional free agency (March 2, 2001). ... Re-signed by Raiders (May 9, 2001).
CHAMPIONSHIP GAME EXPERIENCE: Played in AFC championship game (2000 season).
HONORS: Played in Pro Bowl (1995 and 1996 seasons).
POST SEASON RECORDS: Shares NFL postseason record for most touchdowns by interception return—1 (December 30, 1995, vs. Detroit).
PRO STATISTICS: 1991—Recovered one fumble. 1992—Recovered two fumbles for two yards. 1993—Recovered three fumbles. 1995—Recovered one fumble. 1996—Recovered one fumble for 23 yards and a touchdown. 1997—Recovered one fumble for 37 yards and a touchdown. 1998—Blocked a punt out of end zone for a safety. 1999—Recovered one fumble for nine yards.

			INTERCEPTIONS				SACKS
Year Team	G	GS	No.	Yds.	Avg.	TD	No.
1991—Philadelphia NFL	16	7	0	0	0.0	0	2.0
1992—Philadelphia NFL	16	15	2	4	2.0	0	1.5
1993—Philadelphia NFL	16	16	2	39	19.5	0	6.5
1994—Philadelphia NFL	16	16	1	7	7.0	0	6.0
1995—Philadelphia NFL	16	16	7	104	14.9	1	2.0
1996—Philadelphia NFL	16	16	3	47	15.7	0	5.5
1997—Philadelphia NFL	14	14	2	11	5.5	0	5.0
1998—Philadelphia NFL	16	16	1	21	21.0	0	2.0
1999—Philadelphia NFL	14	13	0	0	0.0	0	2.5
2000—Oakland NFL	16	16	6	68	11.3	1	1.0
Pro totals (10 years)	156	145	24	301	12.5	2	34.0

THOMAS, ZACH   LB   DOLPHINS

PERSONAL: Born September 1, 1973, in Pampa, Texas. ... 5-11/235. ... Full name: Zach Michael Thomas.
HIGH SCHOOL: White Deer (Texas), then Pampa (Texas).
COLLEGE: Texas Tech.

TRANSACTIONS/CAREER NOTES: Selected by Miami Dolphins in fifth round (154th pick overall) of 1996 NFL draft. ... Signed by Dolphins (July 10, 1996). ... Granted free agency (February 12, 1999). ... Re-signed by Dolphins (February 12, 1999).
HONORS: Named linebacker on THE SPORTING NEWS college All-America second team (1994). ... Named linebacker on THE SPORTING NEWS college All-America first team (1995). ... Played in Pro Bowl (1999 and 2000 seasons).
PRO STATISTICS: 1996—Returned one kickoff for 17 yards and recovered two fumbles for seven yards. 1999—Returned one kickoff for 15 yards. 2000—Recovered one fumble.

			INTERCEPTIONS			SACKS
Year Team	G	GS	No.	Yds.	Avg.	TD	No.
1996—Miami NFL	16	16	3	64	21.3	1	2.0
1997—Miami NFL	15	15	1	10	10.0	0	0.5
1998—Miami NFL	16	16	3	21	7.0	▲2	2.0
1999—Miami NFL	16	16	1	0	0.0	0	1.0
2000—Miami NFL	11	11	1	0	0.0	0	1.5
Pro totals (5 years)	74	74	9	95	10.6	3	7.0

THOMASON, JEFF   TE   EAGLES

PERSONAL: Born December 30, 1969, in San Diego. ... 6-5/255. ... Full name: Jeffrey David Thomason.
HIGH SCHOOL: Corona Del Mar (Newport Beach, Calif.).
COLLEGE: Oregon (degree in psychology).
TRANSACTIONS/CAREER NOTES: Signed as non-drafted free agent by Cincinnati Bengals (April 29, 1992). ... On injured reserve with sprained knee (September 1- December 5, 1992). ... Released by Bengals (August 30, 1993). ... Re-signed by Bengals (September 15, 1993). ... Claimed on waivers by Green Bay Packers (August 2, 1994). ... Released by Packers (August 21, 1994). ... Re-signed by Packers (January 20, 1995). ... Granted unconditional free agency (February 13, 1998). ... Re-signed by Packers (March 17, 1998). ... Traded by Packers to Philadelphia Eagles for TE Kaseem Sinceno (March 16, 2000). ... Granted unconditional free agency (March 2, 2001). ... Re-signed by Eagles (May 25, 2001).
CHAMPIONSHIP GAME EXPERIENCE: Played in NFC championship game (1995-1997 seasons). ... Member of Super Bowl championship team (1996 season). ... Played in Super Bowl XXXII (1997 season).
PRO STATISTICS: 1995—Returned one kickoff for 16 yards and recovered one fumble. 1996—Returned one kickoff for 20 yards. 2000—Returned one kickoff for 10 yards.
SINGLE GAME HIGHS (regular season): Receptions—5 (September 1, 1997, vs. Chicago); yards—58 (September 1, 1997, vs. Chicago); and touchdown receptions—1 (November 26, 2000, vs. Washington).

			RECEIVING				TOTALS			
Year Team	G	GS	No.	Yds.	Avg.	TD	TD	2pt.	Pts.	Fum.
1992—Cincinnati NFL	4	0	2	14	7.0	0	0	0	0	0
1993—Cincinnati NFL	3	0	2	8	4.0	0	0	0	0	0
1994—					Did not play.					
1995—Green Bay NFL	16	1	3	32	10.7	0	0	0	0	0
1996—Green Bay NFL	16	1	3	45	15.0	0	0	0	0	0
1997—Green Bay NFL	13	1	9	115	12.8	1	1	0	6	1
1998—Green Bay NFL	16	2	9	89	9.9	0	0	0	0	0
1999—Green Bay NFL	14	2	14	140	10.0	2	2	0	12	0
2000—Philadelphia NFL	16	5	10	46	4.6	5	5	0	30	0
Pro totals (8 years)	98	12	52	489	9.4	8	8	0	48	1

THOMPSON, DERRIUS   WR   REDSKINS

PERSONAL: Born July 5, 1977, in Cedar Hill, Texas. ... 6-2/215. ... Cousin of Reyna Thompson, cornerback with Miami Dolphins (1986-88), New York Giants (1989-92) and New England Patriots (1993-94).
HIGH SCHOOL: Cedar Hill (Texas).
COLLEGE: Baylor.
TRANSACTIONS/CAREER NOTES: Signed as non-drafted free agent by Washington Redskins (April 21, 1999). ... Released by Redskins (September 4, 1999). ... Re-signed by Redskins to practice squad (September 6, 1999). ... Activated (November 16, 1999). ... Released by Redskins (August 27, 2000). ... Re-signed by Redskins to practice squad (August 28, 2000). ... Activated (September 8, 2000). ... Released by Redskins (September 18, 2000). ... Re-signed by Redskins to practice squad (November 16, 2000). ... Activated (December 18, 2000).
PLAYING EXPERIENCE: Washington NFL, 1999 and 2000. ... Games/Games started: 1999 (1/0), 2000 (4/0). Total: 5/0.

THOMPSON, DONNEL   LB   STEELERS

PERSONAL: Born February 17, 1978, in Madison, Wis. ... 5-11/234.
HIGH SCHOOL: West (Madison, Wis.).
COLLEGE: Wisconsin.
TRANSACTIONS/CAREER NOTES: Signed by Pittsburgh Steelers as non-drafted free agent (April 21, 2000).
PLAYING EXPERIENCE: Pittsburgh NFL, 2000. ... Games/Games started: 2000 (8/0).

THOMPSON, KEVIN   QB   BROWNS

PERSONAL: Born July 27, 1977, in Gaithersburg, Md. ... 6-5/236. ... Full name: Kevin James Thompson.
HIGH SCHOOL: Damascus (Md.).
COLLEGE: Penn State.
TRANSACTIONS/CAREER NOTES: Signed by Cleveland Browns as non-drafted free agent (October 20, 2000). ... Released by Browns (September 13, 2000). ... Re-signed by Browns (October 20, 2000). ... On injured reserve with ankle injury (December 11, 2000-remainder of season). ... Assigned by Browns to Frankfurt Galaxy in 2001 NFL Europe enhancement allocation program (February 19, 2000).
PLAYING EXPERIENCE: Cleveland NFL, 2000. ... Games/Games started: 2000 (1/0).
PRO STATISTICS: 2000—Completed only pass attempt for eight yards, fumbled once and recovered one fumble.
SINGLE GAME HIGHS (regular season): Attempts—1 (December 3, 2000, vs. Jacksonville); completions—1 (December 3, 2000, vs. Jacksonville); yards—8 (December 3, 2000, vs. Jacksonville); and touchdown passes—0.

THOMPSON, MICHAEL OT FALCONS

PERSONAL: Born February 11, 1977, in Savannah, Ga. ... 6-4/295. ... Full name: Michael Anthony Thompson.
HIGH SCHOOL: Windsor Forest (Savannah, Ga.).
COLLEGE: Tennessee State.
TRANSACTIONS/CAREER NOTES: Selected by Atlanta Falcons in fourth round (100th pick overall) of 2000 NFL draft. ... Signed by Falcons (May 16, 2000). ... On injured reserve with torn Achilles' tendon (October 10, 2000-remainder of season).
PLAYING EXPERIENCE: Atlanta NFL, 2000. ... Games/Games started: 2000 (2/2).

THOMPSON, MIKE DT BROWNS

PERSONAL: Born December 22, 1971, in Portage, Wis. ... 6-4/296. ... Full name: Michael John Thompson.
HIGH SCHOOL: Portage (Wis.).
COLLEGE: Wisconsin.
TRANSACTIONS/CAREER NOTES: Selected by Jacksonville Jaguars in fourth round (123rd pick overall) of 1995 NFL draft. ... Signed by Jaguars (June 1, 1995). ... Released by Jaguars (August 25, 1996). ... Signed by Green Bay Packers (January 2, 1997). ... Released by Packers (August 18, 1997). ... Signed by Kansas City Chiefs (August 21, 1997). ... Released by Chiefs (August 28, 1997). ... Signed by Cincinnati Bengals (December 15, 1997). ... Inactive for one game (1997). ... Selected by Cleveland Browns from Bengals in NFL expansion draft (February 9, 1999). ... Granted free agency (February 11, 2000). ... Re-signed by Browns (April 14, 2000). ... On injured reserve with knee injury (November 28, 2000-remainder of season). ... Granted unconditional free agency (March 2, 2001). ... Re-signed by Browns (June 6, 2001).
PLAYING EXPERIENCE: Jacksonville NFL, 1995; Cincinnati NFL, 1998; Cleveland NFL, 1999 and 2000. ... Games/Games started: 1995 (2/0), 1998 (9/0), 1999 (10/0), 2000 (12/0). Total: 33/0.
PRO STATISTICS: 1998—Credited with $1/2$ sack. 1999—Recovered two fumbles. 2000—Credited with one sack.

THOMPSON, RAYNOCH LB CARDINALS

PERSONAL: Born November 21, 1977, in New Orleans. ... 6-3/222. ... Full name: Raynoch Joseph Thompson.
HIGH SCHOOL: St. Augustine (New Orleans).
COLLEGE: Tennessee.
TRANSACTIONS/CAREER NOTES: Selected by Arizona Cardinals in second round (41st pick overall) of 2000 NFL draft. ... Signed by Cardinals (June 21, 2000). ... On injured reserve with knee injury (December 15, 2000-remainder of season).
PLAYING EXPERIENCE: Arizona NFL, 2000. ... Games/Games started: 2000 (11/9).

THORNTON, JOHN DT TITANS

PERSONAL: Born October 2, 1976, in Philadelphia. ... 6-2/295. ... Full name: John Jason Thornton.
HIGH SCHOOL: Scotland (Pa.) School for Veterans' Children.
COLLEGE: West Virginia.
TRANSACTIONS/CAREER NOTES: Selected by Tennessee Titans in second round (52nd pick overall) of 1999 NFL draft. ... Signed by Titans (July 26, 1999).
CHAMPIONSHIP GAME EXPERIENCE: Played in AFC championship game (1999 season). ... Played in Super Bowl XXXIV (1999 season).
PRO STATISTICS: 1999—Credited with a safety. 2000—Returned one kickoff for 16 yards and recovered one fumble.

Year Team	G	GS	SACKS
1999—Tennessee NFL	16	3	4.5
2000—Tennessee NFL	16	16	4.0
Pro totals (2 years)	32	19	8.5

THRASH, JAMES WR/KR EAGLES

PERSONAL: Born April 28, 1975, in Denver. ... 6-0/200.
HIGH SCHOOL: Wewoka (Okla.).
COLLEGE: Missouri Southern.
TRANSACTIONS/CAREER NOTES: Signed as non-drafted free agent by Philadelphia Eagles (April 22, 1997). ... Released by Eagles (July 8, 1997). ... Signed by Washington Redskins (July 11, 1997). ... On injured reserve with shoulder injury (December 8, 1998-remainder of season). ... Granted free agency (February 11, 2000). ... Re-signed with Redskins (April 21, 2000). ... Granted unconditional free agency (March 2, 2001). ... Signed by Eagles (March 9, 2001).
PRO STATISTICS: 1999—Rushed once for 37 yards. 2000—Rushed 10 times for 82 yards, returned 10 punts for 106 yards and recovered one fumble.
SINGLE GAME HIGHS (regular season): Receptions—6 (November 5, 2000, vs. Arizona); yards—121 (November 26, 2000, vs. Philadelphia); and touchdown receptions—1 (November 26, 2000, vs. Philadelphia).
STATISTICAL PLATEAUS: 100-yard receiving games: 2000 (2).

Year Team	G	GS	RECEIVING				KICKOFF RETURNS				TOTALS			
			No.	Yds.	Avg.	TD	No.	Yds.	Avg.	TD	TD	2pt.	Pts.	Fum.
1997—Washington NFL	4	0	2	24	12.0	0	0	0	0.0	0	0	0	0	0
1998—Washington NFL	10	1	10	163	16.3	1	6	129	21.5	0	1	0	6	0
1999—Washington NFL	16	0	3	44	14.7	0	14	355	25.4	1	1	0	6	0
2000—Washington NFL	16	9	50	653	13.1	2	45	1000	22.2	0	2	0	12	1
Pro totals (4 years)	46	10	65	884	13.6	3	65	1484	22.8	1	4	0	24	1

TILLMAN, PAT S CARDINALS

PERSONAL: Born November 6, 1976, in Fremont, Calif. ... 5-11/199. ... Full name: Patrick Daniel Tillman.
HIGH SCHOOL: Leland (San Jose, Calif.).
COLLEGE: Arizona State (degree in marketing, 1997).
TRANSACTIONS/CAREER NOTES: Selected by Arizona Cardinals in seventh round (226th pick overall) of 1998 NFL draft. ... Signed by Cardinals for 1998 season. ... Granted free agency (March 2, 2001). ... Re-signed by Cardinals (April 30, 2001).
PLAYING EXPERIENCE: Arizona NFL, 1998-2000. ... Games/Games started: 1998 (16/10), 1999 (16/1), 2000 (16/16). Total: 48/27.
HONORS: Named outside linebacker on THE SPORTING NEWS college All-America first team (1997).
PRO STATISTICS: 1998—Credited with one sack. 1999—Rushed once for four yards, intercepted two passes for seven yards, returned three kickoffs for 33 yards, fumbled once and recovered one fumble. 2000—Intercepted one pass for 30 yards, credited with $1\frac{1}{2}$ sacks and recovered two fumbles.

TILLMAN, TRAVARES S BILLS

PERSONAL: Born October 8, 1977, in Lyons, Ga. ... 6-1/190. ... Full name: Travares Arastius Tillman.
HIGH SCHOOL: Toombs County (Lyons, Ga.).
COLLEGE: Georgia Tech.
TRANSACTIONS/CAREER NOTES: Selected by Buffalo Bills in second round (58th pick overall) of 2000 NFL draft. ... Signed by Bills (July 20, 2000).

| | | | INTERCEPTIONS | | | |
Year Team	G	GS	No.	Yds.	Avg.	TD
2000—Buffalo NFL	15	4	0	0	0.0	0

TIMMERMAN, ADAM G RAMS

PERSONAL: Born August 14, 1971, in Cherokee, Iowa. ... 6-4/300. ... Full name: Adam Larry Timmerman.
HIGH SCHOOL: Washington (Cherokee, Iowa).
COLLEGE: South Dakota State (degree in agriculture business).
TRANSACTIONS/CAREER NOTES: Selected by Green Bay Packers in seventh round (230th pick overall) of 1995 NFL draft. ... Signed by Packers (June 2, 1995). ... Granted free agency (February 13, 1998). ... Re-signed by Packers (April 15, 1998). ... Granted unconditional free agency (February 12, 1999). ... Signed by St. Louis Rams (February 15, 1999).
PLAYING EXPERIENCE: Green Bay NFL, 1995-1998; St. Louis NFL, 1999 and 2000. ... Games/Games started: 1995 (13/0), 1996 (16/16), 1997 (16/16), 1998 (16/16), 1999 (16/16), 2000 (16/15). Total: 93/79.
CHAMPIONSHIP GAME EXPERIENCE: Played in NFC championship game (1995-97 and 1999 seasons). ... Member of Super Bowl championship team (1996 and 1999 seasons). ... Played in Super Bowl XXXII (1997 season).
HONORS: Played in Pro Bowl (1999 season).
PRO STATISTICS: 1999—Recovered one fumble.

TOBECK, ROBBIE C/G SEAHAWKS

PERSONAL: Born March 6, 1970, in Tarpon Springs, Fla. ... 6-4/298. ... Full name: Robert L. Tobeck.
HIGH SCHOOL: New Port Richey (Fla.).
COLLEGE: Washington State.
TRANSACTIONS/CAREER NOTES: Signed as non-drafted free agent by Atlanta Falcons (May 7, 1993). ... Released by Falcons (August 30, 1993). ... Re-signed by Falcons to practice squad (August 31, 1993). ... Activated (January 1, 1994). ... Granted unconditional free agency (February 11, 2000). ... Signed by Seattle Seahawks (March 20, 2000). ... On physically unable to perform list with knee injury (August 20-October 14, 2000).
PLAYING EXPERIENCE: Atlanta NFL, 1994-1999; Seattle NFL, 2000. ... Games/Games started: 1994 (5/0), 1995 (16/16), 1996 (16/16), 1997 (16/15), 1998 (16/16), 1999 (15/15), 2000 (4/0). Total: 88/78.
CHAMPIONSHIP GAME EXPERIENCE: Played in NFC championship game (1998 season). ... Played in Super Bowl XXXIII (1998 season).
PRO STATISTICS: 1996—Caught two passes for 15 yards and a touchdown. 1997—Recovered one fumble. 1998—Recovered one fumble for one yard. 1999—Recovered one fumble.

TOLLIVER, BILLY JOE QB BEARS

PERSONAL: Born February 7, 1966, in Dallas. ... 6-1/217. ... Full name: Billy Joe Tolliver.
HIGH SCHOOL: Boyd (Texas).
COLLEGE: Texas Tech.
TRANSACTIONS/CAREER NOTES: Selected by San Diego Chargers in second round (51st pick overall) of 1989 NFL draft. ... Signed by Chargers (July 30, 1989). ... On injured reserve with broken collarbone (September 5-October 18, 1989). ... On developmental squad (October 19-20, 1989). ... Traded by Chargers to Atlanta Falcons for fifth-round pick (LB Kevin Little) in 1992 draft (August 28, 1991). ... Granted free agency (March 1, 1993). ... Re-signed by Falcons (August 9, 1993). ... Granted unconditional free agency (February 17, 1994). ... Signed by Houston Oilers (September 7, 1994). ... Granted unconditional free agency (February 17, 1995). ... Signed by Falcons (October 23, 1996). ... Inactive for nine games (1996). ... Granted unconditional free agency (February 14, 1997). ... Re-signed by Falcons (March 19, 1997). ... Released by Falcons (October 27, 1997). ... Signed by Kansas City Chiefs (November 5, 1997). ... Released by Chiefs (August 25, 1998). ... Signed by New Orleans Saints (September 9, 1998). ... Released by Saints (August 27, 2000). ... Re-signed by Saints (November 20, 2000). ... Granted unconditional free agency (March 2, 2001). ... Signed by Chicago Bears (May 8, 2001).
PRO STATISTICS: 1989—Fumbled four times and recovered one fumble for minus six yards. 1990—Fumbled six times and recovered two fumbles. 1991—Fumbled three times. 1992—Fumbled five times. 1994—Fumbled seven times. 1997—Fumbled seven times and recovered two fumbles for minus one yard. 1998—Fumbled three times for minus 13 yards. 1999—Fumbled four times and recovered two fumbles for minus 24 yards.

SINGLE GAME HIGHS (regular season): Attempts—51 (December 16, 1990, vs. Denver); completions—28 (October 17, 1999, vs. Tennessee); yards—354 (October 17, 1999, vs. Tennessee); and touchdown passes—3 (December 27, 1998, vs. Buffalo).
STATISTICAL PLATEAUS: 300-yard passing games: 1989 (2), 1990 (1), 1998 (1), 1999 (1). Total: 5.
MISCELLANEOUS: Regular-season record as starting NFL quarterback: 15-32 (.319).

Year Team	G	GS	Att.	Cmp.	Pct.	Yds.	TD	Int.	Avg.	Rat.	Att.	Yds.	Avg.	TD	TD	2pt.	Pts.
					PASSING							RUSHING				TOTALS	
1989—San Diego NFL	5	5	185	89	48.1	1097	5	8	5.93	57.9	7	0	0.0	0	0	0	0
1990—San Diego NFL	15	14	410	216	52.7	2574	16	16	6.28	68.9	14	22	1.6	0	0	0	0
1991—Atlanta NFL	7	2	82	40	48.8	531	4	2	6.48	75.8	9	6	0.7	0	0	0	0
1992—Atlanta NFL	9	5	131	73	55.7	787	5	5	6.01	70.4	4	15	3.8	0	0	0	0
1993—Atlanta NFL	7	2	76	39	51.3	464	3	5	6.11	56.0	7	48	6.9	0	0	0	0
1994—Houston NFL	10	7	240	121	50.4	1287	6	7	5.36	62.6	12	37	3.1	2	2	0	12
1995—								Did not play.									
1996—Atlanta NFL								Did not play.									
1997—Atlanta NFL	6	1	115	63	54.8	685	5	1	5.96	83.4	7	8	1.1	0	0	0	0
—Kansas City NFL	3	0	1	1	100.0	-8	0	0	-8.00	79.2	2	-1	-0.5	0	0	0	0
1998—New Orleans NFL	7	4	199	110	55.3	1427	8	4	7.17	83.1	11	43	3.9	0	0	0	0
1999—New Orleans NFL	10	7	268	139	51.9	1916	7	16	7.15	58.9	26	142	5.5	3	3	0	18
2000—New Orleans NFL								Did not play.									
Pro totals (9 years)	79	47	1707	891	52.2	10760	59	64	6.30	67.7	99	320	3.2	5	5	0	30

TOMICH, JARED   DE

PERSONAL: Born April 24, 1974, in St. John, Ind. ... 6-2/272. ... Full name: Jared James Tomich.
HIGH SCHOOL: Lake Central (St. John, Ind.).
COLLEGE: Nebraska.
TRANSACTIONS/CAREER NOTES: Selected by New Orleans Saints in second round (39th pick overall) of 1997 NFL draft. ... Signed by Saints (July 17, 1997). ... On injured reserve with ankle injury (December 24, 1999-remainder of season). ... Granted free agency (February 11, 2000). ... Re-signed by Saints (June 9, 2000). ... Granted unconditional free agency (March 2, 2001).
PRO STATISTICS: 1997—Returned one kickoff for no yards, fumbled once and recovered one fumble. 1998—Returned one kickoff for no yards and recovered one fumble.

Year Team	G	GS	SACKS
1997—New Orleans NFL	16	1	1.0
1998—New Orleans NFL	16	11	6.0
1999—New Orleans NFL	8	6	3.0
2000—New Orleans NFL	14	0	0.0
Pro totals (4 years)	54	18	10.0

TONGUE, REGGIE   S   SEAHAWKS

PERSONAL: Born April 11, 1973, in Baltimore. ... 6-0/206. ... Full name: Reginald Clinton Tongue.
HIGH SCHOOL: Lathrop (Fairbanks, Alaska).
COLLEGE: Oregon State.
TRANSACTIONS/CAREER NOTES: Selected by Kansas City Chiefs in second round (58th pick overall) of 1996 NFL draft. ... Signed by Chiefs (July 26, 1996). ... Granted unconditional free agency (February 11, 2000). ... Signed by Seattle Seahawks (February 22, 2000).
PRO STATISTICS: 1998—Recovered one fumble. 1999—Ran with lateral from an intercepted pass 46 yards for a touchdown and recovered three fumbles for nine yards.

Year Team	G	GS	No.	Yds.	Avg.	TD	No.
			INTERCEPTIONS				SACKS
1996—Kansas City NFL	16	0	0	0	0.0	0	0.0
1997—Kansas City NFL	16	16	1	0	0.0	0	2.5
1998—Kansas City NFL	15	15	0	0	0.0	0	2.0
1999—Kansas City NFL	16	16	1	80	80.0	1	2.0
2000—Seattle NFL	16	6	0	0	0.0	0	0.0
Pro totals (5 years)	79	53	2	80	40.0	1	6.5

TOOMER, AMANI   WR   GIANTS

PERSONAL: Born September 8, 1974, in Berkely, Calif. ... 6-3/208. ... Name pronounced uh-MAHN-ee.
HIGH SCHOOL: De La Salle Catholic (Concord, Calif.).
COLLEGE: Michigan.
TRANSACTIONS/CAREER NOTES: Selected by New York Giants in second round (34th pick overall) of 1996 NFL draft. ... Signed by Giants (July 21, 1996). ... On injured reserve with knee injury (October 31, 1996-remainder of season). ... Granted free agency (February 12, 1999). ... Re-signed by Giants (July 31, 1999).
CHAMPIONSHIP GAME EXPERIENCE: Played in NFC championship game (2000 season). ... Played in Super Bowl XXXV (2000 season).
PRO STATISTICS: 1996—Recovered two fumbles. 1998—Attempted one pass without a completion. 1999—Rushed once for four yards. 2000—Rushed five times for 91 yards and a touchdown and recovered one fumble.
SINGLE GAME HIGHS (regular season): Receptions—9 (December 10, 2000, vs. Pittsburgh); yards—193 (December 10, 2000, vs. Pittsburgh); and touchdown receptions—3 (December 5, 1999, vs. New York Jets).
STATISTICAL PLATEAUS: 100-yard receiving games: 1999 (4), 2000 (5). Total: 9.

Year Team	G	GS	No.	Yds.	Avg.	TD	No.	Yds.	Avg.	TD	No.	Yds.	Avg.	TD	TD	2pt.	Pts.	Fum.
			RECEIVING				PUNT RETURNS				KICKOFF RETURNS				TOTALS			
1996—New York Giants NFL	7	1	1	12	12.0	0	18	298	16.6	2	11	191	17.4	0	2	0	12	1
1997—New York Giants NFL	16	0	16	263	16.4	1	47	455	9.7	∞1	0	0	0.0	0	2	0	12	0
1998—New York Giants NFL	16	0	27	360	13.3	5	35	252	7.2	0	4	66	16.5	0	5	0	30	0
1999—New York Giants NFL	16	16	79	1183	15.0	6	1	14	14.0	0	0	0	0.0	0	6	0	36	0
2000—New York Giants NFL	16	14	78	1094	14.0	7	0	0	0.0	0	0	0	0.0	0	8	0	48	1
Pro totals (5 years)	71	31	201	2912	14.5	19	101	1019	10.1	3	15	257	17.1	0	23	0	138	2

TOSI, MAO — DE/DT — CARDINALS

PERSONAL: Born December 12, 1976, in Anchorage, Alaska. ... 6-6/305.
HIGH SCHOOL: East Anchorage (Alaska).
JUNIOR COLLEGE: Butler County Community College (Kan.).
COLLEGE: Idaho.
TRANSACTIONS/CAREER NOTES: Selected by Arizona Cardinals in fifth round (136th pick overall) of 2000 NFL draft. ... Signed by Cardinals (June 16, 2000).
PLAYING EXPERIENCE: Arizona NFL, 2000. ... Games/Games started: 2000 (15/10).

TOVAR, STEVE — LB

PERSONAL: Born April 25, 1970, in Elyria, Ohio. ... 6-3/244. ... Full name: Steven Eric Tovar.
HIGH SCHOOL: West (Elyria, Ohio).
COLLEGE: Ohio State.
TRANSACTIONS/CAREER NOTES: Selected by the Cincinnati Bengals in third round (59th pick overall) of 1993 NFL draft. ... Signed by Bengals (July 19, 1993). ... Granted free agency (February 16, 1996). ... Re-signed by Bengals (April 15, 1996). ... On injured reserve with knee injury (December 2, 1996-remainder of season). ... Released by Bengals (August 21, 1998). ... Signed by San Diego Chargers (August 25, 1998). ... Granted unconditional free agency (February 12, 1999). ... Signed by Carolina Panthers (February 15, 1999). ... Released by Panthers (April 27, 2000). ... Signed by San Diego Chargers (July 24, 2000). ... Granted unconditional free agency (March 2, 2001).
PRO STATISTICS: 1993—Recovered one fumble. 1994—Returned one kickoff for eight yards and recovered two fumbles. 1996—Fumbled once.

| | | | INTERCEPTIONS | | | SACKS |
Year Team	G	GS	No.	Yds.	Avg.	TD	No.
1993—Cincinnati NFL	16	9	1	0	0.0	0	0.0
1994—Cincinnati NFL	16	16	1	14	14.0	0	3.0
1995—Cincinnati NFL	14	13	1	13	13.0	0	1.0
1996—Cincinnati NFL	13	13	4	42	10.5	0	3.0
1997—Cincinnati NFL	14	5	0	0	0.0	0	0.0
1998—San Diego NFL	16	2	0	0	0.0	0	1.0
1999—Carolina NFL	16	6	0	0	0.0	0	0.0
2000—San Diego NFL	16	0	0	0	0.0	0	0.0
Pro totals (8 years)	121	64	7	69	9.9	0	8.0

TOWNS, LESTER — LB — PANTHERS

PERSONAL: Born August 28, 1977, in Pasadena, Calif. ... 6-1/252. ... Full name: Lester Towns III.
HIGH SCHOOL: Pasadena (Calif.).
COLLEGE: Washington.
TRANSACTIONS/CAREER NOTES: Selected by Carolina Panthers in seventh round (221st pick overall) of 2000 NFL draft. ... Signed by Panthers (July 14, 2000).
PLAYING EXPERIENCE: Carolina NFL, 2000. ... Games/Games started: 2000 (16/14).
PRO STATISTICS: 2000—Recovered two fumbles.

TOWNSEND, DESHEA — CB — STEELERS

PERSONAL: Born September 8, 1975, in Batesville, Miss. ... 5-10/175. ... Full name: Trevor Deshea Townsend.
HIGH SCHOOL: South Panola (Batesville, Miss.).
COLLEGE: Alabama.
TRANSACTIONS/CAREER NOTES: Selected by Pittsburgh Steelers in fourth round (117th pick overall) of 1998 NFL draft. ... Signed by Steelers (July 6, 1998). ... Granted free agency (March 2, 2001).
PLAYING EXPERIENCE: Pittsburgh NFL, 1998-2000. ... Games/Games started: 1998 (12/0), 1999 (16/4), 2000 (16/0). Total: 44/4.
PRO STATISTICS: 2000—Credited with $3^1/_2$ sacks.

TRAPP, JAMES — CB — RAVENS

PERSONAL: Born December 28, 1969, in Greenville, S.C. ... 6-0/190. ... Full name: James Harold Trapp.
HIGH SCHOOL: Lawton (Okla.).
COLLEGE: Clemson.
TRANSACTIONS/CAREER NOTES: Selected by Los Angeles Raiders in third round (72nd pick overall) of 1993 NFL draft. ... Signed by Raiders (July 13, 1993). ... Raiders franchise moved to Oakland (July 21, 1995). ... Granted free agency (February 16, 1996). ... Re-signed by Raiders (March 30, 1996). ... Granted unconditional free agency (February 11, 1999). ... Signed by Baltimore Ravens (April 23, 1999). ... Granted unconditional free agency (February 11, 2000). ... Re-signed by Ravens (March 16, 2000).
PLAYING EXPERIENCE: Los Angeles Raiders NFL, 1993 and 1994; Oakland NFL, 1995-1998; Baltimore NFL, 1999 and 2000. ... Games/Games started: 1993 (14/2), 1994 (16/2), 1995 (14/2), 1996 (12/4), 1997 (16/16), 1998 (16/0), 1999 (16/0), 2000 (16/1). Total: 120/27.
CHAMPIONSHIP GAME EXPERIENCE: Played in AFC championship game (2000 season). ... Member of Super Bowl championship team (2000 season).
PRO STATISTICS: 1993—Intercepted one pass for seven yards. 1994—Credited with one sack. 1995—Recovered one fumble. 1996—Intercepted one pass for 23 yards. 1997—Intercepted two passes for 24 yards and recovered two fumbles. 1999—Credited with one sack. 2000—Credited with two sacks.

TRAYLOR, KEITH DT BEARS

PERSONAL: Born September 3, 1969, in Little Rock, Ark. ... 6-2/304. ... Full name: Byron Keith Traylor. ... Cousin of Isaac Davis, guard with San Diego Chargers (1994-97) and New Orleans Saints (1997).
HIGH SCHOOL: Malvern (Ark.).
JUNIOR COLLEGE: Coffeyville (Kan.) Community College.
COLLEGE: Oklahoma, then Central Oklahoma.
TRANSACTIONS/CAREER NOTES: Selected by Denver Broncos in third round (61st pick overall) of 1991 NFL draft. ... Signed by Broncos for 1991 season. ... Released by Broncos (June 7, 1993). ... Signed by Los Angeles Raiders (June 1993). ... Released by Raiders (August 30, 1993). ... Signed by Green Bay Packers (September 14, 1993). ... Released by Packers (November 9, 1993). ... Signed by Kansas City Chiefs (January 7, 1994). ... Released by Chiefs (January 14, 1994). ... Re-signed by Chiefs (May 18, 1994). ... Released by Chiefs (August 28, 1994). ... Re-signed by Chiefs (February 28, 1995). ... Granted unconditional free agency (February 14, 1997). ... Signed by Broncos (March 10, 1997). ... Released by Broncos (March 14, 2001). ... Signed by Chicago Bears (March 23, 2001).
CHAMPIONSHIP GAME EXPERIENCE: Played in AFC championship game (1991, 1997 and 1998 seasons). ... Member of Super Bowl championship team (1997 and 1998 seasons).
PRO STATISTICS: 1992—Returned one kickoff for 13 yards. 1995—Recovered one fumble. 1997—Intercepted one pass for 62 yards and a touchdown. 1998—Recovered one fumble. 2000—Recovered one fumble.

Year Team	G	GS	SACKS
1991—Denver NFL	16	2	0.0
1992—Denver NFL	16	3	1.0
1993—Green Bay NFL	5	0	0.0
1994—	Did not play.		
1995—Barcelona W.L.	8	3	0.0
—Kansas City NFL	16	0	1.5
1996—Kansas City NFL	15	2	1.0
1997—Denver NFL	16	16	2.0
1998—Denver NFL	15	14	2.0
1999—Denver NFL	15	15	1.5
2000—Denver NFL	16	16	1.0
W.L. totals (1 year)	8	3	0.0
NFL totals (9 years)	130	68	10.0
Pro totals (10 years)	138	71	10.0

TREU, ADAM C RAIDERS

PERSONAL: Born June 24, 1974, in Lincoln, Neb. ... 6-5/300. ... Name pronounced TRUE.
HIGH SCHOOL: Pius X (Lincoln, Neb.).
COLLEGE: Nebraska.
TRANSACTIONS/CAREER NOTES: Selected by Oakland Raiders in third round (72nd pick overall) of 1997 NFL draft. ... Signed by Raiders for 1997 season.
PLAYING EXPERIENCE: Oakland NFL, 1997-2000. ... Games/Games started: 1997 (16/0), 1998 (16/0), 1999 (16/0), 2000 (16/0). Total: 64/0.
CHAMPIONSHIP GAME EXPERIENCE: Played in AFC championship game (2000 season).
PRO STATISTICS: 1999—Returned one kickoff for six yards and fumbled once.

TROTTER, JEREMIAH LB EAGLES

PERSONAL: Born January 20, 1977, in Hooks, Texas. ... 6-1/261.
HIGH SCHOOL: Hooks (Texas).
COLLEGE: Stephen F. Austin State.
TRANSACTIONS/CAREER NOTES: Selected after junior season by Philadelphia Eagles in third round (72nd pick overall) of 1998 NFL draft. ... Signed by Eagles (July 14, 1998). ... Granted free agency (March 2, 2001). ... Re-signed by Eagles (April 27, 2001).
PLAYING EXPERIENCE: Philadelphia NFL, 1998-2000. ... Games/Games started: 1998 (8/0), 1999 (16/16), 2000 (16/16). Total: 40/32.
HONORS: Played in Pro Bowl (2000 season).
PRO STATISTICS: 1999—Intercepted two passes for 30 yards, credited with $2^{1}/_{2}$ sacks and recovered one fumble. 2000—Intercepted one pass for 27 yards and a touchdown and credited with three sacks.

TUBBS, WINFRED LB

PERSONAL: Born September 24, 1970, in Fairfield, Texas. ... 6-4/254. ... Full name: Winfred O'Neal Tubbs.
HIGH SCHOOL: Fairfield (Texas).
COLLEGE: Texas (degree in psychology, 1993).
TRANSACTIONS/CAREER NOTES: Selected by New Orleans Saints in third round (79th pick overall) of 1994 NFL draft. ... Signed by Saints (July 20, 1994). ... On injured reserve with knee injury (December 22, 1995-remainder of season). ... Granted free agency (February 14, 1997). ... Re-signed by Saints (July 17, 1997). ... Granted unconditional free agency (February 13, 1998). ... Signed by San Francisco 49ers (February 18, 1998). ... Released by 49ers (March 1, 2001).
HONORS: Played in Pro Bowl (1998 season).
PRO STATISTICS: 1995—Recovered one fumble. 1996—Recovered one fumble. 1997—Recovered two fumbles. 1998—Recovered one fumble. 1999—Recovered one fumble. 2000—Recovered one fumble.

Year Team	G	GS	INTERCEPTIONS No.	Yds.	Avg.	TD	SACKS No.
1994—New Orleans NFL	13	7	1	0	0.0	0	1.0
1995—New Orleans NFL	7	6	1	6	6.0	0	1.0
1996—New Orleans NFL	16	13	1	11	11.0	0	1.0
1997—New Orleans NFL	16	16	2	21	10.5	0	2.5
1998—San Francisco NFL	16	16	1	7	7.0	0	1.0
1999—San Francisco NFL	16	15	1	8	8.0	0	2.0
2000—San Francisco NFL	14	14	1	11	11.0	0	2.0
Pro totals (7 years)	98	87	8	64	8.0	0	10.5

TUCKER, JASON   WR/KR   COWBOYS

PERSONAL: Born June 24, 1976, in Waco, Texas. ... 6-1/182.
HIGH SCHOOL: Robinson (Waco, Texas).
COLLEGE: Texas Christian.
TRANSACTIONS/CAREER NOTES: Selected after junior season by Cincinnati Bengals in sixth round (167th pick overall) of 1998 NFL draft. ... Signed by Bengals (July 19, 1998). ... Released by Bengals (August 19, 1998). ... Signed by Green Bay Packers to practice squad (October 28, 1998). ... Released by Packers (December 15, 1998). ... Signed by Dallas Cowboys (January 7, 1999). ... Assigned by Cowboys to Rhein Fire in 1999 NFL Europe enhancement allocation program (February 22, 1999).
PRO STATISTICS: NFL: 1999—Rushed once for eight yards and recovered one fumble. 2000—Rushed four times for 42 yards and a touchdown.
SINGLE GAME HIGHS (regular season): Receptions—7 (December 24, 1999, vs. New Orleans); yards—128 (December 24, 1999, vs. New Orleans); and touchdown receptions—1 (January 2, 2000, vs. New York Giants).
STATISTICAL PLATEAUS: 100-yard receiving games: 1999 (2).

				RECEIVING			PUNT RETURNS				KICKOFF RETURNS				TOTALS			
Year Team	G	GS	No.	Yds.	Avg.	TD	No.	Yds.	Avg.	TD	No.	Yds.	Avg.	TD	TD	2pt.	Pts.	Fum.
1999—Rhein NFLE	...	...	26	454	17.5	3	0	0	0.0	0	0	0	0.0	0	3	0	18	0
—Dallas NFL	15	4	23	439	19.1	2	4	52	13.0	0	22	613	27.9	0	2	0	12	1
2000—Dallas NFL	16	7	13	126	9.7	0	4	9	2.3	0	51	1099	21.5	0	1	0	6	3
NFL Europe totals (1 year)	...	...	26	454	17.5	3	0	0	0.0	0	0	0	0.0	0	3	0	18	0
NFL totals (2 years)	31	11	36	565	15.7	2	8	61	7.6	0	73	1712	23.5	0	3	0	18	4
Pro totals (3 years)	...	...	62	1019	16.4	5	8	61	7.6	0	73	1712	23.5	0	6	0	36	4

TUCKER, REX   G   BEARS

PERSONAL: Born December 20, 1976, in Midland, Texas ... 6-5/315. ... Full name: Rex Truman Tucker. ... Brother of Ryan Tucker, offensive tackle, St. Louis Rams.
HIGH SCHOOL: Robert E. Lee (Midland, Texas).
COLLEGE: Texas A&M.
TRANSACTIONS/CAREER NOTES: Selected in third round by Chicago Bears (66th pick overall) of 1999 NFL draft. ... Signed by Bears (July 21, 1999).
PLAYING EXPERIENCE: Chicago NFL, 1999 and 2000. ... Games/Games started: 1999 (2/1), 2000 (6/0). Total: 8/1.
PRO STATISTICS: 2000—Returned one kickoff for no yards.

TUCKER, RYAN   OT   RAMS

PERSONAL: Born June 12, 1975, in Midland, Texas. ... 6-5/305. ... Full name: Ryan Huey Tucker. ... Brother of Rex Tucker, guard, Chicago Bears.
HIGH SCHOOL: Robert E. Lee (Midland, Texas).
COLLEGE: Texas Christian.
TRANSACTIONS/CAREER NOTES: Selected by St. Louis Rams in fourth round (112th pick overall) of 1997 NFL draft. ... Signed by Rams (July 3, 1997). ... On physically unable to perform list with knee injury (August 19-October 29, 1997). ... Granted free agency (February 11, 2000). ... Tendered offer sheet by Miami Dolphins (February 17, 2000). ... Offer matched by Rams (February 22, 2000).
PLAYING EXPERIENCE: St. Louis NFL, 1997-2000. ... Games/Games started: 1997 (7/0), 1998 (4/0), 1999 (16/0), 2000 (16/16). Total: 43/16.
CHAMPIONSHIP GAME EXPERIENCE: Played in NFC championship game (1999 season). ... Member of Super Bowl championship team (1999 season).
PRO STATISTICS: 1999—Caught one pass for two yards and a touchdown.

TUGGLE, JESSIE   LB   FALCONS

PERSONAL: Born April 4, 1965, in Spalding County, Ga. ... 5-11/230. ... Full name: Jessie Lloyd Tuggle Jr.
HIGH SCHOOL: Griffin (Ga.).
COLLEGE: Valdosta (Ga.) State.
TRANSACTIONS/CAREER NOTES: Signed as non-drafted free agent by Atlanta Falcons (May 2, 1987). ... Granted free agency (February 1, 1991). ... Re-signed by Falcons (August 7, 1991). ... On reserve/did not report list (July 23-August 30, 1993). ... Granted roster exemption (August 30-September 3, 1993). ... Granted unconditional free agency (February 11, 2000). ... Re-signed by Falcons (February 14, 2000). ... On injured reserve with knee injury (October 25, 2000-remainder of season).
CHAMPIONSHIP GAME EXPERIENCE: Played in NFC championship game (1998 season). ... Played in Super Bowl XXXIII (1998 season).
HONORS: Played in Pro Bowl (1992, 1994, 1995, 1997 and 1998 seasons).
RECORDS: Holds NFL career record for most touchdowns by recovery of opponents' fumbles—5; and most touchdowns by fumble recovery—5.
PRO STATISTICS: 1988—Recovered one fumble for two yards and one touchdown. 1989—Recovered one fumble. 1990—Recovered two fumbles for 65 yards and a touchdown. 1991—Recovered two fumbles for 18 yards and one touchdown. 1992—Recovered one fumble for 69 yards and one touchdown. 1993—Recovered one fumble. 1994—Recovered one fumble. 1998—Recovered one fumble for one yard and one touchdown.

			INTERCEPTIONS				SACKS
Year Team	G	GS	No.	Yds.	Avg.	TD	No.
1987—Atlanta NFL	12	4	0	0	0.0	0	1.0
1988—Atlanta NFL	16	8	0	0	0.0	0	0.0
1989—Atlanta NFL	16	16	0	0	0.0	0	1.0
1990—Atlanta NFL	16	14	0	0	0.0	0	5.0
1991—Atlanta NFL	16	16	1	21	21.0	0	1.0
1992—Atlanta NFL	15	15	1	1	1.0	0	1.0
1993—Atlanta NFL	16	16	0	0	0.0	0	2.0

T

Year—Team	G	GS	No.	Yds.	Avg.	TD	No.
			INTERCEPTIONS				**SACKS**
1994—Atlanta NFL	16	16	1	0	0.0	0	0.0
1995—Atlanta NFL	16	16	3	84	28.0	1	1.0
1996—Atlanta NFL	16	16	0	0	0.0	0	1.0
1997—Atlanta NFL	16	15	0	0	0.0	0	1.5
1998—Atlanta NFL	16	16	0	0	0.0	0	3.0
1999—Atlanta NFL	14	14	0	0	0.0	0	3.5
2000—Atlanta NFL	8	7	0	0	0.0	0	0.0
Pro totals (14 years)	209	189	6	106	17.7	1	21.0

TUINEI, VAN   DE   BEARS

PERSONAL: Born February 16, 1971, in Garden Grove, Calif. ... 6-4/290. ... Full name: Vaega Van Tuinei. ... Name pronounced TU-en-a.
HIGH SCHOOL: Westminster (Calif.).
JUNIOR COLLEGE: Golden West College (Calif.).
COLLEGE: Arizona.
TRANSACTIONS/CAREER NOTES: Signed as non-drafted free agent by San Diego Chargers (April 21, 1997). ... Released by Chargers (August 25, 1998). ... Re-signed by Chargers (August 27, 1998). ... Released by Chargers (August 30, 1998). ... Signed by Indianapolis Colts (September 16, 1998). ... Claimed on waivers by Chicago Bears (September 6, 1999). ... Granted free agency (February 11, 2000). ... Re-signed by Bears (April 26, 2000). ... Granted unconditional free agency (March 2, 2001). ... Re-signed by Bears (March 2, 2001).
PLAYING EXPERIENCE: San Diego NFL, 1997; Indianapolis NFL, 1998; Chicago NFL, 1999 and 2000. ... Games/Games started: 1997 (3/0), 1998 (12/0), 1999 (16/8), 2000 (14/2). Total: 45/10.
PRO STATISTICS: 1998—Credited with two sacks and recovered one fumble. 1999—Returned one kickoff for no yards, credited with 2½ sacks and recovered two fumbles. 2000—Returned one kickoff for two yards and credited with one sack.

TUITELE, MAUGAULA   LB   PATRIOTS

PERSONAL: Born May 26, 1978, in San Bernardino, Calif. ... 6-2/255. ... Full name: Maugaula Norman Tuitele.
HIGH SCHOOL: Pacific (Calif.).
COLLEGE: Colorado State.
TRANSACTIONS/CAREER NOTES: Signed by New England Patriots as non-drafted free agent (April 19, 2000). ... Released by Patriots (August 27, 2000). ... Re-signed by Patriots (November 22, 2000). ... Released by Patriots (December 1, 2000). ... Re-signed by Patriots to practice squad (December 6, 2000).
PLAYING EXPERIENCE: New England NFL, 2000. ... Games/Games started: 2000 (1/0).

TUMAN, JERAME   TE   STEELERS

PERSONAL: Born March 24, 1976, in Liberal, Kan. ... 6-3/250. ... Full name: Jerame Dean Tuman. ... Name pronounced Jeremy TOO-man.
HIGH SCHOOL: Liberal (Kan.).
COLLEGE: Michigan.
TRANSACTIONS/CAREER NOTES: Selected by Pittsburgh Steelers in fifth round (136th pick overall) of 1999 NFL draft. ... Signed by Steelers (July 19, 1999). ... On injured reserve with knee injury (October 27, 1999-remainder of season).
PLAYING EXPERIENCE: Pittsburgh NFL, 1999 and 2000. ... Games/Games started: 1999 (7/0), 2000 (16/1). Total: 23/1.
HONORS: Named tight end on THE SPORTING NEWS college All-America third team (1997).
PRO STATISTICS: 2000—Returned one kickoff for minus one yard.

TUPA, TOM   P/QB   JETS

PERSONAL: Born February 6, 1966, in Cleveland. ... 6-4/225. ... Full name: Thomas Joseph Tupa Jr.
HIGH SCHOOL: Brecksville (Broadview Heights, Ohio).
COLLEGE: Ohio State.
TRANSACTIONS/CAREER NOTES: Selected by Phoenix Cardinals in third round (68th pick overall) of 1988 NFL draft. ... Signed by Cardinals (July 12, 1988). ... Granted free agency (February 1, 1991). ... Re-signed by Cardinals (July 17, 1991). ... Granted unconditional free agency (February 1, 1992). ... Signed by Indianapolis Colts (March 31, 1992). ... Released by Colts (August 30, 1993). ... Signed by Cleveland Browns (November 9, 1993). ... Released by Browns (November 24, 1993). ... Re-signed by Browns (March 30, 1994). ... Granted unconditional free agency (February 16, 1996). ... Signed by New England Patriots (March 15, 1996). ... Granted unconditional free agency (February 12, 1999). ... Signed by New York Jets (February 15, 1999).
CHAMPIONSHIP GAME EXPERIENCE: Played in AFC championship game (1996 season). ... Played in Super Bowl XXXI (1996 season).
HONORS: Played in Pro Bowl (1999 season).
PRO STATISTICS: 1988—Attempted six passes with four completions for 49 yards. 1989—Rushed 15 times for 75 yards, attempted 134 passes with 65 completions for 973 yards (three touchdowns and nine interceptions), fumbled twice and recovered one fumble for minus six yards. 1990—Rushed once for no yards and fumbled once for minus seven yards. 1991—Rushed 28 times for 97 yards and a touchdown, attempted 315 passes with 165 completions for 2,053 yards (six touchdowns and 13 interceptions), fumbled eight times and recovered two fumbles. 1992—Rushed three times for nine yards, attempted 33 passes with 17 completions for 156 yards (one touchdwon and two interceptions), fumbled once and recovered one fumble for minus one yard. 1995—Rushed once for nine yards, attempted one pass with a completion for 25 yards. 1996—Attempted two passes without a completion. 1998—Rushed twice for minus two yards. 1999—Rushed twice for eight yards, attempted 11 passes with six completions for 165 yards and two touchdowns and fumbled once.
STATISTICAL PLATEAUS: 300-yard passing games: 1991 (1).
MISCELLANEOUS: Regular-season starting record as starting NFL quarterback: 4-9 (.308).

Year	Team	G		PUNTING				
			No.	Yds.	Avg.	Net avg.	In. 20	Blk.
1988—Phoenix NFL		2	0	0	0.0	.0	0	0
1989—Phoenix NFL		14	6	280	46.7	39.7	2	0
1990—Phoenix NFL		15	0	0	0.0	.0	0	0
1991—Phoenix NFL		11	0	0	0.0	.0	0	0
1992—Indianapolis NFL		3	0	0	0.0	.0	0	0
1993—Cleveland NFL					Did not play.			
1994—Cleveland NFL		16	80	3211	40.1	35.3	27	0
1995—Cleveland NFL		16	65	2831	43.6	36.2	18	0
1996—New England NFL		16	63	2739	43.5	36.0	14	0
1997—New England NFL		16	78	3569	§45.8	36.1	24	1
1998—New England NFL		16	74	3294	44.5	35.4	13	0
1999—New York Jets NFL		16	81	3659	45.2	38.2	25	0
2000—New York Jets NFL		16	83	3714	44.7	33.2	18	0
Pro totals (12 years)		157	530	23297	44.0	35.8	141	1

TURK, MATT — P — DOLPHINS

PERSONAL: Born June 16, 1968, in Greenfield, Wis. ... 6-5/250. ... Brother of Dan Turk, center with five NFL teams (1985-99).
HIGH SCHOOL: Greenfield (Wis.).
COLLEGE: Wisconsin-Whitewater.
TRANSACTIONS/CAREER NOTES: Signed as non-drafted free agent by Green Bay Packers (July 13, 1993). ... Released by Packers (August 4, 1993). ... Signed by Los Angeles Rams (April 1994). ... Released by Rams (August 22, 1994). ... Signed by Washington Redskins (April 5, 1995). ... Traded by Redskins to Miami Dolphins for seventh-round pick (traded to San Francisco) in 2001 draft (March 9, 2000).
HONORS: Played in Pro Bowl (1996-1998 seasons). ... Named punter on THE SPORTING NEWS NFL All-Pro team (1997).
PRO STATISTICS: 1996—Rushed once for no yards and fumbled once. 1997—Rushed once for no yards and fumbled once for minus 16 yards. 1998—Rushed twice for minus 12 yards and fumbled once. 1999—Fumbled once.

Year	Team	G		PUNTING				
			No.	Yds.	Avg.	Net avg.	In. 20	Blk.
1995—Washington NFL		16	74	3140	42.4	37.7	†29	0
1996—Washington NFL		16	75	3386	*45.1	*39.2	25	0
1997—Washington NFL		16	84	3788	45.1	*39.2	32	1
1998—Washington NFL		16	93	4103	44.1	‡39.0	∞33	∞1
1999—Washington NFL		14	62	2564	41.4	35.6	16	0
2000—Miami NFL		16	92	3870	42.1	36.2	25	0
Pro totals (6 years)		94	480	20851	43.4	37.9	160	2

TURLEY, KYLE — OT — SAINTS

PERSONAL: Born September 24, 1975, in Provo, Utah. ... 6-5/300. ... Full name: Kyle John Turley.
HIGH SCHOOL: Valley View (Moreno Valley, Calif.).
COLLEGE: San Diego State.
TRANSACTIONS/CAREER NOTES: Selected by New Orleans Saints in first round (seventh pick overall) of 1998 NFL draft. ... Signed by Saints (July 23, 1998).
PLAYING EXPERIENCE: New Orleans NFL, 1998-2000. ... Games/Games started: 1998 (15/15), 1999 (16/16), 2000 (16/16). Total: 47/47.
HONORS: Named offensive tackle on THE SPORTING NEWS college All-America first team (1997).
PRO STATISTICS: 2000—Recovered four fumbles for minus six yards and caught one pass for 16 yards.

TURNER, SCOTT — CB

PERSONAL: Born February 26, 1972, in Richardson, Texas. ... 5-10/180.
HIGH SCHOOL: J.J. Pearce (Richardson, Texas).
COLLEGE: Illinois (degree in speech communications, 1994).
TRANSACTIONS/CAREER NOTES: Selected by Washington Redskins in seventh round (226th pick overall) of 1995 NFL draft. ... Signed by Redskins (July 18, 1995). ... On injured reserve with ankle injury (December 11, 1997-remainder of season). ... Granted free agency (February 13, 1998). ... Re-signed by Redskins (April 30, 1998). ... Claimed on waivers by San Diego Chargers (August 31, 1998). ... Granted unconditional free agency (February 11, 2000). ... Re-signed by Chargers (April 3, 2000). ... Granted unconditional free agency (March 2, 2001).
PRO STATISTICS: 1995—Returned one punt for no yards, credited with one sack, fumbled once and recovered one fumble. 1996—Recovered one fumble in end zone for a touchdown. 1998—Credited with one sack. 1999—Returned one punt for no yards and recovered one fumble.

Year	Team	G	GS	INTERCEPTIONS			
				No.	Yds.	Avg.	TD
1995—Washington NFL		16	0	1	0	0.0	0
1996—Washington NFL		16	0	2	16	8.0	0
1997—Washington NFL		9	0	0	0	0.0	0
1998—San Diego NFL		16	1	1	0	0.0	0
1999—San Diego NFL		15	0	0	0	0.0	0
2000—San Diego NFL		16	2	1	75	75.0	1
Pro totals (6 years)		88	3	5	91	18.2	1

TUTEN, MELVIN — OT — PANTHERS

PERSONAL: Born November 11, 1971, in Washington, D.C. ... 6-6/305. ... Full name: Melvin Eugene Tuten Jr.
HIGH SCHOOL: Woodrow Wilson (Washington, D.C.).
COLLEGE: Syracuse.
TRANSACTIONS/CAREER NOTES: Selected by Cincinnati Bengals in third round (69th pick overall) of 1995 NFL draft. ... Signed by Bengals (July 18, 1995). ... Released by Bengals (August 18, 1997). ... Signed by Denver Broncos (February 5, 1998). ... Released by Broncos (August 25, 1998). ... Re-signed by Broncos (December 30, 1998). ... Assigned by Broncos to Barcelona Dragons in 1999 NFL Europe enhancement allocation program (February 22, 1999). ... Released by Broncos (September 5, 1999). ... Re-signed by Broncos (November 10, 1999). ... Released by Broncos (August 27, 2000). ... Re-signed by Broncos (September 12, 2000). ... Released by Broncos (October 14, 2000). ... Re-signed by Broncos (October 16, 2000). ... Claimed on waivers by Carolina Panthers (October 23, 2000).
PLAYING EXPERIENCE: Cincinnati NFL, 1995 and 1996; Barcelona NFLE, 1999; Denver NFL, 1999; Carolina NFL, 2000. ... Games/Games started: 1995 (16/2), 1996 (16/7), NFLE 1999 (games played unavailable), NFL 1999 (2/0), 2000 (3/0). Total NFL: 37/9.
PRO STATISTICS: 1995—Caught two passes for 12 yards and one touchdown.

TYLSKI, RICH — G — STEELERS

PERSONAL: Born February 27, 1971, in San Diego. ... 6-5/308. ... Full name: Richard Lee Tylski. ... Name pronounced TILL-skee.
HIGH SCHOOL: Madison (San Diego).
COLLEGE: Utah State (degree in sociology, 1994).
TRANSACTIONS/CAREER NOTES: Signed as non-drafted free agent by New England Patriots (April 25, 1994). ... Released by Patriots (August 20, 1994). ... Re-signed by Patriots to practice squad (August 30, 1994). ... Claimed on waivers by Jacksonville Jaguars (July 26, 1995). ... Released by Jaguars (August 27, 1995). ... Re-signed by Jaguars to practice squad (August 28, 1995). ... Granted free agency (February 12, 1999). ... Re-signed by Jaguars (May 5, 1999). ... Granted unconditional free agency (February 11, 2000). ... Signed by Pittsburgh Steelers (February 28, 2000).
PLAYING EXPERIENCE: Jacksonville NFL, 1996-1999; Pittsburgh NFL, 2000. ... Games/Games started: 1996 (16/7), 1997 (13/13), 1998 (11/8), 1999 (10/8), 2000 (16/16). Total: 66/52.
CHAMPIONSHIP GAME EXPERIENCE: Played in AFC championship game (1999 season).

ULBRICH, JEFF — LB — 49ERS

PERSONAL: Born February 17, 1977, in San Jose, Calif. ... 6-0/249.
HIGH SCHOOL: Live Oak (Morgan Hill, Calif.).
JUNIOR COLLEGE: Gavilan College (Calif.).
COLLEGE: San Jose State, then Hawaii.
TRANSACTIONS/CAREER NOTES: Selected by San Francisco 49ers in third round (86th pick overall) of 2000 NFL draft. ... Signed by 49ers (July 13, 2000). ... On injured reserve with shoulder injury (November 20, 2000-remainder of season).
PLAYING EXPERIENCE: San Francisco NFL, 2000. ... Games/Games started: 2000 (4/0).

ULMER, ARTIE — LB — FALCONS

PERSONAL: Born July 30, 1973, in Rincon, Ga. ... 6-3/247. ... Full name: Charles Artie Ulmer.
HIGH SCHOOL: Effingham County (Springfield, Ga.).
COLLEGE: Georgia Southern, then Valdosta (Ga.) State.
TRANSACTIONS/CAREER NOTES: Selected by Minnesota Vikings in seventh round (220th pick overall) of 1997 NFL draft. ... Signed by Vikings (June 17, 1997). ... On suspended list for violating league substance abuse policy (August 19-September 23, 1997). ... Assigned by Vikings to Frankfurt Galaxy in 1998 NFL Europe enhancement allocation program (February 18, 1998). ... Released by Vikings (August 24, 1998). ... Signed by Denver Broncos (January 14, 1999). ... On injured reserve with knee injury (November 4, 1999-remainder of season). ... Granted free agency (February 11, 2000). ... Signed by San Francisco 49ers to practice squad (September 14, 2000). ... Activated (September 19, 2000). ... Released by 49ers (February 19, 2001). ... Signed by Atlanta Falcons (April 16, 2001).
PLAYING EXPERIENCE: Frankfurt NFLE, 1998; Denver NFL, 1999; San Francisco NFL, 2000. ... Games/Games started: 1998 (games played unavailable), 1999 (7/0), 2000 (12/2). Total NFL: 19/2.
PRO STATISTICS: NFLE: 1998—Credited with three sacks. 2000—Credited with one sack.

UNDERWOOD, DIMITRIUS — DL — COWBOYS

PERSONAL: Born March 29, 1977, in Philadelphia. ... 6-6/276.
HIGH SCHOOL: E.E. Smith (Fayetteville, N.C.).
COLLEGE: Michigan State.
TRANSACTIONS/CAREER NOTES: Selected after junior season by Minnesota Vikings in first round (29th pick overall) of 1999 NFL draft. ... Signed by Vikings (August 1, 1999). ... Left team and decided not to play football (August 11, 1999). ... Claimed on waivers by Miami Dolphins (August 16, 1999). ... On non-football injury list with neck injury (September 28-December 17, 1999). ... Released by Dolphins (December 17, 1999). ... Signed by Dallas Cowboys (March 10, 2000).

Year Team	G	GS	SACKS
2000—Dallas NFL	15	0	4.0

UNUTOA, MORRIS — C

PERSONAL: Born March 10, 1971, in Torrance, Calif. ... 6-1/284. ... Full name: Morris Taua Unutoa. ... Name pronounced oo-nuh-TOE-uh.
HIGH SCHOOL: Carson (Calif.).
COLLEGE: Brigham Young.

TRANSACTIONS/CAREER NOTES: Signed as non-drafted free agent by Philadelphia Eagles (April 26, 1996). ... Granted free agency (February 12, 1999). ... Re-signed by Eagles (March 24, 1999). ... Released by Eagles (September 8, 1999). ... Signed by Tampa Bay Buccaneers (October 5, 1999). ... Granted unconditional free agency (March 2, 2001).
PLAYING EXPERIENCE: Philadelphia NFL, 1996-1998; Tampa Bay NFL, 1999 and 2000. ... Games/Games started: 1996 (16/0), 1997 (16/0), 1998 (16/0), 1999 (12/0), 2000 (16/0). Total: 76/0.
CHAMPIONSHIP GAME EXPERIENCE: Played in NFC championship game (1999 season).
PRO STATISTICS: 1996—Fumbled once.

UPSHAW, REGAN — DE — RAIDERS

PERSONAL: Born August 12, 1975, in Barrien Springs, Mich. ... 6-4/260. ... Full name: Regan Charles Upshaw.
HIGH SCHOOL: Pittsburg (Calif.).
COLLEGE: California.
TRANSACTIONS/CAREER NOTES: Selected after junior season by Tampa Bay Buccaneers in first round (12th pick overall) of 1996 NFL draft. ... Signed by Buccaneers (July 21, 1996). ... Traded by Buccaneers to Jacksonville Jaguars for sixth-round pick (RB Jameel Cook) in 2001 draft (October 19, 1999). ... Granted unconditional free agency (February 11, 2000). ... Signed by Oakland Raiders (March 1, 2000).
CHAMPIONSHIP GAME EXPERIENCE: Played in AFC championship game (1999 and 2000 seasons).
PRO STATISTICS: 1996—Recovered one fumble. 1997—Recovered one fumble. 1998—Intercepted one pass for 26 yards. 2000—Recovered two fumbles for eight yards.

Year Team	G	GS	SACKS
1996—Tampa Bay NFL	16	16	4.0
1997—Tampa Bay NFL	15	15	7.5
1998—Tampa Bay NFL	16	16	7.0
1999—Tampa Bay NFL	1	0	0.0
—Jacksonville NFL	6	0	0.0
2000—Oakland NFL	16	7	6.0
Pro totals (5 years)	70	54	24.5

URLACHER, BRIAN — LB — BEARS

PERSONAL: Born May 25, 1978, in Pasco, Wash. ... 6-3/244. ... Full name: Brian Keith Urlacher.
HIGH SCHOOL: Lovington (N.M.).
COLLEGE: New Mexico.
TRANSACTIONS/CAREER NOTES: Selected by Chicago Bears in first round (ninth pick overall) of 2000 NFL draft. ... Signed by Bears (June 16, 2000).
HONORS: Named strong safety on THE SPORTING NEWS college All-America second team (1999). ... Named NFL Rookie of the Year by THE SPORTING NEWS (2000). ... Played in Pro Bowl (2000 season).
PRO STATISTICS: 2000—Recovered one fumble.

			INTERCEPTIONS				SACKS
Year Team	G	GS	No.	Yds.	Avg.	TD	No.
2000—Chicago NFL	16	14	2	19	9.5	0	8.0

UWAEZUOKE, IHEANYI — WR

PERSONAL: Born July 24, 1973, in Lagos, Nigeria ... 6-2/198. ... Name pronounced ee-HAHN-ee oo-WAY-zoo-kay.
HIGH SCHOOL: Harvard (North Hollywood, Calif.).
COLLEGE: California (degree in political science, 1995).
TRANSACTIONS/CAREER NOTES: Selected by San Francisco 49ers in fifth round (160th pick overall) of 1996 NFL draft. ... Signed by 49ers (July 18, 1996). ... Claimed on waivers by Miami Dolphins (November 9, 1998). ... Granted free agency (February 12, 1999). ... Signed by Carolina Panthers (April 7, 1999). ... Released by Panthers (September 5, 1999). ... Signed by Detroit Lions (September 15, 1999). ... Granted unconditional free agency (February 11, 2000). ... Signed by Oakland Raiders (August 16, 2000). ... Released by Raiders (August 22, 2000). ... Signed by Panthers (October 4, 2000). ... Granted unconditional free agency (March 2, 2001).
CHAMPIONSHIP GAME EXPERIENCE: Played in NFC championship game (1997 season).
PRO STATISTICS: 1997—Recovered two fumbles.
SINGLE GAME HIGHS (regular season): Receptions—3 (November 2, 1997, vs. Dallas); yards—41 (September 21, 1997, vs. Atlanta); and touchdown receptions—1 (November 10, 1996, vs. Dallas).

			RECEIVING				PUNT RETURNS				KICKOFF RETURNS				TOTALS			
Year Team	G	GS	No.	Yds.	Avg.	TD	No.	Yds.	Avg.	TD	No.	Yds.	Avg.	TD	TD	2pt.	Pts.	Fum.
1996—San Francisco NFL	14	0	7	91	13.0	1	0	0	0.0	0	1	21	21.0	0	1	0	6	0
1997—San Francisco NFL	14	0	14	165	11.8	0	34	373	11.0	0	6	131	21.8	0	0	0	0	4
1998—San Francisco NFL	7	0	3	67	22.3	0	0	0	0.0	0	0	0	0.0	0	0	0	0	0
—Miami NFL	4	0	0	0	0.0	0	0	0	0.0	0	0	0	0.0	0	0	0	0	0
1999—Detroit NFL	10	0	1	5	5.0	0	18	150	8.3	0	0	0	0.0	0	0	0	0	1
2000—Carolina NFL	11	2	4	46	11.5	0	10	173	17.3	1	0	0	0.0	0	1	0	6	0
Pro totals (5 years)	60	2	29	374	12.9	1	62	696	11.2	1	7	152	21.7	0	2	0	12	5

VAN DYKE, ALEX — WR — RAIDERS

PERSONAL: Born July 24, 1974, in Sacramento. ... 6-0/205. ... Full name: Franklin Alexander Van Dyke.
HIGH SCHOOL: Luther Burbank (Sacramento).
JUNIOR COLLEGE: Sacramento City College.
COLLEGE: Nevada.

U
V

TRANSACTIONS/CAREER NOTES: Selected by New York Jets in second round (31st pick overall) of 1996 NFL draft. ... Signed by Jets (July 15, 1996). ... Traded by Jets to Pittsburgh Steelers for sixth-round pick (LB Marc Megna) in 1999 draft (March 25, 1999). ... Released by Steelers (September 5, 1999). ... Signed by Philadelphia Eagles (October 12, 1999). ... Released by Eagles (December 7, 2000). ... Signed by Oakland Raiders (February 12, 2001).

CHAMPIONSHIP GAME EXPERIENCE: Played in AFC championship game (1998 season).

HONORS: Named wide receiver on THE SPORTING NEWS college All-America second team (1995).

SINGLE GAME HIGHS (regular season): Receptions—4 (October 13, 1996, vs. Jacksonville); yards—35 (December 7, 1997, vs. Indianapolis); and touchdown receptions—2 (December 7, 1997, vs. Indianapolis).

			RECEIVING				KICKOFF RETURNS				TOTALS			
Year Team	G	GS	No.	Yds.	Avg.	TD	No.	Yds.	Avg.	TD	TD	2pt.	Pts.	Fum.
1996—New York Jets NFL	15	1	17	118	6.9	1	15	289	19.3	0	1	0	6	0
1997—New York Jets NFL	5	0	3	53	17.7	2	6	138	23.0	0	2	0	12	0
1998—New York Jets NFL	16	0	5	40	8.0	0	0	0	0.0	0	0	0	0	0
1999—Philadelphia NFL	2	0	0	0	0.0	0	0	0	0.0	0	0	0	0	0
2000—Philadelphia NFL	4	0	1	8	8.0	0	0	0	0.0	0	0	0	0	0
Pro totals (5 years)	42	1	26	219	8.4	3	21	427	20.3	0	3	0	18	0

VAN PELT, ALEX — QB — BILLS

PERSONAL: Born May 1, 1970, in Pittsburgh. ... 6-1/220. ... Full name: Gregory Alexander Van Pelt.

HIGH SCHOOL: Grafton (W.Va.), then Winston Churchill (San Antonio).

COLLEGE: Pittsburgh.

TRANSACTIONS/CAREER NOTES: Selected by Pittsburgh Steelers in eighth round (216th pick overall) of 1993 NFL draft. ... Signed by Steelers for 1993 season. ... Released by Steelers (August 30, 1993). ... Signed by Kansas City Chiefs to practice squad (November 3, 1993). ... Activated (November 8, 1993); did not play. ... Released by Chiefs (November 17, 1993). ... Re-signed by Chiefs (May 18, 1994). ... Released by Chiefs (August 23, 1994). ... Signed by Buffalo Bills to practice squad (December 14, 1994). ... Activated (December 17, 1994); did not play. ... Granted unconditional free agency (February 11, 2000). ... Re-signed by Bills (July 31, 2000). ... Granted unconditional free agency (March 2, 2001). ... Re-signed by Bills (March 19, 2001).

PRO STATISTICS: 1997—Fumbled three times and recovered three fumbles for minus seven yards.

SINGLE GAME HIGHS (regular season): Attempts—44 (December 20, 1997, vs. Green Bay); completions—23 (December 20, 1997, vs. Green Bay); yards—255 (December 20, 1997, vs. Green Bay); and touchdown passes—2 (October 26, 1997, vs. Denver).

MISCELLANEOUS: Regular-season record as starting NFL quarterback: 1-2 (.333).

			PASSING								RUSHING				TOTALS		
Year Team	G	GS	Att.	Cmp.	Pct.	Yds.	TD	Int.	Avg.	Rat.	Att.	Yds.	Avg.	TD	TD	2pt.	Pts.
1993—Kansas City NFL								Did not play.									
1994—Buffalo NFL								Did not play.									
1995—Buffalo NFL	1	0	18	10	55.6	106	2	0	5.89	110.0	0	0	0.0	0	0	0	0
1996—Buffalo NFL	1	0	5	2	40.0	9	0	0	1.80	47.9	3	-5	-1.7	0	0	0	0
1997—Buffalo NFL	6	3	124	60	48.4	684	2	10	5.52	37.2	11	33	3.0	1	1	0	6
1998—Buffalo NFL	1	0	0	0	0.0	0	0	0	0.0	...	1	-1	-1.0	0	0	0	0
1999—Buffalo NFL	1	0	1	1	100.0	9	0	0	9.00	104.2	1	-1	-1.0	0	0	0	0
2000—Buffalo NFL	1	0	8	4	50.0	67	0	0	8.38	78.6	0	0	0.0	0	0	0	0
Pro totals (6 years)	11	3	156	77	49.4	875	4	10	5.61	48.4	16	26	1.6	1	1	0	6

VANCE, ERIC — S — BUCCANEERS

PERSONAL: Born July 14, 1975, in Tampa. ... 6-2/218.

HIGH SCHOOL: L.D. Bell (Hurst, Texas).

COLLEGE: Vanderbilt.

TRANSACTIONS/CAREER NOTES: Signed as non-drafted free agent by Carolina Panthers (April 25, 1997). ... Released by Panthers (September 1, 1997). ... Signed by San Diego Chargers to practice squad (December 3, 1997). ... Granted free agency after 1997 season. ... Signed by Tampa Bay Buccaneers (December 30, 1997). ... Released by Buccaneers (August 25, 1998). ... Signed by Indianapolis Colts to practice squad (August 31, 1998). ... Signed by Buccaneers off Colts practice squad (October 28, 1998). ... On injured reserve with foot injury (November 10-December 7, 1999). ... Released by Buccaneers (December 7, 1999). ... Signed by San Diego Chargers (February 22, 2000). ... Released by Chargers (August 27, 2000). ... Signed by Buccaneers (August 28, 2000).

PLAYING EXPERIENCE: Tampa Bay NFL, 1998-2000. ... Games/Games started: 1998 (3/1), 1999 (6/0), 2000 (14/0). Total: 23/1.

VANDERJAGT, MIKE — K — COLTS

PERSONAL: Born March 24, 1970, in Oakville, Ont. ... 6-5/210. ... Name pronounced vander-JAT.

HIGH SCHOOL: White Oaks (Ont.).

JUNIOR COLLEGE: Allan Hancock College (Calif.).

COLLEGE: West Virginia.

TRANSACTIONS/CAREER NOTES: Signed by Saskatchewan Roughriders prior to 1993 season. ... Signed by Toronto Argonauts of CFL (February 15, 1994). ... Released by Argonauts (June 13, 1994). ... Signed by Hamilton Tiger-Cats of CFL (June 24, 1994). ... Released by Tiger-Cats (July 11, 1994). ... Signed by Argonauts of CFL (March 16, 1995). ... Released by Argonauts (June 25, 1995). ... Re-signed by Argonauts of CFL (May 10, 1996). ... Signed as non-drafted free agent by Indianapolis Colts (March 4, 1998).

CHAMPIONSHIP GAME EXPERIENCE: Member of CFL Championship team (1996 and 1997).

HONORS: Named Most Outstanding Canadian Player in Grey Cup (1996). ... Named to CFL All-Star team (1997).

PRO STATISTICS: CFL: 1996—Attempted two passes with one completion for 28 yards. 1997—Attempted one pass without a completion, rushed twice for 25 yards and fumbled once.

			PUNTING						KICKING						
Year	Team	G	No.	Yds.	Avg.	Net avg.	In. 20	Blk.	XPM	XPA	FGM	FGA	Lg.	50+	Pts.
1993—Saskatchewan CFL		2	17	672	39.5	32.1	0	0	0	0	0	0	0	0-0	0
1994—									Did not play.						
1995—									Did not play.						
1996—Toronto CFL		18	103	4459	43.3	35.1	0	0	59	59	40	56	51	0-0	179
1997—Toronto CFL		18	118	5303	44.9	37.4	0	0	77	77	33	43	51	0-0	176
1998—Indianapolis NFL		14	0	0	0.0	.0	0	0	23	23	27	31	53	6-9	104
1999—Indianapolis NFL		16	0	0	0.0	0	0	0	43	43	34	38	53	1-2	*145
2000—Indianapolis NFL		16	0	0	0.0	0	0	0	46	46	25	27	48	0-1	121
CFL totals (3 years)		38	238	10434	43.8	36.0	0	0	136	136	73	99	51	0-0	355
NFL totals (3 years)		46	0	0	0.0	0.0	0	0	112	112	86	96	53	7-12	370
Pro totals (6 years)		84	238	10434	43.8	36.0	0	0	248	248	159	195	53	7-0	725

VAUGHN, DARRICK CB/KR FALCONS

PERSONAL: Born October 2, 1978, in Houston. ... 5-11/193.
HIGH SCHOOL: Aldine Nimitz (Houston).
COLLEGE: Southwest Texas State.
TRANSACTIONS/CAREER NOTES: Selected by Atlanta Falcons in seventh round (211th pick overall) of 2000 NFL draft. ... Signed by Falcons (May 17, 2000).
PRO STATISTICS: 2000—Recovered one fumble.

			INTERCEPTIONS				KICKOFF RETURNS				TOTALS			
Year	Team	G	GS	No.	Yds.	Avg.	TD	No.	Yds.	Avg.	TD	TD	2pt.	Pts.	Fum.
2000—Atlanta NFL		16	0	0	0	0.0	0	39	1082	*27.7	*3	3	0	18	1

VERBA, ROSS OL BROWNS

PERSONAL: Born October 31, 1973, in Des Moines, Iowa. ... 6-4/308. ... Full name: Ross Robert Verba.
HIGH SCHOOL: Dowling (West Des Moines, Iowa).
COLLEGE: Iowa.
TRANSACTIONS/CAREER NOTES: Selected by Green Bay Packers in first round (30th pick overall) of 1997 NFL draft. ... Signed by Packers (July 31, 1997). ... Granted unconditional free agency (March 2, 2001). ... Signed by Cleveland Browns (March 23, 2001).
PLAYING EXPERIENCE: Green Bay NFL, 1997-2000. ... Games/Games started: 1997 (16/11), 1998 (16/16), 1999 (11/10), 2000 (16/16). Total: 59/53.
CHAMPIONSHIP GAME EXPERIENCE: Played in NFC championship game (1997 season). ... Played in Super Bowl XXXII (1997 season).
PRO STATISTICS: 1999—Recovered one fumble for two yards.

VICKERS, KIPP OL RAVENS

PERSONAL: Born August 27, 1969, in Tarpon Springs, Fla. ... 6-2/300. ... Full name: Kipp Emmanuel Vickers.
HIGH SCHOOL: Tarpon Springs (Fla.).
COLLEGE: Miami (Fla.).
TRANSACTIONS/CAREER NOTES: Signed as non-drafted free agent by Indianapolis Colts (April 30, 1993). ... Released by Colts (August 30, 1993). ... Re-signed by Colts to practice squad (September 1, 1993). ... Activated (December 21, 1993); did not play. ... Released by Colts (August 28, 1994). ... Re-signed by Colts to practice squad (August 31, 1994). ... Released by Colts (November 1, 1994). ... Re-signed by Colts to practice squad (November 16, 1994). ... Activated (December 24, 1994); did not play. ... Assigned by Colts to Frankfurt Galaxy in 1995 World League enhancement allocation program (February 20, 1995). ... Released by Colts (February 4, 1997). ... Re-signed by Colts for 1997 season. ... Granted free agency (February 13, 1998). ... Re-signed by Colts (February 24, 1998). ... Released by Colts (August 24, 1998). ... Signed by Washington Redskins (November 24, 1998). ... Inactive for five games (1998). ... Granted free agency (February 12, 1999). ... Re-signed by Redskins (February 23, 1999). ... Granted unconditional free agency (February 11, 2000). ... Signed by Baltimore Ravens (February 17, 2000).
PLAYING EXPERIENCE: Frankfurt W.L., 1995; Indianapolis NFL, 1995-1997; Washington NFL, 1999; Baltimore NFL, 2000. ... Games/Games started: W.L. 1995 (games played unavailable), NFL 1995 (9/0), 1996 (10/6), 1997 (9/0), 1999 (11/0), 2000 (12/2). Total NFL: 51/8.
CHAMPIONSHIP GAME EXPERIENCE: Played in AFC championship game (1995 and 2000 seasons). ... Member of Super Bowl championship team (2000 season).

VILLARRIAL, CHRIS G BEARS

PERSONAL: Born June 9, 1973, in Hummelstown, Pa. ... 6-4/308. ... Name pronounced vuh-LAR-ree-uhl.
HIGH SCHOOL: Hershey (Pa.).
COLLEGE: Indiana University (Pa.).
TRANSACTIONS/CAREER NOTES: Selected by Chicago Bears in fifth round (152nd pick overall) of 1996 NFL draft. ... Signed by Bears (July 11, 1996). ... Granted free agency (February 12, 1999). ... Re-signed by Bears (April 16, 1999).
PLAYING EXPERIENCE: Chicago NFL, 1996-2000. ... Games/Games started: 1996 (14/8), 1997 (11/11), 1998 (16/16), 1999 (15/15), 2000 (16/15). Total: 72/65.
PRO STATISTICS: 1998—Recovered one fumble. 1999—Recovered two fumbles.

VINATIERI, ADAM K PATRIOTS

PERSONAL: Born December 28, 1972, in Yunkton, S.D. ... 6-0/200. ... Full name: Adam Matthew Vinatieri. ... Name pronounced VIN-a-TERRY.
HIGH SCHOOL: Rapid City (S.D.) Central.
COLLEGE: South Dakota State (degree in fitness and wellness).
TRANSACTIONS/CAREER NOTES: Signed by Amsterdam Admirals of World League for 1996 season. ... Signed as non-drafted free agent by New England Patriots (June 28, 1996). ... Granted free agency (February 12, 1999). ... Re-signed by Patriots (March 12, 1999).
CHAMPIONSHIP GAME EXPERIENCE: Played in AFC championship game (1996 season). ... Played in Super Bowl XXXI (1996 season).
PRO STATISTICS: 1996—Punted once for 27 yards. 1998—Credited with a two-point conversion.

Year Team	G	KICKING						
		XPM	XPA	FGM	FGA	Lg.	50+	Pts.
1996—Amsterdam W.L.	10	4	4	9	10	43	0-0	31
—New England NFL	16	39	42	27	35	50	1-2	120
1997—New England NFL	16	40	40	25	29	52	1-1	115
1998—New England NFL	16	32	32	31	39	55	2-2	127
1999—New England NFL	16	29	30	26	33	51	1-2	107
2000—New England NFL	16	25	25	27	33	53	1-3	106
W.L. totals (1 year)	10	4	4	9	10	43	0-0	31
NFL totals (5 years)	80	165	169	136	169	55	6-10	573
Pro totals (6 years)	90	169	173	145	179	55	6-0	604

VINCENT, TROY   CB   EAGLES

PERSONAL: Born June 8, 1971, in Trenton, N.J. ... 6-1/200. ... Full name: Troy D. Vincent. ... Nephew of Steve Luke, safety with Green Bay Packers (1975-80).

HIGH SCHOOL: Pennsbury (Fairless Hills, Pa.).

COLLEGE: Wisconsin.

TRANSACTIONS/CAREER NOTES: Selected by Miami Dolphins in first round (seventh pick overall) of 1992 NFL draft. ... Signed by Dolphins (August 8, 1992). ... Designated by Dolphins as transition player (February 25, 1993). ... On injured reserve with knee injury (December 15, 1993-remainder of season). ... Tendered offer sheet by Philadelphia Eagles (February 24, 1996). ... Dolphins declined to match offer (March 3, 1996).

CHAMPIONSHIP GAME EXPERIENCE: Played in AFC championship game (1992 season).

HONORS: Named defensive back on THE SPORTING NEWS college All-America first team (1991). ... Played in Pro Bowl (1999 and 2000 seasons).

RECORDS: Holds NFL record for longest interception return for a touchdown—104 yards (November 3, 1996; with lateral from LB James Willis).

PRO STATISTICS: 1992—Returned five punts for 16 yards and recovered two fumbles. 1993—Recovered one fumble. 1994—Ran 58 yards with lateral from interception for a touchdown. 1996—Ran minus two yards with lateral from punt return. 1997—Returned one punt for minus eight yards, fumbled once and recovered two fumbles for five yards. 1998—Credited with one sack. 1999—Credited with one sack. 2000—Credited with one sack recovered two fumbles.

Year Team	G	GS	INTERCEPTIONS			
			No.	Yds.	Avg.	TD
1992—Miami NFL	15	14	2	47	23.5	0
1993—Miami NFL	13	13	2	29	14.5	0
1994—Miami NFL	13	12	5	113	22.6	1
1995—Miami NFL	16	16	5	95	19.0	▲1
1996—Philadelphia NFL	16	16	3	144	*48.0	1
1997—Philadelphia NFL	16	16	3	14	4.7	0
1998—Philadelphia NFL	13	13	2	29	14.5	0
1999—Philadelphia NFL	14	14	†7	91	13.0	0
2000—Philadelphia NFL	16	16	5	34	6.8	0
Pro totals (9 years)	132	130	34	596	17.5	3

VOLEK, BILLY   QB   TITANS

PERSONAL: Born April 28, 1976, in Fresno, Calif. ... 6-2/210.

HIGH SCHOOL: Clovis West (Fresno, Calif.).

COLLEGE: Fresno State.

TRANSACTIONS/CAREER NOTES: Signed as non-drafted free agent by Tennessee Titans (April 18, 2000).

PLAYING EXPERIENCE: Tennessee NFL, 2000. ... Games/Games started: 2000 (1/0).

V

VON OELHOFFEN, KIMO   DL   STEELERS

PERSONAL: Born January 30, 1971, in Kaunakaki, Hawaii. ... 6-4/305. ... Full name: Kimo K. von Oelhoffen. ... Name pronounced KEE-moe von OHL-hoffen.

HIGH SCHOOL: Molokai (Hoolehua, Hawaii).

JUNIOR COLLEGE: Walla Walla (Wash.) Community College.

COLLEGE: Hawaii, then Boise State.

TRANSACTIONS/CAREER NOTES: Selected by Cincinnati Bengals in sixth round (162nd pick overall) of 1994 NFL draft. ... Signed by Bengals (May 9, 1994). ... Granted unconditional free agency (February 11, 2000). ... Signed by Pittsburgh Steelers (February 14, 2000).

PLAYING EXPERIENCE: Cincinnati NFL, 1994-1999; Pittsburgh NFL, 2000. ... Games/Games started: 1994 (7/0), 1995 (16/0), 1996 (11/1), 1997 (13/12), 1998 (16/16), 1999 (16/5), 2000 (16/16). Total: 95/50.

PRO STATISTICS: 1995—Returned one kickoff for 10 yards. 1996—Credited with one sack. 1999—Credited with four sacks and recovered one fumble. 2000—Credited with one sack.

VRABEL, MIKE   LB   PATRIOTS

PERSONAL: Born August 14, 1975, in Akron, Ohio. ... 6-4/250. ... Full name: Michael George Vrabel.

HIGH SCHOOL: Walsh Jesuit (Cuyahoga Falls, Ohio).

COLLEGE: Ohio State.

TRANSACTIONS/CAREER NOTES: Selected by Pittsburgh Steelers in third round (91st pick overall) of 1997 NFL draft. ... Signed by Steelers (July 15, 1997). ... Granted free agency (February 11, 2000). ... Re-signed by Steelers (April 20, 2000). ... Granted unconditional free agency (March 2, 2001). ... Signed by New England Patriots (March 13, 2001).

CHAMPIONSHIP GAME EXPERIENCE: Played in AFC championship game (1997 season).

PRO STATISTICS: 1997—Returned one kickoff for no yards and recovered one fumble. 1999—Returned one kickoff for six yards and recovered one fumble. 2000—Recovered one fumble.

Year Team	G	GS	SACKS
1997—Pittsburgh NFL	15	0	1.5
1998—Pittsburgh NFL	11	0	2.5
1999—Pittsburgh NFL	10	0	2.0
2000—Pittsburgh NFL	15	0	1.0
Pro totals (4 years)	**51**	**0**	**7.0**

WADE, JOHN　　　　　C　　　　　JAGUARS

PERSONAL: Born January 25, 1975, in Harrisonburg, Va. ... 6-5/300. ... Full name: John Robert Wade.
HIGH SCHOOL: Harrisonburg (Va.).
COLLEGE: Marshall (degree in business management, 1997).
TRANSACTIONS/CAREER NOTES: Selected by Jacksonville Jaguars in fifth round (148th pick overall) of 1998 NFL draft. ... Signed by Jaguars (June 1, 1998). ... On injured reserve with broken foot (September 27, 2000-remainder of season).
PLAYING EXPERIENCE: Jacksonville NFL, 1998-2000. ... Games/Games started: 1998 (4/0), 1999 (16/16), 2000 (2/2). Total: 22/18.
CHAMPIONSHIP GAME EXPERIENCE: Played in AFC championship game (1999 season).
PRO STATISTICS: 1999—Fumbled once for minus 14 yards.

WADE, TODD　　　　　OT　　　　　DOLPHINS

PERSONAL: Born October 30, 1976, in Greenwood, Miss. ... 6-8/325. ... Full name: Todd McLaurin Wade.
HIGH SCHOOL: Jackson (Miss.) Prep.
COLLEGE: Mississippi.
TRANSACTIONS/CAREER NOTES: Selected by Miami Dolphins in second round (53rd pick overall) of 2000 NFL draft. ... Signed by Dolphins (July 24, 2000).
PLAYING EXPERIENCE: Miami NFL, 2000. ... Games/Games started: 2000 (16/16).

WADSWORTH, ANDRE　　　　　DE

PERSONAL: Born October 19, 1974, in St. Croix, Virgin Islands (U.S.) ... 6-4/272.
HIGH SCHOOL: Florida Christian (Miami).
COLLEGE: Florida State (degree in marketing, 1997).
TRANSACTIONS/CAREER NOTES: Selected by Arizona Cardinals in first round (third pick overall) of 1998 NFL draft. ... Signed by Cardinals (September 5, 1998). ... Granted free agency (March 2, 2001).
HONORS: Named defensive end on THE SPORTING NEWS college All-America first team (1997).
PRO STATISTICS: 1998—Recovered three fumbles. 1999—Intercepted one pass for 23 yards.

Year Team	G	GS	SACKS
1998—Arizona NFL	16	15	5.0
1999—Arizona NFL	11	7	2.0
2000—Arizona NFL	9	8	1.0
Pro totals (3 years)	**36**	**30**	**8.0**

WAHLE, MIKE　　　　　G/OT　　　　　PACKERS

PERSONAL: Born March 29, 1977, in Portland, Ore. ... 6-6/310. ... Full name: Michael James Wahle. ... Name pronounced WALL.
HIGH SCHOOL: Rim of the World (Lake Arrowhead, Calif.).
COLLEGE: Navy.
TRANSACTIONS/CAREER NOTES: Selected by Green Bay Packers in second round of 1998 supplemental draft (July 9, 1998). ... Signed by Packers (August 6, 1998). ... Granted free agency (March 2, 2001). ... Re-signed by Packers (May 31, 2001).
PLAYING EXPERIENCE: Green Bay NFL, 1998-2000. ... Games/Games started: 1998 (1/0), 1999 (16/13), 2000 (16/6). Total: 33/19.
PRO STATISTICS: 1999—Recovered one fumble.

WAINRIGHT, FRANK　　　　　TE

PERSONAL: Born October 10, 1967, in Peoria, Ill. ... 6-3/255. ... Full name: Frank Wesley Wainright.
HIGH SCHOOL: Pomona (Arvada, Colo.).
COLLEGE: Northern Colorado.
TRANSACTIONS/CAREER NOTES: Selected by New Orleans Saints in eighth round (210th pick overall) of 1991 NFL draft. ... Signed by Saints (July 14, 1991). ... Released by Saints (August 26, 1991). ... Re-signed by Saints to practice squad (August 28, 1991). ... Activated (September 14, 1991). ... Granted unconditional free agency (February 1-April 1, 1992). ... Re-signed by Saints for 1992 season. ... On injured reserve with foot injury (August 23, 1994-entire season). ... Granted unconditional free agency (February 17, 1995). ... Signed by Denver Broncos (April 17, 1995). ... Released by Broncos (August 22, 1995). ... Signed by Philadelphia Eagles (August 29, 1995). ... Released by Eagles (October 25, 1995). ... Signed by Miami Dolphins (November 15, 1995). ... Granted unconditional free agency (February 16, 1996). ... Re-signed by Dolphins (March 5, 1996). ... Granted unconditional free agency (February 14, 1997). ... Re-signed by Dolphins (February 27, 1997). ... On injured reserve with chest injury (December 9, 1997-remainder of season). ... Granted unconditional free agency (February 12, 1999). ... Signed by Baltimore Ravens (February 25, 1999). ... On injured reserve with back injury (October 25, 2000-remainder of season). ... Granted unconditional free agency (March 2, 2001).
PRO STATISTICS: 1995—Recovered one fumble. 1996—Returned one kickoff for 10 yards.
SINGLE GAME HIGHS (regular season): Receptions—2 (December 3, 1992, vs. Atlanta); yards—42 (December 3, 1992, vs. Atlanta); and touchdown receptions—1 (September 15, 1996, vs. New York Jets).

V
W

Year Team	G	GS	RECEIVING No.	Yds.	Avg.	TD	TOTALS TD	2pt.	Pts.	Fum.
1991—New Orleans NFL	14	2	1	3	3.0	0	0	0	0	0
1992—New Orleans NFL	13	4	9	143	15.9	0	0	0	0	0
1993—New Orleans NFL	16	2	0	0	0.0	0	0	0	0	0
1994—New Orleans NFL					Did not play.					
1995—Philadelphia NFL	7	0	0	0	0.0	0	0	0	0	0
—Miami NFL	6	0	0	0	0.0	0	0	0	0	0
1996—Miami NFL	16	0	1	2	2.0	1	1	0	6	0
1997—Miami NFL	9	0	0	0	0.0	0	0	0	0	0
1998—Miami NFL	16	1	0	0	0.0	0	0	0	0	0
1999—Baltimore NFL	16	0	0	0	0.0	0	0	0	0	0
2000—Baltimore NFL	8	0	0	0	0.0	0	0	0	0	0
Pro totals (9 years)	121	9	11	148	13.5	1	1	0	6	0

WALENDY, CRAIG · RB

PERSONAL: Born July 11, 1977, in Westlake, Calif. ... 6-2/228. ... Full name: Craig H. Walendy.
HIGH SCHOOL: Westlake (Calif.).
COLLEGE: UCLA.
TRANSACTIONS/CAREER NOTES: Signed by New York Giants as non-drafted free agent (June 13, 2000). ... Released by Giants (March 14, 2001). ... Signed by St. Louis Rams (May 3, 2001). ... Released by Rams (June 6, 2001).
PLAYING EXPERIENCE: New York Giants NFL, 2000. ... Games/Games started: 2000 (12/0).
CHAMPIONSHIP GAME EXPERIENCE: Member of Giants for NFC Championship game (2000 season); inactive. ... Member of Giants for Super Bowl XXXV (2000 season); inactive.

WALKER, BRACEY · S · CHIEFS

PERSONAL: Born June 11, 1970, in Spring Lake, N.C. ... 6-0/206. ... Full name: Bracey Wordell Walker.
HIGH SCHOOL: Pine Forest (Fayetteville, N.C.).
COLLEGE: North Carolina.
TRANSACTIONS/CAREER NOTES: Selected by Kansas City Chiefs in fourth round (127th pick overall) of 1994 NFL draft. ... Signed by Chiefs (July 20, 1994). ... Claimed on waivers by Cincinnati Bengals (October 12, 1994). ... Granted free agency (February 14, 1997). ... Re-signed by Bengals (April 18, 1997). ... Claimed on waivers by Miami Dolphins (August 20, 1997). ... On injured reserve with leg injury (December 2, 1997-remainder of season). ... Granted unconditional free agency (February 13, 1998). ... Re-signed by Dolphins (April 27, 1998). ... Released by Dolphins (August 19, 1998). ... Signed by Chiefs (November 3, 1998). ... Granted unconditional free agency (February 11, 2000). ... Re-signed by Chiefs (February 24, 2000).
HONORS: Named defensive back on THE SPORTING NEWS college All-America second team (1993).
PRO STATISTICS: 1995—Recovered two fumbles. 1997—Recovered one fumble.

Year Team	G	GS	INTERCEPTIONS No.	Yds.	Avg.	TD
1994—Kansas City NFL	2	0	0	0	0.0	0
—Cincinnati NFL	7	0	0	0	0.0	0
1995—Cincinnati NFL	14	14	4	56	14.0	0
1996—Cincinnati NFL	16	16	2	35	17.5	0
1997—Miami NFL	12	0	0	0	0.0	0
1998—Kansas City NFL	8	0	0	0	0.0	0
1999—Kansas City NFL	16	1	0	0	0.0	0
2000—Kansas City NFL	15	0	0	0	0.0	0
Pro totals (7 years)	90	31	6	91	15.2	0

WALKER, BRIAN · S · DOLPHINS

PERSONAL: Born May 31, 1972, in Colorado Springs, Colo. ... 6-1/205.
HIGH SCHOOL: Widefield (Colorado Springs, Colo.).
JUNIOR COLLEGE: Snow College (Utah).
COLLEGE: Washington State.
TRANSACTIONS/CAREER NOTES: Signed as non-drafted free agent by Washington Redskins (May 1, 1996). ... Released by Redskins (October 9, 1997). ... Signed by Miami Dolphins (December 9, 1997). ... Active for two games with Dolphins (1997); did not play. ... Claimed on waivers by Seattle Seahawks (September 6, 1999). ... Released by Seahawks (September 14, 1999). ... Re-signed by Seahawks (September 30, 1999). ... On injured reserve with hamstring injury (January 8, 2000-remainder of 1999 playoffs). ... Granted unconditional free agency (February 11, 2000). ... Signed by Dolphins (February 16, 2000).
PLAYING EXPERIENCE: Washington NFL, 1996 and 1997; Miami NFL, 1998 and 2000; Seattle NFL, 1999. ... Games/Games started: 1996 (16/4), 1997 (5/0), 1998 (16/0), 1999 (5/0), 2000 (16/16). Total: 58/20.
PRO STATISTICS: 1996—Credited with one sack. 1998—Intercepted four passes for 12 yards. 1999—Intercepted one pass for 21 yards and recovered one fumble. 2000—Intercepted seven passes for 80 yards and credited with two sacks.

WALKER, DARNELL · CB

PERSONAL: Born January 17, 1970, in St. Louis. ... 5-8/168. ... Full name: Darnell Robert Walker. ... Brother of Marquis Walker, defensive back with four teams (1996-2000).
HIGH SCHOOL: Sumner (St. Louis).
JUNIOR COLLEGE: Coffeyville (Kan.) Community College.
COLLEGE: Oklahoma.

TRANSACTIONS/CAREER NOTES: Selected by Atlanta Falcons in seventh round (178th pick overall) of 1993 NFL draft. ... Signed by Falcons (July 14, 1993). ... Granted free agency (February 16, 1996). ... Re-signed by Falcons (June 12, 1996). ... Granted unconditional free agency (February 14, 1997). ... Signed by San Francisco 49ers (March 28, 1997). ... Released by 49ers (February 7, 2000). ... Signed by Minnesota Vikings (August 15, 2000). ... Released by Vikings (August 27, 2000). ... Signed by Detroit Lions (September 19, 2000). ... Granted unconditional free agency (March 2, 2001).
CHAMPIONSHIP GAME EXPERIENCE: Played in NFC championship game (1997 season).
PRO STATISTICS: 1994—Credited with one sack. 1996—Recovered one fumble. 1997—Credited with one sack. 1999—Credited with one sack and recovered two fumbles for 71 yards and one touchdown.

Year Team	G	GS	INTERCEPTIONS				TOTALS			
			No.	Yds.	Avg.	TD	TD	2pt.	Pts.	Fum.
1993—Atlanta NFL	15	8	3	7	2.3	0	0	0	0	0
1994—Atlanta NFL	16	5	3	105	35.0	1	1	0	6	0
1995—Atlanta NFL	16	7	0	0	0.0	0	0	0	0	0
1996—Atlanta NFL	15	9	1	0	0.0	0	0	0	0	0
1997—San Francisco NFL	16	11	3	49	16.3	0	0	0	0	0
1998—San Francisco NFL	16	16	4	78	19.5	0	0	0	0	0
1999—San Francisco NFL	15	8	1	27	27.0	1	2	0	12	0
2000—Detroit NFL	10	2	1	5	5.0	0	0	0	0	0
Pro totals (8 years)	119	66	16	271	16.9	2	3	0	18	0

WALKER, DARWIN   DT   EAGLES

PERSONAL: Born June 15, 1977, in Walterboro, S.C. ... 6-3/294. ... Full name: Darwin Jamar Walker.
HIGH SCHOOL: Walterboro (S.C.).
COLLEGE: North Carolina State, then Tennessee.
TRANSACTIONS/CAREER NOTES: Selected by Arizona Cardinals in third round (71st pick overall) of 2000 NFL draft. ... Signed by Cardinals (June 19, 2000). ... Claimed on waivers by Philadelphia Eagles (September 12, 2000).
PLAYING EXPERIENCE: Arizona NFL, 2000. ... Games/Games started: 2000 (1/0).
HONORS: Named defensive tackle on THE SPORTING NEWS college All-America second team (1999).

WALKER, DENARD   CB   BRONCOS

PERSONAL: Born August 9, 1973, in Dallas. ... 6-1/190. ... Full name: Denard Antuan Walker.
HIGH SCHOOL: South Garland (Texas), than Harlingen (Texas) Military Institute.
COLLEGE: Louisiana State.
TRANSACTIONS/CAREER NOTES: Selected by Houston Oilers in third round (75th pick overall) of 1997 NFL draft. ... Oilers franchise moved to Tennessee for 1997 season. ... Signed by Oilers (July 18, 1997). ... Oilers franchise renamed Tennessee Titans for 1999 season (December 26, 1998). ... Granted free agency (February 11, 2000). ... Re-signed by Titans (June 3, 2000). ... On suspended list (September 3-5, 2000). ... Granted unconditional free agency (March 2, 2001). ... Signed by Denver Broncos (March 19, 2001).
CHAMPIONSHIP GAME EXPERIENCE: Played in AFC championship game (1999 season). ... Played in Super Bowl XXXIV (1999 season).
PRO STATISTICS: 2000—Returned one punt for no yards and fumbled once.

Year Team	G	GS	INTERCEPTIONS			
			No.	Yds.	Avg.	TD
1997—Tennessee NFL	15	11	2	53	26.5	1
1998—Tennessee NFL	16	16	2	6	3.0	0
1999—Tennessee NFL	15	14	1	27	27.0	0
2000—Tennessee NFL	15	14	2	4	2.0	0
Pro totals (4 years)	61	55	7	90	12.9	1

WALKER, GARY   DT   JAGUARS

PERSONAL: Born February 28, 1973, in Royston, Ga. ... 6-2/301. ... Full name: Gary Lamar Walker.
HIGH SCHOOL: Franklin County (Carnesville, Ga.).
JUNIOR COLLEGE: Hinds Community College (Miss.).
COLLEGE: Auburn.
TRANSACTIONS/CAREER NOTES: Selected by Houston Oilers in fifth round (159th pick overall) of 1995 NFL draft. ... Signed by Oilers (July 10, 1995). ... Oilers franchise moved to Tennessee for 1997 season. ... Granted free agency (February 13, 1998). ... Re-signed by Oilers (July 15, 1998). ... Granted unconditional free agency (February 12, 1999). ... Signed by Jacksonville Jaguars (February 15, 1999).
CHAMPIONSHIP GAME EXPERIENCE: Played in AFC championship game (1999 season).
PRO STATISTICS: 1996—Recovered one fumble.

Year Team	G	GS	SACKS
1995—Houston NFL	15	9	2.5
1996—Houston NFL	16	16	5.5
1997—Tennessee NFL	15	15	7.0
1998—Tennessee NFL	16	16	1.0
1999—Jacksonville NFL	16	16	10.0
2000—Jacksonville NFL	15	14	5.0
Pro totals (6 years)	93	86	31.0

W

WALKER, MARQUIS   CB

PERSONAL: Born July 6, 1972, in St. Louis. ... 5-10/175. ... Full name: Marquis Roshe Walker. ... Brother of Darnell Walker, cornerback with Atlanta Falcons (1993-96), San Francisco 49ers (1997-99) and Detroit Lions (2000).
HIGH SCHOOL: Berkeley (St. Louis).
JUNIOR COLLEGE: Blinn College (Texas), then Cisco (Texas) Junior College.
COLLEGE: Southeast Missouri State.

TRANSACTIONS/CAREER NOTES: Signed as non-drafted free agent by St. Louis Rams (April 24, 1996). ... Released by Rams (September 4, 1996). ... Signed by Washington Redskins to practice squad (September 4, 1996). ... Signed by Rams off Redskins practice squad (November 6, 1996). ... Released by Rams (November 19, 1997). ... Selected by Frankfurt Galaxy in 1998 NFL Europe draft (February 18, 1998). ... Signed by Oakland Raiders (May 5, 1998). ... Granted free agency (February 12, 1999). ... Re-signed by Raiders (March 5, 1999). ... Granted unconditional free agency (February 11, 2000). ... Re-signed by Raiders (April 25, 2000). ... Released by Raiders (June 29, 2000). ... Signed by Detroit Lions (July 17, 2000). ... Granted unconditional free agency (March 2, 2001).

PLAYING EXPERIENCE: St. Louis (8)-Washington (1) NFL, 1996; St. Louis NFL, 1997; Oakland NFL, 1998 and 1999; Detroit NFL, 2000. ... Games/Games started: 1996 (St.L-8/4; Wash.-1/0; Total: 9/4), 1997 (10/0), 1998 (16/7), 1999 (16/0), 2000 (12/2). Total: 63/13.

PRO STATISTICS: 1997—Recovered one fumble. 1998—Intercepted two passes for 28 yards and recovered one fumble for three yards. 1999—Intercepted one pass for no yards and credited with one sack. 2000—Intercepted one pass for 12 yards, fumbled once and recovered two fumbles.

WALLS, WESLEY　　　　　TE　　　　　PANTHERS

PERSONAL: Born February 26, 1966, in Pontotoc, Miss. ... 6-5/250. ... Full name: Charles Wesley Walls.

HIGH SCHOOL: Pontotoc (Miss.).

COLLEGE: Mississippi.

TRANSACTIONS/CAREER NOTES: Selected by San Francisco 49ers in second round (56th pick overall) of 1989 NFL draft. ... Signed by 49ers (July 26, 1989). ... Granted free agency (February 1, 1992). ... Re-signed by 49ers (July 18, 1992). ... On injured reserve with shoulder injury (September 1, 1992-January 16, 1993). ... On injured reserve with shoulder injury (October 27, 1993-remainder of season). ... Granted unconditional free agency (February 17, 1994). ... Signed by New Orleans Saints (April 27, 1994). ... Granted unconditional free agency (February 16, 1996). ... Signed by Carolina Panthers (February 21, 1996). ... On injured reserve with knee injury (October 31, 2000-remainder of season).

CHAMPIONSHIP GAME EXPERIENCE: Played in NFC championship game (1989, 1990 and 1996 seasons). ... Member of Super Bowl championship team (1989 season).

HONORS: Named tight end on THE SPORTING NEWS college All-America second team (1988). ... Played in Pro Bowl (1996-1999 seasons).

PRO STATISTICS: 1989—Recovered one fumble. 1990—Returned one kickoff for 16 yards. 1993—Recovered one fumble. 1995—Returned one kickoff for six yards, fumbled once and recovered one fumble.

SINGLE GAME HIGHS (regular season): Receptions—8 (November 15, 1998, vs. Miami); yards—147 (September 7, 1997, vs. Atlanta); and touchdown receptions—2 (January 2, 2000, vs. New Orleans).

STATISTICAL PLATEAUS: 100-yard receiving games: 1997 (2), 2000 (1). Total: 3.

MISCELLANEOUS: Holds Carolina Panthers all-time records for most touchdown receptions (35) and touchdowns (35).

				RECEIVING			TOTALS			
Year　Team	G	GS	No.	Yds.	Avg.	TD	TD	2pt.	Pts.	Fum.
1989—San Francisco NFL	16	0	4	16	4.0	1	1	0	6	1
1990—San Francisco NFL	16	0	5	27	5.4	0	0	0	0	0
1991—San Francisco NFL	15	0	2	24	12.0	0	0	0	0	0
1992—San Francisco NFL						Did not play.				
1993—San Francisco NFL	6	0	0	0	0.0	0	0	0	0	0
1994—New Orleans NFL	15	7	38	406	10.7	4	4	1	26	0
1995—New Orleans NFL	16	10	57	694	12.2	4	4	1	26	1
1996—Carolina NFL	16	15	61	713	11.7	10	10	0	60	0
1997—Carolina NFL	15	15	58	746	12.9	6	6	0	36	0
1998—Carolina NFL	14	14	49	506	10.3	5	5	0	30	0
1999—Carolina NFL	16	16	63	822	13.0	12	12	0	72	1
2000—Carolina NFL	8	8	31	422	13.6	2	2	0	12	0
Pro totals (11 years)	153	85	368	4376	11.9	44	44	2	268	3

WALSH, CHRIS　　　　　WR

PERSONAL: Born December 12, 1968, in Cleveland. ... 6-1/199. ... Full name: Christopher Lee Walsh.

HIGH SCHOOL: Ygnacio Valley (Concord, Calif.).

COLLEGE: Stanford (degree in quantitative economics, 1991).

TRANSACTIONS/CAREER NOTES: Selected by Buffalo Bills in ninth round (251st pick overall) of 1992 NFL draft. ... Signed by Bills (July 22, 1992). ... Released by Bills (August 31, 1992). ... Re-signed by Bills to practice squad (September 1, 1992). ... Activated (September 19, 1992). ... Released by Bills (October 2, 1992). ... Re-signed by Bills to practice squad (October 2, 1992). ... Released by Bills (March 10, 1994). ... Signed by Minnesota Vikings (May 6, 1994). ... Granted unconditional free agency (February 16, 1996). ... Re-signed by Vikings (March 4, 1996). ... Granted unconditional free agency (February 13, 1998). ... Re-signed by Vikings (March 4, 1998). ... Granted unconditional free agency (March 2, 2001).

CHAMPIONSHIP GAME EXPERIENCE: Member of Bills for AFC championship game (1993 season); inactive. ... Member of Bills for Super Bowl XXVIII (1993 season); inactive. ... Played in NFC championship game (1998 and 2000 seasons).

PRO STATISTICS: 1994—Returned one kickoff for six yards. 1995—Returned three kickoffs for 42 yards. 1996—Attempted one pass without a completion and credited with one two-point conversion. 1997—Returned one kickoff for 10 yards. 2000—Returned one punt for 11 yards and returned two kickoffs for nine yards.

SINGLE GAME HIGHS (regular season): Receptions—4 (December 24, 2000, vs. Indianapolis); yards—44 (December 17, 2000, vs. Green Bay); and touchdown receptions—1 (October 10, 1999, vs. Chicago).

				RECEIVING			TOTALS			
Year　Team	G	GS	No.	Yds.	Avg.	TD	TD	2pt.	Pts.	Fum.
1992—Buffalo NFL	2	0	0	0	0.0	0	0	0	0	0
1993—Buffalo NFL	3	0	0	0	0.0	0	0	0	0	0
1994—Minnesota NFL	10	0	0	0	0.0	0	0	0	0	0
1995—Minnesota NFL	16	0	7	66	9.4	0	0	0	0	0
1996—Minnesota NFL	15	0	4	39	9.8	1	1	1	8	0
1997—Minnesota NFL	14	0	11	114	10.4	1	1	0	6	0
1998—Minnesota NFL	15	0	2	46	23.0	0	0	0	0	0
1999—Minnesota NFL	16	1	2	24	12.0	1	1	0	6	0
2000—Minnesota NFL	16	0	18	191	10.6	0	0	0	0	0
Pro totals (9 years)	107	1	44	480	10.9	3	3	1	20	0

W

WALTER, KEN — P

PERSONAL: Born August 15, 1972, in Cleveland. ... 6-1/195. ... Full name: Kenneth Matthew Walter Jr.
HIGH SCHOOL: Euclid (Ohio).
COLLEGE: Kent.
TRANSACTIONS/CAREER NOTES: Signed as non-drafted free agent by Carolina Panthers (April 14, 1997). ... Released by Panthers (April 24, 2001).
PRO STATISTICS: 1997—Rushed once for minus five yards. 1998—Rushed three times for no yards, attempted one pass without a completion, fumbled twice and recovered two fumbles for minus 20 yards. 2000—Rushed once for no yards, attempted one pass without a completion, fumbled twice and recovered two fumbles for minus 11 yards.

		PUNTING					
Year Team	G	No.	Yds.	Avg.	Net avg.	In. 20	Blk.
1997—Carolina NFL	16	85	3604	42.4	36.4	29	0
1998—Carolina NFL	16	77	3131	40.7	38.1	20	0
1999—Carolina NFL	16	65	2562	39.4	36.7	18	0
2000—Carolina NFL	16	64	2459	38.4	33.8	19	†2
Pro totals (4 years)	64	291	11756	40.4	36.3	86	2

WALTERS, TROY — WR/KR — VIKINGS

PERSONAL: Born December 15, 1976, in College Station, Texas. ... 5-7/173.
HIGH SCHOOL: A&M Consolidated (College Station, Texas).
COLLEGE: Stanford.
TRANSACTIONS/CAREER NOTES: Selected by Minnesota Vikings in fifth round (165th pick overall) of 2000 NFL draft. ... Signed by Vikings (July 12, 2000).
CHAMPIONSHIP GAME EXPERIENCE: Played in NFC championship game (2000 season).
HONORS: Named wide receiver on THE SPORTING NEWS college All-America first team (1999). ... Fred Biletnikoff Award winner (1999).
PRO STATISTICS: 2000—Rushed once for three yards, caught one pass for five yards and recovered one fumble.
SINGLE GAME HIGHS (regular season): Receptions—1 (October 1, 2000, vs. Tampa Bay); yards—5 (October 1, 2000, vs. Tampa Bay); and touchdown receptions—0.

			PUNT RETURNS				KICKOFF RETURNS				TOTALS			
Year Team	G	GS	No.	Yds.	Avg.	TD	No.	Yds.	Avg.	TD	TD	2pt.	Pts.	Fum.
2000—Minnesota NFL	12	0	15	217	14.5	0	30	692	23.1	0	0	0	0	2

WALZ, ZACK — LB — CARDINALS

PERSONAL: Born February 3, 1976, in Mountain View, Calif. ... 6-4/229. ... Full name: Zachary Christian Walz.
HIGH SCHOOL: Saint Francis (San Jose, Calif.).
COLLEGE: Dartmouth (degree in government and economics, 1998).
TRANSACTIONS/CAREER NOTES: Selected by Arizona Cardinals in sixth round (158th pick overall) of 1998 NFL draft. ... Signed by Cardinals (June 4, 1998). ... On injured reserve with knee injury (November 17, 1999-remainder of season). ... On injured reserve with broken leg (November 24, 2000-remainder of season). ... Granted free agency (March 2, 2001). ... Re-signed by Cardinals (June 5, 2001).
PLAYING EXPERIENCE: Arizona NFL, 1998-2000. ... Games/Games started: 1998 (16/0), 1999 (9/9), 2000 (6/5). Total: 31/14.
PRO STATISTICS: 1998—Recovered one fumble. 1999—Credited with one sack. 2000—Intercepted one pass for no yards.

WARD, DEDRIC — WR/PR — DOLPHINS

PERSONAL: Born September 29, 1974, in Cedar Rapids, Iowa. ... 5-9/185. ... Full name: Dedric Lamar Ward. ... Name pronounced DEE-drick.
HIGH SCHOOL: Washington (Cedar Rapids, Iowa).
COLLEGE: Northern Iowa (degree in psychology).
TRANSACTIONS/CAREER NOTES: Selected by New York Jets in third round (88th pick overall) of 1997 NFL draft. ... Signed by Jets (July 17, 1997). ... Granted free agency (February 11, 2000). ... Re-signed by Jets (May 3, 2000). ... Granted unconditional free agency (March 2, 2001). ... Signed by Miami Dolphins (April 18, 2001).
CHAMPIONSHIP GAME EXPERIENCE: Played in AFC championship game (1998 season).
PRO STATISTICS: 1997—Rushed twice for 25 yards. 1998—Rushed twice for seven yards. 1999—Rushed once for minus one yard. 2000—Rushed four times for 23 yards.
SINGLE GAME HIGHS (regular season): Receptions—8 (December 24, 2000, vs. Baltimore); yards—147 (December 24, 2000, vs. Baltimore); and touchdown receptions—1 (December 24, 2000, vs. Baltimore).
STATISTICAL PLATEAUS: 100-yard receiving games: 1997 (1), 2000 (3). Total: 4.

			RECEIVING				PUNT RETURNS				KICKOFF RETURNS				TOTALS			
Year Team	G	GS	No.	Yds.	Avg.	TD	No.	Yds.	Avg.	TD	No.	Yds.	Avg.	TD	TD	2pt.	Pts.	Fum.
1997—New York Jets NFL	11	1	18	212	11.8	1	8	55	6.9	0	2	10	5.0	0	1	0	6	1
1998—New York Jets NFL	16	2	25	477	19.1	4	8	72	9.0	0	3	60	20.0	0	4	0	24	0
1999—New York Jets NFL	16	10	22	325	14.8	3	38	288	7.6	0	0	0	0.0	0	3	0	18	2
2000—New York Jets NFL	16	16	54	801	14.8	3	27	214	7.9	0	0	0	0.0	0	3	0	18	1
Pro totals (4 years)	59	29	119	1815	15.3	11	81	629	7.8	0	5	70	14.0	0	11	0	66	4

W

WARD, HINES — WR — STEELERS

PERSONAL: Born March 8, 1976, in Forest Park, Ga. ... 6-0/197. ... Full name: Hines Ward Jr.
HIGH SCHOOL: Forest Park (Ga.).
COLLEGE: Georgia.
TRANSACTIONS/CAREER NOTES: Selected by Pittsburgh Steelers in third round (92nd pick overall) of 1998 NFL draft. ... Signed by Steelers (July 20, 1998). ... Granted free agency (March 2, 2001).

PRO STATISTICS: 1998—Rushed once for 13 yards and attempted one pass with a completion for 17 yards. 1999—Rushed twice for minus two yards, returned one punt for two yards and returned one kickoff for 24 yards. 2000—Rushed four times for 53 yards, returned seven kickoffs for 186 yards and recovered one fumble.

SINGLE GAME HIGHS (regular season): Receptions—7 (November 28, 1999, vs. Cincinnati); yards—91 (October 15, 2000, vs. Cincinnati); and touchdown receptions—1 (November 26, 2000, vs. Cincinnati).

				RECEIVING				TOTALS		
Year Team	G	GS	No.	Yds.	Avg.	TD	TD	2pt.	Pts.	Fum.
1998—Pittsburgh NFL	16	0	15	246	16.4	0	0	0	0	0
1999—Pittsburgh NFL	16	14	61	638	10.5	7	7	†1	44	1
2000—Pittsburgh NFL	16	15	48	672	14.0	4	4	0	24	2
Pro totals (3 years)	48	29	124	1556	12.5	11	11	1	68	3

WARD, PHILLIP — LB

PERSONAL: Born November 11, 1974, in Gardena, Calif. ... 6-3/230.
HIGH SCHOOL: Pius X (Downey, Calif.).
COLLEGE: UCLA.
TRANSACTIONS/CAREER NOTES: Signed as non-drafted free agent by Indianapolis Colts (April 25, 1997). ... On injured reserve with leg injury (August 5-November 4, 1997). ... Released by Colts (November 4, 1997). ... Signed by Detroit Lions (March 26, 1998). ... Released by Lions (August 30, 1998). ... Signed by St. Louis Rams to practice squad (November 12, 1998). ... Activated (November 30, 1998). ... Assigned by Rams to Berlin Thunder in 1999 NFL Europe enhancement allocation program (February 22, 1999). ... Released by Rams (September 3, 1999). ... Signed by New Orleans Saints (April 7, 2000). ... Released by Saints (August 27, 2000). ... Re-signed by Saints to practice squad (August 29, 2000). ... Activated (December 3, 2000). ... Released by Saints (December 5, 2000). ... Re-signed by Saints (December 10, 2000). ... Released by Saints (December 12, 2000).
PLAYING EXPERIENCE: St. Louis NFL, 1998; New Orleans NFL, 2000. ... Games/Games started: 1998 (2/0), 2000 (2/0). Total: 4/0.

WARFIELD, ERIC — CB — CHIEFS

PERSONAL: Born March 3, 1976, in Vicksburg, Miss. ... 6-0/198. ... Full name: Eric Andrew Warfield.
HIGH SCHOOL: Arkansas (Texarkana, Ark.).
COLLEGE: Nebraska.
TRANSACTIONS/CAREER NOTES: Selected by Kansas City Chiefs in seventh round (216th pick overall) of 1998 NFL draft. ... Signed by Chiefs (May 27, 1998).
PLAYING EXPERIENCE: Kansas City NFL, 1998-2000. ... Games/Games started: 1998 (12/0), 1999 (16/1), 2000 (13/3). Total: 41/4.
PRO STATISTICS: 1999—Intercepted three passes for no yards.

WARNER, KURT — QB — RAMS

PERSONAL: Born June 22, 1971, in Burlington, Iowa. ... 6-2/220. ... Full name: Kurtis Eugene Warner.
HIGH SCHOOL: Regis (Cedar Rapids, Iowa).
COLLEGE: Northern Iowa (degree in communications).
TRANSACTIONS/CAREER NOTES: Signed as non-drafted free agent by Green Bay Packers (April 28, 1994). ... Released by Packers prior to 1994 season. ... Played for Iowa Barnstormers of Arena Football League (1995-97). ... Signed by St. Louis Rams (December 26, 1997). ... Assigned by Rams to Amsterdam Admirals in 1998 NFL Europe enhancement allocation program (February 18, 1998).
CHAMPIONSHIP GAME EXPERIENCE: Played in NFC championship game (1999 season). ... Member of Super Bowl championship team (1999 season).
HONORS: Named NFL Player of the Year by THE SPORTING NEWS (1999). ... Named quarterback on THE SPORTING NEWS NFL All-Pro team (1999). ... Named Most Valuable Player of Super Bowl XXXIV (1999 season). ... Played in Pro Bowl (1999 season). ... Named to play in Pro Bowl (2000 season); replaced by Donovan McNabb due to injury.
RECORDS: Shares NFL single-season record for most games with 300 or more yards passing—9 (1999). ... Shares NFL record for most consecutive games with 300 or more yards passing—6 (September 4-October 15, 2000).
POST SEASON RECORDS: Holds Super Bowl single-game record for most yards passing—414 (January 30, 2000, vs. Tennessee).
PRO STATISTICS: 1999—Fumbled nine times for minus four yards. 2000—Fumbled four times for minus eight yards.
SINGLE GAME HIGHS (regular season): Attempts—47 (September 10, 2000, vs. Seattle); completions—35 (September 10, 2000, vs. Seattle); yards—441 (September 4, 2000, vs. Denver); and touchdown passes—5 (October 10, 1999, vs. San Francisco).
STATISTICAL PLATEAUS: 300-yard passing games: 1999 (9), 2000 (8). Total: 17.
MISCELLANEOUS: Regular-season record as starting NFL quarterback: 21-6 (.778). ... Postseason record as starting NFL quarterback: 3-1 (.750).

					PASSING						RUSHING				TOTALS		
Year Team	G	GS	Att.	Cmp.	Pct.	Yds.	TD	Int.	Avg.	Rat.	Att.	Yds.	Avg.	TD	TD	2pt.	Pts.
1998—Amsterdam NFLE	10	...	326	165	50.6	2101	15	6	6.44	78.8	19	17	0.9	1	1	0	6
—St. Louis NFL	1	0	11	4	36.4	39	0	0	3.55	47.2	0	0	0.0	0	0	0	0
1999—St. Louis NFL	16	16	499	325	*65.1	4353	*41	13	*8.72	*109.2	23	92	4.0	1	1	0	6
2000—St. Louis NFL	11	11	347	235	*67.7	3429	21	18	*9.88	98.3	18	17	0.9	0	0	0	0
NFL Europe totals (1 year)	10	...	326	165	50.6	2101	15	6	6.44	78.8	19	17	0.9	1	1	0	6
NFL totals (3 years)	28	27	857	564	65.8	7821	62	31	9.13	104.0	41	109	2.7	1	1	0	6
Pro totals (4 years)	38	...	1183	729	61.6	9922	77	37	8.39	97.0	60	126	2.1	2	2	0	12

WARREN, CHRIS — RB

PERSONAL: Born January 24, 1968, in Silver Spring, Md. ... 6-2/227. ... Full name: Christopher Collins Warren Jr.
HIGH SCHOOL: Robinson Secondary (Fairfax, Va.).
COLLEGE: Virginia, then Ferrum, Va. (degree in psychology).
TRANSACTIONS/CAREER NOTES: Selected by Seattle Seahawks in fourth round (89th pick overall) of 1990 NFL draft. ... Signed by Seahawks (July 24, 1990). ... Granted free agency (March 1, 1993). ... Tendered offer sheet by New York Jets (April 23, 1993). ... Offer matched by

Seahawks (April 23, 1993). ... Released by Seahawks (March 13, 1998). ... Signed by Dallas Cowboys (April 13, 1998). ... Claimed on waivers by Philadelphia Eagles (December 7, 2000). ... Granted unconditional free agency (March 2, 2001).

HONORS: Played in Pro Bowl (1993-1995 seasons).

PRO STATISTICS: 1990—Fumbled three times and recovered one fumble. 1991—Fumbled three times and recovered one fumble. 1992—Fumbled twice and recovered two fumbles. 1993—Fumbled three times. 1994—Fumbled five times and recovered two fumbles. 1995—Fumbled five times and recovered two fumbles. 1996—Fumbled three times and recovered two fumbles for four yards. 1997—Fumbled twice. 1998—Recovered one fumble. 1999—Fumbled four times. 2000—Fumbled three times.

SINGLE GAME HIGHS (regular season): Attempts—36 (September 19, 1993, vs. New England); yards—185 (December 11, 1994, vs. Houston); and rushing touchdowns—3 (December 17, 1995, vs. Oakland).

STATISTICAL PLATEAUS: 100-yard rushing games: 1992 (3), 1993 (3), 1994 (7), 1995 (8), 1996 (3), 1998 (1). Total: 25.

MISCELLANEOUS: Holds Seattle Seahawks all-time record for most yards rushing (6,706).

			RUSHING				RECEIVING				PUNT RETURNS				KICKOFF RETURNS				TOTALS		
Year Team	G	GS	Att.	Yds.	Avg.	TD	No.	Yds.	Avg.	TD	No.	Yds.	Avg.	TD	No.	Yds.	Avg.	TD	TD	2pt.	Pts.
1990—Seattle NFL	16	0	6	11	1.8	1	0	0	0.0	0	28	269	9.6	0	23	478	20.8	0	1	0	6
1991—Seattle NFL	16	1	11	13	1.2	0	2	9	4.5	0	§32	298	9.3	▲1	32	792	24.8	0	1	0	6
1992—Seattle NFL	16	16	223	1017	4.6	3	16	134	8.4	0	34	252	7.4	0	28	524	18.7	0	3	0	18
1993—Seattle NFL	14	14	273	1072	3.9	7	15	99	6.6	0	0	0	0.0	0	0	0	0.0	0	7	0	42
1994—Seattle NFL	16	15	333	§1545	§4.6	9	41	323	7.9	2	0	0	0.0	0	0	0	0.0	0	11	1	68
1995—Seattle NFL	16	16	310	1346	4.3	§15	35	247	7.1	1	0	0	0.0	0	0	0	0.0	0	16	0	96
1996—Seattle NFL	14	14	203	855	4.2	5	40	273	6.8	0	0	0	0.0	0	0	0	0.0	0	5	1	32
1997—Seattle NFL	15	13	200	847	4.2	4	45	257	5.7	0	0	0	0.0	0	0	0	0.0	0	4	0	24
1998—Dallas NFL	9	0	59	291	4.9	4	13	66	5.1	1	2	11	5.5	0	5	90	18.0	0	5	0	30
1999—Dallas NFL	16	1	99	403	4.1	2	34	224	6.6	0	0	0	0.0	0	0	0	0.0	0	2	0	12
2000—Dallas NFL	13	0	59	254	4.3	2	31	302	9.7	1	0	0	0.0	0	0	0	0.0	0	3	0	18
—Philadelphia NFL	1	1	15	42	2.8	0	1	1	1.0	0	0	0	0.0	0	0	0	0.0	0	0	0	0
Pro totals (11 years)	162	91	1791	7696	4.3	52	273	1935	7.1	5	96	830	8.6	1	88	1884	21.4	0	58	2	352

WARREN, STEVE — DT — PACKERS

PERSONAL: Born January 22, 1978, in Lawton, Okla. ... 6-1/298. ... Full name: Steven Jerome Warren.

HIGH SCHOOL: Kickapoo (Springfield, Mo.).

COLLEGE: Nebraska.

TRANSACTIONS/CAREER NOTES: Selected by Green Bay Packers in third round (74th pick overall) of 2000 NFL draft. ... Signed by Packers (June 5, 2000).

PLAYING EXPERIENCE: Green Bay NFL, 2000. ... Games/Games started: 2000 (13/0).

WARRICK, PETER — WR — BENGALS

PERSONAL: Born June 19, 1977, in Bradenton, Fla. ... 5-11/195.

HIGH SCHOOL: Southeast (Bradenton, Fla.).

COLLEGE: Florida State.

TRANSACTIONS/CAREER NOTES: Selected by Cincinnati Bengals in first round (fourth pick overall) of 2000 NFL draft. ... Signed by Bengals (June 4, 2000).

HONORS: Named wide receiver on The Sporting News college All-America first team (1998 and 1999).

PRO STATISTICS: 2000—Recovered one fumble.

SINGLE GAME HIGHS (regular season): Receptions—7 (November 19, 2000, vs. New England); yards—80 (September 10, 2000, vs. Cleveland); and touchdown receptions—1 (December 24, 2000, vs. Philadelphia).

			RUSHING				RECEIVING				PUNT RETURNS				TOTALS			
Year Team	G	GS	Att.	Yds.	Avg.	TD	No.	Yds.	Avg.	TD	No.	Yds.	Avg.	TD	TD	2pt.	Pts.	Fum.
2000—Cincinnati NFL	16	16	16	148	9.3	2	51	592	11.6	4	7	123	17.6	1	7	0	42	2

WASHINGTON, DAMON — RB — GIANTS

PERSONAL: Born February 20, 1977, in Lockney, Texas. ... 5-11/193. ... Full name: Damon Keane Washington.

HIGH SCHOOL: Southwest (San Diego, Calif.).

COLLEGE: Colorado State.

TRANSACTIONS/CAREER NOTES: Signed as non-drafted free agent by Chicago Bears (April 23, 1999). ... Released by Bears (September 6, 1999). ... Re-signed by Bears to practice squad (October 20, 1999). ... Released by Bears (November 8, 1999). ... Signed by St. Louis Rams (April 25, 2000). ... Released by Rams (August 28, 2000). ... Signed by New York Giants to practice squad (September 12, 2000). ... Activated (November 22, 2000).

PLAYING EXPERIENCE: New York Giants NFL, 2000. ... Games/Games started: 2000 (3/0).

CHAMPIONSHIP GAME EXPERIENCE: Member of Giants for NFC Championship game (2000 season); inactive. ... Member of Giants for Super Bowl XXXV (2000 season); inactive.

W

WASHINGTON, DEWAYNE — CB — STEELERS

PERSONAL: Born December 27, 1972, in Durham, N.C. ... 6-0/193. ... Full name: Dewayne Neron Washington.

HIGH SCHOOL: Northern (Durham, N.C.).

COLLEGE: North Carolina State.

TRANSACTIONS/CAREER NOTES: Selected by Minnesota Vikings in first round (18th pick overall) of 1994 NFL draft. ... Signed by Vikings (July 14, 1994). ... Granted unconditional free agency (February 13, 1998). ... Signed by Pittsburgh Steelers (February 25, 1998).

HONORS: Was a high school All-America selection by The Sporting News (1989).

PRO STATISTICS: 1994—Recovered two fumbles for 17 yards and one touchdown. 1998—Recovered two fumbles.

Year Team	G	GS	INTERCEPTIONS			
			No.	Yds.	Avg.	TD
1994—Minnesota NFL	16	16	3	135	45.0	2
1995—Minnesota NFL	15	15	1	25	25.0	0
1996—Minnesota NFL	16	16	2	27	13.5	1
1997—Minnesota NFL	16	16	4	71	17.8	0
1998—Pittsburgh NFL	16	16	5	§178	35.6	▲2
1999—Pittsburgh NFL	16	16	4	1	0.3	0
2000—Pittsburgh NFL	16	16	5	59	11.8	0
Pro totals (7 years)	111	111	24	496	20.7	5

WASHINGTON, KEITH — DE — BRONCOS

PERSONAL: Born December 18, 1972, in Dallas. ... 6-4/275. ... Full name: Keith L. Washington.
HIGH SCHOOL: Wilmer-Hutchins (Dallas).
COLLEGE: UNLV.
TRANSACTIONS/CAREER NOTES: Signed as non-drafted free agent by Minnesota Vikings (April 9, 1995). ... Released by Vikings (August 27, 1995). ... Re-signed by Vikings to practice squad (August 28, 1995). ... Activated (October 9, 1995); did not play. ... On injured reserve with ankle injury (November 15, 1995-remainder of season). ... Released by Vikings (August 25, 1996). ... Signed by Detroit Lions (August 26, 1996). ... Released by Lions (August 26, 1997). ... Signed by Baltimore Ravens (October 15, 1997). ... Granted free agency (February 13, 1998). ... Re-signed by Ravens (April 14, 1998). ... Granted unconditional free agency (February 11, 2000). ... Re-signed by Ravens (March 31, 2000). ... Released by Ravens (March 13, 2001). ... Signed by Denver Broncos (April 6, 2001).
PLAYING EXPERIENCE: Detroit NFL, 1996; Baltimore NFL, 1997-2000. ... Games/Games started: 1996 (12/0), 1997 (10/1), 1998 (16/0), 1999 (16/0), 2000 (16/0). Total: 70/1.
CHAMPIONSHIP GAME EXPERIENCE: Played in AFC championship game (2000 season). ... Member of Super Bowl championship team (2000 season).
PRO STATISTICS: 1996—Returned one kickoff for 14 yards. 1997—Credited with two sacks. 1998—Credited with one sack. 1999—Returned one kickoff for 12 yards, credited with one sack, fumbled once and recovered one fumble. 2000—Returned one kickoff for 17 yards and recovered one fumble.

WASHINGTON, MARCUS — LB — COLTS

PERSONAL: Born October 17, 1977, in Auburn, Ala. ... 6-3/255. ... Full name: Marcus Cornelius Washington.
HIGH SCHOOL: Auburn (Ala.).
COLLEGE: Auburn.
TRANSACTIONS/CAREER NOTES: Selected by Indianapolis Colts in second round (59th pick overall) of 2000 NFL draft. ... Signed by Colts (July 13, 2000).
PRO STATISTICS: 2000—Intercepted one pass for one yard.

Year Team	G	GS	SACKS
2000—Indianapolis NFL	16	0	2.0

WASHINGTON, TED — DT — BEARS

PERSONAL: Born April 13, 1968, in Tampa. ... 6-5/330. ... Full name: Theodore Washington. ... Son of Ted Washington, linebacker with New York Jets (1973) and Houston Oilers (1974-82).
HIGH SCHOOL: Tampa Bay Vocational Tech Senior.
COLLEGE: Louisville.
TRANSACTIONS/CAREER NOTES: Selected by San Francisco 49ers in first round (25th pick overall) of 1991 NFL draft. ... Signed by 49ers (July 10, 1991). ... Traded by 49ers to Denver Broncos for fifth-round pick (traded to Green Bay) in 1994 draft (April 19, 1994). ... Granted unconditional free agency (February 17, 1995). ... Signed by Buffalo Bills (February 25, 1995). ... Designated by Bills as franchise player (February 13, 1998). ... Free agency status changed from franchise to transitional (February 27, 1998). ... Re-signed by Bills (March 2, 1998). ... Released by Bills (February 22, 2001). ... Signed by Chicago Bears (April 10, 2001).
CHAMPIONSHIP GAME EXPERIENCE: Played in NFC championship game (1992 and 1993 seasons).
HONORS: Played in Pro Bowl (1997, 1998 and 2000 seasons).
PRO STATISTICS: 1993—Recovered one fumble. 1994—Intercepted one pass for five yards. 1997—Recovered one fumble. 1998—Intercepted one pass for no yards and credited with a safety.

Year Team	G	GS	SACKS
1991—San Francisco NFL	16	0	1.0
1992—San Francisco NFL	16	6	2.0
1993—San Francisco NFL	12	12	3.0
1994—Denver NFL	15	15	2.5
1995—Buffalo NFL	16	15	2.5
1996—Buffalo NFL	16	16	3.5
1997—Buffalo NFL	16	16	4.0
1998—Buffalo NFL	16	16	4.5
1999—Buffalo NFL	16	16	2.5
2000—Buffalo NFL	16	16	2.5
Pro totals (10 years)	155	128	28.0

W

WASHINGTON, TODD — C/G — BUCCANEERS

PERSONAL: Born July 19, 1976, in Nassawadox, Va. ... 6-3/324. ... Full name: Todd Page Washington.
HIGH SCHOOL: Nandua (Onley, Va.).
COLLEGE: Virginia Tech (degree in physical education and health, 1998).
TRANSACTIONS/CAREER NOTES: Selected by Tampa Bay Buccaneers in fourth round (104th pick overall) of 1998 NFL draft. ... Signed by Buccaneers (June 11, 1998). ... Granted free agency (March 2, 2001).
PLAYING EXPERIENCE: Tampa Bay NFL, 1998-2000. ... Games/Games started: 1998 (4/0), 1999 (6/0), 2000 (10/0). Total: 20/0.
CHAMPIONSHIP GAME EXPERIENCE: Played in NFC championship game (1999 season).

WATERS, BRIAN — C — CHIEFS

PERSONAL: Born February 18, 1973, in Waxahachie, Texas. ... 6-3/293. ... Full name: Brian Demond Waters.
HIGH SCHOOL: Waxahachie (Texas).
COLLEGE: North Texas.
TRANSACTIONS/CAREER NOTES: Signed as non-drafted free agent by Dallas Cowboys (April 23, 1999). ... Released by Cowboys (September 5, 1999). ... Signed by Kansas City Chiefs (January 11, 2000).
PLAYING EXPERIENCE: Kansas City NFL, 2000. ... Games/Games started: 2000 (6/0).

WATSON, CHRIS — CB/PR/KR — BILLS

PERSONAL: Born June 30, 1977, in Chicago. ... 6-1/192.
HIGH SCHOOL: Leo (Chicago).
COLLEGE: Eastern Illinois.
TRANSACTIONS/CAREER NOTES: Selected by Denver Broncos in third round (67th pick overall) of 1999 NFL draft. ... Signed by Broncos (June 15, 1999). ... Traded by Broncos to Buffalo Bills for fourth-round pick (traded back to Buffalo) in 2001 draft (August 27, 2000).
PRO STATISTICS: 1999—Recovered three fumbles. 2000—Recovered two fumbles.

			PUNT RETURNS				KICKOFF RETURNS				TOTALS		
Year Team	G	GS	No.	Yds.	Avg.	TD	No.	Yds.	Avg.	TD	TD	2pt.	Pts.	Fum.
1999—Denver NFL	14	1	44	334	7.6	1	48	1138	23.7	0	1	0	6	5
2000—Buffalo NFL	16	4	33	163	4.9	0	44	894	20.3	0	0	0	0	4
Pro totals (2 years)	30	5	77	497	6.5	1	92	2032	22.1	0	1	0	6	9

WATSON, JUSTIN — RB/FB — RAMS

PERSONAL: Born January 7, 1975, in Bronx, N.Y. ... 6-0/220. ... Full name: Justin Sean Watson.
HIGH SCHOOL: Marshall (Pasadena, Calif.).
COLLEGE: San Diego State (degree in criminal justice).
TRANSACTIONS/CAREER NOTES: Signed as non-drafted free agent by San Diego Chargers (April 20, 1998). ... Released by Chargers (August 24, 1998). ... Re-signed by Chargers to practice squad (November 25, 1998). ... Assigned by Chargers to Berlin Thunder in 1999 NFL Europe enhancement allocation program (February 22, 1999). ... Released by Chargers (April 22, 1999). ... Signed by St. Louis Rams (July 1, 1999).
CHAMPIONSHIP GAME EXPERIENCE: Member of Rams for NFC championship game (1999 season); inactive. ... Member of Super Bowl championship team (1999 season); inactive.
SINGLE GAME HIGHS (regular season): Attempts—17 (November 12, 2000, vs. New York Giants); yards—102 (Ocotber 1, 2000, vs. San Diego); and rushing touchdowns—1 (December 10, 2000, vs. Minnesota).
STATISTICAL PLATEAUS: 100-yard rushing games: 2000 (1).

			RUSHING				RECEIVING				TOTALS		
Year Team	G	GS	Att.	Yds.	Avg.	TD	No.	Yds.	Avg.	TD	TD	2pt.	Pts.	Fum.
1998—San Diego NFL								Did not play.						
1999—Berlin NFLE	...	...	81	333	4.1	2	18	188	10.4	1	3	0	18	0
—St. Louis NFL	8	0	47	179	3.8	0	0	0	0.0	0	0	0	0	2
2000—St. Louis NFL	14	2	54	249	4.6	4	10	56	5.6	0	4	0	24	0
NFL Europe totals (1 year)	...	...	81	333	4.1	2	18	188	10.4	1	3	0	18	0
NFL totals (1 year)	22	2	101	428	4.2	4	10	56	5.6	0	4	0	24	2
Pro totals (2 years)	...	...	182	761	4.2	6	28	244	8.7	1	7	0	42	2

WATTERS, RICKY — RB — SEAHAWKS

PERSONAL: Born April 7, 1969, in Harrisburg, Pa. ... 6-1/217. ... Full name: Richard James Watters.
HIGH SCHOOL: Bishop McDevitt (Harrisburg, Pa.).
COLLEGE: Notre Dame (degree in design, 1990).
TRANSACTIONS/CAREER NOTES: Selected by San Francisco 49ers in second round (45th pick overall) of 1991 NFL draft. ... Signed by 49ers (July 11, 1991). ... On injured reserve with foot injury (August 27, 1991-entire season). ... Designated by 49ers as transition player (February 15, 1994). ... Tendered offer sheet by Philadelphia Eagles (March 18, 1995). ... 49ers declined to match offer (March 25, 1995). ... Granted unconditional free agency (February 13, 1998). ... Signed by Seattle Seahawks (March 4, 1998).
CHAMPIONSHIP GAME EXPERIENCE: Played in NFC championship game (1992-1994 seasons). ... Member of Super Bowl championship team (1994 season).
HONORS: Played in Pro Bowl (1992-1996 seasons).
POST SEASON RECORDS: Shares Super Bowl single-game records for most points—18; and most touchdowns—3 (January 29, 1995, vs. San Diego). ... Holds NFL postseason single-game records for most points—30; most touchdowns—5; and most rushing touchdowns—5 (January 15, 1994, vs. New York Giants).
PRO STATISTICS: 1992—Attempted one pass without a completion and recovered one fumble. 1993—Recovered one fumble. 1994—Recovered two fumbles. 1997—Recovered one fumble. 1998—Completed one pass for one yard and a touchdown and recovered one fumble. 2000—Recovered two fumbles.
SINGLE GAME HIGHS (regular season): Attempts—33 (December 10, 1995, vs. Dallas); yards—178 (December 20, 1998, vs. Indianapolis); rushing touchdowns—3 (December 5, 1993, vs. Cincinnati).
STATISTICAL PLATEAUS: 100-yard rushing games: 1992 (4), 1993 (3), 1994 (2), 1995 (4), 1996 (6), 1997 (2), 1998 (4), 1999 (4), 2000 (2). Total: 31. ... 100-yard receiving games: 1994 (1), 2000 (1). Total: 2.
MISCELLANEOUS: Active AFC leader for career rushing yards (10,325), rushing touchdowns (77) and touchdowns (90).

W

			RUSHING				RECEIVING				TOTALS			
Year Team	G	GS	Att.	Yds.	Avg.	TD	No.	Yds.	Avg.	TD	TD	2pt.	Pts.	Fum.
1991—San Francisco NFL								Did not play.						
1992—San Francisco NFL	14	13	206	1013	4.9	9	43	405	9.4	2	11	0	66	2
1993—San Francisco NFL	13	13	208	950	4.6	‡10	31	326	10.5	1	11	0	66	5
1994—San Francisco NFL	16	16	239	877	3.7	6	66	719	10.9	5	11	0	66	8
1995—Philadelphia NFL	16	16	337	1273	3.8	11	62	434	7.0	1	12	0	72	6
1996—Philadelphia NFL	16	16	*353	1411	4.0	13	51	444	8.7	0	13	0	78	5
1997—Philadelphia NFL	16	16	285	1110	3.9	7	48	440	9.2	0	7	0	42	3
1998—Seattle NFL	16	16	319	1239	3.9	9	52	373	7.2	0	9	1	56	4
1999—Seattle NFL	16	16	325	1210	3.7	5	40	387	9.7	2	7	0	42	4
2000—Seattle NFL	16	16	278	1242	4.5	7	63	613	9.7	2	9	0	54	5
Pro totals (9 years)	139	138	2550	10325	4.0	77	456	4141	9.1	13	90	1	542	42

WAYNE, NATE   LB   PACKERS

PERSONAL: Born January 12, 1975, in Chicago. ... 6-0/230.
HIGH SCHOOL: Noxubee County (Macon, Miss.).
COLLEGE: Mississippi.
TRANSACTIONS/CAREER NOTES: Selected by Denver Broncos in seventh round (219th pick overall) of 1998 NFL draft. ... Signed by Broncos (June 9, 1998). ... Assigned by Broncos to Barcelona Dragons in 1999 NFL Europe enhancement allocation program (February 22, 1999). ... Released by Broncos (September 19, 1999). ... Re-signed by Broncos to practice squad (September 21, 1999). ... Activated (September 22, 1999). ... Traded by Broncos to Green Bay Packers for conditional future draft pick (August 15, 2000).
PLAYING EXPERIENCE: Denver NFL, 1998 and 1999; Barcelona NFLE, 1999; Green Bay NFL, 2000. ... Games/Games started: 1998 (1/0), NFLE 1999 (games played unavailable); NFL 1999 (15/0), 2000 (16/13). Total NFL: 32/13.
CHAMPIONSHIP GAME EXPERIENCE: Member of Broncos for AFC championship game (1998 season); inactive. ... Member of Super Bowl championship team (1998 season); inactive.
PRO STATISTICS: NFLE: 1999—Intercepted one pass for 31 yards and credited with one sack. NFL: 1999—Credited with two sacks. 2000—Credited with two sacks and recovered one fumble for nine yards.

WEARY, FRED   CB   SAINTS

PERSONAL: Born April 12, 1974, in Jacksonville. ... 5-10/181. ... Full name: Joseph Fredrick Weary.
HIGH SCHOOL: Mandarin (Jacksonville).
COLLEGE: Florida.
TRANSACTIONS/CAREER NOTES: Selected by New Orleans Saints in fourth round (97th pick overall) of 1998 NFL draft. ... Signed by Saints (July 10, 1998). ... On injured reserve with knee injury (November 29, 2000-remainder of season). ... Granted free agency (March 2, 2001).
HONORS: Named cornerback on THE SPORTING NEWS college All-America first team (1997).
PRO STATISTICS: 1999—Recovered four fumbles for 60 yards. 2000—Credited with two sacks.

			INTERCEPTIONS			
Year Team	G	GS	No.	Yds.	Avg.	TD
1998—New Orleans NFL	14	1	2	64	32.0	1
1999—New Orleans NFL	16	11	2	49	24.5	0
2000—New Orleans NFL	12	12	2	27	13.5	0
Pro totals (3 years)	42	24	6	140	23.3	1

WEATHERS, ANDRE   CB   GIANTS

PERSONAL: Born August 6, 1976, in Flint, Mich. ... 6-0/190. ... Full name: Andre Le'Melle Weathers.
HIGH SCHOOL: Flint (Mich.) Central.
COLLEGE: Michigan.
TRANSACTIONS/CAREER NOTES: Selected by New York Giants in sixth round (205th pick overall) of 1999 NFL draft. ... Signed by Giants (July 27, 1999). ... On injured reserve with knee injury (November 27, 1999-remainder of season). ... On injured reserve with knee injury (November 2, 2000-remainder of season).
PLAYING EXPERIENCE: New York Giants NFL, 1999 and 2000. ... Games/Games started: 1999 (9/0), 2000 (1/0). Total: 10/0.
PRO STATISTICS: 1999—Intercepted one pass for eight yards and a touchdown and recovered one fumble.

WEAVER, JED   TE   DOLPHINS

W

PERSONAL: Born August 11, 1976, in Bend, Ore. ... 6-4/246. ... Full name: Timothy Jed Weaver. ... Cousin of Jeff Weaver, pitcher, Detroit Tigers.
HIGH SCHOOL: Redmond (Ore.).
COLLEGE: Oregon.
TRANSACTIONS/CAREER NOTES: Selected by Philadelphia Eagles in seventh round (208th pick overall) of 1999 NFL draft. ... Signed by Eagles (July 16, 1999). ... Claimed on waivers by Miami Dolphins (August 23, 2000).
PRO STATISTICS: 2000—Returned one kickoff for 15 yards.
SINGLE GAME HIGHS (regular season): Receptions—5 (December 24, 2000, vs. New England); yards—63 (December 24, 2000, vs. New England); and touchdown receptions—0.

			RECEIVING				TOTALS			
Year Team	G	GS	No.	Yds.	Avg.	TD	TD	2pt.	Pts.	Fum.
1999—Philadelphia NFL	16	10	11	91	8.3	0	0	†1	2	0
2000—Miami NFL	16	0	10	179	17.9	0	0	0	0	1
Pro totals (2 years)	32	10	21	270	12.9	0	0	1	2	1

WEBB, RICHMOND   OT   BENGALS

PERSONAL: Born January 11, 1967, in Dallas. ... 6-6/320. ... Full name: Richmond Jewel Webb Jr.
HIGH SCHOOL: Franklin D. Roosevelt (Dallas).
COLLEGE: Texas A&M (degree in industrial distribution).
TRANSACTIONS/CAREER NOTES: Selected by Miami Dolphins in first round (ninth pick overall) of 1990 NFL draft. ... Signed by Dolphins (July 27, 1990). ... Designated by Dolphins as franchise player (February 12, 1999). ... Designated by Dolphins as franchise player (February 11, 2000). ... Granted unconditional free agency (March 2, 2001). ... Signed by Cincinnati Bengals (April 30, 2001).
PLAYING EXPERIENCE: Miami NFL, 1990-2000. ... Games/Games started: 1990 (16/16), 1991 (14/14), 1992 (16/16), 1993 (16/16), 1994 (16/16), 1995 (16/16), 1996 (16/16), 1997 (16/16), 1998 (9/9), 1999 (15/14), 2000 (14/14). Total: 164/163.
CHAMPIONSHIP GAME EXPERIENCE: Played in AFC championship game (1992 season).
HONORS: Named NFL Rookie of the Year by THE SPORTING NEWS (1990). ... Played in Pro Bowl (1990-1996 seasons). ... Named offensive tackle on THE SPORTING NEWS NFL All-Pro team (1992 and 1994).
PRO STATISTICS: 1995—Recovered one fumble.

WEBSTER, JASON   CB   49ERS

PERSONAL: Born September 8, 1977, in Houston. ... 5-9/180.
HIGH SCHOOL: Willowridge (Houston).
COLLEGE: Texas A&M.
TRANSACTIONS/CAREER NOTES: Selected by San Francisco 49ers in second round (48th pick overall) of 2000 NFL draft. ... Signed by 49ers (July 18, 2000).
PRO STATISTICS: 2000—Recovered one fumble for one yard.

			INTERCEPTIONS			
Year Team	G	GS	No.	Yds.	Avg.	TD
2000—San Francisco NFL	16	10	2	78	39.0	1

WEBSTER, LARRY   DT   RAVENS

PERSONAL: Born January 18, 1969, in Elkton, Md. ... 6-5/288. ... Full name: Larry Melvin Webster Jr.
HIGH SCHOOL: Elkton (Md.).
COLLEGE: Maryland.
TRANSACTIONS/CAREER NOTES: Selected by Miami Dolphins in third round (70th pick overall) of 1992 NFL draft. ... Signed by Dolphins (July 10, 1992). ... Granted free agency (February 17, 1995). ... Signed by Cleveland Browns (May 4, 1995). ... On suspended list for violating league substance abuse policy (September 4-26, 1995). ... Browns franchise moved to Baltimore and renamed Ravens for 1996 season (March 11, 1996). ... On suspended list for violating league substance abuse policy (August 20, 1996-July 13, 1997). ... Granted unconditional free agency (February 13, 1998). ... Re-signed by Ravens (February 16, 1998). ... Granted unconditional free agency (February 11, 2000). ... Re-signed by Ravens (February 16, 2000). ... On suspended list for violating league substance abuse policy (April 11-November 18, 2000).
PLAYING EXPERIENCE: Miami NFL, 1992-1994; Cleveland NFL, 1995; Baltimore NFL, 1997-2000. ... Games/Games started: 1992 (16/0), 1993 (13/9), 1994 (16/7), 1995 (10/0), 1997 (16/3), 1998 (15/0), 1999 (16/16), 2000 (5/0). Total: 107/35.
CHAMPIONSHIP GAME EXPERIENCE: Played in AFC championship game (1992 and 2000 seasons). ... Member of Super Bowl championship team (2000 season).
PRO STATISTICS: 1992—Credited with 1 1/2 sacks. 1993—Recovered one fumble. 1999—Credited with two sacks. 2000—Recovered one fumble.

WEBSTER, NATE   LB   BUCCANEERS

PERSONAL: Born November 29, 1977, in Miami. ... 5-11/225. ... Full name: Nathaniel Webster Jr.
HIGH SCHOOL: Northwestern (Miami).
COLLEGE: Miami (Fla.).
TRANSACTIONS/CAREER NOTES: Selected after junior season by Tampa Bay Buccaneers in third round (90th pick overall) of 2000 NFL draft. ... Signed by Buccaneers (July 11, 2000).
PLAYING EXPERIENCE: Tampa Bay NFL, 2000. ... Games/Games started: 2000 (16/0).
HONORS: Named linebacker on THE SPORTING NEWS college All-America second team (1999).

WEDDERBURN, FLOYD   OT   SEAHAWKS

PERSONAL: Born May 5, 1976, in Kingston, Jamaica. ... 6-5/333. ... Full name: Floyd E. Wedderburn.
HIGH SCHOOL: Upper Darby (Drexel Hill, Pa.).
COLLEGE: Penn State.
TRANSACTIONS/CAREER NOTES: Selected by Seattle Seahawks in fifth round (140th pick overall) of 1999 NFL draft. ... Signed by Seahawks (July 29, 1999). ... Active for five games (1999); did not play.
PLAYING EXPERIENCE: Seattle NFL, 2000. ... Games/Games started: 2000 (16/16).

W

WEINER, TODD   OT   SEAHAWKS

PERSONAL: Born September 16, 1975, in Bristol, Pa. ... 6-4/300.
HIGH SCHOOL: Taravella (Coral Springs, Fla.).
COLLEGE: Kansas State.
TRANSACTIONS/CAREER NOTES: Selected by Seattle Seahawks in second round (47th pick overall) of 1998 NFL draft. ... Signed by Seahawks (July 15, 1998).
PLAYING EXPERIENCE: Seattle NFL, 1998-2000. ... Games/Games started: 1998 (6/0), 1999 (11/1), 2000 (16/6). Total: 33/7.
HONORS: Named offensive tackle on THE SPORTING NEWS college All-America second team (1997).

WELBOURN, JOHN   OT/G   EAGLES

PERSONAL: Born March 30, 1976, in Torrance, Calif. ... 6-5/318.
HIGH SCHOOL: Palos Verdes Peninsula (Rolling Hills Estate, Calif.).
COLLEGE: California (degree in rhetoric).
TRANSACTIONS/CAREER NOTES: Selected by Philadelphia Eagles in fourth round (97th pick overall) of 1999 NFL draft. ... Signed by Eagles (July 25, 1999). ... On injured reserve with knee injury (September 13, 1999-remainder of season).
PLAYING EXPERIENCE: Philadelphia NFL, 1999 and 2000. ... Games/Games started: 1999 (1/1), 2000 (16/16). Total: 17/17.
PRO STATISTICS: 2000—Recovered one fumble.

WELLS, DEAN   LB   PANTHERS

PERSONAL: Born July 20, 1970, in Louisville, Ky. ... 6-3/248. ... Full name: Donald Dean Wells.
HIGH SCHOOL: Holy Cross (Louisville, Ky.).
COLLEGE: Kentucky (degree in marketing, 1992).
TRANSACTIONS/CAREER NOTES: Selected by Seattle Seahawks in fourth round (85th pick overall) of 1993 NFL draft. ... Signed by Seahawks (July 13, 1993). ... Granted unconditional free agency (February 12, 1999). ... Signed by Carolina Panthers (April 7, 1999).
PLAYING EXPERIENCE: Seattle NFL, 1993-1998; Carolina NFL, 1999 and 2000. ... Games/Games started: 1993 (14/1), 1994 (15/0), 1995 (14/10), 1996 (16/15), 1997 (16/16), 1998 (9/8), 1999 (16/10), 2000 (16/14). Total: 116/74.
PRO STATISTICS: 1995—Recovered one fumble. 1996—Credited with one sack and recovered two fumbles. 1997—Credited with one sack and recovered one fumble. 1998—Intercepted one pass for 25 yards. 1999—Intercepted one pass for one yard and credited with ¹/₂ sack. 2000—Intercepted one pass for 14 yards.

WELLS, MIKE   DT   BEARS

PERSONAL: Born January 6, 1971, in Arnold, Mo. ... 6-3/315. ... Full name: Mike Allan Wells.
HIGH SCHOOL: Fox (Arnold, Mo.).
COLLEGE: Iowa (degree in communication studies, 1994).
TRANSACTIONS/CAREER NOTES: Selected by Minnesota Vikings in fourth round (125th pick overall) of 1994 NFL draft. ... Signed by Vikings (June 24, 1994). ... Released by Vikings (August 28, 1994). ... Signed by Detroit Lions (August 29, 1994). ... Granted free agency (February 14, 1997). ... Re-signed by Lions (June 2, 1997). ... Granted unconditional free agency (February 13, 1998). ... Signed by Chicago Bears (February 17, 1998).
PLAYING EXPERIENCE: Detroit NFL, 1994-1997; Chicago NFL, 1998-2000. ... Games/Games started: 1994 (4/0), 1995 (15/0), 1996 (16/1), 1997 (16/16), 1998 (16/16), 1999 (16/16), 2000 (16/14). Total: 99/63.
PRO STATISTICS: 1994—Credited with ¹/₂ sack. 1996—Recovered one fumble in end zone for a touchdown. 1997—Credited with one sack and recovered one fumble. 1998—Credited with three sacks. 1999—Credited with one sack and recovered one fumble. 2000—Credited with one sack, intercepted one pass for 21 yards and caught one pass for 13 yards.

WESLEY, GREG   S   CHIEFS

PERSONAL: Born March 19, 1976, in England, Ark. ... 6-2/208. ... Full name: Gregory Lashon Wesley.
HIGH SCHOOL: England (Ark.).
COLLEGE: Arkansas-Pine Bluff.
TRANSACTIONS/CAREER NOTES: Selected by Kansas City Chiefs in third round (85th pick overall) of 2000 NFL draft. ... Signed by Chiefs (June 6, 2000).
PRO STATISTICS: 2000—Recovered one fumble.

| | | | INTERCEPTIONS | | | | SACKS |
Year Team	G	GS	No.	Yds.	Avg.	TD	No.
2000—Kansas City NFL	16	16	2	28	14.0	0	1.0

WEST, LYLE   S

PERSONAL: Born December 20, 1976, in Columbus, Ga. ... 6-0/215.
HIGH SCHOOL: Washington (Fremont, Calif.).
JUNIOR COLLEGE: Chabot College (Calif.).
COLLEGE: San Jose State.
TRANSACTIONS/CAREER NOTES: Selected by New York Giants in sixth round (189th pick overall) of 1999 NFL draft. ... Signed by Giants (July 29, 1999). ... On suspended list for violating league substance abuse policy (November 23-December 20, 1999). ... Released by Giants (May 15, 2001).
PLAYING EXPERIENCE: New York Giants NFL, 1999 and 2000. ... Games/Games started: 1999 (6/0), 2000 (16/2). Total: 22/2.
CHAMPIONSHIP GAME EXPERIENCE: Played in NFC championship game (2000 season). ... Played in Super Bowl XXXV (2000 season).
PRO STATISTICS: 2000—Recovered one fumble.

WESTBROOK, BRYANT   CB   LIONS

PERSONAL: Born December 19, 1974, in Charlotte. ... 6-0/198. ... Full name: Bryant Antoine Westbrook.
HIGH SCHOOL: El Camino (Oceanside, Calif.).
COLLEGE: Texas.
TRANSACTIONS/CAREER NOTES: Selected by Detroit Lions in first round (fifth pick overall) of 1997 NFL draft. ... Signed by Lions (August 9, 1997). ... On injured reserve with Achilles' tendon injury (December 4, 2000-remainder of season).
PRO STATISTICS: 1999—Recovered one fumble.

W

Year Team	G	GS	INTERCEPTIONS No.	Yds.	Avg.	TD
1997—Detroit NFL	15	14	2	64	32.0	1
1998—Detroit NFL	16	16	3	49	16.3	1
1999—Detroit NFL	10	8	0	0	0.0	0
2000—Detroit NFL	13	13	6	126	21.0	1
Pro totals (4 years)	54	51	11	239	21.7	3

WESTBROOK, MICHAEL WR REDSKINS

PERSONAL: Born July 7, 1972, in Detroit. ... 6-3/220.
HIGH SCHOOL: Chadsey (Detroit).
COLLEGE: Colorado.
TRANSACTIONS/CAREER NOTES: Selected by Washington Redskins in first round (fourth pick overall) of 1995 NFL draft. ... Signed by Redskins (August 14, 1995). ... On injured reserve with neck injury (December 8, 1998-remainder of season). ... On injured reserve with knee injury (September 12, 2000-remainder of season).
HONORS: Named wide receiver on THE SPORTING NEWS college All-America first team (1994).
PRO STATISTICS: 1999—Recovered one fumble.
SINGLE GAME HIGHS (regular season): Receptions—10 (November 22, 1998, vs. Arizona); yards—159 (September 12, 1999, vs. Dallas); and touchdown receptions—3 (November 22, 1998, vs. Arizona).
STATISTICAL PLATEAUS: 100-yard receiving games: 1996 (1), 1997 (1), 1998 (4), 1999 (5). Total: 11.

Year Team	G	GS	RUSHING Att.	Yds.	Avg.	TD	RECEIVING No.	Yds.	Avg.	TD	TOTALS TD	2pt.	Pts.	Fum.
1995—Washington NFL	11	9	6	114	19.0	1	34	522	15.4	1	2	0	12	0
1996—Washington NFL	11	6	2	2	1.0	0	34	505	14.9	1	1	0	6	0
1997—Washington NFL	13	9	3	-11	-3.7	0	34	559	16.4	3	3	0	18	0
1998—Washington NFL	11	10	1	11	11.0	0	44	736	16.7	6	6	0	36	0
1999—Washington NFL	16	16	7	35	5.0	0	65	1191	18.3	9	9	†1	56	3
2000—Washington NFL	2	2	0	0	0.0	0	9	103	11.4	0	0	0	0	0
Pro totals (6 years)	64	52	19	151	7.9	1	220	3616	16.4	20	21	1	128	3

WETNIGHT, RYAN TE

PERSONAL: Born November 5, 1970, in Fresno, Calif. ... 6-2/236. ... Full name: Ryan Scott Wetnight.
HIGH SCHOOL: Hoover (Fresno, Calif.).
JUNIOR COLLEGE: Fresno (Calif.) City College.
COLLEGE: Stanford.
TRANSACTIONS/CAREER NOTES: Signed as non-drafted free agent by Chicago Bears (April 29, 1993). ... Released by Bears (October 10, 1993). ... Re-signed by Bears to practice squad (October 11, 1993). ... Activated (October 29, 1993). ... Released by Bears (October 7, 1994). ... Re-signed by Bears (October 10, 1994). ... On injured reserve with knee injury (December 7, 1995-remainder of season). ... Granted unconditional free agency (February 14, 1997). ... Re-signed by Bears (April 2, 1997). ... Granted unconditional free agency (February 13, 1998). ... Re-signed by Bears (February 23, 1998). ... Released by Bears (August 27, 2000). ... Signed by Green Bay Packers (September 30, 2000). ... Granted unconditional free agency (March 2, 2001).
PRO STATISTICS: 1997—Returned one kickoff for nine yards. 2000—Returned one kickoff for no yards.
SINGLE GAME HIGHS (regular season): Receptions—6 (October 3, 1999, vs. New Orleans); yards—70 (December 7, 1997, vs. Buffalo); and touchdown receptions—1 (October 31, 1999, vs. Washington).

Year Team	G	GS	RECEIVING No.	Yds.	Avg.	TD	TOTALS TD	2pt.	Pts.	Fum.
1993—Chicago NFL	10	1	9	93	10.3	1	1	0	6	0
1994—Chicago NFL	11	0	11	104	9.5	1	1	0	6	0
1995—Chicago NFL	12	2	24	193	8.0	2	2	0	12	0
1996—Chicago NFL	11	5	21	223	10.6	1	1	0	6	0
1997—Chicago NFL	16	3	46	464	10.1	1	1	0	6	1
1998—Chicago NFL	15	3	23	168	7.3	2	2	0	12	1
1999—Chicago NFL	16	4	38	277	7.3	1	1	0	6	0
2000—Green Bay NFL	10	0	3	20	6.7	0	0	0	0	0
Pro totals (8 years)	101	18	175	1542	8.8	9	9	0	54	2

WHALEN, JAMES TE COWBOYS

PERSONAL: Born December 11, 1977, in Portland, Ore. ... 6-2/228. ... Full name: James Patrick Whalen Jr.
HIGH SCHOOL: La Salle (Portland, Ore.).
JUNIOR COLLEGE: Shasta College (Calif.).
COLLEGE: Kentucky.
TRANSACTIONS/CAREER NOTES: Selected by Tampa Bay Buccaneers in fifth round (157th pick overall) of 2000 NFL draft. ... Signed by Buccaneers (July 10, 2000). ... Released by Buccaneers (August 27, 2000). ... Signed by Dallas Cowboys to practice squad (August 30, 2000). ... Activated (December 7, 2000). ... Assigned by Cowboys to Scottish Claymores in 2001 NFL Europe enhancement allocation program (February 19, 2001).
PLAYING EXPERIENCE: Dallas NFL, 2000. ... Games/Games started: 2000 (3/0).

W

WHEATLEY, AUSTIN TE SAINTS

PERSONAL: Born November 16, 1977, in Milan, Ill. ... 6-5/254.
HIGH SCHOOL: Rock Island (Ill.).
COLLEGE: Iowa.
TRANSACTIONS/CAREER NOTES: Selected by New Orleans Saints in fifth round (158th pick overall) of 2000 NFL draft. ... Signed by Saints (July 11, 2000).
PLAYING EXPERIENCE: New Orleans NFL, 2000. ... Games/Games started: 2000 (4/0).

WHEATLEY, TYRONE   RB   RAIDERS

PERSONAL: Born January 19, 1972, in Inkster, Mich. ... 6-0/235.
HIGH SCHOOL: Robichaud (Dearborn Heights, Mich.).
COLLEGE: Michigan.
TRANSACTIONS/CAREER NOTES: Selected by New York Giants in first round (17th pick overall) of 1995 NFL draft. ... Signed by Giants (August 9, 1995). ... Traded by Giants to Miami Dolphins for seventh-round pick (LB O.J. Childress) in 1999 draft (February 12, 1999). ... Released by Dolphins (August 3, 1999). ... Signed by Oakland Raiders (August 4, 1999).
CHAMPIONSHIP GAME EXPERIENCE: Played in AFC championship game (2000 season).
PRO STATISTICS: 1996—Completed only pass attempt for 24 yards and a touchdown and recovered one fumble for minus 18 yards. 1997—Recovered three fumbles. 1999—Recovered one fumble. 2000—Recovered one fumble.
SINGLE GAME HIGHS (regular season): Attempts—26 (December 16, 2000, vs. Seattle); yards—156 (October 22, 2000, vs. Seattle); and rushing touchdowns—2 (September 24, 2000, vs. Cleveland).
STATISTICAL PLATEAUS: 100-yard rushing games: 1997 (1), 1999 (2), 2000 (3). Total: 6.

				RUSHING				RECEIVING				KICKOFF RETURNS				TOTALS		
Year Team	G	GS	Att.	Yds.	Avg.	TD	No.	Yds.	Avg.	TD	No.	Yds.	Avg.	TD	TD	2pt.	Pts.	Fum.
1995—New York Giants NFL..	13	1	78	245	3.1	3	5	27	5.4	0	10	186	18.6	0	3	0	18	2
1996—New York Giants NFL..	14	0	112	400	3.6	1	12	51	4.3	2	23	503	21.9	0	3	0	18	6
1997—New York Giants NFL..	14	7	152	583	3.8	4	16	140	8.8	0	0	0	0.0	0	4	0	24	3
1998—New York Giants NFL..	5	0	14	52	3.7	0	0	0	0.0	0	1	16	16.0	0	0	0	0	0
1999—Oakland NFL..............	16	9	242	936	3.9	8	21	196	9.3	3	0	0	0.0	0	11	0	66	3
2000—Oakland NFL..............	14	13	232	1046	4.5	9	20	156	7.8	1	0	0	0.0	0	10	0	60	4
Pro totals (6 years)...............	76	30	830	3262	3.9	25	74	570	7.7	6	34	705	20.7	0	31	0	186	18

WHIGHAM, LARRY   S   BEARS

PERSONAL: Born June 23, 1972, in Hattiesburg, Miss. ... 6-2/210. ... Full name: Larry Jerome Whigham.
HIGH SCHOOL: Hattiesburg (Miss.).
COLLEGE: Northeast Louisiana (degree in criminal justice).
TRANSACTIONS/CAREER NOTES: Selected by Seattle Seahawks in fourth round (110th pick overall) of 1994 NFL draft. ... Signed by Seahawks (June 9, 1994). ... Released by Seahawks (August 28, 1994). ... Re-signed by Seahawks to practice squad (August 29, 1994). ... Signed by New England Patriots off Seahawks practice squad (September 13, 1994). ... Granted free agency (February 14, 1997). ... Re-signed by Patriots (May 1, 1997). ... Granted unconditional free agency (February 12, 1999). ... Re-signed by Patriots (April 14, 1999). ... Released by Patriots (March 13, 2001). ... Signed by Chicago Bears (April 18, 2001).
CHAMPIONSHIP GAME EXPERIENCE: Played in AFC championship game (1996 season). ... Played in Super Bowl XXXI (1996 season).
HONORS: Played in Pro Bowl (1997 season).
PRO STATISTICS: 1994—Fumbled once. 1995—Recovered one fumble. 1996—Recovered one fumble. 1997—Credited with two sacks. 1998—Returned one kickoff for no yards. 1999—Credited with three sacks.

			INTERCEPTIONS			
Year Team	G	GS	No.	Yds.	Avg.	TD
1994—New England NFL...	12	0	1	21	21.0	0
1995—New England NFL...	16	0	0	0	0.0	0
1996—New England NFL...	16	1	0	0	0.0	0
1997—New England NFL...	16	0	2	60	30.0	1
1998—New England NFL...	16	0	1	0	0.0	0
1999—New England NFL...	16	0	0	0	0.0	0
2000—New England NFL...	14	4	0	0	0.0	0
Pro totals (7 years)..	106	5	4	81	20.3	1

WHITE, CHRIS   DE   COWBOYS

PERSONAL: Born September 28, 1976, in Shreveport, La. ... 6-3/285. ... Full name: Christopher James White.
HIGH SCHOOL: Captain Shreve (Shreveport, La.).
COLLEGE: Southern (degree in animal science).
TRANSACTIONS/CAREER NOTES: Selected by Jacksonville Jaguars in seventh round (246th pick overall) of 1999 NFL draft. ... Signed by Jaguars (May 26, 1999). ... Released by Jaguars (September 5, 1999). ... Re-signed by Jaguars to practice squad (September 6, 1999). ... Activated (November 29, 1999); did not play. ... Claimed on waivers by Atlanta Falcons (August 24, 2000). ... Released by Falcons (August 28, 2000). ... Re-signed by Falcons to practice squad (August 30, 2000). ... Activated (September 19, 2000). ... Released by Falcons (November 14, 2000). ... Re-signed by Falcons to practice squad (November 16, 2000). ... Released by Falcons (December 1, 2000). ... Signed by Dallas Cowboys (December 14, 2000).
CHAMPIONSHIP GAME EXPERIENCE: Member of Jaguars for AFC championship game (1999 season); inactive.

Year Team	G	GS	SACKS
2000—Atlanta NFL...	5	0	0.0

WHITE, DEZ   WR   BEARS

PERSONAL: Born August 23, 1979, in Orange Park, Fla. ... 6-0/219. ... Full name: Edward Dezmon White. ... Nephew of Adrian White, defensive back with New York Giants (1987-89 and 1991), Green Bay Packers (1992) and New England Patriots (1993).
HIGH SCHOOL: The Bolles School (Jacksonville).
COLLEGE: Georgia Tech.
TRANSACTIONS/CAREER NOTES: Selected after junior season by Chicago Bears in third round (69th pick overall) of 2000 NFL draft. ... Signed by Bears (July 19, 2000).
SINGLE GAME HIGHS (regular season): Receptions—2 (December 24, 2000, vs. Detroit); yards—25 (October 15, 2000, vs. Minnesota); and touchdown receptions—1 (October 15, 2000, vs. Minnesota).

			RECEIVING				TOTALS			
Year Team	G	GS	No.	Yds.	Avg.	TD	TD	2pt.	Pts.	Fum.
2000—Chicago NFL...	15	0	10	87	8.7	1	1	0	6	1

W

WHITE, JAMEL   RB/KR   BROWNS

PERSONAL: Born February 11, 1977, in Los Angeles. ... 5-9/208.
HIGH SCHOOL: Palmdale (Calif.).
COLLEGE: South Dakota.
TRANSACTIONS/CAREER NOTES: Signed as non-drafted free agent by Indianapolis Colts (April 20, 2000). ... Released by Colts (August 27, 2000). ... Signed by Cleveland Browns (August 29, 2000).
SINGLE GAME HIGHS (regular season): Attempts—12 (November 12, 2000, vs. New England); yards—37 (November 12, 2000, vs. New England); and rushing touchdowns—0.

			RUSHING				RECEIVING				KICKOFF RETURNS				TOTALS		
Year Team	G	GS	Att.	Yds.	Avg.	TD	No.	Yds.	Avg.	TD	No.	Yds.	Avg.	TD	TD 2pt.	Pts.	Fum.
2000—Cleveland NFL	13	0	47	145	3.1	0	13	100	7.7	0	43	935	21.7	0	0 0	0	0

WHITE, REGGIE   DE

PERSONAL: Born December 19, 1961, in Chattanooga, Tenn. ... 6-5/304. ... Full name: Reginald Howard White.
HIGH SCHOOL: Howard (Chattanooga, Tenn.).
COLLEGE: Tennessee.
TRANSACTIONS/CAREER NOTES: Selected by Memphis Showboats in 1984 USFL territorial draft. ... Signed by Showboats (January 15, 1984). ... On developmental squad (March 9-24, 1984). ... Selected by Philadelphia Eagles in first round (fourth pick overall) of 1984 NFL supplemental draft. ... Released by Showboats (September 19, 1985). ... Signed by Eagles (September 21, 1985). ... Granted roster exemption (September 21-27, 1985). ... On reserve/did not report list (July 28-August 23, 1989). ... Designated by Eagles as franchise player (February 25, 1993). ... Signed by Green Bay Packers (April 6, 1993); Eagles received first-round pick (G Lester Holmes) in 1993 draft and first-round pick (traded to Cleveland) in 1994 draft as compensation. ... Announced retirement (April 19, 1998); decided to return for 1998 season. ... Announced retirement (January 6, 1999). ... Signed by Carolina Panthers (July 21, 2000). ... Announced retirement (March 1, 2001).
CHAMPIONSHIP GAME EXPERIENCE: Played in NFC championship game (1995-97 seasons). ... Member of Super Bowl championship team (1996 season). ... Played in Super Bowl XXXII (1997 season).
HONORS: Named defensive end on THE SPORTING NEWS college All-America first team (1983). ... Named defensive end on THE SPORTING NEWS USFL All-Star team (1985). ... Played in Pro Bowl (1986-1993, 1995-1998 seasons). ... Named Outstanding Player of Pro Bowl (1986 season). ... Named defensive end on THE SPORTING NEWS NFL All-Pro team (1987, 1988, 1991, 1993, 1995 and 1998). ... Named to play in Pro Bowl (1994 season); replaced by Wayne Martin due to injury.
RECORDS: Holds NFL career records for most sacks—198; and most seasons with 10 or more sacks—12.
POST SEASON RECORDS: Holds Super Bowl single-game record for most sacks (since 1982)—3 (January 26, 1997, vs. New England). ... Shares NFL postseason career record for most sacks—12. ... Shares NFL postseason single-game record for most safeties—1 (January 3, 1993, at New Orleans).
PRO STATISTICS: USFL: 1984—Recovered one fumble. 1985—Credited with one safety and recovered one fumble for 20 yards and a touchdown. NFL: 1985—Recovered two fumbles. 1987—Recovered one fumble for 70 yards and a touchdown. 1988—Recovered two fumbles. 1989—Recovered one fumble for 10 yards. 1990—Intercepted one pass for 33 yards and recovered one fumble. 1991—Intercepted one pass for no yards and recovered three fumbles for eight yards. 1992—Recovered one fumble for 37 yards and a touchdown. 1993—Recovered two fumbles for 10 yards. 1994—Recovered one fumble. 1996—Intercepted one pass for 46 yards, fumbled twice and recovered three fumbles for two yards. 1997—Recovered two fumbles. 2000—Recovered one fumble.
MISCELLANEOUS: Active NFL leader for career sacks (198.0). ... Holds Philadelphia Eagles all-time record for most sacks (124). ... Holds Green Bay Packers all-time record for most sacks (68.5).

Year Team	G	GS	SACKS
1984—Memphis USFL..........................	16	16	12.0
1985—Memphis USFL..........................	18	18	11.5
—Philadelphia NFL..........................	13	12	13.0
1986—Philadelphia NFL..........................	16	16	18.0
1987—Philadelphia NFL..........................	12	12	*21.0
1988—Philadelphia NFL..........................	16	16	*18.0
1989—Philadelphia NFL..........................	16	16	11.0
1990—Philadelphia NFL..........................	16	16	14.0
1991—Philadelphia NFL..........................	16	16	15.0
1992—Philadelphia NFL..........................	16	16	14.0
1993—Green Bay NFL..........................	16	16	‡13.0
1994—Green Bay NFL..........................	16	15	8.0
1995—Green Bay NFL..........................	15	13	12.0
1996—Green Bay NFL..........................	16	16	8.5
1997—Green Bay NFL..........................	16	16	11.0
1998—Green Bay NFL..........................	16	16	‡16.0
2000—Carolina NFL..........................	16	16	5.5
USFL totals (2 years).........................	34	34	23.5
NFL totals (15 years).........................	232	228	198.0
Pro totals (17 years).........................	266	262	221.5

WHITE, STEVE   DE   BUCCANEERS

PERSONAL: Born October 25, 1973, in Memphis, Tenn. ... 6-2/271. ... Full name: Stephen Gregory White.
HIGH SCHOOL: Westwood (Memphis, Tenn.).
COLLEGE: Tennessee (degree in psychology, 1996).
TRANSACTIONS/CAREER NOTES: Selected by Philadelphia Eagles in sixth round (194th pick overall) of 1996 NFL draft. ... Signed by Eagles (July 17, 1996). ... Released by Eagles (August 20, 1996). ... Signed by Tampa Bay Buccaneers to practice squad (August 27, 1996). ... Activated (October 15, 1996). ... Released by Buccaneers (November 9, 1996). ... Re-signed by Buccaneers (November 12, 1996).
PLAYING EXPERIENCE: Tampa Bay NFL, 1996-2000. ... Games/Games started: 1996 (4/0), 1997 (15/1), 1998 (16/0), 1999 (13/13), 2000 (15/0). Total: 63/14.
CHAMPIONSHIP GAME EXPERIENCE: Played in NFC championship game (1999 season).
PRO STATISTICS: 1997—Returned one kickoff for no yards. 1998—Credited with two sacks and recovered one fumble. 1999—Credited with two sacks and recovered one fumble. 2000—Credited with two sacks.

W

WHITEHEAD, WILLIE   DE   SAINTS

PERSONAL: Born January 26, 1973, in Tuskegee, Ala. ... 6-3/285. ... Full name: William Whitehead.
HIGH SCHOOL: Tuskegee (Ala.) Institute.
COLLEGE: Auburn.
TRANSACTIONS/CAREER NOTES: Signed as non-drafted free agent by San Francisco 49ers (April 26, 1995). ... Released by 49ers (July 16, 1995). ... Signed by Baltimore Stallions of CFL (August 1995). ... Signed by Montreal Alouettes of CFL to practice squad (1996). ... Signed by Hamilton Tiger-Cats of CFL (May 14, 1997). ... Signed by Detroit Lions (February 11, 1998). ... Released by Lions (August 25, 1998). ... Signed by New Orleans Saints (January 27, 1999). ... Assigned by Saints to Frankfurt Galaxy in 1999 NFL Europe enhancement allocation program (February 22, 1999).
PRO STATISTICS: 1997—Recovered one fumble.

Year Team	G	GS	SACKS
1995—Baltimore CFL	1	...	0.0
1996—Montreal CFL	Did not play.		
1997—Hamilton CFL	15	...	13.0
1999—Frankfurt NFLE	...	...	2.0
—New Orleans NFL	16	3	7.0
2000—New Orleans NFL	16	2	5.5
NFL Europe totals (1 year)	...	...	2.0
CFL totals (2 years)	16	...	13.0
NFL totals (2 years)	32	5	12.5
Pro totals (5 years)	...	...	27.5

WHITFIELD, BOB   OT   FALCONS

PERSONAL: Born October 18, 1971, in Carson, Calif. ... 6-5/310. ... Full name: Bob Whitfield Jr.
HIGH SCHOOL: Banning (Los Angeles).
COLLEGE: Stanford.
TRANSACTIONS/CAREER NOTES: Selected after junior season by Atlanta Falcons in first round (eighth pick overall) of 1992 NFL draft. ... Signed by Falcons (September 4, 1992). ... Granted roster exemption for one game (September 1992).
PLAYING EXPERIENCE: Atlanta NFL, 1992-2000. ... Games/Games started: 1992 (11/0), 1993 (16/16), 1994 (16/16), 1995 (16/16), 1996 (16/16), 1997 (16/16), 1998 (16/16), 1999 (16/16), 2000 (15/15). Total: 138/127.
CHAMPIONSHIP GAME EXPERIENCE: Played in NFC championship game (1998 season). ... Played in Super Bowl XXXIII (1998 season).
HONORS: Named offensive tackle on THE SPORTING NEWS college All-America first team (1991). ... Played in Pro Bowl (1998 season).
PRO STATISTICS: 1993—Recovered two fumbles. 1996—Recovered one fumble.

WHITING, BRANDON   DT/DE   EAGLES

PERSONAL: Born July 30, 1976, in Santa Rosa, Calif. ... 6-3/285. ... Name pronounced WHITE-ing.
HIGH SCHOOL: Polytechnic (Pasadena, Calif.).
COLLEGE: California.
TRANSACTIONS/CAREER NOTES: Selected by Philadelphia Eagles in fourth round (112th pick overall) of 1998 NFL draft. ... Signed by Eagles (July 14, 1998). ... Granted free agency (March 2, 2001). ... Re-signed by Eagles (March 20, 2001).
PRO STATISTICS: 1998—Recovered one fumble for 24 yards. 1999—Intercepted one pass for 22 yards and a touchdown and returned three kickoffs for 49 yards. 2000—Returned one kickoff for 18 yards and recovered two fumbles.

Year Team	G	GS	SACKS
1998—Philadelphia NFL	16	5	1.5
1999—Philadelphia NFL	13	2	1.0
2000—Philadelphia NFL	16	11	3.5
Pro totals (3 years)	45	18	6.0

WHITTED, ALVIS   WR   JAGUARS

PERSONAL: Born September 4, 1974, in Durham, N.C. ... 6-0/182. ... Full name: Alvis James Whitted.
HIGH SCHOOL: Orange (Hillsborough, N.C.).
COLLEGE: North Carolina State.
TRANSACTIONS/CAREER NOTES: Selected by Jacksonville Jaguars in seventh round (192nd pick overall) of 1998 NFL draft. ... Signed by Jaguars (May 19, 1998).
CHAMPIONSHIP GAME EXPERIENCE: Played in AFC championship game (1999 season).
PRO STATISTICS: 1998—Returned a blocked punt 24 yards for a touchdown. 1999—Returned eight kickoffs for 187 yards and one touchdown. 2000—Returned four kickoffs for 67 yards.
SINGLE GAME HIGHS (regular season): Receptions—4 (December 23, 2000, vs. New York Giants); yards—55 (October 29, 2000, vs. Dallas); and touchdown receptions—2 (October 29, 2000, vs. Dallas).

Year Team	G	GS	RUSHING				RECEIVING				TOTALS			
			Att.	Yds.	Avg.	TD	No.	Yds.	Avg.	TD	TD	2pt.	Pts.	Fum.
1998—Jacksonville NFL	16	0	3	13	4.3	0	2	61	30.5	0	1	0	6	0
1999—Jacksonville NFL	14	1	1	9	9.0	0	0	0	0.0	0	1	0	6	0
2000—Jacksonville NFL	16	3	0	0	0.0	0	13	137	10.5	3	3	0	18	1
Pro totals (3 years)	46	4	4	22	5.5	0	15	198	13.2	3	5	0	30	1

W

WHITTINGTON, BERNARD　　DE

PERSONAL: Born August 20, 1971, in St. Louis. ... 6-5/280. ... Full name: Bernard Maurice Whittington.
HIGH SCHOOL: Hazelwood East (St. Louis).
COLLEGE: Indiana (degree in sports management).
TRANSACTIONS/CAREER NOTES: Signed as non-drafted free agent by Indianapolis Colts (May 5, 1994). ... Granted free agency (February 14, 1997). ... Re-signed by Colts (June 13, 1997). ... Granted unconditional free agency (March 2, 2001).
CHAMPIONSHIP GAME EXPERIENCE: Played in AFC championship game (1995 season).
PRO STATISTICS: 1995—Recovered one fumble. 1998—Recovered two fumbles.

Year Team	G	GS	SACKS
1994—Indianapolis NFL	13	8	0.0
1995—Indianapolis NFL	16	13	2.0
1996—Indianapolis NFL	16	14	3.0
1997—Indianapolis NFL	15	6	0.0
1998—Indianapolis NFL	15	11	4.0
1999—Indianapolis NFL	15	15	1.0
2000—Indianapolis NFL	15	12	1.0
Pro totals (7 years)	105	79	11.0

WHITTLE, JASON　　G　　GIANTS

PERSONAL: Born March 7, 1975, in Springfield, Mo. ... 6-4/305.
HIGH SCHOOL: Camdenton (Mo.).
COLLEGE: Southwest Missouri State.
TRANSACTIONS/CAREER NOTES: Signed as non-drafted free agent by New York Giants (April 24, 1998). ... Released by Giants (August 30, 1998). ... Re-signed by Giants to practice squad (September 1, 1998). ... Activated (December 16, 1998).
PLAYING EXPERIENCE: New York Giants NFL, 1998-2000. ... Games/Games started: 1998 (1/0), 1999 (16/1), 2000 (16/2). Total: 33/3.
CHAMPIONSHIP GAME EXPERIENCE: Played in NFC championship game (2000 season). ... Played in Super Bowl XXXV (2000 season).

WIEGERT, ZACH　　OT　　JAGUARS

PERSONAL: Born August 16, 1972, in Fremont, Neb. ... 6-5/310. ... Full name: Zach Allen Wiegert. ... Name pronounced WEE-gert.
HIGH SCHOOL: Fremont (Neb.) Bergan.
COLLEGE: Nebraska.
TRANSACTIONS/CAREER NOTES: Selected by St. Louis Rams in second round (38th pick overall) of 1995 NFL draft. ... Signed by Rams (July 18, 1995). ... Granted free agency (February 13, 1998). ... Re-signed by Rams (June 17, 1998). ... Designated by Rams as transition player (February 12, 1999). ... Re-signed by Rams (March 24, 1999). ... Released by Rams (April 28, 1999). ... Signed by Jacksonville Jaguars (May 5, 1999). ... On injured reserve with knee injury (October 25, 2000-remainder of season).
PLAYING EXPERIENCE: St. Louis NFL, 1995-1998; Jacksonville NFL, 1999 and 2000. ... Games/Games started: 1995 (5/2), 1996 (16/16), 1997 (15/15), 1998 (13/13), 1999 (16/12), 2000 (8/8). Total: 73/66.
CHAMPIONSHIP GAME EXPERIENCE: Played in AFC championship game (1999 season).
HONORS: Outland Trophy Award winner (1994). ... Named offensive lineman on THE SPORTING NEWS college All-America first team (1994).
PRO STATISTICS: 1996—Recovered two fumbles. 1997—Caught one pass for one yard and recovered four fumbles for no yards and one touchdown. 1998—Recovered one fumble. 1999—Caught one pass for minus three yards and recovered one fumble. 2000—Recovered one fumble.

WIEGMANN, CASEY　　C　　CHIEFS

PERSONAL: Born July 20, 1975, in Parkersburg, Iowa. ... 6-3/285. ... Name pronounced WEG-man.
HIGH SCHOOL: Parkersburg (Iowa).
COLLEGE: Iowa.
TRANSACTIONS/CAREER NOTES: Signed as non-drafted free agent by Indianapolis Colts (April 26, 1996). ... Released by Colts (August 25, 1996). ... Re-signed by Colts to practice squad (August 27, 1996). ... Activated (September 10, 1996); did not play. ... Released by Colts (September 22, 1996). ... Re-signed by Colts to practice squad (September 23, 1996). ... Activated (October 15, 1996); did not play. ... Claimed on waivers by New York Jets (October 29, 1996). ... Released by Jets (September 21, 1997). ... Signed by Chicago Bears (September 24, 1997). ... Granted free agency (February 12, 1999). ... Tendered offer sheet by Miami Dolphins (April 5, 1999). ... Offer matched by Bears (April 8, 1999). ... Granted unconditional free agency (March 2, 2001). ... Signed by Kansas City Chiefs (March 15, 2001).
PLAYING EXPERIENCE: New York Jets (3)-Chicago (1) NFL, 1997; Chicago NFL, 1998-2000. ... Games/Games started: 1997 (NYJ-3/0; Chi.-1/0; Total: 4/0), 1998 (16/16), 1999 (16/0), 2000 (16/10). Total: 52/26.
PRO STATISTICS: 1998—Returned one kickoff for eight yards, fumbled once and recovered one fumble for minus three yards. 1999—Returned one kickoff for two yards. 2000—Recovered one fumble.

WIGGINS, JERMAINE　　TE　　PATRIOTS

PERSONAL: Born January 18, 1975, in East Boston, Mass. ... 6-2/255.
HIGH SCHOOL: East Boston.
COLLEGE: Georgia.
TRANSACTIONS/CAREER NOTES: Signed by New York Jets as non-drafted free agent (April 19, 1999). ... Released by Jets (August 23, 1999). ... Re-signed by Jets to practice squad (August 28, 1999). ... Claimed on waivers by New England Patriots (November 28, 2000). ...
PRO STATISTICS: 2000—Returned one kickoff for 12 yards and fumbled once.
SINGLE GAME HIGHS (regular season): Receptions—5 (December 4, 2000, vs. Kansas City); yards—81 (December 24, 2000, vs. Miami); and touchdown receptions—1 (December 4, 2000, vs. Kansas City).

				RECEIVING		
Year Team	G	GS	No.	Yds.	Avg.	TD
2000—New York Jets NFL	11	0	2	4	2.0	1
—New England NFL	4	2	16	203	12.7	1
Pro totals (1 years)	15	2	18	207	11.5	2

W

WILEY, CHUCK — DE — FALCONS

PERSONAL: Born March 6, 1975, in Baton Rouge, La. ... 6-5/277. ... Full name: Samuel Charles Wiley Jr. ... Cousin of Doug Williams, quarterback with Tampa Bay Buccaneers (1978-82), Oklahoma Outlaws of USFL (1984), Arizona Outlaws of USFL (1985) and Washington Redskins (1986-89).

HIGH SCHOOL: Southern University Lab (Baton Rouge, La.).

COLLEGE: Louisiana State (degree in pre-physical therapy).

TRANSACTIONS/CAREER NOTES: Selected by Carolina Panthers in third round (62nd pick overall) of 1998 NFL draft. ... Signed by Panthers (June 10, 1998). ... On injured reserve with heel injury (August 30, 1998-entire season). ... Claimed on waivers Atlanta Falcons (August 28, 2000).

PLAYING EXPERIENCE: Carolina NFL, 1999; Atlanta NFL, 2000. ... Games/Games started: 1999 (16/16), 2000 (16/0). Total: 32/16.

PRO STATISTICS: 2000—Credited with four sacks.

WILEY, MARCELLUS — DE — CHARGERS

PERSONAL: Born November 30, 1974, in Compton, Calif. ... 6-4/275. ... Full name: Marcellus Vernon Wiley.

HIGH SCHOOL: Santa Monica (Calif.).

COLLEGE: Columbia (degree in sociology, 1997).

TRANSACTIONS/CAREER NOTES: Selected by Buffalo Bills in second round (52nd pick overall) of 1997 NFL draft. ... Signed by Bills (June 20, 1997). ... Granted unconditional free agency (March 2, 2001). ... Signed by San Diego Chargers (March 4, 2001).

PRO STATISTICS: 1997—Returned one kickoff for 12 yards, fumbled once and recovered two fumbles for 40 yards. 1998—Recovered one fumble for 15 yards. 1999—Intercepted one pass for 52 yards. 2000—Recovered one fumble.

Year Team	G	GS	SACKS
1997—Buffalo NFL	16	0	0.0
1998—Buffalo NFL	16	3	3.5
1999—Buffalo NFL	16	1	5.0
2000—Buffalo NFL	16	15	10.5
Pro totals (4 years)	64	19	19.0

WILEY, MICHAEL — RB — COWBOYS

PERSONAL: Born January 5, 1978, in Spring Valley, Calif. ... 5-11/189.

HIGH SCHOOL: Monte Vista (Spring Valley, Calif.).

COLLEGE: Ohio State.

TRANSACTIONS/CAREER NOTES: Selected by Dallas Cowboys in fifth round (143rd pick overall) of 2000 NFL draft. ... Signed by Cowboys (July 14, 2000).

PRO STATISTICS: 2000—Recovered one fumble.

SINGLE GAME HIGHS (regular season): Attempts—11 (December 10, 2000, vs. Washington); yards—38 (December 10, 2000, vs. Washington); and rushing touchdowns—0.

			RUSHING				RECEIVING				KICKOFF RETURNS				TOTALS			
Year Team	G	GS	Att.	Yds.	Avg.	TD	No.	Yds.	Avg.	TD	No.	Yds.	Avg.	TD	TD	2pt.	Pts.	Fum.
2000—Dallas NFL	10	0	24	88	3.7	0	14	72	5.1	1	13	303	23.3	0	1	0	6	3

WILKINS, JEFF — K — RAMS

PERSONAL: Born April 19, 1972, in Youngstown, Ohio. ... 6-2/205. ... Full name: Jeff Allen Wilkins.

HIGH SCHOOL: Austintown Fitch (Youngstown, Ohio).

COLLEGE: Youngstown State (degree in communications, 1993).

TRANSACTIONS/CAREER NOTES: Signed as non-drafted free agent by Dallas Cowboys (April 28, 1994). ... Released by Cowboys (July 18, 1994). ... Signed by Philadelphia Eagles (November 14, 1994). ... Released by Eagles (August 14, 1995). ... Signed by San Francisco 49ers (November 8, 1995). ... Granted unconditional free agency (February 14, 1997). ... Signed by St. Louis Rams (March 6, 1997). ... Granted unconditional free agency (March 2, 2001). ... Re-signed by Rams (March 2, 2001).

CHAMPIONSHIP GAME EXPERIENCE: Played in NFC championship game (1999 season). ... Member of Super Bowl championship team (1999 season).

PRO STATISTICS: 1999—Punted twice for 57 yards.

		KICKING							
Year Team	G	XPM	XPA	FGM	FGA	Lg.		50+	Pts.
1994—Philadelphia NFL	6	0	0	0	0	0		0-0	0
1995—San Francisco NFL	7	27	29	12	13	40		0-0	63
1996—San Francisco NFL	16	40	40	30	34	49		0-0	130
1997—St. Louis NFL	16	32	32	25	∞37	52		2-2	107
1998—St. Louis NFL	16	25	26	20	26	‡57		3-6	§85
1999—St. Louis NFL	16	*64	*64	20	28	51		1-4	‡124
2000—St. Louis NFL	11	38	38	17	17	51		1-1	89
Pro totals (7 years)	88	226	229	124	155	57		7-13	598

WILKINS, TERRENCE — WR/KR — COLTS

PERSONAL: Born July 29, 1975, in Washington, D.C. ... 5-8/178. ... Full name: Terrence Olondo Wilkins.

HIGH SCHOOL: Bishop Denis J. O'Connell (Arlington, Va.).

COLLEGE: Virginia.

TRANSACTIONS/CAREER NOTES: Signed as non-drafted free agent by Indianapolis Colts (April 22, 1999).

PRO STATISTICS: 1999—Rushed once for two yards and recovered one fumble in end zone for a touchdown. 2000—Rushed three times for eight yards and recovered one fumble.

W

SINGLE GAME HIGHS (regular season): Receptions—9 (September 25, 2000, vs. Jacksonville); yards—148 (September 25, 2000, vs. Jacksonville); and touchdown receptions—1 (December 3, 2000, vs. New York Jets).
STATISTICAL PLATEAUS: 100-yard receiving games: 1999 (1), 2000 (2). Total: 3.

				RECEIVING				PUNT RETURNS				KICKOFF RETURNS				TOTALS		
Year Team	G	GS	No.	Yds.	Avg.	TD	No.	Yds.	Avg.	TD	No.	Yds.	Avg.	TD	TD	2pt.	Pts. Fum.
1999—Indianapolis NFL	16	11	42	565	13.5	4	41	388	9.5	1	51	1134	22.2	▲1	7	0	42	3
2000—Indianapolis NFL	14	7	43	569	13.2	3	29	240	8.3	0	15	279	18.6	0	3	0	18	4
Pro totals (2 years)	30	18	85	1134	13.3	7	70	628	9.0	1	66	1413	21.4	1	10	0	60	7

WILKINSON, DAN   DT   REDSKINS

PERSONAL: Born March 13, 1973, in Dayton, Ohio. ... 6-5/313. ... Nickname: Big Daddy.
HIGH SCHOOL: Paul L. Dunbar (Dayton, Ohio).
COLLEGE: Ohio State.
TRANSACTIONS/CAREER NOTES: Selected after sophomore season by Cincinnati Bengals in first round (first pick overall) of 1994 NFL draft. ... Signed by Bengals (May 5, 1994). ... Designated by Bengals as franchise player (February 11, 1998). ... Tendered offer sheet by Washington Redskins (February 25, 1998). ... Bengals declined to match offer (February 26, 1998); Bengals received first-(LB Brian Simmons) and third-round (G Mike Goff) picks as compensation.
HONORS: Named defensive lineman on THE SPORTING NEWS college All-America first team (1993).
PRO STATISTICS: 1996—Intercepted one pass for seven yards, fumbled once and recovered one fumble. 1998—Intercepted one pass for four yards and recovered one fumble. 1999—Intercepted one pass for 88 yards and a touchdown and recovered one fumble.

Year Team	G	GS	SACKS
1994—Cincinnati NFL	16	14	5.5
1995—Cincinnati NFL	14	14	8.0
1996—Cincinnati NFL	16	16	6.5
1997—Cincinnati NFL	15	15	5.0
1998—Washington NFL	16	16	7.5
1999—Washington NFL	16	16	8.0
2000—Washington NFL	16	16	3.5
Pro totals (7 years)	109	107	44.0

WILLIAMS, AENEAS   CB   RAMS

PERSONAL: Born January 29, 1968, in New Orleans. ... 5-11/200. ... Full name: Aeneas Demetrius Williams. ... Name pronounced uh-NEE-us.
HIGH SCHOOL: Fortier (New Orleans).
COLLEGE: Southern (degree in accounting, 1990).
TRANSACTIONS/CAREER NOTES: Selected by Phoenix Cardinals in third round (59th pick overall) of 1991 NFL draft. ... Signed by Cardinals (July 26, 1991). ... Granted free agency (February 17, 1994). ... Cardinals franchise renamed Arizona Cardinals for 1994 season. ... Re-signed by Cardinals (June 1, 1994). ... Granted unconditional free agency (February 16, 1996). ... Re-signed by Cardinals (February 27, 1996). ... Designated by Cardinals as franchise player (February 22, 2001). ... Re-signed by Cardinals (April 21, 2001). ... Traded by Cardinals to St. Louis Rams for second- (DB Michael Stone) and fourth-round (DT Marcus Bell) picks in 2001 draft (April 21, 2001).
HONORS: Named cornerback on THE SPORTING NEWS NFL All-Pro team (1995 and 1997). ... Played in Pro Bowl (1994-1999 seasons).
PRO STATISTICS: 1991—Fumbled once and recovered two fumbles for 10 yards. 1992—Recovered one fumble for 39 yards. 1993—Recovered two fumbles for 20 yards and a touchdown. 1994—Recovered one fumble. 1995—Fumbled once and recovered three fumbles. 1996—Credited with one sack and recovered one fumble. 1998—Credited with one sack. 1999—Recovered two fumbles. 2000—Recovered two fumbles for 104 yards and one touchdown.

				INTERCEPTIONS		
Year Team	G	GS	No.	Yds.	Avg.	TD
1991—Phoenix NFL..	16	15	∞6	60	10.0	0
1992—Phoenix NFL..	16	16	3	25	8.3	0
1993—Phoenix NFL..	16	16	2	87	43.5	1
1994—Arizona NFL	16	16	†9	89	9.9	0
1995—Arizona NFL	16	16	6	86	14.3	†2
1996—Arizona NFL	16	16	6	89	14.8	1
1997—Arizona NFL	16	16	6	95	15.8	∞2
1998—Arizona NFL	16	16	1	15	15.0	0
1999—Arizona NFL	16	16	2	5	2.5	0
2000—Arizona NFL	16	16	5	102	20.4	0
Pro totals (10 years)	160	159	46	653	14.2	6

WILLIAMS, BOBBIE   G   EAGLES

PERSONAL: Born September 25, 1976, in Jefferson, Texas. ... 6-3/320.
HIGH SCHOOL: Jefferson (Texas).
COLLEGE: Arkansas.
TRANSACTIONS/CAREER NOTES: Selected by Philadelphia Eagles in second round (61st pick overall) of 2000 NFL draft. ... Signed by Eagles (July 17, 2000). ... Inactive for all 16 games (2000).

WILLIAMS, BRIAN   LB

PERSONAL: Born December 17, 1972, in Dallas. ... 6-1/257. ... Full name: Brian Marcee Williams.
HIGH SCHOOL: Bishop Dunne (Dallas).
COLLEGE: Southern California (degree in public administration).
TRANSACTIONS/CAREER NOTES: Selected by Green Bay Packers in third round (73rd pick overall) of 1995 NFL draft. ... Signed by Packers (May 9, 1995). ... Granted free agency (February 13, 1998). ... Re-signed by Packers (February 17, 1998). ... On injured reserve with knee

injury (November 9, 1999-remainder of season). ... On injured reserve with knee injury (December 15, 2000-remainder of season). ... Released by Packers (February 23, 2001).

CHAMPIONSHIP GAME EXPERIENCE: Played in NFC championship game (1995-97 seasons). ... Member of Super Bowl championship team (1996 season). ... Played in Super Bowl XXXII (1997 season).

PRO STATISTICS: 1996—Recovered three fumbles. 1997—Intercepted two passes for 30 yards and recovered one fumble. 1999—Intercepted two passes for 60 yards and recovered one fumble. 2000—Recovered one fumble.

Year Team	G	GS	SACKS
1995—Green Bay NFL	13	0	0.0
1996—Green Bay NFL	16	16	0.5
1997—Green Bay NFL	16	16	1.0
1998—Green Bay NFL	16	15	2.0
1999—Green Bay NFL	7	7	2.0
2000—Green Bay NFL	4	3	0.5
Pro totals (6 years)	72	57	6.0

WILLIAMS, CHARLIE   CB

PERSONAL: Born February 2, 1972, in Detroit. ... 6-0/204.
HIGH SCHOOL: Henry Ford (Detroit).
COLLEGE: Bowling Green State.
TRANSACTIONS/CAREER NOTES: Selected by Dallas Cowboys in third round (92nd pick overall) of 1995 NFL draft. ... Signed by Cowboys (July 18, 1995). ... On physically unable to perform list with knee injury (July 18-November 8, 1996). ... Granted free agency (February 13, 1998). ... Re-signed by Cowboys (April 16, 1998). ... Granted unconditional free agency (February 11, 2000). ... Re-signed by Cowboys (May 1, 2000). ... Granted unconditional free agency (March 2, 2001).
PLAYING EXPERIENCE: Dallas NFL, 1995-2000. ... Games/Games started: 1995 (16/0), 1996 (7/0), 1997 (16/0), 1998 (15/3), 1999 (16/8), 2000 (11/0). Total: 81/11.
CHAMPIONSHIP GAME EXPERIENCE: Played in NFC championship game (1995 season). ... Member of Super Bowl championship team (1995 season).
PRO STATISTICS: 1996—Returned two kickoffs for 21 yards and fumbled once. 1997—Credited with two sacks. 1999—Recovered one fumble. 2000—Intercepted one pass for no yards.

WILLIAMS, CLARENCE   RB   CARDINALS

PERSONAL: Born May 16, 1977, in Detroit ... 5-9/193.
HIGH SCHOOL: Cass Tech (Detroit).
COLLEGE: Michigan.
TRANSACTIONS/CAREER NOTES: Signed as non-drafted free agent by Arizona Cardinals (April 23, 1999). ... Released by Cardinals (September 4, 1999). ... Re-signed by Cardinals to practice squad (September 7, 1999). ... Released by Cardinals (August 28, 2000). ... Re-signed by Cardinals to practice squad (August 29, 2000). ... Activated (November 24, 2000).
PLAYING EXPERIENCE: Arizona NFL, 2000. ... Games/Games started: 2000 (2/0).
PRO STATISTICS: 2000—Caught one pass for five yards.

WILLIAMS, DAN   DT   CHIEFS

PERSONAL: Born December 15, 1969, in Ypsilanti, Mich. ... 6-4/288. ... Full name: Daniel Williams II. ... Brother of Lamanzer Williams, defensive end, Kansas City Chiefs.
HIGH SCHOOL: Willow Run (Ypsilanti, Mich.).
COLLEGE: Tennessee State, then Toledo.
TRANSACTIONS/CAREER NOTES: Selected by Denver Broncos in first round (11th pick overall) of 1993 NFL draft. ... Signed by Broncos (July 19, 1993). ... On injured reserve with knee injury (December 19, 1995-remainder of season). ... Released by Broncos (July 18, 1997). ... Signed by Kansas City Chiefs (July 24, 1997). ... Designated by Chiefs as franchise player (February 13, 1998). ... Sat out 1998 season due to contract dispute. ... Granted unconditional free agency (February 12, 1999). ... Re-signed by Chiefs (February 16, 1999).
PRO STATISTICS: 1993—Recovered one fumble. 1994—Intercepted one pass for minus three yards. 1996—Recovered one fumble. 1997—Recovered two fumbles for two yards. 1999—Recovered two fumbles. 2000—Fumbled once and recovered one fumble for nine yards.

Year Team	G	GS	SACKS
1993—Denver NFL	13	11	1.0
1994—Denver NFL	12	7	0.0
1995—Denver NFL	6	6	2.0
1996—Denver NFL	15	15	1.0
1997—Kansas City NFL	15	6	10.5
1998—Kansas City NFL	Did not play.		
1999—Kansas City NFL	14	9	5.0
2000—Kansas City NFL	12	10	7.5
Pro totals (7 years)	87	64	27.0

W

WILLIAMS, DARRYL   S   BENGALS

PERSONAL: Born January 8, 1970, in Miami. ... 6-0/202. ... Full name: Darryl Edwin Williams.
HIGH SCHOOL: American (Hialeah, Fla.).
COLLEGE: Miami (Fla.).
TRANSACTIONS/CAREER NOTES: Selected after junior season by Cincinnati Bengals in first round (28th pick overall) of 1992 NFL draft. ... Signed by Bengals (July 25, 1992). ... Designated by Bengals as transition player (February 15, 1994). ... Free agency status changed by

Bengals from transitional to unconditional (February 16, 1996). ... Signed by Seattle Seahawks (February 21, 1996). ... Released by Seahawks (March 1, 2000). ... Signed by Bengals (March 6, 2000).
HONORS: Named defensive back on THE SPORTING NEWS college All-America second team (1991). ... Played in Pro Bowl (1997 season).
RECORDS: Shares NFL single-game record for most opponents' fumbles recovered—3 (October 4, 1998, vs. Kansas City).
PRO STATISTICS: 1992—Recovered one fumble. 1993—Recovered two fumbles. 1994—Returned one punt for four yards and recovered two fumbles. 1995—Recovered three fumbles. 1996—Recovered one fumble for two yards. 1997—Recovered one fumble. 1998—Recovered three fumbles. 1999—Recovered one fumble.

| Year Team | G | GS | INTERCEPTIONS | | | | SACKS |
			No.	Yds.	Avg.	TD	No.
1992—Cincinnati NFL	16	12	4	65	16.3	0	2.0
1993—Cincinnati NFL	16	16	2	126	63.0	▲1	2.0
1994—Cincinnati NFL	16	16	2	45	22.5	0	1.0
1995—Cincinnati NFL	16	16	1	1	1.0	0	1.0
1996—Seattle NFL	16	16	5	148	29.6	1	0.0
1997—Seattle NFL	16	16	▲8	172	21.5	1	0.0
1998—Seattle NFL	16	16	3	41	13.7	0	0.0
1999—Seattle NFL	13	12	4	41	10.3	0	0.0
2000—Cincinnati NFL	16	16	1	36	36.0	1	0.0
Pro totals (9 years)	141	136	30	675	22.5	4	6.0

WILLIAMS, ELIJAH   CB   FALCONS

PERSONAL: Born August 20, 1975, in Milton, Fla. ... 5-10/180. ... Full name: Elijah Elgebra Williams.
HIGH SCHOOL: Milton (Fla.).
COLLEGE: Florida.
TRANSACTIONS/CAREER NOTES: Selected by Atlanta Falcons in sixth round (166th pick overall) of 1998 NFL draft. ... Signed by Falcons (June 11, 1998). ... Granted free agency (March 2, 2001). ... Re-signed by Falcons (April 16, 2001).
PLAYING EXPERIENCE: Atlanta NFL, 1998-2000. ... Games/Games started: 1998 (15/0), 1999 (15/2), 2000 (15/3). Total: 45/5.
CHAMPIONSHIP GAME EXPERIENCE: Played in NFC championship game (1998 season). ... Played in Super Bowl XXXIII (1998 season).
PRO STATISTICS: 1998—Rushed twice for minus two yards and returned seven kickoffs for 132 yards. 1999—Returned three kickoffs for 37 yards. 2000—Intercepted one pass for one yard and returned two kickoffs for 34 yards.

WILLIAMS, ERIK   OT   COWBOYS

PERSONAL: Born September 7, 1968, in Philadelphia. ... 6-6/311. ... Full name: Erik George Williams.
HIGH SCHOOL: John Bartram (Philadelphia).
COLLEGE: Central State (Ohio).
TRANSACTIONS/CAREER NOTES: Selected by Dallas Cowboys in third round (70th pick overall) of 1991 NFL draft. ... Signed by Cowboys (July 14, 1991). ... Designated by Cowboys as transition player (February 15, 1994). ... On non-football injury list with knee injury suffered in automobile accident (November 21, 1994-remainder of season).
PLAYING EXPERIENCE: Dallas NFL, 1991-2000. ... Games/Games started: 1991 (11/3), 1992 (16/16), 1993 (16/16), 1994 (7/7), 1995 (15/15), 1996 (16/16), 1997 (15/15), 1998 (15/15), 1999 (14/14), 2000 (16/16). Total: 141/133.
CHAMPIONSHIP GAME EXPERIENCE: Played in NFC championship game (1992, 1993 and 1995 seasons). ... Member of Super Bowl championship team (1992, 1993 and 1995 seasons).
HONORS: Named offensive tackle on THE SPORTING NEWS NFL All-Pro team (1993 and 1995). ... Played in Pro Bowl (1993, 1996, 1997 and 1999 seasons).
PRO STATISTICS: 1991—Recovered one fumble.

WILLIAMS, GEORGE   DT

PERSONAL: Born December 8, 1975, in Roseboro, N.C. ... 6-3/298.
HIGH SCHOOL: Rosewood (Goldsboro, N.C.).
COLLEGE: North Carolina State.
TRANSACTIONS/CAREER NOTES: Signed as non-drafted free agent by New York Giants (April 24, 1998). ... Released by Giants (February 19, 2001).
PLAYING EXPERIENCE: New York Giants NFL, 1998-2000. ... Games/Games started: 1998 (2/0), 1999 (16/0), 2000 (13/0). Total: 31/0.
CHAMPIONSHIP GAME EXPERIENCE: Member of Giants for NFC championship game (2000 season); inactive. ... Member of Giants for Super Bowl XXXV (2000 season); inactive.
PRO STATISTICS: 2000—Recovered one fumble.

W

WILLIAMS, GRANT   OT   PATRIOTS

PERSONAL: Born May 10, 1974, in Hattiesburg, Miss. ... 6-7/325.
HIGH SCHOOL: Clinton (Miss.).
JUNIOR COLLEGE: Hinds Community College (Miss.).
COLLEGE: Louisiana Tech (degree in biology, 1995).
TRANSACTIONS/CAREER NOTES: Signed as non-drafted free agent by Seattle Seahawks (April 22, 1996). ... Granted unconditional free agency (February 11, 2000). ... Signed by New England Patriots (March 17, 2000).
PLAYING EXPERIENCE: Seattle NFL, 1996-1999; New England NFL, 2000. ... Games/Games started: 1996 (8/0), 1997 (16/8), 1998 (16/0), 1999 (16/15), 2000 (15/8). Total: 71/31.
PRO STATISTICS: 1997—Recovered two fumbles.

WILLIAMS, JAMAL   DT   CHARGERS

PERSONAL: Born April 28, 1976, in Washington, D.C. ... 6-3/305.
HIGH SCHOOL: Archbishop Carroll (Washington, D.C.).
COLLEGE: Oklahoma State.
TRANSACTIONS/CAREER NOTES: Selected by San Diego Chargers in second round of 1998 supplemental draft (July 9, 1998). ... Signed by Chargers (August 7, 1998). ... Granted free agency (March 2, 2001). ... Re-signed by Chargers (May 11, 2001).
PLAYING EXPERIENCE: San Diego NFL, 1998-2000. ... Games/Games started: 1998 (9/0), 1999 (16/2), 2000 (16/16). Total: 41/18.
PRO STATISTICS: 1998—Intercepted one pass for 14 yards and a touchdown. 1999—Credited with one sack. 2000—Credited with one sack.

WILLIAMS, JAMES   OT   BEARS

PERSONAL: Born March 29, 1968, in Pittsburgh. ... 6-7/331. ... Full name: James Otis Williams.
HIGH SCHOOL: Allderdice (Pittsburgh).
COLLEGE: Cheyney (Pa.) State.
TRANSACTIONS/CAREER NOTES: Signed as non-drafted free agent by Chicago Bears (April 25, 1991). ... Granted free agency (February 16, 1996). ... Re-signed by Bears (March 15, 1996).
PLAYING EXPERIENCE: Chicago NFL, 1991-2000. ... Games/Games started: 1991 (14/0), 1992 (5/0), 1993 (3/0), 1994 (16/15), 1995 (16/16), 1996 (16/16), 1997 (16/16), 1998 (16/16), 1999 (16/16), 2000 (16/16). Total: 134/111.
PRO STATISTICS: 1991—Credited with one sack. 1996—Recovered two fumbles. 2000—Recovered one fumble.
MISCELLANEOUS: Switched from defensive line to offensive line during the 1992 season.

WILLIAMS, JAMES   WR   SEAHAWKS

PERSONAL: Born March 6, 1978, in Raymond, Miss. ... 5-10/180.
HIGH SCHOOL: Warren Central (Vicksburg, Miss.).
JUNIOR COLLEGE: Hinds Community College (Miss.).
COLLEGE: Marshall.
TRANSACTIONS/CAREER NOTES: Selected by Seattle Seahawks in sixth round (175th pick overall) of 2000 NFL draft. ... Signed by Seahawks (June 22, 2000).
PLAYING EXPERIENCE: Seattle NFL, 2000. ... Games/Games started: 2000 (10/0).
PRO STATISTICS: 2000—Rushed once for minus five yards, caught eight passes for 99 yards, returned three kickoffs for 76 yards and credited with one safety.
SINGLE GAME HIGHS (regular season): Receptions—2 (December 3, 2000, vs. Atlanta); yards—31 (October 15, 2000, vs. Indianapolis); and touchdown receptions—0.

WILLIAMS, JAY   DE   PANTHERS

PERSONAL: Born October 13, 1971, in Washington, D.C. ... 6-3/280. ... Full name: Jay Omar Williams.
HIGH SCHOOL: St. John's (Washington, D.C.).
COLLEGE: Wake Forest.
TRANSACTIONS/CAREER NOTES: Signed as non-drafted free agent by Miami Dolphins (April 28, 1994). ... Released by Dolphins (August 28, 1994). ... Signed by Los Angeles Rams to practice squad (September 27, 1994). ... Activated (December 7, 1994); did not play. ... Rams franchise moved from Los Angeles to St. Louis (April 12, 1995). ... On physically unable to perform list with forearm injury (July 31-November 18, 1996). ... Released by Rams (November 20, 1996). ... Re-signed by Rams (December 11, 1996). ... Granted free agency (February 12, 1999). ... Re-signed by Rams (May 4, 1999). ... Granted unconditional free agency (February 11, 2000). ... Signed by Carolina Panthers (February 16, 2000).
CHAMPIONSHIP GAME EXPERIENCE: Played in NFC championship game (1999 season). ... Member of Super Bowl championship team (1999 season).
PRO STATISTICS: 1997—Returned one kickoff for 10 yards.

Year Team	G	GS	SACKS
1994—Los Angeles Rams NFL	Did not play.		
1995—St. Louis NFL	6	0	0.0
1996—St. Louis NFL	2	0	0.0
1997—St. Louis NFL	16	2	1.0
1998—St. Louis NFL	16	1	1.0
1999—St. Louis NFL	16	0	4.0
2000—Carolina NFL	16	14	6.0
Pro totals (6 years)	72	17	12.0

WILLIAMS, JERMAINE   RB

PERSONAL: Born August 14, 1973, in Greenville, N.C. ... 6-0/235.
HIGH SCHOOL: J.H. Rose (Greenville, N.C.).
JUNIOR COLLEGE: Butler County Community College (Kan.).
COLLEGE: Houston.
TRANSACTIONS/CAREER NOTES: Signed as non-drafted free agent by Tampa Bay Buccaneers (April 25, 1997). ... Released by Buccaneers (August 4, 1997). ... Signed by Oakland Raiders (April 25, 1998). ... Released by Raiders (September 1, 1998). ... Re-signed by Raiders to practice squad (September 2, 1998). ... Activated (October 24, 1998). ... Released by Raiders August 22, 2000). ... Signed by Jacksonville Jaguars (October 31, 2000). ... Released by Jaguars (February 19, 2001).
PLAYING EXPERIENCE: Oakland NFL, 1998 and 1999; Jacksonville NFL, 2000. ... Games/Games started: 1998 (10/0), 1999 (15/0), 2000 (7/0). Total: 32/0.
PRO STATISTICS: 1999—Caught one pass for 20 yards. 2000—Rushed two times for eight yards and returned two kickoffs for 50 yards.
SINGLE GAME HIGHS (regular season): Attempts—2 (December 10, 2000, vs. Arizona); yards—8 (December 10, 2000, vs. Arizona); and rushing touchdowns—0.

W

WILLIAMS, JOSH DT COLTS

PERSONAL: Born August 9, 1976, in Denver. ... 6-3/284. ... Full name: Josh Sinclair Williams.
HIGH SCHOOL: Cypress Creek (Houston).
COLLEGE: Michigan.
TRANSACTIONS/CAREER NOTES: Selected by Indianapolis Colts in fourth round (122nd pick overall) of 2000 NFL draft. ... Signed by Colts (June 27, 2000).
PRO STATISTICS: 2000—Credited with one safety and recovered one fumble.

Year Team	G	GS	SACKS
2000—Indianapolis NFL	14	7	3.0

WILLIAMS, K.D. LB PACKERS

PERSONAL: Born April 21, 1973, in Tampa. ... 6-0/235. ... Full name: Kevin Williams. ... Cousin of Juran Bolden, cornerback with four NFL teams (1996-99).
HIGH SCHOOL: Jefferson (Tampa).
JUNIOR COLLEGE: Arizona West Junior College.
COLLEGE: Henderson State (Ark.).
TRANSACTIONS/CAREER NOTES: Signed by Winnipeg Blue Bombers of CFL (January 6, 1995). ... Traded by Blue Bombers of CFL with S Jason Mallett and DE Horace Morris to Sasketchewan Roughriders of CFL for LB Sheldon Benoit, CB Nick Ferguson and G John James (May 5, 1997). ... Traded by Roughriders of CFL with LB Lamar Griggs to Hamilton Tiger-Cats of CFL for second-round pick in 1998 CFL college draft and future considerations (September 4, 1997). ... Released by Tiger-Cats (October 9, 1997). ... Selected by Frankfurt Galaxy in 1998 NFL Europe draft (February 23, 1998). ... Signed as non-drafted free agent by Dallas Cowboys (July 21, 1998). ... Released by Cowboys (August 25, 1998). ... Signed by Kansas City Chiefs to practice squad (September 1, 1998). ... Released by Chiefs (Novmeber 3, 1998). ... Signed by Oakland Raiders (March 1999). ... Released by Raiders (December 14, 1999). ... Signed by New Orleans Saints (March 23, 2000). ... Traded by Saints with third-round pick (traded to San Francisco) in 2001 draft to Green Bay Packers for QB Aaron Brooks and TE Lamont Hall (July 31, 2000).
PRO STATISTICS: CFL: 1995—Recovered three fumbles. 1996—Recovered two fumbles for seven yards. NFL: 1999—Recovered one fumble. 2000—Recovered one fumble.

			INTERCEPTIONS				SACKS
Year Team	G	GS	No.	Yds.	Avg.	TD	No.
1995—Winnipeg CFL	15	...	1	0	0.0	0	5.0
1996—Winnipeg CFL	18	...	4	72	18.0	1	5.0
1997—Saskatchewan CFL	10	...	2	38	19.0	1	3.0
—Hamilton CFL	3	...	1	18	18.0	0	1.0
1998—Frankfurt NFLE	...	...	0	0	0.0	0	2.5
1999—Oakland NFL	9	8	1	14	14.0	0	1.0
2000—Green Bay NFL	16	3	0	0	0.0	0	0.5
NFL Europe totals (1 year)	...	...	0	0	0.0	0	2.5
CFL totals (3 years)	46		8	128	16.0	2	14.0
NFL totals (2 years)	25	11	1	14	14.0	0	1.5
Pro totals (6 years)	...	...	9	142	15.8	2	18.0

WILLIAMS, KARL WR* BUCCANEERS

PERSONAL: Born April 10, 1971, in Albion, Mich. ... 5-10/177.
HIGH SCHOOL: Garland (Texas).
COLLEGE: Texas A&M-Kingsville.
TRANSACTIONS/CAREER NOTES: Signed as non-drafted free agent by Tampa Bay Buccaneers (April 23, 1996).
CHAMPIONSHIP GAME EXPERIENCE: Played in NFC championship game (1999 season).
PRO STATISTICS: 1996—Rushed once for minus three yards and recovered one fumble. 1997—Rushed once for five yards and recovered one fumble. 1999—Recovered one fumble. 2000—Recovered one fumble.
SINGLE GAME HIGHS (regular season): Receptions—6 (September 13, 1998, vs. Green Bay); yards—87 (December 7, 1997, vs. Green Bay); and touchdown receptions—2 (November 2, 1997, vs. Indianapolis).

			RECEIVING				PUNT RETURNS				KICKOFF RETURNS				TOTALS			
Year Team	G	GS	No.	Yds.	Avg.	TD	No.	Yds.	Avg.	TD	No.	Yds.	Avg.	TD	TD	2pt.	Pts.	Fum.
1996—Tampa Bay NFL	16	0	22	246	11.2	0	13	274	21.1	1	14	383	27.4	0	1	0	6	2
1997—Tampa Bay NFL	16	8	33	486	14.7	4	46	‡597	13.0	∞1	15	277	18.5	0	5	0	30	5
1998—Tampa Bay NFL	13	6	21	252	12.0	1	10	83	8.3	0	0	0	0.0	0	1	0	6	0
1999—Tampa Bay NFL	13	4	21	176	8.4	0	20	153	7.7	0	1	15	15.0	0	0	0	0	2
2000—Tampa Bay NFL	13	0	2	35	17.5	0	31	286	9.2	1	19	453	23.8	0	1	0	6	2
Pro totals (5 years)	71	18	99	1195	12.1	5	120	1393	11.6	3	49	1128	23.0	0	8	0	48	11

WILLIAMS, KEVIN WR/KR

PERSONAL: Born January 25, 1971, in Dallas. ... 5-9/195. ... Full name: Kevin Ray Williams.
HIGH SCHOOL: Franklin D. Roosevelt (Dallas).
COLLEGE: Miami (Fla.).
TRANSACTIONS/CAREER NOTES: Selected after junior season by Dallas Cowboys in second round (46th overall) of 1993 NFL draft. ... Signed by Cowboys (April 29, 1993). ... Granted unconditional free agency (February 14, 1997). ... Signed by Arizona Cardinals (July 15, 1997). ... Granted unconditional free agency (February 13, 1998). ... Signed by Buffalo Bills (February 17, 1998). ... Released by Bills (April 14, 2000). ... Signed by San Francisco 49ers (July 19, 2000). ... Granted unconditional free agency (March 2, 2001).
CHAMPIONSHIP GAME EXPERIENCE: Played in NFC championship game (1993-1995 seasons). ... Member of Super Bowl championship team (1993 and 1995 seasons).

PRO STATISTICS: 1993—Fumbled eight times and recovered four fumbles. 1994—Fumbled four times and recovered three fumbles. 1995—Fumbled three times. 1997—Fumbled three times and recovered one fumble. 1998—Fumbled three times and recovered two fumbles. 2000—Fumbled once and recovered one fumble.

SINGLE GAME HIGHS (regular season): Receptions—9 (December 25, 1995, vs. Arizona); yards—203 (December 25, 1995, vs. Arizona); and touchdown receptions—2 (December 25, 1995, vs. Arizona).

STATISTICAL PLATEAUS: 100-yard receiving games: 1995 (1).

Year Team	G	GS	RUSHING				RECEIVING				PUNT RETURNS				KICKOFF RETURNS				TOTALS		
			Att.	Yds.	Avg.	TD	No.	Yds.	Avg.	TD	No.	Yds.	Avg.	TD	No.	Yds.	Avg.	TD	TD	2pt.	Pts.
1993—Dallas NFL	16	1	7	26	3.7	2	20	151	7.6	2	36	381	10.6	†2	31	689	22.2	0	6	0	36
1994—Dallas NFL	15	2	6	20	3.3	0	13	181	13.9	0	39	349	8.9	1	43	1148	26.7	1	2	0	12
1995—Dallas NFL	16	16	10	53	5.3	0	38	613	16.1	2	18	166	9.2	0	49	1108	22.6	0	2	0	12
1996—Dallas NFL	10	9	4	11	2.8	0	27	323	12.0	1	2	17	8.5	0	21	471	22.4	0	1	0	6
1997—Arizona NFL	16	0	1	-2	-2.0	0	20	273	13.7	1	40	462	11.6	0	‡59	*1458	24.7	0	1	0	6
1998—Buffalo NFL	16	0	5	46	9.2	0	29	392	13.5	1	37	369	10.0	0	47	1059	22.5	0	1	0	6
1999—Buffalo NFL	16	0	1	13	13.0	0	31	381	12.3	0	33	331	10.0	0	42	840	20.0	0	0	0	0
2000—San Fran. NFL	16	0	0	0	0.0	0	0	0	0.0	0	26	220	8.5	0	30	536	17.9	0	0	0	0
Pro totals (8 years)	121	28	34	167	4.9	2	178	2314	13.0	7	231	2295	9.9	3	322	7309	22.7	1	13	0	78

WILLIAMS, KEVIN　　　S　　　DOLPHINS

PERSONAL: Born August 4, 1975, in Pine Bluff, Ark. ... 6-0/190.
HIGH SCHOOL: Watson Chapel (Pine Bluff, Ark.).
COLLEGE: Oklahoma State.
TRANSACTIONS/CAREER NOTES: Selected by New York Jets in third round (87th pick overall) of 1998 NFL draft. ... Signed by Jets (July 20, 1998). ... On non-football illness list with viral infection (October 18, 1999-remainder of season). ... Released by Jets (November 7, 2000). ... Signed by Miami Dolphins (November 28, 2000).
CHAMPIONSHIP GAME EXPERIENCE: Played in AFC championship game (1998 season).
PRO STATISTICS: 1998—Intercepted one pass for 34 yards.

Year Team	G	GS	KICKOFF RETURNS				TOTALS			
			No.	Yds.	Avg.	TD	TD	2pt.	Pts.	Fum.
1998—New York Jets NFL	15	6	11	230	20.9	0	0	0	0	0
1999—New York Jets NFL	4	0	6	166	27.7	0	0	0	0	1
2000—New York Jets NFL	9	7	21	551	26.2	▲1	1	0	6	0
—Miami NFL	2	0	3	64	21.3	0	0	0	0	0
Pro totals (3 years)	30	13	41	1011	24.7	1	1	0	6	1

WILLIAMS, MOE　　　RB　　　VIKINGS

PERSONAL: Born July 26, 1974, in Columbus, Ga. ... 6-1/210. ... Full name: Maurice Jabari Williams.
HIGH SCHOOL: Spencer (Columbus, Ga.).
COLLEGE: Kentucky.
TRANSACTIONS/CAREER NOTES: Selected after junior season by Minnesota Vikings in third round (75th pick overall) of 1996 NFL draft. ... Signed by Vikings (July 22, 1996). ... On injured reserve with foot injury (December 8, 1998-remainder of season). ... Granted free agency (February 12, 1999). ... Re-signed by Vikings (April 30, 1999). ... Granted unconditional free agency (February 11, 2000). ... Re-signed by Vikings (March 20, 2000).
CHAMPIONSHIP GAME EXPERIENCE: Played in NFC championship game (2000 season).
PRO STATISTICS: 1998—Recovered one fumble. 2000—Recovered one fumble.
SINGLE GAME HIGHS (regular season): Attempts—19 (November 2, 1997, vs, New England); yards—43 (November 2, 1997, vs. New England); and rushing touchdowns—1 (October 24, 1999, vs. San Francisco).

Year Team	G	GS	RUSHING				RECEIVING				KICKOFF RETURNS				TOTALS			
			Att.	Yds.	Avg.	TD	No.	Yds.	Avg.	TD	No.	Yds.	Avg.	TD	TD	2pt.	Pts.	Fum.
1996—Minnesota NFL	9	0	0	0	0.0	0	0	0	0.0	0	0	0	0.0	0	0	0	0	0
1997—Minnesota NFL	14	0	22	59	2.7	1	4	14	3.5	0	16	388	24.3	0	1	0	6	0
1998—Minnesota NFL	12	1	0	0	0.0	0	1	64	64.0	0	2	19	9.5	0	0	0	0	1
1999—Minnesota NFL	14	0	24	69	2.9	1	1	12	12.0	0	10	240	24.0	1	2	0	12	0
2000—Minnesota NFL	16	0	23	67	2.9	0	4	31	7.8	0	10	214	21.4	0	0	1	2	0
Pro totals (5 years)	65	1	69	195	2.8	2	10	121	12.1	0	38	861	22.7	1	3	1	20	1

W

WILLIAMS, NICK　　　FB　　　BENGALS

PERSONAL: Born March 30, 1977, in Farmington Hills, Mich. ... 6-2/267. ... Full name: James Nicolas Williams.
HIGH SCHOOL: Harrison (Farmington Hills, Mich.).
COLLEGE: Miami (Fla.).
TRANSACTIONS/CAREER NOTES: Selected by Cincinnati Bengals in fifth round (135th pick overall) of 1999 NFL draft. ... Signed by Bengals (May 19, 1999).
PRO STATISTICS: 2000—Recovered one fumble.
SINGLE GAME HIGHS (regular season): Attempts—5 (November 26, 2000, vs. Pittsburgh); yards—18 (October 24, 1999, vs. Indianapolis); and rushing touchdowns—0.

Year Team	G	GS	RUSHING				RECEIVING				KICKOFF RETURNS				TOTALS			
			Att.	Yds.	Avg.	TD	No.	Yds.	Avg.	TD	No.	Yds.	Avg.	TD	TD	2pt.	Pts.	Fum.
1999—Cincinnati NFL	11	0	10	30	3.0	0	10	96	9.6	0	8	109	13.6	0	0	0	0	1
2000—Cincinnati NFL	14	4	10	54	5.4	0	7	84	12.0	0	2	12	6.0	0	0	0	0	2
Pro totals (2 years)	25	4	20	84	4.2	0	17	180	10.6	0	10	121	12.1	0	0	0	0	3

WILLIAMS, PAT · DT · BILLS

PERSONAL: Born October 24, 1972, in Monroe, La. ... 6-3/310. ... Full name: Patrick Williams.
HIGH SCHOOL: Wossman (Monroe, La.).
JUNIOR COLLEGE: Navarro College (Texas).
COLLEGE: Northeast Oklahoma, then Texas A&M.
TRANSACTIONS/CAREER NOTES: Signed as non-drafted free agent by Buffalo Bills (April 25, 1997). ... Granted free agency (February 11, 2000). ... Re-signed by Bills (March 23, 2000).
PRO STATISTICS: 2000—Recovered two fumbles.

Year Team	G	GS	SACKS
1997—Buffalo NFL	1	0	0.0
1998—Buffalo NFL	14	0	3.5
1999—Buffalo NFL	16	0	2.5
2000—Buffalo NFL	16	3	2.5
Pro totals (4 years)	47	3	8.5

WILLIAMS, PAYTON · DB · STEELERS

PERSONAL: Born November 19, 1978, in Riverside, Calif. ... 5-7/170.
HIGH SCHOOL: Moreno Valley (Calif.).
COLLEGE: Fresno State.
TRANSACTIONS/CAREER NOTES: Signed as non-drafted free agent by Indianapolis Colts (April 16, 2000). ... Released by Colts (November 1, 2000). ... Signed by Pittsburgh Steelers to practice squad (December 14, 2000).
PLAYING EXPERIENCE: Indianapolis NFL, 2000. ... Games/Games started: 2000 (7/0).
PRO STATISTICS: 2000—Returned seven punts for 108 yards and returned 12 kickoffs for 238 yards.

WILLIAMS, RICKY · RB · SAINTS

PERSONAL: Born May 21, 1977, in San Diego. ... 5-10/236. ... Full name: Errick Lynne Williams.
HIGH SCHOOL: Patrick Henry (San Diego).
COLLEGE: Texas.
TRANSACTIONS/CAREER NOTES: Selected by New Orleans Saints in first round (fifth pick overall) of 1999 NFL draft. ... Signed by Saints (May 14, 1999).
HONORS: Named running back on THE SPORTING NEWS college All-America first team (1997 and 1998). ... Doak Walker Award winner (1997 and 1998). ... Heisman Trophy winner (1998). ... Walter Camp Award winner (1998). ... Maxwell Award winner (1998). ... Named College Football Player of the Year by THE SPORTING NEWS (1998).
PRO STATISTICS: 1999—Attempted one pass without a completion and recovered one fumble. 2000—Attempted one pass with one completion for 34 yards and recovered two fumbles.
SINGLE GAME HIGHS (regular season): Attempts—40 (October 31, 1999, vs. Cleveland); yards—179 (October 31, 1999, vs. Cleveland); and rushing touchdowns—3 (October 22, 2000, vs. Atlanta).
STATISTICAL PLATEAUS: 100-yard rushing games: 1999 (2), 2000 (5). Total: 7.

			RUSHING				RECEIVING				TOTALS			
Year Team	G	GS	Att.	Yds.	Avg.	TD	No.	Yds.	Avg.	TD	TD	2pt.	Pts.	Fum.
1999—New Orleans NFL	12	12	253	884	3.5	2	28	172	6.1	0	2	0	12	6
2000—New Orleans NFL	10	10	248	1000	4.0	8	44	409	9.3	1	9	0	54	6
Pro totals (2 years)	22	22	501	1884	3.8	10	72	581	8.1	1	11	0	66	12

RECORD AS BASEBALL PLAYER

TRANSACTIONS/CAREER NOTES: Batted right, threw right. ... Selected by Philadelphia Phillies organization in eighth round of free-agent draft (June 1, 1995). ... Selected by Montreal Expos from Phillies organization in Rule 5 major league draft (December 14, 1998). ... Traded by Expos to Texas Rangers for cash considerations (December 15, 1998).

									BATTING					FIELDING			
Year Team (League)	Pos.	G	AB	R	H	2B	3B	HR	RBI	Avg.	BB	SO	SB	PO	A	E	Avg.
1995—Martinsville (Appal.)	OF	36	113	19	27	1	0	0	11	.239	6	32	13	51	5	3	.949
1996—Piedmont (S. Atl.)	OF	84	266	30	50	4	3	3	20	.188	18	87	17	117	9	9	.933
1997—Piedmont (S. Atl.)	OF	37	136	12	28	5	0	1	6	.206	9	44	10	58	5	3	.955
1998—Batavia (NY-Penn)	OF	13	53	7	15	0	0	0	3	.283	2	16	6	17	1	0	1.000

WILLIAMS, ROLAND · TE · RAIDERS

PERSONAL: Born April 27, 1975, in Rochester, N.Y. ... 6-5/269. ... Full name: Roland Lamar Williams.
HIGH SCHOOL: East (Rochester, N.Y.).
COLLEGE: Syracuse (degree in speech communications, 1997).
TRANSACTIONS/CAREER NOTES: Selected by St. Louis Rams in fourth round (98th pick overall) of 1998 NFL draft. ... Signed by Rams (July 13, 1998). ... Granted free agency (March 2, 2001). ... Re-signed by Rams (April 20, 2001). ... Traded by Rams to Oakland Raiders for fourth-round pick (traded to Arizona) in 2001 draft (April 20, 2001).
CHAMPIONSHIP GAME EXPERIENCE: Played in NFC championship game (1999 season). ... Member of Super Bowl championship team (1999 season).
PRO STATISTICS: 1999—Recovered two fumbles.
SINGLE GAME HIGHS (regular season): Receptions—5 (October 24, 1999, vs. Cleveland); yards—50 (October 24, 1999, vs. Cleveland); and touchdown receptions—2 (October 24, 1999, vs. Cleveland).

W

			RECEIVING				TOTALS			
Year Team	G	GS	No.	Yds.	Avg.	TD	TD	2pt.	Pts.	Fum.
1998—St. Louis NFL	13	9	15	144	9.6	1	1	0	6	0
1999—St. Louis NFL	16	15	25	226	9.0	6	6	0	36	0
2000—St. Louis NFL	16	11	11	102	9.3	3	3	1	20	0
Pro totals (3 years)	45	35	51	472	9.3	10	10	1	62	0

WILLIAMS, SAMMY   OL   RAVENS

PERSONAL: Born December 14, 1974, in Magnolia, Miss. ... 6-5/318.
HIGH SCHOOL: Thornton Township (Harvey, Ill.).
JUNIOR COLLEGE: Coffeyville (Kan.) Community College.
COLLEGE: Oklahoma.
TRANSACTIONS/CAREER NOTES: Selected by Baltimore Ravens in sixth round (164th pick overall) of 1998 NFL draft. ... Signed by Ravens (July 21, 1998). ... On injured reserve with knee and ankle injuries (August 30, 1998-entire season). ... Released by Ravens (September 4, 1999). ... Claimed on waivers by Kansas City Chiefs (September 6, 1999). ... Claimed on waivers by Ravens (November 10, 1999). ... Assigned by Ravens to Berlin Thunder in 2001 NFL Europe enhancement allocation program (February 19, 2001).
PLAYING EXPERIENCE: Kansas City NFL, 1999 and 2000. ... Games/Games started: 1999 (1/0), 2000 (1/0). Total: 2/0.
CHAMPIONSHIP GAME EXPERIENCE: Member of Ravens for AFC Championship game (2000 season); inactive. ... Member of Super Bowl championship team (2000 season); inactive.

WILLIAMS, SHAUN   S   GIANTS

PERSONAL: Born October 10, 1976, in Los Angeles. ... 6-2/215. ... Full name: Shaun LeJon Williams.
HIGH SCHOOL: Crespi (Encino, Calif.).
COLLEGE: UCLA.
TRANSACTIONS/CAREER NOTES: Selected by New York Giants in first round (24th pick overall) of 1998 NFL draft. ... Signed by Giants (July 24, 1998).
PLAYING EXPERIENCE: New York Giants NFL, 1998-2000. ... Games/Games started: 1998 (13/0), 1999 (11/0), 2000 (16/16). Total: 40/16.
CHAMPIONSHIP GAME EXPERIENCE: Played in NFC championship game (2000 season). ... Played in Super Bowl XXXV (2000 season).
HONORS: Named free safety on THE SPORTING NEWS college All-America second team (1997).
PRO STATISTICS: 1998—Intercepted two passes for six yards. 2000—Intercepted three passes for 52 yards and recovered one fumble.

WILLIAMS, TONY   DT   BENGALS

PERSONAL: Born July 9, 1975, in Germantown, Tenn. ... 6-1/292. ... Full name: Anthony Demetric Williams.
HIGH SCHOOL: Oakhaven (Memphis, Tenn.), then Germantown (Tenn.).
COLLEGE: Memphis.
TRANSACTIONS/CAREER NOTES: Selected by Minnesota Vikings in fifth round (151st pick overall) of 1997 NFL draft. ... Signed by Vikings (June 17, 1997). ... Granted free agency (February 11, 2000). ... Re-signed by Vikings (May 18, 2000). ... Granted unconditional free agency (March 2, 2001). ... Signed by Cincinnati Bengals (March 6, 2001).
PLAYING EXPERIENCE: Minnesota NFL, 1997-2000. ... Games/Games started: 1997 (6/2), 1998 (14/9), 1999 (16/12), 2000 (14/12). Total: 50/35.
CHAMPIONSHIP GAME EXPERIENCE: Played in NFC championship game (1998 and 2000 season).
PRO STATISTICS: 1998—Credited with one sack and recovered one fumble for six yards. 1999—Credited with five sacks and recovered one fumble. 2000—Credited with four sacks.

WILLIAMS, TYRONE   CB   PACKERS

PERSONAL: Born May 31, 1973, in Bradenton, Fla. ... 5-11/193. ... Full name: Upton Tyrone Williams.
HIGH SCHOOL: Manatee (Bradenton, Fla.).
COLLEGE: Nebraska.
TRANSACTIONS/CAREER NOTES: Selected by Green Bay Packers in third round (93rd pick overall) of 1996 NFL draft. ... Signed by Packers (May 15, 1996). ... Granted free agency (February 12, 1999). ... Re-signed by Packers (May 17, 1999).
CHAMPIONSHIP GAME EXPERIENCE: Played in NFC championship game (1996 and 1997 seasons). ... Member of Super Bowl championship team (1996 season). ... Played in Super Bowl XXXII (1997 season).
PRO STATISTICS: 1996—Recovered one fumble. 1999—Fumbled once and recovered two fumbles for 12 yards.

Year Team	G	GS	No.	Yds.	Avg.	TD
			INTERCEPTIONS			
1996—Green Bay NFL	16	0	0	0	0.0	0
1997—Green Bay NFL	16	15	1	0	0.0	0
1998—Green Bay NFL	16	16	5	40	8.0	0
1999—Green Bay NFL	16	16	4	12	3.0	0
2000—Green Bay NFL	16	16	4	105	26.3	1
Pro totals (5 years)	80	63	14	157	11.2	1

W

WILLIAMS, TYRONE   DE   CHIEFS

PERSONAL: Born October 22, 1972, in Philadelphia. ... 6-4/292. ... Full name: Tyrone M. Williams Jr.
HIGH SCHOOL: LaVista (Papillion, Neb.).
COLLEGE: Wyoming.
TRANSACTIONS/CAREER NOTES: Signed as non-drafted free agent by St. Louis Rams (July 25, 1996). ... Released by Rams (August 25, 1996). ... Re-signed by Rams to practice squad (August 26, 1996). ... Allocated by Rams to Rhein Fire in 1997 World League enhancement allocation program (February 19, 1997). ... Released by Rams (August 19, 1997). ... Signed by Chicago Bears to practice squad (August 27, 1997). ... Released by Bears (September 9, 1997). ... Re-signed by Rams to practice squad (September 25, 1997). ... Signed by Bears off Rams practice squad (October 29, 1997). ... Released by Bears (August 31, 1998). ... Signed by Philadelphia Eagles (July 6, 1999). ... Released by Eagles (September 4, 1999). ... Re-signed by Eagles (October 20, 1999). ... Released by Eagles (September 20, 2000). ... Signed by Kansas City Chiefs (September 27, 2000).
PLAYING EXPERIENCE: Chicago NFL, 1997; Philadelphia NFL, 1999; Philadelphia (3)-Kansas City (10) NFL, 2000. ... Games/Games started: 1997 (3/0), 1999 (4/0), 2000 (Phi.-3/0; K.C.-10/0; Total: 13/0). Total: 17/0.
PRO STATISTICS: 1999—Credited with three sacks and recovered one fumble. 2000—Credited with 1 1/2 sacks.

WILLIAMS, WALLY G/C SAINTS

PERSONAL: Born February 19, 1971, in Tallahassee, Fla. ... 6-2/321. ... Full name: Wally James Williams Jr.
HIGH SCHOOL: James S. Rickards (Tallahassee, Fla.).
COLLEGE: Florida A&M.
TRANSACTIONS/CAREER NOTES: Signed as non-drafted free agent by Cleveland Browns (April 27, 1993). ... Browns franchise moved to Baltimore and renamed Ravens for 1996 season (March 11, 1996). ... Designated by Ravens as franchise player (February 13, 1998). ... Re-signed by Ravens (August 18, 1998). ... Granted unconditional free agency (February 12, 1999). ... Signed by New Orleans Saints (February 15, 1999). ... On injured reserve with neck injury (November 19, 1999-remainder of season).
PLAYING EXPERIENCE: Cleveland NFL, 1993-1995; Baltimore NFL, 1996-1998; New Orleans NFL, 1999 and 2000. ... Games/Games started: 1993 (2/0), 1994 (11/7), 1995 (16/16), 1996 (15/13), 1997 (10/10), 1998 (13/13), 1999 (6/6), 2000 (16/16). Total: 89/81.
PRO STATISTICS: 1994—Recovered one fumble. 1998—Recovered one fumble. 2000—Recovered one fumble.

WILLIAMS, WILLIE CB SEAHAWKS

PERSONAL: Born December 26, 1970, in Columbia, S.C. ... 5-9/180. ... Full name: Willie James Williams Jr.
HIGH SCHOOL: Spring Valley (Columbia, S.C.).
COLLEGE: Western Carolina.
TRANSACTIONS/CAREER NOTES: Selected by Pittsburgh Steelers in sixth round (162nd pick overall) of 1993 NFL draft. ... Signed by Steelers (July 9, 1993). ... Granted free agency (February 16, 1996). ... Re-signed by Steelers (June 12, 1996). ... Granted unconditional free agency (February 14, 1997). ... Signed by Seattle Seahawks (February 18, 1997). ... Granted unconditional free agency (March 2, 2001). ... Re-signed by Seahawks (May 3, 2001).
CHAMPIONSHIP GAME EXPERIENCE: Played in AFC championship game (1994 and 1995 seasons). ... Played in Super Bowl XXX (1995 season).
PRO STATISTICS: 1993—Returned one kickoff for 19 yards. 1996—Credited with one sack and recovered one fumble. 1998—Recovered one fumble. 2000—Credited with one sack and recovered one fumble.

				INTERCEPTIONS		
Year Team	G	GS	No.	Yds.	Avg.	TD
1993—Pittsburgh NFL	16	0	0	0	0.0	0
1994—Pittsburgh NFL	16	1	0	0	0.0	0
1995—Pittsburgh NFL	16	15	§7	122	17.4	▲1
1996—Pittsburgh NFL	15	14	1	1	1.0	0
1997—Seattle NFL	16	16	1	0	0.0	0
1998—Seattle NFL	14	14	2	36	18.0	1
1999—Seattle NFL	15	14	5	43	8.6	1
2000—Seattle NFL	16	15	4	74	18.5	1
Pro totals (8 years)	124	89	20	276	13.8	4

WILLIG, MATT OT 49ERS

PERSONAL: Born January 21, 1969, in La Mirada, Calif. ... 6-8/317. ... Full name: Matthew Joseph Willig.
HIGH SCHOOL: St. Paul (Santa Fe Springs, Calif.).
COLLEGE: Southern California.
TRANSACTIONS/CAREER NOTES: Signed as non-drafted free agent by New York Jets (May 5, 1992). ... Released by Jets (August 24, 1992). ... Re-signed by Jets to practice squad (September 2, 1992). ... Activated (December 24, 1992). ... Active for one game (1992); did not play. ... Signed by Jets (February 14, 1995). ... Released by Jets (April 23, 1996). ... Signed by Atlanta Falcons (May 2, 1996). ... Granted unconditional free agency (February 13, 1998). ... Signed by Green Bay Packers (May 5, 1998). ... Released by Packers (February 23, 1999). ... Signed by Cleveland Browns (August 17, 1999). ... Released by Browns (September 5, 1999). ... Signed by St. Louis Rams (November 30, 1999). ... Granted unconditional free agency (February 11, 2000). ... Signed by San Francisco 49ers (June 7, 2000).
PLAYING EXPERIENCE: New York Jets NFL, 1993-1995; Atlanta NFL, 1996 and 1997; Green Bay NFL, 1998; San Francisco NFL, 2000. ... Games/Games started: 1993 (3/0), 1994 (16/3), 1995 (15/12), 1996 (12/0), 1997 (16/13), 1998 (16/0), 2000 (16/3). Total: 94/31.
CHAMPIONSHIP GAME EXPERIENCE: Member of Rams for NFC championship game (1999 season); inactive. ... Member of Super Bowl championship team (1999 season); inactive.
PRO STATISTICS: 1998—Recovered one fumble.

WILLIS, DONALD G CHIEFS

PERSONAL: Born July 15, 1973, in Goleta, Calif. ... 6-3/330. ... Full name: Donald Kirk Willis.
HIGH SCHOOL: Cabrillo (Lompoc, Calif.).
COLLEGE: Washington, then North Carolina A&T.
TRANSACTIONS/CAREER NOTES: Signed as non-drafted free agent by Seattle Seahawks (April 27, 1995). ... Claimed on waivers by New Orleans Saints (December 1, 1995). ... Inactive for 16 games (1995). ... Released by Saints (September 8, 1997). ... Signed by Tampa Bay Buccaneers (December 30, 1997). ... Released by Buccaneers (August 30, 1998). ... Signed by Kansas City Chiefs (March 12, 1999). ... Released by Chiefs (September 6, 1999). ... Re-signed by Chiefs (March 6, 2000).
PLAYING EXPERIENCE: New Orleans NFL, 1996; Kansas City NFL, 2000. ... Games/Games started: 1996 (4/0), 2000 (16/2). Total: 20/2.

WILSON, AL LB BRONCOS

PERSONAL: Born June 21, 1977, in Jackson, Tenn. ... 6-0/240. ... Full name: Aldra Kauwa Wilson.
HIGH SCHOOL: Central Merry (Jackson, Tenn.).
COLLEGE: Tennessee.
TRANSACTIONS/CAREER NOTES: Selected by Denver Broncos in first round (31st pick overall) of NFL draft. ... Signed by Broncos (July 21, 1999).
PLAYING EXPERIENCE: Denver NFL, 1999 and 2000. ... Games/Games started: 1999 (16/12), 2000 (15/14). Total: 31/26.
HONORS: Named inside linebacker on THE SPORTING NEWS college All-America second team (1998).
PRO STATISTICS: 1999—Credited with one sack and recovered two fumbles. 2000—Intercepted three passes for 21 yards and credited with five sacks.

W

WILSON, ANTONIO   LB   VIKINGS

PERSONAL: Born December 29, 1977, in Seagoville, Texas. ... 6-2/247.
HIGH SCHOOL: Skyline (Dallas).
COLLEGE: Texas A&M-Commerce.
TRANSACTIONS/CAREER NOTES: Selected by Minnesota Vikings in fourth round (106th pick overall) of 2000 NFL draft. ... Signed by Vikings (July 21, 2000). ... Assigned by Vikings to Barcelona Dragons in 2001 NFL Europe enhancement allocation program (February 19, 2001).
PLAYING EXPERIENCE: Minnesota NFL, 2000. ... Games/Games started: 2000 (1/0).
CHAMPIONSHIP GAME EXPERIENCE: Member of Vikings for NFC championship game (2000 season); inactive.

WILSON, JERRY   CB

PERSONAL: Born July 17, 1973, in Alexandria, La. ... 5-10/187. ... Full name: Jerry Lee Wilson Jr.
HIGH SCHOOL: La Grange (Lake Charles, La.).
COLLEGE: Southern (degree in rehabilitation counseling).
TRANSACTIONS/CAREER NOTES: Selected by Tampa Bay Buccaneers in fourth round (105th pick overall) of 1995 NFL draft. ... Signed by Buccaneers (May 9, 1995). ... On injured reserve with knee injury (August 31, 1995-entire season). ... Released by Buccaneers (August 20, 1996). ... Signed by Miami Dolphins to practice squad (October 29, 1996). ... Activated (November 5, 1996). ... Granted unconditional free agency (March 2, 2001).
PLAYING EXPERIENCE: Miami NFL, 1996-2000. ... Games/Games started: 1996 (2/0), 1997 (16/0), 1998 (16/0), 1999 (16/1), 2000 (16/0). Total: 66/1.
PRO STATISTICS: 1997—Credited with two sacks and recovered one fumble. 1998—Intercepted one pass for no yards. 1999—Intercepted one pass for 13 yards, returned three kickoffs for 50 yards and credited with three sacks. 2000—Intercepted one pass for 19 yards and credited with 1/2 sack.

WILSON, REINARD   LB   BENGALS

PERSONAL: Born December 17, 1973, in Lake City, Fla. ... 6-2/266. ... Cousin of Brian Allen, linebacker, St. Louis Rams. ... Name pronounced ruh-NARD.
HIGH SCHOOL: Columbia (Lake City, Fla.).
COLLEGE: Florida State.
TRANSACTIONS/CAREER NOTES: Selected by Cincinnati Bengals in first round (14th pick overall) of 1997 NFL draft. ... Signed by Bengals (July 18, 1997).
HONORS: Named defensive end on THE SPORTING NEWS college All-America second team (1996).
PRO STATISTICS: 2000—Recovered one fumble for three yards.

Year Team	G	GS	SACKS
1997—Cincinnati NFL	16	4	3.0
1998—Cincinnati NFL	16	15	6.0
1999—Cincinnati NFL	15	0	3.0
2000—Cincinnati NFL	14	0	3.0
Pro totals (4 years)	61	19	15.0

WILSON, ROBERT   WR   SAINTS

PERSONAL: Born June 23, 1974, in Tallahassee, Fla. ... 5-11/176.
HIGH SCHOOL: Jefferson County (Monticello, Fla.).
COLLEGE: Florida A&M.
TRANSACTIONS/CAREER NOTES: Signed as non-drafted free agent by Seattle Seahawks (April 25, 1997). ... Released by Seahawks (August 18, 1997). ... Re-signed by Seahawks to practice squad (August 19, 1997). ... Activated (December 17, 1997); did not play. ... Released by Seahawks (September 6, 1999). ... Re-signed by Seahawks (October 20, 1999). ... Released by Seahawks (November 13, 1999). ... Signed by New Orleans Saints (March 6, 2000).
PLAYING EXPERIENCE: Seattle NFL, 1998 and 1999; New Orleans NFL, 2000. ... Games/Games started: 1998 (16/0), 1999 (2/0), 2000 (15/0). Total: 33/0.
PRO STATISTICS: 1998—Returned one kickoff for 16 yards. 2000—Caught 11 passes for 154 yards and ran 11 yards with lateral.
SINGLE GAME HIGHS (regular season): Receptions—8 (December 3, 2000, vs. Denver); yards—122 (December 3, 2000, vs. Denver); and touchdown receptions—0.
STATISTICAL PLATEAUS: 100-yard receiving games: 2000 (1).

W

WILSON, TROY   DE

PERSONAL: Born November 22, 1970, in Topeka, Kan. ... 6-4/257. ... Full name: Troy Ethan Wilson.
HIGH SCHOOL: Shawnee Heights (Tecumseh, Kan.).
COLLEGE: Pittsburg (Kan.) State (degree in business management, 1992).
TRANSACTIONS/CAREER NOTES: Selected by San Francisco 49ers in seventh round (194th pick overall) of 1993 NFL draft. ... Signed by 49ers (May 12, 1993). ... On non-football injury list with back injury (August 24-October 16, 1993). ... Released by 49ers (August 27, 1995). ... Signed by Denver Broncos (September 28, 1995). ... Released by Broncos (October 30, 1995). ... Signed by Kansas City Chiefs (April 1996). ... Released by Chiefs (August 20, 1996). ... Signed by St. Louis Rams (February 6, 1997). ... Released by Rams (August 19, 1997). ... Signed by 49ers (May 26, 1998). ... Claimed on waivers by New Orleans Saints (September 1, 1998). ... Granted free agency (February 12, 1999). ... Re-signed by Saints (May 17, 1999). ... Released by Saints (August 2, 2000). ... Signed by Chicago Bears (August 7, 2000). ... Granted unconditional free agency (March 2, 2001).
CHAMPIONSHIP GAME EXPERIENCE: Played in NFC championship game (1993 and 1994 seasons). ... Member of Super Bowl championship team (1994 season).

Year Team	G	GS	SACKS
1993—San Francisco NFL	10	0	5.5
1994—San Francisco NFL	11	0	2.0
1995—Denver NFL	3	0	0.5
1996—	Did not play.		
1997—	Did not play.		
1998—New Orleans NFL	15	0	1.0
1999—New Orleans NFL	16	4	5.5
2000—Chicago NFL	6	0	1.0
Pro totals (6 years)	61	4	15.5

WILTZ, JASON   DT/DE   JETS

PERSONAL: Born November 23, 1976, in New Orleans. ... 6-4/300.
HIGH SCHOOL: St. Augustine (New Orleans).
COLLEGE: Nebraska.
TRANSACTIONS/CAREER NOTES: Selected by New York Jets in fourth round (123rd pick overall) of 1999 NFL draft. ... Signed by Jets (July 29, 1999).
PLAYING EXPERIENCE: New York Jets NFL, 1999 and 2000. ... Games/Games started: 1999 (12/1), 2000 (15/1). Total: 27/2.
PRO STATISTICS: 1999—Intercepted two passes for five yards and credited with one sack. 2000—Credited with one sack.

WINFIELD, ANTOINE   CB   BILLS

PERSONAL: Born June 24, 1977, in Akron, Ohio. ... 5-9/180. ... Full name: Antoine D. Winfield.
HIGH SCHOOL: Garfield (Ohio).
COLLEGE: Ohio State.
TRANSACTIONS/CAREER NOTES: Selected by Buffalo Bills in first round (23rd pick overall) of 1999 NFL draft. ... Signed by Bills (July 30, 1999). ... On injured reserve list with shoulder injury (November 22, 2000-remainder of season).
HONORS: Named cornerback on THE SPORTING NEWS college All-America second team (1997). ... Jim Thorpe Award winner (1998). ... Named cornerback on THE SPORTING NEWS college All-America first team (1998).

			INTERCEPTIONS			
Year Team	G	GS	No.	Yds.	Avg.	TD
1999—Buffalo NFL	16	2	2	13	6.5	0
2000—Buffalo NFL	11	11	1	8	8.0	0
Pro totals (2 years)	27	13	3	21	7.0	0

WINTERS, FRANK   C   PACKERS

PERSONAL: Born January 23, 1964, in Hoboken, N.J. ... 6-3/305. ... Full name: Frank Mitchell Winters.
HIGH SCHOOL: Emerson (Union City, N.J.).
JUNIOR COLLEGE: College of Eastern Utah.
COLLEGE: Western Illinois (degree in political science administration, 1987).
TRANSACTIONS/CAREER NOTES: Selected by Cleveland Browns in 10th round (276th pick overall) of 1987 NFL draft. ... Signed by Browns (July 25, 1987). ... Granted unconditional free agency (February 1, 1989). ... Signed by New York Giants (March 17, 1989). ... Granted unconditional free agency (February 1, 1990). ... Signed by Kansas City Chiefs (March 26, 1990). ... Granted unconditional free agency (February 1, 1992). ... Signed by Green Bay Packers (March 17, 1992). ... Granted unconditional free agency (February 17, 1994). ... Re-signed by Packers (April 1, 1994). ... Granted unconditional free agency (February 14, 1997). ... Re-signed by Packers (March 26, 1997). ... On injured reserve with leg injury (December 16, 1998-remainder of season). ... Granted unconditional free agency (February 11, 2000). ... Re-signed by Packers (April 4, 2000).
PLAYING EXPERIENCE: Cleveland NFL, 1987 and 1988; New York Giants NFL, 1989; Kansas City NFL, 1990 and 1991; Green Bay NFL, 1992-2000. ... Games/Games started: 1987 (12/0), 1988 (16/0), 1989 (15/0), 1990 (16/6), 1991 (16/0), 1992 (16/11), 1993 (16/16), 1994 (16/16), 1995 (16/16), 1996 (16/16), 1997 (13/13), 1998 (13/13), 1999 (16/16), 2000 (14/14). Total: 211/137.
CHAMPIONSHIP GAME EXPERIENCE: Played in AFC championship game (1987 season). ... Played in NFC championship game (1995-97 seasons). ... Member of Super Bowl championship team (1996 season). ... Played in Super Bowl XXXII (1997 season).
HONORS: Played in Pro Bowl (1996 season).
PRO STATISTICS: 1987—Fumbled once. 1990—Recovered two fumbles. 1992—Fumbled once. 1994—Fumbled once and recovered one fumble for minus two yards. 1996—Recovered one fumble. 1999—Recovered one fumble.

WISNIEWSKI, STEVE   G   RAIDERS

PERSONAL: Born April 7, 1967, in Rutland, Vt. ... 6-4/305. ... Full name: Stephen Adam Wisniewski. ... Brother of Leo Wisniewski, nose tackle with Baltimore/Indianapolis Colts (1982-84). ... Name pronounced wiz-NEWS-key.
HIGH SCHOOL: Westfield (Houston).
COLLEGE: Penn State.
TRANSACTIONS/CAREER NOTES: Selected by Dallas Cowboys in second round (29th pick overall) of 1989 NFL draft. ... Draft rights traded by Cowboys with sixth-round pick (LB Jeff Francis) in 1989 draft to Los Angeles Raiders for second-(RB Darryl Johnston), third-(DE Rhondy Weston) and fifth-round (LB Willis Crockett) picks in 1989 draft (April 23, 1989). ... Signed by Raiders (July 22, 1989). ... Granted free agency (March 1, 1993). ... Re-signed by Raiders for 1993 season. ... Raiders franchise moved to Oakland (July 21, 1995).
PLAYING EXPERIENCE: Los Angeles Raiders NFL, 1989-1994; Oakland NFL, 1995-2000. ... Games/Games started: 1989 (15/15), 1990 (16/16), 1991 (15/15), 1992 (16/16), 1993 (16/16), 1994 (16/16), 1995 (16/16), 1996 (16/16), 1997 (16/16), 1998 (16/16), 1999 (16/16), 2000 (16/16). Total: 191/191.
CHAMPIONSHIP GAME EXPERIENCE: Played in AFC championship game (1990 and 2000 seasons).
HONORS: Named guard on THE SPORTING NEWS college All-America first team (1987 and 1988). ... Named guard on THE SPORTING NEWS NFL All-Pro team (1990-1994). ... Played in Pro Bowl (1990, 1991, 1993, 1995 and 2000 seasons). ... Named to play in Pro Bowl (1992 season); replaced by Jim Ritcher due to injury.
PRO STATISTICS: 1989—Recovered three fumbles. 1995—Recovered one fumble.

W

WISTROM, GRANT DE RAMS

PERSONAL: Born July 3, 1976, in Webb City, Mo. ... 6-4/272. ... Full name: Grant Alden Wistrom.
HIGH SCHOOL: Webb City (Mo.).
COLLEGE: Nebraska.
TRANSACTIONS/CAREER NOTES: Selected by St. Louis Rams in first round (sixth pick overall) of 1998 NFL draft. ... Signed by Rams (July 18, 1998).
CHAMPIONSHIP GAME EXPERIENCE: Played in NFC championship game (1999 season). ... Member of Super Bowl championship team (1999 season).
HONORS: Named defensive end on THE SPORTING NEWS college All-America first team (1996 and 1997).
PRO STATISTICS: 1998—Recovered one fumble for four yards. 1999—Intercepted two passes for 131 yards and two touchdowns, fumbled once and recovered one fumble for 31 yards.

Year Team	G	GS	SACKS
1998—St. Louis NFL	13	0	3.0
1999—St. Louis NFL	16	16	6.5
2000—St. Louis NFL	16	16	11.0
Pro totals (3 years)	45	32	20.5

WITHROW, CORY C VIKINGS

PERSONAL: Born April 5, 1975, in Spokane, Wash. ... 6-2/281.
HIGH SCHOOL: Mead (Spokane, Wash.).
COLLEGE: Washington State.
TRANSACTIONS/CAREER NOTES: Signed as non-drafted free agent by Minnesota Vikings (April 23, 1998). ... Released by Vikings (August 30, 1998). ... Signed by Cincinnati Bengals to practice squad (December 18, 1998). ... Released by Bengals (April 15, 1999). ... Signed by Vikings (April 30, 1999). ... Released by Vikings (September 5, 1999). ... Re-signed by Vikings to practice squad (September 6, 1999). ... Activated (October 26, 1999); did not play. ... Released by Vikings (November 30, 1999). ... Re-signed by Vikings to practice squad (December 1, 1999).
PLAYING EXPERIENCE: Minnesota NFL, 2000. ... Games/Games started: 2000 (12/0).
CHAMPIONSHIP GAME EXPERIENCE: Played in NFC championship game (2000 season).

WITMAN, JON FB STEELERS

PERSONAL: Born June 1, 1972, in Wrightsville, Pa. ... 6-1/240. ... Full name: Jon Doyle Witman.
HIGH SCHOOL: Eastern York (Wrightsville, Pa.).
COLLEGE: Penn State.
TRANSACTIONS/CAREER NOTES: Selected by Pittsburgh Steelers in third round (92nd pick overall) of 1996 NFL draft. ... Signed by Steelers (July 16, 1996). ... Granted free agency (February 12, 1999). ... Re-signed by Steelers (March 10, 1999). ... On injured reserve with broken leg (October 17, 2000-remainder of season). ... Released by Steelers (March 1, 2001). ... Re-signed by Steelers (April 2, 2001).
CHAMPIONSHIP GAME EXPERIENCE: Played in AFC championship game (1997).
PRO STATISTICS: 1996—Returned one kickoff for 20 yards.
SINGLE GAME HIGHS (regular season): Attempts—7 (November 3, 1996, vs. St. Louis); yards—33 (November 3, 1996, vs. St. Louis); and rushing touchdowns—0.

Year Team	G	GS	RUSHING				RECEIVING				TOTALS			
			Att.	Yds.	Avg.	TD	No.	Yds.	Avg.	TD	TD	2pt.	Pts.	Fum.
1996—Pittsburgh NFL	16	4	17	69	4.1	0	2	15	7.5	0	0	0	0	0
1997—Pittsburgh NFL	16	2	5	11	2.2	0	1	3	3.0	0	0	0	0	0
1998—Pittsburgh NFL	16	8	1	2	2.0	0	13	74	5.7	0	0	0	0	0
1999—Pittsburgh NFL	16	11	6	18	3.0	0	12	106	8.8	0	0	0	0	0
2000—Pittsburgh NFL	6	5	3	5	1.7	0	5	33	6.6	0	0	0	0	0
Pro totals (5 years)	70	30	32	105	3.3	0	33	231	7.0	0	0	0	0	0

WOHLABAUGH, DAVE C BROWNS

PERSONAL: Born April 13, 1972, in Hamburg, N.Y. ... 6-3/292. ... Full name: David Vincent Wohlabaugh. ... Name pronounced WOOL-uh-buh.
HIGH SCHOOL: Frontier (Hamburg, N.Y.).
COLLEGE: Syracuse.
TRANSACTIONS/CAREER NOTES: Selected by New England Patriots in fourth round (112th pick overall) of 1995 NFL draft. ... Signed by Patriots (June 26, 1995). ... Granted free agency (February 13, 1998). ... Re-signed by Patriots (May 28, 1998). ... Granted unconditional free agency (February 12, 1999). ... Signed by Cleveland Browns (February 16, 1999).
PLAYING EXPERIENCE: New England NFL, 1995-1998; Cleveland NFL, 1999 and 2000. ... Games/Games started: 1995 (11/11), 1996 (16/16), 1997 (14/14), 1998 (16/16), 1999 (15/15), 2000 (12/12). Total: 84/84.
CHAMPIONSHIP GAME EXPERIENCE: Played in AFC championship game (1996 season). ... Played in Super Bowl XXXI (1996 season).
PRO STATISTICS: 1995—Recovered one fumble. 1996—Recovered two fumbles for one yard.

W

WONG, KAILEE LB VIKINGS

PERSONAL: Born May 23, 1976, in Eugene, Ore. ... 6-2/250.
HIGH SCHOOL: North Eugene (Ore.).
COLLEGE: Stanford.
TRANSACTIONS/CAREER NOTES: Selected by Minnesota Vikings in second round (51st pick overall) of 1998 NFL draft. ... Signed by Vikings (July 25, 1998). ... On injured reserve with leg injury (December 31, 1998-remainder of season). ... Granted free agency (March 2, 2001).
PLAYING EXPERIENCE: Minnesota NFL, 1998-2000. ... Games/Games started: 1998 (15/0), 1999 (13/8), 2000 (16/16). Total: 44/24.
CHAMPIONSHIP GAME EXPERIENCE: Played in NFC championship game (2000 season).
PRO STATISTICS: 1998—Credited with $1\frac{1}{2}$ sacks. 1999—Recovered one fumble for four yards. 2000—Intercepted two passes for 28 yards, credited with two sacks and fumbled once.

WOODALL, LEE — LB — BRONCOS

PERSONAL: Born October 31, 1969, in Carlisle, Pa. ... 6-1/230. ... Full name: Lee Artis Woodall.
HIGH SCHOOL: Carlisle (Pa.).
COLLEGE: West Chester (Pa.) University.
TRANSACTIONS/CAREER NOTES: Selected by San Francisco 49ers in sixth round (182nd pick overall) of 1994 NFL draft. ... Signed by 49ers (July 20, 1994). ... Released by 49ers (February 9, 2000). ... Signed by Carolina Panthers (March 22, 2000). ... Released by Panthers (February 28, 2001). ... Signed by Denver Broncos (May 4, 2001).
CHAMPIONSHIP GAME EXPERIENCE: Played in NFC championship game (1994 and 1997 seasons). ... Member of Super Bowl championship team (1994 season).
HONORS: Played in Pro Bowl (1995 and 1997 seasons).
PRO STATISTICS: 1994—Recovered one fumble. 1995—Recovered two fumbles for 98 yards and one touchdown. 2000—Recovered one fumble.

Year Team	G	GS	INTERCEPTIONS				SACKS
			No.	Yds.	Avg.	TD	No.
1994—San Francisco NFL	15	13	0	0	0.0	0	1.0
1995—San Francisco NFL	16	16	2	0	0.0	0	3.0
1996—San Francisco NFL	16	13	0	0	0.0	0	2.5
1997—San Francisco NFL	16	16	2	55	27.5	0	0.0
1998—San Francisco NFL	15	15	1	4	4.0	0	0.0
1999—San Francisco NFL	16	16	0	0	0.0	0	2.5
2000—Carolina NFL	16	16	1	0	0.0	0	0.0
Pro totals (7 years)	110	105	6	59	9.8	0	9.0

WOODEN, SHAWN — S — BEARS

PERSONAL: Born October 23, 1973, in Philadelphia. ... 5-11/205. ... Full name: Shawn Anthony Wooden.
HIGH SCHOOL: Abington (Pa.).
COLLEGE: Notre Dame (degree in computer science).
TRANSACTIONS/CAREER NOTES: Selected by Miami Dolphins in sixth round (189th pick overall) of 1996 NFL draft. ... Signed by Dolphins (July 10, 1996). ... On injured reserve with knee injury (September 15, 1998-remainder of season). ... Granted free agency (February 12, 1999). ... Re-signed by Dolphins (April 23, 1999). ... Granted unconditional free agency (February 11, 2000). ... Signed by Chicago Bears (March 6, 2000).
PRO STATISTICS: 1996—Recovered two fumbles. 1997—Fumbled once and recovered two fumbles. 1999—Recovered two fumbles. 2000—Recovered one fumble for three yards.

Year Team	G	GS	INTERCEPTIONS			
			No.	Yds.	Avg.	TD
1996—Miami NFL	16	11	2	15	7.5	0
1997—Miami NFL	16	15	2	10	5.0	0
1998—Miami NFL	2	1	0	0	0.0	0
1999—Miami NFL	15	6	0	0	0.0	0
2000—Chicago NFL	11	0	0	0	0.0	0
Pro totals (5 years)	60	33	4	25	6.3	0

WOODS, JEROME — S — CHIEFS

PERSONAL: Born March 17, 1973, in Memphis, Tenn. ... 6-2/207.
HIGH SCHOOL: Melrose (Memphis, Tenn.).
JUNIOR COLLEGE: Northeast Mississippi Community College.
COLLEGE: Memphis.
TRANSACTIONS/CAREER NOTES: Selected by Kansas City Chiefs in first round (28th pick overall) of 1996 NFL draft. ... Signed by Chiefs (August 12, 1996). ... Granted unconditional free agency (February 11, 2000). ... Re-signed by Chiefs (February 11, 2000).
PRO STATISTICS: 1996—Fumbled once and recovered one fumble. 1997—Credited with one sack and recovered two fumbles for 13 yards. 1999—Recovered one fumble for 19 yards. 2000—Credited with two sacks.

Year Team	G	GS	INTERCEPTIONS			
			No.	Yds.	Avg.	TD
1996—Kansas City NFL	16	0	0	0	0.0	0
1997—Kansas City NFL	16	16	4	57	14.3	0
1998—Kansas City NFL	16	16	2	47	23.5	0
1999—Kansas City NFL	15	15	1	5	5.0	0
2000—Kansas City NFL	16	16	2	0	0.0	0
Pro totals (5 years)	79	63	9	109	12.1	0

W

WOODSON, CHARLES — DB — RAIDERS

PERSONAL: Born October 7, 1976, in Fremont, Ohio ... 6-1/205.
HIGH SCHOOL: Ross (Fremont, Ohio).
COLLEGE: Michigan.
TRANSACTIONS/CAREER NOTES: Selected after junior season by Oakland Raiders in first round (fourth pick overall) of 1998 NFL draft. ... Signed by Raiders (July 20, 1998).
CHAMPIONSHIP GAME EXPERIENCE: Played in AFC championship game (2000 season).
HONORS: Named cornerback on The Sporting News college All-America second team (1996). ... Heisman Trophy winner (1997). ... Jim Thorpe Award winner (1997). ... Maxwell Award winner (1997). ... Chuck Bednarik Award winner (1997). ... Named College Football Player of the Year

by THE SPORTING NEWS (1997). ... Named cornerback on THE SPORTING NEWS college All-America first team (1997). ... Played in Pro Bowl (1998-2000 seasons).
PRO STATISTICS: 1999—Caught one pass for 19 yards and recovered one fumble for 24 yards. 2000—Caught one pass for eight yards and recovered one fumble.

			INTERCEPTIONS			
Year Team	G	GS	No.	Yds.	Avg.	TD
1998—Oakland NFL	16	16	5	118	23.6	1
1999—Oakland NFL	16	16	1	15	15.0	1
2000—Oakland NFL	16	16	4	36	9.0	0
Pro totals (3 years)	48	48	10	169	16.9	2

WOODSON, DARREN   S   COWBOYS

PERSONAL: Born April 25, 1969, in Phoenix. ... 6-1/219. ... Full name: Darren Ray Woodson.
HIGH SCHOOL: Maryvale (Phoenix).
COLLEGE: Arizona State (degree in criminal justice).
TRANSACTIONS/CAREER NOTES: Selected by Dallas Cowboys in second round (37th pick overall) of 1992 NFL draft. ... Signed by Cowboys (April 26, 1992). ... On injured reserve with broken forearm (December 14, 2000-remainder of season).
CHAMPIONSHIP GAME EXPERIENCE: Played in NFC championship game (1992-1995 seasons). ... Member of Super Bowl championship team (1992, 1993 and 1995 seasons).
HONORS: Named strong safety on THE SPORTING NEWS NFL All-Pro team (1994-1996 and 1998). ... Played in Pro Bowl (1994-1996 and 1998 seasons). ... Named to play in Pro Bowl (1997 season); replaced by John Lynch due to injury.
PRO STATISTICS: 1993—Recovered three fumbles for three yards. 1994—Recovered one fumble. 1996—Fumbled once and recovered one fumble. 1997—Fumbled once and recovered two fumbles.

			INTERCEPTIONS				SACKS
Year Team	G	GS	No.	Yds.	Avg.	TD	No.
1992—Dallas NFL	16	2	0	0	0.0	0	1.0
1993—Dallas NFL	16	15	0	0	0.0	0	0.0
1994—Dallas NFL	16	16	5	140	28.0	1	0.0
1995—Dallas NFL	16	16	2	46	23.0	1	0.0
1996—Dallas NFL	16	16	5	43	8.6	0	3.0
1997—Dallas NFL	14	14	1	14	14.0	0	2.0
1998—Dallas NFL	16	15	1	1	1.0	0	3.0
1999—Dallas NFL	15	15	2	5	2.5	0	1.0
2000—Dallas NFL	11	11	2	12	6.0	0	0.0
Pro totals (9 years)	136	120	18	261	14.5	2	10.0

WOODSON, ROD   S   RAVENS

PERSONAL: Born March 10, 1965, in Fort Wayne, Ind. ... 6-0/205. ... Full name: Roderick Kevin Woodson.
HIGH SCHOOL: R. Nelson Snider (Fort Wayne, Ind.).
COLLEGE: Purdue.
TRANSACTIONS/CAREER NOTES: Selected by Pittsburgh Steelers in first round (10th pick overall) of 1987 NFL draft. ... On reserve/unsigned list (August 31-October 27, 1987). ... Signed by Steelers (October 28, 1987). ... Granted roster exemption (October 28-November 7, 1987). ... Granted free agency (February 1, 1991). ... Re-signed by Steelers (August 22, 1991). ... Granted unconditional free agency (February 14, 1997). ... Signed by San Francisco 49ers (July 17, 1997). ... Released by 49ers (February 9, 1998). ... Signed by Baltimore Ravens (February 20, 1998). ... Granted unconditional free agency (March 2, 2001). ... Re-signed by Ravens (May 7, 2001).
CHAMPIONSHIP GAME EXPERIENCE: Played in AFC championship game (1994 and 2000 seasons). ... Member of Steelers for AFC championship game (1995 season); inactive. ... Played in Super Bowl XXX (1995 season). ... Played in NFC championship game (1997 season). ... Member of Super Bowl championship team (2000 season).
HONORS: Named defensive back on THE SPORTING NEWS college All-America second team (1985). ... Named kick returner on THE SPORTING NEWS college All-America first team (1986). ... Named kick returner on THE SPORTING NEWS NFL All-Pro team (1989). ... Played in Pro Bowl (1989-1994, 1996, 1999 and 2000 seasons). ... Named cornerback on THE SPORTING NEWS NFL All-Pro team (1990 and 1992-1994).
RECORDS: Shares NFL career record for most touchdowns by interception return—9.
PRO STATISTICS: 1987—Recovered two fumbles. 1988— Recovered three fumbles for two yards. 1989— Recovered four fumbles for one yard. 1990—Recovered three fumbles. 1991— Recovered three fumbles for 15 yards. 1992—Recovered one fumble for nine yards. 1993—Rushed once for no yards and recovered one fumble. 1994—Recovered one fumble. 1996—Recovered three fumbles for 42 yards and a touchdown. 1997—Recovered one fumble. 1999—Recovered two fumbles. 2000—Recovered three fumbles for four yards.
MISCELLANEOUS: Active AFC leader for career interceptions (58). ... Holds Baltimore Ravens all-time record for most interceptions (17).

			INTERCEPTIONS				SACKS	PUNT RETURNS				KICKOFF RETURNS				TOTALS			
Year Team	G	GS	No.	Yds.	Avg.	TD	No.	No.	Yds.	Avg.	TD	No.	Yds.	Avg.	TD	TD	2pt.	Pts.	Fum.
1987—Pittsburgh NFL	8	0	1	45	45.0	1	0.0	16	135	8.4	0	13	290	22.3	0	1	0	6	3
1988—Pittsburgh NFL	16	16	4	98	24.5	0	0.5	33	281	8.5	0	37	850	23.0	0	1	0	6	3
1989—Pittsburgh NFL	15	14	3	39	13.0	0	0.0	29	207	7.1	0	§36	§982	*27.3	†1	1	0	6	3
1990—Pittsburgh NFL	16	16	5	67	13.4	0	0.0	§38	§398	10.5	†1	35	764	21.8	0	1	0	6	3
1991—Pittsburgh NFL	15	15	3	72	24.0	0	1.0	28	§320	§11.4	0	*44	§880	20.0	0	0	0	0	3
1992—Pittsburgh NFL	16	16	4	90	22.5	0	6.0	32	§364	§11.4	1	25	469	18.8	0	1	0	6	2
1993—Pittsburgh NFL	16	16	8	§138	17.3	▲1	2.0	42	338	8.0	0	15	294	19.6	0	1	0	6	2
1994—Pittsburgh NFL	15	15	4	109	27.3	2	3.0	39	319	8.2	0	15	365	24.3	0	2	0	12	2
1995—Pittsburgh NFL	1	1	0	0	0.0	0	0.0	0	0	0.0	0	0	0	0.0	0	0	0	0	0
1996—Pittsburgh NFL	16	16	6	121	20.2	1	1.0	0	0	0.0	0	0	0	0.0	0	2	0	12	1
1997—San Francisco NFL	14	14	3	81	27.0	0	0.0	1	0	0.0	0	0	0	0.0	0	0	0	0	0
1998—Baltimore NFL	16	16	6	108	18.0	▲2	0.0	0	0	0.0	0	0	0	0.0	0	2	0	12	0
1999—Baltimore NFL	16	16	†7	195	27.9	†2	0.0	2	0	0.0	0	0	0	0.0	0	2	0	12	1
2000—Baltimore NFL	16	16	4	20	5.0	0	0.0	0	0	0.0	0	0	0	0.0	0	0	0	0	0
Pro totals (14 years)	196	187	58	1183	20.4	9	13.5	260	2362	9.1	2	220	4894	22.2	2	14	0	84	23

W

WOODY, DAMIEN — C — PATRIOTS

PERSONAL: Born November 3, 1977, in Beaverdam, Va. ... 6-3/315. ... Full name: Damien Michael Woody.
HIGH SCHOOL: Patrick Henry (Beaverdam, Va.).
COLLEGE: Boston College.
TRANSACTIONS/CAREER NOTES: Selected after junior season by New England Patriots in first round (17th pick overall) of 1999 NFL draft. ... Signed by Patriots (July 30, 1999).
PLAYING EXPERIENCE: New England NFL, 1999 and 2000. ... Games/Games started: 1999 (16/16), 2000 (16/16). Total: 32/32.
PRO STATISTICS: 1999—Fumbled once and recovered one fumble for minus 10 yards.

WORTHAM, BARRON — LB

PERSONAL: Born November 1, 1969, in Fort Worth, Texas. ... 5-11/245. ... Full name: Barron Winfred Wortham.
HIGH SCHOOL: Everman (Texas).
COLLEGE: Texas-El Paso.
TRANSACTIONS/CAREER NOTES: Selected by Houston Oilers in sixth round (194th pick overall) of 1994 NFL draft. ... Signed by Oilers (July 12, 1994). ... Granted free agency (February 14, 1997). ... Oilers franchise moved to Tennessee for 1997 season. ... Re-signed by Oilers (July 9, 1997). ... Granted unconditional free agency (February 13, 1998). ... Re-signed by Oilers (February 23, 1998). ... Oilers franchise renamed Tennessee Titans for 1999 season (December 26, 1998). ... Released by Titans (April 25, 2000). ... Signed by Dallas Cowboys (May 4, 2000). ... Granted unconditional free agency (March 2, 2001).
CHAMPIONSHIP GAME EXPERIENCE: Played in AFC championship game (1999 season). ... Played in Super Bowl XXXIV (1999 season).
HONORS: Named linebacker on THE SPORTING NEWS college All-America second team (1993).
PRO STATISTICS: 1994—Recovered one fumble. 1995—Returned one kickoff for minus three yards. 1996—Recovered two fumbles. 1999—Recovered three fumbles for eight yards. 2000—Intercepted two passes for one yard and recovered one fumble.

Year Team	G	GS	SACKS
1994—Houston NFL	16	1	0.0
1995—Houston NFL	16	5	1.0
1996—Houston NFL	15	14	2.0
1997—Tennessee NFL	16	16	0.0
1998—Tennessee NFL	13	0	0.0
1999—Tennessee NFL	16	15	0.5
2000—Dallas NFL	16	11	0.0
Pro totals (7 years)	108	62	3.5

WRIGHT, ANTHONY — QB — COWBOYS

PERSONAL: Born February 14, 1976, in Vanceboro, N.C. ... 6-1/195. ... Cousin of Jesse Campbell, safety with Philadelphia Eagles (1991 and 1992), New York Giants (1992-97) and Washington Redskins (1997 and 1998).
HIGH SCHOOL: West Craven (N.C.).
COLLEGE: South Carolina.
TRANSACTIONS/CAREER NOTES: Signed as non-drafted free agent by Pittsburgh Steelers (April 18, 1999). ... Active for one game (1999); did not play. ... Released by Steelers (August 27, 2000). ... Signed by Cowboys to practice squad (August 30, 2000). ... Activated (November 21, 2000).
PRO STATISTICS: 2000—Fumbled three times and recovered one fumble for minus three yards.
SINGLE GAME HIGHS (regular season): Attempts—25 (December 17, 2000, vs. New York Giants); completions—13 (December 17, 2000, vs. New York Giants); yards—119 (December 17, 2000, vs. New York Giants); and touchdown passes—0.
MISCELLANEOUS: Regular-season record as starting NFL quarterback: 0-2.

Year Team	G	GS	PASSING Att.	Cmp.	Pct.	Yds.	TD	Int.	Avg.	Rat.	RUSHING Att.	Yds.	Avg.	TD	TOTALS TD	2pt.	Pts.
1999—Pittsburgh NFL							Did not play.										
2000—Dallas NFL	4	2	53	22	41.5	237	0	3	4.47	31.7	12	36	3.0	0	0	0	0
Pro totals (1 years)	4	2	53	22	41.5	237	0	3	4.47	31.7	12	36	3.0	0	0	0	0

WRIGHT, KENNY — CB — VIKINGS

PERSONAL: Born September 14, 1977, in Ruston, La. ... 6-1/205.
HIGH SCHOOL: Ruston (La.).
COLLEGE: Arkansas, then Northwestern (La.) State.
TRANSACTIONS/CAREER NOTES: Selected after junior season by Minnesota Vikings in fourth round (120th pick overall) of 1999 NFL draft. ... Signed by Vikings (July 21, 1999).
PLAYING EXPERIENCE: Minnesota NFL, 1999 and 2000. ... Games/Games started: 1999 (16/12), 2000 (16/7). Total: 32/19.
CHAMPIONSHIP GAME EXPERIENCE: Member of Vikings for NFC championship game (2000 season); inactive.
PRO STATISTICS: 1999—Intercepted one pass for 11 yards. 2000—Recovered one fumble for 11 yards.

W

WRIGHT, KENYATTA — LB — BILLS

PERSONAL: Born February 19, 1978, in Vian, Okla. ... 6-0/238.
HIGH SCHOOL: Vian (Okla.).
COLLEGE: Oklahoma State.
TRANSACTIONS/CAREER NOTES: Signed as non-drafted free agent by Buffalo Bills (April 23, 2000).
PLAYING EXPERIENCE: Buffalo NFL, 2000. ... Games/Games started: 2000 (16/0).

WUERFFEL, DANNY · QB

PERSONAL: Born May 27, 1974, in Fort Walton Beach, Fla. ... 6-1/208. ... Full name: Daniel Carl Wuerffel. ... Name pronounced WER-ful.
HIGH SCHOOL: Fort Walton Beach (Fla.).
COLLEGE: Florida.
TRANSACTIONS/CAREER NOTES: Selected by New Orleans Saints in fourth round (99th pick overall) of 1997 NFL draft. ... Signed by Saints (July 17, 1997). ... Released by Saints (February 11, 2000). ... Signed by Green Bay Packers (July 5, 2000). ... Granted unconditional free agency (March 2, 2001).
HONORS: Davey O'Brien Award winner (1995 and 1996). ... Heisman Trophy winner (1996). ... Named College Player of the Year by THE SPORTING NEWS (1996). ... Named quarterback on THE SPORTING NEWS college All-America first team (1996).
PRO STATISTICS: 1997—Fumbled twice and recovered two fumbles. 1998—Fumbled once and recovered one fumble.
SINGLE GAME HIGHS (regular season): Attempts—47 (October 4, 1998, vs. New England); completions—25 (October 4, 1998, vs. New England); yards—278 (October 4, 1998, vs. New England); and touchdown passes—2 (October 4, 1998, vs. New England).
MISCELLANEOUS: Regular-season record as starting NFL quarterback: 2-4 (.333).

				PASSING							RUSHING				TOTALS		
Year Team	G	GS	Att.	Cmp.	Pct.	Yds.	TD	Int.	Avg.	Rat.	Att.	Yds.	Avg.	TD	TD	2pt.	Pts.
1997—New Orleans NFL	7	2	91	42	46.2	518	4	8	5.69	42.3	6	26	4.3	0	0	0	0
1998—New Orleans NFL	5	4	119	62	52.1	695	5	5	5.84	66.3	11	60	5.5	0	0	0	0
1999—New Orleans NFL	4	0	48	22	45.8	191	0	3	3.98	30.8	2	29	14.5	1	1	0	6
2000—Rhein NFLE	...	...	260	161	61.9	2042	25	7	7.85	107.2	24	80	3.3	2	0	0	0
—Green Bay NFL	1	0	0	0	0.0	0	0	0	0.0	...	2	-2	-1.0	0	0	0	0
NFL Europe totals (1 year)	...	...	260	161	61.9	2042	25	7	7.85	107.2	24	80	3.3	2	0	0	0
NFL totals (4 years)	17	6	258	126	48.8	1404	9	16	5.44	51.2	21	113	5.4	1	1	0	6
Pro totals (5 years)	...	...	518	287	55.4	3446	34	23	6.65	79.4	45	193	4.3	3	1	0	6

WUNSCH, JERRY · OT · BUCCANEERS

PERSONAL: Born January 21, 1974, in Eau Claire, Wis. ... 6-6/339. ... Full name: Gerald Wunsch. ... Name pronounced WUNCH.
HIGH SCHOOL: West (Wausau, Wis.).
COLLEGE: Wisconsin (degree in history).
TRANSACTIONS/CAREER NOTES: Selected by Tampa Bay Buccaneers in second round (37th pick overall) of 1997 NFL draft. ... Signed by Buccaneers (July 18, 1997). ... Granted unconditional free agency (March 2, 2001). ... Re-signed by Buccaneers (April 9, 2001).
PLAYING EXPERIENCE: Tampa Bay NFL, 1997-2000. ... Games/Games started: 1997 (16/0), 1998 (16/1), 1999 (16/13), 2000 (16/16). Total 64/30.
CHAMPIONSHIP GAME EXPERIENCE: Played in NFC championship game (1999 season).
PRO STATISTICS: 1997—Recovered one fumble.

WYCHECK, FRANK · TE · TITANS

PERSONAL: Born October 14, 1971, in Philadelphia. ... 6-3/250. ... Name pronounced WHY-check.
HIGH SCHOOL: Archbishop Ryan (Philadelphia).
COLLEGE: Maryland.
TRANSACTIONS/CAREER NOTES: Selected after junior season by Washington Redskins in sixth round (160th pick overall) of 1993 NFL draft. ... Signed by Redskins (July 15, 1993). ... On suspended list for anabolic steroid use (November 29, 1994-remainder of season). ... Released by Redskins (August 17, 1995). ... Signed by Houston Oilers (August 18, 1995). ... Granted free agency (February 16, 1996). ... Re-signed by Oilers (June 28, 1996). ... Oilers franchise moved to Tennessee for 1997 season. ... Oilers franchise renamed Tennessee Titans for 1999 season (December 26, 1998).
CHAMPIONSHIP GAME EXPERIENCE: Played in AFC championship game (1999 season). ... Played in Super Bowl XXXIV (1999 season).
HONORS: Played in Pro Bowl (1998-2000 seasons).
PRO STATISTICS: 1993—Recovered one fumble. 1995—Rushed once for one yard and a touchdown and recovered one fumble. 1996—Rushed twice for three yards. 1997—Recovered one fumble. 1998—Recovered two fumbles. 1999—Completed only pass attempt for 61 yards and a touchdown. 2000—Attempted two passes with two completions for 53 yards and a touchdown.
SINGLE GAME HIGHS (regular season): Receptions—10 (December 5, 1999, vs. Baltimore); yards—87 (December 5, 1999, vs. Baltimore); and touchdown receptions—2 (October 1, 2000, vs. New York Giants).

			RECEIVING				KICKOFF RETURNS				TOTALS			
Year Team	G	GS	No.	Yds.	Avg.	TD	No.	Yds.	Avg.	TD	TD	2pt.	Pts.	Fum.
1993—Washington NFL	9	7	16	113	7.1	0	0	0	0.0	0	0	0	0	1
1994—Washington NFL	9	1	7	55	7.9	1	4	84	21.0	0	1	0	6	0
1995—Houston NFL	16	11	40	471	11.8	1	0	0	0.0	0	2	0	12	0
1996—Houston NFL	16	16	53	511	9.6	6	2	5	2.5	0	6	0	36	2
1997—Tennessee NFL	16	16	63	748	11.9	4	1	3	3.0	0	4	1	26	0
1998—Tennessee NFL	16	16	70	768	11.0	2	1	10	10.0	0	2	0	12	2
1999—Tennessee NFL	16	16	69	641	9.3	2	0	0	0.0	0	2	0	12	0
2000—Tennessee NFL	16	16	70	636	9.1	4	0	0	0.0	0	4	0	24	2
Pro totals (8 years)	114	99	388	3943	10.2	20	8	102	12.8	0	21	1	128	7

WYNN, RENALDO · DE · JAGUARS

PERSONAL: Born September 3, 1974, in Chicago. ... 6-3/288. ... Full name: Renaldo Levalle Wynn.
HIGH SCHOOL: De La Salle Institute (Chicago).
COLLEGE: Notre Dame (degree in sociology, 1996).
TRANSACTIONS/CAREER NOTES: Selected by Jacksonville Jaguars in first round (21st pick overall) of 1997 NFL draft. ... Signed by Jaguars (July 21, 1997). ... On injured reserve with groin injury (December 25, 1998-remainder of season).

W

CHAMPIONSHIP GAME EXPERIENCE: Played in AFC championship game (1999 season).
PRO STATISTICS: 1997—Recovered one fumble. 1998—Recovered one fumble. 1999—Recovered one fumble.

Year Team	G	GS	SACKS
1997—Jacksonville NFL	16	8	2.5
1998—Jacksonville NFL	15	15	1.0
1999—Jacksonville NFL	12	10	1.5
2000—Jacksonville NFL	14	14	3.5
Pro totals (4 years)	57	47	8.5

WYNN, SPERGON　　QB　　BROWNS

PERSONAL: Born August 10, 1978, in Houston. ... 6-3/226.
HIGH SCHOOL: Episcopal (Bellaire, Texas).
COLLEGE: Minnesota, then Southwest Texas State.
TRANSACTIONS/CAREER NOTES: Selected by Cleveland Browns in sixth round (183rd pick overall) of 2000 NFL draft. ... Signed by Browns (July 11, 2000). ... On injured reserve with knee injury (December 8, 2000-remainder of season). ... Assigned by Browns to Amsterdam Admirals in 2001 NFL Europe enhancement allocation program (February 19, 2001).
PRO STATISTICS: 2000—Fumbled twice.
SINGLE GAME HIGHS (regular season): Attempts—16 (December 3, 2000, vs. Jacksonville); completions—7 (October 29, 2000, vs. Cincinnati); yards—82 (October 29, 2000, vs. Cincinnati); and touchdown passes—0.
MISCELLANEOUS: Regular-season record as starting NFL quarterback: 0-1.

					PASSING							RUSHING				TOTALS	
Year Team	G	GS	Att.	Cmp.	Pct.	Yds.	TD	Int.	Avg.	Rat.	Att.	Yds.	Avg.	TD	TD	2pt.	Pts.
2000—Cleveland NFL	7	1	54	22	40.7	167	0	1	3.09	41.2	3	15	5.0	0	0	0	0

WYRICK, JIMMY　　CB　　LIONS

PERSONAL: Born December 31, 1976, in DeSoto, Texas. ... 5-9/179.
HIGH SCHOOL: DeSoto (Texas).
COLLEGE: Minnesota.
TRANSACTIONS/CAREER NOTES: Signed as non-drafted free agent by Detroit Lions (April 28, 2000). ... On injured reserve with ankle injury (October 16, 2000-remainder of season).
PLAYING EXPERIENCE: Detroit NFL, 2000. ... Games/Games started: 2000 (6/0).

YAMINI, BASHIR　　WR　　COWBOYS

PERSONAL: Born September 10, 1977, in Dolton, Ill. ... 6-3/190.
HIGH SCHOOL: Thornridge (Ill.).
COLLEGE: Iowa.
TRANSACTIONS/CAREER NOTES: Signed as non-drafted free agent by Denver Broncos (April 17, 2000). ... Claimed on waivers by Tennessee Titans (August 28, 2000). ... Released by Titans (November 4, 2000). ... Re-signed by Titans to practice squad (November 8, 2000). ... Granted free agency following 2000 season. ... Signed by Dallas Cowboys (March 20, 2001).
PLAYING EXPERIENCE: Tennessee NFL, 2000. ... Games/Games started: 2000 (6/0).

YEAST, CRAIG　　WR/KR　　BENGALS

PERSONAL: Born November 20, 1976, in Danville, Ky. ... 5-7/165. ... Full name: Craig Nelson Yeast.
HIGH SCHOOL: Harrodsburg (Ky.).
COLLEGE: Kentucky.
TRANSACTIONS/CAREER NOTES: Selected by Cincinnati Bengals in fourth round (98th pick overall) of 1999 NFL draft. ... Signed by Bengals (July 28, 1999).
PRO STATISTICS: 1999—Fumbled twice and recovered one fumble. 2000—Fumbled three times and recovered one fumble.
SINGLE GAME HIGHS (regular season): Receptions—4 (November 19, 2000, vs. New England); yards—57 (November 19, 2000, vs. New England); and touchdown receptions—0.

			RUSHING			RECEIVING				PUNT RETURNS				KICKOFF RETURNS				TOTALS	
Year Team	G	GS	Att.	Yds.	Avg.	TD	No.	Yds.	Avg.	TD	No.	Yds.	Avg.	TD	No.	Yds.	Avg.	TD	TD	2pt.	Pts.
1999—Cincinnati NFL	9	0	2	-16	-8.0	0	3	20	6.7	0	10	209	20.9	†2	3	50	16.7	0	2	0	12
2000—Cincinnati NFL	15	7	1	15	15.0	0	24	301	12.5	0	34	225	6.6	0	7	106	15.1	0	0	0	0
Pro totals (2 years)	24	7	3	-1	-0.3	0	27	321	11.9	0	44	434	9.9	2	10	156	15.6	0	2	0	12

YODER, TODD　　TE　　BUCCANEERS

PERSONAL: Born March 18, 1978, in New Palestine, Ind. ... 6-4/234.
HIGH SCHOOL: New Palestine (Ind.).
COLLEGE: Vanderbilt.
TRANSACTIONS/CAREER NOTES: Signed as non-drafted free agent by Tampa Bay Buccaneers (April 17, 2000).
PLAYING EXPERIENCE: Tampa Bay NFL, 2000. ... Games/Games started: 2000 (9/0).
PRO STATISTICS: 2000—Caught one pass for one yard, returned one punt for no yards and fumbled once.
SINGLE GAME HIGHS (regular season): Receptions—1 (September 10, 2000, vs. Chicago); yards—1 (September 10, 2000, vs. Chicago); and touchdown receptions—0.

W
Y

YOUNG, BRIAN　　　DE　　　RAMS

PERSONAL: Born July 8, 1977, in Lawton, Okla. ... 6-2/290.
HIGH SCHOOL: Andress (El Paso, Texas).
COLLEGE: Texas-El Paso.
TRANSACTIONS/CAREER NOTES: Selected by St. Louis Rams in fifth round (139th pick overall) of 2000 NFL draft. ... Signed by Rams (July 7, 2000).
PLAYING EXPERIENCE: St. Louis NFL, 2000. ... Games/Games started: 2000 (11/0).

YOUNG, BRYANT　　　DT　　　49ERS

PERSONAL: Born January 27, 1972, in Chicago Heights, Ill. ... 6-3/291. ... Full name: Bryant Colby Young.
HIGH SCHOOL: Bloom (Chicago Heights, Ill.).
COLLEGE: Notre Dame.
TRANSACTIONS/CAREER NOTES: Selected by San Francisco 49ers in first round (seventh pick overall) of 1994 NFL draft. ... Signed by 49ers (July 26, 1994). ... On injured reserve with broken leg (December 2, 1998-remainder of season). ... On physically unable to perform list with leg injury (July 30-August 10, 1999).
CHAMPIONSHIP GAME EXPERIENCE: Played in NFC championship game (1994 and 1997 seasons). ... Member of Super Bowl championship team (1994 season).
HONORS: Named defensive tackle on THE SPORTING NEWS NFL All-Pro team (1996 and 1998). ... Played in Pro Bowl (1996 and 1999 season).
PRO STATISTICS: 1994—Recovered one fumble. 1995—Recovered two fumbles. 1996—Recovered one fumble for 43 yards. 1998—Recovered one fumble. 1999—Credited with a safety. 2000—Recovered one fumble.

Year　Team	G	GS	SACKS
1994—San Francisco NFL	16	16	6.0
1995—San Francisco NFL	12	12	6.0
1996—San Francisco NFL	16	16	11.5
1997—San Francisco NFL	12	12	4.0
1998—San Francisco NFL	12	12	9.5
1999—San Francisco NFL	16	16	11.0
2000—San Francisco NFL	15	15	9.5
Pro totals (7 years)	99	99	57.5

YOUNG, FLOYD　　　CB

PERSONAL: Born November 23, 1975, in New Orleans. ... 6-0/179. ... Full name: Floyd Alexander Young.
HIGH SCHOOL: Clark (New Orleans).
JUNIOR COLLEGE: Scottsdale (Ariz.) Community College.
COLLEGE: Texas A&M-Kingsville.
TRANSACTIONS/CAREER NOTES: Signed as non-drafted free agent by Tampa Bay Buccaneers (May 5, 1997). ... Released by Buccaneers (July 18, 1997). ... Re-signed by Buccaneers (July 22, 1997). ... Released by Buccaneers (August 17, 1997). ... Re-signed by Buccaneers to practice squad (August 26, 1997). ... Activated (September 27, 1997). ... Granted free agency (February 11, 2000). ... Re-signed by Buccaneers (May 30, 2000). ... Granted unconditional free agency (March 2, 2001).
PLAYING EXPERIENCE: Tampa Bay NFL, 1997-2000. ... Games/Games started: 1997 (12/1), 1998 (11/0), 1999 (6/0), 2000 (7/0). Total: 36/1.
CHAMPIONSHIP GAME EXPERIENCE: Played in NFC championship game (1999 season).
PRO STATISTICS: 1998—Recovered one fumble.

YOUNG, RYAN　　　OT　　　JETS

PERSONAL: Born June 28, 1976, in St. Louis. ... 6-5/320.
HIGH SCHOOL: Parkway Central (Chesterfield, Mo.).
COLLEGE: Kansas State.
TRANSACTIONS/CAREER NOTES: Selected by New York Jets in seventh round (223rd pick overall) of 1999 NFL draft. ... Signed by Jets (June 25, 1999).
PLAYING EXPERIENCE: New York Jets NFL, 1999 and 2000. ... Games/Games started: 1999 (15/7), 2000 (16/16). Total: 31/23.

ZAHURSKY, STEVE　　　G　　　BROWNS

PERSONAL: Born September 2, 1976, in Euclid, Ohio. ... 6-6/305. ... Name pronounced za-HER-ski.
HIGH SCHOOL: Euclid (Ohio).
COLLEGE: Kent.
TRANSACTIONS/CAREER NOTES: Signed as non-drafted free agent by Jacksonville Jaguars (April 23, 1998). ... Released by Jaguars (August 30, 1998). ... Signed by Philadelphia Eagles to practice squad (December 7, 1998). ... Granted free agency following 1998 season. ... Signed by Cleveland Browns (February 11, 1999).
PLAYING EXPERIENCE: Cleveland NFL, 1999 and 2000. ... Games/Games started: 1999 (9/7), 2000 (16/16). Total: 25/23.
PRO STATISTICS: 2000—Recovered three fumbles.

ZEIER, ERIC　　　QB　　　FALCONS

PERSONAL: Born September 6, 1972, in Pensacola, Fla. ... 6-1/214. ... Full name: Eric Royce Zeier. ... Name pronounced ZIRE.
HIGH SCHOOL: Heidelberg (West Germany), then Marietta (Ga.).
COLLEGE: Georgia.

TRANSACTIONS/CAREER NOTES: Selected by Cleveland Browns in third round (84th pick overall) of 1995 NFL draft. ... Signed by Browns (July 14, 1995). ... Browns franchise moved to Baltimore and renamed Ravens for 1996 season (March 11, 1996). ... Granted free agency (February 13, 1998). ... Tendered offer sheet by Atlanta Falcons (March 5, 1998). ... Offer matched by Ravens (March 10, 1998). ... Traded by Ravens to Tampa Bay Buccaneers for sixth-round pick (traded to Minnesota) in 1999 draft (April 17, 1999). ... Granted unconditional free agency (February 11, 2000). ... Re-signed by Buccaneers (March 2, 2000). ... Traded by Buccaneers to Falcons for seventh-round pick (TE Dauntae' Finger) in 2001 draft (March 6, 2001).
CHAMPIONSHIP GAME EXPERIENCE: Member of Buccaneers for NFC championship game (1999 season); did not play.
HONORS: Named quarterback on The Sporting News college All-America second team (1994).
PRO STATISTICS: 1995—Fumbled three times. 1996—Fumbled twice and recovered one fumble. 1997—Fumbled three times for minus 14 yards. 1998—Fumbled twice and recovered one fumble. 1999—Fumbled once.
SINGLE GAME HIGHS (regular season): Attempts—54 (November 5, 1995, vs. Houston); completions—29 (October 31, 1999, vs. Detroit); yards—349 (December 21, 1997, vs. Cincinnati); and touchdown passes—3 (December 14, 1997, vs. Tennessee).
STATISTICAL PLATEAUS: 300-yard passing games: 1995 (1), 1997 (2). Total: 3.
MISCELLANEOUS: Regular-season record as starting NFL quarterback: 5-7 (.417).

			PASSING								RUSHING				TOTALS		
Year Team	G	GS	Att.	Cmp.	Pct.	Yds.	TD	Int.	Avg.	Rat.	Att.	Yds.	Avg.	TD	TD	2pt.	Pts.
1995—Cleveland NFL	7	4	161	82	50.9	864	4	9	5.37	51.9	15	80	5.3	0	0	1	2
1996—Baltimore NFL	1	0	21	10	47.6	97	1	1	4.62	57.0	2	8	4.0	0	0	0	0
1997—Baltimore NFL	5	3	116	67	57.8	958	7	1	8.26	101.1	10	17	1.7	0	0	0	0
1998—Baltimore NFL	10	4	181	107	59.1	1312	4	3	7.25	82.0	11	17	1.5	0	0	0	0
1999—Tampa Bay NFL	2	1	55	32	58.2	270	0	1	4.91	63.4	3	7	2.3	0	0	0	0
2000—Tampa Bay NFL	3	0	3	3	100.0	19	0	0	6.33	93.1	2	-2	-1.0	0	0	0	0
Pro totals (6 years)	28	12	537	301	56.1	3520	16	15	6.55	74.4	43	127	3.0	0	0	1	2

ZEIGLER, DUSTY   C   GIANTS

PERSONAL: Born September 27, 1973, in Savannah, Ga. ... 6-5/303. ... Full name: Curtis Dustin Zeigler. ... Name pronounced ZIG-ler.
HIGH SCHOOL: Effingham County (Springfield, Ga.).
COLLEGE: Notre Dame.
TRANSACTIONS/CAREER NOTES: Selected by Buffalo Bills in sixth round (202nd pick overall) of 1996 NFL draft. ... Signed by Bills (June 25, 1996). ... Granted free agency (February 12, 1999). ... Re-signed by Bills (April 15, 1999). ... Granted unconditional free agency (February 11, 2000). ... Signed by New York Giants (March 6, 2000).
PLAYING EXPERIENCE: Buffalo NFL, 1996-1999; New York Giants NFL, 2000. ... Games/Games started: 1996 (2/0), 1997 (13/13), 1998 (16/16), 1999 (15/15), 2000 (16/16). Total: 62/60.
CHAMPIONSHIP GAME EXPERIENCE: Played in NFC championship game (2000 season). ... Played in Super Bowl XXXV (2000 season).
PRO STATISTICS: 1997—Fumbled once and recovered one fumble for minus 12 yards. 1998—Fumbled three times for minus 19 yards.

ZELENKA, JOE   TE

PERSONAL: Born March 9, 1976, in Cleveland. ... 6-3/280. ... Full name: Joseph John Zelenka.
HIGH SCHOOL: Benedictine (Cleveland).
COLLEGE: Wake Forest.
TRANSACTIONS/CAREER NOTES: Signed as non-drafted free agent by San Francisco 49ers (April 23, 1999). ... Traded by 49ers to Washington Redskins for seventh-round pick (TE Eric Johnson) in 2001 draft (April 17, 2000). ... Released by Redskins (March 9, 2001).
PLAYING EXPERIENCE: San Francisco NFL, 1999; Washington NFL, 2000. ... Games/Games started: 1999 (13/0), 2000 (16/0). Total: 29/0.
PRO STATISTICS: 1999—Fumbled once and recovered one fumble for minus 15 yards.

ZELLNER, PEPPI   DE   COWBOYS

PERSONAL: Born March 14, 1975, in Forsythe, Ga. ... 6-5/257. ... Full name: Hunndens Guiseppi Zellner.
HIGH SCHOOL: Mary Persons (Forsythe, Ga.).
JUNIOR COLLEGE: Georgia Military College.
COLLEGE: Fort Valley (Ga.) State.
TRANSACTIONS/CAREER NOTES: Selected by Dallas Cowboys in fourth round (132nd pick overall) of 1999 NFL draft. ... Signed by Cowboys (July 27, 1999). ... On injured reserve with knee injury (December 12, 2000-remainder of season).
PLAYING EXPERIENCE: Dallas NFL, 1999 and 2000. ... Games/Games started: 1999 (13/0), 2000 (12/0). Total: 25/0.
PRO STATISTICS: 1999—Credited with one sack. 2000—Credited with one sack.

ZEREOUE, AMOS   RB   STEELERS

PERSONAL: Born October 8, 1976, in Ivory Coast. ... 5-8/202. ... Name pronounced zer-O-way.
HIGH SCHOOL: W.C. Mepham (Hempstead, N.Y.).
COLLEGE: West Virginia.
TRANSACTIONS/CAREER NOTES: Selected after junior season by Pittsburgh Steelers in third round (95th pick overall) of 1999 NFL draft. ... Signed by Steelers (July 30, 1999).
HONORS: Named running back on The Sporting News college All-America third team (1997).
SINGLE GAME HIGHS (regular season): Attempts—17 (September 12, 1999, vs. Cleveland); yards—44 (September 12, 1999, vs. Cleveland); and rushing touchdowns—0.

			RUSHING				RECEIVING				KICKOFF RETURNS				TOTALS			
Year Team	G	GS	Att.	Yds.	Avg.	TD	No.	Yds.	Avg.	TD	No.	Yds.	Avg.	TD	TD	2pt.	Pts.	Fum.
1999—Pittsburgh NFL	8	0	18	48	2.7	0	2	17	8.5	0	7	169	24.1	0	0	0	0	0
2000—Pittsburgh NFL	12	0	6	14	2.3	0	0	0	0.0	0	0	0	0.0	0	0	0	0	0
Pro totals (2 years)	20	0	24	62	2.6	0	2	17	8.5	0	7	169	24.1	0	0	0	0	0

ZGONINA, JEFF   DT   RAMS

PERSONAL: Born May 24, 1970, in Chicago. ... 6-2/300. ... Full name: Jeffrey Marc Zgonina. ... Name pronounced ska-KNEE-na.
HIGH SCHOOL: Mount Carmel (Chicago).
COLLEGE: Purdue (degree in community health promotion, 1992).
TRANSACTIONS/CAREER NOTES: Selected by Pittsburgh Steelers in seventh round (185th pick overall) of 1993 NFL draft. ... Signed by Steelers (July 16, 1993). ... Claimed on waivers by Carolina Panthers (August 28, 1995). ... Granted free agency (February 16, 1996). ... Re-signed by Panthers (April 11, 1996). ... Released by Panthers (August 19, 1996). ... Signed by Atlanta Falcons (October 8, 1996). ... Granted unconditional free agency (February 14, 1997). ... Signed by St. Louis Rams (March 17, 1997). ... Released by Rams (August 30, 1998). ... Signed by Oakland Raiders (October 13, 1998). ... Released by Raiders (October 18, 1998). ... Signed by Indianapolis Colts (November 25, 1998). ... Granted unconditional free agency (February 12, 1999). ... Signed by Rams (April 5, 1999).
PLAYING EXPERIENCE: Pittsburgh NFL, 1993 and 1994; Carolina NFL, 1995; Atlanta NFL, 1996; St. Louis NFL, 1997, 1999 and 2000; Indianapolis NFL, 1998. ... Games/Games started: 1993 (5/0), 1994 (16/0), 1995 (2/0), 1996 (8/0), 1997 (15/0), 1998 (2/0), 1999 (16/0), 2000 (16/11). Total: 80/11.
CHAMPIONSHIP GAME EXPERIENCE: Played in AFC championship game (1994 season). ... Played in NFC championship game (1999 season). ... Member of Super Bowl championship team (1999 season).
PRO STATISTICS: 1993—Recovered one fumble. 1994—Returned two kickoffs for eight yards, fumbled once and recovered one fumble. 1996—Credited with one sack and recovered one fumble. 1997—Returned one kickoff for five yards and credited with two sacks. 1999—Credited with $4^1/_2$ sacks. 2000—Credited with two sacks and recovered three fumbles.

ZIEMANN, CHRIS   OT   GIANTS

PERSONAL: Born September 20, 1976, in Aurora, Ill. ... 6-7/315.
HIGH SCHOOL: Waubonsie Valley (Aurora, Ill.).
COLLEGE: Michigan.
TRANSACTIONS/CAREER NOTES: Signed as non-drafted free agent by New York Giants (April 20, 2000). ... On injured reserve with knee injury (November 2, 2000-remainder of season).
PLAYING EXPERIENCE: New York Giants NFL, 2000. ... Games/Games started: 2000 (8/0).

2001 DRAFT PICKS

ADAMS, KEITH   LB   TITANS

PERSONAL: Born November 22, 1979, in College Park, Ga. ... 5-11/223.
HIGH SCHOOL: Westlake (Atlanta).
COLLEGE: Clemson.
TRANSACTIONS/CAREER NOTES: Selected after junior season by Tennessee Titans in seventh round (232nd pick overall) of 2001 NFL draft.
HONORS: Named linebacker on THE SPORTING NEWS college All-America third team (1999). ... Named linebacker on THE SPORTING NEWS college All-America first team (2000).
COLLEGE NOTES: Recovered two fumbles (1999); intercepted one pass (2000).

Year Team	G	SACKS
1998—Clemson	11	0.0
1999—Clemson	12	16.0
2000—Clemson	12	7.0
College totals (3 years)	35	23.0

AKBAR, HAKIM   S   PATRIOTS

PERSONAL: Born August 11, 1980, in Riverside, Calif. ... 6-0/211.
HIGH SCHOOL: Polytechnic (Riverside, Calif.).
COLLEGE: Washington.
TRANSACTIONS/CAREER NOTES: Selected after junior season by New England Patriots in fifth round (163rd pick overall) of 2001 NFL draft.
COLLEGE NOTES: Recovered one fumble (1998); recovered two fumbles (1999); recovered two fumbles (2000).

Year Team	G	No.	Yds.	Avg.	TD
			INTERCEPTIONS		
1998—Washington	11	1	17	17.0	0
1999—Washington	11	1	4	4.0	0
2000—Washington	11	2	31	15.5	0
College totals (3 years)	33	4	52	13.0	0

ALEXANDER, DAN   RB   TITANS

PERSONAL: Born March 17, 1978, in Wentzville, Mo. ... 6-0/244.
HIGH SCHOOL: Wentzville (Mo.).
COLLEGE: Nebraska.
TRANSACTIONS/CAREER NOTES: Selected by Tennessee Titans in sixth round (192nd pick overall) of 2001 NFL draft.

Year Team	G	Att.	Yds.	Avg.	TD	No.	Yds.	Avg.	TD	TD	Pts.
		RUSHING				RECEIVING				TOTALS	
1997—Nebraska	6	16	68	4.3	0	0	0	0.0	0	0	0
1998—Nebraska	9	70	369	5.3	4	0	0	0.0	0	4	24
1999—Nebraska	12	134	865	6.5	8	4	56	14.0	0	8	48
2000—Nebraska	11	182	1154	6.3	8	2	17	8.5	0	8	48
College totals (4 years)	38	402	2456	6.1	20	6	73	12.2	0	20	120

ALLEN, BRIAN   LB   RAMS

PERSONAL: Born April 1, 1978, in Lake City, Fla. ... 6-1/238. ... Cousin of Reinard Wilson, defensive end, Cincinnati Bengals.
HIGH SCHOOL: Columbia (Lake City, Fla.).
COLLEGE: Florida State.
TRANSACTIONS/CAREER NOTES: Selected by St. Louis Rams in third round (83rd pick overall) of 2001 NFL draft. ... Signed by Rams (June 5, 2001).
COLLEGE NOTES: Recovered two fumbles (1998); recovered two fumbles (2000).

Year Team	G	No.	Yds.	Avg.	TD	No.
		INTERCEPTIONS				SACKS
1997—Florida State	11	0	0	0.0	0	0.0
1998—Florida State	11	0	0	0.0	0	1.0
1999—Florida State	11	1	-3	-3.0	0	5.0
2000—Florida State	12	1	0	0.0	0	1.0
College totals (4 years)	45	2	-3	-1.5	0	7.0

ALLEN, WILL   CB   GIANTS

PERSONAL: Born August 5, 1978, in Syracuse, N.Y. ... 5-10/192. ... Full name: Will D. Allen.
HIGH SCHOOL: Corcoran (Syracuse, N.Y.).
COLLEGE: Syracuse.
TRANSACTIONS/CAREER NOTES: Selected by New York Giants in first round (22nd pick overall) of 2001 NFL draft.
HONORS: Named cornerback to THE SPORTING NEWS college All-America third team (2000).
COLLEGE NOTES: Recovered one fumble (1998).

Year Team	G	No.	Yds.	Avg.	TD	No.	Yds.	Avg.	TD	TD	Pts.
		INTERCEPTIONS				KICKOFF RETURNS				TOTALS	
1997—Syracuse	12	0	0	0.0	0	0	0	0.0	0	0	0
1998—Syracuse	9	0	0	0.0	0	0	0	0.0	0	0	0
1999—Syracuse	11	2	33	16.5	0	18	382	21.2	0	0	0
2000—Syracuse	11	2	9	4.5	0	19	458	24.1	0	0	0
College totals (4 years)	43	4	42	10.5	0	37	840	22.7	0	0	0

ANDERSON, SCOTTY   WR   LIONS

PERSONAL: Born November 24, 1979, in Jonesboro, La. ... 6-2/184. ... Brother of Stevie Anderson, wide receiver with New York Jets (1994) and Arizona Cardinals (1995 and 1996); and brother of Anthony Anderson, defensive back with San Diego Chargers (1987).
HIGH SCHOOL: Jonesboro-Hodge (Jonesboro, La.).
COLLEGE: Grambling State.
TRANSACTIONS/CAREER NOTES: Selected by Detroit Lions in fifth round (148th pick overall) of 2001 NFL draft.

			RECEIVING			
Year Team	G	No.	Yds.	Avg.	TD	
1998—Grambling State	10	54	874	16.2	9	
1999—Grambling State	11	65	1162	17.9	15	
2000—Grambling State	12	76	1298	17.1	11	
College totals (3 years)	33	195	3334	17.1	35	

ARCHULETA, ADAM   S   RAMS

PERSONAL: Born November 27, 1977, in Chandler, Ariz. ... 6-0/215. ... Full name: Adam J. Archuleta.
HIGH SCHOOL: Chandler (Ariz.).
COLLEGE: Arizona State.
TRANSACTIONS/CAREER NOTES: Selected by St. Louis Rams in first round (20th pick overall) of 2001 NFL draft.

		INTERCEPTIONS				SACKS
Year Team	G	No.	Yds.	Avg.	TD	No.
1997—Arizona State	12	0	0	0.0	0	0.0
1998—Arizona State	11	0	0	0.0	0	5.0
1999—Arizona State	11	1	4	4.0	0	5.0
2000—Arizona State	12	1	0	0.0	0	4.0
College totals (4 years)	46	2	4	2.0	0	14.0

BABER, BILLY   TE   CHIEFS

PERSONAL: Born January 17, 1979, in Charlottesville, Va. ... 6-3/248. ... Full name: William F. Baber.
HIGH SCHOOL: Western Albermarle (Va.).
COLLEGE: Virginia.
TRANSACTIONS/CAREER NOTES: Selected by Kansas City Chiefs in fifth round (141st pick overall) of 2001 NFL draft.

			RECEIVING			
Year Team	G	No.	Yds.	Avg.	TD	
1997—Virginia	11	8	93	11.6	1	
1998—Virginia	11	11	117	10.6	0	
1999—Virginia	11	17	118	6.9	4	
2000—Virginia	11	18	216	12.0	0	
College totals (4 years)	44	54	544	10.1	5	

BACKUS, JEFF   OT   LIONS

PERSONAL: Born September 21, 1977, in Midland, Mich. ... 6-5/308. ... Full name: Jeffrey Carl Backus.
HIGH SCHOOL: Norcross (Ga.).
COLLEGE: Michigan.
TRANSACTIONS/CAREER NOTES: Selected by Detriot Lions in first round (18th pick overall) of 2001 NFL draft.
COLLEGE PLAYING EXPERIENCE: Michigan, 1997-2000. ... Games: 1997 (12), 1998 (13), 1999 (12), 2000 (12). Total: 49.

BAILEY, RODNEY   DE   STEELERS

PERSONAL: Born October 7, 1979, in Cleveland. ... 6-3/270.
HIGH SCHOOL: St. Edwards (Cleveland).
COLLEGE: Ohio State.
TRANSACTIONS/CAREER NOTES: Selected by Pittsburgh Steelers in sixth round (181st pick overall) of 2001 NFL draft.

Year Team	G	SACKS
1997—Ohio State	13	3.0
1998—Ohio State	12	6.0
1999—Ohio State	11	1.0
2000—Ohio State	12	8.0
College totals (4 years)	48	18.0

BANNISTER, ALEX   WR   SEAHAWKS

PERSONAL: Born April 23, 1979, in Cincinnati. ... 6-5/201.
HIGH SCHOOL: Hughes Center (Cincinnati).
COLLEGE: Eastern Kentucky.
TRANSACTIONS/CAREER NOTES: Selected by Seattle Seahawks in fifth round (140th pick overall) of 2001 NFL draft.
COLLEGE NOTES: Rushed two times for eight yards (2000).

			RECEIVING			
Year Team	G	No.	Yds.	Avg.	TD	
1997—Eastern Kentucky	5	6	43	7.2	0	
1998—Eastern Kentucky	11	23	320	13.9	2	
1999—Eastern Kentucky	11	44	661	15.0	8	
2000—Eastern Kentucky	11	71	1122	15.8	12	
College totals (4 years)	38	144	2146	14.9	22	

BARLOW, KEVAN   RB   49ERS

PERSONAL: Born January 7, 1979, in Pittsburgh. ... 6-1/238. ... Full name: Kevan C. Barlow.
HIGH SCHOOL: Peabody (Pittsburgh).
COLLEGE: Pittsburgh.
TRANSACTIONS/CAREER NOTES: Selected by San Francisco 49ers in third round (80th pick overall) of 2001 NFL draft.
COLLEGE NOTES: Attempted two passes with an interception (1997); completed only pass attempt for 13 yards and touchdown (1999).

| | | RUSHING | | | | RECEIVING | | | | TOTALS | |
Year Team	G	Att.	Yds.	Avg.	TD	No.	Yds.	Avg.	TD	TD	Pts.
1997—Pittsburgh	7	27	108	4.0	2	6	140	23.3	1	3	18
1998—Pittsburgh	9	121	533	4.4	4	11	140	12.7	1	5	30
1999—Pittsburgh	10	141	630	4.5	6	6	94	15.7	1	7	42
2000—Pittsburgh	11	197	1053	5.3	8	13	134	10.3	1	9	54
College totals (4 years)	37	486	2324	4.8	20	36	508	14.1	4	24	144

BARNES, CHRIS   RB   RAVENS

PERSONAL: Born July 31, 1978, in Avon Park, Fla. ... 6-0/209. ... Full name: Christopher Jeremiah Barnes.
HIGH SCHOOL: Hardee (Wauchula, Fla.).
JUNIOR COLLEGE: Monterey (Calif.) Peninsula College.
COLLEGE: New Mexico State.
TRANSACTIONS/CAREER NOTES: Selected by Baltimore Ravens in fifth round (161st pick overall) of 2001 NFL draft.

| | | RUSHING | | | | RECEIVING | | | | TOTALS | |
Year Team	G	Att.	Yds.	Avg.	TD	No.	Yds.	Avg.	TD	TD	Pts.
1998—Monterey Peninsula Lobos	9	222	1363	6.1	13	0	0	0.0	0	13	98
1999—New Mexico	9	104	519	5.0	6	3	26	8.7	0	6	36
2000—New Mexico	11	171	1131	6.6	5	8	72	9.0	0	5	30
Junior college totals (1 year)	9	222	1363	6.1	13	0	0	0.0	0	13	98
College totals (2 years)	20	275	1650	6.0	11	11	98	8.9	0	11	66

BASHIR, IDREES   DB   COLTS

PERSONAL: Born December 7, 1978, in Decatur, Ga. ... 6-2/206.
HIGH SCHOOL: Dunwoody (Calif.).
COLLEGE: Memphis.
TRANSACTIONS/CAREER NOTES: Selected by Indianapolis Colts in second round (37th pick overall) of 2001 NFL draft. .
COLLEGE NOTES: Returned kickoff for 21 yards (1999).

| | | INTERCEPTIONS | | | |
Year Team	G	No.	Yds.	Avg.	TD
1997—Memphis			Redshirted.		
1998—Memphis	9	0	0	0.0	0
1999—Memphis	11	1	17	17.0	0
2000—Memphis	11	2	100	50.0	1
College totals (3 years)	31	3	117	39.0	1

BAXTER, GARY   DB   RAVENS

PERSONAL: Born November 24, 1978, in Tyler, Texas. ... 6-2/204. ... Full name: Gary Wayne Baxter.
HIGH SCHOOL: John Tyler (Tyler, Texas).
COLLEGE: Baylor.
TRANSACTIONS/CAREER NOTES: Selected by Baltimore Ravens in second round (62nd pick overall) of 2001 NFL draft.
COLLEGE NOTES: Returned four kickoffs for 30 yards and recovered two fumbles (1998); returned four kickoffs for 30 yards and credited with sack (1999).

| | | INTERCEPTIONS | | | |
Year Team	G	No.	Yds.	Avg.	TD
1997—Baylor	8	0	0	0.0	0
1998—Baylor	11	4	87	21.8	0
1999—Baylor	11	2	30	15.0	0
2000—Baylor	11	0	0	0.0	0
College totals (4 years)	41	6	117	19.5	0

BEISEL, MONTY   DE   CHIEFS

PERSONAL: Born August 20, 1978, in Douglass, Kan. ... 6-3/270.
HIGH SCHOOL: Douglass (Kan.).
COLLEGE: Kansas State.
TRANSACTIONS/CAREER NOTES: Selected by Kansas City Chiefs in fourth round (107th pick overall) of 2001 NFL draft.
COLLEGE NOTES: Recovered one fumble (1997); recovered one fumble and intercepted one pass (1998); recovered two fumbles (1999).

Year Team	G	SACKS
1997—Kansas State	9	1.0
1998—Kansas State	11	4.0
1999—Kansas State	11	6.5
2000—Kansas State	13	10.5
College totals (4 years)	44	22.0

BELL, KENDRELL   LB   STEELERS

PERSONAL: Born July 17, 1980, in Augusta, Ga. ... 6-1/236.
HIGH SCHOOL: Laney (August, Ga.).
JUNIOR COLLEGE: Middle Georgia College.
COLLEGE: Georgia.
TRANSACTIONS/CAREER NOTES: Selected by Pittsburgh Steelers in second round (39th pick overall) of 2001 NFL draft.
COLLEGE NOTES: Played fullback (1997). ... Returned two punts for 21 yards (1999).

			INTERCEPTIONS				SACKS
Year Team	G	No.	Yds.	Avg.	TD		No.
1997—Middle Georgia College	...	0	0	0.0	0		0.0
1998—Middle Georgia College	11	0	0	0.0	0		6.0
1999—Georgia	11	3	18	6.0	0		5.0
2000—Georgia	10	1	5	5.0	0		2.0
Junior college totals (2 years)	...	0	0	0.0	0		6.0
College totals (2 years)	21	4	23	5.8	0		7.0

BELL, MARCUS   LB   SEAHAWKS

PERSONAL: Born July 19, 1977, in St. John's, Ariz. ... 6-1/237. ... Full name: Marcus Udall Bell.
HIGH SCHOOL: St. John's (Ariz.).
COLLEGE: Arizona.
TRANSACTIONS/CAREER NOTES: Selected by Seattle Seahawks in fourth round (116th pick overall) of 2001 NFL draft. ... Signed by Seahawks (June 13, 2000).
COLLEGE NOTES: Intercepted one pass (1999).

			INTERCEPTIONS		
	G	No.	Yds.	Avg.	TD
1996—Arizona			Redshirted.		
1997—Arizona	11	0	0	0.0	0
1998—Arizona	11	0	0	0.0	0
1999—Arizona	12	0	0	0.0	0
2000—Arizona	12	1	0	0.0	0
College totals (4 years)	46	1	0	0.0	0

BELL, MARCUS   DT   CARDINALS

PERSONAL: Born June 1, 1979, in Memphis, Tenn. ... 6-1/319.
HIGH SCHOOL: Kingsbury (Tenn.).
COLLEGE: Memphis.
TRANSACTIONS/CAREER NOTES: Selected by Arizona Cardinals in fourth round (123rd pick overall) of 2001 NFL draft. ... Signed by Cardinals (June 4, 2001).

			INTERCEPTIONS			SACKS
Year Team	G	No.	Yds.	Avg.	TD	No.
1997—Memphis	9	0	0	0.0	0	1.0
1998—Memphis	11	0	0	0.0	0	0.0
1999—Memphis	11	1	2	2.0	0	5.0
2000—Memphis	11	1	4	4.0	0	4.0
College totals (4 years)	42	2	6	3.0	0	10.0

BENNETT, MICHAEL   RB   VIKINGS

PERSONAL: Born August 13, 1978, in Milwaukee, Wis. ... 5-9/211.
HIGH SCHOOL: Milwaukee Tech.
COLLEGE: Wisconsin.
TRANSACTIONS/CAREER NOTES: Selected after junior season by Minnesota Vikings in first round (27th pick overall) of 2001 NFL draft.
COLLEGE NOTES: Caught one pass for 29 yards (1999); caught four passes for 23 yards and returned seven kickoffs for 173 yards (2000).

			RUSHING			TOTALS	
	G	Att.	Yds.	Avg.	TD	TD	Pts.
1998—Wisconsin			Did not play.				
1999—Wisconsin	12	57	298	5.2	4	4	24
2000—Wisconsin	11	310	1681	5.4	11	11	66
College totals (2 years)	23	367	1979	5.4	15	15	90

BERLIN, EDDIE   WR   TITANS

PERSONAL: Born January 14, 1978, in Urbandale, Iowa. ... 5-11/186.
HIGH SCHOOL: Urbandale (Iowa).
COLLEGE: Northern Iowa.
TRANSACTIONS/CAREER NOTES: Selected by Tennessee Titans in fifth round (159th pick overall) of 2001 NFL draft.
COLLEGE NOTES: Returned four kickoffs for 58 yards (1997); returned five kickoffs for 94 yards and rushed once for no yards (1999); rushed once for five yards (2000).

			RECEIVING		
Year Team	G	No.	Yds.	Avg.	TD
1997—Northern Iowa	11	46	640	13.9	8
1998—Northern Iowa	11	65	962	14.8	4
1999—Northern Iowa	11	64	938	14.7	6
2000—Northern Iowa	11	74	1195	16.1	16
College totals (4 years)	44	249	3735	15.0	34

BIRD, CORY   DB   COLTS

PERSONAL: Born August 10, 1978, in Atlantic City, N.J. ... 5-10/216. ... Full name: Cory James Bird.
HIGH SCHOOL: Oakcrest (Mays Landing, N.J.).
COLLEGE: Virginia Tech.
TRANSACTIONS/CAREER NOTES: Selected by Indianapolis Colts in third round (91st pick overall) of 2001 NFL draft.
COLLEGE NOTES: Recovered two fumbles (1999); recovered two fumbles (2000).

			INTERCEPTIONS				SACKS
Year	Team	G	No.	Yds.	Avg.	TD	No.
1997—Virginia Tech		10	0	0	0.0	0	2.0
1998—Virginia Tech		11	0	0	0.0	0	1.0
1999—Virginia Tech		11	0	0	0.0	0	6.0
2000—Virginia Tech		11	2	11	5.5	0	3.0
College totals (4 years)		43	2	11	5.5	0	12.0

BLACKMON, HAROLD   CB   SEAHAWKS

PERSONAL: Born May 20, 1978, in Chicago. ... 5-11/210. ... Full name: Harold Gene Blackmon.
HIGH SCHOOL: Leo (Chicago).
COLLEGE: Northwestern.
TRANSACTIONS/CAREER NOTES: Selected by Seattle Seahawks in seventh round (210th pick overall) of 2001 NFL draft.
COLLEGE NOTES: Recovered one fumble (1999).

			INTERCEPTIONS			
Year	Team	G	No.	Yds.	Avg.	TD
1997—Northwestern		12	1	0	0.0	0
1998—Northwestern		12	2	10	5.0	0
1999—Northwestern		11	2	75	37.5	1
2000—Northwestern		12	5	18	3.6	0
College totals (4 years)		47	10	103	10.3	1

BLADE, WILLIE   DT   COWBOYS

PERSONAL: Born February 7, 1979, in Landstuel, Germany. ... 6-3/319.
HIGH SCHOOL: Warner Robins (Ga.).
JUNIOR COLLEGE: Butler County Community College (Kan.).
COLLEGE: Mississippi State.
TRANSACTIONS/CAREER NOTES: Selected by Dallas Cowboys in third round (93rd pick overall) of 2001 NFL draft.
COLLEGE NOTES: Recovered two fumbles (1998); recovered one fumble (1999); recovered two fumbles (2000).

Year	Team	G	SACKS
1998—Butler County CC		11	6.0
1999—Mississippi		11	1.0
2000—Mississippi		11	4.0
Junior college totals (1 year)		11	6.0
College totals (2 years)		22	5.0

BLAYLOCK, DERRICK   RB   CHIEFS

PERSONAL: Born August 23, 1979, in Atlanta, Texas. ... 5-9/188.
HIGH SCHOOL: Atlanta (Texas).
COLLEGE: Stephen F. Austin State.
TRANSACTIONS/CAREER NOTES: Selected by Kansas City Chiefs in fifth round (150th pick overall) of 2001 NFL draft.

			RUSHING				RECEIVING				TOTALS	
Year	Team	G	Att.	Yds.	Avg.	TD	No.	Yds.	Avg.	TD	TD	Pts.
1997—Stephen F. Austin State		8	68	353	5.2	4	1	13	13.0	0	4	24
1998—Stephen F. Austin State		5	34	247	7.3	0	2	11	5.5	0	0	0
1999—Stephen F. Austin State		7	36	109	3.0	2	14	210	15.0	0	2	12
2000—Stephen F. Austin State		11	202	1382	6.8	8	10	60	6.0	0	8	48
College totals (4 years)		31	340	2091	6.2	14	27	294	10.9	0	14	84

BOOTY, JOSH   QB   SEAHAWKS

PERSONAL: Born April 29, 1975, in Shreveport, La. ... 6-2/221.
HIGH SCHOOL: Evangel Academy (Shreveport, La.).
COLLEGE: Louisiana State.
TRANSACTIONS/CAREER NOTES: Selected after junior season by Seattle Seahawks in sixth round (172nd pick overall) of 2001 NFL draft.

			PASSING							RUSHING				TOTALS	
Year	Team	G	Att.	Cmp.	Pct.	Yds.	TD	Int.	Avg.	Rat.	Att.	Yds.	Avg.	TD	TD	Pts.
1999—Louisiana State		10	333	162	48.6	1830	7	19	5.50	90.3	27	-83	-3.1	0	0	0
2000—Louisiana State		10	290	145	50.0	2121	17	15	7.31	120.4	26	0	0.0	0	0	0
College totals (2 years)		20	623	307	49.3	3951	24	34	6.34	104.3	53	-83	-1.6	0	0	0

RECORD AS BASEBALL PLAYER

TRANSACTIONS/CAREER NOTES: Selected by Florida Marlins organization in first round (fifth pick overall) of free-agent draft (June 2, 1994). ... On Kane County suspended list (May 10-13, 1995). ... On Kane County disabled list (May 17-June 12, 1995). ... On Charlotte disabled list (June 10-21, 1998). ... Placed on voluntary retired list (January 22, 1999).
STATISTICAL NOTES: Led Eastern League third basemen with 361 total chances and 38 double plays in 1997.

Year — Team (League)	Pos.	G	AB	R	H	2B	3B	HR	RBI	Avg.	BB	SO	SB	PO	A	E	Avg.
								BATTING								FIELDING	
1994— GC Marlins (GCL).......	IF	10	36	5	8	0	0	1	2	.222	5	8	1	13	32	6	.882
— Elmira (NY-Penn)	SS	4	16	1	4	1	0	0	1	.250	0	4	0	11	8	1	.950
1995— Kane County (Midw.)..	3B	31	109	6	11	2	0	1	6	.101	11	45	1	23	71	9	.913
— Elmira (NY-Penn)	3B	74	287	33	63	18	1	6	37	.220	19	85	4	56	173	26	.898
1996— Kane County (Midw.)..	3B-DH	128	475	62	98	25	1	21	87	.206	46	*195	2	62	252	28	.918
— Florida (N.L.).............	3B	2	2	1	1	0	0	0	0	.500	0	0	0	0	0	0	...
1997— Portland (East.)	3B-DH	122	448	42	94	19	2	20	69	.210	27	166	2	*75	*262	24	.934
— Florida (N.L.).............	3B	4	5	2	3	0	0	0	1	.600	1	1	0	1	5	1	.857
1998— Florida (N.L.).............	3B	7	19	0	3	1	0	0	3	.158	3	8	0	4	11	3	.833
— Charlotte (I.L.)...........	3B	38	127	9	18	3	0	3	11	.142	7	44	0	20	94	10	.919
— Portland (East.)	3B-DH	71	247	28	50	8	3	10	39	.202	20	74	1	43	159	15	.931
Major League totals (3 years)		13	26	3	7	1	0	0	4	.269	4	9	0	5	16	4	.840

BOYD, JAMES — S — JAGUARS

PERSONAL: Born October 17, 1977, in Chesapeake, Va. ... 5-11/208. ... Full name: James Aaron Boyd.
HIGH SCHOOL: Indian River (Chesapeake, Va.).
COLLEGE: Penn State.
TRANSACTIONS/CAREER NOTES: Selected by Jacksonville Jaguars in third round (94th pick overall) of 2001 NFL draft.
HONORS: Named strong safety on THE SPORTING NEWS college All-America third team (2000).
COLLEGE NOTES: Recovered two fumbles (2000).

Year — Team	G	No.	Yds.	Avg.	TD
		INTERCEPTIONS			
1997— Penn State	11	0	0	0.0	0
1998— Penn State	11	0	0	0.0	0
1999— Penn State	12	3	0	0.0	0
2000— Penn State	12	3	24	8.0	0
College totals (4 years)	46	6	24	4.0	0

BREES, DREW — QB — CHARGERS

PERSONAL: Born January 15, 1979, in Austin, Texas. ... 6-0/221. ... Full name: Drew Christopher Brees.
HIGH SCHOOL: Westlake (Austin, Texas).
COLLEGE: Purdue.
TRANSACTIONS/CAREER NOTES: Selected by San Diego Chargers in second round (32nd pick overall) of 2001 NFL draft.
HONORS: Named quarterback to THE SPORTING NEWS college All-America third team (2000). ... Maxwell Award winner (2000).
COLLEGE NOTES: Caught two passes for minus five yards (1998); caught two passes for 13 yards (1999); caught two passes for six yards (2000).

Year — Team	G	Att.	Cmp.	Pct.	Yds.	TD	Int.	Avg.	Rat.	Att.	Yds.	Avg.	TD	TD	Pts.
		PASSING								RUSHING				TOTALS	
1997— Purdue............................	7	43	19	44.2	232	0	1	5.40	84.9	10	9	0.9	2	2	12
1998— Purdue............................	13	569	361	63.4	3983	39	20	7.00	137.8	69	193	2.8	3	3	18
1999— Purdue............................	12	554	337	60.8	3909	25	12	7.06	130.7	79	177	2.2	4	4	24
2000— Purdue............................	12	512	309	60.4	3668	26	12	7.16	132.6	95	521	3.6	5	5	30
College totals (4 years)............	44	1678	1026	61.1	11792	90	45	7.03	132.5	253	900	3.6	14	14	84

BREWER, SEAN — TE — BENGALS

PERSONAL: Born October 5, 1977, in Riverside, Calif. ... 6-4/255.
HIGH SCHOOL: Polytechnic (Riverside, Calif.).
JUNIOR COLLEGE: Riverside.
COLLEGE: San Jose State.
TRANSACTIONS/CAREER NOTES: Selected by Cincinnati Bengals in third round (66th pick overall) of 2001 NFL draft.
COLLEGE NOTES: Played defensive end (1998).

Year — Team	G	No.	Yds.	Avg.	TD
		RECEIVING			
1997— Riverside Community College...............................	10	7	76	10.9	3
1998— San Jose State	11	7	56	8.0	1
1999— San Jose State	10	20	152	7.6	3
2000— San Jose State	12	29	372	12.8	1
Junior college totals (1 year)..	10	7	76	10.9	3
College totals (3 years)	33	56	580	10.4	5

BROWN, DEE — RB — PANTHERS

PERSONAL: Born May 12, 1979, in Orlando, Fla. ... 5-10/209. ... Full name: Dadrian L. Brown.
HIGH SCHOOL: Lake Brantley (Fla.).
COLLEGE: Syracuse (degree in psychology).
TRANSACTIONS/CAREER NOTES: Selected by Carolina Panthers in sixth round (175th pick overall) of 2001 NFL draft.

Year — Team	G	Att.	Yds.	Avg.	TD	No.	Yds.	Avg.	TD	TD	Pts.
		RUSHING				RECEIVING				TOTALS	
1997— Syracuse	12	118	555	4.7	8	5	53	10.6	0	8	48
1998— Syracuse	11	58	299	5.2	7	2	11	5.5	0	7	42
1999— Syracuse	11	145	741	5.1	4	13	52	4.0	0	4	24
2000— Syracuse	11	172	1031	6.0	9	14	90	6.4	2	11	66
College totals (4 years)	45	493	2626	5.3	28	34	206	6.1	2	30	180

BUCKHALTER, CORRELL — RB — EAGLES

PERSONAL: Born October 6, 1978, in Collins, Miss. ... 6-0/222.
HIGH SCHOOL: Collins (Miss.).
COLLEGE: Nebraska.
TRANSACTIONS/CAREER NOTES: Selected by Philadelphia Eagles in fourth round (121st pick overall) of 2001 NFL draft. ... Signed by Eagles (May 24, 2001).
COLLEGE NOTES: Returned kickoff for 19 yards (2000).

		RUSHING				RECEIVING				TOTALS	
Year Team	G	Att.	Yds.	Avg.	TD	No.	Yds.	Avg.	TD	TD	Pts.
1997—Nebraska	12	54	311	5.8	6	3	6	2.0	0	6	36
1998—Nebraska	12	142	799	5.6	8	13	88	6.8	0	8	48
1999—Nebraska	11	111	662	6.0	6	3	21	7.0	0	6	36
2000—Nebraska	11	196	750	3.8	7	5	85	17.0	1	8	48
College totals (4 years)	46	503	2522	5.0	27	24	200	8.3	1	28	168

BURGESS, DERRICK — DE — EAGLES

PERSONAL: Born August 12, 1978, in Riverdale, Md. ... 6-2/266.
HIGH SCHOOL: Eleanor Roosevelt (Greenbelt, Md.).
COLLEGE: Mississippi.
TRANSACTIONS/CAREER NOTES: Selected by Philadelphia Eagles in third round (63rd pick overall) of 2001 NFL draft.
COLLEGE NOTES: Intercepted two passes (2000).

Year Team	G	SACKS
1997—Mississippi	11	2.0
1998—Mississippi	10	1.5
1999—Mississippi	11	4.5
2000—Mississippi	11	9.5
College totals (4 years)	43	17.5

BUTLER, JERAMETRIUS — CB — RAMS

PERSONAL: Born November 28, 1978, in Dallas. ... 5-10/181.
HIGH SCHOOL: Carter (Dallas).
COLLEGE: Kansas State.
TRANSACTIONS/CAREER NOTES: Selected after junior season by St. Louis Rams in fifth round (145th pick overall) of 2001 NFL draft.

		INTERCEPTIONS			
Year Team	G	No.	Yds.	Avg.	TD
1997—Kansas State			Redshirted.		
1998—Kansas State	12	2	14	7.0	0
1999—Kansas State	10	2	7	3.5	0
2000—Kansas State	13	6	47	7.8	0
College totals (3 years)	35	10	68	6.8	0

CAPEL, JOHN — WR — BEARS

PERSONAL: Born October 27, 1978, in Brooksville, Fla. ... 5-11/170. ... Full name: John Capel Jr.
HIGH SCHOOL: Hernando (Fla.).
COLLEGE: Florida.
TRANSACTIONS/CAREER NOTES: Selected after sophomore season by Chicago Bears in seventh round (208th pick overall) of 2001 NFL draft.

		RUSHING				RECEIVING				PUNT RETURNS				KICKOFF RETURNS				TOTALS	
Year Team	G	Att.	Yds.	Avg.	TD	No.	Yds.	Avg.	TD	No.	Yds.	Avg.	TD	No.	Yds.	Avg.	TD	TD	Pts.
1998—Florida	11	11	80	7.3	1	2	4	2.0	0	8	77	9.6	0	10	274	27.4	0	1	6
1999—Florida	12	0	0	0.0	0	9	84	9.3	0	2	-3	-1.5	0	9	141	15.7	0	0	0
2000—Florida								Did not play.											
College totals (2 years)	23	11	80	7.3	1	11	88	8.0	0	10	74	7.4	0	19	415	21.8	0	1	6

CARSWELL, ROBERT — S — CHARGERS

PERSONAL: Born October 26, 1978, in Lithion, Ga. ... 5-11/215. ... Full name: Robert L. Carswell.
HIGH SCHOOL: Stone Mountain (Ga.).
COLLEGE: Clemson.
TRANSACTIONS/CAREER NOTES: Selected by San Diego Chargers in seventh round (244th pick overall) of 2001 NFL draft.
HONORS: Named free safety on THE SPORTING NEWS college All-America third team (2000).
COLLEGE NOTES: Recovered one fumble (1999); recovered one fumble and credited with one sack (2000).

		INTERCEPTIONS			
Year Team	G	No.	Yds.	Avg.	TD
1997—Clemson	12	0	0	0.0	0
1998—Clemson	11	0	0	0.0	0
1999—Clemson	12	6	72	12.0	0
2000—Clemson	12	2	29	14.5	0
College totals (4 years)	47	8	101	12.6	0

CARTER, ANDRE   DE   49ERS

PERSONAL: Born May 12, 1979, in Denver, Colo. ... 6-4/265.
HIGH SCHOOL: Oak Grove (San Jose, Calif.).
COLLEGE: California.
TRANSACTIONS/CAREER NOTES: Selected by San Francisco 49ers in first round (seventh pick overall) of 2001 NFL draft.
HONORS: Named defensive end on The Sporting News college All-America first team (2000).

Year Team	G	SACKS
1997—California	11	3.5
1998—California	10	4.0
1999—California	11	10.0
2000—California	11	13.0
College totals (4 years)	43	30.5

CARTER, JONATHAN   WR   GIANTS

PERSONAL: Born March 20, 1979, in Anniston, Ala. ... 6-0/182.
HIGH SCHOOL: Lineville (Ala.).
COLLEGE: Troy State.
TRANSACTIONS/CAREER NOTES: Selected by New York Giants in fifth round (162nd pick overall) of 2001 NFL draft.

Year Team	G	RUSHING Att.	Yds.	Avg.	TD	RECEIVING No.	Yds.	Avg.	TD	KICKOFF RETURNS No.	Yds.	Avg.	TD	TOTALS TD	Pts.
1997—Troy State						Did not play.									
1998—Troy State						Did not play.									
1999—Troy State	11	0	0	0.0	0	6	237	39.5	0	2	20	10.0	0	3	18
2000—Troy State	12	9	94	10.4	0	44	737	16.8	9	10	286	28.6	1	10	60
College totals (2 years)	23	9	94	10.4	0	50	974	19.5	9	12	306	25.5	1	13	78

CARTER, QUINCY   QB   COWBOYS

PERSONAL: Born October 13, 1977, in Decatur, Ga. ... 6-2/225.
HIGH SCHOOL: Southwest DeKalb (Decatur, Ga.).
COLLEGE: Georgia.
TRANSACTIONS/CAREER NOTES: Selected after junior season by Dallas Cowboys in second round (53rd pick overall) of 2001 NFL draft.
HONORS: Named College Football Player of the Year by The Sporting News (1998).

Year Team	G	PASSING Att.	Cmp.	Pct.	Yds.	TD	Int.	Avg.	Rat.	RUSHING Att.	Yds.	Avg.	TD	TOTALS TD	Pts.
1998—Georgia	11	290	176	60.7	2484	12	9	8.57	140.1	99	284	2.9	0	4	24
1999—Georgia	11	380	216	56.8	2713	17	9	7.14	128.4	102	255	2.5	5	5	30
2000—Georgia	7	183	91	49.7	1250	6	10	6.83	107.0	50	67	1.3	0	2	12
College totals (3 years)	29	853	483	56.6	6447	35	25	7.56	127.8	251	606	2.4	5	11	66

CAVER, QUINTON   LB   EAGLES

PERSONAL: Born August 22, 1978, in Anniston, Ala. ... 6-4/230.
HIGH SCHOOL: Anniston (Ala.).
COLLEGE: Arkansas.
TRANSACTIONS/CAREER NOTES: Selected by Philadelphia Eagles in second round (55th pick overall) of 2001 NFL draft.
COLLEGE NOTES: Recovered one fumble (1998); recovered one fumble (1999); recovered one fumble and intercepted pass for 33 yards and one touchdown (2000).

Year Team	G	SACKS
1997—Arkansas	11	1.0
1998—Arkansas	11	2.0
1999—Arkansas	11	1.0
2000—Arkansas	11	2.0
College totals (4 years)	44	6.0

CHAMBERS, CHRIS   WR   DOLPHINS

PERSONAL: Born August 12, 1977, in Bedford, Ohio. ... 5-11/212.
HIGH SCHOOL: Bedford (Ohio).
COLLEGE: Wisconsin.
TRANSACTIONS/CAREER NOTES: Selected by Miami Dolphins in second round (52nd pick overall) of 2001 NFL draft.
COLLEGE NOTES: Returned kickoff for 15 yards, returned five punts for two yards and rushed twice for 17 yards (1997).

Year Team	G	RECEIVING No.	Yds.	Avg.	TD
1997—Wisconsin	10	6	50	8.3	0
1998—Wisconsin	13	28	563	20.1	7
1999—Wisconsin	11	41	578	14.1	4
2000—Wisconsin	9	52	813	15.6	5
College totals (4 years)	43	127	2004	15.8	16

CHUKWURAH, PATRICK   LB   VIKINGS

PERSONAL: Born March 1, 1979, in Nigeria. ... 6-2/238.
HIGH SCHOOL: MacArthur (Texas).
COLLEGE: Wyoming.
TRANSACTIONS/CAREER NOTES: Selected by Minnesota Vikings in fifth round (157th pick overall) of 2001 NFL draft.
COLLEGE NOTES: Intercepted one pass for 60 yards and a touchdown (1999).

Year Team	G	SACKS
1997—Wyoming	12	4.0
1998—Wyoming	11	7.0
1999—Wyoming	11	9.0
2000—Wyoming	11	7.0
College totals (4 years)	45	27.0

CLEMENTS, NATE   CB   BILLS

PERSONAL: Born December 12, 1979, in Shaker Heights, Ohio. ... 5-11/191.
HIGH SCHOOL: Shaker Heights (Ohio).
COLLEGE: Ohio State.
TRANSACTIONS/CAREER NOTES: Selected after junior season by Buffalo Bills in first round (21st pick overall) of 2001 NFL draft.
COLLEGE NOTES: Returned four kickoffs for 147 yards (2000).

Year Team	G	INTERCEPTIONS No.	Yds.	Avg.	TD	PUNT RETURNS No.	Yds.	Avg.	TD	TOTALS TD	Pts.
1998—Ohio State	12	1	0	0.0	0	1	7	7.0	0	0	0
1999—Ohio State	12	2	36	18.0	0	18	175	9.7	0	0	0
2000—Ohio State	12	4	47	11.8	0	39	513	13.2	1	1	6
College totals (3 years)	36	7	83	11.9	0	58	695	12.0	1	1	6

CODY, TAY   CB   CHARGERS

PERSONAL: Born October 6, 1977, in Blakely, Ga. ... 5-9/180.
HIGH SCHOOL: Earl County (Blakely, Ga.).
COLLEGE: Florida State.
TRANSACTIONS/CAREER NOTES: Selected by San Diego Chargers in third round (67th pick overall) of 2001 NFL draft.
HONORS: Named cornerback on THE SPORTING NEWS college All-America first team (2000).
COLLEGE NOTES: Recovered one fumble (1997); recovered one fumble (1998); credited with one sack (2000).

Year Team	G	INTERCEPTIONS No.	Yds.	Avg.	TD
1997—Florida State	11	3	2	0.7	0
1998—Florida State	12	1	1	1.0	0
1999—Florida State	10	2	18	9.0	0
2000—Florida State	12	6	200	33.3	1
College totals (4 years)	45	12	221	18.4	1

COMBS, DEREK   RB   RAIDERS

PERSONAL: Born February 28, 1979, in Urbancrest, Ohio. ... 5-11/197.
HIGH SCHOOL: Grove City (Urbancrest, Ohio).
COLLEGE: Ohio State.
TRANSACTIONS/CAREER NOTES: Selected by Oakland Raiders in seventh round (228th pick overall) of 2001 NFL draft.
COLLEGE NOTES: Caught one pass for one yard (1998); caught one pass for 16 yards (1999); caught nine passes for 78 yards (2000).

	G	RUSHING Att.	Yds.	Avg.	TD	TOTALS TD	Pts.
1997—Ohio State	10	25	82	3.3	0	0	0
1998—Ohio State	9	31	89	2.9	1	1	6
1999—Ohio State	10	43	173	4.0	4	4	24
2000—Ohio State	11	175	888	5.1	5	5	30
College totals (4 years)	40	274	1232	4.5	10	10	60

COOK, JAMEEL   FB   BUCCANEERS

PERSONAL: Born February 8, 1979, in Miami. ... 5-10/227.
HIGH SCHOOL: Southridge (Miami).
COLLEGE: Illinois.
TRANSACTIONS/CAREER NOTES: Selected after junior season by Tampa Bay Buccaneers in sixth round (174th pick overall) of 2001 NFL draft.
COLLEGE NOTES: Returned four kickoffs for 40 yards (1999); returned one kickoff for 18 yards (2000).

Year Team	G	RUSHING Att.	Yds.	Avg.	TD	RECEIVING No.	Yds.	Avg.	TD	TOTALS TD	Pts.
1998—Illinois	10	48	190	4.0	0	4	0	0.0	0	0	0
1999—Illinois	12	19	121	6.4	0	26	288	11.1	5	5	30
2000—Illinois	10	49	215	4.4	0	34	218	6.4	1	1	6
College totals (3 years)	32	116	526	4.5	0	64	506	7.9	6	6	36

COOPER, CHRIS — DT — RAIDERS

PERSONAL: Born December 27, 1977, in Lincoln, Neb. ... 6-6/270.
HIGH SCHOOL: Lincoln Southeast (Neb.).
COLLEGE: Nebraska-Omaha.
TRANSACTIONS/CAREER NOTES: Selected by Oakland Raiders in sixth round (184th pick overall) of 2001 NFL draft.

Year—Team	G	SACKS
1996—Nebraska-Omaha	Redshirted.	
1997—Nebraska-Omaha	11	4.0
1998—Nebraska-Omaha	11	7.0
1999—Nebraska-Omaha	11	9.0
2000—Nebraska-Omaha	11	11.0
College totals (4 years)	44	31.0

COOPER, JARROD — S — PANTHERS

PERSONAL: Born March 31, 1978, in Pearland, Texas. ... 6-0/210.
HIGH SCHOOL: Pearland (Texas).
COLLEGE: Kansas State.
TRANSACTIONS/CAREER NOTES: Selected by Carolina Panthers in fifth round (143rd pick overall) of 2001 NFL draft.
COLLEGE NOTES: Recovered one fumble (1997); recovered three fumbles and intercepted one pass (1998); recovered one fumble (1999).

Year—Team	G	SACKS
1997—Kansas State	11	2.0
1998—Kansas State	12	1.5
1999—Kansas State	11	0.0
2000—Kansas State	9	0.0
College totals (4 years)	43	3.5

CROWELL, RICK — LB — DOLPHINS

PERSONAL: Born May 21, 1977, in Chula Vista, Calif. ... 6-2/238. ... Full name: Rick James Crowell.
HIGH SCHOOL: Castle Park (Chula Vista, Calif.).
COLLEGE: Colorado State.
TRANSACTIONS/CAREER NOTES: Selected by Miami Dolphins in sixth round (188th pick overall) of 2001 NFL draft.
COLLEGE NOTES: Recovered two fumbles (1998); caught one pass for four yards and touchdown (2000).

Year—Team	G	INTERCEPTIONS No.	Yds.	Avg.	TD	SACKS No.
1996—Colorado State	12	0	0	0.0	0	0.0
1997—Colorado State	12	0	0	0.0	0	3.0
1998—Colorado State	12	1	22	22.0	1	4.0
1999—Colorado State	5	1	54	54.0	1	1.0
2000—Colorado State	10	3	44	14.7	1	1.0
College totals (5 years)	51	5	120	24.0	3	9.0

CRUMPLER, ALGE — TE — FALCONS

PERSONAL: Born December 23, 1977, in Wilmington, N.C. ... 6-2/264. ... Full name: Algernon Darius Crumpler.
HIGH SCHOOL: New Hanover (Wilmington, N.C.).
COLLEGE: North Carolina.
TRANSACTIONS/CAREER NOTES: Selected by Atlanta Falcons in second round (35th pick overall) of 2001 NFL draft. ... Signed by Falcons (May 29, 2001).

Year—Team	G	RECEIVING No.	Yds.	Avg.	TD
1996—North Carolina	11	1	4	4.0	0
1997—North Carolina	11	24	278	11.6	4
1998—North Carolina	Redshirted.				
1999—North Carolina	11	20	191	9.6	0
2000—North Carolina	11	23	287	12.5	1
College totals (4 years)	44	68	760	11.2	5

DAVIS, ENNIS — DT — SAINTS

PERSONAL: Born December 2, 1977, in Los Angeles. ... 6-4/303.
HIGH SCHOOL: Reseda (Calif.).
COLLEGE: Southern California.
TRANSACTIONS/CAREER NOTES: Selected by New Orleans Saints in seventh round (221st pick overall) of 2001 NFL draft.
HONORS: Named defensive tackle on THE SPORTING NEWS college All-America third team (2000).
COLLEGE NOTES: Recovered one fumble (1998); recovered two fumbles and intercepted two passes for 30 yards and one touchdown (1999).

Year—Team	G	SACKS
1997—Southern California	11	1.0
1998—Southern California	13	3.0
1999—Southern California	12	5.0
2000—Southern California	12	6.0
College totals (4 years)	48	15.0

DAVIS, LEONARD — OT — CARDINALS

PERSONAL: Born September 5, 1978, in Wortham, Texas. ... 6-6/370. ... Full name: Leonard Barnett Davis.
HIGH SCHOOL: Wortham (Texas).
COLLEGE: Texas.
TRANSACTIONS/CAREER NOTES: Selected by Arizona Cardinals in first round (second pick overall) of 2001 NFL draft.
HONORS: Named offensive tackle on THE SPORTING NEWS college All-America first team (2000).
COLLEGE NOTES: Played defensive tackle (1997). ... Recovered one fumble (1997).
COLLEGE PLAYING EXPERIENCE: Texas, 1997-2000. ... Games: 1997 (11) 1998 (11), 1999 (11), 2000 (11). Total: 44.

DeMULLING, RICK — G — COLTS

PERSONAL: Born July 21, 1977, in Cheney, Wash. ... 6-4/313.
HIGH SCHOOL: Cheney (Wash.).
COLLEGE: Idaho.
TRANSACTIONS/CAREER NOTES: Selected by Indianapolis Colts in seventh round (220th pick overall) of 2001 NFL draft.
COLLEGE PLAYING EXPERIENCE: Idaho, 1997-2000. ... Games: 1997 (8), 1998 (11), 1999 (9), 2000 (11). Total: 39.

DENMAN, ANTHONY — LB — JAGUARS

PERSONAL: Born October 30, 1979, in Lufkin, Texas. ... 6-1/237. ... Full name: Anthony R. Denman.
HIGH SCHOOL: Rusk (Texas).
COLLEGE: Notre Dame.
TRANSACTIONS/CAREER NOTES: Selected by Jacksonville Jaguars in seventh round (213th pick overall) of 2001 NFL draft.
HONORS: Named linebacker on THE SPORTING NEWS college All-America second team (2000).
COLLEGE NOTES: Recovered three fumbles and intercepted one pass (1999).

Year Team	G	SACKS
1997—Notre Dame	11	0.0
1998—Notre Dame	11	3.0
1999—Notre Dame	12	1.0
2000—Notre Dame	11	5.0
College totals (4 years)	45	9.0

DIEM, RYAN — G — COLTS

PERSONAL: Born July 1, 1979, in Carol Stream, Ill. ... 6-6/332.
HIGH SCHOOL: Glenbard North (Carol Stream, Ill.).
COLLEGE: Northern Illinois.
TRANSACTIONS/CAREER NOTES: Selected by Indianapolis Colts in fourth round (118th pick overall) of 2001 NFL draft.
COLLEGE PLAYING EXPERIENCE: Northern Illinois, 1997-2000. ... Games: 1997 (9), 1998 (11), 1999 (11), 2000 (11). Total: 42.

DIXON, TONY — S — COWBOYS

PERSONAL: Born June 18, 1979, in Reform, Ala. ... 6-1/213.
HIGH SCHOOL: Pickens County (Reform, Ala.).
COLLEGE: Alabama (degree in management).
TRANSACTIONS/CAREER NOTES: Selected by Dallas Cowboys in second round (56th pick overall) of 2001 NFL draft.

Year Team	G	INTERCEPTIONS				SACKS
		No.	Yds.	Avg.	TD	No.
1997—Alabama	11	0	0	0.0	0	1.0
1998—Alabama	10	1	1	1.0	0	0.0
1999—Alabama	12	0	0	0.0	0	0.0
2000—Alabama	10	2	13	6.5	0	1.0
College totals (4 years)	43	3	14	4.7	0	2.0

DOERING, JASON — DB — COLTS

PERSONAL: Born April 22, 1978, in Rhinelander, Wis. ... 6-0/200.
HIGH SCHOOL: Rhinelander (Wis.).
COLLEGE: Wisconsin.
TRANSACTIONS/CAREER NOTES: Selected by Indianapolis Colts in sixth round (193rd pick overall) of 2001 NFL draft.
COLLEGE NOTES: Credited with one sack (1998).

Year Team	G	INTERCEPTIONS			
		No.	Yds.	Avg.	TD
1996—Wisconsin		Redshirted.			
1997—Wisconsin	13	0	0	0.0	0
1998—Wisconsin	12	3	22	7.3	0
1999—Wisconsin	11	0	0	0.0	0
2000—Wisconsin	11	3	0	0.0	0
College totals (4 years)	47	6	22	3.7	0

DORSEY, CHAR-RON   OT   COWBOYS

PERSONAL: Born November 5, 1977, in Jacksonville. ... 6-7/367.
HIGH SCHOOL: The Bolles School (Jacksonville).
COLLEGE: Florida State.
TRANSACTIONS/CAREER NOTES: Selected by Dallas Cowboys in seventh round (242nd pick overall) of 2001 NFL draft.
COLLEGE NOTES: Played defensive tackle (1997). ... Credited with one sack (1997).
COLLEGE PLAYING EXPERIENCE: Florida State, 1997-2000. ... Games: 1997 (5), 1998 (did not play), 1999 (11), 2000 (11). Total: 27.

DOWNING, ERIC   DT   CHIEFS

PERSONAL: Born September 16, 1978, in Ahoskie, N.C. ... 6-4/294. ... Full name: Eric Lamont Downing.
HIGH SCHOOL: John F. Kennedy (Paterson, N.J.).
JUNIOR COLLEGE: Coffeyville (Kan.) Community College.
COLLEGE: Syracuse.
TRANSACTIONS/CAREER NOTES: Selected by Kansas City Chiefs in third round (75th pick overall) of 2001 NFL draft.

Year Team	G	SACKS
1997—Coffeyville CC	12	6.0
1998—Syracuse	10	0.0
1999—Syracuse	12	2.0
2000—Syracuse	11	0.5
Junior college totals (1 year)	12	6.0
College totals (3 years)	33	2.5

DRAPER, SHAWN   OT   DOLPHINS

PERSONAL: Born July 5, 1979, in Huntsville, Ala. ... 6-3/294.
HIGH SCHOOL: Butler (Huntsville, Ala.).
COLLEGE: Alabama.
TRANSACTIONS/CAREER NOTES: Selected by Miami Dolphins in fifth round (156th pick overall) of 2001 NFL draft.
COLLEGE NOTES: Played defensive tackle (1998-99). ... Played left tackle and tight end (2000). ... Credited with $1/2$ sack (1999). ... Caught three passes for 90 yards and one touchdown (2000).
COLLEGE PLAYING EXPERIENCE: Alabama, 1997-2000. ... Games: 1997 (11), 1998 (11), 1999 (12), 2000 (10). Total: 44.

DRIVER, TONY   S   BILLS

PERSONAL: Born August 4, 1977, in Louisville, Ky. ... 6-1/211.
HIGH SCHOOL: Male (Louisville, Ky.).
COLLEGE: Notre Dame.
TRANSACTIONS/CAREER NOTES: Selected by Buffalo Bills in sixth round (178th pick overall) of 2001 NFL draft.
COLLEGE NOTES: Recovered one fumble (1998); recovered one fumble (1999); credited with one sack (2000).

		RUSHING				INTERCEPTIONS				RECEIVING				KICKOFF RETURNS				TOTALS	
Year Team	G	Att.	Yds.	Avg.	TD	No.	Yds.	Avg.	TD	No.	Yds.	Avg.	TD	No.	Yds.	Avg.	TD	TD	Pts.
1997—Notre Dame	12	35	125	3.6	3	0	0	0.0	0	1	2	2.0	0	11	214	19.5	0	3	18
1998—Notre Dame	11	1	2	2.0	0	2	54	27.0	0	0	0	0.0	0	23	512	22.3	0	0	0
1999—Notre Dame	7	49	187	3.8	4	0	0	0.0	0	1	6	6.0	0	3	101	33.7	0	4	24
2000—Notre Dame	11	0	0	0.0	0	2	62	31.0	0	0	0	0.0	0	9	232	25.8	0	6	36
College totals (4 years)	41	85	314	3.7	7	4	116	29.0	0	2	8	4.0	0	46	1059	23.0	0	13	78

DYSON, ANDRE   CB   TITANS

PERSONAL: Born May 25, 1979, in Layton, Utah. ... 5-10/177.
HIGH SCHOOL: Clearfield (Utah).
COLLEGE: Utah.
TRANSACTIONS/CAREER NOTES: Selected by Tennessee Titans in second round (60th pick overall) of 2001 NFL draft.
COLLEGE NOTES: Recovered one fumble (1998); recovered one fumble (1999); recovered one fumble and returned five punts for 73 yards (2000).

		INTERCEPTIONS			
Year Team	G	No.	Yds.	Avg.	TD
1997—Utah	11	0	0	0.0	0
1998—Utah	10	3	0	0.0	0
1999—Utah	11	6	57	9.5	1
2000—Utah	11	4	115	28.8	3
College totals (4 years)	43	13	172	13.2	4

EDWARDS, RON   DT   BILLS

PERSONAL: Born July 12, 1979, in Houston. ... 6-2/298.
HIGH SCHOOL: Klein Forest (Houston).
COLLEGE: Texas A&M.
TRANSACTIONS/CAREER NOTES: Selected by Buffalo Bills in third round (76th pick overall) of 2001 NFL draft. ... Signed by Bills (June 1, 2001).

Year Team	G	SACKS
1997—Texas A&M	11	0.0
1998—Texas A&M	13	5.0
1999—Texas A&M	11	4.0
2000—Texas A&M	11	1.0
College totals (4 years)	46	10.0

EVANS, HEATH   FB   SEAHAWKS

PERSONAL: Born December 30, 1978, in West Palm Beach, Fla. ... 6-0/246. ... Full name: Bryan Heath Evans.
HIGH SCHOOL: Kings Academy (Miami).
COLLEGE: Auburn.
TRANSACTIONS/CAREER NOTES: Selected by Seattle Seahawks in third round (82nd pick overall) of 2001 NFL draft.
COLLEGE NOTES: Returned one kickoff 15 yards (1999).

		RUSHING				RECEIVING				TOTALS	
Year Team	G	Att.	Yds.	Avg.	TD	No.	Yds.	Avg.	TD	TD	Pts.
1997—Auburn						Redshirted.					
1998—Auburn	5	14	36	2.6	2	7	151	21.6	1	3	18
1999—Auburn	11	93	330	3.5	2	8	97	12.1	0	2	12
2000—Auburn	12	42	260	6.2	2	15	107	7.1	0	2	12
College totals (3 years)	28	149	626	4.2	6	30	355	11.8	1	7	42

FATAFEHI, MARIO   DT   CARDINALS

PERSONAL: Born January 27, 1979, in Honolulu, Hawaii. ... 6-2/307.
HIGH SCHOOL: Ferrington (Honolulu, Hawaii).
JUNIOR COLLEGE: Snow College (Utah).
COLLEGE: Kansas State.
TRANSACTIONS/CAREER NOTES: Selected by Arizona Cardinals in fifth round (133rd pick overall) of 2001 NFL draft. ... Signed by Cardinals (June 5, 2001).
COLLEGE NOTES: Recovered one fumble (1999); recovered two fumbles (2000).

Year Team	G	SACKS
1999—Kansas State	11	3.5
2000—Kansas State	13	8.5
College totals (2 years)	24	12.0

FEELEY, A.J.   QB   EAGLES

PERSONAL: Born May 16, 1977, in Caldwell, Idaho. ... 6-4/220. ... Full name: Adam Joshua Feeley.
HIGH SCHOOL: Ontario (Ore.).
COLLEGE: Oregon.
TRANSACTIONS/CAREER NOTES: Selected by Philadelphia Eagles in fifth round (155th pick overall) of 2001 NFL draft. ... Signed by Eagles (June 6, 2001).

		PASSING								RUSHING				TOTALS	
Year Team	G	Att.	Cmp.	Pct.	Yds.	TD	Int.	Avg.	Rat.	Att.	Yds.	Avg.	TD	TD	Pts.
1996—Oregon							Redshirted.								
1997—Oregon	4	10	8	80.0	137	1	0	13.70	228.1	1	2	2.0	0	0	0
1998—Oregon	6	6	0	0.0	0	0	0	0.0	0.0	1	-1	-1.0	0	0	0
1999—Oregon	10	259	136	52.5	1951	14	6	7.53	129.0	31	-5	-0.2	0	0	0
2000—Oregon	2	13	5	38.5	87	0	0	6.69	94.7	4	4	1.0	0	0	0
College totals (4 years)	22	288	149	51.7	2175	15	6	7.55	128.2	37	0	0.0	0	0	0

FERGUSON, ROBERT   WR   PACKERS

PERSONAL: Born December 17, 1979, in Houston. ... 6-1/209.
HIGH SCHOOL: Spring Woods (Houston).
JUNIOR COLLEGE: Tyler (Texas) Junior College.
COLLEGE: Texas A&M.
TRANSACTIONS/CAREER NOTES: Selected after junior season by Green Bay Packers in second round (41st pick overall) of 2001 NFL draft.

		RECEIVING			
Year Team	G	No.	Yds.	Avg.	TD
1999—Tyler JC	10	36	539	15.0	3
2000—Texas A&M	10	58	888	15.3	6
Junior college totals (1 year)	10	36	539	15.0	3
College totals (1 years)	10	58	888	15.3	6

FERRARIO, BILL   G   PACKERS

PERSONAL: Born September 22, 1978, in Scranton, Pa. ... 6-2/313. ... Full name: William Ferrario.
HIGH SCHOOL: West (Scranton, Pa.).
COLLEGE: Wisconsin.
TRANSACTIONS/CAREER NOTES: Selected by Green Bay Packers in fourth round (105th pick overall) of 2001 NFL draft.
HONORS: Named guard on THE SPORTING NEWS college All-America third team (2000).
COLLEGE PLAYING EXPERIENCE: Wisconsin, 1996-2000. ... Games: 1996 (redshirted), 1997 (13), 1998 (12), 1999 (12), 2000 (13). Total: 50.

FLETCHER, JAMAR   CB   DOLPHINS

PERSONAL: Born August 28, 1979, in St. Louis. ... 5-9/177.
HIGH SCHOOL: Hazelwood East (St. Louis).
COLLEGE: Wisconsin.
TRANSACTIONS/CAREER NOTES: Selected after junior season by Miami Dolphins in first round (26th pick overall) of 2001 NFL draft.
HONORS: Named cornerback on THE SPORTING NEWS college All-America first team (1999). ... Named cornerback on THE SPORTING NEWS college All-America second team (2000). ... Jim Thorpe Award winner (2000).

Year Team	G	INTERCEPTIONS No.	Yds.	Avg.	TD
1998—Wisconsin	10	7	145	20.7	3
1999—Wisconsin	12	7	135	19.3	2
2000—Wisconsin	10	7	179	25.6	0
College totals (3 years)	32	21	459	21.9	5

FLOWERS, RICHMOND WR JAGUARS

PERSONAL: Born May 4, 1978, in Birmingham, Ala. ... 5-11/192. ... Full name: Richmond McDavid Flowers III.
HIGH SCHOOL: Vestavia Hills (Birmingham, Ala.).
COLLEGE: Duke, then Tennessee-Chattanooga.
TRANSACTIONS/CAREER NOTES: Selected by Jacksonville Jaguars in seventh round (235th pick overall) of 2001 NFL draft.

Year Team	G	RUSHING Att.	Yds.	Avg.	TD	RECEIVING No.	Yds.	Avg.	TD	PUNT RETURNS No.	Yds.	Avg.	TD	KICKOFF RETURNS No.	Yds.	Avg.	TD	TOTALS TD	Pts.
1996—Duke	11	0	0	0.0	0	5	51	10.2	1	0	0	0.0	0	27	512	19.0	0	1	6
1997—Duke	2	0	0	0.0	0	3	62	20.7	1	0	0	0.0	0	0	0	0.0	0	1	6
1998—Duke	9	1	9	9.0	0	48	704	14.7	4	0	0	0.0	0	20	457	22.9	0	4	24
1999—Duke	11	5	20	4.0	0	42	649	15.5	5	0	0	0.0	0	7	154	22.0	0	5	30
2000—Tennessee-Chattanooga	11	3	28	9.3	0	86	1035	12.0	2	16	98	6.1	0	25	568	22.7	0	2	12
College totals (5 years)	44	9	57	6.3	0	184	2501	13.6	13	16	98	6.1	0	79	1691	21.4	0	13	78

FORNEY, KYNAN G FALCONS

PERSONAL: Born September 8, 1978, in Nacogdoches, Texas. ... 6-3/304.
HIGH SCHOOL: Nacogdoches (Texas).
JUNIOR COLLEGE: Trinity Valley Community College (Texas).
COLLEGE: Hawaii.
TRANSACTIONS/CAREER NOTES: Selected by Atlanta Falcons in seventh round (219th pick overall) of 2001 NFL draft. ... Signed by Falcons (May 21, 2001).
COLLEGE PLAYING EXPERIENCE: Trinity Valley Community College, 1996-97. ... Hawaii, 1998-2000. ... Games: 1998 (12), 1999 (redshirted), 2000 (11). Total: 23.

FULLER, CURTIS S SEAHAWKS

PERSONAL: Born July 25, 1978, in North Richland Hill, Texas. ... 5-10/186.
HIGH SCHOOL: Christian (Fort Worth, Texas).
JUNIOR COLLEGE: Trinity Valley Community College (Texas).
COLLEGE: Texas Christian (degree in psychology).
TRANSACTIONS/CAREER NOTES: Selected by Seattle Seahawks in fourth round (127th pick overall) of 2001 NFL draft.
COLLEGE NOTES: Credited with one sack (2000).

Year Team	G	INTERCEPTIONS No.	Yds.	Avg.	TD
1996—Trinity Valley			Did not play.		
1997—Trinity Valley	...	9	0	0.0	0
1998—Texas Christian	11	1	26	26.0	1
1999—Texas Christian	11	1	0	0.0	0
2000—Texas Christian	11	1	0	0.0	0
Junior college totals (1 year)	...	9	0	0.0	0
College totals (3 years)	33	3	26	8.7	1

GANDY, MIKE G BEARS

PERSONAL: Born January 3, 1979, in Rockford, Ill. ... 6-4/313. ... Full name: Michael Joseph Gandy.
HIGH SCHOOL: Garland (Texas).
COLLEGE: Notre Dame (degree in sociology and computer applications).
TRANSACTIONS/CAREER NOTES: Selected by Chicago Bears in third round (68th pick overall) of 2001 NFL draft.
HONORS: Named guard on THE SPORTING NEWS college All-America first team (2000).
COLLEGE PLAYING EXPERIENCE: Notre Dame, 1996-2000. ... Games: 1996 (redshirted), 1997 (did not play), 1998 (11), 1999 (12), 2000 (11). Total: 34.

GARDNER, ROD WR REDSKINS

PERSONAL: Born October 26, 1977, in Jacksonville, Fla. ... 6-2/216. ... Full name: Roderick F. Gardner.
HIGH SCHOOL: Raines (Jacksonville, Fla.).
COLLEGE: Clemson.
TRANSACTIONS/CAREER NOTES: Selected by Washington Redskins in first round (15th pick overall) of 2001 NFL draft.
COLLEGE NOTES: Attempted two passes with two completions for 15 yards and rushed once for one yard (1999); attempted one pass without a completion, rushed four times for minus one yard and returned eight kickoffs for 168 yards (2000).

Year Team	G	RECEIVING No.	Yds.	Avg.	TD
1997—Clemson	12	8	101	12.6	1
1998—Clemson	11	20	263	13.2	1
1999—Clemson	12	80	1084	13.6	4
2000—Clemson	12	58	1050	18.1	7
College totals (4 years)	47	166	2498	15.0	13

GARNER, RANDY   DE   FALCONS

PERSONAL: Born November 28, 1977, in Douglasville, Texas. ... 6-4/273.
HIGH SCHOOL: Atlanta (Texas).
COLLEGE: Arkansas.
TRANSACTIONS/CAREER NOTES: Selected by Atlanta Falcons in sixth round (167th pick overall) of 2001 NFL draft. ... Signed by Falcons (May 29, 2001).
COLLEGE NOTES: Intercepted one pass (1999).

Year Team	G	SACKS
1997—Arkansas	11	2.0
1998—Arkansas	11	5.0
1999—Arkansas	11	5.5
2000—Arkansas	9	2.0
College totals (4 years)	42	14.5

GARZA, ROBERT   C   FALCONS

PERSONAL: Born March 26, 1979, in Rio Hondo, Texas. ... 6-2/292.
HIGH SCHOOL: Rio Hondo (Texas).
COLLEGE: Texas A&M-Kingsville.
TRANSACTIONS/CAREER NOTES: Selected by Atlanta Falcons in fourth round (99th pick overall) of 2001 NFL draft. ... Signed by Falcons (May 21, 2001).
COLLEGE PLAYING EXPERIENCE: Texas A&M-Kingsville, 1997-2000. ... Games: 1997 (4), 1998 (14), 1999 (10), 2000 (11). Total: 39.

GERMANY, REGGIE   WR   BILLS

PERSONAL: Born March 19, 1978, in Hazelwood, Mo. ... 6-1/196.
HIGH SCHOOL: Hazelwood East (St. Louis).
COLLEGE: Ohio State.
TRANSACTIONS/CAREER NOTES: Selected by Buffalo Bills in seventh round (214th pick overall) of 2001 NFL draft.

Year Team	G	RECEIVING			
		No.	Yds.	Avg.	TD
1997—Ohio State	8	1	17	17.0	0
1998—Ohio State	10	14	229	16.4	4
1999—Ohio State	12	43	656	15.3	1
2000—Ohio State	10	22	366	16.6	1
College totals (4 years)	40	80	1268	15.9	6

GIBSON, DERRICK   S   RAIDERS

PERSONAL: Born March 22, 1979, in Miami. ... 6-1/211.
HIGH SCHOOL: Killian (Miami).
COLLEGE: Florida State.
TRANSACTIONS/CAREER NOTES: Selected by Oakland Raiders in first round (28th pick overall) of 2001 NFL draft.
COLLEGE NOTES: Credited with two sacks (1999).

Year Team	G	INTERCEPTIONS			
		No.	Yds.	Avg.	TD
1997—Florida State	11	0	0	0.0	0
1998—Florida State	12	1	10	10.0	0
1999—Florida State	11	4	40	10.0	0
2000—Florida State	12	2	25	12.5	0
College totals (4 years)	46	7	75	10.7	0

GLENN, JASON   LB   LIONS

PERSONAL: Born August 20, 1979, in Aldine, Texas. ... 6-0/231.
HIGH SCHOOL: Nimitz (Aldine, Texas).
COLLEGE: Texas A&M.
TRANSACTIONS/CAREER NOTES: Selected by Detroit Lions in sixth round (173rd pick overall) of 2001 NFL draft.
COLLEGE NOTES: Recovered two fumbles (1997); recovered one fumble (2000).

Year Team	G	INTERCEPTIONS				SACKS
		No.	Yds.	Avg.	TD	No.
1997—Texas A&M	12	0	0	0.0	0	0.0
1998—Texas A&M	12	0	0	0.0	0	1.0
1999—Texas A&M	9	0	0	0.0	0	5.0
2000—Texas A&M	10	3	36	12.0	0	5.0
College totals (4 years)	43	3	36	12.0	0	11.0

GORIN, BRANDON   OT   CHARGERS

PERSONAL: Born July 17, 1978, in Muncie, Ind. ... 6-6/304. ... Full name: Brandon Michael Gorin.
HIGH SCHOOL: Southside (Ind.).
COLLEGE: Purdue.
TRANSACTIONS/CAREER NOTES: Selected by San Diego Chargers in seventh round (201st pick overall) of 2001 NFL draft.
COLLEGE PLAYING EXPERIENCE: Purdue, 1996-2000. ... Games: 1996 (redshirted), 1997 (12), 1998 (13), 1999 (12), 2000 (12). Total: 49.

GRAMATICA, BILL   K   CARDINALS

PERSONAL: Born July 10, 1978, in Argentina. ... 5-10/192. ... Full name: Guillermo Gramatica. ... Brother of Martin Gramatica, kicker, Tampa Bay Buccaneers.
HIGH SCHOOL: LaBelle (Fla.).
COLLEGE: Florida State, then South Florida.
TRANSACTIONS/CAREER NOTES: Selected by Arizona Cardinals in fourth round (98th pick overall) of 2001 NFL draft. ... Signed by Cardinals (June 4, 2001).

Year Team	G	KICKING						
		XPM	XPA	FGM	FGA	Lg.	50+	Pts.
1997—Florida State	...	10	12	2	4	34	0-0	16
1998—South Florida	...	46	47	16	24	44	0-0	94
1999—South Florida	...	10	11	4	5	44	0-0	22
2000—South Florida	...	29	30	16	24	63	0-0	77
College totals (4 years)	...	95	100	38	57	63	0-0	209

GRANT, DeLAWRENCE   DE   RAIDERS

PERSONAL: Born November 18, 1979, in Compton, Calif. ... 6-2/267. ... Full name: DeLawrence Grant Jr.
HIGH SCHOOL: Centennial (Compton, Calif.).
JUNIOR COLLEGE: El Camino College (Calif.).
COLLEGE: Oregon State.
TRANSACTIONS/CAREER NOTES: Selected by Oakland Raiders in third round (89th pick overall) of 2001 NFL draft.
HONORS: Named defensive end on THE SPORTING NEWS college All-America second team (2000).
COLLEGE NOTES: Recovered two fumbles (1997); recovered three fumbles (1998); recovered three fumbles and intercepted one pass (2000).

Year Team	G	SACKS
1997—El Camino College	11	6.0
1998—El Camino College	10	8.0
1999—Oregon State	11	6.0
2000—Oregon State	12	7.0
Junior college totals (2 years)	21	14.0
College totals (2 years)	23	13.0

GREENWOOD, MORLON   LB   DOLPHINS

PERSONAL: Born July 17, 1978, in Jamaica, West Indies. ... 6-0/239. ... Full name: Morlon Owen Greenwood.
HIGH SCHOOL: Freeport (N.Y.).
COLLEGE: Syracuse.
TRANSACTIONS/CAREER NOTES: Selected by Miami Dolphins in third round (88th pick overall) of 2001 NFL draft.

Year Team	G	SACKS
1997—Syracuse	12	2.0
1998—Syracuse	11	3.0
1999—Syracuse	11	1.0
2000—Syracuse	11	0.0
College totals (4 years)	45	6.0

HAAYER, ADAM   OT   TITANS

PERSONAL: Born February 22, 1977, in Wyoming, Minn. ... 6-6/297.
HIGH SCHOOL: Forest Lake (Minn.).
COLLEGE: Minnesota.
TRANSACTIONS/CAREER NOTES: Selected by Tennessee Titans in sixth round (199th pick overall) of 2001 NFL draft.
COLLEGE PLAYING EXPERIENCE: Minnesota, 1996-2000. ... Games: 1996 (redshirted), 1997 (12), 1998 (11), 1999 (11), 2000 (12). Total: 46.

HALL, COREY   DB   FALCONS

PERSONAL: Born January 17, 1979, in Athens, Ga. ... 6-4/190.
HIGH SCHOOL: Clarke General (Ga.).
COLLEGE: Appalachian State.
TRANSACTIONS/CAREER NOTES: Selected by Atlanta Falcons in seventh round (215th pick overall) of 2001 NFL draft.

Year Team	G	INTERCEPTIONS			
		No.	Yds.	Avg.	TD
1997—Appalachian State	11	2	0	0.0	0
1998—Appalachian State	13	3	33	11.0	0
1999—Appalachian State		Statistics unavailable.			
2000—Appalachian State	14	3	28	9.3	0
College totals (3 years)	38	8	61	7.6	0

HAMILTON, BEN   C   BRONCOS

PERSONAL: Born August 18, 1977, in Plymouth, Minn. ... 6-4/283. ... Son of Wes Hamilton, guard with Minnesota Vikings (1976-84).
HIGH SCHOOL: Wayzata (Minn.).
COLLEGE: Minnesota.
TRANSACTIONS/CAREER NOTES: Selected by Denver Broncos in fourth round (113th pick overall) of 2001 NFL draft.
HONORS: Named center on THE SPORTING NEWS college All-America first team (1999 and 2000).
COLLEGE PLAYING EXPERIENCE: Minnesota, 1996-2000. ... Games: 1996 (redshirted), 1997 (12), 1998 (11), 1999 (11), 2000 (12). Total: 46.

HAMPTON, CASEY — DT — STEELERS

PERSONAL: Born September 3, 1977, in Galveston, Texas. ... 6-1/321.
HIGH SCHOOL: Ball (Galveston, Texas).
COLLEGE: Texas.
TRANSACTIONS/CAREER NOTES: Selected by Pittsburgh Steelers in first round (19th pick overall) of 2001 NFL draft.
HONORS: Named defensive tackle on THE SPORTING NEWS college All-America second team (1999). ... Named defensive tackle on THE SPORTING NEWS college All-America first team (2000).
COLLEGE NOTES: Recovered one fumble (1998); recovered two fumbles (1999).

Year Team	G	SACKS
1996—Texas	12	1.0
1997—Texas	3	0.0
1998—Texas	11	2.0
1999—Texas	13	3.0
2000—Texas	11	3.5
College totals (5 years)	50	9.5

HARRIS, NICK — P — BRONCOS

PERSONAL: Born July 28, 1976, in Phoenix. ... 6-2/221.
HIGH SCHOOL: Westview (Phoenix).
COLLEGE: California (degree in business administration).
TRANSACTIONS/CAREER NOTES: Selected by Denver Broncos in fourth round (120th pick overall) of 2001 NFL draft.
COLLEGE NOTES: Rushed two times for 28 yards (1997); rushed two times for minus 19 yards (2000).

Year Team	G	PUNTING					
		No.	Yds.	Avg.	Net avg.	In. 20	Blk.
1997—California	...	77	3250	42.2	36.6	8	0
1998—California	...	87	3546	40.8	33.3	27	3
1999—California	...	85	3744	44.0	40.0	21	1
2000—California	...	73	3030	41.5	37.7	36	3
College totals (4 years)	...	322	13570	42.1	36.9	92	7

HARTS, SHAUNARD — DB — CHIEFS

PERSONAL: Born August 4, 1978, in Pittsburg, Calif. ... 6-0/200.
HIGH SCHOOL: Pittsburg (Calif.).
COLLEGE: Boise State.
TRANSACTIONS/CAREER NOTES: Selected by Kansas City Chiefs in seventh round (212th pick overall) of 2001 NFL draft.
COLLEGE NOTES: Caught 12 passes for 246 yards and one touchdown (1997); rushed 90 times for 406 yards and three touchdowns and caught 19 passes for 203 yards and two touchdowns (1998).

Year Team	G	INTERCEPTIONS				SACKS
		No.	Yds.	Avg.	TD	No.
1997—Boise State	11	0	0	0.0	0	0.0
1998—Boise State	11	0	0	0.0	0	0.0
1999—Boise State			Statistics unavailable.			
2000—Boise State	13	2	39	19.5	1	7.0
College totals (3 years)	35	2	39	19.5	1	7.0

HARTWELL, EDGERTON — LB — RAVENS

PERSONAL: Born May 27, 1978, in Las Vegas, Nev. ... 6-1/244.
HIGH SCHOOL: Cheyenne (Las Vegas, Nev.).
COLLEGE: Wisconsin, then Western Illinois.
TRANSACTIONS/CAREER NOTES: Selected by Baltimore Ravens in fourth round (126th pick overall) of 2001 NFL draft.
COLLEGE NOTES: Recovered two fumbles (1998); recovered one fumble (1999); recovered four fumbles (2000).

Year Team	G	INTERCEPTIONS				SACKS
		No.	Yds.	Avg.	TD	No.
1996—Wisconsin			Redshirted.			
1997—Wisconsin	13	0	0	0.0	0	0.0
1998—Western Illinois	14	1	42	42.0	0	1.0
1999—Western Illinois	11	1	41	41.0	1	6.0
2000—Western Illinois	12	1	6	6.0	0	5.0
College totals (4 years)	50	3	89	29.7	1	12.0

HAYWARD, REGGIE — DE — BRONCOS

PERSONAL: Born March 14, 1979, in Dolton, Ill. ... 6-5/255.
HIGH SCHOOL: Thornridge (Dolton, Ill.).
COLLEGE: Iowa State.
TRANSACTIONS/CAREER NOTES: Selected by Denver Broncos in third round (87th pick overall) of 2001 NFL draft.
COLLEGE NOTES: Recovered one fumble (1998); recovered two fumbles (1999); recovered two fumbles (2000).

Year Team	G	SACKS
1997—Iowa State	11	0.0
1998—Iowa State	11	5.5
1999—Iowa State	11	4.0
2000—Iowa State	11	7.0
College totals (4 years)	44	16.5

HEAP, TODD — TE — RAVENS

PERSONAL: Born March 16, 1980, in Mesa, Ariz. ... 6-5/252. ... Full name: Todd Benjamin Heap.
HIGH SCHOOL: Mountain View (Mesa, Ariz.).
COLLEGE: Arizona State.
TRANSACTIONS/CAREER NOTES: Selected after junior season by Baltimore Ravens in first round (31st pick overall) of 2001 NFL draft.
HONORS: Named tight end on THE SPORTING NEWS college All-America first team (2000).
COLLEGE NOTES: Rushed once for two yards (2000).

			RECEIVING		
Year Team	G	No.	Yds.	Avg.	TD
1998—Arizona State	11	12	209	17.4	4
1999—Arizona State	12	55	832	15.1	3
2000—Arizona State	12	48	644	13.4	3
College totals (3 years)	35	115	1685	14.7	10

HENDERSON, JAMIE — CB — JETS

PERSONAL: Born January 1, 1979, in Carrolton, Ga. ... 6-2/202. ... Full name: Jamie Concepcion Henderson.
HIGH SCHOOL: Carrolton (Ga.).
JUNIOR COLLEGE: Mississippi Gulf Coast Junior College.
COLLEGE: Georgia.
TRANSACTIONS/CAREER NOTES: Selected by New York Jets in fourth round (101st pick overall) of 2001 NFL draft.

			INTERCEPTIONS		
Year Team	G	No.	Yds.	Avg.	TD
1997—Mississippi Gulf Coast		Statistics unavailable.			
1998—Mississippi Gulf Coast		Statistics unavailable.			
1999—Georgia	11	5	77	15.4	1
2000—Georgia	11	3	35	11.7	1
College totals (2 years)	22	8	112	14.0	2

HENRY, ANTHONY — CB — BROWNS

PERSONAL: Born March 29, 1979, in Fort Myers, Fla. ... 6-0/205. ... Full name: Anthony Daniel Henry.
HIGH SCHOOL: Bayshore (Fla.).
COLLEGE: South Florida.
TRANSACTIONS/CAREER NOTES: Selected by Cleveland Browns in fourth round (97th pick overall) of 2001 NFL draft.

			INTERCEPTIONS		
Year Team	G	No.	Yds.	Avg.	TD
1997—South Florida	11	2	11	5.5	0
1998—South Florida	11	0	0	0.0	0
1999—South Florida	9	3	27	9.0	1
2000—South Florida	11	5	88	17.6	0
College totals (4 years)	42	10	126	12.6	1

HENRY, TRAVIS — RB — BILLS

PERSONAL: Born October 29, 1978, in Frostproof, Fla. ... 5-9/221. ... Full name: Travis Deion Henry.
HIGH SCHOOL: Frostproof (Fla.).
COLLEGE: Tennessee.
TRANSACTIONS/CAREER NOTES: Selected by Buffalo Bills in second round (58th pick overall) of 2001 NFL draft.

		RUSHING				RECEIVING				TOTALS	
Year Team	G	Att.	Yds.	Avg.	TD	No.	Yds.	Avg.	TD	TD	Pts.
1997—Tennessee	6	2	4	2.0	0	0	0	0.0	0	0	0
1998—Tennessee	12	176	970	5.5	7	4	31	7.8	0	7	42
1999—Tennessee	11	125	790	6.3	8	3	3	1.0	0	8	48
2000—Tennessee	11	253	1314	5.2	11	13	65	5.0	0	11	66
College totals (4 years)	40	556	3078	5.5	26	20	99	5.0	0	26	156

HEUPEL, JOSH — QB — DOLPHINS

PERSONAL: Born March 22, 1978, in Aberdeen, S.D. ... 6-1/216.
HIGH SCHOOL: Aberdeen Central (S.D.).
JUNIOR COLLEGE: Snow College (Utah).
COLLEGE: Weber State, then Oklahoma.
TRANSACTIONS/CAREER NOTES: Selected by Miami Dolphins in sixth round (177th pick overall) of 2001 NFL draft.
HONORS: Named College Football Player of the Year by THE SPORTING NEWS (2000). ... Named quarterback on THE SPORTING NEWS college All-America first team (2000).

		PASSING								RUSHING				TOTALS	
Year Team	G	Att.	Cmp.	Pct.	Yds.	TD	Int.	Avg.	Rat.	Att.	Yds.	Avg.	TD	TD	Pts.
1997—Weber State	4	82	40	48.8	461	1	2	5.62	95.2	10	-1	-0.1	0	0	0
1998—Snow Junior College	10	258	153	59.3	2308	28	5	8.95	166.4	37	47	1.3	4	4	24
1999—Oklahoma	11	500	310	62.0	3460	30	15	6.92	133.9	47	-98	-2.1	5	5	30
2000—Oklahoma	12	433	280	64.7	3392	20	14	7.83	139.2	70	144	2.1	7	7	42
Junior college totals (1 year)	10	258	153	59.3	2308	28	5	8.95	166.4	37	47	1.3	4	4	24
College totals (3 years)	27	1015	630	62.1	7313	51	31	7.20	133.1	127	45	0.4	12	12	72

HILL, RENALDO   DB   CARDINALS

PERSONAL: Born November 12, 1978, in Detroit. ... 5-11/182.
HIGH SCHOOL: Chadsey (Mich.).
COLLEGE: Michigan State.
TRANSACTIONS/CAREER NOTES: Selected by Arizona Cardinals in seventh round (202nd pick overall) of 2001 NFL draft. ... Signed by Cardinals (May 30, 2001).
COLLEGE NOTES: Credited with one sack (1998).

| | | INTERCEPTIONS | | | |
Year Team	G	No.	Yds.	Avg.	TD
1997—Michigan State			Did not play.		
1998—Michigan State	12	5	23	4.6	0
1999—Michigan State	12	1	-2	-2.0	0
2000—Michigan State	11	3	7	2.3	0
College totals (3 years)	35	9	28	3.1	0

HOCHSTEIN, RUSS   G   BUCCANEERS

PERSONAL: Born October 7, 1977, in Hartington, Neb. ... 6-3/288.
HIGH SCHOOL: Cedar Catholic (Hartington, Neb.).
COLLEGE: Nebraska.
TRANSACTIONS/CAREER NOTES: Selected by Tampa Bay Buccaneers in fifth round (151st pick overall) of 2001 NFL draft.
HONORS: Named guard on THE SPORTING NEWS college All-America first team (2000).
COLLEGE PLAYING EXPERIENCE: Nebraska, 1996-2000. ... Games: 1996 (redshirted), 1997 (5), 1998 (11), 1999 (12), 2000 (11). Total: 39.

HODGE, SEDRICK   LB   SAINTS

PERSONAL: Born September 13, 1978, in Fayettesville, Ga. ... 6-3/235. ... Full name: Sedrick Jamaine Hodge.
HIGH SCHOOL: Westminster (Atlanta).
COLLEGE: North Carolina.
TRANSACTIONS/CAREER NOTES: Selected by New Orleans Saints in third round (70th pick overall) of 2001 NFL draft. ... Signed by Saints (June 4, 2001).

| | | INTERCEPTIONS | | | | SACKS |
Year Team	G	No.	Yds.	Avg.	TD	No.
1997—North Carolina	11	0	0	0.0	0	0.0
1998—North Carolina	11	1	5	5.0	0	3.5
1999—North Carolina	11	1	19	19.0	0	0.0
2000—North Carolina	11	0	0	0.0	0	7.0
College totals (4 years)	44	2	24	12.0	0	10.5

HOLLOWAY, JABARI   TE   PATRIOTS

PERSONAL: Born December 18, 1978, in Atlanta. ... 6-3/255. ... Full name: Jabari Jelani Holloway.
HIGH SCHOOL: Sandy Creek (Tyrone, Ga.).
COLLEGE: Notre Dame.
TRANSACTIONS/CAREER NOTES: Selected by New England Patriots in fourth round (119th pick overall) of 2001 NFL draft.

| | | RECEIVING | | | |
Year Team	G	No.	Yds.	Avg.	TD
1997—Notre Dame	11	8	144	18.0	1
1998—Notre Dame	11	15	262	17.5	2
1999—Notre Dame	12	12	189	15.8	4
2000—Notre Dame	10	6	97	16.2	0
College totals (4 years)	44	41	692	16.9	7

HOLLOWAY, MENSON   DE   49ERS

PERSONAL: Born July 12, 1978, in El Paso, Texas. ... 6-2/270.
HIGH SCHOOL: Andress (Texas).
COLLEGE: Texas-El Paso.
TRANSACTIONS/CAREER NOTES: Selected by San Francisco 49ers in sixth round (191st pick overall) of 2001 NFL draft.
COLLEGE NOTES: Played tight end (1996).

Year Team	G	SACKS
1996—Texas-El Paso	11	0.0
1997—Texas-El Paso		Redshirted.
1998—Texas-El Paso	11	0.0
1999—Texas-El Paso	12	2.0
2000—Texas-El Paso	11	10.5
College totals (4 years)	45	12.5

HOLMAN, RASHAD — CB — 49ERS

PERSONAL: Born January 17, 1978, in Louisville, Ky. ... 5-11/190.
HIGH SCHOOL: Male (Louisville, Ky.).
COLLEGE: Louisville.
TRANSACTIONS/CAREER NOTES: Selected by San Francisco 49ers in sixth round (179th pick overall) of 2001 NFL draft.

Year Team	G	INTERCEPTIONS No.	Yds.	Avg.	TD
1996—Louisville		Redshirted.			
1997—Louisville	10	1	0	0.0	0
1998—Louisville	11	2	0	0.0	0
1999—Louisville	12	5	57	11.4	0
2000—Louisville	...	6	32	5.3	0
College totals (4 years)	...	14	89	6.4	0

HOUSHMANDZADEH, T.J. — WR — BENGALS

PERSONAL: Born August 26, 1977, in Victor Valley, Calif. ... 6-2/205. ... Full name: Touraj Houshmandzadeh.
HIGH SCHOOL: Barstow (Calif.).
JUNIOR COLLEGE: Cerritos College (Calif.).
COLLEGE: Oregon State.
TRANSACTIONS/CAREER NOTES: Selected by Cincinnati Bengals in seventh round (204th pick overall) of 2001 NFL draft.

Year Team	G	RECEIVING No.	Yds.	Avg.	TD	PUNT RETURNS No.	Yds.	Avg.	TD	KICKOFF RETURNS No.	Yds.	Avg.	TD	TOTALS TD	Pts.
1997—Cerritos College	10	33	622	18.8	5	0	0	0.0	0	7	342	48.9	1	6	36
1998—Cerritos College	8	32	530	16.6	4	6	142	23.7	1	14	386	27.6	1	6	36
1999—Oregon State	11	24	378	15.8	2	21	181	8.6	0	13	250	19.2	0	2	12
2000—Oregon State	12	48	730	15.2	7	28	278	9.9	0	2	20	10.0	0	7	42
Junior college totals (2 years)	18	65	1152	17.7	9	6	142	23.7	1	21	728	34.7	2	12	72
College totals (2 years)	23	72	1108	15.4	9	49	459	9.4	0	15	270	18.0	0	9	54

HOWARD, WILLIE — DE — VIKINGS

PERSONAL: Born December 26, 1977, in Mountain View, Calif. ... 6-3/298.
HIGH SCHOOL: Los Altos (Mountain View, Calif.).
COLLEGE: Stanford.
TRANSACTIONS/CAREER NOTES: Selected by Minnesota Vikings in second round (57th pick overall) of 2001 NFL draft.
COLLEGE NOTES: Recovered one fumble (1997); recovered one fumble (1998); recovered two fumbles (1999); recovered one fumble and intercepted one pass for 17 yards (2000).

Year Team	G	SACKS
1997—Stanford	11	2.0
1998—Stanford	11	5.5
1999—Stanford	11	10.0
2000—Stanford	11	5.0
College totals (4 years)	44	22.5

HOWELL, JOHN — S — BUCCANEERS

PERSONAL: Born April 28, 1978, in North Platte, Neb. ... 5-11/196. ... Full name: John Thomas Howell.
HIGH SCHOOL: Mullen (Neb.).
COLLEGE: Colorado State.
TRANSACTIONS/CAREER NOTES: Selected by Tampa Bay Buccaneers in fourth round (117th pick overall) of 2001 NFL draft.

Year Team	G	INTERCEPTIONS No.	Yds.	Avg.	TD	SACKS No.
1996—Colorado State	7	0	0	0.0	0	0.0
1997—Colorado State	12	0	0	0.0	0	0.0
1998—Colorado State		Redshirted.				
1999—Colorado State	11	1	0	0.0	0	4.0
2000—Colorado State	11	2	0	0.0	0	5.0
College totals (4 years)	41	3	0	0.0	0	9.0

HUFF, ORLANDO — LB — SEAHAWKS

PERSONAL: Born August 14, 1978, in Mobile, Alabama. ... 6-2/245.
HIGH SCHOOL: Upland (Calif.).
JUNIOR COLLEGE: Eastern Arizona Junior College.
COLLEGE: Fresno State.
TRANSACTIONS/CAREER NOTES: Selected by Seattle Seahawks in fourth round (104th pick overall) of 2001 NFL draft.

Year Team	G	SACKS
1998—Fresno State		Redshirted.
1999—Fresno State	13	4.0
2000—Fresno State	12	10.0
College totals (2 years)	25	14.0

HUTCHINSON, STEVE — G — SEAHAWKS

PERSONAL: Born November 1, 1977, in Coral Springs, Fla. ... 6-5/306.
HIGH SCHOOL: Coral Springs (Fla.).
COLLEGE: Michigan.
TRANSACTIONS/CAREER NOTES: Selected by Seattle Seahawks in first round (17th pick overall) of 2001 NFL draft.
HONORS: Named guard on THE SPORTING NEWS college All-America first team (2000).
COLLEGE PLAYING EXPERIENCE: Michigan, 1997-2000. ... Games: 1997 (12), 1998 (12), 1999 (11), 2000 (12). Total: 47.

JACKSON, JAMES — RB — BROWNS

PERSONAL: Born August 4, 1976, in Belle Glade, Fla. ... 5-10/209. ... Full name: James Shurrate Jackson.
HIGH SCHOOL: Glades Central (Belle Glade, Fla.).
COLLEGE: Miami.
TRANSACTIONS/CAREER NOTES: Selected by Cleveland Browns in third round (65th pick overall) of 2001 NFL draft.

		RUSHING				RECEIVING				TOTALS	
Year Team	G	Att.	Yds.	Avg.	TD	No.	Yds.	Avg.	TD	TD	Pts.
1996—Miami (Fla.)	2	8	25	3.1	0	1	7	7.0	0	0	0
1997—Miami (Fla.)	9	81	595	7.3	6	10	52	5.2	0	6	36
1998—Miami (Fla.)	10	82	545	6.6	5	5	30	6.0	0	5	30
1999—Miami (Fla.)	9	169	782	4.6	7	13	133	10.2	1	8	48
2000—Miami (Fla.)	11	201	1006	5.0	11	9	56	6.2	2	13	78
College totals (5 years)	41	541	2953	5.5	29	38	278	7.3	3	32	192

JAMES, CEDRIC — WR — VIKINGS

PERSONAL: Born March 19, 1976, in Fort Worth, Texas. ... 6-1/199.
HIGH SCHOOL: Kennedale (Texas).
COLLEGE: Texas Christian.
TRANSACTIONS/CAREER NOTES: Selected by Minnesota Vikings in fourth round (131st pick overall) of 2001 NFL draft.
COLLEGE NOTES: Rushed one time for minus seven yards (1997); rushed three times for one yard (1998).

		RECEIVING				KICKOFF RETURNS				TOTALS	
Year Team	G	No.	Yds.	Avg.	TD	No.	Yds.	Avg.	TD	TD	Pts.
1997—Texas Christian	10	4	51	12.8	0	0	0	0.0	0	0	0
1998—Texas Christian	11	13	167	12.8	1	0	0	0.0	0	1	6
1999—Texas Christian	10	4	52	13.0	0	5	141	28.2	0	0	0
2000—Texas Christian	11	19	310	16.3	3	4	78	19.5	0	3	18
College totals (4 years)	42	40	580	14.5	4	9	219	24.3	0	4	24

JAMESON, MICHAEL — DB — BROWNS

PERSONAL: Born July 14, 1979, in Killeen, Texas. ... 5-11/187.
HIGH SCHOOL: Ellison (Killeen, Texas).
COLLEGE: Texas A&M.
TRANSACTIONS/CAREER NOTES: Selected by Cleveland Browns in sixth round (165th pick overall) of 2001 NFL draft.
COLLEGE NOTES: Credited with one sack (1998); returned two punts for 20 yards (1999); returned one punt for 39 yards (2000). ... Signed by Browns (May 24, 2001).

		INTERCEPTIONS			
Year Team	G	No.	Yds.	Avg.	TD
1997—Texas A&M	12	0	0	0.0	0
1998—Texas A&M	13	0	0	0.0	0
1999—Texas A&M	11	5	151	30.2	3
2000—Texas A&M	9	2	88	44.0	0
College totals (4 years)	45	7	239	34.1	3

JENKINS, KRIS — DT — PANTHERS

PERSONAL: Born August 3, 1979, in Ypsilanti, Mich. ... 6-4/305. ... Full name: Kristopher Rudy-Charles Jenkins.
HIGH SCHOOL: Belleville (Ypsilanti, Mich.).
COLLEGE: Maryland.
TRANSACTIONS/CAREER NOTES: Selected by Carolina Panthers in second round (44th pick overall) of 2001 NFL draft.
COLLEGE NOTES: Recovered one fumble (1999); recovered one fumble (2000).

Year Team	G	SACKS
1997—Maryland	11	0.0
1998—Maryland	8	1.0
1999—Maryland	11	1.0
2000—Maryland	11	8.0
College totals (4 years)	41	10.0

JENNINGS, JONAS   OT   BILLS

PERSONAL: Born November 21, 1977, in College Park, Ga. ... 6-3/320.
HIGH SCHOOL: Tri-Cities (East Point, Ga.).
COLLEGE: Georgia.
TRANSACTIONS/CAREER NOTES: Selected by Buffalo Bills in third round (95th pick overall) of 2001 NFL draft.
COLLEGE PLAYING EXPERIENCE: Georgia, 1996-2000. ... Games: 1996 (redshirted), 1997 (11), 1998 (11), 1999 (11), 2000 (11). Total: 44.

JOHNSON, CHAD   WR   BENGALS

PERSONAL: Born January 9, 1978, in Los Angeles. ... 6-1/192.
HIGH SCHOOL: Miami Beach (Fla.).
JUNIOR COLLEGE: Santa Monica College (Calif.).
COLLEGE: Oregon State.
TRANSACTIONS/CAREER NOTES: Selected by Cincinnati Bengals in second round (36th pick overall) of 2001 NFL draft.
COLLEGE NOTES: Rushed two times for minus five yards (2000).

| | | | RECEIVING | | |
Year Team	G	No.	Yds.	Avg.	TD
1997—Santa Monica College	10	57	1238	21.7	17
1998—Santa Monica College		Did not play.			
1999—Santa Monica College	10	63	862	13.7	6
2000—Oregon State	12	37	806	21.8	8
Junior college totals (2 years)	20	120	2100	17.5	23
College totals (1 years)	12	37	806	21.8	8

JOHNSON, ERIC   TE   49ERS

PERSONAL: Born August 15, 1979, in Needham, Mass. ... 6-3/230.
HIGH SCHOOL: Needham (Mass.).
COLLEGE: Yale.
TRANSACTIONS/CAREER NOTES: Selected by San Francisco 49ers in seventh round (224th pick overall) of 2001 NFL draft.
COLLEGE NOTES: Punted 11 times for 402 yards and rushed once for no gain (1998); punted 44 times for 1805 yards (1999); punted 53 times for 2026 yards and rushed once for 12 yards (2000).

| | | | RECEIVING | | |
Year Team	G	No.	Yds.	Avg.	TD
1997—Yale	10	4	55	13.8	0
1998—Yale	8	24	224	9.3	0
1999—Yale	10	67	858	12.8	9
2000—Yale	10	86	1007	11.7	14
College totals (4 years)	38	181	2144	11.8	23

JOHNSON, RIALL   LB   BENGALS

PERSONAL: Born April 20, 1978, in Lynnwood, Wash. ... 6-3/240.
HIGH SCHOOL: Mariner (Wash.).
COLLEGE: Stanford.
TRANSACTIONS/CAREER NOTES: Selected by Cincinnati Bengals in sixth round (168th pick overall) of 2001 NFL draft.

Year Team	G	SACKS
1996—Stanford		Redshirted.
1997—Stanford	11	2.0
1998—Stanford	10	6.0
1999—Stanford	11	13.0
2000—Stanford	11	15.0
College totals (4 years)	43	36.0

JOHNSON, RUDI   RB   BENGALS

PERSONAL: Born October 1, 1979, in Ettrick, Va. ... 5-10/230. ... Full name: Rudi Ali Johnson.
HIGH SCHOOL: Thomas Dale (Ettrick, Va.).
JUNIOR COLLEGE: Butler County Community College.
COLLEGE: Auburn.
TRANSACTIONS/CAREER NOTES: Selected by Cincinnati Bengals in fourth round (100th pick overall) of 2001 NFL draft.
HONORS: Named running back on THE SPORTING NEWS college All-America second team (2000).
COLLEGE NOTES: Returned four kickoffs for 62 yards and attempted seven passes with five completions for 65 yards and one touchdown (1999).

| | | RUSHING | | | | RECEIVING | | | | TOTALS | |
Year Team	G	Att.	Yds.	Avg.	TD	No.	Yds.	Avg.	TD	TD	Pts.
1999—Butler County CC	12	306	2224	7.3	31	10	207	20.7	4	35	210
2000—Auburn	12	324	1567	4.8	13	9	70	7.8	0	13	78
Junior college totals (1 year)	12	306	2224	7.3	31	10	207	20.7	4	35	210
College totals (1 years)	12	324	1567	4.8	13	9	70	7.8	0	13	78

JONES, KENYATTA   OL   PATRIOTS

PERSONAL: Born January 18, 1979, in Gainesville, Fla. ... 6-3/315. ... Full name: Kenyatta Lapoleon Jones.
HIGH SCHOOL: Eastside (Gainesville, Fla.).
COLLEGE: South Florida.
TRANSACTIONS/CAREER NOTES: Selected by New England Patriots in fourth round (96th pick overall) of 2001 NFL draft.
COLLEGE PLAYING EXPERIENCE: South Florida, 1997-2000. ... Games: 1997 (10), 1998 (10), 1999 (11), 2000 (11). Total: 42.

JORDAN, LAMONT   RB   JETS

PERSONAL: Born November 11, 1978, in Forestville, Md. ... 5-10/230.
HIGH SCHOOL: Suitland (Forestville, Md.).
COLLEGE: Maryland.
TRANSACTIONS/CAREER NOTES: Selected by New York Jets in second round (49th pick overall) of 2001 NFL draft.
HONORS: Named running back on THE SPORTING NEWS college All-America third team (1999).
COLLEGE NOTES: Attempted one pass and returned five kickoffs for 76 yards (1997); attempted two passes with two completions for 83 yards and one touchdown (1998); attempted three passes with two completions for 60 yards and one touchdown (1999); attempted five passes with one completion for minus six yards and one interception (2000).

| | | RUSHING | | | | RECEIVING | | | | TOTALS | |
Year Team	G	Att.	Yds.	Avg.	TD	No.	Yds.	Avg.	TD	TD	Pts.
1997—Maryland	11	159	689	4.3	3	22	155	7.0	0	3	18
1998—Maryland	10	169	906	5.4	6	14	87	6.2	0	6	36
1999—Maryland	11	266	1632	6.1	16	19	208	10.9	1	17	102
2000—Maryland	11	213	920	4.3	11	21	287	13.7	0	11	66
College totals (4 years)	43	807	4147	5.1	36	76	737	9.7	1	37	222

JUE, BHAWOH   CB   PACKERS

PERSONAL: Born May 24, 1979, in Liberia. ... 6-0/197. ... Full name: Bhawoh Papi Jue.
HIGH SCHOOL: Chantilly (Va.).
COLLEGE: Penn State.
TRANSACTIONS/CAREER NOTES: Selected by Green Bay Packers in third round (71st pick overall) of 2001 NFL draft.

| | | INTERCEPTIONS | | | |
Year Team	G	No.	Yds.	Avg.	TD
1997—Penn State	7	0	0	0.0	0
1998—Penn State	10	2	25	12.5	0
1999—Penn State	12	2	51	25.5	1
2000—Penn State	12	3	31	10.3	0
College totals (4 years)	41	7	107	15.3	1

KASPER, KEVIN   WR   BRONCOS

PERSONAL: Born December 23, 1977, in Burr Ridge, Ill. ... 6-0/193.
HIGH SCHOOL: Hinsdale South (Burr Ridge, Ill.).
COLLEGE: Iowa.
TRANSACTIONS/CAREER NOTES: Selected by Denver Broncos in sixth round (190th pick overall) of 2001 NFL draft. ... Signed by Broncos (May 17, 2001).
COLLEGE NOTES: Rushed one time for minus nine yards (1999); rushed one time for minus 11 yards (2000).

| | | RECEIVING | | | |
Year Team	G	No.	Yds.	Avg.	TD
1996—Iowa			Redshirted.		
1997—Iowa	11	1	19	19.0	0
1998—Iowa	11	14	281	20.1	1
1999—Iowa	10	60	664	11.1	3
2000—Iowa	12	82	1010	12.3	7
College totals (4 years)	44	157	1974	12.6	11

KELLY, ERIC   CB   VIKINGS

PERSONAL: Born January 15, 1977, in Milwaukee. ... 5-10/197.
HIGH SCHOOL: Bay (Panama, Fla.).
COLLEGE: Kentucky.
TRANSACTIONS/CAREER NOTES: Selected by Minnesota Vikings in third round (64th pick overall) of 2001 NFL draft.

| | | INTERCEPTIONS | | | |
Year Team	G	No.	Yds.	Avg.	TD
1997—Kentucky	10	0	0	0.0	0
1998—Kentucky	11	0	0	0.0	0
1999—Kentucky	10	3	52	17.3	0
2000—Kentucky	11	1	20	20.0	0
College totals (4 years)	42	4	72	18.0	0

KING, ANDRE — WR — BROWNS

PERSONAL: Born November 26, 1973, in Fort Lauderdale, Fla. ... 6-0/200.
HIGH SCHOOL: Stranahan (Fla.).
COLLEGE: Miami.
TRANSACTIONS/CAREER NOTES: Selected by Cleveland Browns in seventh round (245th pick overall) of 2001 NFL draft.

			RECEIVING		
Year Team	G	No.	Yds.	Avg.	TD
1997—Miami (Fla.)	8	5	66	13.2	0
1998—Miami (Fla.)	11	28	397	14.2	1
1999—Miami (Fla.)	12	20	220	11.0	1
2000—Miami (Fla.)	11	11	151	13.7	1
College totals (4 years)	42	64	834	13.0	3

KNIGHT, ROGER — LB — STEELERS

PERSONAL: Born October 11, 1978, in Queens Village, N.Y. ... 6-2/234.
HIGH SCHOOL: Brooklyn Tech (N.Y.).
COLLEGE: Wisconsin.
TRANSACTIONS/CAREER NOTES: Selected by Pittsburgh Steelers in sixth round (182nd pick overall) of 2001 NFL draft.

			INTERCEPTIONS			SACKS
Year Team	G	No.	Yds.	Avg.	TD	No.
1997—Wisconsin	12	0	0	0.0	0	0.0
1998—Wisconsin	6	0	0	0.0	0	0.0
1999—Wisconsin	12	1	11	11.0	0	1.0
2000—Wisconsin	13	0	0	0.0	0	4.0
College totals (4 years)	43	1	11	11.0	0	5.0

KOCUREK, KRIS — DT — SEAHAWKS

PERSONAL: Born November 15, 1978, in Rockdale, Texas. ... 6-5/293.
HIGH SCHOOL: Caldwell (Texas).
COLLEGE: Texas Tech.
TRANSACTIONS/CAREER NOTES: Selected by Seattle Seahawks in seventh round (237th pick overall) of 2001 NFL draft.

Year Team	G	SACKS
1997—Texas Tech	10	1.5
1998—Texas Tech	11	0.0
1999—Texas Tech	10	1.0
2000—Texas Tech	12	3.0
College totals (4 years)	43	5.5

KOLODZIEJ, ROSS — DT — GIANTS

PERSONAL: Born May 11, 1978, in Stevens Point, Wis. ... 6-3/286.
HIGH SCHOOL: Stevens Point (Wis.).
COLLEGE: Wisconsin.
TRANSACTIONS/CAREER NOTES: Selected by New York Giants in seventh round (230th pick overall) of NFL draft.
COLLEGE NOTES: Granted medical redshirt (1996).

Year Team	G	SACKS
1996—Wisconsin	3	0.0
1997—Wisconsin	13	1.0
1998—Wisconsin	12	2.0
1999—Wisconsin	12	3.0
2000—Wisconsin	12	3.0
College totals (5 years)	52	9.0

LAYNE, GEORGE — FB — CHIEFS

PERSONAL: Born October 9, 1978, in Alvin, Texas. ... 5-11/243.
HIGH SCHOOL: Alvin (Texas).
COLLEGE: Texas Christian.
TRANSACTIONS/CAREER NOTES: Selected after junior season by Kansas City Chiefs in fourth round (108th pick overall) of 2001 NFL draft.
COLLEGE NOTES: Returned one kickoff for eight yards (1998); returned two kickoffs for 19 yards (1999); returned one kickoff for 12 yards (2000).

		RUSHING				RECEIVING				TOTALS	
Year Team	G	Att.	Yds.	Avg.	TD	No.	Yds.	Avg.	TD	TD	Pts.
1997—Texas Christian					Redshirted.						
1998—Texas Christian	9	7	17	2.4	0	0	0	0.0	0	0	0
1999—Texas Christian	11	44	186	4.2	2	5	79	15.8	0	2	12
2000—Texas Christian	11	46	279	6.1	6	8	151	18.9	2	8	48
College totals (3 years)	31	97	482	5.0	8	13	230	17.7	2	10	60

LEAVERTON, DAVID   P   JAGUARS

PERSONAL: Born April 1, 1978, in Midland, Texas. ... 6-3/211.
HIGH SCHOOL: Midland (Texas).
COLLEGE: Tennessee (degree in finance).
TRANSACTIONS/CAREER NOTES: Selected by Jacksonville Jaguars in fifth round (142nd pick overall) of 2001 NFL draft.

					PUNTING			
Year Team	G	No.	Yds.	Avg.	Net avg.	In. 20	Blk.	
1996—Tennessee			Redshirted.					
1997—Tennessee	...	8	291	36.4	31.0	2	0	
1998—Tennessee	...	56	2178	38.9	32.1	13	1	
1999—Tennessee	...	57	2427	42.6	39.8	17	0	
2000—Tennessee	...	59	2415	40.9	38.0	20	2	
College totals (4 years)	...	180	7311	40.6	36.4	52	3	

LEHR, MATT   C   COWBOYS

PERSONAL: Born April 25, 1979, in Jacksonville. ... 6-2/292. ... Full name: Matthew Steven Lehr.
HIGH SCHOOL: Woodbridge (Va.).
COLLEGE: Virginia Tech.
TRANSACTIONS/CAREER NOTES: Selected by Dallas Cowboys in fifth round (137th pick overall) of 2001 NFL draft.
COLLEGE PLAYING EXPERIENCE: Virginia Tech, 1997-2000. ... Games: 1997 (4), 1998 (10), 1999 (12), 2000 (12). Total: 38.

LEVERETTE, OTIS   DE   DOLPHINS

PERSONAL: Born May 31, 1978, in Americus, Ga. ... 6-7/275.
HIGH SCHOOL: Americus (Ga.).
JUNIOR COLLEGE: Middle Georgia College.
COLLEGE: Alabama-Birmingham.
TRANSACTIONS/CAREER NOTES: Selected by Miami Dolphins in sixth round (187th pick overall) of 2001 NFL draft.

Year Team	G	SACKS
1996—Middle Georgia	Statistics unavailable.	
1997—Middle Georgia	Statistics unavailable.	
1998—Alabama-Birmingham	Did not play.	
1999—Alabama-Birmingham	11	0.0
2000—Alabama-Birmingham	...	3.5
College totals (2 years)	...	3.5

LEWIS, DAMIONE   DT   RAMS

PERSONAL: Born March 1, 1978, in Sulphur Springs, Texas. ... 6-2/301. ... Full name: Damione Ramon Lewis.
HIGH SCHOOL: Sulphur Springs (Texas).
COLLEGE: Miami.
TRANSACTIONS/CAREER NOTES: Selected by St. Louis Rams in first round (12th pick overall) of 2001 NFL draft.
HONORS: Named defensive tackle on THE SPORTING NEWS college All-America third team (2000).
COLLEGE NOTES: Recovered one fumble (1999).

Year Team	G	SACKS
1997—Miami (Fla.)	11	4.0
1998—Miami (Fla.)	11	2.0
1999—Miami (Fla.)	12	6.5
2000—Miami (Fla.)	9	3.0
College totals (4 years)	43	15.5

LEYVA, VICTOR   G   BENGALS

PERSONAL: Born December 18, 1977, in Porteville, Calif. ... 6-3/322.
HIGH SCHOOL: Monache (Porterville, Calif.).
COLLEGE: Arizona State (degree in sociology).
TRANSACTIONS/CAREER NOTES: Selected by Cincinnati Bengals in fifth round (135th pick overall) of 2001 NFL draft.
COLLEGE PLAYING EXPERIENCE: Arizona State, 1997-2000. ... Games: 1997 (12), 1998 (11), 1999 (12), 2000 (12). Total: 47.

LIGHT, MATT   OT   PATRIOTS

PERSONAL: Born June 23, 1978, in Greenville, Ohio. ... 6-4/305. ... Full name: Matthew Charles Light.
HIGH SCHOOL: Greenville (Ohio).
COLLEGE: Purdue.
TRANSACTIONS/CAREER NOTES: Selected by New England Patriots in second round (48th pick overall) of 2001 NFL draft.
HONORS: Named offensive tackle on THE SPORTING NEWS college All-America third team (2000).
COLLEGE NOTES: Played tight end (1996). ... Caught one pass for 16 yards (1996).
COLLEGE PLAYING EXPERIENCE: Purdue, 1996-2000. ... Games: 1996 (7), 1997 (redshirted), 1998 (13), 1999 (12), 2000 (12). Total: 44.

LINCOLN, ALEX   LB   49ERS

PERSONAL: Born November 17, 1977, in Meridian, Miss. ... 6-0/237. ... Full name: Alex Richard Lincoln.
HIGH SCHOOL: Murphy (Mobile, Ala.).
COLLEGE: Mississippi, then Auburn.
TRANSACTIONS/CAREER NOTES: Selected by San Francisco 49ers in seventh round (209th pick overall) of 2001 NFL draft.
COLLEGE NOTES: Recovered two fumbles (1997); recovered one fumble (2000).

| Year Team | G | INTERCEPTIONS | | | | SACKS |
		No.	Yds.	Avg.	TD	No.
1997—Mississippi	10	0	0	0.0	0	7.0
1998—Auburn				Redshirted.		
1999—Auburn	11	1	20	20.0	1	1.5
2000—Auburn	12	1	0	0.0	0	0.0
College totals (3 years)	33	2	20	10.0	1	8.5

LOVE, ARTHER   TE   PATRIOTS

PERSONAL: Born September 18, 1977, in Soperton, Ga. ... 6-4/252.
HIGH SCHOOL: Montgomery County (Soperton, Ga.).
COLLEGE: South Carolina State.
TRANSACTIONS/CAREER NOTES: Selected by New England Patriots in sixth round (180th pick overall) of 2001 NFL draft.
COLLEGE NOTES: Returned one kickoff eight yards (2000).

| Year Team | G | RECEIVING | | | |
		No.	Yds.	Avg.	TD
1997—South Carolina State	11	1	13	13.0	0
1998—South Carolina State	11	6	98	16.3	1
1999—South Carolina State	9	7	109	15.6	1
2000—South Carolina State	10	20	342	17.1	2
College totals (4 years)	41	34	562	16.5	4

LUCAS, KEN   CB   SEAHAWKS

PERSONAL: Born January 23, 1979, in Cleveland, Miss. ... 6-0/200.
HIGH SCHOOL: East Side (Cleveland, Miss.).
COLLEGE: Mississippi.
TRANSACTIONS/CAREER NOTES: Selected by Seattle Seahawks in second round (40th pick overall) of 2001 NFL draft.
COLLEGE NOTES: Caught nine passes for 96 yards, rushed one time for three yards (1997); caught 12 passes for 152 yards, rushed two times for 75 yards (1998); returned 11 kickoffs for 185 yards and returned one punt for 17 yards (1998); returned one kickoff for 26 yards (1999).

| Year Team | G | INTERCEPTIONS | | | |
		No.	Yds.	Avg.	TD
1997—Mississippi	11	0	0	0.0	0
1998—Mississippi	11	0	0	0.0	0
1999—Mississippi	10	2	24	12.0	0
2000—Mississippi	11	5	60	12.0	0
College totals (4 years)	43	7	84	12.0	0

MAESE, JOE   C   RAVENS

PERSONAL: Born December 2, 1978, in Morenci, Ariz. ... 6-0/235.
HIGH SCHOOL: Cortez (Ariz.).
JUNIOR COLLEGE: Phoenix College.
COLLEGE: New Mexico.
TRANSACTIONS/CAREER NOTES: Selected by Baltimore Ravens in sixth round (194th pick overall) in 2001 NFL draft.
COLLEGE NOTES: Phoenix College, 1997 and 1998; New Mexico, 1999 and 2000. ... Games: 1997 (games played unavailable), 1998 (games played unavailable), 1999 (11), 2000 (12). Total NCAA: 23.

MANUMALEUNA, BRANDON   TE   RAMS

PERSONAL: Born January 4, 1980, in Torrance, Calif. ... 6-2/288. ... Full name: Brandon Michael Manumaleuna.
HIGH SCHOOL: Narbonne (Calif.).
COLLEGE: Arizona.
TRANSACTIONS/CAREER NOTES: Selected by St. Louis Rams in fourth round (129th pick overall) of 2001 NFL draft.
COLLEGE NOTES: Rushed once for no yards (1998).

| Year Team | G | RECEIVING | | | |
		No.	Yds.	Avg.	TD
1997—Arizona	9	1	45	45.0	0
1998—Arizona	12	6	22	3.7	0
1999—Arizona	12	20	316	15.8	2
2000—Arizona	11	13	161	12.4	1
College totals (4 years)	44	40	544	13.6	3

MARKHAM, JOHN   K   GIANTS

PERSONAL: Born April 27, 1979, in Brentwood, Tenn. ... 6-1/212.
HIGH SCHOOL: Montgomery Bell (Tenn.).
COLLEGE: Vanderbilt.
TRANSACTIONS/CAREER NOTES: Selected by New York Giants in fifth round (160th pick overall) of 2001 NFL draft.
COLLEGE NOTES: Attempted one pass without a completion (1998); attempted one pass with completion for 17 yards (1999).

			PUNTING						KICKING				
	No.	Yds.	Avg.	Net avg.	In. 20	Blk.	XPM	XPA	FGM	FGA	Lg.	50+	Pts.
1997—Vanderbilt	0	0	0.0	.0	0	0	13	10	8	13	49	0-0	37
1998—Vanderbilt	6	262	43.7	43.3	3	0	13	15	13	21	49	0-0	52
1999—Vanderbilt	60	2446	40.8	37.5	17	2	26	27	12	16	49	0-0	62
2000—Vanderbilt	0	0	0.0	.0	0	0	19	21	14	18	52	0-0	61
College totals (4 years)	66	2708	41.0	38.0	20	2	71	73	47	68	52	0-0	212

MARSHALL, TORRANCE   LB   PACKERS

PERSONAL: Born June 12, 1977, in Miami. ... 6-2/245.
HIGH SCHOOL: Sunset (Miami).
JUNIOR COLLEGE: Kemper Military Junior College (Mo.), then Miami-Dade Community College.
COLLEGE: Oklahoma.
TRANSACTIONS/CAREER NOTES: Selected by Green Bay Packers in third round (72nd pick overall) of 2001 NFL draft.
HONORS: Named linebacker on The Sporting News college All-America third team (2000).
COLLEGE NOTES: Recovered one fumble (1996); recovered two fumbles (1997).

			INTERCEPTIONS			SACKS
Year Team	G	No.	Yds.	Avg.	TD	No.
1996—Kemper Military	10	0	0	0.0	0	6.0
1997—Kemper Military	10	1	0	0.0	0	6.0
1998—Miami-Dade Community College				Did not play.		
1999—Oklahoma	11	0	0	0.0	0	7.0
2000—Oklahoma	11	2	65	32.5	1	5.0
Junior college totals (2 years)	20	1	0	0.0	0	12.0
College totals (2 years)	22	2	65	32.5	1	12.0

MARTIN, DAVID   WR   PACKERS

PERSONAL: Born March 13, 1979, in Norfolk, Va. ... 6-3/214. ... Full name: David Earl Martin.
HIGH SCHOOL: Norview (Norfolk, Va.).
COLLEGE: Tennessee.
TRANSACTIONS/CAREER NOTES: Selected by Green Bay Packers in sixth round (198th pick overall) of 2001 NFL draft.

			RECEIVING		
Year Team	G	No.	Yds.	Avg.	TD
1997—Tennessee	5	1	22	22.0	0
1998—Tennessee	10	3	59	19.7	0
1999—Tennessee	10	13	177	13.6	2
2000—Tennessee	11	29	285	9.8	3
College totals (4 years)	36	46	543	11.8	5

McALLISTER, DEUCE   RB   SAINTS

PERSONAL: Born December 27, 1978, in Morton, Miss. ... 6-1/222. ... Full name: Dulymus McAllister.
HIGH SCHOOL: Morton (Miss.).
COLLEGE: Mississippi.
TRANSACTIONS/CAREER NOTES: Selected by New Orleans Saints in first round (23rd pick overall) of 2001 NFL draft.
COLLEGE NOTES: Attempted two passes with two completions for 32 yards (1999); attempted one pass with one completion for 20 yards and a touchdown (2000).

		RUSHING				RECEIVING				PUNT RETURNS				KICKOFF RETURNS				TOTALS	
Year Team	G	Att.	Yds.	Avg.	TD	No.	Yds.	Avg.	TD	No.	Yds.	Avg.	TD	No.	Yds.	Avg.	TD	TD	Pts.
1997—Mississippi	11	94	402	4.3	4	7	71	10.1	0	0	0	0.0	0	0	0	0.0	0	4	0
1998—Mississippi	11	212	1082	5.1	7	18	154	8.6	0	0	0	0.0	0	0	0	0.0	0	7	42
1999—Mississippi	10	151	809	5.4	12	20	201	10.1	0	3	30	10.0	0	25	652	26.1	1	13	78
2000—Mississippi	11	159	767	4.8	14	18	190	10.6	2	17	191	11.2	1	20	340	17.0	0	17	102
College totals (4 years)	43	616	3060	5.0	37	63	616	9.8	2	20	221	11.1	1	45	992	22.0	1	41	222

McCANTS, DAMERIEN   WR   REDSKINS

PERSONAL: Born August 1, 1977, in Odenton, Md. ... 6-4/210.
HIGH SCHOOL: Arundel (Md.).
COLLEGE: Delaware State.
TRANSACTIONS/CAREER NOTES: Selected by Washington Redskins in fifth round (154th pick overall) of 2001 NFL draft.
COLLEGE NOTES: Returned one punt for 12 yards (1999); returned one punt for 28 yards and returned one kickoff for 71 yards and a touchdown (2000).

Year Team		RECEIVING			
	G	No.	Yds.	Avg.	TD
1997—Delaware State Hornets	7	20	380	19.0	4
1998—Delaware State Hornets	8	18	251	13.9	2
1999—Delaware State Hornets	11	9	299	33.2	2
2000—Delaware State Hornets	11	36	692	19.2	18
College totals (4 years)	37	83	1622	19.5	26

PERSONAL: Born December 11, 1978, in Naperville, Ill. ... 6-2/200.
HIGH SCHOOL: Naperville (Ill.) North.
COLLEGE: Northern Illinois.
TRANSACTIONS/CAREER NOTES: Selected by Tennessee Titans in fourth round (124th pick overall) of 2001 NFL draft.
COLLEGE NOTES: Rushed two times for 37 yards (1998); rushed four times for 52 yards (1999); rushed eight times for 73 yards (2000).

Year Team		RECEIVING				PUNT RETURNS				KICKOFF RETURNS				TOTALS	
	G	No.	Yds.	Avg.	TD	No.	Yds.	Avg.	TD	No.	Yds.	Avg.	TD	TD	Pts.
1997—Northern Illinois	11	27	431	16.0	4	0	0	0.0	0	6	103	17.2	0	4	24
1998—Northern Illinois	11	54	486	9.0	5	28	234	8.4	0	4	76	19.0	0	5	30
1999—Northern Illinois	11	57	906	15.9	10	2	13	6.5	0	1	15	15.0	0	10	60
2000—Northern Illinois	11	66	1168	17.7	10	19	362	19.1	1	18	411	22.8	0	11	66
College totals (4 years)	44	204	2991	14.7	29	49	609	12.4	1	29	605	20.9	0	30	180

PERSONAL: Born March 17, 1977, in Orlando, Fla. ... 5-10/187. ... Full name: Marlon Tarron McCree.
HIGH SCHOOL: Atlantic (Daytona, Fla.).
COLLEGE: Kentucky (degree in finance).
TRANSACTIONS/CAREER NOTES: Selected by Jacksonville Jaguars in seventh round (233rd pick overall) of 2001 NFL draft. ... Signed by Jaguars (June 4, 2001).
COLLEGE NOTES: Recovered one fumble (1998); recovered three fumbles (1999); recovered two fumbles (2000).

Year Team		INTERCEPTIONS				SACKS
	G	No.	Yds.	Avg.	TD	No.
1997—Kentucky	11	0	0	0.0	0	0.0
1998—Kentucky	11	0	0	0.0	0	7.0
1999—Kentucky	11	2	49	24.5	0	2.0
2000—Kentucky	11	0	0	0.0	0	5.5
College totals (4 years)	44	2	49	24.5	0	14.5

PERSONAL: Born May 24, 1979, in Willingboro, N.J. ... 6-6/327. ... Full name: Kareem Michael McKenzie.
HIGH SCHOOL: Willingboro (N.J.).
COLLEGE: Penn State.
TRANSACTIONS/CAREER NOTES: Selected by New York Jets in third round (79th pick overall) of 2001 NFL draft.
COLLEGE PLAYING EXPERIENCE: Penn State, 1997-2000. ... Games: 1997 (5), 1998 (10), 1999 (12), 2000 (11). Total: 38.

PERSONAL: Born February 8, 1979, in Wexford, Pa. ... 6-2/213. ... Full name: Michael Edward McMahon.
HIGH SCHOOL: North Allegheny (Pa.).
COLLEGE: Rutgers.
TRANSACTIONS/CAREER NOTES: Selected by Detroit Lions in fifth round (149th pick overall) of 2001 NFL draft.

Year Team		PASSING								RUSHING				TOTALS	
	G	Att.	Cmp.	Pct.	Yds.	TD	Int.	Avg.	Rat.	Att.	Yds.	Avg.	TD	TD	Pts.
1997—Rutgers	9	212	104	49.1	1259	6	12	5.94	97.0	49	17	0.3	2	2	12
1998—Rutgers	11	276	143	51.8	2203	12	16	7.98	121.6	62	-67	-1.1	2	2	12
1999—Rutgers	5	146	66	45.2	989	5	7	6.77	103.8	35	-8	-0.2	0	1	6
2000—Rutgers	10	340	169	49.7	2157	18	17	6.34	110.5	68	243	3.6	3	3	18
College totals (4 years)	35	974	482	49.5	6608	41	52	6.78	109.7	214	185	0.9	7	8	48

PERSONAL: Born June 7, 1978, in Pittsburgh, Kan. ... 6-4/250.
HIGH SCHOOL: Pittsburgh (Kan.).
COLLEGE: Kansas State.
TRANSACTIONS/CAREER NOTES: Selected by Tennessee Titans in third round (90th pick overall) of 2001 NFL draft.

Year Team		RECEIVING			
	G	No.	Yds.	Avg.	TD
1997—Kansas State	8	1	19	19.0	0
1998—Kansas State	11	0	0	0.0	0
1999—Kansas State	11	8	105	13.1	0
2000—Kansas State	11	9	103	11.4	1
College totals (4 years)	41	18	227	12.6	1

MERRILL, THAN   DB   BUCCANEERS

PERSONAL: Born December 12, 1977, in Fresno, Calif. ... 6-1/225.
HIGH SCHOOL: Fresno (Calif.).
COLLEGE: Stanford, then Yale.
TRANSACTIONS/CAREER NOTES: Selected by Tampa Bay Buccaneers in seventh round (223rd pick overall) of 2001 NFL draft.
COLLEGE NOTES: Returned six punts for 88 yards (1998).

			INTERCEPTIONS		
Year Team	G	No.	Yds.	Avg.	TD
1996—Stanford			Redshirted.		
1997—Stanford	11	2	34	17.0	0
1998—Yale	10	1	12	12.0	0
1999—Yale	10	4	2	0.5	0
2000—Yale	8	2	2	1.0	0
College totals (4 years)	39	9	50	5.6	0

MIDDLEBROOKS, WILLIE   CB   BRONCOS

PERSONAL: Born February 12, 1979, in Florida City, Fla. ... 6-1/200.
HIGH SCHOOL: Homestead (Fla.).
COLLEGE: Minnesota.
TRANSACTIONS/CAREER NOTES: Selected after junior season by Denver Broncos in first round (24th pick overall) of 2001 NFL draft.

			INTERCEPTIONS		
Year Team	G	No.	Yds.	Avg.	TD
1998—Minnesota	11	2	0	0.0	0
1999—Minnesota	11	1	26	26.0	1
2000—Minnesota	8	1	29	29.0	0
College totals (3 years)	30	4	55	13.8	1

MINNIS, MARVIN   WR   CHIEFS

PERSONAL: Born February 6, 1977, in Miami. ... 6-1/171.
HIGH SCHOOL: Nortwestern (Miami).
COLLEGE: Florida State.
TRANSACTIONS/CAREER NOTES: Selected by Kansas City Chiefs in third round (77th pick overall) of 2001 NFL draft. ... Signed by Chiefs (May 25, 2001).
HONORS: Named wide receiver on THE SPORTING NEWS college All-America first team (2000).

			RECEIVING		
Year Team	G	No.	Yds.	Avg.	TD
1997—Florida State	11	11	163	14.8	1
1998—Florida State	12	22	338	15.4	2
1999—Florida State	9	19	257	13.5	3
2000—Florida State	11	63	1340	21.3	11
College totals (4 years)	43	115	2098	18.2	17

MINOR, TRAVIS   RB   DOLPHINS

PERSONAL: Born June 30, 1979, in Gretna, La. ... 5-10/194.
HIGH SCHOOL: Catholic (Baton, La.).
COLLEGE: Florida State.
TRANSACTIONS/CAREER NOTES: Selected by Miami Dolphins in third round (85th pick overall) of 2001 NFL draft.
COLLEGE NOTES: Returned four kickoffs for 85 yards (2000).

		RUSHING				RECEIVING				TOTALS	
Year Team	G	Att.	Yds.	Avg.	TD	No.	Yds.	Avg.	TD	TD	Pts.
1997—Florida State	11	112	623	5.6	9	27	207	7.7	2	11	66
1998—Florida State	10	191	857	4.5	7	21	189	9.0	1	8	48
1999—Florida State	11	180	815	4.5	7	16	102	6.4	0	7	42
2000—Florida State	11	181	923	5.1	5	42	333	7.9	0	5	30
College totals (4 years)	43	664	3218	4.8	28	106	831	7.8	3	31	186

MISSOURI, DWAYNE   DE   RAVENS

PERSONAL: Born December 23, 1978, in San Antonio. ... 6-5/265. ... Full name: Dwayne Anthony Missouri.
HIGH SCHOOL: Roosevelt (San Antonio).
COLLEGE: Northwestern.
TRANSACTIONS/CAREER NOTES: Selected by Baltimore Ravens in seventh round (231st pick overall) of 2001 NFL draft.
COLLEGE NOTES: Recovered one fumble (1997).

Year Team	G	SACKS
1997—Northwestern	7	0.0
1998—Northwestern	12	3.0
1999—Northwestern	11	5.0
2000—Northwestern	11	9.0
College totals (4 years)	41	17.0

MITCHELL, FREDDIE   WR   EAGLES

PERSONAL: Born November 28, 1978, in Lakeland, Fla. ... 5-11/184. ... Full name: Freddie Lee Mitchell II.
HIGH SCHOOL: Kathleen (Lakeland, Fla.).
COLLEGE: UCLA.
TRANSACTIONS/CAREER NOTES: Selected after junior season by Philadelphia Eagles in first round (25th pick overall) of 2001 NFL draft.
HONORS: Named wide receiver on THE SPORTING NEWS college All-America first team (2000).
COLLEGE NOTES: Returned four kickoffs for 125 yards, returned three punts for 17 yards, rushed one time for 30 yards and attempted two passes with two completions for 95 yards and two touchdowns (1998); returned seven kickoffs for 122 yards, returned four punts for 28 yards, rushed five times for 37 yards and attempted two passes with one completion for 18 yards (1999); returned one punt for no yards, rushed two times for negative one yard and attempted two passes with two completions for 76 yards and two touchdowns (2000).

		RECEIVING			
Year Team	G	No.	Yds.	Avg.	TD
1998—UCLA	3	4	108	27.0	1
1999—UCLA	11	38	533	14.0	0
2000—UCLA	12	77	1494	19.4	9
College totals (3 years)	26	119	2135	17.9	10

MONDS, MARIO   DT   REDSKINS

PERSONAL: Born November 10, 1976, in Pierce, Fla. ... 6-4/331.
HIGH SCHOOL: Westwood (Fla.).
JUNIOR COLLEGE: Hutchinson (Kan.) Community College.
COLLEGE: Cincinnati.
TRANSACTIONS/CAREER NOTES: Selected by Washington Redskins in sixth round (186th pick overall) of 2001 NFL draft.

Year Team	G	SACKS
1997—Hutchinson CC	Statistics unavailable.	
1998—Hutchinson CC	Statistics unavailable.	
1999—Cincinnati	10	5.0
2000—Cincinnati	10	5.0
College totals (2 years)	20	10.0

MORENO, ZEKE   LB   CHARGERS

PERSONAL: Born October 10, 1978, in Chula Vista, Calif. ... 6-2/246. ... Full name: Ezekiel Moreno.
HIGH SCHOOL: Castle Park (Chula Vista, Calif.).
COLLEGE: Southern California.
TRANSACTIONS/CAREER NOTES: Selected by San Diego Chargers in fifth round (139th pick overall) of 2001 NFL draft.
COLLEGE NOTES: Recovered two fumbles (1999); recovered two fumbles (2000).

		INTERCEPTIONS				SACKS
Year Team	G	No.	Yds.	Avg.	TD	No.
1997—Southern California	10	1	19	19.0	0	1.0
1998—Southern California	13	1	6	6.0	0	1.0
1999—Southern California	12	3	76	25.3	0	4.0
2000—Southern California	12	0	0	0.0	0	3.0
College totals (4 years)	47	5	101	20.2	0	9.0

MORGAN, DAN   LB   PANTHERS

PERSONAL: Born December 19, 1978, in Coral Springs, Fla. ... 6-2/233. ... Full name: Daniel Thomas Morgan Jr.
HIGH SCHOOL: Taravella (Coral Springs, Fla.).
COLLEGE: Miami.
TRANSACTIONS/CAREER NOTES: Selected by Carolina Panthers in first round (11th pick overall) of 2001 NFL draft.
HONORS: Named linebacker on THE SPORTING NEWS college All-America first team (2000). ... Butkus Award winner (2000). ... Chuck Bednarik Award winner (2000).
COLLEGE NOTES: Returned one kickoff for 14 yards (1998).

		INTERCEPTIONS				SACKS
Year Team	G	No.	Yds.	Avg.	TD	No.
1997—Miami (Fla.)	11	0	0	0.0	0	3.0
1998—Miami (Fla.)	11	0	0	0.0	0	2.0
1999—Miami (Fla.)	12	0	0	0.0	0	5.0
2000—Miami (Fla.)	11	2	34	17.0	0	4.0
College totals (4 years)	45	2	34	17.0	0	14.0

MORGAN, QUINCY   WR   BROWNS

PERSONAL: Born September 23, 1977, in Garland, Texas. ... 6-1/209.
HIGH SCHOOL: South Garland (Texas).
COLLEGE: Kansas State.
TRANSACTIONS/CAREER NOTES: Selected by Cleveland Browns in second round (33rd pick overall) of 2001 NFL draft.
HONORS: Named wide receiver on THE SPORTING NEWS college All-America third team (2000).
COLLEGE NOTES: Rushed three times for 11 yards (2000).

		RECEIVING				KICKOFF RETURNS				TOTALS	
Year Team	G	No.	Yds.	Avg.	TD	No.	Yds.	Avg.	TD	TD	Pts.
1999—Kansas State	11	42	1007	24.0	9	3	44	14.7	0	9	54
2000—Kansas State	13	64	1166	18.2	14	7	160	22.9	0	14	84
College totals (2 years)	24	106	2173	20.5	23	10	204	20.4	0	23	138

MOSS, SANTANA　　　WR　　　JETS

PERSONAL: Born June 1, 1979, in Miami. ... 5-10/185. ... Full name: Santana Terrell Moss.
HIGH SCHOOL: Carol City (Miami).
COLLEGE: Miami.
TRANSACTIONS/CAREER NOTES: Selected by New York Jets in first round (16th pick overall) of 2001 NFL draft.
HONORS: Named kick returner on THE SPORTING NEWS college All-America first team (2000).
COLLEGE NOTES: Rushed one time for 39 yards and a touchdown (1997); rushed three times for 35 yards (1998); rushed two times for two yards (1999); and rushed six times for 201 yards and two touchdowns (2000).

		RECEIVING				PUNT RETURNS				KICKOFF RETURNS				TOTALS	
Year Team	G	No.	Yds.	Avg.	TD	No.	Yds.	Avg.	TD	No.	Yds.	Avg.	TD	TD	Pts.
1997—Miami (Fla.)	8	14	269	19.2	0	0	0	0.0	0	7	168	24.0	0	0	0
1998—Miami (Fla.)	10	30	631	21.0	8	8	74	9.3	0	3	73	24.3	0	8	48
1999—Miami (Fla.)	12	54	899	16.6	6	33	467	14.2	2	6	134	22.3	0	8	48
2000—Miami (Fla.)	11	45	748	16.6	5	36	655	18.2	4	0	0	0.0	0	9	54
College totals (4 years)	41	143	2547	17.8	19	77	1196	15.5	6	16	375	23.4	0	25	150

MYERS, LEONARD　　　CB　　　PATRIOTS

PERSONAL: Born December 18, 1978, in Fort Lauderdale, Fla. ... 6-0/201. ... Full name: Leonard Bernard Myers.
HIGH SCHOOL: Dillard (Fort Lauderdale, Fla.).
COLLEGE: Miami.
TRANSACTIONS/CAREER NOTES: Selected by New England Patriots in sixth round (200th pick overall) of 2001 NFL draft.
COLLEGE NOTES: Recovered one fumble and returned three kickoffs for 81 yards (1997); returned one kickoff for 32 yards (1999).

		INTERCEPTIONS				PUNT RETURNS				TOTALS	
Year Team	G	No.	Yds.	Avg.	TD	No.	Yds.	Avg.	TD	TD	Pts.
1997—Miami (Fla.)	11	2	64	32.0	0	1	11	11.0	0	0	0
1998—Miami (Fla.)	10	2	0	0.0	0	9	73	8.1	0	0	0
1999—Miami (Fla.)	12	3	62	20.7	1	0	0	0.0	0	1	6
2000—Miami (Fla.)	9	2	34	17.0	0	0	0	0.0	0	0	0
College totals (4 years)	42	9	160	17.8	1	10	84	8.4	0	1	6

NEWCOMBE, BOBBY　　　WR　　　CARDINALS

PERSONAL: Born August 8, 1979, in Sierra Leone, Africa. ... 5-11/189. ... Full name: Robert Wundu Sowa Newcombe.
HIGH SCHOOL: Highland (Albuquerque, N.M.).
COLLEGE: Nebraska.
TRANSACTIONS/CAREER NOTES: Selected by Arizona Cardinals in sixth round (166th pick overall) of 2001 NFL draft. ... Signed by Cardinals (May 30, 2001).
COLLEGE NOTES: Returned 12 punts for 244 yards and one touchdown and returned one kickoff for 16 yards (1997); returned 16 punts for 294 yards and one touchdown and returned one kickoff for 18 yards (1999); returned 20 punts for 291 yards and one touchdown and returned one kickoff for 20 yards (2000).

		PASSING					RUSHING				RECEIVING				TOTALS	
Year Team	G	Att.	Cmp.	Pct.	Yds.	TD	Int.	Avg.	Att.	Yds.	Avg.	TD	No.	Yds.	Avg.	TD	TD	Pts.
1997—Nebraska	12	1	1	100.0	15	0	0	15.00	16	156	9.8	1	7	173	24.7	1	2	12
1998—Nebraska	6	79	50	63.3	712	1	1	9.01	83	228	2.7	8	0	0	0.0	0	8	48
1999—Nebraska	12	19	11	57.9	246	2	1	12.95	37	87	2.4	3	19	238	12.5	3	6	36
2000—Nebraska	11	0	0	0.0	0	0	0	0.0	9	18	2.0	0	19	249	13.1	0	0	0
College totals (4 years)	41	99	62	62.6	973	3	2	9.83	145	489	3.4	12	45	660	14.7	4	16	96

NIX, JOHN　　　DT　　　COWBOYS

PERSONAL: Born November 24, 1976, in Lucendale, Miss. ... 6-2/278.
HIGH SCHOOL: George County (Miss.).
COLLEGE: Southern Mississippi.
TRANSACTIONS/CAREER NOTES: Selected by Dallas Cowboys in seventh round (240th pick overall) of 2001 NFL draft.

Year Team	G	SACKS
1997—Southern Mississippi	11	1.5
1998—Southern Mississippi	0	1.5
1999—Southern Mississippi	10	2.0
2000—Southern Mississippi	11	4.0
College totals (4 years)	32	9.0

NKWENTI, MATHIAS　　　OT　　　STEELERS

PERSONAL: Born May 11, 1978, in Younda, Cameroon, Africa. ... 6-3/300.
HIGH SCHOOL: Thomas S. Wootton (Rockville, Md.).
COLLEGE: Temple.
TRANSACTIONS/CAREER NOTES: Selected by Pittsburgh Steelers in fourth round (111th pick overall) of 2001 NFL draft. ... Signed by Steelers (May 19, 2001).
COLLEGE NOTES: Credited with one sack (1997); credited with three sacks (1998).
COLLEGE PLAYING EXPERIENCE: Temple, 1996-2000. ... Games: 1996 (redshirted), 1997 (10), 1998 (10), 1999 (4), 2000 (11). Total: 35. ... Played defensive tackle (1997-1999). ... Played defensive tackle and offensive tackle (2000).

NORRIS, TORRANCE RB SAINTS

PERSONAL: Born June 16, 1978, in Houston. ... 6-1/244. ... Full name: Torrance Moran Norris.
HIGH SCHOOL: James Madison (Houston).
COLLEGE: Kansas.
TRANSACTIONS/CAREER NOTES: Selected by New Orleans Saints in fourth round (115th pick overall) of 2001 NFL draft.

			RUSHING				RECEIVING				TOTALS	
Year Team	G	Att.	Yds.	Avg.	TD	No.	Yds.	Avg.	TD	TD	Pts.
1996—Kansas						Redshirted.					
1997—Kansas	3	0	0	0.0	0	0	0	0.0	0	0	0
1998—Kansas	11	5	14	2.8	0	4	-3	-0.8	0	0	0
1999—Kansas	12	107	537	5.0	8	10	64	6.4	1	9	54
2000—Kansas	7	87	313	3.6	2	3	26	8.7	0	2	12
College totals (4 years)	33	199	864	4.3	10	17	87	5.1	1	11	66

OFAHENGAUE, TEVITA TE CARDINALS

PERSONAL: Born July 9, 1975, in Tonga, Hawaii. ... 6-2/250.
HIGH SCHOOL: Kahuku (Hawaii).
COLLEGE: Brigham Young.
TRANSACTIONS/CAREER NOTES: Selected by Arizona Cardinals in seventh round (246th pick overall) of 2001 NFL draft. ... Signed by Cardinals (May 30, 2001).

		RECEIVING			
Year Team	G	No.	Yds.	Avg.	TD
1997—Brigham Young			Redshirted.		
1998—Brigham Young	12	19	264	13.9	2
1999—Brigham Young	11	21	284	13.5	2
2000—Brigham Young	12	22	305	13.9	0
College totals (3 years)	35	62	853	13.8	4

OJO, ONOME WR SAINTS

PERSONAL: Born June 3, 1977, in Vallejo, Calif. ... 6-6/265.
HIGH SCHOOL: Urban (Calif.).
COLLEGE: UC-Davis.
TRANSACTIONS/CAREER NOTES: Selected by New Orleans Saints in fifth round (153rd pick overall) of 2001 NFL draft.

			RUSHING				RECEIVING				TOTALS	
Year Team	G	Att.	Yds.	Avg.	TD	No.	Yds.	Avg.	TD	TD	Pts.
1997—California-Davis						Statistics unavailable.					
1998—California-Davis						Statistics unavailable.					
1999—California-Davis						Statistics unavailable.					
2000—California-Davis	13	1	-5	-5.0	0	33	865	26.2	11	11	66

OKOBI, CHUKKY C STEELERS

PERSONAL: Born October 18, 1978, in Hamden, Conn. ... 6-2/310. ... Full name: Chukwunweze Sonume Okobi.
HIGH SCHOOL: Trinity Prawling (N.Y.).
COLLEGE: Purdue.
TRANSACTIONS/CAREER NOTES: Selected by Pittsburgh Steelers in fifth round (146th pick overall) of 2001 NFL draft. ... Signed by Steelers (May 17, 2001).
COLLEGE PLAYING EXPERIENCE: Purdue, 1996-2000. ... Games: 1996 (redshirted), 1997 (12), 1998 (13), 1999 (6), 2000 (12). Total: 43.

O'LEARY, DAN TE BILLS

PERSONAL: Born September 1, 1977, in Cleveland. ... 6-3/260. ... Full name: Daniel Edward O'Leary.
HIGH SCHOOL: St. Ignatius (Ohio).
COLLEGE: Notre Dame.
TRANSACTIONS/CAREER NOTES: Selected by Buffalo Bills in sixth round (195th pick overall) of 2001 NFL draft.

		RECEIVING			
Year Team	G	No.	Yds.	Avg.	TD
1997—Notre Dame	6	6	81	13.5	0
1998—Notre Dame	11	3	32	10.7	1
1999—Notre Dame	12	13	183	14.1	2
2000—Notre Dame	11	10	87	8.7	1
College totals (4 years)	40	32	383	12.0	4

PALMER, JESSE QB GIANTS

PERSONAL: Born October 5, 1979, in Toronto. ... 6-2/219. ... Full name: Jesse James Palmer.
HIGH SCHOOL: St. Pius X (Ottawa).
COLLEGE: Florida.
TRANSACTIONS/CAREER NOTES: Selected by New York Giants in fourth round (125th pick overall) of 2001 NFL draft.

Year Team	G	PASSING								RUSHING				TOTALS	
		Att.	Cmp.	Pct.	Yds.	TD	Int.	Avg.	Rat.	Att.	Yds.	Avg.	TD	TD	Pts.
1997—Florida	6	38	21	55.3	291	4	3	7.66	138.5	2	4	2.0	0	0	0
1998—Florida	6	123	73	59.3	1246	14	5	10.13	173.9	17	-57	-3.4	0	0	0
1999—Florida	5	95	44	46.3	565	2	5	5.95	92.7	12	-20	-1.7	0	0	0
2000—Florida	10	223	116	52.0	1653	11	4	7.41	127.0	36	-51	-1.4	6	6	36
College totals (4 years)	27	479	254	53.0	3755	31	17	7.84	133.1	67	-124	-1.9	6	6	36

PEKO, TUPE   C   JETS

PERSONAL: Born August 19, 1978, in Whittier, Calif. ... 6-4/300. ... Full name: Siitupe Peko.
HIGH SCHOOL: La Serna (Calif.).
JUNIOR COLLEGE: Cerritos College (Calif.).
COLLEGE: Michigan State.
TRANSACTIONS/CAREER NOTES: Selected by New York Jets in seventh round (217th pick overall) in 2001 NFL draft.
COLLEGE NOTES: Caught six passes for 106 yards and one touchdown (1997). ... Played tight end (1997).
COLLEGE PLAYING EXPERIENCE: Cerritos College, 1997 and 1998; Michigan State, 1999 and 2000. ... Games: 1997 (10), 1998 (11), 1999 (11), 2000 (10). Total Junior College: 21. Total NCAA: 21

PERRYMAN, RAYMOND   DB   RAIDERS

PERSONAL: Born November 27, 1978, in Phoenix. ... 6-0/200.
HIGH SCHOOL: South Mountain (Phoenix).
COLLEGE: Northern Arizona.
TRANSACTIONS/CAREER NOTES: Selected by Oakland Raiders in fifth round (158th pick overall) of 2001 NFL draft.

Year Team	G	INTERCEPTIONS				SACKS
		No.	Yds.	Avg.	TD	No.
1997—Northern Arizona	11	0	0	0.0	0	0.0
1998—Northern Arizona	11	1	26	26.0	0	2.5
1999—Northern Arizona	11	0	0	0.0	0	4.5
2000—Northern Arizona	11	1	0	0.0	0	1.0
College totals (4 years)	44	2	26	13.0	0	8.0

PETERSON, WILL   CB   GIANTS

PERSONAL: Born June 15, 1979, in Uniontown, Pa. ... 6-0/197. ... Full name: William James Peterson Jr.
HIGH SCHOOL: Laurel Highlands (Pa.).
COLLEGE: Michigan, then Western Illinois.
TRANSACTIONS/CAREER NOTES: Selected by New Yorks Giants in third round (78th pick overall) of 2001 NFL draft.

Year Team	G	INTERCEPTIONS				SACKS
		No.	Yds.	Avg.	TD	No.
1997—Michigan	12	0	0	0.0	0	0.0
1998—Michigan	9	4	76	19.0	1	0.0
1999—Western Illinois				Redshirted.		
2000—Western Illinois	10	5	161	32.2	1	2.0
College totals (3 years)	31	9	237	26.3	2	2.0

PHARMS, JEREMIAH   LB   BROWNS

PERSONAL: Born June 24, 1978, in Sacramento. ... 6-0/251.
HIGH SCHOOL: Valley (Sacramento).
COLLEGE: Washington.
TRANSACTIONS/CAREER NOTES: Selected by Cleveland Browns in fifth round (134th pick overall) of 2001 NFL draft.
COLLEGE NOTES: Recovered three fumbles (1999); recovered one fumble (2000).

Year Team	G	SACKS
1996—Washington		Redshirted.
1997—Washington	11	3.0
1998—Washington	11	8.0
1999—Washington	11	2.0
2000—Washington	0	5.5
College totals (4 years)	33	18.5

PICKETT, RYAN   DT   RAMS

PERSONAL: Born October 8, 1979, in Zephyrhills, Fla. ... 6-2/310.
HIGH SCHOOL: Zephyrhills (Fla.).
COLLEGE: Ohio State.
TRANSACTIONS/CAREER NOTES: Selected after junior season by St. Louis Rams in first round (29th pick overall) of 2001 NFL draft.

Year Team	G	SACKS
1998—Ohio State	13	2.0
1999—Ohio State	12	3.0
2000—Ohio State	12	3.0
College totals (3 years)	37	8.0

POCHMAN, OWEN   K   PATRIOTS

PERSONAL: Born August 2, 1977, in Renton, Wash. ... 5-11/179.
HIGH SCHOOL: Mercer Island (Wash.).
COLLEGE: Brigham Young.
TRANSACTIONS/CAREER NOTES: Selected by New England Patriots in seventh round (216th pick overall) of 2001 NFL draft.

			KICKING					
Year Team	G	XPM	XPA	FGM	FGA	Lg.	50+	Pts.
1997—Brigham Young	...	29	30	9	15	47	0-0	56
1998—Brigham Young	...	41	42	20	27	47	0-0	101
1999—Brigham Young	...	36	38	18	25	47	0-0	90
2000—Brigham Young	...	29	29	19	24	56	0-0	86
College totals (4 years)	...	135	139	66	91	56	0-0	333

POLK, CARLOS   LB   CHARGERS

PERSONAL: Born February 22, 1977, in Rockford, Ill. ... 6-2/250.
HIGH SCHOOL: Guilford (Rockford, Ill.).
COLLEGE: Nebraska (degree in sociology).
TRANSACTIONS/CAREER NOTES: Selected by San Diego Chargers in fourth round (112th pick overall) of 2001 NFL draft.
HONORS: Named linebacker on THE SPORTING NEWS college All-America third team (2000).
COLLEGE NOTES: Recovered one fumble (1998).

		INTERCEPTIONS				SACKS
Year Team	G	No.	Yds.	Avg.	TD	No.
1997—Nebraska	12	0	0	0.0	0	1.0
1998—Nebraska	12	1	16	16.0	0	1.0
1999—Nebraska	12	0	0	0.0	0	6.5
2000—Nebraska	11	1	39	39.0	1	1.0
College totals (4 years)	47	2	55	27.5	1	9.5

POLLEY, TOMMY   LB   RAMS

PERSONAL: Born January 11, 1978, in Baltimore. ... 6-3/240.
HIGH SCHOOL: Dunbar (Baltimore).
COLLEGE: Florida State.
TRANSACTIONS/CAREER NOTES: Selected by St. Louis Rams in second round (42nd pick overall) of 2001 NFL draft.
HONORS: Named linebacker on THE SPORTING NEWS college All-America third team (2000).
COLLEGE NOTES: Recovered one fumble (1998); recovered two fumbles (1999); recovered three fumbles (2000).

		INTERCEPTIONS				SACKS
Year Team	G	No.	Yds.	Avg.	TD	No.
1997—Florida State	11	0	0	0.0	0	1.0
1998—Florida State	10	1	3	3.0	0	1.0
1999—Florida State	11	0	0	0.0	0	3.0
2000—Florida State	12	1	4	4.0	1	2.0
College totals (4 years)	44	2	7	3.5	1	7.0

RABACH, CASEY   C   RAVENS

PERSONAL: Born September 24, 1977, in Sturgeon Bay, Wis. ... 6-4/301.
HIGH SCHOOL: Sturgeon Bay (Wis.).
COLLEGE: Wisconsin.
TRANSACTIONS/CAREER NOTES: Selected by Baltimore Ravens in third round (92nd pick overall) of 2001 NFL draft.
COLLEGE PLAYING EXPERIENCE: Wisconsin, 1997-2000. ... Games: 1997 (12), 1998 (11), 1999 (12), 2000 (13). Total: 48.

RAIOLA, DOMINIC   C   LIONS

PERSONAL: Born December 30, 1978, in Honolulu, Hawaii. ... 6-1/303.
HIGH SCHOOL: St. Louis (Honolulu, Hawaii).
COLLEGE: Nebraska (degree in communication studies).
TRANSACTIONS/CAREER NOTES: Selected by Detroit Lions in second round (50th pick overall) of 2001 NFL draft.
HONORS: Named center on THE SPORTING NEWS college All-America second team (2000).
COLLEGE PLAYING EXPERIENCE: Nebraska, 1997-2000. ... Games: 1997 (redshirted), 1998 (12), 1999 (12), 2000 (11). Total: 35.

RAMBO, KEN-YON   WR   RAIDERS

PERSONAL: Born October 4, 1978, in Cerritos, Calif. ... 6-0/191.
HIGH SCHOOL: Polytechnic (Long Beach, Calif.).
COLLEGE: Ohio State.
TRANSACTIONS/CAREER NOTES: Selected by Oakland Raiders in seventh round (229th pick overall) of 2001 NFL draft.

		RUSHING				RECEIVING				PUNT RETURNS				KICKOFF RETURNS				TOTALS	
Year Team	G	Att.	Yds.	Avg.	TD	No.	Yds.	Avg.	TD	No.	Yds.	Avg.	TD	No.	Yds.	Avg.	TD	TD	Pts.
1997—Ohio State	13	2	2	1.0	0	7	145	20.7	1	0	0	0.0	0	4	100	25.0	0	1	6
1998—Ohio State	10	0	0	0.0	0	5	77	15.4	0	19	128	6.7	0	12	237	19.8	0	0	0
1999—Ohio State	12	5	34	6.8	0	41	833	20.3	6	3	20	6.7	0	31	653	21.1	0	6	36
2000—Ohio State	12	6	19	3.2	0	53	794	15.0	2	1	-3	-3.0	0	17	478	28.1	0	2	12
College totals (4 years)	47	13	55	4.2	0	106	1849	17.4	9	23	145	6.3	0	64	1468	22.9	0	9	54

REED, JAMES — DT — JETS

PERSONAL: Born February 3, 1977, in Saginaw, Mich. ... 6-0/285. ... Full name: James Reed Jr.
HIGH SCHOOL: Saginaw (Mich.).
COLLEGE: Iowa State.
TRANSACTIONS/CAREER NOTES: Selected by New York Jets in seventh round (206th pick overall) of 2001 NFL draft.

Year Team	G	SACKS
1996—Iowa State	Redshirted.	
1997—Iowa State	11	6.0
1998—Iowa State	11	4.0
1999—Iowa State	11	1.0
2000—Iowa State	11	3.0
College totals (4 years)	44	14.0

REYNOLDS, JAMAL — DE — PACKERS

PERSONAL: Born February 20, 1979, in Aiken, S.C. ... 6-3/266.
HIGH SCHOOL: Aiken (S.C.).
COLLEGE: Florida State.
TRANSACTIONS/CAREER NOTES: Selected by Green Bay Packers in first round (10th pick overall) of 2001 NFL draft.
HONORS: Named defensive end on THE SPORTING NEWS college All-America first team (2000). ... Lombardi Trophy winner (2000).

Year Team	G	SACKS
1997—Florida State	8	0.0
1998—Florida State	11	4.5
1999—Florida State	12	7.0
2000—Florida State	0	12.0
College totals (4 years)	31	23.5

RILEY, KARON — DE — BEARS

PERSONAL: Born June 18, 1980, in Detroit. ... 6-2/251.
HIGH SCHOOL: Martin Luther King (Detroit).
COLLEGE: Southern Methodist, then Minnesota.
TRANSACTIONS/CAREER NOTES: Selected by Chicago Bears in fourth round (103rd pick overall) of 2001 NFL draft.
HONORS: Named defensive end on THE SPORTING NEWS college All-America third team (2000).
COLLEGE NOTES: Recovered one fumble (1998); recovered one fumble and intercepted one pass (2000).

Year Team	G	SACKS
1996—SMU	5	0.0
1997—SMU	9	3.0
1998—Minnesota	Redshirted.	
1999—Minnesota	12	16.0
2000—Minnesota	12	13.0
College totals (4 years)	38	32.0

ROBERG, MIKE — TE — PANTHERS

PERSONAL: Born September 18, 1977, in Kent, Wash. ... 6-4/263.
HIGH SCHOOL: University (Spokane, Wash.).
COLLEGE: Idaho.
TRANSACTIONS/CAREER NOTES: Selected by Carolina Panthers in seventh round (227th pick overall) of 2001 NFL draft.
COLLEGE NOTES: Played defensive tackle (1997). ... Credited with $1/2$ sack and recovered one fumble (1997).

Year Team	G	RECEIVING			
		No.	Yds.	Avg.	TD
1997—Idaho	11	0	0	0.0	0
1998—Idaho	11	13	157	12.1	2
1999—Idaho	9	17	165	9.7	4
2000—Idaho	11	34	400	11.8	4
College totals (4 years)	42	64	722	11.3	10

ROBERTSON, BERNARD — C — BEARS

PERSONAL: Born June 9, 1979, in New Orleans. ... 6-3/297. ... Full name: Bernard Robertson Jr.
HIGH SCHOOL: Karr (New Orleans).
COLLEGE: Tulane.
TRANSACTIONS/CAREER NOTES: Selected by Chicago Bears in fifth round (138th pick overall) of 2001 NFL draft.
COLLEGE PLAYING EXPERIENCE: Tulane, 1997-2000. ... Games: 1997 (11), 1998 (11), 1999 (10), 2000 (11). Total: 43.

ROBERTSON, TYRONE — DT — BILLS

PERSONAL: Born August 15, 1979, in Danville, Va. ... 6-4/287.
HIGH SCHOOL: George Washington (Va.).
JUNIOR COLLEGE: Hinds Community College (Miss.).
COLLEGE: Georgia.
TRANSACTIONS/CAREER NOTES: Selected by Buffalo Bills in seventh round (238th pick overall) of 2001 NFL draft.

Year Team	G	SACKS
1998—Georgia		Redshirted.
1999—Georgia	12	9.5
2000—Hinds CC	10	9.5
College totals (1 year)	12	9.5
Junior college totals (1 year)	10	9.5

ROBINSON, KOREN — WR — SEAHAWKS

PERSONAL: Born March 19, 1980, in Belmont, N.C. ... 6-1/211.
HIGH SCHOOL: South Point (N.C.).
COLLEGE: North Carolina State.
TRANSACTIONS/CAREER NOTES: Selected after sophomore season by Seattle Seahawks in first round (ninth pick overall) of 2001 NFL draft.

Year Team	G	RUSHING				RECEIVING				PUNT RETURNS				KICKOFF RETURNS				TOTALS	
		Att.	Yds.	Avg.	TD	No.	Yds.	Avg.	TD	No.	Yds.	Avg.	TD	No.	Yds.	Avg.	TD	TD	Pts.
1999—North Carolina State	11	13	15	1.2	0	48	853	17.8	2	14	94	6.7	1	4	54	13.5	0	3	18
2000—North Carolina State	11	15	95	6.3	0	62	1061	17.1	13	14	218	15.6	1	20	506	25.3	0	14	84
College totals (2 years)	22	28	110	3.9	0	110	1914	17.4	15	28	312	11.1	2	24	560	23.3	0	17	102

ROGERS, SHAUN — DT — LIONS

PERSONAL: Born March 12, 1979, in Houston. ... 6-4/331.
HIGH SCHOOL: LaPorte (Texas).
COLLEGE: Texas.
TRANSACTIONS/CAREER NOTES: Selected by Detroit Lions in second round (61st pick overall) of 2001 NFL draft.

Year Team	G	SACKS
1997—Texas	8	2.0
1998—Texas	11	3.0
1999—Texas	13	5.5
2000—Texas	9	3.5
College totals (4 years)	41	14.0

ROSENFELS, SAGE — QB — REDSKINS

PERSONAL: Born March 6, 1978, in Maquoketa, Iowa. ... 6-4/221.
HIGH SCHOOL: Maquoketa (Iowa).
COLLEGE: Iowa State.
TRANSACTIONS/CAREER NOTES: Selected by Washington Redskins in fourth round (109th pick overall) of 2001 NFL draft.

Year Team	G	PASSING								RUSHING				TOTALS	
		Att.	Cmp.	Pct.	Yds.	TD	Int.	Avg.	Rat.	Att.	Yds.	Avg.	TD	TD	Pts.
1996—Iowa State							Redshirted.								
1997—Iowa State	4	10	4	40.0	37	0	2	3.70	31.1	2	20	10.0	0	0	0
1998—Iowa State	3	9	3	33.3	48	0	1	5.33	55.9	4	34	8.5	0	0	0
1999—Iowa State	11	235	127	54.0	1781	10	11	7.58	122.4	80	225	2.8	4	4	24
2000—Iowa State	11	333	172	51.7	2298	12	12	6.90	114.3	78	381	4.9	10	10	60
College totals (4 years)	29	587	306	52.1	4164	22	26	7.09	115.2	164	660	4.0	14	14	84

SANDS, TERDELL — DT — CHIEFS

PERSONAL: Born October 31, 1979, in Chattanooga, Tenn. ... 6-6/280. ... Full name: Terdell Duane Sands.
HIGH SCHOOL: Howard (Chattanooga, Tenn.).
COLLEGE: Tennessee, then Tennessee-Chattanooga.
TRANSACTIONS/CAREER NOTES: Selected by Kansas City Chiefs in seventh round (243rd pick overall) of 2001 NFL draft.

Year Team	G	SACKS
1997—Tennessee		Statistics unavailable.
1998—Tennessee		Statistics unavailable.
1999—Tennessee-Chattanooga	11	0.0
2000—Tennessee-Chattanooga		Did not play.
College totals (1 years)	11	0.0

SCHOBEL, AARON — DE — BILLS

PERSONAL: Born April 1, 1977, in Columbus, Texas. ... 6-3/261.
HIGH SCHOOL: Columbus (Texas).
COLLEGE: Texas Christian.
TRANSACTIONS/CAREER NOTES: Selected by Buffalo Bills in second round (46th pick overall) of 2001 NFL draft.
HONORS: Named defensive end on THE SPORTING NEWS college All-America second team (2000).

Year Team	G	SACKS
1997—Texas Christian	11	7.0
1998—Texas Christian	11	7.5
1999—Texas Christian	11	10.0
2000—Texas Christian	11	6.5
College totals (4 years)	44	31.0

SCOTT, CAREY — CB — VIKINGS

PERSONAL: Born August 11, 1978, in Savannah, Ga. ... 6-0/180.
HIGH SCHOOL: Beach (Ga.).
COLLEGE: Kentucky State.
TRANSACTIONS/CAREER NOTES: Selected by Minnesota Vikings in sixth round (189th pick overall) of 2001 NFL draft.
COLLEGE NOTES: Returned two kickoffs for 34 yards (1998).

			INTERCEPTIONS			
Year Team	G	No.	Yds.	Avg.	TD	
1996—Kentucky State			Redshirted.			
1997—Kentucky State	11	2	...	...	...	
1998—Kentucky State	10	4	...	...	...	
1999—Kentucky State	8	3	...	...	...	
2000—Kentucky State	9	0	...	...	...	
College totals (4 years)	38	9	...	...	...	

SCOTT, CEDRIC — DE — GIANTS

PERSONAL: Born October 19, 1977, in Gulfport, Miss. ... 6-5/274.
HIGH SCHOOL: Gulfport (Miss.).
COLLEGE: Southern Mississippi (degree in exercise physiology).
TRANSACTIONS/CAREER NOTES: Selected by New York Giants in fourth round (114th pick overall) of 2001 NFL draft.
COLLEGE NOTES: Recovered two fumbles (1999); recovered two fumbles (2000).

Year Team	G	SACKS
1997—Southern Mississippi	11	1.0
1998—Southern Mississippi	11	9.5
1999—Southern Mississippi	11	4.0
2000—Southern Mississippi	11	12.0
College totals (4 years)	44	26.5

SEYMOUR, RICHARD — DT — PATRIOTS

PERSONAL: Born October 6, 1979, in Gadsden, S.C. ... 6-6/300.
HIGH SCHOOL: Lower Richland (S.C.).
COLLEGE: Georgia.
TRANSACTIONS/CAREER NOTES: Selected by New England Patriots in first round (sixth pick overall) of 2001 NFL draft.
HONORS: Named defensive tackle on THE SPORTING NEWS college All-America second team (2000).
COLLEGE NOTES: Recovered one fumble (1998).

		INTERCEPTIONS				SACKS
Year Team	G	No.	Yds.	Avg.	TD	No.
1997—Georgia	9	0	0	0.0	0	0.0
1998—Georgia	11	0	0	0.0	0	4.0
1999—Georgia	11	1	1	1.0	0	4.0
2000—Georgia	10	0	0	0.0	0	1.5
College totals (4 years)	41	1	1	1.0	0	9.5

SILVERS, ELLIOT — OT — CHARGERS

PERSONAL: Born February 19, 1978, in Agoura, Calif. ... 6-7/321.
HIGH SCHOOL: Agoura (Calif.).
COLLEGE: Washington.
TRANSACTIONS/CAREER NOTES: Selected by San Diego Chargers in fifth round (132nd pick overall) of 2001 NFL draft.
COLLEGE PLAYING EXPERIENCE: Washington, 1996-2000. ... Games: 1996 (redshirted), 1997 (4), 1998 (11), 1999 (11), 2000 (11). Total: 37.

SMITH, DWIGHT — CB — BUCCANEERS

PERSONAL: Born August 13, 1978, in Atlanta. ... 5-10/201.
HIGH SCHOOL: Central (Detroit).
COLLEGE: Akron.
TRANSACTIONS/CAREER NOTES: Selected by Tampa Bay Buccaneers in third round (84th pick overall) of 2001 NFL draft.
HONORS: Named cornerback on THE SPORTING NEWS college All-America third team (2000).
COLLEGE NOTES: Credited with $1/2$ sack, recovered one fumble and rushed three times for seven yards (1999); caught three passes for 94 yards and recovered three fumbles (2000).

		INTERCEPTIONS				PUNT RETURNS				KICKOFF RETURNS				TOTALS	
Year Team	G	No.	Yds.	Avg.	TD	No.	Yds.	Avg.	TD	No.	Yds.	Avg.	TD	TD	Pts.
1997—Akron	5	1	0	0.0	0	4	38	9.5	0	8	147	18.4	0	0	0
1998—Akron	11	2	0	0.0	0	5	35	7.0	0	17	381	22.4	0	0	0
1999—Akron	11	2	53	26.5	1	5	22	4.4	0	11	261	23.7	0	1	6
2000—Akron	11	10	208	20.8	2	2	5	2.5	0	2	37	18.5	0	2	12
College totals (4 years)	38	15	261	17.4	3	16	100	6.3	0	38	826	21.7	0	3	18

SMITH, JUSTIN   DE   BENGALS

PERSONAL: Born September 30, 1979, in Jefferson City, Mo. ... 6-4/270.
HIGH SCHOOL: Jefferson City (Mo.).
COLLEGE: Missouri.
TRANSACTIONS/CAREER NOTES: Selected after junior season by Cincinnati Bengals in first round (fourth pick overall) of 2001 NFL draft.
HONORS: Named defensive end on THE SPORTING NEWS college All-America third team (2000).
COLLEGE NOTES: Recovered one fumble (1998). ... Recovered two fumbles (1999). ... Recovered two fumbles (2000).

Year Team	G	SACKS
1998—Missouri	11	3.5
1999—Missouri	11	8.0
2000—Missouri	11	11.0
College totals (3 years)	33	22.5

SMITH, KENNY   DT   SAINTS

PERSONAL: Born September 8, 1977, in Meridian, Miss. ... 6-3/289.
HIGH SCHOOL: Meridian (Miss.).
COLLEGE: Alabama.
TRANSACTIONS/CAREER NOTES: Selected by New Orleans Saints in third round (81st pick overall) of 2001 NFL draft.
COLLEGE NOTES: Recovered one fumble (2000).

Year Team	G	SACKS
1997—Alabama	11	2.0
1998—Alabama	11	2.0
1999—Alabama	9	3.0
2000—Alabama	11	3.5
College totals (4 years)	42	10.5

SMITH, STEVE   WR   PANTHERS

PERSONAL: Born May 12, 1979, in Lynwood, Calif. ... 5-9/179. ... Full name: Stevonne Smith.
HIGH SCHOOL: University (Los Angeles).
JUNIOR COLLEGE: Santa Monica Junior College.
COLLEGE: Utah.
TRANSACTIONS/CAREER NOTES: Selected by Carolina Panthers in third round (74th pick overall) of 2001 NFL draft.
COLLEGE NOTES: Rushed three times for 21 yards (1999); rushed five times for 31 yards (2000).

Year Team	G	RECEIVING No.	Yds.	Avg.	TD	PUNT RETURNS No.	Yds.	Avg.	TD	KICKOFF RETURNS No.	Yds.	Avg.	TD	TOTALS TD	Pts.
1997—Santa Monica JC									Statistics unavailable.						
1998—Santa Monica JC									Statistics unavailable.						
1999—Utah	11	43	860	20.0	8	29	495	17.1	3	6	169	28.2	0	11	66
2000—Utah	10	35	743	21.2	4	43	365	8.5	1	17	336	19.8	0	5	30
College totals (2 years)	21	78	1603	20.6	12	72	860	11.9	4	23	505	22.0	0	16	96

SMOOT, FRED   CB   REDSKINS

PERSONAL: Born April 17, 1979, in Jackson, Miss. ... 5-11/179. ... Full name: Fredrick D. Smoot.
HIGH SCHOOL: Provine (Jackson, Miss.).
JUNIOR COLLEGE: Hinds Community College (Miss.).
COLLEGE: Mississippi State.
TRANSACTIONS/CAREER NOTES: Selected by Washington Redskins in second round (45th pick overall) of 2001 NFL draft.
HONORS: Named cornerback on THE SPORTING NEWS college All-America first team (2000).
COLLEGE NOTES: Credited with one sack (1998).

Year Team	G	INTERCEPTIONS No.	Yds.	Avg.	TD
1997—Hinds CC	11	6	86	14.3	1
1998—Hinds CC	10	7	43	6.1	0
1999—Mississippi State	11	5	13	2.6	0
2000—Mississippi State	11	5	31	6.2	0
Junior college totals (2 years)	21	13	129	9.9	1
College totals (2 years)	22	10	44	4.4	0

SPOON, BRANDON   LB   BILLS

PERSONAL: Born July 5, 1978, in Burlington, N.C. ... 6-2/244. ... Full name: Thomas Brandon Spoon.
HIGH SCHOOL: Williams (Burlington, N.C.).
COLLEGE: North Carolina.
TRANSACTIONS/CAREER NOTES: Selected by Buffalo Bills in fourth round (110th pick overall) of 2001 NFL draft.
COLLEGE NOTES: Recovered one fumble (1996); recovered one fumble (1998).

Year Team	G	SACKS
1996—North Carolina	11	0.0
1997—North Carolina	11	3.5
1998—North Carolina	11	5.0
1999—North Carolina	2	0.0
2000—North Carolina	11	1.0
College totals (5 years)	46	9.5

ST. PAUL, FRANCIS   WR   RAMS

PERSONAL: Born March 25, 1979, in Los Angeles. ... 5-9/175.
HIGH SCHOOL: Murphy (Calif.).
COLLEGE: Northern Arizona.
TRANSACTIONS/CAREER NOTES: Selected by St. Louis Rams in sixth round (197th pick overall) of 2001 NFL draft. ... Signed by Rams (June 2, 2001).

		RECEIVING				PUNT RETURNS				KICKOFF RETURNS				TOTALS	
Year Team	G	No.	Yds.	Avg.	TD	No.	Yds.	Avg.	TD	No.	Yds.	Avg.	TD	TD	Pts.
1997—Northern Arizona	5	2	83	41.5	1	0	0	0.0	0	7	140	20.0	0	1	6
1998—Northern Arizona	11	46	767	16.7	7	0	0	0.0	0	10	200	20.0	0	7	42
1999—Northern Arizona	10	67	987	14.7	13	0	0	0.0	0	0	0	0.0	0	13	78
2000—Northern Arizona	5	29	230	7.9	2	5	78	15.6	1	4	62	15.5	0	3	18
College totals (4 years)	31	144	2067	14.4	23	5	78	15.6	1	21	402	19.1	0	24	144

STEELE, MARKUS   LB   COWBOYS

PERSONAL: Born July 24, 1979, in Cleveland. ... 6-3/240.
HIGH SCHOOL: Chanel (New Bedford, Ohio).
JUNIOR COLLEGE: Long Beach City College.
COLLEGE: Southern California.
TRANSACTIONS/CAREER NOTES: Selected by Dallas Cowboys in fourth round (122nd pick overall) of 2001 NFL draft.
COLLEGE NOTES: Recovered one fumble (1997); recovered one fumble (1998); recovered two fumbles and intercepted one pass (1999); recovered one fumble (2000).

Year Team	G	SACKS
1997—Long Beach JC	12	8.0
1998—Long Beach JC	11	8.0
1999—Southern California	12	3.0
2000—Southern California	10	3.0
Junior college totals (2 years)	23	16.0
College totals (2 years)	22	6.0

STEWART, DALEROY   DT   COWBOYS

PERSONAL: Born November 1, 1978, in Vero Beach, Fla. ... 6-3/298. ... Full name: Daleroy Andrew Stewart.
HIGH SCHOOL: Vero Beach (Fla.).
COLLEGE: Southern Mississippi.
TRANSACTIONS/CAREER NOTES: Selected by Dallas Cowboys in sixth round (171st pick overall) in 2001 NFL draft.

Year Team	G	SACKS
1997—Southern Mississippi	8	8.0
1998—Southern Mississippi	10	0.5
1999—Southern Mississippi	Statistics unavailable.	
2000—Southern Mississippi	11	4.0
College totals (3 years)	29	12.5

STEWART, MATT   LB   FALCONS

PERSONAL: Born August 31, 1979, in Columbus, Ohio. ... 6-3/232.
HIGH SCHOOL: DeSales (Columbus, Ohio).
COLLEGE: Vanderbilt.
TRANSACTIONS/CAREER NOTES: Selected by Atlanta Falcons in fourth round (102nd pick overall) of 2001 NFL draft. ... Signed by Falcons (May 30, 2001).
COLLEGE NOTES: Recovered one fumble (1998); recovered four fumbles (2000).

		INTERCEPTIONS				SACKS
Year Team	G	No.	Yds.	Avg.	TD	No.
1997—Vanderbilt	11	0	0	0.0	0	0.0
1998—Vanderbilt	11	0	0	0.0	0	2.0
1999—Vanderbilt	11	0	0	0.0	0	6.5
2000—Vanderbilt	11	3	60	20.0	0	6.5
College totals (4 years)	44	3	60	20.0	0	15.0

STEWART, TONY   TE   EAGLES

PERSONAL: Born August 9, 1979, in Lohne, Germany. ... 6-5/255. ... Full name: Tony Alexander Stewart.
HIGH SCHOOL: Allentown Central (Pa.).
COLLEGE: Penn State.
TRANSACTIONS/CAREER NOTES: Selected by Philadelphia Eagles in fifth round (147th pick overall) of 2001 NFL draft. ... Signed by Eagles (May 22, 2001).
COLLEGE NOTES: Returned three kickoffs for 15 yards (1997).

		RECEIVING			
Year Team	G	No.	Yds.	Avg.	TD
1997—Penn State	11	0	0	0.0	0
1998—Penn State	10	7	144	20.6	0
1999—Penn State	12	14	266	19.0	1
2000—Penn State	12	38	451	11.9	2
College totals (4 years)	45	59	861	14.6	3

STONE, MICHAEL — CB — CARDINALS

PERSONAL: Born February 13, 1978, in Southfield, Mich. ... 5-11/191. ... Full name: Michael Ahmed Stone.
HIGH SCHOOL: Southfield-Lathrup (Southfield, Mich.).
COLLEGE: Memphis.
TRANSACTIONS/CAREER NOTES: Selected by Arizona Cardinals in second round (54th pick overall) of 2001 NFL draft.
COLLEGE NOTES: Recovered one fumble (1998); recovered one fumble (1999); recovered one fumble (2000).

			INTERCEPTIONS				SACKS
Year	Team	G	No.	Yds.	Avg.	TD	No.
1998—Memphis		9	0	0	0.0	0	0.0
1999—Memphis		11	1	0	0.0	0	1.0
2000—Memphis		11	2	28	14.0	0	0.0
College totals (3 years)		31	3	28	9.3	0	1.0

STROUD, MARCUS — DT — JAGUARS

PERSONAL: Born June 25, 1978, in Barney, Ga. ... 6-6/317.
HIGH SCHOOL: Brooks County (Barney, Ga.).
COLLEGE: Georgia.
TRANSACTIONS/CAREER NOTES: Selected by Jacksonville Jaguars in first round (13th pick overall) of 2001 NFL draft.
COLLEGE NOTES: Recovered one fumble (2000).

Year	Team	G	SACKS
1997—Georgia		11	2.0
1998—Georgia		11	1.0
1999—Georgia		10	2.0
2000—Georgia		11	1.5
College totals (4 years)		43	6.5

SULFSTED, ALEX — OT — CHIEFS

PERSONAL: Born December 21, 1977, in Loveland, Ohio. ... 6-5/310.
HIGH SCHOOL: Mariemont (Ohio).
COLLEGE: Miami of Ohio.
TRANSACTIONS/CAREER NOTES: Selected by Kansas City Chiefs in sixth round (176th pick overall) of 2001 NFL draft.
COLLEGE PLAYING EXPERIENCE: Miami of Ohio, 1996-2000. ... Games: 1996 (redshirted), 1997 (3), 1998 (11), 1999 (8), 2000 (11). Total: 33.

SULLIVAN, MARQUES — OT — BILLS

PERSONAL: Born February 2, 1978, in Oak Park, Ill. ... 6-5/323.
HIGH SCHOOL: Fenwick (Oak Park, Ill.).
COLLEGE: Illinois.
TRANSACTIONS/CAREER NOTES: Selected by Buffalo Bills in fifth round (144th pick overall) of 2001 NFL draft.
COLLEGE PLAYING EXPERIENCE: Illinois, 1997-2000. ... Games: 1997 (11), 1998 (11), 1999 (12), 2000 (11). Total: 45.

SUTHERLAND, VINNY — WR — FALCONS

PERSONAL: Born April 22, 1978, in West Palm Beach, Fla. ... 5-8/188. ... Full name: Vincent Joseph Sutherland.
HIGH SCHOOL: Palm Beach Lakes (Fla.).
COLLEGE: Purdue.
TRANSACTIONS/CAREER NOTES: Selected by Atlanta Falcons in fifth round (136th pick overall) of 2001 NFL draft. ... Signed by Falcons (May 29, 2001).

			RUSHING				RECEIVING				PUNT RETURNS				KICKOFF RETURNS				TOTALS	
Year	Team	G	Att.	Yds.	Avg.	TD	No.	Yds.	Avg.	TD	No.	Yds.	Avg.	TD	No.	Yds.	Avg.	TD	TD	Pts.
1997—Purdue		12	13	111	8.5	2	34	357	10.5	2	15	147	9.8	0	1	19	19.0	0	4	24
1998—Purdue		13	9	58	6.4	0	31	301	9.7	3	10	82	8.2	0	0	0	0.0	0	3	18
1999—Purdue		12	18	163	9.1	0	39	698	17.9	7	18	296	16.4	2	1	13	13.0	0	9	54
2000—Purdue		11	10	52	5.2	1	72	1014	14.1	13	16	159	9.9	0	22	535	24.3	0	14	84
College totals (4 years)		48	50	384	7.7	3	176	2370	13.5	25	59	684	11.6	2	24	567	23.6	0	30	180

TAFOYA, JOE — DE — BUCCANEERS

PERSONAL: Born September 6, 1977, in Pittsburg, Calif. ... 6-4/258. ... Full name: Joseph Peter Tafoya.
HIGH SCHOOL: Pittsburg (Calif.).
COLLEGE: Arizona.
TRANSACTIONS/CAREER NOTES: Selected by Tampa Bay Buccaneers in seventh round (234th pick overall) of 2001 NFL draft.
COLLEGE NOTES: Recovered two fumbles (1998); recovered one fumble (2000).

Year	Team	G	SACKS
1997—Arizona		10	4.0
1998—Arizona		10	4.5
1999—Arizona		12	10.0
2000—Arizona		11	6.0
College totals (4 years)		43	24.5

TAYLOR, CHRIS — WR — STEELERS

PERSONAL: Born April 25, 1979, in Madisonville, Texas. ... 5-10/176.
HIGH SCHOOL: Madisonville (Texas).
COLLEGE: Texas A&M.
TRANSACTIONS/CAREER NOTES: Selected by Pittsburgh Steelers in seventh round (218th pick overall) of 2001 NFL draft. ... Signed by Steelers (May 30, 2001).

		RUSHING				RECEIVING				PUNT RETURNS				KICKOFF RETURNS				TOTALS	
Year Team	G	Att.	Yds.	Avg.	TD	No.	Yds.	Avg.	TD	No.	Yds.	Avg.	TD	No.	Yds.	Avg.	TD	TD	Pts.
1997—Texas A&M	12	0	0	0.0	0	3	29	9.7	0	6	68	11.3	0	6	83	13.8	0	0	0
1998—Texas A&M	13	4	63	15.8	1	15	306	20.4	2	37	285	7.7	0	6	162	27.0	0	3	18
1999—Texas A&M	11	1	4	4.0	0	33	591	17.9	4	16	103	6.4	0	5	105	21.0	0	4	24
2000—Texas A&M	11	1	2	2.0	0	32	390	12.2	1	17	125	7.4	0	0	0	0.0	0	1	6
College totals (4 years)	47	6	69	11.5	1	83	1316	15.9	7	76	581	7.6	0	17	350	20.6	0	8	48

TERRELL, DAVID — WR — BEARS

PERSONAL: Born March 13, 1979, in Richmond, Va. ... 6-3/215.
HIGH SCHOOL: Huguenot (Richmond, Va.).
COLLEGE: Michigan.
TRANSACTIONS/CAREER NOTES: Selected after junior season by Chicago Bears in first round (eighth pick overall) of 2001 draft.
HONORS: Named wide receiver on THE SPORTING NEWS college All-America second team (2000).
COLLEGE PLAYING EXPERIENCE: Played defensive back (1998-99). ... Intercepted one pass (1999).

		RECEIVING				PUNT RETURNS				TOTALS	
Year Team	G	No.	Yds.	Avg.	TD	No.	Yds.	Avg.	TD	TD	Pts.
1998—Michigan	13	14	149	10.6	2	2	15	7.5	0	2	12
1999—Michigan	12	71	1038	14.6	7	0	0	0.0	0	8	48
2000—Michigan	12	67	1130	16.9	14	2	11	5.5	0	14	84
College totals (3 years)	37	152	2317	15.2	23	4	26	6.5	0	24	144

THOMAS, ANTHONY — RB — BEARS

PERSONAL: Born November 11, 1977, in Winnfield, La. ... 6-1/226. ... Full name: Anthony Jermaine Thomas.
HIGH SCHOOL: Winnfield (La.).
COLLEGE: Michigan.
TRANSACTIONS/CAREER NOTES: Selected by Chicago Bears in second round (38th pick overall) of 2001 NFL draft.
HONORS: Named running back to THE SPORTING NEWS college All-America third team (2000).

		RUSHING				RECEIVING				KICKOFF RETURNS				TOTALS	
Year Team	G	Att.	Yds.	Avg.	TD	No.	Yds.	Avg.	TD	No.	Yds.	Avg.	TD	TD	Pts.
1997—Michigan	12	137	549	4.0	5	22	219	10.0	0	8	200	25.0	0	5	30
1998—Michigan	12	167	893	5.3	15	16	152	9.5	0	12	304	25.3	0	15	90
1999—Michigan	12	301	1297	4.3	17	33	168	5.1	0	11	216	19.6	0	17	102
2000—Michigan	12	319	1733	5.4	18	17	271	15.9	1	0	0	0.0	0	19	114
College totals (4 years)	48	924	4472	4.8	55	88	810	9.2	1	31	720	23.2	0	56	336

TOMLINSON, LaDAINIAN — RB — CHARGERS

PERSONAL: Born June 23, 1979, in Dallas. ... 5-10/221.
HIGH SCHOOL: Waco University (Texas).
COLLEGE: Texas Christian.
TRANSACTIONS/CAREER NOTES: Selected by San Diego Chargers in first round (fifth pick overall) of 2001 NFL draft.
HONORS: Named running back on THE SPORTING NEWS college All-America third team (1999). ... Named running back on THE SPORTING NEWS college All-America first team (2000). ... Doak Walker Award winner (2000).

		RUSHING				RECEIVING				KICKOFF RETURNS				TOTALS	
Year Team	G	Att.	Yds.	Avg.	TD	No.	Yds.	Avg.	TD	No.	Yds.	Avg.	TD	TD	Pts.
1997—Texas Christian	11	126	538	4.3	6	12	107	8.9	0	20	386	19.3	0	6	36
1998—Texas Christian	11	144	717	5.0	8	6	34	5.7	0	17	383	22.5	0	8	48
1999—Texas Christian	11	268	1850	6.9	18	12	55	4.6	0	2	69	34.5	0	18	108
2000—Texas Christian	11	369	2158	5.8	22	10	40	4.0	0	0	0	0.0	0	22	132
College totals (4 years)	44	907	5263	5.8	54	40	236	5.9	0	39	838	21.5	0	54	324

TOVIESSI, PAUL — DE — BRONCOS

PERSONAL: Born February 26, 1978, in Alexandria, Va. ... 6-6/260. ... Full name: Paul Zinssou Setondji Toviessi.
HIGH SCHOOL: West Potomac (Alexandria, Va.).
COLLEGE: Marshall.
TRANSACTIONS/CAREER NOTES: Selected by Denver Broncos in second round (51st pick overall) of 2001 NFL draft.
COLLEGE NOTES: Recovered one fumble (1997); recovered one fumble (1999); recovered one fumble and intercepted one pass (2000).

Year Team	G	SACKS
1997—Marshall	13	4.0
1998—Marshall	1	1.0
1999—Marshall	13	3.5
2000—Marshall	13	7.0
College totals (4 years)	40	15.5

TUIASOSOPO, MARQUES　　QB　　RAIDERS

PERSONAL: Born March 22, 1979, in Woodinville, Wash. ... 6-1/219.
HIGH SCHOOL: Woodinville (Wash.).
COLLEGE: Washington.
TRANSACTIONS/CAREER NOTES: Selected by Oakland Raiders in second round (59th pick overall) of 2001 NFL draft.

Year Team	G	Att.	Cmp.	Pct.	Yds.	TD	Int.	Avg.	Rat.	Att.	Yds.	Avg.	TD	TD	Pts.
					PASSING						RUSHING			TOTALS	
1997—Washington	9	64	37	57.8	650	3	1	10.16	155.5	39	112	2.9	0	1	6
1998—Washington	11	79	40	50.6	484	2	5	6.13	97.8	43	327	7.6	7	7	42
1999—Washington	11	295	171	58.0	2221	12	11	7.53	127.2	138	541	3.9	0	6	36
2000—Washington	11	323	170	52.6	2146	14	11	6.64	115.9	126	394	3.1	6	6	36
College totals (4 years)	42	761	418	54.9	5501	31	28	7.23	121.7	346	1374	4.0	13	20	120

TURNER, T.J.　　LB　　PATRIOTS

PERSONAL: Born October 1, 1978, in Hillsboro, Ohio. ... 6-2/252.
HIGH SCHOOL: Hillsboro (Ohio).
COLLEGE: Michigan State.
TRANSACTIONS/CAREER NOTES: Selected by New England Patriots in seventh round (239th pick overall) of 2001 NFL draft.
COLLEGE NOTES: Recovered two fumbles (1999).

Year Team	G	No.	Yds.	Avg.	TD	No.
		INTERCEPTIONS				SACKS
1997—Michigan State	12	0	0	0.0	0	0.0
1998—Michigan State	10	0	0	0.0	0	2.0
1999—Michigan State	12	5	105	21.0	1	2.0
2000—Michigan State	4	0	0	0.0	0	0.0
College totals (4 years)	38	5	105	21.0	1	4.0

VANDEN BOSCH, KYLE　　DE　　CARDINALS

PERSONAL: Born November 17, 1978, in Larchwood, Iowa. ... 6-4/270.
HIGH SCHOOL: West Lyon (Larchwood, Iowa).
COLLEGE: Nebraska (degree in finance).
TRANSACTIONS/CAREER NOTES: Selected by Arizona Cardinals in second round (34th pick overall) of 2001 NFL draft.

Year Team	G	SACKS
1997—Nebraska	12	1.0
1998—Nebraska	12	2.0
1999—Nebraska	11	4.5
2000—Nebraska	11	5.5
College totals (4 years)	46	13.0

VICK, MICHAEL　　QB　　FALCONS

PERSONAL: Born June 26, 2080, in Newport News, Va. ... 6-0/214. ... Full name: Michael Dwayne Vick.
HIGH SCHOOL: Warwick (Newport News, Va.).
COLLEGE: Virginia Tech.
TRANSACTIONS/CAREER NOTES: Selected after sophomore season by Atlanta Falcons in first round (first pick overall) of 2001 NFL draft. ... Signed by Falcons (May 9, 2001).
HONORS: Named College Football Freshman of the Year by THE SPORTING NEWS (1999). ... Named quarterback on THE SPORTING NEWS college All-America first team (1999).

Year Team	G	Att.	Cmp.	Pct.	Yds.	TD	Int.	Avg.	Rat.	Att.	Yds.	Avg.	TD	TD	Pts.
					PASSING						RUSHING			TOTALS	
1999—Virginia Tech	10	152	90	59.2	1840	12	5	12.11	180.4	108	585	5.4	8	8	48
2000—Virginia Tech	10	161	87	54.0	1234	8	6	7.66	127.4	104	617	5.9	8	8	48
College totals (2 years)	20	313	177	56.5	3074	20	11	9.82	153.1	212	1202	5.7	16	16	96

WALKER, KENYATTA　　OT　　BUCCANEERS

PERSONAL: Born February 1, 1979, in Meridian, Miss. ... 6-5/302. ... Full name: Idrees Kenyatta Walker.
HIGH SCHOOL: Meridian (Miss.).
COLLEGE: Florida.
TRANSACTIONS/CAREER NOTES: Selected after junior season by Tamap Bay Buccaneers in first round (first pick overall) of 2001 NFL draft.
COLLEGE PLAYING EXPERIENCE: Florida, 1998-2000. ... Games: 11 (1998), 11 (1999), 11 (2000). Total: 33.

WALLS, RAYMOND   CB   COLTS

PERSONAL: Born July 24, 1979, in Kentwood, La. ... 5-10/175. ... Full name: Raymond Omoncial Tyshone Walls.
HIGH SCHOOL: Kentwood (La.).
COLLEGE: Southern Mississippi.
TRANSACTIONS/CAREER NOTES: Selected by Indianapolis Colts in fifth round (152nd pick overall) of 2001 NFL draft.
COLLEGE NOTES: Caught two passes for 18 yards (1997); caught ten passes for 127 yards and one touchdown (1998); returned 18 kickoffs for 329 yards (2000).

		INTERCEPTIONS			
Year Team	G	No.	Yds.	Avg.	TD
1997—Southern Mississippi	11	0	0	0.0	0
1998—Southern Mississippi	11	0	0	0.0	0
1999—Southern Mississippi	11	2	0	0.0	0
2000—Southern Mississippi	11	2	54	27.0	1
College totals (4 years)	44	4	54	13.5	1

WARD, CHAD   G   JAGUARS

PERSONAL: Born January 12, 1977, in Kennewick, Wa. ... 6-4/339.
HIGH SCHOOL: Riverview (Kennewick, Wa.).
COLLEGE: Washington.
TRANSACTIONS/CAREER NOTES: Selected by Jacksonville Jaguars in sixth round (170th pick overall) of 2001 NFL draft. ... Signed by Jaguars (June 4, 2001).
HONORS: Named offensive tackle on THE SPORTING NEWS college All-America first team (2000).
COLLEGE PLAYING EXPERIENCE: Washington, 1997-2000. ... Games: 1997 (11), 1998 (11), 1999 (11), 2000 (11). Total: 44.

WARREN, GERALD   DT   BROWNS

PERSONAL: Born July 25, 1978, in Lake City, Fla. ... 6-4/322. ... Full name: Gerald T. Warren.
HIGH SCHOOL: Union City (Raiford, Fla.).
COLLEGE: Florida.
TRANSACTIONS/CAREER NOTES: Selected by Cleveland Browns in first round (third pick overall) of 2001 NFL draft.
COLLEGE NOTES: Recovered one fumble (1998).

Year Team	G	SACKS
1997—Florida	3	1.0
1998—Florida	10	2.0
1999—Florida	10	2.0
2000—Florida	12	4.5
College totals (4 years)	35	9.5

WAYNE, REGGIE   WR   COLTS

PERSONAL: Born November 17, 1978, in Marrero, La. ... 6-0/197.
HIGH SCHOOL: Ehret (La.).
COLLEGE: Miami.
TRANSACTIONS/CAREER NOTES: Selected by Indianapolis Colts in first round (30th pick overall) of 2001 NFL draft.
COLLEGE NOTES: Rushed two times for 15 yards (2000).

		RECEIVING			
Year Team	G	No.	Yds.	Avg.	TD
1997—Miami (Fla.)	11	48	640	13.3	2
1998—Miami (Fla.)	9	42	629	15.0	4
1999—Miami (Fla.)	12	40	486	12.2	4
2000—Miami (Fla.)	11	43	755	17.6	10
College totals (4 years)	43	173	2510	14.5	20

WEATHERINGTON, COLSTON   DE   COWBOYS

PERSONAL: Born October 29, 1977, in Graceville, Fla. ... 6-5/270.
JUNIOR COLLEGE: Fort Scott (Kan.) Community College, then Northwest Mississippi Community College.
COLLEGE: Central Missouri State.
TRANSACTIONS/CAREER NOTES: Selected by Dallas Cowboys in seventh round (207th pick overall) of 2001 NFL draft.

Year Team	G	SACKS
1997—Fort Scott	Statistics unavailable.	
1997—Northwest Mississippi	Statistics unavailable.	
1997—Central Missouri State	Statistics unavailable.	
2000—Central Missouri State	11	6.5

WEINKE, CHRIS   QB   PANTHERS

PERSONAL: Born July 31, 1972, in St. Paul, Minn. ... 6-4/238.
HIGH SCHOOL: Cretin-Derham (St. Paul, Minn.).
COLLEGE: Florida State (degree in sports management).
TRANSACTIONS/CAREER NOTES: Selected by Carolina Panthers in fourth round (106th pick overall) of 2001 NFL draft.
HONORS: Named quarterback on THE SPORTING NEWS college All-America second team (2000). ... Heisman Trophy winner (2000). ... Davey O'Brien Award winner (2000).

			PASSING							RUSHING				TOTALS	
Year Team	G	Att.	Cmp.	Pct.	Yds.	TD	Int.	Avg.	Rat.	Att.	Yds.	Avg.	TD	TD	Pts.
1997—Florida State	3	13	7	53.8	82	2	1	6.31	142.2	2	8	4.0	0	0	0
1998—Florida State	10	286	145	50.7	2487	19	6	8.70	141.5	47	-168	-3.6	0	1	6
1999—Florida State	11	377	232	61.5	3103	25	14	8.23	145.1	40	-109	-2.7	0	0	0
2000—Florida State	12	431	266	61.7	4167	33	11	9.67	163.1	30	-97	-3.2	1	1	6
College totals (4 years)	36	1107	650	58.7	9839	79	32	8.89	151.1	119	-366	-3.1	2	2	12

RECORD AS BASEBALL PLAYER

TRANSACTIONS/CAREER NOTES: Selected by Toronto Blue Jays organization in second round of free-agent draft (June 4, 1990).

			BATTING											FIELDING			
Year Team (League)	Pos.	G	AB	R	H	2B	3B	HR	RBI	Avg.	BB	SO	SB	PO	A	E	Avg.
1991—St. Cath. (NY-Penn)	1B	75	272	31	65	9	1	3	40	.239	41	61	12	56	132	21	.900
1992—Myrtle Beach (S.Atl.)	1B	135	458	61	110	16	2	13	63	.240	70	89	4	1141	85	26	.979
1993—Dunedin (FSL)	1B	128	476	68	135	16	2	17	98	.284	66	78	8	1142	101	20	.984
1994—Knoxville (Sou.)	1B	139	526	61	133	23	2	8	87	.253	45	121	12	1173	93	9	.993
1995—Syracuse (I.L.)	1B-3B	113	341	42	77	12	2	10	41	.226	44	74	4	1173	93	9	.993
1996—Syracuse (I.L.)	1B	51	161	21	30	8	1	3	18	.186	19	49	0	321	36	9	.975
—Knoxville (Sou.)	1B	75	265	48	70	18	2	15	55	.264	52	74	2	78	13	0	1.000

WESTMORELAND, ERIC   LB   JAGUARS

PERSONAL: Born March 11, 1977, in Jasper, Tenn. ... 5-11/236. ... Full name: Eric Lebron Westmoreland.
HIGH SCHOOL: Marion County (Tenn.).
COLLEGE: Tennessee.
TRANSACTIONS/CAREER NOTES: Selected by Jacksonville Jaguars in third round (73rd pick overall) of 2001 NFL draft.
COLLEGE NOTES: Recovered one fumble (1996); recovered one fumble (1998); recovered two fumbles (1999); recovered one fumble (2000).

		INTERCEPTIONS				SACKS
Year Team	G	No.	Yds.	Avg.	TD	No.
1996—Tennessee	11	0	0	0.0	0	0.0
1997—Tennessee	2	0	0	0.0	0	1.0
1998—Tennessee	12	1	0	0.0	0	0.0
1999—Tennessee	9	0	0	0.0	0	0.0
2000—Tennessee	11	0	0	0.0	0	5.0
College totals (5 years)	45	1	0	0.0	0	6.0

WHITE, MITCH   OT   SAINTS

PERSONAL: Born March 25, 1978, in Phoenix ... 6-5/308. ... Full name: Mitchell Eugene White.
HIGH SCHOOL: Rancho Bernardo (San Diego).
JUNIOR COLLEGE: Palomar College (Calif.).
COLLEGE: Oregon State.
TRANSACTIONS/CAREER NOTES: Selected by New Orleans Saints in sixth round (185th pick overall) of 2001 NFL draft.
COLLEGE PLAYING EXPERIENCE: Palomar College, 1997 and 1998; Oregon State, 1999 and 2000. ... Games: 1997 (games played unavailable), 1998 (games played unavailable), 1999 (12), 2000 (12). Total NCAA: 24

WILLIAMS, BROCK   CB   PATRIOTS

PERSONAL: Born August 12, 1979, in Hammond, La. ... 5-10/185.
HIGH SCHOOL: Hammond (La.).
COLLEGE: Notre Dame.
TRANSACTIONS/CAREER NOTES: Selected by New England Patriots in third round (86th pick overall) of 2001 NFL draft.
COLLEGE NOTES: Recovered one fumble (1998); credited with one sack (2000).

		INTERCEPTIONS			
Year Team	G	No.	Yds.	Avg.	TD
1997—Notre Dame	7	0	0	0.0	0
1998—Notre Dame	11	1	3	3.0	0
1999—Notre Dame			Redshirted.		
2000—Notre Dame	11	1	0	0.0	0
College totals (3 years)	29	2	3	1.5	0

WILLIAMS, JIMMY — CB — BILLS

PERSONAL: Born March 10, 1979, in Baton Rouge, La. ... 5-10/184.
HIGH SCHOOL: Episcopal (Baton Rouge, La.).
COLLEGE: Vanderbilt.
TRANSACTIONS/CAREER NOTES: Selected by Buffalo Bills in sixth round (196th pick overall) of 2001 NFL draft.
COLLEGE NOTES: Caught 23 passes for 189 yards and one touchdown and recovered one fumble (1997); caught seven passes for 76 yards (1998); recovered one fumble (2000).

		RUSHING				INTERCEPTIONS				PUNT RETURNS				KICKOFF RETURNS				TOTALS	
Year Team	G	Att.	Yds.	Avg.	TD	No.	Yds.	Avg.	TD	No.	Yds.	Avg.	TD	No.	Yds.	Avg.	TD	TD	Pts.
1997—Vanderbilt	11	98	527	5.4	2	0	0	0.0	0	0	0	0.0	0	20	476	23.8	0	4	24
1998—Vanderbilt	11	3	7	2.3	0	4	59	14.8	0	0	0	0.0	0	29	678	23.4	1	1	6
1999—Vanderbilt	11	1	8	8.0	0	2	35	17.5	0	38	285	7.5	1	17	376	22.1	0	1	6
2000—Vanderbilt	9	0	0	0.0	0	4	64	16.0	0	15	118	7.9	0	7	147	21.0	0	0	0
College totals (4 years)	42	102	542	5.3	2	10	158	15.8	0	53	403	7.6	1	73	1677	23.0	1	6	36

WILLIAMS, LOUIS — C — PANTHERS

PERSONAL: Born April 11, 1979, in Fort Walton Beach, Fla. ... 6-4/291. ... Full name: Louis Randall Williams Jr.
HIGH SCHOOL: Choctawhatchee (Fla.).
COLLEGE: Louisiana State.
TRANSACTIONS/CAREER NOTES: Selected by Carolina Panthers in seventh round (211th pick overall) of 2001 NFL draft.
COLLEGE PLAYING EXPERIENCE: Louisiana State, 1997-2000. ... Games: 1997 (7), 1998 (11), 1999 (11), 2000 (11). Total 40.

WILLIAMS, MAURICE — OT — JAGUARS

PERSONAL: Born January 26, 1979, in Detroit. ... 6-5/307. ... Full name: Maurice Carlos Williams.
HIGH SCHOOL: Pershing (Detroit).
COLLEGE: Michigan.
TRANSACTIONS/CAREER NOTES: Selected by Jacksonville Jaguars in second round (43rd pick overall) of 2001 NFL draft.
COLLEGE NOTES: Played defensive lineman (1997).
COLLEGE PLAYING EXPERIENCE: Michigan, 1997-2000. ... Games: 1997 (5), 1998 (5), 1999 (13), 2000 (13). Total: 39.

WILSON, ADRIAN — DB — CARDINALS

PERSONAL: Born October 12, 1979, in High Point, N.C. ... 6-2/213.
HIGH SCHOOL: T.W. Andrews (High Point, N.C.).
COLLEGE: North Carolina State.
TRANSACTIONS/CAREER NOTES: Selected after junior season by Arizona Cardinals in third round (64th pick overall) of 2001 NFL draft.
COLLEGE NOTES: Returned four kickoffs for 66 yards (1998); Recovered two fumbles, returned one kickoff for three yards and caught one pass for 81 yards and one touchdown (2000).

		INTERCEPTIONS				SACKS
Year Team	G	No.	Yds.	Avg.	TD	No.
1998—North Carolina State	10	1	0	0.0	0	1.0
1999—North Carolina State	12	1	0	0.0	0	1.0
2000—North Carolina State	11	1	3	3.0	0	0.0
College totals (3 years)	33	3	3	1.0	0	2.0

WILSON, CEDRICK — WR/KR — 49ERS

PERSONAL: Born December 17, 1978, in Memphis, Tenn. ... 5-9/179.
HIGH SCHOOL: Melrose (Memphis, Tenn.).
COLLEGE: Tennessee.
TRANSACTIONS/CAREER NOTES: Selected by San Francisco 49ers in sixth round (169th pick overall) of 2001 NFL draft.
COLLEGE NOTES: Returned one punt for no gain (1997); returned one punt for 12 yards (1999).

		RECEIVING				KICKOFF RETURNS				TOTALS	
Year Team	G	No.	Yds.	Avg.	TD	No.	Yds.	Avg.	TD	TD	Pts.
1997—Tennessee	12	7	71	10.1	2	4	88	22.0	0	2	12
1998—Tennessee	12	33	558	16.9	6	4	84	21.0	0	6	36
1999—Tennessee	11	57	827	14.5	4	3	50	16.7	0	4	24
2000—Tennessee	11	62	681	11.0	12	1	14	14.0	0	12	72
College totals (4 years)	46	159	2137	13.4	24	12	236	19.7	0	24	144

WINBORN, JAMIE — LB — 49ERS

PERSONAL: Born May 14, 1979, in Wetumpka, Ala. ... 6-0/242.
HIGH SCHOOL: Wetumpka (Ala.).
COLLEGE: Vanderbilt.
TRANSACTIONS/CAREER NOTES: Selected after junior season by San Francisco 49ers in second round (47th pick overall) of 2001 NFL draft.
COLLEGE NOTES: Recovered one fumble (1998); recovered one fumble (1999).

Year Team	G	SACKS
1998—Vanderbilt	11	8.0
1999—Vanderbilt	11	5.5
2000—Vanderbilt	9	3.0
College totals (3 years)	31	16.5

WINEY, BRANDON   OT   DOLPHINS

PERSONAL: Born January 27, 1978, in Lake Charles, La. ... 6-7/294.
HIGH SCHOOL: Washington-Marion (Lake Charles, La.).
COLLEGE: Louisiana State.
TRANSACTIONS/CAREER NOTES: Selected by Miami Dolphins in sixth round (164th pick overall) of 2001 NFL draft.
HONORS: Named offensive tackle on THE SPORTING NEWS college All-America third team (2000).
COLLEGE PLAYING EXPERIENCE: Louisiana State, 1996-2000. ... Games: 1996 (redshirted), 1997 (2), 1998 (11), 1999 (9), 2000 (9). Total: 31.

WOMACK, FLOYD   OT   SEAHAWKS

PERSONAL: Born November 15, 1978, in Cleveland, Miss. ... 6-4/345. ... Full name: Floyd Seneca Womack.
HIGH SCHOOL: East Side (Cleveland, Miss.).
COLLEGE: Mississippi State.
TRANSACTIONS/CAREER NOTES: Selected by Seattle Seahawks in fourth round (128th pick overall) of 2001 NFL draft.
COLLEGE PLAYING EXPERIENCE: Mississippi State, 1997-2000. ... Games: 1997 (3), 1998 (12), 1999 (11), 2000 (6). Total: 32.

WORTHEN, SHAWN   DT   VIKINGS

PERSONAL: Born September 12, 1978, in San Antonio. ... 6-0/316.
HIGH SCHOOL: Alamo Heights (San Antonio).
COLLEGE: Texas Christian.
TRANSACTIONS/CAREER NOTES: Selected by Minnesota Vikings in fourth round (130th pick overall) of 2001 NFL draft.

Year Team	G	SACKS
1997—Texas Christian	7	0.0
1998—Texas Christian	11	1.0
1999—Texas Christian	11	4.0
2000—Texas Christian	11	2.5
College totals (4 years)	40	7.5

WYMS, ELLIS   DE   BUCCANEERS

PERSONAL: Born April 12, 1979, in Indianola, Miss. ... 6-3/279. ... Full name: Ellis Rashad Wyms.
HIGH SCHOOL: Gentry (Indianola, Miss.).
COLLEGE: Mississippi State.
TRANSACTIONS/CAREER NOTES: Selected by Tampa Bay Buccaneers in sixth round (183rd pick overall) of 2001 NFL draft.
COLLEGE NOTES: Recovered two fumbles (2000).

Year Team	G	SACKS
1997—Mississippi State	8	1.0
1998—Mississippi State	12	1.0
1999—Mississippi State	11	5.0
2000—Mississippi State	9	3.0
College totals (4 years)	40	10.0

WYNN, MILTON   WR   RAMS

PERSONAL: Born August 21, 1978, in Mission Hills, Calif. ... 6-3/205.
HIGH SCHOOL: Antelope Valley (Calif.).
JUNIOR COLLEGE: Bakersfield (Calif.) College, then Los Angeles Valley College.
COLLEGE: Washington State.
TRANSACTIONS/CAREER NOTES: Selected by St. Louis Rams in fourth round (116th pick overall) of 2001 NFL draft.
COLLEGE NOTES: Returned nine punts for 169 yards (1998).

Year Team	G	RUSHING Att.	Yds.	Avg.	TD	RECEIVING No.	Yds.	Avg.	TD	TOTALS TD	Pts.
1997—Bakersfield					Statistics unavailable.						
1998—Los Angeles Valley	10	1	-1	-1.0	0	44	751	17.1	7	7	42
1999—Washington State	1	0	0	0.0	0	3	20	6.7	0	0	0
2000—Washington State	11	2	32	16.0	1	52	964	18.5	5	6	36
Junior college totals (1 year)	10	1	-1	-1.0	0	44	751	17.1	7	7	42
College totals (2 years)	12	2	32	16.0	1	55	984	17.9	5	6	36

ZUKAUSKAS, PAUL   G   BROWNS

PERSONAL: Born July 12, 1979, in Weymouth, Mass. ... 6-6/318. ... Full name: Paul Malcolm Zukauskas.
HIGH SCHOOL: Boston College (Ma.).
COLLEGE: Boston College.
TRANSACTIONS/CAREER NOTES: Selected by Cleveland Browns in seventh round (203rd pick overall) of 2001 NFL draft.
HONORS: Named guard on THE SPORTING NEWS college All-America second team (2000).
COLLEGE PLAYING EXPERIENCE: Boston College, 1997-2000. ... Games: 1997 (7), 1998 (11), 1999 (11), 2000 (10). Total: 39.

HEAD COACHES

BELICHICK, BILL — PATRIOTS

PERSONAL: Born April 16, 1952, in Nashville. ... Full name: William Stephen Belichick. ... Son of Steve Belichick, fullback with Detroit Lions (1941); head coach at Hiram (Ohio) College (1946-49); assistant coach, Vanderbilt (1949-53); assistant coach, North Carolina (1953-56); assistant coach, Navy (1956-83); and administrative assistant, Navy (1983-89).

HIGH SCHOOL: Annapolis (Md.) and Phillips Academy (Andover, Mass.).

COLLEGE: Wesleyan University (degree in economics, 1975).

HEAD COACHING RECORD

BACKGROUND: Assistant special teams coach, Baltimore Colts NFL (1975). ... Assistant special teams coach, Detroit Lions NFL (1976 and 1977). ... Assistant special teams coach/assistant to defensive coordinator, Denver Broncos NFL (1978). ... Special teams coach, New York Giants NFL (1979 and 1980). ... Linebackers coach, Giants (1981 and 1982). ... Defensive coordinator/linebackers coach, Giants (1983-1988). ... Defensive coordinator/secondary coach, Giants (1989 and 1990). ... Assistant head coach/secondary coach, New England Patriots NFL (1996). ... Assistant head coach/secondary coach, New York Jets NFL (1997-1999).

				REGULAR SEASON		POST-SEASON	
	W	L	T	Pct.	Finish	W	L
1991—Cleveland NFL	6	10	0	.375	3rd/AFC Central Division	0	0
1992—Cleveland NFL	7	9	0	.438	3rd/AFC Central Division	0	0
1993—Cleveland NFL	7	9	0	.438	3rd/AFC Central Division	0	0
1994—Cleveland NFL	11	5	0	.688	2nd/AFC Central Division	1	1
1995—Cleveland NFL	5	11	0	.313	4th/AFC Central Division	0	0
2000—New England NFL	5	11	0	.313	5th/AFC Eastern Division	0	0
Pro totals (6 years)	**41**	**55**	**0**	**.427**	**Pro totals (6 years)**	**1**	**1**

NOTES:

1994—Defeated New England, 20-13, in first-round playoff game; lost to Pittsburgh, 29-9, in conference playoff game.

BILLICK, BRIAN — RAVENS

PERSONAL: Born February 28, 1954, in Fairborn, Ohio. ... Full name: Brian Harold Billick. ... Played tight end.

HIGH SCHOOL: Redlands (Calif.).

COLLEGE: Air Force, then Brigham Young.

TRANSACTIONS/CAREER NOTES: Selected by San Francisco 49ers in 11th round of 1977 NFL draft. ... Signed by 49ers for 1977 season. ... Released by 49ers (August 30, 1977). ... Signed by Dallas Cowboys (May 1978). ... Released by Cowboys before 1978 season.

HEAD COACHING RECORD

BACKGROUND: Assistant coach, University of Redlands (1977). ... Graduate assistant, Brigham Young (1978). ... Assistant public relations director, San Francisco 49ers NFL (1979 and 1980). ... Assistant coach and recruiting coordinator, San Diego State (1981-1985). ... Offensive coordinator, Utah State (1986-1988). ... Assistant coach, Stanford (1989-1991). ... Tight ends coach, Minnesota Vikings (1992). ... Offensive coordinator, Minnesota Vikings (1993-1998).

				REGULAR SEASON		POST-SEASON	
	W	L	T	Pct.	Finish	W	L
1999—Baltimore NFL	8	8	0	.500	3rd/AFC Central Division	0	0
2000—Baltimore NFL	12	4	0	.750	2nd/AFC Central Division	4	0
Pro totals (2 years)	**20**	**12**	**0**	**.625**	**Pro totals (2 years)**	**4**	**0**

NOTES:

2000—Defeated Denver, 21-3, in first-round playoff game; defeated Tennessee, 24-10, in conference playoff game; defeated Oakland, 16-3, in AFC championship game; defeated New York Giants, 34-7, in Super Bowl XXXV.

CAMPO, DAVE — COWBOYS

PERSONAL: Born July 18, 1947, in New London, Conn. ... Full name: David Cross Campo.

HIGH SCHOOL: Robert E. Fitch (Groton, Conn.).

COLLEGE: Central Connecticut State.

HEAD COACHING RECORD

BACKGROUND: Coach, Central Connecticut State (1971 and 1972). ... Coach, Albany State (1973). ... Coach, Bridgeport (1974). ... Coach, University of Pittsburgh (1975). ... Coach, Washington State (1976). ... Coach, Boise State (1977-1979). ... Coach, Oregon State (1980). ... Coach, Weber State (1981 and 1982). ... Coach, Iowa State (1983). ... Coach, Syracuse (1984-1986). ... Secondary coach, Miami, Fla. (1987 and 1988). ... Secondary coach, Dallas Cowboys NFL (1989-1994). ... Defensive coordinator, Cowboys (1995-1999).

				REGULAR SEASON		POST-SEASON	
	W	L	T	Pct.	Finish	W	L
2000—Dallas NFL	5	11	0	.313	4th/NFC Eastern Division	0	0

PERSONAL: Born August 31, 1946, in Waterloo, N.Y. ... Full name: Thomas Richard Coughlin.
HIGH SCHOOL: Waterloo (N.Y.) Central.
COLLEGE: Syracuse (bachelor's degree in education, 1968; master's degree in education, 1969).

HEAD COACHING RECORD

BACKGROUND: Graduate assistant, Syracuse (1969). ... Quarterbacks/offensive backfield coach, Syracuse (1974-1976). ... Offensive coordinator, Syracuse (1977-1980). ... Quarterbacks coach, Boston College (1980-1983). ... Receivers coach, Philadelphia Eagles NFL (1984 and 1985). ... Receivers coach, Green Bay Packers NFL (1986 and 1987). ... Receivers coach, New York Giants NFL (1988-1990).

	W	L	T	Pct.	REGULAR SEASON Finish	POST-SEASON W	L
1970—Rochester Tech	4	3	0	.571	Eastern College Athletic Conference	0	0
1971—Rochester Tech	5	2	1	.688	Eastern College Athletic Conference	0	0
1972—Rochester Tech	4	5	0	.444	Eastern College Athletic Conference	0	0
1973—Rochester Tech	3	5	1	.389	Eastern College Athletic Conference	0	0
1991—Boston College	4	7	0	.364	7th/Big East Conference	0	0
1992—Boston College	8	2	1	.773	3rd/Big East Conference	0	1
1993—Boston College	8	3	0	.727	3rd/Big East Conference	1	0
1995—Jacksonville NFL	4	12	0	.250	5th/AFC Central Division	0	0
1996—Jacksonville NFL	9	7	0	.563	2nd/AFC Central Division	2	1
1997—Jacksonville NFL	11	5	0	.688	T1st/AFC Central Division	0	1
1998—Jacksonville NFL	11	5	0	.688	1st/AFC Central Division	1	1
1999—Jacksonville NFL	14	2	0	.875	1st/AFC Central Division	1	1
2000—Jacksonville NFL	7	9	0	.438	4th/AFC Central Division	0	0
College totals (7 years)	**36**	**27**	**3**	**.568**	**College totals (2 years)**	**1**	**1**
Pro totals (6 years)	**56**	**40**	**0**	**.583**	**Pro totals (5 years)**	**4**	**4**

NOTES:

1992—Lost to Tennessee, 38-23, in Hall of Fame Bowl.
1993—Defeated Virginia, 31-13, in CarQuest Bowl.
1996—Defeated Buffalo, 30-27, in first-round playoff game; defeated Denver, 30-27, in conference playoff game; lost to New England, 20-6, in AFC championship game.
1997—Lost to Denver, 42-17, in first-round playoff game.
1998—Defeated New England, 25-10, in first-round playoff game; lost to New York Jets, 34-24, in conference playoff game.
1999—Defeated Miami, 62-7, in conference playoff game; lost to Tennessee, 33-14, in AFC championship game.

PERSONAL: Born May 8, 1957, in Pittsburgh. ... Full name: William Laird Cowher. ... Played linebacker.
HIGH SCHOOL: Carlynton (Carnegie, Pa.).
COLLEGE: North Carolina State (bachelor of science degree in education, 1979).
TRANSACTIONS/CAREER NOTES: Signed as non-drafted free agent by Philadelphia Eagles (May 8, 1979). ... Released by Eagles (August 14, 1979). ... Signed by Cleveland Browns (February 27, 1980). ... On injured reserve with knee injury (August 20, 1981-entire season). ... Traded by Browns to Eagles for ninth-round pick (WR Don Jones) in 1984 draft (August 21, 1983). ... On injured reserve with knee injury (September 25, 1984-remainder of season).
PLAYING EXPERIENCE: Cleveland NFL, 1980 and 1982; Philadelphia NFL, 1983 and 1984. ... Games: 1980 (16), 1982 (9), 1983 (16), 1984 (4). Total: 45.
PRO STATISTICS: 1983—Recovered one fumble.

HEAD COACHING RECORD

BACKGROUND: Special teams coach, Cleveland Browns NFL (1985 and 1986). ... Defensive backs coach, Browns (1987 and 1988). ... Defensive coordinator, Kansas City Chiefs NFL (1989-1991).
HONORS: Named NFL Coach of the Year by The Sporting News (1992).

	W	L	T	Pct.	REGULAR SEASON Finish	POST-SEASON W	L
1992—Pittsburgh NFL	11	5	0	.688	1st/AFC Central Division	0	1
1993—Pittsburgh NFL	9	7	0	.563	2nd/AFC Central Division	0	1
1994—Pittsburgh NFL	12	4	0	.750	1st/AFC Central Division	1	1
1995—Pittsburgh NFL	11	5	0	.688	1st/AFC Central Division	2	1
1996—Pittsburgh NFL	10	6	0	.625	1st/AFC Central Division	1	1
1997—Pittsburgh NFL	11	5	0	.688	T1st/AFC Central Division	1	1
1998—Pittsburgh NFL	7	9	0	.438	3rd/AFC Central Division	0	0
1999—Pittsburgh NFL	6	10	0	.375	4th/AFC Central Division	0	0
2000—Pittsburgh NFL	9	7	0	.563	3rd/AFC Central Division	0	0
Pro totals (9 years)	**86**	**58**	**0**	**.597**	**Pro totals (8 years)**	**5**	**6**

NOTES:

1992—Lost to Buffalo, 24-3, in conference playoff game.
1993—Lost to Kansas City, 27-24 (OT), in first-round playoff game.
1994—Defeated Cleveland, 29-9, in conference playoff game; lost to San Diego, 17-13, in AFC championship game.
1995—Defeated Buffalo, 40-21, in conference playoff game; defeated Indianapolis, 20-16, in AFC championship game; lost to Dallas, 27-17, in Super Bowl XXX.
1996—Defeated Indianapolis, 42-14, in first-round playoff game; lost to New England, 28-3, in conference playoff game.
1997—Defeated New England, 7-6, in conference playoff game; lost to Denver, 24-21, in AFC championship game.

*Vertical left margin:* HEAD COACHES

DAVIS, BUTCH — BROWNS

PERSONAL: Born November 17, 1951, in Tahlequah, Okla. ... Full name: Paul Hilton Davis.
HIGH SCHOOL: Bixby (Okla.).
COLLEGE: Arkansas (degree in biology and life science).

HEAD COACHING RECORD

BACKGROUND: Assistant coach, Fayetteville (Ark.) High School (1973). ... Assistant coach, Pawhuska (Okla.) High School (1974 and 1975). ... Assistant coach, Sand Springs (Okla.) High School (1976 and 1977). ... Head coach, Rogers High School, Tulsa, Okla. (1978). ... Assistant coach, Oklahoma State (1979-1983). ... Assistant coach, University of Miami (1984-1988). ... Assistant coach, Dallas Cowboys NFL (1989-1992). ... Defensive coordinator, Cowboys (1993 and 1994).

			REGULAR SEASON			POST-SEASON	
	W	L	T	Pct.	Finish	W	L
1995—Miami (Fla.)	8	3	0	.727	T1st/Big East Conference	0	0
1996—Miami (Fla.)	9	3	0	.750	T1st/Big East Conference	1	0
1997—Miami (Fla.)	5	6	0	.455	T5th/Big East Conference	0	0
1998—Miami (Fla.)	9	3	0	.750	T2nd/Big East Conference	1	0
1999—Miami (Fla.)	9	4	0	.692	2nd/Big East Conference	1	0
2000—Miami (Fla.)	11	1	0	.917	1st/Big East Conference	1	0
College totals (6 years)	**51**	**20**	**0**	**.718**	**College totals (6 years)**	**4**	**0**

NOTES:
1996—Defeated Virginia, 31-21, in CarQuest Bowl.
1998—Defeated North Carolina State, 46-23, in Micron PC Bowl.
1999—Defeated Georgia Tech, 28-13, in Gator Bowl.
2000—Defeated Florida, 37-20, in Sugar Bowl.

DUNGY, TONY — BUCCANEERS

PERSONAL: Born October 6, 1955, in Jackson, Mich. ... Full name: Anthony Kevin Dungy. ... Played defensive back and quarterback. ... Name pronounced DUN-gee.
HIGH SCHOOL: Parkside (Jackson, Mich.).
COLLEGE: Minnesota (degree in business administration, 1978).
TRANSACTIONS/CAREER NOTES: Signed as non-drafted free agent by Pittsburgh Steelers (May 1977). ... Traded by Steelers to San Francisco 49ers for 10th-round pick in 1980 draft (August 21, 1979). ... Traded by 49ers with RB Mike Hogan to New York Giants for WR Jimmy Robinson and CB Ray Rhodes (March 27, 1980).
CHAMPIONSHIP GAME EXPERIENCE: Played in AFC championship game (1978 season). ... Played in Super Bowl XIII (1978 season).
PRO STATISTICS: 1977—Attempted eight passes with three completions for 43 yards and two interceptions, rushed three times for eight yards and fumbled once. 1978—Recovered two fumbles for eight yards. 1979—Recovered two fumbles.

			INTERCEPTIONS			
Year Team	G	No.	Yds.	Avg.	TD	
1977—Pittsburgh NFL	14	3	37	12.3	0	
1978—Pittsburgh NFL	16	6	95	15.8	0	
1979—San Francisco NFL	15	0	0	0.0	0	
Pro totals (3 years)	45	9	132	14.7	0	

HEAD COACHING RECORD

BACKGROUND: Defensive backs coach, University of Minnesota (1980). ... Defensive assistant, Pittsburgh Steelers NFL (1981). ... Defensive backs coach, Steelers (1982 and 1983). ... Defensive coordinator, Steelers (1984-1988). ... Defensive backs coach, Kansas City Chiefs NFL (1989-1991). ... Defensive coordinator, Minnesota Vikings NFL (1992-1995).

			REGULAR SEASON			POST-SEASON	
	W	L	T	Pct.	Finish	W	L
1996—Tampa Bay NFL	6	10	0	.375	4th/NFC Central Division	0	0
1997—Tampa Bay NFL	10	6	0	.625	2nd/NFC Central Division	1	1
1998—Tampa Bay NFL	8	8	0	.500	3rd/NFC Central Division	0	0
1999—Tampa Bay NFL	11	5	0	.688	1st/NFC Central Division	1	1
2000—Tampa Bay NFL	10	6	0	.625	2nd/NFC Central Division	0	1
Pro totals (5 years)	**45**	**35**	**0**	**.563**	**Pro totals (3 years)**	**2**	**3**

NOTES:
1997—Defeated Detroit, 20-10, in first-round playoff game; lost to Green Bay, 21-7, in conference playoff game.
1999—Defeated Washington, 14-13, in conference playoff game; lost to St. Louis, 11-6, in NFC championship game.
2000—Lost to Philadelphia, 21-3, in first-round playoff game.

EDWARDS, HERMAN — JETS

PERSONAL: Born April 27, 1954, in Fort Monmouth, N.J. ... Full name: Herman Lee Edwards. ... Played cornerback.
HIGH SCHOOL: Monterey (Calif.).
JUNIOR COLLEGE: Monterey (Calif.) Peninsula College.
COLLEGE: California, then San Diego State (degree in criminal justice).
TRANSACTIONS/CAREER NOTES: Signed as non-drafted free agent by Philadelphia Eagles (May 1977). ... Released by Eagles (September 8, 1986). ... Signed by Los Angeles Rams (September 15, 1986). ... Released by Rams (October 20, 1986). ... Signed by Atlanta Falcons (November 3, 1986). ... Announced retirement (November 24, 1986).

CHAMPIONSHIP GAME EXPERIENCE: Played in NFC championship game (1980 season). ... Played in Super Bowl XV (1980 season).

PRO STATISTICS: 1977—Recovered two fumbles and fumbled once. 1978—Recovered one fumble for 26 yards and a touchdown and fumbled once. 1979—Recovered one fumble. 1981—Recovered one fumble for four yards. 1985—Recovered one fumble for four yards.

			INTERCEPTIONS			
Year	Team	G	No.	Yds.	Avg.	TD
1977—Philadelphia NFL		14	6	9	1.5	0
1978—Philadelphia NFL		16	7	59	8.4	0
1979—Philadelphia NFL		16	3	6	2.0	0
1980—Philadelphia NFL		16	3	12	4.0	0
1981—Philadelphia NFL		16	3	1	0.3	0
1982—Philadelphia NFL		9	5	3	0.6	0
1983—Philadelphia NFL		16	1	0	0.0	0
1984—Philadelphia NFL		16	2	0	0.0	0
1985—Philadelphia NFL		16	3	8	2.7	1
1986—Los Angeles Rams NFL		4	0	0	0.0	0
—Atlanta NFL		3	0	0	0.0	0
Pro totals (10 years)		142	33	98	3.0	1

HEAD COACHING RECORD
BACKGROUND: Defensive backs coach, San Jose State (1987-1989). ... Scout, Kansas City Chiefs NFL (1990, 1991 and 1995). ... Defensive backs coach, Chiefs (1992-1994). ... Assistant head coach/defensive back coach, Tampa Bay Buccaneers NFL (1996-2000).

FASSEL, JIM — GIANTS

PERSONAL: Born August 31, 1949, in Anaheim. ... Full name: James Fassel. ... Played quarterback.

HIGH SCHOOL: Anaheim (Calif.) High.

JUNIOR COLLEGE: Fullerton (Calif.) College.

COLLEGE: Southern California, then Long Beach State (degree in physical education, 1972).

TRANSACTIONS/CAREER NOTES: Selected by Chicago Bears in seventh round of 1972 NFL draft.

HEAD COACHING RECORD
BACKGROUND: Coach, Fullerton College (1973). ... Player/coach, Hawaii Hawaiians WFL (1974). ... Quarterbacks/receivers coach, Utah (1976). ... Offensive coordinator, Weber State (1977 and 1978). ... Offensive coordinator, Stanford (1979-1983). ... Offensive coordinator, New Orleans Breakers USFL (1984) ... Quarterbacks coach, New York Giants NFL (1991). ... Offensive coordinator, Giants (1992) ... Assistant head coach/offensive coordinator, Denver Broncos NFL (1993 and 1994). ... Quarterbacks coach, Oakland Raiders NFL (1995). ... Offensive coordinator/quarterbacks coach, Arizona Cardinals NFL (1996).

HONORS: Named NFL Coach of the Year by THE SPORTING NEWS (1997).

				REGULAR SEASON		POST-SEASON	
	W	L	T	Pct.	Finish	W	L
1985—Utah	8	4	0	.667	2nd/Western Athletic Conference	0	0
1986—Utah	2	9	0	.182	9th/Western Athletic Conference	0	0
1987—Utah	5	7	0	.417	7th/Western Athletic Conference	0	0
1988—Utah	6	5	0	.545	4th/Western Athletic Conference	0	0
1989—Utah	4	8	0	.333	7th/Western Athletic Conference	0	0
1997—New York Giants NFL	10	5	1	.656	1st/NFC Eastern Division	0	1
1998—New York Giants NFL	8	8	0	.500	3rd/NFC Eastern Division	0	0
1999—New York Giants NFL	7	9	0	.438	3rd/NFC Eastern Division	0	0
2000—New York Giants NFL	12	4	0	.750	1st/NFC Eastern Division	2	1
College totals (5 years)	25	33	0	.431			
Pro totals (4 years)	37	26	1	.586	**Pro totals (3 years)**	2	2

NOTES:

1997—Lost to Minnesota, 23-22, in first-round playoff game.

2000—Defeated Philadelphia, 20-10, in conference playoff game; defeated Minnesota, 41-0, in NFC championship game; lost to Balitmore, 34-7, in Super Bowl XXXV.

FISHER, JEFF — TITANS

PERSONAL: Born February 25, 1958, in Culver City, Calif. ... Full name: Jeffrey Michael Fisher. ... Played safety.

HIGH SCHOOL: Taft (Woodland Hills, Calif.).

COLLEGE: Southern California (degree in public administration, 1981).

TRANSACTIONS/CAREER NOTES: Selected by Chicago Bears in seventh round (177th pick overall) of 1981 NFL draft. ... On injured reserve with broken leg (October 24, 1983-remainder of season). ... On injured reserve with ankle injury entire 1985 season.

CHAMPIONSHIP GAME EXPERIENCE: Played in NFC championship game (1984 season).

PRO STATISTICS: 1981—Recovered one fumble. 1984—Recovered one fumble.

		INTERCEPTIONS				PUNT RETURNS				KICKOFF RETURNS				TOTALS			
Year	Team	G	No.	Yds.	Avg.	TD	No.	Yds.	Avg.	TD	No.	Yds.	Avg.	TD	TD	2pt.	Pts.	Fum.
1981—Chicago NFL	16	2	3	1.5	0	43	509	11.8	1	7	102	14.6	0	1	0	6	3
1982—Chicago NFL	9	3	19	6.3	0	7	53	7.6	0	7	102	14.6	0	0	0	0	2
1983—Chicago NFL	8	0	0	0.0	0	13	71	5.5	0	0	0	0.0	0	0	0	0	0
1984—Chicago NFL	16	0	0	0.0	0	57	492	8.6	0	0	0	0.0	0	0	0	0	4
1985—Chicago NFL								Did not play.									
Pro totals (4 years)	49	5	22	4.4	0	120	1125	9.4	1	14	204	14.6	0	1	0	6	9

HEAD COACHING RECORD

BACKGROUND: Defensive backs coach, Philadelphia Eagles NFL (1986-1988). ... Defensive coordinator, Eagles (1989 and 1990). ... Defensive coordinator, Los Angeles Rams NFL (1991). ... Defensive backs coach, San Francisco 49ers NFL (1992 and 1993). ... Defensive coordinator, Houston Oilers NFL (February 9-November 14, 1994). ... Oilers franchise moved to Tennessee for 1997 season.

	W	L	T	Pct.	REGULAR SEASON Finish	POST-SEASON W	L
1994—Houston NFL	1	5	0	.167	4th/AFC Central Division	0	0
1995—Houston NFL	7	9	0	.438	T2nd/AFC Central Division	0	0
1996—Houston NFL	8	8	0	.500	T3rd/AFC Central Division	0	0
1997—Tennessee NFL	8	8	0	.500	3rd/AFC Central Division	0	0
1998—Tennessee NFL	8	8	0	.500	2nd/AFC Central Division	0	0
1999—Tennessee NFL	13	3	0	.813	2nd/AFC Central Division	3	1
2000—Tennessee NFL	13	3	0	.813	1st/AFC Central Division	0	1
Pro totals (7 years)	**58**	**44**	**0**	**.569**	**Pro totals (3 years)**	**3**	**2**

NOTES:
1994—Replaced Jack Pardee as head coach (November 14) with 1-9 record and club in fourth place.
1999—Defeated Buffalo, 22-16, in first-round playoff game; defeated Indianapolis, 19-16, in conference playoff game; defeated Jacksonville, 33-14 in AFC championship game; lost to St. Louis, 23-16, in Super Bowl XXXIV.
2000—Lost to Baltimore, 24-10, in conference playoff game.

GREEN, DENNIS   VIKINGS

PERSONAL: Born February 17, 1949, in Harrisburg, Pa.
HIGH SCHOOL: John Harris (Harrisburg, Pa.).
COLLEGE: Iowa (degree in recreation education, 1971).

HEAD COACHING RECORD

BACKGROUND: Graduate assistant, University of Iowa (1972). ... Running backs/receivers coach, Dayton (1973). ... Running backs/receivers coach, Iowa (1974-1976). ... Running backs coach, Stanford (1977 and 1978). ... Special teams coach, San Francisco 49ers NFL (1979). ... Offensive coordinator, Stanford (1980). ... Receivers coach, 49ers (1986-1988).

	W	L	T	Pct.	REGULAR SEASON Finish	POST-SEASON W	L
1981—Northwestern	0	11	0	.000	10th/Big Ten Conference	0	0
1982—Northwestern	3	8	0	.273	T8th/Big Ten Conference	0	0
1983—Northwestern	2	9	0	.182	T8th/Big Ten Conference	0	0
1984—Northwestern	2	9	0	.182	9th/Big Ten Conference	0	0
1985—Northwestern	3	8	0	.273	T9th/Big Ten Conference	0	0
1989—Stanford	3	8	0	.273	T7th/Pacific-10 Conference	0	0
1990—Stanford	5	6	0	.455	T6th/Pacific-10 Conference	0	0
1991—Stanford	8	3	0	.727	T2nd/Pacific-10 Conference	0	1
1992—Minnesota NFL	11	5	0	.688	1st/NFC Central Division	0	1
1993—Minnesota NFL	9	7	0	.563	2nd/NFC Central Division	0	1
1994—Minnesota NFL	10	6	0	.625	1st/NFC Central Division	0	1
1995—Minnesota NFL	8	8	0	.500	4th/NFC Central Division	0	0
1996—Minnesota NFL	9	7	0	.563	2nd/NFC Central Division	0	1
1997—Minnesota NFL	9	7	0	.563	T3rd/NFC Central Division	1	1
1998—Minnesota NFL	15	1	0	.938	1st/NFC Central Division	1	1
1999—Minnesota NFL	10	6	0	.625	2nd/NFC Central Division	1	1
2000—Minnesota NFL	11	5	0	.688	1st/NFC Central Division	1	1
College totals (8 years)	**26**	**62**	**0**	**.295**	**College totals (1 year)**	**0**	**1**
Pro totals (9 years)	**92**	**52**	**0**	**.639**	**Pro totals (8 years)**	**4**	**8**

NOTES:
1991—Lost to Georgia Tech, 18-17, in Aloha Bowl.
1992—Lost to Washington, 24-7, in first-round playoff game.
1993—Lost to New York Giants, 17-10, in first-round playoff game.
1994—Lost to Chicago, 35-18, in first-round playoff game.
1996—Lost to Dallas, 40-15, in first-round playoff game.
1997—Defeated New York Giants, 23-22, in first-round playoff game; lost to San Francisco, 38-22, in conference playoff game.
1998—Defeated Arizona, 41-21, in conference playoff game; lost to Atlanta, 30-27, in NFC championship game.
1999—Defeated Dallas, 27-10, in first-round playoff game; lost to St. Louis, 49-37, in conference playoff game.
2000—Defeated New Orleans, 34-16, in conference playoff game; lost to New York Giants, 41-0, in NFC championship game.

GRUDEN, JON   RAIDERS

PERSONAL: Born August 17, 1963, in Sandusky, Ohio. ... Son of Jim Gruden, scout, San Francisco 49ers; and brother of Jay Gruden, quarterback with Tampa Bay Storm of Arena League (1991-96) and current head coach, Orlando Predators of Arena League.
HIGH SCHOOL: Clay (South Bend, Ind.).
COLLEGE: Dayton, then Tennessee (degree in communications, 1985).

HEAD COACHING RECORD

BACKGROUND: Graduate assistant, Tennessee (1986 and 1987). ... Passing game coordinator, Southeast Missouri State (1988). ... Wide receivers coach, Pacific (1989). ... Assistant coach, San Francisco 49ers NFL (1990) ... Wide receivers coach, University of Pittsburgh (1991). ... Offensive/quality control coach, Green Bay Packers NFL (1992). ... Wide receivers coach, Packers (1993 and 1994). ... Offensive coordinator, Philadelphia Eagles NFL (1995-1997).

	REGULAR SEASON					POST-SEASON	
	W	L	T	Pct.	Finish	W	L
1998—Oakland NFL......................	8	8	0	.500	T2nd/AFC Western Division	0	0
1999—Oakland NFL......................	8	8	0	.500	T3rd/AFC Western Division	0	0
2000—Oakland NFL......................	12	4	0	.750	1st/AFC Western Division	1	1
Pro totals (3 years)	**28**	**20**	**0**	**.583**	**Pro totals (1 year)**	**1**	**1**

NOTES:
2000—Defeated Miami, 27-0, in conference playoff game; lost to Baltimore, 16-3, in AFC championship game.

HASLETT, JIM — SAINTS

PERSONAL: Born December 9, 1957, in Pittsburgh. ... Full name: James Donald Haslett. ... Cousin of Hal Stringert, defensive back with San Diego Chargers (1974-80). ... Played linebacker.
HIGH SCHOOL: Avalon (Pittsburgh).
COLLEGE: Indiana University, Pa. (degree in elementary education).
TRANSACTIONS/CAREER NOTES: Selected by Buffalo Bills in second round (51st pick overall) of 1979 NFL draft. ... On injured reserve with back injury (September 13-November 17, 1983). ... On injured reserve with broken leg (September 1, 1986-entire season). ... Released by Bills (September 7, 1987). ... Signed by New York Jets as replacement player (September 30, 1987). ... On injured reserve with back injury (October 20, 1987-remainder of season).
HONORS: Played in Pro Bowl (1980 and 1981 seasons).
PRO STATISTICS: 1979—Recovered two fumbles. 1980—Recovered one fumble. 1982—Recovered one fumble and caught one pass for four yards. 1984—Recovered three fumbles for ten yards. 1985—Recovered three fumbles and fumbled once. 1987—Recovered one fumble.

		INTERCEPTIONS			
Year Team	G	No.	Yds.	Avg.	TD
1979—Buffalo NFL	16	2	15	7.5	0
1980—Buffalo NFL	16	2	30	15.0	0
1981—Buffalo NFL	16	0	0	0.0	0
1982—Buffalo NFL	6	0	0	0.0	0
1983—Buffalo NFL	5	0	0	0.0	0
1984—Buffalo NFL	15	0	0	0.0	0
1985—Buffalo NFL	16	1	40	40.0	0
1986—Buffalo NFL			Did not play.		
1987—New York Jets NFL.................................	3	1	9	9.0	0
Pro totals (8 years)	93	6	94	15.7	0

HEAD COACHING RECORD

BACKGROUND: Linebackers coach, University of Buffalo (1988). ... Defensive coordinator, University of Buffalo (1989 and 1990). ... Defensive coordinator, Sacramento Surge W.L. (1991 and 1992). ... Linebackers coach, Oakland Raiders NFL (1993 and 1994). ... Linebackers coach, New Orleans Saints NFL (1995). ... Defensive coordinator, Saints (1996). ... Defensive coordinator, Pittsburgh Steelers NFL (1997-1999).

	REGULAR SEASON					POST-SEASON	
	W	L	T	Pct.	Finish	W	L
2000—New Orleans NFL................	10	6	0	.625	1st/NFC Western Division	1	1

NOTES:
2000—Defeated St. Louis, 31-28, in first-round playoff game; lost to Minnesota, 34-16, in conference playoff game.

HOLMGREN, MIKE — SEAHAWKS

PERSONAL: Born June 15, 1948, in San Francisco. ... Full name: Michael George Holmgren. ... Played quarterback.
HIGH SCHOOL: Lincoln (San Francisco).
COLLEGE: Southern California (degree in business finance, 1970).
TRANSACTIONS/CAREER NOTES: Selected by St. Louis Cardinals in eighth round of 1970 NFL draft. ... Released by Cardinals (1970).

HEAD COACHING RECORD

BACKGROUND: Assistant coach, Sacred Heart Cathedral Prep School, San Francisco (1972 and 1973). ... Assistant coach, Oak Grove High School, San Jose, Calif. (1975-1980). ... Offensive coordinator/quarterbacks coach, San Francisco State (1981). ... Quarterbacks coach, Brigham Young (1982-1985). ... Quarterbacks coach, San Francisco 49ers NFL (1986-1988). ... Offensive coordinator, 49ers (1989-1991).

	REGULAR SEASON					POST-SEASON	
	W	L	T	Pct.	Finish	W	L
1992—Green Bay NFL	9	7	0	.563	2nd/NFC Central Division	0	0
1993—Green Bay NFL	9	7	0	.563	T2nd/NFC Central Division	1	1
1994—Green Bay NFL	9	7	0	.563	T2nd/NFC Central Division	1	1
1995—Green Bay NFL	11	5	0	.688	1st/NFC Central Division	2	1
1996—Green Bay NFL	13	3	0	.813	1st/NFC Central Division	3	0
1997—Green Bay NFL	13	3	0	.813	1st/NFC Central Division	2	1
1998—Green Bay NFL	11	5	0	.688	2nd/NFC/Central Division	0	1
1999—Seattle NFL	9	7	0	.563	T1st/AFC Western Division	0	1
2000—Seattle NFL	6	10	0	.375	4th/AFC Western Division	0	0
Pro totals (9 years)	**90**	**54**	**0**	**.625**	**Pro totals (7 years)**	**9**	**6**

NOTES:
1993—Defeated Detroit, 28-24, in first-round playoff game; lost to Dallas 27-17, in conference playoff game.
1994—Defeated Detroit, 16-12, in first-round playoff game; lost to Dallas, 35-9, in conference playoff game.

HEAD COACHES

1995—Defeated Atlanta, 37-20, in first-round playoff game; defeated San Francisco, 27-17, in conference playoff game; lost to Dallas, 38-27, in NFC championship game.
1996—Defeated San Francisco, 35-14, in conference playoff game; defeated Carolina, 30-13, in NFC championship game; defeated New England, 35-21, in Super Bowl XXXI.
1997—Defeated Tampa Bay, 21-7, in conference playoff game; defeated San Francisco, 23-10, in NFC championship game; lost to Denver, 31-24, in Super Bowl XXXII.
1998—Lost to San Francisco, 30-27, in first-round playoff game.
1999—Lost to Miami, 20-17, in first-round playoff game.

JAURON, DICK   BEARS

PERSONAL: Born October 7, 1950, in Swampscott, Mass. ... Full name: Richard Manuel Jauron. ... Played defensive back.
COLLEGE: Yale (degree in history).
TRANSACTIONS/CAREER NOTES: Selected by Detroit Lions in fourth round of 1973 NFL draft. ... Released by Lions (August 23, 1978). ... Signed by Cincinnati Bengals (August 29, 1978). ... On injured reserve with knee injury (November 12, 1980-remainder of season).
HONORS: Played in Pro Bowl (1974 season).

		INTERCEPTIONS			PUNT RETURNS				KICKOFF RETURNS				TOTALS			
Year Team	G	No.	Yds.	Avg.	TD	No.	Yds.	Avg.	TD	No.	Yds.	Avg.	TD	TD	2pt.	Pts.	Fum.
1973—Detroit NFL	14	4	208	52.0	1	6	49	8.2	0	17	405	23.8	0	1	0	6	0
1974—Detroit NFL	14	1	26	26.0	0	17	286	16.8	0	2	21	10.5	0	0	0	0	0
1975—Detroit NFL	10	4	39	9.8	0	6	29	4.8	0	0	0	0.0	0	0	0	0	0
1976—Detroit NFL	6	2	0	0.0	0	0	0	0.0	0	0	0	0.0	0	0	0	0	0
1977—Detroit NFL	14	3	55	18.3	0	11	41	3.7	0	0	0	0.0	0	0	0	0	0
1978—Cincinnati NFL	16	4	52	13.0	1	3	32	10.7	0	0	0	0.0	0	1	0	6	0
1979—Cincinnati NFL	16	6	41	6.8	0	1	10	10.0	0	0	0	0.0	0	0	0	0	0
1980—Cincinnati NFL	10	1	11	11.0	0	0	0	0.0	0	0	0	0.0	0	0	0	0	0
Pro totals (8 years)	100	25	432	17.3	2	44	447	10.2	0	19	426	22.4	0	2	0	12	0

HEAD COACHING RECORD

BACKGROUND: Secondary coach, Buffalo Bills NFL (1985). ... Defensive backs coach, Green Bay Packers NFL (1986-94). ... Defensive coordinator, Jacksonville Jaguars NFL (1995-1998).

		REGULAR SEASON					POST-SEASON	
	W	L	T	Pct.	Finish		W	L
1999—Chicago NFL	6	10	0	.375	5th/NFC Central Division		0	0
2000—Chicago NFL	5	11	0	.313	5th/NFC Central Division		0	0
Pro totals (2 years)	11	21	0	.344				

LeBEAU, DICK   BENGALS

PERSONAL: Born September 9, 1937, in London, Ohio. ... Full name: Charles Richard LeBeau. ... Name pronounced luh-BO.
HIGH SCHOOL: London (Ohio).
COLLEGE: Ohio State (degree in education, 1963).
TRANSACTIONS/CAREER NOTES: Selected by Cleveland Browns in fifth round of NFL draft (1959). ... Released by Browns (1959). ... Signed by Detroit Lions (1959).
HONORS: Played in Pro Bowl (1964-1966 seasons).
PRO STATISTICS: 1960—Returned two kickoffs for 16 yards. 1962—Recovered one fumble for a touchdown.

		INTERCEPTIONS			
Year Team	G	No.	Yds.	Avg.	TD
1959—Detroit NFL	6	0	0	0.0	0
1960—Detroit NFL	12	4	58	14.5	0
1961—Detroit NFL	14	3	45	15.0	0
1962—Detroit NFL	14	4	67	16.8	!1
1963—Detroit NFL	14	5	158	31.6	1
1964—Detroit NFL	14	5	45	9.0	0
1965—Detroit NFL	14	7	84	12.0	1
1966—Detroit NFL	14	4	66	16.5	0
1967—Detroit NFL	14	4	29	7.3	0
1968—Detroit NFL	14	5	23	4.6	0
1969—Detroit NFL	14	6	15	2.5	0
1970—Detroit NFL	14	9	96	10.7	0
1971—Detroit NFL	13	6	76	12.7	0
1972—Detroit NFL	14	0	0	0.0	0
Pro totals (14 years)	185	62	762	12.3	3

HEAD COACHING RECORD

BACKGROUND: Special teams coach, Philadelphia Eagles NFL (1973-1975). ... Defensive backs coach, Green Bay Packers NFL (1976-1979). ... Defensive backs coach, Cincinnati Bengals NFL (1980-1983). ... Defensive coordinator, Bengals (1984-1991). ... Assistant coach, Pittsburgh Steelers NFL (1991-1994). ... Defensive coordinator, Steelers (1995 and 1996). ... Assistant head coach/defensive coordinator, Bengals (1997-September 25, 2000).

		REGULAR SEASON					POST-SEASON	
	W	L	T	Pct.	Finish		W	L
2000—Cincinnati NFL	4	9	0	.308	5th/AFC Central Division		0	0

NOTES:
2000—Replaced Bruce Coslet as head coach (September 25), with 0-3 record and club in sixth place.

HEAD COACHES

MARIUCCI, STEVE   49ERS

PERSONAL: Born November 4, 1955, in Iron Mountain, Mich. ... Full name: Steven Mariucci. ... Played quarterback.
HIGH SCHOOL: Iron Mountain (Mich.).
COLLEGE: Northern Michigan.
TRANSACTIONS/CAREER NOTES: Signed with Hamilton Tiger-Cats of CFL for 1978 season.

HEAD COACHING RECORD

BACKGROUND: Quarterbacks/running backs coach, Northern Michigan (1978 and 1979). ... Quarterbacks/special teams coordinator, Cal State Fullerton (1980-1982). ... Assistant head coach, Louisville (1983 and 1984). ... Receivers coach, Orlando Renegades USFL (1985). ... Quality control coach, Los Angeles Rams NFL (fall 1985). ... Wide receivers/special teams coach, University of California (1987-1989). ... Offensive coordinator/quarterbacks coach, University of California (1990 and 1991). ... Quarterbacks coach, Green Bay Packers NFL (1992-1995).

	W	L	T	Pct.	REGULAR SEASON Finish	POST-SEASON W	L
1996—California	6	6	0	.500	T5th/Pacific-10 Conference	0	1
1997—San Francisco NFL	13	3	0	.813	1st/NFC Western Division	1	1
1998—San Francisco NFL	12	4	0	.750	2nd/NFC Western Division	1	1
1999—San Francisco NFL	4	12	0	.250	4th/NFC Western Division	0	0
2000—San Francisco NFL	6	10	0	.375	4th/NFC Western Division	0	0
College totals (1 year)	6	6	0	.500	**College totals (1 year)**	0	1
Pro totals (4 years)	35	29	0	.547	**Pro totals (2 years)**	2	2

NOTES:

1996—Lost to Navy, 42-38, in Aloha Bowl.
1997—Defeated Minnesota, 38-22, in conference playoff game; lost to Green Bay, 23-10, in NFC championship game.
1998—Defeated Green Bay, 30-27, in first-round playoff game; lost to Atlanta, 20-18, in conference playoff game.

MARTZ, MIKE   RAMS

PERSONAL: Born May 13, 1951, in Sioux Falls, S.D.
HIGH SCHOOL: Madison (San Diego).
JUNIOR COLLEGE: San Diego Mesa Community College.
COLLEGE: UC Santa Barbara, then Fresno State.

HEAD COACHING RECORD

BACKGROUND: Coach, Bullard High School, Fresno, Calif. (1973). ... Coach, San Diego Mesa Community College (1974, 1976 and 1977). ... Coach, San Jose State (1975). ... Coach, Santa Ana College (1978). ... Coach, Fresno State (1979). ... Coach, Pacific University (1980 and 1981). ... Running backs coach, University of Minnesota (1982). ... Quarterbacks/receivers coach, Arizona State (1983, 1986 and 1987). ... Offensive coordinator, Arizona State (1984 and 1988-1991). ... Offensive assistant, Los Angeles Rams NFL (1992 and 1993). ... Quarterbacks coach, Rams (1994). ... Offensive assistant, St. Louis Rams NFL (1995 and 1996). ... Quarterbacks coach, Washington Redskins NFL (1997 and 1998). ... Offensive coordinator, Rams (1999).

	W	L	T	Pct.	REGULAR SEASON Finish	POST-SEASON W	L
2000—St. Louis NFL	10	6	0	.625	2nd/NFC Western Division	0	1

NOTES:

2000—Lost to New Orleans, 31-28, in first-round playoff game.

McGINNIS, DAVE   CARDINALS

PERSONAL: Born August 7, 1951, in Independence, Kan.
HIGH SCHOOL: Snyder (Texas).
COLLEGE: Texas Christian (degree in business administration).

HEAD COACHING RECORD

BACKGROUND: Freshman coach, Texas Christian (1973 and 1974). ... Linebackers/secondary coach, University of Missouri (1975-1977). ... Secondary coach, Indiana State (1978-1981). ... Defensive backfield coach, Texas Christian (1982). ... Defensive ends/linebackers coach, Kansas State (1983-1985). ... Linebackers coach, Chicago Bears NFL (1986-1995). ... Defensive coordinator, Arizona Cardinals (1996-October 23, 2000).

	W	L	T	Pct.	REGULAR SEASON Finish	POST-SEASON W	L
2000—Arizona NFL	1	8	0	.111	5th/NFC Eastern Division	0	0

NOTES:

2000—Replaced Vince Tobin as head coach (October 23), with 2-5 record and club in fifth place.

MORA, JIM   COLTS

PERSONAL: Born May 24, 1935, in Los Angeles. ... Full name: James Ernest Mora.
HIGH SCHOOL: University (Los Angeles).
COLLEGE: Occidental College (bachelor degree in physical education, 1957), then Southern California (master's degree in education, 1967).
MISCELLANEOUS: Played for U.S. Marines at Quantico (1957) and Camp Lejeune (1958 and 1959).

HEAD COACHING RECORD

BACKGROUND: Assistant coach, Occidental College (1960-1963). ... Linebackers coach, Stanford (1967). ... Defensive assistant, University of Colorado (1967-1973). ... Linebackers coach, UCLA (1974). ... Defensive coordinator, University of Washington (1975-1977). ... Defensive line coach, Seattle Seahawks NFL (1978-1981). ... Defensive coordinator, New England Patriots NFL (1982).

HONORS: Named USFL Coach of the Year by THE SPORTING NEWS (1984). ... Name NFL Coach of the Year by THE SPORTING NEWS (1987).

						POST-SEASON	
		REGULAR SEASON					
	W	L	T	Pct.	Finish	W	L
1964—Occidental	5	4	0	.556	3rd/Southern Calif. Intercollegiate Conference	0	0
1965—Occidental	8	1	0	.889	1st/Southern Calif. Intercollegiate Conference	0	0
1966—Occidental	5	4	0	.556	4th/Southern Calif. Intercollegiate Conference	0	0
1983—Philadelphia USFL	15	3	0	.833	1st/Atlantic Division	1	1
1984—Philadelphia USFL	16	2	0	.889	1st/Eastern Conference Atlantic Division	3	0
1985—Baltimore USFL	10	7	1	.583	4th/Eastern Conference	3	0
1986—New Orleans NFL	7	9	0	.438	4th/Western Division	0	0
1987—New Orleans NFL	12	3	0	.800	2nd/Western Division	0	1
1988—New Orleans NFL	10	6	0	.625	T1st/Western Division	0	0
1989—New Orleans NFL	9	7	0	.563	3rd/Western Division	0	0
1990—New Orleans NFL	8	8	0	.500	2nd/Western Division	0	1
1991—New Orleans NFL	11	5	0	.688	1st/Western Division	0	1
1992—New Orleans NFL	12	4	0	.750	2nd/Western Division	0	1
1993—New Orleans NFL	8	8	0	.500	2nd/Western Division	0	0
1994—New Orleans NFL	7	9	0	.438	T2nd/Western Division	0	0
1995—New Orleans NFL	7	9	0	.438	T3rd/Western Division	0	0
1998—Indianapolis NFL	3	13	0	.188	5th/AFCWestern Division	0	0
1999—Indianapolis NFL	13	3	0	.813	1st/AFC Eastern Division	0	1
2000—Indianapolis NFL	10	6	0	.625	2nd/AFC Eastern Division	0	1
College totals (3 years)	**18**	**9**	**0**	**.667**			
USFL totals (3 years)	**41**	**12**	**1**	**.769**	**USFL totals (3 years)**	**7**	**1**
NFL totals (13 years)	**117**	**90**	**0**	**.565**	**NFL totals (6 years)**	**0**	**6**
Pro totals (16 years)	**158**	**102**	**1**	**.607**	**Pro totals (9 years)**	**7**	**7**

NOTES:

1983—Defeated Chicago, 44-38 (OT), in divisional playoff game; lost to Michigan, 24-22, in USFL championship game.

1984—Defeated New Jersey, 28-7, in conference playoff game; defeated Birmingham, 20-10, in conference championship game; defeated Arizona, 23-3, in USFL championship game.

1985—Defeated New Jersey, 20-17, in conference playoff game; defeated Birmingham, 28-14, in conference championship game; defeated Oakland, 28-24, in USFL championship game.

1987—Lost to Minnesota, 44-10, in wild-card playoff game.

1990—Lost to Chicago, 16-6, in conference playoff game.

1991—Lost to Atlanta, 27-20, in first-round playoff game.

1992—Lost to Philadelphia, 36-20, in first-round playoff game.

1999—Lost to Tennessee, 19-16, in conference playoff game.

2000—Lost to Miami, 23-17, in first-round playoff game.

MORNHINWEG, MARTY — LIONS

PERSONAL: Born March 29, 1962, in Edmond, Okla.

HIGH SCHOOL: Oak Grove (San Jose, Calif.).

COLLEGE: Montana.

HEAD COACHING RECORD

BACKGROUND: Receivers coach, University of Montana (1985). ... Graduate assistant/quarterbacks coach, University of Texas-El Paso (1986 and 1987). ... Running backs coach, Northern Arizona (1988). ... Offensive coordinator/quarterbacks coach, Southeast Missouri State (1989 and 1990). ... Tight ends coach, University of Missouri (1991). ... Offensive line coach, Missouri (1992 and 1993). ... Offensive coordinator, Northern Arizona (1994). ... Offensive assistant/quality control, Green Bay Packers NFL (1995). ... Quarterbacks coach, Packers (1996). ... Offensive coordinator, San Francisco 49ers NFL (1997-2000).

REEVES, DAN — FALCONS

PERSONAL: Born January 19, 1944, in Rome, Ga. ... Full name: Daniel Edward Reeves. ... Played running back.

HIGH SCHOOL: Americus (Ga.).

COLLEGE: South Carolina.

TRANSACTIONS/CAREER NOTES: Signed as non-drafted free agent by Dallas Cowboys for 1965 season.

CHAMPIONSHIP GAME EXPERIENCE: Played in NFL championship game (1966 and 1967 seasons). ... Played in NFC championship game (1970 and 1971 seasons). ... Played in Super Bowl V (1970 season). ... Member of Super Bowl championship team (1971 season).

HONORS: Named halfback on THE SPORTING NEWS NFL Eastern Conference All-Star team (1966).

PRO STATISTICS: 1965—Returned two kickoffs for 45 yards. 1966—Returned two punts for minus one yard, returned three kickoffs for 56 yards and fumbled six times. 1967—Fumbled seven times. 1969—Fumbled twice. 1970—Fumbled four times. 1971—Fumbled once.

		PASSING							RUSHING				RECEIVING				TOTALS		
Year Team	G	Att.	Cmp.	Pct.	Yds.	TD	Int.	Avg.	Att.	Yds.	Avg.	TD	No.	Yds.	Avg.	TD	TD	2pt.	Pts.
1965—Dallas NFL	13	2	1	50.0	11	0	0	5.50	33	102	3.1	2	9	210	23.3	1	3	0	18
1966—Dallas NFL	14	6	3	50.0	48	0	0	8.00	175	757	4.3	8	41	557	13.6	8	16	0	96
1967—Dallas NFL	14	7	4	57.1	195	2	1	27.86	173	603	3.5	5	39	490	12.6	6	11	0	66
1968—Dallas NFL	4	4	2	50.0	43	0	0	10.75	40	178	4.5	4	7	84	12.0	1	5	0	30
1969—Dallas NFL	13	3	1	33.3	35	0	1	11.67	59	173	2.9	4	18	187	10.4	1	5	0	30
1970—Dallas NFL	14	3	1	33.3	14	0	1	4.67	35	84	2.4	2	12	140	11.7	0	2	0	12
1971—Dallas NFL	14	5	2	40.0	24	0	1	4.80	17	79	4.6	0	3	25	8.3	0	0	0	0
1972—Dallas NFL	14	2	0	0.0	0	0	0	0.0	3	14	4.7	0	0	0	0.0	0	0	0	0
Pro totals (8 years)	100	32	14	43.8	370	2	4	11.56	535	1990	3.7	25	129	1693	13.1	17	42	0	252

HEAD COACHING RECORD

BACKGROUND: Player/coach, Dallas Cowboys NFL (1970 and 1971). ... Offensive backs coach, Cowboys (1972 and 1974-1976). ... Offensive coordinator, Cowboys (1977-1980).

HONORS: Named NFL Coach of the Year by THE SPORTING NEWS (1993 and 1998).

	REGULAR SEASON					POST-SEASON	
	W	L	T	Pct.	Finish	W	L
1981—Denver NFL	10	6	0	.625	T1st/AFC Western Division	0	0
1982—Denver NFL	2	7	0	.222	12th/AFC	0	0
1983—Denver NFL	9	7	0	.563	T2nd/AFC Western Division	0	1
1984—Denver NFL	13	3	0	.813	1st/AFC Western Division	0	1
1985—Denver NFL	11	5	0	.688	2nd/AFC Western Division	0	0
1986—Denver NFL	11	5	0	.688	1st/AFC Western Division	2	1
1987—Denver NFL	10	4	1	.700	1st/AFC Western Division	2	1
1988—Denver NFL	8	8	0	.500	2nd/AFC Western Division	0	0
1989—Denver NFL	11	5	0	.688	1st/AFC Western Division	2	1
1990—Denver NFL	5	11	0	.313	5th/AFC Western Division	0	0
1991—Denver NFL	12	4	0	.750	1st/AFC Western Division	1	1
1992—Denver NFL	8	8	0	.500	3rd/AFC Western Division	0	0
1993—New York Giants NFL	11	5	0	.688	2nd/NFC Eastern Division	1	1
1994—New York Giants NFL	9	7	0	.563	2nd/NFC Eastern Division	0	0
1995—New York Giants NFL	5	11	0	.313	4th/NFC Eastern Division	0	0
1996—New York Giants NFL	6	10	0	.375	5th/NFC Eastern Division	0	0
1997—Atlanta NFL	7	9	0	.438	T2nd/NFC Western Division	0	0
1998—Atlanta NFL	14	2	0	.875	1st/NFC Western Division	2	1
1999—Atlanta NFL	5	11	0	.313	3rd/NFC Western Division	0	0
2000—Atlanta NFL	4	12	0	.250	5th/NFC Western Division	0	0
Pro totals (20 years)	**171**	**140**	**1**	**.550**	**Pro totals (8 years)**	**10**	**8**

NOTES:

1983—Lost to Seattle, 31-7, in wild-card playoff game.

1984—Lost to Pittsburgh, 24-17, in conference playoff game.

1986—Defeated New England, 22-17, in conference playoff game; defeated Cleveland, 23-20 (OT), in AFC championship game; lost to New York Giants, 39-20, in Super Bowl XXI.

1987—Defeated Houston, 34-10, in conference playoff game; defeated Cleveland, 38-33, in AFC championship game; lost to Washington, 42-10, in Super Bowl XXII.

1989—Defeated Pittsburgh, 24-23, in conference playoff game; defeated Cleveland, 37-21, in AFC championship game; lost to San Francisco, 55-10, in Super Bowl XXIV.

1991—Defeated Houston, 26-24, in conference playoff game; lost to Buffalo, 10-7, in AFC championship game.

1993—Defeated Minnesota, 17-10, in first-round playoff game; lost to San Francisco, 44-3, in conference playoff game.

1998—Defeated San Francisco, 20-18, in conference playoff game; defeated Minnesota, 30-27, in NFC championship game; lost to Denver, 34-19, in Super Bowl XXXIII.

REID, ANDY   EAGLES

PERSONAL: Born March 19, 1958, in Los Angeles. ... Full name: Andrew Walter Reid.

HIGH SCHOOL: John Marshall (Los Angeles).

COLLEGE: Brigham Young (bachelor's degree in physical education; master's degree in professional leadership, physical education and athletics).

HEAD COACHING RECORD

BACKGROUND: Graduate assistant, Brigham Young University (1982). ... Offensive coordinator, San Francisco State (1983-1985). ... Offensive line coach, Northern Arizona University (1986). ... Offensive line coach, University of Texas-El Paso (1987 and 1988). ... Offensive line coach, University of Missouri (1989-1992). ... Tight ends coach, Green Bay Packers NFL (1993-1996). ... Quarterbacks coach, Packers (1997 and 1998).

HONORS: Named NFL Coach of the Year by THE SPORTING NEWS (2000).

	REGULAR SEASON					POST-SEASON	
	W	L	T	Pct.	Finish	W	L
1999—Philadelphia NFL	5	11	0	.313	5th/NFC Eastern Division	0	0
2000—Philadelphia NFL	11	5	0	.688	2nd/NFC Eastern Division	1	1
Pro totals (2 years)	**16**	**16**	**0**	**.500**	**Pro totals (1 year)**	**1**	**1**

NOTES:

2000—Defeated Tampa Bay, 21-3, in first-round playoff game; lost to New York Giants, 20-10, in conference playoff game.

RILEY, MIKE   CHARGERS

PERSONAL: Born July 6, 1953, in Wallace, Idaho ... Full name: Michael Joseph Riley.

HIGH SCHOOL: Corvallis (Ore.).

COLLEGE: Alabama (degree in social science), then Whitworth College, Wash. (master's degree).

HONORS: Named CFL Coach of the Year (1988 and 1990).

HEAD COACHING RECORD

BACKGROUND: Graduate assistant, University of California (1975). ... Graduate assistant, Whitworth College (1976). ... Defensive coordinator/secondary, Linfield College (1977-1982). ... Secondary coach, Winnipeg Blue Bombers of CFL (1983-1985). ... Defensive coordinator, Northern Colorado University (1986). ... Offensive coordinator/quarterbacks coach, University of Southern California (1993-1996).

	REGULAR SEASON					POST-SEASON	
	W	L	T	Pct.	Finish	W	L
1987—Winnipeg CFL	12	6	0	.667	1st/Eastern Division	0	1
1988—Winnipeg CFL	9	9	0	.500	2nd/Eastern Division	3	0
1989—Winnipeg CFL	7	11	0	.389	3rd/Eastern Division	1	1
1990—Winnipeg CFL	12	6	0	.667	1st/Eastern Division	2	0
1991—San Antonio W.L.	4	6	0	.400	—	0	0
1992—San Antonio W.L.	7	3	0	.700	—	0	0
1997—Oregon State	3	8	0	.273	10th/Pacific 10 Conference	0	0
1998—Oregon State	5	6	0	.455	T8th/Pacific 10 Conference	0	0
1999—San Diego NFL	8	8	0	.500	T3rd/AFC Western Division	0	0
2000—San Diego NFL	1	15	0	.063	5th/AFC Western Division	0	0
College totals (2 years)	8	14	0	.364			
W.L. totals (2 years)	11	9	0	.550			
CFL totals (4 years)	40	32	0	.556	**CFL totals (4 years)**	6	2
NFL totals (2 years)	9	23	0	.281			
Pro totals (8 years)	60	64	0	.484	**Pro totals (4 years)**	6	2

NOTES:

1987—Lost to Toronto Argonauts, 19-3, in Divisional Finals of Grey Cup.

1988—Defeated Hamilton, 35-28, in Divisional Semi-finals of Grey Cup; defeated Toronto, 27-11, in Divisional Finals of Grey Cup; defeated B.C., 22-21, in Grey Cup Finals.

1989—Defeated Toronto, 30-7, in Divisional Semifinals of Grey Cup; lost to Hamilton, 14-10, in Divisional Finals of Grey Cup.

1990—Defeated Toronto, 20-17, in Divisional Finals of Grey Cup; defeated Edmonton, 50-11, in Grey Cup finals.

SCHOTTENHEIMER, MARTY   REDSKINS

PERSONAL: Born September 23, 1943, in Canonsburg, Pa. ... Full name: Martin Edward Schottenheimer. ... Played linebacker. ... Brother of Kurt Schottenheimer, defensive coordinator, Washington Redskins.

HIGH SCHOOL: McDonald (Pa.).

COLLEGE: Pittsburgh (degree in English, 1964).

TRANSACTIONS/CAREER NOTES: Selected by Buffalo Bills in seventh round of 1965 AFL draft. ... Released by Bills (1969). ... Signed by Boston Patriots (1969). ... Patriots franchise renamed New England Patriots for 1971 season. ... Traded by New England Patriots to Pittsburgh Steelers for OT Mike Haggerty and a draft choice (July 10, 1971). ... Released by Steelers (1971).

CHAMPIONSHIP GAME EXPERIENCE: Member of AFL championship team (1965 season). ... Played in AFL championship game (1966 season).

HONORS: Played in AFL All-Star Game (1965 season).

PRO STATISTICS: 1969—Returned one kickoff for 13 yards. 1970—Returned one kickoff for eight yards.

		INTERCEPTIONS			
Year Team	G	No.	Yds.	Avg.	TD
1965—Buffalo AFL	14	0	0	0.0	0
1966—Buffalo AFL	14	1	20	20.0	0
1967—Buffalo AFL	14	3	88	29.3	1
1968—Buffalo AFL	14	1	22	22.0	0
1969—Boston AFL	11	1	3	3.0	0
1970—Boston NFL	12	0	0	0.0	0
AFL totals (5 years)	67	6	133	22.2	1
NFL totals (1 year)	12	0	0	0.0	0
Pro totals (6 years)	79	6	133	22.2	1

HEAD COACHING RECORD

BACKGROUND: Linebackers coach, Portland Storm WFL (1974). ... Linebackers coach, New York Giants NFL (1975 and 1976). ... Defensive coordinator, Giants (1977). ... Linebackers coach, Detroit Lions NFL (1978 and 1979). ... Defensive coordinator, Cleveland Browns NFL (1989-October 22, 1984).

	REGULAR SEASON					POST-SEASON	
	W	L	T	Pct.	Finish	W	L
1984—Cleveland NFL	4	4	0	.500	3rd/AFC Central Division	0	0
1985—Cleveland NFL	8	8	0	.500	3rd/AFC Central Division	0	1
1986—Cleveland NFL	12	4	0	.750	1st/AFC Central Division	1	1
1987—Cleveland NFL	10	5	0	.667	1st/AFC Central Division	1	1
1988—Cleveland NFL	10	6	0	.625	T2nd/AFC Central Division	0	1
1989—Kansas City NFL	8	7	1	.531	2nd/AFC Western Division	0	0
1990—Kansas City NFL	11	5	0	.688	2nd/AFC Western Division	0	1
1991—Kansas City NFL	10	6	0	.625	2nd/AFC Western Division	1	1
1992—Kansas City NFL	10	6	0	.625	2nd/AFC Western Division	0	1
1993—Kansas City NFL	11	5	0	.688	1st/AFC Western Division	2	1
1994—Kansas City NFL	9	7	0	.563	T2nd/AFC Western Division	0	1
1995—Kansas City NFL	13	3	0	.813	1st/AFC Western Division	0	1
1996—Kansas City NFL	9	7	0	.563	2nd/AFC Western Division	0	0
1997—Kansas City NFL	13	3	0	.813	1st/AFC Western Division	0	1
1998—Kansas City NFL	7	9	0	.438	4th/AFC Western Division	0	0
Pro totals (15 years)	145	85	1	.630	**Pro totals (11 years)**	5	11

NOTES:

1984—Replaced Sam Rutigliano as coach of Cleveland (October 22), with 1-7 record and in third place.

1985—Lost to Miami, 24-21, in conference playoff game.

1986—Defeated Ney York Jets, 23-20 (2 OT), in conference playoff game; lost to Denver, 23-20 (OT), in AFC championship game.

HEAD COACHES

1987—Defeated Indianapolis, 38-21, in conference playoff game; lost to Denver, 38-33, in AFC championship game.
1988—Lost to Houston, 24-23, in wild-card playoff game.
1990—Lost to Miami, 17-16, in conference playoff game.
1991—Defeated Los Angeles Raiders, 10-6, in first-round playoff game; lost to Buffalo, 37-14, in conference playoff game.
1992—Lost to San Diego, 17-0, in first-round playoff game.
1993—Defeated Pittsburgh, 27-24 (OT), in first-round playoff game; defeated Houston, 28-20, in conference playoff game; lost to Buffalo, 30-13, in AFC championship game.
1994—Lost to Miami, 27-17, in first-round playoff game.
1995—Lost to Indianapolis, 10-7, in conference playoff game.
1997—Lost to Denver, 14-10, in conference playoff game.

SEIFERT, GEORGE — PANTHERS

PERSONAL: Born January 22, 1940, in San Francisco. ... Full name: George Gerald Seifert. ... Name pronounced SEE-fert.
HIGH SCHOOL: Polytechnic (Pasadena, Calif.).
COLLEGE: Utah (bachelor's degree in zoology, 1963; master's degree in physical education, 1966).
MISCELLANEOUS: Served six months in U.S. Army after college.

HEAD COACHING RECORD
BACKGROUND: Graduate assistant, Utah (1964). ... Assistant coach, Iowa (1966). ... Defensive backs coach, Oregon (1967-1971). ... Defensive backs coach, Stanford (1972-1974 and 1977-1979). ... Defensive backs coach, San Francisco 49ers NFL (1980-1982). ... Defensive coordinator, 49ers (1983-1988).
HONORS: Named NFL Coach of the Year by THE SPORTING NEWS (1990 and 1994).

		REGULAR SEASON				POST-SEASON	
	W	L	T	Pct.	Finish	W	L
1965—Westminster College (Utah)	3	3	0	.500	Independent	0	0
1975—Cornell	1	8	0	.111	8th/Ivy League	0	0
1976—Cornell	2	7	0	.222	T7th/Ivy League	0	0
1989—San Francisco NFL	14	2	0	.875	1st/NFC Western Division	3	0
1990—San Francisco NFL	14	2	0	.875	1st/NFC Western Division	1	1
1991—San Francisco NFL	10	6	0	.625	T2nd/NFC Western Division	0	0
1992—San Francisco NFL	14	2	0	.875	1st/NFC Western Division	1	1
1993—San Francisco NFL	10	6	0	.625	1st/NFC Western Division	1	1
1994—San Francisco NFL	13	3	0	.813	1st/NFC Western Division	3	0
1995—San Francisco NFL	11	5	0	.688	1st/NFC Western Division	0	1
1996—San Francisco NFL	12	4	0	.750	T1st/NFC Western Division	1	1
1999—Carolina NFL	8	8	0	.500	2nd/NFC Western Division	0	0
2000—Carolina NFL	7	9	0	.438	3rd/NFC Western Division	0	0
College totals (3 years)	6	18	0	.250			
Pro totals (10 years)	113	47	0	.706	**Pro totals (7 years)**	10	5

NOTES:
1989—Defeated Minnesota, 41-13, in conference playoff game; defeated Los Angeles Rams, 30-3, in NFC championship game; defeated Denver, 55-10, in Super Bowl XXIV.
1990—Defeated Washington, 28-10, in conference playoff game; lost to New York Giants, 15-13, in NFC championship game.
1992—Defeated Washington, 20-13, in conference playoff game; lost to Dallas 30-20 in NFC championship game.
1993—Defeated New York Giants, 44-3, in conference playoff game; lost to Dallas 38-21, in NFC championship game.
1994—Defeated Chicago, 44-15, in conference playoff game; defeated Dallas, 38-28, in NFC championship game; defeated San Diego, 49-26, in Super Bowl XXIX.
1995—Lost to Green Bay, 27-17, in conference playoff game.
1996—Defeated Philadelphia; 14-0, in first-round playoff game; lost to Green Bay, 35-14, in conference playoff game.

SHANAHAN, MIKE — BRONCOS

PERSONAL: Born August 24, 1952, in Oak Park, Ill. ... Full name: Michael Edward Shanahan.
HIGH SCHOOL: Franklin Park (East Leyden, Ill.).
COLLEGE: Eastern Illinois (bachelor's degree in physical education, 1974; master's degree in education, 1975).

HEAD COACHING RECORD
BACKGROUND: Graduate assistant, Eastern Illinois (1973 and 1974). ... Running backs/wide receivers coach, Oklahoma (1975 and 1976). ... Backfield coach, Northern Arizona (1977). ... Offensive coordinator, Eastern Illinois (1978). ... Offensive coordinator, University of Minnesota (1979). ... Offensive coordinator, University of Florida (1980-1983). ... Quarterbacks coach, Denver Broncos NFL (1984, 1989 and 1990). ... Offensive coordinator, Broncos (1985-1987 and 1991). ... Offensive coordinator, San Francisco 49ers NFL (1992-1994).

		REGULAR SEASON				POST-SEASON	
	W	L	T	Pct.	Finish	W	L
1988—Los Angeles Raiders NFL	7	9	0	.438	3rd/AFC Western Division	0	0
1989—Los Angeles Raiders NFL	1	3	0	.250	—	0	0
1995—Denver NFL	8	8	0	.500	T3rd/AFC Western Division	0	0
1996—Denver NFL	13	3	0	.813	1st/AFC Western Division	0	1
1997—Denver NFL	12	4	0	.750	2nd/AFC Western Conference	4	0
1998—Denver NFL	14	2	0	.875	1st/AFC Western Division	3	0
1999—Denver NFL	6	10	0	.375	5th/AFC Western Division	0	0
2000—Denver NFL	11	5	0	.688	2nd/AFC Western Division	0	1
Pro totals (8 years)	72	44	0	.621	**Pro totals (5 years)**	7	2

NOTES:

1989—Replaced as Raiders coach by Art Shell (October 3) with club tied for fourth place.
1996—Lost to Jacksonville, 30-27, in conference playoff game.
1997—Defeated Jacksonville, 42-17, in first-round playoff game; defeated Kansas City, 14-10, in conference playoff game; defeated Pittsburgh, 24-21, in AFC championship game; defeated Green Bay, 31-24, in Super Bowl XXXII.
1998—Defeated Miami, 38-3, in conference playoff game; defeated New York Jets, 23-10, in AFC championship game; defeated Atlanta, 34-19, in Super Bowl XXXIII.
2000—Lost to Baltimore, 21-3, in first-round playoff game.

SHERMAN, MIKE — PACKERS

PERSONAL: Born December 19, 1954, in Norwood, Mass.
COLLEGE: Central Connecticut State.

HEAD COACHING RECORD

BACKGROUND: Head coach, Stamford High School, Stamford, Conn. (1979 and 1980). ... Coach, University of Pittsburgh (1981 and 1982). ... Coach, Tulane (1983 and 1984). ... Offensive coordinator, Holy Cross (1985-1988). ... Offensive line coach, Texas A&M (1989-1993). ... Offensive line coach, UCLA (1994). ... Offensive line coach, Texas A&M (1995-1996). ... Tight ends coach, Green Bay Packers NFL (1997-1998). ... Offensive coordinator/tight ends coach, Seattle Seahawks NFL (1999).

	REGULAR SEASON					POST-SEASON	
	W	L	T	Pct.	Finish	W	L
2000—Green Bay NFL	9	7	0	.563	3rd/NFC Central Division	0	0

VERMEIL, DICK — CHIEFS

PERSONAL: Born October 30, 1936, in Calistoga, Calif. ... Full name: Richard Albert Vermeil. ... Brother of Al Vermeil, conditioning coach with San Francisco 49ers (1979-82) and brother-in-law of Louie Giammona, running back with Philadelphia Eagles (1978-82).
HIGH SCHOOL: Calistoga (Calif.).
JUNIOR COLLEGE: Napa College (degree in physical education, 1958).
COLLEGE: San Jose State (master's degree in physical education, 1959).

HEAD COACHING RECORD

BACKGROUND: Assistant coach, Del Mar High School, San Jose, Calif. (1959). ... Head coach, Hillsdale High School, San Mateo, Calif. (1960-1962; record: 17-9-1). ... Assistant coach, College of San Mateo (1963). ... Assistant coach, Stanford (1965-1968). ... Assistant coach, Los Angeles Rams NFL (1969 and 1971-1973). ... Assistant coach, UCLA (1970).
HONORS: Named NFL Coach of the Year by THE SPORTING NEWS (1979 and 1999).

	REGULAR SEASON					POST-SEASON	
	W	L	T	Pct.	Finish	W	L
1964—Napa College	8	1	0	.889	2nd/Golden Valley Conference	0	0
1974—UCLA	6	3	2	.636	T3rd/Pacific-8 Conference	0	0
1975—UCLA	8	2	1	.773	T1st/Pacific-8 Conference	1	0
1976—Philadelphia NFL	4	10	0	.286	4th/NFC Eastern Division	0	0
1977—Philadelphia NFL	5	9	0	.357	T4th/NFC Eastern Division	0	0
1978—Philadelphia NFL	9	7	0	.563	2nd/NFC Eastern Division	0	1
1979—Philadelphia NFL	11	5	0	.688	T1st/NFC Eastern Division	1	1
1980—Philadelphia NFL	12	4	0	.750	T1st/NFC Eastern Division	2	1
1981—Philadelphia NFL	10	6	0	.625	2nd/NFC Eastern Division	0	1
1982—Philadelphia NFL	3	6	0	.333	5th/NFC Eastern Division	0	0
1997—St. Louis NFL	5	11	0	.313	5th/NFC Western Division	0	0
1998—St. Louis NFL	4	12	0	.250	T4th/NFC Western Division	0	0
1999—St. Louis NFL	13	3	0	.813	1st/NFC Western Division	3	0
College totals (3 years)	22	6	3	.758	**College totals (1 year)**	1	0
Pro totals (10 years)	76	73	0	.510	**Pro totals (5 years)**	6	4

NOTES:

1975—Defeated Ohio State, 23-10, in Rose Bowl.
1978—Lost to Atlanta, 14-13, in conference playoff game.
1979—Defeated Chicago, 27-17, in first-round playoff game; lost to Tampa Bay, 24-17, in conference playoff game.
1980—Defeated Minnesota, 31-16, in conference playoff game; defeated Dallas, 20-7, in NFC championship game; lost to Oakland, 27-10, in Super Bowl XV.
1981—Lost to New York Giants, 27-21, in conference playoff game.
1982—Only nine of 16 games were played due to the cancellation of games because of a players strike.
1999—Defeated Minnesota, 49-37, in conference playoff game; defeated Tampa Bay, 11-6, in NFC championship game; defeated Tennessee, 23-16, in Super Bowl XXXIV.

WANNSTEDT, DAVE — DOLPHINS

PERSONAL: Born May 21, 1952, in Pittsburgh. ... Full name: David Raymond Wannstedt.
HIGH SCHOOL: Baldwin (Pittsburgh).
COLLEGE: Pittsburgh (bachelor of science degree in physical education, 1974; master's degree in education, 1975).
TRANSACTIONS/CAREER NOTES: Selected by Green Bay Packers in 15th round (376th pick overall) of 1974 NFL draft. ... On injured reserve with neck injury for entire 1974 season.

HEAD COACHES

HEAD COACHING RECORD

BACKGROUND: Graduate assistant, University of Pittsburgh (1975). ... Defensive line coach, University of Pittsburgh (1976-1978). ... Defensive line coach, Oklahoma State (1979 and 1980). ... Defensive coordinator, Oklahoma State (1981 and 1982). ... Defensive line coach, Southern California (1983-1985). ... Defensive coordinator, Miami, Fla. (1986-1988). ... Defensive coordinator, Dallas Cowboys NFL (1989-1992). ... Assistant head coach, Miami Dolphins NFL (1999).

		REGULAR SEASON				POST-SEASON	
	W	L	T	Pct.	Finish	W	L
1993—Chicago NFL	7	9	0	.438	4th/NFC Central Division	0	0
1994—Chicago NFL	9	7	0	.563	T2nd/NFC Central Division	1	1
1995—Chicago NFL	9	7	0	.563	3rd/NFC Central Division	0	0
1996—Chicago NFL	7	9	0	.438	3rd/NFC Central Division	0	0
1997—Chicago NFL	4	12	0	.250	5th/NFC Central Division	0	0
1998—Chicago NFL	4	12	0	.250	5th/NFC Central Division	0	0
2000—Miami NFL	11	5	0	.688	1st/AFC Eastern Division	1	1
Pro totals (7 years)	**51**	**61**	**0**	**.455**	**Pro totals (2 years)**	**2**	**2**

NOTES:
1994—Defeated Minnesota, 35-18, in first-round playoff game; lost to San Francisco, 44-15, in conference playoff game.
2000—Defeated Indianapolis, 23-17, in first-round playoff game; lost to Oakland, 27-0, in conference playoff game.

WILLIAMS, GREGG   BILLS

PERSONAL: Born July 15, 1958, in Excelsior Springs, Mo.
COLLEGE: Northeast Missouri, then Central Missouri (master's degree in education).

HEAD COACHING RECORD

BACKGROUND: Assistant coach, Excelsior Springs (Mo.) High School (1980-1983). ... Head coach, Belton (Mo.) High School (1984-1987). ... Graduate Assistant, University of Houston (1988 and 1989). ... Quality control coach, Houston Oilers NFL (1990-1992). ... Special teams coach, Oilers (1993). ... Linebackers coach, Oilers (1994-1996). ... Defensive coordinator, Tennessee Oilers NFL (1997 and 1998). ... Defensive coordinator, Tennessee Titans NFL (1999 and 2000).